ENCYCLOPEDIA OF AMERICAN LIVES

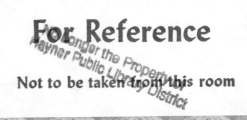

The SCRIBNER ENCYCLOPEDIA *of*

AMERICAN LIVES

The SCRIBNER ENCYCLOPEDIA *of*

AMERICAN LIVES

VOLUME FOUR

1994–1996

KENNETH T. JACKSON
EDITOR IN CHIEF

KAREN MARKOE
GENERAL EDITOR

ARNOLD MARKOE
EXECUTIVE EDITOR

CHARLES SCRIBNER'S SONS
AN IMPRINT OF THE GALE GROUP
NEW YORK   DETROIT   SAN FRANCISCO   LONDON   BOSTON   WOODBRIDGE, CT

Copyright © 2001 Charles Scribner's Sons

Charles Scribner's Sons
An imprint of The Gale Group
1633 Broadway
New York, NY 10019

Library of Congress Cataloging-in-Publication Data

The Scribner encyclopedia of American lives / Kenneth T. Jackson,
    editor in chief ; Karen Markoe, general editor ; Arnold Markoe,
    executive editor.
        p.   cm.
    Includes bibliographical references and index.
    Contents: v. 1. 1981–1985
    ISBN 0-684-80492-1 (v. 1 : alk. paper)
    1. United States—Biography—Dictionaries.   I. Jackson, Kenneth
T.   II. Markoe, Karen.   III. Markoe, Arnie.
CT213.S37   1998
920.073—dc21   98-33793
                                                            CIP

ISBN 0-684-80644-4 (v. 4 : alk. paper)

1 3 5 7 9 11 13 15 17 19 20 18 16 14 12 10 8 6 4 2
PRINTED IN THE UNITED STATES OF AMERICA

The paper in this publication meets the minimum requirements of the American National Standard for Information Services—Permanence of Paper for Printed Library Materials, ANSI Z39.48-1992.

EDITORIAL *and* PRODUCTION STAFF

Managing Editor
TIMOTHY J. DeWERFF

Project Editor
TARA M. STRICKLAND

Editorial Assistants
MICHELLE BECKER   SARAH FEEHAN
LEE ANN FULLINGTON   KASY MOON   CHARLES SCRIBNER IV

Editors
CAROL J. CIASTON   JOHN FITZPATRICK   KATHY MOREAU   CARYN RADICK

Copy Editors, Researchers
GRETCHEN GORDON   JEAN F. KAPLAN   LOUISE B. KETZ   JUDSON KNIGHT
MICHAEL LEVINE   LINDA SANDERS   NEIL SCHLAGER
JANET BALE   HELEN A. CASTRO   ELEANOR R. HERO   JOSH LAUER   ANNA LOVE LEHRE
CHERYL MacKENZIE   MARCIA MERRYMAN MEANS   MARK MIKULA
MARTHA SCHÜTZ   CINDI SHERMAN   INGRID STERNER

Proofreaders
MARCEL CHOUTEAU   MARGIE DUNCAN   THERESA FRITZGES   MARK GOLDMAN
ERICH J. KAISER   MATTHEW KOHUT   KIM A. NIR   BARBARA A. SOMOGYI

Picture Researchers
KATHLEEN DROSTE
MARGARET CHAMBERLAIN   DEAN DAUPHINAIS   DOUGLAS PUCHOWSKI

Designer
BRADY McNAMARA

Compositor
IMPRESSIONS BOOK AND JOURNAL SERVICES, INC.

Publisher
KAREN DAY

PREFACE

This fourth volume in the *Scribner Encyclopedia of American Lives (SEAL)* series contains the biographies of 313 persons who died in the three-year period between 1 January 1994 and 31 December 1996. It also includes cumulative name and occupations indexes containing the names of all the 1,619 biographees in the entire series.

The format of this book is alphabetical. Each essay in it appraises the circumstances and influences that shaped the life of an individual subject. Each entry also includes the full dates of birth and death, the full names and occupations of parents, the number of siblings, the educational institutions attended and degrees granted, the names of spouses and the dates of marriages and divorces, and the number of children. Wherever possible, the book also includes information on residences, cause of death, and place of burial. The length of an article was determined both by the relative significance of the subject and by the completeness of biographical material available.

In selecting a few hundred subjects from the millions of Americans who died in 1994, 1995, and 1996, the editors followed a rigorous process. First, they compiled a list of several thousand candidates from a variety of sources. Second, they classified the names according to profession or occupation. Third, they submitted the lists to specialists or groups of specialists who helped to rank the potential biographees. The final list, however, is solely the responsibility of the editors, who weighed the relative significance of particular politicians and poets, chemists and criminals, business leaders and baseball players.

The 313 individuals who are profiled in this book obviously lived extraordinary lives and in conspicuous ways set themselves apart from the rest of us. Some won fame on the battlefield or in the halls of government. Others distinguished themselves by their books, their research efforts, or their creative genius. Still others became household names because of their achievements as performing artists or sports heroes. But taken together, these unusual individuals reflect the diversity of the nation they called home. They came from every race, ethnic group, socioeconomic class, and region of the United States. Many were born to privilege; others were born to poor parents. All took advantage of their natural gifts to leave a permanent mark on a continental nation. In general, the editors have included individuals, such as Joseph Brodsky, who made major professional or artistic contributions while living in the United States, whether or not they ever actually became American citizens.

Some of the choices of subjects were easy, and many of the names in this book, such as President Richard Nixon, Supreme Court Justice Warren Burger, comedian George Burns, novelist Ralph Ellison, singer Ella Fitzgerald, Nobel laureate Linus Pauling, Secretary of State Dean Rusk, scientist Jonas Salk, slugging outfielder Mickey Mantle, Speaker of the House Tip O'Neill, and First Lady Jacqueline Kennedy Onassis, will be familiar to almost everyone. Similarly, Jerry Garcia of the Grateful Dead will attract wide interest. But this volume also includes persons who were not much in the news during their lifetimes and who are only now receiving the recognition they deserve.

As is the case in any large-scale research effort, *SEAL* depended on the hard work and cooperation of hundreds of contributors, many new to this venture. We acknowledge again the diligent research efforts undertaken by our 229 writers. Resourceful photo editors located photographs for almost every subject. Happily, the editors of this volume all had worked together on similar ventures and chose to do so again. The result of this collaboration is a book that we trust will be useful, reliable, and enjoyable.

In particular, we wish to thank Tara M. Strickland of the Visual Education Corporation in Princeton, New Jersey, who as project editor oversaw the copyediting and proofreading of this volume. Her cooperative spirit, cheerfulness under pressure, and high standards were essential in moving this book to publication. We also wish to thank our longtime collaborator Timothy J. DeWerff, who managed the entire effort from his office at Scribners with his unique combination of wide intelligence, superb judgment, meticulous organization, and reliable good humor. Similarly, Richard H. Gentile has provided valuable insight and advice throughout our many years of collaboration as he has demonstrated time and again his encyclopedic knowledge of American history. Finally, we wish to record our continuing gratitude to Karen Day, the publisher of Charles Scribner's Sons. Her personal commitment to this project has always been the essential ingredient in its success, and everyone who uses this volume will be in her debt.

Kenneth T. Jackson, Editor in Chief
Karen E. Markoe, General Editor
Arnold Markoe, Executive Editor

CONTENTS

The SCRIBNER ENCYCLOPEDIA *of*
AMERICAN LIVES

A

ABBOTT, George Francis (*b*. 25 June 1887 in Forestville, New York; *d*. 31 January 1995 in Miami, Florida), actor, playwright, producer, and director who contributed to more than 100 plays and musicals in his almost eighty-year-long career on the Broadway stage.

Abbott was one of three children born to George Burwell Abbott, who ran a uniform-making business in Salamanca, New York, and May McLaury, a homemaker. In 1898 the family moved to Cheyenne, Wyoming, where Abbott's father, who had gone bankrupt, was appointed a government land agent. Young George (called "Francis" in those days) became familiar with cowboy life. Because of his unruly behavior he was sent to a military academy in Kearney, Nebraska, which straightened his posture and eliminated his antisocial ways. Another setback forced Abbott's father to move the family back east to Hamburg, New York, where Abbott was active in school sports and theatricals at Hamburg High School, from which he graduated in 1907.

In 1911 he graduated from the University of Rochester, where he was again involved in sports and dramatics. He even wrote and staged his own farce, *Perfectly Harmless* (1910). After graduating he studied playwriting from 1911 to 1912 at George Pierce Baker's famous Harvard workshop. The Harvard Dramatic Club later produced one of his student plays. He also won a $100 prize for a one-act play, *The Man in the Manhole* (1912), successfully produced by Boston's Bijou Theatre, which hired him as assistant

manager. After a year, he left to pursue a Broadway career and in 1913 landed a role in *The Misleading Lady,* but the lack of additional opportunities led him to work in vaudeville and as a movie extra. He married his former high school teacher, Ednah Levis, three years his senior, in 1914; she died in 1930, leaving him with one daughter.

The struggling young actor-playwright began working in 1918 as a general factotum for the producer John Golden. With his success as a cowboy named Tex in *Zander the Great* (1923), named one of the year's ten best performances, Abbott began to get noticed as a character actor. His playwriting efforts, usually in collaboration with others, paid off in 1925 with *The Fall Guy,* a breezy hit comedy about New Yorkers cowritten with James Gleason. *The Fall Guy* also launched Abbott's directing career when he took over the staging from Gleason, who was busy elsewhere. Moreover, Abbott was already a respected play doctor for ailing scripts.

Abbott hit pay dirt in 1926 with his staging of *Broadway,* cowritten with Philip Dunning. This hard-boiled, fast-paced, backstage-at-a-nightclub comedy-melodrama, with its local color and 200-plus entrances and exits, established the slick professionalism that came to be called "the Abbott touch." Journalist Maurice Zolotow later described this as "speed. Curtains rise and fall quickly. Actors enter and exit on the run. . . . Lines of dialogue are spit out feverishly. Characters cross in front of one another with dizzying rapidity. Doors are forever being jerked open and slammed

George Abbott, 1954. © BETTMANN/CORBIS

shut." Despite the often frenetic pacing, the actors provided a bedrock of realistic behavior. A royalty conflict with *Broadway's* argumentative producer, Jed Harris, inspired Abbott—despite his lack of taste for the job—to become his own producer on many subsequent projects.

Abbott continued acting until 1934, after which he did not apply greasepaint until a 1955 revival of Thornton Wilder's *The Skin of Our Teeth,* which toured in the USSR. Meanwhile, Hollywood beckoned, and Abbott directed his first film, *The Devil's Candlesticks,* in 1928, but he disliked the tedium of movie directing. In all, he directed or worked as a screenwriter on eleven movies, the best known being *All Quiet on the Western Front* (1930), *Too Many Girls* (1940), *Kiss and Tell* (1945), *Damn Yankees* (1957), and *The Pajama Game* (1958).

Abbott directed many Broadway melodramas in the 1920s and 1930s, including *Chicago* (1926), *Four Walls* (cowritten with Dana Burnet, 1927), *Spread Eagle* (1927), *Lilly Turner* (cowritten with Philip Dunning, 1932), *Heat Lightning* (cowritten with Leon Abrams, 1933), *Small Miracle* (1934), Abbott's own *Ladies' Money* (1934), *Angel Island* (1937), and *Goodbye in the Night* (1940). But he became even more successful with farce and comedy, coauthoring (with John Cecil Holm) and staging the extremely popular

Three Men on a Horse (1935) and directing such hits as *Boy Meets Girl* (1935), *Jumbo* (1935), *Brother Rat* (1936), *Room Service* (1937), and *What a Life* (1938).

Despite these achievements, Abbott's greatest productions of the 1930s and 1940s were musical comedies (although he could not read music). These included his direction of such Richard Rodgers and Lorenz Hart collaborations as *On Your Toes* (musical book coauthored by Abbott, 1936), *The Boys from Syracuse* (book coauthored by Abbott, 1938), *Too Many Girls* (1939), and *Pal Joey* (1940). Other memorable musicals he directed were *Best Foot Forward* (book coauthored with John Cecil Holm, 1941), *On the Town* (1944), *High Button Shoes* (1947), *Where's Charley?* (book by Abbott, 1948), and *Call Me Madam* (1950). The next decade included *A Tree Grows in Brooklyn* (book coauthored with Betty Smith, on whose novel the show was based, 1951), *Me and Juliet* (1953), *The Pajama Game* (codirected with Jerome Robbins; book coauthored with Richard Bissell, 1954), *Damn Yankees* (book coauthored with Douglass Wallop, 1955), *Once upon a Mattress* (1959), and *Fiorello!* (1959), for which he shared the Tony Award and Pulitzer Prize with Jerome Weidman as coauthor of the book. Abbott helped to further the process of integration of elements—book, score, choreography, design—that marks the development of the post–1920s American musical theater.

His work on straight plays was less frequent during the 1940s and 1950s, and only a few were hits. Abbott's only successful musical in the 1960s was *A Funny Thing Happened on the Way to the Forum* (1962), which garnered him his first directing Tony. He remained relatively prolific and directed two hit comedies, *Take Her, She's Mine* (1961) and *Never Too Late* (1962), but most of his shows flopped. Still, his lifetime contributions were significant enough for the Fifty-fourth Street Theater to be named for him in 1965. (It was subsequently demolished).

Abbott's Broadway presence was minimal during the 1970s, and it was during this decade that he directed his first regional theater production—a 1973 revival of *Life with Father* in Seattle—and his first off-off-Broadway play, Lee Kalcheim's *Winning Isn't Everything* (1978). Prior to the latter, he had temporarily left the theater in disgust following the failure of *Music Is,* his 1976 musical adaptation of Shakespeare's *Twelfth Night.* During his absence he wrote a backstage novel, *Tryout* (1979).

Abbott, who in 1982 had been presented with a Kennedy Center Honors Award by President Ronald Reagan, astonished the theater world and earned his second directing Tony in 1983 with his vigorous revival of *On Your Toes,* even overseeing its 1986 production in Los Angeles. He continued to write and direct even as a centenarian. This included a new version of *Broadway* called *Speakeasy* (1987), staged for Cleveland's Great Lakes Theater Festival, which presented a weekend conference in his honor called "Classic Broadway." *Speakeasy*'s move to Broadway, though, failed. Abbott was further feted in 1987 when he received a special Tony honoring his 100th birthday. His final project was *Frankie* (1989), an unsuccessful off-off-Broadway musicalization of the Frankenstein story, although, at 106, he participated as an adviser on the 1994 revival of *Damn Yankees*.

From 1924 to 1972, Broadway never was without at least one, and sometimes as many as seven, Abbott shows. Not until very late in his career did he stage a revival. He was responsible in one way or another for nearly 120 Broadway shows, thirteen of which ran for more than 500 performances, once a sign of hit status.

Abbott epitomized the totally-in-control professional. Blue-eyed, with slicked-down thinning blond hair; six feet, two inches tall; slender; he was always tastefully dressed—even at rehearsals—in a suit and tie. This nonsmoking, near-teetotaler, who made millions at his trade, presented a picture of confidence and ability that helped him in his business and artistic dealings as well as in his active social life, with wealthy Long Islanders, where this advocate of healthy living was a highly reputed croquet player. He also socialized with denizens of Miami, Florida, where he had a home and liked to spend his winters swimming and playing tennis and golf. After his wife's death, he became one of New York's most eligible bachelors, and he was considered an outstanding ballroom dancer, with a flair for the rumba. He married Mary Sinclair in 1946 but the marriage ended in divorce in 1951. In November 1983, at age ninety-five, he married Joy Valderrama, over forty years his junior.

Because of Abbott's aloof demeanor, he was generally referred to as "Mr. Abbott," even among close collaborators, and the term was used as the title of his 1963 autobiography. Despite his towering reputation, he remained open to advice from coworkers; the work came before his ego. He rehearsed with calm and efficiency, treating actors with courtesy but never releasing his autocratic control. Stars who tested his limits were tactfully put in their place. When pushed too far, however, he could be a severe whip cracker. His rehearsals were businesslike affairs devoid of the intellectual probing that Abbott dismissed as phony in other directors' work. To grab attention in large theaters, he often stopped rehearsals by blowing a whistle; its relative volume signaled the level of his disturbance.

His productions were known for excellent taste, well-considered musical accompaniment, expert typecasting, rapid but well-balanced pacing, comprehensible speech (he insisted on audible line endings), naturalness of dialogue and action, lack of sentimentality, consistently motivated behavior unmarred by unnecessary emotional introspection, and a deadpan approach to even the most broadly comical material. His primary instincts were commercial

and he was never known for arty effects or intellectual themes. Theater, to Abbott, was a business creating a product that had to earn an income. Abbott's shows offered colorful characters and situations, with smoothly written dialogue that often delighted in clever repartee. He removed whatever threatened to slow down the action or split the audience's focus.

Abbott's plays, whether from his own pen or others, reveled in topical appeal aimed at the widest theatergoing public. Controversial material was usually avoided or toned down. Still, he sometimes broke new ground, as with *On Your Toes*, the first musical comedy to seriously introduce ballet (choreographed by George Balanchine); *The Boys from Syracuse*, Broadway's first musical comedy based on Shakespeare (*The Comedy of Errors;* 1938); *Pal Joey*, which had an amoral nightclub rogue for its hero; *The Pajama Game*, with its subject of labor unrest; *New Girl in Town* (1957), inspired by Eugene O'Neill's dark drama about a prostitute; and *A Funny Thing Happened on the Way to the Forum*, a faithful musicalization of classical Roman comedy.

When he was producing, he sought to keep costs low—he was a notorious penny-pincher—and preferred actors whose salary demands were reasonable. This often led him to bypass stars in favor of lesser-known players, thereby benefiting the play by removing the distraction of the star's charisma while also furthering various young actors' careers. In fact, the youth factor in his casts was one of his chief characteristics. Among the many actors who went on to stardom after being discovered by Abbott—who confessed to a "Pygmalion complex"—were Bob Fosse, Gene Kelly, Nancy Walker, Shirley Booth, Carol Haney, Eddie Bracken, Kirk Douglas, Eddie Albert, Garson Kanin, Shirley MacLaine, Liza Minelli, and Sam Levene, among others. In the 1930s, so many actors were used regularly by Abbott that they came to be considered part of an informal Abbott Acting (or "Stock") Company. He was similarly prone to giving new writers, composers, designers, and choreographers career-generating opportunities. One of the most prominent of his protégés was director-producer Hal Prince, with whom he long shared an office in Rockefeller Center.

It is unlikely that anyone will ever approach the length and abundance of George Abbott's career on Broadway, which lasted close to eighty years. When he died in his sleep of a stroke, he was 107. By this time, Broadway had moved in new directions, but Abbott's legacy continued to survive.

★

Abbott's autobiography is *"Mister Abbott"* (1963). The most comprehensive surveys of his work are in Samuel L. Leiter, *From Belasco to Brook: Representative Directors of the English-Speaking*

Stage (1991); Samuel L. Leiter, *The Great Stage Directors: 100 Distinguished Careers of the Theatre* (1994); Tom Mikotowicz's essay in John W. Frick and Stephen M. Vallillo, eds., *Theatrical Directors: A Biographical Dictionary* (1994); and Lewis Shelton, "George Abbott and the Total Theatre Perspective of Directing," *Journal of American Theatre and Drama* (winter 2000). Earlier articles include Maurice Zolotow, "Broadway's Most Successful Penny-Pincher," *Saturday Evening Post* (29 Jan. 1955). Doctoral dissertations include Dean William Hess, *A Critical Analysis of the Musical Theatre Productions of George Abbott* (1976), and Robert MacLennan, *The Comedy of George Abbott* (1975). An obituary is in the *New York Times* (1 Feb. 1995).

SAMUEL L. LEITER

AGNEW, Spiro Theodore   (*b.* 9 November 1918 in Baltimore, Maryland; *d.* 17 September 1996 in Berlin, Maryland), vice president of the United States who resigned and pleaded no contest to charges of tax evasion.

Agnew grew up in a Democratic household. His father, Theodore Spiro Agnew, whose name was originally Anagnostopolous, emigrated from Greece in 1897, and his mother, Margaret Akers, was a native of Virginia. Theodore

Spiro T. Agnew. LIBRARY OF CONGRESS

Agnew owned a large restaurant, the Piccadilly, in downtown Baltimore and was a national leader in the American Hellenic Educational Progressive Association. In his youth Spiro Agnew was a member of the Sons of Pericles, which was affiliated with his father's Greek fraternal organization.

Attending Baltimore public schools, including Public School 69, Garrison Junior High School, and Forest Park High School, Agnew graduated in February 1937. He then studied as a chemistry major at Johns Hopkins University until 1939, when he transferred to the University of Baltimore Law School, taking night classes while working as a clerk and assistant underwriter for the Maryland Casualty Company.

In September 1941 Agnew was drafted into the U.S. Army. After training at Camp Croft, South Carolina, he attended Officer Candidate School at Fort Knox, Kentucky, where he was commissioned a second lieutenant on 24 May 1942. Serving as a company commander in the Tenth Armored Division, Agnew spent almost half of the war in combat and earned a Bronze Star. On 27 May 1942 he married Elinor Isabel Judefind. They had four children.

Upon returning from World War II in 1945, Agnew completed his law studies in 1947. He passed the bar in the same year and moved with his family to the Baltimore suburb of Towson, where he opened a law office. Like many other second-generation Americans of this era, Agnew distanced himself from the Old Country. He converted from the Greek Orthodox religion of his parents to Episcopalian. When he moved to the suburbs, Agnew asked others to address him as "Ted" rather than his given name.

It was in the suburbs that Agnew became politically active. At the urging of a senior law associate, who advised that the minority party would offer less competition and more opportunity for political advancement, he switched to the Republican party. He became active in the local Kiwanis Club, the Veterans of Foreign Wars post, and the Towson Parent Teacher Association. In 1956 he played a leadership role in the success of a referendum that established home rule for Baltimore County. As a result of these efforts, in 1957 Agnew was named to the county's zoning board of appeals, which dealt with the suburbs but not the city of Baltimore. His reappointment to the board in 1961 was denied by the county council's Democratic majority, but the slight attracted public sympathy for Agnew. Running for Baltimore County executive in 1962, he prevailed despite a Democratic registration edge of about four to one.

As the first Republican county executive in sixty-seven years, Agnew gained statewide prominence. During his four-year term he improved the county's water and sewage systems, built new schools, approved higher salaries for teachers, established a human rights commission, and enacted a public accommodations law. Agnew ran for governor of Maryland in 1966 and defeated the segregationist

Democrat George M. Mahoney to become only the fifth Republican chief executive in the state's history. Many African Americans and liberal white Democrats crossed party lines to support Agnew.

In his first year as governor Agnew fulfilled most of his campaign promises. He obtained a graduated income tax, enacted the first statewide open housing law south of the Mason-Dixon line, repealed the state law banning racial intermarriage, increased state aid to antipoverty programs, signed a more liberal abortion law, and promoted tough water pollution regulations. He appointed more blacks to senior governmental roles than any previous Maryland governor.

Agnew also became a player in national politics. An early leader of the movement to draft Nelson Rockefeller for the 1968 Republican presidential nomination, Agnew was embarrassed when the New York governor dropped out of the race on 21 March without giving him advance notice. After this snub Agnew began positioning himself to the right. In April he had more than 200 black students arrested for refusing to leave the state capitol. During the rioting in Baltimore in 1968 following the assassination of the Reverend Martin Luther King, Jr., Agnew rebuked the city's moderate black leadership for their silence. Agnew also renounced the Reverend Ralph Abernathy's march on Washington, D.C., that year. In the process Agnew moved from liberal Republican to law-and-order conservative.

When Rockefeller changed his mind and became an active candidate, Agnew shunned him and delivered the nominating speech for Nixon at the Republican National Convention on 7 August 1968. His speech hailed Nixon as "the one man whom history has so clearly thrust forward, the one whom all America will recognize as a man whose time has come." The next day Nixon chose Agnew as his running mate. Agnew acknowledged that his name was "not exactly a household word" and said that Nixon's phone call was "a bolt from the blue." Agnew, tall and well-groomed, was chosen partly because of his ethnic background and crossover appeal to traditionally Democratic constituencies.

In the fall campaign Agnew was Nixon's hatchet man. Agnew attacked the Democratic presidential nominee Hubert H. Humphrey as "soft on communism" and "squishy soft" on Vietnam. Agnew, who was unaccustomed to national press coverage, was embarrassed by reports that he used ethnic slurs while traveling on his campaign plane. The Democrats, seeking to make Agnew's inexperience a campaign issue, aired a television commercial in which a voice asked, "Spiro Agnew for vice president?" This was followed by laughter, then the narrator's voice said, "This would be serious if it wasn't so funny."

After Nixon's victory, Agnew became the administration's most visible and controversial spokesperson. Law and order was a recurring theme in his speeches. "I will not lower my voice until the restoration of sanity and order will allow a quiet voice to be heard again," he told a Philadelphia, Pennsylvania, audience in November 1969. That same month he delivered a speech in Des Moines, Iowa, that labeled television commentators "a tiny fraternity of privileged men elected by no one and enjoying a monopoly sanctioned and licensed by the government." He later referred to critics of the Vietnam War as "an effete corps of impudent snobs" and "sunshine patriots."

Agnew's attacks on political opponents were harsh and personal. During the 1970 midterm election he referred to the liberal New York senator Charles E. Goodell as "the Christine Jorgensen of Republican politics" (Jorgensen had gained notoriety for a sex-change operation). He denounced the Republican representative from California Paul McCloskey as "a Benedict Arnold" for challenging Nixon's renomination in the 1972 New Hampshire primary. In November 1972 Nixon and Agnew were easily reelected. As Nixon became entangled in the Watergate controversy, Agnew loomed as the heir apparent.

Early in his second term, in 1973, Agnew became the subject of a federal investigation. The Justice Department obtained evidence that Agnew had been accepting illegal cash payments from contractors for more than a decade, while he was county executive, governor, and vice president. With Nixon's future in doubt because of Watergate, Attorney General Elliot Richardson plea-bargained with Agnew to prevent him from moving up to the presidency. On 10 October 1973 Agnew resigned as vice president. He soon pleaded no contest to a single count of tax evasion in a federal courtroom in Baltimore. Agnew was placed on three years probation and was fined $10,000. He was disbarred in May 1974. Even though the government released overwhelming proof that he took bribes and kickbacks, Agnew vehemently denied all charges except tax evasion.

"My decision to resign and enter a plea of nolo contendere rests on my firm belief that the public interest requires swift disposition of the problems which are facing me," Agnew said in the courtroom. "I admit that I did receive payments during the year 1967, which were not expended for political purposes and that, therefore, these payments were income taxable to me in that year and that I so knew."

Agnew blamed Nixon for his downfall. "We were never close," he said in 1976. "I haven't seen him and have no desire to see him." But when Nixon died in 1994, Agnew went to his funeral. "I decided after twenty years of resentment to put it all aside," he said.

After leaving office Agnew split his time between homes in Rancho Mirage, California, and Ocean City, Maryland, working as an international business broker. Among his chief benefactors was King Faisal of Saudi Arabia. In May 1995 Agnew returned to the Capitol for the unveiling of his vice presidential bust outside the Senate chamber. He said he understood that some people felt it was "an honor I don't deserve." But, he continued, the sculpture "has less to do with Spiro Agnew than the office I held." Agnew died of leukemia at the age of seventy-seven and is buried in Delaney Valley Memorial Gardens in Timonium, Maryland.

★

Agnew's political memoir is *Go Quietly . . . or Else* (1980). Jules Witcover, *White Knight: The Rise of Spiro Agnew* (1972), is the most authoritative biography, and Richard M. Cohen and Witcover, *A Heartbeat Away: The Investigation and Resignation of Vice President Spiro T. Agnew* (1974), is the best study of Agnew's fall from grace. Agnew is profiled in the *Philadelphia Inquirer* (11 Oct. 1973). An obituary is in the *New York Times* (18 Sept. 1996).

STEVE NEAL

ALLEN, Mel(vin) (*b.* 14 February 1913 in Johns, Alabama; *d.* 16 June 1996 in Greenwich, Connecticut), Hall of Fame sports broadcaster whose decades-long association with the New York Yankees baseball franchise made him known as the "voice of the Yankees."

Melvin Allen Israel was the son of Julius Israel and Anna Lieb, Russian immigrants who owned a general store. He had one brother and one sister. Allen was an excellent student, graduating at age fifteen from Philips High School in Birmingham, Alabama. There he played both football and baseball. He might have become a professional athlete,

but a childhood accident broke both legs and left him a slow runner.

At age nineteen Allen received his B.A. degree in political science from the University of Alabama. He was student manager of the football team and public-address announcer at football games. He admired the radio style of Graham McNamee. In his senior year he was awarded a speech "gradership," which later became a teaching position when his professor became ill. After graduation Allen attended law school at the University of Alabama. He received his LL.B. in 1936 at the age of twenty-three. In 1935, while still in law school, he taught speech at the university. During this time he was also the radio announcer of football games for the University of Alabama's Crimson Tide on a Birmingham station that was an affiliate of CBS in New York City.

On a Christmas vacation in New York in 1936, Allen met a friend at CBS who talked him into auditioning for a radio job with the network. He won the job over a field of twenty other applicants, and he began working as a staff announcer the next year. At the request of CBS, he shortened his name to Mel Allen; he had the change legalized in 1943. Allen was assigned to various jobs at CBS, including disk jockey, news announcer, and announcer for the bands of Tommy Dorsey, Glenn Miller, and Benny Goodman, when these bands performed in New York hotels.

Allen's career received a boost in 1939 when he covered the Vanderbilt Cup boat races from an airplane for radio audiences, displaying impressive knowledge of the races and a quick wit. He also reported on tennis matches being

Mel Allen, in the broadcast booth at New York's Yankee Stadium, 1990. AP/WIDE WORLD PHOTOS

held on Long Island, New York, while in an airplane, further enhancing his reputation as a promising announcer. Ironically, Allen was leery of flying; he would read detective novels to divert his attention on commercial flights for years to come.

Allen's association with baseball began in 1939, when he began broadcasting New York Yankee baseball games with Arch McDonald and New York Giant games with Joe Bolton. By 1943 he had broadcast three World Series and had become one of the most popular broadcasters in baseball. His career was interrupted by World War II. In 1943 Allen entered the U.S. Army as a private. He eventually rose to the rank of staff sergeant. Nevertheless, Allen continued to hone his broadcasting skills during the war, as he was assigned to the Armed Forces Radio Service and became a featured announcer for the "Army Hour" broadcasts.

In 1946 Allen became a full-time broadcaster for the Yankees. He quickly perfected his unique style of broadcasting. Showing an emotional and infectious enthusiasm, he began each game with an energetic "Hello everybody!" He gave nicknames to players that quickly captured the imagination of fans: Phil Rizzuto was "Scooter," for his quickness; Joe DiMaggio was the "Yankee Clipper," a reference to fast and majestic sailing ships; Tommy Henrich was "Old Reliable," for clutch hitting. Allen also developed numerous expressions that would be associated with him for years after, such as "How about that?," which he used to highlight surprisingly good plays, and "Going, going, gone!," his call for home runs.

Although Allen openly rooted for the Yankees, he gave due praise to players of other teams. Allen also showed enthusiasm for the Yankee broadcast sponsors. For instance, a home run would be called a "Ballantine blast" or a "White Owl wallop," sayings that served to increase sales of beer and cigars, respectively. Allen's response to criticism of his display of emotion was that he was showing fans his appreciation for being at the ballpark and his respect for those at home or work who could only listen to the game.

Allen was known for his accuracy in describing people or events. Rizzuto, who became a broadcaster after his playing career ended, noted that Allen would correct any broadcaster, even while on the air, if he thought a mistake had been made. Another hallmark of his announcing style was his copious use of statistics, which were usually provided by his brother Larry, who worked as Allen's longtime statistician.

By the 1940s Allen, having been involved in many of the team's most memorable events, was known as the "voice of the Yankees." For instance, on two occasions he introduced famed ballplayers who were saying goodbye to Yankee fans. The first of these took place on 4 July 1939, when beloved first baseman Lou Gehrig, who had recently retired and who had just learned that he was dying of amyotrophic lateral sclerosis (ALS), was honored in a ceremony at Yankee Stadium. The second took place in 1948 when legendary player Babe Ruth announced his retirement. Allen also witnessed notable on-the-field events during his tenure, such as DiMaggio's fifty-six game hitting streak in 1941 and the home-run duel in 1961 between Roger Maris and Mickey Mantle. In all, Allen was the announcer for twenty World Series and twenty-four all-star games.

Allen worked well with others who joined him in the broadcast booth. For example, he helped Rizzuto make the transition from Yankee shortstop to broadcaster, and his energetic style meshed well with the unemotional approach of Walter "Red" Barber when Barber came from the Brooklyn Dodgers to the Yankees. Allen and Barber, who worked together on Yankee broadcasts from 1954 to 1964, were known as "fire and ice," respectively. In 1978 the pair became the first two inductees into the Baseball Hall of Fame's broadcasting wing.

Allen was personally impressive. He stood over six-feet, one-inch tall, weighed 195 pounds, and had perfect posture, engaging speech, and a warm smile. He often said he would like to marry if he "found the right girl," but that never happened. He was a lifelong bachelor.

After the 1964 season, the Yankees did not renew Allen's contract. Controversy clouds this incident. Close observers note that the Yankees were in the process of being sold; therefore, many high-salaried coaches, managers, administrators, and broadcasters saw their contracts go unrenewed, perhaps to make the price of the team more affordable to prospective buyers. Between 1965 and 1978 Allen was absent from the broadcast booth for all but one year—1968, when he was the announcer for the Cleveland Indians.

But Allen's broadcast career was not yet finished. In 1977 he was hired to host the syndicated TV show *This Week in Baseball*, a job he would hold until his death in 1996. Then, in 1978 George Steinbrenner bought the Yankees and immediately brought Allen back on the Yankees' payroll. Allen subsequently broadcast forty games a year for eight years over SportsChannel, a local cable channel. From 1986 to 1996 Allen also hosted the TV show *Yankees Magazine,* which aired on the Madison Square Garden regional television network.

Allen lived with his sister, Ester Kaufman, after her husband's death in 1977. He died of natural causes on 16 June 1996 and was buried in Temple Beth El cemetery in Stamford, Connecticut.

On 27 August 1950 the Yankees honored him with a day of appreciation at Yankee Stadium; he donated his entire financial award to college-scholarship funds. It was a fitting gesture from a man whose gracious air and colorful commentary made him synonymous with Yankee baseball during the middle decades of the twentieth century. A plaque in Yankee Stadium, in its old center field region, honors Allen's contribution to Yankee history.

★

Allen wrote two memoirs that offer a wealth of information about his life and career: *It Takes Heart,* written with Frank Graham, Jr. (1959), and *You Can't Beat the Hours: A Long, Loving Look at Big-League Baseball, Including Some Yankees I Have Known,* written with Ed Fitzgerald. Details about his career are also on view at the National Baseball Hall of Fame in Cooperstown, New York. Obituaries are in the *New York Times* and *Los Angeles Times* (both 17 June 1996).

LAWRENCE ROCKS

ANDREWS, Maxene Angelyn (*b.* 3 January 1916 in Minneapolis, Minnesota; *d.* 21 October 1995 in Hyannis, Massachusetts), singer who had a long recording and performing career as a member of the Andrews Sisters.

Andrews was the second daughter of Peter Andrews and Olga Sollie, café owners in Minneapolis. She was four and a half years younger than her sister LaVerne Sophie and two years older than her sister Patricia Marie. The sisters began singing together at talent contests, and after winning a contest at the Orpheum Theater in Minneapolis in April 1931, they were hired by the bandleader Larry Rich. They toured with Rich from the summer of 1931 to the summer of 1932, after which they sang with big bands. While working with Leon Belasco's Orchestra, they made their first recordings in March 1937, but when Belasco disbanded his group, the sisters were stranded in New York City. They

planned to give up show business and return to Minnesota, but a one-night job singing over the radio earned them a contract with Decca Records. Their first Decca single flopped, but their second, a novelty recording of an English-language version of the Yiddish show tune "Bei Mir Bist du Schoen," became a surprise hit, topping the charts in January 1938.

On the strength of their hit the sisters began performing live and in 1939 were being broadcast on the radio. Their next major hit came in early 1939 with the nonsense song "Hold Tight"; during that year they also scored with a series of upbeat tunes, many of which had an ethnic flavor, including "Beer Barrel Polka," "Well All Right," "Yodelin' Jive" (on which they were paired with Bing Crosby), and "Say 'Si, Si.'" In 1940 they signed with Universal Pictures, which used them in a series of low-budget films through 1945, starting with *Argentine Nights* (1940). In their second film, *Buck Privates* (1941), they performed "Boogie Woogie Bugle Boy," which became a signature song for them, and revived "(I'll Be with You) In Apple Blossom Time," their next major hit.

In March 1941 Maxene married Lou Levy, the group's personal manager. She and Levy adopted two children and divorced in 1951. With the U.S. entry into World War II in December 1941, the Andrews Sisters began making frequent appearances at military bases. When their recording activities were curtailed by the ban called by the musicians union in August 1942, they spent more time in Hollywood, appearing in three films in 1942 and another three in 1943. In the fall of 1943, a year ahead of its competitors RCA Victor and Columbia, Decca settled with the union, freeing its artists to record, and the Andrews Sisters were again paired with Bing Crosby for the million-selling "Pistol

Maxene Andrews *(left)* and her sisters Patty *(center)* and LaVerne *(right)*. ARCHIVE PHOTOS

Packin' Mama." Their own "Shoo-Shoo Baby" topped the charts in January 1944, and they scored a series of hits with Crosby throughout the year, including "(There'll Be a) Hot Time in the Town of Berlin (When the Yanks Go Marching In)" (number one in October), "Is You Is or Is You Ain't (Ma' Baby)," and "Don't Fence Me In" (number one in December and a million-seller). They also released three films and, in December, began starring in their own radio series, *The Andrews Sisters' Eight-to-the-Bar Ranch.*

Their success continued in 1945, with the million-selling "Rum and Coca-Cola" hitting number one in February and becoming the year's biggest hit; they also had two more major hits with Crosby, "Ac-Cent-Tchu-Ate the Positive" and "Along the Navajo Trail." After the end of the war they turned their attention largely away from movies and toward personal appearances abroad and on the emerging nightclub circuit, while continuing to work in radio. Their recording career cooled slightly, but they still scored major hits during the late 1940s, including the million-selling "South America, Take It Away" with Crosby, "Rumors Are Flying" with Les Paul, and the million-selling "Christmas Island" with Guy Lombardo and His Royal Canadians (all in 1946); "Near You" and "Civilization (Bongo, Bongo, Bongo)" with Danny Kaye (both in 1947); "Toolie Oolie Doolie (The Yodel Polka)" and "Underneath the Arches" (both in 1948); and the million-selling number-one song "I Can Dream, Can't I?" (1949). Their final number-one hit came with "I Wanna Be Loved" in June 1950.

The Andrews Sisters' success as a recording act declined in the early 1950s, and when they left Decca at the end of 1953, Patty, who had been recording solo in recent years, formally left the group and launched her own career, signing with Capitol Records. Maxene and LaVerne persevered as a duo for a time, then each tried performing solo. During this period Maxene worked with the composer Frank Loesser on songs he was writing for his musical *The Most Happy Fella.* Her recordings of several of these songs, her first as a soloist, eventually were released on the compact disc *An Evening with Frank Loesser* in 1992.

The Andrews Sisters reunited in 1956. They recorded for Capitol Records until 1961, when they moved to Dot Records, where they stayed until 1965, but their main income came from live appearances. LaVerne was stricken with cancer in 1966 (she died in 1967), and a substitute was hired to perform in her place. In 1968 the Andrews Sisters broke up again. Patty continued to perform, but Maxene retired from music and began teaching at the Lake Tahoe Paradise College of Fine Arts.

The Andrews Sisters enjoyed renewed popularity after Bette Midler revived "Boogie Woogie Bugle Boy" as a hit in 1973, and Maxene reunited with Patty for the Broadway musical *Over Here!,* which opened on 6 March 1974 and ran for 341 performances. The sisters permanently sepa-

rated after the show closed, but Maxene stayed in music, launching a solo career. In 1985 she released her debut solo album, *Maxene: An Andrews Sister.* With Bill Gilbert she wrote a memoir, *Over Here, Over There: The Andrews Sisters and the USO Stars in World War II,* which was published in 1993. She returned to musical theater with the off-Broadway musical *Swingtime Canteen,* which opened on 14 March 1995, but while on vacation from the show she died of a heart attack. She is buried in Forest Lawn Cemetery in Glendale, California.

Maxene Andrews's accomplishments are inevitably combined with those of her sisters. Employing a distinctive vocal harmony style that drew upon the exuberant, dance-oriented arrangements of swing music, and with a frisky sense of humor, the Andrews Sisters helped popularize a variety of musical genres within popular music, including many ethnic forms as well as boogie-woogie. As entertainers, they defined the exuberant 1940s style that maintained morale and helped win World War II. Though she never achieved widespread popularity apart from the group, Maxene, the most articulate and personable of the sisters, successfully forged a career as a singer, musical-comedy performer, and author long after the group's heyday.

★

Over Here, Over There: The Andrews Sisters and the USO Stars in World War II (1993), written by Maxene Andrews with Bill Gilbert, is, as its title suggests, not merely a memoir of a particular period in the Andrews Sisters' career but also an examination of other entertainers; nevertheless, it contains useful biographical information about Maxene Andrews. John Sforza, *Swing It! The Andrews Sisters Story* (2000), is a long overdue biography of the sisters that is thorough and sympathetic. The longest and most comprehensive article on them is William J. Ruhlmann, "The Andrews Sisters: Three Sides to Every Story," Goldmine (20 Jan. 1995), which is based on interviews with Maxene and Patty, Lou Levy, and the Andrews Sisters' musical director, Vic Schoen. A more succinct version is in the liner notes to the Andrew Sisters' CD *Their All-Time Greatest Hits* (1994). There is an obituary in the *New York Times* (23 Oct. 1995).

WILLIAM J. RUHLMANN

ANFINSEN, Christian Boehmer (*b.* 26 March 1916 in Monessen, Pennsylvania; *d.* 14 May 1995 in Randallstown, Maryland), biochemist who shared the 1972 Nobel Prize in chemistry with Sanford Moore and William Stein for his discovery of the connection between the primary and tertiary structure of enzymes.

Anfinsen was born in a small town near Pittsburgh to Christian Anfinsen, an engineer and immigrant from Norway, and Sophie Rasmussen, a homemaker also of Norwegian heritage. After attending local schools, Anfinsen re-

Christian Anfinsen. AP/WIDE WORLD PHOTOS

ceived a bachelor's degree at Swarthmore College in 1937 and a master's degree at the University of Pennsylvania in 1939. After completing his master's degree, he received a fellowship from the American Scandinavian Foundation to spend a year at the Carlsberg Laboratory in Copenhagen, Denmark. Returning to the United States in 1940, he entered Harvard University, where he earned his doctorate in biochemistry in 1943. On 29 November 1941 he married Florence Bernice Kenenger, with whom he had three children.

In 1943 Anfinsen became an assistant professor of biological chemistry at Harvard. Taking a leave from Harvard from 1944 to 1946, he worked in the U.S. Office of Scientific Research and Development, then in the biochemical division of the Medical Nobel Institute in Sweden as an American Cancer Society senior fellow. In 1946 he returned to Harvard to take a position as associate professor, remaining until 1950. Anfinsen joined the staff of the National Institutes of Health in Bethesda, Maryland, in 1950 and until 1962 was the director of the Laboratory of Cellular Physiology and Metabolism. From 1962 to 1982 he headed the Laboratory of Chemical Biology at the National Institute of Arthritis, Metabolism, and Digestive Diseases in Bethesda, Maryland.

Anfinsen received the Rockefeller Foundation Public Service Award in 1954 and a Guggenheim fellowship for

research at the Weizmann Institute of Science in Israel in 1958. Between 1962 and 1982 he received several honorary degrees and held professorships at several universities. He was a member of the Royal Danish Academy, president of the American Society of Biological Chemistry, a member of the Board of Governors of the Weizmann Institute of Science, a member of the U.S. National Academy of Sciences, and a member of the American Academy of Arts and Sciences. He was an editor of the magazine *Advances in Protein Chemistry* and served on the editorial boards of the *Journal of Biological Chemistry, Biopolymers,* and the *Proceedings of the National Academy of Sciences.*

Anfinsen's primary research was devoted to studying the structure and function of enzymes, the proteins that promote biochemical reactions. He was the quintessential protein chemist, a man acutely aware of both the chemical and biological sides of the field. He began an experimental study of protein biosynthesis in the late 1940s, before the structure of DNA was known. He later diversified his activities in a more chemical direction in the mid-1950s, when a large supply of the bovine enzyme pancreatic ribonuclease became available. In the late 1960s he studied the structure and function of many proteins with a particular interest in nuclease, the enzyme that breaks down nucleic acids. His research determined how a particular set of amino acids configure in a way that results in the active form of the enzyme.

Anfinsen shared the Nobel Prize in chemistry with Sanford Moore and William Stein in 1972 while Anfinsen was chief of the Laboratory of Chemical Biology at the National Institutes of Health. The prize was awarded for pioneering work relating to the structure and biological function of the enzyme ribonuclease. Stein and Moore concentrated on the sequencing of the ribonuclease chain, only the second complete sequence of a protein yet determined at that time. Anfinsen and his team concentrated on the effects of the enzyme's structure on its catalytic properties. He ascertained how the ribonuclease molecule folds to form the characteristic three-dimensional structure that is compatible with its function. In other words, he discovered the connection between the primary and tertiary structures of enzymes.

To accomplish this Anfinsen observed a complete ribonuclease molecule under a variety of conditions, establishing that the tertiary structure of active ribonuclease arises because it is the most stable arrangement of its amino acids under normal physiological conditions. One modification he experimented with was the reduction of the four disulfide bonds in the native molecule to eight sulphydryl groups, with the understanding that sulphydryl groups can be reoxidized back to the disulphide form. Anfinsen left the reduced enzyme solution out in the air overnight. By the following day almost all of the catalytic activity had returned, meaning that the protein had reformed its native structure unaided. He concluded that all the information necessary to conserve the randomly coiled peptide chain into its unique, biologically active structure was contained in the sequence of amino-acids residue in the chain. This was the final answer to the last step in protein biosynthesis. Anfinsen's result was confirmed later in dozens of papers from his own laboratories and in thousands of papers from other laboratories.

Anfinsen authored some 200 original scientific articles. His seminal work, *The Molecular Basis of Evolution,* published in 1959, laid out the general outline and basic requirements for the complexity of the evolutionary process. A tall and pleasant-looking man, he divorced his first wife in 1978 and in 1979 married Libby Esther Schulman. With that marriage, he became stepfather to three sons and one daughter.

Anfinsen was a professor of biology at Johns Hopkins University from 1982 until his death. During his later years at Johns Hopkins he began experimenting with proteins of hyperthermophillic (extreme heat-loving) bacteria taken from hydrothermal vents on the floors of the Mediterranean Sea and the Pacific Ocean. He died at the age of seventy-nine of an apparent heart attack at the Northwest Hospital Center in Randallstown.

The work of Anfinsen, Moore, and Stein laid a pathway for future investigations in protein chemistry and opened the door for major breakthroughs involving hundreds of enzymes. Their conclusions have been used in research on various diseases, including cancer, and have provided a prototype for many studies.

★

For brief biological information on Anfinsen see *American Men and Women of Science* (19th ed., 1995–1996). Emily J. McMurray, ed., *Notable Twentieth-Century Scientists,* vol. 1 (1995), includes details on his research work; and Charles R. Cornell, ed., *Biography Index: A Cumulative Index to Biographical Material in Books and Magazines, September 1995 to August 1996* (1996), provides a brief summary of Anfinsen's life and work. An obituary is in the *New York Times* (16 May 1995) and *Nature* (6 July 1995).

MARIA PACHECO

ARCEL, Ray (*b.* 30 August 1899 in Terre Haute, Indiana; *d.* 7 March 1994 in New York City), boxing trainer who handled twenty-two world champions, including Benny Leonard, Barney Ross, Jim Braddock, Tony Zale, Billy Soose, Ezzard Charles, and Roberto Duran.

Arcel was one of two children of David Arcel, a Russian-born Jewish immigrant who worked as a peddler in the fruit and candy business, and Rose Wachsman, a homemaker from Brooklyn, New York. Arcel's mother suffered

Ray Arcel, 1983. AP/WIDE WORLD PHOTOS

from diabetes and died when Arcel was four years old. The family, who had moved to New York City's Lower East Side prior to Rose's death, next moved to East 106th Street in East Harlem, then a predominantly Italian neighborhood. The multiethnic streets of Harlem were where Arcel was introduced to fisticuffs. "You had to fight in those days," he later recalled. "We were the only Jewish family there." Arcel graduated from the academically elite Stuyvesant High School in Manhattan in 1917.

While learning to box at Grupp's Gymnasium on 116th Street near Eighth Avenue, Arcel became the protégé of the Welsh-born trainer Dai Dollings, who worked with champions Ted ("Kid") Lewis, Jack Britton, and Johnny Dundee. Dollings preached the importance of treating each fighter as an individual. "That was the one thing he inspired me with," Arcel recalled. "Everyone's style is different." Arcel's other key mentor was Frank ("Doc") Bagley, manager of heavyweight champion Gene Tunney. Bagley, a legendary "cut man," taught Arcel the art of closing a boxer's wounds during the one-minute break between rounds.

Following the 1920 passage of the Walker Law, which legalized professional boxing in the state of New York, Arcel became one of the city's leading trainers. He seconded three champions in three years: flyweight Frankie Genaro in 1923, bantamweight Abe Goldstein in 1924, and bantamweight Charley Phil Rosenberg in 1925.

From 1925 through 1934, Arcel was partners with the trainer Whitey Bimstein. Stillman's Gym, on Eighth Avenue between Fifty-fourth and Fifty-fifth Streets, near Madison Square Garden, became their headquarters. Together, they handled junior welterweight champion Jackie ("Kid") Berg, middleweight champion Lou Brouillard, and bantamweight champion Sixto Escobar, among countless other champions and contenders. While Bimstein was gregarious, Arcel was, as A. J. Liebling put it, "severe and decisive, like a teacher in a Hebrew school."

In 1931, when former lightweight champion Benny Leonard, age thirty-five, was forced out of a six-year retirement by financial setbacks suffered as a result of the stock market crash of 1929, Leonard asked Arcel to train him for a comeback. Arcel always considered Leonard the epitome of a great boxer. "His main asset was his ability to think," said Arcel, for whom boxing was always the triumph of "brains over brawn." Arcel seconded Leonard in over a dozen fights in small venues, building to Leonard's 1932 loss in Madison Square Garden at the hands of future welterweight champion Jimmy McLarnin.

Arcel handled thirteen opponents of the heavyweight champion Joe Louis, earning the nickname "The Meat Wagon" because he so frequently dragged Louis's unconscious victims from the ring. After looking across at Arcel for the fifth or sixth time, Louis famously asked before the start of a bout: "You here again?" Arcel simply burst out laughing. While working in heavyweight champion Ezzard Charles's corner in 1950, Arcel finally earned a victory over Louis. "As glad as I was that Ezzard beat Joe," Arcel recalled, "I was sad for Joe."

Moving into the promotional end of boxing, Arcel, in partnership with two of his colleagues, created *The Saturday Night Fights,* which aired weekly on the ABC television network, starting in January 1953. This put Arcel and his partners in competition with the International Boxing Club (IBC), controlled by Jim Norris of Madison Square Garden. Norris's group, which ran boxing shows on rival networks, was associated with the organized crime elements that had a stranglehold on boxing in the 1950s. Returning from Yom Kippur services at a Boston synagogue on 19 September 1953, Arcel was struck on the head with a lead pipe by an unseen assailant. He had round-the-clock police protection during the nineteen days he was hospitalized following the attack. Arcel soon returned to work on his television series, but it went off the air in January 1955 when he lost his sponsor. Discouraged by the state of boxing, Arcel accepted a job offer from the referee Harry Kessler, founder of the Meehanite Metal Corporation where

Arcel worked as a purchasing agent for the next seventeen years.

In 1972 Arcel, age seventy-three, was lured back into boxing by the wealthy Panamanian manager Carlos Eleta, whose fighter, Alfonso ("Peppermint") Frazer, was challenging for the junior welterweight title. Arcel traveled to Panama, where he donned a disguise to spy on the secret training sessions of Frazer's opponent. After Frazer won the crown, Eleta called on Arcel to help with a young lightweight named Roberto Duran. Together with the veteran trainer Freddie Brown, Arcel took Duran to the lightweight championship in 1972 and a highly publicized June 1980 victory over Sugar Ray Leonard for the welterweight championship. Arcel was also in Duran's corner in November 1980 when Duran, after being ridiculed by Leonard in the ring, quit in the middle of the eighth round, saying, "No más!" (Spanish for "no more!"). Arcel's ring career ended on a high note in June 1982 when he worked in heavyweight champion Larry Holmes's corner during Holmes's victory over challenger Gerry Cooney.

Arcel's first wife, Hazel Masterson, whom he had married in the mid-1930s, died in 1946. Their adopted daughter died in 1990. On 12 August 1954, Arcel married Stephanie Howard, an actress who later worked in the fashion industry; they did not have children. In his later years Arcel lived on Lexington Avenue in Manhattan. Arcel died of leukemia at the Beth Israel Medical Center in Manhattan. His ashes were spread on a hillside in Bucks County, Pennsylvania.

Dapper, soft-spoken, and scholarly, Arcel was a rare gentleman in a brutal sport. Serving as his fighters' psychologist, father figure, friend, and teacher, Arcel often said, "There wasn't one fighter I worked with that ever got hurt. At least not with me in his corner." With six decades at the pinnacle of his profession, Arcel was a gifted storyteller and a living encyclopedia of boxing whose intimate recollections of ring legends from Jack Dempsey and Joe Louis to Benny Leonard and Roberto Duran were incomparable in their range and insight.

★

Arcel wrote an unpublished memoir that is the source for much of the personal information cited. Ronald K. Fried, *Corner Men: Great Boxing Trainers* (1991), devotes a chapter to Arcel, as does Dave Anderson, *In This Corner: Great Boxing Trainers Talk About Their Art* (1991). *New York Times* columns by Anderson and Red Smith during the 1970s and early 1980s also capture much of Arcel's personal story and accounts of boxing history. A description of Arcel's influence on Roberto Duran can be found in Jerry Izenberg, "Boxing's Last Great Trainer," *Sport* (Jan. 1979). An obituary of Arcel is in the *New York Times* (8 Mar. 1994).

RONALD K. FRIED

ASPIN, Les(lie), Jr. (*b.* 21 July 1938 in Milwaukee, Wisconsin; *d.* 21 May 1995 in Washington, D.C.), congressman and noted expert on defense matters who became secretary of defense under President Bill Clinton.

Aspin was the son of Leslie and Marie (Orth) Aspin, immigrants from Yorkshire, England. He attended public schools in Milwaukee, then went to Yale University, graduating with a B.A. degree in 1960. A Rhodes scholarship took him to Oxford University, where he received his M.A. in 1962, and he earned his Ph.D. in economics from the Massachusetts Institute of Technology in 1965. Meanwhile, he had already begun to pursue his interest in politics, working as a staff member to Senator William Proxmire in 1960 and managing his reelection campaign in 1964. He also served as staff assistant to Walter Heller, chair of the President's Council of Economic Advisers (1963).

Having joined the Army Reserve Officers Training Corps (ROTC), Aspin became one of Secretary of Defense Robert McNamara's "whiz kids" during the Vietnam War, rising to the rank of captain and working as a systems analyst for the Pentagon (1966–1968). He then taught economics at Marquette University (1969–1970). He married Maureen Shea in 1969; they had no children and divorced in 1979.

Les Aspin. ARCHIVE PHOTOS

In 1970, Aspin ran for and won election to the U.S. House of Representatives. He transformed Wisconsin's First Congressional District from a safe Republican seat into a Democrat stronghold through twelve consecutive victories (1970–1992). Aspin focused on defense, intelligence, and environmental issues and served on several House committees: Government Operations, Budget, District of Columbia, and Armed Services.

As a member of the House Armed Services Committee for twenty-two years, he earned a reputation as a muckraking gadfly, attacking waste, fraud, and mismanagement at the Pentagon. Aspin's colleagues recognized his expertise on Pentagon policy when they disregarded the seniority system to elect him committee chair (1985–1992). His nonpartisan approach on defense matters did not please House Democrats, however. He nearly lost his chair because of his support for the Reagan administration's military buildup in the 1980s, particularly its development of the MX missile and policy of aiding the Nicaraguan Contras. Aspin took advantage of the end of the cold war and a bold prediction of a quick victory with limited casualties in the Gulf War to solidify his leadership of the committee and defense policymaking process in the House.

In selecting Aspin as his first secretary of defense (20 January 1993–3 February 1994), President Bill Clinton hoped that Aspin would apply his knowledge of the budget process at the Pentagon and on Capitol Hill to achieve substantial savings on defense spending. The president also saw Aspin's commitment to military reform as essential for reshaping U.S. military strategy in the post–cold war era. Aspin, however, failed to live up to his billing. His "bottom-up" review of the military structure and limited cuts in his defense budget for 1994 fell far short of congressional and White House demands. His recommendations for reductions in overall personnel strength caused Pentagon officials to doubt whether the military could fight and win two regional conflicts simultaneously.

Aspin's handling of volatile social issues produced further criticism of his leadership at the Pentagon. He awkwardly mediated a highly divisive public debate between Clinton and the military brass over ending discrimination against homosexuals in the military. The final compromise, a policy dubbed "Don't Ask, Don't Tell," satisfied no one. Under pressure from the Tailhook scandal, in which male naval officers at a Las Vegas convention sexually harassed many female officers, Aspin allowed women to compete for combat roles and appointed the first female service secretary in the U.S. armed forces.

Aspin's inability to determine how to project U.S. power in Bosnia, Haiti, and Somalia contributed to his failure as secretary of defense. After witnessing the dangers of military intervention in Vietnam, Aspin opposed deploying military force in areas that the United States did not understand or on terrain that nullified its firepower; he also was aware that no military operation should be undertaken without broad domestic and international support. Yet he could not distill these lessons into strategy. While he believed that American force could be used effectively to buttress diplomacy, he was never sure of when or where to apply it. He opposed the use of force to help President Jean-Bertrand Aristide assume power in Haiti after local mobs resisted the landing of U.S. troops assigned to restore order at Port-au-Prince. He also opposed the use of ground troops to separate Bosnian Muslims, Serbs, and Croats but favored using high-technology weapons as a feasible option. In Somalia, Aspin's greatest headache, he defended the Clinton administration's decision to change the scope of Operation Restore Hope from humanitarian assistance to nation building. This necessitated disarming rival clans, notably that led by the Somali warlord Mohammed Farah Aideed. In October 1993, eighteen U.S. troops were killed, seventy-eight wounded, and one helicopter pilot captured in a firefight with Aideed's forces. This might have been avoided had Aspin agreed to a request to send armored reinforcements to Somalia a month earlier. As members of Congress called for Aspin's resignation, the beleaguered secretary sparred with the Office of Management and Budget over defense spending cuts. Under the strain of these pressures and health problems, Aspin resigned his post in mid-December 1993.

Aspin left his post on 4 February 1994 and joined the faculty of Marquette University's international studies program in Washington, D.C. In 1994 he served on the Commission on Roles and Missions and chaired the President's Foreign Intelligence Advisory Board. The following year Aspin presided over another commission, Roles and Capabilities of the Intelligence Community. He died in Washington, D.C., from a stroke, a month before his fifty-seventh birthday. He is buried at Wisconsin Memorial Park in Brookfield, Wisconsin.

Aspin's inability to translate his knowledge of defense matters into military strategy and manage the Pentagon can be attributed to three key factors. He lacked the discipline and management skills necessary to control the Pentagon bureaucracy. His overanalysis in rationalizing defense policy, focusing on ambiguities and contractions of policymaking rather than making decisions, undermined his relationship with the Joint Chiefs of Staff, who favored policy formulation and execution based on clear objectives and endgame strategies (Powell Doctrine). No doubt, Aspin's appearance—his stooped shoulders, ill-fitting clothes, thinning hair, and glasses constantly slipping from his nose—reinforced his image as an indecisive university professor unable to satisfy the needs of the nation's top brass. Lastly, Aspin's failure to develop close relationships with

President Clinton, Secretary of State Warren Christopher, and National Security Adviser Anthony Lake limited his clout in the White House and thus cost him the respect of the military. Consequently Aspin, once considered a "thoughtful and prescient" defense expert, left the Pentagon with a reputation as perhaps the worst secretary of defense since James Forrestal.

★

Aspin's papers concentrating on his work in Congress and at the Pentagon are collected at the State Historical Society of Wisconsin at Madison. This compilation, combined with committee reports and articles on defense policy penned by Aspin as well as the *Congressional Quarterly Almanac* and the *Congressional Record,* is extremely helpful in studying Aspin's public career but offers few insights into his private life. For Aspin's thoughts on reshaping American military strategy in the post–cold war era see *The Aspin Papers: Sanctions, Diplomacy, and the War in the Persian Gulf* (1991) and *Defense for a New Era: Lessons on the Gulf War* (1992). Studies that address the confusion and perils regarding military intervention in Haiti, Bosnia, and Somalia during the first year of the Clinton administration include Les Aspin, *Challenges to Values-Based Military Intervention* (1995); Richard N. Haass, *Intervention: The Use of American Military Force in the Post–Cold War World* (1994); Walter Clarke and Jeffrey Herbst, "Somalia and the Future of Humanitarian Intervention," *Foreign Affairs* 75 (Mar.–Apr. 1996): 70–85; and John R. Bolton, "Wrong Turn in Somalia," *Foreign Affairs* 73 (Jan.–Feb. 1994): 56–66. Michael Masiello Curtis, "Phoenix: The House Armed Services Committee Under Les Aspin (1985–1992)" (Ph.D. diss., Johns Hopkins University, 1995), examines Aspin's leadership in the defense policymaking process in the House during the Reagan and Bush administrations. An obituary is in the *New York Times* (22 May 1995).

DEAN FAFOUTIS

ATANASOFF, John Vincent (*b.* 4 October 1903 in Hamilton, New York; *d.* 15 June 1995 in Monrovia, Maryland), inventor of the first automatic digital computer whose breakthrough concepts were critical to the subsequent development of the general-purpose computer during World War II.

Atanasoff was the first of nine children born to Bulgarian immigrant Ivan (John) Atanasoff and Iva Purdy. His father was a college graduate and largely self-taught electrical engineer. His American-born mother was a mathematics teacher. In Atanasoff's youth, the family moved frequently, before relocating to Brewster, Florida, where he attended public school. At a young age, he showed a keen interest in mathematics, stimulated by an obsession with understanding the workings of his father's slide rule.

Atanasoff completed high school in two years, graduating from Mulberry High School in 1920. He spent a year

John Atanasoff. AP/WIDE WORLD PHOTOS

phosphate prospecting to earn money to attend the University of Florida in Gainesville. There he studied electrical engineering and graduated in 1925. He earned a master's degree at Iowa State College in 1926 and married Lura Meeks. The couple had three children.

Atanasoff, a handsome man with bright eyes and wavy hair, of medium height and build, taught at Iowa State College and prepared for his doctorate by studying physics and mathematics. He earned his Ph.D. in theoretical physics at the University of Wisconsin in 1930 while studying the dielectric constant of helium. The project involved solving complicated mathematical problems on a desk calculator.

Atanasoff returned to the Iowa State faculty in 1930 with a new interest: creating a better device to solve complicated mathematical problems. He had the requisite background for the project—degrees in electrical engineering, mathematics, and theoretical physics. His initial work focused on existing mechanical calculators, though he quickly realized their limitations. Attention shifted to the emerging field of electronics and new experiments with vacuum tubes. In 1937 Atanasoff gravitated to an entirely new approach. The device would be electric and it would record in its memory whether a current was on or off. That made it possible to compute using binary numbers instead of the traditional ten-digit decimal system. In 1939 Atanasoff and his graduate student Clifford Berry built a prototype machine in two months. A full-scale machine followed in 1940. Numbers were entered onto punch cards. Vacuum tubes performed the calculations. Capacitors stored the numbers on a memory drum.

The inexpensive device cost less than $6,000 to build and was the size of an office desk. The computer received little public or scientific notice, with one notable exception. John W. Mauchly, a physicist from Ursinus College, visited Atanasoff in 1941 and spent several days reading and viewing Atanasoff's notes and seeing demonstrations of the machine known as the Atanasoff Berry Computer (ABC). The original machine was delicate and had a few problems, although it worked and could solve simultaneous algebraic equations with up to thirty variables. Patent applications were fumbled by university officials and attorneys and not aggressively pushed by Atanasoff. Further work was dropped with the outbreak of World War II.

In 1942 Atanasoff took a scientific job at the Naval Ordnance Laboratory in Washington, D.C., working mostly on ship dynamics. Meanwhile, Mauchly and his graduate student J. Presper Eckert, Jr. sold the U.S. Army on the potential military uses of a computer, and it gave the Mauchly team a contract to build a computer that could quickly calculate ballistic missile trajectories. Work began in July 1943 and was completed two years later. In February 1946, the War Department publicly announced the "first all-electronic general purpose computer ever developed." The machine was known as ENIAC (Electronic Numerical Integrator and Computer). ENIAC was huge, filling an entire room and weighing over thirty tons. It solved in hours problems that previously took years to calculate. Industrial and commercial applications were obvious. Atanasoff was crushed at this development. Since 1941, Mauchly regularly had sought him out for advice, information, and assistance on computer development. Atanasoff believed many of his ideas were incorporated into ENIAC, but could not get details because of national security classifications. The Navy had wanted Atanasoff to build a computer, but the project was dropped with the public announcement of ENIAC.

Atanasoff continued his government career after the war. He received the Navy Distinguished Public Service Award in 1945. In 1949 he became chief scientist for the Army Field Forces in Fort Monroe, Maryland. That year he divorced his wife and married Alice Crosby. In 1952 he became president of his own company, the Ordnance Engineering Corporation in Frederick, Maryland, which was sold to Aerojet General Corporation in 1957. In 1961 he formed Cybernetics, where he pursued a long-time interest of a phonetic alphabet for computers.

Questions emerged over patent rights in the growing computer industry. In 1973 the U.S. Federal Court in Minnesota decided a landmark case that pitted the industry giants Sperry Rand and Honeywell against each other over ENIAC royalties. Sperry Rand, a major computing company that had absorbed a failed company begun by Mauchly and Eckert, was charging others millions in royalties to use ENIAC patents. Honeywell went to federal court to challenge the patents, hiring as a consultant Atanasoff, who saw the lawsuit as an opportunity to legally establish himself as the inventor of the digital computer despite having never filed a patent. The court ruled that Atanasoff invented the first automatic electric computer and that Mauchly and Eckert had derived ideas from him. The decision rendered the ENIAC patents invalid.

The case was important in establishing Atanasoff's initial contributions to a major invention, though he continued to live in relative obscurity. Public recognition was slow to follow, though it was enhanced with the publication of books on the controversy. His awards include several honorary degrees, membership in the Bulgarian Academy of Science (1970), the Computer Pioneer Medal from the Institute of Electrical and Electronic Engineers (1981), and the National Medal of Technology, presented by President George Bush (1990).

Atanasoff died of a stroke at the age of ninety-one. He is buried in Pine Grove Cemetery in Mount Airy, Maryland.

Atanasoff's contributions to the development of the computer were almost forgotten. He built a simple computing machine based on using electricity and binary numbers. His purpose was simple: build a better calculator. It took a war and a government-funded research team three years to take those ideas and build the first general-purpose computer. Who invented the computer is arguable, but Atanasoff's critical contribution is not.

★

Atanasoff's papers, technical notes, invention records, and federal trial documents are in the Special Collections Department, Iowa State University, Ames, Iowa. Several books established Atanasoff's pioneering role, especially Clark R. Mollenhoff, *Atanasoff: Forgotten Father of the Computer* (1988), and Alice R. Burks and Arthur W. Burks, *The First Electronic Computer: The Atanasoff Story* (1988). A contrary view is found in Scott McCartney's *ENIAC: The Triumphs and Tragedies of the World's First Computer* (1999). The Annals of the History of Computing, the leading scholarly journal on the history of computing, has written extensively on the dispute between Atanasoff and Mauchly. An obituary is in the *New York Times* (17 June 1995). Oral history tapes are in the Computer Oral History Collection at the Smithsonian Institution in Washington, D.C.

BRENT SCHONDELMEYER

B

BAKER, George Pierce (*b*. 1 November 1903 in Cambridge, Massachusetts; *d*. 25 January 1995 in Phoenix, Arizona), transportation economist who, as the dean of the Harvard Graduate School of Business Administration, played a pivotal role in its development.

Baker was the son of George Pierce Baker and Christina Hopkinson. He grew up in Cambridge, Massachusetts, where his father was a distinguished professor of dramatic literature at Harvard and his mother was a homemaker. After finishing high school at the preparatory school Brown and Nichols (now called Buckingham, Brown, and Nichols) in Cambridge, Baker worked for one year for the Boston & Maine Railroad, confirming his fascination with railroads and transportation. In 1921 he began attending Harvard College, graduating in 1925 with an A.B. degree. On 4 September 1924 he married Ruth P. Bremer; they had four children.

After a year working as an investment counselor at Scudder, Stevens, and Clark, based in Boston, Baker returned to Harvard for graduate work in economics. In 1928, while working on his master's degree, Baker began teaching economics in Harvard's division of history, government, and economics. Completing his master's in 1930 and his doctorate in 1934, he continued to teach at Harvard until 1936. He published *The Formation of the New England Railroad Systems* the following year. In 1957 he coauthored with Gayton E. Germane *Case Problems in Transportation Management*.

In 1936 the Harvard Graduate School of Business Administration recognized the need to incorporate instruction on transportation economics and management into its curriculum, and the school invited Baker to join the faculty as an assistant professor of transportation. Baker then introduced the school's first course on the burgeoning business of airline transportation. The school promoted Baker to associate professor in 1939.

Baker's work on transportation and his research and teaching on airline management won him an invitation to join the Civil Aeronautics Board (CAB) in 1940. He accepted the position, taking a leave of absence from Harvard. In 1942 he became the vice chairman of the CAB, but the demands of World War II led him to resign within months to assume the position of director of requirements in the office of the U.S. Army's quartermaster general. The next year Baker joined the General Staff with the rank of colonel. In 1945 he was awarded the Legion of Merit for his military service.

Following the war Baker directed the U.S. State Department's Office of Transport and Communications Policy. In 1946 he headed the U.S. delegation to the Bermuda Civil Aviation Conference, where he negotiated with the United Kingdom the first bilateral agreement on international air rights. This agreement established the framework that governed most international air traffic into the twenty-first century. In 1947 President Harry S. Truman appointed Baker vice chairman of the Findletter Air Policy Commission, whose purpose was to consider the nation's air defense

George Baker. AP/WIDE WORLD PHOTOS

strategy. The commission played a central role in articulating the concept of mutual deterrence that dominated much strategic thinking during the cold war and gave a central strategic role to the air force. From 1946 to 1956 Baker served on the United Nations Transport and Communications Commission.

In 1946 Baker resumed his teaching position, initially in a joint appointment at the Fletcher School of Law and Diplomacy and at the Harvard Business School as the James J. Hill Professor of Transportation. From 1948 to 1963 he taught exclusively at Harvard. Baker served from 1953 to 1958 as the director of the school's doctoral program. He led a substantial reorganization and expansion of the program, looking to provide appropriately trained faculty for the rapidly expanding schools of business in the country. He also participated in two major evaluations and revisions of the M.B.A. curriculum.

When Stanley F. Teele retired as the dean of the school in 1962, Baker served as the acting dean from March to October. In 1963 Baker accepted appointment as the dean of the school and moved to the George Fisher Baker Professorship of Administration. (Baker was not related to the namesake of this chair.) He believed that his seven-year tenure, lasting to December l969, was marked by three ma-

jor accomplishments. First, he restructured the organization of the faculty. With the school's growth, the faculty had reached 130 but had remained nominally "generalists." Baker recognized that the faculty was both too numerous to operate effectively as a single unit and needed to have some moderate specialization around which to organize its activities. He required the entire faculty to affiliate with one of six areas. This facilitated the second major achievement, a major reorganization of the curriculum, which had begun in 1959 under his predecessor. Contrary to some expectations, the curricular reform confirmed Harvard's commitment to relying on the "case method" of instruction, which emphasized problem solving, in contrast to the increasingly popular discipline-based approach to training. The third major accomplishment in Baker's view was the completion of the "Andrew Report" that laid out a ten-year strategic plan for using the school's resources.

Baker was also remarkably effective at raising money for the school. During his tenure he created twenty-two endowed chairs, more than had been created in the previous fifty years, and for the first time since 1953 the school began building new facilities. He dramatically expanded the school's executive training programs, and Harvard named its first facility dedicated to this activity after Baker. He significantly expanded the international activities of the school, and in 1963 he ended the male-only admissions policy and expanded opportunities for minority students. In recognition of his broad contributions to its growth and improvement, the Harvard Graduate School of Business presented Baker with its highest award, the Distinguished Service Award. Two portraits of Baker—tall, of medium build, with light brown hair—hang in the school's Baker Library. He retired from the school in 1970.

Baker had remained professionally active throughout these years. From 1954 to 1962 he was president of the Transportation Association of America, and he then served as its chairman from 1962 to 1968. He was also the president of the Transportation Research Foundation. He was elected a fellow of the American Academy of Arts and Sciences and was a member of the Council on Foreign Relations. In 1964, at the request of President John F. Kennedy, he brought together a group of Harvard faculty members to advise Central American countries on economic integration. In 1969 President Richard Nixon asked Baker to serve on an advisory panel seeking to make the executive branch "a more effective instrument of public policy." Baker was one of "ten distinguished Americans" appointed to the President's Commission on Postal Organization. After he retired from the Harvard deanship, he served as one of four court-appointed trustees for the bankrupt Pennsylvania New York Central Railroad.

Baker served on numerous corporate boards, including those of United Parcel Service (UPS), Mobil Oil, Lockheed,

Jewel Companies, and First National Bank of Boston. He did extensive consulting with both corporate clients and government agencies. Numerous institutions awarded him honorary degrees, including Clarkson College of Technology, Suffolk University, Allegheny College, Bowling Green State University, Pace College, and the University of Western Ontario.

Baker moved to Phoenix in 1978. His first wife died in March that same year, and on 1 November 1978 he married Mary Elizabeth Osher. He died in Phoenix from complications following a stroke. He is buried in Rindge, New Hampshire, near the vacation home that he built in the 1960s.

In addition to his influential role in shaping air transportation policy, Baker played a pivotal role in sustaining, even revitalizing, Harvard's Graduate School of Business. He reoriented its curriculum and programs to the changing needs of the American and international business community, including the opening of its program to women and minorities.

★

Baker's papers, 1938–1970, in the Harvard Business School Archives in the Baker Library include office files and papers on outside activities, including his United Nations work, 1946–1947. For further information see "Tailoring the B-School to New Business World," *Business Week* (19 Jan. 1963): 72–74, and "Dean Baker Views Recent Accomplishments," *Harvard Business School Bulletin* (9 Apr. 1968). Obituaries are in the *Phoenix Gazette* (27 Jan. 1995) and the *New York Times* (28 Jan. 1995).

FRED CARSTENSEN

BALL, George Wildman (*b.* 21 December 1909 in Des Moines, Iowa; *d.* 26 May 1994 in New York City), lawyer, government official, and writer who urged the importance of a united Europe.

The son of Amos Ball, Jr., a Standard Oil of Indiana vice president and director, and the former Edna Wildman, a teacher, George Ball grew up in Des Moines and in Evanston, Illinois. Ball was born into a family that included two older brothers, and he graduated from Northwestern University in 1930 and its law school in 1933. He joined the Franklin D. Roosevelt administration in Washington as a member of the Farm Credit administration, about which subject he knew nothing, he later wrote, having never spent a night on a farm. When his superior, Henry Morgenthau, Jr., transferred to the treasury department, Ball accompanied him, and upon Morgenthau's becoming secretary in 1934 the young lawyer found himself in the midst of major New Deal events. It was an exciting time. But in 1935, having discovered that handling a kaleidoscope of projects was doing little for his training as a lawyer, he resigned and moved to Chicago to learn the details of practice.

George Ball. LIBRARY OF CONGRESS

In 1942, another landmark year, Ball went back to Washington during a second time of national emergency, initially working with the Lend-Lease Administration and in 1944 with what became the U.S. Strategic Bombing Survey. The survey's sponsor, the U.S. Army Air Forces, sought to defend the bombing of the European continent as crucial to the defeat of Germany. Ball's report concluded that bombing failed to play a decisive role.

In the war's last months Ball became a close friend and disciple of the French economist Jean Monnet, who advocated European integration in a common market and a coal and steel community. During Ball's tenure as undersecretary of state from 1961 to 1966, he supported a "Europe first" agenda, expressing little interest in that decade's consuming subject of American foreign relations, Vietnam.

In the latter 1940s and in the 1950s, Ball engaged in legal work, in large part concerning international economics. In the administration of President John F. Kennedy (1961–1963), he was appointed undersecretary of economic affairs and then, upon the resignation of Chester Bowles, of political affairs, both positions under Secretary of State Dean Rusk. The first two political issues that the lawyer-turned-diplomatist addressed were Laos and Cuba. To the former he brought skepticism, believing American interests in the Southeast Asian nation's civil strife to be minuscule. Cuba, close at hand, was something else. As U.S. involvement deepened after the abortive Bay of Pigs invasion (1961), developing into the Cuban missile crisis in 1962, Ball became one of the key figures in the administration's decision to prevent Soviet ships from bringing war matériel into Cuba and to insist that the Soviets withdraw their missiles from Cuban soil.

As Ball was not a part of "the Harvard crowd," his relations with President Kennedy were close but not intimate. Moreover, for one involved in government during the Depression and World War II, 1961 represented a less momentous experience. His relations with Kennedy's successor, Lyndon B. Johnson, were far more complicated, he wrote years later. Continuing as undersecretary of state, Ball privately sought to balance Johnson's patriotism and mastery of congressional arm-twisting with the weaknesses and insecurities that he felt derived from the president's sensitivity over having graduated from a Texas teachers' college.

Vietnam was the central foreign policy issue of the Johnson years, and from the beginning Ball opposed escalation. He did not hesitate to present his views to the president. Although Johnson thanked him for them, he went in the opposite direction by following the advice of Ball's chief, Secretary Rusk, and Secretary of Defense Robert S. McNamara.

In 1966 Ball resigned and chose not to go public with his Vietnam dissent until the beginning of the Richard M. Nixon administration in 1969. After leaving the Department of State, he was associated with the New York investment banking firm of Lehman Brothers Kuhn Loeb and maintained a residence in Princeton, New Jersey, with his wife, the former Ruth Murdoch, whom he had married on 16 September 1932 and with whom he had two sons.

Ball was a tall, powerfully built man who was well read and closely connected to a number of important people. He believed himself the champion of lost causes. Among these causes were Adlai Stevenson's 1952 and 1956 presidential campaigns, with which he was closely associated; Vietnam; and also efforts to lessen U.S. involvement with the shah Reza Pahlavi's regime in Iran. In another area of foreign policy, he favored reduced support of Israel. Monnet once told him that his basic fault was having an interest in too many things. The advice may have been unfair, considering the complexity of American foreign relations during his time of government service. His policy positions on the major issues have sparked debate, both over the issues themselves and his approaches to them. He died of abdominal cancer at the age of eighty-four.

★

Ball was the author of a half-dozen books, the most important of which is *The Past Has Another Pattern: Memoirs* (1982). Other significant books by Ball include *The Discipline of Power* (1968), *Diplomacy for a Crowded World* (1976), and *Passionate Attachment: America's Involvement with Israel* (1992). See also David L. DiLeo, *George Ball, Vietnam, and the Rethinking of Containment* (1991). An obituary is in the *New York Times* (28 May 1994).

ROBERT H. FERRELL

BALLANTINE, Ian Keith (*b.* 15 February 1916 in New York City; *d.* 9 March 1995 in Bearsville, New York), publisher and pioneer of the paperback book industry whose companies published authors ranging from H. G. Wells to John Steinbeck to J. R. R. Tolkien.

Ballantine was one of two children born to Edward James Ballantine, a Scottish actor and sculptor, and Stella Commins, a publicist. His father was an immigrant to the United States by way of the Shaw Repertory Company, while his mother was an American citizen who worked for the Ben Greet Players and Jesse L. Lasky.

Ian Ballantine, 1982. COURTESY OF MRS. BETTY BALLANTINE

In 1933 Ballantine completed his secondary education at the prestigious Stuyvesant High School in New York City. Prior to his enrollment at Stuyvesant High School, he attended fourteen schools due to his father's career. He entered Columbia University in New York City in 1933, receiving his A.B. degree in economics in 1938 and earning Phi Beta Kappa honors. He then studied at the London School of Economics and Political Science for one year. There, he wrote a thesis that dealt with the provision within the American copyright law that created a market for low-cost British reprints in the United States. Sir Allan Lane, owner of Penguin Books Ltd. of Britain, became interested in the concept, and Ballantine persuaded Lane to establish an American branch. Ballantine and his new bride, Elizabeth ("Betty") Norah Jones, whom he had married on 22 June 1939 and with whom he had one child, opened Penguin Books in the United States in 1939, with Ian serving as general manager. Only twenty-three years of age at the time, Ballantine's first list of titles consisted of twenty British reprints. He operated Penguin until June 1945, at which time the company was sold to New American Library (NAL).

During this time the paperback market grew rapidly because of its flexibility and practicality. For its part, Penguin was successful in delivering books to American soldiers during World War II. These included the *Infantry Journal*, various manuals, and "how to" military books. Paperbacks were given to soldiers at the front lines and sold in military commissaries. After leaving Penguin, Ballantine established Bantam Books, Inc. in 1945, offering paperbacks for twenty-five cents. He extensively researched the reading trends of the American public and developed the "Bantam Best Seller Plan" in 1949. His idea was to obtain an accurate count of books sold per title on a monthly basis. Ballantine used a sampling technique of twenty-two representative cities to determine sales patterns over a ten-day period and came up with a monthly list of eight best-sellers. In preparing the list, Ballantine was also able to determine that his company's return rate—the number of unsold books returned by booksellers—was less than one percent, an enviable statistic (*Publishers Weekly*, 9 July 1949). Wide exposure of the accurate, up-to-date best-seller list led to increased sales. Ballantine continued his research in mass communications, including magazines, radio, and television, as a part-time faculty member in sociology at Columbia University. In 1951 he assisted in organizing Transworld Books, a branch of Bantam located in London and devoted to the British market.

In 1952 the Ballantines left Bantam because of their interest in original publishing. They established Ballantine Books with the specific plan of simultaneously publishing original fiction and nonfiction in both hardcover and paperback. For the first six months, the new company operated out of the Ballantines' home at 440 West Twenty-fourth Street in New York City. With Ian as president and Betty working as secretary and office administrator, they were gradually able to hire other essential personnel, including Richard Powers to design book covers. Powers adopted a surrealist style that became the trademark of Ballantine Books during the 1950s.

The "Ballantine Plan" made it possible for small firms to handle important titles on a large scale. Farrar, Straus and Young and Houghton-Mifflin were the first two publishers to participate in the plan. Ballantine released its first four titles on 10 November 1952, followed by three titles each month thereafter. *Executive Suite* by Cameron Hawley, jointly published in hardcover by Houghton-Mifflin, was the first to be published. Paperback sales of *Executive Suite* soared to 800,000 after the movie based on the book was released in 1954.

Ballantine Books' distribution contract with the Hearst Corporation was canceled in 1954 due to "an intramural battle" that did not involve Ballantine but deeply affected it, costing $600,000 and putting the company near bankruptcy. The company was able to regain its production schedule by slowly adding one title at a time. The first title added was *The Power and the Prize* (1954) by Howard Swiggett. In October of the same year the company was able to increase its production to three titles per month.

Ballantine mentored the careers of authors such as Ray Bradbury, Arthur C. Clarke, and Carlos Castaneda. He was particularly influential in the genres of science fiction, fantasy, westerns, and mysteries. He published the only official edition of J. R. R. Tolkien's *Lord of the Rings* (1965), and his most successful title was Tolkien's *The Hobbit* (1966), which sold more than eight million copies.

In 1974 the Ballantines sold Ballantine Books to Random House and launched Rufus Publications. In their latter years they worked on books by celebrity authors such as astronaut Chuck Yeager and actress Shirley MacLaine. They also established a trade paperback division called Peacock Press at Bantam.

The Ballantines had a year-round weekend home in Woodstock, New York. Ian Ballantine's main interest was helping young authors get published. He read manuscripts up until the day before he died in his home from a heart attack at the age of seventy-nine. About her partnership with her husband, Betty Ballantine stated, "He was brilliant at marketing. While I had a broad range of responsibilities working within the firm, Ian was out on the road marketing and inspiring authors to write. It is my belief that we created successful experiences for our authors. Our desire was to do original printing in paperback format." Betty stated that she felt their greatest contribution to paperback publishing was introducing books that addressed environmental and ecological issues during the 1960s and

1970s. Among the environmental titles they released during this period was the influential *Population Bomb* (1968) by Paul Ehrlich.

Ian Ballantine's inexpensive, mass-produced paperbacks revolutionized publishing. During his five-decade career, he created and expanded reading opportunities for a large segment of the American population. His influence on the industry was symbolized by the lifetime achievement award he and his wife were given by Literary Market Place a month before his death.

★

For an interesting perspective on Ballantine's career, see his letter within John Ciardi's American Literary Collection titled "To J. Vernon Shea, Jr." (1955); the collection is an archival manuscript of thirty-four letters discussing various problems and successes in publishing anthropological works. For a description of Ballantine's best-seller plan for Bantam Books, see "Best Sellers at a Quarter: Bantam Books' New Marketing Program," *Publishers Weekly* (9 July 1949). An extensive biographical sketch can be found in *Current Biography* (1954). Obituaries are in the *New York Times* (10 Mar. 1995) and *Publishers Weekly* (20 Mar. 1995).

JOHNNIEQUE B. ("JOHNNIE") LOVE

BELL, Terrel Howard (*b.* 11 November 1921 in Lava Hot Springs, Idaho; *d.* 22 June 1996 in Salt Lake City, Utah), career educator who as secretary of education institutionalized the department and placed school reform on the national agenda.

Bell was one of nine children born to Willard Dewain Bell and Alta Martin, an Idaho farm couple. Known as "Ted" to his family, he was only nine when his father died; he learned the value of education from his mother. As high school valedictorian in a one-building school system, Bell delivered his address in a suit donated by his teachers. Two subsequent years at Albion State Normal School, at $11.50 a term, were idyllic. Dedicated teachers taught him to love learning and made Bell a lifelong advocate of "open access" community colleges. An energetic man who stood five feet, five inches tall, he enlisted in the United States Marine Corps during World War II and spent three and a half years in the Pacific theater, returning as a first sergeant eager to take advantage of the GI bill. After receiving his B.A. degree from Southern Idaho College of Education (1946), Bell worked as a high school science teacher and athletic coach in rural Idaho before becoming administrator of the Rockland Valley school district (1947–1954). He received an M.S. in educational administration from the University of Idaho (1954) and was a Ford Foundation scholar at Stanford University (1954–1955). His 1 August 1957 marriage to Elizabeth Ruth Fitzgerald lasted until his death and produced four sons. Bell headed school districts in Wyoming and Utah while earning his doctorate at the University of Utah (1961).

Terrel Bell. AP/WIDE WORLD PHOTOS

In 1962 Bell became professor and chairman of the department of educational administration at Utah State University. A year later he was appointed superintendent of public instruction for the state of Utah, serving also on the state's vocational education board. He was appalled when teachers declared a two-day "recess" from their jobs in May 1964, but he later became a supporter of collective bargaining rights for instructional staff. Bell's national career began in April 1970, when he was named associate commissioner for regional office coordination at the Office of Education in the Department of Health, Education, and Welfare (HEW); when his superior resigned, he became acting commissioner of education as the nation fought over segregation and busing. Little in Bell's background seemed to prepare him for the rigors of the capital, and his Mormon religion made him suspect to civil rights leaders. Bell opposed busing as the sole means to ensure integration, but his total lack of bias and his placement of federal fiscal monitors in southern school districts accused of violating educational assistance programs won him vast respect. He was commissioner for seven crucial months during confirmation proceedings for a successor, and then became deputy commissioner for school systems. After September 1971 he headed the Granite School District in Salt Lake City, where his innovations included home-based preschool training; night courses in health, child psychology, and "skills of parenting"; and family counseling. *Your Child's*

Intellect (1972) attempted to mobilize parents and schools in the service of young people.

Selected by President Richard Nixon to become commissioner of education, Bell won easy Senate confirmation on 5 June 1974. He worked well with HEW secretary Caspar Weinberger, and both later served in President Ronald Reagan's cabinet. Bell believed that inequities in funding public school districts could be alleviated by restructuring districts to create reasonably comparable tax bases. He argued that zoning, urban renewal, economic isolation, and social pathology in ghetto areas were all factors determining school performance, and that racial balance without social change was meaningless. Although federal money could encourage innovation, he believed that responsibility for educational excellence lies primarily with state and local leaders, with parents being the ultimate authority. Bell continued to serve the administration of President Gerald Ford before returning to professorial life in Utah.

The U.S. Department of Education, created by the administration of President Jimmy Carter in May 1980, immediately became a target for Republican conservatives who charged that it improperly expanded the national government's role over a local prerogative. One theme of Ronald Reagan's 1980 presidential campaign was abolition of the "great bureaucratic joke," and on 8 January 1981 Bell was offered the position of secretary of education with the implicit task of fulfilling Reagan's pledge. Bell, however, believed the federal government played a limited yet vital role in education. The only nonmillionaire in the cabinet, Bell arrived in the capital prepared to battle "movement conservatives" who sought to destroy the department. His memoir, *The Thirteenth Man* (1988), chronicles four unpleasant years in the cabinet as Bell defended his department against those who sought to abolish it. He tenaciously fought bureaucratic battles with the Office of Management and Budget for sufficient funding, continued aid to handicapped students, and opposed a "mean-spirited" Justice Department reluctant to press civil rights enforcement. Liberals feared Bell's intentions while conservatives found him wanting in fervor, but he believed he could streamline the department and make Reagan appreciate the federal role in education. As early as the summer of 1981 he was rated the fifth most effective cabinet member, "doing a good job of working himself out of a job."

Because the Reagan administration opposed any national study of education, Bell independently ordered an examination of schools in the United States. His National Commission on Excellence in Education produced *A Nation at Risk* (26 April 1983) and began the movement for educational reform in America. It was "difficult to find a compliment on any page" of a report that discovered "a rising tide of mediocrity" threatening national survival. The United States had fallen behind other nations in education and had "masses of illiterate and unemployable" youths; if a foreign power had done to Americans what they did to themselves it would have been an act of war. The report demanded system-wide change: emphasis on basics in primary grades, higher requirements for high school graduation, stricter college admission standards, better teacher pay including merit awards, and a longer school year. Within a year forty-eight states had toughened standards, and the tireless secretary began to issue lists of high-achieving schools and comparative charts rating state performance. Bell denounced publishers for "dumbing down" textbooks, and his crusade transformed education into a winning Reagan campaign theme in 1984.

In November 1984 Bell discovered that despite his efforts the Department of Education was targeted for additional budget cuts. He resigned. But he had successfully institutionalized the department, and Reagan praised the "Secretary of Excellence" when Bell returned to the University of Utah. There he collected numerous honorary doctorates (forty-four), spoke out for equal educational opportunity, and managed a consulting firm, T. H. Bell and Associates. Bell also taught Sunday school, performed community service, and enjoyed his growing family. He died of pulmonary fibrosis and is buried in Salt Lake City. His skill preserved a federal role in education against the "most anti-education administration in this century."

★

Bell's writings detail his educational philosophy. *Effective Teaching: How to Recognize and Reward Competence* (1962) and *A Performance Accountability System for School Administrators* (1972) approach schools from the top, while *A Philosophy of Education for the Space Age: A Guide to Practical Thinking about the Aims and Purposes of Education Today* (1963), *Your Child's Intellect: A Guide to Home-based Preschool Education* (1972), written with Arden R. Thorem, and *Active Parent Concern: A New Home Guide to Help Your Child Do Better in School* (1976) advocate increased parental involvement in education. His battle to maintain the Department of Education is presented in *The Thirteenth Man: A Reagan Cabinet Memoir* (1988). *How to Shape Up Our Nation's Schools: Three Crucial Steps for Renewing American Education* (1991), written with Donna L. Elmquist, distills his ideas, but *A Nation at Risk* (1983) offers an as-yet-unfulfilled platform. Obituaries may be found in the *New York Times* and *Deseret News* (both 24 June 1996).

GEORGE J. LANKEVICH

BELLI, Melvin Mouron (*b.* 29 July 1907 in Sonora, California; *d.* 9 July 1996 in San Francisco, California), attorney whose extravagant private life and flamboyant courtroom behavior often overshadowed formidable legal skills that, over time, reshaped the trial tactics of lawyers across the country, won his clients substantial settlements, and earned him the title "king of torts" in the second half of the twentieth century.

Melvin Belli, 1985. © SANDRO TUCCI/GAMMA LIAISON

Belli was the only child of Leonie Mouron Belli, a house-wife, and Caesar Arthur Belli, a well-to-do banker and rancher whose Swiss-Protestant forebears had settled in the American West after the Civil War. Raised in Sonora and then in Stockton, California, he was named class valedictorian at Stockton High School in 1925, only to be expelled two weeks before graduation for being drunk on school grounds. His father successfully sued the school administration for his diploma, teaching him, he said, the power of the law and of lawyers to transform lives.

Belli entered the University of California, Berkeley, where he gained a reputation as a campus cutup and free spirit. Earning mostly B's and C's, he graduated with a B.A. in 1929. He then traveled to Europe and Asia as a licensed ordinary seaman on tramp steamers and returned home in the autumn of 1930 to enroll in Boalt Hall, Berkeley's law school, graduating with an LL.B. in 1933 at the height of the Great Depression.

He found temporary work as an undercover investigator for the National Recovery Administration, riding boxcars and reporting on radical activities among the wandering homeless throughout the Southwest. Often chased, sometimes jailed, and once beaten by railroad and local police, Belli said he developed a "strong sympathy for the under-dog and the outcast" and became determined to pursue a career as a trial lawyer to defend the rights of the powerless.

He squeaked through the California bar exam in August 1933 and immediately eloped to Reno, Nevada, with Eliz-abeth Ballantine, the first of his six wives, who worked as a secretary for Traveler's Aid in San Francisco. The marriage lasted eighteen years and produced two sons and two daughters.

Beginning in 1933 Belli cobbled together a series of legal jobs. For a time he represented without pay a number of death-row prisoners at San Quentin as counsel to the prison's Roman Catholic chaplain. By 1940 he had organized his own firm of Belli, Ashe & Gerry; the firm was transformed over the years into Belli, Belli, Brown, Monzione, Fabbro & Zakaria. A tireless self-promoter who later boasted that he had gone to his office seven days a week for more than fifty years, he built his legal reputation on the use of "demonstrative evidence" and the concept of "the more adequate award," two elements of trial practice that he pioneered and popularized. Using whatever means he could to make jurors see how an injury had changed a plaintiff's life, he employed films, skeletons, charts, and graphs to support his claim for substantial damages. During one summation, in a case involving the loss of a limb, he dropped an artificial leg onto the lead juror's lap, asking her to pass it on so that all the jurors could feel what his client was forced to wear every day.

Belli dominated a courtroom by his mere presence. Standing well over six feet tall, he was always impeccably dressed, his square-jawed face framed with black-rimmed glasses and topped in later years by a thick, flowing mane of white hair. One reporter wrote that listening to him was like hearing a great symphonic orchestra, so deep and resonating was his voice. His trial tactics and remarks to the press touched the outer edge of accepted legal decorum, and he was often threatened with disciplinary proceedings by judges, the Association of Trial Lawyers of America—an organization he had helped found—and the American Bar Association, which he dismissed as a protective society for corporate lawyers.

Belli's appetite for food, drink, and good times was legendary. He appeared in several movies, including *Wild in the Streets* (1968) and *Gimme Shelter* (1970). Divorced from his first wife in 1951, he was married within six months to Toni Nichols, a reporter, whom he divorced in 1954. On 3 May 1956 he married Joy Maybelle Turney, a stewardess, with whom he had a son; they divorced in 1965. His 1966 marriage to Pat Montandon, a model, was annulled within a matter of months. On 3 June 1972 he married Lia G. T. Triff, a twenty-three-year-old college graduate; they had a daughter and divorced in 1991.

His flamboyance was reflected in the Belli Building at 722 Montgomery Street in San Francisco. A regular stop for tour buses, the historic building, purchased in 1959, had lush gardens and a rooftop flagpole where Belli hoisted a Jolly Roger flag and fired two small signal guns at sunset to announce any courtroom victory. His office was decorated "in early bordertown bordello," a critic said, and featured flame-red wallpaper, deep-piled Persian rugs, and four crystal chandeliers. At the side of his desk stood "Elmer," a skeleton he brought to trial whenever a jury needed instruction in human anatomy. The desk itself was placed before a plate glass window at street level so passersby could wave at him when he was at work and he could wave back.

His client list included stars of the entertainment world, ranging from Errol Flynn and Mae West to the Rolling Stones, and some of the most notorious criminals of his time, including Jack Ruby, who murdered Lee Harvey Oswald in 1963, and a Nevada nurse known as the "Angel of Death." He represented the families of black inmates killed or injured in a 1975 riot at Soledad State Prison. But he earned the title "king of torts" (assigned him by *Life* magazine in 1954) for his numerous victories in civil court, gaining huge settlements for the plaintiff in a broad range of individual and class cases, covering medical malpractice, product liability, personal injury, and divorce. He once claimed that he had recovered more than $700 million for his clients. In its heyday his firm had offices in eight California cities and in Washington, D.C.

In collaboration with a number of writing associates, Belli wrote or edited more than sixty books over thirty years, including several multivolume legal texts. The best known was the five-volume *Modern Trials* (1954–1960, rev. 1981), which became a standard text in a number of law schools and a bible for personal-injury lawyers nationwide. Other

professional titles included: *The Adequate Award* (1953); *The Modern Trial Lawyer* (1954); the four-volume *Trial and Tort Trends* (1954, rev. 1960); *Trial Tactics* (1967); and *Product Liability: The Blue Chip of Damages* (1981).

Several of Belli's books were popular accounts of his courtroom work, most notably *Dallas Justice: The Real Story of Jack Ruby and His Trial* (1964), written with Maurice C. Carroll. His other books for a lay audience included *Blood Money: Ready for the Plaintiff* (1956), an examination of personal injury law, and (with Danny R. Jones) *Belli Looks at Life and Law in Japan* (1960) and *Belli Looks at Life and Law in Russia* (1963). Over the years, he wrote a syndicated column for the *San Francisco Chronicle* and was an editor or contributor to several professional law journals, including *Torts* and the *American Trial Lawyers Association Journal*. Of all his books, only two were still in print after his death: *Everybody's Guide to the Law: The First Place to Look for the Legal Information You Need Most* (1987), written with Allen P. Wilkinson, and *Divorcing: The Complete Guide for Men and Women* (1988), coauthored by Mel Krantzler, a psychologist, and Christopher S. Taylor, an attorney.

In the 1980s Belli entered a number of high-profile class-action suits that included the Union Carbide chemical spill in Bhopal, India, the downing of a Korean airliner by Soviet fighter planes, the MGM Grand Hotel fire in Las Vegas, Nevada, the Exxon *Valdez* oil spill in Alaska, and the Dow Corning breast implant cases. All of them produced millions of dollars in settlements or judgments, but because of drawn-out appeals, payments were not immediately forthcoming. For Belli, the delays proved disastrous because he was otherwise unable to meet the costs of litigation.

In the first of a series of setbacks in the final years of Belli's life, the Belli Building sustained serious damage in the Loma Prieta earthquake of 1987 and had to be abandoned until structural upgrades, costing millions of dollars, made it safe for occupancy. Belli lacked the capital for such an undertaking, so the building was still in disrepair at the time of his death—and for years afterward—while his heirs and creditors struggled in court to determine who among them could claim ownership.

In 1991 Belli's fifth marriage ended acrimoniously with a multimillion-dollar settlement that further strained his dwindling resources. Through the next five years he battled ill health, dissolved his law partnership (1993), reorganized his practice as The Law Offices of Melvin Belli, Sr., and fought in court with his former partners over the old firm's client list and finances. He faced malpractice suits from clients and more than thirty suits from creditors. Both the state and federal governments made him the target of tax-evasion charges. In December 1995, months after Dow Corning defaulted on a $200 million settlement due him,

Belli filed for bankruptcy protection. Six months later a federal judge placed his law firm in the hands of an independent examiner.

On 29 May 1996 he married Nancy Ho, a longtime friend who had earlier lent him money from her substantial real estate holdings in San Francisco. Within six weeks he was dead from a combination of pneumonia, a stroke, and pancreatic cancer. His son Caesar Belli demanded an autopsy and asked the district attorney to bring murder charges against Nancy Belli, hinting that a painkilling drug may have been misused. A week after the memorial service at Grace (Episcopal) Cathedral, the coroner ruled that the autopsy showed Belli had died from natural causes.

No charges were brought against Nancy Belli, but in an ironic ending to a storied law career, Belli's death opened the way to dozens of lawsuits that dragged on for years, as clients, creditors, ex-wives, children, and former partners sued each other and the estate for what they believed was rightfully theirs. As many as 150 lawyers in three countries were engaged in untangling the legal mess Belli's last years had created. It was exactly the kind of litigation he had found so exhilarating in his own career and was—some of his contemporaries suggested—exactly the kind of legacy he would have hoped to leave behind.

★

As a general rule Belli's legal papers are protected in perpetuity by the attorney-client privilege and are not accessible to researchers; his personal papers are held by his estate. In addition to his autobiography, *My Life on Trial* (1976), written with Robert Kaiser, Belli scattered personal anecdotes throughout his books for a general audience, commenting on his marriages in *Divorcing* (1988) and on his law career in *Blood Money: Ready for the Plaintiff* (1956); *The Belli Files: Reflections on the Wayward Law* (1983); and *Belli for Your Malpractice Defense* (1986). See also the brief profile in *Life* magazine (18 Oct. 1954); the "Playboy Interview," conducted by Alex Haley, *Playboy* (July 1965); and an interview with Digby Diehl, *Supertalk* (1974). Belli's books also include *The Use of Demonstrative Evidence in Achieving the More Adequate Award* (1955); *Modern Trial Law* (1957); *Modern Damages,* 6 vols. (1959); *Tort and Medical Yearbook,* 2 vols. (1961); *The Urologist and the Law* (1979); and *The Successful Opening Statement* (1981). There are two early popular biographies: Robert Wallace, *Life and Limb: An Account of the Career of Melvin M. Belli, Personal-Injury Trial Lawyer* (1955), and Norman Sheresky, *On Trial: Masters of the Courtroom* (1977). See also Krysten Crawford, "Tortious Maximus," *American Lawyer* (2 Dec. 1999). The family squabbles and legal entanglements following Belli's death are described by Lisa Davis in "Battle Belli," *SF Weekly* (12 Apr. 2000). Obituaries are in the *San Francisco Chronicle* (10 July 1996) and *New York Times* (11 July 1996).

ALLAN L. DAMON

BENSON, Ezra Taft (*b.* 4 August 1899 in Whitney, Idaho; *d.* 30 May 1994 in Salt Lake City, Utah), secretary of agriculture during the administration of Dwight D. Eisenhower and president of the Church of Jesus Christ of Latter-day Saints, known for his outspoken conservative views.

Benson was the eldest of eleven children of George Taft Benson and Sarah S. Dunkley, farmers. At an early age he was busy with farm chores: herding cattle, milking cows, and digging potatoes. At age sixteen he received from a neighbor the arduous task of thinning an acre of sugar beets, which he finished in a day.

In his teens, Benson attended Oneida State Academy. He enrolled at Utah State Agricultural College at Logan, now Utah State University, in 1918. After three years there he spent two years as a Mormon missionary to England. He then returned to Idaho, where he and a younger brother bought their father's farm. They managed the farm and attended Brigham Young University, where Benson was awarded his B.S. degree in 1926. He then enrolled at Iowa State College and obtained an M.S. in agricultural economics. During this period of farming and study he married Flora Smith Amussen on 10 September 1926. The two had four daughters and two sons: Barbara, Beverly, Bonnie, Flora Beth, Reed, and Mark.

In 1929 Benson became a county extension agent in Idaho and later that year became a marketing specialist and economist for the University of Idaho. Benson was to have a long-term association with the farm cooperative movement. In 1933 he helped found the Idaho Cooperative

Ezra Taft Benson as U.S. Secretary of Agriculture, 1954. © BETTMANN/ CORBIS

Council, which he served in an executive capacity, and from 1939 to 1944 he was executive secretary of the National Council of Farmer Cooperatives.

President Franklin D. Roosevelt appointed Benson to the National Agricultural Advisory Commission during World War II. The appointment did not prevent him from criticizing farm policy. In late 1942 he signed a statement protesting the increasing regulation of farmers. He also issued a stunning rebuke to the administration's crop-subsidy program.

During this time he was active in the Mormon Church. He became president of the Boise stake in 1938 and the following year moved to the nation's capital, where he served as president of the Washington, D.C., stake from 1940 to 1943. He was ordained an apostle of the church in 1943 and became a member of the Council of Twelve, the church's second-highest ruling body. In 1946 Benson headed the Mormon Church's European mission and was in charge of distributing supplies to a war-shattered continent.

President-elect Dwight D. Eisenhower named Benson as his secretary of agriculture in 1952. It was a difficult time to take on that post, with crop surpluses mounting and dragging down farmers' incomes. Benson believed that the high, fixed price supports in place since World War II had caused the surpluses, and with Eisenhower's blessing he advanced a program for flexible supports, lowered during crop surpluses to encourage farmers to cut back production, and raised in time of need. The plan met stiff resistance in Congress. Most farm-bloc legislators, both Democrats and Republicans, wanted supports high and fixed. Benson and the administration won approval for the plan in 1954 only after agreeing to limit the lower end of the plan's range.

Later that year Democrats regained control of Congress in the midterm elections, and in 1955 the House approved a return to high, rigid supports. This fight became entangled with an administration proposal for a Soil Bank. Benson had mixed feelings about what emerged from Congress. The idea had been to pay farmers to retire land dedicated to surplus crops. The so-called Acreage Reserve was limited to four years. The other part of the program was the Conservation Reserve, which would pay farmers to switch certain amounts of land for longer periods to conservation purposes. Benson liked the idea of the Conservation Reserve but was not enthusiastic about the Acreage Reserve, seeing it as a necessary evil to reduce the surplus. The problem was that the Democrat-controlled Congress insisted upon tying the Soil Bank to a return to high, fixed supports. Benson strongly urged a veto, and President Eisenhower agreed. A new Soil Bank bill was passed by Congress. Although Benson still had reservations, he did not recommend another veto, and the bill was signed by the president.

The other major agricultural legislation during the Benson years came in 1958. Benson had argued for an increase in acreage allotments for most basic crops and for an end to restrictions for corn. He wanted to widen the range of supports to allow for lowering them still further. Because of technological advances, Benson believed acreage allotments were ineffective and that other methods to reduce surpluses had to be tried. The administration won approval of its plan to eliminate acreage allotments for corn, but limitations remained for most other basic crops.

Leaving office in 1961, Benson returned to his post in the Council of Twelve. In 1973 he became president of the council, and in 1985 he became president and prophet of the church, a post in which he served until his death in 1994.

During his tenure as secretary of agriculture, there were many calls from the farm bloc and others for Benson to resign. In 1957, in Sioux Falls, South Dakota, eggs were thrown at the secretary during a speech. Eisenhower remained loyal to Benson, who was one of only two cabinet members to stay for the entire eight years of the administration. At the end of Benson's time in office, crop surpluses were still high. He ardently believed that what had been needed to solve the surplus was less, not more, government intervention, and here was the source of his major disagreements with the congressional farm bloc. In the years after the Eisenhower presidency Benson was outspoken in behalf of conservative ideas and became associated with the John Birch Society. He denounced liberalism, including the civil rights movement, progressive income taxes, the welfare state, and feminism. In his later years Benson was beset by health problems, and he died of congestive heart failure in Salt Lake City at the age of ninety-five.

★

Benson wrote about his time as secretary of agriculture in *Cross Fire: The Eight Years with Eisenhower* (1962). His conservative idealism is detailed in his books *The Red Carpet* (1962), *Title of Liberty* (1964), *The Constitution: A Heavenly Banner* (1986), and *The Teachings of Ezra Taft Benson* (1988). A full treatment of Benson's life is *Ezra Taft Benson: A Biography* (1987) by Sheri L. Dew; shorter summaries include an entry in *Current Biography 1953* and Frederick J. Simonelli, "Benson, Ezra Taft," *American National Biography* (1999). A study of Benson's time as secretary is Edward L. Schapsmeier and Frederick H. Schapsmeier, *Ezra Taft Benson and the Politics of Agriculture: The Eisenhower Years, 1953–1961* (1975). Helpful information about agricultural legislation during Benson's years as secretary can be found in *Congressional Quarterly*'s *Congress and the Nation, 1945–1964: A Review of Government and Politics* (1965). An obituary is in the *New York Times* (31 May 1994).

TRACY STEVEN UEBELHOR

BERMAN, Pandro Samuel (*b.* 28 March 1905 in Pittsburgh, Pennsylvania; *d.* 13 July 1996 in Beverly Hills, California), producer whose 118 films included many of Hollywood's most literate and distinguished pictures, including the Fred Astaire–Ginger Rogers musicals and memorable films of Katharine Hepburn, Bette Davis, Elizabeth Taylor, Paul Newman, and Elvis Presley.

Berman was the oldest of three children born to Harry Michael Berman (formerly Pandrowitz) and Julie Epstein, Russian-Jewish immigrants. After unsuccessful ventures selling real estate, hats, and furs, Harry Berman, like others in his family, became a film salesman, joining World Films in Newcastle, Pennsylvania, shortly after Pandro's birth. In 1914 he became branch manager for Metro Film Corporation in Kansas City, Missouri, taking Pandro in the evenings to sell films at neighborhood theaters. In 1916, when the family settled in New York City, Harry worked for Carl Laemmle, Sr.'s Universal Company, where he rose to the position of General Sales Manager for the United States. Before Harry became a film salesman, Julie Berman opened and operated a successful fur store. Once the family became prosperous, she became a homemaker.

In New York, Berman attended DeWitt Clinton High School; following graduation in 1923 he left school to pursue the film business in California. In 1922 his father had

Pandro Berman (*left*) with Vicente Minnelli on the set of *Tea and Sympathy*. THE KOBAL COLLECTION

joined a partnership to organize the Film Booking Office, and Pandro was hired by the new studio as a script clerk, working on silent two-reel comedies. By 1926 he had risen to first assistant director to Tod Browning, Ralph Ince, Al Santell, and others, eventually becoming a film cutter.

Harry Berman died in 1925, and in 1927 Berman left the F.B.O. to join Columbia Pictures as head of the cutting department. He arrived just as the sound revolution was transforming production and editing. The same year, on 24 July, he married Viola Newman, a childhood friend; they had three children.

After six months Berman left Columbia, and with his new knowledge of sound filmmaking, he became chief film editor at the F.B.O.—now reorganized as Radio-Keith-Orpheum Corporation, makers of RKO Radio Pictures. By 1931 Berman had become the assistant to studio head William Le Baron, who gave Berman his first job as a producer. David O. Selznick became production head in 1931, firing most of Le Baron's personnel but retaining Berman as his assistant. When trouble developed in making *What Price Hollywood?* (1932), Berman again was called on to produce. He continued as a producer at RKO until 1939, making sixty-eight pictures.

Selznick's successor in 1933 was Merian C. Cooper, who during periods of illness left Berman in charge of the studio. Having seen Fred Astaire and Ginger Rogers in supporting roles in *Flying Down to Rio* (1933), Berman reunited them as stars of *The Gay Divorcee* (1934). The six Astaire-Rogers films that followed in the 1930s, especially *Top Hat* (1935), are generally believed to have saved the studio from insolvency. Many of Berman's less financially successful pictures in this period are now considered classics, including *Morning Glory* (1933), with Katharine Hepburn, and *Of Human Bondage* (1934), with Bette Davis. For her role, Hepburn won an Academy Award.

At Cooper's resignation in 1934, Berman, only twenty-nine years old, became RKO's head of production. But he left the post after six months, preferring to develop his own pictures. Late in 1937, after the studio had gone through two more production chiefs, Berman reluctantly took up the task again. Under his leadership, RKO made some of its most memorable films, including *Gunga Din* (1939); *Room Service* (1938), with the Marx Brothers; and *The Hunchback of Notre Dame* (1939), with Charles Laughton.

Tired of continual shake-ups and disagreements with management, Berman left RKO in 1939, despite the studio's offer of twenty-five percent of the profits from his pictures. In 1940 he signed with Louis B. Mayer to become a salaried producer for Metro-Goldwyn-Mayer (MGM), where he remained for twenty-seven years.

MGM provided Berman not only independence and stability but the production resources of Hollywood's major studio. Mayer trusted him to undertake films even when the studio management doubted their prospects. Beginning with a string of moneymakers in the early 1940s, Berman moved to more artistically ambitious features like *The Picture of Dorian Gray* (1945) and *Madame Bovary* (1949).

As at RKO and most other Hollywood studios, the producer exercised the artistic control that was sought (but rarely achieved) by directors, including final editing. In the late 1940s, to preserve the creative authority of producers, he supported the organization of the Screen Producers Guild (later the Producers Guild of America) and later served on its Board of Directors. Berman argued that every picture needed the "stamp" of a particular artist; however, the artist might not be the director but the producer, the writer, or even the actor.

Elizabeth Taylor's career developed largely through films that Berman produced, beginning with her juvenile role in *National Velvet* (1944) and continuing through *Father of the Bride* (1950), *Cat on a Hot Tin Roof* (1958), and *Butterfield 8* (1960), for which Taylor won an Academy Award. Taylor also appeared in Berman's *Ivanhoe* (1952), one of a series of English medieval romances that also included *Knights of the Round Table* (1953) with Ava Gardner and Robert Taylor.

The increasing sexual frankness of Elizabeth Taylor's later films reflected Berman's understanding of the social changes taking place among filmgoers. He had gauged audience desire for sophistication in the 1930s and domestic values of the 1940s. Now, he sought new subjects: realistic social issues like juvenile delinquency in *Blackboard Jungle* (1955), interracial romance in *Bhowani Junction* (1956) and *A Patch of Blue* (1965), sexual awareness in *Tea and Sympathy* (1956), and even the controversial pop-star magnetism of Elvis Presley in *Jailhouse Rock* (1957).

Berman's associate producer on *Jailhouse Rock* and some later films was Kathryn Hereford Buchman, whom he married 10 July 1960, following a 1959 divorce from his first wife. Berman and Kathryn had no children.

Following a corporate shake-up at MGM, Berman joined veteran producer Lawrence Weingarten to form an independent company, Avon Productions, and began again to collect a percentage of the profits from his MGM films. By this time, however, the studio system was growing moribund. After 1957, Berman produced only ten pictures, although these included such important releases as Tennessee Williams's *Sweet Bird of Youth* (1962), for which actor Ed Begley won an Academy Award. His association with MGM ended when he moved in 1967 to Twentieth Century–Fox; there, futilely hoping to avoid corporate bureaucracy, he made his last two films.

Berman retired in 1970, citing the diminished artistic role of producers and what he saw as a pervasive exploitation of sex in films. He pursued interests in real estate, construction, and oil; presented master classes in film at the University of Southern California; and participated in film retrospectives and seminars. In 1977 the Motion Picture Academy presented him with the Irving Thalberg Memorial Award, and in 1992 he received the David O. Selznick Lifetime Achievement Award from the Producers Guild of America. He died at his home of congestive heart failure and is buried in Hillside Memorial Park in Los Angeles.

Though Berman claimed that he made "more failures than successes," he produced at least forty films that were widely regarded as classics. His career spanned a Hollywood era when producers exercised artistic control, from the choice of literary properties, to casting, to details of art direction and editing. Berman saw to all of these with an intelligence and taste, in both his films and his personal manner, for which he was renowned. Soft-spoken and restrained, he demanded the best technical and production values to entertain audiences. He regarded the core of his job as script development, and in an interview with the *Hollywood Reporter* suggested this might be the result of his mother's influence: "She used to make me read Shakespeare and Rudyard Kipling's poems," he said, "and I think this really got me interested in the film business."

★

Berman's papers are collected at the University of Wisconsin at Madison. The Academy of Motion Picture Arts and Sciences, Beverly Hills, California, also maintains an archive. Berman's films are surveyed in John Douglas Eames, *The MGM Story: The Complete History of Fifty Roaring Years* (2d ed., 1989), and Richard B. Jewell and Vernon Harbin, *The RKO Story* (1982). See also Betty Lasky, *RKO: The Biggest Little Major of Them All* (1984). Obituaries are in the *Los Angeles Times* (14 July 1996), *New York Times* (15 July 1996), and the London *Times* (17 July 1996). Berman was the subject of two oral history projects: Mike Steen, *American Film Institute Oral History of Pandro S. Berman* (1972), and Ronald L. Davis, *Southern Methodist University Oral History Project: Pandro S. Berman* (1978). The former was partially published in Mike Steen, *Hollywood Speaks!: An Oral History* (1974). After his retirement, Berman gave occasional interviews for television documentaries, including *George Stevens: A Filmmaker's Journey* (1984).

ALAN BUSTER

BERNARDIN, Joseph Louis (*b.* 2 April 1928 in Columbia, South Carolina; *d.* 14 November 1996 in Chicago, Illinois), cardinal archbishop of Chicago for fourteen years; at the center of almost every major development of post–Vatican II American Catholicism.

Bernardin was one of two children born to Joseph ("Bepi") Bernardin, a stonecutter, and Maria M. Simion, immigrants from Tonadico di Primiero in the Dolomite Moun-

Joseph Bernardin. LIBRARY OF CONGRESS

tains of northern Italy, near Austria. Bepi died of cancer in 1934. Maria banked his insurance for education and worked as a seamstress, and for the Works Progress Administration (WPA), to support her family. Bernardin cared for his younger sister and learned to prepare dinner. The family lived in a public housing project until 1951. He attended Catholic and public elementary schools, public high school, and one year of pre-med at the University of South Carolina. Upon acceptance as a candidate for the priesthood, Bernardin entered St. Mary's College, St. Mary, Kentucky, to study Latin in a special makeup course. He graduated summa cum laude with a B.A. degree in philosophy from St. Mary's Seminary, Baltimore (1948). Invited to complete his studies at the North American College (the traditional training ground for church leaders) in Rome, he declined because of his mother's health.

Bernardin studied theology and received an M.A. in education from the Catholic University of America in Washington, D.C. (1952). Ordained to the priesthood by Bishop John J. Russell for the diocese of Charleston (26 April 1952), Bernardin spent fourteen years there, serving four bishops in many capacities. These included the offices of chancellor, vicar general, diocesan counselor, administrator of the diocese when the see was vacant, and chaplain at the Citadel, a military college in Charleston. He was named a papal chamberlain in 1959 and a domestic prelate in 1962 by Pope John XXIII. On 9 March 1966, Monsignor Bernardin was appointed Auxiliary Bishop of Atlanta by

Pope Paul VI. Upon his episcopal ordination (26 April 1966, with Archbishop Paul J. Hallinan of Atlanta as principal consecrator), he became the youngest bishop in the country. In Atlanta he served as vicar general and rector of the cathedral. After the death of Archbishop Hallinan in March 1968, Bernardin served as administrator of the archdiocese until the installation of the new archbishop.

On 10 April 1968, Bishop Bernardin was elected the first general secretary of the National Conference of Catholic Bishops (NCCB) and its social action agency, the United States Catholic Conference (USCC), because of his administrative skills, energy, and ability as a mediator. During this period, the bishops were reorganizing according to the norms established by Vatican II, with emphasis on the collective role of the bishops, along with the pope, in governing the church. As general secretary, he served as coordinator of the reorganization until the latter part of 1972. During this term, he undertook a major study of the priesthood, which caused a great deal of controversy. (The study, in which psychological findings were written up by Eugene Kennedy and sociological findings by Andrew Greeley, was the best study ever done on the priesthood, according to priests consulted thirty years later. However, the nervous bishops did not appear eager to learn or reveal that much about themselves.)

On 21 November 1972, Bernardin was appointed archbishop of Cincinnati by Pope Paul VI, and was installed by the Most Rev. Luigi Raimondi, apostolic delegate to the United States, in ceremonies at the Cathedral of St. Peter in Chains (19 December 1972). He served the Ohio Metropolitan see for almost ten years. Here he joined a prayer group of younger priests, who challenged his priorities. Of swarthy complexion, he was balding and stocky and relished good food and wine. He dieted, lost the weight, and never regained it. He also began to devote the first hour of his day to prayer and meditation. Bernardin also gave away money and art objects as he went through a complete conversion.

From November 1974 to November 1977, Bernardin served as NCCB/USCC president, essentially head of the American Catholic hierarchy. On 10 July 1982, Pope John Paul II appointed him archbishop of Chicago, the see left vacant by the death of John Cardinal Cody. His installation by the Most Rev. Pio Laghi, apostolic delegate, took place at Holy Name Cathedral on 24 August 1982. He was elevated to the Sacred College of Cardinals on 2 February 1983, making him the first Italian-American cardinal.

Cardinal Bernardin oversaw the NCCB's drafting of *The Challenge of Peace,* a pastoral letter on nuclear arms and American defense policy. This put him on the cover of *Time* on 29 November 1982. He received the Albert Einstein Peace Prize for this work in 1983. As chairman of the Committee for Pro-Life Activities, he gave an address at Fordham University in December 1983, recasting the church's opposition to abortion as part of a "consistent ethic of life" that also opposed war and capital punishment. His expression "seamless garment," meaning that all life is sacred and deserving of a mantle of protection, helped change the terms of the national debate on abortion.

In Chicago, Cardinal Bernardin inherited an archdiocese in chaos. Several hundred priests had resigned, vocations were down, population shifts had decimated many parishes, and morale was low. He had to close or consolidate churches and schools, many of which were more than 100 years old. Sexual abuse of young parishioners by some priests became a matter of public knowledge. In 1991 he took action and established Policies and Procedures to be Followed in Cases of Accusations of Sexual Abuse. A fitness review board for priests was also instituted. Many other dioceses adopted this program. Then, in November 1993, the cardinal himself became the target of sexual abuse charges. He turned the allegation over to the review committee and, standing alone, answered every question asked him at two news conferences, denying the charges. His accuser later recanted, and Bernardin traveled to Philadelphia to pray with the man just before he died of AIDS at the end of 1994.

In March 1995, Bernardin made his first pilgrimage to the Holy Land, with a delegation of Catholic and Jewish leaders from Chicago. There he met with Israeli and Palestinian officials and spoke out against his church's silence on the Holocaust. In May 1995 he received the University of Notre Dame's Laetare Medal, considered by many to be the most prestigious Catholic award given in the United States.

Bernardin was diagnosed with pancreatic cancer, and underwent surgery in June 1995. In an interview, he said that he had grown up with three fears: fear of death, fear of being falsely accused of something serious, and fear of cancer. Then, all three things threatened him at the same time. After speaking with his friend and fellow priest Henri Nouwen, Bernardin began to look upon death as a friend. "You begin to talk with your friend, and some of the fears dissipate." As he underwent chemotherapy, he began an additional ministry to hundreds of cancer patients and to the dying.

In August 1996, Cardinal Bernardin announced the Catholic Common Ground Project to promote dialogue among American Catholics who disagree on church issues. Severely criticized for this by the cardinal archbishops of New York, Boston, Philadelphia, and Washington, D.C., he responded, "Who says there is no dissent in the church?" Two weeks later, he learned that his cancer had returned and was terminal. His doctors informed him that the chemotherapy was not working, and he stopped the treatments.

President Clinton awarded Bernardin the Medal of Freedom, the government's highest civilian honor, in Sep-

tember 1996, saying "in a time of transition in his church, his community, his nation, and the world, he has held fast to his mission to bring out the best in humanity and to bring people together. Without question, he is both a remarkable man of God and a man of the people."

Shortly before his death, Bernardin wrote to the United States Supreme Court about doctor-assisted suicide: "Our legal and ethical tradition has held consistently that suicide, assisted-suicide, and euthanasia are wrong because they involve a direct attack on innocent human life." But, he continued, an individual has the right to avoid extraordinary medical treatment when it is futile or unduly burdensome.

Under Pope Paul VI, Bernardin was appointed to the Sacred Congregation for Bishops (1973); to the Pontifical Commission for Social Communications (1974); and consultor for the Sacred Congregation for Catholic Education (1978). Pope John Paul II appointed him to the following curial groups: the Pontifical Commission for the Revision of the Code of Canon Law (1983); the Congregation for the Evangelization of Peoples (1983–1988); and the Congregation for Sacraments and Divine Worship and the Secretariat for Promoting Christian Unity (1984). He was a delegate to, and served on the council of, the Synod of Bishops from 1974 to 1990.

Joseph Cardinal Bernardin was a skilled mediator and troubleshooter. Cool in controversy, he was warm and affable in his personal contacts, with a good sense of humor. He spoke Italian, Latin, English, and Spanish and liked to walk, cook, swim, and attend the symphony and baseball games. A careful planner, he slept only six hours a night, using the other hours for his writing. The post–Vatican II church was often divided over issues such as human sexuality, the role of women in the church, and priestly celibacy. The Vietnam War, the encyclical *Humanae Vitae,* which condemned contraception, the abortion struggle, and racial tensions, were major issues during his tenure. His was a strong voice on pro-life issues, nuclear weapons, peace, and the politics of wealth and poverty. He developed models for cutbacks in the schools and churches of Chicago, dealing with clerical abuse, and dialogue between priests and laity. And he supervised the reorganization of the National Conference of Catholic Bishops. Without him, the American Catholic Church would have been vastly different. Bernardin died of pancreatic and liver cancer, at the age of sixty-eight. He is buried in the bishops' chapel at Mount Carmel Cemetery in Chicago.

★

Cardinal Bernardin's papers are in the Archdiocese of Chicago's Joseph Cardinal Bernardin Archives and Records Center, Chicago, Illinois. *The Consistent Ethic of Life* (1988), includes ten of his major addresses, as well as response papers from a symposium. *The Gift of Peace: Personal Reflections* (1997), was finished two weeks before his death. *The Word of Cardinal Bernardin,* edited by Paolo Magagnotti (1996), is a collection of his works and addresses. John H. White's photographs of the Cardinal, with text by Eugene Kennedy, are contained in *This Man Bernardin* (1996). Kennedy, a long-time friend, also wrote *Bernardin: Life to the Full* (1997) and *My Brother Joseph: The Spirit of a Cardinal and the Story of a Friendship* (1997). See also Tim Unsworth, *I Am Your Brother Joseph: Cardinal Bernardin of Chicago* (1997). Magazine and journal articles include Kenneth L. Woodward and John McCormick, "The Art of Dying Well," *Newsweek* (25 Nov. 1996); Jeffrey L. Sheler, "I See Death as a Friend," *U.S. News and World Report* (25 Nov. 1996); an interview in the *New York Times Magazine* on "Death as a Friend" (1 Dec. 1996). Obituaries are in the *New York Times, Boston Globe,* and *Chicago Tribune* (all 15 Nov. 1996).

MARY NAHON GALGAN

BERNAYS, Edward L. (*b.* 22 November 1891 in Vienna, Austria; *d.* 9 March 1995 in Cambridge, Massachusetts), public relations practitioner who profoundly influenced the professions of public relations, advertising, and marketing as well as the modern realm of the "spinmeister."

Bernays was the son of Ely Bernays, a moody and strident man born in Austria who came to America in 1892 and earned his living as a grain exporter on the Manhattan Product Exchange, and Anna Freud, who managed the home and raised Edward and his four sisters. Ely's younger sister Martha married Sigmund Freud. There was a second bond between the Freuds and Bernayses: Edward's mother was Sigmund's younger sister. Edward celebrated his first birthday on the steamer to America and spent his early years living in relative prosperity in a series of brownstones in fashionable neighborhoods of New York City. Summers meant trips to the spas of Sharon Springs, New York; to the Adirondack Mountains; or, on one special occasion, to Ossiacher Lake in Austria, where Uncle Sigmund paid a visit and took his young nephew on long walks that Edward would remember and recount for the next eighty years. At home, Edward's typical setting was center stage, with his two older sisters and two younger ones playing supporting roles.

Bernays enrolled at Cornell University's august College of Agriculture and graduated with a B.S. degree in 1912, fulfilling his parents' dreams if not his own. He devoted most of his energies in school to picking up communication and marketing skills that would ensure he never again had to set foot on a farm. After school he took a series of jobs that let him indulge his desire for good living, but it was not until he went to work as a promoter that he was able to engage his creative energies. His clients ranged from the Ballet Russe to the greatest tenor of his time, Enrico Caruso, from the makers of Ivory soap to the U.S. propaganda agency during World War I. For each, he began with con-

Edward Bernays. LIBRARY OF CONGRESS

ventional techniques of blanketing the media with press releases, but in each case he went further, pioneering techniques that became trademarks for himself and his evolving public relations (PR) profession. With the ballet he enticed manufacturers of jewelry, handbags, lampshades, and other products to introduce models inspired by the color and design of Ballet Russe sets and costumes. With Ivory he enticed millions of American youth to carve its big white bars into soap sculptures, in the process helping shape the Procter & Gamble product into the all-American soap. And with Caruso he coined the irresistible sobriquet "man with the orchid-lined voice"; in one of the many stories he crafted on the tenor's tour of America, Bernays was promoted as "the Caruso of press agents and the press agent of Caruso."

Over time the notion of promotion, and self-promotion, became so much a part of Bernays's personality that it even seeped into his wedding plans. He and his bride-to-be, Doris E. Fleischman, had settled on a modern marriage, one that would take place in the austere chapel in the New York Municipal Building, with no family or friends to bear witness, no gown or tuxedo, and no band or bouquet. There was not even a wedding ring—a symbol, to such freethinking youth in 1922, of the spousal slavery they were determined to resist. Even the timing was designed to ensure secrecy, with the couple turning up at the chapel minutes before it was to close, ensuring the wedding could not be reported in the next day's papers. In the end, however, the young publicity agent could not keep the secret. He had his young bride sign the register at the Waldorf-Astoria Hotel using her maiden name, which he knew would trigger an immediate notification of the press—a policy that he as hotel PR man had instituted himself. In this case the result was headlines, in America and overseas, proclaiming "Bride Registers Under Her Maiden Name." Why save the surprise, Bernays reasoned, when the marriage could become a major story, helping not only him but his hotel client and the women's movement as well?

Those same powers of persuasion were put to use for hundreds of other Bernays clients. In 1930 he went to work for America's biggest book publishers, who were desperate to increase sales. Rather than cutting prices, which was the approach other promoters took, Bernays reasoned that "where there are bookshelves there will be books." So he got respected public figures to endorse the importance of books to civilization, then persuaded architects and decorators to put up shelves to store the precious volumes—which is why so many homes from that era have built-in bookshelves. Shortly afterwards he signed on with the Multiple Sclerosis Society, convincing its leaders that the name of their illness was more of a mouthful than most Americans could digest. He got them to prune it back to MS, which helped make the obscure ailment into a favorite cause. His most famous campaign was one he waged in the 1920s and 1930s on behalf of tobacco tycoons, climaxing in a parade of cigarette-smoking debutantes down New York City's Fifth Avenue on Easter Sunday. Bernays managed to recast smoking as an act of female liberation, in the process helping to convince a generation of women to light up the cigarettes that he suspected were deadly.

His tactics differed from client to client, but his philosophy remained the same. Hired to sell a product or service, Bernays instead sold whole new ways of behaving that reaped huge rewards for his clients and redefined the very texture of American life. Sometimes his campaigns involved strategies so complex and oblique that even he had trouble following the script, which often involved front groups, letter-writing campaigns, and alliance after alliance. At other times his approach was artfully simple, like reducing a name to its initials. Sometimes he appealed to the best instincts of clients and consumers; at other times he launched schemes he knew were wrong and willfully deceived the public. Always, however, there was a grand concept, the brash, bold, big thinking that grew out of his being more ingenious than his competitors, more cocksure, and generally more expensive. His big fees made Bernays rich, but more important, they helped convince his clients that his advice was worth its cost and that, since he was earning

as much as their chief executive officer, it was with the CEO that he should be plotting strategy. His way of doing things was part P. T. Barnum and part J. P. Morgan, blended in a way that was uniquely E. L. Bernays.

Bernays was short and plain, with a paunch that increased over time and that he accentuated by patting. But as soon as he entered a room, his audience realized how much he knew about almost everything and understood that he was worth listening to. That electric personality allowed Bernays to compete successfully on his own, with a small group of junior associates, when others in the public relations world were forming enormous companies. It also captivated his two daughters, Anne and Doris, although over time they resented what they felt were their father's attempts to manipulate and stage-manage their lives with the same techniques he masterminded for his clients. Bernays gave up his formal practice in 1962 when he and his wife moved to Cambridge, Massachusetts, where their daughters lived with their families. But Bernays continued offering advice to a range of public and corporate clients during his thirty-three years of "retirement." He died at home in Cambridge at age 103 of natural causes and was cremated.

Bernays's impact on his profession and on American society was profound and at times troubling. Much as his uncle Sigmund Freud had revolutionized the way the world thought about individual behavior, so Bernays was able to transform attitudes toward group action. He used his uncle's ideas in the commercial realm to predict, then adjust, the way people believed and behaved. Never mind that they did not realize it. In fact, all the better. And just as Freud was rewarded with the title of "Father of Psychoanalysis," so Bernays became known around the world as the "Father of Public Relations."

That was an image Bernays carefully sculpted in the 14 books he wrote on the profession and its practices, along with hundreds of articles, an 849-page autobiography (1965), the 774-page annotated bibliography he commissioned on his writings (1978), and the nearly 1,000 boxes of papers he left to the Library of Congress. Bernays was not the first modern PR practitioner, but he was the profession's first philosopher and intellectual. He saw the big picture when few others did, and he was the first to appreciate the nexus between theory and practice. In doing so, he was the first to demonstrate how powerful the profession could be in shaping America's economic, political, and cultural life, for better as well as for worse.

★

Bernays's personal and professional papers are at the manuscript division of the Library of Congress, Washington, D.C. His autobiography, *Biography of an Idea: Memoirs of Public Relations Counsel Edward L. Bernays* (1965), traces his personal and professional life until he was seventy. The only full-length biography is

Larry Tye, *The Father of Spin: Edward L. Bernays and the Birth of Public Relations* (1998). There are scores of long articles on his life, along with in-depth obituaries in the *New York Times* (10 Mar. 1995), *Boston Globe* (10 Mar. 1995), and other major American newspapers.

LARRY TYE

BLACK, Fischer Sheffey (*b.* 11 January 1938 in Washington, D.C.; *d.* 30 August 1995 in New Canaan, Connecticut), investment adviser and finance professor who helped lay down the theoretical foundations of stock-option pricing.

Black was the son of Fischer Sheffey Black and Elizabeth Zemp; he had two siblings. While attending Harvard College, Black switched majors several times before graduating with a bachelor's degree in physics in 1959. Five years later Harvard conferred on him a doctorate in applied mathematics.

With strong academic training in quantitative analysis and computer technology, Black easily found employment in 1965 with the management-consulting firm of Arthur D. Little, Inc., in Cambridge, Massachusetts. With the advent of complex quantitative methods in business management and the introduction of computers into the decision-making process in the early 1960s, Black's expertise was in high demand.

While working with computers and processing information at Arthur D. Little, Black became good friends with Jack Treynor. A Harvard Business School alumnus, Treynor was deeply involved in stock market research. He was trying to formulate a relationship between a stock's rate of return and the stock market risk. This idea of analyzing the seemingly chaotic world of the stock market caught the interest of the mathematically minded Black. The friends soon became colleagues in pursuit of a workable scientific model of the market.

Black stayed with Arthur D. Little until 1969. By this time he had learned enough about the financial market to start his own financial consulting business: Associates in Finance of Belmont, Massachusetts. Making money depended on providing sound financial advice, which, in turn, was dependent on a thorough knowledge of the complex relationships among the underlying economic variables. Because Treynor had already moved on to a more lucrative position with Merrill Lynch in New York City, Black looked to the finance faculty at the nearby Massachusetts Institute of Technology (MIT) for academic support. As the field of finance was increasingly becoming quantitative, Black's overture of cooperation was readily accepted by an MIT faculty in need of mathematicians to help with the formulation and testing of their theories. Additionally, Black had the advantage of providing the practical expertise necessary to bridge the academic and business worlds.

Black developed a special friendship with two MIT finance scholars: Myron Scholes and Robert Merton. What brought these three men together was the search for a valuation formula for "options." Options are a type of financial instrument that gives their holders the right to buy (calls) or the right to sell (puts) another financial instrument (usually corporate stock) at a predetermined price (strike price) within a specified time period. Options had been around for quite a long time. However, interest in them surged during the 1960s. Black and his MIT colleagues were fascinated by the complex relationship that seemed to exist between the value of an option and the movements in the price of its underlying financial instrument. Figuring out a price formula for options was not only an academic exercise; it would also help the practitioners to predict the future option prices.

In 1971 Black accepted a visiting professorship at the University of Chicago. A year later he was appointed head of the university's Center for Research in Security Prices. In 1973 he and Scholes published "The Pricing of Options and Corporate Liabilities" in the *Journal of Political Economy*. They had figured out the formula just in time. By coincidence, the Chicago Board of Options Exchange had commenced operations exactly one month before the paper was published. The "Black-Scholes Formula" was received enthusiastically by both the practitioners and the academicians. Within a brief period of time Fischer Black became a familiar name in all academic and business circles dealing with options.

In 1975 Black took a teaching position at MIT. His third wife (his previous two marriages had ended in divorce), Catherine Tawes, had never liked living in Chicago. While at MIT, Black continued to work on his research agenda. Some of his publications were, of course, related to his favorite topic of the options market. Others, such as "The Ins and Outs of Foreign Investment" (*Financial Analysts Journal,* May–June 1978), were on quite different subjects. In addition to teaching and research, Black also managed to run a lucrative consulting business.

In 1984 Black accepted a partnership at the prestigious Goldman Sachs investment banking firm in New York City. The business world always appealed to him. He was designated vice president for trading and arbitrage and was expected to be the expert in residence on all aspects of the company's business. Despite his busy schedule at the firm, Black made sure he had time for academic endeavors. For example, in 1985 he became the president of the American Finance Association. Later, he wrote "How We Came Up with the Option Formula" (*Journal of Portfolio Management,* winter 1989) and coauthored "Asset Allocation:

Combining Investor Views with Market Equilibrium" (*Journal of Fixed Income,* September 1991).

At the age of fifty-six, this fair, blue-eyed, tall, soft-spoken, quiet and polite man was at the peak of his career. He and his wife Catherine, together with their daughters Alethea, Melissa, Ashley, and Paige, a stepdaughter (Kristen Tawes), a stepson (Kevin Tawes), and his son, Terry Linton, seemed to have it all. Then suddenly, Black was afflicted with cancer of the throat. He died at home after one year of battling the disease.

The discovery of a valuation formula by Fischer Black and his colleagues proved to be an important breakthrough in the field of finance. The Black-Scholes Formula, as it later came to be known, paved the way for finance theoreticians to develop new models to meet the needs of an ever expanding options market. Without his seminal work, the financial markets would be a much riskier environment for investors in general and options speculators in particular.

★

The most extensive coverage of Fischer Black is in Peter L. Bernstein's *Capital Ideas: The Improbable Origins of Modern Wall Street* (1992). Good biographical summaries are "Fischer Black," *Economist* (9 Sept. 1995); Elizabeth Corcoran, "Fischer Black: Calculated Risks Enable Mathematician to Turn a Profit," *Scientific American* (Mar. 1990); and Jeffrey M. Laderman, "Fischer Black Is Practicing What He Teaches," *Business Week* (6 Aug. 1984). For an excellent account and analysis of his academic contributions, see G. L. Gastineau, "Fischer Black: Describing an Elephant," *Journal of Portfolio Management* (Dec. 1996): 25–28. Obituaries are in the *New York Times* (31 Aug. 1995).

MOJTABA SEYEDIAN

BLAINE, Vivian (*b.* 21 November 1921 in Newark, New Jersey; *d.* 9 December 1995 in Century City, California), actress and singer in films and plays, best remembered for her role as the long-suffering, perpetually engaged Miss Adelaide in the musical *Guys and Dolls.*

Born Vivian Stapleton, Blaine was the only child of a hairdresser and a theatrical agent. When she was only three years old, her father recognized the early signs of her talent and booked her into a vaudeville act. While still in elementary school, Blaine was playing dollar-a-night singing dates at nightclubs, company parties, and police benefits. At fourteen, she began singing with the Halsey Miller Orchestra, and after graduating from Southside High School in Newark, she went on the road as a singer with little-known bands. Each band gave her a different name.

In 1941, while she was singing at the Governor Clinton hotel in New York City, Blaine's photograph appeared in a newspaper, and a talent scout for Twentieth Century-

Vivian Blaine, 1971. AP/WIDE WORLD PHOTOS

Fox invited her to take a screen test. The studio's head, Darryl F. Zanuck, was impressed by the test and signed her to a contract. At first she was given small roles in minor films such as *Girl Trouble* (1942) and *He Hired the Boss* (1943), and she played the female lead in the Laurel and Hardy comedy *Jitterbugs* (1943). During World War II she spent much of her time touring the USO circuit, entertaining the troops.

Unhappy about her film career, Blaine stormed into Zanuck's office, insisting on better roles and threatening to quit. She won a leading role in the musical *Greenwich Village* (1944) opposite Don Ameche. Her subsequent roles in lightweight musicals, including *Something for the Boys* (1944), *Doll Face* (1945), and *Three Little Girls in Blue* (1946), gave her scant opportunities to make a lasting impression. She fared somewhat better as a band singer who has a romance with farm boy Dick Haymes in the diverting Rodgers and Hammerstein musical *State Fair* (1945). To bolster her box office appeal, the studio's publicity department labeled her the "Cherry Blonde" because of the unusual color of her hair. Still, Blaine sensed that her film career was waning, especially when the studio cast her in a minor black-and-white musical entitled *If I'm Lucky* (1946).

Blaine's big career break came with the casting of *Guys and Dolls,* the Frank Loesser–Abe Burrows stage musical based on Damon Runyon's stories of life among New York's endearing lowlife characters. At first Blaine auditioned for the role of Sarah Brown, but she was told that her personality was too strong to play the demure Salvation Army girl. Several months later she met the musical's producers, Cy Feuer and Ernest Martin, who were having casting problems, and auditioned successfully for the role of Miss Adelaide. Speaking in a squeaky, nasal New York voice, Blaine was delightful as the nightclub chanteuse who was long engaged to Nathan Detroit, operator of "the oldest established permanent floating crap game in New York." Her rendition of "Adelaide's Lament," in which she mournfully proclaimed that "a person could develop a cold" if she remained unmarried for too long, brought her acclaim at every performance. She was equally engaging singing "A Bushel and a Peck" and "Take Back Your Mink" in the Hot Box nightclub. The musical, which opened on 24 November 1950, ran for 1,200 performances, and Blaine received a Donaldson Award as best newcomer of the year. Although many actresses, including Betty Grable and Marilyn Monroe, were considered for the 1955 film version, Blaine was chosen to repeat the role opposite Frank Sinatra. She played Miss Adelaide again in a 1966 stage revival.

Although she cherished the role of Miss Adelaide, Blaine found that it was so closely identified with her that it hindered other opportunities for employment. Nevertheless, she continued her stage career after leaving *Guys and Dolls,* starring opposite David Wayne in the 1958 musical play *Say Darling.* She also replaced Shelley Winters as the desperate wife of a drug addict in *A Hatful of Rain* (1956), played an actress in the comedy *Enter Laughing* (1963), and took over Elaine Stritch's role as the caustic wife who sings "The Ladies Who Lunch" in the musical *Company* in 1971. In 1984, she played the aging courtesan in a short-lived revival of *Zorba.*

After the 1950s her roles in films were sporadic. She played a WAVE in the musical *Skirts Ahoy* (1952) and starred opposite comedian Red Skelton in *Public Pigeon No. One* (1957). In later years she appeared in a few low-budget films such as *Parasite* (1981). On television, she costarred in 1951 and 1952 with comedian Pinky Lee in a situation comedy with music called *Those Two.* Over the years she had guest roles in television series such as *Mary Hartman, Mary Hartman* and *Fantasy Island* and also appeared in television plays including *Katie: Portrait of a Centerfold* (1978), *The Cracker Factory* (1979), and *I'm Going to Be Famous* (1981). Blaine was married three times: to talent agent Manuel George Frank in 1945 (divorced in 1956); to film executive Milton Rackmil in 1959 (divorced in 1961); and to theatrical manager Stuart Clark in 1973. She had no children. She died in New York City of congestive heart failure.

Few actresses are fortunate enough to be identified for all time with even a single role. Although her "cherry blonde" hair, broad, winning smile, and exuberant style brightened many films and plays, Vivian Blaine achieved theatrical immortality by playing the perennially hopeful, endearing Miss Adelaide in the classic musical *Guys and Dolls.* With her sneezes, her wheezes, and "a sinus that's really a pip," that Hot Box chanteuse, and Blaine herself, remain lodged in our collective memory.

★

A clippings file on Vivian Blaine can be found in the Performing Arts Library at Lincoln Center in New York City. References to Blaine can be found in Susan Loesser, *A Most Remarkable Fella: Frank Loesser and the Guys and Dolls in His Life* (1993). Two interviews with Blaine are Stuart Oderman, *Film Fan Monthly,* no. 130 (Apr. 1972) and Rex Reed, *New York Sunday News* (16 Mar. 1980). Obituaries are in the *New York Times* (14 Dec. 1995) and *Variety* (1 Jan. 1996).

TED SENNETT

BLANTON, (Leonard) Ray (*b.* 10 April 1930 in Hardin County, Tennessee; *d.* 22 November 1996 in Jackson, Tennessee), governor of Tennessee (1975–1979) whose scandal-plagued administration led to his conviction on criminal charges of conspiracy to sell liquor licenses to his friends.

Blanton was born on a farm in western Tennessee, the second of three children of Leonard A. Blanton and Ora Delaney Blanton, who were sharecroppers. Despite the family's Great Depression–era poverty, Blanton always recalled a happy upbringing. The Blantons bettered their lot in the late 1930s by acquiring a small farm of their own. Book learning was not a priority of families in these circumstances, but Blanton was a good student and won a Danforth Foundation Award for outstanding scholarship at Old Shiloh High School. He earned a degree in agriculture at the University of Tennessee and taught this subject for a few years at a high school in Indiana.

In 1949, while still an undergraduate, he married Betty Littlefield, his high-school sweetheart. During his years away from home, Blanton's father and younger brother, Gene, borrowed enough money to start a road-building company in nearby Adamsville. The business thrived, and Blanton decided to leave teaching and join the family enterprise. The construction business in Tennessee in those years was riddled with corrupt practices including bid rigging and political kickbacks. This way of life was bred into the Blanton brothers as their route to realizing financial success and stature in their community. Blanton's father was elected mayor of Adamsville, and, from their humble beginnings, the Blanton family became one of the most prominent in the community. However, Ray Blanton and

Ray Blanton, 1978. AP/WIDE WORLD PHOTOS

his wife and children lived for the next decade in a mobile home, traveling from one job site to another.

In 1964 the incumbent state representative for the Adamsville district did not stand for reelection. Urged by a number of people to run, Blanton agreed, easily winning the Democratic primary, which was tantamount to election. Two years later he opted for a tougher race, for the U.S. House of Representatives. The incumbent was a popular twelve-term veteran and dean of the Tennessee delegation. Blanton and his family spent the summer of 1966 on a bus, traveling from town to town, shaking hands and talking to voters one-on-one. Although tending to stoutness, the dark-haired Blanton was a good-looking man when he smiled. Unfortunately, his distaste for the media usually induced the scowl that many people recall from news photographs and television interviews. With strong financial backing from his family and from various business groups, Blanton pulled off a startling upset victory, winning by barely three hundred votes. He also faced an unusually strong opponent in the general election, a former chairman of the Tennessee Republican Party, who had public support and financial backing. Again, he won narrowly.

Blanton's record of his three terms in Congress reflected the conservative rural attitudes of the district he represented. He worked successfully for major industrial development in farm areas and job training for Vietnam veter-ans. He opposed busing for racial balance and, in general, was not responsive to the concerns of black voters. Blanton believed in staying in touch with his district, mandating to his staff that constituent mail be answered within twenty-four hours. In 1972 Blanton took on another uphill race. He ran for the U.S. Senate, opposing the Republican senator Howard Baker. This time, he suffered a stinging defeat, losing by 300,000 votes, in part because he was unable to muster the black support normally available to a Democratic candidate. However, the race gave him statewide name recognition and resulted in a campaign organization that could be called upon again.

In 1974, after the Republican Party had been devastated by the Watergate scandal in Washington, D.C., Blanton ran for governor, defeating eleven other candidates in the Democratic primary. Facing the Republican Lamar Alexander in the general election, Blanton successfully linked Alexander to President Richard Nixon and Watergate and won by a handy margin. Soon after his inauguration, Ray Blanton learned that a political career cannot be run the same way as a small-town construction company. The Federal Bureau of Investigation began an investigation following allegations that he had violated campaign finance laws during his run against Howard Baker.

Blanton named advisory committees in all ninety-five Tennessee counties; critics immediately derided these committees as nothing more than old-fashioned patronage conduits. Media reports surfaced of other questionable activities including state purchasing irregularities involving a firm owned by Blanton's family. In December 1975 Republicans began an investigation in the hope of garnering enough evidence to impeach Blanton. The most notorious scandal of the Blanton administration involved the sale of pardons and sentence commutations for prisoners. Two of Blanton's aides were found guilty of these charges as well as illegally selling surplus state property.

Blanton declined to run for reelection, citing family reasons, but concerns about his honesty had discredited him as a public official. In his final days in office, he scandalized the state by pardoning fifty-two inmates, including convicted murderers. Governor-elect Lamar Alexander was sworn into office three days early at the behest of federal officials hoping to head off further pardons and commutations. Throughout, Blanton denied any wrongdoing.

In 1981 Blanton was convicted on federal charges of mail fraud, conspiracy, and extortion. He spent twenty-two months in prison from 1984 to 1986. He devoted the rest of his life to trying to clear his name by getting the convictions overturned. In 1988 he was successful in getting the mail fraud conviction reversed. After his release from prison, Blanton became a radio commentator for a time and later sold prefabricated metal buildings and used cars and trucks. Long rumored to be an alcoholic, Blanton died of liver disease while awaiting a liver transplant. He is buried in Shiloh Church Cemetery in Shiloh National Park, Tennessee.

Blanton's achievements as governor are frequently overshadowed by the scandals that flourished during his administration. However, he did succeed in extending civil-service protection to state workers, raised the state Department of Tourism to a cabinet-level agency, and encouraged foreign business investments in Tennessee, paving the way for the Nissan Motor Company of Japan to open an assembly plant for light trucks in Tennessee in 1980. By most accounts, Blanton was an able administrator with a warm personality. But the clannishness bred into him during his small-town upbringing made him suspicious of those outside his circle and unable to say no to those within it.

★

The seamier aspects of the Blanton administration are detailed in Peter Maas's *Marie—A True Story* (1983), which was the basis for a 1985 motion picture of the same name starring Sissy Spacek, and *FBI Code Name TENNPAR* by former FBI agent Hank Hillin (1985). Blanton's record in Congress is analyzed by Richard Sandler in "Ray Blanton, Democratic Representative from Tennessee" (1972), a part of the Ralph Nader Congress Project *Citizens Look at Congress.* Extensive coverage of Blanton's years as governor appeared in Tennessee newspapers, notably the Nashville *Tennessean* and Memphis *Commercial Appeal.* An obituary is in the *New York Times* (23 Nov. 1996).

NATALIE B. JALENAK

BLOCH, Robert Albert   (*b.* 5 April 1917 in Chicago, Illinois; *d.* 23 September 1994 in Los Angeles, California), author and screenwriter specializing in suspense-mystery and supernatural horror, best known for the novel *Psycho.*

Robert Bloch (called "Bob") was the elder of two children of Raphael A. Bloch (known as Ray or Ralph) and Stella Loeb. During Bob's childhood the family lived in Maywood, Illinois, a Chicago suburb, where he attended Emerson Grammar School. A bright child, he was skipped four semesters, advancing from first to fourth grade in one year. The family was culturally but not religiously Jewish, attending the Methodist church for social reasons.

Bob enjoyed Chicago's Art Institute and Lincoln Park Zoo. He read copiously, including the Tom Swift novels and the dime-novel adventures of Buffalo Bill and others; later he relished the Oz books and stories about Tarzan and Dr. Fu Manchu. He also enjoyed early films, especially *The Phantom of the Opera* starring Lon Chaney, Sr. Most importantly, in 1927 Bloch discovered *Weird Tales* magazine, a showcase of supernatural horror fiction.

His father worked as a banker in Chicago but lost two jobs after each bank closed due to bad management; though

Robert Bloch. ARCHIVE PHOTOS

the fault was not his, he had difficulty finding work. When Bob was in his early teens the family moved to Milwaukee, Wisconsin, where his mother, a teacher and social worker before her marriage, had been invited to return to her former job, working with immigrant families and their children at Abraham Lincoln House. His father found sporadic work, but the mother's job supported the family. Bloch attended Steuben Junior High School and Washington High School, then graduated from Lincoln High School in June 1934.

By then Bloch's life as a writer had begun. In 1933 he had written to H. P. Lovecraft, whose short fiction in *Weird Tales* he admired; Lovecraft, a voluminous correspondent, encouraged his teenage friend to write fiction. Bloch was not paid for his first two published short stories ("Lilies" and "The Black Lotus"), but by July 1934 he had sold two stories to *Weird Tales,* "The Feast in the Abbey" and "The Secret in the Tomb." Within eighteen months his fiction was selling regularly.

Bloch supported himself by writing, in many forms, for the rest of his life. He joined the Milwaukee Fictioneers, which included science fiction writers and editors, and wrote for *Amazing Stories.* Moving away from the deep in-fluence of Lovecraft's style on his fiction, Bloch consciously turned to mainstream influences—Somerset Maugham, Aldous Huxley, Thomas Mann—and other popular writers, such as Damon Runyon, James M. Cain, and Thorne Smith. In the late 1930s, Bloch sold jokes to the radio comics Stoopnagle and Budd.

In 1939, with his high school friend Harold Gauer, Bloch wrote publicity releases and speeches for a dark-horse Milwaukee mayoral candidate, Carl Zeidler. However, when Zeidler won, Bloch and Gauer were considered too young and uneducated for positions in the administration. Bloch married Marion Ruth Holcombe on 2 October 1940 and made a living primarily by writing fiction for magazines including *Unknown Worlds, Imaginative Tales, Fantastic Adventures,* and *Rogue.* They had a daughter, Sally, on 28 July 1943. Because he had to assist his wife, who suffered aftereffects of tuberculosis of the bone, Bloch did not serve in World War II.

From 1942 to 1953, Bloch wrote copy for the Gustav Marx Advertising Agency and continued to write fiction. The first collection of his stories, *The Opener of the Way,* was published in 1945 by August Derleth's Arkham House (founded to publish Lovecraft's works). His first novel was *The Scarf,* published in 1947; Bloch also began writing scripts—mainly adaptations of his short stories—for the radio show *Stay Tuned for Terror.* In 1953 the Bloch family moved to Marion's hometown, Weyauwega, Wisconsin, where Bloch wrote novels and commuted to Milwaukee to appear as a regular panelist on a cartoon quiz show, *It's a Draw.* In the 1950s landmark short stories such as "Yours Truly, Jack the Ripper" and "Water's Edge" were published, reprinted repeatedly, and adapted for radio and later television.

Bloch's most famous novel, *Psycho,* was published in 1959; this story of a mother-obsessed, murderous motel manager was inspired by the rural Wisconsin ghoul and murderer Ed Gein. While the novel was still being made into an award-winning film (1960) by Alfred Hitchcock, Bloch and his family moved to Los Angeles. Bloch began screenwriting—including *Strait-Jacket* (1964), starring Joan Crawford—and adapting his own and others' work for television. Personable and genuinely nice, Bloch made many friends, including such film greats as Buster Keaton, Boris Karloff, and Fritz Lang, as well as fellow-writers Charles Beaumont, Fritz Leiber, Ray Bradbury, and others.

Marion never fully adapted to Los Angeles, and she and Bloch were divorced. During the long proceedings, the writer met and fell in love with Eleanor Alexander, whose writer-producer husband had recently died. Bloch and Elly married on 16 October 1964, a sound marriage that lasted until his death.

During his last three decades, Bloch produced screen-plays for movies and television, short stories, novels, and an endearing volume of memoirs. He won the Hugo Award from the World Science Fiction Convention in 1959 for his story "That Hellbound Train." In 1975 he was guest of honor at the First World Fantasy Convention, where he was given the Life Achievement Award, and in 1991 he won the Bram Stoker Award from the Horror Writers of America for lifetime contribution to the field. Even when terminally ill with cancer of the esophagus and kidneys, Bloch thought first of his friends, graciously saying goodbye to distant friends and joking until the end. His ashes, in a book-shaped urn, are kept by the University of Wyoming.

The epitome of a professional writer, Bloch took seriously every job, always seeking to entertain and thrill the reader, viewer, or listener as well as to make money practicing his craft. Moreover, he was kind and thoughtful, reaching out to new writers, and an honest gentleman even in as competitive a milieu as Hollywood. The combination of humor and horror gives his work unique appeal—a combination seen in his oft-quoted self-description, "I have the heart of a child. I keep it in a jar on my desk."

★

Bloch's manuscripts, correspondence, and personal memorabilia are in the American Heritage Center at the University of Wyoming in Laramie. His "unauthorized autobiography," *Once Around the Bloch* (1993), is indispensable, charming, and informative. Works about Bloch tend to be from small publishers and hard to find but worthwhile, such as Graeme Flanagan's *Robert Bloch: A Bio-Bibliography* (1979); Harold Lee Prosser's *The Man Who Walked Through Mirrors: Robert Bloch as Social Critic* (1989); and *The Complete Robert Bloch: An Illustrated, Comprehensive Bibliography* (1986) and *Robert Bloch* (1986), both by Randall D. Larson. *Robert Bloch: Appreciations of the Master* (1995), edited by Richard Matheson and Ricia Mainhardt, includes factual pieces and emotional tributes and reprints of some of Bloch's best short fiction. An obituary is in the *New York Times* (25 Sept. 1994).

BERNADETTE LYNN BOSKY

BOMBECK, Erma Louise Fiste (*b.* 21 February 1927 in Dayton, Ohio; *d.* 22 April 1996 in San Francisco, California), newspaper columnist and best-selling author who poked gentle fun at suburban life, housework, marriage, and parenthood.

Bombeck was the only child of Cassius Fiste, a crane operator for the city of Dayton who died when his daughter was nine years old, and Erma Haines, a homemaker who went to work in a General Motors factory after her husband's death. In order to survive her family problems, Erma developed a whimsical approach to life. By the time she was thirteen years old she was writing a humor column for her junior high school paper, which she continued at Patterson Vocational High School in Dayton. When she

Erma Bombeck. AP/WIDE WORLD PHOTOS

Bombeck's columns featured a gentle self-deprecating wit based upon her experiences cleaning house, shopping, raising children, and being a wife, roles she continued to hold even after the family moved in 1971 to Paradise Valley, Arizona, a suburb of Phoenix, where her husband became a high school principal. She once noted, "I spend ninety percent of my life living scripts and ten percent writing them." Her tart comments were welcomed by millions of suburban wives and mothers weary of striving for illusory perfection. Bombeck told a reporter, "My type of humor is almost pure identification. A housewife reads my column and says, 'But that's what happened to ME! I know just what she's talking about.'" Her writings dealt with the mundane realities of a homemaker's world. These included ironing—her "second favorite household chore," the first being "hitting my head on the top of the bunk bed until I faint"—and dirty ovens: "If it won't catch fire today, clean it tomorrow." She also wrote about the problems of family relationships including sibling rivalry ("Who gets the fruit cocktail with the one cherry on top?") and male obsessions ("If a man watches sixteen consecutive quarters of football, he can be declared legally dead.") "No one knows what her life expectancy is," she once joked, "but I have a horror of leaving this world and not having anyone in the entire family know how to replace a toilet tissue spindle." Amused by the popularity of Robert James Waller's novel *The Bridges of Madison County* (1992), she commented that housewives all over America were fantasizing about their romantic ideal man, "hiding bottles of wine behind the bleach in the utility room just in case. The other day, an exterminator knocked on my door asking for directions and I wondered, 'Is he the one?'"

Bombeck was also the author of more than a dozen books. These included such best-sellers as *The Grass Is Always Greener Over the Septic Tank* (1976), *If Life is a Bowl of Cherries, What Am I Doing in the Pits?* (1978), *Motherhood: The Second Oldest Profession* (1983), and *A Marriage Made in Heaven: or, Too Tired for an Affair* (1993). After sales of more than 15 million books, Bombeck signed a three-book deal with Harper & Row in 1988 that experts valued at $12 million. In addition to her writing, Bombeck appeared regularly on the ABC television show *Good Morning America* from 1975 to 1986. She also lectured widely; contributed to several magazines; created and produced *Maggie,* a television series that ran briefly in 1981; and saw *The Grass Is Greener* made into a television movie in 1978, with Carol Burnett playing Bombeck's harried alter ego.

In 1992 Bombeck underwent a mastectomy after being diagnosed with breast cancer. The following year her kidneys began to fail as a result of a hereditary disorder, polycystic kidney disease, that had been diagnosed when she was twenty years old. She began dialysis at home. She was touched when more than thirty fans offered her their kid-

graduated from high school in 1944, she took a job as a copygirl for the Dayton *Journal-Herald.* After graduating from the University of Dayton in 1949, she became a reporter for the same paper and eventually a feature writer for the women's page. In 1949 she married William Bombeck, a sportswriter on the paper who became a public school administrator in Dayton.

When her first child, Betsy, was born in 1953, Bombeck left her job to take on the role of homemaker and mother. The couple had two other children. In the era of the idealized suburban wife and mother, Bombeck recalled, "we knew what we were supposed to do: Snap those beans. Iron those shoelaces." She read about famous women who had fashioned their own careers and concluded that "it wasn't fulfilling to clean chrome faucets with a toothbrush." In 1964, when her youngest child started school, Bombeck decided that, at the age of thirty-seven, she was "too old for a paper route, too young for Social Security, and too tired for an affair." She convinced the editor of a small suburban weekly, the *Kettering-Oakwood Times,* to let her write a humorous column for $3 a week on what she termed the "utility room beat." By the following year the column, titled "At Wit's End," was appearing twice weekly in the *Journal-Herald.* Its popularity grew rapidly, and by 1970 the column was syndicated on a three-times-a-week basis. By the time of her death, it appeared twice weekly in more than 600 newspapers with an estimated 30 million readers.

neys. She responded to those who expressed sadness about her illness by remarking, "Never feel sorry for a humorist." She continued to work on her column and books, refusing to worry about other goals. "Miss America took all the good ones," she joked. "I wanted to cure world hunger and have world peace. I wanted to do that, but she took it." After a long wait for a kidney transplant, a suitable donor was found, and she underwent the operation at the University of California at San Francisco Medical Center in April 1996. The hospital announced that she died "from medical complications following a kidney transplant."

Erma Bombeck once told an interviewer about her work, "I would rather hang from one hundred refrigerator doors than in the Louvre." She exceeded that goal.

★

Books by Erma Bombeck not mentioned in the text include *At Wit's End* (1967), a collection of columns; *"Just Wait Till You Have Children of Your Own!"* (1971); *I Lost Everything in the Post-Natal Depression* (1973); *Aunt Erma's Cope Book* (1979); *Family: The Ties That Bind—And Gag!* (1987); *I Want to Grow Hair, I Want to Grow Up, I Want to Go to Boise: Children Surviving Cancer* (1989); *When You Look Like Your Passport Photo, It's Time to Go Home* (1991); and *All I Know About Animal Behavior I Learned in Loehmann's Dressing Room* (1995). Obituaries are in the *New York Times* and *USA Today* (both 23 Apr. 1996).

LOUISE A. MAYO

BOORDA, Jeremy Michael ("Mike") (*b.* 26 November 1939 in South Bend, Indiana; *d.* 16 May 1996 in Washington, D.C.), four-star admiral who was the only person in American naval history to rise from the lowest rank to the highest office. He committed suicide while serving as chief of naval operations.

The middle of three children of Herman Boorda and Gertrude Frank Wallis, corner-store clothing merchants, Jeremy Boorda had a difficult youth. The family, which moved several times before finally settling in Momence, Illinois, was troubled as neither parent had much time for their children. Herman was diagnosed with paranoid schizophrenia after trying to commit suicide when Jeremy was thirteen.

An indifferent student and a loner at school, Jeremy quit high school during his junior year, and in early 1956, lying about his age, he enlisted in the navy at sixteen. Following basic training, he attended the Naval Air Technical Training School in Norman, Oklahoma, where he specialized in personnel administration. On 13 March 1957 Boorda married Bettie May Moran, a student at the University of Oklahoma; they had four children. Naval service had a focusing effect on Boorda, and by 1961 he had advanced to the rank of petty officer first class, serving primarily in aviation commands at Miramar, California.

U.S. Navy Admiral Mike Boorda aboard the aircraft carrier *Theodore Roosevelt*, 1993. ASSOCIATED PRESS AP

After completing officer candidate school in 1962, Boorda was commissioned an ensign, and during the next two decades he rose to the rank of captain while holding a variety of assignments. They included service aboard the destroyer *Porterfield;* attendance at the naval destroyer school; a stint as weapons officer on the destroyer *John R. Craig,* which engaged in fire support missions for American and South Vietnamese troops in Vietnam in 1965; command of the minesweeper *Parrot;* instructor at the naval destroyer school; attendance at the Naval War College at Newport, Rhode Island, and the University of Rhode Island, where he earned a bachelor's degree in 1971; service as executive officer of the destroyer *Brooke,* which in 1972–1973 escorted aircraft carriers operating against North Vietnam; a tour in the bureau of naval personnel; command of the destroyer *Farragut* from 1975 to 1977; service as executive assistant in the naval secretariat for manpower and reserve affairs; command of Destroyer Squadron 22 from 1981 to 1983; and service as executive assistant to the chief of naval personnel from 1983 to 1984. In these posts Boorda earned a reputation as an outstanding gunnery officer and seaman and as a politically savvy officer who was a strong advocate for the navy on Capitol Hill. He also earned a reputation as "a sailor's sailor" because of his efforts to improve the welfare of enlisted men.

In 1984 Boorda was appointed executive assistant to the chief of naval operations, his first "flag" assignment (that is, one filled by an admiral), and two years later he became commander of Cruiser-Destroyer Group 8, followed shortly afterward by stints as commander of an aircraft carrier battle group and later as commander of the Battle Force Sixth Fleet. From 1988 to 1991 Boorda was chief of naval personnel, and in December 1991, now a four-star admiral, he became commander in chief, Allied Forces Southern Europe and commander in chief, U.S. Naval Forces Europe. In the former role, Boorda commanded North Atlantic Treaty Organization (NATO) forces enacting United Nations sanctions against the warring factions in the Balkans, and in February 1994 he ordered air strikes in Bosnia against Serbian forces, the first offensive military action ever by NATO forces.

Boorda was appointed chief of naval operations in April 1994, the first "mustang"—an officer commissioned from the enlisted ranks—to be named chief and the first chief from the surface fleet in more than two decades. He had little combat experience, yet President Bill Clinton and Secretary of Defense William Perry thought his political skills and popularity with sailors made him a good choice to restore the morale and image of a service that had been buffeted by troubles in recent years. These troubles included the crashes of a number of costly F-14 aircraft and dealing with the lingering effects of the Tailhook scandal, which involved the molestation of female naval officers at the 1991 convention of the Tailhook Association, a group of current and former naval aviators. Few had been satisfied by the navy's handling of the scandal. Aviators charged that the probe to identify and punish offenders had degenerated into a witch-hunt, while others charged that Tailhook symbolized a prevailing hostility against women in the navy that needed to be completely rooted out.

Boorda took a number of steps to improve the navy and burnish its public standing. He intensified long-range strategic planning to make the most of the navy's dollars at a time when defense budgets were dwindling because of the end of the cold war, lobbied Congress for new ships, submarines, and aircraft, insisted upon improved aviation-maintenance and pilot-training programs, worked to convince members of Congress that the navy had put Tailhook behind it, and attempted to address the concerns of ordinary sailors over matters like housing and family problems, even if it meant personally bending a rule to benefit a sailor in need.

Boorda's actions were popular with Congress and sailors; however, he was soon entangled in troubles. There were continuing controversies over the treatment of women, scandals at the U.S. Naval Academy, and more aircraft crashes. In addition, some in the naval community began to criticize his leadership. They complained that he was too liberal on gender issues, too ready to ignore the chain of command in personnel matters, and too willing to curry the favor of politicians by failing to fight for the careers of good officers who had been unfairly stigmatized by the sexual scandals. Under Boorda's leadership, they charged, the navy was emphasizing "political correctness" to the detriment of naval traditions and warrior virtues.

By the spring of 1996 some of Boorda's critics were saying that he had lost the respect of senior officers and should resign. At the same time, *Newsweek* magazine began to look into reports that for a number of years before 1995 Boorda had wrongly worn combat valor pins on two Vietnam War decorations. Perhaps fearing that a dispute over the legitimacy of his wartime decorations would further harm the battered reputation of the navy, or perhaps distraught by the attacks from his critics, Boorda killed himself on 16 May 1996 at his quarters in the Washington Navy Yard. He is buried at Arlington National Cemetery.

The wearing of a decoration to which one is not entitled is a serious violation of navy rules and difficult to explain away for a senior commander, even if it is in error. The valor pins worn by Boorda signified being fired at in combat, and like many naval officers at the time of the Vietnam War, Boorda believed that his service in the war zone qualified him to wear them. Navy rules about medals were not always clear during the war, and it was not uncommon, especially in the surface fleet, to leave it up to the individual's interpretation as to whether he should wear a valor pin. But according to regulations that went into effect in 1969, one was entitled to wear the pin only if it had been specifically authorized in the medal citation. Boorda's citations did not include the authorizations, and in 1995 the navy's Office of Awards and Special Projects advised him that he did not rate the pins. In a suicide note Boorda said he had made "an honest mistake" in wearing them, although some noted that as an experienced personnel officer and a senior commander he should have been fully aware of the rules. After a request from Boorda's widow for an official ruling from the navy on the appropriateness of the pins, Secretary of the Navy John Dalton in April 1998 placed "a memorandum for the record" in Boorda's service file certifying that he was entitled to wear them. He cited the authority of Admiral Elmo Zumwalt, commander of U.S. naval forces in Vietnam and later chief of naval operations, who in a memorandum also placed in Boorda's file stated that wearing the pins was "appropriate, justified, and proper." Dalton's action did not change the official record, however, which requires an appeal to the Board for Correction of Naval Records, a long and complicated process that was not initiated.

A diminutive, gregarious, and energetic man, Boorda stood out for his efforts to guide the trouble-plagued navy into the post–cold war era of reduced budgets and across the divide between an old navy secure in its verities and a new navy caught up in the nation's cultural wars.

★

Boorda's tenure as chief of naval operations is described within the larger context of the navy's travails in Gregory L. Vistica, *Fall from Glory: The Men Who Sank the U.S. Navy* (1997). Magazine articles offer the best source of information about Boorda. They include Tom Philpott, "Can Mike Boorda Salvage the Navy?," *Washingtonian* (Feb. 1995); "A Matter of Honor," *Newsweek* (27 May 1996); Richard Zoglin, "A Question of Honor," *Time* (27 May 1996); Peter J. Boyer, "Admiral Boorda's War," *New Yorker* (16 Sept. 1996); Nick Kotz, "Breaking Point," *Washingtonian* (Dec. 1996); Nick Kotz, "A Matter of Honor," *Washingtonian* (July 1998); and "Another Chapter in the Boorda Matter," *Newsweek* (6 July 1998). Obituaries are in the *New York Times* and *Washington Post* (both 17 May 1996).

JOHN KENNEDY OHL

BOYER, Ernest LeRoy, Sr. (*b.* 13 September 1928 in Dayton, Ohio; *d.* 8 December 1995 in Princeton, New Jersey), educator, author, and foundation executive who had a profound influence on American education in the last quarter of the twentieth century.

Boyer was the second of three sons born to Clarence W. Boyer, a Dayton businessman, and Ethel French Boyer, who helped with the family business. Boyer's grandfather, the Reverend William Boyer, at age forty, moved his family into the Dayton slums, where he ran a Brethren in Christ mission for more than forty years, setting an example that inspired Ernest Boyer's commitment to a life of public service. In grade school his family's pacifist tradition set Boyer apart by preventing him from helping his classmates in war bond drives, a popular form of competition among schoolchildren during World War II. In 1944 he transferred from public schools in Dayton to Messiah Academy at Messiah Bible College in Grantham, Pennsylvania, on a small campus operated by the Brethren in Christ Church. At Messiah, Boyer excelled in academics, sports, chorus, government, and publications.

After graduating in 1946, Boyer sailed to Poland with "Operation Heifer," a postwar project to replenish that country's decimated livestock. Exposed to war-ravaged Europe, he made his first attempts to communicate across culture and language barriers. He returned to Messiah Bible College and graduated with a two-year degree in Bible studies in 1948.

In 1950 Boyer completed a bachelor's degree at Greenville College (Illinois), where he had developed into a formidable debater. Marriage to Kathryn Garis Tyson, a classmate at Messiah Academy, took place on 26 August 1950. The Boyers had four children. Kathryn , a registered nurse-midwife, later delivered most of their grandchildren.

Ernest Boyer, 1970. AP/WIDE WORLD PHOTOS

Boyer took a few graduate courses at Ohio State University. At the University of Southern California, Boyer earned M.A. and Ph.D. degrees in speech pathology in 1956. The following year he was a postdoctoral fellow in medical audiology at University of Iowa Hospital. In 1960, after brief teaching and administrative posts at Loyola University (Los Angeles) and Upland College, he directed the Western College Association Commission to Improve the Education of Teachers. From 1962 to 1965 he was director of the Center for Coordinated Education at the University of California, Santa Barbara.

In 1965 he became vice president for university-wide activities of the State University of New York (SUNY). On 30 July 1970, Boyer succeeded Samuel B. Gould as chancellor of the youngest, largest, and most complex public university system in the nation. With continual encouragement from Governor Nelson Rockefeller, the 1960s and 1970s were years of remarkable growth for SUNY. For Chancellor Boyer the times were complicated by the geographic dispersion of sixty-four semi-autonomous campuses and the need for system cooperation and by the increase in student activism and campus unrest. Nonetheless, Boyer oversaw many innovative programs.

In 1971 the creation of Empire State College, based in

Saratoga Springs, freed adult students from the demands of campus residency and class attendance. Through tutorials and learning contracts, they were able to work and earn degrees. Empire State College, which Boyer was key in creating, has served as a model for adult learners for much of higher education. As chancellor, Boyer exemplified academic and political statesmanship. He imbued large meetings with a sense of intimacy. He was quick to summarize complex issues and propose effective solutions. Boyer remained the contemplative professional at the center of controversies such as antiwar protests, sit-ins, and demonstrations. Even though SUNY was a volatile, sprawling multiversity, Boyer worked to ensure that it remained, at its core, a community.

In 1977 President Jimmy Carter called Boyer to Washington, D.C., to serve as Commissioner of education under the Department of Health, Education, and Welfare (HEW). Here Boyer encountered a large and dispirited bureaucracy. In a brief two years he was able to streamline much of the work of HEW. He reinvigorated his colleagues by founding the Horace Mann Center, an internal professional development program. Commissioner Boyer struggled to address widespread problems of basic literacy and promote equity of educational opportunity.

In 1979 Boyer accepted the presidency of the Carnegie Foundation for the Advancement of Teaching in Princeton. For Boyer this was a difficult choice; he and President Carter were close. But, as HEW secretary Joseph A. Califano, Jr., observed, federal regulations were anticipated that could prevent Boyer from becoming a foundation executive. (Boyer had to leave before 1 July 1979, when the Ethics in Government Act took effect.)

Under Boyer's direction, the Carnegie Foundation systematically examined the full spectrum of American education for more than fifteen years (1979–1995). Boyer initiated major studies that argued for critical restructuring of primary, secondary, and college education. He participated in the studies as well as in the writing and meticulous editing of the reports, which advocated reform in university governance, general education, concepts of scholarship, and public service. Boyer's quest was to return education to the center of American life and to restore transformational powers to the nation's schools. Boyer cherished the potential of the spoken and written word. Each report that bears Boyer's name is suffused with his communitarian philosophy expressed through an exquisitely crafted prose style. In *College: The Undergraduate Experience in America* (1987), he wrote: "We proceed, then, with the conviction that if a balance can be struck between individual interests and shared concerns, a strong learning community will result. And perhaps it is not too much to hope that the college, as a vital community of learning, can be a model for society at large—a society where private and public purposes also

must be joined." Boyer's other major works are *Quest for Common Learning* (1981) with Arthur Levine, *The Control of the Campus* (1982), *High School: A Report on Secondary Education in America* (1983), *Campus Life: In Search of Community* (1990), *Scholarship Reconsidered: Priorities of the Professoriate* (1990), *Ready to Learn* (1991), *The Basic School: A Community for Learning* (1995), *Building Community: A New Future for Architecture Education and Practice* (1996) with Lee Mitang.

From 1979 to 1995 Ernest Boyer was a tireless advocate for American education. His commitment to educators was unparalleled. His archives contain more than 1,500 speeches, lectures, and articles. Boyer crisscrossed the country continuously, sometimes making more than fifteen appearances in as many states in one month. The nation's colleges responded by awarding him more than 150 honorary degrees.

During the closing years of his life, Boyer had a running battle with cancer. The day before he died, he worked from his home in Princeton. A few days later he was laid to rest in the cemetery of the Perkiomen Valley Brethren in Christ Church near Graterford, Pennsylvania, the church where he was married forty-five years earlier.

Ernest Boyer captured best the spirit of his own life in a 1984 address commemorating the seventy-fifth anniversary of Messiah College: "The tragedy of life is not death; it is destined for us all. The tragedy of life is to die with convictions undeclared and service unfulfilled."

★

Extensive archival materials covering Boyer's personal and professional life are housed at the Boyer Center of Messiah College in Grantham, Pennsylvania. There is no biography of Boyer. Obituaries are in the *New York Times* (9 and 10 Dec. 1995).

JOSEPH G. FLYNN

BROCCOLI, Albert Romolo ("Cubby") (*b.* 5 April 1909 in New York City; *d.* 27 June 1996 in Beverly Hills, California), film producer best known for the James Bond series of motion pictures.

The younger of two children born to Giovanni Broccoli and Christina Vence, immigrants from the Calabria region of southern Italy, Broccoli was born in the borough of Queens in New York City. When he was a young child his cousin Patrick DiCiccio started calling him "Kabbible," after a popular comic strip character of the day. The nickname was soon shortened to "Kubbie," then changed to "Cubby," the name that family, friends, and acquaintances called him for the rest of his life. Broccoli and his older brother attended P.S. 107 in Queens. Later, he attended elementary school in suburban Rye, New York, and public schools in Astoria, Queens. His mother was employed as a

Albert "Cubby" Broccoli with his grandchildren at the Hollywood Walk of Fame, 1990. ASSOCIATED PRESS AP

cook and housekeeper. His father, a laborer who worked on construction projects, eventually obtained promotion to supervisor. When Broccoli was in high school, his parents purchased a twenty-five-acre farm at Garden Lake on Long Island. He dropped out of high school to work full-time on the farm. Later, Broccoli and his brother purchased their own farm in eastern Florida. After two years the venture failed. He returned to New York and found employment selling coffins.

In 1934 DiCiccio, now a Hollywood agent, invited Broccoli to stay with him in Los Angeles. On his first day in Hollywood, Broccoli met Cary Grant, who became a life-long friend. The following evening, a chance meeting with Howard Hughes led to a more influential friendship. Through his friendship with Hughes, Broccoli became a fixture at social events in Hollywood, Palm Springs, and the new resort of Las Vegas. He remained in Hollywood for the next eighteen years, pursuing a career in the film industry. Starting as an assistant director at Twentieth Century–Fox, he worked in various capacities on several Fox productions prior to World War II. His connections within the Hollywood community further improved during

the war. Enlisting in the navy, he spent the entire war booking America's most popular entertainers in benefit shows. By 1948 he had acquired a position of influence in the industry, working as an agent for the Famous Artists agency. He left the agency in 1952, however, to form a production company with the filmmaker Irving Allen.

Taking advantage of tax incentives offered by the British government, Broccoli and Allen based their new venture, Warwick Films, in the United Kingdom. For the next twenty-five years, Broccoli was an independent filmmaker based in London. The producers scored a major coup by signing Alan Ladd to star in their first three films. While profitable in its early years, the company foundered when Broccoli and Allen attempted to distribute their own films. In 1960, the commercial failure of *The Trials of Oscar Wilde* (U.S. title: *The Man with the Green Carnation*), a critical success but a box-office disaster, ended the Broccoli-Allen partnership.

Broccoli married three times. He married his first wife, Gloria Blondell, in 1940; their brief union ended in divorce. In 1951 he married a widow, Nedra Clark. The marriage produced two children. Nedra Broccoli died of cancer in 1958. In 1959 Broccoli married a divorcée, the writer Dana Wilson. The marriage made her son, Michael Wilson, a member of Broccoli's family, and the couple's daughter, Barbara, was born in 1960.

In 1961 Broccoli teamed with the Canadian producer Harry Saltzman to bring Ian Fleming's suave master spy, James Bond, to the screen. Naming their new company Eon Productions, the producers obtained the backing of United Artists for an initial Bond film. Despite the objections of United Artists executives, they cast a then little-known Scottish actor, Sean Connery, as Bond. Both *Dr. No* (1962) and *From Russia with Love* (1963) provided United Artists with major hits; the third Bond film, *Gold-finger* (1964), made James Bond an international phenom-enon. Broccoli and Saltzman's escapist entertainment, a mixture of sex and violence, exotic locales, beautiful women, megalomaniacal villains, and implausible techno-logical gadgets, inspired a host of imitators on movie and television screens for the next several years. The fourth Bond film, *Thunderball,* ranked number one in U.S. box office receipts for 1965.

Eon Productions released twelve more Bond films be-tween 1967 and 1989. Four different actors portrayed Bond during this period, with the English actor Roger Moore proving the most durable of Connery's replacements. The Broccoli-Saltzman partnership ended in 1976. Investment failures forced Saltzman to sell his half of Eon to United Artists, which became Broccoli's new partner in the series. After the Broccolis moved to Beverly Hills in 1977, Michael Wilson began to play a prominent role in Eon Productions. By 1985 Broccoli was coproducing films with his stepson, and in the late 1980s he also started grooming his daughter Barbara, an associate producer on *The Living Daylights* (1987), as his replacement.

At the 1982 Academy Awards ceremony, Broccoli received the Academy's highest honor, the Irving G. Thalberg Award. In 1986 Queen Elizabeth II named him a member of the Order of the British Empire (OBE). The following year the French government named him a Commandeur de l'Ordre des Artes et des Lettres.

In 1990 the series was discontinued while Broccoli sued a new partner in Eon, MGM-Pathé, over the proposed price of international television rights. In 1994 an out-of-court settlement made it possible to start production on a new Bond movie, *GoldenEye.* Broccoli cast the Irish actor Pierce Brosnan as Bond and named Michael Wilson and Barbara Broccoli as the film's producers.

In May 1994 Broccoli was diagnosed with an aortal aneurysm. An operation repaired the damaged blood vessel, but continuing coronary problems left him an invalid. He died at his home in Beverly Hills on 27 June 1996. He is buried at Forest Lawn Cemetery in Los Angeles.

At the time of Broccoli's death, the Bond films had grossed more than $2 billion, and it was estimated that half the world's population had seen at least one Bond movie. The Bond films remained the most profitable series in the history of motion pictures, and the genre that Broccoli pioneered, the big-budget action film, had become a Hollywood staple. Although Ian Fleming created James Bond, Broccoli's films made Bond one of the best-known fictional characters of the twentieth century.

★

Broccoli's posthumous autobiography, *When the Snow Melts: The Autobiography of Cubby Broccoli* (1998), written with the British journalist Donald Zec, remains the only full-length account of the producer's life. Other sources include Raymond Benson, *The James Bond Bedside Companion* (1988); Ephraim Katz, *The Film Encyclopedia* (2d ed., 1994); and Grace Jermoski, ed., *The International Dictionary of Films and Filmmakers* (1997). In addition to wire-service obituaries published by Reuters and the Associated Press (both 28 June 1996), obituaries of Broccoli are in the London *Times, New York Times,* and *Los Angeles Times* (all 29 June 1996).

THOMAS SCHAFFER

BRODSKY, Joseph (Iosif or Josip Alexandrovich) (*b.* 24 May 1940 in Leningrad, Soviet Union [now Russia]; *d.* 28 January 1996 in New York City), Russian poet who immigrated to the United States in 1972, won the Nobel Prize for literature in 1987, and became the fifth U.S. poet laureate in 1991.

Brodsky's father, Alexander I. Brodsky, an officer in the Russian navy until his rank was stripped by the government

Joseph Brodsky. ARCHIVE PHOTOS

because he was Jewish, was a sometime commercial photographer and storyteller. His mother, Maria M. Volpert, often supported the family as a linguist and interpreter. The middle-class family lived in a communal apartment, and Joseph attended schools in Leningrad (now St. Petersburg), where he suffered from the anti-Semitism of his teachers and began developing a philosophy of dissent. At the age of fifteen, he quit school and took a variety of jobs: farm laborer, metal worker, stoker in a boiler house, milling machine operator in a factory, photographer, sailor, assistant to a coroner and to a geologist on expeditions across the Soviet Union and Central Asia (1956–1962), and translator. During this period, he began an intensive program of self-education, reading literary classics and studying English and Polish in order to translate into Russian the works of poets John Donne and Czesław Miłosz.

In 1955, Brodsky began to write poetry, which became known through mimeographed "samizdat" (self-published) sheets for friends, publication in the underground journal *Sintaksis,* and his recitations on street corners. His immediate circle of friends in Leningrad included Evgeny Rein, Anatoly Naiman, Lev Loseff, Vladimir Uflyand, and Yakov Gordin. His work impressed the poet Anna Akhmatova, one of Russia's leading literary figures, and other prominent Soviet cultural personalities.

Brodsky's powerful, individualistic writing troubled the Communist and literary establishments and led to official harassment. He suffered various arrests between 1959 and 1964. In 1963 he was attacked by a Leningrad newspaper as a "vagrant" and "semiliterary parasite," writing gibberish and devoted to translating and writing poetry instead of being a socially useful citizen with a steady job. He was placed in Kashchenko Psychiatric Hospital in Moscow from December 1963 to January 1964. In February 1964, he was arrested, tried, found guilty, and sentenced to five years at a labor camp in Norinskaya, a small village in the far north of Arkhangelsk province near the Arctic Circle, where he chopped wood, hauled manure, and crushed rocks. His case became a cause célèbre when one supporter and member of the Leningrad writers' union, Frieda Vigdorova, made available to the outside world her stenographic record of the trial. His poems and translations were also circulated outside the Soviet Union. The resulting protest against his incarceration by leading writers inside and outside of Russia forced his release after eighteen months. After his return to Leningrad, however, the harassment by the secret police resumed. In 1965 his son, Andrei, was born to Leningrad artist Martina Basmanova. Dmitry Bobyshev, a rival Leningrad poet and friend, also had an affair with Martina, and they lived in a ménage à trois.

Despite the translation of many of his works into English, German, and French and publication abroad, Brodsky was not permitted to attend international writers' conferences. In 1971 he received and declined two invitations to Israel, but in May 1972 the Ministry of the Interior questioned his refusal. Ten days later, authorities searched his apartment, confiscated his poems, and forced his involuntary exile to Vienna, Austria. There he met the American poet W. H. Auden, who arranged for him to serve as poet-in-residence at the University of Michigan for a year. After teaching at Queens College in New York from 1973 to 1974, he returned to the University of Michigan from 1974 to 1980. He became an American citizen in 1977. He moved to the Greenwich Village neighborhood of New York City in 1980 and taught poetry and literature as an adjunct professor at Columbia University and New York University. In 1981 he accepted a chair at Mount Holyoke College, where he taught Russian and comparative literature and served as the Andrew Mellon Professor of Literature for fifteen years until his death.

Brodsky was described shortly after his immigration as tall and well built, with reddish hair and sharp, gray-green eyes. Although he was a chain smoker, he was also a vigorous and volatile man whose deep, rumbling voice recited his powerful lyrics in Russian in a liturgical chant with the force of an organ bellows. His immense industriousness, self-confidence, ready irony, insouciance, and cunning eased his transition in America, but he remained viscerally and expressively Russian. He was active in Russian émigré affairs and had ties to prominent Russian and Eastern European figures in exile, such as Mikhail Baryshnikov, Czesław Miłosz, and Tomas Venclova, as well as Western intellectuals such as Robert Lowell, Derek Walcott, Richard Wilbur, and Susan Sontag. He traveled widely but never back to his homeland, even after the collapse of the Soviet government in 1991. He was never allowed to visit his parents in the twelve years before they died (they had repeatedly been denied exit permits by the Soviet government), nor did he ever see his son or Andrei's mother again.

Brodsky composed his poems in Russian and translated many of them into English himself. Some translations by others have been considered less successful in language and form. His poetry was influenced by his mentor and friend Anna Akhmatova; the English poet John Donne, for whom he wrote an elegy; and W. H. Auden, who wrote a foreword for Brodsky's *Selected Poems, Joseph Brodsky* (1977) prior to his death in 1973. Brodsky's other personal literary antecedents included Virgil, Aleksandr Pushkin, Marina Tsvetaeva, Osip Mandelstam, Eugenio Montale, Constantine Cavafy, T. S. Eliot, Fyodor Dostoyevsky, Lev Shestov, and Isaiah Berlin.

In the 1960s Brodsky's preoccupation with time, death, faith, and the power of language struck a chord with his readers in Russia. Over time his focus was not on political matters but on the contrast between the bleakness of life and the brilliance of language. His recurrent themes were the traditional and timeless concerns of lyric poets: man and nature, love and death, the ineluctability of anguish, the fragility of human achievements and attachments, the preciousness of the privileged moment, the "unrepeatable." He saw the role of poetry, or accelerated thinking, as exploring the capacity of language to travel farther, faster; and he considered rhyme essential to this process. In the original Russian, the technical virtuosity of his brilliant rhyming is rich and inventive and works in tandem with often complex meters and a great deal of enjambment. His metaphors, a key device, are bold, often multilayered, and ingeniously constructed. The considerable length of some poems ("Great Elegy to John Donne" runs 308 lines) is a trademark.

Brodsky, who considered the elegy "the most fully developed genre in poetry," became one of the most famous elegists of his time. His physical exile and resulting estrangement added spatial disjunctiveness to the elegy's traditional temporal disjunctiveness. To him, any "on the death of . . ." poem contains an element of self-portrait, although he insisted that readers focus on poetry and language rather than the poet.

His work, including plays, essays, and criticism as well as poetry, has been published in anthologies in twelve languages and in magazines and journals such as the *New Yorker, New York Review of Books, Russian Review, Nouvelle Revue Française,* and the *New Leader.* Brodsky received a poetry nomination from the National Book Critics Circle in 1980 and the MacArthur Fellowship in 1981, both for *A*

Part of Speech (1977). In 1986 the National Book Critics Circle honored him with the award for nonfiction prose for *Less than One: Selected Essays* (1986). He was also well known for *To Urania: Selected Poems 1965–1985* (1988). In 1987 he was awarded the Nobel Prize in literature after the Swedish Academy read his work in English and cited its "great breadth in time and space." In 1991 he was named poet laureate of the United States. He was awarded an honorary D.Litt. degree from Yale University in 1978, an honorary doctorate of literature from Oxford University, the Mondello Prize (Italy) in 1979, and a Guggenheim fellowship in 1987. Brodsky also created drawings, particularly portraits of other poets, one of which appeared on the cover of the poet's book of poetry.

In 1990 Brodsky married Maria Sozzani, of Italian and Russian descent, with whom he had a daughter, Anna. On 28 January 1996 he succumbed to a sudden heart attack at their apartment in Brooklyn Heights, New York. He had been in frail health for two decades, having had open-heart surgery in 1979 and two bypass operations. His wife and daughter were with him when he died. Brodsky is buried on San Michele Cemetery Island in the Venetian lagoon. In a unique memorial service at the Cathedral of St. John the Divine in New York City on 8 March 1996, Brodsky was eulogized in his own words, in the words of other poets, and with music. His essays on Robert Frost were published in *Homage to Frost* after his death.

Joseph Brodsky's unique achievements and contributions to world literature, particularly poetry and the elegy, are heightened by his personal struggles and his relative youth in gaining significant recognition. For a Russian immigrant in exile to have become a major writer in the English as well as Russian language and recipient of major literary honors in so few years is an unusual accomplishment. He was an extraordinarily gifted writer who combined the roles of poet and educator in his creative years in the United States. His work continues to be recognized and read today worldwide.

★

Brodsky's works include *Verses and Poems* (1965), *Elegy to John Donne and Other Poems* (1967), *A Stop in the Desert* (1970), *Poems by Joseph Brodsky* (1972), and the essay "Watermark" (1992). See also David M. Bethea, *Joseph Brodsky and the Creation of Exile* (1994); Mikhail Lemkhin, *Joseph Brodsky, Leningrad: Fragments* (1998); Lev Loseff and Valentina Polukhins, *Joseph Brodsky: Portrait of a Poet* (1998); Solomon Volkov, *Conversations with Joseph Brodsky: A Poet's Journey Through the Twentieth Century* (1998); and David Rigsbee, *Styles of Ruin: Joseph Brodsky and the Postmodernist Elegy* (1999). An obituary is in the *New York Times* (29 Jan. 1996).

PHYLLIS BADER-BOREL

BROOKS, Cleanth (*b.* 16 October 1906 in Murray, Kentucky; *d.* 10 May 1994 in New Haven, Connecticut), literary critic, author, and educator who was a leading member of the New Criticism movement in American literature.

Brooks was the son of Cleanth Brooks, a minister, and Bessie Lee Witherspoon Brooks, a homemaker. Brooks's father encouraged his son to read widely in literature. This habit was further developed by his attendance at the McTyeire School, a small private institution in Tennessee, which gave him grounding in classical Greek and Latin.

In 1924 Brooks entered Vanderbilt University in Nashville, Tennessee, where he was exposed to the prominent southern literary group known as the Fugitives, a cadre of writers and literary critics—among them Donald Davidson, John Crowe Ransom, Robert Penn Warren, Allen Tate, and Randall Jarrell—who laid the foundations for the New Criticism movement, in which Brooks himself would later be a leading light. Abandoning his youthful desire to become a lawyer, Brooks threw himself into the study of literature. "The thing that I got most out of

Cleanth Brooks. AP/WIDE WORLD PHOTOS

Vanderbilt," he recalled later, "was to discover suddenly that literature was not a dead thing to be looked at through the glass of a museum case, but was very much alive."

After receiving his A.B. degree from Vanderbilt in 1928, Brooks earned an M.A. degree at Tulane University in New Orleans in 1929. Winning a Rhodes scholarship, he studied at Exeter College, Oxford University, in England, earning another B.A. in 1931 and a B.Litt. degree in 1932. He then began a fifteen-year career (1932–1947) at Louisiana State University (LSU), rising from lecturer to professor of English. Meanwhile, on 12 September 1934 he married Edith Amy Blanchard. They had no children.

Robert Penn Warren joined the LSU faculty soon after Brooks. This renewal of their earlier relationship at Vanderbilt would prove fruitful personally and professionally for both men. Brooks launched his literary career in 1935 with his first book, *The Relation of the Alabama-Georgia Dialect to the Provincial Dialects of Great Britain.* That same year he and Warren founded the *Southern Review,* which Brooks edited until 1942.

Frustrated at the dearth of decent textbooks for undergraduate literature courses, Brooks, Warren, and John Thibaut Purser produced *An Approach to Literature: A Collection of Prose and Verse with Analyses and Discussions* (1936). This work foreshadowed Brooks and Warren's *Understanding Poetry: An Anthology for College Students* (1938), which went through several editions and may be characterized as one of the bibles of the New Criticism movement. With its detailed analyses, the book revolutionized the teaching of poetry.

Even as a student, Brooks later described himself as "appalled at the fact that so much of the conventional graduate study seemed to have nothing to do with the interior life of the poem. . . . Graduate training at that time didn't pay much attention to it. It was all purely historical and biographical." The New Criticism sought to remedy this defect with an emphasis on the inner meaning and structure of a piece of literature, wholly apart from the biographical background of the author or the cultural setting of the work. A poem, for example, must be examined for its internal metaphor, irony, and paradox. As life itself is infinitely complex, only a poem can fully capture this complexity. To paraphrase a poem was for Brooks the highest form of heresy. The critic must never let his description of the poem act as a substitute for the work itself; his only duty is to explicate its meaning for the modern reader, regardless of the age of the poem.

The Well-Wrought Urn: Studies in the Structure of Poetry (1947) brilliantly illustrated this last fact, as Brooks drew on poetry from the Elizabethan Age to modern times to illustrate New Critical techniques. Regardless of the historical milieu of a poem, in each case Brooks teased out similar qualities of metaphorical complexity. As he stated in the opening essay, "The language of poetry is the language of paradox."

Brooks continued to produce landmark college texts, with *Understanding Fiction* (1943), in collaboration with Warren; *Understanding Drama* (1945), coauthored with Robert Heilman; and *Modern Rhetoric* (1949), also with Warren. A long-running editorial project was *The Percy Letters* (1944–1988), a nine-volume compilation of the works of English bishop and scholar Thomas Percy (1729–1811), in collaboration with A. F. Falconer and David Nichol Smith.

In 1947 Brooks moved to Yale University, where he was professor of English for the next thirteen years and then Gray Professor of Rhetoric until his retirement in 1975. He spent a decade (1953–1963) as a Library of Congress fellow, and two years (1964–1966) as the cultural attaché at the American embassy in London, providing him an opportunity to lecture widely throughout England. From 1980 to 1981 he was a senior fellow at the National Humanities Center in North Carolina.

After his retirement from Yale, Brooks's scholarship remained as fruitful and productive as ever. He lectured widely and continued to publish prolifically. As a southerner he was almost inevitably drawn to the works of William Faulkner. In 1963 he had produced *William Faulkner: The Yoknapatawpha Country,* which one reviewer called "the best single critical work on the novels of Faulkner's fictional saga." *William Faulkner: Toward Yoknapatawpha and Beyond* (1978) was a study of Faulkner's non-Yoknapatawpha novels. *William Faulkner: First Encounters* (1983), intended especially for undergraduates, provided brilliant explanations of some of Faulkner's more difficult works. In *The Language of the American South* (1985), based on his Lamar Memorial Lectures at Mercer University, Brooks returned to his earliest scholarly interest in American dialects.

Brooks was widely honored by his colleagues, with numerous visiting professorship appointments and eighteen honorary degrees. He died of cancer of the esophagus at age eighty-seven and is buried in suburban Hamden, Connecticut.

Brooks authored or edited more than thirty books and scores of articles. As early as 1940, John Crowe Ransom hailed him as "very likely, the most expert living 'reader' or interpreter of difficult verse," and the historian of criticism René Wellek labeled him nothing less than "the critic of critics." James J. Sosnoski perhaps summed up his contributions best: "[Brooks's] two greatest achievements are that he made difficult modern writers accessible to a generation of scholars for whom it was inconceivable that a great writer could exist in the twentieth century, and he taught the next generation of critics how to read closely." No less significant were his textbooks, which have continued to illuminate modern literature for generations of students.

★

Brooks's papers are at the University of Kentucky, Yale University, the Newberry Library in Chicago, and the University of Tennessee. Modern studies of Brooks are Lewis P. Simpson, ed., *The Possibilities of Order: Cleanth Brooks and His Work* (1975), and Mark Royden Winchell, *Cleanth Brooks and the Rise of Modern Criticism* (1996). Lewis P. Simpson, ed., *Cleanth Brooks and Robert Penn Warren: A Literary Correspondence* (1998), details the rich relationship between the two men. See also John Michael Walsh, *Cleanth Brooks: An Annotated Bibliography* (1990). John Paul Pritchard, *Criticism in America* (1956); Murray Krieger, *The New Apologists for Poetry* (1956); and René Wellek, *Concepts of Criticism* (1963), all have sections on Brooks. James G. Lesniak, ed., *Contemporary Authors,* vol. 35 (1992), has a revealing interview with Brooks. An obituary is in the *New York Times* (12 May 1994).

WILLIAM F. MUGLESTON

BROWN, Edmund Gerald ("Pat") (*b.* 21 April 1905 in San Francisco, California; *d.* 16 February 1996 in Beverly Hills, California), lawyer, attorney general, and governor of California who led the Democratic party's revival in California in the 1950s and 1960s, and whose accomplishments in two terms as governor included creation of a statewide water-pumping system, reform of the state's higher education system, and massive freeway construction.

Brown was the eldest of four children born to Ida Schuckman and Edmund Joseph Brown, a small business owner and sometime bookmaker. Raised in the Catholic Church of his father, he attended public schools in San Francisco, graduating from Lowell High School, where he held several elective offices, played basketball, and was head of the debating society. His nickname, "Pat," derived from a competition-winning speech on war bonds that he delivered as a seventh-grader, which he concluded with Patrick Henry's ringing phrase "Give me liberty or give me death." As a schoolboy, he worked in his father's cigar store, laundry, and penny arcades.

Following graduation from high school, Brown took night courses at the San Francisco College of Law, while working days for Milton Schmitt, an attorney and former member of the state assembly. In 1927 Brown received his LL.B. degree and passed the California bar. When Schmitt died the following year, Brown inherited his practice and, inviting his brother Harold and two other partners to join him, established a firm that became one of the most prosperous in San Francisco. In 1928 he first tried for public office, running unsuccessfully as the Republican candidate for a seat in the state assembly. Two years later he eloped to Reno, Nevada, with his high school sweetheart, Bernice

Layne, the daughter of a San Francisco police captain. Married on 30 October 1930, they had three daughters and one son, Edmund G. ("Jerry") Brown, who eventually also served as governor of California.

In 1934 Brown joined the Democratic party and was promptly elected to the San Francisco Democratic party's central committee. Inspired by the successes of Earl Warren, the young, crime-busting district attorney in neighboring Oakland, Brown set his sights on becoming his city's district attorney. After losing badly to five-time incumbent Matthew Brady in 1939, he came back to defeat Brady in 1943. As district attorney, Brown crafted a strong "law and order" record by cracking down on gambling, prostitution, and juvenile delinquency, while at the same time establishing solid liberal credentials that would serve him well later. A staunch defender of civil liberties and civil rights, he opposed President Franklin D. Roosevelt's 1942 decision to intern Japanese Americans during World War II and championed the cause of improved housing for the many African Americans who had moved west during the war to work in the shipyards. He also appointed the city's first black and Asian assistant district attorneys. Although unsuccessful in his candidacy for the position of state attorney general in 1946, he was easily reelected to a second four-year term as district attorney in 1947.

Brown's string of statewide political victories began in 1950, when he was the lone Democrat to survive a Republican sweep led by Governor Earl Warren, winning the attorney general's post by nearly a quarter-million votes over Republican Ed Shattuck. The popular Warren, who had won the gubernatorial nomination of both parties in the state's open primaries, played a pivotal role in Brown's electoral success by permitting him to link their names in the latter's political advertisements. Brown was reelected attorney general in 1954, the last candidate to win the nomination of both parties by cross-filing in California's open primaries before that possibility was ended by a change in state law. As attorney general he continued to attack organized crime, investigated scandals in the State Liquor Commission, exposed mistreatment of patients in the state's mental hospitals, and conducted raids on illegal gambling houses and bordellos. His staff also fought hard to protect the state's share of royalties from offshore oil drilling. As the only Democrat holding statewide office, Brown was the titular leader of the California Democratic Council (CDC), a progressive organization that was created in the mid-1950s to advance the liberal agenda within the party. He was also the favorite-son candidate of the California delegation at the 1952 and 1956 Democratic conventions. His successes and visibility as attorney general made him the logical choice of his party for the 1958 gubernatorial nomination. In the general election, campaigning on a platform he labeled "responsible liberalism,"

Pat Brown, 1964. ASSOCIATED PRESS AP

Brown became only the second Democrat in the twentieth century to win the California governorship, trouncing Senator William F. Knowland by more than a million votes. His victory was aided considerably by organized labor, due to Knowland's endorsement of the antiunion "right to work" ballot initiative known as Proposition 18.

Brown's chief legacies as governor were products of his first two years in office. His record of legislative success in that brief period rivaled that of the progressive governor Hiram Johnson in the early twentieth century. His victories included gaining approval of a master plan for higher education in California that expanded and integrated the state's community colleges, state college, and the University of California, substantially increased funding for public schools, and the end of cross-filing by candidates in the state's party primaries. Expansion of state services was paid for by a set of significant tax increases. Perhaps most important, Brown's tireless campaigning on behalf of a bond referendum to fund a $1.75 billion plan for diversion of water from the northern part of the state to the south was approved by California voters in November 1960, even while the Republican presidential candidate, Richard Nixon, carried the state. The resulting California Water Plan symbolized Brown's commitment to unify his large and diverse state. On the negative side, his vacillation before finally allowing the execution of longtime death-row inmate Caryl Chessman in May 1959 earned him the derisive nickname "Tower of Jello." On the whole, however, "re-

sponsible liberalism" was popular with the voters, and in 1962 Brown was reelected by nearly 300,000 votes, this time defeating former vice president Nixon after a campaign that drew national attention.

Brown's second term as governor was less productive than his first. A 1963 fair housing act was virtually the last liberal measure to be approved by the legislature during his tenure, and that law was repealed by the state's voters via Proposition 14 in 1964 (though the Supreme Court later overturned the referendum). Brown's stock fell sharply as the mood of California's voters shifted to the right in the face of the "free speech" protests at the University of California, Berkeley, and growing racial tensions in the cities, capped by the deadly rioting in the Watts neighborhood of Los Angeles in August 1965. The governor's conduct in the face of these unhappy events did not help his cause. Accepting inaccurate reports that the Berkeley student protesters had turned violent, Brown in December 1964 sent in state police who turned aggressively on the students. When the Watts riots broke out, his ability to manage the state was further questioned. As Brown's popularity and effectiveness declined, he became uncharacteristically testy. In 1966, running for reelection against the rising conservative Republican star Ronald Reagan, he descended to bitter criticisms during the campaign and lost his "good guy" image. He also lost the election by nearly a million votes.

Following his defeat, Brown returned to the practice of law, joining the prestigious Los Angeles law firm of Ball,

Hunt, Hart, Brown, and Baerwitz. Having left the governor's mansion with meager savings, he became a millionaire through his practice and shrewd investments in Indonesian oil. Once returned to private life, he helped to raise money to advance his son Jerry's successful election campaigns for governor of California in 1974 and 1978. Later in his life, another of his children, Kathleen, came close to following the example of her father and brother; she lost the 1994 gubernatorial election to the incumbent Republican Pete Wilson. Brown remained vigorous until the last few years of his life—a popular stump speaker and the recognized "father figure" of the California Democratic party. He died at his home in Beverly Hills of a heart attack and was buried in Holy Cross Cemetery in San Francisco.

Though somewhat owlish behind his spectacles, Brown was a personable, funny, and jaunty fellow—in many ways the stereotype of the old-time Irish "pol." Sometimes seemingly bumbling, he was honest and direct. Much of his political success derived from his accessible, "nice guy" persona. He loved swimming, golf, and spending time with his family. Almost alone among leading California politicians of his generation, he never sought national office, and no one ever questioned his commitment to his beloved home state. An opponent of the death penalty who permitted more than forty executions during his tenure as governor, Brown was a pragmatist who accepted the limits imposed by public opinion and statutory authority. He reflected the politics of the possible in the 1950s and 1960s, bobbing and weaving through the ideological waves to bring the Democratic party to respectability in California, and he led his state to the forefront of national attention.

★

Brown's voluminous personal and political papers are housed in the Bancroft Library of the University of California, Berkeley. In addition, a number of oral history transcripts in the Regional Oral History Office of the Bancroft Library relate to Brown's gubernatorial years. The best treatment of his life and political contributions is Roger O. Rapoport, *California Dreaming: The Political Odyssey of Pat and Jerry Brown* (1982). Detailed discussions of his gubernatorial achievements also appear in Ansel Adams et al., *California: The Dynamic State* (1966); Royce D. Delmatier et al., *The Rumble of California Politics, 1848–1970* (1970); and Jackson K. Putnam, *Modern California Politics*, 3d ed. (1990). Useful articles include: Totton Anderson, "The 1958 California Election," *Western Political Quarterly* 12 (1959): 276–300; Roger O. Rapoport, "The Political Odyssey of Pat Brown," *California History* 64 (winter 1985): 2–9; Kurt Schupparra, "Freedom vs. Tyranny: The 1958 California Election and the Origins of the State's Conservative Movement," *Pacific Historical Review* 63 (Nov. 1994): 537–560; and Gerard J. DeGroat, "Ronald Reagan and Student Unrest in California, 1966–1970," *Pacific Historical Review* 65 (Feb.

1996): 107–129. An obituary is in the *New York Times* (18 Feb. 1996).

GARY W. REICHARD

BROWN, Ron(ald) Harmon   (*b*. 1 August 1941 in Washington, D.C.; *d*. 3 April 1996 near Dubrovnik, Croatia), lawyer, first African American leader of a national political party, and secretary of commerce.

Brown, the only child of William Harmon Brown, a hotel manager, and Gloria Elexine Osborne, a salesperson, grew up amid the expanding black middle class that emerged during World War II. His father graduated from Howard University in 1941 and worked for the federal government until 1947, when he became the manager of the Hotel Theresa in New York City, which was just down the block from Harlem's world-famous Apollo Theatre. Thus Brown's formative years were spent in the Theresa, the favorite hotel of visiting black entertainers, sports figures, and politicians.

Brown grew up in Harlem, which was almost exclusively black. However, the student bodies of the prestigious schools he attended, Hunter Elementary School for Gifted

Ron Brown. LIBRARY OF CONGRESS

Children, the Walden School, and finally the Rhodes School, from which he graduated in June 1958, contained only a few African American children. When his parents separated in early 1958, Brown continued to live with his father at the Theresa until September, when he enrolled in Middlebury College, a small school in Vermont. One of three African Americans in the entire student body, Brown became the first black ever admitted to a fraternity at Middlebury. Both of his parents remarried, and Brown gained a half brother by his father's second marriage.

In June 1962 Brown received a B.A. degree in political science and a Reserve Officers' Training Corps (ROTC) commission as a second lieutenant in the U.S. Army. As he was not to report for active duty until March 1963, he took courses at St. John's University Law School in Queens, New York. On 11 August 1962 he married Alma Arrington, a graduate of Fisk University. The couple had two children.

Brown served with the U.S. Army in Virginia, Germany (where he was the first black officer in his unit), and Korea, attaining the rank of captain before his discharge in June 1967. He immediately enrolled in night school at St. John's University Law School, where he was the only black student. During the day he worked for the National Urban League.

After graduating from law school in June 1970, Brown advanced to ever more responsible positions with the National Urban League, becoming its general counsel in January 1972. In October 1973 he was named the director of the league's Washington, D.C., bureau. He acted as a liaison between the league and government agencies, lobbying for funds and legislation on key issues, such as equal opportunity. He testified before committees, drafted legislation, published reports, and slowly developed the political connections that eventually gained him the chairmanship of the Democratic National Committee (DNC).

In December 1979 Brown left the league to work on Senator Edward Kennedy's 1980 presidential campaign. Kennedy lost the Democratic nomination to the incumbent, President Jimmy Carter, but in September 1980 Kennedy, chairman of the Senate Judiciary Committee, named Brown the chief counsel to the committee. The appointment was not effective until the end of the year, so in the interim Brown served as a consultant to the committee and was a fellow at the Harvard Institute of Politics, where he taught a weekly seminar.

When the Republicans took control of the Senate in January 1981, Kennedy lost his chairmanship, and Brown became the minority counsel. Brown left that position to join Kennedy's staff until he was named the general counsel to the DNC in April. In July 1981 Brown, who always appeared in public impeccably dressed and sported a large mustache that could not hide his "baby face" and impish

smile, resigned to become the first African American partner at the prestigious Washington lobbying law firm of Patten, Boggs & Blow.

Brown maintained ties to the DNC but turned his energies to lobbying the government on behalf of his clients, including Haiti, then under the dictatorship of Jean-Claude "Baby Doc" Duvalier. Many black leaders opposed any dealings with Haiti because of its numerous human rights violations, but Brown claimed the Haitian people would be helped through "commercial diplomacy," which he hoped would force the Duvalier regime to reform its human rights policies in return for U.S. aid.

In 1984 Brown declined to work on the presidential campaign of the reverend Jesse Jackson, and in 1988 he declined to become Jackson's campaign manager. However, in May 1988 Brown reluctantly agreed to be Jackson's convention manager. Brown was later credited with brokering a deal between Jackson and the Democratic nominee, Governor Michael Dukakis of Massachusetts, that helped prevent a breakup of the party and a split in the black leadership over Jackson's candidacy.

In December 1988 Paul Kirk, chairman of the DNC, announced he would not seek reelection. Despite opposition from many southern Democrats, some of it blatantly racist, Brown sought the post. One by one his rivals withdrew, and Brown was elected by acclamation on 10 February 1989. He declared that his chairmanship would not be about race but about winning races for the Democratic party. He fulfilled his promise when he refused to support a black candidate running as an independent in a special mayoral election in Chicago in 1989. Instead he worked for the Democratic nominee and eventual winner of the contest, Richard M. Daley.

As the chair of the DNC, Brown, who remained a full though nonworking partner at Patten, Boggs & Blow, raised money for the Democratic party with the ultimate goal of capturing the White House in 1992. During the primary campaign he concluded that Arkansas governor Bill Clinton was the candidate most likely to defeat the incumbent George Bush. Despite scandals that plagued Clinton during the campaign, Brown devised a winning strategy. The Democrats attacked Bush as too interested in foreign affairs to the neglect of domestic problems, which gave birth to the slogan "It's the economy, stupid."

Although Brown would have preferred to be the secretary of state, he accepted Clinton's offer of the Department of Commerce. To win Senate confirmation Brown agreed to sever all ties with his lucrative law practice. He also gave up the chairmanship of the DNC on 23 January 1993. Brown took a tremendous cut in pay to become the first African American secretary of commerce, and the job also took a toll on his reputation. In August 1993 he was accused of accepting $700,000 from the government of Vietnam in exchange for pushing the Clinton administration to normalize U.S.–Vietnamese relations. The Justice Department formally cleared Brown of those charges in February 1994.

Meanwhile Brown pressed ahead with efforts to "grow" the economy and provide jobs for American workers by securing foreign contracts for American companies. He led trade missions to numerous countries, and American businesspeople scrambled for inclusion. Republicans, who took control of both houses of Congress in January 1995, charged that Brown "sold" places on trade missions in return for contributions to the Democratic party, and they called for the abolishment of the Commerce Department.

Congressman William Clinger, Jr., the new chairman of the House Governmental Oversight and Reform Committee, accused Brown of violating financial disclosure rules and claimed to have uncovered questionable dealings from which Brown profited. On 16 May 1995 Attorney General Janet Reno asked for the appointment of an independent counsel to investigate the allegations. On 6 July 1995 a federal judicial panel appointed Daniel Pearson to the post. Pearson assembled a staff and began his investigation, but he declined to pursue the matter after Brown's death in a plane crash in Croatia. Brown had been leading a trade mission composed largely of American business executives who were seeking contracts for projects aimed at reconstructing the war-torn region. Brown's plane, an Air Force version of a Boeing 737, missed the approach to Cilipi Airport in stormy weather and crashed into a nearby mountain. All thirty-five people aboard were killed.

Brown's body was returned to Washington, D.C. After a funeral service at Washington National Cathedral on 10 April 1996, Brown was buried in Arlington National Cemetery in Arlington, Virginia.

Brown, who compiled a remarkable list of African American "firsts," was a controversial figure. His supporters contended that he was the victim of unwarranted attacks, often racially motivated, and that he was a surrogate for the enmity of the enemies of his boss. Unable to get at Clinton, they unjustly attacked the man who helped put him in the presidency. On the other hand, Brown's detractors charged that he was corrupt and used his position for personal gain. In addition, the circumstances of his death have led to several conspiracy theories, including the allegation that Brown died of a gunshot wound to the head before his plane crashed. Adherents to this theory appear to believe Brown was murdered to silence him, and his plane was destroyed to cover the crime.

★

Tracey L. Brown's loving memoir of her father, *The Life and Times of Ron Brown* (1998), tends toward the filiopietistic; however, it is invaluable for personal details about Brown's family, life,

and career. More critical is Steven A. Holmes, *Ron Brown: An Uncommon Life* (2000), a "warts-and-all" portrait of a smooth political operator. Nicholas A. Guarino, *Murder in the First Degree: An Interim Report on the Death of Commerce Secretary Ron Brown and 34 Other United States Citizens* (1996), contends that Brown, who "knew too much," had to be silenced before he brought down the Clinton presidency, and his plane was deliberately crashed to cover his murder. Daniel Pearson, *Final Report of the Independent Counsel in Re: Ronald H. Brown* (1996), sets forth the rationale for shutting down the investigation of the allegations against Brown because of his death. Sean Wilentz, "The Fixer as Statesman: Ron Brown and the Perils of Public Service," *New Yorker* (15 Apr. 1996), provides a brief but perceptive assessment of Brown's services to the Democratic Party and the nation. See also *Memorial Tributes Delivered in Congress: Ronald H. Brown, 1941–1996, Secretary of Commerce* (1997). Obituaries are in the *New York Times* and *Washington Post* (both 4 Apr. 1996), *Time* (15 Apr. 1996), and *Ebony* (June 1996).

ROMAN ROME

BROWNELL, Herbert, Jr. (*b.* 20 February 1904 in Peru, Nebraska; *d.* 1 May 1996 in New York City), attorney general of the United States, presidential adviser, and Republican party official who was noted for his commitment to civil rights.

Brownell was one of seven children of Herbert Brownell and May A. Miller. He spent his early years in Peru, Nebraska, where his father taught the physical sciences at the Nebraska State Normal School. In 1910 the family moved to Lincoln upon his father's appointment as a professor of science education in the teacher's college of the University of Nebraska. Following his elementary and secondary education in the Lincoln public schools, Brownell entered the University of Nebraska in 1920, gaining his bachelor's degree in 1924. During his college years, he served as editor of the student newspaper, was president of the Delta Upsilon fraternity, and was elected to Phi Beta Kappa. During his senior year, he also taught journalism at Doane College in Crete, Nebraska.

Initially undecided between a career in journalism and the law, Brownell chose the latter following his admission to Yale Law School. During his second year he was elected editor in chief of the *Yale Law Journal*. He received his LL.B. in 1927 and was elected to the Order of the Coif. He later received honorary degrees from American University, the University of Notre Dame, Lafayette College, Hamilton College, Fordham University, Union College, Dickinson College, Peru State College, the National University of Ireland, and the University of Nebraska.

From 1927 to 1929 Brownell was an associate at the law firm of Root, Clark, Buckner & Ballantine in New York City. In 1929 he moved to Lord, Day & Lord, where he

Herbert Brownell as U.S. Attorney General. CORBIS CORPORATION (BELLEVUE)

became a partner in 1932. When not in government service, Brownell remained affiliated with that firm until its dissolution shortly before his death.

In 1931 Brownell embarked on his political career, seeking election as the Republican and reform candidate for the Tenth New York State Assembly District, which encompassed the Greenwich Village, Gramercy Park, Murray Hill, and theater district areas of Manhattan. Another young Republican reformer, Thomas E. Dewey, served as his campaign manager. While on the campaign trail, Brownell met Doris A. McCarter, who would become his wife on 16 June 1934 and the mother of their four children; she would remain by his side until her death in 1979. His marriage commencing on 23 December 1987 to Marion (Riki) Taylor ended in divorce.

Although unsuccessful in his first bid, Brownell ran again in 1932 and was elected. It was the first of five elections (1932–1936) he would win to the then-yearly terms of the state assembly. While in Albany, Brownell was a key linkage between New York City reformers, Mayor Fiorello La Guardia most notably, and the upstate Republican leadership of the state assembly. He sponsored legislation

strengthening child labor laws and antigangster and racketeering bills, revising the New York City charter, liberalizing the state pension system, and establishing a citywide parks department. He served on the Judiciary Committee, was chair of the Social Welfare Committee, and was one of four Republican members of the powerful Rules Committee.

Following his decision not to seek reelection, Brownell was asked to serve as general counsel for the New York World's Fair of 1939–1940. In 1940 state Republican leaders appointed Brownell as legal counsel to the Republican State Party Committee. During this period, he also began preparations for Dewey's 1942 bid for governor of New York and was appointed his campaign manager. Following Dewey's victory, Brownell turned down offers to join the Dewey administration, but he remained an influential member of Dewey's "kitchen cabinet." As the 1944 presidential election approached, Brownell became Dewey's chief strategist in securing the Republican nomination that year. Dewey was defeated in the general presidential election by Franklin Delano Roosevelt. However, following the Republican party convention, Brownell was appointed chairman of the Republican National Committee, a position he would hold until 1946. During his tenure as chair of the party, Brownell strengthened the national party's organization and developed its first direct-mail fundraising efforts. In 1948 Brownell again served as Dewey's campaign manager in the presidential campaign. But, as in 1944, Dewey lost the election, this time to Harry Truman.

In 1952 Brownell was a key participant in a group of business and political leaders who were urging General Dwight D. Eisenhower to run for president. It was an effort that led to a secret visit by Brownell to Eisenhower's North Atlantic Treaty Organization (NATO) headquarters in Paris to press upon him the need to mount an active campaign to secure the Republican nomination. Prior to the 1952 Republican convention, Brownell also devised the successful "fair play" strategy that would deprive Senator Robert Taft of a number of contested delegates to the convention and that would prove instrumental in securing Eisenhower's nomination. Following the revelation of vice presidential candidate Richard Nixon's "secret fund," Brownell was enlisted to advise Eisenhower on how to deal with the scandal, and thereafter he served as an informal adviser to the candidate.

Following the election, Brownell and General Lucius Clay headed up Eisenhower's transition to office. Brownell was then tapped by Eisenhower to serve as attorney general, a position he held until 1957. Brownell's great-uncle William H. H. Miller had served as attorney general under President Benjamin Harrison, and Miller's portrait graced Brownell's office.

During his tenure as attorney general, Brownell reorganized the Justice Department and sought to remedy the corruption and morale problems that had plagued it during the Truman years. Along with others in the administration, Brownell worked behind the scenes to curb the excesses of Senator Joseph McCarthy. Brownell's efforts to develop more effective internal security policies proved more controversial, especially following a speech Brownell delivered in which he alleged that the Truman administration had been lax in dealing with suspected Communists, most notably Treasury Department official Harry Dexter White. Although former president Truman denied the charges against White at the time, materials that were declassified years later bore out Brownell's charges.

Following Eisenhower's 1955 heart attack, Brownell was instrumental in drafting a proposal for dealing with presidential disability that would eventually become the Twenty-fifth Amendment to the Constitution. Brownell, however, was not the only member of his family to have an imprint on that document; a distant relative, Susan Brownell Anthony, was an active force in advocating the women's suffrage amendment.

Brownell's greatest achievements as attorney general were in the area of civil rights. He successfully persuaded Eisenhower to let the Justice Department support the efforts at school desegregation in the landmark 1954 case *Brown* v. *Board of Education*. In 1955 he crafted the first major civil rights legislation since Reconstruction, although the bill that would eventually pass in 1957 did not include crucial enforcement provisions that Brownell had drafted. Brownell was also a strong voice for other federal efforts at enforcing civil rights, most notably in urging Eisenhower to take a strong stand during the Little Rock, Arkansas, school crisis of 1957. He was especially instrumental in recommending the appointments of federal district and appeals court judges, particularly in the South, who were committed to carrying out the Supreme Court's civil rights rulings.

In the years following his tenure as attorney general, Brownell returned to his law practice. He served on the board of directors of the Dia Art Foundation, the Ludwig Foundation for Cancer Research, and the Miller Center for Public Affairs at the University of Virginia, where he participated in a number of its commissions on the study of policy issues. He also served as president of the New York City Bar Association from 1962 to 1963, as the first chairman of the Institute for Court Management, for which he was appointed by Chief Justice Warren Burger, and as an adviser to New York City mayor John Lindsay, who had been Brownell's executive assistant at the Justice Department.

In 1969 Brownell was a leading candidate for appointment as chief justice of the United States Supreme Court by President Nixon, a post that went instead to his longtime friend Warren Burger. He was later appointed by Nixon to serve as special ambassador to Mexico to deal with Colorado River issues. He was appointed by President Gerald Ford to serve as chairman of the National Study Commission on Records and Documents of Federal Officials. During the Jimmy Carter administration, he was called upon for counsel regarding the president's constitutional powers to abrogate the Mutual Defense Treaty of 1954 with Taiwan. President Ronald Reagan appointed him vice chairman of the Commission on the Bicentennial of the U.S. Constitution. It was a fitting capstone to his long and dedicated career of service to the law and to his nation. Brownell died of cancer in May 1996 in New York City.

Brownell's character and accomplishments are best summed up by an entry that President Eisenhower made in his personal diary on 14 May 1953:

> Herb Brownell. Here is a man with long experience in politics, especially in the conduct of political campaigns. It would be natural to suppose that he would become hard-boiled, and that the code by which he lives could hardly be classified as one of high moral quality. The contrary seems to be true—certainly he has never suggested or proposed to me any action which could be considered in the slightest degree dishonest or unethical. His reputation with others seems to match my own high opinion of his capabilities as a lawyer, his qualities as a leader, and his character as a man. I am devoted to him and am perfectly confident that he would make an outstanding president of the United States.

★

Brownell's personal and official papers are located at the Eisenhower Presidential Library in Abilene, Kansas. His memoir, written with John P. Burke, is *Advising Ike* (1993). Accounts of his association with Governor Thomas E. Dewey are quite limited but the best can be found in Richard Norton Smith, *Thomas E. Dewey and His Times* (1982). On his service as attorney general, Eisenhower's own memoirs, *Mandate for Change* (1963) and *Waging Peace* (1965), are useful, as is Stephen Ambrose, *Eisenhower*, vol. 2 (1983), and John T. Elliff, *The United States Department of Justice and Individual Rights, 1937–1962* (1987). An obituary is in the *New York Times* (3 May 1996).

JOHN P. BURKE

BUKOWSKI, Charles (*b.* 16 August 1920 in Andernach, Germany; *d.* 9 March 1994 in San Pedro, California), hard-drinking novelist, poet, and short-story writer best known for his autobiographical screenplay *Barfly* (1987).

Christened Henry Charles Bukowski, Jr., in the Roman Catholic faith, Bukowski was the only child of Henry Charles Bukowski, an American sergeant stationed in occupied Germany, and his wife, Katherine Fett, a German seamstress. The family left for the United States in April

Charles Bukowski. ARCHIVE PHOTOS

1923, living briefly in Baltimore, Maryland and Pasadena, California, before settling permanently in Los Angeles, where Bukowski, Sr., found work as a milkman.

Bukowski's childhood was a living nightmare. His father beat him regularly with a razor strop and he was teased and bullied by his classmates at the Virginia Road Elementary School and later at Mount Vernon Junior High. In 1936 Bukowski entered Los Angeles High School, where he continued to feel unpopular and out of place. Living under constant stress, he developed one of the worst cases of *acne vulgaris* his doctors had ever seen. As a teenager Bukowski discovered two remedies for his pain: alcohol and literature. Along with playing the horses and classical music, they were to remain lifelong comforts.

In 1939 Bukowski enrolled in Los Angeles City College, but he took little interest in his studies and in 1941 dropped out to pursue a writing career. Exempted from military service for psychological reasons, he spent the war years writing and traveling, supporting himself at a variety of menial jobs including stock boy, dishwasher, elevator operator, and Red Cross orderly.

Writing under his middle name, Charles, Bukowski had some early success. "Aftermath of a Lengthy Rejection Slip" appeared in the March-April issue of *Story* in 1944, and "20 Tanks from Kasseldown" was published in Caresse Crosby's *Portfolio III* (1946), alongside work by Henry Miller, Federico García Lorca, Jean Genet, and Jean-Paul Sartre. A steady stream of rejection slips discouraged Bukowski, however, causing him to abandon the pen in favor

of the bottle. For the next ten years he devoted himself to boozing and barroom brawling.

Back in Los Angeles in 1946, Bukowski met Jane Cooney Baker in the Glenview Bar. The tempestuous love affair that followed was dramatized in the Barbet Schroeder film *Barfly* (1987), with Faye Dunaway playing Wanda Wilcox (Baker's role) and Mickey Rourke starring as Henry Chinaski, Bukowski's literary doppelgänger. Their constant drinking and carousing proved too much for Bukowski, who in the spring of 1955 awoke one morning in the charity ward of Los Angeles County Hospital, having narrowly escaped death from a bleeding ulcer.

Upon his release from the hospital, Bukowski began writing poetry. After breaking up with Baker, he met Barbara Frye, the editor of *Harlequin,* who had accepted some of his poems. They married in Las Vegas, Nevada, on 29 October 1955. Following a brief visit with Frye's relatives in Wheeler, Texas, they returned to Los Angeles, where they published a special issue of *Harlequin* containing eight Bukowski poems. Temperamentally unsuited for each other, they divorced on 18 March 1958 and had no children. Bukowski found an apartment at 1623 North Mariposa Avenue and began seeing Jane Baker off and on again. Baker's death on 22 January 1962 inspired his moving poem "For Jane, with all the love I had, which was not enough."

With the exception of Jane's death, the 1960s were good to Bukowski. A $15,000 inheritance and a steady, if stultifying, job sorting mail with the U.S. Postal Service gave him financial security. His first collection of poems, *Flower, Fist and Bestial Wail,* appeared in 1960. In 1963 the Loujon Press edition of *It Catches My Heart in Its Hands* received high praise from Kenneth Rexroth in the *New York Times Book Review.* It was John Martin, however, the founder of Black Sparrow Press, who was to change Bukowski's life forever. After publishing several books by Bukowski, Martin agreed to give him a stipend of $100 a month if he would leave the post office and devote himself to writing full-time. About to be fired anyway, Bukowski gratefully accepted the offer.

The 1970s and 1980s were Bukowski's most productive years. In February 1971 Black Sparrow published *Post Office,* Bukowski's novel based on eleven grueling years with the postal service. A critical and financial success, it sold 75,000 copies in the United States and more than half a million copies abroad. It was followed by three autobiographical novels in the same vein: *Factotum* (1975), *Women* (1978), and *Ham On Rye* (1982). In 1978, Bukowski read to packed auditoriums in Germany and was lionized by the European media. With the release of the film *Barfly* in 1987, he became famous at home.

Success changed Bukowski's lifestyle dramatically. By 1984 he was earning more than $100,000 a year. He bought a BMW 320i and an $80,000 house in San Pedro. He was able to drink expensive wines and spend afternoons at the racetrack in the company of movie stars like Sean Penn and Madonna. On 18 August 1985, he married Linda Lee Beighle at the Church of the People in Los Feliz, California. Beighle, a health-store owner he first met in 1976, proved to be a stabilizing influence on Bukowski, encouraging him to lose weight and drink more moderately. Bukowski's novel *Hollywood* (1989) captures the essence of his life at this time.

In the winter of 1987 Bukowski contracted tuberculosis. The disease took its toll on him physically but he continued to work on *Hollywood* as well as *The Roominghouse Madrigals: Early Selected Poems 1946–1966* (1988). These were followed by *Septuagenarian Stew* (1990), an anthology of new as well as previously published stories and poems, and *The Last Night of the Earth Poems* (1992). Bukowski's health continued to deteriorate. He had cataract surgery in the summer of 1992 and was diagnosed with leukemia in the spring of 1993. During a brief remission, he finished *Pulp* (1994), his tongue-in-cheek detective novel. He died in San Pedro Peninsula Hospital on 9 March 1994, attended by his wife and his daughter, Marina, the child he fathered with Frances ("FrancEye") Smith, a fan whom he lived with from 1963 to 1965. He was buried at the Green Hills cemetery in San Pedro on 14 March 1994, following a Buddhist service. The epitaph on his gravestone reads, "DON'T TRY."

In spite of his reputation as a drunken brawler, a womanizer, and a gambler, Bukowski was a prolific writer, producing six novels, five collections of short stories, and thirty-two volumes of poetry, most of which were written after his fortieth birthday. At the time of his death two million copies of his books were in print. Bukowski's detractors charged him with being crude, vulgar and sexist; his fans praised him for his wit, candor, and hard-edged realism. Because his work focused on the lower strata of society, drunks, whores, and manual laborers, the media tended to dismiss Bukowski as the "poet laureate of Los Angeles low life" or "bard of the barroom and the brothel." Widely translated, Bukowski has received serious scholarly attention abroad but in the United States he remains "the dirty old man of American letters," a cult figure renowned more for his raucous lifestyle than for his art.

★

Libraries containing manuscripts and papers relating to Bukowski include the University of California, Santa Barbara; the University of Southern California; the University of California, Long Beach; Temple University; and the University of Arizona, Tucson. Seamus Cooney has edited four volumes of correspondence: *The Bukowski/Purdy Letters* (1983), *Screams from the Balcony: Selected Letters 1960–1970* (1993), *Living On Luck: Selected Letters 1960s–1970s* (1995), and *Reach for the Sun: Selected Letters*

1978–1994 (1999). There are two major biographies: Howard Sounes, *Charles Bukowski: Locked in the Arms of a Crazy Life* (1998), and Neeli Cherkovski, *Bukowski: A Life* (1997), actually a revised edition of his earlier book *Hank: The Life of Charles Bukowski* (1991). Both are sympathetic portraits, with Cherkovski having both the advantage and disadvantage of having known Bukowski personally. A profile by Paul Ciotti is in the *Los Angeles Times Magazine* (22 March 1977). Special issues of journals devoted to Bukowski include *The Review of Contemporary Fiction* 3 (Fall 1983) and the memorial issue of *Beat Scene 20* (1994). Obituaries are in the *Los Angeles Times* (10 Mar. 1994) and the *New York Times* (11 Mar. 1994). Audio recordings include *Charles Bukowski Reads His Poetry* (1980), *Hostage* (1994), and *Bukowski at Bellevue* (1998). Barbet Schroeder's *Charles Bukowski Tapes* is a four-hour video of interviews and readings shot during the filming of *Barfly*.

WILLIAM M. GARGAN

BUNDY, McGeorge (*b.* 30 March 1919 in Boston, Massachusetts; *d.* 16 September 1996 in Boston, Massachusetts), dean of the Faculty of Arts and Sciences at Harvard University, national security adviser to Presidents John F. Kennedy and Lyndon B. Johnson, and president of the Ford Foundation.

The Bundy saga is an emblematic story of the "American century." Smart and gifted, this Boston Brahmin family endowed their sons with all the privileges and opportunities of the American establishment. Bundy was one of five children born to Harvey Hollister Bundy, a Yale- and Harvard-trained lawyer, and Katharine Lawrence Putnam, a homemaker and niece of Harvard President A. Lawrence Lowell. Like his elder brothers, Harvey and William, McGeorge Bundy was sent to the elite Groton School in Groton, Massachusetts, from the age of twelve until he graduated in 1936. He then followed his father and brothers to Yale University, where he was tapped as a member of Skull and Bones, a secret society. Graduating from Yale in 1940, Bundy traveled in South America for a year and then was selected as a junior fellow at Harvard.

During World War II, Bundy's father served as the executive assistant to Secretary of War Henry L. Stimson. Bundy and his brother William were both trained as signal intelligence officers. Assigned to Bletchley Park outside of London, William Bundy became one of America's leading cryptographers, privy to the war's most closely guarded secret, the German military cipher, code-named ULTRA. McGeorge Bundy served as Admiral Alan Kirk's "one-time-pad" man, decoding similar intelligence intercepts during the 1944 Normandy invasion. The experience left the Bundy brothers with an appreciation for what an important weapon intercept intelligence could be to those who had to make decisions about war and peace in a dangerous age.

McGeorge Bundy. LIBRARY OF CONGRESS

In February 1947 Bundy ghost-wrote Stimson's classic defense of the decision to drop the atomic bomb on Japan. Published in *Harper's* magazine in February 1947, the Stimson-Bundy essay helped to convince a generation of Americans that the atomic bombing was a justifiable act of war. Four decades later, in a scholarly book titled *Danger and Survival: Choices About the Bomb in the First Fifty Years* (1988), Bundy quietly retracted many of the arguments he had advanced in Stimson's name to defend the destruction of Hiroshima and Nagasaki.

A year later he was a coauthor of Stimson's memoirs, *On Active Service in Peace and War*. Published in 1948, just as the cold war was unfolding, the book became a bible of the establishment's worldview, an argument for an activist foreign policy. As a young man in his early thirties, Bundy's mentors included Supreme Court Justice Felix Frankfurter, the poet Archibald MacLeish, Henry Lewis Stimson, Walter Lippmann, Dean Acheson, Judge Learned Hand, John J. McCloy, Joseph Alsop, J. Robert Oppenheimer, and Allen Dulles.

In 1949, having established himself as an up-and-coming young policy intellectual, Bundy began teaching government and world affairs at Harvard. Though he lacked a doctorate in any field, he quickly received tenure, and by 1953, at the precocious age of thirty-four, he was appointed dean of Harvard's Faculty of Arts and Sciences. By then, Bundy had married Mary Buckminster Lothrop (on 10 June 1950), an associate director of admissions at Radcliffe. The couple had four sons.

At Harvard throughout the 1950s, Dean Bundy had to defend the university from Senator Joseph McCarthy's political witch-hunts. He protected those few tenured Harvard professors who had once been members of the Communist Party and who refused to "name names." But as a cold war anticommunist liberal, Bundy also felt compelled to sacrifice some of the untenured scholars who refused to cooperate with the FBI.

When John F. Kennedy occupied the White House in 1961, McGeorge Bundy was named the president's special assistant for national security affairs and William Bundy became a deputy assistant secretary of defense. In the early 1960s, Bundy managed one crisis after another: the Bay of Pigs, Laos, Berlin, and the most dangerous nuclear confrontation of the entire cold war—the Cuban Missile Crisis. He also supervised numerous covert intelligence operations, including Operation Mongoose, which aimed to destabilize Fidel Castro's Cuba. But it was Bundy's role as an early architect of the war in Vietnam that engulfed his career in controversy. At every stage of the war—from the assassination of South Vietnamese president Ngo Dinh Diem in 1963 to the Gulf of Tonkin affair in 1964, from the bombing campaign of Operation Rolling Thunder to President Johnson's July 1965 decision to send hundreds of thousands of American combat troops to Vietnam—Bundy helped to fashion a policy of gradual escalation.

When Bundy initially recommended a sustained bombing campaign to Johnson in February 1965, he warned the president, "We cannot assert that a policy of sustained reprisal will succeed in changing the course of the contest in Vietnam. It may fail, and we cannot estimate the odds of success with any accuracy—they may be somewhere between 25 percent and 75 percent. What we can say is that even if it fails, the policy will be worth it. At a minimum it will dampen down the charge that we did not do all that we could have done, and this charge will be important in many countries, including our own."

During the critical decisions of 1964–1965, Bundy urged President Johnson not to make an open-ended commitment of American ground troops. In June 1965, Bundy warned Defense Secretary Robert S. McNamara that his proposal to introduce large numbers of troops was "rash to the point of folly." The president's national security adviser clearly understood the risks associated with any attempt to wage a ground war in Southeast Asia.

When the conflict nevertheless escalated into a major land war, Bundy persevered in a policy that he had known from the beginning was dubious. But like Robert McNamara, he now defended the war in public even while in private he increasingly acknowledged that it was not going well. In November 1965, Bundy informed President Johnson that he had decided to accept the presidency of the Ford Foundation.

Two weeks before he finally left the White House in early 1966, Bundy wrote a memorandum for his files in which he took issue with what he called the "Lippmann Thesis." Contrary to syndicated columnist Walter Lippmann's assumption that the United States didn't belong in Southeast Asia, Bundy noted that "we have been the dominant power" for twenty years. "The truth is that in Southeast Asia we are stronger than China." The war's casualties were terrible, but the "danger to one man's life, as such, is not a worthy guide. . . . If the basic questions of interest, right, and power are answered, the casualties and costs are to be accepted." As to Lippmann's frequent argument that where the French had failed, the Americans were no more likely to succeed, Bundy retorted, "There has been no serious proof of French political effectiveness since 1919."

How could Bundy warn against the "folly" of intervention and then barely nine months later tell himself that the "casualties and costs are to be accepted"? One explanation seems to rest in the fact that as a liberal he feared the conservative alternative. Bundy knew he could hold his own in any debating forum with the antiwar students and his critics in the academy. Indeed, some of the war's critics included his Cambridge friends and former colleagues, intellectuals like David Riesman, John Kenneth Galbraith, Stanley Hoffmann, and Hans Morgenthau.

If opposition to the war came from the left, Bundy understood that the real threat lay to their right. Once President Johnson had decided to take a stand in South Vietnam, the job of men like Bundy was to contain the war. If not managed by liberals, he felt this war could easily have become a Chinese-American war, a rerun of the Korean War. If the Chinese communists intervened with large numbers of ground troops, Bundy knew that the pressures from the Joint Chiefs to use tactical nuclear weapons would become irresistible. There were, as Bundy said, "wild men waiting in the wings."

Caricatured as a war criminal by the New Left in the 1960s," Bundy in the decades afterward remained a liberal in every sense of the word. As president of the Ford Foundation, he lent intellectual and financial support to a whole range of liberal causes, including affirmative action, the environment, arms control, public television, and public interest law. He became an eloquent critic of institutionalized white racism. It was, he wrote in 1968, the "white man's fears and hates that must have first place" in explaining the condition of the American Negro.

In 1982 Bundy—together with George Kennan, Gerard Smith, and Robert McNamara—wrote a major essay in *Foreign Affairs* arguing that the United States should abandon its policy of "first use" of nuclear weapons in the event of a Soviet invasion of Western Europe. The essay made headlines around the globe.

Even in his twilight years, Bundy helped to frame the debate on arms control negotiations with the Soviets, the future of NATO, and the nature of the national security state at the end of the cold war. And yet, on the issue of the war that will forever be associated with his name, he remains an enigma.

Bundy died in Boston of heart failure at the age of seventy-seven. His funeral service was held in St. John's Church in Beverly Farms, Massachusetts. His old Harvard friend Arthur Schlesinger, Jr., wistfully noted that Bundy represented "the last hurrah of the Northeast Establishment. He was the final executor of the grand tradition of Henry Stimson, Dean Acheson, Averell Harriman, Robert Lovett, John J. McCloy—patricians who, combining commitment to international responsibility with instinct for command and relish in power, served the republic pretty well in the global crises of the twentieth century." On a personal level, Schlesinger remembered his friend as a man of "sparkling personality, witty and elegant." Bundy, he said, had displayed the courage to "transcend the politics and the complacencies of his class." Born a privileged Republican, he had become a liberal Democrat. "A single tragic error," Schlesinger concluded, "prevented him from achieving his full promise as a statesman."

★

Some of Bundy's papers are in the John F. Kennedy Presidential Library and the Lyndon Baines Johnson Presidential Library together with numerous oral history interviews. Kai Bird wrote the only biography of McGeorge Bundy: *The Color of Truth: McGeorge Bundy and William Bundy, Brothers in Arms* (1998). Many books on the Vietnam War feature Bundy, including Milton Viorst, *Hustlers and Heroes: An American Political Panorama* (1971); David Halberstam, *The Best and the Brightest* (1972); Larry Berman, *Planning a Tragedy: The Americanization of the War in Vietnam* (1982); John Ranelagh, *The Agency: The Rise and Decline of the CIA from Wild Bill Donovan to William Casey* (1986); Raymond L. Garthoff, *Reflections on the Cuban Missile Crisis* (1987); Sigmund Diamond, *Compromised Campus: The Collaboration of Universities with the Intelligence Community, 1945–1955* (1992); H. W. Brands, *The Devil We Knew: Americans and the Cold War* (1993); Lloyd C. Gardner, *Pay Any Price: Lyndon Johnson and the Wars for Vietnam* (1995); *Hiroshima's Shadow: Writings on the Denial of History and the Smithsonian Controversy,* an anthology on the atomic bomb edited by Kai Bird and Lawrence Lifschultz

(1998); and Fredrik Logevall, *Choosing War: The Lost Chance for Peace and the Escalation of the War in Vietnam* (1999). Bundy himself is the author of *Danger and Survival: Choices About the Bomb in the First Fifty Years* (1988), and the editor of *The Pattern of Responsibility: From the Record of Dean Acheson* (1952). An obituary is in the *New York Times* (17 Sept. 1996).

KAI BIRD

BURGER, Warren Earl (*b.* 17 September 1907 in Saint Paul, Minnesota; *d.* 25 June 1995 in Washington, D.C.), lawyer, jurist, and chief justice of the United States (1969–1986) who helped to move the Supreme Court away from its liberalism of the 1960s.

Burger was one of seven children of Charles Joseph Burger, a farmer, rail-cargo inspector, and traveling salesman, and Katharine Schnittger, a homemaker. Burger graduated from John A. Johnson High School in Saint Paul in 1925 and attended night school at the University of Minnesota for two years. In 1927 he enrolled in night classes at the Saint Paul College of Law (now the William Mitchell College of Law); he supported himself by selling insurance during the day and received his LL.B. degree in 1931 with high honors. While practicing with the law firm of Boyesen, Otis, and Faricy, Burger served on the faculty of the Saint

Warren Burger. LIBRARY OF CONGRESS

Paul College of Law for twelve years. Between 1935 and 1953 he was a partner in the successor firm of Faricy, Burger, Moore, and Costello, arguing more than a dozen cases before the U.S. Supreme Court. He married Elvera Stromberg on 8 November 1933; they had one son and one daughter.

A large, handsome man with a baritone voice and a pleasant demeanor, Burger became actively involved in politics and community affairs while practicing law in Saint Paul. Associating with the moderate wing of the Republican Party, he began a close affiliation with Harold Stassen in 1938, when Stassen was elected governor of Minnesota. Burger was a Stassen adviser and fund-raiser for fifteen years. He managed Stassen's unsuccessful bids for the Republican presidential nomination in 1948 and again in 1952. At the 1948 National Republican Convention, Burger impressed several party leaders, including Richard M. Nixon and Herbert Brownell, both of whom later boosted his judicial career.

When Stassen failed to gain the 1952 Republican nomination, Burger helped to throw the crucial support of the Minnesota delegation to Dwight D. Eisenhower instead of Robert A. Taft. This influenced Burger's appointment in 1953 as assistant attorney general in charge of the Justice Department's Civil Division. In Washington he earned a reputation for dealing with maritime and labor-law litigation. One highly publicized case before the Supreme Court involved the dismissal of a government consultant, Dr. John P. Peters, on loyalty grounds.

Although he enjoyed his experience at the Justice Department, Burger resigned after two years to return to St. Paul. He soon went back to Washington, D.C., however, when in 1956 he accepted a seat on the U.S. Court of Appeals for the District of Columbia Circuit, often called the second most important court in the country. A hardworking conservative jurist over the next thirteen years, he was an outspoken critic of some of the Supreme Court's most famous criminal procedure decisions of the 1960s, while Chief Justice Earl Warren presided over the High Court. Burger was also often in disagreement with his more liberal court of appeals colleagues, especially on criminal procedure. In one case he censured his brethren by writing:

> The seeming anxiety of judges to protect every accused person from every consequence of his voluntary utterances is giving rise to myriad rules, sub-rules, variations, and exceptions, which even the most sophisticated lawyers and judges are taxed to follow. . . . Guilt or innocence becomes irrelevant in the criminal trial as we flounder in a morass of artificial rules poorly conceived and often impossible of application.

Burger's views on criminal law and procedure squared with the Republican conservatism of the late 1960s. "Law and order" was a hotly debated issue because of the growth in crime in the United States and controversial Supreme Court decisions extending the rights of criminal defendants. The accent on criminal justice in the 1968 presidential election year reflected the concerns of many Americans and leading Republicans, and opinion polls showed that voters saw Richard Nixon as the candidate who could most effectively deal with the nation's crime problems. Nixon openly criticized Warren Court decisions in his 1968 campaign, arguing that a major way to handle problems involving crime was to appoint "strict constructionists" to the Supreme Court.

During the summer of 1967, Burger delivered a law-and-order speech at Wisconsin's Ripon College that caught Nixon's attention. In it, Burger maintained that "governments exist chiefly to foster the rights and interests of their citizens—to protect their homes and property, their persons and their lives. If a government fails in this basic duty, it is not redeemed by providing even the most perfect system for the protection of the rights of defendants in the criminal courts." These views closely matched Nixon's, leading them to talk at length early in 1969 and remain in touch until Burger's nomination to the Supreme Court.

President Nixon announced his choice for chief justice on 21 May 1969. Speaking to the press, he portrayed the sixty-two-year-old Burger as a man of integrity who had worked his way from a modest background to success, as a man with extensive legal experience and great intelligence, and, most important, as an experienced strict-constructionist judge who would interpret the law, not make it. Saying the appointment of a Supreme Court justice was one of the most important actions of a president, Nixon expected Burger to interpret the Constitution narrowly, especially as it pertained to criminal suspects.

On 3 June 1969 the Senate Judiciary Committee handled the nomination of Warren Burger in less than two hours. The hearings underscored Burger's views on constitutional interpretation, and the committee unanimously approved his nomination. The Senate completed its deliberations six days later. In the less than three weeks between his nomination and confirmation, Burger went from a little-known court of appeals judge to Earl Warren's successor. He was sworn in as the fifteenth chief justice of the United States on 24 June 1969.

Chief Justice Burger's legacy is primarily understood through his contributions to U.S. constitutional law, including several landmark decisions in which he spoke for the Supreme Court. The first, *Swann* v. *Charlotte-Mecklenburg Board of Education,* was handed down on 20 April 1971. Here the Court addressed for the first time the issue of busing students to bring about a racial balance in public schools. Charlotte, North Carolina, had always required white and African American children to attend separate schools until *Brown* v. *Board of Education* (1954) declared segregation unconstitutional. After that, Charlotte failed to integrate its schools, and a federal court ordered the busing of Charlotte schoolchildren as a last resort. Burger's majority opinion in *Swann* approved of busing as one means of bringing about desegregation unless it presented a risk to a child's health or significantly impinged upon the educational process. In addition, he concluded that school-district lines could be gerrymandered by a school board to enhance desegregation on an interim basis. Quotas should not be used, however, to require an exact racial balance in individual schools.

On 28 June 1971, Burger delivered another prominent decision in *Lemon* v. *Kurtzman,* establishing the basic standard courts should apply in guaranteeing separation of church and state. He announced in this case that a law permitting state subsidies to parochial schools to help pay teachers' salaries in secular courses violated the First Amendment. In reaching his decision, Burger indicated that a threefold test would henceforth be used in resolving whether a law abridged the establishment clause: It must have a secular purpose, its primary effect could not advance or inhibit religion, and it could not foster an "excessive entanglement with religion."

Miller v. *California* was a leading ruling in obscenity law, and Burger delivered the opinion for the Court in that case on 21 June 1973. There he revised some of the law's prior definitions of obscenity and stressed that local community standards must determine what is obscene for each community. In the future, Burger observed, a conviction for obscenity should be based on "(a) whether 'the average person, applying contemporary community standards' would find that the work, taken as a whole, appeals to the prurient interest; (b) whether the work depicts or describes, in a patently offensive way, sexual conduct specifically defined by the applicable state law; and (c) whether the work, taken as a whole, lacks serious literary, artistic, political, or scientific value."

Perhaps the most famous Supreme Court opinion written by Chief Justice Burger was *United States* v. *Nixon,* announced on 24 July 1974. This case grew out of the Watergate scandal, in which President Nixon faced the threat of impeachment because of the illegal cover-up of the Watergate break-in. A central issue concerned the president's assertions that the doctrine of separation of powers prevented the judiciary from reviewing his claim of executive privilege—the exemption of a president from disclosure requirements to protect confidentiality in carrying out critical governmental functions. Burger held against the president, responding that the courts must ultimately determine the meaning of the Constitution. On the other hand, deferring to the executive, Burger for the first time bestowed Supreme Court recognition of an executive privilege against disclosure. Such a privilege is necessary to promote confidentiality and candor when the president and his key advisers make decisions, but Burger rejected Nixon's contention that executive privilege is absolute, because, in this case, an absolute privilege in a criminal prosecution would interfere with the judiciary's responsibility to do justice. Nixon resigned seventeen days after Burger's opinion was released, knowing he would otherwise be impeached.

Chief Justice Burger delivered another critical school desegregation opinion, *Milliken* v. *Bradley,* on 25 July 1974. There a federal judge had ordered schoolchildren bused between Detroit and surrounding suburban school districts to correct unconstitutional segregation in Detroit alone. Burger contended, however, that court-ordered busing across city and suburban school lines was constitutionally permissible only where illegal segregation was proven in each school district to undergo busing or where illegal segregation in one school district had a significant segregative effect on another district. This holding, widely criticized by liberals, reduced the likelihood that America's schools would be desegregated, because minorities tended to live in cities, whereas whites increasingly resided in the suburbs.

Nixon appointed Burger to the Supreme Court with criminal justice in mind, but Burger's opinions in that field were not among his best known. Indeed, not a single one reversed a major Warren Court precedent. Still, they usually exhibited a conservative theme. In *United States* v. *Harris* (1971), Burger spoke for the majority in ruling that probable cause for a search warrant could be based on a tip from an anonymous informant who was not proven to be reliable. The same year, in *Harris* v. *New York* (1971), he held that even though the warnings required by *Miranda* v. *Arizona* (1966) were not properly given to a criminal suspect, incriminating statements made to the police could nevertheless be introduced at trial to impeach the credibility of a suspect's statements made on the witness stand. Burger's most notable fair-trial opinion came in *Chandler* v. *Florida* (1981), in which he announced that televising a state criminal trial does not inherently abridge the rights to fair trial and due process. Perhaps most indicative of Burger's sense of criminal justice, *Nix* v. *Williams* (1984) decided that if evidence would have been inevitably discovered by legal means, it could not be excluded at trial because of an illegal search.

Two leading separation-of-powers opinions also contributed to Burger's legacy in constitutional law: *Immigration and Naturalization Service* v. *Chadha* (1983) and *Bowsher* v. *Synar* (1986). He held in *Chadha* that the legislative veto provision of the federal Immigration and Nationality Act was unconstitutional and, as a result, cast doubt on the legality of the legislative veto generally. The decision ostensibly weakened congressional oversight of the executive branch when many observers called for more checks on the executive establishment. In *Bowsher,* Burger struck down a major provision of the Balanced Budget and Emergency Deficit Control Act of 1985, which sought to control the growth of the federal budget deficit and eliminate it. He maintained that the provision violated the doctrine of separation of powers because it assigned to the comptroller general, an agent of Congress, functions that properly belonged to the executive branch.

While Burger penned several historic opinions, he was not considered one of the more outstanding justices on the modern Supreme Court. Legal commentators have concluded that Burger failed to provide adequate leadership as chief justice, that he used his power as chief justice in questionable ways to try to influence the Court's decisions, that he lacked an overarching constitutional philosophy, that his opinions were often unimaginative and narrowly written, and that he was too conservative on some issues. On the other hand, even critics concede that Burger made valuable contributions to judicial administration during his years on the Court, especially through his pivotal role in the creation of the National Center for State Courts and the Institute for Court Management.

On 26 September 1986, at the age of seventy-nine, Warren Burger unexpectedly retired from the Supreme Court to become the chairman of the Bicentennial Commission, thus allowing President Ronald Reagan to elevate William H. Rehnquist to the Court's center seat. Continuing to live in his farmhouse in McLean, Virginia, Burger directed the Bicentennial Commission's myriad activities for five years with all the energy he could muster. On 25 June 1995, he died of congestive heart failure in Washington, D.C., and was buried in Arlington National Cemetery.

★

Burger's papers are located at the College of William and Mary School of Law in Williamsburg, Virginia. While no autobiography or biography has been written, Burger and his Court are the focus of several books, including Vincent Blasi, ed., *The Burger Court: The Counter-Revolution That Wasn't* (1983), which probes developments in several areas of constitutional law during the first decade or so of the Burger Court; Charles M. Lamb and Stephen C. Halpern, eds., *The Burger Court: Political and Judicial Profiles* (1991), which contains individual studies of each justice who served on the Burger Court; and Bernard Schwartz, ed., *The Burger Court: Counter-Revolution or Confirmation?* (1998), which examines the Burger Court from various legal and historical perspectives.

Various articles have specifically focused on Burger. See, for example, Joseph F. Kobylka, "Leadership on the Supreme Court of the United States: Chief Justice Burger and the Establishment Clause," *Western Political Quarterly* 42 (Dec. 1989): 545–568, which explores Burger's inability to shape the Court's doctrine of separation of church and state; Charles M. Lamb, "The Making of a Chief Justice: Warren Burger on Criminal Procedure, 1956–1969," *Cornell Law Review* 60 (June 1975): 743–788, which surveys Burger's lower court and early Supreme Court decisions on criminal procedure; Edward A. Tamm and Paul C. Reardon, "Warren E. Burger and the Administration of Justice," *Brigham Young University Law Review* 1981, no. 3 (1981): 447–521, which examines the changes in the administration of justice generated by Burger. The *Oklahoma Law Review* published a symposium on Burger in its spring 1992 issue, with articles on his views and decisions on criminal justice, school desegregation, freedom of press, separation of church and state, and administrative law, among others topics. Obituaries are in the *New York Times* and *Washington Post* (both 26 June 1995).

CHARLES M. LAMB

BURKE, Arleigh Albert   (*b.* 19 October 1901 near Boulder, Colorado; *d.* 1 January 1996 in Bethesda, Maryland), four-star admiral and three-term chief of naval operations.

Burke was raised in a Swedish farming family, the oldest of six children of Oscar Burke and Clara Moklar. His father

Chief of Naval Operations Arleigh Burke, 1955. ASSOCIATED PRESS U.S. NAVY

was born August Bjorkgren, but Americanized his name when he emigrated to the United States from Sweden in 1855. Disliking farming, Burke opted for a military career and in 1919 was admitted to the U.S. Naval Academy. At graduation he ranked an unremarkable seventy-first in a class of 412. On the afternoon of his commissioning as an ensign, 7 June 1923, he wed Roberta ("Bobbie") Gorsuch; the marriage lasted until Burke's death seventy-two years later. They had no children.

After serving for five years (1923–1928) on the battleship *Arizona,* in January 1929 Burke entered a postgraduate course in ordnance offered in Annapolis, Maryland, and in 1931 received an M.S.E. degree in chemical engineering and explosives from the University of Michigan. After serving for five years as the main battery officer of the heavy cruiser *Chester,* he worked as an analyst of fleet gunnery exercises for the Bureau of Ordnance. His request for destroyer duty, first made in 1934, was finally answered in June 1937, when he became the executive officer of the new *Craven.* On 5 June 1939 he assumed command of the destroyer *Mugford,* which excelled in gunnery under Burke.

In July 1940 Burke was assigned to inspect gun mounts built at the Naval Gun Factory in Washington, D.C., although he hungered for sea duty in the Pacific. His repeated requests were finally approved, and after a promotion to captain he commanded several destroyer squadrons in the South Pacific from January to October 1943. He became known for his aggressive and innovative tactics and his preference for fighting at night. Transferred to the command of Destroyer Squadron 23, the "Little Beavers," in October 1943, Burke garnered the nickname "Thirty-one-Knot Burke" when boiler trouble caused one of his destroyers to make only thirty-one rather than thirty-four or more knots. Destroyer Squadron 23 participated in twenty-two engagements in the next few months, including the nighttime Battle of Empress Augusta Bay in the Solomon Islands in early November and the destruction of three Japanese transports and two destroyer escorts off Cape Saint George, New Ireland, on 25 November.

Burke was initially angry when he was ordered to leave his destroyer command and report on 24 March 1944 as chief of staff to Admiral Marc A. Mitscher, who commanded Task Force 58, the fast carriers in the Pacific. But Burke ultimately served closely with Mitscher during the rest of World War II and, later, as Mitscher's chief of staff while he commanded the Eighth—later Sixth—Fleet that would counter communism in the Mediterranean. Burke was also with Mitscher while he commanded the Atlantic Fleet, until Mitscher's unexpected death from a heart attack early in 1947.

In July 1948 Burke assumed command of the light cruiser *Huntington,* but in October he was recalled to Washington to head Op-23, the organizational research and policy division of the Office of the Chief of Naval Operations (CNO). His assignment was to advise about problems arising from the power struggle between the air force and the navy as the result of proposed unification of these branches of the service within a single Department of Defense. Burke supported the importance of naval aviation and thus fell out of favor with some members of the administration of Harry S. Truman, who wished to rely more heavily on the air force's B-36 bombers. Burke's garnering of opposition against air force supremacy prompted Secretary of the Navy Francis P. Matthews to impound his files and have him arrested. No improprieties were found, and he was released, but Op-23 was disestablished. Burke's name was also removed from the list of captains selected for promotion. This action aroused such a public outcry, however, that Truman overruled it. Burke became a rear admiral on 15 July 1950.

By 1950 Burke had been appointed navy secretary of the Defense Research and Development Board, and he was well versed in the latest information on guided missiles and nuclear weapons. With the outbreak of the Korean War in June 1950, he became deputy chief of staff to the commander of naval forces in the Far East, Admiral Turner C. Joy. After a short-lived cruiser division command during the spring of 1951 off the coast of Korea, Burke joined the United Nations delegation to the truce talks for six months. Among other accomplishments he defined the military demarcation line and demilitarized zone as a condition for the cessation of hostilities.

After a cease-fire line was established in November 1951, Burke returned to Washington and began a two-year tour as the director of the Strategic Plans Division in the Office of the CNO. He also helped the CNO, Admiral Robert B. Carney, prepare the navy's criticism of President Dwight D. Eisenhower's "New Look" defense policy, which was based on "massive retaliation" with nuclear weapons rather than conventional forces. In January 1955 Burke was named commander of the destroyer force of the U.S. Atlantic Fleet, and on 17 August 1955, after Secretary of the Navy Charles S. Thomas declined to appoint Carney for a second term, Burke was chosen over nearly 100 more senior admirals to serve as Eisenhower's naval operations chief.

As CNO, Burke upheld the navy's role in the military establishment and acquired new weapons to counter the Soviets, including intermediate-range and long-range guided missiles, strategic aircraft, and nuclear-powered submarines fitted with atom-tipped missiles. Burke also ordered nuclear-powered submarines to operate under the Arctic ice, which dominated 3,000 miles of the Russian coastline. However, between 1957 and 1961 the number of American warships dropped from 409 to 386. Burke adamantly disagreed with Eisenhower's Defense Reorganization Act of 1958; he maintained that concentrating power

in the secretary of defense served to deny the CNO effective control of the navy, making him merely a military adviser to civilians.

With liquid fuel too dangerous to use in ships, Burke asked the army to cooperate in improving a solid-fueled missile with greater range. However, in September 1955 he made the most important decision he made in his six years as CNO: he created a Special Projects Office and directed Rear Admiral William Francis ("Red") Raborn to produce a nuclear-powered guided missile submarine by 1963. In 1957 he stopped cooperating with the army. Raborn's work resulted in the first Polaris missile submarine, commissioned on 1 January 1960.

As a member of the Joint Chiefs of Staff, Burke participated in solving various international crises in Egypt, Jordan, Lebanon, and Taiwan. Burke was willing to initiate the use of tactical nuclear weapons in addressing communist aggression, but in each case the situations were resolved without major incident. At the end of the Eisenhower administration, when U.S. Air Force General Thomas L. Power requested that Polaris submarines be placed under his command, Burke fought with the Joint Chiefs of Staff, testified in Congress, and made his case in the press for retaining navy control, but ultimately a compromise was enforced. A Joint Strategic Target Planning Staff was created with the commander of the Strategic Air Command as its director and a vice admiral as his deputy, despite Burke's vociferous protests.

With John F. Kennedy as president, Burke observed that Secretary of Defense Robert S. McNamara did not understand the military well but made himself in effect the chief of staff of the U.S. armed forces. In Burke's view, McNamara undercut the services by having a group of young "whiz kids" determine the defense budget, which would be allotted on the basis of "function" rather than service. McNamara approved increasing the Polaris program by ten units in 1962, for a total of forty-one, but Burke had to pay for them by taking funds from other programs. Burke also disapproved of the 1961 Bay of Pigs invasion planned by the Central Intelligence Agency. After the failure of the Cuban invasion, in part due to the lack of American aerial support, Kennedy had Burke represent the Joint Chiefs of Staff in a study group that reviewed the operation and recommended how to avoid similar mistakes. The June 1961 report stressed that the secrecy attending the planning for the operation prevented adequate staffing, good communications, and written plans. That same year, Burke refused Kennedy's request that he continue as CNO. He also declined Kennedy's offer to name him ambassador to Australia. Kennedy awarded him a Gold Star in lieu of a third Distinguished Service Medal on 23 July 1961, and on 1 August, Burke vacated his office after forty-two years of service to the navy.

After his military retirement Burke sat on the boards of directors of a number of prominent corporations, a defense policy institute, and numerous patriotic and veterans' organizations. In 1989 he and his wife were at the Bath Iron Works in Maine for the launching of the Aegis guided missile destroyer *Arleigh Burke*, the first of an entire class.

Burke excelled at commanding destroyers and served memorably as Admiral Mitscher's chief of staff. His knowledge of technology brought the navy into the nuclear age, and he made tremendous contributions to post–World War II strategic planning and policymaking. Upon news of Burke's death—from complications of pneumonia, in 1996 at the age of ninety-four—one admiral remembered him as "relentless in combat, resourceful in command, and revered by his crews. He was the sailor's sailor." Burke was buried at Annapolis Naval Academy Cemetery in Annapolis, Maryland.

★

See the biography by E. B. Potter, *Admiral Arleigh Burke* (1990). John Kenneth Jones, *Destroyer Squadron 23: Combat Exploits of Arleigh Burke's Gallant Force* (1959), and Ken Jones and Hubert Kelley, Jr., *Admiral Arleigh (31-Knot) Burke: The Story of a Fighting Sailor* (1962), cover Burke's service in World War II and as CNO. Also see David Alan Rosenberg, "Officer Development in the Interwar Navy: The Making of a Naval Professional, 1919–1940," *Pacific Historical Review* 44 (Nov. 1975): 503–26, and David Alan Rosenberg, "Arleigh A. Burke," in Robert W. Love, Jr., ed., *The Chiefs of Naval Operations* (1980). Paolo E. Coletta, *Admiral Marc A. Mitscher and U.S. Naval Aviation* (1997), includes Burke's wartime and postwar service with Admiral Mitscher to February 1947. Jeffrey G. Barlow, *Revolt of the Admirals: The Fight for Naval Aviation, 1945–1950* (1994), and Paolo E. Coletta, *The United States Navy and Defense Unification, 1947–1953* (1981), cover Burke's role as head of Op-23. An obituary is in the *New York Times* (2 Jan. 1996).

PAOLO E. COLETTA

BURKE, Selma Hortense (*b.* 31 December 1900 in Mooresville, North Carolina; *d.* 29 August 1995 in New Hope, Pennsylvania), sculptor noted for creating a relief plaque of President Franklin D. Roosevelt housed in the Recorder of Deeds Building in Washington, D.C.

Selma Burke was the seventh of ten children born to the African American Methodist minister Neal Burke, who died when she was twelve, and Mary Jackson Burke, an educator and homemaker. She became interested in the arts at a very early age. Interviews regularly mentioned her discovery that the clay she and her siblings used to whitewash the fireplace could be molded into shapes, and that it would accept and hold the impressions of objects such as coins.

Burke became even more interested in art by studying

Selma Burke, with her bronze plaque of Franklin D. Roosevelt. AP/WIDE WORLD PHOTOS

objects her father collected on his travels as a cruise-ship chef and also when he worked on the railroad. He encouraged her appreciation of art and her talent, and when the Burke household received trunks full of African carvings left to them by two missionary uncles, the artworks were given to Selma. Her mother considered them "graven images" and kept them in the attic, which is where Burke spent her time learning about African art.

Her mother, a practical woman, felt that Burke should pursue a more stable career and insisted that her daughter receive an education. Burke began her studies at the Slater Industrial and State Normal School and went on to graduate from the St. Agnes Training School for Nurses in Raleigh, North Carolina, in 1924 and from the Women's Medical College in Philadelphia in 1928. Meanwhile she rekindled a relationship with a childhood friend, Durant Woodward, whom she married in 1928 and who died tragically of blood poisoning the following year.

In 1929 she began working as a private nurse for an Otis Elevator heiress, Mrs. Amelia Waring, in New York City. Burke was paid well enough so that by the time Mrs. Waring died, four years later, she had built up sufficient savings to avoid the hardships of the Great Depression. She decided to make art her life, so impressing a teacher at Columbia with some small clay figurines that she had crafted that she won a scholarship to the school. She also took classes at Sarah Lawrence College (where she also modeled) and immersing herself in the artistic awakening that would become known as the Harlem Renaissance. She met and later married the famed poet Claude McKay. In 1935 she won a $1,500 Julius Rosenwald Award and in 1936 a Boehler Foundation Award, which allowed her to study in Europe for a year. While abroad, Burke studied sculpture with Aristide Maillol and ceramics with Michael Powolney, and was critiqued by the painter Henri Matisse. She left Austria at the end of 1937. Initially returning to her studies, she founded the Selma Burke School of Sculpture in Greenwich Village in 1940. In 1942 she enlisted in the navy to help in the war effort by working in an airplane plant in New Jersey and driving a truck at the Brooklyn Navy Yard.

The next year, Burke entered a competition sponsored by the Fine Arts Commission in Washington, D.C., to sculpt a relief portrait of President Franklin D. Roosevelt. While working at the Brooklyn Navy Yard, Burke hurt her back and was recovering in the hospital when she found out she had been selected for the commission. She was instructed to base her work on photographs of the president. Unfortunately, all of the photographs she could find were full-frontal or three-quarter views, making it difficult to capture Roosevelt's profile. This was not an acceptable way for her to achieve what she hoped "to be the best piece of sculpture I had ever done." The White House granted her request for a sitting on 22 February 1944. She had a second sitting with the president and scheduled a third, which was forestalled by Roosevelt's sudden death in April 1945. The finished plaque was installed in the Recorder of Deeds Building on 24 September 1945, presented by President Harry S. Truman and unveiled by Frederick Weaver, great-grandson of Frederick Douglass, the first African American to hold the office of Recorder of Deeds.

Controversy has always surrounded Burke's portrait and its relationship to the image of Roosevelt that later appeared on the U.S. ten-cent coin on Roosevelt's birthday (30 January) in 1946. John Sinnock, the chief engraver of the United States Mint at that time, was recognized as the designer of the coin—his initials appear on the face. But strong evidence suggests that he used Burke's image as a model. Hers was the most recent and was considered the best likeness of the president at the time, and several documents in the Roosevelt archives mention Burke's image as the basis for the portrait on the dime. In 1990, after years of controversy, the Bush administration recognized Burke as the artist of the profile on the coin. The rendering on the dime differs slightly from Burke's plaque, with a lower forehead and adjustment of the hair (presumably to oblige Eleanor Roosevelt's criticism that Burke made his forehead too high).

Burke's second husband, Claude McKay, died in 1947, and on 30 September 1949 she married the architect Herman Kobbé, who died in 1955. They lived in New Hope,

Pennsylvania, where she was very active in the art community. (Burke never had any children.) After Kobbé's death, she moved to Pittsburgh, where she founded the Selma Burke Art Center (1968–1981), but she returned to New Hope for the final years of her life.

Prolific in stone and wood, Burke's work is in many museum, university, and community collections. Along with making art, she was extremely involved in teaching art. She wanted children to have opportunities that had not been available to her as a child. The recipient of numerous awards and honorary degrees, she has had streets named after her, and both Pennsylvania and North Carolina have proclaimed a "Selma Burke Day" in her honor. She died of cancer in New Hope, and her ashes were scattered over the Delaware River.

Burke always worked in a representational manner, with her noncommissioned, personal works more emotive than her portrait busts. She created likenesses of Martin Luther King, Jr., John Brown, Booker T. Washington, Wendell Willkie, Charles Schwab, and Mary McLeod Bethune. In 1979 she earned one of the first Annual Women's Caucus for Art Awards along with Alice Neel, Isabel Bishop, Louise Nevelson, and Georgia O'Keeffe.

★

Burke's personal papers were donated to Spelman College in Atlanta, Georgia, with plans to be open to the public in 2001. There is no full-length biography. An interview with the artist, conducted by Robert J. Gangewere, appears in *Carnegie Magazine* 49, no. 1 (Jan. 1975). Burke receives attention in several reference books about women artists and African American women, notably Phoebe M. Harris, ed., *Women Artists of Color: A Bio-Critical Sourcebook to Twentieth Century Artists in the Americas* (1999); Darlene Clark Hine, ed., *Black Women in America: An Historical Encyclopedia* (1993); and Jessie Carney Smith, ed., *Notable Black American Women* (1992). Obituaries are in the *Pittsburgh Post-Gazette* (30 Aug. 1995) and *Philadelphia Inquirer* and *Seattle Times* (both 1 Sept. 1995).

CYNTHIA L. CAMPBELL

BURNS, George (*b.* 20 January 1896 in New York City; *d.* 9 March 1996 in Los Angeles, California), comedian who acquired celebrity as half of the George Burns and Gracie Allen comedy team and, after Allen's death, achieved a highly successful solo career.

George Burns was born Nathan Birnbaum, the tenth of twelve children of Louis Birnbaum, an Austrian immigrant, and Dora Bluth, a Polish immigrant. The family lived in a three-room apartment on the Lower East Side of Manhattan, where many Jewish immigrants had settled after arriving from Eastern Europe. Louis Birnbaum earned so little as a butcher's helper that Dora took in wash to

George Burns. THE KOBAL COLLECTION

support the household. Things grew desperate when Louis died at the age of forty-seven, a victim of the 1904 influenza epidemic.

That same year, at the age of eight, Burns—who would forever be "Nat" to his intimates—joined a street-corner singing group called "The Peewee Quartet." After that, show business became his consuming interest. Three years later, economic need and academic boredom caused him to quit school in the fifth grade. Consequently, he was almost illiterate for the rest of his life.

Burns abandoned the quartet when a friend taught him the basics of tap dancing, after which he decided to make a career of song and dance on the vaudeville stage. He took the name, George Burns, borrowing "George" from a favorite brother and Burns—so he said—from the local "Burns Brothers Coal Yard." More likely, he simply anglicized "Birnbaum."

In the following years Burns acquired a vast collection of names as he joined countless acts in a frantic effort to break into vaudeville. He was Jackson in "Jackson and Malone," Harris in "Harris and Dunlop," Jose in "Jose and Dolores," and first Brown and then Williams of "Brown and Williams." Everything in his life was grist for a vaudevillian view of life. He even married a dance partner named Hermosa Jose (whose real name was Hannah Siegel) because that was the only way her parents would allow her

to tour with him, according to Burns. He would put a "vaudeville shine" on life's mundane events because, as he would always say, he preferred show business to everyday drabness.

The marriage to Hannah Siegel was as short-lived as their stage act, but neither failure upset him. In later years, Burns recalled both the wife and the act as comedy material. Indeed, most of his banter was based on personal history as he chose to reinvent it, not for his own psychological advantage but for laughs. Burns's most striking characteristic was good humor—a boundless optimism and a love of his life. Financial circumstances may have sometimes forced the young man to take the occasional job—as a garment worker, for instance—but he would quit as soon as he earned enough money to buy a new auditioning outfit. Then he was on to the next third-rate vaudeville theater and the next failed act.

The turning point for Burns came in 1923. He was playing a final engagement as half of a disbanding impressionist act called "Burns and Lorraine," when he was visited backstage by a beautiful young singer-dancer named Grace Allen, who was looking for a new partner. She, too, had performed since childhood, but in every other respect these two could not have been more different. Burns was a product of New York's teeming Lower East Side, a first-generation American, and a Jew. Allen, who was ten years younger than Burns, was an Irish Catholic from San Francisco. His parents were poor immigrants who had never heard of show business, while she came from a theatrical family. And although Burns had known nothing but failure, Allen had been successful from the outset, dancing with her sisters as part of "The Four Colleens."

By 1923, however, the last of Allen's sisters had quit the act, leaving the seventeen-year-old performer in search of a new partner and a new act. That fortuitous night, she found both the partner and the act on the stage of a small-time vaudeville theater in suburban Union City, New Jersey, while attending a friend's performance. Within weeks, Burns and Allen were rehearsing a new routine, described by Burns as a "street-corner comedy act." It was his first attempt at comedy, and Allen was the "straight man," providing the cues for Burns's punch lines.

At their first performance, Burns's losing streak remained intact. He was no more successful at comedy than he'd been at singing and dancing. But also intact was Allen's winning streak; she got more laughs with her set-ups than he got with his punch lines. "I didn't have to be a genius," Burns later recalled, "to understand that there was something wrong with a comedy act when the straight lines got more laughs than the punch lines." His friend and fellow vaudevillian Jack Benny, who was in that first audience, agreed. And so, between the first and second shows, Burns—more interested in being a hit than in being a star—revised the routine, giving Allen some of the funnier material.

ALLEN: My sister had a baby.
BURNS: Boy or girl?
ALLEN: I don't know, and I can't wait to find out if I'm an uncle or an aunt.

The audience rewarded his efforts by making them a smash hit, and Burns realized that his gift was indeed a sense of humor—a sense of Allen's humor and the know-how to deliver it to an audience. His talent was for directing and writing—for capitalizing on Allen's sincerity and vulnerability, and for focusing the audience's attention on what he called her "illogical logic." He made her endearingly hilarious, and she became a Galatea to his Pygmalion.

The duo's act quickly rose through the ranks of vaudeville, and only two years later they were starring on the big time (vaudeville status was described as the "big," "medium," or "small" time). While reviews were often dismissive of Burns, he knew how essential he was to the team, and so did Allen. Moreover, she had fallen in love with him, as he already had with her. They were married, with Jack Benny as best man, on 7 January 1926, while on the road, in Cleveland, Ohio. They later adopted two children.

Burns was not only the mastermind behind the act but also its canny business manager. By 1928, he and Allen were headlining at vaudeville's mecca, the Palace Theater in New York City. And he was smart enough to keep out of the stock market, whose crash devastated some of their colleagues—Eddie Cantor, for instance, and Al Jolson. Moreover, Burns anticipated the death of vaudeville, quitting it to take himself and Allen into movies and the new medium of radio.

In Hollywood the couple was paid huge fees for short films and bit parts. The only movie in which they played characters other than themselves was "Damsel in Distress" (1937), in which they also can be seen dancing brilliantly with their close friend Fred Astaire. The picture is the only remaining evidence of Burns's considerable ability as a dancer.

The team's greater success was in radio, where they quickly rose to top popularity, as did their pal Benny. This lasted from 1932 into the 1950s, when they took the half hour "George Burns and Gracie Allen Show" into television. As in radio, it always began with their theme music, "The Love Nest," and always ended with the lines:

BURNS: Say good night, Gracie.
ALLEN: Good night.

Many people would insist that her final line was to mindlessly repeat, "Good night, Gracie," but in so doing she would have appeared a "Dumb Dora" (as such acts were sometimes called). Burns knew that her appeal was based instead on innocence and dearness. The character she played was literal minded and blithe, but not stupid. It was one of several strict rules he followed. For instance, Allen would never look at the audience—not even a radio studio audience—but only at George. Then he would glance at the audience, in effect pointing out the way to find her funny in an endearing way, rather than laughing at her expense.

Likewise, Burns would never be mean or sarcastic with her, would never even touch her, and the cigar that he used for a prop would always be kept away from her face. These were sacrosanct rules, for he knew how thoroughly the act depended on the character she was playing, just as it depended on his timing, shaping, writing, and direction. He was convinced that without her, his act would be finished.

By 1958, Allen had become weary of performing and wished to pursue a life beyond show business that focused on her children as well as her family and friends. She was also suffering from agonizing migraine headaches. But with every contract renewal, Burns convinced Allen to go on, both to take them into the new medium of television and to perpetuate his own career. She went along with him until suffering a heart attack in 1958.

With the final broadcast of "The George Burns and Gracie Allen Show" on 4 June 1958, they never worked as a team again. At first, Burns attempted to be a solo performer, but the television audience wanted Allen, and the CBS weekly "The George Burns Show" (1958–1959) was canceled after one season. Then he tried to re-create the act, giving Allen's old material to such new partners as Carol Channing or Ann-Margret. Their imitations only reminded audiences of the beloved original.

Finally, Burns seemed broken beyond repair by Allen's death in 1964, at the age of fifty-four. Photographs of the funeral depict him leaning on Jack Benny, and for ten years afterward, Burns was a virtual nonentity in show business. Having produced not only the Burns and Allen television show, but also several other series, such as *No Time for Sergeants* (1964), he was a wealthy man. But retirement was the same as death to him, and in 1974, he suffered a near-fatal heart attack. However, with the new development of open-heart surgery, Burns became the oldest patient to undergo a triple-bypass operation.

While still recovering from surgery, Burns was asked by an ailing Jack Benny to substitute at a one-night hotel engagement and Benny gave him more than the brief assignment. When Benny's illness proved to be pancreatic cancer, he recommended—on his deathbed—that Burns replace him in the movie *The Sunshine Boys*.

This proved to be the second miracle in Burns's life. Just as Allen's partnership had enabled him to become a hit, now Benny made it possible for him to be a star on his own. He showed up for the movie audition with apparent confidence ("I'm perfect for the part," he told a friend. "They're looking for an old Jewish vaudevillian and I'm an old Jewish vaudevillian."), but in fact, having never learned to read fluently and fearful of being handed an unexpected scene, he had memorized his character's entire part. He got the role, and not only accepted minimum pay, but leapt at the opportunity.

With *The Sunshine Boys,* Burns won in 1976 the Academy Award for Best Supporting Actor. The movie began a second life for him—a second career in show business, even more successful than the first. In 1977 he starred in the phenomenally successful movie, *Oh, God!* playing a deity of unexpected whimsy. Audiences took the wisely comic God to their hearts, and Burns became America's favorite old man. Between 1975 and 1979, he wrote two books, appeared in five movies (including *Just You and Me, Kid; Going in Style;* and two sequels to *Oh, God!*), and starred in countless television specials. Appearing in Las Vegas and Atlantic City nightclubs, he earned between $25,000 and $50,000 a week. Entering his eighties, he became a symbol of optimism and productivity. He was perhaps the most famous and popular old man America had ever known, surely the funniest, and his appeal crossed all age boundaries. For the elderly, he represented vitality, for the young he stood for wisdom. Still the canny vaudevillian, he perfected his old performing trademarks, and they faithfully served the same purposes. His stammer, for instance, gave him time to set up the next line, while his puffs on a burning cigar allowed the audience to laugh, and the length of its ash let him know how long he had been on stage.

Burns had always specialized in unexpected comedy, but even he had never figured on age as a gold mine of humor. It proved to be exactly that. Instead of concealing his interest in younger women, he would tell audiences, "I would go out with women my age, but there are no women my age." He made it clear, however, that he still loved Allen, reminding audiences of his "chats" with her during regular visits to her grave. The "God" movies had lent him an aura of sagacity so that he could play the role of benign grandfather. "You can't help getting older," he would say, "but you don't have to get old." With his courtly manner and elfin glee, he was able to talk straight to the elderly about overcoming infirmities. "When I walk," he would tell them, "I take steps, and not little ones. Little steps, you'll never get there."

As he entered his middle nineties, it seemed as if Burns would continue to perform forever, certainly to the magic number of 100 years. The country cheered him on toward the mark. He continued to star in television specials and perform in casinos. Plans were made for his centennial— a television special, a show at the London Palladium, and an appearance in Las Vegas that sold out immediately upon its announcement. "I can't die now," Burns said, "because I'm booked." But those centennial engagements were canceled when, in 1994, he fell in his bathroom and suffered a concussion. He recovered enough to resume his habit of drinking at least one martini every day. Although now wheelchair-bound, he continued his regular lunches at Hillcrest, the Hollywood country club. Already shrunken and wizened, he seemed determined to make it to 100 years of age, and he did, but just barely; Burns died two months later at his home. He is buried in Forest Lawn Cemetery in Glendale, California.

Burns was a phenomenon in American cultural as well as entertainment history. In show business, he had two distinct careers, first as the partner of Gracie Allen in a comedy team that spanned vaudeville, radio, movies, and television. Although they reached the top in all of these fields, Burns surpassed it after his wife's death, winning an Academy Award at the age of eighty. For the next twenty years he was America's favorite grandfather, a raconteur and comic philosopher starring in movies, nightclubs, and television specials. It was a long, rich life spanning and celebrating all the periods and styles of American entertainment, and he lived it with such zest and relish that he became an icon, symbolizing affirmation and continued productivity for the elderly.

★

Burns's autobiographies include *I Love Her, That's Why!* (1955), *The Third Time Around* (1980), *How to Live to Be 100— Or More* (1983), *Prescription for Happiness* (1984), *Gracie: A Love Story* (1988), and *All My Best Friends* (1989). See also Cynthia Hobart Lindsay (with George Burns), *Living It Up (Or, They Still Love Me in Altoona)* (1976), and Martin Gottfried, *In Person: The Great Entertainers* (1985). An obituary is in the *New York Times* (10 Mar. 1996).

MARTIN GOTTFRIED

C

CAESAR, Irving (*b.* 4 July 1895 in New York City; *d.* 17 December 1996 in New York City), important Tin Pan Alley lyricist who collaborated with some of the industry's most famous composers and who wrote such classic songs as "Tea for Two" and "Swanee."

Caesar was the son of Morris Caesar, a teacher and book dealer, and Sofia Selinger. Born on the Lower East Side of Manhattan in New York City and originally named "Isidore," Caesar received his early musical training at the Music School Settlement in Manhattan. He purchased his first piano as a young boy for $5 and with the help of neighbors got it to the upper floor of the tenement he called home. After graduating in 1914 from Townsend Harris Hall (a high school for advanced students that compressed four years into three), Caesar spent one year at City College of New York pursuing a business major.

In 1915 Caesar answered a newspaper advertisement and found himself appointed secretary to Henry Ford's Peace Ship, whose ill-fated mission was to try to stop World War I. On board, Caesar wrote a series of short songs telling the Germans to stop the war. He tried to no avail to convince Ford to translate the lyrics into German and drop them over the troops in the trenches. Nevertheless, he formed a friendship with Ford, and Ford asked Caesar to work on the assembly line in order to prepare for running his own branch of Ford's export business.

Caesar's life, however, was destined to go in another direction. While continuing to work on the assembly line during 1916 and 1917, Caesar enjoyed going to the publishing house of Jerome Remick to hear a young man named George Gershwin play the piano. Within a short time, Gershwin began to set Caesar's lyrics to music in songs like "You-oo, Just You," "There's More to the Kiss than the X-X-X," and "I Was So Young." These songs appeared on Broadway in the Gershwin shows *Hitchy-Koo* (1918) and *Good Morning, Judge* (1919).

Gershwin and Caesar became good friends and could often be seen going to concerts, shows, and clubs together. While riding on the top level of a double-decker bus, the two friends composed their first huge hit, "Swanee." It was first heard in the stage show that opened the Capitol Theatre movie house in New York City on 24 October 1919. "Swanee" might have faded away had it not been for Al Jolson. The song was introduced at the Winter Garden Theatre as part of Jolson's act and became his signature song. Thanks in no small part to Jolson, Caesar's first-year royalties for the song were $10,000, a significant amount in 1920. Caesar earned money from the song for years afterward.

The 1920s proved to be one of the most prolific decades in Caesar's long life. With Eddie Cantor, Caesar wrote the song "I Love Her, She Loves Me." In 1922 Cantor both recorded the song and used it in his show *Make It Snappy.* For the W. C. Fields show *Poppy,* Caesar put new lyrics to a Viennese song, "Wien, du Stadt der Lieder," retitling it

Irving Caesar *(right)* with fellow songwriters Ray Henderson *(left)* and Jack Yellen *(center)*, 1933. © BETT-MANN/CORBIS

"Someone Will Make You Smile," and wrote lyrics for the Stephen Jones melody "What Do You Do Sunday?" Between 1922 and 1925 the show *Greenwich Village Follies* teamed Caesar with Cole Porter, Lew Fields, and John Murray Anderson. During this decade, Caesar and Gershwin also collaborated for "The Yankee Doodle Blues" (1922) and "Nashville Nightingale" (1923). *No, No, Nanette,* which proved to be the most successful play of Caesar's life, was produced in 1925. This show paired Caesar with the esteemed composer Vincent Youmans and included two huge hits that have become American standards, "Tea for Two" and "I Want to Be Happy."

Caesar's most famous song, "Tea for Two," had an inauspicious beginning. As legend has it, late one night Youmans played the just-composed melody to Caesar. After performing the song, Youmans became agitated and insisted on having lyrics written that evening. As a way to calm Youmans down and get some sleep, Caesar wrote a quick set of silly improvised lyrics, with the intention of writing better lyrics in the morning. Youmans, however, thought the improvised lyrics were perfect for the show, and they were left untouched and added to *No, No, Nanette.* Thus the "silly" lyrics "Picture you upon my knee / Just tea for two / and two for tea" became part of Americana.

By the mid- to late 1930s the focus of Caesar's career had shifted away from the Broadway stage toward the classroom. His *Songs of Safety* were sung by children across the nation. "Let the Ball Roll," "Ice Skating Is Nice Skating," and "Sing a Song of Friendship" were some of the most widely popularized. Caesar's governmental work also included a musical setting for "The Pledge of Allegiance" that was accepted as an official government document. In the 1930s and 1940s Caesar also wrote songs for motion pictures such as George White's *Scandals* and *Curly Top.*

In the 1950s he offered *Songs of Friendship* to the federal government to promote international goodwill. The collection included "Thomas Jefferski," "Election Day," and "There's Something About America." It was rejected by the government and the New York City Board of Education but was finally printed by the Anti-Defamation League of B'nai Brith.

Caesar was also a well-known practical joker and wit. When once asked what came first, the music or the lyrics, Caesar made his famous reply, "What comes first is the contract." Caesar spent his final years in his huge Manhattan apartment, having years before grown disgusted with the direction modern music had taken. He complained that "good lyrics and tunes are no longer wanted" and that "we have a form of musical juvenile delinquency abetted by adult delinquency." He was always ready, it seemed, to burst into every verse of almost every song he had ever written. He died at Mount Sinai Hospital in New York City and was survived by his wife, Christina A. Ballesteros.

★

Information about Caesar's life and work is included in the following: David Ewen, *American Popular Songs from the Revolutionary War to the Present* (1966) and *American Songwriters* (1987); Roger Kinkle, ed., *The Complete Encyclopedia of Popular Music and Jazz, 1900–1950* (1974); Peter Gammond, *Oxford Companion to Popular Music* (1991); and Colin Larkin, ed., *The Encyclopedia of Popular Music* (1998). An obituary is in the *New York Times* (18 Dec. 1996).

ROBERT PISPECKY

CALLOWAY, Cab (*b.* 25 December 1907 in Rochester, New York; *d.* 18 November 1994 in Hockessin, Delaware), musical artist and master entertainer who combined musical virtuosity with broad popular appeal and never lost popularity with his worldwide audience.

Born Cabell Calloway III, he was the second of six children of Cabell Calloway II, a lawyer, and Martha Eulalia Reed, a teacher and a church organist. In 1918 the Calloways moved from Rochester, New York, back to their original home in Baltimore, where Cab studied voice with Ruth Macabee, a concert artist whom Cab later credited for instructing him in professional vocal technique and diction. As a high school student, Cab excelled at singing, acting, dancing, and sports. He played professional basketball

Cab Calloway, 1930. AP/WIDE WORLD PHOTOS

briefly with the Baltimore Athenians of the Negro Professional League. Torn between professional athletics and music, in 1927 Cab yielded to his parents' wishes and enrolled at Crane College in Chicago as a prelaw student. His singing in the Chicago musical review "Plantation Days," in which his sister Blanche also appeared, seems to have been Cab's principal artistic influence in his early years. (Blanche Calloway had her own career as a fine jazz singer and bandleader.) In 1928 he married Wenonah "Betty" Conacher, with whom he had two daughters. They were separated in 1943 and divorced in 1949.

Within a year of enrolling at Crane, Calloway was appearing as the emcee and lead singer at Chicago's Dreamland Cafe. In 1929 he quit school and signed on as bandleader at the prestigious Sunset Cafe. The house band styled themselves the Alabamians and signed with Calloway to record and tour that year for MCA Records. The band toured well throughout the Northeast but was received poorly by New Yorkers more accustomed to the orchestral and improvisational powerhouse bands of Fletcher Henderson and Charles Johnson. Calloway quit the Alabamians when the New York press dubbed them "too square," but not before meeting Louis Armstrong, who was visiting New York with his Hot Seven. Armstrong arranged an audition for Calloway for a Broadway review called *Connie's Hot Chocolates*. Cab won it and began a renowned stage career.

In 1930 Calloway agreed to lead the house band, the Missourians, at the Savoy Ballroom in New York City. He was a startling success. His onstage gyrations and antics matched his eccentric zoot suits, knee-draped jackets, floor-length key chains, and white satin tuxedos. His year on Broadway had taught him how to entertain and provoke. Astoundingly, his sartorial and theatrical hype (what a sideman called "all that whoopin' and hollerin'") never overwhelmed his music. In Calloway's own slang, he was the "hipster with the twister to the slammer," which translated roughly as the cool guy with the key to the door. It was in 1930 that Calloway opened that door to his enduring success.

Late in 1930, Duke Ellington asked Calloway to appear at the popular Cotton Club in Harlem as his touring replacement. Calloway obliged, and he and his band brought the house down with "Kickin' the Gong Around," a thinly veiled song about opium. A young, upward-bound singer named Bing Crosby caught that show and immediately recommended him for the Paramount Theater and the *Lucky Strike Hit Parade* radio show. Calloway became the first African American musician to be broadcast on a previously all-white show on network radio.

By 1931 Cab Calloway and His Orchestra had succeeded Duke Ellington at the Cotton Club. They also began to record the first of several hundred Calloway songs.

One of the first and most famous was "Minnie the Moocher," which debuted without its trademark "Hi-de-hi-de-hi" call-and-response. That unforgettable hook was improvised by Calloway during a radio appearance in 1931, when he apparently forgot his own lyrics to the second verse and scatted a last-second melody. The band loved it and joined in, as did a half century of audiences. Few seemed concerned that "Minnie" was a barely disguised song about cocaine.

For the next ten years, Calloway headlined at the Cotton Club. His first appearance in a motion picture was in *The Big Broadcast*, in 1932, and he also performed in three animated cartoons for the Max Fleischer Studios: *Snow White, The Old Man of the Mountain,* and *Minnie the Moocher.* For these cartoons, Calloway was filmed and then rotoscoped, every frame hand traced and then reanimated. Dozens of his scores accompanied the Betty Boop cartoons.

Cab had a sharp ear for talent. He helped develop many of the next generations of jazz greats: Doc Cheatham, Milt Hinton, Dizzy Gillespie, Mario Bauzá, Cozy Cole, Reuven Reeves, Jonah Jones, and Chu Berry. He paid his musicians top dollar and treated his band well, always traveling first class, often with a private Pullman car. The band toured Europe for the first time in 1935.

In 1936 he appeared in the film *The Singing Kid* with Al Jolson. Two years later he published *Cab Calloway's Hepster's Dictionary: The Language of Jive.* More cartoon caricatures of Calloway followed from 1937 to 1944, most for Warner Brothers. He recorded the hit single "Blues in the Night" in 1942. The following year, Calloway starred with Lena Horne in the box-office success *Stormy Weather,* singing two songs superbly, "Geechy Joe" and "Sunday in Savannah." Calloway possessed an extraordinary, complex vocal style: part jive and scat, part opera, part melodrama, part testimonial.

As America's pop music modulated from swing to rock and roll in the late 1940s, Calloway's career changed. He disbanded his orchestra in 1948, touring with a septet or a trio, which he called his Cab Jivers. In 1949 he married Nuffie Macneal, with whom he had three daughters. In 1950 he starred as the character Sportin' Life in a Broadway revival of George Gershwin's *Porgy and Bess.* Calloway was perfect for the role, because he was Gershwin's model for the character in the original production. In 1957 he appeared with Louis Armstrong, Ruby Dee, Eartha Kitt, Pearl Bailey, and Ella Fitzgerald in the film *St. Louis Blues.* Ten years later Calloway was back on Broadway, with Pearl Bailey in a revival of *Hello, Dolly* with an African American cast. In 1973 he costarred with Barbara McNair in *The Pajama Game.* He toured nationally with *Bubblin' Brown Sugar* (1978) and *Eubie* (1980.)

Late in his life, Calloway endeared himself to new generations of listeners. Three episodes of *Sesame Street* in 1978 featured an avuncular Calloway as the "Hi-De-Ho" Man. In 1980 he made a dazzling, high-energy appearance (at the age of seventy-three) in the film *The Blues Brothers.* In 1989 Calloway "did his thing" in Janet Jackson's music video "Alright." He was awarded the National Arts Medal by President Bill Clinton at a formal White House ceremony in 1993. In June 1994 he suffered a stroke at a retirement home in Delaware. He slowly weakened and died in November.

Calloway left an unequaled legacy in entertainment—concerts, recordings, film, animation, musical theater, radio, and television.

★

The Calloway papers are in the archives of the Boston University Library. The Schomburg Center for Research in Black Culture in New York City houses the Cab Calloway Portrait Collection, and a clippings file is in the New York Public Library for the Performing Arts. Calloway wrote an autobiography, *Of Minnie the Moocher and Me,* with Bryant Rollins (1976). An obituary is in the *New York Times* (20 Nov. 1994). See also Jay Popa, *Cab Calloway and His Orchestra* (rev. ed. 1987), for a discography.

JAMES MCELWAINE

CANDY, John Franklin (*b.* 31 October 1950 in Newmarket, Ontario, Canada; *d.* 4 March 1994 in Durango, Mexico), Emmy-winning, affable, rotund comedian best known for his *SCTV* performances and starring roles in such films as *Splash; Planes, Trains and Automobiles; Uncle Buck;* and *Only the Lonely.*

Candy's early years were spent in King City, Ontario, the younger son of working-class parents. His father, Sidney James Candy, a war veteran and car salesman, died from a heart attack at the age of thirty-five. (Candy's fatherless youth would later figure in one of *SCTV*'s most popular skits, a parody of *Leave It to Beaver.* Candy, as Beaver, comments, "Life stinks, Wally.") After his father's death, his mother, Evangeline Aker, moved her two children to her parents' bungalow in East York, Ontario, and worked as a clerk in a retail store. John attended Holy Cross Catholic School and was an altar boy. He sold bottle caps to see films. Candy said, "I would come home and re-create every movie. . . . I think I may have become an actor to hide from myself."

Candy, a first-generation TV viewer, feared he might become a television addict from watching so much TV; his early favorites included *Jack Benny, Jack Paar,* and *The Honeymooners.* Nevertheless, Candy told *Playboy,* "I wasn't interested in any one show. I was influenced by the medium."

Candy created shows in neighbors' garages. After finishing the eighth grade, he attended Neil McNeil Catholic

John Candy, 1991. THE KOBAL COLLECTION

School in the four-year diploma stream, making passing grades. Self-conscious because of his large size, he preferred to be on the gym team that wore shirts rather than on the one that did not. He played clarinet, served as student council treasurer, and was tackle for the football team. Although gentle in manner, he was also an aggressive team player. A knee injury ended his football career, but he later co-owned the Toronto Argonauts team in the Canadian Football League.

Despite Candy's innocent demeanor, he smoked cigarettes at school, tried marijuana, and drank. His drama teacher claimed that Candy took drama because the typing class was full. In a production of *Julius Caesar and Burning Effigy,* Candy drew laughs with his role as a dog. His friend Jonathon O'Mara said of Candy, "At first he would just strike you as a fun guy to be around, . . . but he also had a side to him that a lot of people didn't see. He was very sensitive, and eager to be liked." Candy worked at various part-time jobs and drove people to bingo and stores in his "White Knight" Chevrolet. When he left home, Candy said, "It was quite traumatic for everyone."

He entered Centennial Community College in Scarborough, Ontario, confessing, "I didn't know what I wanted to be." Candy quit during his second year to become an actor. In 1970 Toronto talent agent Catherine McCartney auditioned him for a toothpaste commercial. Art Linkletter corrected Candy for smoking on the set. Candy, who was six feet, three inches tall and later weighed more than 275 pounds, retorted, "Yeah, it might stunt my growth."

In a local theater group, he received $40 a week for a part in *Creeps* (1971), costarring Dan Aykroyd, who would later figure prominently in Candy's career. During this time Candy met Rosemary Margaret Hobor. They married in 1979 and had two children. Also during this period, Candy worked for Perkins Paper as a door-to-door salesman, claiming, "I was terrible at it. Out of forty salesmen, I was number forty. I was having so much fun doing theater my heart just wasn't in flogging napkins." His boss agreed. "Candy, you're fired. I should never have hired a damned actor."

He joined a children's troupe, the Caravan Theater, in 1972. Candy and Gale Garnett were yoked together as toadstools. Despite close proximity, Garnett said Candy was professional and supportive but someone "whom I didn't know at all." That summer, Candy met Marcus O'Hara and his girlfriend, Gilda Radner, who would achieve fame herself as a comedian and who would become close friends with Candy.

Candy's career entered a promising new phase when he joined Chicago's Second City theater troupe in 1973. In 1974 he moved back to Toronto to help establish a local Second City troupe, and it was here that he would land his first breakthrough part. The venue was *SCTV,* a television program created and performed by the Second City troupe. The program ran in syndication between 1977 and 1979 as *SCTV* and again between 1981 and 1983 as *SCTV Network 90.* Candy both wrote for and performed on the show, and his memorable characters included Johnny LaRue, Mayor Tommy Shanks, the Guy with the Snake on His Face, Orson Welles, Luciano Pavarotti, and Yosh Schmenge. For his work on *SCTV,* Candy won Emmy Awards in 1982 and 1983.

Candy performed in or directed at least one film a year beginning in 1974, but it was after his success with *SCTV* that his most notable roles occurred. The films in which he acted included *Stripes* (1981), *Summer Rental* (1985), *Little Shop of Horrors* (1986), *Spaceballs* (1987), *Speed Zone!* (1989), *Who's Harry Crumb?* (1989), *The Rescuers Down Under* (1991), *Delirious* (1991), *Only the Lonely* (1991), *Nothing but Trouble* (1991), and *Once upon a Crime* (1992). The careers of Candy, Tom Hanks, Daryl Hannah, and the director Ron Howard took off with *Splash* (1984), in which Candy played the brother of Hanks's mermaid-smitten character. After *Planes, Trains and Automobiles* (1987), the stress of fame made him long for the old days with friends at Second City. In *The Great Outdoors* (1988), in which he starred with Aykroyd, Candy played opposite a 1,400-pound grizzly bear in "one of the most frightening experiences of my life." He enjoyed pleasing his fans but disliked personal attention. At one point Toronto producer John Brunton arranged a television tribute for Candy at Toronto's Sky Dome, but Candy refused. "It's too embarrassing to have all this attention directed at me."

Cool Runnings (1993) was Candy's last popular movie. In November 1993 Candy made his final public appearance with his friend Eugene Levy at a benefit performance at the Sky Dome. Troubled by anxiety and lack of sleep, Candy said his deceased friend Gilda Radner had appeared in a dream. "Don't worry, John," she said, "everything is going to be all right." Within months, Candy died of a heart attack in his sleep in Durango, Mexico, while filming *Wagons East.* He is buried in Holy Cross Cemetery and Mausoleum in Culver City, California.

John Candy lived out his childhood dream as a film star. More important, he discovered himself. Candy said, "It took me a long time to learn what is really valuable in life. I went through a period of real acquisitiveness . . . as if owning lots of stuff said a damn about who you really are and what your life really means. Maybe I've finally learned what happiness is: my family, my wife, my kids. We're only here a short time. Let's enjoy it, whatever happens. We love each other. That's all that matters."

★

Martin Knelman, *Laughing on the Outside: The Life of John Candy* (1996), provides an intimate chronological study of Candy's life. Steven A. LuKanic, ed., *Film Actors Guide* (1991), offers complete release information about Candy's movies through 1991. David Inman, *The T.V. Encyclopedia* (1991), contains information about thousands of television personalities and discusses Candy's Emmy Awards. Ronald L. Smith, *Who's Who in Comedy: Comedians, Comics, and Clowns from Vaudeville to Today's Stand-ups* (1992), follows Candy's career in narrative and by films, television, and on video. Ephraim Katz, ed., *The Film Encyclopedia* (1994), is a comprehensive one-volume encyclopedia of world cinema that includes information about Candy's film roles. Larry Langman and Paul Gold, *Comedy Quotes from the Movies* (1994), cover more than 4,000 humorous quotes from film genres, topically arranged and indexed. Everett Grant Jarvis, *Final Curtain: Deaths of Noted Movie and Television Personalities 1912–1996* (1996), references original birth records and death statistics through 3 May 1996 and locations of cemeteries. Biographical information about Candy, photos, and fan letters are available at www.john-candy.com. An obituary is in the *New York Times* (5 Mar. 1994).

SANDRA REDMOND PETERS

CANNON, Sarah Ophelia Colley. *See* Pearl, Minnie.

CHADWICK, Florence May (*b.* 9 November 1918 in San Diego, California; *d.* 15 March 1995 in San Diego, California), champion marathon swimmer who gained worldwide acclaim in 1950 when she swam the English Channel one hour faster than any previous woman swimmer.

Chadwick was the second child and the only daughter of Richard William Chadwick, a San Diego police detective,

and Mary Lacko, the owner of a downtown restaurant. Florence Chadwick was encouraged by her uncle, Mike Lacko, to enter competitive swimming when she was six years old and growing up at 2120 Warrington Street in Point Loma on San Diego Bay. The youngster set her sights on emulating Gertrude Ederle's 1926 record English Channel swim, and at age ten she became the first child to swim the six-mile San Diego Bay Channel. Soon afterward she won her first trophy in the city's annual 2.5-mile rough-water night swim off Hermosa Beach, the first of dozens of Pacific Coast amateur open-water titles she captured over the next nineteen years. While growing up, Chadwick was trained by her father, who set up a gym in the family's garage, where she sawed wood to develop both her stamina and her shoulders. In 1930 the local swimming coach Henry Gunther took over, and he remained her coach throughout Chadwick's amateur career. She failed to break into the national ranks while swimming with the Los Angeles Athletic Club with teammates Eleanor Holm and Esther Williams. Chadwick did little better than a second-place finish to Holm in the 1932 U.S. Nationals. She realized that her forte was in outdoor swimming.

Chadwick attended Loma Portal Elementary School and in 1936 graduated from Point Loma Senior High School, where she swam competitively, was elected president of the associated high school student body, and was a member of the Girl Reserves, a junior branch of the YWCA. She attended San Diego State College (1937), Southwestern University of Law at Los Angeles (1938), and Balboa Law School in San Diego (1939). In 1940 she entered the local Dickenson Business College for eighteen months and became a trainee at the comptometer school of San Diego's Felt and Tarrant Manufacturing Company. Vacillating between an athletic career and show business, she produced and performed in aquacades, an entertainment rage of the time. She also appeared in *Bathing Beauty,* a 1945 MGM swimming film extravaganza, with her former teammate Williams. She was briefly married twice. She first married Alex Balich in 1939; they divorced in 1940. In 1942 she married Bob Warner, a San Diego policeman; they divorced in 1946. Chadwick referred to both marriages as "detours" from her swimming career.

After two years as aquatic director at nearby La Jolla Beach and Tennis Club, Chadwick left in June 1948 for Saudi Arabia and an office job with the giant Arabian-American Oil Company. Committed to her childhood goal of swimming the English Channel, she banked her salary and trained daily. When transferred to Ras al Mishah in the Persian Gulf, she trained in the gulf's redolent, oil-slicked waters, which she later said felt like swimming in "hot soup." A strict conditioning regime made her "swim until tired, then swim until exhausted, and then swim an extra half-mile." She saved $5,000 toward her Channel ex-

Florence Chadwick. ARCHIVE PHOTOS

become the first woman to swim the Channel from England (Saint Margaret's Bay, Dover) to France (Sangatte) on 11 September 1951. She made that swim in sixteen hours and twenty-two minutes, a record she would shatter twice before retiring in 1960.

Known as the "channel barnstormer," Chadwick set swimming records for California's Catalina (1952), the English Channel, the Strait of Gibraltar, the Bosporus, and the Dardanelles (all in fall 1953). The once-impoverished Californian who had exhausted her nest egg for her first Channel swim now commanded fees ranging from $5,000 to $20,000 an exhibition, made frequent appearances on radio and television, and traveled nationwide on behalf of her sponsor, Catalina Bathing Suits. Between "channels" she worked for Grossinger's Resort in New York's Catskills Mountains as aquatics director (1952–1963). Her annual income was well in excess of $50,000, making her the highest paid woman athlete in the country. As late as 1957 she was still setting records, swimming the fourteen-mile Bristol Channel (England to Wales) in six hours and seven minutes. Three years later, after several failed efforts to cross the treacherous North Channel between Ireland and Scotland, Chadwick retired. In her forty-year career she had set seventeen world records in long-distance swimming, leading *Sports Illustrated* to name her the "best woman long-distance swimmer the world has ever known" (7 November 1960). She was inducted into San Diego's Hall of Champions in 1962, the International Swimming Hall of Fame in 1970, and the International Women's Sports Hall of Fame in 1996.

Chadwick remained in New York City, her home since 1950, where she taught swimming until 1966. At that time she joined Manufacturers Hanover Bank as a credit counselor and public relations representative in its Wall Street branch. Her mother was ailing, so Chadwick moved back to the pink house on Warrington Street in 1970. Equipped with a broker's license earned in 1969, she spent her remaining years as a stockbroker and financial consultant and continued to work with a new generation of marathon swimmers. She died of leukemia at age seventy-six in San Diego's Mercy Hospital. Her body was cremated and her ashes scattered in the Pacific Ocean.

Chadwick was one of the world's great marathon swimmers. At 5 feet 6 inches and 140 pounds, her physique was more that of a swimsuit model than an endurance swimmer and helped dispel the myth that only well-padded women could withstand the rigors of marathon swimming. Johnny Weissmuller, the Olympic champion and motion picture star, once said of Chadwick, "She's the greatest swimmer of all time—maybe of either sex." Her achievements came at a time when most Americans viewed marathon swimming as comparable to flagpole sitting or Niagara Falls barrel sailing. Few regarded the endeavor as much more

penses and in June 1950 headed for Wissant, France, where she trained for another two months.

At 2:37 A.M. on 8 August 1950 Chadwick entered the Channel's choppy, frigid waters, nowhere warmer than 60 degrees Fahrenheit, at Cape Gris-Nez on the coast of France. Escorted by the *Marcel Nicole* fishing boat carrying her father, two Saudi friends, and officials, she swam through the night, starting off at a blistering sixty strokes a minute. She reached Dover, England, in thirteen hours and twenty minutes, lopping more than an hour off Ederle's twenty-four-year-old record. She was the twelfth woman and the thirty-second swimmer to complete the nineteen-mile swim since England's Matthew Webb first swam the route seventy-five years earlier. In a dramatic finish, British artillery forces suspended fire as Chadwick swam into their gunnery practice area. Wading ashore through a bed of kelp she announced, "I feel fine and I am quite prepared to swim back."

Chadwick did swim back, but not until a year later. She overcame strong tides, winds, heavy fog, and icy waters to

than a publicity stunt. Chadwick's career changed that perception. Her records all have been superseded, but she was among the first to lend credibility to the sport of endurance swimming.

★

Both the Henning Library and Archive at the International Swimming Hall of Fame in Fort Lauderdale, Florida, and the San Diego Hall of Champions maintain a collection of photographs, articles, and memorabilia pertaining to Chadwick's career. Gail Campbell, *Marathon: The World of the Long-Distance Athlete* (1977), places Chadwick in the context of the history of marathon swimming and devotes a short chapter to her achievements. "Whatever Happened to Florence Chadwick?" *San Francisco Sunday Examiner and Chronicle* (13 Sept. 1970), recounts events in the swimmer's early career and her training methods. "Florence Chadwick Still Dreams of Channel Swim," *San Diego Union* (22 Mar. 1970), offers a glimpse of the aging swimmer's regrets and hopes as well as her outlook on swimming. Obituaries are in the *San Diego Union-Tribune* (18 Mar. 1995) and the *New York Times* (19 Mar. 1995).

MARTHA MONAGHAN CORPUS

Roy Chalk, 1967. AP/WIDE WORLD PHOTOS

CHALK, (Oscar) Roy (*b.* 7 June 1907 in London, England; *d.* 1 December 1995 in New York City), flamboyant businessman with diverse holdings in transportation, real estate, and publishing.

Chalk was one of three children of a Russian father, Bennett Chalk, and a Polish mother, Sophie Stern Clark. When Chalk was three years old, his family moved to the United States, where they settled in the Bronx, New York. Bennett Chalk was a shopkeeper who moonlighted as a cantor at the synagogue near the family home. The Chalks soon moved to Manhattan's Upper West Side, where Chalk attended public school and insisted that his friends call him Roy. (Throughout his life, calling him Oscar was an invitation to rebuke). Chalk played stickball with boys from the neighborhood, including George and Ira Gershwin and Lou Gehrig.

Bestowed with a sense of self-sufficiency at an early age, he entered night school at New York University after graduating from the High School of Commerce and worked at odd jobs during the day. He received his law degree in 1931 and was admitted to the New York State bar in 1932. Specializing in real estate transactions and landlord-tenant disputes, Chalk opened an office in midtown Manhattan.

In 24 December 1931, Chalk married Claire Cole; they had one child. His marriage was a key event in his rise up the social ladder. With the financial help of his father-in-law, Herman Cole, a prominent New York real estate investor, Chalk bought a sixteen-story apartment house on Fifth Avenue for one million dollars. The investment proved wise and launched Chalk into construction and real estate. He soon owned an array of valuable properties in Manhattan and the Bronx. The son of an immigrant, Chalk was a millionaire at thirty.

Despite his success, Chalk was constantly striving, reinventing himself. During World War II, he worked with the military, first as a civilian lawyer, then as an aeronautical training consultant. In the latter position he saw an opportunity, and founded a lucrative company, Metal Associates, Inc., to make electronic training devices for the army and navy. When the war ended, Chalk bought two ragged DC-3 airplanes and started Trans Caribbean Airways. He operated nonscheduled flights between New York City and San Juan, Puerto Rico, and was able to offer lower fares and better service than his competitors, Pan American and Eastern. Subsidiary to the airline, he acquired International Railways, a 795-mile railroad line that hauled bananas across Central America. Chalk even owned a banana plantation for a brief time.

When the Korean War broke out in 1950, Chalk saw another opportunity. The army was short of transport planes for cargo and troops, and turned to the nonscheduled airlines' association, the Air Coach Transport Association (ACTA), which parceled out business to its constituent airlines on an equal basis. Chalk formed a competing association, the Independent Military Air Transport Association

(IMATA), allowing his airline, Trans Caribbean, a larger share of business than if it had remained in the ACTA. In this and other exploits, Chalk revealed an ability to cultivate politicians. In 1957 Trans Caribbean Airways was certified by the Civil Aeronautics Board to fly scheduled routes, making it the first nonscheduled airline in two decades to gain certification.

Turning his attention from the air to the ground, Chalk in 1956 bought the broken-down Washington, D.C., Transit System from a private financier, edging out a competitor's bid by trading on his political connections. He succeeded in lobbying for a fare increase of five cents, exemptions on fuel taxes, and a subsidy for carrying schoolchildren at reduced fares. Chalk repaid the support of his political friends and investors, rejuvenating the company by sprucing up the buses and adding air-conditioned coaches, express routes, and service to the suburbs. Net income nearly doubled, and Chalk paid off a $9 million loan in two years, well before it was due.

In 1962 Chalk entered the publishing world by acquiring the Spanish-language daily newspaper *El Diario de Nueva York*, with a large circulation among New York's Puerto Rican population. Soon Chalk set out to undercut the rival newspaper *La Prensa* by dropping El *Diario*'s newsstand price. Within six months, Chalk bought out *La Prensa* and merged the two papers. The newly merged *El Diario–La Prensa* became a powerful voice in city and national politics. Although Chalk had been a supporter of Republican President Dwight Eisenhower at the time he bought D.C. Transit, his editorials praised Democrats and blistered Republicans. During the 1960s he became a prominent fund-raiser for the Democratic Party. He also bought an advertising agency, three television stations in Puerto Rico, and a number of radio stations, in addition to his ever-expanding portfolio of real estate holdings.

In the latter part of the 1960s and early 1970s, however, Chalk's fortunes began to wane. Trans Caribbean Airways was running large deficits and was sold to American Airlines for stock spin-offs and a consulting contract. D.C. Transit also turned unprofitable and lost favor with the public. Chalk himself became a controversial figure in Washington and a lightning rod for public dissatisfaction with privately owned urban transit. Repeated fare increases, coupled with large dividends for shareholders, brought on lawsuits and boycotts (one led by the youthful Marion Barry, later controversial in his own right as Washington's mayor), prompting calls in Congress that the government take over the system, which it did in 1973.

Chalk sold *El Diario–La Prensa* to Gannett Company in 1981, but he refused to slow down. He helped found the American-Korean Foundation to foster closer ties between the United States and South Korea, earning the National Medal of Honor from the South Korean government and honorary citizenship. He was also chairman of the American Jewish Committee and the United Nations Finance Committee.

At the age of eighty-three, Chalk's life seemed to come full circle. He was hired by the Russian president Boris Yeltsin and prime minister Ivan Silaev as a lobbyist and financier to raise money for the Russian Republic while forging ties throughout the United States. The job allowed him to wed his Russian roots, his jet-setting lifestyle, and his ferocious cultivation of the American political and business establishment.

A throwback to the nineteenth-century era of self-made tycoons, Chalk was famed for his large fortune and flamboyant tastes. In addition to a twelve-room apartment on Fifth Avenue in Manhattan, Chalk and his wife owned a thirty-acre estate in Falls Church, Virginia, and a home in Palm Beach, Florida. They traveled frequently to London and Monaco, where he moored his 165-foot yacht, the *Blue Horizon*. He indulged his fondness for art and fashion, owning paintings by Renoir and expensive suits by the dozen. Chalk died of cancer at New York Hospital. An aggressive businessman, Chalk often acted first and considered the consequences later. "A lack of knowledge is a great advantage," he once said. "With ignorance, you proceed with confidence where you would otherwise proceed with trepidation."

★

The best overview of Chalk's life is in *Current Biography* (1971). He was also a frequent subject for reporters and magazine writers and was featured in *Coronet* (Aug. 1966), *Forbes* (1 June 1965), *New York Herald Tribune* (8 Dec. 1962), *Newsweek* (4 June 1962 and 17 July 1967), *Status* (Jan.–Feb. 1966), *Time* (4 May 1970), and, especially, articles in the *Washington Post* from 1962 to 1991. Obituaries are in the *New York Times* and *Washington Post* (both 2 Dec. 1995).

TIMOTHY KRINGEN

CHAMBERLAIN, John Rensselaer (*b.* 28 October 1903 in New Haven, Connecticut; *d.* 9 April 1995 in New Haven, Connecticut), author, critic, and editor whose gradual conversion from radicalism to conservatism represented the political odyssey of many intellectuals in the decades following the Great Depression.

Chamberlain was the son of Robert Rensselaer Chamberlain, a furniture retailer, and Emily Davis. From 1916 to 1920 he attended Loomis Institute at Windsor, Connecticut, graduating at age sixteen. After spending a year as an itinerant laborer in California, he enrolled at Yale University, where he served on the board of the *Yale Literary Magazine,* wrote a column for the *Yale Daily News,* and chaired the *Yale Record.*

After receiving his B.Phil. degree in 1925, Chamberlain briefly worked for a New York advertising agency. He was a city reporter for the *New York Times* from 1926 to 1928, at which point he was made assistant editor of the *Times's* book review section, a post he held until 1933.

In 1932 Chamberlain published *Farewell to Reform: A History of the Rise, Life, and Decay of the Progressive Mind in America,* a well-received critical survey of the American reform tradition in literature that contained deftly drawn portraits of personalities and movements. He found populists burdened by their focus on free silver, muckrakers impotent to hinder corporate power, progressives accomplishing "minimal results," and Woodrow Wilson betraying his own principles by leading his nation into war. In a second edition (1933), he predicted that Franklin D. Roosevelt would be driven to the right, which would substantiate Chamberlain's claim that New Deal reforms were bound to fail.

In April 1933 Chamberlain became associate editor of the *Saturday Review of Literature,* but that September he returned to the *New York Times* as book columnist, in which capacity he wrote five reviews a week in a "Books of the *Times*" column. From 1936 to 1938 he was book editor of the monthly *Scribner's Magazine,* and in 1936 he began summarizing books as well for *Current History.* From 1939 to 1947 he was book editor of the monthly *Harper's Magazine.* During this time he contributed frequently to such publications as the *New York Herald Tribune, New Republic, Common Sense, Yale Review,* and *Commonweal.*

In 1936 Chamberlain became an editor at *Fortune,* a business monthly, where he remained until 1941. By reporting firsthand on industrial developments throughout the nation, Chamberlain became more sympathetic to business. *Fortune* publisher Henry Luce let Chamberlain be something of a maverick, permitting him to endorse a third term for Franklin Roosevelt and write a dissent on the famous "American Century" editorial published in Luce's weekly *Life* in February 1941.

In 1933 Chamberlain had defined himself as a Marxist "in the Bernard Shaw sense," but by the mid-1930s he was intensely critical of communism at home and abroad. In 1940 he published *The American Stakes,* as persuasive a plea for gradualism as *Farewell to Reform* had been an attack upon it. Drawing upon his magazine articles, he defended much of the New Deal, welcomed a mixed economy, and advocated consumer cooperatives. Strongly anti-interventionist, he claimed that the United States should limit military involvement to the Western Hemisphere. In 1940 and 1941 he served on the editorial board of *Uncensored,* a mimeographed weekly sponsored by the Writers Anti-War Bureau.

From 1942 to 1944 Chamberlain was again the *Times* book columnist, splitting daily assignments with Orville

Prescott. From 1945 to 1950 he was a senior editor at *Life.* At first he worked out of Washington, D.C., writing articles on such matters as the findings of the Pearl Harbor congressional investigation, the failures of Britain's new Labour government, and the need to contain the Soviets in Asia as well as Europe. From 1948 to 1950 he contributed biweekly editorials, sharing the task with John Osborne. He was also on the editorial staff of *Plain Talk,* a militant anti-Soviet monthly stressing the dangers of domestic communism and lasting from 1946 to 1950.

From 1950 to 1952 Chamberlain reviewed politics, economics, and the arts for a journal that was in some sense *Plain Talk*'s officially designated successor, the biweekly *Freeman,* which he first coedited with Henry Hazlitt and Suzanne La Follette, themselves former radicals of the 1930s. In his articles and book reviews, Chamberlain defended the brand of anticommunism espoused by Senator Joseph McCarthy. He also supported conservative senator Robert Taft's bid for the 1952 Republican presidential nomination, and he accused the Truman administration of appeasing communism, particularly in China. Chamberlain resigned from the board of the *Freeman* in 1953, along with La Follette and editor Forrest Davis, when such wealthy backers as the du Ponts and the oil magnate J. Howard Pew sought a more pro-Eisenhower stance. When, in January 1956, the Foundation for Economic Education converted the *Freeman* into a monthly, however, Chamberlain became a frequent contributor. In 1955, when the *National Review* was founded, Chamberlain appeared on its masthead as an editorial writer and fortnightly book reviewer. From 1953 to 1955 he was associate editor of *Barron's National Financial Weekly,* after which he became staff writer for the *Wall Street Journal* until 1960. For twenty-five years, ending in 1985, he wrote a daily column, "These Days," for Hearst's King Features Syndicate, assuming the slot once designated to George Sokolsky. There was hardly a conservative journal to which Chamberlain did not contribute, be it the tabloid weekly *Human Events* or the more intellectual monthly *Modern Age.*

Chamberlain continued to write books as well. His book *MacArthur, 1941–1951* (1954) is a spirited defense of every major move undertaken by the flamboyant general. Although Douglas MacArthur's intelligence chief, General Charles Willoughby, was listed as first author, Chamberlain wrote the working text. In 1959 he published *The Roots of Capitalism,* a popularized economic history beginning with a discussion of Adam Smith's *Wealth of Nations* and stressing the virtues of "supply-side" economics. In 1963 his book *The Enterprising Americans: A Business History of the United States,* a condensation of a series originally running in *Fortune,* challenged the "robber baron" thesis. In his lively narrative, he defended such maligned figures as

J. P. Morgan, John D. Rockefeller, and "Commodore" Cornelius Vanderbilt.

Despite his lifetime of heavy writing commitments, Chamberlain had time to teach budding apprentices. In 1934 and 1935 he was lecturer at the Columbia University School of Journalism; he was later associate professor at Columbia from 1941 to 1944. From 1972 to 1977 he was dean of the Troy (Alabama) State University School of Journalism, conducting a seminar on investigative journalism every three weeks.

On 22 April 1926 he married Margaret Sterling, who died in 1955. They had two daughters. On 29 June 1956 he married Ernestine Stodelle. They had one son. Chamberlain died of natural causes at age ninety-one.

Throughout his career, Chamberlain was noted for his lucid style, breadth of knowledge, and conciliatory personality. Though his political odyssey was marked by a radical shift from the left to the right, he always saw himself as the foe of entrenched power, be it business or the state.

★

The papers of John Chamberlain are located in the Hoover Institution of War, Revolution and Peace, Stanford University. Chamberlain's autobiography is titled *A Life with the Printed Word* (1982). For scholarly treatment of Chamberlain, see Louis Filler, "John Chamberlain and American Liberalism," *Colorado Quarterly* 6 (autumn 1957): 200–211, and Frank Annunziata, "The Political Thought of John Chamberlain," *South Atlantic Quarterly* 74 (winter 1975): 53–73. For a collection of his *Freeman* reviews, see his book *The Turnabout Years: America's Cultural Life, 1900–1950* (1991). Obituaries are in the *New York Times* (13 Apr. 1995) and *National Review* (1 May 1995).

JUSTUS D. DOENECKE

CHANCELLOR, John William (*b.* 14 July 1927 in Chicago, Illinois; *d.* 12 July 1996 in Princeton, New Jersey), respected television journalist best known for his work as anchorman and commentator for *NBC Nightly News.*

The only child of the Chicago hotel executives E. M. J. Chancellor and Mary Barrett, Chancellor spent much of his youth working at odd jobs, including turns as carpenter's helper, hospital attendant, and riverboat deckhand. Although distinctively studious in manner and tone, Chancellor had little formal education, only briefly attending the University of Illinois following his discharge from the U.S. Army, in which he served as a public relations specialist from 1945 to 1947. That same year he married Constance Herbert; they had one daughter before their divorce in 1956. (A second marriage, to Barbara Upshaw, took place in 1958; they had a daughter and a son.)

In 1948 Chancellor was hired as a copyboy by the *Chicago Sun-Times;* he remained in the news business for the

John Chancellor, 1976. © BETTMANN/CORBIS

rest of his career. Learning his trade on the job, he quickly moved through the ranks to proofreader, reporter, and feature writer. In 1952, at age twenty-five, Chancellor was recruited by NBC's Chicago television station, then known as WNBQ. Television news operations were in their infancy during the early 1950s, as stations recruited a mixture of print and radio reporters to develop the emerging form of television journalism. Chancellor was a member of this pioneer cohort; his career closely paralleled the evolution of TV reporting. "When I started at NBC, I was one of its first television reporters. We had only three or four," he recalled in an interview.

As a local TV correspondent he was charged with covering Chicago police-blotter stories, which meant chasing his share of ambulances around the city. Initially unhappy with the clutter of cumbersome 1950s television equipment as well as with the brevity of TV news pieces, he expressed a desire to return to "real" journalism (that is, newspaper work). However, Chancellor showed imagination and talent on the screen, winning an award from Sigma Delta Chi, the national journalism fraternity, for his coverage of the capture of a murderer—a story he had reported in the midst of a crossfire of bullets on the street. NBC soon promoted him to national assignments as its chief midwestern correspondent.

Chancellor first gained significant national attention

with his coverage of the Central High School desegregation case in Little Rock, Arkansas, in 1957. The national media were generally despised by segregationists for their perceived "Yankee biases." Chancellor found himself the object of hostility and threats of physical violence as an on-site representative of what some citizens, including some police, called to his face, "the Nigger Broadcasting Company." His persistence and professionalism, however, led to several NBC scoops in the complex and inflammatory story, and this was not lost on network management. It was in Little Rock that Chancellor realized the enormous power that could be wielded by television news—as well as the personal risks involved in having access to that power.

Another landmark moment in his career occurred in San Francisco in 1964. While covering the Republican National Convention, he once again found himself in trouble for alleged "liberal bias" in reporting. Partisans of Senator Barry Goldwater had him forcibly removed from the convention hall for blocking an aisle during a floor demonstration. Still on the air as he was led away by armed police, he told viewers, "I've been promised bail, ladies and gentlemen. . . . This is John Chancellor, somewhere in custody." His cool-headed, poker-faced wit endeared him to viewers who disdained the robotlike protocols that were becoming standard in most network reporting during this period.

Chancellor served briefly as a European correspondent, but the network was anxious to develop him as a household name and face and reassigned him to become host of its daily wake-up program, *Today,* broadcast live from Rockefeller Center in New York City. Under previous hosts, *Today* had been a hodgepodge of entertainment and news, with an emphasis on the former. A chimpanzee named J. Fred Muggs, for example, had been the show's regular "co-host." To reverse the balance, NBC called on Chancellor and shifted responsibility for *Today* from its Entertainment to its News Division.

The newsman-emcee took decisive steps to quickly accomplish this task. Refusing to participate in comic stunts or to announce on-air commercials, he moderated the entertainment element by presenting fewer performances and more celebrity interviews. He soon managed to establish a dignified identity for both host and show. Despite his success at recasting *Today* into a respected news magazine that would later be copied by the other networks, Chancellor was unhappy with the job, preferring to return to "pure news," which NBC reluctantly allowed him to do after little more than a year. But the purposes of the *Today* assignment had been fulfilled. The show was saved and, whether he wanted the distinction or not, Chancellor had indeed proved to be a nationally marketable TV personality.

An on-air correspondent once again, Chancellor hopscotched around NBC news operations during the second half of the 1960s, heading bureaus in Brussels and West Berlin before moving to Washington, D.C., as White House correspondent during the presidency of Lyndon Johnson. This brought about an unexpected turn of events. Johnson greatly admired Chancellor, both professionally and personally, and offered him the directorship of Voice of America, the international radio service of the U.S. Information Agency. The VOA had developed a reputation as a mouthpiece for bluntly biased cold war rhetoric. Chancellor was asked to reestablish it as a dependable source of news for a worldwide listenership. He accepted the job at a 50 percent reduction from his NBC salary.

As he had with the *Today* show, Chancellor showed quick results in restoring credibility to the troubled radio service. The harsh propagandistic tone of its programming was softened, as network-style "evenhandedness" was instituted. Chancellor mandated more use of contemporary music and introduced such features as cuts from comedy albums by such rising performers as Bill Cosby and Bob Newhart. He added his NBC colleague David Brinkley as an analyst and commentator. When he quit the position in 1967, he told the *New York Times* he was satisfied that the public could now have confidence that "the government is engaged in honest journalism."

Returning to NBC, Chancellor once again took up his maverick role in the News Division. His documentary *Israel: Victory or Else,* concerning the Six-Day War of 1967, was described by the critic George Gent as "finely detailed and frequently elegant." He was able to interview both the Israeli prime minister Yitzhak Rabin and the Egyptian president Anwar Sadat for another of his documentaries, *Rabin and Sadat: War or Peace?* Over the course of his career he conducted interviews with every sitting president of the United States, from Dwight Eisenhower to Bill Clinton.

In 1970, upon the retirement of NBC news anchor Chet Huntley, the network again turned to John Chancellor for a solution. Chancellor had often expressed his preference for reporting over anchor-desk newsreading, but he was persuaded to participate in an NBC news experiment. Huntley had coanchored a very successful daily evening news program with David Brinkley. Brinkley would be kept, but Huntley would be replaced by two new co-anchors, Frank McGee and Chancellor. The three-anchor format proved to be a flop, however, and Chancellor was appointed as sole anchor within a year. For the next two decades he was the public face of NBC News.

For a dozen of those years Chancellor's *NBC Nightly News* was in daily competition with Walter Cronkite's *CBS Evening News.* Cronkite is often remembered as the leading network anchor and "America's most trusted man." It is worth noting, however, that during this period predating the proliferation of cable channels, all three network news programs had enormous audiences by later standards, and Cronkite's ratings were often only a tiny fraction higher than Chancellor's. This is all the more remarkable for the fact that Chancellor was restless in the anchor chair throughout, wishing he could return to the field. Reuven Frank, the two-time president of NBC News, described him this way:

> He was born to be a reporter. That's what he wanted to do. He was always wanting to go somewhere and cover something. He would say dumb things like, "I would do it even if I weren't paid." I said, "No, you wouldn't." I've worked with a lot of reporters. Several were truly born reporters. He was one. That's all he ever wanted to do. When he became an anchorman, he'd try and explain things, with the pointer and the glasses. It's all he ever wanted to do. It was his whole being.

Along with Cronkite, Edward R. Murrow, Howard K. Smith, Robert Trout, and others, Chancellor was part of the founding generation of television newspeople who were originally trained on the job at newspapers, wire services, and radio stations. These pioneers brought personal identities as journalists with them when they chose to make the switch to television. By contrast, most on-air figures of later generations were little more than actors, trained and cast specifically to read prepared copy to a camera.

Chancellor was extremely protective of his private life. He enjoyed reading, listening to classical music, and walking. In 1995 he narrated the nine-hour PBS documentary series *Baseball* produced by Ken Burns. The following year he died of stomach cancer at his Princeton home.

★

Chancellor's papers and effects are in the custody of his family. For further reading on Chancellor's views on American politics and the news business, see his *Peril and Promise: A Commentary on America* (1990) and, with Walter Mears, *The News Business* (1983). Obituaries are in the *New York Times* and *Los Angeles Times* (both 13 July 1996).

DAVID MARC

CHANDRASEKHAR, Subrahmanyan ("Chandra") (*b.* 19 October 1910 in Lahore, British India [later Pakistan]; *d.* 21 August 1995 in Chicago, Illinois), Nobel laureate and one of the foremost scientists of the twentieth century, known for his wide-ranging contributions to physics, astrophysics, and applied mathematics.

Chandrasekhar, known simply as "Chandra" in the scientific world, was one of ten children of Chandrasekhara Subrahmanya Ayyar, an officer in the British government service, and Sitalakkshmi Balakrishnan, a woman of great talent and intellectual attainments who played a pivotal role in Chandrasekhar's career. Chandrasekhar's early educa-

Subrahmanyan "Chandra" Chandrasekhar. AP/WIDE WORLD PHOTOS

tion took place at home under the tutelage of his parents and private tutors. When he was twelve, his family moved to Madras, where he began his regular schooling at the Hindu High School in Triplicane, which he attended from 1922 to 1925. Chandrasekhar then received his university education at the Presidency College in Madras. He earned a bachelor of science degree with honors in physics in 1930, and was awarded a Government of India scholarship for graduate studies at Cambridge University in England.

Chandrasekhar left India for England in July 1930. At Cambridge he became a research student under the supervision of the pioneering theoretical astrophysicist Ralph Howard Fowler. He spent the third year of his graduate scholarship in Copenhagen, Denmark, at Niels Bohr's Institute for Theoretical Physics before completing work on his Cambridge Ph.D. in the summer of 1933. In October he was elected a fellow of Trinity College, Cambridge, which he attended from 1933 to 1937. The only Indian previously elected to this prestigious fellowship was the mathematics prodigy Srinivasa Ramanujan, sixteen years before. Chandrasekhar visited the United States for the first time from January to March 1936. His stay at Harvard University in Cambridge, Massachusetts, was at the invitation of the director of the Harvard College Observatory, Dr. Harlow Shapley. In the late summer of 1936, Chandrasekhar returned to his native country for a short visit to marry Lalitha Doraiswamy, whom he had met while both were undergraduates at Presidency College. They wed on 11 September 1936 and did not have children.

In January 1937 Chandrasekhar joined the faculty of the University of Chicago at the Yerkes Observatory in Williams Bay, Wisconsin. Chandrasekhar and his wife lived in Williams Bay for the next twenty-seven years. In 1964 they moved to Chicago, living in the Hyde Park neighborhood near the university. Elected a fellow of the Royal Society of London in 1944 and named the Morton D. Hull Distinguished Service Professor in 1946, Chandrasekhar remained at the University of Chicago until his death. Chandrasekhar and Lalitha became citizens of the United States in 1953.

Chandrasekhar's scientific career began while an undergraduate at the Presidency College, when he published his first paper, "The Compton Scattering and the New Statistics," in the *Proceedings of the Royal Society* in 1929. In 1930, during his voyage from India to England, he made the fundamental discovery that came to be known as the "Chandrasekhar limit," the upper limit on the mass of a star that could become a white dwarf (that limit being 1.44 times the mass of the sun). Its significance, however, was undermined for a time as the result of an unexpected encounter during the January 1935 meeting of the Royal Astronomical Society in London, between Chandrasekhar and the internationally famous Sir Arthur Stanley Eddington, who dismissed the limit as "Reductio ad absurdum behaviour" of a star. More than twenty years passed before the Chandrasekhar limit became an accepted fact. It was hailed as one of the most important discoveries of the twentieth century, because it paved the way to the discovery of the other two terminal stages of a star: neutron stars and black holes.

Chandrasekhar's distinctive pattern of research encompassed diverse areas, each of which occupied Chandrasekhar for a period of five to ten years. Each period of study resulted in a series of long papers and ended with a monograph. Speaking about his monographs and his motivation for research, Chandrasekhar, in the autobiographical account published with his Nobel lecture, said:

> After the early years, my scientific work has followed a certain pattern motivated, principally, by a quest after perspectives. In practice, this quest consists in my choosing (after some trials and tribulations) a certain area, which appears amenable to cultivation and compatible with my taste, ability, and temperament. And when after some years of study, I feel that I have accumulated a sufficient body

of knowledge and achieved a view of my own, I have the urge to present my point of view *ab initio* [from the beginning], in a coherent account with order, form, and structure.

Chandrasekhar's major contributions to twentieth-century astrophysics were in the studies of the structures and stability problems during stellar evolution; stellar dynamics dealing with distribution of matter and motion in the aggregation of stars, star clusters, and galaxies; the principles of radiation transfer and radiation equilibrium in stellar atmospheres, particularly the theory of the illumination and the polarization of the sunlit sky; and the theory of the negative ion of hydrogen that resolved a long-standing controversy of the 1930s pertaining to the solar spectrum and the abundance of hydrogen in the sun. Beginning in 1960, Chandrasekhar focused his attention mainly on Albert Einstein's general relativity and bringing it into its "natural home," astronomy. In his first paper on relativity in 1964, he made a major discovery in the relativistic theory of stellar pulsations: the relativistic instability against gravitational collapse. He developed the theory to take into account relativistic effects systematically and to establish beyond doubt, at least theoretically, the existence of black holes in the universe. His contributions to the mathematical theory of black holes and his studies of the exact solutions of Einstein's equations provided new and important physical and mathematical insights into the richness and beauty of Einstein's theory. During the last decade of his life, Chandrasekhar was devoted to the study of Sir Isaac Newton's *Principia* (1687) and in 1995, just before he died of a heart attack, his monumental treatise, *Newton's Principia for the Common Reader,* was published. His remains were cremated. Among the numerous prizes, honors, and medals bestowed on Chandrasekhar for his scientific accomplishments were the Nobel Prize in physics (1983) and the Copley Medal of the Royal Society of London (1984). He was elected to the National Academy of Sciences in 1955, and was also the recipient of National Medal of Science awarded by President Lyndon Johnson (1966) and Padma Vibhusana (the highest honor that the Indian government bestows on a noncitizen) by the president of India (1968).

Teaching was an integral part of Chandrasekhar's research. A superb teacher and lecturer, well known for elegance and scholarship, he made a lasting impression on the students who came from all over the world to do graduate work under his supervision. He was the sole editor of the *Journal of Astronomy and Astrophysics* for almost twenty years and was chiefly responsible for making it the foremost journal of its kind in the world. Chandrasekhar was a strong advocate of the pursuit of science in all countries and resented any suggestion that developing countries should abandon pure science in favor of what some believed were more practical needs. His life stood for singular dedication to the pursuit of science, and to practicing its precepts and living up to its values to the furthest possible limit in one's life.

★

Some two-thirds of Chandrasekhar's research papers are collected together in his *Selected Papers,* 7 vols. (1989–1997). The end of the sixth volume contains a complete bibliography of his publications. While his six monographs are technical in nature, his *Truth and Beauty: Aesthetics and Motivations in Science* (1987) is a collection of seven lectures in which he explores, in a semipopular way, the motivations in the pursuit of science and the patterns of scientific creativity. See also Kameshwar C. Wali, *Chandra: A Biography of S. Chandrasekhar* (1991), and Kameshwar C. Wali, ed., *S. Chandrasekhar: The Man Behind the Legend* (1997), a collection of essays by some of his students and close associates. An obituary is in the *New York Times* (22 Aug. 1995).

KAMESHWAR C. WALI

CHEN, Joyce (*b.* 14 September 1917 in Beijing, China; *d.* 23 August 1994 in Lexington, Massachusetts), chef and restaurateur who introduced authentic Mandarin Chinese cooking in the United States.

Chen was born Liao Jia Ai, the youngest of nine children. She was given the name Joyce by a teacher because of her

Joyce Chen. COURTESY OF JOYCE CHEN, INC.

"good grades and joyous disposition." Her father, Liao Hsin-shih, was a railroad administrator and city executive. Chen referred to her mother as Mrs. Hsin-shih Liao. Her grandfather and his brothers held high-ranking positions in the Chin Dynasty. Despite being born into a well-to-do family, Chen was taught culinary skills "so I wouldn't eat raw rice in case I couldn't afford a family cook." When she was sixteen years old her family moved to Shanghai, where in 1942 she married Thomas Chen (Chen Da Zhong). The couple had three children: two were born in Shanghai, and the third was born in Cambridge, Massachusetts, where the family settled after fleeing China in 1949 just before the Communist revolution.

In Cambridge, Chen cooked in her home for Chinese students who were unable to find authentic Mandarin (Northern) cuisine in any Chinese restaurants. Her career was launched when the egg rolls she made for a fund-raiser at her children's school quickly sold out and she was asked to make more. In 1958 she opened the first Joyce Chen Restaurant, featuring Mandarin Chinese cooking. She hoped the restaurant, located in Cambridge near Harvard University, would "serve as a cultural exchange center." In 1960 she began to teach Chinese cooking at home and at adult-education centers. She eventually opened four restaurants in Boston, Cambridge, and Cape Cod, serving the Harvard and Massachusetts Institute of Technology communities and such well-known figures as John Kenneth Galbraith, James Beard, Henry Kissinger, and Julia Child. She introduced Americans to moo-shu dishes and hot-and-sour soup and invented the term "Peking ravioli" to describe dumplings, also known as pot stickers, to Italian customers. She did not put chow mein, chop suey, or French bread on her menus or tables, and she did not have a different menu for non-Asian customers, a common practice at that time. At first she served a lunch buffet with Chinese dishes alongside Western foods but eventually "did away with the ham and turkey." She often sponsored cultural culinary events like "Breakfast in Shanghai" to talk about Chinese food and culture.

In 1962 she self-published the first edition of the *Joyce Chen Cook Book* because publishers refused to print color pictures or the grid index she had devised for classifying recipes according to levels of cost, difficulty, and preparation and cooking time. She created uncomplicated Chinese recipes, meticulously tested, including American substitutes for hard-to-find ingredients, with pictures and detailed descriptions of spices, sauces, and ingredients. The book even included a tear-out shopping list in English with Chinese characters. Her text clearly explained the differences among regional styles of Chinese cooking. She also substituted oil for lard and was proud that the noted cardiologist Dr. Paul Dudley White wrote a laudatory introduction to the book.

Chen revolutionized Chinese restaurant menus by devising the now-common numbering system. Because her cooks did not read English, and the customers did not read Chinese, she simply numbered the menu items. In 1966 she created *Joyce Chen Cooks* for WGBH TV, the Public Broadcasting System outlet in Boston, sharing a cooking studio with Julia Child. Chen, who was five-feet, two-inches tall, had to wear high heels to work comfortably at the counters that were built for the six-foot tall Child. The twenty-six-episode series won the *Reader's Digest* new show award. She was the first person of Asian ancestry to have her own television program. In 1972 she traveled to China and made the PBS documentary *Joyce Chen's China.*

Chen was called the "godmother" of authentic Chinese cooking. Unable to find enough knowledgeable or experienced cooks in the United States, she brought over many chefs from China. Despite immigration quotas, Chen lobbied politicians who had been her customers to help her bring in the people she needed. A 1974 genealogy of Chinese restaurants nationwide shows the cooks Chen brought into the country who then established restaurants of their own, including the famous Uncle Tai's in Manhattan.

An entrepreneur as well as a chef, Chen founded Joyce Chen Products, selling specialty cookware. She was the first to import polyethylene cutting boards into the United States. She designed and patented a flat-bottom wok with a long handle that could be used on electric stoves, and marketed specially designed cooking shears and cleavers. In 1984 Joyce Chen Specialty Foods began to sell prepared sauces, oils, and condiments as a subsidiary—along with Joyce Chen Products—of Joyce Chen, Inc.

In 1985 multi-infarct dementia, or possibly Alzheimer's disease, forced her to retire. Her daughter Helen Chen, also a noted chef and cookbook author, succeeded Joyce as chief executive officer of the company. (Joyce and Thomas Chen had divorced in the mid-1960s.) Joyce's children cared for her at home until 1993, when she entered the Fairlawn nursing home in Lexington. She died there of cardiac arrest at the age of seventy-six. She is buried in Mount Auburn Cemetery in Cambridge.

In February 1996 Chen was elected to the hall of fame of the *Nation's Restaurant News,* called the "NRN Fifty," joining James Beard, Julia Child, Wolfgang Puck, Thomas Jefferson (who is listed as "America's first gourmet"), Howard Johnson, and Ray Kroc. In 1998 she was inducted into the James Beard Foundation Hall of Fame, "created to pay tribute to culinary figures who made lasting contributions to America's culinary scene." In the foundation's words, Chen was a chef who "set the standards for Asian cuisine in America."

★

Autobiographical information is in the *Joyce Chen Cook Book* (1962) and *Helen Chen's Chinese Home Cooking* (1994). Bo Bur-

lingham, "Joyce Chen and the Szechuan-Cambridge Connection," *The Real Paper* [Cambridge] (1974), traces the genealogy of Chinese cooks who started their careers in Joyce Chen's restaurants. *Nation's Restaurant News* (Feb. 1996) has biographical information, as does an article by Nina Simonds in *News from the Beard House* (Oct. 1994). Obituaries are in the *Boston Globe* (25 Aug. 1994) and *New York Times* (26 Aug. 1994).

JANE BRODSKY FITZPATRICK

CHERRY, Don(ald) Eugene (*b.* 18 November 1936 in Oklahoma City, Oklahoma; *d.* 19 October 1995 in Málaga, Spain), pocket-trumpet and cornet player who was a leading figure in free (also called avant-garde) jazz.

Cherry's father was a nightclub manager and bartender and his mother, Daisy McKee, was a homemaker. In 1940 the family moved to Los Angeles. Cherry began taking piano lessons at the age of seven and acquired a trumpet when he was thirteen. He attended Freemont High School but cut classes to play in the bands Samuel Browne led at nearby Jefferson High. By 1954 Cherry was playing professionally.

In 1956 Cherry met Ornette Coleman, thus beginning a musical relationship that would revolutionize jazz. Cherry had a reputation as a fine young jazz trumpet player. Coleman was an outcast too radical for the jazz scene of the time. Coleman and Cherry began intensive rehearsals. Their music was innovative. Whereas most jazz of the period used popular-music song forms with improvisations based on standard chord-pattern harmonies, Coleman created directly from the emotions of his compositions: new rhythmic and harmonic patterns were freely created in solo improvisations. In its rhythmic swing and emotional rawness it was a logical development from earlier jazz, Afro-American blues, and gospel music. And Cherry became perhaps the best interpreter of it.

With Coleman as leader, their first album was *Something Else!!!* (recorded on 10 and 22 February 1958). In October 1958, with pianist Paul Bley as leader, Coleman and Cherry began an engagement at the Hillcrest nightclub in Los Angeles; they worked for six weeks before being fired. John Lewis, the pianist with the Modern Jazz Quartet, heard the group and helped arrange a scholarship for Coleman and Cherry to the School of Jazz in Lenox, Massachusetts, and a contract with Atlantic Records. Cherry was now playing a small cornet he called a pocket trumpet. The more conical bore of the cornet gave a plaintive, raw, and brassy sound as compared to the more brilliant tone of the standard trumpet. With *Tomorrow Is the Question* (1959), *The Shape of Jazz to Come* (1959), *Change of the Century* (1959), and *This Is Our Music* (1960), a new style of jazz was firmly established.

Their engagement at the New York City jazz club the

Don Cherry playing a pocket trumpet. ARCHIVE PHOTOS

Five Spot in November 1959 caused a furious controversy. Some critics, fans, and fellow musicians claimed the music was a hoax, too radical a departure to be authentic jazz. Others, such as the composers Gunther Schuller and Leonard Bernstein, were ecstatic about the music. What was supposed to be a two-week gig stretched into two-and-a-half months.

After appearing on Coleman's first seven records, Cherry left the Ornette Coleman Quartet in the spring of 1961. Over the next three decades the band occasionally reformed for concerts and recording sessions. From 1976 to 1987 Cherry, along with other ex-Coleman band members including Charlie Haden, Dewey Redman, and Ed Blackwell, sporadically played in a band called Old and New Dreams, which featured their former leader's compositions. It was like an Ornette Coleman Quartet without Coleman.

Throughout the early 1960s Cherry continued in the role of musical partner to many of the best jazz saxophonists. As leader in 1960 he recorded *The Avant-Garde* with John Coltrane and in 1961 recorded *Evidence* with Steve Lacy. For eight months beginning in July 1962 he was with Sonny Rollins. At the end of 1963 he formed the short-lived New York Contemporary Five with Archie Shepp and John Tchicai. He was hired by Albert Ayler, often held to be the most radical of free-jazz players, to record the soundtrack for the film *New York Eye and Ear Control,* which led to a European tour with Ayler in the fall of 1964.

When the other Ayler band members returned to the United States, Cherry moved to Paris and formed a band to play his music. Cherry's compositional genius is appar-

ent on the critically acclaimed *Complete Communion* (1965) and *Symphony For Improvisers* (1966). He used chantlike repetitive themes with open improvisations to create extended jazz suites. This new approach was to influence the work of other jazz musicians including John Coltrane and Cecil Taylor.

Cherry married his first wife, Carletta, in 1955. They had two children, both musicians, David Ornette and his sister, Jan. Cherry met his second wife, the Swedish artist Moki (sometimes spelled Mocqui) Karlsson when he was touring with Sonny Rollins. Cherry said that he fell in love with her when he awoke one morning to find she had dyed his long underwear yellow. They had a son, Eagle Eye, and Moki's daughter from an earlier marriage, Neneh. Both became famous pop music singer-songwriters. (Cherry also fathered another child with a different woman at the beginning of his marriage to Moki.) The family had a house in Tagarp, Sweden, beginning in the early 1970s but often led a nomadic life, driving a beat-up camper through Europe, Africa, the Middle East, and even India. Cherry immersed himself in non-Western ethnic music. He played exotic folk instruments such as the African guitarlike doussoun'gouni, or the Mayan bird flute. In an interview with *Option* magazine he said, "I wanted music to be an organic experience; a natural part of life that I woke up with every day." His interests in world music are documented on the recordings *Eternal Rhythm* (1968), *Mu, Parts 1 & 2* (1969), and *Relativity Suite* (1973), and in his bands Codona and Multikulti.

In July 1989 Cherry moved to the San Francisco area;

Moki had returned to Sweden. Cherry's health began to fail, and his playing suffered. He died of complications caused by hepatitis at the home of his stepdaughter, Neneh Cherry, in southern Spain. He is buried in Fuengirola, Spain.

Throughout his life Don Cherry had an all-encompassing, childlike, creative personality. He was tall with a wiry, slender build and an elfin face. As a jazz musician and composer his work was outstanding. With Ornette Coleman he brought a new approach to improvisation. He also created a new compositional style that became part of the vocabulary of avant-garde jazz. He went on to incorporate instruments and songs of world music into his uniquely individualistic style.

★

Further information on Cherry's life and music is in *Notes and Tones: Musician to Musician Interviews* (rev. ed., 1982); Ben Sidran, *Talking Jazz: An Illustrated Oral History* (1992); interviews in *Down Beat* (21 Nov. 1963, 28 July 1966, 13 July 1978, and June 1983); and Joseph Hooper, "Not Your Average Family," *The New York Times Magazine* (10 Dec. 1989), which deals with Don, Moki, Neneh, and Eagle Eye Cherry. A helpful booklet is in *The Complete Blue Note Recordings of Don Cherry,* released in a limited edition by Mosaic Records in 1993, which includes original text by Michael Cuscuna and quotes from Art Taylor. Ekkehard Jost, *Free Jazz* (rev. ed., 1981), has a technical analysis of Ornette Coleman's and Cherry's music. See also Andrew Jones, "Global Villager: Don Cherry's Musical Journey," *Option* (Nov.–Dec. 1990): 64, 66–67, 166. An obituary is in the late New York edition of the *New York Times* (21 Oct. 1995).

JOHN VOIGT

CHILDRESS, Alice Herndon (*b.* 12 October 1916 in Charleston, South Carolina; *d.* 14 August 1994 in New York City), novelist and the first African-American woman playwright to have her work professionally produced.

In 1925, after the separation of her parents, Alonzo and Florence White Herndon, Childress was sent from Charleston to the Harlem neighborhood of New York City to be raised by her maternal grandmother, Eliza Campbell White. She attended New York's Public School 81, Julia Ward Howe Junior High School, and Wadleigh High School (she did not graduate). Her grandmother encouraged her to write, telling her that her thoughts were "worth keeping," but Childress credited a public school teacher for specifically encouraging her interest in drama during her formative years. She married Alvin Childress (who played Amos in *Amos 'n' Andy*) in her late teens and in November 1935 gave birth to her only child, a daughter. She wrote an unpublished play, *Hell's Alley,* with her husband in 1938, but it was several years before she turned to writing full-time.

Alice Childress. PHOTOGRAPH BY JERRY BAUER; REPRODUCED BY PERMISSION

In 1940 she became a member of the American Negro Theatre (ANT), a pioneering black theater company founded in Harlem, where her colleagues included Harry Belafonte, Ruby Dee, and Sidney Poitier. Childress recalled that although her primary role with the company was as an actor, she also painted scenery, coached other actors, and assisted directors. As an actor, her roles included Polly Ann in *Natural Man* by Theodore Browne and her Tony-nominated role as Blanche in Philip Yordan's *Anna Lucasta* (which moved to Broadway's Mansfield Theatre on 30 August 1944 and ran for 957 performances).

Childress's first play, a one-act titled *Florence,* was produced by ANT in 1949 with Childress as the director and star. In 1950 Childress opened her own theater with Paul Robeson, but the venture was short-lived. That same year she wrote a musical revue adaptation of Langston Hughes's satirical short-story collection *Simple Speaks His Mind.* Titled *Just a Little Simple,* the show ran for two months at the Club Baron Theatre in Harlem. Childress's female counterpart to Hughes's Jesse B. Simple was an insightful New York domestic named Mildred. The column "Here's Mildred," serialized in the *Baltimore Afro-American,* culminated in a published book, *Like One of the Family: Conversations from a Domestic's Life* (1956).

On 7 April 1952 *Gold Through the Trees* was produced at the Club Baron in Harlem by the Committee for the Negro in the Arts/Council on the Harlem Theatre; this musical revue was the first play written by a black woman to be professionally produced on the American stage. Childress's first full-length play, *Trouble in Mind*, opened on 4 November 1955 at the Greenwich Mews Theatre. She had been obliged to change the play's ending when her producer threatened cancellation if the play did not end happily, but she insisted that the original ending be published in the anthology *Black Theatre*, edited by Lindsay Patterson in 1957.

Childress was active in the civil rights movement during the 1950s and 1960s. She also acted, notably as Mrs. Thurston in *The Cool World* on Broadway (1960). Some time after divorcing her first husband, she married the musician Nathan Woodard on 17 July 1957.

Wedding Band: A Love/Hate Story in Black and White, with a cast that included Ruby Dee, Abbey Lincoln, Moses Gunn, and Clarice Taylor, opened in December 1966 at the University of Michigan at Ann Arbor. A Chicago production in 1971 drew black audiences for a sold-out six-week run. On 26 November 1972, *Wedding Band* opened at the New York Shakespeare Festival Public Theater with Ruby Dee and James Broderick in the leading roles. Childress directed this production through previews, before Joseph Papp took over as director. In 1973 the Public Theater's production was televised nationally during prime time by ABC, but many affiliates refused to broadcast the depiction of an interracial relationship. *Wedding Band* gave voice to a black woman's experience of antimiscegenation laws and, like all of Childress's work, subverted images of working-class black complacency.

Rejuvenated by a two-year residency at Radcliffe College (1966–1968) as a playwright and scholar, in 1968 Childress staged a tribute to Martin Luther King, Jr., *The Freedom Drum* (later retitled *Young Martin Luther King, Jr.*), with music by her husband. While this Performing Arts Repertory Theatre production was touring, she produced three one-act plays on interracial themes between 1969 and 1970: *Wine in the Wilderness, String,* and *Mojo: A Black Love Story.* Childress wrote *Wine in the Wilderness* and *Mojo* as a means of commenting upon the growing classism and sexism developing in tangent with the politicization of the black community and also in response to the need for love scenes for black actors. In her 1971 anthology *Black Scenes* (1971), Childress demonstrated her interest in combining a breadth of useful working material for the black stage with historical depth, for instance by including a piece by Theodore Ward, who was at that time the oldest living black playwright in America.

In 1973 Childress published the young adult novel *A Hero Ain't Nothin' but a Sandwich,* the story of a thirteen-year-old inner-city boy addicted to drugs. She was thrown into the spotlight when the Board of Education for the Island Trees Union Free School District in New York banned *Hero,* along with nine other books from school libraries; the ban was eventually rejected by the U.S. Supreme Court. *Hero* went on to win the American Library Association's award for the best young adult book of 1975 and was nominated for the Newbery Medal and the National Book Award. Childress also wrote the screenplay for a 1978 film adaptation of the book starring Cicely Tyson and Paul Winfield. Around the same time, Childress wrote two children's plays—*When the Rattlesnake Sounds* (1975) and *Let's Hear It for the Queen* (1976).

In 1977 Childress teamed up with her musician husband to write a play commissioned by the South Carolina Commission for the Arts in celebration of "Alice Childress Week." *Sea Island Song* toured through public schools in Charleston and Columbia for a week in October 1977. In subsequent years Childress wrote two more works of adolescent fiction—*Rainbow Jordan* (1981) and *Those Other People* (1989)—and one adult novel (*A Short Walk,* 1979). Her last play, *Moms: A Praise Play for a Black Comedienne* (1986), was a tribute to Jackie "Moms" Mabley (Loretta Mary Aiken). Childress died of cancer in New York City at the age of seventy-seven.

Childress once said that artistically she focused "on portraying have-nots in a *have* society, those seldom singled out by mass media, except as source material for derogatory humor and condescending clinical social analysis." A pivotal dramatist bridging the Harlem Renaissance and the post–civil rights era, Childress was tenacious in representing ordinary people's struggles.

★

Childress's manuscripts are collected at the New York Public Library Schomburg Center for Research in Black Culture. The Hatch-Billops Collection in New York holds an extensive 1972 interview. The most complete biographical source is La Vinia Delois Jennings, *Alice Childress* (1995). Obituaries are in the *Los Angeles Times, New York Times,* and *Washington Post* (all 19 Aug. 1994) and the *Chicago Tribune* (21 Aug. 1994).

TINA REDD

CHURCH, Alonzo (*b.* 14 June 1903 in Washington, D.C.; *d.* 11 August 1995 in Hudson, Ohio), mathematician, logician, philosopher of mathematics, and computer scientist best known for three contributions to mathematical logic: Church's thesis, Church's theorem, and the lambda calculus.

Church was the son of Samuel Robbins Church, a judge, and Mildred Hannah Letterman Parker, a homemaker.

Among his namesake ancestors were Alonzo Church (1793–1862), president of the University of Georgia from 1829 to 1859, and Alonzo Webster Church (*b.* 1829), a librarian and bibliographer. His brother, Randolph Warner Church (1907–1984), was the state librarian of Virginia from 1947 to 1972.

After graduating from Ridgefield High School, Connecticut, in 1920, Church entered Princeton University. During his sophomore year he won the prestigious Class of 1861 prize in mathematics. He became the protégé of Oswald Veblen, who urged him to pursue graduate study in mathematics. Among his other teachers were Luther Eisenhart, Henry Burchard Fine, Joseph H. M. Wedderburn, James W. Alexander II, and Einar Hille. On 25 August 1925 he married Mary Julia Kuczinski, a nurse. They had a son and two daughters.

Princeton awarded Church his A.B. in 1924 and his Ph.D. in 1927, both in mathematics. His doctoral dissertation, "Alternatives to Zermelo's Assumption," was published in 1927 in *Transactions of the American Mathematical Society*. From 1927 to 1929 he held a National Research Fellowship, spending the first year at Harvard University, the next half year in Göttingen, Germany, studying with David Hilbert, and the last half year in Amsterdam, Netherlands, studying with Luitzen Egbertus Jan Brouwer. Upon completing his fellowship, he returned to Princeton as assistant professor of mathematics. He was promoted to associate professor in 1939, full professor in 1947, and professor of mathematics and philosophy in 1961. He remained at Princeton until 1967. It was the perfect home for him. With the newly founded Institute for Advanced Study and the presence of such thinkers as Albert Einstein, Hermann Weyl, Eugene Paul Wigner, Oskar Morgenstern, Alan Turing, Kurt Gödel, Stephen C. Kleene, John Kemeny, Solomon Lefschetz, John von Neumann, Robert Oppenheimer, and Leon Henkin, Princeton in the 1930s and 1940s was the world's most fertile environment for mathematical and scientific research.

Church began developing the lambda calculus in the late 1920s and published his earliest version in "A Set of Postulates for the Foundation of Logic," *Annals of Mathematics* 33 (1932). After several more papers on this topic, he put the whole system into a book, *The Calculi of Lambda-Conversion* (1941). In the lambda calculus there are no logical constants and all mathematical objects are functions. A term is lambda-definable if and only if it is definable as a function in the lambda calculus. Lambda-definability was a prerequisite to the invention of digital computers, and the lambda calculus is a linchpin of computer science.

Church first proposed the thesis that bears his name at the meeting of the American Mathematical Society in April 1935. He first published it in "Abstract 205," *Bulletin of the American Mathematical Society* (May 1935), and more fully in "An Unsolvable Problem in Elementary Number Theory," *American Journal of Mathematics* 58 (1936). It argues that a mechanical or rule-governed algorithm for computing a function is possible just in case the function is recursive. As of 2000, it had not been proved, but a great deal of evidence had been presented to support it. Named "Church's thesis" by Kleene in 1952, it is sometimes called the "Church-Turing thesis" because Turing, who in 1935 was Maxwell Herman Alexander Newman's graduate student at Cambridge University, independently and simultaneously achieved the same result as Church. Newman assured the mathematical community that Turing had not stolen anything from Church, and Turing became Church's graduate student at Princeton in 1936. Another expression of Church's thesis is that a function is computable if and only if it is lambda-definable, that is, if and only if it is computable in a Turing machine.

Church's theorem is not to be confused with Church's thesis. Church published the theorem in "A Note on the Entscheidungsproblem," *Journal of Symbolic Logic* 1 (1936). It is sometimes called the "Church-Turing undecidability theorem" because there is some overlap between Church's result and what Turing wrote in "On Computable Numbers, with an Application to the Entscheidungsproblem," *Proceedings of the London Mathematical Society* 42 (1936). Church and Turing were each studying decidability and undecidability in the wake of Gödel's two incompleteness proofs (1931), which show that for every consistent formal system adequate for arithmetic, there is at least one well-formed sentence in that system that cannot be proved within the system. Church's theorem proves that first-order predicate logic is undecidable.

In 1936 Church cofounded the Association for Symbolic Logic; he was an editor of its major periodical, the *Journal of Symbolic Logic,* from 1936 to 1979. The first edition of his *Introduction to Mathematical Logic,* which became a standard text, appeared in 1944. In 1967 he became professor of philosophy at the University of California at Los Angeles (UCLA). In 1978 he was elected to the National Academy of Sciences. In 1984 his revised and expanded *Bibliography of Symbolic Logic, 1666–1935* appeared, reprinted from the *Journal of Symbolic Logic.*

Church retired from UCLA in 1990. Two years later, in order to be near his son, Alonzo, Jr., he moved to Hudson, Ohio, where he died of natural causes. His funeral was in the Marquand Transept of the Princeton University Chapel, 14 August 1995, with burial in Princeton Cemetery.

Church was preeminent among twentieth-century logicians. Colleagues admired the painstaking care he took in every aspect of his life. His devotion to exactitude in teaching, editing, writing, and theorizing sometimes manifested itself as fastidiousness. He would, for example, use different colors of ink to express different ideas in his correspondence.

★

Information about Church's life and work is available in the Princeton University archives and through the Princeton department of mathematics. Especially useful among these papers is the transcript of William Aspray's 1984 interview with Church. The second edition of the *Cambridge Dictionary of Philosophy* (1999) includes John Corcoran's clear assessment of Church's place in the history of logic. Obituaries are in the *New York Times* (5 Sept. 1995); the *History of Logic Newsletter* 19 (1995): 1–2; *Modern Logic* 5 (1995): 408–412; and the *Bulletin of Symbolic Logic* 1 (1995): 486–488.

ERIC V. D. LUFT

CLAMPITT, Amy Kathleen (*b.* 15 June 1920 in New Providence, Iowa; *d.* 10 September 1994 in Lenox, Massachusetts), editor, lecturer, and poet whose verse is characterized by complex syntax and sophisticated imagery.

The oldest of five children of Roy Justin Clampitt, a farmer, and Lutie Pauline Felt, Clampitt grew up on a 125-acre farm. She loved the outdoors and her earliest memories

Amy Clampitt. AP/WIDE WORLD PHOTOS

were of violets that grew like a "cellarhole of pure astonishment." Encouraged by her grandfather, she read voluminously as a child. She started writing poetry at age eight, but her earliest ambition was to be a painter. When Clampitt was ten, her family was forced to move to another farm because of economic problems brought on by the Great Depression; the sense of dislocation and loss would remain with her throughout her life.

In high school Clampitt wrote a few sonnets that "weren't bad," as she said in an interview with *New York* magazine in 1984, but she had no desire to become a poet. Thanks to an English assignment, she discovered the poetry of John Keats and was attracted to his descriptions and evocation of physical sensations. The influence of Keats would be apparent in her future work. At Grinnell College in Iowa, Clampitt majored in English and "fell in love" with the poetry of Gerard Manley Hopkins, a nineteenth-century English poet and Jesuit priest. Hopkins's celebration of the spiritual nature of the physical world and his intensity appealed to Clampitt. He, too, would influence her poetry, particularly in her intricate use of words. Clampitt wrote little poetry during her college years and graduated in 1941 with honors and a B.A. degree in English. She was also elected to Phi Beta Kappa.

Living in the Midwest, Clampitt had always felt a sense of cultural isolation. In 1941, with a graduate fellowship to Columbia University, she relocated to New York City. Except for occasional visits, she never returned to the Midwest. However, the life of a graduate student was not for her; she saw Columbia as a "mill for getting advanced degrees" and dropped out during her first year. In 1943 she went to work as a secretary for Oxford University Press, where she eventually became promotion director for college textbooks.

In 1949 Clampitt won an essay contest; the prize was a trip to England. Clampitt always felt that she had missed a sense of history growing up in the Midwest. The trip to England provided her with a connection to the past. While there she had the opportunity to visit Oxford and see the university. It was just as described in Hopkins's poem "Duns Scotus's Oxford." At Christ Church Hall she felt she could "smell" the presence of the past. Two years later in 1951, she quit her job at Oxford University Press and used her savings to tour Great Britain, Italy, and Greece. After five months Clampitt returned to New York City and wrote the first of three novels; not one was accepted for publication.

Clampitt went to work as a reference librarian for the National Audubon Society in 1952, a position she would hold until 1959. She spent her lunch hours bird-watching in Central Park, wrote book reviews for *Audubon* magazine, and continued to produce novels. The seven years she spent at Audubon were not happy ones. Nevertheless, Clampitt liked learning about biology and was entranced by a biography of Charles Darwin, whose theory of evolution became a recurrent theme in her poetry. During this period Clampitt did not write poetry; "I was paralyzed," she said in her interview in *New York* magazine. She lacked the self-confidence necessary to take a chance and create.

A family problem caused her to resign from her job at Audubon, and she returned to Iowa for six months, working in a contractor's office. While there she wrote another novel that was never published, but she did resolve years of miscommunication with her family. Buoyed by her reconciliation with her family, Clampitt returned to New York City to a new job and a new decade. She worked as a freelance editor, earning a reputation for her ability to fix difficult manuscripts. Clampitt, who grew up as a Quaker, also became deeply involved in the peace movement from 1967 to 1970. She participated in the action known as the "daily death toll," in which protestors lay in front of the White House gates to symbolize the number of Vietnamese killed that day. All protestors wore Vietnamese hats and had to designate their occupations on a banner. Clampitt chose "poet." It was the first time she had thought of herself as a poet, and in fact she was now writing poetry. But like her novels, her poetry was not being accepted for publication.

In 1974 at her own expense, Clampitt contracted with Washington Street Press to publish a collection of her poems, *Multitudes, Multitudes.* Although this volume lacks her later precision, polish, and assurance, it includes those themes she continually reiterated in subsequent work: war, the past, mythology, love, nature. In 1977 Clampitt went to work for the publishing house E. P. Dutton as an editor. She stayed with Dutton until 1982. Clampitt continued to send out her poems, hoping to get published, and in 1978 her poem "The Sun Underfoot Among the Sundews" was accepted for the 14 August issue of the *New Yorker.* Poetry editor Howard Moss was charmed by the poem and stated in *New York* magazine, "I fell in love with it immediately. We were all waiting for someone like Amy to come along, someone who didn't pretend that life was simple. Right away I knew she was the real thing."

When she received a check for the poem, the first significant money she had earned as a writer, she sent her mother flowers. Clampitt was in her late fifties, and from this point her poems appeared regularly in the *New Yorker, Nation, New Republic, Atlantic Monthly, Kenyon Review, Prairie Schooner,* and *Yale Review.* In 1981 she was invited to participate in a workshop project sponsored by the nonprofit Coalition of Publishers for Employment. The result was *The Isthmus,* which contains fifteen poems. Some of the poems are about the coast of Maine ("The Isthmus," "The Lighthouse," "Surf"); others are mediations on death or reflections on design in nature ("Saint Audrey's Necklace").

In 1982 Clampitt won a Guggenheim Foundation Fellowship and became a full-time poet. Future jobs would include teaching appointments as writer in residence at the College of William and Mary, Amherst College, and Smith College. Clampitt's first major collection of poetry, *The Kingfisher* (1983), published when she was sixty-three, established her as a major poet. This collection of fifty poems, many previously published in various magazines, was praised by poets and critics alike. The title is an allusion to a line in a poem by Hopkins that reads, "As Kingfishers catch fire, dragonflies draw flame." Divided into six sections, the collection is organized around the four elements of fire, water, earth, and air. The poems' subjects are diverse, ranging from marine life and wildflowers to John Lennon's murder, the Vietnam War, and the Holocaust. Some poems are about her parents: "A Procession at Candlemas" describes the death of her mother, and "Beethoven Opus 111" draws a comparison between her father's struggle to cultivate the land and Beethoven's battle to create music despite his deafness. Making connections between seemingly disparate subjects is typical of her style. Although some of the poems are humorous, the general tone is somber. *The Kingfisher* was nominated for a National Book Critics Circle Award.

Clampitt's next collection, *What the Light Was Like* (1985), centers on images of light and darkness. It consists of forty poems grouped into five sections; the section titles refer to locales such as "The Shore," "The Hinterland," and "The Metropolis." The poems shift not just in location but also in time and perspective. From a cottage on the Maine coast to a scene set in an Iowa farmhouse in the past to an apartment in Manhattan, the movement echoes the relocations in Clampitt's own life. As in the previous volume, this book includes poems about her family and is dedicated to her brother Richard, whose death is described in the poem "The Curfew." The centerpiece of the book, literally and thematically, is "Voyages: A Homage to John Keats," a sequence of eight poems. "Voyages" is a pastiche, drawing from Keats's life, letters, and poems. *Voyages* was published separately in a limited edition in 1984.

In her next volume, *Archaic Figure* (1987), Clampitt explores the consciousness of women from Greek mythology to modern times. The first two sections of the book, "Hellas" and "The Mirror of the Gorgon," were inspired by her travels in Greece. The third section, "A Gathering of Shades," is a series of biographical poems focusing on writers such as William and Dorothy Wordsworth, with a particular emphasis on Dorothy. This section of ten poems is the core of the volume and includes "An Anatomy of Migraine," which unifies the section since all the writers described suffered severe headaches.

In *Westward* (1990) Clampitt's central thematic concern is of men and women traveling and arriving. Journeys include those of the present and past as well as imaginary journeys, such as "John Donne in California." The title poem is based on Clampitt's own journey from London west to Iona off the coast of Scotland. A poem about the past is "The Prairie," a long, eight-part narrative detailing the journey of Clampitt's grandparents to the prairie and their struggle to make a life for themselves; it includes a comparison with the experience of the playwright Anton Chekhov on the Russian steppes.

The heart of Clampitt's fifth volume of poetry, *A Silence Opens* (1994), is "A Silence," which the critic Harold Bloom described as the "crown of Clampitt's poetic life's work." Clampitt was aware she was dying while writing most of this volume. Fellow poet and friend Mary Jo Salter wrote about "A Silence" that Clampitt "had chosen at the end to open spaces between words, to allow for all the things poetry cannot say, and to respect the silence she believed was waiting for each of us." *The Collected Poems of Amy Clampitt* was published posthumously in 1997.

In addition to her poetry, Clampitt edited *The Essential Donne* (1988) and wrote *Predecessors, Et Cetera* (1991), a collection of essays. Her unpublished play about Dorothy Wordsworth, *Mad with Joy,* was given a staged reading at the Poets' Theatre in Cambridge, Massachusetts, in 1992. Clampitt won a number of prizes, including the award in literature from the American Academy and Institute of Arts and Letters in 1984, a fellowship from the Academy of American Poets in 1984, and a MacArthur fellowship in 1992 that allowed her to purchase a cottage in the Berkshire Mountains of western Massachusetts.

Clampitt's unofficial critic and companion for twenty-six years was Harold L. Korn, a law professor at Columbia University. Opposed to marriage and childbearing for most of her life because she felt they depleted creative energy, Clampitt married Korn in the spring of 1994, three months before her death. She had no children. Clampitt died in her home of cardiac arrest, following a battle with ovarian cancer.

As a poet, Clampitt struggled for years to find her voice and an audience. The stunning success of *The Kingfisher* was a shock to her. Although some found her poetry difficult to read and were confused by the dense literary allusions and the involuted syntax of her poetry, others were thrilled by the richness of her vocabulary, her wide range of subjects, and her perception and evocation of the natural world.

★

An additional small volume of Clampitt's poetry, *The Summer Solstice* (1983), was published in a limited edition (thirty-three copies, to be exact), as well as *Manhattan: An Elegy, and Other Poems* (1990), another very limited edition. For good background material see Patricia Morrisroe, "The Prime of Amy Clampitt: A Major Poet Makes a Late Arrival," *New York* (15 Oct. 1984). Interviews include: Laura Fairchild, "Amy Clampitt: An Interview," *American Poetry Review* (July/Aug. 1987): 17–20, and Robert E. Hosmer, Jr., "Amy Clampitt: The Art of Poetry XLV," *Paris Review* 35, no. 126 (spring 1993): 76–109. Critical reviews of her poetry that include some biographical information are: Helen Vendler, "On the Thread of Language," *New York Review of Books* (3 Mar. 1983); J. D. McClatchy, "Earthbound and Fired-Up," *New Republic* (22 Apr. 1985); Christina Robb, "Amy Clampitt Reveals the Poetry of Nature," *Boston Globe* (6 Apr. 1990); Phoebe Pettingell, "Amy Clampitt's Pilgrimage," *New Leader* (16 Apr. 1990): 16–17; Robert B. Shaw, "Review of *A Silence Opens,*" *Poetry* (Dec. 1994): 161–166; Harold Bloom, "Poetry in Review," *Yale Review* 86, no. 1 (Jan. 1998): 179–185; and Willard Spiegelman, "What to Make of an Augmented Thing," *Kenyon Review* 21, no. 1 (winter 1999): 172–182. A tribute by Mary Jo Salter is in the *New Republic* (6 Mar. 1995). Obituaries are in the *New York Times* (12 Sept. 1994); *Los Angeles Times* (13 Sept. 1994); *Boston Globe* (14 Sept. 1994); London *Times* (20 Sept. 1994); and London *Independent* (23 Sept. 1994).

MARCIA B. DINNEEN

CLAVELL, James duMaresq (*b.* 10 October 1924 in Sydney, Australia; *d.* 6 September 1994 in Vevey, Switzerland), screenwriter, director, producer, and novelist, best known for *Shogun,* which established him as a master of modern fictional multicultural analysis.

Self-defined as a "half-Irish Englishman with Scots overtones," Clavell was the son of the Royal British Navy Captain Richard Charles Clavell and homemaker Eileen Collis, who instilled in him a sense of duty and propriety, and pride in his family's naval heritage and Norman descent. He initially attended Portsmouth Grammar School in England, but his father's military duty stations in Commonwealth port cities such as Hong Kong assured him a varied education, including foreign languages and first-hand acculturation. On completing public school in England at age seventeen in 1940, Clavell joined the British Royal Artillery, serving in Malaysia from 1940 to 1946.

Wounded in 1941 and captured in 1942, Clavell spent three-and-a-half years in two Japanese prisoner-of-war camps, one in Java, the other the notorious Changi prison near Singapore, where 140,000 out of 150,000 inmates died. His experiences in Changi taught Clavell to value individuals over class or duty, free enterprise and capitalistic ventures over socialism, and loyalty to a small, interdependent group of friends over loyalty to groupthink or religious abstractions. Suffering from what came to be called post-traumatic stress disorder, he could not face his memories of the camps for fourteen years—until nightmares, chills, and other signs of deep-rooted psychological stress led him to write his first novel, *King Rat* (1962), as a therapeutic coming-to-terms with the costs of surviving. In his character Peter Marlowe, Clavell paints a self-portrait of an adaptable, resilient youth who finds British military values unsuited for the brutal conditions of Changi. This cathartic working out of the choices facing humans reduced to sub-human conditions renewed him spiritually.

In 1946, after a motorcycle accident left him lame in one leg, Clavell received a disability discharge at the rank of captain and entered the University of Birmingham in England for a year. He married April Stride, an aspiring ballerina and actress, on 20 February 1951, and they had two daughters. A visit to a movie set gave him a new career direction, first in film distribution and next in television production in New York City (1953). He then worked as a carpenter in Hollywood, California, while searching for a screenwriting position. A collaborative screenwriting of *Far Alert* began his movie/writing career, although the movie was never released. His early screenplays include *The Fly* (1958), *Watusi* (1958), and *The Great Escape* (1963), for which Clavell received a Screen Writers Award. In 1963 Clavell—whose wartime experiences made him appreciate American enterprise, ingenuity, individualism, and strength of will—became a naturalized American citizen. In addition to the screenplays *633 Squadron* (1964) and *The Satan Bug* (1965), he wrote, produced, and directed films like *Five Gates to Hell* (1959), *Walk Like a Dragon* (1960), *To Sir with Love* (1966), *Where's Jack?* (1968), and *The Last Valley* (1969), the latter a haunting anti-war action film.

Writing screenplays gave Clavell the confidence and a 1960 Hollywood screenwriters' strike provided the free time to write *King Rat*. Five other Asian-themed novels followed. To write *Tai-Pan* (1966) and its sequel *Noble House* (1981), Clavell took his family to Hong Kong in 1963, where he refamiliarized himself with the city, its history, and its rich local color. Writing about Changi instilled in Clavell an appreciation of cultural relativism as expressed in his most popular work, *Shogun* (1975), and its sequel, *Gai-Jin* (1993). Clavell's horror at the Islamic Revolution in Iran and his personal sympathy for expatriate British and Iranian friends inspired his novel *Whirlwind* (1986). Clavell's novels, which take place in time periods ranging from 1606 to 1979, argue the value of cultural interaction to promote understanding and change, the dangers of ethnic homogeneity, the importance of continued contact with the East for the long-term interests of East and West, and the value of individualism, competition, and capitalism.

Clavell was the executive producer of two television miniseries of his novels: *Shogun* (broadcast in September 1980) and *Noble House* (1988). An estimated 130 million viewers tuned in to the twelve-hour *Shogun*, shot in Japan; a two-and-a-half-hour movie version of the miniseries was released in 1981. Clavell worked on casting, script revisions, and footage cuts to assure authenticity and to capture on

James Clavell. © SHELLEY GAZIN/CORBIS

film the cultural and psychological nuances of his books. He courageously insisted that the Japanese characters speak in their native language, without subtitles, making *Shogun* one of the first films in which extended multilingual exchanges occur. His miniseries taught millions worldwide about the history and culture of Japan, China, Macao, and Hong Kong. Unfortunately, Clavell died before he could do a planned miniseries on *Whirlwind*. While producing his novels, Clavell wrote the play *Countdown to Armageddon: E = mc²* (1966), some poetry, and two children's books, *The Children's Story . . . But Not Just For Children* (1981) and *Thrump-O-Moto: A Fantasy* (1986).

Clavell was over six feet tall and solidly built, with broad shoulders, a strong Scottish chin, brown eyes, and a ruddy complexion. During his moviemaking and writing career, he traveled a great deal and resided in many places, including England, California, British Columbia, the south of France, and Switzerland. Because of increased prices and taxes when President François Mitterand's government came to power, he and his family left France in 1981 for Gstaad, a wealthy mountain resort in Switzerland. There Clavell became close friends with a neighbor, the actor Roger Moore. The well-known conservative William F. Buckley, Jr. was another friend.

Clavell read widely, conversed with people from the cultures he was interested in, and then used his imagination to build a visual image, one sensitive to cross-cultural interaction. Suffering from cancer, he died of a stroke at age sixty-nine, and was survived by his wife of forty-three years and two daughters. Eric Major of the London publishing house of Hodder and Stoughton called him "one of the great epic storytellers of our age." Clavell's life-long defense of capitalistic free enterprise as the best hope for developing nations and his promotion of binding international ties to undercut nationalistic differences directly resulted from his surviving Changi; his psychologically complex, multicultural novels and films opened up new cultures and points of view while exploring past conflicts.

★

Gina Macdonald, *James Clavell: A Critical Companion* (1996), is the only full-length treatment of his novels. Published interviews with James Clavell include those of Archer Winsten, "Novelist James Clavell," *New York Post* (17 May 1971), Cynthia Gorney, "Interview," *Washington Post* (4 February 1979), Edwin McDowell, "Behind the Best Sellers," *New York Times Book Review* (17 May 1981), Stella Dong, "James Clavell," *Publishers Weekly* (24 October 1987), and Cathy Nolan, "Talking with . . . James Clavell; The Rising Sun Never Sets on His Empire," *People Weekly* (10 May 1993). Obituaries are in the *Washington Post, New York Times, Los Angeles Times, Wall Street Journal, USA Today,* and a London Associated press release (all on 8 Sept. 1994).

GINA MACDONALD

CLAY, Lucius DuBignon, Jr. (*b.* 6 July 1919 in Alexandria, Virginia; *d.* 7 February 1994 in Alexandria, Virginia), air force general who rose to the command of all air defenses in North America.

Clay was the elder of two sons of Lucius DuBignon Clay, Sr., one of the leading U.S. Army generals of World War II, and Marjorie McKeown, a homemaker. Growing up an "army brat," Clay moved frequently during his youth as his father moved from assignment to assignment in the United States and Panama. After graduating from Western High School in Washington, D.C., in 1937, Clay entered the United States Military Academy at West Point, New York, where he had lived as a child while his father was an instructor at the school between 1924 and 1928. Although Clay entered West Point with the class of 1941, he was held back in his plebe (freshman) year and graduated with the class of 1942. Thus Clay's younger brother, Frank Butner Clay, who entered West Point in 1938, was his classmate, and the two men graduated together on 29 May 1942.

After receiving his commission Clay entered the United States Army Air Forces (USAAF), which was created in June 1941 with autonomous status within the army. He attended flight school at Lubbock Field, Texas, received his pilot's wings in December 1942, and went on for more training with bombers. In June 1943 he was assigned to the

Lucius D. Clay. NORTH AMERICAN AEROSPACE DEFENSE COMMAND

616th Bombardment Squadron at MacDill Field, Florida. In August he joined the 495th Bombardment Squadron as the assistant operations officer and was eventually shipped to England with the unit. While in Florida he met and on 6 December 1943 married Betty Rose Commander of Tampa, Florida. The couple had four children.

In June 1944 Clay was assigned to the 344th Bombardment Group in England. First as a squadron leader and then as group commander, he flew some sixty combat missions over Europe. After Germany's surrender in May 1945, Clay remained in Europe and eventually became the deputy commander and deputy for base services at the European Air Depot in Erding, Germany.

Clay returned to the United States in February 1947 for staff duty with the USAAF just as the National Security Act of 1947 (26 June 1947) cleared the way for the establishment of the U.S. Air Force as an independent branch of the armed services. Clay transferred from the army and served on the staff of the deputy chief of staff, Operations for Atomic Energy, Headquarters, U.S. Air Force at the Pentagon. Thus Clay, although only a lieutenant colonel at the time, was present at the creation of a new branch of the U.S. armed forces and would rise in rank and responsibilities with its expansion.

In 1949 Clay was assigned to the Air University and Air

War College at Maxwell Air Force Base, Alabama. In June 1952 he returned to the Pentagon to become an Air Force member of the Joint Strategic Plans Group of the Joint Chiefs of Staff. From 1954 to 1956 he served on the staff of Headquarters, U.S. Air Force. In July 1956 he became deputy commander of the Seventy-second Bombardment Wing at Ramey Air Force Base, Puerto Rico. In 1958 he returned to staff work at Headquarters, Strategic Air Command at Offutt Air Force Base, Nebraska. In 1961 he was reassigned to the Joint Chiefs of Staff at the Pentagon, where he was first a member of the Joint War Games Control Group and later the deputy director for operations. He was promoted to brigadier general in August 1962.

In August 1964 Clay was named the vice commander of the Twelfth Air Force at James Connelly Air Force Base, Texas. In January 1966 he took over command of the unit and was promoted to major general. In July 1966 he returned to the Pentagon and served in a series of increasingly important staff positions until August 1969, when he became deputy chief of staff for plans and operations, and was promoted to lieutenant general. In February 1970 Clay left staff work once again to assume the position of the vice commander in chief, Pacific Air Forces, but in September of that year he was named the commander of the Seventh Air Force at Tan Son Nhut Airfield in the former Republic of Vietnam (South Vietnam). He also served as the deputy commander for air operations, United States Military Assistance Command Vietnam (MACV). Thus Clay, who was awarded his fourth star and raised to the rank of full general, was responsible for directing all air force combat, support, and air-defense operations in Southeast Asia, advising the MACV commander on matters relating to tactical air support of ground forces in South Vietnam, and coordinating the efforts of the South Vietnamese air forces.

In August 1971 he became the commander in chief, Pacific Air Forces, with headquarters at Hickam Air Force Base, Hawaii, which gave him overall command of U.S. air power in the Pacific during the closing years of America's direct involvement in the Vietnam War.

Clay reached the pinnacle of his career in October 1973 when he became the commander in chief of the North American Air Defense Command/Continental Air Defense Command as well as the commander of the United States Air Force Aerospace Defense Command at Ent Air Force Base, Colorado. In these capacities Clay was responsible for the air defenses of the North American continent and for global aerospace surveillance to provide warning of hostile attack from outer space.

Upon his retirement on 1 September 1975, he remained in Colorado Springs, Colorado. Uncomfortable with the idea of trading on his service connections, Clay chose not to enter a new career in the private sector. Instead he devoted himself to working with a number of charitable organizations and was active in several Air Force associations.

In 1990 a deteriorating lung condition exacerbated by the high altitude of Colorado led Clay to return to the place of his birth, Alexandria. After the death of his wife in 1992, he moved to a military retirement community at Fort Belvoir, Virginia. He died at Alexandria Hospital of emphysema and cardiac arrest, and is buried in Arlington National Cemetery in Arlington, Virginia.

In his many staff positions, Clay played an important role in the transformation of the USAAF from an arm of the army into the new and separate service known as the U.S. Air Force. In his various command positions, he aided in the development of American air power both as a tactical and a strategic force.

★

No biography of Clay exists. However, Jean Edward Smith's biography of Clay's father, *Lucius D. Clay: An American Life* (1990), gives an idea of what Clay's early years were like, although it provides little specific biographical information about him. "General Lucius D. Clay Jr.," *United States Air Force Biography*, Secretary of the Air Force, Office of Information (1974), provides a résumé of his career. Obituaries are in the *Washington Post* (9 Feb. 1994), *New York Times* (14 Feb. 1994), *Air Force Times* (16 May 1994), and *Assembly* (May 1995). A transcript of an oral history interview is in Columbia University, Oral History Research Office, Butler Library, New York City.

ROMAN ROME

CLURMAN, Richard Michael (*b.* 10 March 1924 in New York City; *d.* 15 May 1996 in Quogue, New York), journalist and longtime executive for Time Inc., and its first chief of correspondents.

Clurman was one of three children of Will N. Clurman, a prominent builder and real estate developer, and Emma Hertzberg, a homemaker. His father was from New York's Lower East Side and began building homes and apartment houses on suburban Long Island in the late 1930s. Richard's uncle, Harold ("Edgar") Clurman, was a famous Broadway and motion picture director, author, and critic. His grandfather, Samuel Michael Clurman, was a prominent physician who wrote a medical column in the newspaper the *Jewish Day*. Clurman had longed to be a journalist since he was a boy growing up on Long Island. He edited newspapers for his grammar school, high school, college, and the U.S. Army, where he served during World War II in the Information and Education Division. After graduating from the University of Chicago in 1946 with a Ph.B. in political science, he became an editor for *Commentary* magazine in New York. In 1949 he joined the staff

Richard Clurman, 1972. AP/WIDE WORLD PHOTOS

of *Time* magazine, editing its press section ("Judgments and Prophecies") and opinion section.

During his sixth year there, Clurman wrote a 4,000-word cover story for *Time* titled "Alicia in Wonderland" (13 September 1954). Alicia Patterson, editor-publisher of the Long Island–based tabloid *Newsday,* the most successful daily newspaper of the post–World War II era, had just won a Pulitzer Prize for an investigation of corrupt labor leader William DeKoning, Sr. A child of the famed Patterson-McCormick newspaper publishing dynasty, her father, Captain Joseph Medill Patterson, had invented tabloid journalism in America. In September 1955 she hired Clurman, aged thirty-one, away from *Time* as her editorial director and assistant, hoping he would offer a "more cosmopolitan view of the world."

In April 1957 Clurman married Shirley Potash, who had variously been an assistant public-relations director for Time Inc., assistant to Oscar Hammerstein, and a public-relations staffer for Twentieth Century–Fox and the Rockefeller family. This was his second marriage; they had one son. (His first marriage had produced two daughters and ended in divorce.) Their uptown apartment was the scene of fascinating, star-studded dinner parties where Clurman, who disdained small talk, told people he "refused to be bored," tapped a spoon against a glass to rouse everyone's attention, and announced a topic for discussion.

Clurman returned to Time Inc. in 1958 as deputy chief of domestic correspondents. One year later he was named chief of domestic correspondents. In 1962, Time Inc.'s founder and editor-in-chief, Henry R. Luce, appointed Clurman chief of correspondents of the Time-Life News Service. This was the first time all thirty of the company's domestic and foreign news bureaus were combined into one operation. Clurman was in charge of 105 staff correspondents and 300 part-time correspondents, stationed in thirty-four cities around the world. He traveled constantly, visiting different bureaus and meeting the leading figures of the day. Before he took this position, he underwent a crash course in foreign affairs since he had only been overseas for three days.

In 1968 Clurman, at age forty-four, was named board chairman of the New York City Center of Music and Drama by Mayor John V. Lindsay, the center's president, who had urged the selection committee to choose someone with a fresh perspective. The center, which pioneered the concept of civic art centers in America, had outgrown its current sites. Included among its seven constituents were the New York City Opera, New York City Ballet, Joffrey Ballet, and Alvin Ailey City Center Dance Theater. Although Clurman soon recruited experts in the fields of business, real estate, city planning, law, and the arts and announced a plan for four new theaters on the old Madison Square Garden site, the scheme failed because he was remiss at fund-raising and did not solicit enough from affluent patrons.

In 1969, Clurman assumed a new post at Time Inc. as vice president in charge of editorial development and acquisitions. In 1970, toward the end of his career, Clurman was made head of Time-Life Video to develop programming for the fledgling cable television industry. He also was appointed chairman of the board of Time-Life Broadcast Inc.

In November 1972, Mayor Lindsay prevailed upon Clurman to become commissioner of parks and administrator of parks, recreation, and cultural affairs. He took a year's leave of absence from his Time Inc. job, and in January 1973 he announced a shake-up of the agency's top echelon, warned of firings, and threatened to withhold maintenance funding from those parks excessively violated by vandalism, unless the surrounding community helped stop it.

When Clurman retired from Time Inc., he had devoted twenty-three years to his field. By the end of his life, the onetime slim and sandy-haired six-footer, who was seldom seen without a cigarette dangling from his mouth, had given of his expertise to the cultural and civic betterment of New York City. The Richard M. Clurman Award ($5,000) is presented to young journalists in his memory.

Clurman died of a heart attack at age seventy-two at his

summer home in Quogue, Long Island; his remains were cremated. A memorial service held in June at Manhattan's Temple Emanu-El attracted the media's elite: Barbara Walters, David Halberstam, David Greenway (editorial-page editor of the *Boston Globe*), and Harry Evans (president and publisher of Random House). One eulogist, Clurman's best friend Oz Elliott, a former editor of *Newsweek* who had been with him at *Time,* said, "While Dick made himself an expert at many things, his true specialty was friendship." William F. Buckley, Jr., said, "I have always subconsciously looked out for the total Christian, and when I found him, he turned out to be a non-practicing Jew." Mike Wallace said Clurman called him every Sunday after viewing the *60 Minutes* television show to discuss how the segment had gone. *Time* writer Hugh Sidey said, "He never panicked in a crisis, was always instructive when correcting you, and there was always laughter when he was around."

★

Clurman wrote *Beyond Malice: The Media's Years of Reckoning* (1988) while doing pro bono work as board chairman of Columbia University's Seminars on Media and Society. It examines sensational front-page stories that had elicited hostile public reaction, which he blamed on the media's propensity to invade privacy and emphasize bad news. He decided to write another book, *To the End of Time: The Seduction and Conquest of a Media Empire* (1992), two weeks after he heard the first incredulous merger announcement about Time Inc.—the world's largest combined magazine and book publisher—and Warner Communications Inc.—an entertainment conglomerate of films, records, and cable television. An obituary is in the *New York Times* (17 May 1996).

MELANI SUE BOULTIER

COBAIN, Kurt Donald (*b.* 20 February 1967 in Hoquiam, Washington; *d.* 5 April 1994 in Seattle, Washington), singer and guitarist for the grunge rock group Nirvana, whose music of alienation and angst became wildly popular and helped define 1990s youth culture.

Cobain was born in the small logging community of Hoquiam, where Cobain's father, Donald Leland Cobain, was a car mechanic; he had moved to Washington State after marrying Wendy Fradenburg. When Cobain was six months old the family moved to neighboring Aberdeen, another small and economically depressed logging and fishing community. Cobain had one sister.

By all accounts, Cobain's childhood was a happy one until 1975, when his parents divorced. From the moment his parents separated Cobain became withdrawn, depressive, and sullen. His grades at Aberdeen Elementary suffered. He lived with his mother for a year before her remarriage sent him to live with his single father in the

Kurt Cobain. © KEN SETTLE

neighboring town of Montesano. However, his father also remarried and Cobain felt displaced again. Cobain eventually spent his preadolescence being moved among three sets of aunts and uncles and his paternal grandparents. For the rest of his education he shuffled between schools in Montesano and Aberdeen.

Cobain received a secondhand electric guitar and amplifier for his fourteenth birthday. He had been attracted to the melodic rock of the Beatles as a child, and as an adolescent his tastes moved to heavy rock from the late 1970s and 1980s by bands such as Kiss and AC/DC. In the summer before he entered high school, Cobain heard of the exploits of the British punk band the Sex Pistols. The rebellion of punk rock intrigued him; but the small record shops in Aberdeen did not carry the Sex Pistols album.

Cobain hated high school, but the people he met there moved him toward the music he was to create. At Montesano High he met Matt Lukin and Buzz Osbourne, two musicians who formed a band called the Melvins. Cobain attended their practice sessions and was astounded by their energy and the punk-inspired music they produced. Around this time Osbourne gave Cobain a tape with the first punk rock he had ever heard, by such bands as Black Flag and Flipper.

In 1984 Cobain moved back into his mother's house in Aberdeen, where he attended Aberdeen High and met one of the future members of Nirvana. Krist Novoselic had a great deal in common with Cobain: they both felt trapped in provincial Aberdeen and sought refuge in music. The two decided to form a band with Cobain playing guitar and singing and Novoselic playing bass.

Cobain left his mother's home after dropping out of high school in 1985, first living with friends and eventually renting a series of dilapidated houses. He was homeless for a period and slept under a bridge near the Wishka River. He worked as a janitor. Cobain and Novoselic hired a drummer by the name of Aaron Burckhard, and the group started to perform at small parties in the neighboring college town of Olympia. The band, which went under several different names, quickly developed a repertory of songs all written by Cobain. With titles such as "Hairspray Queen," "Floyd the Barber," and "Downer," the band became known for high-energy performances often tinged with humor and anger at life in Aberdeen. However, Burckhard did not display the kind of dedication Cobain and Novoselic were putting into the music, and they searched for a replacement.

In 1987 Cobain met Tracy Marander and moved into her apartment in Olympia, thus escaping the claustrophobic world of Aberdeen. In 1988 Cobain and Novoselic, with the help of Dale Crover, the drummer for the Melvins, made a demo tape at the Seattle studio Reciprocal Recording. Reciprocal and its engineer, Jack Endino, were vital elements in the evolution of the "underground" music of the Pacific Northwest that would later be classified as grunge. The demo that Endino recorded of Cobain and his band—they had not yet settled on the name Nirvana—cost $152.44. Endino was very impressed with the music and passed on a copy of the tape to Jonathan Poneman, cofounder of Sub Pop, the independent record label responsible for issuing the first grunge recordings. Sub Pop immediately asked the band to record a single. After going through a succession of drummers, the band settled on Chad Channing and went back to Reciprocal to record its first single, "Love Buzz/Big Cheese." By this time the band was called Nirvana and by the end of the year it was back in the studio recording its first album, *Bleach*. Made for $606.17, the album featured many of the songs Cobain had written earlier but also included new work such as the melodic, pop-influenced "About a Girl." *Bleach* was released in 1989 and Nirvana did extensive touring to promote it.

Nirvana's members became infamous for smashing all of their instruments after successful performances.

Sub Pop asked for a follow-up to *Bleach,* but Cobain and Novoselic were unhappy with the promotion and distribution of Nirvana's first album. They were also unhappy with Channing, whom they replaced in 1990 with Dave Grohl, an extremely hard-hitting drummer in the mold of Led Zeppelin's John Bonham. With Grohl behind them, Cobain and Novoselic broke with Sub Pop and signed with a major commercial label, Geffen/DGC. They released their second album, *Nevermind,* at the end of 1991. It was a stunning progression from *Bleach.* They retained their driving, punk-influenced sound, but the music was more melodic and filled with catchy hooks. Songs such as "Polly" and "Something in the Way" displayed Cobain's ability to juggle melody and frenzied guitar playing. The first song on the album, "Smells Like Teen Spirit," tapped into the zeitgeist; the song's final words, "a denial," seemed to speak for post–cold war youth culture. The astounding success of the album shocked the band and its record company. The music video for "Smells Like Teen Spirit" became a staple on MTV. By January of 1992, Nirvana had the best-selling album in the world.

Cobain was slight of stature and often wore layers of T-shirts on stage. His performances were often filled with energy and humor. On off nights he would be sullen and inattentive to his playing. Cobain's drug use had primarily consisted of marijuana, but by the time of *Nevermind*'s shocking success he had begun to use heroin regularly. He always claimed to have violent stomach pains, and heroin was one way of battling this discomfort. In 1992 Cobain married Courtney Love, who was involved with her own band, Hole; the two had a daughter, Frances Bean Cobain, the same year. The pressure of having a best-selling album started to weigh on Cobain; his private life was scrutinized in the press and the band's constant touring to huge crowds all over the world started to wear him down. During her pregnancy, Love had given an interview in *Vanity Fair* that incorrectly intimated that Love had been using heroin during her pregnancy. This eventually caused the Los Angeles County Department of Children's Services to attempt to take custody of their daughter away from the couple. After a costly legal battle Frances Bean remained with her parents, but the story was played up in the press and the pressure upon Cobain mounted. His problems with heroin escalated, and he tried several times to go through a detoxification program. To meet the demands for more Nirvana music, the band released a compilation of rare tracks and B-sides called *Incesticide* at the end of 1992.

The next two years of Cobain's life were a downward spiral consisting of his fight against heroin and the rigors of fame. In spite of personal problems, the final years of Cobain's life were filled with music. In 1993 he provided backing guitar for a recording with his literary hero, William S. Burroughs, on *The "Priest" They Called Him*. Nirvana also released its third album, *In Utero*. This last work was an attempt to return to the band's punk origins but at the same time displayed some of Cobain's most intense songwriting in "Heart-Shaped Box" and "All Apologies." The band also delivered a breathtaking performance on *MTV Unplugged* that was issued as a recording a year later.

In March of 1994 Cobain attempted suicide in Rome by overdosing on pills and alcohol. The event was reported as an accident in the press, but Cobain's personal life began to spin out of control. Love coordinated a drug intervention for him and he agreed to go into a rehabilitation program. He spent two days in a rehab center in Los Angeles before escaping and secretly flying back to his Seattle home. His friends and family searched for him, but he had locked himself in a small room above his garage where he injected heroin for the last time and then killed himself with a shotgun.

Reaction to Cobain's suicide was immediate, intense, and worldwide. His death at twenty-seven was a staggering blow to rock. The music critic David Fricke called Cobain the John Lennon of his generation. Cobain's songs of pain and loss had a remarkable beauty that became a part of millions of lives at the same time they altered the history of popular music.

★

Michael Azerrad, *Come As You Are: The Story of Nirvana* (1993), is an important chronicle of Cobain's life and work. *Rolling Stone*'s coverage of the work of Cobain has been compiled in *Cobain* (1994); Dave Thompson, *Never Fade Away: The Kurt Cobain Story* (1994), focuses on Cobain's death; and Christopher Sandford, *Kurt Cobain* (1996), is a full biography. The cultural importance of Cobain's music is analyzed in John Rocco, ed., *The Nirvana Companion* (1998). Jim Berkenstadt and Charles Cross have discussed the creation of Nirvana's most famous album in *Nevermind* (1998). Gina Arnold, *Route 666: On the Road to Nirvana* (1993), concerns itself with the growth of the "underground" music that led to Nirvana. Clark Humphrey, *Loser: The Real Seattle Music Story* (1995), also focuses on the music scene. An obituary is in the *New York Times* (9 Apr. 1994).

JOHN ROCCO

COHEN, Audrey C. (*b.* 14 May 1931 in Pittsburgh, Pennsylvania; *d.* 10 March 1996 in New York City), innovative educator, social activist, and businesswoman whose belief in "purpose-centered" education lead her to found Audrey Cohen College in New York City and to trademark a system of education used in elementary and high schools throughout the United States.

Cohen was born to Abe Cohen and Esther Morgan in Pittsburgh and attended local schools. As a high school student she was chosen to attend a seminar sponsored by the Young Men's Christian Association in Washington, D.C., where she saw firsthand the segregation endured by the black students in her group. She later said this was a seminal experience in her life. She went to the University of Pittsburgh, graduating magna cum laude in 1953 with a bachelor of arts degree in secondary education. In 1957 and 1958 she did postgraduate work in political science and education at George Washington University in Washington, D.C. She married Ralph Wharton, a physician, and they had two daughters.

In 1958, seeing an opportunity for women in the newly emerging field of social research, Cohen founded PartTime Research Associates, employing college-educated women who needed flexible work schedules. During this era, U.S. corporations would not have ordinarily hired women for projects within the company, but they were happy, as Cohen said, to come knocking at her door. PartTime Research Associates became the first U.S. corporation to employ only women. Its clients included the Department of State, New York's governor Nelson Rockefeller, and Union Carbide.

PartTime Associates helped college-educated women, but Cohen was looking for ways to help lower-income women. During the 1960s she noticed the nation's shift

Audrey Cohen, 1971. © BETTMANN/CORBIS

from a manufacturing to a service economy and recognized the need for worker training in this new economy. In 1964 she secured a federal grant to found the Women's Talent Corps, which trained workers for such emerging occupations as paralegals, teachers' aides, mental health workers, occupational therapists, and social workers. Later named the Talent Corps and opened to men, this organization filled a need that was not being met by existing social programs and the traditional educational system. Through the Talent Corps, Cohen found a way to provide new educational and employment opportunities for thousands of unemployed and underemployed people. The Talent Corps, located on Varick Street in Manhattan, eventually transitioned into the College of Human Services, and was later renamed Audrey Cohen College. In 1970 the college trademarked the term "Human Service" and held the first professional conference in this new professional field.

By then Cohen, who felt that the traditional education system was not meeting societal needs, began a quest to design a more practical and useful educational system. She began phasing out her college's associate degree programs in order to redesign them. During the next four years she studied the U.S. labor market and global economic trends and worked closely with employers to find out what they wanted to see in their employees. She suggested that in order to rethink education one should start from scratch and ask, as if no schools existed, "What kind of schools would we want to build if we could look at our needs, without any presuppositions?"

By 1974 Cohen had designed and (always the businesswoman) trademarked her "Purpose-Centered System of Education." Her central idea was that education must never be abstract but instead must be closely linked to clearly understood purposes. She saw two main goals of education: teaching students job skills and teaching them to be better citizens. Other facets of "purpose-centered" education came out of Cohen's concerns for social justice. She maintained that there are five dimensions of knowledge and action: a socially useful purpose; values and ethics; self and others; systems; and skills. These five dimensions became a central core of her system.

During the 1980s Cohen expanded the college's mission to reform what she saw as failing public schools. She designed a curriculum for school-aged children, using two themes for each grade. She considered the intellectual maturity of different age groups and what she thought children needed to know about the world and their place in it, and coupled these themes with the five dimensions of learning. For example, in kindergarten the themes are "we build a family-school partnership" and "we care for living things." For eighth graders the themes are "I earn responsibility at my internship" and "we bring our community together."

In 1983 Cohen, working with local public school officials, established the College for Human Services Junior High School. Later an elementary school and a high school also linked up with the college.

In 1983 the college, led by Cohen, received a $1 million grant from the Hasbro Children's Foundation to expand its pioneering curriculum design into the nation's public schools, an endeavor that occupied Cohen through the 1980s. In 1992 the college received a $4.5 million grant from the New American Schools Development Corporation, a private, nonprofit organization based in Arlington, Virginia, that supports research toward improving public education. Cohen's group was one of nine design teams out of 700 to win an NASDC grant.

In 1996 the college was selected for support by the influential Education Commission of the States, a nonprofit organization that advises the states on education policy. That year, Audrey Cohen schools, as they are called, enrolled about twenty thousand elementary and secondary school students in five states. Audrey Cohen College requires that public schools that want to use the Cohen system undertake an intensive self-examination, sometimes taking a year or more, before signing on. Then there is no turning back, and no picking and choosing what aspects of the system to use. Cohen was fiercely protective that her trademarked system be used in its entirety, exactly as she designed it. At the time of Cohen's death from cancer at the age of sixty-four, the system was being used in schools throughout the country, from kindergarten to high school levels.

Throughout her life, Cohen displayed a keen awareness of social and economic trends, and she used this awareness to help train and employ people otherwise left out of the economic mainstream: minority group members, immigrants, and the poor. Her social activism was successful because of her drive and determination, sharp business skills, and her ability to work with business leaders. Always a powerhouse of ideas, energy, and social commitment, Cohen believed that education must empower individuals to take charge of their lives and help them make positive changes in their communities.

★

Information about Cohen's life and work can be found through Audrey Cohen College in New York. Her views of public education and a description of her purpose-centered system of education can be found in her article "A New Educational Paradigm," *Phi Delta Kappan* 74, no. 10 (June 1993):791–795. Two views of her schools project are Mark Pitsch, "The Outsider" (in the series "Breaking the Mold: The Shape of Schools to Come"), *Education Week* (25 Jan. 1995): 23–25; and Julie L. Nicklin, "Education with a Purpose," *Chronicle of Higher Education* 41 (14 July

1995): A13–A15. An obituary is in the *New York Times* (12 Mar. 1996).

JULIANNE CICARELLI

COLBERT, Claudette   (*b.* 3 September 1903 in Paris, France; *d.* 30 July 1996 in Barbados, West Indies), actor of stage, screen, television, and radio who won the Academy Award for best actress for the comedy classic *It Happened One Night.*

Colbert was born Lily Claudette Chauchoin. When the financial situation in France adversely affected her father, Georges Chauchoin, a banker, he and his wife, Jeanne Loew Chauchoin, brought Colbert and her brother to New York City in 1912. Colbert attended Public School #15 and graduated from Washington Irving High School in 1923. Her first high school role was Rosalind in Shakespeare's *As You Like It.* After graduation, Colbert attended the Art Students League, gave French lessons, and worked in dress shops, aspiring to a career in fashion design.

Colbert made her first Broadway appearance in 1923 in a small role as Sybil Blake in Anne Morrison's *The Wild Westcotts.* One story about this role says that Colbert so impressed Morrison at a social function that the playwright inserted a few lines for Colbert to speak, and that during the pre-Broadway run the director felt compelled to en-

Claudette Colbert. THE KOBAL COLLECTION

hance her role. In any event, the bubbly five-foot-four, hazel-eyed Colbert resolved to become an actress. She adopted "Claudette Colbert" as her stage name—"Colbert" being her paternal grandmother's maiden name.

She performed in almost a dozen plays between 1924 and 1926 in New York, Chicago, and Washington, D.C. Although Colbert never took any formal acting lessons, she educated herself in acting techniques by observing well-established actors as she stood in the wings during performances. Al Woods, producer at New York's Eltinge Theatre, gave her a five-year contract, which began in the 1925–1926 season. Greater financial responsibilities intensified her drive toward a successful acting career when her father died in 1926. When Colbert starred in Kenyon Nicholson's melodrama *The Barker* in 1927, she impressed audiences and critics with the development of her character, Lou, the seductive snake charmer. The play became the vehicle for her London debut on 7 May 1928. She performed in several other Broadway plays from the fall of 1928 through 1929, including Eugene O'Neill's *Dynamo* and Elmer Rice's *See Naples and Die,* her final Broadway appearance until 1955.

Colbert secretly married Norman Foster, her costar in *The Barker,* on 13 March 1928 in London. The couple preferred to live apart for much of the first year of their marriage and, even when the press disclosed the marriage, they generally lived at separate addresses in California. A Mexican divorce dissolved the marriage in August 1935. On 24 December 1935, in Yuma, Arizona, Colbert married Dr. Joel J. Pressman, who had been her overseeing physician during some of her (lifelong) sinus problems. Pressman died of liver cancer on 26 February 1968. Colbert had no children.

Colbert's first and only silent film, which was directed by Frank Capra, was *For the Love of Mike,* which she filmed in 1927 while still starring in *The Barker.* The film demanded so much studio time that Colbert could barely make her first entrance in the play. Colbert was so displeased with the entire experience and the resulting film that she resolved never to act on the screen again. Yet within two years, perhaps in part due to the effect the Great Depression had on the finances of Broadway, she agreed to a fourteen-year contract (1930–1944) with Paramount. Colbert worked through 1931 at the Paramount studios in the borough of Queens in New York City before moving to Hollywood with her mother and brother. In 1929 she starred with Edward G. Robinson in her first talking picture, *The Hole in the Wall.* Colbert's early films were melodramas or sophisticated comedies. She appeared with Walter Huston in *The Lady Lies* (1929), joined Foster in *Young Man of Manhattan* (1930), and acted with her French compatriots Maurice Chevalier (*The Big Pond,* 1930; *The Smiling Lieutenant,* 1931) and Charles Boyer (*The Man from Yesterday,* 1932; *Private Worlds,* 1935; and *Tovarich,* 1937).

During her peak years, some of Colbert's costars included Fredric March, Herbert Marshall, Melvyn Douglas, John Barrymore, Ray Milland, Robert Young, Ronald Colman, David Niven, James Stewart, Henry Fonda, and Spencer Tracy. The motion picture high points of these years were Ernst Lubitsch's *The Smiling Lieutenant;* two films directed by Cecil B. DeMille, *The Sign of the Cross* (1932) and *Cleopatra* (1934); Mitchell Leisen's outstanding comedy, *Midnight* (1939); Colbert's first Technicolor film, John Ford's *Drums Along the Mohawk* (1939); and Preston Sturges's *The Palm Beach Story* (1942).

The pinnacle of Colbert's motion-picture career was Frank Capra's *It Happened One Night* (1934). She was not overly impressed with the script, and at the time was preparing for a ski trip to Sun Valley, Idaho. Unable to secure his first choice for the role, Capra coaxed Colbert into accepting the lead by promising to double her current salary at Paramount ($25,000 per film) and to squeeze the filming into several weeks to finish in time for Christmas. Colbert won the 1935 Academy Award for best actress for her role in the film. It was so unusual for a comedy to win a top Academy Award that Colbert, attired in a traveling suit and ready to board a train, had to be rushed by studio personnel to the Los Angeles Biltmore Hotel, where she proudly accepted her award. Her two subsequent Academy Award nominations were for *Private Worlds* (1935), about the staff in a mental institution, and *Since You Went Away* (1944), a home-front World War II drama, in which she played the mother of Jennifer Jones and Shirley Temple. Colbert's final film with Paramount was *Practically Yours* (1944) with Fred MacMurray. During her years with Paramount, Colbert made more than forty films.

In the late 1930s and 1940s Colbert engaged in occasional radio work for DeMille's Lux Radio Theatre on CBS: *Hands Across the Sea* and *The Awful Truth.* During her freelancing period from the mid-1940s through 1961, Colbert worked with at least six American studios, as well as studios in England and France. She made two more films at United Artists with Don Ameche, a comedy, *Guest Wife* (1945), and a thriller, *Sleep, My Love* (1948); her last two of seven films with MacMurray at Universal, *The Egg and I* (1947) and *Family Honeymoon* (1948); some unusual war-related films at RKO-International, *Tomorrow Is Forever* (1946) with Orson Welles and George Brent; and at Twentieth Century-Fox, *Three Came Home* (1950) with Sessue Hayakawa. Colbert made her last comedy in 1951 (*Let's Make It Legal,* Twentieth Century-Fox) and her final film in 1961 (*Parrish,* Warner Brothers).

During the early 1950s Colbert continued performances on *Lux Radio Theatre* and appeared in the theater and the new medium of television. She returned to Broadway in

1956 to replace Margaret Sullavan in *Janus.* On 29 October 1958 Colbert opened in the first of over 450 performances of *The Marriage-Go-Round,* a comedy with Boyer for which she received a nomination for the Tony Award for best actress.

Colbert made her first television appearance in April 1951 on CBS's *The Jack Benny Show* and the first of her many dramatic television roles in September 1954 in *The Royal Family* for CBS's *The Best of Broadway.* Among her numerous television appearances were Noel Coward's *Blithe Spirit* (1956), *General Motors Fiftieth Anniversary Show* (1957), and *The Bells of St. Mary's* (1959). In 1987, almost thirty years after *The Bells of St. Mary's,* Colbert appeared with Ann-Margaret in *The Two Mrs. Grenvilles* on NBC, for which she was nominated for an Emmy (1987) and awarded a Golden Globe (1988). At the 1988 American Festival in Deauville, France, Colbert was presented with the medal of the French Legion of Honor. In 1984 she was honored by the Film Society of Lincoln Center, and in 1989 she was presented with a Lifetime Achievement Honor from the Kennedy Center for the Performing Arts in Washington, D.C.

In the mid-1970s Colbert embarked upon a third phase of her stage career, beginning in 1974 with *Community of Two* in Philadelphia. For her role in *The Kingfisher* (1978), she won the Sarah Siddons Society Award for best actress. Her final stage performance was in Frederick Lonsdale's *Aren't We All?,* which opened in London in the summer of 1984 and subsequently toured in the United States and Australia.

In addition to property in California, two apartments in Manhattan (at 136 East Sixty-fourth Street) and an apartment in the Passy district of Paris, Colbert and her husband owned an estate in Saint Peter, Barbados, West Indies, which they named "Bellerive." After they sold the estate in California where Colbert had lived with her mother for many years, they made Bellerive their permanent residence. Colbert enjoyed painting portraits, swimming daily in her pool, and entertaining friends. Even after a stroke in March 1993 left her confined to a wheelchair, she was still able to visit with her friends. Colbert died at the age of ninety-two; her remains were cremated and divided between New York and Barbados. Her cremated remains in Barbados are placed near her husband, who is buried in St. Peter's Cemetery.

Claudette Colbert sparkled in the spotlight of theatrical fame, first during the late 1920s and again over fifty years later. She also reigned as one of Hollywood's highest-salaried stars from the mid-1930s through the 1940s. Because of her professional perfectionism and earnest approach to her dramatic craft —whether on stage, screen, radio, or television—she created vibrant personalities that ranged from queens of antiquity, to seventeenth- and eighteenth-century Americans, to contemporary sophisticated ladies, to modern wartime internees, that captivated and sustained the interest of the audience. Colbert always gave an interesting screen performance, even when the rest of a film was mediocre. She excelled in screwball comedies such as *It Happened One Night,* and that film has become an enduring classic.

★

The Billy Rose Theatre Collection at the New York Public Library for the Performing Arts at Lincoln Center holds some clippings, photographs, and scrapbooks about Colbert's career. Colbert never wrote an autobiography. She did give interviews to Lawrence J. Quirk for parts of *Claudette Colbert: An Illustrated Biography* (1985), which covers her personal and professional life on stage and screen and contains an excellent selection of photographs, a filmography, and an index. There are interviews in the *New York Times,* such as 24 Mar. 1935, 17 Feb. 1946, and 27 Feb. 1955. Other works focusing on Colbert are: Joseph B. Pacheco, Jr., "Claudette Colbert: Projected a Cheery Insouciance During Depression and War," *Films in Review* (21 May 1970), with stills and filmography; James Robert Parish, "Claudette Colbert," in *The Paramount Pretties* (1972), a discussion of her stage, screen, radio, and television credits, with some interesting quotes, a summarizing essay, a biographical section, filmography, and photographs; Parish, "Fred MacMurray-Claudette Colbert," in *Hollywood's Great Love Teams* (1974), a discussion of their films, along with film synopses and commentary; David Shipman, "Claudette Colbert," in *The Great Movie Stars: The Golden Years* (1979), a succinct summary of her career; and Annette Tapert, *The Power of Glamour* (1998), a discussion of her style, personality, sense of fashion, disciplined routine, and an insight into her lifestyle, with a collection of spectacular photographs. For extensive bibliographies see Mel Schuster, *Motion Picture Performers: A Bibliography of Magazine and Periodical Articles, 1900–1969* (1971) and *Supplement No. 1, 1970–1974* (1976). Obituaries are in the *New York Times* and *Los Angeles Times* (both 31 July 1996) and London *Times* (1 Aug. 1996). Many of Colbert's sixty-four films are available on commercial videocassettes; the Library of Congress has a sound recording of some of *The Barker.*

MADELINE SAPIENZA

COLBY, William Egan   (*b.* 4 January 1920 in Saint Paul, Minnesota; *d.* 6 May 1996 near Rock Point, Maryland), covert operations specialist who served as director of the Central Intelligence Agency during the turbulent 1970s.

The only child of Elbridge Colby, a teacher of English literature who became a career U.S. Army officer, and Margaret Mary Egan, William Colby grew up on military posts in Panama, China, and North America. After graduating from high school in Burlington, Vermont, at age sixteen he entered Princeton University. Far from the typical Prince-

William Colby. ARCHIVE PHOTOS

ton student of the era, Colby waited tables in the dining hall and served as an altar boy in the Roman Catholic chapel. He graduated in 1940 with a Phi Beta Kappa key and a commission in the Reserve Officers' Training Corps.

Colby then enrolled at Columbia University Law School, hoping to become a labor lawyer with President Franklin D. Roosevelt's New Deal. Concerned about the rise of fascism, he applied for active military duty in August 1941. After completing artillery training at Fort Sill, Oklahoma, he remained at the post as an instructor at the Field Artillery Officer Candidate School. Anxious to see combat, he volunteered for parachute training. When a recruiter from the Office of Strategic Services (OSS) sought qualified parachute officers for a hazardous mission, Colby seized the opportunity to join the wartime intelligence organization.

Colby underwent commando training in Scotland and England during the early months of 1944 and then was assigned to the Jedburgh program. In August 1944, as part of the program, he parachuted into German-occupied France as part of a three-man team to coordinate resistance units. He returned to England at the beginning of 1945 and was given command of the OSS's Norwegian Special Operations Group. In March he led a group of Norwegian Americans on a ski-parachute mission to disrupt enemy communications in the area south of Trondheim, Norway.

A highly decorated major, Colby returned to the United States after the war ended in Europe, married Barbara Heinzen on 15 September 1945, and reentered Columbia Law School. After receiving his LL.B. in 1947, he accepted the invitation of William Donovan, head of the wartime OSS, to join the Manhattan law firm Donovan, Leisure, Newton, Lombard and Irvine. In 1949 he left the firm for the staff of the National Labor Relations Board in Washington, D.C.

Shortly after the outbreak of the Korean War in June 1950, Colby took up a long-standing invitation to join the Central Intelligence Agency (CIA). Specializing in covert operations, he was assigned to the Scandinavian Branch in the Western European Division of the Office of Policy Coordination. Based in Stockholm, Sweden, he set up stay-behind networks that would come into being should the Soviet Union overrun Scandinavia. In 1953 the CIA sent him to Rome, where he conducted covert political operations against Italian communists.

A new phase of Colby's intelligence career began in 1958, when he was assigned to the Far East Division of the Clandestine Service (also known as the Directorate of Plans and, later, the Directorate of Operations). Posted to Saigon in 1959, he acted as liaison between the CIA and Ngo Dinh Diem, the president of South Vietnam. The following year he became chief of the agency's Saigon station.

Colby returned to Washington in 1962. For the next five years he was centrally involved in the evolution of U.S. policy toward Vietnam as deputy chief, then chief from 1963 on, of the Far East Division in the Directorate of Plans. At the request of President Lyndon B. Johnson, Colby took a leave of absence from the CIA in 1968 and went to Vietnam as head of the U.S. State Department's Civil Operations and Rural Development Support (CORDS) program. Holding the rank of ambassador, he supervised the Phoenix Intelligence Program, a controversial scheme to expose the Vietcong's infrastructure throughout South Vietnam. Although largely successful, the program was criticized for its use of torture and assassination.

Concerned about the health of his eldest daughter (one of his five children) who was slowly dying of anorexia nervosa, Colby returned to the United States in 1971, rejoined the CIA, and became the agency's executive director–comptroller, a position he used to streamline budgetary procedures. In May 1973 after a brief tour as head of the Clandestine Service, he was selected by President Richard Nixon to become director of the CIA.

Colby took over the intelligence agency during a time of troubles. Under attack for its involvement in assassination plots and other alleged misuses of power, the CIA became the target of numerous investigations. Colby spent most of his time responding to official inquiries about the agency's activities. Criticized by many intelligence officers for his openness, Colby believed that candor was necessary to ensure the survival of the CIA. His forthright cooperation with Congress caused President Gerald Ford to request his resignation late in 1975.

Colby declined an offer to become an ambassador to the North Atlantic Treaty Organization (NATO) and instead opened a law office in Washington, D.C. In November 1984 he divorced Heinzen and on 20 November 1984 married Sally Shelton, a high-ranking official at the U.S. Agency for International Development. Still vigorous and active in his senior years, he disappeared on 27 April 1996 while on a solo canoe trip from his weekend home in Rock Point, Maryland. His body was discovered nine days later (the official date of his death); the cause of death was drowning. He is buried at Arlington National Cemetery in Arlington, Virginia.

Colby joined the CIA during the early years of the cold war, when the agency attracted the "best and the brightest" of the nation in a crusade against communism. He never doubted that the CIA was an organization of honorable men who stood in the forefront of the battle for freedom. An individual of courage and integrity, Colby became a consummate practitioner of covert operations. Although his candor in the 1970s may have inflicted short-term damage on the CIA, his conduct likely saved the agency from being dismantled by an angry Congress.

★

Colby wrote two books during his retirement: *Honorable Men: My Life in the CIA* (1978) and *Lost Victory: A Firsthand Account of America's Sixteen-Year Involvement in Vietnam* (1989). His obituary is in the *New York Times* (7 May 1996).

WILLIAM M. LEARY

COLEMAN, James Samuel (*b.* 12 May 1926 in Bedford, Indiana; *d.* 25 March 1995 in Chicago, Illinois), sociologist and scholar at Johns Hopkins University and the University of Chicago whose studies and reports were used in determining social policy related to education.

Coleman was one of two children born to Maurine Lappin, a homemaker, and James Fox Coleman, a foreman. Raised in Ohio and Kentucky, Coleman graduated from Manual High School in Louisville, Kentucky, in 1944. He briefly attended Emory and Henry College in Emory, Virginia, after which he served in the U.S. Navy from 1944 through 1946, entering as an apprentice seaman. After his discharge as a seaman second class, Coleman attended Indiana University for one year and then studied at Purdue University,

James S. Coleman, 1975. AP/WIDE WORLD PHOTOS

from which he graduated in 1949 with a B.S. degree in chemical engineering. He worked for Eastman-Kodak in Rochester, New York, from 1949 until 1951, when he decided to study sociology at Columbia University. On 2 February 1949 he married Lucille Richey; they had three sons.

Coleman's four years at Columbia University changed him profoundly, turning him from a chemical engineer into a social scientist. In addition to taking courses for his doctorate, which he received in 1955, Coleman worked as a research associate for the Bureau of Applied Social Research and with Seymour Lipset on a study of the typesetters' union in New York City. When he left Columbia for a fellowship at the Center for Advanced Study in the Behavioral Sciences at Palo Alto, California, Coleman was a seasoned social scientist. He had set habits of research, collegial work patterns, and publications in process, including, with Lipset and Martin A. Trow, *Union Democracy* (1956) and, without collaboration, *Community Conflict* (1957). He had begun to research topics that occupied a lot of his scholarly energy—adolescents and education.

From 1956 to 1959 Coleman was an assistant professor of sociology at the University of Chicago. He joined the faculty of Johns Hopkins University in Baltimore as an associate professor in 1959 and was promoted to a full professor of sociology in 1961. During his tenure at Johns Hopkins, Coleman became prominent outside the scholarly community by leading the group that produced *Equality of Educational Opportunity* (1966), often referred to as the Coleman Report. Coleman and his associates surveyed 60,000 teachers and 570,000 students for this study commissioned by the U.S. Department of Education to fulfill a requirement of the Civil Rights Act of 1964. Coleman and his associates concluded that education in the United States was not equal, that parents had the greatest influence on the educational success of their children, and that poor, minority children were more successful when educated in an economically mixed environment. The conclusions of the report were highly controversial, but further research supported them. Coleman always claimed that the results of the report were misinterpreted. Civil rights advocates used the information to justify busing as the main means of integrating schools.

Coleman rejoined the faculty of the sociology department at the University of Chicago in 1973. That year he and his first wife divorced. On 27 August 1973 he married Zdzislawa Walaszek; they had one son. In 1975 he issued a number of papers and reports detailing the failure of busing to rectify the inequalities of the American education system. In 1981, with *Coleman Report on Public and Private Schools,* the draft of *Public and Private Schools* (1982) issued by the National Center for Educational Statistics, Coleman once again found himself embroiled in controversy. Although he later amended this study, citing fallacies in the data collection and interpretation, it started a decade of discourse and research on the success of parochial schools in the education of minority children. As early as 1978 Coleman proposed granting tax credits to parents with low incomes who sent their children to private schools. In reports, books, and papers published in the 1980s he advocated providing educational vouchers to low-income parents to give them choices in educating their children. Coleman argued that this type of program would provide competition for the public schools and would in turn pressure those schools to improve educational practices for all poor and minority children.

Coleman was a tall man with gray eyes and a fringe of hair that changed over the years from gray to white. He was a disciplined and highly focused worker whose brilliance and innovative thinking helped direct the course of educational policy over a period of thirty years. He had the courage to confront pertinent issues even though his conclusions would be controversial and his work would be attacked, often viciously. By all accounts, his own included, Coleman was an indifferent public speaker. His ideas, expressed in print with such lucidity, were complex and not particularly appropriate for oral presentation.

Coleman died of prostate cancer in the University of Chicago Hospitals. He was sixty-eight years of age. Coleman is buried in a family plot in the Riverside Cemetery in Hopkinsville, Christian County, Kentucky.

Coleman applied his scientific background and cross-disciplinary interests to sociological studies over a broad range of topics. The Coleman Report, with its impact on busing in the late 1960s and early 1970s, was chosen by the Museum of Education as one of the most influential educational books of the twentieth century. Coleman's research in the 1980s contributed to dialogues on public funding for private education, educational standards, and curriculum content. Coleman's most lasting legacy may be in the practice of sociology, where his work furthered research and analytical techniques as well as an examination of social theory at the end of the twentieth century.

★

Coleman's autobiographical essay "Columbia in the Fifties" in Bennett M. Berger, *Authors of Their Own Lives* (1990), provides insight into his development as a sociologist as well as a fascinating glimpse at the sociology department at Columbia University in the 1950s. A short, precise article, David J. Hoff, "Echoes of the Coleman Report," *Education Week* 18 (24 Mar. 1999): 33–35, evaluates the study's long-term influence on education in the United States. Andrew Greeley, "Community as Social Capital: James S. Coleman on Catholic Schools," *America* 157 (1987): 110–112, describes Coleman's study comparing schools in the public and private sectors and its implications for Catholic schools. Daniel Patrick Moynihan, "The Lives They Lived: James S. Coleman," *New York Times Magazine* (31 Dec. 1995), is a touching and personal appreciation of Coleman and his work. Obituaries are in the *New York Times* (28 Mar. 1995) and *Education Week* 14 (5 Apr. 1995): 15.

ELLEN LOUGHRAN

COLLINS, John Frederick (*b.* 20 July 1919 in Boston, Massachusetts; *d.* 23 November 1995 in Brighton, Massachusetts), lawyer and politician, who as the mayor of Boston from 1960 to 1968 provided political leadership and worked with the business community to support urban redevelopment that left a revitalized Boston positioned to take advantage of the new information-based economy.

Collins was the oldest of three children born to Frederick B. Collins, a mechanic for the Boston Elevated Railway, and Margaret Mellyn, a homemaker. Educated in the Boston public schools, he graduated from Roxbury Memorial High School in 1937. He attended Suffolk University Law School from 1937 to 1941, earning a bachelors of law degree cum laude and graduating first in his class. He was admitted to the Massachusetts bar in 1941, and later that year ran unsuccessfully for the Boston City Council. He enlisted in the U.S. Army in 1942, served in the counterintelligence corps, and was discharged in 1946 with the rank of captain.

John Collins in 1959, stricken with polio before becoming mayor of Boston. ASSOCIATED PRESS AP

On 6 September 1947 Collins married Mary Patricia Cunniff; they had four children.

Collins, who lived in the Roxbury section of Boston, was elected as a Democrat to the Massachusetts House of Representatives in November 1946 and served two terms from 1947 to 1951. Elected to the Massachusetts Senate in November 1950, he served two terms from 1951 to 1955. In the Senate Collins sponsored anti-Communist legislation and bills to control narcotics. In 1954 he was the Democratic nominee for Massachusetts's attorney general, but was defeated by the Republican incumbent George Fingold.

In 1955 Collins ran for the Boston City Council. Ten days before the September primary, he and three of his children were stricken with polio. His children recovered, but Collins was almost totally paralyzed and nearly died. Recovery was slow, although after ten years in a wheelchair he was able to walk with crutches. His physicians thought he should withdraw from the campaign, but he refused and his wife managed the campaign. Collins finished eleventh among the eighteen finalists in the primary, but few thought he could win one of the nine seats in the November election. During a televised speech he predicted victory and promised to attend the first meeting of the city council in January. He finished third among the nine winners, took the oath of office at his home, and was present for the first council meeting.

Collins served on the city council from 1956 to 1957. He resigned to accept an appointment as the registrar of probate and insolvency for Suffolk County from Governor Foster Furcolo. In 1958 he was elected to a full six-year term as registrar.

When Collins announced his candidacy for mayor of Boston in 1959, most observers doubted he could prevail over the state senate president John E. Powers in the contest to succeed the retiring mayor John B. Hynes. Powers, a legislator for twenty-one years, had a large campaign war chest and the support of most Boston and state political groups and leaders. Collins ran his campaign as a political outsider and underdog. He used television to present a clean-cut, wholesome, nonpolitical image. He generated sympathy and respect because, like former president Franklin D. Roosevelt, he had not been defeated by polio. His well-run campaign played on his opponent's name, pledging to "stop power politics." He supported a limited state sales tax to help cut property taxes, a more efficient municipal government, and urban renewal. In the September primary Collins received twenty-two percent of the vote, second to Powers, who received only thirty-four percent. Four days before the November election, Collins capitalized on a federal raid on a Boston bookmaker whom he said had ties to Powers. Collins captured fifty-six percent of the ballots, defeating his opponent by more than 24,000 votes.

On 4 January 1960 Collins was inaugurated as the mayor of Boston. As the city's chief executive, this blunt, articulate, hard-working veteran of Boston politics was not fooled or frightened by anyone. He even had a private phone line installed in the mayor's office, gave its number to only selected individuals, and answered it himself.

As mayor, Collins met with a group of Boston's business leaders every other week. Collins set the agenda and used these contacts to convince the business community to loan technically trained individuals to help him reorganize the city, recruit experts to work for the city, lobby the legislature, and, perhaps most importantly, demonstrate to the business leaders that their mayor was competent and honest and would work with them to develop the city.

Collins selected effective legislative lobbyists and was willing to call and visit with state legislators in support of pending bills. He also lobbied the federal government to provide funds for renewal projects. Toward the end of his administration, however, the federal government began to reduce assistance because of increased spending for the Vietnam War.

To supervise urban renewal Collins hired Edward J. Logue, a lawyer and urban planner who had been directing New Haven, Connecticut's, redevelopment since 1954 and who had a reputation for attracting federal funds. Collins had the board of the Boston Redevelopment Authority (BRA) name Logue as development administrator. Although most of his salary came from the BRA, some came from the mayor's office, so Logue worked directly under Collins. The mayor instructed Logue to prepare a comprehensive development plan for Boston and then carry it out.

Collins worked with Logue to get favorable court rulings, federal funds, and the necessary legislation to enable the BRA to carry out urban redevelopment. He also worked with local business leaders to plan the reconstruction of the downtown business district. New construction began with the fifty-two-story Prudential Tower, followed by completion of the Boston Common underground garage, demolition of Scollay Square and its replacement with a new Government Center including a new Boston City Hall, and reconstruction of the waterfront including a new aquarium. Highways were built, historic Quincy Market behind Faneuil Hall was restored, and some housing was rehabilitated. The BRA publicized its accomplishments nationally and invited private business to locate and build in Boston. By 1966 new construction occupied about one quarter of the city's land and was called by many the "New Boston."

Promising to "complete the job we have started," Collins ran for reelection in 1963, basing his campaign on four years of property tax cuts, a three percent reduction in the city budget, and the urban renewal program that he said produced more construction, more jobs, and more family income. He won with sixty percent of the vote.

Collins discovered that while business leaders, tourists, and urban planners hailed the New Boston, the working-class residents of the surrounding neighborhoods opposed redevelopment as they saw residences and communities demolished and replaced by upscale housing developments. Also, the African American community perceived Collins as an unfriendly executive who did not do enough to respond to its needs. In 1966 Collins sought the Democratic nomination for the U.S. Senate, but lost both the convention endorsement and the primary. On 6 June 1967 Collins announced that he would not seek a third term as mayor. Although the new City Hall would not be ready for use until the middle of 1968, Collins moved to the mayor's office in December 1967, where he met with his successor, Kevin H. White. Then he developed a case of pneumonia that prevented him from attending White's inauguration.

Collins served as a visiting professor of urban affairs at the Alfred P. Sloan School of Management of the Massachusetts Institute of Technology (MIT) from 1968 to 1980. While there he served as chief advisor to the MIT Fellows in the Urban Affairs Program. The program sponsored junior faculty who worked full time for a year with city officials on urban problems. He resumed his law practice, maintaining an office in Boston until 1990. He served as a consultant, wrote occasional articles on political and moral issues, and was a television panelist on *Five on Five,* a program on Boston's Channel 5. He chaired the Massachusetts Democrats and Independents for Nixon in 1972 while serving as co-vice chairman of the national organization and was an unofficial advisor to Governor Edward King from 1979 to 1983. Hospitalized with pneumonia in July 1995, Collins died of a myocardial infarction four months later, and is buried in Saint Joseph's Cemetery in West Roxbury.

Collins was a large man, six-feet, two-inches tall and weighing 190 pounds. He was intelligent, hardworking, knowledgeable, articulate, tough, and straightforward. If he did not like an article in a newspaper, he would call the reporter, not the editor. He understood the ins and outs of Boston politics. That understanding, combined with his independence from other political leaders, enabled him to pursue his goals of efficient city government and urban redevelopment. Although successful in rebuilding the downtown business district, he did not have the support of the residents in the poorer neighborhoods, who saw redevelopment as destroying their homes and communities. The rebuilt New Boston, however, attracted high technology, finance, and service industries that made the city a leader in the world economy.

★

Collins's papers are in Special Collections, Boston Public Library, Copley Square, Boston, Massachusetts. The papers cover his two terms as mayor as well as his campaigns for mayor and for the U.S. Senate. For a detailed analysis of Boston's 1959 mayoral election and Collins's victory, see Murray B. Levin, *The Alienated Voter: Politics in Boston,* (1960). Lawrence W. Kennedy, *Planning the City upon a Hill: Boston Since 1630* (1992), discusses Collins's role as a municipal leader who was essential to Boston's urban planning and redevelopment. Thomas H. O'Connor, *Building a New Boston: Politics and Urban Renewal, 1950–1970* (1993), covers extensively the mayor's contributions to Boston's redevelopment. O'Connor's *The Boston Irish: A Political History* (1995), places Collins in the context of the Boston Irish community. Mark I. Gelfand, *Trustee for a City: Ralph Lowell of Boston* (1998), contains information about Collins and his relationship with leaders of the Boston business community. Walter McQuade, "Boston: What Can a Sick City Do?" in *Fortune* (June 1964), is a contemporary view of Boston's redevelopment. For a critical view of Boston's redevelopment during Collins's administration see Jack Tager, "Urban Renewal in Boston: Municipal Entrepreneurs and Urban Elites," *Historical Journal of Massachusetts* 21 (winter 1993): 1–32. Obituaries are in the *Boston Globe, Boston Herald,* and *New York Times* (all 24 Nov. 1995).

WILLIAM A. HASENFUS

CONDON, Richard Thomas (*b.* 18 March 1915 in New York City; *d.* 9 April 1996 in Dallas, Texas), writer best known for his conspiratorial novels of government and organized crime, such as *The Manchurian Candidate* (1959) and *Prizzi's Honor* (1982).

Condon was the older of two children of Richard Aloysius Condon, a naval officer, and Martha Irene Pickering, a stenographer and homemaker. Growing up in New York City's Washington Heights, Condon graduated from De Witt Clinton High School in 1934, but his grades were so poor that he was not admitted to college. He worked as an elevator operator, a hotel clerk, and a waiter. In 1935 he took a job as an advertising copywriter with the New York firm Kelly, Nason, and Roosevelt. This work led to his first career, as a movie publicist. In 1936 he began working for Walt Disney, where he handled the publicity for such films as *Pinocchio* (1940), *Fantasia* (1940), and *Dumbo* (1941).

On 14 January 1938 Condon married Evelyn Rose Hunt, a model he had met during his copywriting days. They remained married for the rest of his life and had two daughters. In 1942 Hal Horne, who had hired Condon, moved to Twentieth Century–Fox, and Condon, who had been exempted from the World War II draft as a stutterer, followed

Richard Condon. © JERRY BAUER

him. Condon opened his own agency, Richard Condon Inc., in 1945 and, by his own account, worked for all the major companies except Warner Brothers and MGM. In 1953 he took a job with United Artists as European publicity director, and he and his family moved to Paris.

In 1957 disillusion and two duodenal ulcers led Condon to leave the film business. He returned to New York City and embarked on his second, more successful career as a novelist. His first novel, *The Oldest Confession* (1958), a tale of art theft, was an immediate success; it was filmed as *The Happy Thieves* (1962).

It was Condon's second novel, however, that made his reputation and may be the work for which he will be most remembered. In *The Manchurian Candidate* (1959), an American soldier is captured and brainwashed by the Chinese communists and then returned to America to take part in an assassination plot. The novel's conspiratorial view of the highest circles of government, interwoven with a fast-moving suspense plot and a tale of family tragedy, captivated readers. It, too, was made into a movie, released in 1962.

In August 1959 Condon moved with his family to Mexico so he could research *A Talent for Loving,* a comic Western novel published in 1961. From there the Condons moved to Paris, where they stayed for six months in 1961, and then to Switzerland, where they lived at Anières and then at Monte de Trinita. In 1970 the Condons moved again, to the town of Rossenarra in Ireland. At this point Condon's literary reputation had fallen into desuetude. Although such novels as *Some Angry Angel* (1960), *Any God Will Do* (1966), and *Mile High* (1969) won a devoted cult following, Condon's baroque plotting, fascination with trivia, and often thinly-disguised loathing for those in power led critics to wonder if he would ever return to the high standard set by *The Manchurian Candidate.*

Winter Kills (1974) was widely viewed as such a comeback. Its subject, the assassination of John F. Kennedy presented in thin fictional disguise, had the grandeur needed for its dramatic, even tragic, treatment, and the complexities of plot were under firm auctorial control. Reviewers hailed it as a return to former glories. In 1979 *Winter Kills* was made into a movie that gained favorable reviews but soon disappeared from theaters. Condon praised the movie as faithful to his vision and blamed its disappearance on the same powerful forces he was attacking in the book.

Condon again fell from critical favor. He was seen as shrill and repetitive, airing his hatreds and obsessions, as in *Death of a Politician* (1978), which seemed little more than an unremitting attack on Richard Nixon, a frequent Condon target. In 1980 Condon returned to the United States, specifically Dallas, to be near his grandchildren. Perhaps reenergized by the return to his native soil, he produced another major work. In *Prizzi's Honor* (1982) Condon audaciously set a tale of tragically doomed love in an organized crime family, with hired killers as protagonists.

The novel received popular and critical acclaim and was made into a successful film in 1985, with Condon himself working on the screenplay. Condon returned to the Prizzi family with a prequel, *Prizzi's Family* (1986), and sequels, *Prizzi's Glory* (1988) and *Prizzi's Money* (1994). Later novels, such as *Emperor of America* (1990), were not well received. Condon died of heart and kidney ailments in Presbyterian Hospital, Dallas.

Condon saw himself as an entertainer, not as a serious creator of great literature; he once compared his work with that of a saloon singer, reminding people of sorrows, pleasures, and corruption. His best novels juxtapose complex tales of conspiracy in the circles of power with personal obsession, usually romantic and/or familial. His major works—*The Manchurian Candidate, Winter Kills,* and *Prizzi's Honor*—have elements of classical tragedy, with heroic protagonists determining their own destinies and finally being brought down by their flaws and forced to kill what they love. At its worst, the grandeur becomes grandiosity, tragedy becomes sitcom coincidence, and righteous indignation turns to strident and repetitive complaining. But even the failures have some saving graces of wit and characterization.

The conspiratorial vision that made *The Manchurian Candidate* so shocking came to seem almost tame, as books like those of Thomas Pynchon and Robert Anton Wilson, movies like Oliver Stone's *JFK* (1991), and television shows like *The X-Files* offered even more horrifying visions. But they all built on Condon's foundation.

★

Condon recounted his life story, with particular attention to his moves, in the memoir *And Then We Moved to Rossenarra* (1973). In 1984 he updated the account of his life with a contribution to the *Contemporary Authors Autobiography Series.* His fiction has received little academic and critical attention. Leo Braudy's review of *Winter Kills* in the *New York Times Book Review,* (26 May 1974; reprinted in his collection, *Native Informant,* 1991), called attention to this important revival of Condon's career. Carolyn See's essay-review of *Emperor of America,* "Words—and Satire—Fail in Novel," *Los Angeles Times* (26 Feb. 1990) offers a considered statement of the case that the fiction of Condon's later years was fatally flawed by its shrillness. An obituary is in the *New York Times* (10 Apr. 1996).

ARTHUR D. HLAVATY

CONERLY, Charles Albert, Jr. ("Charlie") (*b.* 19 September 1921 in Clarksdale, Mississippi; *d.* 13 February 1996 in Memphis, Tennessee), college football player, combat marine in World War II, and championship professional quarterback with the New York Giants of the National Football League (NFL) at the time the sport was capturing national attention.

Conerly was one of three children born in the Mississippi Delta to Charles Albert Conerly, Sr., a police officer turned farmer, and Winford Fite, a nurse. Like many young boys in the rural South and elsewhere during the 1920s and 1930s, Conerly participated in a variety of sports and games. He was good at all of them and by the time he got to Clarksdale High School, where he starred in football, basketball, baseball, and tennis, he was an accomplished athlete. Additionally, after three months of playing golf Conerly was breaking eighty, and he scored more than two hundred the fourth time he bowled. But it was football that earned him a scholarship to the University of Mississippi in Oxford ("Ole Miss") in the fall of 1941. In 1942 after Conerly's sophomore season, he enlisted in the U.S. Marine Corps and saw combat on several occasions, most notably during the horrific battle for the island of Iwo Jima. Early in 1945 he was discharged in time for the 1946 college football season, but it was a repeat of the 1942 season at Ole Miss: their team, the Rebels, won two games while losing seven.

In 1947, Conerly's senior season, the twenty-six-year-old single-wing tailback blossomed. Conerly and the team's end Barney Poole were a formidable pass-catch combination, and Ole Miss—ranked tenth in the Southeastern Conference (SEC) in pre-season—had an 8–2 season and won the SEC championship, including a 13–9 victory over Texas Christian in the newly inaugurated Delta Bowl in Memphis.

Chunkin' Charlie ("in the South we 'chunk' a rock or a ball," explained his widow) was a consensus All-America and led the nation in every meaningful passing category: attempts (233), completions (133), completion percentage (.571), and touchdowns (eighteen). In addition, he ran for 417 yards and passed for 1,367. He finished fourth in the balloting for the Heisman Trophy, awarded to the nation's outstanding college football player. Before leaving Ole Miss, Conerly batted .467 for the Rebels's baseball team and fielded several offers to sign a major league contract in that sport.

While Conerly was fighting with the marines in the South Pacific, he was selected in the 1945 NFL draft by the Washington Redskins (he was eligible because his entering freshman class at Mississippi had been graduated by that time). Since the Redskins already had the legendary Slingin' Sammy Baugh at quarterback and would subsequently acquire University of Alabama All-America Harry Gilmer, their need for a third passer was slight. They traded the rights to Conerly to the New York Giants. He started in the College All-Star Game in Chicago and then at twenty-seven—in those days an age when many were retiring from pro football—reported as a rookie to the Giants's training camp. Before reporting, Conerly was involved in a minor flap. The baseball executive Branch Rickey, who was involved with the Brooklyn Dodgers's

Charlie Conerly. COURTESY PRO FOOTBALL HALL OF FAME

football team of the rival All-America Football Conference, offered Conerly a four-year contract for $95,000, a huge sum for the time. He then bemoaned the fact that Conerly would sign "an inferior" offer, five years with the Giants at $72,500. Later it was determined that Rickey's offer was a publicity stunt. Conerly was quoted in the New York Times as saying, "The Brooklyn offer came after the Dodgers were sure I had decided to play for the Giants."

Although the Giants were only 4–8 in 1948 and Conerly was pressured constantly by opposing defenses, his individual play was outstanding. He passed for 2,175 yards and won Rookie of the Year honors. After the season he married Perian (pronounced Perry Ann) Collier on 23 June 1949. Perian Conerly gained recognition as a journalist and author. Her book, *Backseat Quarterback* (1963), about life as the wife of an NFL player, was critically acclaimed and sold well. The couple did not have children.

Conerly continued to perform well but for several succeeding seasons the Giants were mediocre. As the offensive leader, Conerly was the focal point of the Giants fans' vocal displeasure. He had decided to retire after the 1953 season, in which the Giants' record was 3–9, but new head coach Jim Lee Howell and his assistant, Vince Lombardi, talked Conerly out of it.

With a rejuvenated offense built around Frank Gifford and Kyle Rote and a smothering defense, the Giants were champions of the professional football world in 1956. Conerly—after fighting off competition from Paul Governali, Travis Tidwell, Arnold Galiffa, Fred Benners, Bobby Clatterbuck, George Shaw, Don Heinrich, and Lee Grosscup—was finally appreciated as the Giants contended annually for an NFL title. Through the years, the stoic Conerly endured the wrath of fickle fans in silence.

In 1958 and 1959 the Giants battled to the NFL Championship game, only to lose twice to the Baltimore Colts, who were led by legendary quarterback Johnny Unitas. The 1958 "sudden death" overtime game is still widely regarded as the "Greatest Game Ever Played." Nationally televised, it captured the country's attention. More specifically, the Madison Avenue advertising agencies became aware of the drawing power of NFL athletes, especially the successful, hometown Giants.

Conerly's thick southern drawl precluded him from radio and television opportunities like those that his teammates Gifford, Rote, and Pat Summerall received. However, his rugged, weathered, masculine looks did gain him some fame and fortune as the first Marlboro man in Philip Morris's cigarette print ads. Conerly stood at six feet, one inch tall with a playing weight of 185 pounds.

During the later stages of his Giants career, Conerly and Don Heinrich formed a unique quarterback combination. Heinrich, although second team, would actually start the game. Conerly would observe the opponent's defense from the bench for the first quarter of the game and then go in as the beneficiary of what he had seen earlier. The system worked so well that in 1959 Conerly was awarded the Jim Thorpe Trophy as NFL's Most Valuable Player.

During Conerly's final season in 1961, the Giants acquired future Pro Football Hall of Fame quarterback Y. A. Tittle and Conerly became a backup. Coach Allie Sherman said of his forty-year-old quarterback's final season, "Four times I called on Charlie during the season, and all four times he came through for us." Conerly retired after the 1961 championship game loss, and the Giants officially retired his number forty-two jersey the following year.

Conerly operated a chain of shoe stores in Mississippi and played in many charity golf tournaments in his later years. After an illness, Conerly died of heart disease in a Memphis hospital at the age of seventy-four. He is buried in Oakridge Cemetery in Clarksdale. Each year the Charlie Conerly Memorial Trophy is presented to the outstanding college football player in the state of Mississippi.

As a man and a player, Charlie Conerly typified many men of the World War II generation. He saw what needed to be done and without fanfare simply did it. He was so highly thought of by his Giants teammates that when his old roommate Frank Gifford was inducted into the Pro Football Hall of Fame in Canton, Ohio, he said, almost apologetically, "Chuck, you belong here, too." Giants owner Wellington Mara often remarked, "Charlie is the best player *not* in the Pro Football Hall of Fame." Conerly was, however, voted into the College Football Hall of Fame in 1966.

★

While there is no full-length biography of Conerly, information can be found in Don Smith, *New York Giants* (1960); Perian Conerly, *Backseat Quarterback* (1963); Barry Gottehrer, *The Giants of New York: The History of Professional Football's Most Fabulous Dynasty* (1963); Dave Klein, *The New York Giants: Yesterday, Today, and Tomorrow* (1973); Dave Klein, *The Game of Their Lives* (1976); and Frank Gifford with Harry Waters, *The Whole Ten Yards* (1993). An obituary is in the *New York Times* (14 Feb. 1996).

JIM CAMPBELL

CONOVER, Willis Clark, Jr. (*b.* 18 October 1920 in Buffalo, New York; *d.* 17 May 1996 in Alexandria, Virginia), host of Voice of America's *Music USA Jazz Hour* from 1955 to 1996, bringing jazz to an estimated 30 million listeners worldwide as "America's Jazz Ambassador."

Conover was the oldest of three children of a career army officer, Willis Clark Conover, Sr., and Frances Estelle Harris, an elementary schoolteacher. Because his family moved often, Conover attended many schools before graduating from Cambridge High School in Cambridge, Maryland, where the family settled when his father retired. He attended Salisbury State Teachers College in Salisbury, Maryland, in 1938, leaving after one year. He was married and divorced five times but had no children.

Willis Conover in his Voice of America Studio in Washington, D.C., broadcasting *Music USA,* 1959. ASSOCIATED PRESS AP

In 1939 Conover began working at WSAL, an AM radio station in Salisbury, as a writer and announcer. That same year he won an amateur announcing contest and was hired at WTBO-AM in Cumberland, Maryland, working until he was drafted into the army in 1942. He served as a technical sergeant at Fort George C. Meade in Maryland, interviewing recruits.

Beginning in 1944 Conover hosted a weekend jazz show at WWDC-AM in Washington, D.C., working at the station full-time after his army discharge in February 1946. He promoted jazz at clubs at the Howard Theatre in Washington, where he helped to desegregate the city by bringing together black and white musicians. He emceed the Band, a popular integrated jazz orchestra that could not play at segregated clubs.

In 1954 Conover applied to Voice of America (VOA), the radio station of the United States Information Agency (USIA), to host a jazz radio program. He was hired as an independent contractor, at his insistence, to retain control over the content of his programs. Initially, there was some opposition by some who felt that jazz was not appropriate music to export to (mostly) communist countries, but Conover saw jazz as the ultimate representation of American freedom, describing it as "a liberating kind of music . . . with the vitality and spirit that characterize our country at its best." His first broadcast was on 6 January 1955. The two-hour show began with fifteen minutes of news, then forty-five minutes of popular music, followed by forty-five minutes of jazz. His signature opening was "This is Willis Conover in Washington, D.C, with the Voice of America Jazz Hour," and the show's theme song was Billy Strayhorn's recording of Duke Ellington's "Take the 'A' Train." Conover taped the shows using his own collection of about 60,000 records. From 1958 to 1960 Conover also worked for WCBS in New York City. Deciding that the VOA shows were more important, he gave up the higher paying WCBS job and moved to Washington. He also produced the VOA's weekly show *Music with Friends* for broadcast in Poland. Over the years he interviewed all the jazz greats, including Duke Ellington, Louis Armstrong, Billie Holiday, Erroll Garner, and Dizzy Gillespie.

Conover traveled to Brussels, Belgium, in 1958 to emcee American jazz concerts. In 1959 the USIA sent Conover on a five-week trip, beginning in Tunisia and including Norway and Poland. In all countries he was greeted by hundreds of adoring fans. He emceed the Newport Jazz Festival from 1951 to 1964 and hosted and produced numerous jazz concerts at the Kennedy Center for the Performing Arts in Washington, D.C., from 1969 to 1972; at Carnegie Hall in New York City; and for Public Television. He produced and emceed the New Orleans Jazz Festival (1969) and hosted or spoke at events in Istanbul, Turkey (1960); Moscow (1970); Oslo, Norway (1976); and Bombay, India

(1978), among other places. On 29 April 1970 Conover arranged and hosted Duke Ellington's seventieth birthday party at the White House. In the same year he received the Recording Industry Association of America's annual cultural award. He served on the Jazz Panel (which he created) of the National Endowment for the Arts from 1968 to 1972. In 1977 he received the Order of Merit from the Polish Ministry of Culture for "outstanding contributions to Polish culture" and was honored again in 1991 by the Polish president Lech Walesa. He accompanied the first live American music tour of the Soviet Union in 1982.

In 1990 Conover was awarded an honorary doctorate of music from Berklee College of Music in Boston, where he was a trustee and trustee emeritus. Berklee also established the Willis Conover Award for Excellence in Jazz Broadcasting. He was elected to the prestigious Cosmos Club in Washington, D.C., on 6 August 1991. The U.S. House of Representatives passed a resolution praising Conover's "unique and important contribution to the cause of international understanding and good will" and "for the unique contribution of Mr. Conover to expanding the understanding of American culture around the world through his thirty-eight years of jazz broadcast." Conover received *Down Beat's* Lifetime Achievement Award in 1995. On the fortieth anniversary of *Music USA Jazz Hour* (1995), Conover traveled to Poland for a tribute concert.

Conover was an author as well as a jazz aficionado. From 1936 to 1938 he created and published *Science-Fantasy Correspondent,* a magazine with stories and articles about the science-fantasy genre. He wrote *Lovecraft at Last* in 1975, a memoir of his correspondence with the writer H. P. Lovecraft, which began when Conover was only fourteen years old. The book received a special professional award in 1976 from the World Fantasy Convention in New York City. He also wrote jazz reviews and profiles for the *Saturday Review* and wrote songs, poetry, and liner notes for many jazz recordings.

Conover's famous smooth voice and impeccable slow diction, perfect for cutting through the static of short-wave radio, brought jazz to listeners in communist countries the world over, and many learned English from listening to the show. He played standard popular songs in the nonjazz portion of the show, but he disliked rock and roll music. He was virtually unknown in the United States, where it is illegal to broadcast VOA programs. He hated the label "disk jockey," preferring to say, "I conduct a music show." The pretaped shows usually revolved around a theme, with commentary from Conover. His legacy includes more than 15,000 tapes of his shows, which were rerun for about six months after his death. Enthusiastic fans, always there when he traveled abroad, saw Conover as America's "greatest ambassador." It would be hard to overestimate his influence on the estimated 30 million listeners in the Soviet

Union and Eastern Europe (and as many as 100 million worldwide) that he introduced to jazz, including many working as musicians today. To quote *Down Beat* (1995): "If you had to identify a single voice . . . that has changed the course of jazz history, it would certainly be . . . Willis Conover."

Conover, six feet tall with dark hair and black-framed eyeglasses, had throat cancer surgery and radiation therapy in 1985, but he continued working until shortly before his death. He died of lung cancer after two weeks at Alexandria Hospital in Alexandria. Conover's ashes are in the Columbarium at Arlington National Cemetery in Virginia. The VOA produced a memorial concert on 4 June 1996 in its Washington headquarters. Willis Conover was an intensely private man. His jazz friends and coworkers knew virtually nothing about his private life, and his family knew little about his professional life. Private even in death, the plaque at the Columbarium reads simply "Willis C. Conover, Jr., TSG USA 1920–1996."

★

Conover's tapes and papers are at the University of North Texas Music Library in Denton, Texas. The VOA and Berklee College of Music's Office of Public Information have clipping files on Conover. Berklee's Stan Getz Media Center and Library has cataloged many of the records with Conover's liner notes. Some autobiographical material can be found in *Lovecraft at Last* (1975). Fred Bouchard wrote about Conover in September 1995 for *Down Beat*'s lifetime achievement award. Dave Burns's article in *World Monitor* (Feb. 1993) was read into the *Congressional Record*, as was the *Reader's Digest* article "The World's Favorite American" (July 1985). Obituaries are in the *New York Times*, *Washington Post*, and *Boston Globe* (all 19 May 1996). Other obituaries are in the *Miami Herald* (20 May 1996), London *Independent* and *Guardian* (both 22 May 1996), and *Down Beat* (Aug. 1996).

JANE BRODSKY FITZPATRICK

CORNFELD, Bernard ("Bernie") (*b.* 17 August 1927 in Istanbul, Turkey; *d.* 27 February 1995 in London, England), entrepreneur who founded Investors Overseas Services, a financial conglomerate that became a powerful but controversial force in the mutual fund industry before its spectacular collapse in 1970.

Cornfeld—originally named Benno but known to friends and critics alike simply as Bernie—was the son of Leon and Sophie Cornfeld, who met in Vienna and immigrated to the United States in 1930. They eventually settled in Brooklyn, where Cornfeld's father, a Romanian Jewish actor and film impresario (who had four sons from a previous marriage), died three years later. Sophie Cornfeld, the daughter of a once-prosperous Russian Jewish family,

worked in an international freight-forwarding office and as a nurse to support herself and her young son.

Cornfeld, who was built like a fireplug and spoke with a pronounced stutter as a boy, was educated in New York public schools and graduated from Abraham Lincoln High School in the Brighton Beach section of Brooklyn. After serving two years as an assistant purser in the merchant marine, he enrolled in Brooklyn College, where he dabbled in socialist politics before graduating with a major in psychology in 1950. His interest in psychology was sparked in 1947 when Willard Beecher, a New York therapist and a disciple of the Austrian psychologist Alfred Adler, successfully treated his childhood stammer.

In late 1954 after a nine-month stint working as a youth counselor for B'nai B'rith in Philadelphia, Cornfeld signed on to sell mutual funds for Investors Planning Corporation, a small sales organization set up to capitalize on the reviving interest in mutual funds in the United States. While working there he displayed the personal charisma and extravagant living habits that would characterize the rest of his career.

In the fall of 1955 Cornfeld sailed for France to explore mutual fund sales opportunities in Paris. His prospects included military personnel and corporate executives who were in the vanguard of American industry's postwar invasion of global markets. He soon gathered a motley team of bright but bohemian salespeople, using the recruiting gambit that became his trademark: "Do you sincerely want to be rich?" He spoke in an evangelical manner at sales meetings and whispered intensely in private conversations, making him highly successful in motivating his sales force.

The riches Cornfeld promised were generated by the controversial product he sold: contractual plans in which customers paid for their fund purchases in monthly installments over a long span of time, paying high sales commissions in the early years of fund ownership.

In 1958 Cornfeld moved his sales organization, which he called Investors Overseas Services (IOS), from Paris to Geneva. Two years later he registered IOS in Panama, codifying a financial empire that would ultimately encompass a secretive Swiss bank, an insurance company, scattered real estate interests, and a stable of offshore investment funds, all operating beyond the reach of any single country's securities laws.

By the early 1960s, with IOS channeling hundreds of millions of dollars into American mutual funds, Cornfeld had enough financial power to attract the attention of the U.S. Securities and Exchange Commission, which soon accused him of violating American mutual fund laws. In 1967 he settled the commission's complaint out of court by agreeing to shed his American operations and limit the size of his investments in American mutual funds.

By then Cornfeld's colorful flaunting of the fund in-

Bernie Cornfeld, 1974. © Hulton-Deutsch Collection/Corbis

dustry's gray-flannel traditions had made him a national celebrity. Photographs from that era show him striding across the lobby of a New York City hotel, leading his pet ocelot on a leash; playing backgammon on his luxurious personal jet; and relaxing at the Château de Pelly, his thirteenth-century castle near Geneva, with a bevy of attractive young women. In March 1968 *Fortune* magazine reported that Cornfeld had once appeared to address an assembly of dark-suited Swiss bankers wearing a sport jacket and escorting a beautiful woman on his arm. "It was a very good sport jacket. . . . And it was also, as always, a very good blond. But neither helped the image," the magazine observed.

By the end of the decade IOS was managing roughly $2.5 billion of its customers' money and Cornfeld's private fortune was reported to be as much as $100 million. But as Cornfeld paraded his apparent wealth, IOS was succumbing to weak management and careless, if not outright illegal, financial practices. In May 1970, with the company's affairs in disarray and its stock price plunging, Cornfeld's board of directors forced him out. Within the year the company was in the hands of the American financier Robert Vesco, who later became a fugitive after being accused of looting what remained of the IOS empire.

In 1973 Cornfeld was accused by Swiss prosecutors of defrauding employees who purchased IOS stock; he spent eleven months in a Swiss jail before being freed on bond. He was acquitted of the charges in 1979. Cornfeld's remaining years were marked by tax wrangles in the United States, various international business speculations, and an embarrassing conviction in California in 1976 for using an electronic device to make long-distance telephone calls without paying for them.

In 1978 Cornfeld married Lorraine Dillon in California; they were divorced in 1986 but amicably shared the upbringing of their daughter. Cornfeld also supported a second child, a daughter born out of wedlock. Additionally, he adopted a child, the daughter of a close friend.

By the 1990s Cornfeld had moved his base of operations to London. In mid-1994 he suffered a severe stroke while visiting in Tel Aviv; he was later transferred to a London hospital, where he remained until his death from pneumonia nearly eight months later. He is buried at the Edgewarebury Cemetery, outside London.

Cornfeld's headline-making reputation as a jet-setter as well as his regulatory troubles obscured his genuine talent for financial innovation. He created the first rough prototype of a mutual fund with check-writing privileges, years before American funds offered that service. He developed one of the first "country funds," an Israel fund that he opened in 1962. But perhaps his best-known innovation was the Fund of Funds, an offshore fund created in 1962, whose sole purpose was to invest in the shares of American mutual funds, a concept that was widely copied in the fund industry.

★

Cornfeld's personal papers, according to his former wife, remained in the Château de Pelly when it was sold after his death and were disposed of by the new owners. An account of Cornfeld's business life can be found in *The Bernie Cornfeld Story* (1970), by

Bert Cantor. A less sympathetic but more complete account is provided in *Do You Sincerely Want to Be Rich?: The Full Story of Bernard Cornfeld and IOS, an International Swindle* (1971), by Charles Raw, Bruce Page, and Godfrey Hodgson. More limited information can be found in *The '70s Crash and How to Survive It* (1970), by John F. Lawrence and Paul E. Steiger; *The Go-Go Years* (1973), by John Brooks; and *Fidelity's World: The Secret Life and Public Power of the Mutual Fund Giant* (1995), by Diana B. Henriques. Obituaries are in the (London) *Independent* (1 Mar. 1995), (London) *Daily Telegraph, Guardian* (Manchester, England), *New York Times,* and London *Times* (all 2 March 1995). A brief commentary by Cornfeld is in *The Way It Was: An Oral History of Finance 1967–1987* (1988), by the editors of *Institutional Investor.*

DIANA B. HENRIQUES

CORRIGAN, Douglas ("Wrong-Way Corrigan") (*b.* 22 January 1907 in Galveston, Texas; *d.* 9 December 1995 in Orange, California), aviator famous for his 1938 solo flight from New York to Ireland, instead of California, his intended destination.

Corrigan was the eldest son of railroad civil engineer Clyde Sinclair Corrigan, a native of Oakland, California, and Evelyn Groce Nelson, a schoolteacher from Tarentum, Pennsylvania. In 1913 the family moved to San Antonio, Texas, and in 1919 after his parents divorced, Corrigan relocated with his mother to Los Angeles. Up until then Corrigan's first name had been Clyde, but to avoid any reminders of her ex-husband, Evelyn renamed her son Douglas, after the popular movie star Douglas Fairbanks. Corrigan's formal education ended with the ninth grade, which he completed at Public School 69 in New York City, where he lived briefly with his father when his mother was ill with cancer. Douglas Corrigan returned to Los Angeles in June 1921 shortly before his mother died.

Corrigan worked odd jobs on home construction sites around Los Angeles until one day in October 1925, when he stopped at a makeshift airfield near Mesa Drive and Exposition Boulevard. He was curious enough to climb aboard a converted World War I biplane for a ten-minute flight. He was immediately hooked on aviation. Six months later on 25 March 1926 he flew solo for the first time, "the biggest day in my life," he later recalled. Corrigan moved to San Diego in February 1927 to work at the Ryan Aircraft Factory, where he helped build the airplane Charles Lindbergh flew across the Atlantic on 21 May 1927. In the early 1930s Corrigan "barnstormed" up and down the East Coast, selling airplane rides for a few dollars a person at air shows and fairs.

In 1933 Corrigan purchased a used airplane, the Curtiss Model 50 "Robin," for $325. By 1936, dissatisfied with work in aircraft factories and with "life in general," he decided to attempt a nonstop solo transatlantic flight. He outfitted his Robin with extra fuel tanks and installed a more pow-

Douglas "Wrong-Way" Corrigan, 1938. © MUSEUM OF FLIGHT/CORBIS

erful engine, the Wright model J6–5. The U.S. Department of Commerce, at that time in charge of aviation, would not accept that Corrigan's plane was capable of such a journey and refused to grant him a license for a transatlantic voyage, but in June 1938 it did issue him the license to attempt a cross-country flight. He completed the Los Angeles–New York leg of his trip in twenty-seven hours and fifty minutes on 9 July 1938 and received a license for the return flight to California.

Corrigan recounted his famous return flight in countless newspaper articles and in his 1938 autobiography, *That's My Story*. In the book, he described how he left from Floyd Bennett Field in Brooklyn, New York, at dawn on 17 July 1938. With his forward vision obscured by the extra gasoline tanks and only two boxes of fig cookies and two chocolate bars for food and a quart bottle of water, Corrigan took off in an easterly direction to avoid buildings to the west of the airfield that he might not clear with his gasoline-heavy aircraft. Planning to turn westward, he had to set his course according to a compass mounted on the cockpit floor after he discovered that the compass in his instrument panel was malfunctioning. After two hours he flew over a city that he assumed was Baltimore. Heavy cloud cover and fog obscured his vision for the next twenty-four hours; when the weather cleared, expecting the Rocky Mountains to loom ahead, he saw only water. Looking down at his compass in the floor in the brighter light, he realized that he had misread it and had been heading eastward, over the Atlantic Ocean. The city he had flown over was Boston, not Baltimore. He then noticed "some nice green hills" that he decided must be Ireland. He landed at the first airport he encountered, Baldonnel Field in Dublin, twenty-eight hours and thirteen minutes after leaving Brooklyn. Walking up to an official, Corrigan announced: "My name's Corrigan. I left New York yesterday morning headed for California, but I got mixed up in the clouds and must have flown the wrong way." And as improbable as it was, he stuck to this story for the rest of his life. But in 1988 at an event marking the fiftieth anniversary of the flight, when asked by reporters whether he made an honest navigational error, he repeated his famous statement, "I made a mistake," and then added, "I was never really too honest, you know."

The story of the little second-hand "flying jalopy," with its shy, smiling pilot who was told he could not fly the Atlantic but did anyway greatly appealed to Depression-weary Americans. Upon Corrigan's return to the United States via steamship (as "punishment" his pilot's license was suspended for the exact length of the sea journey), he was feted in New York City with a ticker-tape parade up Broadway (the "Canyon of Heroes"), from Battery Park to City Hall. As Corrigan and his plane, which he had dubbed *Sunshine,* toured the country, they were greeted with laugh-

ter and great affection. Medals, awards, and products named after him, including a watch that ran backward, came in the wake of his famous "wrong-way" flight. He even starred in a 1939 motion picture of his life, *The Flying Irishman.*

Corrigan resumed a private life after his moment of fame. On 17 July 1939, the first anniversary of the flight, Douglas Corrigan married Elizabeth Marvin, a schoolteacher. They had three sons. During World War II Corrigan joined the Army Air Corps Ferry Command where he was a transport and test pilot, and after the war he operated an air freight service. In the 1950s he bought a citrus grove in Santa Ana, California, but the farm failed and he sold most of the property to developers, with the exception of the house and garage where the Robin was stored. He was devastated by the deaths of his wife on 9 May 1966 and later his son in the crash of a light plane on Catalina Island in 1972.

In 1988 Corrigan briefly returned to the limelight and appeared in ceremonies marking the fiftieth anniversary of his flight. He reassembled the Robin for an air show at Hawthorne, California, but his plan to fly it once again was never realized. Corrigan died of prostate cancer at Saint Joseph's Hospital in Orange. His remains are buried in Fairhaven Memorial Park in Santa Ana, California.

Douglas Corrigan was a uniquely American-style hero. The diffident loner who defies authority to triumph over adversity has always been a popular figure in American folklore. Corrigan never wavered from his story that he had intended to fly to California but made a mistake and wound up in Ireland. Somehow no one ever really believed him, but they loved him all the more for it.

★

Corrigan's autobiography, *That's My Story* (1938), provides a detailed account of his early life and the famous flight. There is relatively little information about his subsequent life except a few newspaper feature articles, notably in the *Los Angeles Times.* These include: Paul Dean, "Return of 'Wrong Way': Fifty Years Later, Douglas Corrigan Talks About His Famous 'Mistake' and, at 81, His Plans to Fly Again," (16 Aug. 1988), and Joseph N. Bell, "Sure, He Flew the Wrong Way, But Everyone Loved It," (10 July 1990). Obituaries are in the *Los Angeles Times* (13 Dec. 1995), *New York Times* (14 Dec. 1995), (London) *Independent* (15 Dec. 1995), and *Washington Post* (18 Dec. 1995).

KENNETH R. COBB

COSELL, Howard (*b.* 25 March 1920 in Winston-Salem, North Carolina; *d.* 23 April 1995 in New York City), radio and television sportscaster best known for his caustic, verbose commentary.

Cosell was born Howard William Cohen, one of two children of Isadore Cohen, an accountant, and Nellie Cohen.

Howard Cosell. ARCHIVE PHOTOS

Before Howard's third birthday Isadore Cohen moved his family to Brooklyn, New York, where Howard attended public schools. Reared in an immigrant Jewish family, Howard strove to succeed. He played varsity basketball and ran track at Alexander Hamilton High School, where he also edited the sports section of the school newspaper. After graduating in 1938, Cosell wanted to become a journalist, but his parents convinced him to study law. By age twenty-one he had earned a B.A. in English literature and an LL.B., both from New York University. As an undergraduate he changed his last name to Cosell, which was closer to the family's original name in Polish.

Cosell eventually returned to his first love, journalism. During World War II he graduated from Officer Candidate School and served in the U.S. Army Transportation Corps at the New York Port of Embarkation. He became an important transport planner and attained the rank of major. In 1944 he married Mary Edith "Emmy" Abrams, the daughter of an industrialist. They had two daughters. Following World War II, Cosell opened a law practice in New York, where his clients included the baseball player Willie Mays and the Little League of New York. In 1953 he signed with the ABC radio network to host a public affairs program on which little leaguers questioned major league baseball stars. Beginning in 1956 he reported on sports for ABC radio and during the succeeding two years hosted *Sports Focus,* a television show that allowed Cosell to explore the relationships among athletics and wider social concerns.

Cosell's reputation as a maverick journalist began with his reporting on boxing. Starting in 1959 he called the action and provided commentary for world championship bouts over ABC radio and television. When the heavyweight champion Cassius Clay, a Black Muslim, changed his name to Muhammad Ali, Cosell respected the decision and never used Ali's "slave" name. The two men forged a close association that abetted their careers. When in 1967 the New York State Boxing Commission stripped Ali of his title for refusing military service on grounds of conscientious objection, Cosell lambasted the move as "imbecilic" and "illegal under the Fifth and Fourteenth Amendments." His stand generated hate mail and some death threats. During the 1968 Olympics in Mexico City, Cosell offended white racists when he sympathetically interviewed Tommie Smith, the gold medal–winning sprinter who raised his clenched fist in a Black Power salute at the victory ceremony. Cosell defended another African American athlete, Curt Flood of the St. Louis Cardinals, when Flood successfully challenged major league baseball's reserve clause, commencing the era of free agency.

In the 1960s Cosell's activities expanded. Between 1961 and 1971 he reported nightly on sports for WABC-TV, ABC's outlet in New York City. During 1962 and 1963 Cosell covered New York Mets baseball games for ABC radio until the Mets management dismissed him, partly because he declined to cheer for the hometown team. Cosell formed his own company, Legend Productions, which released a series of documentaries (1963). *A Look behind the Legend,* narrated by Cosell, examined the life of Babe Ruth and drew praise, as did *Run to Daylight,* the story of the Green Bay Packers football team and their coach Vince Lombardi, whom Cosell admired. A proponent of racial equality, Cosell especially liked *One Hundred Yards to Glory,* which profiled Grambling College, a small, historically black school in Louisiana with a potent football team coached by Eddie Robinson.

Cosell's career skyrocketed in 1970, when ABC inaugurated *Monday Night Football.* In weekly, prime-time telecasts of National Football League (NFL) games, Keith Jackson and later Frank Gifford provided play-by-play coverage, Don Meredith analyzed videotaped replays, and Cosell offered commentary. In tapping Cosell, Roone Arledge, president of ABC Sports, went against the wishes of the NFL commissioner Pete Rozelle, who opposed the inclusion of such an iconoclastic reporter. Nevertheless, during its first season *Monday Night Football* captured a 32 percent share of the television audience, and Arledge credited Cosell's "spice" with enlivening each telecast, "particularly when a game wasn't very good." *Monday Night Football* remained one of the decade's most popular television programs.

During the 1970s Cosell emerged as America's most entertaining and most infuriating sportscaster. His high-pitched Brooklyn twang, staccato delivery, and supercilious vocabulary ("I have lived on the precipice of professional peril every day of my career") inspired both impersonation and derision. Cosell parodied himself during an appearance in Woody Allen's film *Bananas* (1971) and in guest shots on such television comedies as *The Odd Couple, Nanny and the Professor, The Partridge Family,* and *Saturday Night Live.* "Arrogant, pompous, obnoxious, vain, cruel, verbose, a show-off," he wrote, "I have been called all of these. Of course, I am." He labeled the autocratic Avery Brundage, chair of the International Olympic Committee, "William of Orange." According to Cosell, most baseball players seemed "afflicted with tobacco-chewing minds." He chided "carpet-bagging" owners who removed sports franchises from cities with loyal fans and denounced "jockocracy," the promotion of former athletes with little journalistic training to broadcast booths. As early as 1971 Cosell attacked major league baseball owners for failing to hire even one African American manager.

Nevertheless, Cosell tired of sports. After witnessing a brutal bout in 1982, he announced that he would no longer comment on professional boxing for ABC's *Wide World of Sports.* In 1983 Cosell's liberal credentials came under fire when, during a *Monday Night Football* telecast, he referred to Alvin Garrett, a wide receiver for the Washington Redskins, as "that little monkey." Cosell explained that the allusion was to Garrett's diminutive size, not his race, and he never apologized. Dubbing professional football "a stagnant bore," he left *Monday Night Football* following the 1983 season. He had grown weary of press criticism and the gaffes of his coworkers Gifford and Meredith, two former NFL stars whom he disparaged in his book *I Never Played the Game* (1985). In 1984 ABC canceled Cosell's talk show *SportsBeat,* which had drawn poor ratings. Cosell's wife died in 1990. He continued his weekly radio program *Speaking of Sports* until he retired in 1992. Cosell died of a heart embolism in Manhattan three years later.

Cosell lived in Pound Ridge, New York, and in New York City. Known as a prankster, he was given to joshing and flirting in his inimitably grandiloquent style. His hobby was his career; to him, professional sport was "the toy department of life." Cosell was the first sportscaster to achieve celebrity status. Unlike many earlier journalists, he

refused to treat either games or athletes as sacrosanct, and he reminded Americans that sports reflected the values of their society. Yet Cosell's ego overshadowed his ideas. He once asserted that talent had no place in sportscasting, adding: "That's why I don't belong. I lack mediocrity."

★

Cosell's books include *Cosell* (1973), *Like It Is* (1974), and *I Never Played the Game* (1985). An insightful profile is Robert Lipsyte, "He Was One of a Kind in a Booth of His Own," *New York Times* (24 Apr. 1995). For Cosell's role at ABC, see Bert Randolph Sugar, *"The Thrill of Victory": The Inside Story of ABC* (1978). His relationship with Muhammad Ali receives attention in Jeffrey T. Scammon, *Beyond the Ring: The Role of Boxing in American Society* (1988). An obituary is in the *New York Times* (24 Apr. 1995).

DEAN J. KOTLOWSKI

COTTEN, Joseph Cheshire (*b.* 15 May 1905 in Petersburg, Virginia; *d.* 6 February 1994 in Los Angeles, California), stage, radio, and screen actor who worked with the Mercury Theatre and appeared in such films as *Citizen Kane* (1941), *A Portrait of Jennie* (1948), and *The Third Man* (1949).

Cotten, the eldest of three sons born to Joseph Cheshire Cotten, a postal employee, and Sally Willson, a homemaker, grew up in the Tidewater region of Virginia and spent many summers at his uncle's cottage at Virginia

Joseph Cotten. THE KOBAL COLLECTION

Beach. After attending Petersburg High School, where he played center for the football team for three years and acted in drama productions, he moved to Washington, D.C., in 1923. An aunt who resided there encouraged him to sign up for elocution lessons at the Hickman School of Expression with English-born Robert Nugent Hickman. While studying at the school, Cotten supplemented financial assistance from his family by working as a professional football player (at $25 per quarter-game) and as a lifeguard. After receiving a certificate in the summer of 1923, he went to New York City in 1924 to seek acting roles; meanwhile, he worked at various jobs, including selling paint. When he relocated to Miami two years later, his jobs included packaging potato salad for the Tip-Top Salad Company, selling advertisements for the *Miami Herald,* and contributing theatrical reviews about the Miami Civic Theatre.

At the Miami Civic Theatre, Cotten acted in five plays and met his first wife, Lenore Kipp La Mont, and her daughter from her first marriage. On returning to New York, Cotten presented a letter of introduction to David Belasco, who hired him as assistant stage manager and understudy to Lynne Overman in *Dancing Partner* (1930) and then to Melvyn Douglas in *Tonight or Never* (1930). From 1931 to 1932 Cotten acted in numerous productions with Boston's Copley Square Theatre. During the summer of 1932 he worked in summer stock at Richmond, Virginia, and Bar Harbor, Maine. He married La Mont on 18 October 1931.

Cotten made his Broadway debut in a minor role in the short-lived *Absent Father* (1932); subsequent New York performances included Dick Ashley in *Jezebel* (1933) and a policeman in *The Postman Always Rings Twice* (1936). Cotten auditioned for radio, a medium most suitable to his unique voice, which was calm and firm, resonant and mellifluous. During one assignment for CBS Radio's *School of the Air,* Cotten worked with the up-and-coming actor-director genius of radio, stage, and screen, Orson Welles. Welles went on to assign Cotten a lead in the Federal Theatre Project production of *Horse Eats Hat* (1936). When Welles and John Houseman established the Mercury Theatre in 1937, Cotten appeared in most of the productions: Welles's fascinating rendering of William Shakespeare's *Julius Caesar* (1937), as Publius; the period-dress comedy *The Shoemaker's Holiday* (1938), with Vincent Price; and *Danton's Death* (1938), which closed the Mercury Theatre. Cotten also appeared in *Too Much Johnson* (1938), for which Welles shot silent-film footage.

Cotten's first true stage hit was his role as C. K. Dexter Haven in *The Philadelphia Story* (1939–1940), starring Katharine Hepburn and Van Heflin. For that role the six-foot, two-inch, blue-eyed actor darkened his blond curly hair. Before the cast's national tour, however, his agent sent him to Hollywood in 1940. There, Welles arranged with

RKO Pictures for Cotten to star as Jedediah Leland (from a young man through his octogenarian years) with other Mercury Theatre actors in Welles's first and perhaps greatest film as actor and director, *Citizen Kane* (1941).

Cotten's next roles with Welles were Eugene Morgan in *The Magnificent Ambersons* (1942) and Howard Graham in *Journey into Fear* (1942). Before the end of the decade Cotten again appeared with Welles as Holly Martins in Carol Reed's *The Third Man* (1949). Welles remained one of Cotten's closest professional and personal friends, and Cotten took small roles in several of Welles's later films, including *Touch of Evil* (1958) and *Vérités et mensonges (F for Fake,* 1974).

Other motion picture work in the 1940s included *Lydia* (1941), Alfred Hitchcock's *Shadow of a Doubt* (1943), in which Cotten played the murderous Uncle Charlie, the award-winning *Gaslight* (1944), and home-front war films such as *Since You Went Away* (1944) and *I'll Be Seeing You* (1944). In 1942 Cotten signed a seven-year contract with David O. Selznick. From 1943 to 1944 Cotten performed many Sundays on CBS Radio's *Ceiling Zero/Rigdan Amazon-Ceiling Unlimited* program. During September and October 1943 Cotten, appearing as Jo-Jo the Great, joined Welles, Rita Hayworth, and later her replacement Marlene Dietrich, and others in *The Mercury Wonder Show,* a ninety-minute magic show performed for U.S. troops in the Los Angeles area under a huge tent in Hollywood.

The immediate postwar years saw Cotten costarring with Jennifer Jones and Gregory Peck in a Western, *Duel in the Sun* (1946); with Loretta Young and Ethel Barrymore in *The Farmer's Daughter* (1947); and with Jones in William Dieterle's surrealistic romance *A Portrait of Jennie* (1948). For this film, Cotten was recognized as best actor with the Volpi Cup at the Venice Film Festival in 1949.

Cotten acted in more than sixty films through the early 1980s (including Italian, German, and Japanese productions), but those from the 1950s on, though he always gave solid, attractive performances, usually lacked high-quality scripts and rarely became popular successes. Among these later films, *The Steel Trap* (1952), *Niagara* (1953), *Hush . . . Hush, Sweet Charlotte* (1965), *Petulia* (1968), *Tora! Tora! Tora!* (1970), and *A Delicate Balance* (1973) deserve special attention.

Cotten returned to Broadway as Linus Larrabee, Jr., in the hit *Sabrina Fair* (1953) and as Victor Fabian in the moderately successful *Once More with Feeling* (1958) with Arlene Francis.

During the filming in Italy of *The Angel Wore Red* (1960), his wife, who arrived for Christmas, was diagnosed with leukemia and died in Rome on 7 January 1960. Cotten then married the English-born actress Patricia Medina on 20 October 1960. After honeymooning, they returned to Cotten's home, Villa Tramonto, overlooking the ocean in the Pacific Palisades, California. They never had children. Occasionally they appeared together on stage.

Cotten had returned to radio in 1953 as narrator and actor on ABC's *Philco Radio Playhouse* and acted in the Mutual Broadcasting System's *The Private Files of Dr. Matthew Bell*. Within a few years he tried television, which provided him with a wide range of projects over the next decades as performer, host, and narrator. His dramatic television debut was in "The High Green Wall," an episode of *General Electric Theater* (1954). He acted in *State of the Union* (1954) and hosted and narrated CBS's *The Twentieth Century-Fox Hour* during its first season in 1955. He also hosted the dramatic anthology series *On Trial*, which premiered in 1956; the title was changed to *The Joseph Cotten Show* on 1 February 1957, and it ran off and on until September 1959. From the 1950s through the early 1980s Cotten starred in other dramatic anthologies and various specials and made guest appearances on prime-time weekly series; the years 1956–1957 and 1967–1972 were particularly busy for him on television. He also hosted the National Broadcasting Company's weekly half-hour documentary series *Hollywood and the Stars* (1963–1964) and played Dr. Joseph Francis Condon in *The Lindbergh Kidnapping Case* (1976) and General George C. Marshall in *Churchill and the Generals* (1979).

In the early 1970s Cotten and his wife sold Villa Tramonto. While on tour in Phoenix with *The Reluctant Debutante* (1974–1975), Cotten consulted doctors about throat problems. As he battled cancer of the vocal cords, he suffered a heart attack at home on 8 June 1981, followed by a stroke that ultimately required speech therapy. After he had a laryngectomy in April 1989, his entire larynx was eventually removed and a prosthesis inserted. The immediate cause of death was pneumonia. Cotten is buried at Blandford Cemetery in Petersburg.

Whether on radio or screen, Cotten's most distinctive asset was his voice, as he himself admitted. His handsome, gentlemanly appearance was, of course, no hindrance to his portrayals in motion pictures or television. He was one of those many Hollywood actors whose outstanding interpretations of various roles can be so vividly recalled—as in *Citizen Kane, The Magnificent Ambersons, Shadow of a Doubt, Since You Went Away, The Farmer's Daughter, A Portrait of Jennie,* and *The Third Man.*

★

The Joseph Cotten Collection at the University of Southern California, Cinema-Television Library contains photographs and scrapbooks from stage and screen through the 1940s that Cotten donated during his lifetime. Cotten wrote an autobiography, *Vanity Will Get You Somewhere* (1987); his widow, Patricia Medina, also wrote some anecdotes, emphasized her late husband's charitable nature, and detailed the sufferings of his final years with

cancer in *Laid Back in Hollywood: Remembering* (1998); the photographs in both books are excellent. Discussions of Cotten are in Ronald Bowers, "Joseph Cotten," in his *The Selznick Players* (1976), pp. 174–195, excellent with its format of essay, biography, photographs, and filmography; and David Shipman, "Joseph Cotten," in his *The Great Movie Stars: The International Years,* vol. 2 (1995), pp. 111–115. For extensive bibliographies primarily in Hollywood journals, see Mel Schuster, *Motion Picture Performers: A Bibliography of Magazine and Periodical Articles, 1900–1969* (1971), and *Supplement No. 1, 1970–1974* (1976). For a focus on his association with the Mercury Theatre and with Orson Welles, see Bret Wood, *Orson Welles: A Bio-Bibliography* (1990). Obituaries are in the *New York Times* and *Los Angeles Times* (both 7 Feb. 1994), and *Variety* (14 Feb. 1994). Joseph Cotton was interviewed on 28 August 1980 as part of a project on the Mercury Theatre/Theater Union; the interview is available at the Columbia University Oral History Collection, New York City.

MADELINE SAPIENZA

CRAY, Seymour Roger (*b.* 28 September 1925 in Chippewa Falls, Wisconsin; *d.* 5 October 1996 in Colorado Springs, Colorado), major figure and pioneer in the design and engineering of supercomputers, whose technological genius was responsible for a series of innovations in the building of very fast computers.

Cray was one of two children born to Seymour Roger Cray, a civil engineer who worked for an electric power company and as a city manager in northwestern Wisconsin, and Lillian Scholer, the daughter of a Methodist minister and a

Seymour Cray. AP/WIDE WORLD PHOTOS

homemaker. While growing up Cray exhibited a talent and passion for science and mathematics and tinkered extensively with electrical apparatus around his home. After graduating from Chippewa Falls High School in 1943, Cray entered the U.S. Army, spending time in Europe and south Asia during World War II as a radio communications specialist.

After returning from military service Cray entered the University of Minnesota to study engineering, like his father before him. In 1947 he married Verene Voll, the daughter of a Methodist minister. The couple had two daughters and one son and divorced in 1975. Cray completed a B.S. degree in electrical engineering in 1950 and an M.S. degree in applied mathematics in 1951. His seemingly innate talent for both the practical and the applied, nurtured by combined study in both engineering and mathematics, would later serve him well in the field of computer science.

Cray's first job after completing college was in Minneapolis with Engineering Research Associates (ERA), a company formed after World War II to perpetuate the U.S. Navy's cryptography operation. The cold war push to build ever more complex weapons and defense systems—which began after the war and continued without diminution until the early 1990s—was a persistent stimulus to the designing and building of fast computers. The first head of ERA was William Norris, also an electrical engineer, who had worked during the war with the navy's cryptography laboratory.

Soon after Cray began work with ERA in 1951 the company was sold to Remington Rand, and within four years Remington Rand merged with the Sperry Corporation to form Sperry-Rand. Cray's first experience in building marketable computers was with Remington Rand's UNIVAC computers. The culture of this large corporation was not conducive to the innovation that both Norris and Cray thought was necessary to engineer computing machines, so Norris left Sperry-Rand in 1957 to found Control Data Corporation (CDC) in Minneapolis/St. Paul. Cray followed within a few months. Cray, with his rapidly developing command of all aspects of computer design and engineering, quickly became the mastermind of CDC's computers, and the CDC 1604 reached the market in 1960 as the fastest computer in the world. One major innovation in the 1604 was the use of transistors, which had been introduced about ten years earlier by Fairchild Electronics, to replace the vacuum tubes that had been the standard in computers up to that time.

In 1962, because of his desire for independence and freedom from interference, Cray reached an agreement with CDC that allowed him to move his project to Chippewa Falls, about eighty miles from company headquarters. This was to remain his base of operations for more than twenty-

five years. The CDC 6600, now generally recognized as the first supercomputer, was completed and marketed during 1963. The CDC 6600 introduced several innovations, including the use of Freon as a coolant and the use of silicon-based transistors. This computer, the fastest in the world at the time, could carry out 3 million interactions per second. However, to give a perspective on the ephemeral nature of the description "supercomputer," the desktop computer of the late 1990s could perform more than 1 billion interactions per second.

With the success of its CDC 1604, CDC 6600, and CDC 7600, Control Data Corporation quickly became the third largest computer manufacturer in the world (IBM was first, Sperry-Rand second). Supercomputers were required in the advancing fields of high technology and science, and they were especially in demand by U.S. military laboratories. In a relatively short time Cray had led this start-up company to beat far larger and more established companies in the race to make the most advanced computing machines of the time. The CDC 7600, which was marketed in 1969, became a widely used supercomputer during the early 1970s. In 1972 Cray was awarded the Harry Goode Memorial Award for outstanding achievement in the field of information processing.

Cray left CDC the same year, discontented with actions of the company that he perceived to be intervention, to form his own company, Cray Research Corporation (CRC), also in Chippewa Falls. The new company's first computer, the CRAY–1 introduced in 1976, brought CRC success and recognition as the leader in producing supercomputers. One of its notable innovations was the use of vector processing, which replaced the earlier technique of scalar processing and allowed faster simultaneous calculation rather than series operations. Cray Research was the leading producer of fast computers through the late 1970s and early 1980s. Once again Cray's engineering genius had taken another company to the top. In 1980 Cray married his second wife, Geri M. Harrand, and became stepfather to her three children.

The CRAY X–MP, introduced in 1982 and engineered by a team led by Steve Chen, had multiple processors and was a faster version of the CRAY–1. The commercial success of the CRAY X–MP boosted Cray Research during a period when the company was struggling to complete its next project, the CRAY–2. However, Cray believed the CRAY–2 had become too encumbered with the "upgrade" image as an improvement of the CRAY–1. He tended to create everything from a blank page, and this led him to look beyond the CRAY–2 to the CRAY–3, allowing others to complete the CRAY–2. Straying from his normal pattern of using only tested materials and components, Cray attempted to use gallium arsenide, rather than silicon, for the circuits in his next computer. Gallium arsenide was known to permit an increased rate of transfer of electrons at switches and a concomitant reduction in heat generation, compared with silicon. But Cray never succeeded with gallium arsenide and returned to silicon.

In 1989, feeling that fresh surroundings and a new start were needed to sustain his drive to complete the next supercomputers, Cray, along with his wife, moved a branch of Cray Research from Chippewa Falls to Colorado Springs, Colorado. The following year he reached an agreement with Cray Research to partially finance a new company, Cray Computer Corporation, whose immediate goal would be to complete the CRAY–3 project. Although the CRAY–3 supercomputer was completed in the new company, it was not marketable and none were sold. Cray Computer filed for protection under bankruptcy law in 1995.

The supercomputer industry was changing, in no small part because the demand for such machines had lessened with the end of the cold war, an event signaled in late 1989 by the fall of the Berlin Wall. In the early 1990s Cray Computer and Cray Research were the only companies producing supercomputers. The wide availability and low cost of microprocessors also brought revolutionary changes in the use of personal computers (PCs), especially the capacity of PCs for integrated uses through connections with other, large-capacity computers. The industry was thus drawn in new directions.

Even after the failure of Cray Computer Corporation in 1995 Cray still believed there was a market for supercomputers. In 1996 at the age of seventy he began to raise capital to found a new company. But this new venture ended when Cray was seriously injured in an automobile accident in Colorado Springs on 22 September 1996. He died two weeks later. His remains were cremated and scattered in the Colorado mountains at an undisclosed location.

Seymour Cray is recognized as the single most successful designer and builder of supercomputers during the first thirty years of the development of the computer industry. A number of traits contributed to his success, among which was his facility with both the applied and the theoretical. Cray insisted upon personally knowing and working on every detail of a project, and his single-minded dedication and concentration to the tasks at hand led him to resist any interruption. He was frequently in conflict with management in attempting to protect his time and that of his staff. In 1989 Cray declined to accept the National Medal of Technology because it would have required his taking a day or two from his work to go to Washington, D.C., for a ceremony with President George Bush.

Another characteristic conducive to Cray's creativity was his personal belief that innovation must begin with a clean slate and not be encumbered by existing ways of doing things. This penchant for starting anew on every venture,

and for restarting some projects by clearing out everything and starting from ground zero, has been called "The Cray-Way" by Charles J. Murray. Cray's desire to pursue original engineering on every project was in interesting contrast to his aversion to using newly discovered materials or invented components (the gallium arsenide effort being an exception). For instance, he delayed the use of transistors, silicon-based transistors, and integrated circuits until they had been tested for years in other products. Cray is the undisputed major figure in the history of supercomputer architecture and engineering. His technological genius remains the hallmark of the supercomputer era.

★

Cray's professional life, as well as a history of the development of supercomputers, is given by Charles J. Murray in *The Supermen: The Story of Seymour Cray and the Technical Wizards Behind the Supercomputer* (1997). R. Slater, *Portraits in Silicon* (1989), presents additional biographical information. An account of the role of supercomputing and Cray's contributions in the advancement of science and high technology is provided by William J. Kaufmann III and Larry L. Smarr in *Supercomputing and the Transformation of Science* (1993). See also Philip Elmer-Dewitt, "Computer Chip off the Old Block: Genius Seymour Cray and the Company He Founded Split Up," *Time* (29 May 1989); Russell Mitchell, "The Genius," *Business Week* (30 Apr. 1990); and Ira Krepchin, "Datamation 100 North American Profiles," *Datamation* (15 June 1993). Obituaries are in the *New York Times* (6 Oct. 1996) and *Washington Post* (6 and 7 Oct. 1996).

W. HUBERT KEEN

CURTI, Merle Eugene (*b.* 15 September 1897 in Papillion, Nebraska; *d.* 9 March 1996 in Madison, Wisconsin), one of the most influential and prolific of U.S. intellectual and social historians, who passionately espoused liberal causes and social justice as a public intellectual.

Curti was the son of a Swiss American, John Eugene Curti, and a New Englander, Alice Hunt. Moving with his family to Omaha, Nebraska, as a boy, his understanding of how the frontier shaped life was enriched by his exposure to how small cities had been influenced by immigration. After graduating from South High School in 1916, he served briefly during World War I in the Student Army Training Corps. He received his B.A. degree summa cum laude in 1920 from Harvard, where he was influenced by the distinguished historians Frederick Jackson Turner, Samuel Eliot Morison, and Edward Channing. He went on to received his M.A. degree in 1921, also from Harvard. From 1924 to 1925 he studied under the cultural historian Charles Cestre at the Sorbonne as part of a fellowship. He received his Ph.D. from Harvard in 1927.

In 1925 he married the prominent child psychologist,

Merle Curti. STATE HISTORICAL SOCIETY OF WISCONSIN WHi (X3) 506902

pacifist, and socialist Margaret Wooster. She edited many of his written works and influenced his sense that race, ethnicity, and gender had less to do with intelligence and accomplishment than with the socioeconomic environment of peoples. This sharpened his passion for improving the economic and educational circumstances of America's poor through liberal government programs.

Curti taught at Smith College (1925–1937), Columbia University Teachers College (1937–1942), and the University of Wisconsin at Madison (1942–1968). During Curti's long teaching career, he directed more than eighty doctoral dissertations, including those of the distinguished historians Richard Hofstadter, John Higham, and Warren Susman. Curti also lectured frequently in Europe, Japan, Australia, and India. He served as president of the Mississippi Valley Historical Society from 1951 to 1952 and the American Historical Association from 1953 to 1954. Early in his professional career Curti was strongly influenced by the educator John Dewey's instrumentalism, the dominant American philosophy of the interwar years. Although his own interests were wide-ranging and diverse, Curti is loosely grouped with the progressive school of American historiography, which included the like-minded Turner, Carl Becker, and Charles Beard, all of whom were influenced by Dewey's methods and assumptions about truth.

For the progressive interwar historians, history was not regarded as a static subject that through careful empirical enquiry and the compiling of facts could yield objective and absolute Truth. They opposed the nineteenth-century view of the historian, who in pursuing truth could be impartial and disinterested, much as a natural scientist. Progressives challenged the faith that the same historical truths were obtainable regardless of the historian's cultural or temporal environment. Curti and his fellow progressive historians emphasized the historian's problematic and tentative access to truth. From the theories historians adopt to the facts they select and the questions they ask of the data, historical understanding was partial and reflected socioeconomic interests.

If historical understanding was partial and relative to deeply embedded cultural values and interests for the progressives, it nonetheless provided provisional answers to important questions. For Curti and progressives such as Merrill Jensen, William Hesseltine, Fred Shannon, Becker, and Beard, the historian might use historiography to raise useful questions and provide partial answers that could be employed to improve society. Progressives, particularly in the 1930s, saw historians as properly engaged in social, political, and economic issues of the day. Although Curti was dubious that historians alone could build a more equitable society, he felt that historians served to either sustain or undermine extant social arrangements by the questions they raised.

In *Growth of American Thought* (1943), for which he won the Pulitzer Prize in 1944, and much of his other writing, Curti viewed ideas in their economic and social context. In this classic historical survey of the United States, Curti helped establish American intellectual history as a distinct field. Viewing ideas as functional, reflective of the social and economic environment, and pragmatic in effecting real change, the book surveys the social history of leading American ideas and the relations of those ideas to today's intellectual environment. The book remains a standard reference book in American studies and intellectual history.

Curti is also remembered for his several books on antiwar movements in the United States. These sympathetic books included *Bryan and World Peace* (1931), *Peace or War: The American Struggle* (1936), and *The American Peace Crusade* (1929), based on his dissertation. His efforts helped to establish peace studies as a viable subfield of American history.

Curti's other efforts tie ideas to social, economic, and political environments found expression in his classic history of education, *The Social Ideas of American Educators* (1935). His book *The University of Wisconsin: A History* (1949), written with Vernon Carstensen, set a new standard for institutional histories by placing the university's history in a socioeconomic and cultural context. His interest in philanthropy as a force in U.S. intellectual life found expression in *American Philanthropy Abroad: A History* (1963), one of the first studies of its kind. A late effort was his book *Human Nature in American Thought: A History* (1980), which reveals the changing relationship between politics and economics to assumptions about human nature.

Curti was also a leader in applying social science methods to the study of history. Chairing the influential Committee on Historiography of the Social Science Research Council, he was a primary author (with Beard) of the famous "Bulletin 54," *Theory and Practice in Historical Studies* (1946). A paradigmatic methodological work, it called for a wedding of sophisticated social scientific methods with historiography. It boldly argued that history had general social significance, adequate objective validity, and substantial diagnostic and prognostic value. Its varied essays emphasized that the selection of facts reflected social and cultural influences as well as the historian's interests.

In the 1950s, which ushered in a new era of more conservative, consensus historiography, Curti was attacked in some circles for being too liberal and too wedded to the social sciences. The famous Harvard intellectual historian Perry Miller found Curti's style of intellectual history to be shallow and neglectful of the autonomy of ideas themselves. A few others, inside and outside academia, decried his "radical" high school textbook *The Rise of the American Nation*, coauthored with Lewis Paul Todd (1950), and his relativism, denunciation of McCarthyism and loyalty oaths, and sympathy for transformative social justice causes. In 1961 his first wife died.

Curti married Frances B. Becker in 1968, the same year that he retired from teaching. He continued to write books. He died from a stroke at the Methodist Retirement Center and is buried in Madison. He left a legacy of historiographical innovation, a host of devoted former students, and a bold legacy of advocacy for liberal social change. Few historians have had a greater impact on intellectual history and American studies in the twentieth century. His memory is honored by an annual book prize awarded by the Organization of American Historians for the best new book on American intellectual or social history. He is also honored by the annual Curti Lectures and Curti professorship at the University of Wisconsin.

★

Curti's papers are located at the Wisconsin State Historical Society. They are rich in his correspondence, lectures, newspaper and journal articles, manuscripts, and books. The papers are particularly insightful about the changing nature of the historical profession during Curti's lifetime. Although there is no full-length biography of Curti, an assessment and bibliography of his writing can be found in "Merle Curti: An Appraisal and Bibliography of His Writings," *Wisconsin Magazine of History* (winter 1970–1971). For Curti's relationship to the progressive school of history and his positions in historical objectivity, see Peter Novick, *That Noble Dream: The Objectivity Question and the American Historical Profession* (1988); David W. Levy, "Merle Curti's Place in American Scholarship: A Consideration of the Controversy," *Journal of Thought* 6 (1971); and John Higham, "The Schism in American Scholarship," *American Historical Review* 72 (1966). A memorial is Allen F. Davis, "Memorial to Merle E. Curti," *American Studies Association Newsletter* (June 1996). An obituary is in the *New York Times* (17 Mar. 1996).

ALFRED L. CASTLE

D

DABNEY, Virginius (*b*. 8 February 1901 in University [now part of Charlottesville], Virginia; *d*. 28 December 1995 in Richmond, Virginia), newspaperman, historian, and author.

Dabney was the only son and second of three children of Richard Heath Dabney, a historian who for forty-nine years was on the faculty at the University of Virginia, and Lily Heath Davis, a homemaker. Virginius was named for his grandfather, the first male in the family to be named after his native state. He attended the Episcopal High School in Alexandria, graduating at age sixteen, then completed his undergraduate studies at the University of Virginia in 1920. He earned a master's degree there the following year. He taught French at Episcopal High School for a year, then began his newspaper career as a cub reporter at the *Richmond News-Leader* in 1922. He soon began specializing in stories on state politics. During his six years with the *News-Leader,* he regularly contributed pieces on southern regional topics to the *New York Times* and such national periodicals as the *Saturday Evening Post, Saturday Review of Literature, New Republic, The Nation*, and *Harper's*. A vigorous man, standing just over six feet, two inches and weighing 200 pounds, his hobbies were walking and tennis; he called the latter a "most contributing factor in my writing."

On 10 October 1923 Dabney married Douglas Harrison Chelf; they had three children. In 1928 Dabney moved to the *Richmond Times-Dispatch* as an editorial writer, rising to chief editorial writer in 1934 and to editor in 1936. For thirty-three years he had full responsibility for the editorial page. He was also a lecturer at Princeton University in 1940 and at Cambridge University in England in 1954. Dabney was an early supporter of the New Deal but later came to view much of it as "specious and wasteful." Nevertheless, Dabney and the *Richmond Times-Dispatch* endorsed Franklin D. Roosevelt for the presidency four times, albeit with "diminishing enthusiasm each time."

Early on, Dabney himself took moderately progressive positions on national issues as they affected the South, as in his first two books, *Liberalism in the South* (1932) and *Below the Potomac* (1942), a distillation of his Princeton lectures. Dabney argued in 1936 that the political views of most southerners were too much influenced by racial prejudice. Too often, he said, the southern viewpoint was "shaped . . . on the basis of attitudes inherited from our grandfathers." This would have to change, he said, lest the region fall permanently behind other parts of the country. In 1937 he gave his support to the National Association for the Advancement of Colored People (NAACP)-sponsored anti-lynching legislation in Congress, and he continued to press this issue until its final enactment many years later. He consistently urged that reforms be made in the South's racial policies, notably repeal of the poll tax and the desegregation of public transportation. During World War II he urged the defense industry to employ blacks and pay them the same salaries as white workers. In the 1950s he opposed

Virginius Dabney, in front of the church where Patrick Henry demanded liberty or death in 1775. AP/WIDE WORLD PHOTOS

closing the public schools when the state's Democratic Party leadership advocated massive resistance to the Supreme Court's *Brown* vs. *Board of Education of Topeka* decision. In 1938 he urged the Roosevelt administration to provide healthcare for the poor. He also frequently took issue with conservative positions taken by his state's influential senator, Harry Flood Byrd, not only on matters affecting race, but also on a variety of other social and political questions. Dabney spoke out on many domestic and foreign issues, including shorter working hours for women, farm tenancy reform in the South, and Hitler's rise in Germany.

During his thirty-five year tenure as editorial director at the *Richmond Times-Dispatch*, Dabney took a principled stand on a wide range of issues. He was frequently critical of the American presidents who served from Franklin D. Roosevelt to Lyndon B. Johnson and was not afraid to condemn a leader's position on an issue or question his integrity. He considered Senator Joseph R. McCarthy of Wisconsin "a disgrace to American civilization," and he also thought that the Senator's importance had been blown out of proportion. Dabney objected to the close association of John and Robert Kennedy to McCarthy, and did not un-

derstand the adulation given to these men by the American public. He did not trust Johnson, believing him too prone to reverse himself on major issues.

The issue of race was a challenging one for Dabney during his editorship. He felt strongly that the white and black races should "strive to maintain their racial identities and cultural heritages." He contended that immediate enforcement of the Supreme Court's 1954 desegregation decision would be "premature, unwise, and productive of much trouble." Fearing white Virginians' immoderate resistance to interracial contests for political office and other shows of equality, he editorially proposed "slow but certain" steps that could be taken in race relations. In general, however, most of Virginia's political leaders showed little inclination to follow his lead. Dabney urged that Virginia school districts be allowed local option in the matter of school desegregation, but from 1954 to 1959, the state's senior senator, Harry F. Byrd, pressed instead for a policy of "massive resistance." Inasmuch as both the owner and then editor of the *Richmond Times-Dispatch* supported Byrd, Dabney did not attack the prevailing view, though he later wrote that he would have "liked to do so."

In 1948 Dabney was awarded a Pulitzer Prize for his editorial writing. He retired from full-time newspaper work in 1969. Of Dabney's fifteen books, several focused on the history of his state, including *Virginia: The New Dominion* (1971); *Richmond: The Story of a City* (1976); and *Mr. Jefferson's University* (1981), a history of his alma mater. His autobiography, *Across the Years,* appeared in 1978. Dabney's health declined in later years and he died at age ninety-four of natural causes. He is buried at Hollywood Cemetery in Richmond.

★

A number of Dabney's typed and handwritten manuscript articles, papers, correspondences, and other materials are in the Virginius Dabney Papers, Special Collections Department, Alderman Library, University of Virginia, Charlottesville. This same repository holds additional Dabney materials in the papers of Harry Flood Byrd Sr., Sarah-Patton Boyle, and Frederick Nolting Jr. Dabney's autobiography, *Across The Years: Memories of a Virginian* (1978), is a valuable resource, providing many useful details. An obituary is in the *Richmond Times-Dispatch* (29 Dec. 1995).

KEIR B. STERLING

DAHMER, Jeffrey Lionel (*b.* 21 May 1960 in Milwaukee, Wisconsin; *d.* 28 November 1994 near Milwaukee, Wisconsin), serial killer and cannibal convicted of fifteen murders and responsible for seventeen or more. The racial aspects of his killings and the poor performance of the police caused investigations and protests.

Dahmer's father, Lionel Herbert Dahmer, a research chemist with a reputation as hard working, earned a Ph.D. in

Jeffrey Dahmer. AP/WIDE WORLD PHOTOS

chemistry from Iowa State University in 1966. Dahmer's mother, Joyce Annette Flint, exhibited emotional disturbances and odd physical symptoms. A second son, David, was born when Jeffrey was seven. The marriage was troubled, and both pregnancies were difficult physically and emotionally. Lionel Dahmer later wondered if Jeffrey Dahmer's dark future was influenced by the prescription drugs Joyce Dahmer used during these years, and various writers have speculated that Jeffrey felt abandoned when David was born. Until his preteen years Jeffrey Dahmer seemed shy and fearful of new situations but happy, even ebullient when secure with his family. Rumors later circulated that Jeffrey was sexually abused by a neighbor when he was eight, but both Dahmer and his father disputed this.

Dahmer attended Hazel Harvey Elementary School near Akron, Ohio, beginning in 1966. Between the ages of ten and fifteen he withdrew emotionally, and his interests darkened. He collected roadkill and dissolved the animals in acid. Even his posture changed, becoming stiff, and his nervous shyness was uncontrollable. He also discovered alcohol, and by the time of his graduation from Revere High School in Bath, Ohio, in 1978, he was a full-fledged alcoholic. Emboldened by drink, he was a class clown. His classmates referred to any outrageous prank as "doing a Dahmer."

In 1978, after years of arguments and unhappiness, Dahmer's parents divorced bitterly. Because Dahmer was legally an adult, both the court and the parents showed great concern for David but little for Jeffrey. In fact Joyce Dahmer and David Dahmer moved out, leaving the eighteen-year-old Jeffrey Dahmer alone. His father, with a new partner, Shari Jordan, moved back in but spent most of the next months locating David. Jeffrey's alcoholism caused tensions with his father and Shari. He attended Ohio State University for one quarter in the fall of 1978, then dropped out. Forced to support himself, he joined the U.S. Army in January 1979.

Dahmer served three years in the army, including time in Baumholder, Germany, before his discharge for excessive drinking. Considered brilliant, he was an adequate soldier but spent much time quietly drunk in the barracks listening to heavy metal music. Tall, blond, and clean-cut, Dahmer was good-looking except for his blank stare. Although he could be violent, he was usually passive.

Unbeknownst to everyone, Dahmer had already killed his first victim on 18 June 1978, soon after his graduation from high school and his parents' divorce. The crime was clearly sexual. Dahmer picked up a hitchhiking fellow teenager, took him home, had sex with him, and murdered him. Dahmer reported sexual fantasies at age fourteen, when he realized he was homosexual. He also explored scenarios of power, control, and violence. He killed the hitchhiker for wanting to leave.

When questioned about unsolved homicides, Dahmer insisted he killed no one while in the army or while he drifted in south Florida following his discharge from military service. The murders began again, however, after he moved in with his paternal grandmother, Catherine Dahmer, at 2357 South Fifty-seventh Street in West Allis, Wisconsin, in 1982. Dahmer was arrested for indecent exposure at the Wisconsin State Fair in 1982 and for exposing himself to two small boys in 1986, later insisting he simply had been urinating. Some gay bathhouses in Milwaukee barred Dahmer for drugging other patrons. In 1985 Dahmer took a night-shift job mixing ingredients at the Ambrosia Chocolate Company in Milwaukee.

Dahmer later explained that he could not stand to be abandoned, so he killed to keep his pickup partners with him. He often saved their cleaned skulls as souvenirs and even cut off chunks of their flesh to eat. Wanting to make zombies who would be living sex toys incapable of independent thought, he conducted gruesome experiments, injecting acid into his victims' brains. This killed some, and others he stabbed or strangled. He photographed the men before and after death.

While living with his grandmother, Dahmer killed three men. His grandmother complained of odors, which Dahmer attributed to chemical experiments. In 1988 he rented his own apartment in Milwaukee, and in 1990 he moved to 213 Oxford Apartments, 924 North Twenty-fifth Street.

Convicted of sexually assaulting minors in August 1988 and again in January 1989, Dahmer was only sentenced to work release, not to prison. In vain, Dahmer's father pleaded for help, including the alcoholism treatment promised as part of parole. Dahmer killed once in 1989, but then the murders gained momentum. He committed four in 1990 and eight in 1991, including two murders within three days after he lost his job. Those murders may also have been triggered by a phone call in March 1991 from Dahmer's mother, who had been absent for five years. On 26 May 1991 a fourteen-year-old Laotian boy escaped Dahmer's apartment, but incredibly the police returned the frightened child to Dahmer, who told the officers they were quarreling lovers. The police did not investigate, despite the apartment's odors. Dahmer killed the boy, then performed oral sex on his corpse.

Finally, on 22 July 1991 a victim escaped Dahmer and convinced police to investigate. Officers carried out body parts, a heavily locked refrigerator containing the head of a previous victim, and vats of acid as a numbed public and the media watched.

Dahmer found many of his victims, all in their teens or twenties, in gay bars or public places such as malls. After inviting them home for a drink, or promising pay for nude photo modeling, he drugged them. The murderer's confessions led to his conviction, and he was sentenced by a jury to fifteen consecutive life sentences with no parole eligibility for 936 years. While serving his sentence at the Columbia Correctional Institution near Milwaukee, Dahmer was killed on 28 November 1994 by Christopher Scarver, a psychotic fellow inmate. In a macabre aftermath reminiscent of his upbringing, his parents legally fought over Dahmer's cremated remains and whether their son's brain, preserved after autopsy, should be studied or destroyed. The brain was cremated. In a legal decision evocative of Solomon, Dahmer's ashes were divided, half going to each parent.

Dahmer's legacy is dual: horror at the outer reaches of human consciousness and behavior and shock at the social and political flaws his story illuminates. Because many victims were nonwhite and the police had returned the Laotian boy to Dahmer and made crude jokes afterward, protesters accused Milwaukee officials of racial discrimination and homophobia. Three officers responsible for the return were suspended without pay, and the police department was investigated. Nevertheless, the public outcry continued. Commentators also sadly noted how many opportunities to stop Dahmer the police and the justice system had wasted. More basic is a gruesome fascination with the sexual nature of the crimes, the cannibalism, and the macabre motive of zombie making. Starting his murders so young, Dahmer seems both pitiful and peculiarly repugnant.

★

Books about Dahmer include Edward Baumann, *Step into My Parlor: The Chilling Story of Serial Killer Jeffrey Dahmer* (1991); Richard Tithecott and James Kincaid, *Of Men and Monsters: Jeffrey Dahmer and the Construction of the Serial Killer* (1997); Don Davis, *The Milwaukee Murders* (1997); and Robert J. Dvorchak and Lisa Holewa, *Milwaukee Massacre* (1991). Lionel Dahmer, *A Father's Story* (1994), provides insight colored by a father's sense of responsibility. Moira Martingale, *Cannibal Killers* (1994), contains a detailed chapter on Dahmer. Robert K. Ressler and Tom Shachtman, *I Have Lived in the Monster* (1997), includes a lengthy interview with Dahmer.

BERNADETTE LYNN BOSKY

DANDRIDGE, Raymond Emmett ("Squatty") (*b.* 31 August 1913 in Richmond, Virginia; *d.* 12 February 1994 in Palm Bay, Florida), infielder in the Negro baseball leagues and Latin American leagues who was elected to the National Baseball Hall of Fame in 1987 and to the Mexican Baseball Hall of Fame in 1989.

Dandridge was one of three children born to Archie Dandridge, a semiprofessional pitcher who also worked in a cigarette and textile manufacturing company, and Alberta Thompson. Dandridge attended George Mason School in Richmond until he was ten years old, when he and his two sisters went to live with their mother in Buffalo, New York. There Dandridge attended Public School 28 and played all

Ray "Squatty" Dandridge. AP/WIDE WORLD PHOTOS

sports, including softball and baseball. He dropped out of school in the ninth grade but continued to attend vocational classes part-time at Elm High School for four years while playing softball for a local team. Soon after dropping out of high school, Dandridge began to play softball for the Jacobson and Pharmacy team.

At age eighteen the five-foot, seven-inch Dandridge, who was easily recognizable because of the bowlegged gait that earned him the nickname "Squatty," moved back to his father's home. In Richmond he played semiprofessional baseball for the All-Stars, the Violets, and the Paramounts. Dandridge played against other players, like Buck Leonard and Dave Barnhill, who also had distinguished careers in the Negro Leagues.

In 1933 the Detroit Stars came to Richmond to play an exhibition game against the Paramounts. The right-handed Dandridge impressed the Stars manager, who offered him a position on the team. However, the young baseball player was reluctant to accept the position until his father convinced him to do so. He received $60 a month plus a food allowance of $2 a day.

In his first season Dandridge experienced moderate success on the field. But the Stars organization went bankrupt, and Dandridge returned to Richmond. In the 1934 season he joined the Newark Dodgers. With that team he hit .333 from the right side of the plate and for the first time played third base, the infield position for which he became best known. Recognized on the field by his pillow-sized third base glove, he earned a place in the Negro Leagues All-Star East-West Game.

After his successful 1935 season Dandridge joined a team that barnstormed the East Coast. Including players like Satchel Paige and Josh Gibson, this team played against a team headlined by Dizzy Dean and his brother Paul Dean. During the off-season Dandridge for the first time traveled with a group of Negro Leagues all-star players to Latin America to play on a team that called itself the Brooklyn Eagles in the Puerto Rican winter league.

From 1936 to 1938 Dandridge played for the Newark Eagles during the regular season and returned to Latin America to play in the winter season. In 1936 he played in thirty-one games and finished the season with a .301 batting average. For the 1937 season Dandridge played in twenty-five games and compiled a .354 batting average. Also in 1937 he married Florence Copper on 1 October. The couple had three children.

Dandridge's 1938 stint with the Eagles was brief, and he accepted an offer to play baseball in Caracas, Venezuela, for $350 a month. He stayed for two years and in 1939 led the Caracas team to a baseball title. He also played on the Mexican team in Veracruz and on the Cuban team in Cienfuegos during that year.

In 1940 the Mexican millionaire Jorge Pasquel recruited Dandridge to play for the Mexican league and paid him a $10,000 bonus. Dandridge used the bonus to purchase the home his family had rented in Newark, New Jersey. In 1942 he returned to the Eagles for a partial season, appearing in only twenty-seven games, and he remained in Mexico throughout the 1943 season. In 1944 Dandridge decided to return to the United States, and once again he spent a brief time with the Newark Eagles, playing in twenty-eight games. He finished the season with a batting average of .320 and again earned a place on the Negro Leagues all-star team. In 1945, Dandridge's last year with the Newark Eagles, he made twenty-six appearances and completed the season with a .313 average.

Dandridge asked for a raise after the 1945 season, and the owner of the Eagles refused, not the first time Dandridge's plea for a raise was turned down. Returning to the Mexican league, he served as a player-coach for the Mexico City Reds until 1948. He hit safely in thirty-two consecutive games and set a new Mexican league record. That year he returned to the United States to play briefly for the New York Cubans. In 1949 Dandridge entered the regular minor leagues, where he played four seasons with Minneapolis in the American Association and one year in the Pacific Coast League. In 1950, when Dandridge was thirty-seven years old, he hit .311 with eleven home runs and eighty runs batted in, which earned him the most valuable player award for the American Association. He spent the 1951 and 1952 seasons with Sacramento and Oakland in the Pacific Coast League. In Oakland he injured his arm in a collision with a catcher while both were chasing a foul ball and had to sit out the 1953 season. He joined a club in Bismarck, North Dakota, for the following two seasons and served as a player-manager. Dandridge retired following the 1955 season knowing he would never play in the major leagues.

In the 1950s and 1960s Dandridge lived in Newark, where he managed Dave's Long Bar and two other establishments before serving as director of the John F. Kennedy Recreation Center in Newark for eight years. On 10 July 1966 he married Henrietta Newman. The Newark City Council on 14 August 1980 honored Dandridge with a resolution thanking him for his work with the city's children. Five years later a ball diamond in Newark's Westside Park was named the Raymond E. Dandridge, Sr., Baseball Field. In 1996 he was posthumously elected to the New Jersey Sports Hall of Fame.

In 1984 Dandridge and his wife retired to Palm Bay, Florida. On 3 March 1987 he received the news that he was selected for induction to the National Baseball Hall of Fame. Two years later, in 1989, he was elected to the Mexican Baseball Hall of Fame. Dandridge died of prostate cancer and is buried in Fountainhead Memorial Park in Palm Bay.

Dandridge has been compared to the third basemen

Brooks Robinson and William Julius "Judy" Johnson, Robinson's counterpart in the Negro Leagues. Dandridge played in the Negro Leagues at a time when baseball was a segregated sport, therefore most experts never saw his on-field excellence. Unfortunately, when baseball was integrated, Dandridge's age had become a factor. While he excelled in the integrated minor leagues, he never made it to the integrated major leagues. Baseball's color line, which compensated white players more than black players, drove players like Dandridge from the Negro Leagues to Latin America, where the pay was better and racism was less prevalent. Dandridge's memberships in two baseball halls of fame honor his achievements and his contributions to the sport in both North America and Latin America.

★

A biographical file at the National Baseball Hall of Fame in Cooperstown, New York, contains Dandridge's personal information sheet, a record of his playing experiences and the teams he played for. *The Baseball Encyclopedia* (1996) lists the Negro Leagues records of Dandridge and other players. James A. Riley, *Dandy, Day, and the Devil* (1987), and John B. Holway, *Blackball Stars: Negro League Pioneers* (1988), each devotes an entire chapter to Dandridge's Negro Leagues and Latin American playing careers. An obituary is in the *New York Times* (13 Feb. 1994).

JON E. TAYLOR

DAY, Leon (*b.* 30 October 1916 in Alexandria, Virginia; *d.* 13 March 1995 in Baltimore, Maryland), baseball pitcher in the Negro Leagues who is regarded by some as the best all-around player and was elected to the National Baseball Hall of Fame in 1995.

Day was one of two children born to Ellis Day, a glass factory worker, and Hattie Lee. Shortly after Leon's birth, the family moved to Mount Winans, Maryland, where Day grew up watching the Black Sox of the Negro Leagues play. At the age of twelve he played sandlot baseball for the Mount Winans Athletic Club. Then he joined a semiprofessional team, the Silver Moons, playing second base and pitching.

After one year of high school in Mount Winans, the five-foot, nine-inch, 175-pound Day dropped out in 1931 to play baseball. In 1934 one of Day's teammates on the Silver Moons told the Black Sox manager, Rap Dixon, about him. After seeing Day play, Dixon immediately offered him $50 a month to play for the team. Day readily accepted. He distinguished himself on the mound by establishing a right-handed, no-windup delivery to the plate, and he became known for his fastball. Famed for his quiet demeanor, he was called "the gentleman of the box" by his teammates. When he was not called on to pitch, he sometimes played either second base or a position in the outfield. However,

Leon Day. NATIONAL BASEBALL HALL OF FAME LIBRARY, COOPERSTOWN, N.Y.

the Black Sox failed to pay him the agreed-upon salary, and Day joined the Brooklyn Eagles in New York for the 1935 season. With the Eagles he received the first of seven invitations to play in the Negro Leagues All-Star East-West Game.

At the end of the 1935 season Day, like many other Negro Leagues players, traveled to Puerto Rico to play winter ball. He hit .307 from the right side of the plate. In 1936 Day returned to the Eagles, which during the off-season had left Brooklyn for New Jersey to become the Newark Eagles. Day continued to play for the Eagles until he injured his arm playing in the winter league in Cuba and had to miss the 1938 season. He returned to the Eagles in 1939 and was selected again to play in the all-star game. On 17 July 1939 Day married Helen Elizabeth Johnson. They had one daughter. Shortly after her birth in 1952, the couple separated, but their divorce was not finalized until the early 1970s.

In 1940 Day and his Newark Eagles teammate Ray Dandridge played in the Mexican league, but Day returned for the 1941, 1942, and 1943 seasons with the Eagles. Day finished the 1941 season with a .331 batting average, and in 1942 he set a Negro Leagues record of eighteen strikeouts in one game. He was elected to play in the 1942 all-star game and pitched against Satchel Paige, defeating Paige 5 to 2. At the end of the season Day was picked up by the Homestead Grays to pitch against the Kansas City Monarchs in the World Series. Day faced Paige once again and won 4 to 1. Day struck out twelve batters and surrendered only one walk and five hits in the game. The owners of the Monarchs protested the Grays' use of Day's pitching arm. The victory was disallowed, and Day was sent home.

Midway through the 1943 season Day was drafted into the U.S. Army. He served in the segregated 818th Amphibious Battalion that landed in Normandy, six days after D Day. At the conclusion of the war, Day was a pitcher with his army unit baseball team, which defeated General George Patton's Third Army team for the European theater of operations baseball championship. The two teams played in Nürnberg before a crowd of more than 100,000. Day's unit then played the Mediterranean theater champs and soundly defeated them also.

Returning to the United States in 1946, Day picked up the ball for the Newark Eagles and immediately hurled a no-hitter against the Philadelphia Stars. He played in twenty-two games and batted an impressive .385. Unfortunately, Day injured his arm again at the end of the season. Nevertheless, the Eagles defeated the Kansas City Monarchs for the Negro Leagues championship that year. Dandridge convinced him to return to Mexico, and Day spent the 1947 and 1948 seasons playing in the Mexican baseball league for the Mexico City Reds.

Day returned to the United States in 1949 and joined the Baltimore Elite Giants, who won the pennant that year. Day played in fifty-seven games, the most of any season of his career, and finished the season with a respectable .271 batting average. He declined to play for the team a second year and signed with the Winnipeg Buffalos in the Canadian league. The following year he pitched for Toronto in the International League, and in 1952 he played for Scranton of the Eastern League, a farm team of the Boston Red Sox. He batted .314 and compiled a thirteen-to-nine pitching record for 1952. In 1953 Day returned to Canada to play for the Edmonton Eskimos in the AAA Western International League that season and the next. He finished his career with Brandon of the same Canadian league in the 1955 season.

After he retired, Day settled in Newark and managed a bar called Hodes. In 1970 he moved to Baltimore, where he took a position as a security guard with a transfer company. He retired from that position in 1979 and remained

in Baltimore the rest of his life. In November 1980 he married Geraldine Ingram.

In 1993 Day was inducted into the Puerto Rican Professional Baseball Hall of Fame. On 30 July 1995 Day learned of his election to the National Baseball Hall of Fame. Unfortunately, before his induction ceremony, he died at St. Agnes Hospital in Baltimore from complications associated with heart disease and diabetes. Day is buried in Arbutus Memorial Park in Baltimore. Posthumously, in 1998, he was elected to the New Jersey Sports Hall of Fame.

Day was one of the Negro Leagues' greatest pitchers. Some have compared his abilities to Paige, while others have argued that Day's talent surpassed those of Paige. Day's performance on the field may be debated, but the impact of segregation on and off the field during the era in which he played is not. The color line in baseball prevented Day from showcasing his pitching talent before a wider audience. Later, when baseball was integrated, his age prevented Day from moving on to the major leagues. Day's induction into the Baseball Hall of Fame validated his contributions not only to Negro Leagues baseball but to the entire sport.

★

A file of biographical clippings is in the Baseball Hall of Fame in Cooperstown, New York. *The Baseball Encyclopedia* (1996) has a section on Negro Leagues players that lists Day's baseball statistics by year. James A. Riley, *Dandy, Day, and the Devil* (1987), and John B. Holway, *Blackball Stars: Negro League Pioneers* (1988), each devote an entire chapter to Day's baseball career. Frazier "Slow" Robinson, Day's teammate on the Baltimore Elite Giants, discussed Day's performance as a player in *Catching Dreams* (1999). The *Baltimore Sun* (24 Sept. 1992) features an article about Day's experiences in the Negro Leagues. Articles regarding his death and his induction into the Baseball Hall of Fame are in the *Baltimore Evening Sun* (14 Mar. 1995) and the *New York Times* (14 Mar. 1995). In addition to the above materials, the present article is based on the author's interview with Day's daughter, Barbara Jean Hart.

Jon E. Taylor

DeBARTOLO, Edward John, Sr. (*b.* 17 May 1919 in Youngstown, Ohio; *d.* 19 December 1994 in Youngstown, Ohio), pioneer in the shopping-mall industry and one of the most influential shapers of American retail development in the second half of the twentieth century.

DeBartolo's father, Anthony Paonessa, an Italian immigrant, died the year DeBartolo was born. His widowed mother, the former Rose Villani, later married Michael DeBartolo, who had immigrated to the United States from Bari, Italy, at the age of twenty-three. His stepfather was a mason and general contractor and had a construction com-

Edward DeBartolo, 1985. AP/WIDE WORLD PHOTOS

pany in Youngstown, where DeBartolo worked from an early age. While in high school DeBartolo took his stepfather's last name as a tribute. After graduating from South High School in 1927, DeBartolo drove a truck and worked at construction sites, but his mother insisted he go to college, so in 1928 he entered the University of Notre Dame. Even as a young man, DeBartolo displayed the work ethic that was to frame his life. His energy would not be confined to a normal college schedule, so while pursuing a major in civil engineering, DeBartolo worked at various Indiana construction sites during evenings and weekends. In the summers he returned home to Youngstown to write contracting bids for his stepfather's company.

After DeBartolo graduated from Notre Dame in 1932 with a degree in civil engineering, he spent the next five years working for the family construction company. In 1937 he set out on his own, building a series of innovative single-family residences in the Youngstown area. In 1941 he enlisted in the U.S. Army, earning the rank of second lieutenant in the Army Corp of Engineers. DeBartolo married Marie Patricia Montani on 18 December 1943. They had two children, Edward J. DeBartolo, Jr., who later served as president and chief administration officer of the DeBartolo Corporation, and Marie D. (DeBartolo) York, who was executive vice president of personnel and public relations. Following a tour of duty in Korea during World War II, he went back to Youngstown and founded the Edward J. DeBartolo Corporation in Boardman, Ohio, a suburb of Youngstown.

DeBartolo quickly recognized that the postwar population shift to the suburbs was a business opportunity. While William and Alfred Levitt and others were constructing subdivisions for the burgeoning suburban population, DeBartolo was busy building strip plazas and malls where they would go to shop. "Stay out in the country," was his motto, "that's the new downtown."

In 1949 the Edward J. DeBartolo Corporation built its first shopping strip in the Youngstown area, the Belmont Avenue Shopping Plaza. In 1950 the company constructed the Boardman Plaza, a retail strip center eight miles from the company's main office. According to his brother-in-law Frank Mastriana, DeBartolo purchased the property at a sheriff's sale: "he . . . bought that corner for $75,000, and he didn't have a dime. Then he went to the banks and said, 'Lend me money, I just bought that corner.' I guess they admired his guts." Over the next twenty-five years banks became enamored with DeBartolo's drive and ingenuity, financing the construction of numerous retail centers, including the construction of what was then the world's largest mall at Richmond Park, near Cleveland in 1976.

In 1997, having already acquired the Thistledown racetrack in Cleveland (1959), the DeBartolo family purchased the San Francisco 49ers football team. The DeBartolos were among the nation's largest single investors in professional sports teams and businesses. Eventually their holdings included hockey and soccer teams as well as two more racetracks, Louisiana Downs in Bossier City, Louisiana, and Remington Park in Oklahoma City, Oklahoma. The profitability of sports businesses made them attractive investments, but the political side of these enterprises, particularly the racetracks, involved DeBartolo in some controversial business practices. In Oklahoma City, for instance, the DeBartolo Corporation consented to build a racetrack only after the state legislature passed a law effectively prohibiting the construction of new tracks, insulating DeBartolo's Remington Park from competition.

In the late 1980s the real-estate market in the United States declined and so did the value of the DeBartolo Corporation. Banks became increasingly reluctant to lend money for big construction projects, and DeBartolo had to rely more and more on self-financing. This led to cash flow problems that forced the company to sell assets to raise cash, including the Pittsburgh Penguins hockey team. An ill-advised loan to Robert Campeau in 1989 for the doomed takeover of the Federated Department Stores chain saddled the DeBartolo Corporation with a mountain of debt that forced the company to go public in 1994 as the only way to survive. The once-mighty family that had owned and operated businesses became just another real-estate investment trust listed on the New York Stock Exchange.

The downturn in real estate deflated DeBartolo's net worth, but not his generosity. In 1989 he donated $33 million to the University of Notre Dame, the largest gift ever made to that institution at the time. The money was used to build the DeBartolo Quadrangle, a complex of buildings dedicated in 1992. DeBartolo also helped to establish the National Italian Sports Hall of Fame in Chicago and was often honored for his achievements and generosity. In 1984 Youngstown State University presented him with an honorary doctorate and designated the College of Arts and Sciences Building "DeBartolo Hall."

A man of irrepressible energy, DeBartolo for years worked fifteen hours a day on weekdays, ten to twelve hours on Saturdays, and seven hours on Sundays. The shy dynamo could function with only four hours of sleep and would often be at his desk at 5 A.M. when he wasn't visiting a construction site or closing a deal. "I love the action," he said in 1973, when his company was in various stages of thirty-five different projects, "It stopped being work a long time ago." By 1983 when *Forbes* magazine published its first list of richest Americans, the man who loved his work was listed as the forty-third richest man in the nation and the first richest in Ohio.

Despite his enormous wealth and the high-profile stake his family had in the world of professional sports, DeBartolo was a shy, complex, and intensely private person who shunned the limelight. His lifestyle was truly modest and unassuming. He could have lived anywhere and been one of the most famous, if not the most flamboyant, business professionals of his era. Instead he chose to spend most of his working life in his hometown, close to his family,

living in a modest twelve-room ranch-style home. DeBartolo died at home of complications from pneumonia at the age of eighty-five. He is buried in Youngstown.

At its peak, DeBartolo's retail development empire owned or operated nearly one-tenth of all the shopping mall space in America and was one of the world's largest developers of shopping malls, orchestrating the opening of more than 200 centers in twenty states. In October 1994 just weeks before DeBartolo's death, *Forbes* magazine listed him as the ninety-fifth richest American, with a personal fortune of around $850 million.

However, there was a downside to DeBartolo's otherwise stellar career in real estate. DeBartolo was, inadvertently to be sure, one of the architects of the "malling of America" and in his own way a major contributor to suburban sprawl. This was painfully evident in his own hometown, where the success of the DeBartolo Corporation's Boardman Plaza, coupled with the demise of the steel industry in the late 1970s, reduced the once-thriving central business district of Youngstown into a virtual ghost town.

★

Jonathan R. Laing, "King of Malls," *Barrons* (12 June 1989), gives a critical perspective on DeBartolo. S. Lubove, "The Disney Touch," *Forbes* (16 Apr. 1990), is the story of how DeBartolo built and operated Remington Park racetrack in Oklahoma City. Steve Phillips, "Veil Lifted on DeBartolo Real Estate, Mall Empire," Cleveland *Plain Dealer* (23 Nov. 1993), describes the magnitude of DeBartolo's holdings and why his company had to go public. For a profile of DeBartolo when his company was near its peak constructing malls, see Isadore Barmash, "No. 1 Builder of Shopping Malls: A Shy Dynamo," the *New York Times* (29 Apr. 1993). A brief obituary is in the *New York Times* (20 Dec. 1994), and a far more detailed and insightful obituary is in the Youngstown *Vindicator* (19 Dec. 1994).

JAMES CICARELLI

DELANY, Annie Elizabeth ("Bessie") (*b.* 3 September 1891 in Raleigh, North Carolina; *d.* 25 September 1995 in Mount Vernon, New York), dentist, civil rights activist, and coauthor of the best-selling memoir *Having Our Say: The Delany Sisters' First 100 Years* (1993).

Bessie was the third of ten children born to Henry Beard Delany, Sr., a former slave who became the first elected African American bishop of the Episcopal Church, U.S.A., and vice principal of Saint Augustine's College in Raleigh, North Carolina, and Nanny James Logan, a matron at Saint Augustine's. Henry Delany's family were house slaves of a family named Mock, who taught them to read and write. Nanny Logan was born free. Brought up on the Saint Augustine campus, Bessie and her siblings were reared in a household that emphasized education, religion, and ser-

Bessie Delany *(right)*, with her sister Sadie, 1993. © JACQUES CHENET/ GAMMA LIAISON

vice. The Delany children were raised with the motto, "your job is to help someone." Growing up on a college campus provided them a somewhat sheltered experience, but no black children in the Jim Crow South were completely immune from the harsh racial realities of the time. Feisty throughout her life, Bessie lashed into anyone who slighted her on the basis of her race or sex. She considered herself dark-skinned and said, "the darker you are, honey, the harder it is." She knew that dark-skinned blacks often bore the brunt of racial prejudice and developed an aggressive attitude in response. As a five-year-old on the way to Pullen Park in Raleigh, Bessie was introduced to racism by a trolley driver who forced her family to the back of the car. She and her siblings protested loudly, but to no avail. When they arrived at the park and found segregated water fountains, Bessie drank from the one reserved for whites.

Delany received her primary and secondary education at Saint Augustine's in nontraditional classrooms, where her classmates were both children and adults. She graduated from Saint Augustine's in 1911 with the equivalent of a two-year degree and then worked as a teacher in Boardman, North Carolina, earning forty dollars a month. In 1913 she moved to Brunswick, Georgia, and taught at the Saint Athanasius School, with the goal of saving money to

continue her education. Once while traveling to her job, Bessie was almost lynched for telling a drunken white man at the Waycross train station to "shut up" and go away. She escaped, and the incident did not deter her from speaking her mind whenever she felt slighted.

In 1915, traveling with their mother, Delany and her older sister Sarah (Sadie) visited New York City. The sisters decided to move to New York to continue their education. Sadie arrived in 1916 and Bessie joined her in 1917. At a time when many blacks headed North for greater opportunity, nine of the ten Delany children moved to New York City and all ten finished college. Delany had aspirations of becoming a doctor but entered Columbia University's School of Dental and Oral Surgery in 1919, one of eleven women and the only black woman in a class of about 200. She graduated in June 1923. Known as "Dr. Bessie," Delany, only the second licensed black woman dentist in New York State, was renowned for providing free care to the poor at her office on Seventh Avenue and 135th Street. In twenty-seven years of practice she never raised her rates of two dollars for a cleaning and five dollars for a silver filling. When business suffered during the Great Depression, Delany supplemented her income by running a dental clinic near City Hall in Lower Manhattan.

Harlem was a lively place in the 1920s, and Delany rubbed shoulders with such luminaries as the poet James Weldon Johnson, who was a patient of hers, the bandleader Cab Calloway, and the singer Paul Robeson. By the middle of the 1920s Dr. Delany's office was a meeting place for activists in Harlem, including E. Franklin Frazier. She enthusiastically participated in civil rights marches in Manhattan. Around 1925 she had a run-in with the Ku Klux Klan on Long Island, New York, which only furthered her resolve to fight for civil rights. Reflecting upon that incident, she recalled, "All you had to do was say the word 'protest' and I was there!" While her sister Sadie preferred Booker T. Washington's theory of gradual advancement through practical education, Delany was more confrontational and embraced the philosophy of her friend W. E. B. Du Bois. Bessie and Sadie rented their first apartment together in Harlem around 1919 before moving to a Bronx cottage and finally settling into a home they bought in Mount Vernon in 1957. Nanny Logan Delany joined the two sisters in New York in April 1928, following the death of her husband. In 1950 Dr. Delany retired prematurely from her dental practice to care for her ailing mother, who died on 2 June 1956.

In 1991 Amy Hill Hearth, a reporter for the *New York Times,* interviewed Sadie and Bessie, as the two had just celebrated their 102nd and 100th birthdays. Readers immediately fell in love with the Delany sisters, who teamed with the reporter to write *Having Our Say: The Delany Sisters' First 100 Years* (1993), which sold millions of copies and maintained a spot on the *New York Times* paperback best-seller list for seventy-seven weeks. In 1995 their story was turned into a Broadway play that earned three Tony Award nominations. At the ages of 103 and 105, Bessie and Sadie again collaborated with Hearth to produce *The Delany Sisters' Book of Everyday Wisdom* (1995). Bessie died in her sleep in her Mount Vernon home and is buried between her parents in Raleigh's Mount Hope Cemetery. On 18 April 1999 *Having Our Say* aired as a CBS made-for-television movie.

Spurning traditional societal norms, Bessie Delany blazed a fiercely independent trail. Neither Bessie nor her sister Sadie ever married, and over the years the two became inseparable, referring to themselves as "maiden ladies." Prideful and stubborn, Delany was well ahead of her time. She soared to professional heights that few women, let alone African American women, were able to reach. Her continuous battles against racism and sexism might have broken the spirits of someone with less determination. However, this adversity only made Delany work harder and set her sights higher. Fighting through tremendous obstacles, she never lost her "urge to change the world."

★

Henry Beard Delany's personal papers are in the Delany Collection at St. Augustine's College. Bessie Delany's memoir, with Sarah Delany and Amy Hill Hearth, is *Having Our Say: The Delany Sisters' First 100 Years* (1993). Their second book with Hearth is *The Delany Sisters' Book of Everyday Wisdom* (1995). Following Bessie's death, Sadie wrote *On My Own: Life Without Bessie* (1997). "Two 'Maiden Ladies' With Century-Old Stories to Tell," the article that generated public interest in the Delany sisters, is in the *New York Times* (22 Sept. 1991). An obituary is in the *New York Times* (26 Sept. 1995).

DANIEL MASSEY

DICKEY, William Malcolm ("Bill") (*b.* 6 June 1907 in Bastrop, Louisiana; *d.* 12 November 1993 in Little Rock, Arkansas), baseball player, manager, and coach and member of the National Baseball Hall of Fame who bridged the New York Yankees dynasty eras of Babe Ruth through Mickey Mantle.

One of seven children born to John Dickey, a railroad worker, and his wife, Laura, Dickey received his first baseball instruction from his father, a former minor league catcher. As a youngster Dickey dreamed of becoming a major league catcher and in a twenty-year professional career never played any other position. He grew up in Kensett, Arkansas, and was the star high school catcher in nearby Searcy until his family moved to Little Rock when he was sixteen. He spent one year at Little Rock Junior College in 1924 and played semipro baseball for one year before sign-

Bill Dickey, 1942. AP/WIDE WORLD PHOTOS

ing a professional contract in 1925 when he was seventeen. He then spent four seasons as a minor league catcher in Arkansas, Oklahoma, Minnesota, and Buffalo, New York.

The New York Yankees purchased the contract of the six-foot, one-inch, 185-pound catcher, who threw right-handed and batted left, in 1927, and he was promoted to the big league club at the end of the 1928 season. The following year Dickey began a string of catching more than 100 games a season for thirteen consecutive years (1929–1941), a major league record. Although he played in lineups that featured such great hitters as Babe Ruth, Lou Gehrig, and Joe DiMaggio, Dickey was one of the most feared clutch hitters on the team. Dickey had unusually high batting averages for a catcher, beginning with .324 in his rookie year, and he hit over .300 in ten of his first eleven seasons. His .362 batting average in 1936 established a record for catchers. In 1943 he hit .351 in his final season as a starting catcher.

During his first seven seasons he hit seventy-six home runs and was not considered a long-ball threat, but from 1936 to 1939 he blossomed into a slugger, and in that four-year period he drove in more than 100 runs each season and slammed 102 home runs, more than half his career total, while guiding his team to four consecutive world championships. In 1937 his twenty-nine home runs established an American League record for catchers, and he tied a major league record by slugging grand-slam home runs in two consecutive games. Dickey played in eight World Series (1932, 1936–1939, 1941–1943), and his team was victorious seven times. Although the All-Star Game was not created until his fifth year as a starting catcher, he was selected to the American League team eleven times.

As a defensive player Dickey had an uncanny memory for hitters' weaknesses, possessed a strong, accurate throwing arm, and was a masterful handler of all types of pitchers: fireballers, spitballers, and curveballers. In 1931 he set an American League fielding record by not allowing a single passed ball in 125 games. He led the league in putouts six times, fielding average four times, assists three times, and once in double plays. In 1929 he became one of only four American League catchers ever to record three assists in one inning and made a rare catcher's unassisted double play in 1941. The legendary Connie Mack said Dickey was the game's greatest catcher.

Dickey was celebrated for his modesty, dignity, and composure. Although quiet and reserved off the field, he was fiercely competitive once the game started and said, "If you haven't got that competitive fire, you may stay in the big leagues for a few years, but you're not going too far. The competitive spirit means the difference between great and mediocre." Only once did Dickey display explosive anger on the field. During a close game on 4 July 1932, the Washington Senators outfielder Carl Reynolds came barreling with spikes high into Dickey, who was blocking home plate. Dickey picked himself up off the ground and with one punch broke Reynolds's jaw. The American League fined him $1,000 (his salary was only $14,000), and he was suspended for one month. In his first game back he blasted a grand-slam home run and smacked three singles. Later that year, on 5 October 1932, he married Violet Arnold. Their daughter, Lorraine, was born in 1935.

Dickey's even temperament was much like that of his roommate and closest friend with the club, Lou Gehrig. He was the only teammate invited to Gehrig's wedding in 1933 and was the first on the ball club to learn of Gehrig's terminal illness. Dickey was also the only active player to play himself in the 1942 film biography of Gehrig, *Pride of the Yankees,* starring Gary Cooper.

After batting .351 in 1943 and hitting a two-run home run in the fifth game of the 1943 World Series to give the Yankees another world championship, Dickey enlisted in the navy and served during 1944 and 1945. In 1946 he returned to the Yankees and played his final season as a backup catcher. He became the Yankees interim manager that May after Joe McCarthy became ill. Dickey then guided the Yankees to a 57–48 record before resigning in September. He claimed that he did not have the proper temperament for managing a team. In 1949 he returned to the Yankees as a coach under manager Casey Stengel and

was instrumental in turning young Yogi Berra into an outstanding catcher. He coached the club until 1957 and was a Yankees scout in 1959.

In 1954 Dickey was elected to the National Baseball Hall of Fame. Over his career he batted .313 in 1,789 games, stroking 1,969 hits, including 202 home runs while scoring 930 times and driving in 1,209 runs. Dickey was voted the game's greatest living catcher during major league baseball's centenary celebration in 1969. He died in Little Rock and is buried there at Roselawn Cemetery.

Dickey's brilliance as a ballplayer is easily documented by his statistics, but on the most famous and successful baseball team in history he was especially beloved for his team spirit, loyalty, and sportsmanship. In 1939 after Lou Gehrig's illness was made public, Dickey insisted on rooming the entire year with his best friend despite the growing hysteria fueled by ignorant newspaper accounts that claimed Gehrig's rare disease was contagious. When his protégé Yogi Berra hit his thirtieth home run in 1952 to break Dickey's American League record for catchers, Dickey was in the first base coaching box jumping for joy as Berra rounded the bases.

★

An in-depth evaluation of Dickey's career comparing him to Berra is found in *The Bill James Historical Baseball Abstract* (1985); Larry Klein's insightful chapter about Dickey, "Bill Dickey: Baseball's Immortal Catcher," is in *Sports Magazine's All Time All Stars,* edited by Tim Murray (1977); also see Lowell Reidenbaugh, *Cooperstown: Where Baseball's Legends Live Forever* (1983); Christy Walsh, *Baseball's Greatest Lineup* (1952); and Ray Robinson, "Dickey: Calm but Combative," in the *New York Times* (14 Nov. 1993). An obituary is in the *New York Times* (13 Nov. 1993).

MARK A. BLICKLEY

DUKE, Angier Biddle (*b.* 30 November 1915 in New York City; *d.* 29 April 1995 in Southampton, New York), diplomat, public servant, and heir to the American Tobacco Company fortune whose charm, energy, and social skill set a new standard for relations with foreign officials.

Duke was the older son of Angier Buchanan Duke, a wealthy executive of the American Tobacco Company, founded by his grandfather. Duke's mother, Cordelia Drexel Biddle, was a descendant of prominent Philadelphia banking and finance families. Shortly after the birth of their second son, Anthony Drexel Duke, Duke's parents separated. In 1921 they were divorced, and Duke's father died two years later, leaving a fortune in trust to his sons. Their mother and stepfather, T. Markoe Robertson, an architect, raised the boys. Duke attended St. Paul's School in Concord, New Hampshire, and entered Yale College in 1934. Called "Bunny" by his family and "Angie" by his friends,

Angier Biddle Duke, 1968. AP/WIDE WORLD PHOTOS

Duke, "a restless, tobacco-rich playboy," excelled at languages.

He left Yale in 1936 without receiving a degree and married Priscilla St. George on 2 January 1937 in a lavish society wedding. The couple separated after the birth of their son and were divorced on 27 August 1940. Duke, who had worked as a sportswriter for a small magazine, joined the Citizens Military Training Corps in the summer of 1940. Later that year, he married Margaret Screven White. In February 1941 Duke enlisted in the army; he attended Officer Candidate School at Fort Lee, Virginia, and was commissioned a second lieutenant in January 1942. His success in the military shifted his life's focus from social excess to social responsibility. During World War II he served with the Air Transport Command in North Africa and Europe, achieving the rank of major. He followed the D-Day invasion into France, saw the liberation of Paris, and witnessed the opening of the death camp at Buchenwald. He understood his years in the service to have been his formative education: "Nothing so illuminating had ever happened to me before." In 1946 Duke established the Duke International Corporation to handle foreign and domestic investments. During the late 1940s he began to contribute and then to participate in New York State Democratic Party politics.

Eager to make use of Duke's facility with languages and his business experience in Latin America, A. Stanford Griffis, a friend and the ambassador to Argentina, invited Duke to accompany him as a special assistant. Slim, tall, and elegantly dressed, Duke enthusiastically assumed the responsibilities of consular work. President Harry Truman then assigned Griffis with Duke to the Madrid Embassy in 1951. The following year, impressed by his work in Argentina and Spain, Truman named Duke the ambassador to El Salvador. Duke was so popular a public figure in El Salvador that when President Dwight Eisenhower's election signaled a change of ambassadors, Salvadorans petitioned Washington unsuccessfully in an attempt to retain him. Duke's marriage to Margaret White ended with divorce in early 1952. Christened in the Methodist church, Duke became a Roman Catholic in October and on 11 December 1952 married Maria-Luisa de Arana. They had two children.

Although Duke's career in foreign service was interrupted with the election of a Republican president, he continued to represent the United States by chairing the International Rescue Committee (IRC). He traveled to Southeast Asia in 1955 to coordinate relief work in Vietnam following its partition, and he made several trips to Europe to negotiate on behalf of refugees from the 1956 Hungarian Revolution. His administrative work for the IRC was extended by fundraising for related organizations such as American Friends of Vietnam, the Emergency Committee of the United Nations, and the American Immigration and Citizenship Conference. In addition to humanitarian work, Duke continued to spend time and money supporting Democratic Party endeavors. In 1960 he chaired the Democratic Nationalities Committee, reaching out to engage Hispanic voters. In late 1960 the president-elect John F. Kennedy nominated Duke for the position of chief of protocol and raised him to the personal rank of ambassador. Duke's responsibilities involved greeting and caring for visiting heads of state as well as for the nearly 40,000 people living in the United States who were connected to foreign consulates.

During previous administrations visitors representing foreign governments met with the secretary of state for substantive exchanges and with the president for social and public relations purposes. Duke, whose skill, efficiency, and unfailing good manners were valued by Kennedy, managed to streamline the formal, full-dress meetings so that Kennedy himself could meet officials privately and informally while maintaining dignity and the attention to protocol expected by heads of state. In Duke's role as chief of protocol, he was often called on to protect dignitaries from African and Asian countries from embarrassing insults in racially segregated Washington, D.C. Duke interceded on the behalf of diplomats seeking housing or service in public facilities and in August 1961 publicly resigned from the prestigious Metropolitan Club to protest its policy of exclusion.

In July 1961 Duke's third wife, Maria-Luisa, died when a small plane taking her to their summer home in Southampton, New York, crashed. On 12 May 1962 Duke married Robin Chandler Lynn; they had a son, and Duke assumed the role of stepfather to her two children from a previous marriage. In November 1963 Duke helped Jacqueline Kennedy plan the state events to honor her assassinated husband. The country had never before witnessed such an elaborate and moving public funeral. Duke researched other presidential funerals, organized the reception, and planned for the participation of heads of state, former presidents, congressional and state leaders, and the ordinary Americans who streamed into Washington to pay their respects to Kennedy. Duke continued to serve as chief of protocol in President Lyndon Johnson's administration until 1964. Named ambassador to Spain in 1965, Duke calmed international fears in 1966 by swimming in the Mediterranean after a U.S. Air Force B-52 crashed and lost four 25-megaton hydrogen bombs in the sea. In late 1967 Duke returned to Washington, acting as Johnson's chief of protocol. Between 1968 and 1969 he was ambassador to Denmark. With the Democrats out of national office, Duke agreed to serve without pay as New York City mayor John Lindsay's commissioner of civic affairs and public events. Under President Jimmy Carter, Duke served as ambassador to Morocco from 1979 to 1981. At his retirement in 1981, Henry Kissinger presented him with the Hans J. Morgenthau Award for "exemplary foreign policy contributions to the United States."

Never one to be inactive, Duke became a trustee of Southampton Center of Long Island University. He served as chancellor from 1986 until 1990. On 29 April 1995 Duke was hit by a car and killed at age seventy-nine while rollerblading near his home in Southampton. The funeral at the Cathedral of St. John the Divine in Manhattan brought together more than 1,000 mourners who came to celebrate Duke's verve, creativity, and vision. He is buried in Southampton. A man of enormous energy, Angier Duke used his wealth, intellect, courtesy, and tact in the service of his country.

★

A collection of papers relating to Duke's career is on file at the Southampton Center of Long Island University. A lengthy portrait of him by E. J. Kahn, "Good Manners and Common Sense," centering on his work as chief of protocol and providing biographical information, appeared in the *New Yorker* (15 Aug. 1964). Duke was featured in *Current Biography Yearbook, 1962–1963,* and in *Political Profiles: The Kennedy Years* (1976). Articles in *Time* (25 May 1953) and *Newsweek* (11 Jan. 1965) cover events in his political and foreign service career. An obituary and portraits are in the *New York Times* (30 April, 1 May, 2 May, 4 May 1995). *The Washington Post* (2 May 1995) published an obituary and a remembrance, as did the *Los Angeles Times* (1 May 1995) and the *Southampton Press* (4 May 1995).

WENDY HALL MALONEY

DZUBAS, Friedel Alfred (*b.* 20 April 1915 in Berlin, Germany; *d.* 14 December 1994 in Newton, Massachusetts), artist in the style of abstract expressionism known as the New York School whose paintings have endured through the birth and demise of many artistic trends.

Dzubas was the youngest of three sons born to Martin Dzubas, a clothing designer and textile factory manager, and Martha Schmidt Dzubas, a homemaker. An indifferent student, Dzubas was encouraged to paint and draw by his grandmother and drawing teacher in the local school. His parents did not approve of art as Dzubas's career path, but they did arrange an apprenticeship to an established Berlin decorative arts firm in 1933 when he was seventeen. Until he fled Germany in August 1939 to avoid conscription in Hitler's army, Dzubas threw himself into his painting, attended lectures, was an extra in the State Opera Company, and briefly joined a Communist youth organization. During this period of heady youthful exploration and self-education, he painted landscapes in watercolor and social scenes in oil paint. He visited museums and learned about contemporary art, particularly the German expressionists.

On 22 June 1939 he married Dorothea Brasch in Frankfurt. They later had one child. Two months later he fled Germany by train and stayed in London with an uncle until he booked passage on a ship for Montreal, Canada. Dzubas then made his way to the United States. His wife joined him in Virginia, where he was working on a farm. From 1940 until 1952 he painted while making frequent moves and working at a wide variety of jobs, including jobs as a busboy, housepainter, and graphic designer for the Chicago firm of Ziff-Davis. After a divorce from Dorothea in 1945, he moved to New York City, where he continued to free-lance as a graphic designer.

In 1948 he met the art critic Clement Greenberg, who introduced him to abstract expressionists such as Jackson Pollock, Willem de Kooning, and Franz Klein. Dzubas became a member of the Eighth Street Club, an artists' group that met at the Cedar Bar in Greenwich Village to discuss and argue about contemporary art. Initially, Dzubas painted works of expressionistic color held together by a style of energetic line drawing that was influenced by Paul Klee. After meeting Jackson Pollock, Dzubas, in interviews, spoke of the powerful influence Pollock exerted on him, not so much in technique but in the potential for artistic freedom that Pollock explored.

Friedel Dzubas at the Castelli Gallery, 1959. COPYRIGHT © BY FRED W. McDARRAH

In 1952 Dzubas shared a studio with another rising abstract expressionist, Helen Frankenthaler. In November of that year he had his first one-man show at New York's Tibor de Nagy gallery. The exhibit, while not a financial success, provided Dzubas with the exposure he needed to build his reputation as an artist. Unfortunately his personal life was disintegrating. He had married Marilyn Morgan in 1946 and had two children, but this marriage was breaking up. His divorce left him with serious self doubts, and he withdrew from painting for two years.

Dzubas returned to painting in 1955, and gave free rein to his expressionism by using color in partnership with a frenetic black linear calligraphy. This style of work reached its peak in 1959, when Dzubas completed a number of paintings with titles and influences from baroque architecture and religious sentiment. He credited this "baroque" period to ten months of travel in Austria and Germany, and to his obsession with baroque paintings. Dzubas was naturalized as a U.S. citizen in May 1959.

In the early 1960s Dzubas purged himself of the dense black calligraphic compositions and began to consider a canvas as a place to assemble simple, meaningful forms. Color became a tool for reaching a new emotional and expressive level, and Dzubas balanced big blocks of thinly washed color on large canvases. He hit a level of artistic maturity with this direction. His personal life was changing, too. He married Allison Gray in 1963 and had one child, but they divorced in 1970. By 1973 he had married again, this time to Mary Kelsey, but they divorced in 1978. They had no children.

Dzubas began a period of intense activity during the 1960s and 1970s, teaching at a number of colleges and universities. He received recognition for his work, sold paintings, won two Guggenheim Fellowships (1966 and 1968) and a National Endowment for the Arts Painting Fellowship (1968), was positively reviewed in numerous newspaper and magazine articles, and showed his paintings at major galleries and museums in the United States and Europe. In 1990 the André Emmerich Gallery in New York mounted a retrospective of four decades of his paintings, from 1950 through 1990. Dzubas died at his home in Newton, Massachusetts, from complications of Parkinson's disease at the age of seventy-nine, and was buried in Mount Auburn Cemetery in Boston.

Dzubas did not receive the wide public recognition given to other important painters in the New York School, peers such as Pollock, de Kooning, or Frankenthaler. While other artists changed painting styles, Dzubas held fast to his philosophy of creating nonobjective, color-saturated paintings that are recognized by critics and art collectors as some of the finest abstract paintings produced in this period. His work has endured through the birth and demise of many artistic trends because of its aesthetic excellence. While Dzubas retained a sensibility that was grounded in the richness of the old masters, as his fraying blocks of color swirled and bumped across the canvas, he was engaged in the only reliable constant in his life, his art.

★

Dzubas's personal papers and correspondence are in the care of his daughter Hannele Dzubas of Martha's Vineyard, Massachusetts. For information about Dzubas's life and work, see catalogs prepared for exhibitions such as Charles W. Millard, *Friedel Dzubas,* for the Hirshhorn Museum, Washington, D.C. (1983); Karen Wilkin (introduction), *Friedel Dzubas, New Paintings,* for the André Emmerich Gallery, New York City (1987); *Works by Friedel Dzubas,* for the Nassau County Museum of Art, Long Island, New York (1987); and Karen Wilkin, *Friedel Dzubas: Four Decades, 1950–1990,* for the André Emmerich Gallery (1991). Dzubas was interviewed by Charles Millard on 25 Aug. 1982 in Washington, D.C., and on 17 Aug. 1982 in Cambridge, Massachusetts. The original tapes of these interviews are on deposit at the Archives of American Art, Smithsonian Institution, Washington, D.C. An obituary is in the *New York Times* (14 Dec. 1994).

ROSEMARIE S. CARDOSO

E

ECKERT, J(ohn Adam) Presper, Jr. (*b.* 9 April 1919 in Philadelphia, Pennsylvania; *d.* 3 June 1995 in Bryn Mawr, Pennsylvania), electrical engineer who invented and built the computers that initiated the digital age.

Eckert was the only child of John P. Eckert, Sr., a self-made millionaire builder of parking garages and apartment buildings, and Ethel Hallowell, a homemaker whose grandfather had been a successful inventor and manufacturer of confectionery equipment. As a boy, Eckert traveled extensively with his family throughout the United States, Europe, and the Middle East. He was five when his father brought home one of the earliest radio sets, and he was instantly captivated, building a succession of radios and other electronic sound devices throughout his school years. One of his most ambitious tinkerings was a table-top pond on which boats were manipulated by magnets on tracks underneath the table—when he was twelve the toy won him first prize in a Philadelphia hobby fair. While in high school at the William Penn Charter School, Eckert was able to do odd jobs in the nearby laboratory where Philo Farnsworth was developing electronic television.

After graduating from high school in 1937, Eckert enrolled at the University of Pennsylvania, where he ultimately received both a B.S. degree (1941) and an M.S. degree (1943) in electrical engineering. As an undergraduate, Eckert demonstrated his brilliance during summer consulting jobs more than he did in the classroom, and he

learned how to build reliability into fragile instruments. While a first-year graduate student at Penn in 1941, he happened to meet John Mauchly, twelve years his senior, a small-college physics professor with a long interest in the possibility of electronic computing. Mauchly's interest had been heightened and focused more on digital technology by a recent trip to see a desk-sized device to solve simultaneous equations that John Atanasoff was attempting to build at Iowa State College. Mauchly had been told by experts that vacuum tubes blew out too often for thousands of them to be combined in a single device. Eckert—with a youthful confidence bolstered by years of past engineering successes—assured him that it could be done, and the two began swapping ideas.

After the United States entered World War II, the U.S. Army began building new artillery pieces faster than it could produce the voluminous firing tables needed to aim them under varying conditions. Eckert and Mauchly proposed the development of a general-purpose electronic digital computer to calculate the tables, and in the spring of 1943 the army agreed to back the project at Penn. The twenty-four-year-old Eckert was named chief engineer. With Mauchly as an invaluable consultant, Eckert tirelessly drove a project that eventually involved dozens of engineers and technicians. His style could be brusque, but he was universally respected for his engineering genius.

Eckert and Mauchly's digital calculating machine, called ENIAC (electronic numerical integrator and computer),

J. Presper Eckert *(left)* with Dr. John W. Mauchly and a tape recording-transmitting machine. AP/WIDE WORLD PHOTOS

was completed in the fall of 1945, only two and a half years after it had been authorized but too late to play any role in the war. Covering as much floor space as a small house, with 18,000 vacuum tubes and endless plug-in cables, ENIAC could compute in thirty seconds a table that would take a person twenty hours.

Meanwhile, early in 1944, once the ENIAC design had been frozen but technicians were still building it, Eckert and Mauchly began to explore the concepts for a second machine, called EDVAC (electronic discrete variable automatic computer), which would incorporate memory and stored programs. As the essential memory device, Eckert proposed a mercury-delay line he had helped invent while working on radar projects early in the war. Later in 1944 the renowned mathematician John von Neumann visited the project and joined in the periodic discussions of the small EDVAC design group. (In 1945, while ENIAC was still shrouded in wartime secrecy, von Neumann drafted a summary of the group's thinking that was circulated under his name. Ever since, the stored program concept has been popularly, but erroneously, attributed to von Neumann alone.) That same year, Eckert married Hester Caldwell; they had two children.

In February 1946 the army and the University of Penn-

sylvania publicly demonstrated ENIAC, informing the world of the birth of a new technology of "electronic brains." Penn also organized a summer lecture program in which Eckert, Mauchly, and others of the ENIAC team transmitted its secrets to two dozen key engineers, several of whom subsequently built important new machines. Indeed, virtually all of the new British and American computer projects of the late 1940s had important links to ENIAC and EDVAC. ENIAC itself performed valuable calculations for the military for a decade.

By then the two inventors had left Penn to found a company soon known as the Eckert-Mauchly Computer Corporation, the first in the world to build electronic digital computers, for which they proposed a wide range of business, governmental, and research applications. Mauchly concentrated on sales, while Eckert began designing UNIVAC (universal automatic computer) as a stored-program computer with mercury-delay lines for internal memory and specially-developed magnetic tape for data storage.

The machine took more time and money than the partners had estimated, and in 1950 they were forced to sell their company to the Remington-Rand Corporation—soon to be Sperry-Rand and ultimately Unisys. There Eckert led the completion of UNIVAC, and the first machine was turned over to the U.S. Census Bureau in March 1951. It was the first general-purpose electronic computer manufactured for the commercial market.

Some twenty UNIVACs were sold over the next three years, demonstrating that computers could play an important role in business as well as science. For its coverage of the 1952 presidential election, the CBS television network had Eckert feed the earliest returns to a UNIVAC, and the machine quickly produced the unexpected, but accurate, results that Dwight D. Eisenhower's victory would be a landslide. Overnight "UNIVAC" became synonymous with "computer" in the American mind. Sperry-Rand, however, was more attuned to mass-producing typewriters and electric razors than investing millions in developing new technology. By contrast, IBM, jolted by UNIVAC's threat to its traditional line of mechanical punch-card processors, mobilized its capital and sales force to enter and eventually dominate the field of electronic computing.

At Sperry, Eckert continued to lead the development of several new generations of UNIVAC and other computers. In later years he continued to advise the company on computer development, but his best ideas—in such areas as personal computers and optical character recognition—were too visionary to find favor in a large commercial organization. Trying to get them accepted was, he complained, like "swimming in molasses."

Eckert's wife Hester died in 1952; in 1962 he married Judith Rewalt, and they had two children. Eckert was awarded the National Medal of Science in 1969. In 1973 a federal judge invalidated the broad patent that Eckert and Mauchly had obtained on the electronic digital computer and many specifics of the ENIAC design. While acknowledging ENIAC as a "pioneering achievement," the judge found that the claim had been filed too late and that it owed too much to Atanasoff's relatively unsophisticated and never-completed machine. Patent issues aside, historians recognize ENIAC as a landmark in computer technology that owed much to Eckert's inventive genius. Eckert died of leukemia in Bryn Mawr. He is buried at Valley Forge Memorial Gardens in King of Prussia, Pennsylvania.

Eckert was the master engineer of the dawn of the computer revolution. Together with Mauchly he demonstrated to the world the feasibility and applicability of electronic digital computers and founded the computer industry.

★

There is no full-length biography. Scott McCartney, *ENIAC: The Triumphs and Tragedies of the World's First Computer* (1999), does an excellent job of describing the accomplishments of Eckert and Mauchly. An earlier popular overview is in chapters 5–8 of Joel Shurkin, *Engines of the Mind: A History of the Computer* (1984). A more academic evaluation is Nancy Stern, *From ENIAC to UNIVAC: An Appraisal of the Eckert-Mauchly Computers* (1981). The only full treatment of Eckert's early life is Peter Eckstein, "J. Presper Eckert," *IEEE Annals of the History of Computing* 18, no. 1 (spring 1996): 25–44, ending with the beginning of his work on ENIAC. Records from the UNIVAC Division of Remington-Rand are at the Hagley Museum and Library in Wilmington, Delaware. An obituary is in the *New York Times* (7 June 1995). A 1988 oral history is in the Smithsonian Videohistory Program.

PETER ECKSTEIN

EISENSTAEDT, Alfred   (*b*. 6 December 1898 in Dirschau [now Tczew], West Prussia [now Poland]; *d*. 24 August 1995 in Oak Bluffs, Massachusetts), photographer whose work for *Life* magazine from its inception in 1936 helped define photojournalism in the United States.

Eisenstaedt was the son of Joseph Eisenstaedt, a successful retailer, and Regina Schoen. His parents moved with their three sons to Wilmersdorf in Berlin in 1906, where Eisenstaedt stayed until his departure from Nazi Germany in 1935. Educated at the Hohenzollern Gymnasium from 1906 to 1912, Eisenstaedt graduated with a baccalaureate the same year an uncle gave him his first camera, an Eastman Kodak No. 3 folding camera. In 1913 he enrolled in the University of Berlin, but his education was interrupted by World War I. Drafted into the German army's Fifty-fifth Field Artillery Regiment in 1916, Eisenstaedt suffered shrapnel wounds in both legs on 12 April 1918 in an offensive in Dieppe, France. He was one of two survivors from his regiment.

Alfred Eisenstaedt. CORBIS-BETTMANN

Eisenstaedt began his career as a photojournalist in 1927, when the illustrated weekly *Der Weltspeigel* purchased his photograph of a tennis match. He soon began freelancing for Pacific and Atlantic Photo (which became the Associated Press in 1931) while working as a button and belt salesman. On 3 December 1929 Pacific and Atlantic hired him to be the primary photographer in its Berlin office. His first professional assignment took him in 1929 to the Nobel Prize ceremony in Stockholm, Sweden, where he photographed laureate Thomas Mann. For the next six years Eisenstaedt established himself as a documentary photographer adept at capturing significant moments and figures of history. He toured Europe creating portraits of luminaries ranging from Max Schmeling, Marlene Dietrich, and Richard Strauss to Adolf Hitler and Benito Mussolini. The young Jewish photographer was present on 13 June 1934 in Venice when the two fascist dictators met for the first time. In 1935 the political situation in Europe forced his immigration to New York City where he resided until his death. Upon his arrival in the United States, Eisenstaedt freelanced for *Harper's Bazaar, Vogue,* and *Town and Country.* In 1936 the publisher Henry R. Luce hired Eisenstaedt to be one of four photographers to staff his new *Magazine X.* Upon publication eight months later Eisenstaedt shared the masthead of the now titled *Life* with photographers Margaret Bourke-White, Thomas McAvoy, and Peter Stackpole. Of the group, Eisenstaedt wrote, "we were no-nonsense people, part of an elite group, pioneers of photojournalism in America." Not yet possessing U.S. citizenship, Eisenstaedt, now called "Eisie," was obliged to spend the war years on the home front. The task of uplifting American spirits fit the outgoing, sunny disposition of the photographer. Even after being naturalized in 1942, Eisenstaedt continued to favor examinations of life in the United States rather than events abroad. In the more than eighty-five covers Eisenstaedt shot for *Life,* Americans went to school, college, ski slopes, tennis courts, the movies, and to war.

His most famous photograph, "V.J. Day at Times Square, New York City, August 14, 1945," showed Americans celebrating the end of the war. The image of a sailor kissing a young nurse in a full embrace displays the exuberant catharsis of the moment while presenting a thesis on Eisenstaedt's approach to photojournalism. He captured candid moments that displayed the benevolence of humanity. Among the *Life* photographers, Eisie was known as an "undershooter." It took him only four shots to create "V.J. Day at Times Square." Not a formal stylist like his friend Bourke-White, Eisenstaedt created photographs that reveal as little of the hand and personality of the artist as was possible. "There is no Eisenstaedt picture," he explained.

In 1949 Eisenstaedt married a young South African, Alma Kathy Kaye; she lived with her husband until her death in 1972. The couple had no children. Eisenstaedt's sister-in-law, Lucy (Lulu) Kaye, was his companion from 1972 until his death. In his final years, Lulu helped him navigate the few blocks to the office in the Time-Life Building to which he reported daily.

Eisenstaedt's portraits after World War II depict the lives of notables from the Kennedys to the queen of England, from Charlie Chaplin to Ernest Hemmingway. His camera also caught the pleasures, and on occasion the pain, of less distinguished people; children playing at the beach or gasping at a puppet show, street vendors, and beggars all appear in his work. In 1966 Eisenstaedt published the first of his thirteen books, *Witness to Our Time,* a collection of photos from his career in photojournalism. In his third and fourth books, *Martha's Vineyard* (1970) and *Witness to Nature* (1971), Eisenstaedt revealed an interest in life apart from paparazzi and current events.

In 1972 *Life* stopped publication and, although Eisenstaedt was retained by Time, Inc., he worked only intermittently for *Life* when it began publishing again in 1978. Key publications from the period include *Eisenstaedt's Guide to Photography* (1978); *Eisenstaedt: Germany* (1980), an album pairing photographs taken before he left Germany with ones taken on his first return in 1979; *Eisenstaedt on Eisenstaedt* (1985); and *Eisenstaedt: Remembrances* (1990), a retrospective volume dedicated to his late wife. In his work after 1932 Eisenstaedt favored Leica or Nikon 35mm cameras for their flexibility.

Eisenstaedt received numerous honors and awards. The first came in 1951 when the *Encyclopaedia Britannica Yearbook* named him "Photographer of the Year." The International Museum of Photography in Rochester, New York, gave the photographer his first one-person exhibition in 1954. Eisenstaedt was named one of the world's ten great photographers in an international poll conducted by *Popular Photography* in 1968. In 1986 the International Center of Photography mounted a retrospective exhibition entitled "Eisie at 88." Two years later he received the Presidential Medal of Arts and the International Center of Photography Master of Photography Award. In 1997 *Life* established the Alfred Eisenstaedt Awards of Magazine Photography, which are administered by the Columbia University School of Journalism.

Eisenstaedt died of a heart attack while on Martha's Vineyard, a favorite vacation spot of the artist since the 1930s. He is buried in Mount Hebron Cemetery in the borough of Queens in New York City.

Questioned about the striking lack of commentary in his photography, particularly his German work, Eisenstaedt explained, "I don't see Germany with political eyes. I see pictures." Although his posture of neutrality dates his art, Eisenstaedt's often startling success at absenting himself from his work has left us with images that transcribed the voices of another age with considerable clarity. He possessed a cunning ability to capture fleeting moments of genuine feeling and a keen sense of anecdote. In the best and also the most fallible sense, Eisenstaedt's photographs are eminently human.

★

No biography exists of Eisenstaedt, although his own publications often include autobiographical notes and essays. *Eisenstaedt on Eisenstaedt* is the most complete of these. The 1980 reprinting of *Witness to Our Time* with an essay by Henry R. Luce is of particular interest. An interview with the photographer, "A Conversation with Alfred Eisenstaedt," appeared in *Print* 33 (July–Aug. 1979): 33–38, 104. Shorter interviews published in the *British Journal of Photography* include Tom Ang, "Eisenstaedt in London," 133 (28 Feb. 1986): 244–247, and Michael Hallett, "A Lifetime with Life," 139 (28 May 1992): 10–11. See also the critical biographical essay by James Traub, "A Wonderful Life," *American Photographer* 17 (Dec. 1986): 45–59. An obituary is in the *New York Times* and *Washington Post* (both 25 Aug. 1995).

PETER R. KALB

ELGART, Les(ter) Elliot (*b.* 3 August 1917 in New Haven, Connecticut; *d.* 29 July 1995 in Dallas, Texas), trumpeter and dance-band leader.

Elgart's father, Arthur Max Elgart, worked as a mechanic, electrician, and salesman. His mother, Bess Aisman, was a talented amateur pianist who taught music prior to her marriage. Elgart's only sibling, Lawrence ("Larry") Elgart, born in 1922 in New London, Connecticut, also gained fame as a saxophonist and bandleader.

By 1927 the family had moved to Morristown, New Jersey, where Les learned to play the bugle as a Cub Scout. In 1929, with their parents' encouragement, Les began playing trumpet, and Larry took up the clarinet, later switching to saxophone. During the 1930s the family moved several times, finally settling in Pompton Lakes, New Jersey, where the brothers attended Pompton Lakes High School. Although Les was a fine athlete and pitched well enough in grammar school to attract the attention of a minor league baseball scout, his greatest ambition was to be a bandleader. He began playing trumpet with local groups and left high school in 1933 to pursue his career.

Elgart's idol was the trumpeter Bunny Berigan. In 1939 he won the lead trumpet chair in Berigan's band, but the band went bankrupt in 1940. Between 1940 and 1942 Elgart played in various bands, including those led by Harry James and Charlie Spivak, who said: "He was one of the best sidemen I ever had." On 2 April 1942 he enlisted in the navy in Newport, Rhode Island, but was discharged on 29 May 1942 due to an unspecified physical disability. Shortly thereafter, he joined Woody Herman's band and appeared with the band in the movie *Wintertime* (1943), starring Sonja Henie.

In 1945 the brothers organized their own big band ensemble, the Les Elgart Orchestra. Les fronted the band and played trumpet; Larry led the saxophone section on alto sax. Using arrangements by Bill Finegan and Nelson Riddle, they played at ballrooms in New York and New Jersey, but big bands faced economic difficulties due to a postwar recession and the growing popularity of television. In 1948, after recording two singles for Bullet Records that garnered little attention, the Les Elgart Orchestra disbanded. Between 1948 and 1952 Les worked as a freelance trumpeter, and Larry freelanced in New York City and immersed himself in the new recording technologies. The use of more sensitive microphones allowed subtle sounds to emerge with greater clarity and reduced the need for a heavy rhythm section.

In 1952 the brothers organized another band, distinctive for what came to be known as the "Elgart sound": silky-smooth saxophone playing and a rich, brilliant brass section, featuring bass trombone. Arrangements by Charles Albertine showcased the tightly synchronized saxophone and brass sections and a rhythm section with guitar instead of piano, with few improvised solos.

Intent on landing a recording contract, Larry took a demo recording of the band to George Avakian at Columbia Records. "I liked the light swinging beat and straight ahead sound," Avakian said, " . . . and thought it would have youth appeal. . . . Les had all the qualities for success

Les Elgart. ARCHIVE PHOTOS

as a bandleader, good-looking, fine musician, warm and friendly, and his sidemen were carefully chosen to fit the sound." Columbia issued three singles late in 1952, which did not sell well; however, *Sophisticated Swing,* an album issued in 1953, was a smash hit, winning a five-star review in *Down Beat* from Jack Tracy, who wrote: "It's difficult to see how Elgart can miss with this new band." A second album, *Just One More Dance* (1954), was equally popular, which led to a coveted booking at the Hotel Astor in New York in August 1954. Thereafter, the band toured the country, using "Heart of My Heart" from the *Sophisticated Swing* album as its theme song.

While playing a date in Philadelphia in 1953 the Elgart brothers saw a local television show, *American Bandstand,* hosted by Bob Horn. Les contacted Horn and offered to record a theme song for the show. Horn agreed. In a collaborative effort, Larry Elgart created a melody, Charles Albertine arranged it, and the Les Elgart Orchestra recorded it as "Bandstand Boogie" in 1954. Dick Clark kept the theme when he took over as host, and *American Bandstand* later became ABC's longest running show for teenagers (1957 to 1987).

In 1955 a *Variety* reviewer wrote: "Elgart's band . . . manages to generate some unusual sounds [with] interesting experimentation going on in the interplay of the various sections. The result is an overall fresh approach in a conventional dance band format." The big-band historian George Simon later wrote: "It was a very musical band and Les was a good lead trumpeter."

Although the band continued to tour and record for Columbia, the brothers had different artistic goals. Les preferred to front the band and concentrate on the dancers, whereas Larry was concerned with musical style and perfecting their recordings. The brothers split up in 1959. Larry remained on the East Coast and formed the Larry Elgart Orchestra, which recorded for RCA and MGM. Les moved to California and recorded eight more albums for Columbia, including *Les Elgart on Tour* (1959), *Half Satin–Half Latin* (1961), and *Best Band On Campus* (1962).

In 1963 Larry rejoined the band, renamed the Les and Larry Elgart Orchestra, which recorded eight more albums for Columbia. The band did several network radio broadcasts between 1964 and 1966 and appeared on a Jackie Gleason television special featuring big bands on 21 November 1966. Their last album for Columbia was *Wonderful World of Today's Hits* (1967). Due to changing musical tastes, Columbia released many of its longtime artists in 1968, including the Elgart band, and the brothers again went their separate ways.

During the early 1970s Les moved to San Antonio, Texas, and continued touring with his band, using a core group of musicians augmented with local players. On 17 October 1977 in Dallas, he married Joerene (Williams) Ingram, who had three children from a previous marriage. She and Elgart had no children. She became manager of the band, which played at colleges, at conventions, and on cruises. Elgart's final performance was on Long Island, New York, shortly before he died of a heart attack at his stepdaughter's home in Dallas. He is buried at Hillcrest Memorial Park in Dallas.

Although some critics felt the "Elgart sound" was so consistent as to be tiresome, Les Elgart's goal was to lead a big band that provided danceable music with a distinctly different sound. In this he succeeded, and his band survived at a time when many big-name bands did not, leaving a recorded legacy of two dozen albums.

★

Some of Elgart's personal papers and big-band arrangements are held by his brother, Larry, in Florida; others are with his widow, Joerene Elgart, in Texas. Richard F. Palmer and Charles Garrod, *Les and Larry Elgart and Their Orchestras* (1992), a Joyce Record Club publication, contains an extensive discography, dates and locations of band appearances, and some biographical material. Several articles about the Les Elgart Orchestra are in *Down Beat* (6 Oct. 1954), including Nat Hentoff, "Les Elgart: The Band That Didn't Imitate Glenn Miller." Some of Elgart's Columbia recordings have been reissued on the compact discs *Best of Big*

Bands: *Les & Larry Elgart* (1990) and *Sentimental Swing: All-Star Dance Classics* (1993). An audiotape, *Les Elgart at the Pelham Heath Inn,* is available from the Joyce Record Club, Portland, Oregon. Obituaries are in the *New York Times* and *Dallas Morning News* (both 31 July 1995).

SUSAN FLEET

ELKIN, Stanley Lawrence (*b.* 11 May 1930 in New York City; *d.* 30 May 1995 in St. Louis, Missouri), novelist, essayist, and educator known for his innovative prose style, his extravagant humor, and his driven, obsessive characters.

Elkin was one of two children born to Philip Elkin, a salesman, and Zelda Feldman, a homemaker. When he was three years old the family moved to Chicago, where his father accepted a job as a traveling salesman selling costume jewelry throughout the Midwest. Elkin fondly remembered his father's material success and his pitchman's rhetoric in his autobiographical essay "My Father's Life" (1987; reprinted in *Pieces of Soap,* 1992), and many of his early works were concerned with consumer culture in ways that are rare in American literature. Although the family had moved to Chicago, Elkin's bar mitzvah took place in New York City on 17 July 1943. He attended school in Chicago, then majored in English literature at the University of Illinois.

Stanley L. Elkin. © MIRIAM BERKLEY

From that institution he received an A.B. degree in 1952 and his M.A. degree in 1953. He married Joan Marion Jacobsen on 1 February 1953. An artist, Joan's portraits of her husband adorn the dust jackets of several of his later works, most notably the collection of essays and autobiographical reminiscences *Pieces of Soap.* They had three children.

Elkin served in the United States Army from 1955 to 1957. During this time he cultivated a lifelong interest in interactive radio as a means of communicating among the alienated, a theme that organized his third novel, *The Dick Gibson Show* (1971). In "Where I Read What I Read" (printed in *Antaeus,* 1982, and in *Pieces of Soap*), Elkin reminisced about the reading opportunities his stay in the army provided, both during a bivouac in Colorado in 1955 and in the Army Reserves during 1958. After he was discharged from the army in 1957, Elkin returned to the University of Illinois, where he defended his Ph.D. dissertation, "Religious Themes and Symbols in the Novels of William Faulkner," in 1961. While completing the thesis Elkin joined the faculty of Washington University in St. Louis, where he taught for the rest of his academic career. At Washington he knew and appreciated such literary colleagues as William H. Gass, Howard Nemerov, and Mona van Duyn. He became Merle Kling Professor of Modern Letters in 1983, an endowed chair that permitted him to limit his teaching and concentrate on writing. He was honored by a star in the St. Louis Walk of Fame in May 1991. In 1999 Washington University, supported by a Danforth grant, established the Stanley Elkin Professorship in the Humanities.

Before he left Illinois in 1960, Elkin worked on the staff of *Accent* magazine, which published his early story "In the Alley," for which he received the Longview Foundation Award in 1962. "The Great Sandusky," a selection-in-progress from his first novel, *Boswell: A Modern Comedy* (1964), won the *Paris Review* humor prize that year, although it garnered mixed reviews from the critics. He was also nominated four times for National Book Awards. Two novels, *George Mills* (1982) and the posthumous *Mrs. Ted Bliss* (1995), won National Book Critics Circle Awards. His first novel, *Boswell* (1964), was subsidized by his mother, who sponsored Elkin and his wife as they traveled through Italy and England, during which time Elkin completed the novel.

After collecting his short stories in *Criers and Kibitzers, Kibitzers and Criers* (1966), Elkin became an important new voice in American fiction with his second, more controversial novel, *A Bad Man* (1967). A study of incarceration and obsession, this novel challenges many assumptions Americans have about the penal system and the nature of guilt. By the end of the 1960s Elkin's position in American letters was secure. He had been a visiting professor at two universities and earned a Guggenheim fellowship and a Rockefeller Foundation grant.

However, in 1968 when Elkin was only thirty-eight, he had his first heart attack, and the health concerns that plagued him for the rest of his life began. Formerly a robust individual, Elkin had to reassess his active life and his work. He continued with and even refined the rhetoric of aggression that had been his trademark, but the prophetic obsession with mortality that animated the protagonist of *Boswell* soon took a more central role in his fiction. His novel about talk radio, *The Dick Gibson Show* (1971), consolidated his reputation and he was awarded a grant by the National Endowment for the Arts and Humanities. While he was in Great Britain in 1972 however, he experienced tingling sensations that led first to physical therapy, then to a diagnosis of multiple sclerosis in that same year. The disease eventually limited his mobility as well as his tactile sensation and control. While he adjusted to the diagnosis, his awards and honors multiplied. He was invited to prestigious universities as a visiting professor and was recognized by the American Academy of Arts and Letters. The hero of his next novel, *The Franchiser* (1976), suffers through a series of progressively deteriorating episodes of multiple sclerosis. In that novel Elkin cleverly associated the disease attacking his hero's body with the breakdown of America's infrastructure during the 1970s, especially that decade's oil crises.

From *The Franchiser* on, much of Elkin's fiction exhibited a more serious tone. The aggressive syntax and the fascination with style and rhetoric for their own sake remained, as did the love of telling a good story. In many novels, however, the concern with health and the fragility of the human condition became a central preoccupation. The blue-collar hero of Elkin's favorite book, *George Mills* (1982), suffers from chronic back ailments and serves briefly as chaperone to a rich woman seeking a miracle cure for cancer. His masterpiece, *The Magic Kingdom* (1985), published the year of Elkin's first heart bypass surgery, treats a despairing effort, based on a variation on the "grant-a-wish" theme, to provide a diversion for children dying from horrid, terminal conditions. His final novels, *The Mac-Guffin* (1991) and *Mrs. Ted Bliss* (1995), are respectively about a chronically ill minor politician and about a widow adjusting to life after her husband's death. Elkin died of heart failure in Jewish Hospital in St. Louis.

In the decade before he died, Elkin saw his own work subject to specialization among the American literary community, meaning that his readers were a primarily specialized audience of students, critics of postmodern American fiction, and fellow writers. Although many writers and several critics saw him as an extraordinarily original writer and a craftsman of great skill, his work was not widely received in popular circles. In addition, some readers reacted adversely to his triptych, *The Living End* (1979), because of its satiric portrayal of God and the Holy Family. However, during the same period as Elkin's popularity as a novelist and cultural commentator went into a temporary decline, he was eagerly sought after by magazines and journals for his crotchety, eccentric views on pubic life. His essays on the Academy Awards and the California culture are marvelous revivals of the familiar essay genre and he established himself as one of the most astute commentators o the work we do, the things we consume, the culture we inhabit, and the way we live. Since Elkin's death there have been indications that he will be restored to his rightful place as one of the most original, if idiosyncratic, fiction writers of the second half of the twentieth century and one of the most astute commentators on the work we do, the things we consume, the culture we inhabit, and the ways these things shape our character and our fate.

★

Elkin's personal papers are archived at Washington University in St. Louis. No formal biography of Elkin exists at this time, but autobiographical essays appear in *Early Elkin* (1985) and *Pieces of Soap* (1992). For brief descriptions of Elkin's life story, see Doris G. Bargen, *The Fiction of Stanley Elkin* (1980), and David C. Dougherty, *Stanley Elkin* (1991). An obituary appears in the Chicago *Tribune* (1 June 1995).

DAVID C. DOUGHERTY

ELLINGTON, Mercer Kennedy (*b.* 11 March 1919 in Washington, D.C.; *d.* 8 February 1996 in Copenhagen, Denmark), trumpet player, composer, and bandleader who took over the orchestra of his father, Duke Ellington, after the elder man's death in 1974.

Mercer Ellington was the only surviving child of the noted composer and pianist Edward Kennedy ("Duke") Ellington and his wife, Edna Thompson, a pianist and homemaker. A second child, a girl, died in infancy. The couple separated when their son was nine. Thereafter, the boy spent half of each year with his mother, who taught him to read music and play the piano. He also took trumpet lessons. Father and son were not close, however, and during the part of each year Mercer spent with his father, the members of the Ellington band served as his surrogate extended family in helping him to mature. In *Duke Ellington in Person* (1978), Mercer's biography of his father, the younger Ellington points out that while his father never did anything overt to hurt his son and his aspirations, whenever the younger Ellington did slip in some fashion Duke let his son suffer and recover on his own when some parental help should have been called for or at least offered.

Ellington's family moved to New York in 1930. After graduating from Evander Childs High School in the Bronx,

Mercer Ellington. ARCHIVE PHOTOS

young Ellington studied at the prestigious Juilliard School of Music in Manhattan. During World War II he was in the U.S. Army and worked at Republic Aircraft, meanwhile taking composition and orchestration classes at New York University. He also attended Columbia University. Following his military service he formed his own band, which included the vocalist Carmen McRae. This group was the house band at the Savoy Ballroom in New York City. At different times, Ellington organized other big bands for special performances, employing such musicians as Dizzy Gillespie, Cat Anderson, Chico Hamilton, and Clark Terry.

The younger Ellington worked as an arranger for his father's band as well as those of Charlie Barnet, Cootie Williams, and Count Basie. He also composed numbers including "Things Ain't What They Used to Be," "Blue Serge," and "Jumpin' Punkins." ("Pigeons and Peppers," which he wrote at the age of eighteen, was the first of his pieces recorded by Duke, at a 1937 session with Cootie Williams presiding.)

From 1950 to 1952, young Ellington operated his own company, Mercer Records; in 1954 he was with the trumpeter Cootie Williams as a sideman and band manager. From 1955 to 1959 he was the chief assistant to his father, and in the 1960s, Mercer led the Duke Ellington band and recorded with all-star musicians taken from the latter organization. He was musical director for the singer Della Reese from 1960 to 1962, prior to becoming a disc jockey on New York City radio station WLIB for two years. At this point in his career, the elder Ellington induced him to join the main band as a trumpet player and manager. In that capacity (from 1965 to 1974) he gained more status within the band as he helped bring stability to the organization, which had been in financial disarray.

Following his father's death, Mercer took over the band on a regular basis. As leader and his father's replacement, young Ellington made European tours in 1975 and 1977. The Ellington revue *Sophisticated Ladies* (1981–1983), a Broadway musical comprised of Duke's tunes, was a successful venture with the younger Ellington conducting the score. He also expanded the orchestra's repertoire to include such works as *Queenie Pie* (Duke's only opera) and *Three Black Kings,* upon which he had worked with his father. At the 1982 Kool Jazz Festival he conducted the original score for *Black, Brown, and Beige*. In addition, he made occasional recordings. One of these, *Digital Duke,* received a Grammy Award in 1988 as best jazz instrumental album. The CD *Music Is My Mistress* received a 1990 Grammy nomination.

In 1974, following Duke's death, Mercer moved to Holte, north of Copenhagen, continuing a practice begun by some jazz musicians in the 1970s. At that time Denmark was a center for European jazz, and many African American jazz greats, such as Dexter Gordon and Ben Webster, found a refuge there from their nonrecognition in American jazz circles and an escape from the racism they experienced in their home country. Beginning in the late 1980s, while living in Copenhagen, Ellington booked only occasional band engagements. He met and married a Danish woman, Lena Margrethe Anderson, who survived him. They had four children.

With Mercer living in Denmark, the band was not often seen in the United States. The Duke Ellington Orchestra, with Mercer Ellington conducting, did, however, tour in the United States during the early 1990s. It also performed at the New Orleans Super Bowl and made annual visits to Japan and Europe.

Ellington died of a heart attack at the age of seventy-six. After his death, his son Paul (b. 1978) took over the Ellington band.

Mercer Ellington was a success in virtually every undertaking, with or without his father's assistance. Seemingly, there was space for only one male at a time in the Ellington family, and for most of Mercer's life this was Duke. The characterization of son by father in Duke's *Music Is My Mistress* as "dedicated to maintaining the luster of his father's image" is accurate. In retrospect, it may have been this goal that Duke was striving to accomplish throughout Mercer's career. That Mercer succeeded is evident from the awards and recognition he received following his father's death.

Mercer Ellington was a talented musician, composer, and businessman who was seldom given a chance by his father to succeed.

★

There is no full-length biography of Mercer Ellington, though with Stanley Dance he wrote a biography of his father, *Duke Ellington in Person: An Intimate Memoir* (1978). Duke Ellington, *Music Is My Mistress* (1973), provides little information about Mercer. Ian Carr et al., *Jazz the Rough Guide* (1995), and Roger D. Kinkle, *The Complete Encyclopedia of Popular Music and Jazz: 1900–1950* (1974), contain both biographical and brief discographical material. Burt Korell, "Mercer Ellington: And the Beat Goes On," *International Musician* (Apr. 1975), is a critic's assessment of Mercer's succession to Duke's band. Michiko Kakutani's "Life as Ellington's Son Was Mostly 'Mood Indigo,'" *New York Times* (29 Mar. 1981), is a brief but accurate evaluation of the father-son relationship. John McDonough, "Mercer Ellington: 1919–1996," *Down Beat* (May 1996), is a memorial including considerable detail. *Jet* (26 February 1996) also contains a memorial with interesting information. An obituary is in the *New York Times* (9 Feb. 1996). A standard musical example is 1989's *Music Is My Mistress: The Duke Ellington Orchestra Conducted by Mercer Ellington* (CD Music Masters no. CIJD-60–185), with personnel from various Ellington groups.

BARRETT G. POTTER

ELLISON, Ralph Waldo (*b.* 1 March 1914 in Oklahoma City, Oklahoma; *d.* 16 April 1994 in New York City), novelist, essayist, and man of letters best known for *Invisible Man* (1952), the first novel by an African American to win the National Book Award.

Ellison was the elder of two sons born to Lewis Alfred Ellison, the owner of a small ice and coal business who died when the older boy was three years old, and Ida Millsap, a domestic who canvassed for the Socialist Party and was later jailed several times for breaking the segregated housing ordinance in Oklahoma City during the early 1930s. After remarrying in the early 1920s, Ellison's mother and her husband, John Bell, raised Ralph and his brother in Oklahoma City.

Ellison attended the Frederick Douglass School for twelve years, graduating in 1931. As a boy he was drawn to music; his mother bought him a used cornet, and by the age of eight he was a member of the school band. Encouraged by his mother, who often brought home *Vanity Fair,*

Literary Digest, and other magazines from the houses she cleaned, Ellison became an insatiable reader at a young age. In 1933 the state of Oklahoma awarded him a scholarship (a means of keeping black students out of state colleges), and Ellison used it to study music at the Tuskegee Institute in Alabama. A music major, Ellison worked part-time in the library, where he discovered modern writers such as James Joyce, Ezra Pound, Gertrude Stein, Ernest Hemingway, and F. Scott Fitzgerald. T. S. Eliot's *The Waste Land* (1922) especially intrigued him; he found similarities between the literary techniques of Eliot and the jazz techniques of Louis Armstrong, which he later pursued in his fiction.

In July 1936, after his junior year at Tuskegee, Ellison went to New York City to earn money for his senior year and to study sculpture, and he stayed. Once in New York, he met and was befriended by the poet Langston Hughes. A meeting with the author Richard Wright in June of 1937 and subsequent friendship led Ellison toward becoming a writer. Wright encouraged him to review a novel for the radical journal *New Challenge,* which Wright edited, and to try his hand at writing a short story. During this period Ellison agitated on behalf of Republican Spain and was involved in the campaign for the release of the Scottsboro boys, nine young black men convicted and sentenced to death on trumped-up charges of raping two white women in a boxcar in Alabama.

In October 1937 Ellison was called to his mother's bedside in Dayton, Ohio, where she had moved in 1935 or 1936 after John Bell's death. She passed away the morning after he arrived, and penniless, he stayed in Dayton with his brother for almost seven months. There Ellison earned his living by shooting wild game and selling it to General Motors executives. These months proved a turning point for Ellison, as he began seriously to write fiction after hours in the law offices of W. O. Stokes, one of the first black attorneys in Dayton. Until April 1938 when a Works Progress Administration (WPA) job allowed him to return to New York, Ellison wrote drafts or partial drafts of several stories, two or three sketches, and a novel referred to as "Slick," which he later abandoned.

From 1938 until World War II, Ellison worked on the New York Federal Writers Project of the WPA. Starting in the late 1930s, he contributed reviews, essays, and short fiction to *New Masses, Tomorrow, The Negro Quarterly* (of which for a time he was managing editor), *The New Republic, Saturday Review, The Antioch Review, The Reporter,* and other periodicals. Ellison married Rose Poindexter on 16 September 1938. They were divorced in 1945, and a year later he married Fanny McConnell with whom he lived until his death in 1994. They had no children.

From 1943 until 1945, Ellison, preferring not to serve in the segregated U.S. Army, served in the merchant ma-

Ralph Ellison. ARCHIVE PHOTOS

rine. He worked as a cook on ships transporting arms across the Atlantic to the Allies in Great Britain and the Soviet Union. On sick leave back in the United States, he began *Invisible Man* in July 1945 at a friend's place in Waitsfield, Vermont. While working on what he called his "prison camp novel," Ellison found his fingers typing a strange, apparently unrelated sentence: "I am an invisible man." Intrigued, he resisted the impulse to destroy the page, and his mind began to fill in the lineaments of the character who would say such a thing. Soon he had a novel going, and Ellison wrote *Invisible Man* over the next seven years. During these years Ellison lived and worked in New York City, except for occasional forays to Bennington College in Vermont, where he met and discussed literature and literary form with Kenneth Burke, Stanley Edgar Hyman, Shirley Jackson, and R. W. B. Lewis.

Upon its publication in 1952, *Invisible Man* was recognized as one of the most important works of fiction of its time. In the journal *Commentary,* Saul Bellow called it a "book of the very first order, a superb book . . . a brilliant individual victory." Foreshadowing trouble to come for Ellison in the 1960s, defenders of Black Nationalism and the Communist Party were harshly critical. But negative responses were few; more typical was the verdict of the National Book Award jury. Noting that "Mr. Ellison has the courage to take many literary risks," the jury awarded *In-*

visible Man its prize for fiction in 1953. In years to come the stature of Ellison's novel only increased. A 1965 *Book Week* poll of over 200 authors, critics, and editors named *Invisible Man* "the most distinguished single work" published in the previous twenty years.

The acclaim given to *Invisible Man* opened up new horizons and opportunities for Ellison. In 1954 he was invited to lecture in Germany and at the Salzburg Seminar in Austria. In 1955 the American Academy of Arts and Letters awarded him the Prix de Rome, enabling him to spend two years in residence at the American Academy from 1955 to 1957. During this time he was earnestly at work on the novel that he hoped would soon follow *Invisible Man*. But first in Rome and later in New York, he found himself torn between fiction and a critical prose that explored themes similar to those he pursued in fiction: "the word and the contradiction of the word" of the American ideal as well as the discovery and "the evasion of identity." Important essays from this period include "Society, Morality and the Novel," written for *The Living Novel* (1957), a book of critical essays edited by Granville Hicks, and "Change the Joke and Slip the Yoke," published as an exchange with Stanley Edgar Hyman in *Partisan Review* in 1958. While he was at the American Academy in Rome, Ellison also served as American representative at literary conferences in London, Mexico City, and Tokyo.

Returning to the United States, Ellison taught Russian and American literature at Bard College in New York from 1958 to 1961; for most of that time he lived in Saul Bellow's house in Tivoli not far from the Hudson River, where he hunted with his black Labrador retriever, Tucka Tarby. In 1960 the first and longest excerpt from his novel-in-progress to be published in his lifetime appeared in print in *Noble Savage*, a new journal edited by Bellow. Additional selections from the work were published in 1960 and 1963. However, the next book of Ellison's to appear was not the novel but *Shadow and Act*, a collection of essays published in 1964. This volume established Ellison as an essayist and an American man of letters to be reckoned with, as well as a formidable novelist.

In the middle to late 1960s, as he continued to struggle with his second novel, Ellison began to feel the heat of criticism from black militants and exponents of the Black Arts movement, who resented his continued stance in favor of racial integration. At the same time he fell into conflict with some of his literary colleagues, both black and white, because of his support for President Lyndon B. Johnson's policy in Vietnam. Ellison defended the Vietnam War "less out of patriotic enthusiasm than tragic necessity." The United States, he felt, had "certain responsibilities to the Vietnamese and the structure of power in the world."

Meanwhile, the rewritten contract for Ellison's long-awaited second novel was signed on 17 August 1965, stip-ulating delivery by 1 September 1967. In his mind Ellison was moving toward completion in the summer or fall of 1967. Then, on 29 November, a fire at Ellison's summer home in the Berkshires destroyed what Ellison described as both "a section of my work-in-progress" and "a year's worth of revisions." Although Ellison may have reimagined and reconstructed the lost material, arguably he never attained a full, sure-handed grasp of the totality of his ambitious saga of racial complexity and American identity. Between 1969 and 1977 he published four more excerpts from the work in literary quarterlies. On and off for the rest of his life, he stayed at work on his ever expanding novel-in-progress, but he never finished. In one of the paradoxes of Ellison's literary life, during each year and each of the four decades in which his second novel failed to appear, his first novel, *Invisible Man,* continued to grow in critical reputation and popularity.

Despite only one novel and a single book of essays to his credit, the influence and importance of Ellison's work was such that he was awarded the Presidential Medal of Freedom in 1969; the Chevalier de l'Ordre des Arts et des Lettres in 1970 by the French minister of culture, André Malraux, whose novel *La condition humaine* (*Man's Fate*, 1933) had inspired Ellison in the 1930s; the Langston Hughes Medallion for contributions in arts and letters by City College of New York in 1984; and the National Medal of Arts in 1985. Ellison was a charter member of the National Council on the Arts and Humanities, and he received honorary degrees from Tuskegee, Rutgers University, the University of Michigan, Williams College, Harvard University, and Wesleyan University.

From 1970 to 1979 Ellison held the Albert Schweitzer Chair in the Humanities at New York University. After his retirement he published *Going to the Territory* (1986), a second collection of essays. Although he worked steadily on the second novel, Ellison published no further excerpts in his lifetime. Close to his eightieth birthday, he told an interviewer that "there will be something very soon." But within a month he was stricken with a virulent, rapidly accelerating case of pancreatic cancer. When Ellison died on 16 April 1994, at his home on Riverside Drive in Manhattan, the novel and other literary projects were left unfinished. He is buried in Trinity Cemetery in New York City.

Ellison left behind a remarkable array of rich manuscripts, correspondence, and papers. Between 1995 and 2000 four volumes were posthumously published, including *The Collected Essays of Ralph Ellison* (1995); *Flying Home and Other Stories* (1996); *Juneteenth* (1999), the central narrative of his unfinished novel; and *Trading Twelves: The Selected Letters of Ralph Ellison and Albert Murray* (2000). Yet to be published were a scholarly edition of the fragments of the unfinished second novel, a volume of letters, and memoirs of Ellison's early life in Oklahoma and his experience in New York in the 1930s. Since Ellison's death, interest in his work and his life has accelerated in the United States and abroad, where foreign language editions of his fiction and, to a lesser extent his essays, sprout like dragon's teeth. The publication of the posthumous *Juneteenth,* edited by his literary executor, John F. Callahan, prompted reconsideration of Ellison's place in literary history. By virtue of *Invisible Man* and the rest of his oeuvre, a consensus is forming that he occupies a place of preeminence not only in American and African American literature but also in twentieth-century world literature.

★

Ralph Ellison's papers and correspondence are in the Manuscript Division of the Library of Congress. There is also Ellison material in the James Weldon Johnson Collection of the Beinecke Library at Yale University and in the archives of New York University. Maryemma Graham and Amritjit Singh, eds., *Conversations with Ralph Ellison* (1995), is a collection of his interviews. Collections of critical essays by Ellison and others, and interviews with Ellison, include John Hersey, ed., *Ralph Ellison: A Collection of Critical Essays* (1970); Michael S. Harper and John Wright, eds., the *Carleton* Miscellany (winter 1980); Kimberly W. Benston, ed., *Speaking for You: The Vision of Ralph Ellison* (1987); and Robert J. Butler, ed., *The Critical Response to Ralph Ellison* (2000). Among several noteworthy books about Ellison and his work are Robert G. O'Meally, *The Craft of Ralph Ellison* (1980), and Mark Busby, *Ralph Ellison* (1991). Eric J. Sundquist, *Cultural Contexts for Ralph Ellison's* Invisible Man (1995), is a useful casebook on that novel. There is an obituary in the *New York Times* (17 Apr. 1994).

JOHN F. CALLAHAN

ERIKSON, Erik Homburger (*b.* 15 June 1902 in Frankfurt, Germany; *d.* 12 May 1994 in Harwich, Massachusetts), psychoanalyst who theorized that psychological development is best understood in the context of social, geographical, and historical circumstances and is best known for his study of the adolescent "identity crisis" and as a founder of the discipline of psychohistory.

Erikson was the son of Karla Abrahamsen, a member of a prominent Jewish family in Copenhagen, Denmark. Karla's first husband had abandoned her four years before she became pregnant and she was sent to live with relatives in Germany for the birth of her first child. In Germany, Abrahamsen met the pediatrician Theodore Homburger, and the couple was married in 1905. Erik was told that Homburger was his biological father and carried his name beginning in 1905. Until 1911, when Erik was legally adopted by Homburger, his birth certificate listed his father as Valdemar Salomonsen, Karla's first husband, but the true identity of Erikson's biological father is unknown. He

Erik Erikson. ARCHIVE PHOTOS

and his two half sisters were raised in the upper-middle-class Jewish neighborhood of Karlsruhe. (Another child died at age two.) Erikson attended the local gymnasium, where, according to Erikson's own account, his tall, blond, blue-eyed physical appearance often marked him as different from other Jewish children, just as his name and family marked him as different from the dominant German Gentile culture. Later in life, Erikson often noted that his early years as an immigrant and as an adopted child placed him on the margins of multiple cultural identities and prompted his lifelong concern with the nature of identity formation in individuals and groups.

Beginning in 1922, the young Erikson undertook a *Wandhershaft,* an extended period of wandering, reading, reflection, and journal writing typical of many middle-class European youths of his day. As he traveled around Europe, he occasionally found employment as a portrait sketch artist. In 1927 he accepted a life-changing invitation from his friend Peter Blos to work with children at the Hietzing School in Vienna, Austria, established primarily for children of the psychoanalytic patients of Sigmund Freud and associates. Erikson's exceptional skills with children quickly caught the attention of Sigmund Freud's daughter, Anna, who invited the young man to enter analysis. Anna

Freud's goal was to train Erikson as one of the first child analysts in the Vienna psychoanalytic circle. At her urging, Erikson also completed Montessori training in 1932, the only official diploma he ever earned. During this period of his life, he met and married Canadian-born Joan Serson, a student of dance and crafts, on 27 September 1930. The couple settled into domestic life in Vienna while Erikson completed his psychoanalytic training with the Vienna Psychoanalytic Society. Their first son was born in 1930. In 1933, after a second son was born, Erik was admitted as a full member of the society, which gave him the credentials to practice psychoanalysis internationally. By 1933 the Eriksons had become wary of Adolf Hitler's power and influence over Austria. Anti-Semitism was on the rise in the region, and the family left that year for Denmark and later for the United States.

Soon after arriving in America, Erikson opened a private practice in psychoanalysis in Boston, which provided a simple but adequate income for the young family's basic needs. In 1938 Joan gave birth to a daughter. Erikson's psychoanalytic practice began to grow, and he soon found himself called upon to consult with members of the Boston Psychoanalytic Society and the prestigious Judge Baker Clinic. He also obtained research fellowships at the Harvard Psychological Clinic and Massachusetts General Hospital's department of psychiatry. In 1939, with the encouragement of his older children and wife, Erikson applied for U.S. citizenship, and the family name was officially changed from Homburger to Erikson.

During his long career, Erikson taught at Harvard, Yale, and the University of California at Los Angeles and served in a variety of research and clinical settings. He also had an extended clinical appointment at the Austin Riggs Center in Stockbridge, Massachusetts, for the treatment of psychoanalytic patients. Erikson became well known among psychoanalytic practitioners in the nation as a gifted analyst with children, and they often referred their most difficult cases to him. In 1935 he began an association with Yale University, where he pioneered studies in the use of toys in the psychoanalysis of children. During this time Erikson also engaged in a number of anthropological studies with Native Americans in the American West. While at UCLA in 1951, in protest of the extremes of McCarthy era politics, Erikson refused to sign the loyalty oath required of faculty members employed by California universities and resigned his position.

In 1944, Joan Erikson gave birth to a fourth child, who was born with Down's syndrome. The child was immediately institutionalized and his existence kept secret. It was a traumatic experience for Erikson, and the boy's birth and absence from the home seemed to establish a backdrop and shadowy context for his work on "normal" childhood development. In 1950 Erikson published a collection of essays,

Childhood and Society, which included case studies, historical reflection, theoretical constructions, and anthropological studies. Perhaps the most penetrating essay was a study of Hitler's psychological development as a child and adolescent, in which Erikson anticipated much current thought on "gang" behavior among adolescents and adults. After the publication of *Childhood and Society,* Erikson gradually began to shift his emphasis from clinical work to writing, speaking, and teaching. He always gave credit to his wife as coauthor of his work. By 1970 Erikson was a well-known figure in American cultural life. In that year, his picture appeared on the cover of *Time* magazine, and his work and career were featured in numerous national publications. Erikson's study of the sixteenth-century church reformer Martin Luther (*Young Man Luther,* 1958) and of Mohandas Gandhi (*Gandhi's Truth,* 1969) were popular among social critics of the time, and the work on Gandhi won the Pulitzer Prize. In 1973 he was selected from more than 200 nominees to present the Jefferson Lectures sponsored by the National Endowment for the Humanities.

Erikson's primary contribution to American intellectual and cultural history came through his writings. When *Childhood and Society* was published in 1950 it received respectable but limited attention. The work was rediscovered, however, during the civil rights movement of the 1960s and again during the Vietnam War. Erikson's mapping of the human life cycle and particular emphasis on the identity crisis struck a chord with those who saw America suffering from its own version of a collective identity crisis. New notice was also given to Erikson's work on Martin Luther, wherein Erikson combined psychoanalysis and history in a particularly vivid fashion, sparking an ongoing interest in the use of psychology within the disciplines of historical and cultural studies. His work on Gandhi, completed shortly after the assassination of Martin Luther King, Jr., provided an alternative perspective on violence, political oppression, and the psychology of human freedom.

In 1975 the critic Marshall Berman published an article in the *New York Times Book Review* that accused Erikson of denying his Jewish heritage by changing his name and by de-emphasizing the significance of ethnic identity. While most who knew the complexity of Erikson's personality thought the accusation was overly harsh, it did raise questions that troubled the aging Erikson deeply. He chose not to respond, aside from reminding his public that he had retained his stepfather's name as his middle name throughout his life. It is also worth noting that Erikson's final major literary effort was a largely unknown psychohistorical essay on Jesus of Nazareth, "The Galilean Sayings and the Sense of 'I'" (Yale Review, 1982). In this complex essay, Erikson drew together the breadth of his psychoanalytic and historical interests, with particular emphasis on the contribution of Jewish culture in the development of a moral alternative to the mechanized violence of the modern world. Speaking from the "margins of psychology and theology," Erikson framed a vision, informed by the disciplines of history and psychoanalysis, of a universal "table fellowship" in which human beings might find peace and mutual affirmation. In the end, however, Erikson did not commit himself in this essay or anywhere else to a particular religious or ideological position. Erikson was a sought-after speaker until frailty and illness began to lessen his vigor. He died peacefully at age ninety-two in a nursing home. He is buried in the Cemetery of the First Congregational Church in Harwich.

Erikson's work on human psychological and social development is imbedded in the very language by which Americans and others discuss and analyze individual and collective identity formation. The subject of "identity crisis" has worked its way into countless research and therapeutic projects. His work on the stages of the human life cycle has shaped the conversation in our culture about life passages from infancy to old age. He pioneered "psychohistory" in his works on Luther, Hitler, Thomas Jefferson, Gandhi, and others. While psychohistory as a specific discipline has never flourished, it is commonplace now for historians to use some measure of psychological analysis in their writing, particularly in biographical work.

Erikson's primary contribution to American intellectual culture was his insistence that individual psychological development should always be studied and understood in the context of human social, geographical and historical realities. He was also a subtle but radical reformer of psychoanalytic thought and practice. Although he never launched a public critique of his Freudian heritage, he quietly set about upending the Freudian emphasis on pathology. By contrast, Erikson recast psychoanalysis with a particularly upbeat American flavor that emphasized the adaptability of ego development.

★

Harvard University's Houghton Library holds many of Erikson's more important manuscripts and papers. The most accurate and authoritative biography of Erikson is Lawrence J. Friedman, *Identity's Architect: A Biography of Erik H. Erikson* (1999), which is also the best overview of Erikson's writings. The Harvard psychiatrist and teacher Robert Coles wrote an extended commentary, *Erik H. Erikson: The Growth of His Work* (1970), but it is limited by its lack of critical perspective. Noteworthy critical examinations of Erikson are Paul Roazen, *The Power and Limits of a Vision* (1976), which takes Erikson to task for lack of experimental rigor; Frederick Crews, *Skeptical Engagements* (1986), which charges that Erikson was a particularly subtle and dangerous representative of Freudian orthodoxy; Hetty Zock, *A Psychology of Ultimate Concern: Erik H. Erikson's Contribution to the Psychology of Religion* (1990), a more positive examination of the existentialist force of Erikson's work and a summary of Erikson's work without re-

sorting to excessive reductionism; and Stephen Schlein, *A Way of Looking at Things: Selected Papers from 1930 to 1980. Erik H. Erikson* (1987), a collection of important essays. An obituary is in the *Washington Post* (14 May 1994).

DAVID C. ANDERSEN

EVERSON, William Oliver (Brother Antoninus) (*b.* 10 September 1912 in Sacramento, California; *d.* 3 June 1994 in Santa Cruz, California), poet and printer known as the "Beat friar."

Everson was the second of three children born to Louis Waldemar Everson, a native of Norway, the composer of "Selma, the Home of the Peach!," and a printer, and Francelia Marie Herber, a Roman Catholic from Minnesota who converted to Christian Science. Soon after William was born, the Eversons moved from Sacramento to Selma, California, fifteen miles southeast of Fresno in the central San Joaquin Valley.

The Everson Printery was a source of modest income for the family, supplemented by the elder Everson's service as justice of the peace and bandmaster. During summer vacations from Selma Union High School, beginning in 1924, William worked at the Libby cannery, which he continued to do throughout high school. In his senior year he fell in love with Edwa Poulson, a junior. After graduation

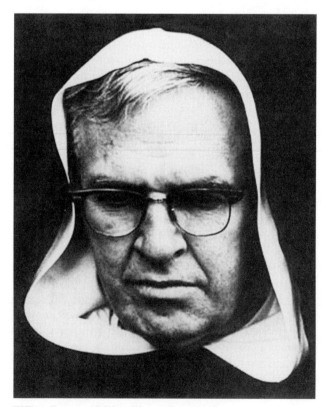

William Everson. AP/WIDE WORLD PHOTOS

from high school he enrolled in Fresno State College in 1931, but after one semester he dropped out, went back to work at the cannery, then took a job in New Mexico harvesting pine nuts. The pine nut project failed, and he returned to Selma. Working once again at the cannery, he was promoted to syrup maker. In November 1933 he enlisted in the Civilian Conservation Corps.

In the fall of 1934 Everson returned to Fresno State, where he discovered in the library a volume of Robinson Jeffers's poetry, which affected him deeply, persuading him to become a poet. After another semester at the college he dropped out again and returned to Selma to write poetry about the San Joaquin Valley, "to become a poet in my own right, to plant a vineyard, to commune with nature, and marry my high school sweetheart."

After a courtship of eight years Everson and Poulson were married in 1938, when she graduated from Fresno State and got a job as a schoolteacher in Dinuba, California. They leased the Wenty family ranch near Selma and planted muscat grapes. Everson found work in construction, first in building a new post office, then in laying concrete irrigation pipe. The Libby cannery in Selma moved to Sunnyvale, California, where he had seasonal work, again as a syrup maker. While there, he made a pilgrimage to Robinson Jeffers's Tor House in Carmel, California. In 1935 Everson published his first book of poetry, *These Are the Ravens,* an eleven-page issue in the Pamphlet Series of Western Poets printed by the Greater West Publishing Company in San Leandro, California, with partial subsidy from the author.

During 1938 he finished writing *The Masculine Dead* and *War Elegies* and began *The Residual Years* and *Poems MCMXLII.* In 1939 the fine printer Ward Ritchie published *San Joaquin,* with an introduction by Lawrence Clark Powell, a librarian at the University of California, Los Angeles, and author who became a good friend to Everson and influenced his development during the next decade. *San Joaquin* was a handsomely designed book and Everson's first major publication.

As the threat of war grew in Europe, Everson's pacifist convictions were reflected in a number of poems. Many of these he discarded, but with a loan from his friend Kenneth Carothers he sent *The Masculine Dead* to the publisher James Decker in November 1941. Decker was in financial trouble, so although the book did appear, Everson was disappointed at the number of typographical errors in it.

After a year of uncertainty about his draft status, Everson was summoned to Civilian Public Service Camp Number 56 in Waldport, Oregon, a former Civilian Conservation Corps camp to which conscientious objectors were sent to do forest-reclamation work. One of his poems appeared in the camp newsletter, *The Tide,* and he was enthusiastically involved in establishing an alternative weekly called *Untide,*

in which his "War Elegies," among other verses, appeared.

By March 1943 Everson had adjusted to his new surroundings. He wrote to Powell: "Of the 150 men here I have found one affinity, one near affinity, and a host of swell eggs. This is a most marvellous place to be cooped up in. And I suffer a deep sense of guilt that the situation is one I can enjoy while Edwa suffers in Selma."

Actually, Edwa's suffering was somewhat alleviated by the companionship of Carothers, who had loved her since high school; Carothers had been discharged from the army (after a nervous breakdown and the discovery in his pocket of a homosexual love letter) within weeks of Everson's induction into the Civilian Public Service.

Everson did not learn of the liaison for a year, but he accepted it. His only response was his long "Chronicle of Division." In 1944 the Untide Press published an enlarged version of *War Elegies* as well as *Waldport Poems,* which reflects his separation from Edwa. The Waldport Press published *The Residual Years: Poems, 1940–1941* in 1944 and *Poems MCMXLII* in 1945. On 23 March 1946 Everson was discharged from the Civilian Public Service, bought a Washington handpress, and moved to Ham and Mary Tyler's Treesbank Farm, near Sebastopol, California, where he spent time with Robert Duncan, Kenneth Rexroth, and other poets later called the Beats. He also met and fell in love with the artist and poet Mary Fabilli.

Everson next moved to Berkeley, where he installed his big press in Fabilli's home and took a custodial job at the University of California Press. Everson and Fabilli were married in Reno, Nevada, on 12 June 1948, after Everson's divorce in February of that same year; later they produced *A Privacy of Speech* (1949), which he wrote and set in type and she illustrated with wood-block prints. In 1948 Everson's first major collection of poems, *The Residual Years* (which included the poems from the earlier title of the same name), was published by James Laughlin at New Directions to predominantly favorable reviews.

Everson's marriage ended on 30 June 1949, when the Roman Catholic Church announced it would not recognize the union because Fabilli had been divorced while she and her first husband were members of the church. In late July 1949 Everson was baptized in Saint Augustine's Church in Oakland, California. That same summer he received a Guggenheim fellowship. He wrote poetic tributes to Fabilli in *Springing of the Blade* and "The Falling of the Grain." *Springing of the Blade* was produced in a handsome edition in 1968 by Kenneth J. Carpenter's Black Rock Press in Reno.

In 1951 Everson was accepted as a lay brother in the Dominican order and given the name "Brother Antoninus" at Saint Albert's College in Oakland. There the Seraphim Press published his *Triptych for the Living* on the Nativity. He devoted most of his time and energy to printing *Novum*

Psalterium Pii XII, of which he completed seventy-two pages over the next seven years. But he was still writing poetry, committing to verse his inner conflicts between Eros and Thanatos and between art and religion. In 1955 he had the seventy-two finished pages of the Psalter bound, and they were distributed in a limited edition by Countess Estelle Doheny of Los Angeles, a well-known collector of fine-press books.

In 1957 in *Evergreen Review* Rexroth published his "San Francisco Letter," in which he described the work of the Beat poets, conspicuously including Brother Antoninus. Antoninus published *The Crooked Lines of God* in 1959 and *The Hazards of Holiness* in 1962, both of which were well received. Reviews of his religious verse had stirred interest in the Beat friar—as well as the disapproval of the archbishop in San Francisco.

In 1959 Antoninus met Rose Moreno Tannlund, with whom he shared a brief but "intense relationship" that inspired his *Rose of Solitude,* which was published by Doubleday in 1967. In 1963 he was legally divorced from Fabilli, and he entered the novitiate in the Kentfield Priory.

At the end of 1969, however, at a poetry reading at the University of California, Davis, he read a love poem written to Susanna Rickson, "Tendril in the Mesh," and shed his Dominican robes. He married Rickson the following Saturday, 13 December 1969, and moved with her and her infant son to Stinson Beach, California. Their marriage ended in divorce in 1990.

From 1971 to 1981 Everson was poet in residence at the Santa Cruz campus of the University of California and lived at Kingfisher Flat, in the mountains north of Santa Cruz, where he installed his Washington press. He also taught printing at the university library's Lime Kiln Press, which produced two handsomely crafted Jeffers volumes, *Tragedy Has Obligations* (1973) and *Granite and Cypress* (1975). During his final years Everson suffered increasingly from Parkinson's disease, which with pneumonia was the cause of his death at Kingfisher Flat in 1994.

★

A major portion of Everson's correspondence, tapes, and other papers is in the Bancroft Library of the University of California, Berkeley. The Black Sparrow Press has published the most comprehensive collection of his poetry, *The Crooked Lines of God: A Life Trilogy,* which consists of *The Residual Years: Poems, 1934–1948* (1997), *The Veritable Years: Poems, 1949–1966* (1998), and *The Integral Years: Poems, 1966–1994* (2000). Albert Gelpi's biographical afterword to *The Blood of the Poet* (1994) is a good source, as are his introduction to *The Veritable Years* and Allan Campo's foreword to the same volume. Obituaries are in the *San Francisco Chronicle* (4 June 1994) and the *New York Times* (6 June 1994).

DAVID W. HERON

EWELL, Tom (*b.* 29 April 1909 in Owensboro, Kentucky; *d.* 12 September 1994 in Woodland Hills, California), actor whose starring appearance opposite Marilyn Monroe in *The Seven Year Itch* (1953) associated him with one of the twentieth century's most enduring sex symbols.

Ewell was born Samuel Yewell Tompkins, the son of Samuel William Tompkins, an attorney, and Martine Yewell, a homemaker. Nicknamed Straw because of his red hair, Yewell grew up fascinated with the showboats on the nearby Ohio River. He acted in grade-school theatricals and helped found the Rose Curtain Players at Owensboro Senior High School, from which he graduated in 1927. Later that year he entered the University of Wisconsin to study law but after four years decided, along with his college friend Don Ameche, to move to New York City to be an actor. At this point Yewell changed his name to Tom Ewell.

During his first decade in show business, Ewell appeared in a string of failures. His initial Broadway role, which he won because of his red hair, was a bit part as Red in *They Shall Not Die* (1934), which is based on the Scottsboro case involving nine black boys accused of raping two Alabama white women. As Ewell moved from flop to flop, he worked in odd jobs that ranged from elevator operator to street photographer. "I didn't do these crazy things because I wanted to—I had to," he said after he became successful.

Tom Ewell, 1971. THE KOBAL COLLECTION

World War II interrupted Ewell's theatrical career. He enlisted in the navy in 1942, served in the Atlantic and the Mediterranean, and had risen to the rank of lieutenant by the time of his discharge in 1945. On 18 March 1946 he married Judith Ann Abbott, the daughter of the theatrical producer George Abbott. The couple divorced soon afterward. Ewell next married Marjorie Sanborn on 29 April 1948; they had one son.

Ewell's theatrical fortunes improved in the late 1940s. He did well in *Apple of His Eye* in 1946 and then had his first hit in *John Loves Mary* (1947) as the hero's friend. He received accolades from *Variety*'s Poll of Drama Critics and a Donaldson Award. Ewell's success took him to Hollywood, where he appeared as the wayward husband in *Adam's Rib* (1949), starring Spencer Tracy and Katharine Hepburn. He made a number of other films, including *Up Front* (1951), based on the Bill Mauldin GI cartoon characters, and *Willie and Joe Back at the Front* (1952), which he claimed to have done "just for the money."

His greatest professional success came in November 1952, when he opened on Broadway as Richard Sherman in *The Seven Year Itch*. While his wife and child are away for the summer, Sherman, who has been married for seven years, pursues the attractive woman who lives above his apartment. The play featured Ewell soliloquizing to the audience about his thoughts, a technique that he repeated in the movie version of the play and other films. The role of the bumbling but earnest philanderer was perfectly suited to Ewell's rumpled stage persona of the lecherous, ineffectual middle-class male. "I've never read a part that gives an actor an opportunity for such variety," he told an interviewer. This part garnered Ewell a Tony Award in 1953 for best dramatic actor.

The Seven Year Itch was such a hit, running for 730 performances on Broadway and a national tour, that a screen version became the logical next step for its author, George Axelrod. Billy Wilder was hired to direct, and Marilyn Monroe, then at the height of her popularity as a sex goddess, was cast as the alluring woman upstairs. Although he was identified with the role of Richard Sherman, Ewell was not the first choice of the movie's producers. "Billy Wilder wanted me," Ewell said. He knew that Wilder had also considered Gary Cooper and William Holden for the part, but he did not know that Wilder had really hoped to sign Walter Matthau. In the end it became clear that Ewell was the best choice because Monroe's star power would determine the success or failure of the film at the box office. Ewell received $25,000 for his performance in the film, which was released in 1955.

Ewell found Monroe easy to work with, though in later life he told curious fans that he had no idea what she was really like. The film was not as funny as the play, but it contains one enduring image. Ewell stands next to Monroe when her skirt is blown upward by a blast of air from a New York City subway grate. Reproduced on countless posters and a seller on the Internet four decades later, the image gave Ewell a notoriety that overshadowed the rest of his career.

Through the rest of the 1950s and into the 1960s, Ewell stayed active in film and theater. His movies included two more roles with Hollywood's most glamorous starlets, *The Lieutenant Wore Skirts* (1956) with Sheree North and *The Girl Can't Help It* (1956) with Jayne Mansfield. He returned to Broadway in *The Thurber Carnival* (1960) and then appeared once again in his harried-husband role as the star of the short-lived *Tom Ewell Show* from 1960 to 1961. For the next two decades Ewell toured with stock companies and had character parts in movies such as *State Fair* (1962) and *The Last Tycoon* (1976). He was Robert Blake's sidekick, Billy Truman, in the television police drama *Baretta* (1975–1978). By that time Ewell had put on a good deal of weight. Beset with a drinking problem early in his stage career, he confined himself to soft drinks later in life. By the 1980s he had retired to California, where he died after a long series of illnesses.

Ewell was a talented, competent actor who performed well in a variety of roles, but he was most comfortable as the 1950s male with libidinous urges that conflict with the middle-class lifestyle. In the right part, which *The Seven Year Itch* provided for him, he was a master of timing and the hilarious pause. When he crossed paths with Marilyn Monroe, he became a residual part of her legend and will be linked with her as long as *The Seven Year Itch* is shown and the photograph of Monroe's windswept dress is displayed.

★

There are a few documents relating to Ewell in the Phyllis McGinley Papers at Syracuse University. The *New York Herald Tribune* morgue at the Center for American History at the University of Texas at Austin contains a small file of clippings under the title "Mrs. Tom Ewell." The Kentucky Historical Society also has some clippings about him. A useful sketch is in *Current Biography Yearbook, 1961* (1962): 149–151. John S. Wilson, "Tom Ewell's Twenty-Year Pitch," *Theatre Arts* (May 1953): 18–22, and Herbert Mitgang, "Tom Ewell's Twenty-Year Itch," *New York Times Magazine* (19 Sept. 1954), are lively contemporary evaluations. Ewell's role in *The Seven Year Itch* is discussed in Donald Spoto, *Marilyn Monroe: The Biography* (1993), and Ed Sikov, *On Sunset Boulevard: The Life and Times of Billy Wilder* (1998). An obituary is in the *New York Times* (13 Sept. 1994). Ewell gave an informative interview in 1974 to the Southern Methodist University Oral History Project on the Performing Arts, which is available on microfiche (1978).

LEWIS L. GOULD

F

FACTOR, Max, Jr. (*b*. 18 August 1904 in St. Louis, Missouri; *d*. 7 June 1996 in Los Angeles, California), cosmetic chemist and businessman noted for inventing makeup products, formulating perfumes, and innovating marketing practices.

Factor was the youngest of four children of Max Factor, a wig maker and cosmetologist, and Esther Rosa Factor, a homemaker whose maiden name is not known. Factor also had two half brothers, each from one of his father's previous marriages. Given the name Francis at birth and called Frank, Factor changed his name to Max, Jr., on his father's death in 1938. The Factor family emigrated from Russia to St. Louis in 1902 so that Max Factor, Sr., could take advantage of the business opportunities at the World's Fair in 1904. Soon thereafter the family moved to Los Angeles, where the senior Factor hoped his skills in wig-making and cosmetic composition would be useful to the movie industry. Factor grew up in Los Angeles, attending local public schools until he left school in tenth grade to join the family business full time. After school and during holidays Factor and his brothers and sisters worked in the family cosmetics and wig-making business. He and his older brother Davis Factor made deliveries and took parts as extras in movies so they could make sure all the wigs were returned at the end of each day's shooting.

Factor worked with his father in the laboratory to develop new cosmetic products that solved problems caused by technological improvements in cameras and other equipment. During the 1920s the Factors developed improved greasepaints that gave actors and actresses a more natural appearance in black and white films. With the advent of color photography in the 1930s, actors and actresses turned the color of the surroundings. Addressing this problem, the Factors produced Pan-Cake makeup, which was so popular with the actresses that they took it home from the studios. Consequently the Factor family began to market their product to the general public. On 26 March 1933 Factor married Mildred ("Milly") Cohen. They had two sons.

By the time his father died in 1938, Max Factor cosmetics were sold throughout the United States and Europe. The company was characterized by innovative practices in product development and in marketing techniques. Family members continued the company's operations. Max Factor, Jr., president of the company, and Davis Factor, company chair, worked tirelessly to promote the company's creativity and growth.

After the end of World War II the company's fortunes burgeoned. In the company laboratories Factor experimented with perfumes and cosmetics for the movie studios and then marketed the successful ones to the general public. He is credited with inventing nonallergenic lipstick and waterproof mascara and was known for his sensitive nose.

Factor was a quiet, modest man of great kindness. He remained married to Milly until her death in 1969, something of a feat in Hollywood circles. A short, dapper man

Max Factor, Jr., with actress-model Perry Sheehan, 1950. ASSOCIATED PRESS

with wavy hair and an engaging smile, Factor was known for remembering the names of the people who waited on him in restaurants. After the Factor family sold the company to the Norton Simon Company in 1973, Factor retired and devoted his time to his favorite charities, including Cedars-Sinai Medical Center in Los Angeles and the Devereaux Foundation for the mentally disabled in Santa Barbara, California. He died of congestive heart failure in Los Angeles at ninety-one years of age. He is buried in Hillside Cemetery in Los Angeles.

Although it is difficult to separate Factor's contributions from those of the rest of the family, his innovations affected many women in the 1950s and 1960s. When Max Factor, Sr., began to sell cosmetics to the general public in the 1920s, societal attitudes toward the use of cosmetics were negative. The Factor family's marketing efforts contributed to a dramatic change in applications and attitudes toward cosmetics. Although Max Factor, Jr., did not invent lipstick, his improvements made the product an important part of many women's attire.

★

Facets of Factor's career are detailed in Fred E. Bosten, Robert A. Salvatore, and Paul A. Kaufman, *Max Factor's Hollywood* (1995), a lavishly illustrated book about the family company. Mary Tannen provides a description of Factor with personal tributes

from family and friends as well as details of his long and successful career in the *New York Times Magazine* (29 Dec. 1996). Obituaries are in the *Los Angeles Times* (9 June 1996), *New York Times* (14 June 1996), and *Economist* (15 July 1996).

ELLEN LOUGHRAN

FAUBUS, Orval Eugene   (*b.* 7 January 1910 near Combs, Arkansas; *d.* 14 December 1994 in Conway, Arkansas), governor of Arkansas who precipitated a constitutional crisis over school desegregation in 1957.

Faubus was the oldest of seven children born to John Samuel Faubus, an Ozarks farmer and Socialist, and Addie Joslen, a homemaker. His father barely escaped imprisonment for organizing opposition to U.S. involvement in World War I. At age eighteen Orval became a teacher, though he had only an eighth-grade education, a common practice in the rural South during the early twentieth century. He moved to Huntsville, the Madison County seat, twenty-five miles from his home, to attend high school. When he graduated he was twenty-four and had been married for three years to Alta Haskins, the daughter of a rural clergyman. For eleven years Faubus alternated between teaching in the winter and working as a migrant laborer in the summer. He traveled to the upper reaches of the Midwest to pick fruit and vegetables. He went to Washington State to burn brush in the timber woods.

His only experience with higher education became an issue after he entered politics. At his father's urging he spent three months in 1935 at Commonwealth College, a school with strong Socialist party connections in western Arkansas. The Communist party edged out the Socialists during the late 1930s and became the dominant force at the school. Nineteen years after Faubus enrolled at Commonwealth, in his first race for governor, his opponent tried to portray him as a dangerous left-wing radical. Faubus actually had already turned his back on his father's socialism and become a New Deal Democrat by the time he decided to run for office. He campaigned unsuccessfully for the state legislature in 1936, then ran for and won the office of Madison County circuit clerk and recorder in 1938.

Faubus served as an intelligence officer during World War II and took part in some of the heaviest fighting of the European theater, including the Battle of the Bulge. He attained the rank of major in army intelligence. He returned home a hero but somewhat hardened by the war, and as a personable man with dark good looks, he appeared to be a promising politician. He was disappointed when he lost an election for the coveted office of county judge in 1946 to a man who had stayed home and advanced his political career instead of going to war. A friend in Congress rescued Faubus and had him appointed postmaster of

Orval Faubus. LIBRARY OF CONGRESS

Huntsville. In March 1947, regaining his confidence, Faubus bought the weekly *Madison County Record*. He used the newspaper's influence to promote a statewide group of reformist war veterans, and he became friendly with the movement's leader, Sidney McMath.

McMath became governor in 1949 and appointed Faubus to the state highway commission and later made him an assistant in his own office. In those positions Faubus came to know the leading political figures of Arkansas. Those associations gave him an advantage in his ambitious challenge of a respected incumbent governor in the Democratic primary of 1954. It was that governor, Francis A. Cherry, who revealed Faubus's Commonwealth College connection, which until then was known by only a few friends in the Ozarks. Faubus was defended by a strong liberal faction that included the state's most influential newspaper, the *Arkansas Gazette*. He narrowly won the primary and went on to defeat a Republican in the general election, taking office as governor in 1955.

Faubus's early years as governor were progressive in the tradition of the Upper South. He continued McMath's work of removing racial barriers in the state Democratic party. He acquiesced in the desegregation of several Arkansas schools in districts that had small black enrollments. He muscled a tax increase through the legislature to raise salaries for teachers. He improved highways, cleaned up a scandalously inadequate hospital for the mentally ill, and built a model institution for retarded children. Before leaving office he would become a powerful environmentalist on one critical issue. He faced down the U.S. Corps of Engineers and stopped the construction of a dam across one of the most beautiful free-flowing rivers in the South,

making possible the creation of the Buffalo National River. All those accomplishments, however, were overshadowed by a single event that branded Faubus as a racial demagogue and soured the name of Little Rock around the world for at least a generation.

Little Rock, the state's largest school district, had arranged to desegregate one school, Central High, with a token number of black students in the fall of 1957, three years after the Supreme Court, in *Brown* v. *Board of Education of Topeka, Kansas,* had declared segregated schools to be unconstitutional. The plan had been endorsed by a federal judge over the objections of the National Association for the Advancement of Colored People, which favored more extensive integration. But even token dismantling of racial segregation in the schools was bitterly opposed by the Arkansas Citizens Council, part of the South's leading organization of white supremacists. Segregationist leaders portrayed integration as a communist plot and vowed resistance at every level. Those leaders had been buoyed in 1956 by the publication of an extraordinary document from Washington, D.C., known as the Southern Manifesto, which challenged the legality of the Supreme Court's school decision and urged southerners to resist it. Virtually every southern member of Congress, including all six members of the Arkansas delegation, signed the manifesto.

Faced with growing white resistance to the Little Rock plan during his second term, Faubus sent the Arkansas National Guard to surround Central High School on the night of 2 September 1957. The troops had orders to keep nine black students out of the school the next morning. The governor went on television to explain that he had received reports that caravans of armed men were headed for Little Rock to block integration by violence. He said there were further reports that white and black youths had been buying large numbers of knives and other weapons. A subsequent investigation by the Federal Bureau of Investigation revealed no unusual sale of weapons. Years later a leader of the segregationist movement claimed that he and his followers had deceived the governor and school authorities into believing that violence was imminent.

On 20 September a federal court ordered Governor Faubus to stop blocking desegregation of the school. He withdrew the National Guard, but when the nine black students entered Central High School three days later, they were greeted by a mob that seemed intent on harming them. Policemen spirited them out a back entrance. The mob included many Citizens Council members and sympathizers. There was evidence that people close to the governor had encouraged the turnout. In fact, one of the governor's friends was observed inciting the crowd.

President Dwight D. Eisenhower responded to Arkansas's challenge to federal authority by sending units of the U.S. Army to Little Rock to restore order and escort the black students into the school. The soldiers remained for much of the school year. Meanwhile, Eisenhower also ordered the Arkansas National Guard into federal service, making those troops reluctant enforcers of the court order.

Faubus continued to speak out against what he called "forcible integration," but he was careful to avoid the risk of contempt of court. The governor encouraged an eager state legislature to pass a series of laws designed to thwart or slow down integration. He used one of those laws to close Little Rock's four high schools for a year. That rash action galvanized Little Rock's cowed leaders into a successful citywide campaign to reopen the schools with token integration. The governor made no further attempt to stop integration and turned his attention to other matters.

Faubus's opponents, led by the *Arkansas Gazette,* denounced his anti-integration actions for years afterward as cynical and opportunistic. He insisted for the rest of his life that he had acted to protect life and property. He also maintained that he would have been defeated by a radical segregationist in the next election if he had not acted as he did, and there is some evidence that he would have been.

Faubus rode his new popularity to four more two-year terms and, after twelve years in office, became the longest-serving governor in the state's history. He left office in 1967. With his longevity came unprecedented power over state government. The last years of his administration were marred by scandals, as a few of his underlings used their connections to enrich themselves. Faubus had little interest in money except for gifts from friends to build an expensive house and loans to pay substantial medical bills and other debts that he incurred after he left office.

His later life was tragic. Faubus divorced Alta in 1969 to marry a younger woman, Elizabeth Westmoreland. Farrell Faubus, Orval and Alta's only child, committed suicide in 1976. Elizabeth was murdered in her home at Houston in March 1983 while a divorce action against Faubus was pending. Faubus tried to regain the governor's office in 1970, 1974, and 1986. The voters rejected him soundly each time. In 1986 he married Jan Hines Wittenburg, a teacher in Conway, and achieved a measure of consolation. He spent the rest of his life writing essays and memoirs and responding to increasingly rare invitations for public appearances. He died of complications from prostate cancer. He is buried in Combs Cemetery, a short distance from the ruins of the log cabin where he was born.

Faubus's views became more conservative during his later years, as if he were trying to match his beliefs with the defining moment of his public life. He continued to insist that his controversial action in 1957 not only protected life and property but also kept the governor's office out of the hands of a radical white supremacist. His critics took the view that it came to the same thing if a moderate like Faubus did the work of the radicals. Whatever the case, the inadvertent result of his action was to hasten the end of the

southern campaign of massive resistance to integration by forcing President Eisenhower to take a firm stand against state-led obstruction.

★

Faubus's personal and official papers are in the Special Collections Department of the University of Arkansas Library at Fayetteville, Arkansas. He wrote three books of autobiography: *In This Faraway Land* (1971), a memoir of his early life and his World War II experiences; *Down from the Hills,* 2 vols. (1980 and 1985), which uses newspaper clippings to trace his political career; and *Man's Best Friend: The Little Australian and Others* (1991), a collection of essays about dogs he had owned and the periods of his life that each represented. He is the subject of one full-length biography, *Faubus: The Life and Times of an American Prodigal,* by Roy Reed (1997). His 1957 actions on school desegregation are the subject of extensive commentary in books on civil rights and twentieth-century southern history, including: Virgil T. Blossom, *It Has Happened Here* (1959); Ernest Q. Campbell and Thomas F. Pettigrew, *Christians in Racial Crisis* (1959); Daisy Bates, *The Long Shadow of Little Rock* (1962); Elizabeth Jacoway and David R. Colburn, eds., *Southern Businessmen and Desegregation* (1982); Tony Freyer, *The Little Rock Crisis* (1984); Diane D. Blair, *Arkansas Politics and Government* (1988); Harry S. Ashmore, *Civil Rights and Wrongs* (1994); Melba Pattillo Beals, *Warriors Don't Cry* (1994); Numan V. Bartley, *The New South, 1945–1980* (1995); Sara Alderman Murphy, *Breaking the Silence* (1997); and William H. Cobb, *Radical Education in the Rural South: Commonwealth College, 1922–1940* (2000). Faubus is the subject of an entry in *Arkansas Biography: A Collection of Notable Lives* (2000). About seventy-five tape-recorded interviews with him can be found in the Roy Reed Papers at the University of Arkansas Library. Other recorded interviews, audio and video, are among the Faubus Papers in the same library. An obituary is in the *New York Times* (15 Dec. 1994).

ROY REED

FEATHER, Leonard Geoffrey (*b.* 13 September 1914 in London, England, *d.* 22 September 1994 in Encino, California), jazz musician and author, often called the dean of American jazz critics.

Leonard Feather was one of two children of Nathan Feather, who was in the real estate business, and Felicia Zelinski, a homemaker. Feather was educated at St. Paul's School and University College, London, where he graduated in 1932. His parents expected him to follow his father into real estate, but music intervened. He took up clarinet and piano at an early age and then began arranging. His interest in jazz began after hearing Louis Armstrong's recording of "West End Blues." After graduating from college he became involved in London's jazz culture and started to write about the music as well as to compose and perform. His first article was published in 1933 in the English mag-

Leonard Feather *(right)* with Woody Herman *(left)* and Nat King Cole *(center)*. © BETTMANN/CORBIS

azine *Melody Maker,* and it was the saxophonist Benny Carter who, while in England during the early 1930s, told Feather to write. Carter and Feather maintained a lifelong friendship.

Feather's affiliation with the American music magazine *Down Beat* began in October 1935, the year he made the first of several visits to the United States. He moved to New York in 1939. On 18 May 1945, Feather married Jane Larabee; the couple had a daughter, Lorraine. He became a U.S. citizen in 1948.

One of Feather's early accomplishments was to persuade Robert Goffin of *Esquire* to have that magazine poll sixteen jazz critics concerning the condition of jazz in 1943. This led to what was called the "First *Esquire* All-American Jazz Concert," held at the Metropolitan Opera House in January 1944. One of the greatest gatherings of musical talent on one stage at any single time, it included performances by Art Tatum, Coleman Hawkins, Jack Teagarden, Billie Holiday, Roy Eldridge, and Mildred Bailey. There were other *Esquire* concerts as well as the publication for several years of the annual *Esquire Jazz Book,* to which Feather contributed several features. The magazine also sponsored a series of all-star recording sessions for RCA, Commodore, and Continental. Much of the resulting music was produced by Feather, who in subsequent years produced music both for other composers and under his own name.

Feather was a composer and lyricist who sometimes worked in collaboration with his wife, Jane. He played piano and composed the tunes for a number of recording sessions, including "Evil Gal Blues" and "Blowtop Blues"

for the first record by the vocalist Dinah Washington. Other noted jazz artists who performed his compositions were B. B. King and Mel Tormé, along with such famous leaders of the swing era as Duke Ellington (who hired Feather as his press agent), Benny Carter, Lionel Hampton, and Louis Armstrong. In 1954 Feather toured Europe with a program called "Jazz Club USA" after his Voice of America radio series. Billie Holliday was the initial headliner. He also provided arrangements for bands, including Count Basie's, and wrote music for *The Weary Blues,* a reading of poems by Langston Hughes and produced by Metro-Goldwyn-Mayer in 1958.

During the late 1940s and the 1950s, Feather became embroiled in the discussion about the then-new style referred to as bop or bebop, espoused by Parker, Dizzy Gillespie, and others. Feather's first important book, published in 1949, was *Inside BeBop,* which in later editions was called *Inside Jazz.* This volume formed the background for much writing on bop over the next twenty years. Feather's truly great publication appeared in 1955: *The Encyclopedia of Jazz,* a catalog of biographical and other data assembled with the help of his fellow jazz critic Ira Gitler. The material was revised several times over the years. At the time Feather died the two were working on a new edition, *The Biographical Encyclopedia of Jazz,* published in 1999. In all, Feather produced eleven books on his chosen subject, in addition to album notes for thousands of LP records.

Even as he grew older, Feather's views on jazz continued to be of importance to his audience. While at *Metronome* in the mid-1940s, he created the "blindfold test" for judging music. On the air, Feather and other authorities would try to identify musicians and styles from blind listening to recordings. Although he did not embrace the jazz-fusion movement of the 1960s and 1970s, he continued to have the support of his readers. For more than fifty years there were few events relating to jazz that he did not observe and comment upon for *Down Beat, Esquire, Metronome, Playboy, Jazz Times,* or the *Los Angeles Times.* These events ranged from the classic jazz of the 1930s to the first Newport Jazz Festival in 1954 to the 1993 jazz concert at the White House of President Bill Clinton. In 1964 he earned the first Grammy for journalism ever awarded, and in August 1983 Feather received the *Down Beat* Lifetime Achievement Award.

Feather was the New York editor of *Down Beat* until the late 1950s, when he moved to Los Angeles and became a contributor to the *Los Angeles Times.* He also lectured at Marymount College and later taught at the University of California at Riverside and at Los Angeles, and at California State University at Northridge. During the course of his career he served as historian of the National Association of Jazz Educators, as a member of the Newport Jazz Festival Advisory Board, and as a member of the governing board of the National Academy of Recording Arts and Sciences. Feather's other activities included such jobs as jazz program director (1950–1952) and host of a weekly series (1967–1969) for the Voice of America. He hosted an ABC Radio musical quiz show called *Platter-Brains* from 1953 to 1958 and produced music broadcasts for the BBC (1959) and KNBC-TV (1971).

Feather died in Encino, California, nine days after his eightieth birthday, from complications caused by pneumonia. Thoroughly familiar with the music business, Feather used his knowledge to support varied styles of jazz in an even-handed way for over a half-century. A slim person of medium height, he believed in racial integration long before the practice became socially acceptable. Always "reliably professional," he viewed jazz as a long-term development in the performing arts. In a *Down Beat* tribute, John McDonough noted that Leonard Feather, "through his consistency, . . . achieved a rare passage for a working reporter: He evolved from journalist to historian."

★

Leonard Feather's scrapbooks are at the Lionel Hampton School of Music at the University of Idaho and, together with other material, are summarized on the website www.jazzcentral station.com. In Leonard Feather and Ira Gitler, *The Biographical Encyclopedia of Jazz* (1999), the citation for Feather is unusually detailed and marks the first time the writer appeared in one of his works. See also Feather's *The Jazz Years: Earwitness to an Era* (1987). Ian Carr et al., *Jazz, the Rough Guide* (1995), contains biographical and discographic material as does Roger D. Kinkle,

The Complete Encyclopedia of Popular Music and Jazz: 1900–1950 (1974). *Contemporary Authors,* vols. 61–64 and 146, contains extensive details on Feather's career. His recording activities are represented by *Dinah Washington's Greatest Hits* (LP, Pickwick International, no. SPC-3536), which contains numbers by Feather, his wife, Jane, and Lionel Hampton, recorded about 1960; *Night Blooming Jazzmen* (CD, Jazz Heritage, no. 513182A), a 1971 disk that features Feather as pianist, arranger, composer, and session director; and *The First Esquire Concert* (CD, Laserlight, no. 15723), a recording of the 1944 performance. An obituary by Peter Watrous is in the *New York Times* (24 Sept. 1994), and John McDonough's tribute is in *Down Beat* (Dec. 1994).

BARRETT G. POTTER

FEYERABEND, Paul Karl (*b.* 13 January 1924 in Vienna, Austria; *d.* 11 February 1994 in Genolier, Switzerland), philosopher best known for the "epistemological anarchism" of his book *Against Method* (1975).

Feyerabend was the only child of Rosa Witz, a seamstress, and Paul Feyerabend, a civil servant. Drafted at the age of sixteen, he served in the German army until 1945, when he was wounded while retreating from the Russian Army on the Eastern Front. As a result of this injury he suffered from chronic pain and walked with crutches or a stick for

Paul Feyerabend. DR. GRAZIA BORRINI-FEYERABEND

the rest of his life. In 1947 after studying singing and theater at the music academy in Weimar, Germany, he returned to Vienna and entered the university, studying history and physics. He became secretary of the Austrian College Society in Alpbach in 1948, attending summer seminars on the arts, sciences, and philosophy and quickly winning admission to the philosopher Karl Popper's inner circle. Feyerabend received his Ph.D. in 1951 with a dissertation on observation statements supervised by Victor Kraft. The following year he moved to London and studied with Popper after his first choice, Ludwig Wittgenstein, died before he arrived. He returned to Vienna in 1953 and acted as Arthur Pap's research assistant before taking up a position as lecturer in philosophy at the University of Bristol, England, in 1955.

An academic nomad, Feyerabend held positions at many universities, often concurrently. After moving to the United States in 1958 and visiting for a year at the University of California, Berkeley, he was hired with tenure in 1959 (the year he was naturalized), became associate professor in 1962, and taught there intermittently until resigning in 1990. The Minnesota Center for the Philosophy of Science gave him a fellowship three times between 1957 and 1961. Between 1965 and 1975 he lectured at the University of Hamburg, University College of London, the Free University of Berlin, Yale University, the University of Auckland (New Zealand), and the University of Sussex at Brighton, England. Some of these positions were tenured, but none lasted more than three years. Beginning in 1980 Feyerabend divided his time between Berkeley and the Federal Institute of Technology in Zurich, from which he was pensioned in 1991 due to age limits. He received the Austrian President's Award for science and fine arts in 1952 and Italy's Premio Fregene in 1990.

The bullet that lodged in his spine during World War II left Feyerabend impotent, but he nonetheless married four times, including Edultrud (married in 1948, divorced in 1949) and Mary O'Neill (married in 1956, divorced in 1958), and Barbara (married 1970, died 1972). He married his fourth wife Grazia Borrini on 10 January 1989 and with her seemed finally to achieve the intimacy and happiness that had eluded him throughout his life. Feyerabend died of an inoperable brain tumor on 11 February 1994 and was buried at the family gravesite in the Sud-West Friedhof of Vienna.

The controversy around Feyerabend surfaced in the wake of his 1962 essay "Explanation, Reduction, and Empiricism," which illustrated criticisms of the dominant philosophy of science with colorful historical portraits of key scientific advances. In the mid-1960s encounters with colleagues, especially Imre Lakatos, and student radicals stimulated Feyerabend to explore the relations between science and democracy, which he described provocatively in *Against*

Method: Outline of an Anarchistic Theory of Knowledge, first published in essay form in 1970. There and elsewhere, Galileo's conflict with the Catholic Church provided a central example of the irreducible complexity of scientific change. Responding to his critics, Feyerabend defended political relativism in *Science in a Free Society* (1978) and *Farewell to Reason* (1987). He finished his autobiography, *Killing Time* (1995), weeks before his death, and left a nearly complete manuscript, now published as *The Conquest of Abundance* (1999).

Feyerabend criticized "rationalist" accounts of science, which he thought were intended to elevate science above other forms of knowledge. For example, in the 1930s and 1940s logical empiricists such as Rudolf Carnap and Carl Hempel had distinguished science from metaphysics by arguing that even abstract theoretical terms (such as "atom") could be interpreted observationally, and that theory choice depends only on experience. In "Explanation, Reduction, and Empiricism," Feyerabend turned this view on its head. He argued that since the meanings of observation terms depend on theory and may differ from one theory to the next, experience is not a neutral medium for deciding between theories. Interestingly, he and his Berkeley colleague Thomas Kuhn claimed independently that competing theories may be "incommensurable": differences between their observation terms may preclude direct comparison. Many philosophical critics took this point to be indefensible or incoherent.

"Explanation, Reduction, and Empiricism" also reflects the influence of Karl Popper's critical rationalism, which Feyerabend later rejected. Reflecting on the relation between theory and observation, Popper distinguished science from metaphysics on two grounds: insistence on testable theories and rejection of theories that fail experimental tests. By 1970 Feyerabend was arguing that even theories that fail such tests should be developed, since the new methodological rules they embody may ultimately prove useful. Thus, in the sense that progress may depend on breaking rules, he wrote in *Against Method* that "science is an essentially anarchistic enterprise" and that "both an examination of historical episodes and an abstract analysis of the relation between idea and action show that the only principle that does not inhibit human progress is the principle: *anything goes.*"

Feyerabend's later works developed the political consequences of theoretical pluralism. In the absence of distinguishing criteria of the kind sought by rationalism, science falls into place as one tradition among many. From the standpoint of other traditions, its accomplishments may or may not seem worthwhile. Thus Feyerabend defended the right of the minority students entering Berkeley in the mid-1960s to make up their own minds about the cultural value of science and to develop alternative worldviews. More generally, even in later writings where he moved away from relativism, he hoped to challenge the unquestioned authority of the sciences over the opinions, values, and lifestyles of ordinary people.

This iconoclastic stance made Feyerabend unpopular with many scientists, but those who dubbed him "the worst enemy of science" failed to grasp his commitment to encouraging creativity in science. By the same token, the historians and sociologists of science who happily appealed to his relativism underestimated the attraction realism held for him. His early scientific realism, pluralist critique of rationalism, and historical writings all helped revitalize the philosophy of science, despite the trenchant criticisms of the notion of incommensurability. Both with philosophers who declare the disunity of the sciences, and with general readers who value the complexity and ambiguity of history above abstractions such as "truth," "reality," and "objectivity," Feyerabend's influence remains strong.

★

Cambridge University Press published Feyerabend's philosophical papers (vols. 1–2, 1981; vol. 3, 1999). His unpublished works are housed at the University of Konstanz, with microfilms at the University of Pittsburgh. For information about Feyerabend's life and career, see his autobiography *Killing Time* (1995). The lengthy introduction in Frederick Suppe, ed., *The Structure of Scientific Theories* (1977), puts Feyerabend's views in the context of mid-century philosophy of science. John Preston, *Feyerabend: Philosophy, Science and Society* (1997), provides a unified introduction to Feyerabend's central preoccupations. For a range of perspectives, see John Preston, Gonzalo Munevar, and David Lamb, eds., *The Worst Enemy of Science? Essays in Memory of Paul Feyerabend* (2000). Articles in the scientific press include William J. Broad, "Paul Feyerabend: Science and the Anarchist," *Science* (2 Nov. 1979); and John Horgan, "Profile: Paul Karl Feyerabend: The Worst Enemy of Science," *Scientific American* (May 1993), which uses the "worst enemy" trope ironically. Ian Hacking, "Paul Feyerabend, Humanist," *Common Knowledge* 3, no. 2 (spring 1994), is a moving tribute by a preeminent philosopher. An obituary is in the *New York Times* (8 Mar. 1994).

DAVID S. BULLWINKLE

FINCH, Robert Hutchinson (*b.* 9 October 1925 in Tempe, Arizona; *d.* 10 October 1995 in Pasadena, California), politician and presidential adviser who served as secretary of health, education, and welfare in 1969 and 1970.

Robert Finch was the son of Robert L. Finch, a politician, and Gladys Hutchinson, a homemaker. In 1932 his family moved from Arizona to Inglewood, California, where Finch attended public schools. He learned the importance of shrewd campaigning from his father, who, as a Republican, had won a seat in Arizona's predominantly Demo-

Robert Finch, 1986. ARCHIVE PHOTOS

cratic legislature. His father's death forced Finch to spend his adolescence working after school and during summers to support his family. After briefly serving in the Marine Corps during World War II, Finch enrolled in Occidental College in Los Angeles, where he formed the campus Young Republicans club and during his senior year served as president of the student body. In 1947 Finch received his B.A. degree in political science.

Finch's interest in politics never waned. In 1946 he campaigned for Norris Poulson, the Republican congressional candidate for California's Twelfth District, and became Representative Poulson's administrative assistant a year later. In Washington, Finch met Representative Richard M. Nixon, another California Republican, who urged him to study law. In 1951 Finch earned his LL.B. degree from the University of Southern California Law School. He ran strongly but unsuccessfully for Congress in 1952 and 1954. From 1956 to 1958 he chaired the Republican Central Committee of Los Angeles County.

In 1958 Finch moved to Washington, D.C., to become administrative assistant to Vice President Nixon, beginning a long association. Finch helped set the strategy and implement the tactics that earned Nixon the Republican presidential nomination in 1960. He managed the vice president's unsuccessful campaign against the Democrat John F. Kennedy. In 1962, when Nixon rejected his protégé's counsel and sought the California governorship against the Democrat Edmund G. ("Pat") Brown, Finch played a supporting role in the campaign. Following Brown's triumph, with Nixon's star descending, Finch remained one of Nixon's confidants. By the mid-1960s Finch had struck out on his own. In 1964 he managed Republican George Murphy's upset victory over Pierre Salinger for the U.S. Senate from California. Two years later Californians elected Finch lieutenant governor. His margin of victory exceeded, by 355,000 votes, that of fellow Republican Ronald Reagan, who had wrested the governorship from Brown. Finch established a more moderate identity than the conservative Reagan. During the 1966 election he opposed a state proposition, which Reagan backed, allowing any citizen to demand general censorship of material he or she deemed obscene. But Finch dissuaded Reagan from backing a rigid antipornography bill and from pursuing a probe of student unrest at the University of California at Berkeley. Finch, at Reagan's behest, chaired a committee on urban problems, especially those dealing with racial minorities. A pragmatic Republican unafraid to use governmental power to solve social problems, Finch won bipartisan support for legislation enhancing the state's power to loan money to minority businessmen, and he prodded white employers to recruit from disadvantaged groups.

In the late 1960s Finch was nearing political stardom. The columnist William S. White dubbed him in 1966 a "skilled political professional" embodying "mainstream" Republicanism. In 1968 John C. Waugh of the *Christian Science Monitor* wrote of two power centers in California politics, one clustering around Finch, the other around Reagan. There was something reminiscent of Robert Kennedy in Finch. Perhaps it was his youth and handsome, square-jawed appearance, or, more likely, it was his empathy for the plight of the poor and racial minorities. In 1968 he advised Nixon during the latter's successful campaigns for the Republican presidential nomination and his election to the White House.

Although Finch had considered running for the governorship or U.S. Senate in 1970, he agreed to serve as secretary of health, education, and welfare (HEW). As head of the largest federal department and Nixon's confidant, Finch was expected to make a great impact. Here was a young man, the *Chicago Tribune* opined in 1969, "with a potentially lustrous career ahead."

It was not to be. Finch proved unable to assert control over HEW's sprawling, Democrat-oriented bureaucracy. The secretary's indecision emerged when his choice for as-

sistant secretary for health, Dr. John H. Knowles, a moderate Republican, encountered opposition from the conservative American Medical Association (AMA). The dispute dragged on for five months until Nixon, deferring to the AMA, jettisoned the nomination. The president disliked Finch's approach to school desegregation, enforcing guidelines that required schools to desegregate by a certain date or lose federal aid, and opted instead for Attorney General John N. Mitchell's more deliberative approach of filing lawsuits against districts that refused to desegregate. Nixon opposed Finch's tolerant approach to student antiwar demonstrations, reasoning that it conflicted with Mitchell's firmer stance and made the administration appear inconsistent. On the positive side, Finch helped draft the president's welfare reform proposal, the Family Assistance Plan, which promised a minimum income to every American family. But Finch's health was declining, and in 1970 Nixon moved him from HEW to the White House to serve as counselor.

Finch's tenure as counselor proved both a blessing and a curse. The administration's onetime "fair-haired boy" never penetrated the president's inner circle, possibly insulating him from the crimes associated with the Watergate scandal. Finch handled such marginal (to Nixon) issues as recruiting women and Hispanics to federal offices. He did not command the respect of the White House chief of staff H. R. Haldeman or the domestic policy chief John D. Ehrlichman, who defined a "finch" as any example of "superwaffling." Although Finch returned to California late in 1972, following the president's landslide reelection and prior to the investigation of the Watergate scandal, his ties to Nixon shattered his political career. "I couldn't run for dog-catcher without it turning into a referendum on Watergate," he explained in 1974. "But at least I don't have any trouble sleeping at night." In 1976 he ran in California's Republican primary for the U.S. Senate, losing to S. I. Hayakawa.

Finch spent his last years in semiretirement, practicing law in Pasadena. Known for his boundless energy, he enjoyed swimming, tennis, and gardening. Finch passed time with his wife, Carol Crothers, a former teacher whom he had met at Occidental College and married in 1946, and their four children. He died of a heart attack and is buried at Forest Lawn Cemetery in Glendale, California.

Finch represented the Republican party's moderate wing, which viewed the state as the servant of opportunity. His age, energy, and interests placed him within the political mainstream during the 1960s. But Watergate destroyed Nixon's administration and, along with it, Finch's political career. With the onset of Reagan's presidency, Finch's brand of moderate Republicanism went into decline.

★

Finch's personal papers are at the Richard Nixon Library and Birthplace in Yorba Linda, California; his White House files are at the Richard M. Nixon Presidential Materials, National Archives, College Park, Maryland. Firsthand accounts of Finch's service in the Nixon administration include William Safire, *Before the Fall: An Inside View of the Pre-Watergate White House* (1975); John Ehrlichman, *Witness to Power: The Nixon Years* (1982); and H. R. Haldeman, *The Haldeman Diaries: Inside the Nixon White House* (1994). Secondary works include A. James Reichley, *Conservatives in an Age of Change: The Nixon and Ford Administrations* (1981); Joan Hoff, *Nixon Reconsidered* (1994); Dean J. Kotlowski, "Nixon's Southern Strategy Revisited," *Journal of Policy History* 10, no. 2 (1998); and Dean J. Kotlowski, "The Knowles Affair: Nixon's Self-Inflicted Wound," *Presidential Studies Quarterly* 30 (Sept. 2000). An obituary is in the *New York Times* (11 Oct. 1995). An interview between Finch and A. James Reichley is at the Gerald R. Ford Library, Ann Arbor, Michigan. Oral histories are at Butler Library, Columbia University, New York City, and the Oral History Program, California State University, Fullerton.

DEAN J. KOTLOWSKI

FINLEY, Charles Oscar ("Charlie") (*b.* 22 February 1918 in Ensley, Alabama; *d.* 19 February 1996 in Chicago, Illinois), controversial and innovative sports owner who assembled a baseball dynasty in the early 1970s.

Charlie Finley, 1973. AP/WIDE WORLD PHOTOS

Finley was one of the three children of Oscar Finley, a steelworker, and Burmah Fields. Finley attended Emerson High School for three years but graduated from Horace Mann High School in 1936. He played high school and American Legion baseball before beginning work in steel mills at age eighteen. At the outset of World War II, Finley tried to enlist in the U.S. Marines but was classified 4-F because of an ulcer. In 1941 he married Shirley McCartney; they had seven children. At the end of the war he took a sales position with the Travelers Insurance Company. Shortly thereafter Finley endured a bout of tuberculosis, which led to a lengthy hospital stay in 1946–1948. During his recuperation Finley had a conversation with a physician that triggered an idea: health insurance for people in the medical profession. Finley developed his idea into a plan for the American Medical Association; within two years the plan had made him a millionaire.

After making several failed attempts to buy a major league franchise, Finley purchased fifty-two percent of the Kansas City Athletics in December 1960, shortly after the death of the team's owner Arnold Johnson. Two years later Finley renamed the perennial American League doormat the A's. As many other owners had feared, with his radical ideas and forthright manner Finley quickly cemented his reputation as a maverick and a meddler. He continually interfered with his managers, giving them lineup and strategy "suggestions." Ernie Mehl of the *Kansas City Star* wrote that the manager Joe Gordon filled out a lineup card with the words "Approved by C.O.F." scrawled across the bottom. "C.O.F." stood for Charles Oscar Finley.

Although Finley knew little about managing a team, he did show some acumen for assembling one. With a group of excellent scouts, he began identifying young amateur players who formed a nucleus for the A's. In 1964 he targeted Jim Hunter, one of the country's best high school pitchers. Arranging for a police escort and a limousine to transport him to the modest Hunter home, Finley signed Hunter to a $75,000 bonus and contrived the nickname "Catfish" for his new pitching property. In 1966 Finley made the Arizona State University star Reggie Jackson the A's first pick of the amateur draft and personally recruited the slugging outfielder. Overwhelmed by Finley's charm, Jackson surrendered his football scholarship and joined Finley's band of budding stars.

The impact of players like Jackson and Hunter was not felt for several seasons. Yet while Finley's A's trailed the American League in many statistical categories, they became leaders off the field. In 1963 Finley proudly championed multicolored uniforms, the first in major league history. Showing a disdain for traditional colors, which he described as "eggshell white" and "prison gray," the owner introduced his favorite color scheme, green and gold. For home games the A's retained white jerseys but with green undershirts and gold lettering. On the road they donned gold jerseys with green undershirts. The A's eventually started to mix and match colors without regard to home or away status. Although the arrangement angered traditionalists, it satisfied Finley's wish to make the game more appealing in the age of color television. Finley also tinkered with the scheduling of A's games, adjusting start times to accommodate the working class fans. He scheduled weeknight home games at 7:00 P.M., Saturday night games at 6:00 P.M., and Sunday games at 2:00 P.M., with the latter start time giving fans a chance to attend church and eat lunch before heading to the ballpark.

Finley initiated several other gimmicks, including white shoes for his players in lieu of the traditional black; a mechanical rabbit that popped out from behind home plate and delivered baseballs to the umpire; a team mascot (a mule he named Charlie O); and a sheep pasture beyond the outfield. He also took pride in holding a Farmers' Night at Municipal Stadium that included a hog-calling demonstration and a greased-pig competition. On Farmers' Night in 1966 Catfish Hunter nearly lost the use of his hand when, during a milking contest, an angry cow kicked his pail three times.

Unfortunately, Finley's offbeat promotions did little to stimulate attendance in Kansas City. With the A's among the worst drawing cards in the league, Finley repeatedly promised to keep the team in Kansas City but simultaneously tried to move the franchise to other cities. Regularly petitioning other owners for permission to move, in October 1967 he finally received approval to relocate to Oakland, California.

As the A's moved to Oakland, they began to show signs of becoming a pennant-contending team. Still in need of an on-field leader, Finley made another of his frequent managerial moves on 2 October 1970, when he named Dick Williams as skipper. With the fiery Williams at the helm, the A's experienced unprecedented success.

During Williams's first spring training in 1971, the A's experimented with one of Finley's inventions, the three-ball walk. Finley wanted to adopt the rule to stimulate offense and speed up the pace of games. On 6 March 1971 the A's and the Milwaukee Brewers employed Finley's brainchild, and the two pitching staffs combined allowed nineteen walks. Unimpressed, Commissioner Bowie Kuhn ordered an end to the three-ball walk.

In 1972 Finley had more success with his most memorable promotion. After Jackson became the first major leaguer to sport a mustache since 1914, Finley announced plans to hold Mustache Day. All twenty-five players on the A's roster grew mustaches by Father's Day and collected $300 bonuses.

Although Mustache Day proved a public relations success, Finley's other marketing efforts fell flat. "[Many] promotions he draws up are hick-town promotions that don't go over here," explained the Bay Area columnist Glenn Dickey. Finley, whose strangely dark and heavy eyebrows in contrast to his white hair gave him an irritable, almost intimidating appearance, became even more unpopular when he stopped employing ball girls and no longer offered discounts on season ticket purchases. Only twice during Finley's reign in Oakland did the A's draw as many as 1 million fans in a season.

Although fan interest lagged, the quality of the team's play on the field did not. The A's claimed Oakland's first world championship in 1972, as a frenetic Finley engineered sixty-five transactions and employed a whirlwind of forty-seven players. Finley's first world championship did not stunt his thirst for innovation. In the spring of 1973 he introduced orange-colored baseballs, which he believed would be more visible to fans. Yet hitters complained that they could not see the orange balls, and fielders claimed the new balls were hard to grip. Much like the three-ball walk, the orange baseball died off quickly. Finley had more success in advocating another one of his favored concepts: the designated hitter. Although he was not the first to suggest the use of a replacement batter for the pitcher, he repeatedly pushed for the innovation throughout the late 1960s and early 1970s. In 1973 American League owners agreed to adopt the designated hitter rule, which partially appeased Finley's desire to add more offensive excitement to the game.

Finley's personal fortunes also worsened in 1973. On 7 August the overworked Finley suffered a heart attack. After his return from a short hospital stay, his behavior took a turn for the worse. He irrationally badgered Williams and cursed the American League president Joe Cronin during the playoffs. The owner's behavior reached its lowest point during the World Series. Moments after a disheartening defeat in game two, Finley harangued the second baseman Mike Andrews, who had made two critical errors, into signing a statement that he was injured and could no longer play. Oakland players revolted against the "firing" of their teammate, and Kuhn ordered Finley to reinstate Andrews. Infuriated by Finley's treatment of Andrews, Williams resigned as manager. Finley's heart attack seemed responsible for his increasingly cruel demeanor. "Most players—prior to the 1973 season anyhow—would consider Mr. Finley a father figure," explained the team captain Sal Bando. "With his heart attack, things started to change; he became more vindictive." Always penurious, a bitter Finley became especially difficult during contract negotiations with his players.

Finley's erratic behavior began to cripple his team after the 1974 World Series, when a failed insurance payment allowed Catfish Hunter to depart as a free agent. With their staff ace gone, the A's failed to win the pennant in 1975, ending a string of three consecutive world championships. On 15 June 1976 Finley tried to sell three of his best players, Vida Blue, Rollie Fingers, and Joe Rudi, but Kuhn negated the deals. Finley eventually watched most of his stars depart as free agents, destroying the team's fabric.

Unwilling to deal with escalating salaries created by free agency and arbitration, Finley finally sold the A's in 1980, the same year that he and his wife divorced. Finley lived in retirement in La Porte, Indiana, until his death from heart disease at age seventy-seven.

Finley's rash methods frequently made him an enemy of the baseball establishment. For example, he once called Commissioner Kuhn "the village idiot." Nevertheless, Finley succeeded in building one of the game's true dynasties. His creativity also proved visionary. By advocating World Series games at night, the designated hitter rule, and interleague play, he championed radical ideas long before they became fashionable.

★

Numerous clippings and files on Finley are in the National Baseball Hall of Fame Library in Cooperstown, New York. Several books provide detailed information about Finley's life and career, including Herb Michelson, *Charlie O* (1975); Bill Libby, *Charlie O. and the Angry A's* (1975); and Bruce Markusen, *Baseball's Last Dynasty: Charlie Finley's Oakland A's* (1998). Obituaries are in the *New York Post, New York Times,* and *USA Today* (all 20 Feb. 1996).

BRUCE MARKUSEN

FINNEY, Walter Braden ("Jack") (*b.* 2 October 1911 in Milwaukee, Wisconsin; *d.* 14 November 1995 in Greenbrae, California), writer known for his novel of travel into the past, *Time and Again* (1970), and for his novel *The Body Snatchers* (1954), which was adapted into film three times.

Finney was an intensely private, almost reclusive man. He never wrote any memoir pieces; he spoke in public only twice, one of those times to his goddaughter's grade-school class, and he rarely gave interviews. Thus, little is known of his personal life, and his writing is largely left to speak for itself, perhaps as Finney intended. In one interview Finney stated that when he was two years old his father, whose name is unknown, died. Finney and his mother moved to live with his grandparents in Chicago. One on-line biography adds that his stepfather, Frank Berry, was a railroad and telephone worker, and his mother, a homemaker, was also skilled in sewing and woodworking. Another source reports that Finney "amended his name to Jack for writing

Jack Finney. THE NEW YORK TIMES COMPANY

purposes," while the on-line biography states that he was born John Finney and called Jack but was legally renamed for his dead father.

After attending Knox College in Galesburg, Illinois, Finney lived in New York City and worked for an advertising agency sometime in the 1940s. He began writing his first works, suspenseful short stories, in 1946, and around that time he won an award from *Ellery Queen's Mystery Magazine* for "The Widow's Walk." Soon he wrote stories for other magazines, including *Collier's, Saturday Evening Post,* and *McCall's.* Although his short stories often featured fantasy or science-fiction elements, he marketed them to these "slicks" instead of "pulps" such as *Amazing Science-Fiction Stories.*

Around 1950 Finney married Marguerite Guest, who was called "Marg" with a hard *g.* According to an interview, they met in Reno while each was divorcing a previous spouse, but no other source mentions another wife for Finney. Jack and Marg had two children. Sometime between 1947 and 1954 Finney and his family moved to Mill Valley, California, near Sausalito, where he lived for the rest of his life. Finney remained little known, even in his hometown. He avoided friendships with other writers, spending most of his time at home and later visiting his children and his one granddaughter. His marriage with Marg was obviously close and mutually supportive, although he never told her about his stories before they were finished. Finney was careful with money and investments. In early 1995 Don Congdon, his agent for four decades, called Finney "an agent's dream" because he never asked for advances and always delivered a full manuscript for sale.

Doubleday published *Five against the House,* Finney's first novel, in 1954. This story of college students who plan to rob a casino in Reno, Nevada, was made into a movie starring Kim Novak in 1955. Finney disliked the film. The author's reputation rests largely on his next novel, *The Body Snatchers,* which was serialized in *Collier's* in 1954. The novel was adapted for the screen in 1956, 1978, and 1993 as *Invasion of the Body Snatchers.* The earliest adaptation, directed by Don Siegel, is generally considered the best. Finney collaborated on that screenplay.

The Body Snatchers, depicting a small town in which pods from space replace the inhabitants with almost exact duplicates, has been interpreted as an allegory of the perils of communism, of McCarthy-style anticommunism, of consumer conformity, and of fringe-cult obedience. Finney insisted he had no allegory in mind, just a striking suspense story inspired by scientific thought that life may have originated in outer space. The novel's happy ending appears in none of the film adaptations. Finney earned only $15,000 from all three films, $7,500 in the 1950s for selling all rights forever and $3,750 for each of the remakes due to a loophole in the copyright law. The setting of the novel, called Santa Mira in the first editions, was revealed as Mill Valley in later editions.

Finney's one play, *Telephone Roulette,* was published in 1956. The novel *Assault on a Queen,* a thriller about a plot to burglarize the luxury ship *Queen Elizabeth,* and *Good Neighbor Sam,* a humorous novel based on Finney's advertising experience, were published in 1959 and 1963, respectively. Both were made into movies in the 1960s.

Time travel, especially into the past, is a theme in much of Finney's work, both novels and short stories. Many critics find this fiction escapist, too nostalgic, and sentimental. Finney argued that he did show the past as flawed, though overall it is presented as offering a cleaner, gentler way to live. Simon and Schuster published Finney's second best-known novel, *Time and Again,* in 1970. This book tells the story of a New York City advertising illustrator who travels back to the 1880s and falls in love. Its exceptional historical detail, including photographs, made the book a favorite even among readers who dislike fantasy fiction, and the novel garnered critical praise that was unusual for fantastic fiction. Urged by his agent, Finney wrote a somewhat less

successful sequel, *From Time to Time,* published by Simon and Schuster in 1995. It was his last novel. In 1987 he won the World Fantasy Convention Life Achievement Award. He died of pneumonia in Marin General Hospital after a long, if little-publicized, career.

The impression of Finney that remains is of his books—well written, often ingenious, and emotionally effective whether thrilling or nostalgic—and the movies made from them. The Pod People of *Body Snatchers* have become cultural icons, like Frankenstein or Dracula, despite or perhaps because of their many possible interpretations. His time-travel stories, sometimes dismissed as overly sentimental, appeal to even hardheaded readers due to Finney's precise detail and atmospheric power.

★

Despite copious interpretations of films based on Finney's works, especially *Invasion of the Body Snatchers,* little has been written about his life. The *New York Times Magazine* (19 Mar. 1995) and the *Washington Post* (13 Feb. 1994) offer useful facts about and interpretations of Finney the man. Obituaries are in the *New York Times, Washington Post,* and *Los Angeles Times* (all 17 Nov. 1995).

BERNADETTE LYNN BOSKY

FISHER, Avery Robert (*b.* 4 March 1906 in Brooklyn, New York; *d.* 26 February 1994 in New Milford, Connecticut), audio equipment executive, entrepreneur, and patron of the arts for whom Avery Fisher Hall at Lincoln Center is named.

Fisher was the youngest of the six children of Charles Fisher, an owner of a clothing store in Manhattan, New

Avery Fisher, 1983. © BETTMANN/CORBIS

York, and Mary Byrach, a homemaker. His parents had immigrated to New York from Kiev, then a part of Ukraine in 1905. Fisher graduated from DeWitt Clinton High School in New York in 1924 and entered New York University that same year as a prelaw student, but later changed to biology and English. He graduated with a B.A. degree in 1929.

After graduation, the six-foot, stocky Fisher worked at an advertising agency that counted book publishers among its accounts. He left the agency in 1932 for employment with G. P. Putnam's Sons, a publishing company. In 1933 he left Putnam's to become a graphic designer for Dodd, Mead and Company, another publishing organization, for eighteen dollars a week. Leaving that company in 1943, he described book design as "my first love," and he continued to work on projects for Dodd, Mead through the subsequent years. He designed, among other works, *A History of the English-Speaking Peoples* by Sir Winston Churchill (1956) and *The American Seasons* by Edwin Way Teale (1976). Fisher gave his fees for those projects to charities because he felt that "looking at a beautiful typographical design is like listening to music."

In 1937 Fisher established his first entrepreneurial organization while continuing to work as a graphic designer. The Philharmonic Radio Company grew out of his hobby of building radios so he could get better sound than that available with the ready-made models then in use. He made significant improvements in amplifiers, tuners, and speakers. He later remembered that "a number of friends asked me to make for them the kind of equipment I was constructing . . . and before I knew it I had the beginnings of a business."

Fisher sold his first company in 1945 and started Fisher Radio the same year. That company entered the high-fidelity market with a line of components at premium prices. Audio fans acclaimed his products as the "Rolls-Royce of sound equipment." On 8 September 1950 Fisher married Janet Cane; they had three children. Fisher Radio brought out the first transistorized amplifier in 1956 and offered the first stereophonic radio and phonograph combination in 1961. Fisher assembled the engineering staff by hiring the best audio technicians from European companies. "Whenever another company needed an engineer, the first place they came to try to steal somebody was my company. I didn't blame them. I got my engineers from Europe," he said.

Fisher was an amateur violinist whose love of music prompted him to build high-quality radios and phonographs. He considered himself a musician who independently manufactured high quality high-fidelity equipment for music connoisseurs. He had become fascinated with music as a child through his father's large record collection and because everyone in the family played a musical in-

strument. Among his other amusements, he enjoyed tinkering with old automobiles.

Fisher sold Fisher Radio to Emerson for just under $31 million in 1969, when the audio market began to turn toward mass merchandising. The company was eventually sold to Sanyo of Japan. Fisher became a consultant to both companies and, in spite of having no financial interests, regularly attended the annual sales meetings.

After he sold his company Fisher devoted his time to philanthropy. He endowed the Avery Fisher Listening Room in the Bobst Library at New York University, and he donated $10.5 million to Lincoln Center in New York City. Lincoln Center's Philharmonic Hall, built in 1962, was renamed Avery Fisher Hall in his honor in 1973. He initially intended the gift as an endowment fund that would use eighty percent for the maintenance of the hall and the remaining twenty percent for the creation of the Avery Fisher Artist Program. The program offers two different prestigious awards. The larger is the Avery Fisher Prize of $25,000 for young American musicians in recognition of their valuable contributions to their profession. The other prize is the Avery Fisher Career Grant of $10,000 intended to assist with musicians' career-related expenses. Up to five grants are awarded every year. Avery Fisher Hall underwent modifications to address echoes in some areas and dry sound that did not resonate. Fisher became a member of the Board of Directors of Lincoln Center for the Performing Arts in 1975. The following year Avery Fisher Hall was reconstructed to fix its acoustical problems. Of the original gift from Fisher, $4 million was redirected to pay the cost of the reconstruction, which entailed the addition of panels to the ceiling to enhance the acoustics. Fisher took an active, if unofficial interest in the process, conferring with the architect and those responsible for the acoustics as the interior was planned. The renovation solved a number of the original problems.

In 1984 Fisher was elected a director emeritus of Lincoln Center for the Performing Arts. He also sat on the boards of the Chamber Music Society of Lincoln Center and the Marlboro Festival in Marlboro, Vermont. He died in New Milford Hospital of complications of a stroke and was cremated. He had homes in Manhattan and Washington, Connecticut. Fisher's audio designs and philanthropic activities notably contributed to American artistry.

★

An obituary is in the *New York Times* (27 Feb. 1994).

MARTIN JAY STAHL

FITZGERALD, Ella Jane (*b.* 25 April 1917 in Newport News, Virginia; *d.* 15 June 1996 in Beverly Hills, California), jazz singer acclaimed as among the greatest of her time.

Fitzgerald was born into poverty, the illegitimate child of William Fitzgerald and Temperance Williams. Little is known of her father, who separated from her mother when Fitzgerald was still a child, after which her mother moved her to suburban Yonkers, New York. When she was fourteen, her mother died. She was initially under the care of her mother's common-law husband Joseph Da Silva but soon moved in with an aunt in Harlem. Here she was inadequately supervised and was briefly placed in a reformatory, the Riverdale Children's Association. When she came out, she was homeless for a time.

Fitzgerald entered an amateur contest at the Apollo Theatre in Harlem, held on 21 November 1934. She initially intended to dance but changed her mind and sang; she won. When she subsequently won another amateur contest at the Harlem Opera House, the prize was a week's booking at the theater, and she made her professional debut there for the week beginning 15 February 1935. This exposure led to her being hired as a singer with Chick Webb and His Orchestra. She appeared with the Webb band at the Savoy Ballroom, where it had a residency. On 12 June 1935 she first recorded with Webb for Decca Records, singing "I'll Chase the Blues Away" and "Love and Kisses." Her first recording to gain commercial recognition was "Sing Me a Swing Song (and Let Me Dance)," recorded in June 1936. Though her voice and singing technique were not as well-developed here as they would be later on, she

Ella Fitzgerald. ARCHIVE PHOTOS

already exhibited a clear tone, careful articulation, and a supple, buoyant feel for rhythm. That November she sat in with Benny Goodman and His Orchestra on a recording of "Goodnight, My Love" for RCA Victor, subbing for Goodman's usual singer, Helen Ward; the record hit number one in February 1937. Notwithstanding this success, Fitzgerald returned to work with Webb. (Because she was African American, Goodman, who was white, would have had trouble hiring her permanently at the time, although she had attained a level of fame that gave her some autonomy.)

"(If You Can't Sing It) You'll Have to Swing It" (also known as "Mr. Paganini"), which became one of her signature songs, was on the charts in December 1936, and Fitzgerald scored a two-sided chart entry in April 1937 with "Dedicated to You"/"Big Boy Blue," on which she was accompanied by the Mills Brothers. "If You Ever Should Leave" and "All over Nothing at All," both on the charts during the summer of 1937, were issued under her own name, although she was accompanied by members of the Webb orchestra. "Rock It for Me" and "I Got a Guy" both reached the charts under Webb's name in 1938 before "A-Tisket, A-Tasket," which Fitzgerald cowrote with Al Feldman, based on a children's nursery rhyme, became a massive hit, topping the charts in August and selling more than a million copies, making it one of the biggest hits of the decade.

Fitzgerald continued to score hits with the Webb orchestra through the spring of 1939, reaching the top ten with "I Found My Yellow Basket" (a follow-up to "A-Tisket, A-Tasket"), "F. D. R. Jones," and "Undecided." By the time the chronically ill Webb died on 16 June 1939, the twenty-two-year-old singer had gained sufficient prominence to be asked to front the band, which she did, and Ella Fitzgerald and Her Famous Orchestra did their first recording session for Decca less than two weeks later. In January 1941 they scored a top-ten hit with "Five O'Clock Whistle."

Fitzgerald married Benjamin Kornegay on 26 December 1941, but the marriage was annulled. She was married a second time, to Ray Brown, a bass player, on 10 December 1947. They adopted a son and divorced on 28 August 1953.

In July 1942 Fitzgerald gave up the orchestra, opting to perform as a solo act with accompaniment by a small group called the Keys. On the day before the start of the recording ban called by the American Federation of Musicians for 1 August 1942, she recorded "My Heart and I Decided," which reached the top ten of the rhythm and blues (R&B) charts in May 1943. Although her race restricted her opportunities, she had had a network radio show for a few months in 1939 and had made her film debut in *Ride 'Em Cowboy* in 1942. With recordings precluded and travel difficult due to World War II, she returned to radio in August

1942, hosting a twice-a-week show with the Keys through November and then a once-a-week slot on her own through June 1943.

Decca Records settled with the musicians union in the fall of 1943, allowing Fitzgerald to record again, and at her first session she cut "Cow-Cow Boogie (Cuma-Ti-Yi-Yi-Ay)" with the Ink Spots; the disc hit the top ten of the pop charts and number one on the R&B charts. A second pairing with the vocal group in August 1944 was even more successful, producing the two-sided hit "Into Each Life Some Rain Must Fall"/"I'm Making Believe," which topped both the pop and R&B charts and sold a million copies. Fitzgerald continued to chart hits on the pop and R&B charts through the early 1950s, often in combination with other artists. Her popular recordings included "And Her Tears Flowed Like Wine" and "It's Only a Paper Moon" (both in 1945); "I'm Beginning to See the Light" (1945) with the Ink Spots; "You Won't Be Satisfied (Until You Break My Heart)" and "The Frim Fram Sauce" (both in 1946) with Louis Armstrong; "Stone Cold Dead in the Market (He Had It Coming)" and "Petootie Pie" (both in 1946), "Baby, It's Cold Outside" (1949), and "I'll Never Be Free" (1950) with Louis Jordan and His Tympany Five; "(I Love You) For Sentimental Reasons" (1946) with the Delta Rhythm Boys; "That's My Desire" (1947) with the Andy Love Quintet; "My Happiness" (1948) with the Song Spinners; "It's Too Soon to Know" (1948); and "Smooth Sailing" (1951). The last song was an example of Fitzgerald's remarkable scat-singing (wordless vocal improvising) ability, which she also displayed in such memorable 1940s recordings as "Flying Home," "Oh, Lady Be Good," and "How High the Moon."

Such recordings gave the lie to later assertions that Fitzgerald was forced by Decca to record only pop and novelty material and to stay away from jazz singing. Another notable recording from the Decca era was the 1951 album *Ella Fitzgerald Sings Gershwin Songs,* on which she was accompanied only by the pianist Ellis Larkins, a release that preceded the start of her celebrated series of songbook albums by five years.

In February 1949 Fitzgerald had begun to make appearances in the Jazz at the Philharmonic concerts promoted by the impresario Norman Granz, who took over as her manager. Granz also ran various record labels and had strong ideas about Fitzgerald's recording career, but he was at first unable to get her away from Decca. Meanwhile, she made her second film appearance in *Pete Kelly's Blues* (1955), and her album of songs from the soundtrack, also featuring her costar, Peggy Lee, became a top-ten hit.

At this point Granz finally succeeded in ending Fitzgerald's Decca contract, and he immediately signed her to his recently formed Verve Records label. One of his ideas was to have her record a series of two-disc albums backed by an orchestra, each devoted to the work of a great song-

writer. The first of these efforts was *Ella Fitzgerald Sings the Cole Porter Song Book,* recorded and released in 1956, which became a critical and popular success. Fitzgerald and Granz followed it with a Richard Rodgers–Lorenz Hart album in 1957, a Duke Ellington album in 1958, an Irving Berlin album, also in 1958, a massive five-album set of the works of George and Ira Gershwin in 1959, and subsequent collections devoted to Harold Arlen (1961), Jerome Kern (1963), and Johnny Mercer (1965). These albums were celebrated efforts that sold well and earned industry accolades. They were showered with the newly instituted Grammy Awards: the Ellington album won a best jazz performance Grammy; the Berlin album took a best vocal performance Grammy; and "But Not for Me" from the Gershwin set won another best vocal performance Grammy. By bringing together songs that had been scattered among long-forgotten Broadway shows, the albums also had the effect of renewing and consolidating the reputations of the songwriters, who benefited from some of the best interpretations of their work ever done.

The songbook albums were not Fitzgerald's only recordings for Verve in this period. She cut three albums with Louis Armstrong that were popular successes, *Ella and Louis* (1956) and the double LPs *Ella and Louis Again* (1957) and *Porgy and Bess* (1959). The 1959 album *Ella Swings Lightly,* on which she was accompanied by the Marty Paich Dek-Tette, won a Grammy for best jazz performance. At the same time she was performing in the country's top nightclubs and, increasingly, in larger venues, such as Carnegie Hall in New York City and the Hollywood Bowl in California. She also made another film, *St. Louis Blues* (1958), a biography of the musician and composer W. C. Handy, and had guest-star appearances on television. She began to work more frequently overseas, and one of her European shows provided her next record hit. She appeared in Berlin on 13 February 1960, and the show was released on LP as *Mack the Knife—Ella in Berlin.* The title track was a performance of the Kurt Weill standard on which Fitzgerald forgot the lyrics and instead improvised a delightful commentary, turning what could have been an embarrassment into a triumph. The track became a Top 40 hit and won a best vocal performance Grammy, while the album, also a Grammy winner, had a long run in the charts. The same year, Fitzgerald made her last film appearance in *Let No Man Write My Epitaph.*

Fitzgerald continued to earn Grammys and have healthy record sales during the early 1960s. A follow-up live album, *Ella in Hollywood* (1961), was on the charts for much of 1962; *Ella Swings Brightly with Nelson* (Nelson being the conductor and arranger Nelson Riddle) won her another vocal performance Grammy in 1962; *Ella and Basie,* a collaboration with Count Basie's Orchestra, was a chart item in 1963; and her *Hello, Dolly!* album charted in 1964.

Although Fitzgerald still performed successfully in the mid-1960s, her recording career fell into decline. Granz had sold Verve Records to Metro-Goldwyn-Mayer (MGM) at the start of the 1960s but continued to oversee her career at first. Eventually, however, having moved to Europe, he became less involved with her. At the same time the revolution in the recording industry brought about by the arrival of the Beatles threw all non-rock music into the shade. Fitzgerald left Verve in 1966, signing with Capitol Records, where she recorded the religious album *Brighten the Corner,* which reached the charts in 1967. In 1969 she switched to Reprise Records, where she charted with *Ella,* an album of contemporary pop songs. Such recordings dismayed her jazz fans, but in 1972 Granz returned to the record business with his Pablo label. Fitzgerald immediately signed with the company and went back to making jazz records, which she did for the rest of her life. The inauguration of a Grammy Award for best jazz vocal performance in 1976 led to another series of nominations and trophies that trace the highlights of her later discography. She won Grammys for *Fitzgerald and Pass . . . Again* (1976), on which her sole accompaniment was the guitarist Joe Pass; for *Fine and Mellow* (1979); for *A Perfect Match* (1980), a live album with Count Basie; for two songs on *Digital III at Montreux* (1981), from the same 1979 concert that produced *A Perfect Match;* for *The Best Is Yet to Come* (1983); and for *All That Jazz* (1990), which was her thirteenth award.

The bulk of Fitzgerald's time was spent touring the world, often playing at the increasing number of jazz festivals. She was able to work only intermittently in the early 1970s due to recurring eye trouble, but in 1973 she expanded her schedule to include appearances with symphony orchestras. Despite advancing age, she continued to tour extensively in her sixties and seventies. In 1986, suffering from congestive heart failure, she underwent open-heart surgery. When she recovered, she went back on the road. She was finally forced to retire due to ill health in 1992. She died of complications from diabetes three years later and is buried in the Inglewood Park Cemetery in Inglewood, California.

Ella Fitzgerald was an amazing singer with excellent intonation and a range spanning several octaves. Her straight singing rendered service to the songs that brought out their best qualities, and her scatting improvisations were as imaginative as the soloing of any jazz musician. She was also an excellent mimic who could re-create the sounds of various instruments and do spot-on impersonations of everyone from fellow female singers to her gravel-voiced colleague Louis Armstrong.

She was, in addition, an animated performer who spread delight among her listeners. Her only serious rival to the title of the greatest of all female jazz singers is Billie Holiday, and a comparison of the two is instructive. They were close in age (Holiday was two years older), and both suffered enormously as children, subject to dire poverty, broken homes, and stints in reform schools. Both emerged as singers in the Harlem of the 1930s, escaping from their conditions into the rarefied world of recording studios and nightclubs. Holiday, with a limited instrument, focused on an individual interpretative style that gave her performances a haunting quality. She lagged behind the beat and seemed to evoke tragedy with every note. Fitzgerald had a girlish quality; she was full of energy, and her performances were celebrations. It is as hard to imagine Holiday singing "A-Tisket, A-Tasket" as it is to think of Fitzgerald performing Holiday's signature song, the protest lyric "Strange Fruit." Of course, drugs destroyed the voice, career, and life of the one performer and not the other. But no starker contrast between the two greatest female jazz singers of the twentieth century can be heard than that of their separate recordings from the 1957 Newport Jazz Festival released by Verve. (It was reissued on compact disc in 2000.) Holiday, less than two years before her death at forty-four, is ghostlike and almost voiceless; Fitzgerald, at her peak, turns in a typically buoyant performance despite technical glitches. For Fitzgerald it was another in the thousands of performances she gave between her debut in 1934 and her retirement in 1992, one in which she pleased her audience with a display of vocal prowess in the service of sheer joy.

★

Two lesser biographies, Sid Colin's *Ella: The Life and Times of Ella Fitzgerald* (1986) and James Haskins's *Ella Fitzgerald: A Life Through Jazz* (1991), preceded the first major study of her life and career, Stuart Nicholson's *Ella Fitzgerald* (1993). Nicholson, a professional biographer and jazz scholar who also wrote a book about Billie Holiday, is a strong researcher and a good music critic, but his book is written at a distance from its subject. All of the above are British efforts. The only American biography is Geoffrey Mark Fidelman, *First Lady of Song: Ella Fitzgerald for the Record* (1994). As he recounts in his introduction, Fidelman began his book on the advice of an official at Granz's office who gave him the impression he would get greater cooperation than he did. Nevertheless, the book is a reasonable account of Fitzgerald's life, written just before her death when she had stopped performing. Also worth noting are Bud Kliment's well-written biography for young adults, *Ella Fitzgerald* (1988), and editor Leslie Gourse's anthology *The Ella Fitzgerald Companion: Seven Decades of Commentary* (1998). But the definitive book about Ella Fitzgerald has yet to be written. There is an obituary on the front page of the *New York Times* (16 June 1996).

WILLIAM J. RUHLMANN

FONER, Philip Sheldon (*b.* 14 December 1910 in New York City; *d.* 13 December 1994 in Philadelphia, Pennsylvania), Marxist labor historian and prolific author of works on the underclasses in U.S. history.

Foner (with his twin brother, Jack) was the first of four children born to Abraham and Mary Smith Foner. His father was a Jewish immigrant from Russia; his mother emigrated from Poland. During Foner's youth his father was a deliveryman (later a garage owner) and was interested in left-wing causes. Philip worked at odd jobs from an early age and was educated in the New York City public schools. From 1928 to 1932 he attended City College in New York and earned a B.A. degree. In 1933 he was awarded an M.A. degree in history from Columbia University, where he was a student of the noted Civil War historian Allan Nevins. In 1941 Foner earned his Ph.D. at Columbia with a dissertation on the connections between northern businessmen and slavery in the Civil War era.

While working on the doctorate, Foner was an instructor in history at City College, where he was instrumental in founding the college teachers union in 1935. In 1941 the Rapp-Coudert Committee of the New York legislature conducted hearings into possible communist infiltration into the teaching profession. Foner, along with two of his brothers, was among the more than forty teachers and others who were fired for their leftist sympathies. Blacklisted as a result, Foner would not return to the academic world until 1967.

At a May Day demonstration in 1938 Foner became reacquainted with Roslyn Held, a member of the nursery school teachers union. They were married on May Day the following year and had two daughters. Roslyn, who developed a reputation as a book designer, died in 1983. Foner later married Rhoda Lischtash; that marriage ended in divorce in early 1991.

Following his blacklisting, Foner threw himself enthusiastically into liberal causes. He was a founder of the Jefferson School of Social Science, a workers college, in 1942. He also taught classes for a number of labor unions in the Congress of Industrial Organizations. From 1941 to 1945 he served as educational director of the Fur and Leather Workers' Union and regularly contributed a column on labor history to *Tempo*, the union magazine. He also became chief editor and part owner of Citadel Press, which specialized in publishing works that mainstream publishers considered too liberal.

In 1967 Foner returned to academia when he was hired to teach history at Lincoln University (a primarily African American school) near Philadelphia. He retired from Lincoln in 1979. Two years later he was finally vindicated when the Board of Trustees of the City College passed a resolution apologizing for his firing, admitted that his academic freedom had been violated, and vowed that it would not happen again.

Throughout his life Foner was a prolific writer. By the end of his career he had authored or edited more than 110 volumes, as well as several score scholarly articles. Above all else, Foner was a labor historian. In his work on labor history he challenged the position of John R. Commons that organized labor was primarily accommodative and conservative in adapting to conditions in the United States. Based solely on his *The History of the Labor Movement in the United States* (of which ten volumes were published in 1947–1994), Foner's reputation as the outstanding labor historian of the twentieth century is secure.

Foner's legacy is far more extensive, however. He was also the historian of those left out of the American mainstream. He published a number of volumes on African American history, including the three-volume *History of Black Americans* (1975–1983), and dealt with gender issues in the three-volume *Women and the American Labor Movement* (1979–1982) and other works. Foner's interests reached beyond the United States; he published volumes on British workers; on Karl Marx, Karl Liebknecht, and José Martí; and on U.S. imperialism in Latin America. In addition to the numerous works that he wrote, he edited a host of important collections of writings by such figures as Thomas Paine, Frederick Douglass, Mark Twain, and Mother Jones. He also edited *The Factory Girls: A Collection of Writings on Life and Struggles in the New England Factories of the 1840s* (1977). While many of his early works found publication only with radical publishers, the mainstream press was anxious to produce his works as his career blossomed.

Politically committed his entire life, Foner often published relevant and timely major works during periods of controversy. Examples of such are *The Black Panthers Speak* in 1970 and *American Labor and the Indochina War* the following year. He averaged two books and a number of articles and speeches each year for more than a half century. This productivity was possible because of his unusual ability to work on numerous projects at the same time. Moreover, these were not superficial works; professional scholars were impressed by his careful mining of the traditional sources and his talent for uncovering hitherto unused materials. In 1976 he received the Deems Taylor Award from the American Society of Composers, Authors, and Publishers for his *American Labor Songs of the Nineteenth Century* (1975). Along with his three brothers, he was given the Tom Paine Award by the National Emergency Civil Liberties Committee in 1986.

Foner remained a radical to the end of his life. He was always ready to attend a demonstration or a political rally and to lend his voice to an unpopular cause. He was a Marxist, but he saw Marxism as a philosophy and method of analysis rather than as rigid dogma. He also challenged some of the interpretations of the New Left, including its Maoism.

Throughout his life he enjoyed watching tennis, listening to classical music (he played the alto saxophone as a young man), attending the theater, and spending time at his cottage in Maine. He also became a world traveler and was a popular visitor in Cuba, the Soviet Union, and the People's Republic of China.

Following his retirement Foner continued to write, publish, and lecture. After a long illness he died of heart failure in 1994, just one day short of his eighty-fourth birthday. His body was cremated.

Generally categorized as a labor historian, Foner was far more. Few writers have produced a corpus of work as extensive as his. Even scholars who criticize Foner's conclusions find little fault with his thorough research and his penchant for allowing the sources to carry his narrative. Foner combined the instincts of a fighter, a lasting commitment to the forgotten in American life, and a dedication to research and scholarship with a deep and lasting humanitarian outlook.

★

The papers of Philip Foner are in the Tamiment Institute Library in New York City. Those interested in his complete bibliography should consult the pamphlet by Roger Keeran, *Philip Sheldon Foner: A Bibliography,* published by Empire State College/SUNY (1994). An obituary is in the *New York Times* (15 Dec. 1994).

ART BARBEAU

FORTE, Fulvio Chester, Jr. ("Chet") (*b.* 7 August 1935 in Hackensack, New Jersey; *d.* 18 May 1996 in San Diego, California), college basketball star who became director of *Monday Night Football* before his career was virtually destroyed by his addiction to gambling.

Forte, the son of Rosanna and Fulvio Chester Forte, Sr., initially sought to follow his father into medicine before sports altered the direction of his life. Forte first drew attention as a basketball player while at the Fifth Avenue Junior High School in suburban Hackensack, New Jersey, where he stood out in spite of, or perhaps because of, his lack of size. His career blossomed at Hackensack High School on a team whose senior class produced collegiate players for three colleges. One of his teammates, Charles Brown, accompanied him to Columbia University in New York City, although Brown proved to be a better baseball player than basketball player at the collegiate level.

At Columbia, Forte was an immediate sensation, starring for his freshman team. At that time freshmen were not eligible for varsity competition. As a sophomore he was the leading scorer, 22.4 points per game, on a team that finished in a three-way tie for first place in the Eastern Intercollegiate League, forerunner of the Ivy League, but lost the first playoff game and was eliminated. Forte's play was

seemingly effortless. With close-cut dark hair and thin limbs, he possessed a wide variety of shots, creating ways to elude defenders and launch the ball toward the basket in what appeared to be an endless improvisation.

Forte's junior season was curtailed when he did not achieve acceptable grades in chemistry. He sat out the season's final eight games, probably costing his team a chance for the league championship. In the 1956–1957 season Columbia lacked the defensive and rebounding prowess to be a serious contender for league honors. But Forte, the team's captain and a senior, had his finest year, averaging 28.9 points per game and winning the Haggerty Award as the best college player in the New York City area.

Although only five feet, nine inches tall and about 145 pounds, Forte was a dynamo on the court with athletic quickness and ball-handling skills that confounded larger opponents. His performance earned him all-American honors. He was selected College Player of the Year by United Press International in 1957 over such stars as the seven-foot-tall Wilt Chamberlain of Kansas. On 12 February 1951 Forte set a Columbia record against Pennsylvania with 45 points in a single game, a record that stood until 1991. He held more than a dozen school records for game, season, and career performances.

Forte finished his collegiate career with 1,611 points in 65 games (a 24.8 point average) and his three varsity teams won 50 of 73 games. But Forte's size limited his professional potential. Although he was chosen in the National Basketball Association player draft by the Cincinnati Royals (now the Sacramento Kings), he failed to make the team. Forte played in a tour against the Harlem Globetrotters, but the basketball portion of his life was then largely behind him.

In 1962 the Columbia athletic director Ralph Furey contacted Roone Arledge, a young Columbia alumnus whose television career at the American Broadcasting Company was rising fast, about employing Forte, who shortly thereafter joined ABC Sports. At the time Arledge was trying to make ABC-TV competitive with the other networks, and Forte became one of his prime instruments. Forte began working on *Wide World of Sports,* an anthology show that covered a wide range of events, and he shortly proved as creative in the director's seat as he had been on the basketball court, ultimately directing over 300 episodes for *Wide World of Sports.* He branched out into horse racing, auto racing, and basketball, as ABC gradually began competing for live events with CBS and NBC, then the two dominant networks in sports television.

A sea change for both ABC Sports and Forte occurred in 1970, when the National Football League commissioner Pete Rozelle persuaded the network to launch *Monday Night Football,* a part-sports, part-entertainment program wrapped around a football game. Arledge immediately saw it for what it was and assigned Forte as its director. Under Forte's control the event became an American national phenomenon. Forte met Arledge's demands for "up close and personal" coverage with hand-held, sideline cameras and a variety of angles from a dozen other locations. He was also the ringmaster for the three-ring circus in the announcers' booth, where Howard Cosell and Dan Meredith squabbled their way through Frank Gifford's play-by-play call.

Forte directed *Monday Night Football* from its inception until 1986 along with innumerable other major events, including Super Bowl XIX, the World Series, the baseball All-Star Game, and the Olympics. In the 1980s he earned over $900,000 annually. However, underneath this facade of success a gambling addiction was slowly destroying his lifestyle. Following the sale of the ABC network to Capital Cities in 1986, cost-cutting measures reduced what the new owners saw as the production excesses of programs such as *Monday Night Football*. Forte's protests over the new approach cost him his job, despite his eleven Emmy Awards for his sports directing excellence. Some thought his gambling habit, which was well known among ABC executives, contributed to the end of his ABC career.

Forte later admitted to losing more than $4 million in wagers. Once his income declined, Forte, desperate to sustain his habit, lost his million-dollar home in suburban Saddle River, New Jersey, and defrauded a New Jersey businessperson of $100,000. In 1990 Forte pleaded guilty to income tax evasion and wire fraud. He was sentenced in 1992 to 500 hours of community service because the judge determined that he had reformed. In 1990 Forte moved to San Diego and began working as a sports talk-show host on XTRA-AM, an all-sports radio station. His salary was slightly over $1,000 per week, compared to his salad days at ABC Sports, when he earned more than seventeen times that figure. Forte also became a regular at Gamblers Anonymous and frequently appeared on the organization's behalf. He directed some National Football League games for NBC-TV in 1994 and worked as a radio commentator on XTRA's broadcasts of the San Diego Chargers football games in the year before his death.

Forte died in his home at Rancho Santa Fe of a heart attack, survived by his wife, Patricia (whom he married in 1977) and their daughter, Jacqueline. A cardiologist, Steve Gross, failed to respond to phone calls from Forte's wife as her husband experienced classic heart failure symptoms the day he died. Two years later a jury ruled that Gross had been negligent and awarded Forte's wife and daughter $1.7 million in damages.

★

Forte recounted his years with *Monday Night Football* in an article in *Sport* magazine (Feb. 1995). An obituary is in the *New York Times* (19 May 1996).

BILL SHANNON

FOWLER, William Alfred (*b.* 9 August 1911 in Pittsburgh, Pennsylvania; *d.* 14 March 1995 in Pasadena, California), physicist and educator who was foremost in creating the field known as nuclear astrophysics and whose studies of nuclear reactions in stars won a Nobel Prize in 1983.

Fowler was the eldest of three children of John Macleod Fowler, an accountant, and Jennie Summers Watson, a homemaker. Fowler was raised in Lima, Ohio, from the age of two when his father's accounting firm transferred there. His teachers at Lima Central High School encouraged his early interest in engineering and science. An excellent student in academic subjects, Fowler was also active in high school athletics and as a senior won a letter in football. He had an enjoyable youth, observing later in life that near his home was a "running creek and swimming hole. What a wonderful environment it all was for my boyhood!"

While in high school, Fowler won a prize for an essay on the production of cement. Upon graduation in 1929 he selected ceramic engineering as a course of study when he matriculated that fall at Ohio State University in Columbus. As a sophomore he switched his academic focus to engineering physics. During the summer he worked as a recreation director at his boyhood elementary school in Lima, while during the academic year he waited on tables, washed dishes, and fired furnaces at a university sorority. On weekends, he cut and sold ham and cheese in an outdoor stall in a Columbus market.

He spent after-school hours in the electrical engineering department electronics laboratory, where he prepared an undergraduate thesis titled "Focussing of Electron Beams." Graduating with a bachelor of engineering physics degree in 1933, Fowler enrolled as a graduate student at the California Institute of Technology (Caltech). There Fowler came under the supervision of Charles C. Lauritsen, the principal physicist in Caltech's W. K. Kellogg Radiation Laboratory. Fowler viewed Lauritsen as the most important person in his scientific career. Under Lauritsen's direction he wrote his Ph.D. dissertation, "Radioactive Elements of Low Atomic Number," which demonstrated that nuclear forces are symmetric; that is, the interaction forces between two positively charged protons or two neutrons (nuclear particles without charges) are identical once classical electric forces are excluded. Fowler was awarded his doctoral degree in nuclear physics in 1936 with the highest possible academic distinction, summa cum laude.

Fowler was then appointed a research fellow in nuclear physics at Caltech, where he continued his scientific career of nearly fifty years. In 1939 he was appointed an assistant professor of physics and in 1942 was promoted to associate professor. In August 1940 Fowler married Ardiane Foy Olmsted; they had two daughters. That same year, and continuing for most of World War II, Fowler and most of

William Fowler. © BETTMANN/CORBIS

the Kellogg Laboratory staff were engaged in weapons research for the government that included work on proximity fuses for bombs and ordnance rockets for the U.S. Navy. In 1944 he went to the South Pacific in a civilian scientific capacity for three months. During the last two years of the war, Fowler and other Caltech scientists were involved in producing components for the atomic bomb Manhattan project.

After the war, stimulated in large part by the work of the German American physicist Hans Bethe (who won the Nobel Prize in 1967), Fowler and his colleagues turned the primary activities of the Kellogg Laboratory to the study of nuclear reactions that take place in stars. In 1938 Bethe had proposed a detailed mechanism by which energy could be generated inside stars, involving reactions of the nuclei of carbon, nitrogen, and oxygen. These reactions were closely related to the ones being studied in the laboratory by Fowler. Pursuing these investigations at Kellogg and recognizing their important implications, Fowler and Lauritsen designated the focus of their general investigations as "nuclear astrophysics," recognized thereafter as a discipline of its own.

Another of Fowler's collaborators was the English astrophysicist and cosmologist Fred Hoyle, whom Fowler described as the second great influence in his life after Lauritsen. Hoyle in the early 1950s had conjectured that in order for carbon to exist in the universe (and therefore enable the existence of human beings on earth) it must be manufac-

tured in stars. This could only happen if three helium nuclei (each with two protons and two neutrons) fuse together to form the isotope carbon-12 in an excited energy state level above the neutral ground state. Despite theoretical reasons for believing this nuclear reaction could not occur, Hoyle persuaded Fowler to investigate the question experimentally. Fowler then established the validity of Hoyle's hypothesis.

The success of this important experiment led to the conclusion that all elements known in nature, from carbon to uranium, could be produced by nuclear processes in stars, starting with the hydrogen and helium produced at the birth of the universe in the famous "big bang" twelve to fifteen billion years ago. (The term "big bang" was first used by Hoyle in 1950. However, Hoyle rejected this "big bang" concept in favor of a steady-state theory in which the universe had an eternal life.) The theory was presented in *Reviews of Modern Physics* as the landmark article "Synthesis of the Elements in Stars," written by Fowler and Hoyle together with Geoffrey Burbridge and Margaret Burbridge.

Hundreds of related experiments performed by Fowler or his graduate students confirmed nucleosynthesis in stars quantitatively. His research gave impetus to later developments in cosmology by himself and others illuminating difficult questions such as the emanation of radio waves from distant galaxies by gravitational collapse, the occurrence of supernovae, and the origin of the unusual massive stellar objects discovered in 1963 known as quasars. In 1965 he collaborated with Fred Hoyle on the book *Nucleosynthesis in Massive Stars and Supernovae*, and in 1967 his book *Nuclear Astrophysics* was published.

In 1983 Fowler received the Nobel Prize in physics "for his theoretical and experimental studies of the nuclear reactions of importance in the formation of the chemical elements in the universe," which, the Nobel committee said, over the decades since the 1950s had been confirmed in its correctness by more recent progress in nuclear physics. He shared the prize with Subrahmanyan Chandrasekhar of the University of Chicago.

In addition to the Nobel Prize, Fowler won numerous other honors during his career. He was elected to the National Academy of Sciences in 1956. He received the United States Medal for Merit (1948), the National Medal of Science (1974), the Eddington Medal of the Royal Astronomical Society (1978), the Bruce Medal of the Astronomical Society of the Pacific (1979), and the Legion d'Honneur of France (1989). He was named Institute Professor of Physics at Caltech in 1970, a title he held until 1982 when he retired as professor emeritus. Columbia University conferred its 1973 Vetlesen Prize on Fowler, and in 1976 he was elected president of the American Physical Society. He received honorary degrees from the University of Chicago (1976), Ohio State University (1978), the University of Liège in

Belgium (1981), Arizona State University (1985), Georgetown University (1986), and Williams College (1988), among others.

Fowler's first wife died in May 1988 and in December 1989 he married Mary Dutcher, who had been an elementary school teacher on Long Island, New York. Fowler died of kidney failure in a Pasadena hospital at the age of eighty-three. He was cremated and his remains are in a private location in Vermont, where he loved to visit his daughter and only grandchild.

Besides bringing extraordinary personal scientific ability and energy to his work, what emerges clearly from Fowler's distinguished research career was his ability to bring out the best in people. Unlike Nobel Prize–winning scientists Albert Einstein and Paul Dirac, whose exceptional discoveries were uniquely individual and did not depend materially on the efforts of others, Fowler's accomplishments were frequently the result of collaboration, sometimes with his leadership and at other times with the initiative of others.

★

Fowler's papers are in the archives of the California Institute of Technology. An autobiographical essay by Fowler appears in Tore Frängsmyr, ed., *Nobel Lectures in Physics, 1981–1990* (1993). Dennis Overbye, *Lonely Hearts of the Cosmos: The Scientific Quest for the Secret of the Universe* (1991), and a personal reflection by Donald D. Clayton, "William A. Fowler: 1911–1995," *Publications of the Astronomical Society of the Pacific* 108 (Jan. 1996): 1–7, discuss Fowler from the view of those who knew and worked with him. Fowler's Nobel acceptance speech appears in Gösta Ekspong, ed., *Nobel Lectures, Physics 1981–1990* (1993). John F. Gribbin, *Q is for Quantum: An Encyclopedia of Particle Physics* (1998), also discusses Fowler and his work. Hans A. Bethe, "The 1983 Nobel Prize in Physics," *Science* (25 Nov. 1983), and "Nobel Prize to Chandrasekhar and Fowler for Astrophysics," *Physics Today* (Jan. 1984), address the two Nobel Prize winners and their pioneering work in astrophysics. An obituary is in the *New York Times* (16 Mar. 1995).

LEONARD R. SOLON

FRANCIS, Sam(uel) Lewis (*b.* 25 June 1923 in San Mateo, California; *d.* 4 November 1994 in Santa Monica, California), one of the second generation of abstract expressionist artists, highly regarded for his luminous mural-size paintings in which there is constant, energetic interplay between sensuously colored shapes and dazzling white voids.

Francis was the older of two sons of Samuel Francis, a professor of mathematics, and Katherine Lewis, a pianist and teacher of French. Although his first interests were music and literature, he took pre-med and psychology courses at the University of California, Berkeley, where he

Sam Francis. © RICHARD SCHULMAN/GAMMA LIAISON

studied from 1941 to 1943. In 1943 he enlisted in the U.S. Army Air Force. Severe injuries in the crash of a training flight the following year resulted in spinal tuberculosis, and over the months of recovery Francis began to paint as a means of relieving boredom. Lying prone, his attention was caught by the play of light on the ceiling, and by sunrise and sunset effects, which entered into his initial attempts at watercolor. He received his first formal art instruction at a Veterans Administration Hospital in San Francisco. While convalescing at an artists' colony in Carmel, California, in 1947, he began to paint abstract expressionist works that showed the influence of Clyfford Still, Mark Rothko, and Arshile Gorky.

Francis was able to return to Berkeley in 1948. Now majoring in fine arts, he received a B.A. degree in 1949 and an M.A. degree in 1950. Hints of his mature style appear in the large canvas *Opposites,* painted in 1950 before he left for France to study under the G.I. Bill. This painting reveals the influence of Jackson Pollock's "dripped" paintings in its thinly brushed, bloodred cellular forms that circulate against a sparkling white background. Arriving in Paris in 1950, Francis was enrolled briefly at the Académie Fernand

Léger, but his style did not meet with official favor. Two years later, however, he was given his first solo exhibition at a Paris gallery, where he showed huge monochrome oils composed of nebulous layers of subdued colors.

Francis's paintings *Big Red* (1953) and *Red and Black* (1954) marked a return to vibrant, saturated colors. In 1955 they were acquired by, respectively, the Museum of Modern Art and the Solomon R. Guggenheim Museum, both in Manhattan—the first of his paintings to enter public collections. Not until 1956, though, was he given a solo showing in the United States, at the Martha Jackson Gallery in New York. The same year he was included in *Twelve Americans,* an exhibition of second-generation abstract expressionists at the Museum of Modern Art.

After a trip back to California in 1954 Francis returned to Paris, then in 1957 left for a round-the-world trip followed by a long stay in Japan. There he was admired for his gestural manner of painting, his drips and splatters seeming akin to the ancient *haboku* ("flung ink") style. Vacant expanses of white began to appear in his compositions—as in *The Whiteness of the Whale* (1957), one of a number of Francis's visual allusions to Herman Melville's *Moby Dick.* Back in Europe again in 1958 he completed a triptych commissioned by the Basel Kunsthalle, which was later separated and never installed. Painting the clusters of brightly colored cellular shapes that float against white fields on these panels was, the artist commented, "like filling great sails dipped in color." A mural he worked on in New York in 1959 for the Park Avenue branch of Chase Manhattan Bank fared better and was successfully installed.

Between 1960 and 1962, fascinated with the color blue, Francis worked on his *Blue Balls* series, in which viscous balloonlike shapes float or whirl toward the edges of the canvas away from a vacant white central expanse. Some of this series was painted in watercolor or gouache in 1961 while Francis was hospitalized in Bern, Switzerland, for a recurrence of his wartime tuberculosis. After he returned to California later that year, he bought a house in Santa Monica that was formerly owned by Charlie Chaplin. For the rest of his life, this house served as Francis's primary home and studio as he traveled back and forth between studios in California, Paris, Bern, and Tokyo.

Lithography first began to occupy Francis in 1959, when he produced his first prints at Tatyana Grosman's workshop on Long Island, New York. In 1963 he was associated with the Tamarind Lithography Workshop and beginning in 1966 with Gemini G.E.L., both in Los Angeles. In 1967 he established his own press, the Litho Shop, in Santa Monica. His lithographs (and later his monotypes and silk screens) are largely independent of his paintings, but they exhibit the same bold bursts of color. Notable among them are the twelve prints published as *Pasadena Box* by the Art Alliance of the Pasadena Museum in 1966.

During the mid-1960s there was another shift in Francis's painting style. He began to work in acrylics, doing canvases in which narrow streams of color surround and define and play in confrontation with a central white void. He called these his "sail paintings," noting that they reflected his interest in the suction effect of wind on sails. Then came his "edge paintings," in which configurations of color at the edges of the composition play off the vast white center—as in the enormous (twenty-six feet by forty feet) mural commissioned in 1969 for the Neue Nationalgalerie in West Berlin. Francis's lifelong interest in dreams and alchemy, rekindled by sessions with a Jungian psychiatrist in 1971, led to his smaller "mandala paintings" composed of centrally positioned geometric shapes. About 1977 these gave way to gridlike structures and by the 1980s the grids became webs—dense groupings of circular forms and dots of color swirling over a white ground, woven together by sinuous black or colored lines.

Francis's last years were occupied with mural projects, among them *Seafirst* for the Seattle First National Bank (1979); *Spring Thaw* for the U.S. Courthouse in Anchorage, Alaska (1980); and paintings for the San Francisco International Airport (1982) and the San Francisco Museum of Modern Art (1985). In 1992 he received his last commission, to do a monumental painting for the new federal parliament building in Bonn, West Germany, but he did not live to complete it. In 1983 the French government named him a Commander of the Order of Arts and Letters and on 17 November 1999, five years after his death, one of his paintings, *Toward Disappearance* (1958), was auctioned for a record $3,412,500 at Sotheby's New York Contemporary Artists Sale. Francis, whose first four marriages ended in divorce (Vera Miller, 1947–1950; Muriel Goodwin, 1950–?; Teruko Yokoi, 1960–1963; Mako Idemitsu, 1965–?), died of prostate cancer in St. John's Hospital, Santa Monica. He was survived by his fifth wife, the painter Margaret Smith, and his four children.

Francis's prodigiously active career was devoted to exploring what he termed "ceaseless instability," manifested in the restless movement of shapes and colors, and using color so that the painting itself becomes "a source of light." The success of these explorations is attested to by the long list of his solo and group showings and by his representation in major museum collections worldwide.

★

Francis's papers and other archival material are administered by the Sam Francis Estate in Venice, California. Biographies of the artist include articles in *Current Biography* (1973) and Claude Marks, *World Artists: 1950–1980* (1984). These biographies are supplemented by two lavishly illustrated monographs devoted to the artist's work: Peter Selz, *Sam Francis* (1982), which also provides a chronological outline of Francis's life through 1981; and

Karl Gunnar Pontus Hulten, *Sam Francis* (1993), published in conjunction with the artist's 1993 Bonn retrospective. This catalog contains photographs of Francis over the years, photos of his family and friends, and extensive bibliographies of articles and books on Francis through 1981; listings of his exhibitions (1946–1992) and of the catalogs published in connection with these showings; and extracts from his letters and notebooks. An obituary is in the *New York Times* (8 Nov. 1994).

ELEANOR F. WEDGE

FRELENG, Isadore ("Friz") (*b.* 21 August 1906 in Kansas City, Missouri; *d.* 26 May 1995 in Los Angeles, California), animator, director, and producer of animated films and one of the creators of the Warner Brothers style of cartoon animation.

Freleng was one of six children born to Louis Freleng, a Jewish Russian immigrant shoemaker-turned-farmer, and Elka Ribakoff, a homemaker. Because of his diminutive size (as an adult, he only stood five-feet, two-inches tall), Freleng could not participate in sports, so he developed an early talent for sketching. He began a career as an illustrator when he enrolled in the Horner Art School, a private art school in Kansas City that disappeared in the 1930s, and

won a *Kansas City Post* drawing contest, which led to a job with the United Film Advertising Service from 1924 to 1927. United Film specialized in making illustrated cartoons on glass slides and film strips to be run between silent film shorts and features, showcasing local and regional advertising. When fellow illustrator Hugh Harmon left for California to join Walt Disney's new studio, he encouraged Freleng to follow. Disney hired Freleng to work on *Oswald the Rabbit,* but in 1928 producer Charles Mintz fired Disney and took the character and most of Disney's staff, including Freleng, back to work at his own studio in New York. Freleng worked there on the *Krazy Kat* series, but the small budget forced the animators to turn out footage at breakneck speed, and Freleng had little creative input.

Meanwhile back in California, Harmon and Rudolf Ising sold a series called *Looney Tunes,* which starred Bosko the Talk-Ink Kid, to Leon Schlesinger at Warner Brothers. They hired Freleng as head animator on their first entry, *Sinkin' in the Bathtub* (1930). When Ising began a second series of cartoons called *Merrie Melodies* in 1932, Freleng was promoted to animation director. On 4 September 1932 Freleng married Lily Schonfeld, a marriage that lasted until his death. The Frelengs had two daughters.

When Harmon and Ising left for MGM in late 1933,

Friz Freleng, surrounded by some of his cartoon creations at the Hollywood Walk of Fame, 1992. AP/WIDE WORLD PHOTOS

Schlesinger promoted Freleng to head the *Looney Tunes* series. His first decision was to hire animators such as Ben "Bugs" Hardaway, who directed the first Bugs Bunny cartoon, and Tubby Millar. Over the next few years, Freleng coordinated the introduction of animation talent like Tex Avery, Chuck Jones, and Bob Clampett. He introduced Porky Pig, which became his first major success; he hired Joe Dougherty to do Porky's voice in *I Haven't Got a Hat* in 1935 and replaced him with Mel Blanc in 1937. In 1937 Freleng was tempted by a larger paycheck and more creative freedom to join Bill Hanna and Joe Barbera at MGM on their *The Captain and the Kids* series, but he returned to Warner Brothers in 1938 and stayed as one of the head directors until the animation facility closed in 1963.

During the 1940s Freleng worked with all the existing characters at Warner Brothers and created several new ones. In the 1945 Bugs Bunny short *Hare Trigger,* Freleng created Yosemite Sam, a short, hot-tempered, redheaded, mustachioed outlaw he based on his own physical traits and personality. When Freleng became director of the *Tweety Pie* cartoons in 1946, he redesigned the character and added a bird-hungry cat named Sylvester. The success of *Tweety Pie* in 1947 won Freleng the first of four Oscars for best short subject. He would win three more at Warner Brothers: for *Speedy Gonzalez* (1955); for *Birds Anonymous* (1957); and for *Knighty-Knight Bugs* (1958). He was nominated for *Life with Feathers* (1945), *Sandy Claws* (1955), and *Tobasco Road* (1956).

Freleng also directed cartoon segments in feature films in the late 1940s for Warner Brothers. *Two Guys from Texas* (1948) and *My Dream Is Yours* (1949) both showcase Bugs Bunny performing musical numbers with live-action characters. In 1950 Freleng and Chuck Jones were asked to write the studio's eleven-minute 3-D cartoon, *So Much for So Little,* which was commissioned by the U.S. Public Health Service. *So Much for So Little* was the only cartoon ever to win an Academy Award for best documentary.

Speedy Gonzalez was the Warner character most associated with Freleng in the 1950s. Freleng took this mouse character, which first appeared in *Cat-Tails for Two* in 1953, and gave it a name and personality. When Warner animation closed in 1963, Freleng and his partner, David H. DePatie, leased the former Warner facility to produce their own animated shorts. Their first success came in 1964, when producer Blake Edwards asked them to do an animated title sequence for *The Pink Panther,* the film that introduced Inspector Clousseau. The title character received such widespread attention that United Artists approved its use in a cartoon series. DePatie-Freleng's *The Pink Phink* (1964) won Freleng a fifth Academy Award and a contract to produce one Pink Panther cartoon per month for the next six years. The cartoons, inspired by Freleng's love of silent film comedies, made the transition to televi-

sion in 1969 when NBC commissioned a half-hour Saturday-morning series called *The Pink Panther Show.* The Pink Panther character was so popular that it spun off into other programs including *The New Pink Panther Show* (1971–1976), *The Pink Panther Laugh and a Half Hour and a Half* (1976–1977), and *Think Pink Panther!* (1978), as well as three half-hour specials. When NBC tired of the project, Freleng moved over to ABC for *The All-New Pink Panther Show* (1978–1979).

Freleng also produced numerous theatrical cartoons featuring characters like the Inspector (1965–1969), the Ant and the Aardvark (1966–1971), Rolland and Ratfink (1968–1971), the Tijuana Toads (later the Texas Toads, 1969–1971), the Blue Racer (1972–1974), and Hoot Kloot (1973–1974). During the 1970s he developed *The Oddball Couple* (1975–1977), *Return to the Planet of the Apes* (1975–1976), *Baggy Pants & the Nitwits* (1977–1978), and *The Fantastic Four* (1978–1979). In 1977 Freleng was executive producer for an *ABC Afternoon Special,* "My Mom's Having a Baby," which won the Emmy for outstanding informational children's special. In 1978 he won another Emmy, this time for outstanding children's special, with "Halloween Is Grinch Night." Freleng finished his successful television run with an Emmy for the outstanding animated program in the 1981–1982 season for "The Grinch Grinches the Cat in the Hat," which he coproduced with Theodore Geisel.

In the 1970s the popularity of Warner cartoons was revived with the release of *Bugs Bunny, Superstar* (1975), a documentary featuring on-camera interviews with Freleng and his animation peers, Tex Avery and Bob Clampett, along with clips from earlier works. The success of this program led to a series of compilation features that blended new animation with old film clips. Freleng produced and directed three of these features: *Friz Freleng's Looney Looney Bugs Bunny Movie* (1981), *Bugs Bunny's Third Movie— 1001 Rabbit Tales* (1982), and *Daffy Duck's Movie: Fantastic Island* (1983).

Freleng was a workaholic who, despite a Yosemite Sam-type temper, was respected and admired by a great many people in the Hollywood animation community. He was also a devoted family man and a member of both the Masons and the Shriners; he was humble despite the fame and prestige that came to him in his later years. As well as five Oscars and three Emmys, Freleng won the Distinguished Career Award from the Animation Society of International Film Artists in 1976, received awards from the Motion Pictures Screen Cartoonists' Guild and the British Film Institute, and in 1992 his name was placed on the Hollywood Walk of Fame. Freleng's great loves were his family and his work, and he continued to draw and paint the characters he helped popularize until his death from heart failure at the Medical Center of the University of California in Los

Angeles at the age of eighty-nine. He is buried in Forest Lawn Cemetery in Los Angeles.

Freleng, who worked during "The Golden Age of Animation," was a leading architect of animated film for over fifty years. He wrote, animated, and directed more than 300 cartoons, including the most popular and memorable cartoons produced at the Warner Brothers Studio. He created new characters and polished old ones, transforming cartoons from gag-filled strings of loony actions to character-oriented, sophisticated forms of storytelling.

★

The major work on Freleng is Greg Ford, *The Art of Friz Freleng* (1994). Additional information about his role in animation is in Leonard Maltin, *Of Mice and Magic* (1980), and Jeff Lenburg, *The Encyclopedia of Animated Cartoons* (1991). Freleng is also mentioned in Maurice Horn, *The World Encyclopedia of Cartoons* (1980); Danny and Gerald Peary, *The American Animated Cartoon* (1980); Jerry Beck, *I Thought I Saw a Puddy Tat* (1991); and Donald Crafton, *Before Mickey* (1992). *Animazine* (17 Aug. 1984) features an extensive interview with Freleng. An obituary is in the *New York Times* (28 May 1995).

PATRICK A. TRIMBLE

FULBRIGHT, J(ames) William (*b.* 9 April 1905 in Sumner, Missouri; *d.* 9 February 1995 in Washington, D.C.), Arkansas Democratic politician who served for thirty years in the U.S. Senate, exhibiting an independence that infuriated several presidents.

Fulbright was one of six children born to Jay Fulbright and Roberta Waugh Fulbright. The family moved to Fayetteville, Arkansas, in 1906, and his father combined large-scale farming with banking, lumber, and other enterprises that made him one of the richest men in Arkansas when he died in 1923. While his mother struggled to retain control of the family's business empire, he attended the University of Arkansas at Fayetteville, combining average grades with an exceptional talent for football. He graduated with a B.A. degree in political science in 1925. That same year he won a Rhodes scholarship and spent three years studying history and political science at Oxford University in England. After returning to the United States, he met Elizabeth ("Betty") Williams, a vivacious intelligent heiress to a large Philadelphia fortune and married her on 15 June 1932.

After receiving a law degree from George Washington University in 1934, Fulbright went to work in the Antitrust Division of the Justice Department. In 1935 he left this position to teach law at George Washington University, but within a year he returned to Arkansas to teach at the University of Arkansas Law School, participate in the family's businesses, and spend time as a gentleman farmer. Fulbright ended this decade by becoming president of the University of Arkansas at age thirty-four.

J. William Fulbright. AP/WIDE WORLD PHOTOS

His mother's close friendship with the governor of Arkansas, Carl E. Bailey, and her control of an influential newspaper, the *Northwest Arkansas Times,* had much to do with this controversial appointment. Although he was reluctant at first, Fulbright decided to make the most of the job. In his speeches he deplored the negative self-image of Arkansas and became a proponent of inspiring young men to seek political careers. After a heady two years in the limelight, Fulbright's reign came to an abrupt end in 1941, when Governor Bailey lost his bid for a third term. The new governor, Homer Adkins, made firing the young president his first order of business.

This taste of public life was a turning point for Fulbright. In 1942 he ran for Congress in the Third District of Arkansas and was elected in a near-landslide. The voters liked his call for the United States to fight a "creative war," making plans for future peace a vital part of the wartime agenda. In Congress, Fulbright offered a brief resolution calling for an international organization dedicated to preserving peace, and the Fulbright Resolution was passed in June 1943. The resolution made him an instant celebrity, praised by such disparate power centers as the White House and *Life* magazine, and it was a landmark step toward the creation of the United Nations.

In 1944 Fulbright ran for the U.S. Senate and easily defeated Governor Adkins, his opponent for the Senate seat. In his first Senate speech Fulbright criticized the administration of Franklin D. Roosevelt for bypassing Congress in the peace-planning process. When the United Nations took shape in 1945, Fulbright expressed public enthusiasm and private disappointment. He deplored the emphasis on national sovereignty and the great power veto.

In the aftermath of World War II, the United States had large amounts of surplus property abroad. Fulbright proposed a law that would place the money from the sale of this material in a fund to support an international exchange program for "students in . . . education, culture, and science." He won bipartisan backing from figures such as former president Herbert Hoover. On 1 August 1946 the bill became law, launching what would soon be called the Fulbright Program. Expanded by future congresses, it financed the exchange of more than 200,000 foreign and American scholars in Fulbright's lifetime.

When the Republicans won both houses of Congress in the 1946 elections, Fulbright suggested that President Harry S. Truman resign and appoint a Republican president to lead the executive branch and thereby reduce partisan bickering. An infuriated Truman called Fulbright "an overeducated Oxford SOB." Fulbright's relations with the White House did not improve when he undertook an investigation of the Reconstruction Finance Corporation that revealed widespread corruption in the granting of federal loans. Fulbright did support President Truman's decision to resist communist aggression in Korea. But when the People's Republic of China entered the Korean War in late 1950, the senator called for the evacuation of U.S. troops. Fulbright was ignored by the White House and almost everyone else.

In the Senate, Fulbright was among the first to confront Senator Joseph McCarthy's reckless attempts to smear liberals as communist sympathizers. He repeatedly criticized the confrontational anticommunism of President Dwight D. Eisenhower's administration. Fulbright confounded his liberal admirers by signing the 1956 Southern Manifesto, which denounced the Supreme Court for ending segregation and creating "chaos and confusion" in the states of the old Confederacy. Nevertheless, in 1959 the Democratic majority leader of the Senate, Lyndon Johnson, made Fulbright chairman of the Committee on Foreign Relations.

In this powerful role Fulbright at first showed a surprising readiness to support confrontational tactics. During the 1963 Cuban missile crisis, he urged President John F. Kennedy to invade Cuba. He backed the decision to defend South Vietnam against communist insurgency and supported President Lyndon Johnson's expansion of the war. But Fulbright broke with the administration when Johnson used troops to restore order in the Dominican Republic in the spring of 1965, claiming dubious evidence of a communist conspiracy.

The senator's scathing indictment of the president and his advisers inspired savage retaliation from Johnson supporters. Fulbright and his Senate Foreign Relations Committee staff responded by subjecting the war in Vietnam to the same hostile scrutiny. A climax of sorts was the committee's February 1966 hearings on Vietnam, during which Fulbright subjected Secretary of State Dean Rusk to a ferocious cross-examination. His subsequent speech argued that the war was a blunder, which created a national sensation.

Fulbright's criticism coincided with rising disillusionment with the war. He became a spokesman for those Americans who called for a drastic change in U.S. foreign policy vis-à-vis communism. But Fulbright's conservative southern roots made him a flawed leader. Many wondered how the man who called for an end to the war so that the United States could spend more money on social programs for the poor could vote against open housing bills and a rise in the minimum wage.

Republican president Richard Nixon was a more formidable opponent than Lyndon Johnson. Nixon's 1969 appeal to the "silent majority" and his announcement of a gradual withdrawal of American troops outmaneuvered Fulbright and his allies on the Foreign Relations Committee. From 1970 to 1971 Fulbright assailed the "myth" of an international communist conspiracy and called on Americans to accept a communist Vietnam, which offered no threat to America's vital interests. "Fulbright Would Surrender," declared a headline in the *Richmond Times-Dispatch*.

On the domestic front, Fulbright alienated many Arkansans by voting against two Nixon appointees to the Supreme Court, both conservative southerners. An attempt to stage a recall election sputtered into ominous life. But Fulbright continued his offensive against Nixon's policies, especially after the president invaded Cambodia in 1970 to attack communist base camps and after ensuing protests led to the death of four students at Kent State University. Nixon proved to be in closer touch with the majority of Americans. In 1972 the president won a massive victory over the Democratic candidate, Senator George McGovern, a wholehearted advocate of Fulbright's stance on Vietnam.

A few months later Fulbright demonstrated his relative indifference to partisan politics by congratulating Nixon when he announced a settlement with North Vietnam. The precarious peace soon vanished in the quagmire of the Watergate scandal. Nine months after Nixon resigned as president, the Republic of South Vietnam succumbed to a renewed communist offensive in April 1975.

By that time Senator Fulbright had discovered that Arkansans felt little gratitude for his long struggle for a rational foreign policy. He had angered many Jewish voters by calling for an evenhanded approach to the Arab-Israeli conflict and remarking that "the Israelis control the policy in the Congress and the Senate." Running for reelection in 1974 against a popular governor, Dale Bumpers, Fulbright went down to a lopsided two-to-one defeat. His embittered wife refused to go back to Arkansas, and the Fulbrights spent the rest of their lives in Washington, D.C., where he practiced international law and continued to speak out on foreign policy.

Fulbright suffered a severe stroke in 1993 that left him in a wheelchair; he died in his sleep two years later. He was cremated, and his ashes were interred in the Fulbright family plot in Evergreen Cemetery in Fayetteville. President Bill Clinton, who had awarded him the Presidential Medal of Freedom in 1993, delivered a eulogy at Washington's National Cathedral.

A conservative intellectual, Fulbright based his opposition to the Vietnam War on its unconstitutional reliance on undelegated presidential power. He never called the war immoral or advised drafted men to refuse to serve, but he also never apologized for his opposition to civil rights legislation, insisting he remained unconvinced of its effectiveness. Few deny Fulbright's profound impact on a generation of political thinkers. Senator Frank Church of Idaho said, "When all of us are dead, the only one they'll remember is Bill Fulbright."

★

The University of Arkansas has 1,100 linear feet of the Fulbright papers. Additional material is in the files of the Truman, Johnson, Kennedy, Eisenhower, and Nixon libraries. Fulbright's writings include his many speeches, most of which are in the *Congressional Record*, and occasional articles for the *New York Times Magazine* and other publications. Perhaps most noteworthy is his *New Yorker* article "In Thrall to Fear" (8 Jan. 1972), which contains his reflections on U.S. foreign policy since 1945. His books include *Old Myths and New Realities* (1964), *The Arrogance of Power* (1967), *The Pentagon Propaganda Machine* (1970), *The Crippled Giant: American Foreign Policy and Its Domestic Consequences* (1972), and *The Price of Empire* (1989), which he wrote with aide Seth P. Tillman. The papers of aide Carl Marcy in the National Archives are also valuable. By far the best biography is *Fulbright* by Randall Bennett Woods (1995). Also valuable is Woods's *J. William Fulbright, Vietnam, and the Search for a Cold War Foreign Policy* (1998). The best early study is *Fulbright the Dissenter* by Haynes Johnson and Bernard M. Gwertzman (1968). There have been many magazine articles about Senator Fulbright; among the best are Stewart Alsop, "Mr. Dove and Mr. Hawk," *Saturday Evening Post* (18 June 1966), and Charles McCarry, "Mourning Becomes Senator Fulbright," *Esquire* (June 1970). Lengthy obituaries are in the *New York Times* and *Washington Post* (both 10 Feb. 1995).

THOMAS FLEMING

FURCOLO, (John) Foster (*b.* 29 July 1911 in New Haven, Connecticut, *d.* 5 July 1995 in Cambridge, Massachusetts), the first Italian American to win statewide office in Massachusetts and the first Italian American governor of Massachusetts.

Furcolo was the younger of two sons born to Charles Lawrence Furcolo, a neurosurgeon, and Alberta Marie Foster. Furcolo's father was an Italian immigrant who graduated from Yale College in 1910. Foster attended public schools in Longmeadow, Massachusetts, and graduated from New Haven High School. He drove trucks and waited tables to earn his tuition at Yale. As an undergraduate Furcolo played basketball and football, and was captain of the boxing team in 1933. In 1933 he received his B.A. degree. Furcolo's mother and father separated, and his mother changed the spelling of the last name to Furcolowe, which is how Furcolo spelled it when he graduated from Yale. On 18 April 1936 Furcolo married Kathryn Foran; they had five children. While attending Yale Law School, he wrote two plays, *Fancy Free* and *The Grail,* both of which were produced by stock companies. Also in 1936 Furcolo earned his LL.B. degree from Yale Law School. He was admitted to the Massachusetts bar in 1937 and practiced as a trial lawyer in Springfield.

During World War II, Furcolo served in the U.S. Navy

Foster Furcolo, 1954. © BETTMANN/CORBIS

(1943–1945), mainly in the Pacific theater aboard the attack transport *Kershaw* as a lieutenant junior grade. After his discharge Furcolo entered Massachusetts politics. He lost a 1946 bid for the congressional seat from the Second Massachusetts District by only 3,295 votes. However, in 1948 he defeated the Republican incumbent John R. Clason by 15,000 votes to become only the second Democrat elected from western Massachusetts. He served in the Eighty-first Congress and was reelected to a second two-year term in 1950. A member of the House Appropriations Committee, Furcolo generally supported the Truman administration along Democratic party lines.

Furcolo was a member of several other committees, including a special House committee that investigated the 1940 Katyn Forest massacre of Polish army prisoners. In March 1953 he was honored by Free Poland (the Polish government in exile) as knight-commander of the Order of Polonia Restituta for his work. In 1973 he published a novel, *Rendezvous at Katyn,* based on that tragedy. In July 1952 Furcolo resigned his congressional seat to accept appointment by the Massachusetts governor Paul A. Dever as state treasurer and receiver-general. The following November, despite the Eisenhower Republican sweep of national and statewide offices, Furcolo was elected to the position, which he held until 1955.

On 12 December 1953 Furcolo, addressing the liberal Americans for Democratic Action (ADA), shocked the group by suggesting that it disband because it was weakening the Democratic party. As a congressman Furcolo had received high ratings from the ADA on his voting record, but it never supported him again. He was highly rated by the American Federation of Labor (AFL), the Congress of Industrial Organizations (CIO), and *New Republic* magazine. Both the National Radio Press Gallery and *Fortune* magazine praised him as one of the ten best congressmen.

In 1954 Furcolo received the Democratic party's nomination for the Senate seat held by the Republican Leverett Saltonstall since 1944. Without the Democratic senator John F. Kennedy's support, Furcolo lost the election but only by 28,706 votes. In 1956 Furcolo ran for governor and was endorsed by Senator Kennedy. In November, despite another Eisenhower Republican landslide victory in Massachusetts, Furcolo led the Democrats to a sweep of all state offices except that of attorney general. Furcolo beat his Republican opponent, Lieutenant Governor Sumner G. Whittier, by more than 154,000 votes. In 1957, under the quickly unmasked pseudonym John Foster, he wrote *Let George Do It!*, a political satire about ward politics and campaigning for ethnic votes.

Furcolo served two two-year terms as governor (1957–1961). He established a community college system and expanded the University of Massachusetts. He appointed the first African American superior court judge (1958) along with similar firsts for Polish and Portuguese Americans. In 1959 he appointed Jennie Loitman Barron to the Massachusetts Superior Court as the state's first full-time female judge. In 1960, plagued by accusations of corruption in his administration, he lost the Democratic party primary to oppose Saltonstall, ending his elective political career.

In 1960 Furcolo was charged with attempting to bribe the Governor's Council, in order to assure the reappointment of his commissioner of public works, Anthony N. DiNatale. DiNatale himself was indicted on charges of receiving bribes and larceny. Forty other people and ten companies were indicted as a result of investigations by the Massachusetts Crime Commission, headed by the Republican attorney general Edward Brooke. Furcolo's name was cleared in 1965, and those around him deemed him to be honest but surrounded by corrupt people. The charges were felt to have been politically motivated by partisan politics. After leaving elective office Furcolo taught law and government at several colleges. From 1967 to 1972 he was assistant district attorney in Middlesex County, Massachusetts, and from 1975 to 1989 he served as federal administrative judge. His first wife died in 1964. He married Lucy Carra on 16 October 1967. They separated in 1972, and she died in 1979. He married Constance Gleason in 1980.

Furcolo wrote *Law for You* (1975), reissued in 1977 as *Law for the Layman* and revised and updated in 1982 as *Practical Law for the Layman*. In 1982 he wrote *Ballots Anyone? How to Run for Office—and Win!*, a well-reviewed political manual based on his own experiences. He received innumerable honorary awards and honorary degrees during his life.

As governor Furcolo fought unsuccessfully to establish a sales tax, which he considered his biggest failure. He believed the sales tax could both reduce the large budget deficit he had inherited and establish new government-funded programs. He alienated liberals in his 1953 speech to the ADA, in which he implied that they were not anticommunist enough, an inflammatory accusation during the McCarthy era. Furcolo was a staunch anticommunist, but his lasting legacy is the creation of the community college system and the growth of the University of Massachusetts. As a congressman in 1955 he supported federal scholarship loans, and he established a student loan program in Massachusetts. The former U.S. Secretary of Health, Education, and Welfare Joseph A. Califano, Jr., called him "the nation's greatest education governor" in 1982. While Furcolo was governor, Massachusetts ranked first among the states in elder care, civil rights, and education and at the top in health programs. He believed in direct citizen participation and government-funded social programs. Despite a rapid rise to political power, which culminated in his second term as governor, his achievements were relatively unknown at the time of his death. He was outspoken during his life, even before his entrance into electoral politics, and he acknowledged that this may have contributed to his short electoral career.

Furcolo died of heart failure in Youville Hospital in Cambridge, Massachusetts. He is buried in the Holyhood Cemetery in Brookline, Massachusetts.

★

The Massachusetts State Library has two boxes of Furcolo's papers dating from the mid-1940s to 1995. His congressional speeches are in the *Congressional Digest* between 1948 and 1952. A compendium of his speeches and an assessment of his gubernatorial terms is in *Addresses and Messages to the General Court: Public Speeches and Other Papers of General Interest of His Excellency Foster Furcolo,* compiled by Edward Michael O'Brien (1961). *Current Biography 1958* includes an entry on Furcolo. Articles include George McKinnon, "Your New Governor," *Boston Globe* (Dec. 1956 and Jan. 1957); Jack Alexander, "Mr. Unpredictable," *Saturday Evening Post* (9 Aug. 1958); "From Dazzling to Fizzling," *Time* (23 Oct. 1964); and David B. Wilson, "Furcolo's Foresight," *Boston Globe* (10 Feb. 1987). Obituaries are in the *New York Times, Boston Globe, Needham* (Massachusetts) *Times,* and *Needham* (Massachusetts) *Chronicle* (all 6 July 1995), and *Springfield* (Massachusetts) *Union-News* (7 July 1995).

JANE BRODSKY FITZPATRICK

FURNESS, Elizabeth Mary ("Betty") (*b.* 3 January 1916 in New York City; *d.* 2 April 1994 in New York City), film actress who became a pioneer television consumer reporter and government consumer affairs expert.

Furness was the only child of a New York City business family. Her father, George Choate Furness, worked as a Union Carbon and Carbide Corporation executive. Her mother, Florence Sturtevant, was a homemaker. Being a no-nonsense man, her father urged young Betty at age fourteen to do "something useful," so she got a modeling job with the John Robert Powers Modeling Agency. When she was just sixteen, Furness landed a screen test. She would stay in Hollywood for the next several years, performing in thirty-five movies, many of them in the "B" category. "They were appalling," she would later admit, "except for two—*Swing Time* [1936] with Fred Astaire and Ginger Rogers, and the first *Magnificent Obsession* [1935] with Robert Taylor and Irene Dunne."

On 27 November 1937, Furness married bandleader John ("Johnny") Waldo Green. Betty was named in the Society for the Protection of Bandleaders with Hollywood Wives, along with Bette Davis, who was married to Harmon Nelson, and Harriet Nelson, wife of Ozzie Nelson.

Betty Furness, 1967. ASSOCIATE PRESS AP

"The rules were simple," recalled actress Dorothy Lamour in her Hollywood memoir. "The wives had to make at least one weekly phone call to their 'one-nighting' husbands—with reverse charging privileges—and the husbands had to dedicate one or more songs annually to their wives." Those rules, plus the birth of a daughter, Barbara, weren't enough to save Betty Furness's first marriage, and in 1943 she and Green divorced after five years of marriage.

During a slow period in movie work, Furness appeared in a play, *Golden Boy.* She found that she loved the stage so much that she left Hollywood and returned to New York City, where she focused her talent in live theater for a few years. As one of the first women to appear on television, as early as 1945, she earned $50 a week, commentating in a show called "Fashions, Coming and Becoming." Some of her salary was eaten up by the combs she had to replace after they melted under the intense heat of the lamps.

On 1 June 1945, after a one-month courtship, she married Hugh Ernst, Jr. The ceremony, performed in Las Vegas, Nevada, was for "keeps." Their five-year marriage ended in Ernst's death in April 1950.

Living in New York in 1949, Furness took a job with Westinghouse Electric, where she would act as on-air spokesperson for the consumer appliance company. In this role, she would become an instant consumer icon, touting all the new and sparkling labor-saving devices developed to cater to America's postwar homemakers. From time to time between 1949 and 1958, Furness also acted in the *Studio One* television show. Tiring of her limited role with Westinghouse, she left in 1960 and turned to the more serious world of news broadcasting and politics. During this time Furness also hosted a number of television shows. On 15 August 1967, Furness, at age fifty-one, wed Leslie Midgley, to whom she would remain married until her death. Midgley, fifty-two at the time of the marriage, was an executive with the CBS Television Network, a widower, and the father of three children.

During the mid 1960s, Furness became a frontline fighter in the war on poverty. She traveled throughout the United States, recruiting volunteers on VISTA (Volunteers in Service to America). Her enthusiasm caught the eye of President Lyndon B. Johnson, who in March 1967 appointed her as special assistant to the president for consumer affairs. Furness immediately took to this new challenge and went on what would seem to be an endless speaking tour where she would dispense consumer advice to homemakers and chastise diverse consumer industries, from food retailers to furriers. Furness was written about for her style as much as for her consumer advocacy, and she became the darling of the luncheon speech circuit. By September 1967, she was even mentioned by Johnson's advisers as a potential running mate to replace Vice President Hubert Humphrey for an anticipated re-election bid by Johnson in 1968. However, her ardent crusading was looked upon with disfavor in U.S. boardrooms, and several business leaders lobbied President Johnson to jettison her. Furness resigned her position in 1969, after helping secure the passage of a new federal law governing meat inspection.

On 10 August 1970, New York's governor, Nelson Rockefeller, appointed Furness to a newly created post as executive director of the New York State Consumer Protection Board. The appointment lasted less than a year because the state legislature failed to fund the office adequately. An embittered Furness resigned the position on 12 July 1971, stating that it was created by the politicians simply to "throw the ladies a bone. We've got to do a little something for the ladies so we'll put a lady to work here."

As evidence of her ability to do a similar job, in 1973 Furness was appointed New York City's consumer affairs commissioner to replace the retiring Bess Meyerson. Join-

ing New York City's WNBC-TV in 1974, she became a regular on the *Today Show.*

Although Furness's goals were noble, her methods sometimes got her in trouble. In 1977 she became embroiled in a controversy after testing an alcoholic beverage that, she contended, was targeted to appeal to the tastes of underage drinkers. The controversy arose after she tested the beverage on fifteen teenage students of Hartsdale High School. The students' parents complained, and the town's school board considered legal action against her.

After sixteen years with Furness on the *Today Show,* NBC News decided in 1990 not to renew the contract for its consumer reporter, who was then seventy-six years of age. Consumer advocate Ralph Nader then commented that she had "pioneered consumer TV news reporting and she pursued it with intelligence, inquisitiveness and irrepressibility."

Diagnosed with stomach cancer in 1990, Furness died four years later at Manhattan's Sloan-Kettering Memorial Hospital, where she had been undergoing treatment. She was seventy-eight. She is interred at Ferncliff Cemetery in Hartsdale, New York.

Although her career as a screen actress brought her moderate fame and spanned more than three decades, Furness's most important and notable contribution was her television work, which led to her pioneering in consumer advocacy. Furness's fearlessness, knowledge, and effectiveness in these posts are a lasting legacy, which has spawned a number of government and private initiatives in consumer protection and environmental protection.

★

American Weekly magazine (22 July 1951) draws a portrait of Furness's career. See also Dorothy Lamour, *My Side of the Road* (1980), and *Who's Who of American Women* (1982). Videocassettes of Furness's work with Studio One are located in Bowling Green State University Popular Culture Library in Bowling Green, Ohio. Obituaries are in the *Buffalo News* (3 Apr. 1994), *New York Times* (4 Apr. 1994), *Time,* and *People Weekly* (both 11 Apr. 1994).

ROBERT J. SMITH

G

GABOR, Eva (*b.* 11 February 1921[?] in Budapest, Hungary; *d.* 4 July 1995 in Los Angeles, California), youngest of the three famous Gabor sisters and an actress in films, plays, and television.

Gabor was born to Vilmos Gábor and Jolie Tilleman Gábor in 1921. This birth date, like many dates surrounding the family, is not definitive. Her father was a soldier and a jeweler and her mother was an heiress to a Hungarian jewelry fortune. In the late 1930s, Jolie divorced Vilmos, who died in 1962.

Because of an economic downturn in the family, Gabor did not enjoy the finishing-school experience available to her older sisters. Instead, she was tutored by governesses and attended the Forstner Institute in Budapest. In her autobiography, *Orchids and Salami* (1954), Gabor described the sisters' upbringing as one of "cultural ignorance." She remarked that they could speak in four languages, but had nothing of consequence to say. Even at age seventeen, Gabor knew the importance of the "right" marriage. At a party thrown by her sister she met Eric Drimmer, a handsome Swedish doctor who worked in Hollywood. Before the party was over, he had proposed and she had accepted.

Arriving in Hollywood in 1939 as a new bride, Gabor was quickly smitten by the desire to act. Her first attempts were not satisfactory, primarily because of her youthful appearance and difficulty with the language. Nevertheless, Paramount gave her bit parts in two not very success-

ful movies, *Forced Landing* (1941) and *Pacific Blackout* (1942).

Discouraged but not daunted, Gabor continued her quest of acting roles, playing secondary parts in *A Royal Scandal* (1945), *The Wife of Monte Cristo* (1946), and *Song of Surrender* (1949), as well as in plays. Her appearance in a CBS television play, *L'Amour the Merrier* (1949), brought her to the attention of Richard Rodgers, who saw her as a perfect Mignonette in his and Oscar Hammerstein's new production of *The Happy Time* (1950). This play ran for eighteen months and was an undisputed success for Gabor. Concurrent with her appearance in *The Happy Time*, Gabor was hosting the *Eva Gabor Show* (1950–1951) on television. As a result of these performances, she appeared often on television and costarred with Boris Karloff in the television production of Anton Chekhov's masterpiece *Uncle Vanya*. Gabor divorced Eric Drimmer in 1942 and married millionaire Charles Isaacs in 1943. By 1950 they were divorced.

In the 1950s, the Gabor women were in their heyday. The relationship among the sisters was often stormy, fraught by personal and professional rivalry, but the Gabors were never seriously or long estranged. They were often featured in magazines; Eva and Zsa Zsa appeared on the covers of *Life* and *Colliers*. The three sisters also entertained together in a nightclub act in Las Vegas in 1953.

Gabor continued to appear on the stage, on and off-Broadway. She starred in the short-running *Little Glass*

Eva Gabor. THE KOBAL COLLECTION

Clock (1956) and was in Noël Coward's *Present Laughter* (1958). Her second starring role was in *Lulu* (1958), yet another unsuccessful play. Gabor replaced Vivien Leigh as Tatania in *Tovarich* (1963), continuing the role on national tour. She also acted in several films in the 1950s, including, among others, *The Last Time I Saw Paris* (1954), *Artists and Models* (1955), *Don't Go Near the Water* (1957), *Gigi* (1958), and *Youngblood Hawk* (1964).

Gabor, who had long sought stability in her acting roles, finally found stardom through the television series *Green Acres*. With Eddie Albert as Oliver Douglas, she costarred as Lisa Douglas from 1965 to 1971. In the show Jay Somers reversed the premise of *The Beverly Hillbillies,* in which the nouveau riche Clampetts strike it rich and migrate to swanky Beverly Hills. In *Green Acres,* the Douglases move from New York City to rural Hooterville and take up farming. Although the show was sometimes characterized as "fluff and frill," *Green Acres* was consistently in the Nielsen top ten ratings, and Gabor was often cited as television's most popular actress. Gabor never complained about the hours or the work; in her mind she had finally arrived as an actress.

Gabor continued to be professionally active throughout her life. She made more than two dozen television guest appearances. She provided the voice of Bianca in the animated films, *The Rescuers* (1977) and *The Rescuers Down Under* (1990). In her seventies, Gabor repeated her role as

Lisa Douglas in the television movie *Return to Green Acres* (1990).

Despite a busy career, Gabor managed to marry and divorce five husbands. In addition to Eric Drimmer and Charles Isaacs, Gabor married plastic surgeon John Williams in 1956; the alliance lasted eight months. In 1959 she wed Richard Brown, a Wall Street stockbroker to whom she was married for thirteen years, and in 1973 she married Frank Jameson, an aerospace mogul, and Gabor's husband for ten years. Gabor reportedly quipped, "Marriage is too interesting an experiment to be tried only once or twice."

The Gabor sisters, according to the socialite Elsa Maxwell, were "three of the world's true celebrities. . . . [T]hey are famous for being famous." This fame, however, carried a psychological price. In an interview with a *Los Angeles Times* reporter, Gabor once talked about the monetary, physical, and emotional costs of maintaining the appearance necessary to support that fame. According to her, the preparation for the simple act of going out to dinner was a nightmare.

Zsa Zsa was the most famous and flamboyant of the Gabor sisters, but those who knew Eva described her as the most dedicated and industrious. In the foreword to her autobiography, Lawrence Langner describes Gabor's boundless energy, her concentration, and her dedication. In addition to acting, Gabor also created her own successful company, the Eva Gabor Wig Line.

Although the youngest of the Gabor sisters, Eva was the first to die. On 4 July 1995, two years before her mother's death in 1997, Gabor succumbed to a respiratory infection. She is buried in Westfield Memorial Park in Los Angeles. Although her impact was limited to the field of entertainment, Gabor brought joy and delight to her audiences for several decades.

★

Eva Gabor's autobiography, *Orchids and Salami* (1954), is entertaining and informative. However, like Zsa Zsa's *My Story* (1960), cowritten with Gerold Frank, and her mother's *Jolie Gábor as Told to Cindy Adams* (1975), Eva's autobiography is composed primarily of personal anecdotes. A more objective view of all four Gabors is Peter H. Brown's *Such Devoted Sisters: Those Fabulous Gabors* (1985). Brown brings some order to the chaos of the Gabor mystique; he uses varied sources and tries to separate fact from fiction where possible. In addition to the many magazine features on Gabor as well as her family, *Current Biography 1968* has a substantial article, focusing primarily on her acting career. In addition, the *Biographical Encyclopaedia and Who's Who of the American Theatre* (1966) has a shorter piece, detailing Gabor's stage and film performances up to the time of the encyclopedia's publication. An obituary is in the *New York Times* (5 July 1995).

MARY BOYLES

GACY, John Wayne, Jr. (*b.* 17 March 1942 in Chicago, Illinois; *d.* 10 May 1994 in Joliet, Illinois), businessman and small-time community leader who astounded the world with his record serial murders of thirty-three young men, most of whom he buried in the crawl space of his house.

Gacy was one of three children born to John Wayne Gacy, Sr., a machinist, and Marion Elaine Robinson, a homemaker. His father was a harsh disciplinarian and an abusive alcoholic. His mother favored her son, protecting him from his father's alcohol-fueled rages. The elder Gacy, embarrassed by his son's lack of interest in sports and outdoor recreation, condemned the boy as soft and effeminate. Writers find two harbingers in Gacy's childhood. He later stated that when he was eight, a family friend, a contractor, "messed with" him, sexually tickling and wrestling with him. After hitting his head at age eleven, he also suffered blackouts from a blood clot in the brain until the clot was dissolved five years later.

Gacy was bright but undisciplined, his schoolwork uneven. He attended several high schools in Chicago but never graduated: Carl Schurz High School, Providence–St. Mel, Cooley Vocational High, and Charles A. Prosser Vocational. However, desperately seeking approval, he could and did work hard. Still a teenager, he was briefly employed in Las Vegas, Nevada, as a mortuary janitor. After returning to his family, he graduated from Northwestern Business College; he worked as a shoe salesman in Chicago and then in Springfield, Illinois.

In September 1964 Gacy married Marlynn Myers. Marlynn's father invited the Gacys to Waterloo, Iowa, in 1966, asking Gacy to manage three Kentucky Fried Chicken outlets Myers owned. Myers distrusted Gacy, who always courted attention and lied about his accomplishments; but Gacy proved hardworking and competent, if abrasive. Gacy rose in the Waterloo Jaycee hierarchy, as he had done in Springfield. He and his wife had two children.

Then, in late 1968, Gacy was charged with sodomy for paying a sixteen-year-old boy to give him oral sex and with hiring another teenager to beat up the sixteen-year-old. On 2 December 1968 Gacy was sentenced to ten years in the Iowa State Reformatory for Men at Anamosa; the next day Marlynn filed for divorce, which was finalized on 18 September 1969. While in prison Gacy avoided and denigrated homosexual inmates and told his friends he had been framed by envious enemies. Gacy's father died during the 1969 Christmas season, but Gacy was not allowed to attend the funeral.

After release on parole in June 1970 Gacy returned to Chicago, where he worked as a chef. He bought a house at 8213 West Summerdale Avenue in Norwood Park, an address that lives in infamy. Gacy remodeled his home, more enthusiastically than skillfully, and became a respected resident of the quiet family neighborhood. Yet he cruised Chicago for young male pickups; this led to charges of disorderly conduct in February 1971 (dismissed) and charges of aggravated battery and disorderly conduct in June 1972 (never brought to trial).

On 1 July 1972 Gacy married a divorcée named Carole, who was unaware of his other sexuality. Gacy was a good stepfather to Carole's two children, and the couple held lavish theme parties, attended by the entire neighborhood and whatever political and social figures Gacy could persuade to come. Gacy started his own construction business, PDM Contractors, Inc., in 1974. In 1975, too old for the Jaycees, he joined Chicago Democratic politics, becoming secretary-treasurer of the Norwood Park Street Lighting Commission. Gacy began making public appearances as Pogo the Clown and ran large public parades, including the 1978 Polish Day Parade in Chicago, at which he was photographed with First Lady Rosalynn Carter.

Gacy had already committed his first murder on 3 January 1972, stabbing to death a youth he brought home for sex; he later claimed self-defense. This began the thirty-three documented murders, ending only with Gacy's arrest in 1978. His construction company lured young men eager for work; he also cruised for victims in gay bars and the downtown Greyhound bus station. Taking most of them home for sex, he sometimes drugged his victims. Often he

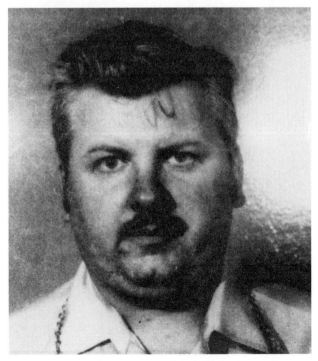

John Wayne Gacy, 1978. ASSOCIATED PRESS AP

talked them into handcuffing themselves as a "magic trick." When they were helpless, he told them, "The trick is, you need the key." Most victims were strangled with a tourniquet device Gacy called "the rope trick." PDM Construction also helped dispose of twenty-nine bodies, burying them on Gacy's own property, especially in the crawl space of his house. Gacy glibly answered complaints about an awful smell, blaming the crawl space's dampness. At least four bodies were dumped in the Des Plaines and Illinois Rivers. Gacy may have killed others during business trips, though that remains unproven and largely uninvestigated.

Carole, though ignorant of the murders, knew their marriage was troubled; she found signs of late-night visits from young men but suspected enough about her husband's sexuality not to ask any questions. The marriage ended amicably in March 1976. Carole continued to visit John, accepting his increased leaning toward homosexuality and unaware of anything darker.

Police remained ignorant as well. Investigations into the disappearances of two victims in 1975 and late 1976 would have tied Gacy to both, but the cases, in different police districts, went unconnected. Many disappearances were ignored as probable runaways.

However, when Robert Piest, a fifteen-year-old from nearby Des Plaines, disappeared on 11 December 1978, witnesses reported having last seen him talking with Gacy. Police harried Gacy with surveillance and got a warrant to excavate: the holiday season of 1978–1979 saw body after body removed from Gacy's house, which was gutted in the process and then destroyed.

Gacy at first cooperated, drawing a meticulous map of the graves. However, he pleaded "not guilty by reason of insanity" and later hinted that others who shared his house may have murdered the victims and buried them there. After a gruesome and arduous trial, in March 1980 the jury quickly returned a verdict of guilty on thirty-three counts of murder, twelve carrying a death sentence, and two charges of sexual assault.

The convict was transferred from Cermak Hospital in the Cook County Jail to the Menard Correctional Center in Chester, Illinois. Once again a model prisoner, Gacy corresponded voluminously and painted—badly—including portraits of clowns and Disney's Seven Dwarfs. He was taken to Stateville Prison in Joliet and just after midnight on 10 May 1994 executed by lethal injection; he is buried in Mayhill Cemetery in Niles, Illinois.

More than most serial killers, Gacy fit the cliché of "such a nice neighbor," the last person one would suspect; but beneath his ingratiating eagerness to please, he harbored a combination of rage, guilt, and sexual loathing. His extreme powers of denial perhaps account for his ability both to murder what was, up until that time, a record number of persons and to live, literally, with the consequences.

★

Tim Cahill, *Buried Dreams* (1986), provides detailed, spooky psychological insight; Clifford L. Linedecker, *The Man Who Killed Boys* (1980), and Harlan Mendenhall, *Fall of the House of Gacy* (1996), provide more facts, as does *Killer Clown*, by Terry Sullivan (a lawyer with Gacy's prosecution) with Peter T. Maiken (1983). An interview with Gacy is in Robert Ressler and Tom Shachtman, *I Have Lived in the Monster* (1997).

BERNADETTE LYNN BOSKY

GARCIA, Hector Perez (*b.* 17 January 1914 in Liera, Tamaulipas, Mexico; *d.* 26 July 1996 in Corpus Christi, Texas), physician and activist most noted for founding the American GI Forum, a veterans and Mexican American civil rights organization.

Garcia was the oldest son of a college professor, José García, and a schoolteacher, Faustina Pérez García. In 1918, during the Mexican Revolution, the family escaped an attack on their village and emigrated to Mercedes, Texas, in the Río Grande Valley. José García purchased a general store, his children learned to pick cotton, and young Hector Gar-

Hector Garcia, 1983. UPI/CORBIS-BETTMANN

cia first came in contact with very poor Mexicans and Mexican American farm laborers.

Although Garcia attended "Mexican only" schools in Mercedes, he excelled as a student in high school and at Edinburg Junior College. Garcia entered the University of Texas in 1934 and received his B.A. degree in zoology two years later, graduating with honors. He immediately entered the University of Texas School of Medicine and earned his M.D. degree in 1940. From 1940 to 1942 Garcia interned at St. Joseph's Hospital of Creighton University in Omaha, Nebraska.

Upon completion of his internship, Garcia volunteered for military service during World War II. He entered the war as a first lieutenant in command of an army infantry company in North Africa. Eventually Garcia transferred to the medical corps and was promoted to the rank of major by the end of the war. In campaigns in North Africa and Europe, he won one bronze star and six battle stars. During the war Garcia met Wanda Fusillo, an Italian doctoral candidate in liberal arts, and they were married on 23 June 1945.

In 1946 Garcia returned with his wife to Texas and settled in Corpus Christi, where they had four children. He soon became aware of the spectrum of social inequities faced by Mexican Americans in the area. He learned of school children still segregated through the eighth grade, of segregated accommodations (signs that read *se sirve solamente a raza blanca* [serving whites only] were commonplace), and, most important, of the high rates of tuberculosis, dysentery, and pneumonia—all treatable conditions—among the Mexican American population in Corpus Christi.

Garcia's outrage at such conditions led him to join the League of United Latin American Citizens (LULAC), a civil rights organization founded in 1929 to fight school segregation. But he worked primarily on his own to bring attention to the appalling health and sanitation conditions in the Corpus Christi area, including those in migrant labor camps, through weekly Spanish-language radio broadcasts and lectures to parent-teacher groups and other volunteer organizations.

At the same time Garcia built a physician's practice that included a substantial number of Mexican American World War II veterans, who were sent to him under an agreement with the local Veterans Administration (VA) office. In treating these patients, Garcia soon learned of a pattern of mistreatment experienced by Mexican American veterans at the hands of the VA. First, Garcia often struggled to get space for patients at the local naval hospital. In addition he discovered that benefits checks sent from Washington, D.C., were often six months late in reaching veterans in Corpus Christi. GI Bill applications for educational benefits frequently were not processed on time (300 veterans who en-

rolled for schooling under the GI Bill in September 1947 did not receive their checks from the government until January 1948). As Garcia learned of such mistreatment and the complete lack of attention paid by the American Legion or Veterans of Foreign Wars, he resolved to take the lead in demanding equal treatment for all veterans.

On 26 March 1948 Garcia gathered more than 700 Mexican American veterans at the Lamar School in Corpus Christi. The veterans took turns voicing grievances and telling stories of apparent betrayal by their own government. At the end of the night, the veterans formed the American GI Forum (AGIF) and elected Garcia its first president.

Garcia believed that the veterans in the AGIF made ideal activists because of their ability, as former soldiers, to follow orders and to stick to an organizing plan. The AGIF proved immediately successful in getting the VA to correct its mistakes and expedite the various claims and applications that it had been neglecting. In addition, it expanded its scope to examine issues concerning housing, education, child welfare, health care, poll taxes, Hispanic representation on draft boards, and employment vis-à-vis the Mexican American population.

Garcia and the AGIF received national attention in 1949 when they came to the aid of the family of Felix Longoria, a Mexican American veteran who was killed on a mission in the Philippines during World War II and whose remains were not recovered and returned to the United States until late 1948. The only funeral director in Three Rivers, Texas, Longoria's hometown, agreed to bury Longoria in the segregated "Mexican" cemetery but would not allow the family to use the chapel for the wake because, he said, "the whites would not like it." Garcia mobilized the AGIF to spark public outrage, and he contacted Senator Lyndon Johnson for assistance. The story made national headlines and led Johnson to make arrangements for Longoria to be laid to rest at Arlington National Cemetery with full military honors.

The controversy established the AGIF as the leading Mexican American civil rights organization several years before mainstream America noticed the growing African American civil rights movement. By the end of 1950 more than 100 AGIF chapters were active throughout Texas. Members came together to write a new state constitution, which announced the organization's mission "to strive for the procurement of all veterans and their families, regardless of race, color, or creed, the equal privileges to which they are entitled under the laws of our country" and for the "preservation of the democratic ideals for which this country has fought in all wars." Any veteran or veteran's spouse was eligible to join the organization.

Garcia continued to be active in the AGIF for the next five decades. In 1999 the AGIF claimed more than 160,000 members in 502 chapters across twenty-four states. President Lyndon Johnson rewarded Garcia's singular contribution by appointing him as a special delegate to the United Nations in 1968. He also made Garcia the first Mexican American member of the UN Commission on Civil Rights. In 1984 President Ronald Reagan awarded Garcia the Medal of Freedom. Garcia died in Corpus Christi following congestive heart failure and pneumonia and was buried in that city.

Garcia tirelessly fought for civil rights and founded the American GI Forum long before Americans had grown accustomed to civil rights as a political issue. He prided himself on working for change within the system. Through assertive grassroots organizing and constant pressure on public officials, Garcia helped advance Mexican American civil rights and paved the way for the Chicano rights movement of the 1960s and 1970s.

★

Hector Garcia's papers are deposited at Texas A&M University at Corpus Christi. Although no full-length biography of Garcia has been written, the American GI Forum is the subject of two useful monographs, both of which examine Garcia's life in some detail: Carl Allsup, *The American GI Forum: Origins and Evolution* (1982), and Henry A. J. Ramos, *A People Forgotten, a Dream Pursued: The History of the American GI Forum.* Julie Leininger Pycior, *LBJ and Mexican Americans: The Paradox of Power* (1997), provides considerable detail on Garcia's relationship with Lyndon Johnson and his place in Texas politics. Also of note is George Norris Green, "The Felix Longoria Affair," *Journal of Ethnic Studies* 19, no. 3 (1991). An obituary appears in the *Corpus Christi Caller-Times* (27 July 1996).

MICHAEL S. FOLEY

GARCIA, Jerome John ("Jerry") (*b.* 1 August 1942 in San Francisco, California; *d.* 9 August 1995 in Forest Knolls, California), lead guitarist, vocalist, and guiding force behind the Grateful Dead, one of the most popular and influential rock bands in history.

Garcia's link with music began when his Spanish immigrant father, Jose "Joe" Garcia, and his mother, Ruth Clifford, named him after the Broadway composer Jerome Kern. Garcia and his younger brother spent their early childhood in San Francisco. Joe Garcia was a professional musician who played the clarinet, but his career was cut short around the time his first son was born due to a dispute with a local musician's union. He quit playing professionally and supported his family by opening a bar in downtown San Francisco.

In the summer of 1946, Jerry Garcia suffered an injury that would later become a world-famous trademark. While helping his brother chop wood at the family's summer cabin, Garcia's middle finger on his right hand was cut so

Jerry Garcia. AP/WIDE WORLD PHOTOS

badly it had to be amputated. A much worse accident was to occur to the Garcia family in 1948: while fishing in deep water, Joe Garcia lost his footing and drowned. Ruth took over running the bar and the brothers were sent to live with their maternal grandparents. Attending the Monroe School, the Garcia brothers continued to live with their grandparents until Ruth remarried in 1953 and took the boys to live with her in suburban Menlo Park, where they attended Menlo-Oaks Middle School.

After a move back to San Francisco, Garcia attended James Denman Middle School and then Balboa High School, two notoriously rough schools. His fifteenth birthday marked the beginning of his interest in playing guitar. He became obsessed with the instrument and practiced constantly. Garcia's early role models were the giants of early electric guitar: Chuck Berry, Buddy Holly, and Bo Diddley. A teacher at Balboa recognized Garcia's artistic ability and encouraged him to take classes in art. By 1958 he was enrolled in the California School of Fine Arts.

After another brief move out of San Francisco and enrollment in Analy High School, Garcia dropped out and joined the army when he was seventeen. He was unable to adapt to military life and went AWOL eight times before receiving a dishonorable discharge at the end of 1960. At the age of eighteen Garcia began the bohemian life he had been yearning for, moving to Palo Alto and immersing himself in Beat culture and folk music. This was an important period of his artistic evolution; he met most of the people who would become prominent in the San Francisco music scene and worked diligently on his guitar playing. One of the more important friendships he made during this period was with Robert Hunter, a musician and poet who would eventually team up with Garcia to become the Grateful Dead's primary songwriting team. Garcia's interest in bluegrass turned into an obsession, and he soon made a name for himself as a banjo player in several local bluegrass combos. Garcia's eclectic interest in several different American musical genres—early rock, blues, folk, country, and bluegrass—formed the background for what would become the repertoire of the Grateful Dead.

In 1963 Garcia met Sara Ruppenthal and the two formed a folk duo called Jerry and Sarah. They were quickly married and their only daughter was born the same year. To support his family, Garcia gave guitar lessons in a music store where he met one of the future drummers of the Grateful Dead, Bill Kreutzmann. On New Year's Eve 1963, Garcia met the sixteen-year-old Bob Weir and they soon formed an ever-evolving jug band with a local bluesman named Ron ("Pigpen") McKernan. They called themselves Mother McCree's Uptown Jug Champions. But in 1965, after seeing the Beatles film *A Hard Day's Night,* the band went electric and called themselves the Warlocks. They soon recruited classically trained Phil Lesh on bass.

The Warlocks played in area clubs and quickly established a small following that appreciated the band's diverse range of music and wild improvisations. In the fall of 1965 the Warlocks started to perform at LSD-fueled parties hosted by the novelist Ken Kesey, author of *One Flew Over the Cuckoo's Nest* (1962). Kesey had volunteered for tests conducted by the federal government on the effects of various psychotomimetic drugs including LSD-25. Kesey believed LSD was the key to a new universal consciousness. A group of others interested in experimenting with LSD, or "acid," gathered around him and called themselves the Merry Pranksters. They gave acid to anyone who would come to their gatherings, which eventually became known as Acid Tests. The Warlocks became the house band for these hallucinogenic revels, and the experience established the band's approach to performing: they never played with a set list and instead relied on improvisation to move them through the music. After discovering that another group was calling themselves the Warlocks, the band searched for another moniker. While flipping through a dictionary, Garcia came across the words "Grateful Dead," the appellation for a series of folktales. The name stuck.

Throughout 1966 the Grateful Dead's popularity grew throughout the Bay Area on the strength of their live performances. Along with other bands such as Jefferson Airplane and Quicksilver Messenger Service, the Grateful Dead became nationally recognized as leaders in the new form of popular music called acid rock. The band played constantly and in the summer of 1966 released its first single, "Don't Ease Me In"/"Stealin'." The venues for their shows grew in size until they were performing at the Fillmore, one of the seats of the acid rock explosion. Garcia and most of the band members moved into a large Victorian house at 710 Ashbury Street, and the place soon became a focal point for the area's music. The Haight-Ashbury section of San Francisco was quickly recognized as ground zero for the counterculture and the music it produced.

During this period of the Grateful Dead's growth in popularity, Garcia's relationship with Sara deteriorated. He moved into 710 Ashbury alone and was soon in a relationship with Carolyn ("Mountain Girl") Adams, a Merry Prankster. Adams and Garcia formed a long-lasting relationship and married on New Year's Eve 1981, evidently for tax purposes. They had two daughters and would divorce years later.

As the Grateful Dead became one of the more popular rock acts in the area, Garcia established himself as a leader of a band that professed no leaders. He guided the band to bluegrass, folk, and country tunes, and his guitar playing became the cynosure of the band's constantly evolving improvisations. Garcia's impact on local music was epitomized by Jefferson Airplane's reference to him as a "Musical and Spiritual Adviser" on the back of their seminal album of the period, *Surrealistic Pillow* (1967). The Grateful Dead's own self-titled first album was released in 1967.

The notoriety of the band put them under official scrutiny, and at the end of 1967 police raided their home at 710 and arrested Weir and McKernan for marijuana possession. But legal troubles did not stop the band from having an incredibly prolific period inside the recording studio and on the road. The band added a second drummer and another keyboardist to record their second album, *Anthem of the Sun,* in 1968. The next year saw the major surge in the band's popularity. They released the albums *Aoxomoxoa* and their first live recording, *Live/Dead.* The band formed a close relationship with concert promoter Bill Graham, who saw to it that the Grateful Dead played to packed houses across the country.

The band became popular and influential; and the dedicated fans who followed them from venue to venue eventually became known as Deadheads. In 1970 Garcia and the band were arrested in New Orleans for drug possession, an incident made famous in the song "Truckin'" on their 1970 album *American Beauty.* From 1969 to 1974 Garcia and Hunter teamed up to produce the songs that would become the heart of the Grateful Dead's repertoire. Although the Dead's touring schedule remained relentless, Garcia always seemed to find time and energy to release solo records and perform in side bands, including the long-lived Jerry Garcia Band.

In 1972 Garcia released his first solo effort, entitled *Garcia*. In 1973 he began to play in a bluegrass band called Old & In the Way. After the Grateful Dead encountered logistical and monetary problems, the band went on a touring hiatus after recording the album *Grateful Dead From the Mars Hotel* in 1974. During this break the band released the album *Blues for Allah* in 1975. They hit the road again a year later. The late 1970s and early 1980s saw Garcia at his most prolific, but at the same time he was developing a drug habit that would plague him for the rest of his life. In addition to using cocaine, Garcia became addicted to a smokable form of heroin known as "Persian." Meanwhile, in addition to the constant touring with the Grateful Dead, Garcia released several more solo albums, including his personal favorite, *Cats Under the Stars* (1978). He also oversaw production of *The Grateful Dead Movie,* released in 1977.

The early 1980s saw the greatest growth in popularity the band would ever experience, and by mid-decade they were playing in football stadiums to accommodate their fans. However, as the decade wore on, Garcia's drug use affected his performances. In 1985 he was arrested in Golden Gate Park when drugs were discovered in his car. The next year saw his first major health scare: he lapsed into a three-day-long diabetic coma. Garcia made a quick recovery but the band was forced to take its longest tour break in ten years. Decades of poor diet, chain smoking, a harsh road schedule, and drug use had reduced Garcia's physical condition to such a level that many doubted that he would return to touring. As it turned out, 1987 became one of the Dead's most prolific years, and Garcia's return was heralded by the band's first studio album in seven years, *In the Dark*. The album did something no other Dead album had ever succeeded in doing: it broke into the Top Ten and received a great deal of exposure on radio and MTV. During this year of enormous growth in the Dead fan base, Garcia played a series of solo shows on Broadway, and Ben & Jerry's Homemade, Inc. unveiled a new flavor of ice cream: Cherry Garcia. The end of the year also saw the birth of Garcia's fourth child with his companion Manasha Matheson.

In 1989 the Dead released their last studio album, *Built to Last*. The Dead continued touring, but in 1992, Garcia had another health scare as he turned fifty: he was diagnosed with exhaustion and an enlarged heart. The band took a break, and Garcia went on a self-described health kick. In 1994 the Rock and Roll Hall of Fame inducted the Grateful Dead, but Garcia was unable to attend the ceremony. In the same year, Garcia married his third wife, Deborah Koons. In 1995, after beginning the Dead's summer tour, Garcia checked himself into Serenity Knolls rehabilitation center to treat his recurring drug addiction. On 9 August he was found dead after suffering a heart attack in his sleep.

The reaction to Garcia's death was worldwide. President Bill Clinton made a public statement about the loss to American music, and flags in San Francisco were ordered to fly at half mast while a tie-dyed flag was raised at City Hall. The man who had epitomized the counterculture was recognized in death as one of the most original, influential, and important contributors to modern American music. Garcia's ashes were scattered in San Francisco Bay and in the Ganges River in India.

★

Garcia described growing up in San Francisco in *Harrington Street* (1995), a slim volume illustrated by his drawings and paintings. The standard biography is Blair Jackson's comprehensive *Garcia* (1999). Other valuable biographical work on Garcia includes Sandy Troy, *Captain Trips* (1994); *Garcia* (1995), a collection of articles put together by the editors of *Rolling Stone;* and Robert Greenfield's "oral" biography *Dark Star* (1996). Garcia's music and the cultural impact of the Grateful Dead have inspired an industry of writing that is cataloged and assessed in David Dodd and Robert Weiner, *The Grateful Dead and the Deadheads: An Annotated Bibliography* (1997). A history of the band is combined with appraisals of their influence on contemporary American culture in John Rocco, ed., *Dead Reckonings: The Life and Times of the Grateful Dead* (1999). Important work on Garcia and the band include Charles Reich and Jann Wenner, *Garcia: Signpost to New Space* (1972); Blair Jackson, *Grateful Dead: The Music Never Stopped* (1983); David Gans, *Conversations with the Dead* (1991); Sandy Troy's *One More Saturday Night* (1991); Blair Jackson, *Goin' Down the Road* (1992); Rock Scully and David Dalton, *Living with the Grateful Dead: Twenty Years on the Bus with Garcia and the Grateful Dead* (1995); and Oliver Trager, *The American Book of the Dead* (1997). Tom Wolfe wrote about early Grateful Dead performances at Ken Kesey's Acid Tests in *The Electric Kool-Aid Acid Test* (1968). Obituaries of Garcia are in the *New York Times* (10 Aug. 1995) and *San Francisco Chronicle* (10 Aug. 1995).

JOHN ROCCO

GARSON, Greer (*b.* 29 September 1903 in London, England; *d.* 6 April 1996 in Dallas, Texas), famed stage and screen actress and philanthropist, nominated for seven Academy Awards and winner as Best Actress for *Mrs. Miniver* (1942).

Born Eileen Evelyn Greer Garson, her parents were George Garson, a Scottish Presbyterian commercial clerk, and his wife, Nancy Sophia Greer, a homemaker. An only child with chronic bronchitis, Garson often missed several weeks at a time after she started Essex Road Elementary School

she played a challenging dual role in George Bernard Shaw's *Too Good to Be True*; the play's hectic routine and costume changes brought on pneumonia, and by spring a tonsillectomy was necessary. Forced to rest the entire summer, she lost her Birmingham contract. Edward Alec Abbot Snelson, a friend from her university days, returned from his career government position in India to be with her and her mother; he and Garson were married on 28 September 1933. After their honeymoon in Germany, Garson, still physically weak, went back to her mother in London and informed Snelson of her decision not to return with him to India. Around Christmas 1937, Garson resolved to seek a divorce; she did so only after she went to Hollywood, where she obtained a divorce on 12 May 1941. Snelson announced in September 1942 that he was suing for divorce on grounds of Garson's desertion, since the United Kingdom did not always recognize American divorces. He was granted in England an uncontested decree *nisi* of divorce on 17 November 1942.

Meanwhile, Garson made her first London stage appearance in Shakespeare's *The Tempest* at the Regent's Park Open Air Theatre on 5 June 1934, and throughout the summer she played walk-ons in other Shakespeare and Shaw plays. She soon attracted critical attention with roles in *The Golden Arrow* (1935), directed by Laurence Olivier, and *Accent on Youth* (1935), for which critics praised both her looks and her rich, resonant speaking voice. Another popular and artistic success for her was Noël Coward's production of *Mademoiselle* (1936–1937). During its London run, Douglas Fairbanks, Jr., and the American film director Tay Garnett approached Garson with screen-test offers for Fairbanks's Criterion Films, but Coward refused to release her. During the summer of 1937 she performed several plays on television for the British Broadcasting Corporation (BBC). After a performance in August 1937 of *Old Music* at the St. James Theatre, Louis B. Mayer arranged for a screen test at Metro-Goldwyn-Mayer's (MGM) Denham studios. The result was a seven-year contract with MGM, at about $500 a week, close to double her weekly salary. In November 1937, accompanied by her mother, Garson set sail on the SS *Normandie* for New York.

About a year after her arrival, Garson accepted the role of Katherine Ellis Chipping opposite Robert Donat in *Goodbye, Mr. Chips* (1939); she earned an Academy Award nomination for best actress. Critical acclaim continued with her performance as Elizabeth Bennet in Robert Z. Leonard's *Pride and Prejudice* (1940), which brought another Academy Award nomination, and as Mrs. Edna Gladney in Mervyn LeRoy's *Blossoms in the Dust* (1941), MGM's first Technicolor drama, with Walter Pidgeon as her costar in this first of eight films together. Garson won an Academy Award for best actress with her portrayal of the heroic title character in the wartime drama *Mrs. Miniver,* which again

Greer Garson. THE KOBAL COLLECTION

at age five. Upon her father's sudden death in 1906, her mother (whom she always called "Nina") inherited several income townhouses. Garson often spent long vacations at County Down, Northern Ireland (which her publicists indicated as her birthplace, also taking five years off her age). She developed powerful memorization skills and at age four reportedly gave a church-hall recitation. She earned a certificate from East Ham Secondary and went to the University of London in September 1921; she won a scholarship and graduated in 1926 with a bachelor's degree and upper-second-class honors. After graduate French courses at the University of Grenoble, France, she returned to London, where she mastered secretarial skills, worked as a researcher for *Encyclopaedia Britannica,* and accepted employment with the advertising branch of Lever Brothers.

Participation in school groups inspired Garson—who was five feet, six inches tall and titian-haired, with blue-green eyes—to become an actress. She had a letter of introduction to Cyril Richards, the general manager of the Birmingham Repertory Theatre, who arranged an audition for her in December 1931. Under contract with the theater, "Eileen Garson" debuted on 30 January 1932 as Shirley Kaplan, a Jewish schoolteacher in *Street Scene*. During a twelve-week tour she adopted the name "Greer Garson" as

costarred her with Pidgeon and premiered at Radio City Music Hall in New York City on 4 June 1942. The role of Mrs. Miniver had been intended for Norma Shearer, still considered MGM's reigning queen; initially, Garson shared Shearer's concern over playing mother to a soldier and his wife. Richard Ney, who played that soldier, married Garson on 24 July 1943; the two honeymooned briefly before Ensign Ney went overseas on wartime naval duty.

Another spectacular success was LeRoy's *Random Harvest* (1942) with Ronald Colman, in which Garson performed a kilted song-and-dance routine called "She's Ma Daisy." She earned Academy Award nominations for her roles in LeRoy's *Madame Curie* (1943) as well as Garnett's *Mrs. Parkington* (1944) and *Valley of Decision* (1945). Offscreen, Garson was active in war bond drives in the United States and Canada. In 1947 Garson signed another seven-year contract with MGM, now worth $5,000 a week, yet the quality of scripts had fallen. Many of her immediate postwar films ended in financial losses for the studio.

Garson's personal life was in turmoil: on 27 January 1947, she announced her separation from Ney; despite a brief reconciliation, they were divorced on 25 September 1947. Fortunately, on the set of *Julia Misbehaves* (1948), her young costars Elizabeth Taylor and Peter Lawford presented one of their mutual friends, U.S. Army Colonel Elijah E. ("Buddy") Fogelson, a millionaire Texas oilman and rancher. Garson and Fogelson began a long and blissful marriage on 15 July 1949; they lived primarily on his ranch in Pecos, New Mexico. Fogelson had long before adopted his nephew as his son; Garson never had any children. On 11 April 1951 she received her final American citizenship papers.

Garson's contract with MGM ended in 1954, after which she made only five more films. Chief among these was Vincent J. Donehue's *Sunrise at Campobello* (1960), which garnered her seventh and final Academy Award nomination for her portrayal of Eleanor Roosevelt. As Mother Prioress opposite Debbie Reynolds in Henry Koster's *The Singing Nun* (1966), Garson acted in one last MGM project. Her final film, *The Happiest Millionaire* (1967), was the last of thirteen Garson films to play at Radio City during the Christmas season. In all, her films played there for a record total of eighty-three weeks, giving her true claim to the title "Queen of Radio City Music Hall." During the same period, Garson performed in a variety of challenging television plays, including *Reunion in Vienna* (1955), *The Little Foxes* (1956), Shaw's *Captain Brassbound's Conversion* (1960), and *The Invincible Mr. Disraeli* (1963). She also relieved Rosalind Russell on Broadway in *Auntie Mame* (1958) and acted in *Captain Brassbound's Conversion* with the Center Theatre Group of Los Angeles in 1968. She was still active during the 1970s and 1980s with appearances on national and public television.

Garson and her husband gave millions to charitable organizations, usually through the E. E. Fogelson and Greer Garson Fogelson Charitable Foundation. At St. John's College (renamed the College of Santa Fe), they established the Greer Garson Theatre in 1975 and the Garson Communications Center and Studios in 1990. Other gifts included Southern Methodist University's Greer Garson Theatre in Dallas (1992); the E. E. Fogelson Visitor Center at the Pecos National Historical Monument (1987); and the Fogelson Forum at the Dallas Presbyterian Hospital (1990). Garson's honors and awards included an honorary degree from the Cleveland Institute of Music (1973), the New Mexico Governor's Award for Excellence and Achievement in the Arts (1987), the Masters Screen Artists Award at the USA Film Festival in Dallas (1988), the Golda Meir Fellowship Award of the Builders of Scopus (1988), and the insignia of Honorary Commander of the Order of the British Empire (1993) for her patriotism, conservation concerns, and university endowments.

Garson developed heart problems in the 1980s and underwent surgery several times, including a quadruple bypass in June 1988; her physicians advised her not to return to the high altitude of Santa Fe, and she finally sold the beloved ranch in 1990. During Christmas week of 1989 a fire destroyed almost everything, including her Academy Award, at her deluxe Wilshire Terrace apartment in Los Angeles; the Academy presented her with a replacement. For about a year prior to her death, Garson resided in the long-term-care unit of the Dallas Presbyterian Hospital, where she died of heart failure. She was buried next to Fogelson at Sparkman-Hillcrest Memorial Park in Dallas. A memorial service was held there at Highland Park Presbyterian Church, and a special memorial service was offered at St. Paul's at Covent Garden in London on 4 July 1996.

One of Hollywood's top box-office attractions from the late 1930s through the war years, Garson had an air of controlled maturity and understated elegance that became especially important during World War II. As her characters endured every trial, inner fortitude and dedication to duty radiated through her comforting voice and graceful demeanor as well as from her reassuring silence. Her characters endured every trial, and that inner fortitude and dedication to duty radiated through her comforting voice and graceful demeanor. The English-born Hollywood actress helped to galvanize public American sentiment in the conflict against Nazism, so that even after the war, a wax figure of Garson as the title character in *Mrs. Miniver* appeared at Madame Tussaud's in London, a film that the British prime minister Winston Churchill assessed to be "propaganda worth a hundred battleships."

★

The Greer Garson Collection of the Bywaters Special Collection, Jake and Nancy Hamon Arts Library, Southern Methodist University, contains scrapbooks, slides, photographs, scripts, awards, correspondence, and other materials and memorabilia from Garson's stage and film career as well as philanthropic activities. Garson never wanted to write an autobiography and was notorious in Hollywood for not liking to grant interviews during her peak years there. (She sometimes wrote articles for specialized journals and newsletters pertaining to cattle and horses.) There is a well-written biography by Michael Troyan, *A Rose for Mrs. Miniver: The Life of Greer Garson* (1999), with complete listings of her plays and films and partial listing of her radio and television work, with bibliography, index, and extensive photographs. Other helpful sources are James Robert Parish and Ronald L. Bowers, *MGM Stock Company* (1973): 268–75, Herbert G. Luft, "Greer Garson: Convinced Audiences That Beauty Is Sometimes Coupled With Selflessness," *Films in Review* (12: Mar. 1961): 152–64, and *Current Biography 1942* (1943). Robert Osborne, *Seventy Years of the Oscar: The Official History of the Academy Awards* (1999), includes extended quotes from Garson's Academy Award acceptance speech, and Anthony Holden, *Behind the Oscar: The Secret History of the Academy Awards* (1994), lists her television credits. For extensive bibliographies primarily covering the Hollywood journals, see Mel Schuster, *Motion Picture Performers: A Bibliography of Magazine and Periodical Articles, 1900–1969* (1971) and *Supplement No. 1, 1970–1974* (1976). Obituaries are in the *New York Times* (7 Apr. 1996), *Los Angeles Times* (7 Apr. 1996), London *Sunday Times* (7 Apr. 1996), and *Current Biography Yearbook 1996* (1997). Many of Garson's films and even some television specials appear on commercial videocassettes; there are audio recordings of some of her narrations and speaking books.

MADELINE SAPIENZA

GELDZAHLER, Henry (*b.* 9 July 1935 in Antwerp, Belgium; *d.* 16 August 1994 in Southampton, New York), art historian, museum curator, and public official whose combination of erudition, personal charm, and flair for showmanship helped ensure the preeminence of New York School artists in the 1960s and 1970s.

Geldzahler was the younger of two sons of Joseph and Charlotte (Gutwirth) Geldzahler, members of Polish Jewish families long resident in the Low Countries. His father was a wealthy diamond broker. Because his mother was a naturalized American, the family was able to escape Belgium and settle in New York shortly before the Nazi invasion in 1940. Geldzahler attended public school prior to going to Horace Mann, a prestigious private high school in the Riverdale section of the Bronx. By the time he entered Yale College, he knew he wanted to be an art museum curator. He later recalled that when he was fifteen, he had seen an Arshile Gorky exhibition at the Whitney Museum

Henry Geldzahler, 1977. AP/WIDE WORLD PHOTOS

and came home "completely knocked out, and that's when I first realized that art could be that moving or upsetting." An art history major at Yale, Geldzahler visited New York museums and galleries on weekends and worked one summer as a volunteer in the Department of European Paintings at the Metropolitan Museum of Art. He spent his junior year in Paris, studying at the École du Louvre and the Sorbonne.

Geldzahler received his B.A. degree, magna cum laude, in 1957, and then went to Harvard to work toward a doctorate. He left Harvard, however, in 1960, without having completed his dissertation (on Henri Matisse's sculpture), when James Rorimer, then director of the Metropolitan, offered him a job as a curatorial assistant responsible for twentieth-century art in the Department of American Painting and Sculpture. For the next two years Geldzahler spent most of his time visiting studios and galleries, seeking out examples of the latest trends for possible acquisition by the museum. Thoroughly grounded as he was in art scholarship, he was often able to defend his proposed purchases, demonstrating to conservative museum officials how works by avant-garde artists actually derived from those of older, established masters. But the fact that the young assistant had become personally involved with some of the artists whose work he was promoting—indeed, had been featured in a "Happening" staged by Claes Oldenburg and a film by Andy Warhol—did not always sit well with the trustees.

On leave from the Metropolitan Museum in 1966 and 1967, Geldzahler served as a program director for the National Endowment for the Arts, awarding grants to artists of his own choosing and recommending disbursements to museums to enable their purchase of works by living American painters and sculptors. Concurrently, he was appointed U.S. commissioner for the 1966 Venice Biennale, charged with selecting artists to be shown in the U.S. pavilion. Instead of the pop artists he had hitherto championed (like Warhol, who once claimed Geldzahler had given him all his ideas), he chose the color-field painters Helen Frankenthaler, Ellsworth Kelly, and Jules Olitski—and one pop painter, the more conservative Roy Lichtenstein. Incensed by the politics and questionable aesthetic judgments involved in the granting of Biennale prizes, Geldzahler raised so strong an objection that two years later the prize system was abolished.

When he returned to the Metropolitan Museum, Geldzahler became curator of the newly established Department of Contemporary Arts (renamed the Department of Twentieth Century Art in 1970), which included drawings, prints, and the decorative arts in addition to paintings and sculptures. In 1970 came the high point of his curatorial career when he put on the monumental—and controversial—exhibition *New York Painting and Sculpture: 1940–1970* (otherwise often referred to as "Henry's show"), designed to celebrate the museum's centennial. For this show, which opened in the fall of 1969 and made use of thirty-five galleries, the curator selected 408 works by forty-three artists whose style had been established by 1965: abstract expressionists and their predecessors, color-field and hard-edge painters, minimalists and pop artists. As he stated in his introductory essay in the exhibition catalog, his guiding principle in selection had been "the extent to which [an artist's] work has commanded critical attention or significantly deflected the course of recent art." Much admired by some critics as stimulating and handsomely presented, more conservative commentators reviled the show as merely an arbitrary assemblage designed to further the reputation of Geldzahler's protégés. The exhibition was also criticized for its exclusion of women artists and black artists. On the whole, however, it was a huge popular success.

In 1977 Geldzahler resigned from the Metropolitan for a variety of reasons: friction with museum executives as a result of some of his curatorial decisions; and his own growing disenchantment with late 1970s trends such as conceptual art, which he felt "didn't do the same for me that the earlier art had: It's the materiality of art . . . the way it's made, that I like." In 1977 New York mayor Edward I. Koch appointed him commissioner of cultural affairs. He took office in January 1978 and for the next five years he raised funds from the city council, the federal government, and private sources for the visual and performing arts. By the time he resigned, he had doubled the Cultural Affairs Department budget.

Thereafter, Geldzahler worked as an independent curator. From 1983 to 1986 he was distinguished guest curator of the Institute for Art and Urban Resources at P.S. 1 Contemporary Art Center, the studio-gallery complex in Long Island City, Queens. After 1987 he was curator for the Dia Art Foundation gallery in Bridgehampton, Long Island, mounting shows of two of his favorites, Warhol and Keith Haring. A book titled *Andy Warhol: Portraits of the Seventies and Eighties* (written with Robert Rosenblum) was published in 1993. Geldzahler never married.

At the age of fifty-nine Geldzahler died of cancer at his home in Southampton just before the publication of a collection of his essays and art criticism, *Making It New: Essays, Interviews, and Talks*. He is buried in Green River Cemetery in Springs, Long Island. A memorial service was held at the Metropolitan Museum of Art in the fall of 1994.

The painter David Hockney, one of several artists who over the years painted affectionate portraits of their friend Henry Geldzahler, paid tribute to him in an introduction to *Making It New*—commenting on his wide range of interests, passionate love of art, and great eye. (Geldzahler himself maintained that his way of looking at art had been formed by the critic Clement Greenberg and the painter Frank Stella.) Geldzahler had been at the center of the city's art world—part impresario, part guru—often quoted and photographed in the press. Masked by his flamboyant persona were the energy and efficiency, political savvy, and business acumen he brought to bear on furthering the cause of art and artists.

★

In addition to the titles mentioned above, Henry Geldzahler put together *American Painting in the Twentieth Century* (1965), a Metropolitan Museum of Art exhibition catalog. *New York Painting and Sculpture: 1940–1970*, with his introductory essay on how the exhibition was assembled, was published by the museum with a 1969 date. *Making It New: Essays, Interviews, and Talks* (1994) includes his capsule history of the New York School. Calvin Tomkins's thirty-one-page profile, "Moving with the Flow," *New Yorker* 47 (6 Nov. 1971), is the most extensive biography of Geldzahler through the time of his Metropolitan exhibition. The record is continued in *Current Biography* (1978). Additional biographical information is found in interviews with the photographer Francesco Scavullo, *Scavullo on Men* (1977), and with the art critic Ingrid Sischy, "Making It New," *Interview* 24 (Apr. 1994), the latter was reprinted in Geldzahler's *Making It New*. Other articles about him are Robert Gerber, "Where Henry Hangs His Hat," *House and Garden* 164 (July 1992); and Julia Szabo, "Regarding Henry," *New York* 28 (16 Jan. 1995). Obituaries are in the *New York Times* (17 Aug. 1994) and *ARTnews* 93 (Oct. 1994).

ELEANOR F. WEDGE

GELLHORN, Walter (*b.* 18 September 1906 in St. Louis, Missouri; *d.* 9 December 1995 in New York City), legal scholar, author, and educator who was a major influence on the practice of administrative law and a staunch proponent of civil rights.

Gellhorn was the eldest of three children born to Edna Fischel, a campaigner for suffrage and a founder of the League of Women Voters, and George Gellhorn, a physician and social activist. (His sister, the writer Martha Gellhorn, was the third wife of Ernest Hemingway.) Gellhorn attended Amherst College in Massachusetts and received a B.A. degree in 1927. He then attended Columbia University Law School, where he edited the *Columbia Law Review* and was granted the LL.B. degree in 1931. Upon graduation he served as law clerk for Supreme Court Justice Harlan Fiske Stone. In 1932 he married Kitty Minus; they had two daughters. He was admitted to the New York bar in 1932 and worked as an attorney for the U.S. Solicitor General from 1932 to 1933, when he left to become a law professor at Columbia University. His connection to the school lasted more than sixty years.

Gellhorn combined teaching with public service from the beginning of his long and distinguished career. In 1935 he joined the New York State Public Works Advisory Council and from 1936 until 1938 was a regional attorney for the U.S. Social Security Board. From 1939 to 1941 he

Walter Gellhorn, 1980. © BETTMANN/CORBIS

was the director of the U.S. Attorney General's Committee on Administrative Procedure. From this last experience came the 1941 publication of *Administrative Law: Cases and Comments,* which has gone through eight editions and is still considered to be the main text on the subject. He also gave the James Schouler Lectures in History and Political Science at Johns Hopkins University. These lectures were published as *Federal Administrative Proceedings* (1941).

During World War II, Gellhorn first served as the assistant general counsel and regional attorney for the Office of Price Administration (OPA) (1942–1943). In keeping with his views on civil liberties, in March 1943 he ordered the OPA investigators not to look for hoarded canned food except in cases of extreme violations, and then only with a search warrant. He left the OPA later that year to become a special assistant to Harold Ickes, secretary of the Interior, then became vice chairman of the National War Labor Board, Second Region. He was named board chairman in July 1945 and held that position until the board ceased its existence on 1 January 1946. He is considered to have been the driving force behind the U.S. Administrative Procedure Act of 1946. This law applies fairness and due process in regard to the rules and regulations administered by federal agencies. He also helped to write the Japanese constitution that was put in place after World War II.

Gellhorn was a member of the American Civil Liberties Union and on its board of directors for twenty-five years. He also was a member of the NAACP Legal Defense Fund. In the late 1940s he reacted strongly against what he saw as excesses of the House Committee on Un-American Activities and published "Report on a Report of the House Committee on Un-American Activities" in the *Harvard Law Review* in 1948. He examined the problem of civil liberties in relation to scientific research and the need for secrecy in *Security, Loyalty, and Science* (1950). He argued rigorously against security regulations that he felt hampered scientific research by keeping discoveries hidden. In "Security, Secrecy, and the Advancement of Science" a chapter in *Civil Liberties Under Attack* (1951), Gellhorn again examined the impact of government control on the flow of scientific data. In 1952 he edited and contributed to *The States and Subversion,* in which he dealt with state laws that concerned subversive activities. In 1953 he headed the New York City Bar Association committee that prepared the *Study of the Administration of Laws Relating to the Family in New York.* The study concluded that a lack of trained investigators and social workers led to great deprivation for children in need of help. This report was published in 1954 as *Children and Families in the Courts of New York City.*

In the 1950s fear of communism grew rapidly in the United States. This led to an atmosphere in which people were unjustly accused of being communist sympathizers, and censorship was promoted as a means of national security. In 1956, when he presented a series of lectures on citizenship at Louisiana State University, he was criticized by the American Legion as being procommunist. The lectures, published as *Individual Freedom and Government Restraint* (1956), dealt with censorship in all its forms and proposed that Americans should have freedom of choice in what they read or watched on television. He continued to champion the preservation of civil rights. In 1957 he contributed to *The Freedom to Read*. He went on to write *American Rights: the Constitution in Action* (1960), *When Americans Complain* (1966), and *Ombudsmen and Others* (1966). The latter two works dealt with methods for handling citizens' grievances both in the United States and abroad. In *When Americans Complain,* he examined the possibilities of having an ombudsman and concluded that, while not possible at the federal level, it was practical at the state and local government level. He is credited with helping to establish the idea of an official mediator to be used in negotiations.

Upon retirement from Columbia University in 1975, Gellhorn was named university professor emeritus, and in 1993 an endowed professorship bearing his name was created in his honor. Gellhorn served as a mediator from the 1960s, when he dealt with a controversy concerning a nuclear-powered vessel as well as the New York City teachers' strike, through the 1980s, when he chaired the mediation panel for the city's transit strike.

During his career he received numerous honors, including the Goldsmith Award in 1951 for *Security, Loyalty, and Science* and the Hillman Award in 1957 for *Individual Freedom and Government Restraints*. He was awarded the Columbia Law Alumni Medal for Excellence in 1971, the Learned Hand Medal in 1979, and the Distinguished Research Award from the American Bar Foundation in 1988, along with ten honorary degrees.

Gellhorn was a tireless champion of individual rights, whose influence on the administrative law of the United States, both as practitioner and teacher, was immeasurable. He died in New York City at age eighty-nine.

★

For further reading of Gellhorn's legal writings see his *Kihonteki Jinken,* a compilation of lectures comparing American and Japanese law presented at the University of Tokyo (1959); *Nihonkoku Kenponi Tsuite No Ronpyo* (1959), a commentary on the Japanese constitution; *Administration of the New York Workmen's Compensation Law* (1962); and *The Sectarian College and the Public Purse* (1970), which deals with church-related institutions and public funds. A memorial to Gellhorn by Peter Strauss appears in *Administrative & Regulatory Law News* (spring 1996). A number of tributes appear in the *Columbia Law Review* (Apr. 1996). An obituary is in the *New York Times* (11 Dec. 1995). The Oral History Research Office of Columbia University holds two Gellhorn reminiscences, from 1955 and 1977, respectively.

ROBERTA PESSAH

GILPATRIC, Roswell Leavitt (*b.* 4 November 1906 in Brooklyn, New York; *d.* 15 March 1996 in New York City), influential lawyer who served in the Department of Defense under Presidents Harry S. Truman, John F. Kennedy, and Lyndon B. Johnson.

Through his parents, Walter Hodges Gilpatric, a New York lawyer, and Charlotte Elizabeth Leavitt, a Congregationalist minister's daughter, Gilpatric counted among his forebears a *Mayflower* pilgrim and a signer of the Declaration of Independence. From 1922 to 1924 he attended on a scholarship the prestigious Hotchkiss School in Lakeville, Connecticut. Scholarships and part-time jobs likewise assisted him through Yale College and Yale Law School, where he earned a B.A. degree with honors in 1928 and an LL.B. in 1931. He was elected Phi Beta Kappa and edited the *Law Journal* for two years.

In 1931 Gilpatric joined the premier New York law firm Cravath, Swaine, and Moore (then Cravath, de Gersdorff, Swaine, and Wood) as an associate, making partner on 1 January 1940. The firm became his permanent professional base, which he left only for periods of government service.

Roswell L. Gilpatric, 1963. ASSOCIATED PRESS AP

From 1966 until he retired in 1977 Gilpatric was the presiding partner. In the depressed 1930s Gilpatric handled corporate bankruptcies and reorganizations and international business; during World War II he advised large industrial clients, notably Fairchild Engine and Airplane Corporation, on defense procurement matters. Until 1944 he also represented the government of Finland, facilitating its purchases of American war supplies, for which he was made a Chevalier of the Order of the White Rose. Among his postwar clients were several defense contractors, including General Dynamics, Olin, and the Fairchild Camera and Instrument Corporation, which Gilpatric chaired from 1975 to 1977.

Gilpatric's wartime activities triggered a lifelong interest in defense policy and government service, which accorded with the Cravath firm's tradition of encouraging such outside occupations. In May 1951, during the Korean War, Gilpatric became assistant secretary of the air force for matériel, directing aircraft procurement and production. In October 1951 his effectiveness brought promotion to undersecretary, a post he held until January 1953. Gilpatric deplored waste and duplication within the armed forces and became a dedicated proponent of enhanced unification and systematic long-term military procurement.

Gilpatric served on the 1956–1957 Rockefeller Brothers Fund defense panel that produced the Gaither report, recommending major increases in weapons research and spending. In the summer of 1960 the Democratic presidential nominee, John F. Kennedy, included Gilpatric in study groups on national security and the defense establishment. The latter group produced a report, to which Gilpatric contributed substantially, that further recommended unifying the armed services' top command structures, abolishing the Joint Chiefs of Staff and enhancing the powers of the secretary of defense.

In January 1961 President Kennedy appointed Robert S. McNamara to the position of secretary of defense, with Gilpatric as his deputy. The two men quickly established a close working relationship; Gilpatric's polish helped to soothe the resentments sometimes created by McNamara's abrasive style. Gilpatric supervised procurement and overseas weapons sales, successfully persuading European allies to strengthen their defenses and narrow the dollar gap— the substantial imbalance in Europe's favor between American spending in Europe and European expenditures in the United States—through massive purchases of American military supplies.

Gilpatric supervised early Defense Department policy planning on Vietnam. In April 1961 he headed a task force that recommended making moderate increases in U.S. aid to Vietnam (which President Kennedy endorsed), contributing some American ground troops, and publicly pledging U.S. intervention if needed to prevent a communist victory.

As Vietnam's significance grew, McNamara largely assumed personal control of Vietnam policy. In his absence, however, on 24 August 1963, Gilpatric approved a State Department cable endorsing a projected internal army coup against South Vietnam's president, Ngo Dinh Diem, a decision about which McNamara later had serious reservations.

During the Cuban missile crisis of October 1962 Gilpatric was a member of the executive committee created by Kennedy to handle the situation. When accompanying McNamara to meetings with the president, Gilpatric habitually said little. On 20 October the committee debated whether to launch direct air strikes on Cuban missile sites or merely impose a naval blockade on Cuba, the more cautious option McNamara and Gilpatric consistently favored. After both sides had spoken, Gilpatric summed up: "Essentially, Mr. President, this is a choice between limited action and unlimited action; and most of us think that it's better to start with limited action." Kennedy followed this advice, and ultimately the crisis was peacefully resolved.

Gilpatric originally intended to resign in mid-1963, but a lengthy Senate investigation into the Pentagon's controversial award of the new TFX fighter contract to General Dynamics rather than Boeing delayed his departure until January 1964. Gilpatric's previous role as lawyer for General Dynamics brought conflict-of-interest allegations, but a 5–4 vote of the Senate Permanent Investigations subcommittee eventually cleared him.

After leaving the Defense Department, Gilpatric wrote extensively on disarmament, military policy, and international affairs, consistently endorsing successive disarmament treaties and urging rationalization and civilian control of the defense establishment. Chairing a panel on nuclear nonproliferation appointed by President Lyndon B. Johnson in November 1964, Gilpatric made the controversial recommendation that the United States consider abandoning its proposed multilateral force. In November 1965 he cochaired a White House citizens' committee that urged both superpowers—the United States and the Soviet Union—to prevent an arms race by instituting a three-year moratorium on producing or deploying defensive missiles. He publicly opposed the Nixon administration's projected antiballistic missile system.

A debonair, though discreet, ladies' man, Gilpatric was married five times. With Margaret Fulton Kurtz (married 18 June 1932; divorced 4 September 1945), Gilpatric had two daughters and a son, his only children. He was subsequently married to Harriet Heywood Wellington (25 October 1946; divorced April 1958); Madelin Thayer Kudner (18 September 1958; divorced February 1970); Paula Melhado Washburn (12 May 1970; divorced January 1985); and Miriam R. Thorne (2 May 1991 until his death). In the 1960s, Gilpatric's frequent appearances escorting Kennedy's widow, Jacqueline, whom he accompanied on a 1968 Mexican vacation, sparked breathless media attention, which was rekindled in 1970 when several affectionate letters she had sent him earlier were stolen and published.

Cultivated, athletic, charming, polished, and impeccably tailored, the incisive and energetic Gilpatric took on numerous directorships and community, philanthropic, and fundraising activities. He was chairman of the Federal Reserve Bank of New York from 1972 to 1975 and a trustee of the New York Public Library, the Metropolitan Museum of Art, and New York University's Institute of Fine Arts. He died of prostate cancer in New York City and is buried on Mount Desert Island in Maine.

Gilpatric epitomized the American "eastern establishment": the elite "in and outers" who, shuttling discreetly between the worlds of government service and corporate finance and law, largely directed the making of U.S. foreign policy in the twentieth century.

★

Gilpatric deposited his papers, covering his public life from 1956 to 1967, in the John F. Kennedy Presidential Library in Boston, Massachusetts. As yet there exists no full biography of Gilpatric. Material on his early legal career is included in Robert T. Swaine, *The Cravath Firm and Its Predecessors, 1819–1947* (1946–1948). Primary source material on Gilpatric's role in Vietnam policy and the Cuban missile crisis is in the relevant volumes of the Government Printing Office series *Foreign Relations of the United States (1870–)*; Mike Gravel, ed., *The Pentagon Papers: The Defense Department History of United States Decision Making on Vietnam* (1971–1972); and Ernest R. May and Philip D. Zelikow, eds., *The Kennedy Tapes: Inside the White House during the Cuban Missile Crisis* (1997). Useful works on the American defense bureaucracy under Truman and in the McNamara years are Carl W. Borklund, *Men of the Pentagon: From Forrestal to McNamara* (1966) and *The Department of Defense* (1968); Doris M. Condit, *History of the Office of the Secretary of Defense*, vol. 2 (1988); Deborah W. Shaplen, *Promise and Power: The Life and Times of Robert McNamara* (1993); and Bernard C. Nalty, ed., *Winged Shield, Winged Sword: A History of the United States Air Force* (1997). Informative summaries of Gilpatric's contributions to successive Democratic presidential administrations are given in Eleanora W. Schoenebaum, ed., *Political Profiles: The Truman Years* (1978) and Nelson Lichtenstein, ed., *Political Profiles: The Kennedy Years* (1976) and *Political Profiles: The Johnson Years* (1976). Obituaries are in the *New York Times* (17 Mar. 1996), *Washington Post* (18 Mar. 1996), and London *Times* (18 Mar. 1996). Arthur M. Schlesinger, Jr., wrote a memorial tribute in the Century Association's *Century Yearbook* for 1997. Cravath, Swaine, and Moore holds an oral history interview with Gilpatric covering his legal career; the Harry S. Truman, John F. Kennedy, and Lyndon B. Johnson presidential libraries hold various oral histories in which Gilpatric reflected on his public service.

PRISCILLA ROBERTS

GINSBERG, Mitchell Irving (*b.* 20 October 1915 in Revere, Massachusetts; *d.* 2 March 1996 in New York City), practitioner and scholar of social welfare policy, commissioner of the New York City Department of Social Services and Human Resources in John Lindsay's mayoral administration, and dean of the Columbia University School of Social Work.

Ginsberg was the son of Harry J. Ginsberg, a maintenance worker, and Rose Harris. He had two siblings, but his older brother died the day Ginsberg was born. When Ginsberg was less than a year old, his family moved to the Dorchester section of the Fourteenth Ward in Boston, an impoverished neighborhood where his father worked as the foreman in an automobile garage. Ginsberg later recalled that his father worked twelve hours a day, seven days a week, for very low wages. The experience of growing up poor profoundly influenced Ginsberg's career choice. A disciplined student, he excelled at the Boston Latin School and earned a scholarship to Tufts College in Medford, Massachusetts.

Ginsberg was admitted to Phi Beta Kappa and graduated summa cum laude with a B.A. degree in history from Tufts in 1937. Upon applying to the School of Foreign Service at Tufts, Ginsberg learned he had little chance of successfully pursuing a career in diplomacy because he was Jewish. Instead, he earned an M.A. degree in education and psychology from Tufts in 1938. He received a national fellowship to the New York School of Social Work (now the Columbia University School of Social Work), graduating with an M.S. degree in social work in 1941. In 1942 Ginsberg entered the U.S. Army, where he served as a supervisor of a psychiatric social work unit at Camp Carson, Colorado, until 1946. After leaving the army as a technical sergeant, he held a variety of social work positions in Boston; Pittsburgh; Manchester, New Hampshire; and finally in New York City at the National Jewish Welfare Board. In 22 August 1948 he married Ida Robbins, an X-ray technician at New York's Memorial Hospital. They had no children. Married for over forty-eight years, they lived in Manhattan until Ginsberg's death in 1996.

Ginsberg joined the Columbia University School of Social Work faculty in 1953 as an assistant professor of social work. Specializing in community relations and group work, he became a full professor in 1956, an associate dean of the School of Social Work in 1960, and the dean of the School of Social Work in 1970.

Serving as the director of the Peace Corps Training Project at Columbia University from 1962 to 1964, Ginsberg initiated programs to instruct Peace Corps and Volunteers in Service to America (VISTA) trainees under the Economic Opportunities Act. He served as a consultant to the Community Action Program of the federal Office for Economic Opportunity in 1965 and was a member of the Steering Committee of the Head Start Program from 1965 to 1968.

Mitchell I. Ginsberg, 1966. © BETTMANN/CORBIS

Taking a leave of absence from Columbia University in 1966, Ginsberg accepted an appointment as the commissioner of the New York City Department of Social Services in Mayor John Lindsay's first term. During what many considered a welfare crisis, New Yorkers welcomed Ginsberg's appointment because of his excellent credentials, and he initiated several important reforms. He instituted an affidavit-like declaration to replace the expensive and often degrading inspections of female welfare recipients traditionally conducted in the middle of the night. Ginsberg experimented with a work incentive program that allowed welfare recipients to retain their benefits while employed. In addition he instituted liberal policies for the dissemination of birth control information and created district advisory boards composed predominantly of welfare recipients.

When the New York City Department of Social Services was brought under the auspices of the newly created Human Resources Administration (HRA), Ginsberg became head of this new agency. As HRA administrator from 1967 to 1970, he often dealt with controversy, underscored by growing budgetary constraints and mounting client demand. HRA was the subject of over a dozen investigations, and while most of the charges resulted from activity that predated Ginsberg's tenure, he was held accountable. Ginsberg capably defended himself against the charges, improved the agency's internal organization, and created auditing procedures to prevent similar problems from threatening the future of the agency.

During his tenure at HRA and later, Ginsberg was a strong proponent of a uniform national welfare policy. His plan emphasized job training and guaranteed employment, and it substituted a national family assistance plan for welfare means testing. He lobbied for these and other reforms in Washington and remained a strong advocate for the poor even after leaving government service.

Ginsberg returned to Columbia University in 1971 to serve as the dean of the School of Social Work and special assistant for community affairs to Columbia's president until 1981. He retired in 1986 after over thirty years at Columbia, but he continued to teach classes and served as codirector of Columbia's Center for the Study of Human Rights. Ginsberg helped create Columbia Community Services, a cooperative project with the university's schools of dentistry, nursing, business, and public health designed to provide health services and social services to residents of homeless shelters.

In 1991 Columbia established the Mitchell I. Ginsberg Professorship in Contemporary Urban Problems, an endowed chair intended to further research on homelessness and other problems of the urban poor. Ginsberg was awarded honorary doctorate degrees from Columbia, Tufts, the University of Maryland, and Adelphi University, and he was the president of the National Association of Social Workers and the National Conference on Social Welfare. Ginsberg died of cardiopulmonary arrest in Manhattan at the age of eighty.

Ginsberg was an individual with strong convictions but a gentle manner. Tall, thin, and gray-haired, he walked with a stoop that made him appear less than his height of six feet, three inches. He was a serious collector of Lincolniana, filling his home with books and memorabilia. He was also an avid gardener and especially loved roses. A member of his college baseball team and captain of its tennis team, Ginsberg was an avid athlete and sports fan, and his childhood dream was to be a professional athlete or sportswriter. However, serious stomach problems and a congenital short esophagus prevented him from pursuing professional sports. Ginsberg's wife noted that the only time she ever saw her often-sick husband run was to get to the stadium to root for his beloved Yankees.

Ginsberg was a welfare scholar and a leader in social reform. Passionate about teaching and devoted to his students, he also found his work in government and policy enormously gratifying. He was committed to the cause of social justice, and his lifework was dedicated to improving conditions for the poor.

★

For further information on Ginsberg see *Current Biography 1971* (1972); Joshua Miller, "A Narrative Interview with Mitchell Ginsberg," *Reflections* (summer 1995); and the *Columbia University Record* (1 Mar. 1991). An obituary is in the *New York Times* (3 Mar. 1996).

NANCY MARKOE

GONZALEZ, Richard Alonzo ("Pancho") (*b.* 9 May 1928 in Los Angeles, California; *d.* 3 July 1995 in Las Vegas, Nevada), tennis champion who dominated professional tennis from the mid-1950s through the early 1960s and continued to play top-caliber tennis into the early 1970s.

Gonzalez, whose last name was frequently spelled "Gonzales" during his playing career, was the eldest of the seven children of Manuel Gonzalez, a movie-set and house painter, and Carmen Alire, a seamstress, both immigrants from Chihuahua, Mexico. His interest in tennis began when he was twelve years old and his mother gave him a tennis racket purchased, legend has it, for fifty-one cents. Gonzalez taught himself the game at the public courts, where he also picked up the nickname "Pancho." He began playing in junior tournaments and did well enough to attract the attention of Perry Jones, who, as secretary of the Southern California Tennis Association, made top-level facilities available to promising youngsters. Unfortunately, Gonzalez had developed a habit of skipping school to practice tennis. When Jones discovered that Gonzalez had not been attending school regularly, he barred Gonzalez from junior tournaments. Gonzalez responded by dropping out of Manual Arts High School entirely at age fifteen, when he was in the eleventh grade. (He had skipped a grade earlier, so he was ahead of this age group.) The result was that he neither played tennis nor attended school but instead hung out on the streets.

Gonzalez entered the U.S. Navy in the fall of 1945, at the age of seventeen, and served as a seaman on transports in the Pacific. After his discharge from the navy in January 1947, he began playing tennis again. In May 1947 he entered the Southern California Tennis Championships. Advancing all the way to the finals, he managed to take a set from Jack Kramer, the top amateur in the United States.

Jones, impressed by that performance, sponsored Gonzalez for an expenses-paid tour of major tournaments in the East. Although Gonzalez did not win any tournaments in 1947, he played impressively. But ignorance about an arcane U.S. Lawn Tennis Association rule almost cost him his amateur standing. Players were only allowed to receive expense money for eight tournaments a year; Gonzalez accepted invitations to ten. Jones interceded on Gonzalez's behalf, and he was given a nominal punishment, suspension from tournament play outside Los Angeles from February to June 1948.

In March 1948 Gonzalez married Henrietta Pedrin; they had three sons. After his suspension Gonzalez won the 1948 clay court nationals, and in September, at the age of twenty, he stunned the tennis world by winning the U.S. National Championships at Forest Hills. Many felt, however, that Gonzalez had won the tournament over a less-than-stellar field, since Ted Schroeder, who had replaced Kramer as the top amateur after Kramer turned professional, had not entered it.

Gonzalez started the 1949 season well, winning the indoor championships in March. He traveled to Europe, and he and Frank Parker won both the French and the Wimbledon doubles championships. In singles, however, Gonzalez lost in the semifinals at the French Championships and in the fourth round at Wimbledon. He was named to the Davis Cup defense team and won both of his matches for the victorious U.S. team. At the U.S. Championships he defeated Schroeder in one of the most closely fought finals in that tournament's history. Gonzalez lost the first two sets, then came back to win the match 16–18, 2–6, 6–1, 6–2, 6–4. Two weeks later he defeated Schroeder at the Pacific Southwest Tournament.

Shortly afterward Bobby Riggs, a tennis champion who had become a promoter, offered Gonzalez the opportunity to turn professional. Gonzalez immediately accepted it. "You can't hold a steady job and hope to be a top amateur player," he later told the *New York Times Magazine*. "You have to keep in competition most of the year to keep your game up with the others' and maintain the physical condition tennis requires. I just managed to get by when I was out of competition, but I had to scrape."

At the time professional opportunities were limited to only a few players. Generally the reigning professional champion and the amateur champion from the previous year would face off against each other at more than 100

Pancho Gonzalez, 1968. CORBIS CORPORATION (BELLEVUE)

stops across the country. Gonzalez proved to be no match for the professional champion, Kramer, who won 96 of their 123 matches. Gonzalez earned close to $85,000, an extraordinarily high salary for an athlete at that time, but he was not signed for the next year's tour. "People only pay to see winners," Riggs told him.

For the next three years few opportunities came Gonzalez's way. He bought and ran a tennis shop in Los Angeles, participated in a few minor tours, and played in the few professional tournaments that existed. In 1954 he got a second chance. Kramer, who had become a tennis promoter, experimented with a minitournament format featuring Gonzalez, Frank Sedgman, Pancho Segura, and Don Budge. The tour was a failure because the public was only interested in seeing the top professional, still Kramer, face a challenger. But Gonzalez established himself as the best in the group.

In 1955 Kramer signed Gonzalez to a seven-year contract, and Gonzalez took over Kramer's role as the top professional, beating Tony Trabert 74 matches to 27 in the 1955–1956 tour. In 1957 he took on another amateur who had recently turned professional, Ken Rosewall, defeating him 50 matches to 26 matches. In 1958 Gonzalez took on Lew Hoad, defeating him 51 to 36. In 1959 they played a round-robin format, with Gonzalez again coming out on top. During that same period he won the World Pro Cham-

pionships, run by Jack March in Cleveland, from 1953 to 1959 and again in 1961.

At six feet, three inches tall, Gonzalez was a striking figure on the court, where he was often likened to a panther. Contributing to the aura were his handsome face and a dangerous-looking scar on his cheek (from a scooter accident when he was seven years old). His biggest weapon was his serve, which, with a wooden racket, was clocked at 112 miles per hour. But he was also known for the sharp angles of his volleys, his court coverage, and his firm grasp of tactics. On court Gonzalez was moody and intense. He glowered at linesmen and was given to angry outbursts. "Pancho gets 50 points on his serve and 50 points on terror," Kramer once said. But Kramer also said, "At 5-all in the fifth, there is no man in the history of tennis that I would bet on against him."

On tour Gonzalez frequently traveled apart from the other players, and to the frustration of Kramer, he rarely saw any point in publicizing his matches. As his remarkable run as top player in the world continued, he grew increasingly bitter that Kramer frequently paid the challengers more than he paid his reigning champion. Gonzalez sued Kramer in an attempt to void his contract, but he lost the case.

In 1959 Gonzalez published an autobiography, *Man with a Racket*. That same year his marriage to Pedrin ended in divorce. In July 1960 he married Madelyn Darrow, a former Miss Rheingold. They had three daughters, one of whom died at age twelve in a horseback riding accident. Darrow preferred that Gonzalez pursue business opportunities rather than tennis, and in 1962 he went into semiretirement. He wrote an instruction book, *Tennis* (1962), with Dick Hawk, coached the U.S. Davis Cup team, and pursued various tennis-related business interests. Periodically he appeared in professional tennis tournaments. He often won, but his occasional losses set off speculation that he would soon retire for good.

In 1968 Gonzalez and Darrow divorced. That same year the major tennis tournaments were finally opened to professionals, and Gonzalez, forty years of age, came out of semiretirement. He reached the semifinals of the French Open, had a disappointing Wimbledon, but made it to the quarterfinals of the U.S. Open.

Gonzalez's opening round match at Wimbledon in 1969 was the longest match in Wimbledon history, a record that the subsequent introduction of the tiebreaker has made virtually impossible to break. Charlie Pasarell, then twenty-five years old, won the first set 24–22. During the second set Gonzalez became increasingly outraged as the light faded and the referee refused to halt the match. After Gonzalez lost the second set 6–1, he threw his racket by the umpire's chair and stormed off the court while the crowd jeered. The match resumed the following day. Gonzalez won the third set 16–14, took the fourth set 6–3, and hung on to win the final set 11–9. This time he walked off the court to a standing ovation. He won more matches that Wimbledon before losing to Arthur Ashe in the fourth round. He reached the fourth round at the U.S. Open that year as well.

In the fall of 1969 Gonzalez announced his retirement and remarried Darrow, but neither the retirement nor the marriage lasted. He and Darrow divorced in 1970. Also that year, in the first round of a series of $10,000 winner-take-all matches, Gonzalez upset Rod Laver, who was coming off a Grand Slam win in 1969. Two weeks later Gonzalez defeated John Newcombe in the same series. In 1970 Gonzalez became tennis director at Caesars Palace in Las Vegas, Nevada, a position he held for seventeen years. His last tournament win was at the Des Moines International in 1972, when he was nearly forty-four years old, making him the oldest man in the open era to win a tournament title. He continued to play in occasional tournaments until 1975.

In December 1972 Gonzalez married Betty Steward. They had one daughter before they divorced in the late 1970s. Gonzalez appeared in occasional Grand Masters tournaments, and he wrote two more instructional books, *Winning Tactics for Weekend Singles,* with Joe Hyams (1974), and *Tennis Begins at 40,* with Jeffrey Bairstow (1976). In 1982 he married Cheryl Duff, but the marriage lasted less than a year. In March 1984 he married Rita Agassi, the older sister of the future tennis champion Andre Agassi. They had one child but divorced in the early 1990s. Gonzalez died of stomach cancer and was buried in Las Vegas.

Comparing athletes across different eras is always difficult, and in Gonzalez's case the difficulties are compounded. In tennis the customary measurement of greatness is the number of Grand Slam tournament victories. Gonzalez had only two, but he was shut out of Grand Slam play from age twenty-two to age thirty-nine. During the time he was shut out, he was unquestionably the best player in the world for eight years, from 1955 to 1962. Gonzalez is not the only player of the years before tournaments were opened whose accomplishments have been obscured because he spent his most productive years as a professional. However, no other player of that era combined such a short amateur career with such a long period in which he dominated the far tougher professional ranks.

★

Pancho Gonzales with Cy Rice, *Man with a Racket* (1959), covers his early life and the first half of his career. Gonzalez's brother Ralph is working on a biography. Jack Kramer with Frank Deford, *The Game: My 40 Years in Tennis* (1979), contains a good deal of information about Gonzalez and gives valuable back-

ground information about professional tennis in the 1950s, as does Will Grimsley, *Tennis: Its History, People, and Events* (1971). Valuable articles include Gene Farmer, "Pancho Gonzales: Amateur Tennis' No. 1 Bad Boy Is Also Its No. 1 Star," *Life* (6 June 1949); Allison Danzig, "Anyone for Tennis? Yes, Gonzales," *New York Times Magazine* (19 May 1957); and Dave Anderson, "The Lone Wolf Faces a Match Point," *New York Times* (12 Mar. 1995). An article on Gonzalez is in *Current Biography 1949.* Obituaries are in the *New York Times* and *Los Angeles Times* (both 5 July 1995).

LYNN HOOGENBOOM

GOODE, Mal(vin) Russell (*b.* 13 February 1908 in White Plains, Virginia; *d.* 12 September 1995 in Pittsburgh, Pennsylvania), newspaper and radio reporter and commentator who became the first black correspondent hired by a major American television network, known as the "dean of black journalism."

The grandson of slaves, Goode grew up in Homestead, Pennsylvania, a steel mill town near Pittsburgh. His father, William Goode, left White Plains, Virginia—and the land his family was given at the time of the Emancipation Proclamation—as a teenager to work in the Pittsburgh steel mills for $1.25 per day. He sent money home but stayed in Homestead and raised his family with his wife, Mary Ellen Hunter, who was a schoolteacher. They had six children.

Even though Homestead had a sizable black population, all of Goode's schoolteachers were white and they

Mal Goode. CORBIS CORPORATION (BELLEVUE)

often made him sit in the back of the class. After graduating from high school in 1927, Goode went to work at U.S. Steel's Homestead Works to pay his way through the pre-law program at the University of Pittsburgh. He worked the night shift while attending classes during the day. In his sophomore year he received a grade of C in a course in which he had earned no lower than a B on any of the assigned work or quizzes. Goode visited the professor to ask about the grade. He recalled the professor saying, "Mr. Goode, you don't expect to get what a white student gets, do you?"

In 1931 he received his bachelor's degree and took the only employment he could find—as a janitor in a clothing store. Subsequent jobs included a position as a counselor at a Pittsburgh YMCA, a probation officer, and a manager for the Pittsburgh Housing Authority.

Goode married Mary Louise Lavelle in 1936. The couple had six children. In 1948 Mary's brother was the top ad salesman at the *Pittsburgh Courier*, the country's largest newspaper serving the black community. Goode was hired by the *Courier* that same year as an assistant to the circulation manager. He also worked in public relations for the paper.

The following year KQV radio offered the *Pittsburgh Courier* a fifteen-minute time slot for two days each week. Goode became the host of "The Courier Speaks," a program on which he discussed issues relevant to the black community. In 1950 the program moved to WHOD, a radio station where Goode's sister Mary Dee was a staff member. The siblings cohosted the show for six years. Goode was news director of WHOD and became the first African American to hold membership in the National Association of Radio and TV News Directors.

It was Goode's friendship with the baseball great Jackie Robinson that led to Goode being hired by ABC's television news division in 1962. Robinson had been critical of the network for not hiring any black reporters. The vice president of ABC News, Jim Hagerty, asked Robinson to recommend a suitable candidate for an on-air position. His suggestion was Goode. The fifty-four-year-old reporter auditioned for fourteen ABC executives and signed a contract on 10 September 1962.

Goode, who made his home in Teaneck, New Jersey, was sent to the United Nations, usually a fairly slow beat, to get acquainted with the new medium. His on-the-job training accelerated when the Cuban missile crisis broke in October 1962. On the first day, he did seven special bulletins on network television and nine on network radio, all without the assistance of a producer. His fair complexion and wavy hair caused some uncertainty among viewers about Goode's race. A woman in the television audience from South Carolina wrote to the network: "I think that was a colored man I saw reporting all day long on the Cuban missile crisis. And although I am white, and although he is a colored man, I want to thank him and I want to thank ABC because this is America, and that's the way it ought to be."

But Goode endured racism on the job. Occasionally, a white cameraman assigned to record Goode's stories would twist the film in the camera to sabotage the endeavor. Goode persevered, however, and went on to cover many of the critical stories of the 1960s, including the Democratic and Republican conventions of 1964 and 1968. He interviewed Malcolm X and Martin Luther King, Jr., and was the sole African American network correspondent assigned to cover King's funeral in April 1968. Goode covered the 1968 funeral of Robert Kennedy and the Poor People's March on Washington, D.C., that same year. He also reported the ABC documentary *It Can Be Done* (1969), which chronicled the resignation of a Ku Klux Klan grand dragon in Atlanta, Georgia, and his eventual support of black voter registration and increased minority employment.

Goode retired from ABC News in 1973, but remained a consultant to the network for fifteen years. As former president of the United Nations Correspondents Association, he maintained an office at the UN building until he was nearly eighty. In his retirement Goode was also active on the lecture circuit. A favorite theme of his talks, particularly to young black audiences, was "I did it. You can do it, too." The Minorities in Broadcast Training Program—a nonprofit organization that selects, trains, and places minority college graduates in news reporting and management jobs—presents an annual Mal Goode Lifetime Achievement Award.

Goode played dual roles in his professional life. He was a reporter and an advocate for civil rights. When he wore his reporter's cap, he was an impartial observer of events. But when he fought for the cause of his people, he was single-minded. Goode died from the complications of a stroke on 12 September 1995, by which time he had witnessed dramatic progress for black reporters in American broadcasting. Prominent African Americans in television news such as the Cable News Network (CNN) anchor Bernard Shaw and the Emmy Award–winning senior correspondent for ABC News, Carole Simpson, have acknowledged the pioneering role of Goode as an inspiration for their own success. He is buried at Saint Peter's Cemetery in East Liberty, Pennsylvania.

★

Goode is included among the subjects in *African Americans Who Were First,* by Joan Potter and Constance Claytor (1997). When Goode was honored with a Racial Justice Award from the YWCA of Greater Pittsburgh, the *New Pittsburgh Courier* carried a synopsis of his accomplishments in an article by Sandy Hamm, "Former Courier Editor Mal Goode Set for Honors" (9 Nov.

1994). Several obituaries profiled the significance of Goode in the history of American journalism, including the *New York Times* (15 Sept. 1995), the *National Association of Black Journalists Journal* (30 Sept. 1995), and the *New York Amsterdam News* (23 Sept. 1995). The most complete story of Mal Goode's life and career is found in the documentary *Pioneer of Color: A Conversation with Mal Goode*, PBS Video (1991).

MARY ANN WATSON

GORDONE, Charles (*b.* 12 October 1925 in Cleveland, Ohio; *d.* 17 November 1995 in College Station, Texas), dramatist, actor, director, and teacher whose 1970 Pulitzer Prize for *No Place to Be Somebody* was the first awarded to an African-American playwright and the first for an off-Broadway production.

Charles Gordone grew up in Elkhart, Indiana, with six brothers and sisters. His father, William Lee Gordone, was an auto mechanic, and his mother, Camille Morgan Gordone, a former dancer in Harlem's Cotton Club and a circus acrobat, taught speech. The light-skinned Gordone was later fond of characterizing himself as "part Indian, part Irish, part French . . . but first of all, we're niggers."

After high school, he enrolled in UCLA but dropped

Charles Gordone. AP/WIDE WORLD PHOTOS

out and joined the U.S. Army Air Forces. Upon leaving the service, he enrolled in California State University, Los Angeles, to study singing but eventually switched to drama, earning a B.A. degree in 1952.

That year he moved to New York City, supporting his stage career by working as a waiter. Among early successes, in 1953 he received recognition for his role in an all-black production of *Of Mice and Men* and played the title role in Wole Soyinka's *The Trials of Brother Jero*. In 1959, Gordone married Jeanne Warner. They were estranged eight years later, but it was during this period that he began and finished *No Place to Be Somebody* (1969). When Jean Genet's *The Blacks* opened off-Broadway in 1961, Gordone was part of the original cast, along with such future notables as Maya Angelou, Roscoe Lee Browne, Godfrey Cambridge, Louis Gossett, Jr., James Earl Jones, Helen Martin, Raymond St. Jacques, and Cicely Tyson. (*No Place to Be Somebody* was dedicated "to the memory of Sidney Bernstein, producer of *The Blacks*.")

Gordone's early and diverse director credits include *Rebels and Bugs, Peer Gynt, Tobacco Road, Faust,* and *Detective Story*. In 1962, he and Cambridge founded the Committee for the Employment of Negro Performers, and he chaired a similar committee for the Congress on Racial Equality. He was associate producer of the 1964 film *Nothing But a Man,* the same year that saw the opening of his play *Little More Light Around the Place,* cowritten with Sidney Easton.

After failing for two years to interest anyone in producing *No Place to Be Somebody,* Gordone managed to persuade the New York Shakespeare Festival's Public Experimental Theater to give the play a chance. The original cast included several actors who would go on to careers in movies: Paul Benjamin, Nathan George, and Ron O'Neal. The play opened 2 May 1969 and was both a critical and a financial success, soon moving to a larger theater. Gordone was likened to Eugene O'Neill and characterized by Walter Kerr as "the most astonishing new American playwright to come along since Edward Albee." The play won numerous writing awards in addition to the Pulitzer Prize.

Subtitled "A Black Black Comedy," *No Place to Be Somebody* examines black-black and black-white relationships and its characters' struggles for identity in a New York bar. The raconteur/chorus Gabe addresses the audience in several extended poetic monologues. Perhaps in part because relationship and identity issues are unresolved and universal, at the end of the twentieth century the play continued to be performed in repertory theaters and colleges and endured in anthologies and course reading lists.

After Gordone's death, some drew parallels to Ralph Ellison and other "one work" early successes. While *No Place to Be Somebody* is evocative of *Invisible Man,* Gordone's involvement with and commitment to the theater was broad, extensive, and eclectic long before winning the

Pulitzer and persisted up to his death a quarter-century later. He continued writing and producing plays: *Worl's Champeen Lip Dansah an' Wahtah Mellon Jooglah* (1969), *Willy Bignigga* (1970), *Chumpanzee* (1970), *Baba-Chops* (1975), *The Last Chord* (1977), *Anabiosis* (1980), and the one-act play "The Cowmen." Screenplays included *No Place to Be Somebody, The W.A.S.P.,* and *From These Ashes.* He also continued to write poetry, releasing a cassette in 1978 that included excerpts from *No Place to Be Somebody.*

In the 1970s, Gordone taught at New York's New School for Social Research (1978–1979) and worked with inmates at New Jersey's Bordentown Correctional Institute to stage Clifford Odets's *Golden Boy* as part of a rehabilitation-therapy program. His work as director included *Cures* (1978) and *Under the Boardwalk* (1979). He had a lead role in Ralph Bakshi's controversial 1975 part-animation film *Coonskin,* re-released as *Streetfight* on video in 1987 (the same year as Gordone's final movie credit, a supporting role in *Angel Heart*).

In the 1980s, Gordone continued to support nontraditional casting of minority actors but without denying the actor's ethnicity or the work's context, casting Latinos as the migrant workers in *Of Mice and Men* and a Creole as Stanley in *A Streetcar Named Desire.* In a San Francisco production in 1982, Gordone met Susan Kouyomjian, his companion for his final thirteen years. In 1985 he obtained a D. H. Lawrence Fellowship in New Mexico, followed by his appointment to Texas A&M University in 1987. There he taught English literature and playwriting until his death, immersing himself in Native American culture and cowboy poetry. Kouyomjian recalled that "cowboys and Indians took him in and seemed to nurture him into a new creativity that was coming full blossom when we discovered his illness."

As early as 1970, Gordone questioned the reality of "black theater." The titular theme of *No Place to Be Somebody* is early evidence of Gordone's belief that blacks are "agrarian." The cowboy-poet Buck Ramsey reminisced, "Chuck believed in a multiracial American theater. It had become black theater, Chicano theater, lesbian theater— he wanted a truly American theater. . . . That essentially left him no place to be."

When Gordone succumbed to liver cancer, memorial services were held at the New York Shakespeare Festival Public Theater, the Canadian River breaks of the Texas Panhandle, the Gene Autry Ranch, and at Texas A&M, where he was eulogized by many of his students. The university subsequently established the annual Gordone Awards in fiction, poetry, and playwriting.

Gordone was survived by Kouyomjian and Warner; daughters Judy and Leah-Carla, sons David and Stephen, and nine grandchildren. The singer and songwriter Leah-Carla Gordone's CD *Butterfly Child* (1998) is dedicated to her father and includes "This Is My Hour (Poppy's Song)."

★

There is not yet a full-length biography of Gordone, but articles in Theressa Gunnels Rush et al., *Black American Writers Past and Present* (1975), Shirelle Phelps, *Contemporary Black Biography* (1992), and Kenneth Estel, ed., *Reference Library of Black America* (1994) each contribute to the picture. Charles Gordone, *No Place to Be Somebody* (1969) contains stills from the original production and an introduction by Joseph Papp. Lindsay Patterson, *Black Theatre: A Twentieth-Century Collection of the Work of Its Best Playwrights* (1971) and Clinton F. Oliver, *Contemporary Black Drama: From* A Raisin in the Sun *to* No Place to Be Somebody (1971) provide additional analysis. An obituary is in the *New York Times* (10 Nov. 1995). The website of Texas A&M's English Department includes an interview with and memorials of Gordone (as well as information on the Gordone Awards).

RICHARD L. COLLIER

GOULD, Morton (*b.* 10 December 1913 in Richmond Hill, New York; *d.* 21 February 1996 in Orlando, Florida), Pulitzer Prize–winning conductor and composer who made classical music accessible to the American public.

Gould was the eldest of four sons born to James Hiram Gould, an Austrian who emigrated to New York in 1907 and worked as a realtor for the American Bankers Association, and Frances Arkin, a homemaker. When Gould's parents realized that he was composing tunes on the piano at age four, he was sent to study piano with Abby Whiteside and composition with Vincent Jones. At age seven he played his own piece, "Just Six," over WOR, a local radio station; a year later he won a scholarship to the New York Institute of Musical Art (now Juilliard). While he did attend Richmond Hill High School, he left at age fifteen to study at New York University's Music School. His father became ill with tuberculosis in 1931, and Gould left school to support his family. This meant having to refuse a scholarship to the prestigious Curtis Institute, recommended by Fritz Reiner, who was impressed with the young Gould's talent. So Gould became, at age eighteen, the house pianist at Rockefeller Center's newly opened Radio City Music Hall, while continuing to study "serious music" with Reiner. Three years later Gould began working as arranger, composer, and conductor for a weekly program called *Music for Today* on the Mutual Radio Network. He would remain in the position from 1934 to 1942, the beginning of a fruitful and eminent career that would span sixty-four years.

Because of national exposure on his radio program, Gould was invited to record his own music as well as that of others; he eventually recorded more than one hundred

Morton Gould. AP/Wide World Photos

albums. His *Second American Symphonette* (1935) clinched Gould's reputation as a popular composer. Considered "lightweight" by some critics because of popular American themes in his music, Gould excelled at combining motifs from jazz, blues, folk ballads, and spirituals with classical symphonic idioms. His *Spirituals for String Choir and Orchestra,* conducted by Leopold Stokowski, was chosen by the New York Music Critics' Circle as a candidate for the best symphonic work of 1942. When Arturo Toscanini conducted *Lincoln Legend* later that year, Gould's career soared, and he never again allowed critics to affect him. In an interview in *Étude* (January 1944), Gould advised the reader who aspired to a musical career to "familiarize himself with as many styles and schools" of music as possible.

In 1942, Gould also composed and arranged music for the enormously popular *Cresta Blanca Carnival* program on NBC, was recruited by CBS in 1943 for *The Chrysler Hour,* and was given his own Thursday night program, *The Music of Morton Gould.* Eventually he conducted every major orchestra in the United States.

Film was Gould's next venture, composing and conducting the music for the United Artists release *Delightfully Dangerous* (1945), which included six original songs and arrangements of several Johann Strauss waltzes in addition to background music. On the Broadway stage Gould pro-

vided the scores for *Billion Dollar Baby* (1945) and *Arms and the Girl* (1952), plus *I'm Old Fashioned,* a 1983 tribute to Fred Astaire. In 1947 Gould composed the score and conducted the orchestra at the Metropolitan Opera House for the opening night of Agnes de Mille's ballet about Lizzie Borden, *Fall River Legend.* When asked to score *Clarinade* (1964), a ballet choreographed by George Balanchine, Gould built on his *Derivations,* written originally for Benny Goodman.

Television also commandeered Gould for numerous programs, most notably the background music for *Verdun* (1963), *World War I* (1964–1965), and *Holocaust* (1978), for which he earned Emmy and Grammy nominations. In the late 1970s and early 1980s, Gould toured Australia, Japan, Mexico, and Israel as a conductor.

In 1983, Gould received the Gold Baton Award, and in 1985, the Medal of Honor for Music from the National Arts Club. In 1986 he was elected president of ASCAP (American Society of Composers, Authors, and Publishers), a position he held until 1994. On Gould's death in 1996, ASCAP renamed its annual "Young Composer Awards" in his honor.

Gould earned a Grammy award in 1966 for his recording, with the Chicago Symphony, of Charles Ives's music. For the 1976 bicentennial celebrations, Gould received three major commissions: from the National Endowment for the Arts for *Symphony of Spirituals,* with the Detroit Symphony; from the New York State Council on the Arts for *American Ballads,* with the Queens Symphony; and from the U.S. Department of Labor for *Something to Do,* with the Kennedy Center Orchestra.

At the Van Cliburn International Piano Competition in Fort Worth in 1993, Gould's piece for piano, *Ghost Waltzes,* was required playing, and his composition for children, *The Jogger and the Dinosaur,* which calls for a rap singer, premiered in Pittsburgh in 1993.

For his lifetime achievement in music, Gould was awarded the prestigious Kennedy Center Honors in 1994, and in 1995 he received the Pulitzer Prize for his tribute to Mstislav Rostropovich, *Stringmusic,* commissioned by the National Symphony in Washington, D.C.

In February 1996 the Disney Institute in Orlando, Florida, invited Gould to be artist-in-residence for a three-day festival of his music; on the second evening, he felt ill and was unable to conduct the U.S. Military Band as planned. The next day, 21 February, the shy, slim, lanky composer died quietly, at age eighty-two, of an aneurysm to the heart.

Married twice, first in the fall of 1936 to Shirley Uzin and then to Shirley Bank on 4 June 1944, Gould had four children—two sons and two daughters, all by his second wife—and lived most of his adult life in suburban Great Neck, New York. Memorial services were held at the Tilles Center for Performing Arts, Long Island, on 25 February and at Carnegie Hall, New York City, on 20 March 1996. Morton Gould is buried in New Montefiore Cemetery on Long Island.

Gould melded typical American motifs with classical idioms to create some of the most popular and accessible works of the twentieth-century symphonic repertoire. Perhaps the following statement, made by Gould upon receiving his Pulitzer Prize, best reflects why his music represents the American scene and soul, and why he became one of the greatest and most loved composers of his era: "I've always felt music should be a normal part of the experience that surrounds us. An American composer should have something to say to a cab driver."

★

A full-length biography is Peter W. Goodman, *Morton Gould: American Salute* (2000). Some of the myriad books and articles about Gould and his music include E. Ruth Anderson, *Contemporary American Composers: A Biographical Dictionary* (1982), Brian Morton and Pamela Collins, eds., *Contemporary Composers* (1992), and Jeffrey H. Renshaw, "The Legacy of Morton Gould," *The Instrumentalist* 51 (July 1996): 17–20. Obituaries are in the *New York Times* (22 Feb. 1996) and *Time* (4 Mar. 1996).

ELAINE MCMAHON GOOD

GRACE, J(oseph) Peter, Jr. (b 25 May 1913 in Manhasset, New York; d .19 April 1995 in New York City), business executive who transformed a thriving family business into a multinational conglomerate in the course of a career whereby he headed a major U.S. corporation for nearly five decades.

Born into wealth as a son of Joseph Peter Grace and Janet Macdonald, J. Peter had two brothers and a sister. The family dynasty began after the Irish potato famine, when Peter's grandfather, William Russell Grace, emigrated to Callao, Peru, where he secured a clerkship with a shipping company that mined and transported guano (bird dung, used as fertilizer) that had accumulated on offshore islands. He soon became a partner, and in 1854 he established W. R. Grace and Company and began shipping cargoes to North America. The company prospered, but for health reasons, Grace relocated to New York City in 1865. As a two-term mayor in the 1880s he accepted the Statue of Liberty from the people of France. In 1907, after his death, his son Joseph Peter Grace became the president of the firm and soon established the Grace National Bank (the predecessor of Marine Midland Bank) and the Grace Line passenger ship service. In 1928 Grace partnered with Pan American Airways to form Panagra, offering the first air service between North and South America.

Meanwhile J. Peter was growing up in Gatsby-style luxury in a Long Island mansion tended by sixty-two servants. He spent summers aboard the family's 150-foot yacht,

J. Peter Grace, Jr., 1982. AP/WIDE WORLD PHOTOS

which had a crew of twenty-eight. He attended Saint Paul's School in Concord, New Hampshire, from 1927 to 1932 and went on to Yale, where he earned letters in three varsity sports and excelled in polo and hockey. Upon earning a B.A. degree in history in 1936, Grace went to work for the family firm; he started his apprenticeship in the mailroom and was shunted from department to department until he became familiar with the entire operation. On 24 May 1941 Grace married Margaret Fennelly, a secretarial student at the Grace Institute, a school founded by the family, designed to provide lower-income young women with marketable skills. The couple eventually had five sons and four daughters. In 1942 Grace served as a lieutenant junior grade in the U.S. Navy. After his father suffered a stroke, he was appointed president of the company in 1945.

Eager to make his mark in the new technological environment and envious of the high profit margins of DuPont, Peter decided to take Grace into the chemical sector. This was a logical move since the firm was already involved in Chilean nitrates, fertilizers, insecticides, and other agricultural chemicals. In order to acquire the capital to implement this decision Grace took the company public in 1953. The infusion of new funds allowed the firm to purchase in 1954 Davison Chemical (which produced petroleum catalysts, silica gels, and superphosphates) and Dewey and Almy Chemical (which made sealing com-

217

pounds and Cryovac, a transparent film used for food packaging). The Dewey and Almy division later developed the twist-off cap and shrink-wrap. Both companies turned out to be astute acquisitions. Grace Chemical added twenty-three more chemical companies within eleven years and became the nation's fifth-largest chemical producer.

In the 1960s and 1970s, Grace further diversified, especially into the energy sector and consumer products markets, where he was much less successful. With the energy crisis of the early 1970s, prospects for Grace Petroleum looked bright, but after the price collapse of the early 1980s, the division was sold off. The foray into retail outlets added home improvement centers, restaurant chains, and stores for leather goods, auto parts, and sporting goods. Grace acquired Herman's in New York and transformed it into the nation's largest sporting goods chain. At one point the company owned about 1,500 retail outlets. By 1990 they had all been sold, and Grace was the world's largest cocoa processor, had a stake in the health care industry, and was wholesaling books.

Through it all, specialty chemicals remained the core business, but nonetheless Grace's erratic corporate strategy resulted in lackluster results for shareholders. In 1992 the former chief executive officer (CEO) turned over the reins to J. P. Bolduc, his handpicked successor, but remained as chairman of the board. Earnings improved, but a sordid internecine battle ensued between Grace and Bolduc. Although no longer CEO, Grace continued to enjoy perquisites such as a personal staff of eleven, a private jet and limousine, and generous maintenance of his Manhattan apartment. Bolduc terminated some of these expenses and the battle was on. After charges against Grace's eldest son of using $1.4 million of corporate money for a personal business venture and countercharges of sexual harassment against Bolduc, both men were ousted from the corporation.

TIAA-CREF, the world's largest pension fund and a major stockholder, became actively involved. It proposed reducing the number of board members and imposing a mandatory retirement age of seventy. In the final showdown, the board approved the proposal and voted Grace out. He died of lung cancer in New York City within two weeks of his ouster. His funeral mass was celebrated by John Cardinal O'Connor at St. Patrick's Cathedral.

Grace may be most remembered for his service from 1982 to 1984 as chairman of President Ronald Reagan's Private Sector Survey on Cost Control, better known as the Grace Commission, created to suggest ways the federal government could save money. Grace was also a philanthropist with a zeal for Roman Catholic causes, donating more than a million dollars each year to favorite charities, most of them Catholic. From the University of Notre Dame, where he was designated a lifetime trustee, he received the Laetare

Medal, one of American Catholicism's highest honors. He was a founding member of Legatus, an international organization of Catholic CEOs devoted to spreading the faith through their professional offices, and he served as president of the Catholic Youth Organization in New York City in the late 1950s and early 1960s. He held honorary degrees from 214 colleges and universities. The fifty-story Grace Building on West Forty-second Street, erected in 1974, has a distinctive light and dark facade that continues upward in a gridlike pattern, and a base that curves outward to the street, causing one to focus on the "Grace" lettering directly above the ground floor.

Peter Grace was five feet, nine inches tall, had blue eyes and brown hair, and spoke with a slight lisp. His image as an outspoken, archconservative curmudgeon was reinforced several times by his public insults of minority groups. A great believer in spreadsheets, the reams of detailed reports he demanded from his managers, and the "numbahs," Grace, paradoxically, often purchased a company on a whim—after a sudden inspiration or after eating at its restaurant. During his career he bought more than 100 companies and sold more than seventy. However, his early decisions to abandon South American operations (later nationalized) and to enter the chemical industry at a propitious moment eventually outweighed his later meandering strategy. When he finally stepped down after forty-seven years, W. R. Grace and Company was ranked number seventy-three on the Fortune 500.

★

There is no book-length biography of Grace. The most comprehensive treatment of his business career is in *International Directory of Company Histories,* vol. 1 (1988). Details of his early career can be found in *Current Biography* (1960). For a later analysis, see the lengthy article that appeared in *USA Today* (31 Dec. 1992), after he resigned as CEO. A front-page article in the *Wall Street Journal* (18 May 1995) is an inside account of the Pyrrhic struggle between Grace and Bolduc. An obituary is in the *New York Times* (21 Apr. 1995).

FRANCIS R. McBRIDE

GRAVES, Nancy Stevenson (*b.* 23 December 1940 in Pittsfield, Massachusetts; *d.* 21 October 1995 in New York City), sculptor, painter, and printmaker whose art drew inspiration from such diverse sources as the natural sciences and the art of Western and non-Western cultures.

Graves, a direct descendent of Cotton Mather, was born into a well-established New England family. She was the older of two daughters of Walter L. Graves, an assistant to the director of the Berkshire Museum of Art and Natural History, and Mary Bates, a secretary. She grew up in Pittsfield and attended public school there until the age of

Nancy Stevenson Graves. AP/WIDE WORLD PHOTOS

twelve. She then attended Miss Hall's School and the Northfield Mount Hermon School for Girls. As a child, Graves took painting classes at the Berkshire museum and spent much time exploring its fine-art and natural-history collections. By age twelve she had decided to be an artist, although her family disapproved and did not encourage her.

After graduating from the Northfield School in 1957, Graves attended Vassar College. She intended to study art, but dismayed by the program's emphasis on art history, she changed to English literature. While at Vassar, she was awarded a fellowship to study painting at the Yale Summer School of Music and Art in Norfolk, Connecticut, which provided her with a grounding in studio skills. After she earned a B.A. degree from Vassar in 1961, she attended the School of Art and Architecture at Yale. She studied painting with Alex Katz and Jack Tworkov, and her classmates included Chuck Close, Richard Serra, and Brice Marden. Taking advantage of Yale's extensive slide collection, Graves looked at as many as 500 to 1,000 works of art a day. She received a B.F.A. degree in 1962 from Yale and an M.F.A. degree in 1964. In 1964 she was awarded a Fulbright-Hayes Fellowship to spend a year in Paris, where she studied painting and printmaking.

In the summer of 1965 Graves married Richard Serra in Paris. (They were divorced in 1970; there were no children.) In 1966 the couple moved to Florence, Italy, where Graves pursued her interest in the study of natural history.

She became fascinated by the meticulously rendered wax models of the eighteenth-century anatomist Clemente Susini, whose slightly surreal, life-size replications of splayed human figures she described as looking as if "Botticelli had been crossed with anatomy." She also studied taxidermy and carpentry, making assemblages of live and stuffed animals juxtaposed with found objects. These investigations led to her first life-sized sculptures of camels, animals she was drawn to because she was intrigued by "the complexity of this ungainly ostrich-like form which was wonderful to draw, and because it was largely outside Western sculpture."

Upon returning to New York City from Europe in 1966, Graves established a studio in lower Manhattan and continued working on her camel sculptures, which she fabricated out of wood, burlap, polyurethane, and animal skin. Although the sculptures were meticulously rendered, she insisted that she was more interested in exploring the metaphoric significance of the animal than its natural depiction. The camel sculptures led to her first solo exhibition, held at New York's Graham Gallery in 1968. The exhibit brought Graves to the attention of two curators from the Whitney Museum of American Art, where she exhibited a one-woman show of her sculpture in 1969. Inspired by the motion studies of the photographer Eadweard Muybridge, she spent several years making short films focused on the perception of motion. In 1970 she traveled to Morocco, where she filmed *Goulimine* (1970) and *Izy Boukir* (1971), studies of the movements of camel herds.

During the early 1970s, a period dominated by minimalism and conceptual art, Graves stayed to her own path. She formulated a new style of sculpture influenced by Pacific Northwest Indian art. In these new works, constructions of bone and fossil elements were invested with ritualistic associations. They were exhibited at the Neue Galerie in Aachen, West Germany, in 1971. In 1972 Graves abandoned sculpture and returned to painting. The paintings in her *Camouflage* series were pointillistic renderings of reptiles, fish, and insects in their natural disguises. Around this time she embarked on another series of paintings based on topographic maps, charts of the ocean floor, and satellite photographs of the moon. The paintings were widely exhibited throughout the United States.

Graves returned to sculpture in 1976, when she was commissioned by the Museum Ludwig in Cologne, West Germany, to create a bronze version of one of her earlier bone sculptures. This led to a major artistic breakthrough for her sculptural work. At the Tallix Foundry in Peekskill, New York, in the late seventies, Graves learned the lost-wax process and experimented with direct casting, which allowed her make molds directly from organic objects (plant and vegetable forms) and inorganic objects (household items and other found materials), greatly enlarging her vocabulary of forms. Drawing from this inventory of found and everyday objects, she assembled disparate elements into strikingly original works of sculpture, often enlivening them by applying rainbow-hued patinas and brightly colored enamel paints. The critic John Russell likened the sculptures to "three dimensional studies in vegetable evolution." Graves maintained that her intention in her work was "to subvert what is logical, what the eye expects."

In the 1980s Graves's work evolved into a fusion of sculpture with painting. In her "shadow series," she attached aluminum sculpture onto the painted canvas. For Graves this was also a period of recognition for her artistic accomplishments (one critic dubbed her "the Renaissance woman of the eighties"). In 1980 the Albright-Knox Art Gallery in Buffalo, New York, held a survey of her work, which traveled internationally. In 1985 she received the New York Dance and Performance Bessie Award for the sets she designed for Trisha Brown's *Lateral Pass,* and the Yale Arts Award for distinguished achievement. In 1986 she received the Vassar College Distinguished Visitor Award, and a traveling exhibit of her work was also organized by Vassar College. For the remainder of her career, Graves continued to fabricate cast-bronze sculptures, incorporating natural forms, found objects, and art-historical fragments. She also produced a substantial body of graphic work that was exhibited posthumously in a retrospective exhibition in 1996. Graves married Avery L. Smith on 15 June 1991. There were no children from this second marriage. In 1992 she received an honorary D.F.A. degree from Yale. Graves died in New York Hospital of cancer at the age of fifty-four. She is buried in Pittsfield.

Likened in appearance to a Henry James heroine, Graves was a tall, patrician woman whose determination and drive was the source of her remarkably versatile creativity and prodigious output (as Trisha Brown described her, "Nancy Graves is a verb"). She traveled extensively, visiting Europe, the Middle East, China, India, Peru, and Australia. With her works in demand by collectors (her sculptures sold upwards of $75,000 in 1986), Graves enjoyed considerable financial success as an artist, enabling her to collect sculpture by Alexander Calder and David Smith, and fine pieces of ancient and primitive art. Her work is on display in many museums, including the Museum of Modern Art, the Whitney Museum of American Art, and in major private collections.

In her approach to art, Nancy Graves brought intellectual rigor and an omnivorous curiosity about art, cultures, and the natural world. Her work, in its melding of diverse subject matter (from scientific sources to what she called the "shards of art"), was among the most iconoclastic and original of her generation. As the critic Thomas Padon wrote of her, Graves was "like an archeologist, [who] sifts through the layers of cultural and geological history to assemble a cache of images drawn from various disciplines, eras, and civilizations."

★

An unpublished interview of Graves in her studio conducted by Paul Cumming on 18 Aug. 1972 is in the Archives of American Art, Smithsonian Institution, Washington, D.C. *Nancy Graves: Sculpture/Drawings/Films: 1969–1971* is the catalogue of an exhibition held at the Neue Galerie in Aachen, West Germany (1971). *Nancy Graves: A Survey 1969/1980* is the catalogue of an exhibition held at the Albright-Knox Art Gallery, Buffalo, New York (1980). The Fort Worth Art Museum's *The Sculpture of Nancy Graves: A Catalogue Raisonné* (1987) is the most thorough overview of her work. Thomas Padon, *Nancy Graves: Excavations in Print: A Catalog Raisonné* (1996) is devoted to her extensive production as a printmaker. Avis Berman, "Nancy Graves' New Age of Bronze," *ARTnews* (Feb. 1986), and Cathleen McGuigan, "Forms of Fantasy," *New York Times Magazine* (6 Dec. 1987), are profiles of Graves and her working methods. An obituary is in the *New York Times* (24 Oct. 1995). "Behind the Scenes with Nancy Graves" (1992) is a videocassette of a television program broadcast on PBS in 1992.

CHRISTINE STENSTROM

GRAY, Barry (*b.* 2 July 1916 in Red Lion, New Jersey; *d.* 21 December 1996 in New York City), New York City announcer credited with creating modern talk radio.

Gray, born Bernard Yaroslaw, was one of four children of Ukrainian Jewish immigrants. His father, Manius Yaroslaw, was an insurance salesman and real estate speculator. Manius's investments failed when he became overextended in Southern California property, anticipating too early the boom that eventually came. His mother, Dora Horowitz, was a homemaker.

Gray moved with his family to Los Angeles when he was seven years old. At age eighteen, while still attending Los Angeles High School, Gray began his career as a radio announcer and local sports reporter. He joined the Civilian Conservation Corps and then enlisted in the army in 1941, just days before the Japanese attack on Pearl Harbor. Gray did not graduate with his high school class, but earned his degree later in life. He did not attend college.

After his army stint with the U.S. Signal Corps in Santa Barbara, California, he returned to the East Coast in 1945 to work for WOR Radio in New York City. At first he hosted live musical performances at various city locales, earning a salary of $59 dollars a week. He then worked as an in-studio, late-night disk jockey on the WOR program *Moonlight Savings Time,* earning $175 a week. As Gray later recalled, he soon realized that late at night, "none of the station executives were listening, so I could say anything I

Barry Gray. CORBIS-BETTMANN

wanted." He expressed his opinions on a wide variety of subjects and then began inviting guests, who also expressed their views. Many but not all were entertainment personalities. An on-air call from the bandleader Woody Herman is reputed to have begun the practice of taking calls from listeners, which he did sporadically; call-ins later became a staple of radio broadcasting. The sponsors believed that the program was becoming too controversial, so WOR dropped the show in the late 1940s.

Gray went to Miami Beach, where he did a program on WKAT Radio from the Copacabana, a famous nightclub. There he again expressed controversial opinions, including his support of civil rights. In 1950 Gray returned to New York City on radio station WMCA, where he entertained listeners for nearly forty years. In the early 1950s he broadcast from Chandler's Restaurant but soon moved to WMCA's studios, then at Fifty-first Street and Broadway. The interview program drew stars such as Paul Newman, Frank Sinatra, Clark Gable, Danny Thomas, Eddie Cantor, and Lenny Bruce to his microphone. He also featured political discussion, interviewing luminaries such as Harry Truman, Eleanor Roosevelt, and later, John and Robert Kennedy. As the years went by, a growing percentage of his guests were political figures. By 1952 Gary was earning $4,000 a week and living with his family in a Fifth Avenue

apartment; later that year he and his family moved to the wealthy suburb of Scarsdale, New York. In 1952 the talk show host locked horns with Walter Winchell, the celebrity columnist and Gray's radio competitor, over an incident at the Stork Club involving Josephine Baker, the African American expatriate entertainer. After Baker was denied a seat at the club, where Winchell held court nightly, she complained on Gray's show that the Stork Club was guilty of race discrimination and that Winchell was a party to it. Winchell, known for his ability to make and break celebrities, was outraged by the charge and fiercely attacked both Gray and Baker in his *New York Daily Mirror* column; he called the radio announcer a Communist sympathizer and orchestrated a campaign to drive sponsors from Gray's show. The feud, in which Gray found an ally in Winchell's competing columnist, Ed Sullivan, lasted for years, until Winchell's influence began to wane in the new television era. In his autobiography, *My Night People* (1975), Gray hinted that thugs hired by Winchell were responsible for beatings he suffered.

Gray occasionally dabbled in television. For example, he was a newscaster on WNEW Channel 5 from 1951 to 1953. He even appeared for a short time in the lead role in an off-Broadway production of the play *Harvey*. But he made his greatest impact on the New York City radio scene.

A liberal early in his career, Gray once remarked self-deprecatingly that in the late 1940s he had regarded the Chinese Communists as agrarian reformers. As the years passed, though, he grew more moderate, his stands becoming a mix of conservative and liberal views. For example, while remaining a strong supporter of civil rights, he publicly backed the New York City police force in its opposition to the creation of a civilian review board to prevent alleged police abuses of minorities. Gray was an auxiliary New York City policeman and once received a commendation from the New York Police Department for coming to the rescue of a police officer during a shootout. A lifetime member of the National Rifle Association, he was a proponent of gun owners' rights.

The image of Gray changed radically over the course of his career. From the perspective of the 1990s, the *Washington Post* journalist Marc Fisher observed that "a style that listeners had found shockingly frank and inquisitive back in the '50s and '60s seemed downright gentlemanly by the time Bob Grant, Howard Stern, and the Greaseman transformed radio a generation later." Although often expressing his views vociferously, Gray maintained an urbane, intimate tone even as many late-twentieth-century talk radio hosts adopted bombastically ideological positions and used vulgarity and shrillness to shock their audiences. He viewed radio as communication not with a mass audience but as a means of talking to thousands of individual listeners. Summing up his broadcasting philosophy in his autobiography, Gary wrote, "Radio is for one pair of ears alone." Gray's style influenced radio and television interviewers such as Larry King and Ted Koppel, both of whom acknowledged his impact on them.

Gray's show was an occasional forum for breaking news. For example, journalist Sidney Zion announced on Gray's program that former Defense Department employee Daniel Ellsberg was the one who had leaked the controversial Pentagon Papers, the secret government study of the Vietnam War excerpted in 1971 by the *New York Times,* which convinced many Americans that the government was deceiving the public about the war. In 1989 Gray left WMCA because a religious broadcaster bought the station and changed the format. He returned to WOR Radio, where he worked until his death.

Gray was skeptical about the influence claimed by talk show hosts of the 1980s and 1990s as the format he pioneered blazed across the AM radio band. Many talk show hosts, Gray said, "take themselves far too seriously. They think they're changing the world. They aren't changing a damn thing." What radio hosts can do, he emphasized, is provide a forum for ideas.

The slim, six-feet, three-inch Gray married Beth Serrao on 14 February 1946. The couple had two children. They were divorced in 1973. Gray married Judith Margot Morris on 24 September 1973; the marriage ended in divorce. He was married to his third wife, Nancy Kellogg, from 5 September 1986 until his death. They had one child.

Over the years, Gray earned considerable recognition for his work. Jack Gould, *New York Times*'s television critic, called Gray's show "a nightly kaffeeklatsch which frequently adds up to extraordinarily different and distinctive radio." In 1996 he was selected Talk Show Host of the Year by the National Association of Talk Show Hosts. Gray died at the age of eighty of complications from back surgery and was cremated.

★

Gray's autobiography, *My Night People* (1975), is short on personal details but vividly describes his radio career, including his long feud with Walter Winchell. His impact on the radio industry is described in Michael Barone and Joannie M. Schrof, "The Changing Voice of Talk Radio," *U.S. News and World Report* (15 Jan. 1990), and Peter Goddard, "A Look into Broadcast's Big Mouths Finds Some Dignity in the Wild West World of Talk Shows," *Toronto Star* (26 July 1997). Upon his death, Gray's impact was described in Marc Fisher, "Talk Radio's Founding Father," *Washington Post* (31 Dec. 1996), and David Hinckley, "Barry Gray: Knight of the Night," *New York Daily News* (23 Dec. 1996). An obituary is in the *New York Times* (22 and 23 Dec. 1996).

PETER FEUERHERD

GREENBERG, Clement (*b.* 16 January 1909 in the Bronx, New York; *d.* 7 May 1994 in New York City), art critic whose influential but often controversial essays on contemporary culture introduced the work of the painter Jackson Pollock and established abstract expressionism as the dominant movement in mid-twentieth-century American art.

The oldest of three sons of well-to-do Lithuanian Jewish immigrants, Joseph Greenberg, a merchant, and Dora Brodwin, Greenberg moved at the age of five to Norfolk, Virginia, where his father had established a business. At the age of eleven, Greenberg and his family moved to Brooklyn, New York, where he attended public schools. From early childhood he liked to draw; when he was sixteen he took a life-drawing class from 1924 to 1925 at the Art Students League in New York City. Languages and literature, however, were his major subjects at Syracuse University, where he received his A.B. degree with honors in 1930 and was elected to Phi Beta Kappa. For the next two years, before going to work for his father, he devoted himself to perfecting his languages (later he did several German translations), reading extensively, and visiting art museums.

Clement Greenberg at the Poindexter Gallery, 1960. COPYRIGHT © BY FRED W. McDARRAH

In 1934 he married Edwina Ewing. They had one son and were divorced in 1936. After a series of clerical jobs with the Civil Service Commission, Greenberg worked from 1937 to 1942 for the U.S. Customs Service, but found time to write stories and poetry (largely unpublished) and to attend lectures at Hans Hofmann's School of Fine Arts in New York, an experience that stimulated his interest in modern painting. A letter Greenberg wrote to Dwight Mac-Donald, editor of *Partisan Review,* led to an invitation to write an article for the journal. The article, "Avant-Garde and Kitsch," ran in the fall 1939 issue. An authoritative discussion of elitist "high art" compared to mass culture (kitsch), it made Greenberg's reputation in New York intellectual circles. The article was reprinted six months later in the British periodical *Horizon.* Greenberg published his first review in the winter of 1939, a comment on Berthold Brecht's "Penny for the Poor."

From 1940 to 1942 Greenberg was one of the editors of *Partisan Review,* for which he continued to write essays on literature, art, and sociopolitical matters (often informed by his then-Trotskyist viewpoint). When the Bollingen/Library of Congress Prize for poetry was awarded in 1948 to Ezra Pound for *The Pisan Cantos*—Pound's pro-Fascist, anti-Semitic stance notwithstanding—Greenberg made a famous protest (*Partisan Review,* May 1949) against excusing an artist's moral failings on the grounds of aesthetic autonomy. His last article for *Partisan Review,* " 'American-Type' Painting," was written in 1955. Considered the definitive statement on abstract expressionism and extensively anthologized, it roused much controversy over Greenberg's omission of the second-generation abstract artists in favor of the new color-field painters. During this period—from 1942 until he resigned around 1950, protesting what he claimed was the magazine's pro-Soviet sympathies—he served also as the first regular art critic at the *Nation.*

Writing and editorship, however, were suspended for eight months in 1943 when Greenberg served in the U.S. Army Air Force before receiving a medical discharge. Shortly thereafter his championship of Jackson Pollock began, with a review in the *Nation* (27 November 1943) of that artist's first solo exhibition. Four years later in "The Present Prospects of American Painting and Sculpture" (*Horizon,* October 1947), Greenberg proclaimed Pollock to be the "most powerful" painter of the day, thus contributing to his phenomenal popularity and alienating supporters of Pollock's rival, Willem de Kooning. Chief among these was Greenberg's one-time friend, the *New Yorker* critic Harold Rosenberg. As for relations with de Kooning, Greenberg—as pugnacious in person as he was in his writing—got into a fistfight with the artist in a Greenwich Village bar in 1961; the altercation is now part of the Greenberg legend.

In August 1944 he became managing editor of the *Contemporary Jewish Record.* When the bimonthly *Record* was replaced by *Commentary,* Greenberg was named associate editor, but he was fired in 1957 after a confrontation with a fellow editor, Norman Podhoretz. From then on the focus of Greenberg's activities changed. He participated more directly in art-world affairs: consulting with museum curators and art dealers throughout the United States and Canada; writing exhibition catalogs; visiting artists' studios (where he often gave advice on work in progress); and teaching. Greenberg was chosen to conduct the prestigious Christian Gauss Seminar in Criticism at Princeton University in 1958 and 1959, and in 1962 he gave his first seminars at Bennington College, where from the early 1950s he had maintained close ties with the art department, organizing exhibitions and critiquing student work. In 1964 Greenberg was guest curator of the landmark show *Post Painterly Abstraction* at the Los Angeles County Museum of Art. He was then appointed by the U.S. Department of State to accompany the exhibition *Two Decades of American Art* and give lectures during its tour of Japan and India in 1966 and 1967.

For a short while between 1958 and 1960, Greenberg had served as a consultant to French & Co., a New York gallery, choosing pictures and arranging exhibitions. Although he earned no commissions and did not deal directly with clients, it was rumored that he was improperly involved in the art market, and there was speculation about his behind-the-scenes influence on artistic reputations. Following these rumors and speculations, Greenberg's own reputation declined. His book *Art and Culture: Critical Essays* (1961), a collection of revised versions of thirty-seven of his critical essays, generated little interest at the time. Many artists and fellow critics, responding to his article "After Abstract Expressionism" in *Art International* (25 October 1962), labeled him a dictatorial elitist for his rejection of postmodern movements such as pop art and minimalism. An article by Rosalind Krauss damaged him further. In "Changing the Work of David Smith," published in *Art in America* (September 1974), Krauss claimed that after Smith's death, Greenberg, who was one of the sculptor's executors and a frequent visitor to his studio, removed the polychrome finish from several of Smith's huge steel sculptures. Greenberg never defended himself from the charge of tampering with the integrity of works of art. But in an interview with his biographer Florence Rubenfeld in 1991, he did admit that "maybe I should have just laid off instead of making his sculpture better."

Greenberg's second marriage, to Janice Elaine Van Horne in 1956, ended in divorce in 1977; they had one daughter. Until 1988, when he returned to his New York City apartment, Greenberg lived in his home in Norwich, New York, lecturing at colleges, making his customary studio visits, and writing a book based on the Bennington seminars he gave in 1971, eventually published as *Homemade Esthetics: Observations on Art and Taste* (1999). He died of emphysema in Lenox Hill Hospital in Manhattan after a four-year illness.

Much reviled by some for his dogmatic opinions, Clement Greenberg was regarded by others as unquestionably the greatest critic of twentieth-century Western art. He was respected for his real passion for art and for his accessible writing style: a concise, fluid prose that was the result of constant rethinking and reworking. Owning to the influence of the philosopher Immanuel Kant and the poet T. S. Eliot (both concerned with the relationship of thought and feeling), Greenberg himself was concerned with discovering how the formal, visible elements of a painting or sculpture "work" to produce an effect, rather than with what a work of art "means." For this reason he is often credited with having introduced the aesthetic approach known as formalism to the study of art.

★

Clement Greenberg's papers are housed in the Getty Research Institute in Los Angeles. Some of his papers are located at the Archives of American Art at the Smithsonian. In addition to his periodical articles, the critic wrote three short monographs: *Joan Miró* (1948); *Henri Matisse* (in the Pocket Library of Great Art series, 1953), an example of his analyses of how paintings "work"; and *Hans Hofmann* (1961). His last book, *Homemade Esthetics: Observations on Art and Taste* (1999), has a foreword by Janice Van Horne Greenberg explaining the composition of the work, which presents both Greenberg's text and excerpts from the Bennington seminars on which it was based. Florence Rubenfeld, *Clement Greenberg: A Life* (1998), is a detailed, candid, balanced account of his place in the art world, but there is no bibliography or chronological summary of his lengthy, complex career. John O'Brian, ed., *Clement Greenberg: The Collected Essays and Criticism,* 4 vols. (vols. 1 and 2, 1986; vols. 3 and 4, 1993), provides the texts of Greenberg's articles from 1939 to 1969, bibliographies of works with reference to the critic, and chronologies. Analyses of Greenberg's opinions are found in Donald Kuspit, *Clement Greenberg, Art Critic* (1979), and J. D. Herbert, *The Political Origins of Abstract-Expressionist Art Criticism: The Early Theoretical and Critical Writings of Clement Greenberg and Harold Rosenberg* (1985). Janice Van Horne, ed., *The Harold Letters, 1928–1943: The Making of an American Intellectual* (2000), is a collection of letters that Greenberg wrote to Harold Lazarus, a classmate at Syracuse. The article on Greenberg in *World Authors: 1900–1950* (1966), revised and updated as of 1992, reprints the critic's autobiographical sketch provided for the 1955 edition of *Twentieth Century Authors.* Adam Gopnik, "The Power Critic," *New Yorker* (16 Mar. 1998), gives a present-day critic's rather dismissive assessment of Greenberg's mid-century contributions and his diminished standing at the end of the century. Obituaries are in the *New York Times* (8 May and 9 May 1994; several inaccuracies were corrected in the 9 May edition), the *Washington Post* (10 May 1994), *Los Angeles Times* (11 May 1994), and Chicago *Tribune* (15 May 1994).

ELEANOR F. WEDGE

GRISWOLD, Erwin Nathaniel (*b.* 14 July 1904 in East Cleveland, Ohio; *d.* 19 November 1994 in Boston, Massachusetts), lawyer, government official, and law school dean who argued the case of the Pentagon Papers in the U.S. Supreme Court, published the first legal casebook on federal taxation, and served as dean of Harvard Law School for twenty-one years.

Griswold was the son of James Harlen Griswold, a lawyer, and Hope Erwin Griswold. He graduated from Cleveland's Shaw High School in 1921 and enrolled in Oberlin College. He graduated from Oberlin in 1925, receiving both an A.B. degree in political science and an M.A. degree. Thinking that "the chances of making a living were probably better in the law" than in astrophysics, Griswold entered Harvard Law School in the fall of 1925. He served as the president of the *Harvard Law Review* and graduated summa cum laude with an LL.B. degree in 1928. He received an S.J.D. degree in 1929. On 30 December 1931 Griswold married Harriet Allena Ford; they had two children.

Erwin Griswold, 1967. © BETTMANN/CORBIS

After practicing for one month at his father's law firm in Cleveland, Griswold moved to Washington, D.C., in October 1929. He had accepted an offer to join the office of the U.S. Solicitor General, which represents the federal government before the Supreme Court. He quickly became its expert on tax law and argued more than twenty-five cases before the Court before he left to join the Harvard Law School faculty in 1934. He won so many that Chief Justice Charles Evans Hughes said that his departure would cost the government a great deal of money.

At Harvard, Griswold taught the first course on federal taxation in the country, and in 1940 he published the first casebook on the subject. Taxation remained his major scholarly interest, although he later said that conflict of laws, which concerns the law that is applied in a particular case, was "really my favorite subject." In 1946 Griswold was named dean of the law school, the first choice of "almost all" faculty members.

As dean, Griswold revamped and upgraded the law school's physical plant, library holdings, and financial holdings. He brought about the admission of women (1949) and a substantial increase in the number of black students. The size of the faculty was doubled and the curriculum was greatly enlarged to include specialized courses such as labor relations, family law, and copyright, and international legal studies became a major focus. Griswold also developed an extensive publications program and strongly encouraged the faculty to perform public service.

A liberal Republican, Griswold publicly opposed President Harry Truman's 1947 executive order reviewing the "loyalty" of all federal employees. At the height of McCarthyism in 1954, he delivered three speeches on the Fifth Amendment, describing the right against self-incrimination as "an old and good friend" and "one of the great landmarks in man's struggle to make himself civilized." Widely reprinted and then published as a book, *The Fifth Amendment Today* (1955), the speeches gave civil libertarians much needed support. In 1961 President John F. Kennedy appointed Griswold to the Civil Rights Commission, and at meetings across the country Griswold forcefully interrogated witnesses to expose lawlessness and injustice. He supported the thrust of the Supreme Court's decisions during the 1950s and 1960s, despite vociferously disagreeing in specific areas such as tax law and school prayer.

In September 1967, after Solicitor General Thurgood Marshall was appointed to the Supreme Court, Griswold's Harvard colleague Archibald Cox recommended him to Attorney General Ramsey Clark as Marshall's successor. Cox, Marshall's predecessor in the post, made this recommendation without Griswold's knowledge, but Cox was aware that Griswold was becoming increasingly frustrated with certain aspects of his role at Harvard. The complexities of federal tax law made teaching the subject less exhilarating,

and Griswold had begun to chafe at the constant fund-raising the law school required. In an address celebrating the school's sesquicentennial, he noted the "inadequacy of many of our premises, and the fact we are often thinking about the wrong things when we are carrying out our intellectual processes. . . . Even in [law] it may be true that 'The letter killeth but the spirit giveth life.'" Griswold felt that law schools should search for the student who "really has fire in his belly." So when Clark asked Griswold if he would be willing to have his name submitted to the president to be solicitor general, he took "15 agonizing seconds, and said yes." Griswold's was the only name on the list. "It was the only job I ever really wanted," he later admitted. Griswold retired from the Harvard deanship, and was confirmed as U.S. Solicitor General on 23 October 1967.

As an advocate before the Supreme Court, Griswold spoke forcefully and carefully. His argument style, noted the distinguished attorney John P. Frank, was "American Gothic snowpile." He moved inexorably ahead without dazzling theoretical leaps or rhetorical flourishes. One justice said he was "like the U.S.S. *Griswold*. Questions from us just bounce off him harmlessly as he cruises through his speeches." In one case that he argued as friend of the court, Griswold placed his chair squarely in the middle of courtroom in order, as he told the court, to make it apparent that he was there as a true friend of the court rather than a friend of one of the parties.

While Griswold upset some Democrats by advocating civil rights less aggressively than they wished, he also annoyed Republicans by refusing to defend federal aid to religious schools or the government's policy of revoking draft deferments of students who demonstrated against conscription for the hostilities in Vietnam. Griswold's most prominent case was in 1971 and involved the Pentagon Papers, a classified government study of American involvement in Vietnam that the *New York Times* and the *Washington Post* published. Griswold wrote a brief defending the government's action to prevent publication on grounds of national security and argued the case in less than twenty-four hours. "It was not my favorite case," he later said. "I had a job to do." The Court ruled decisively against the government, upholding the right of the press to publish the study. In 1989 Griswold wrote that he had "never seen any trace of a threat to the national security from the publication," which was "harmless."

In December 1972 the Nixon administration announced that Griswold would be replaced, and in July 1973, at the end of the Court's term, he left to enter private practice with the Cleveland-based firm of Jones, Day, Reavis and Pogue. He continued arguing cases and engaged in a variety of international peace endeavors. Griswold argued 118 cases before the Supreme Court. He died after a brief illness at the age of ninety.

Griswold served as a trustee of Oberlin College from 1936 to 1980 and as a member of the Council of the American Law Institute from 1953 to 1994. His stiff, sometimes gruff manner and his shyness hid a humane and caring nature. Griswold was a reformer who pursued a philosophy of gradual yet ceaseless change while snared in unrelenting traditionalist garb.

"Built like a granite block" and "just as inflexible in his conceptions of basic rectitude" (there were no divorces on the faculty during his deanship, ran one joke, "because no one would have dared"), Griswold was forthright almost to a fault, ruthlessly plain in language and manner, and often wore a whimsical smile. His humor was generally flat-footed, although it could be understated: he kept on his office wall a plaque that said, "Babe Ruth struck out 1330 times."

★

Griswold's papers are at the Harvard Law School Library and the Harvard University Archives; the former contains a lengthy bibliography. A small collection is at the Oberlin College Archives. Records pertaining to his service as solicitor general are at the National Archives. Griswold's autobiography, *Ould Fields, New Corne: The Personal Memoirs of a Twentieth-Century Lawyer* (1992), is essential reading for anyone interested in his life and career. His role in the Pentagon Papers case is treated in Harrison E. Salisbury, *Without Fear or Favor* (1980), and Roger K. Newman, *Hugo Black: A Biography* (1994). Other sources include the *New York Times,* (14 Nov. 1960, 10 Sept. 1967, 2 Oct. 1967); Joel Seligman, *The High Citadel* (1978); Lincoln Caplan, *The Tenth Justice* (1987); "Dean Erwin Nathaniel Griswold 1904–1994," *Harvard Law Bulletin* (summer 1995); tributes in *Harvard Law Review* (vols. 86 and 108); Ken Gormley, *Archibald Cox* (1997); and Charles Alan Wright, "'A Man May Live Greatly in the Law,'" *Texas Law Review* (vol. 70). Obituaries are in the *Washington Post* and *Boston Globe* (both 20 Nov. 1994), the *New York Times* and *Los Angeles Times* (both 21 Nov. 1994), and the *Times* (London) (23 Nov. 1994). Also see "Interview with Erwin Griswold," University of Connecticut Center for Oral History (1988).

ROGER K. NEWMAN

GRIZZARD, Lewis McDonald, Jr. (*b.* 20 October 1946 in Fort Benning, Georgia; *d.* 20 March 1994 in Atlanta, Georgia), humorist, newspaper columnist for the *Atlanta Journal-Constitution* and a self-proclaimed "quintessential southern male."

Grizzard was the only son of U.S. Army Captain Lewis McDonald Grizzard and schoolteacher Christine Word. Grizzard's father, a coach, teacher, and decorated veteran had served in both World War II and in Korea. Lewis Grizzard was born in Fort Benning while his father was stationed there. After his parents divorced in 1952, his mother and her relatives raised Grizzard in Moreland, Georgia, the scene of many of his future stories. His interest in writing began at an early age, and he gravitated toward sports writing. As a fan of the Atlanta Crackers, a minor-league baseball team, he persuaded his mother to let him stay up late to get the final scores and highlights of the games. His aunt and uncle also fanned this interest by bringing him the daily local newspaper so he could read about the games.

Unlike most people in Moreland, Grizzard was not interested in a career in agriculture; nor did he have a desire to be a teacher like his parents. After graduating from Newnan High School in 1964, he left for Athens and the University of Georgia. He began writing articles and working as sports editor for the *Athens Banner-Herald* and met Nancy Jones, whom he married in July 1966. The next year, just one course short of completing his journalism degree (he eventually completed his degree by correspondence in 1984), Grizzard got a job at the *Atlanta Journal* through Jim Minter, who was then the sports editor. Grizzard made his way up the ranks at the newspaper, becoming the youngest ever executive sports editor of the *Atlanta Journal* at age twenty-three.

Despite his success as an editor, Grizzard's work left him personally unfulfilled. In 1969 he moved to Chicago, where he became sports editor of the *Chicago Sun-Times.* He stayed there through 1976. Depressed over his marital problems (he divorced his first wife, Nancy, in 1969 and his second wife, Fay Rentz, in 1976), Grizzard wrote Minter asking for a writing job. Minter responded by offering a sports column with a cut in pay, and Grizzard agreed. Minter then encouraged him to write his opinions into the column. At first he was hesitant, but Grizzard found that adding in his own thoughts to the column and writing with a southern accent appealed to his readers. Grizzard slowly phased out the sports content (except for talking about his beloved Georgia Bulldogs and their rivals, the Georgia Tech Yellow Jackets and the Florida Gators) and concentrated on giving his opinions on life in general. As Grizzard continued his column, his popularity in the South grew. In February 1979 he met and married his third wife, a former debutante, Kathy Taulman.

Grizzard's mix of satirical humor and unabashed sentimentality made him a hit with his readers. Well-known for his conservative stand on politics, political correctness, and the everyday irritations in life, he had an easygoing, laid-back manner that made his opinions acceptable, even beloved, by some of his fellow southerners.

As his popularity grew, Grizzard was encouraged by Minter to compile some of his best columns in a book. In 1978 he took a grocery sack filled with his best columns to Helen Elliott, founder of Peachtree Publishers. The columns became the basis for his first book, *Kathy Sue Loud-*

ermilk, I Love You, which was published in September 1979. According to Peachtree Press, Elliott gave Grizzard his first advance copy of the book in the same bag. He would publish eight more books with Peachtree, and before his death he published more than twenty books.

Grizzard noted that Taulman tried to bring some "style and sophistication" to his image, but a faulty heart valve that had plagued him since childhood led to the first of his four open-heart operations. The high living had to go, and with it, in 1982, went his third marriage.

As a result of his troublesome relationships with women and his discussion of this topic in his column and on national talk shows such as *Larry King Live,* Grizzard became well known for his stand on marriage. His book *If Love Were Oil, I'd Be About a Quart Low: Lewis Grizzard on Women* (1983) prompted Taulman to write her own book on Grizzard entitled *How to Tame a Wild Bore and Other Facts of Life with Lewis: The Semi-True Confessions of the Third Mrs. Grizzard* (1986), as well as her autobiography, *From Debutante to Doublewide* (1987). Grizzard took both books in stride, but, as he later wrote: "I howled as I read, I cried and I missed her."

Despite having to change some aspects of his lifestyle, Grizzard kept himself busy with his column (which by then was syndicated in 450 newspapers), speaking engagements, public-service announcements, and television appearances, including a guest spot on the show *Designing Women* and a special called "Love, Sex and Romance." He produced video and audio recordings of his comedy routines and songs and by the late 1980s had formed Lewis Grizzard Enterprises to help manage his business affairs. He also helped launch Longstreet Press, which published five of his books. Meanwhile, he found time for golf and tennis.

But unhappy events kept him grounded. His troubled relationship with his father had always bothered Grizzard, and eventually he told of that relationship in the funny and sentimental *My Daddy Was a Pistol and I'm a Son of a Gun* (1986). After his mother's death in 1990, he wrote an equally stirring tribute to his mother, *Don't Forget to Call Your Mama—I Wish I Could Call Mine* (1991).

In 1993 he was forced to undergo a third operation to replace a faulty heart valve. Following the surgery, doctors could not get his heart to beat on its own for several days.

Grizzard survived this ordeal and wrote about it in *I Took a Lickin' and Kept On Tickin' (and Now I Believe in Miracles)* (1993). However, the operation left him with continuing medical problems. At this time he befriended Dedra Kyle, who was at first his caregiver. In March 1994 his continued problems left doctors with little choice but to schedule a fourth operation. Faced with imminent death, Grizzard married Dedra in a bedside ceremony. He did not have children with any of his wives.

On 20 March 1994, Grizzard died at Emory University Hospital after suffering brain damage resulting from the surgery. He was forty-seven years old. In accordance with his wishes, half his ashes were scattered at Sanford Stadium at the University of Georgia and the rest placed in the Word family plot in Moreland.

Recognized by critics as a writer who could charm as well as challenge, Grizzard made his mark in journalism. As noted by his wife Dedra, "He was a bundle of contradictions and a very funny man."

★

Grizzard's own works provide insight into this humorist that cannot be found anywhere else, especially *They Tore Out My Heart and Stomped That Sucker Flat* (1982), *If Love Were Oil, I'd Be About a Quart Low: Lewis Grizzard on Women* (1983), *Elvis Is Dead and I Don't Feel So Good Myself* (1984), *My Daddy Was a Pistol and I'm a Son of a Gun* (1986), *Don't Forget to Call Your Mama—I Wish I Could Call Mine* (1991), *I Took a Lickin' and Kept On Tickin' (and Now I Believe in Miracles)* (1993), and *The Grizzard Sampler: A Collection of the Early Writings of Lewis Grizzard* (1994). His half-brother and fellow humorist, Ludlow Porch, wrote a biographical portrait of his relationship with Grizzard in *Lewis & me & Skipper makes 3* (1991), and friends of Grizzard wrote about their relationship with him in a book called *Don't Fence Me In: An Anecdotal Biography of Lewis Grizzard by Those Who Knew Him Best* (1995). Thomas Kozikowski and Jean W. Ross collaborated on a biographical entry in volume 129 of *Contemporary Authors* (1991). Peter Applebome's article in the *New York Times Magazine* (8 Apr. 1990), provides some additional information on Grizzard's life. *People Weekly* (4 Apr. 1994), contains a one-page tribute to Grizzard. Obituaries are in the *New York Times* (21 Mar. 1994) and *Newsweek* and *Time* (both 4 Apr. 1994).

BRIAN B. CARPENTER

H

HANNAH, John Frederick ("Jack") (*b*. 5 January 1913 in Nogales, Arizona; *d*. 11 June 1994 in Los Angeles, California), film animator and director, painter, and educator who was one of the premier designers for Donald Duck and other Disney characters.

Hannah was one of two sons born to Harry Bradshaw Hannah, who worked for the United States Immigration Office, and Eleanor Marie Brown, a homemaker and switchboard operator for Bethlehem Steel. After attending grammar school in San Ysidro and Sweetwater High School in National City, California, he thought of professional boxing as a career, but a broken nose in a Golden Gloves competition changed his mind. In 1931 Hannah registered for courses at the Art Guild Academy in Los Angeles, supporting himself as an illustrator of theater posters for Foster and Kleiser. He was hired by the Walt Disney Studios in January 1933 as an "in-betweener" (a young artist who fills in the other, less important, drawings of the action, usually following the tracings of the master drawings), earning $16 a week. On 15 September of that same year he married Winifred Marie Meinecke and began a family that included two children.

At Disney, Hannah studied under Norm Ferguson, one of the top animators of the day, and earned extra money as a gag writer. His first full animation scenes were in a Mickey Mouse cartoon, *Shanghaied* (1934). Hannah quickly moved up the studio ladder to first assistant and in 1937 was promoted to full animator on a new cartoon series featuring Donald Duck. In 1938, perceiving limited opportunity in the animation department, Hannah moved to the story department and teamed with Carl Barks to write Donald Duck cartoons.

During the 1930s Disney leased his cartoon characters to the Whitman Publishing Company to reprint the Mickey Mouse and Donald Duck daily comic strips in book form. Whitman, encouraged by their success, wanted to publish original Donald Duck stories. However, because Disney's major illustrators were busy with feature films, the assignment was offered to the story department, and Barks and Hannah took the job. Working with an unproduced Donald cartoon entitled *Morgan's Gold,* Hannah drew interior scenes and Barks did the exteriors. The first original Donald Duck comic book, a sixty-four-page book titled *Donald Duck Finds Pirate's Gold* (1942), was a success. Barks left Disney to work for Whitman, and Hannah took the opportunity to become a full-time director at Disney.

Hannah's first directorial work involved animated training films for the U.S. Navy. He then took over a cartoon unit specializing in Donald Duck shorts, completing his first directorial cartoon with *Donald's Day Off* in December 1944. Hannah's success made him the "duck man" at Disney. Over the next twelve years he directed fifty-one Donald Duck cartoons, as well as the occasional cartoon with Mickey Mouse, Pluto, or Goofy. Hannah introduced numerous comic foils into the series, beginning with Donald's nephews, Huey, Dewey, and Louie, in *Donald's Nephews* in 1938. He also introduced Humphrey the Bear, the Aracuan Bird from *Saludos Amigo* (1943), the Little Ranger, and Bootle Beetle. His greatest success came in a Mickey Mouse/Pluto cartoon, *Squatter's Rights* (1946), when he took two stock background chipmunks and developed them into distinctive personalities. He teamed these chipmunks with Donald Duck for their first appearance in *Chip and Dale* in 1947 and was nominated for an Academy Award for best short subject. The popularity of Chip and Dale spawned an entirely new series, and they became Disney standards. Hannah was nominated for four more Oscars in the next six years: *Tea for Two Hundred* (1948) with Donald Duck; *Toy Tinkers* (1949), another Donald Duck cartoon with Chip and Dale; *Lambert, the Sheepish Lion* (1952), a Disney special; and *Rugged Bear* (1953), which marked the first appearance of Humphrey Bear with Donald Duck.

Hannah changed both the visual and narrative style of the Donald Duck cartoons and was instrumental in turning a one-dimensional secondary character into a fiery individual with a full-blown personality of his own. With Disney's move to feature cartoons and the withdrawal of Mickey Mouse during the World War II years, Donald Duck, under Hannah's direction, became the leading short-film moneymaker of the 1940s. Hannah also directed Donald Duck in Disney's only 3-D cartoon, *Working for Peanuts* (1953), and oversaw the studio's move into CinemaScope, a widescreen process patented during the 1950s that allows for broader screens with enhanced clarity and detail.

Hannah hit his stride in the mid-1950s with the creation of Humphrey Bear and his comic foil, The Little Ranger, but the emphasis at Disney was moving away from cartoon shorts and animation in general toward television. In 1954 Hannah joined the Director's Guild and began directing live action and animation for the studio's television venture, *Disneyland*. The program was the first on ABC's fledgling network to crack Nielson's top twenty ratings, with Hannah directing fourteen episodes over the next five years. After further animation cutbacks at Disney, Hannah decided in 1957 to join Walter Lantz at Universal Pictures, where he directed the live lead-ins to another ABC cartoon program, *The Woody Woodpecker Show* (1957–1958). In 1959 Hannah accepted Lantz's offer to head his animation department. While he was able to attract some of the better illustrators from other major units that were closing down, including Riley Thompson, Tedd Pierce, Dick Kinney, and Milt Schaffer, Hannah's new characters and storylines did not fare well. He introduced Inspector Willoughby in a new series (1960–1965); created a cartoon version of the popular television series *The Life of Riley* entitled *The Beary Family* (1962–1972); and added Gabby Gator to the continuing Woody Woodpecker series. These characters stayed with Lantz, but Hannah did not. Smaller budgets translated into

less creative freedom, and Hannah left Lantz in 1962 to join Bob Clampett Productions, where he animated several unsuccessful pilots and directed some of the popular *Beany and Cecil Shows* (1962–1968).

In the mid-1960s Hannah returned to one of his earliest loves, oil painting, and for the rest of his life produced landscapes that sold in galleries throughout the western United States. He also began a lifelong process of teaching creative art and design. Hannah did return as a part–time script consultant to Disney in the mid-1960s when the studio needed someone to add gags to its live-action comedies, but he was content to spend most of his time oil painting.

In 1975 Disney Studios called Hannah to ask if he would be interested in heading an educational program on character animation at the California Institute of the Arts in Valencia. With funding by the Disney Foundation, Hannah collected a crew of six former Disney animators and began a four-year program teaching drawing and classes in the fine arts as well as animation basics. The program began with sixteen students and blossomed to over 100 by the 1980s, with most of its graduates going directly into the animation field. Hannah headed the program and taught until he retired in 1983.

In 1987 Hannah received a lifetime achievement award, or "Annie," from the International Animated Film Society, and in 1992 was officially named one of the Disney Legends, a title that recognizes past achievement in the production of Disney animation and design. He died of cancer at St. Joseph Medical Center in Los Angeles and is buried in the Forest Lawn Cemetery, also in Los Angeles.

Jack Hannah was one of the most respected directors of animation at the most prestigious animation studio in the world. His creative vision helped shape numerous American icons, and his designs for characters like Donald Duck and Chip and Dale became the standard for countless spinoffs. Audiences continue to enjoy an endless parade of rereleases and new variations on his central ideas. Hannah's influence as a distinguished educator has extended to a whole new generation of animators and illustrators.

★

So far there is no biography about Jack Hannah, but there is an abundance of material on his place in animation and the Disney style of animation. Jeff Lenburg, *The Encyclopedia of Animated Cartoons* (1991), is an excellent source for Hannah's work, as is Leonard Maltin, *Of Mice and Magic: A History of American Animated Cartoons* (1980). There are two extensive interviews with Hannah in *Animania: The Animated Film Quarterly* (1978 and 1982). See also: Christopher Finch, *The Art of Walt Disney* (1973); Leonard Maltin, *The Disney Films* (1984); and Richard Holliss and Brian Sibley, *The Disney Studio Story* (1988). An obituary is in the *New York Times* (17 June 1994).

PATRICK A. TRIMBLE

HANSEN, Al(fred) Earl (*b.* 5 October 1927 in New York City; *d. c.* 21 June 1995 in Cologne, Germany), Fluxus artist, writer, and composer, and one of the first Happening artists.

Hansen, whom fellow artist Allan Kaprow once described as the quintessential "wandering artist [and] the hobo avantgardist," was born in the Richmond Hill section of the borough of Queens, New York, to a working-class family that he referred to as "upper lower class people." One of three sons of Nicholas Hansen, a crane operator of Norwegian descent, and Katherine Lynch, descendant of an Irish Scottish family, Hansen made art and improvised plays in the garage of his Queens home from an early age. He contributed comic strips to a handmade newspaper, *The Daily Flash,* which he produced with his brother Gordon and the future columnist Jimmy Breslin, his friend and next-door neighbor. Hansen, who later called himself an existentialist, believed that, like his parents before him, he alone was responsible for the meaning he brought to his life, and this belief informed his art.

In 1945 Hansen was drafted into the U.S. Army and served in the famed Eighty-second Airborne Division in Europe, where he remained until 1948. While stationed in Frankfurt am Main, Germany, he executed in 1946 what he considered his first "Happening," a form of theater and early example of performance art in which plot is abandoned for a more spontaneous vignette that stresses movement and chance. The 1946 Happening involved pushing a piano from the top floor of a bombed-out building during an armed forces show. Later, Hansen repeated this action in numerous performances around the world, closing the gap between life and art in a dadaist fashion. Ultimately, he called his Happening, "Yoko Ono Piano Drop," referring to his friend and fellow Fluxus artist. (The Fluxus movement was an extension of dadaism launched in the United States during the 1960s. It stressed "conceptual" rather than material or formal aspects of art.)

Between 1948 and 1951, Hansen peripatetically attended art classes at various places, including Tulane University in New Orleans and the Art Students League, New York University, and the Hans Hofmann School of Art, all in Manhattan. He had his first show at the Arts Students League with Jan Groth in 1949. Hansen and Audrey Ostlin Hansen, an actress, model, and bon vivant, had a daughter who later appeared in Hansen's performances.

In December 1951 Hansen reenlisted in the U.S. Air

Al Hansen (*right*) and John Lennon at the Eighth Avant-Garde Festival, 1971. COPYRIGHT © BY FRED W. MCDARRAH

Force, where aside from his regular duties he wrote articles for a military newspaper and painted signs. Meanwhile, he married Marvyne Levy in 1954; the couple had no children and were divorced in 1962. After leaving the military, he returned to New York City late in 1955, supporting himself mainly by working as an art editor and graphic designer for McGraw-Hill while attending evening art classes at Pratt Institute in Brooklyn. The composer John Cage's "Experimental Composition" class at the New School for Social Research in New York City, which Hansen attended in the late 1950s, exposed him to experimental music and performance art as well as to Zen philosophy. Growing tired of traditional art practice, Hansen and a number of other young artists who studied with Cage, such as Kaprow, George Brecht, and Dick Higgins, launched the Happening movement and joined the Fluxus movement.

Hansen's debut as an influential member of the Happening movement was a music Happening called *Alice Denham in 48 Seconds: Percussion Piece* (1958), which was presented in April 1959 to a larger public, along with works of his teacher, John Cage, at the "Concert of Advanced Music." It caused considerable consternation among the more traditional part of the audience at the New York YM-YWHA in April 1959. It was performed with handcrafted rattles following unorthodox musical notations that matched sounds and their duration in seconds to numbers. The same year Hansen, with Larry Poons and Higgs, who called themselves the New York Audio Visual Group, took Happenings to the streets, and Hansen exhibited with Robert Rauschenberg, Claes Oldenburg, Jim Dine, and Kaprow at the Reuben Gallery in New York, the cradle of Happenings in the early 1960s.

By that time Hansen was a major Happening artist in New York City. As Kaprow stated in his "Untitled Guidelines for Happening," Hansen kept the line between art and life "as fluid, and perhaps indistinct, as possible." For Hansen, the fusion of life and art was crucial for the thinking of the "Happening people"; probability and chance were guiding forces for their creative endeavors. In *A Primer of Happenings and Time/Space Art* (1965), Hansen, a true child of the sixties, stressed the unique potential of the Happening to generate "love" that "is going not only from the stage to the audience but from the audience to the stage and back and forth between the people in the happening to each other."

Typical multimedia Happenings by Hansen include *Requiem for W.C. Fields Who Died of Acute Alcoholism,* included in Claes Oldenburg's *Ray Gun Spex* (an evening of Happenings) and performed at the Judson Memorial Church in New York City in 1960. Hansen described his performance in *A Primer of Happenings:* "I projected W. C. Fields movies—flipped upside down and backwards—on my white shirted chest. The movies were spliced with news-

reels and different things." Hansen took part in a number of early Fluxus events, both in the United States and Europe. In the Yam Festival ("Yam" being the anagram for "May"), which took place at the Hardware Poet's Playhouse in New York and at the sculptor George Segal's farm in South Brunswick, New Jersey, in May 1963, Hansen staged a Happening by festooning trees with toilet paper. His volatile Happenings were often performed in a number of alternative art spaces in New York City, including the Café au Go Go, Epitome Coffee Shop, Yoko Ono's loft on Chambers Street, and the Judson Memorial Church.

Hansen's gallery, the Third Rail Gallery of Current Art, opened in 1962 and existed in various incarnations and locations until 1969, showing his and other artists' works. In the heyday of his artistic activities, Hansen also frequented Andy Warhol's Factory, the nightclub Max's Kansas City (known as a favorite nightspot for Warhol and Lou Reed), and appeared on television talk shows hosted by Johnny Carson and Merv Griffin. Throughout the 1960s and during most of the 1970s, Hansen had a reputation of being an innately rebellious bohemian and was a fixture of the neodadaist artistic community in New York City, which included Nam June Paik, John Cage, Yoko Ono, and La Monte Young.

The art dealer Gracie Mansion remembered Hansen as an artist who constantly made art from whatever was at hand and then left it wherever he happened to be. As a result, many of Hansen's early works were lost. Satisfied with making art in a small format, he called himself a "shopping bag guy." Perceiving the process of staging Happenings as analogous to cut-and-paste collaging, Hansen produced a large number of works made of recycled "junk," such as cigarette butts, plastic razors, crushed Coca-Cola cans, burnt matches, and most especially Hershey's chocolate bar wrappers, which Hansen appreciated for their common and perishable qualities that he was able to elevate to the level of a material for making art; the wrappers became known as his "signature material." In the 1960s he incorporated popular imagery into his paintings and made erotic collages using photographs from girlie magazines. He used images of Venus, which took central stage among the motifs in his art, executing them in various forms and materials during the last thirty years of his life.

Hansen taught at Rutgers University in New Brunswick, New Jersey, from 1967 to 1974. Dissatisfied with the lack of attention paid to his art in New York City, starting in the mid-1970s he spent an increasing amount of time in California, where he was involved with the Los Angeles punk scene, and in Europe, where he enjoyed considerable popularity as an artist, particularly in the Scandinavian countries and Germany. Hansen experimented further with performance art after he permanently settled in Cologne, Germany, in 1987, and he and Lisa Cieslik established an art school called the Ultimate Akademie. On 21 June 1995 he was found dead of a heart attack in his Cologne apartment. His body was cremated.

Hansen remains relatively little known in the United States, overshadowed by other members of the neodadaist community in New York City. His pioneering role in launching the Happenings movement and performance art and his contribution to the Fluxus movement await critical examination.

★

Documentation of Hansen's work, along with his personal papers, is kept in the Archiv Sohm at the Staatsgalerie in Stuttgart, Germany; the Henie Onstad Kunstsenter near Oslo, Norway; the Getty Institute for the Arts and Humanities, Santa Monica, California; and the private archives of Francesco Conz in Verona, Italy, and his daughter, Bibbe Hansen, in Los Angeles. Among his major exhibition catalogs are *Al Hansen, Oeuvre/Flashbacks* (1995) and *Al Hansen, An Introspective* (1996). Hansen's grandson, the musician Beck Hansen, edited *Beck and Al Hansen: Playing with Matches* (1998), which is filled with collages, letters, photographs, interviews, and handwritten notes. An obituary is in the *New York Times* (27 June 1995).

MAREK BARTELIK

HANSON Duane Elwood (*b.* 17 January 1925 in Alexandria, Minnesota; *d.* 6 January 1996 in Boca Raton, Florida), internationally renowned superrealist sculptor best known for his trompe l'oeil, life-size polyvinyl casts of ordinary Americans.

Hanson, the only child of Agnes Nelson and Dewey O. Hanson, Swedish-American dairy farmers, grew up in Parkers Prairie, Minnesota. At an early age he showed an aptitude for the arts. He especially loved carving and often fashioned small figures out of candles and firewood using his mother's kitchen knives. One such figure, *The Blue Boy* (1938), copied from a painting by the English portrait painter Thomas Gainsborough, carved when he was thirteen, shows Hanson's early interest in realism. During his years at Parkers High School, Hanson also wrote poetry, acted, and studied music. He graduated in 1944.

Declared ineligible for service in World War II due to an allergic condition, Hanson enrolled briefly at Luther College, in Decorah, Iowa, and at the University of Washington, in Seattle. In 1945 he returned to Minnesota, where he received a bachelor of arts degree from Macalester College in Saint Paul in 1946. While he was in Saint Paul, he met and befriended the established figurative sculptor John Rood, with whom he studied for one year in 1947. Encouraged by this experience, Hanson decided to focus his studies on sculpture. He enrolled in the Cranbrook Academy of Art in Bloomfield Hills, Michigan, where he studied with the internationally known sculptors Bill McVey and

Duane Hanson. AP/WIDE WORLD PHOTOS

Carl Milles. In 1951, after receiving his master of fine arts degree from Cranbrook, he married his first wife, Janice Roche, and moved to Wilton, Connecticut, to teach junior high school. A difficult year followed, as Hanson struggled to develop a language for his work that meshed with the prevailing abstract style that characterized the New York gallery scene. Hanson had his first one-person show at the Wilton Gallery in 1952, but he was unable to secure a show in New York and found it impossible to do nonfigurative work.

Impatient with his progress, Hanson accepted an offer to teach in Munich, West Germany, in 1953 at a United States Army High School. Hanson remained in West Germany until the end of the decade, teaching in Munich until 1957 and then in Bremerhaven from 1957 to 1960. In Bremerhaven, Hanson met the sculptor George Grygo, who introduced him to a polyester resin and fiberglass casting technique. Impressed with the flexibility and lightweight nature of the material, Hanson began his own experiments with it in 1960 when he returned to the United States to teach in Atlanta, Georgia. During his years in Atlanta, Hanson began to make sculptures that addressed social issues such as war, bigotry, and poverty. But his work remained largely unnoticed, and his personal life was deteriorating. In 1965, after the birth of three children, his marriage to Janice Roche ended in divorce, and he moved again, this time to take a teaching job at Miami-Dade Community College in Florida.

In the late 1960s, Hanson abandoned abstraction. Pop art had emerged as the prevailing style, and his cast sculptures began to find a wide audience. Hanson found particular inspiration in the works of the pop artist George Segal, who made castings directly from life and incorporated everyday objects into his sculpture installations. With a newfound confidence, Hanson began creating a series of violent and confrontational sculptures. In 1967, he created several controversial pieces dealing with death. *Abortion,* a graphic depiction of a young woman dead from an illegal abortion procedure, attracted considerable public and critical attention, as did *Welfare-2598* and the horrific battlefield scene *War.* With *War* and other grisly pieces, such as *Gangland Victim* (1967) and *Motorcycle Victim* (1967), both banned from exhibition in Florida, Hanson cast directly from life, utilizing the polyester resin technique he had learned in Germany.

In 1967, Hanson's sculptures caught the attention of the New York gallery director Ivan Karp, who helped arrange a one-person show at the O.K. Harris Gallery in 1970. In 1969, following Karp's suggestion, Hanson left his teaching position in Florida and moved to Greenwich Village in Manhattan with his second wife, Wesla Host, whom he had married in 1968. That marriage produced two children. Hanson remained in New York until 1973, when he returned to live permanently in Davie, Florida. During the New York years, his international reputation was firmly established. In 1972, his work was included in the *Documenta 5* show in Kassel, West Germany, where it received critical acclaim.

The move to New York also brought about a major stylistic shift in Hanson's sculpture. In 1970, he decided to move away from the expressive realism that dealt with the social implications of violence. His new work embodied a more introspective and contemplative type of realism. In such pieces as *Tourists* (1970) and *Hard Hat* (1970), Hanson's subject became the battered and tired lives of the middle class. Painstakingly painted, sculpted, and attired in minute detail, these figures achieved such a high degree of realism that they often fooled museum visitors. Over the next two decades, Hanson's reputation grew steadily. O.K. Harris Gallery continued to represent him into the 1980s, and, in 1978, the Whitney Museum in New York City held a major retrospective. Exhibits of his works were intensely popular with the public, and his sculptures are well represented in both public and private collections around the world.

From the 1970s until his death, Hanson worked steadily, producing three or four figures a year. He continued to portray lower- and middle-class Americans, often choosing "heavyset" people, whom he saw as having "great dignity, or overburdened with despair and fatigue due to the complexities of our time." He continued to cast directly from life, often taking pains to find the right body type. Vastly popular in his adopted home state of Florida, he received the Ambassador of the Arts Award of the State of Florida in 1983 and was awarded the *New York Times* Florida Artist Award in 1985. In 1973, Hanson had been diagnosed with lymphatic cancer. The condition went into remission for more than twenty years, only to resurface in 1995 and take his life the following year. At the time of his death, Hanson had completed more than 100 sculptures.

Hanson saw himself as a "true expressionist," an artist who wanted to give meaning to the lives of the lonely and the marginalized, to the people we pass by without noticing. Despite Hanson's wide popular appeal, his work was criticized for stereotyping and was dismissed by many critics as unsophisticated illustration. But others have found great merit in Hanson's "monstrifications of American types," which can arouse in the viewer alternate feelings of empathy and parody. From a historical perspective, Hanson's superrealist figures connect with a deep interest in realistic depiction in American art that extends backward to nineteenth-century trompe l'oeil painting and forward to the virtual reality of computer-generated imagery.

★

Kirk Varnedoe, *Duane Hanson* (1985), contains a critical essay by the author, an interview with Hanson, and a section on his fabrication process. *Sculptures by Duane Hanson* (1985), by Martin H. Bush, has an extensive bibliography and gives a good chronological account of Hanson's career until 1985. Marco Livingstone, *Duane Hanson* (1997), is a short posthumous publication surveying Hanson's entire professional life. An essay by Joseph Masheck on the sculpture of Duane Hanson and John de Andrea appears in *Super Realism: A Critical Anthology* (1975). An obituary is in the *New York Times* (10 Jan. 1996).

PETER SUCHECKI

HARRIS, (Wanga) Phillip ("Phil") (*b.* 24 June 1904 near Linton, Indiana; *d.* 11 August 1995 in Rancho Mirage, California), bandleader, singer, comedian, and actor, best known for his work in radio and for his recordings of popular novelty songs.

Harris was born in a mining camp outside Linton, Indiana. The date of his birth often is listed as 16 January 1904. His father, Harry Harris, was a circus bandleader and vaudeville musician, and because his mother, Dollie Wright, and Harry frequently traveled, Harris lived with his grandmother during his early childhood. He did not have any siblings. When he was five or six years old, his father relocated the family to Nashville, Tennessee. By the time he

Phil Harris. ARCHIVE PHOTOS

was twelve, Harris was playing drums in his father's band. He attended a military academy in Nashville, where he became active in the school's orchestra.

From 1924 to 1927 he played with the Henry Halstead Orchestra. In 1928 he formed a band with Carol Lofner, and they played for three years at the St. Francis Hotel in San Francisco. That same year, while working in Sydney, Australia, he met Marcia Ralston, an Australian actress, whom he married. They later adopted a boy named Tookie. At the conclusion of the St. Francis Hotel engagement, Lofner departed, and Harris gave up playing the drums in favor of leading his own band, playing for a year in 1932 at the Coconut Grove in Los Angeles and then going on tour. His work with the band attracted the attention of RKO Pictures, who starred him in a three-reel musical directed by Mark Sandrich, entitled *So This Is Harris* (1933). The film, which employed several experimental techniques, won an Academy Award for best short subject. Pleased with the success of this film, the studio signed Harris and Sandrich to do a full-length feature, *Melody Cruise* (1933). Meanwhile, a new band that Harris had formed in 1932 became very popular and was performing on a radio show called *Let's Listen to Harris* (1934).

It was through this radio show that Harris came to the attention of the popular radio comedian Jack Benny. Benny's show, which had premiered on 2 May 1932, featured a new orchestra each year, beginning with George

Olsen and then with Ted Weems, Frank Black, and Don Bestor. However, none of these satisfied Benny, who, among other things, was looking for a bandleader who could be featured in the cast. Phil Harris provided what Benny sought, and he joined the show on 4 October 1936. Harris's band satisfied the national craze for swing music, but particularly important was the character Benny's writers created for Harris. He was portrayed as a happy-go-lucky, bourbon-drinking, gambling, wisecracking bandleader with a southern drawl. He was a likeable character and a perfect foil for Benny. Harris was now a major celebrity. "If it hadn't been for radio," Harris said later, "I would still be a traveling orchestra leader. For seventeen years I played one-night stands, sleeping on buses. I never even voted because I never had a residence." Harris continued to appear on the *Jack Benny Show* until 1952.

In 1940, Harris and Marcia Ralston were divorced, and he renewed an acquaintance with the singer and motion-picture star Alice Faye, whom he had first met in 1933. Faye had been married to the singer Tony Martin, but they, too, had been divorced in 1940. Harris and Faye were married by a judge in Tijuana, Mexico, on 12 May 1941. Later that year they were remarried in a church in Galveston, Texas. Phil Harris and Alice Faye had two daughters, Alice (1942) and Phyllis (1944).

On 29 September 1946, Harris and Faye began to perform together on the *Fitch Bandwagon*, which was aired immediately following the *Jack Benny Show*. The *Phil Harris/Alice Faye Show*, which developed from *Bandwagon*, premiered on NBC on 3 October 1948. Even though Benny had moved to CBS by then, their show continued to follow his, and Harris's portrayal remained the same as it had been with Benny. The *Phil Harris/Alice Faye Show* was very popular, and it was broadcast until 1954.

Throughout these years, Harris recorded popular songs. His specialty was novelty songs, which he delivered in a staccato, talking manner. His most famous releases were "That's What I Like About the South" (1944), "Woodman, Spare That Tree" (release date unknown), "The Preacher and the Bear" (1947), and especially, "The Thing," which was a major hit in 1950, rising to number one on the charts and selling a million copies. He also made television appearances from the 1950s through the 1970s on such shows as *Ben Casey* (1961), *The Andy Williams Show* (1962), *Here's Lucy* (1968), and *Fantasy Island* (1978).

Harris had roles in nearly two dozen motion pictures, but his most celebrated role came in 1967, when he was more or less retired and no longer a major celebrity. In that year, Walt Disney picked him to provide the voice of Baloo the Bear for an animated film based on Rudyard Kipling's *Jungle Book*. Harris's interpretation of the role was so engaging that the entire film script was rewritten to go along with it. Harris was once again catapulted to fame.

Harris's principal recreational interest was golfing; he described himself as a "golfing bum." As his career in comedy faded, he became an increasingly popular figure on the professional-amateur golf circuit, and after the death of his good friend Bing Crosby, he replaced him in doing television commentary for the annual Bing Crosby Pro-Am Pebble Beach Golf Tournament. He particularly enjoyed his home at the Thunderbird Country Club in Rancho Mirage, California, where he died of heart failure on 11 August 1995. He is interred at the Palm Springs Mausoleum in Palm Springs, California, along with Alice Faye, who died in 1998.

Harris had a long and successful career as a musician and radio personality. He is best remembered as the brash character on Jack Benny's radio program, a personality that he enjoyed playing even when he was not on the air. In reality, the hard drinking was an exaggeration, but it was a characteristic that Harris never made any effort to dispel. In his real life, Harris had a reputation for being rather soft-spoken and polite—totally the opposite of his fictional persona.

★

There are no biographies of Phil Harris. Biographical material, focusing particularly on his radio career, appears in John Dunning, *Tune in Yesterday: The Ultimate Encyclopedia of Old-Time Radio, 1925–1976* (1976). Other useful observations may be found in Jack and Joan Benny, *Sunday Nights at Seven: The Jack Benny Story* (1990), and in Gerald Nachman, *Raised on Radio* (1998). A list of Phil Harris's recordings appears in Roger D. Kinkle, *The Complete Encyclopedia of Popular Music and Jazz, 1900–1950* (1974), and his motion-picture and television appearances are listed in volume 24 of *Contemporary Theatre, Film, and Television* (2000). The most useful obituaries are in the New Orleans *Times-Picayune* (13 Aug. 1995), *Los Angeles Times* (13 Aug. 1995), and *New York Times* (14 Aug. 1995).

IVAN D. STEEN

HAWKINS, Frederick ("Erick") (*b.* 23 April 1909 in Trinidad, Colorado; *d.* 23 November 1994 in New York City), dancer and choreographer best known for his pioneering approach to modern dance based on haiku-like metaphor and unstressed, "free-flow" movement.

One of four children, Hawkins was the only son of Eugene Gilbert Hawkins, an inventor, and Myrtle Minnie Cunning. When he was about ten, the family moved from Colorado to Kansas City, Missouri, where he attended public schools including Northeast High School. Encouraged by his teachers, he applied for a scholarship to Harvard University. He was accepted, entering Harvard in 1926 and receiving a B.A. degree in 1932 with a major in Greek studies.

While still in college, Hawkins attended his first dance recital, featuring the German dancer Harald Kreutzberg. The event electrified Hawkins: "Wow! . . . for the first time in my life, I knew what I wanted to do. Dance and make dances." Sometime later he studied with Kreutzberg in Salzburg, Austria. He moved to New York City in 1934 to study ballet at the new School of American Ballet, founded that year by George Balanchine and Lincoln Kirstein. Balanchine pronounced him "very promising" and permitted him, even as a beginner, to teach. He made his dance debut on 9 June 1934 performing in Balanchine's three works, *Serenade, Dreams,* and *Mozartiana.*

In 1936 Kirstein took the best of the Balanchine dancers to form his own Ballet Caravan, for which Hawkins wrote his first piece of choreography, *Show Piece,* which debuted on 15 July 1937. In the summer of 1936 Caravan performed at Bennington College, Vermont, and on opening night, Martha Graham, whose troupe was also there, went backstage to "single" Hawkins out. Hawkins soon decided to switch from ballet to Graham's modern dance because, he said, "I had a continuing desire to do Balanchine's work . . . but at the same time I knew the range of the ballet technique would never let me develop."

Graham had opened her studio in 1926, and she taught only women in her own passionate style that was full of torso contractions. Her attraction to, and later infatuation with, Hawkins was unprecedented, as was her permission to let him attend rehearsals and then dance in the company. He became the first male member of her troupe, making his debut in *American Document* in 1938. While he was with the company, he starred in several other new dances including *El Penitente* (1940), *Appalachian Spring* (1944), and *Dark Meadow* and *Cave of the Heart* (both 1946).

Hawkins also took charge of the administrative and financial affairs of the company, imposing order on its hitherto chaotic business and obtaining grants to underwrite some productions. At the same time, he was beginning to choreograph his own works, including *John Brown* (1945) and *Stephen Acrobat* (1947). These pieces first revealed his stylistic and philosophical differences with Graham.

During one summer, Hawkins traveled through the American West, his birthplace, to study the dances of the Plains Indians, and was struck by the reverence for and harmony with natural phenomena in their dance ceremonies. An intensely thoughtful man, Hawkins combined this reverence with an appreciation of the loveliness of the human body and his studies of Asian philosophy. In addition, an injury that occurred while he was still with Graham made him more aware of his own body and the whole subject of kinesiology (the study of the principles of mechanics and anatomy in relation to human movement) in general.

Hawkins concluded that the locus of movement taught

Erick Hawkins teaching a class in his dance studio, 1962. COPYRIGHT © BY FRED W. McDARRAH

in ballet (the lower back) and by Graham (the torso) was incorrect for proper dance. Instead, he felt its source was from the pelvis, and that dance movement should not fight gravity (as in ballet) but work into it, as did the dances of the Plains Indians. This conviction led him to reject the tensions inherent in both balletic and Graham techniques, calling hers "bound flow" as opposed to his own "free flow."

This free-flow style of movement also fit with his maturing beliefs about the function of art. Influenced by the impersonality of Asian art forms (where the individual artist was not necessarily present), his respect for nature, his belief that art must always show a triumph of life over destructive forces, and his love of metaphor, Hawkins gradually developed a philosophy of dance that differed radically from traditional ballet—with its emphases on conflict, loss, and the individual dancer—as well as from Graham's emphasis on emotion.

Although many critics were unprepared for Hawkins's dances, Edwin Denby already recognized that in his *John Brown* he was performing a kind of "Japanese nō drama," something antithetical to Graham's intense, psychological works. Nevertheless, Hawkins remained with Graham for another five years, and they were married in the summer of 1948. He finally left both Graham and the troupe while on tour in 1950; they divorced in 1954.

On 19 January 1952 Hawkins gave his first concert on his own with *openings of the (eye)*. This work also marked his first of many years of collaboration with the composer Lucia Dlugoszewski, later his second wife, and the sculptor Ralph Dorazio. Hawkins felt strongly about the integration of all aspects of dance, and he commissioned artists and composers for his new works. He abhorred the idea of recorded music for a performance and often positioned the musicians on the stage with the dancers. Dlugoszweski actually created new instruments, including the "timbre piano," for his works. Hawkins later commissioned other composers such as Virgil Thompson, Alan Hovhaness, and Zoltán Kodály, as well as artists such as Isamu Noguchi.

In 1957 Hawkins formed his own troupe, the Erick Hawkins Dance Company, with the dancers he had been working with since leaving Graham. That same year he wrote *Here and Now with Watchers,* which he described as "just pure poetry of movement." However, Hawkins was never interested in movement for its own sake, and in this work, as in many others, he was exploring through metaphor the "suchness" or essence of the elements involved. Don McDonagh later wrote that this piece "may have been the most important one that Hawkins . . . ever made."

Despite McDonagh's observation, for years Hawkins's dances were not popular in New York City, where many critics gave them only pallid praise. They were bothered by the fact that, as Anna Kisselgoff said in a 1968 review, "while there is action on stage, there is rarely anything actually happening." By the early 1970s most Manhattan dance critics had begun to recognize some of what Hawkins was trying to convey, and in 1972 Clive Barnes wrote, "I have in the past always found Hawkins difficult to take. . . . Now for me, at last, enlightenment seems to have come." Barnes added that what he had heretofore regarded as blandness, he now realized was a "kind of Olympian simplicity."

Hawkins continued to dance well into the 1980s and choreographed dances until just before he died. Some of his most well-known pieces were *8 Clear Places* (1960), *Early Floating* (1961), *Dawn Dazzled Door* (1972), *Death Is the Hunter* (1975), *Plains Daybreak* (1979), *God the Reveller* (1987), and *Killer of Enemies* (1991). He received awards from the Mellon Foundation in 1975, *Dance* magazine in 1979, and the Samuel H. Scripps/American Dance Festival in 1988. Western Michigan University awarded him an honorary D.F.A. degree in 1983, and President Clinton presented him with a National Medal of Arts in 1994. Hawkins also wrote essays and gave speeches, some of which appeared in his 1992 book *The Body Is a Clear Place.*

Hawkins was physically fit with a rugged, austere face. He recovered from a stroke in 1988 before dying of prostate cancer at age eighty-five. His memorial service in December 1994 in New York City was attended by many who appreciated his subtle, poetic dances and his own free-flowing dance style. In his persistent, quiet manner, Hawkins changed the way dance could be taught and should be perceived, with his insistence upon a tension-free technique and harmonious, life-affirming messages. Deborah Jowitt noted after his death that to Hawkins "dancing wasn't simply something you did; it was a kind of poetic seeing into the essences of things." As he had always wished, Erick Hawkins had indeed become a "poet of the body."

★

There are modest Hawkins holdings at the New York Public Library Dance Collection and the Harvard University Archives, but the most useful autobiographical material comes from his book *The Body Is a Clear Place and Other Statements on Dance* (1992). No full-length biography exists, but his early life and relationship with Martha Graham are well documented in Agnes de Mille's *Martha: The Life and Work of Martha Graham* (1991). Don McDonagh's *The Complete Guide to Modern Dance* (1976), though old, gives details about some of his earlier dances. There were many reviews of his works and other articles over the years, including: Anna Kisselgoff, "Dance: Hawkins Troupe," *New York Times* (15 Nov. 1968); Clive Barnes, "Hawkins and Tharp—At Home on Broadway," *New York Times* (5 Nov. 1972); Jennifer Dunning, "Blunt Words on Ballet from Erick Hawkins," *New York Times* (11 Feb. 1992), in an interview with Hawkins about his book; and Deborah Jowitt, "Erick Hawkins (1909–1994)," *Village Voice* (13 Dec. 1994). An obituary by Kisselgoff is in the *New York Times* (24 Nov. 1994).

SANDRA SHAFFER VANDOREN

HEMINGWAY, Margaux (*b.* 16 February 1955 in Portland, Oregon; *d.* 28 June 1996 in Santa Monica, California), fashion model and actress who was a granddaughter of the novelist Ernest Hemingway.

Hemingway was the second of three children of John ("Jack") Hadley Nicanor Hemingway, eldest son of the

Margaux Hemingway. THE KOBAL COLLECTION

writer Ernest Hemingway and a stockbroker, writer, conservationist, and sport fisherman, and Byra ("Puck") Whittlesey Whitlock, an airline employee. Her given name at birth was Margot Byra Hemingway. Hemingway's early childhood was lived somewhat in the shadow of her famous grandfather, and, as her father sought to make a career in the securities business, the family moved from Portland, Oregon, to Havana, Cuba; Mill Valley, California; and finally Ketchum, Idaho, where they settled when Margaux was twelve years old.

In 1962, in the aftermath of the sensation caused by the suicide of her grandfather, Margaux was first afflicted with the epilepsy that would trouble her all her life. She also suffered from dyslexia, which made her indifferent about school and more interested in a variety of outdoor activities, including skiing, hiking, and fishing. Learning from her parents that she was conceived over a bottle of Château Margaux champagne, she adopted the *-aux* ending of her name.

Around 1973, having dropped out of high school, she joined a friend in a local public relations firm; during a trip to New York City, her striking looks, six-foot frame, husky voice, and famous name attracted the attention of Errol

Wetson, founder of a hamburger chain. Her star rose quickly: in the fall of 1974, Wetson introduced Hemingway to people in the fashion industry, including the photographer Francesco Scavullo. Acting as her manager, Wetson helped arrange articles, fashion spreads, and cover photos for her in *Vogue, Town and Country, Sports Illustrated, Women's Wear Daily,* and *People* magazine. Wetson and Hemingway also became engaged during this time.

In June 1975, having just turned twenty, Hemingway signed a contract with Fabergé, the cosmetics manufacturer, for $1 million, at that time the largest advertising deal ever offered to a woman, all less than a year after her arrival in New York. This deal attracted an enormous amount of press coverage; one typical article described her as "Viking-woman tall, magnificently Wild West and American ski-slope outdoorsy." She appeared on the cover of *Time* magazine that month as the headliner of a story about "The New Beauties."

She married Wetson in Paris in 1975 and embarked on a round of parties at nightclubs, drinking heavily and making the gossip columns. In 1976 she made her film debut in *Lipstick;* her performance was harshly criticized and the movie bombed, but critics praised the performance of her younger sister Mariel, whom Margaux had suggested for a part in the movie. Ironically, press attention abruptly shifted from Margaux to Mariel, who went on to have a successful career in film and television.

Hemingway divorced Wetson in 1978 and that same year costarred with her father in an ABC documentary about the jungle and wildlife of Venezuela. Her winning the role may have been due to her connection with the Venezuelan film director Bernard Foucher, whom she married the following year. The couple lived lavishly in Paris, and Hemingway appeared on French television. Her film career continued with small roles in mostly second-rate movies such as *Killer Fish* (1978), *They Call Me Bruce?* (1982), and the more mainstream *Over the Brooklyn Bridge* (1984), in which she costarred with Elliott Gould and Sid Caesar.

Hemingway's plans to make a documentary with her husband about her grandfather were eventually abandoned, and she divorced Foucher in 1985. By this time, her alcoholism had advanced to the point where she was having trouble with her memory and was deeply in debt. Meanwhile, her mother, from whom she had grown estranged, died of cancer in 1988, deepening Hemingway's already serious depression. That same year she checked herself into the Betty Ford Clinic to help her in her struggle with alcohol. In an attempt to pay off her debts and restart her modeling and film career, she posed for *Playboy* magazine in 1990. Her newfound sobriety and a live-in relationship with a businessman in Manhattan seemed to have stabilized her for a time, but she had never been good at managing her money and was forced to declare bankruptcy in 1991.

After her appearance in *Playboy* and a role in a French movie failed to have the desired effect, she began to consult a variety of chiropractors and alternative healers in the hope of finding a spiritual solution to her physical problems, which included bulimia as well as epilepsy and dyslexia. This led her to take a trip to India in 1994, where she suffered some sort of breakdown; she was treated at a private psychiatric clinic in Idaho, from which she was released in 1995.

Hemingway moved to California and acted in a half dozen low-budget films in the 1990s, made infomercials, and endorsed a psychic hotline. In the last days of June 1996, she made phone calls to several friends, leaving rambling messages. On 1 July, a friend went to her apartment in Santa Monica and found her body; it was one day short of the thirty-fifth anniversary of the suicide of her grandfather Ernest. Although close friends found it hard to believe, the coroner's report ruled her death a suicide, caused by "acute barbiturate intoxication," making her the fifth member of her family in four generations to commit suicide.

Hemingway was by all accounts warm and trusting, an open and enthusiastic person who made friends easily, and whose naiveté made her a target for unscrupulous people seeking to profit from her celebrity. She was overwhelmed by her sudden rise to fame and her equally rapid descent out of the public gaze. Having never been trained for a career out of the spotlight, and having never sought to develop herself professionally, she did not have a job or skill to fall back on when her novelty wore off. There were some indications that she was working her way back to more solid ground: she had made a series of nature shows to be broadcast on a cable channel, and there was talk of her bringing out a line of signature clothing and cosmetics. Her sister Mariel felt that Margaux's personality was more suited to television comedy than to movie drama, saying, "My sister was a big girl, bold and uninhibited. She had that presence. . . . In comedy, I think she could have really been amazing." Her remains were cremated and interred in the Ketchum Cemetery near her famous grandfather.

★

There is no biography of Margaux Hemingway. Many published sources about her are somewhat gossipy accounts and contain conflicting, inaccurate, or misleading information. The high-water mark of her celebrity was the eight-month period from March to October 1975, when at least a dozen articles about her appeared in *Time, Newsweek,* the *New Yorker, Harper, Esquire, People, Vogue,* and elsewhere. Within five years there was almost no press notice of her at all. She was given to a confessional manner, and in the 1980s and 1990s her struggles with bulimia, alcohol, epilepsy, and dyslexia were very public. In 1988, *People Weekly* published a revealing interview with her (8 Feb. 1988), but her death prompted an outpouring of articles of varying value, the best of which are "A Life Eclipsed," in *People Weekly* (15 July 1996), and Hara Estroff Marano's excellent and probing portrait "What Killed Margaux Hemingway?" *Psychology Today* 29, no. 6 (Nov./Dec. 1996). An obituary is in the *New York Times* (3 July 1996).

PETER COVENEY

HERRNSTEIN, Richard Julius (*b.* 20 May 1930 in New York City; *d.* 13 September 1994 in Belmont, Massachusetts), psychology educator and vigorous advocate of the intelligence quotient (IQ) test as an indicator of future personal development.

Herrnstein was the son of Hungarian immigrant parents, Rezso Herrnstein, a housepainter, and Flora Irene Friedman. Herrnstein attended the High School of Music and Art in Manhattan and City College of New York, graduating with a B.A. in 1952. He went immediately to Harvard University to do graduate work in psychology and received his Ph.D. from Harvard in 1955. His dissertation is entitled "Behavioral Consequences of the Removal of a Discriminative Stimulus Associated with the Variable Interval Re-

Richard J. Herrnstein. COURTESY OF SUSAN HERRNSTEIN

inforcement." On 28 May 1951 he married Barbara Brodo. They had one child before they divorced in February 1961.

Serving as a research psychologist in the U.S. Army from 1955 to 1958, Herrnstein rose to the rank of first lieutenant and was stationed at Walter Reed Army Medical Center in Washington, D.C. While in Washington, in 1957–1958 he was also a lecturer at the University of Maryland, in College Park.

In 1958 Herrnstein returned to Harvard to teach psychology. On 11 November 1961 he married Susan Chalk Gouinlock; they had two sons. Between 1965 and 1967 Herrnstein was the director of Harvard's psychology laboratories. In 1967 he became a full professor of psychology and began a four-year term as the chairman of the Department of Psychology. From 1975 to 1981 he was the editor of *Psychological Bulletin.*

Herrnstein, a prolific writer, published textbooks, scholarly articles, and books for the general public. His three textbooks are *A Source Book in the History of Psychology,* with Edwin G. Boring (1965); *Laboratory Experiments in Psychology,* with Joseph C. Stevens and George S. Reynolds (1965); and *Psychology* (1975). His three books for the general public are *I.Q. in the Meritocracy* (1973); *Crime and Human Nature,* with James Q. Wilson (1985); and *The Bell Curve,* with Charles Murray (1994).

Herrnstein was also the author of two controversial articles in *Atlantic Monthly.* The first, entitled simply "I.Q." (1971), was a somewhat popularized review of the arguments in favor of IQ as the best early indictor of future life achievement. The concept was difficult for many people to accept in an era of radical protest against the Vietnam War and of social policy designed to improve the lot of the disadvantaged. Herrnstein was surprised by the opposition his ideas generated, particularly in the press, and in 1982 he published another article in *Atlantic Monthly* entitled "I.Q. Testing and the Media." In this article he accused the major newspapers and news magazines of reporting stories critical of the value of IQ testing but of failing to report developments that supported the value of such tests.

Herrnstein, who described himself as "incurably addicted to quantification," was a strong advocate of gathering data on various social and psychological indicators that could be used to foretell the outcomes of social interventions for categorized groups. His ideas were closely associated with those advanced by Arthur Jensen of the University of California at Berkeley, who also valued the IQ test as a marker of future outcomes. Jensen and Herrnstein were considered conservative social thinkers for their view that intelligence was largely hereditary. In *Crime and Human Nature,* Herrnstein maintained that IQ was the best indicator of future criminal activity. Those who scored low on IQ tests as young children were substantially more likely to commit crime as juveniles or young adults.

Because these ideas were advanced in an era of social activism, they ran counter to the beliefs of many student protesters as well as the views of the education establishment, which was engaged in numerous programs designed to improve the social outcomes of the disadvantaged. Thus both the student activists and the professional education interests sought to discredit Herrnstein's ideas.

As Herrnstein related in *IQ in the Meritocracy,* he had difficulty presenting his argument to university audiences, and his repeated attempts to publish in large newspapers were rebuffed. Yet the reaction of the early 1970s was mild compared to the firestorm that erupted with the publication, within a month of Herrnstein's death, of *The Bell Curve.* After Herrnstein died of lung cancer and was buried in Warsaw, New York, his coauthor, the sociologist Charles Murray, was forced to defend the book alone. It was assaulted both in the press and in various professional publications and conclaves especially for its suggestion that black Americans were less intellectually endowed than white Americans. Much of the criticism dealt with the implications of Herrnstein and Murray's findings for social policy, but a good deal also accused them of manipulating the quantitative data. A number of books were published specifically to refute the conclusions and the methodology of *The Bell Curve.*

Herrnstein's passionate belief in the value of quantification underlay many of his views. He had investigated virtually all the data sets that had been gathered both in the United States and in Europe in great quantity in the era following World War II, and he believed they justified the conclusions he and his various collaborators drew from them. That his conclusions tended to coincide with conservative political opinions at a time when liberal positions dominated the intellectual world left Herrnstein open to verbal assault and occasionally to physical constraints on his ability to express his opinions. The issues he raised remained controversial at the onset of the twenty-first century in the academic and public policy worlds, where the question of "nature versus nurture," or genetic endowment versus environment, had not been conclusively decided.

★

Personal details about Herrnstein are in his entry in *Who's Who in America 1992–1993* (1992). The preface in *I.Q. in the Meritocracy* (1973), details the battles Herrnstein fought with the radicals and the liberal establishment in the early 1970s. Charles Murray, in "The Bell Curve and Its Critics," *Commentary* (May 1995), defends his and Herrnstein's book. Chief among the books that attack Herrnstein's dedication to IQ tests as indicative measurements are Stephen Jay Gould, *The Mismeasure of Man* (1981, 1996); Steve Fraser, ed., *The Bell Curve Wars: Race, Intelligence, and the Future of America* (1995); Russell Jacoby and Naomi Glauberman, *The Bell Curve Debate: History, Documents, Opinions*

(1995); and Bernie Devlin et al., eds., *Intelligence, Genes, and Success* (1997). The most balanced critique of *The Bell Curve* is provided by the economist and Nobel laureate James J. Heckman in "Lessons from the Bell Curve," *Journal of Political Economy* 103, no. 5 (October 1995). Obituaries are in the *Boston Globe* (15 Sept. 1994) and the *New York Times* (16 Sept. 1994).

NANCY M. GORDON

HEXTER, J. H. ("Jack")   (*b.* 25 May 1910 in Memphis, Tennessee; *d.* 8 December 1996 in St. Louis, Missouri), historian and educator who specialized in the Renaissance period, developed historical methodology, and studied the growth of freedom in the West.

Hexter, whose given name was Milton Kaufman, always called himself Jack. The first of two sons born to Milton Jacobs Hexter, a cotton broker, and Alma Marks, a homemaker, he was taken to Cincinnati, Ohio, as a young boy. Raised there by his grandmother Fannie Marks, he received his education in the city's public schools before entering the University of Cincinnati in 1928. Hexter earned his B.A. degree after only three years. He then pursued his graduate studies at Harvard University, where he took an M.A. (1933) and Ph.D. (1937). Under the direction of Wilbur C. Abbott, an authority on Oliver Cromwell, he completed a doctoral dissertation, "The Rise of the Independent Party," which examined the critical role John Pym played in organizing parliamentary opposition to King Charles I. Revised and published in 1941 as *The Reign of King Pym,* it earned him recognition as a specialist in Stuart-era history.

Meanwhile, Hexter had begun his academic career, giving classes at the University of Cincinnati (1936), Harvard University (1937), and Massachusetts Institute of Technology (1938). He then accepted a position as an instructor at Queens College in New York City. His teaching was interrupted by service in the U.S. Army during World War II, when he worked in military intelligence. On 29 March 1942 he married Ruth Mullin; they had four children.

Discharged from the army in 1945, Hexter returned to Queens College. In 1957, having established his scholarly credentials, he moved to Washington University in St. Louis, Missouri, where he spent seven years as a full professor. Drawn to Yale University in 1964, Hexter became director of the Center for Parliamentary History before retiring in 1978. Still energetic and productive, Hexter rejoined Washington University as a distinguished historian in residence and from 1986 to 1990 as John M. Olin Professor of the History of Freedom.

A voracious reader rather than an archival researcher, Hexter wrote, edited, and translated a dozen books and contributed thirty articles and fifty reviews to various scholarly journals. His work often challenged long-held views concerning English history. In *More's* Utopia: *The Biography of an Idea* (1952), Hexter placed the famed humanist in the context of early sixteenth-century political conditions as well as Thomas More's own family situation. He co-edited a new version of *Utopia* (1965), offering a fresh interpretation of the text and More's purpose in writing it. Finally, in *The Vision of Politics on the Eve of the Reformation: More, Machiavelli, and Seyssel* (1973), he compared the political theories set forth in *Utopia, The Prince,* and *The Monarchy of France.*

Hexter's provocative articles, collected in *Reappraisals in History* (1961), stirred considerable controversy. In "The Myth of the Middle Class in Tudor England" he denied the traditional belief that the Tudor monarchs favored wealthy merchants and financiers. His "Storm over the Gentry" challenged the prevalent interpretations concerning rural landowners and their participation in the English Civil War. Heated replies from scholars whose judgments Hexter had questioned soon followed. He used lengthy review-essays to analyze major works by Lawrence Stone, Christopher Hill, and Fernand Braudel. Republishing these in *On Historians: Reappraisals of Some of the Makers of Modern History* (1979), Hexter praised the authors' contributions but critiqued their methodology. The sole scholar Hexter genuinely admired was Garrett Mattingly, whose *Armada* (1959) he lauded for its sound scholarship and elegant prose.

Even as Hexter engaged in historical polemics, he formulated his own philosophy of history and methodology. Beginning with *Reappraisals in History* and continuing with *Doing History* and *The History Primer* (both 1971), he assailed the "analytical philosophers" who, he claimed, misunderstood the true nature of historical writing. He rejected their claim that "scientific" laws could be applied to his discipline. Rather, in "doing history," the trained specialist should employ "common sense" rules to construct a narrative. Hexter also insisted that words be carefully weighed, since the rhetoric of historical writing embodies the structure of an historian's thinking. Using personal experiences instead of far-reaching theories like Marxism, the professional could better grasp the thoughts and actions of historical figures. Hexter proposed a series of simple rules, the most important being to "render the best and most likely account of the human past that can be sustained by the relevant evidence." Ultimately the historian's peers would judge the quality of a work. Puckishly, Hexter used the 1951 baseball pennant race to illustrate his concept of historical narration.

During his second stay at Washington University, he founded and directed the Center for the History of Freedom. Its purpose was to trace the development of liberty in the West between the seventeenth and twentieth centuries. The collapse of Soviet communism gave added impetus to the project, which included annual conferences, each dealing with a different phase of freedom, and subsequent publication of the proceedings. To its initial volume, *Parliament and Liberty from the Reign of Elizabeth to the English Civil War* (1992), Hexter contributed an essay on the freedom of elections under King James I, seeing in this small episode the first efforts to challenge royal prerogative, a step toward the growth of modern freedom.

In later years, Hexter, who was short and stocky, gained considerable weight because he loved fine cuisine. Suffering from a chronic heart condition, he died at his home in St. Louis at the age of eighty-six. He is buried there in Bellefontaine Cemetery.

Hexter's importance resides not only in his conscientious scholarship and advocacy of good writing. Ever the gadfly, he enjoyed questioning received ideas about the past and demolishing unsound philosophical attitudes toward it. He firmly believed that by applying "common language, common sense, and credibility" to historical studies, professional historians could "advance knowledge, understanding, and truth."

★

Hexter's papers remain in his family's possession, but a collection of his correspondence is held at the Center for the History of Freedom at Washington University. In a humorous essay, "Call Me Ishmael, or a Rose by Any Other Name," *American Scholar* 52 (summer 1983), Hexter explains how he adopted the name Jack. An extensive bibliography of his writings is presented in Barbara C. Malament, ed., *After the Reformation: Essays in Honor of J. H. Hexter* (1980), which also offers a discussion by Louis O. Mink of Hexter's philosophy of history. Appreciations are found in the American Historical Association's *Perspectives* (Mar. 1997), *Journal of the History of Ideas* (Apr. 1997), and *Proceedings of the American Philosophical Society* 143 (June 1999). An obituary is in the *New York Times* (16 Dec. 1996).

JAMES FRIGUGLIETTI

HIGHSMITH, (Mary) Patricia (*b.* 19 January 1921 in Fort Worth, Texas; *d.* 4 February 1995 in Locarno, Switzerland), author of twenty-two superb suspense novels, five of which feature her most famous character, Tom Ripley.

Highsmith was the only child of Jay Bernard Plangman and Mary Coates. Her parents separated five months before her birth, and Highsmith did not meet her father until she was twelve. Her mother, a commercial artist, married Stanley Highsmith, a fashion illustrator for *Women's Wear Daily,* who moved his family to New York City. Although Highsmith took her stepfather's name, her mother's second marriage floundered with separations occurring when the child was twelve, sixteen, and nineteen years old. High-

Patricia Highsmith. © JERRY BAUER

smith was deeply alienated from her mother and avoided her for the last two decades of the parent's life. Highsmith's earliest years were spent in Texas with her maternal grandmother, who taught her to read at age two. She finished secondary school at Julia Richman High School in Manhattan, then graduated from Barnard College in 1942 with a B.A. degree in literature and zoology. She was already writing stories; "The Heroine" was first published in *Harper's Bazaar* and then included in the O. Henry Prize Stories of 1946. Highsmith spent much of the 1940s living in Greenwich Village in Manhattan, writing comic books for cash and novels on the weekends. The writer Truman Capote supported her application to Yaddo, the artist colony in upstate New York, where she wrote *Strangers on a Train*. Rejected by six publishers, it was published by Harper Brothers in 1950 and soon made into a classic motion picture directed by Alfred Hitchcock. In this story, two men, Bruno and Guy, meet on a train and make an implicit pact to kill each other's enemies (a former lover and a parent). As with many Highsmith tales, this brief encounter and a seemingly juvenile agreement result in irrational terror, ruined lives, and murder.

Highsmith traveled to Europe in the early 1950s, returned to Manhattan, then journeyed to Mexico and the American Southwest. In 1952 she published *The Price of Salt* under the pen name Claire Morgan. In this pathbreaking novel of lesbian love, the protagonists reunite rather than die as required in standard gay novels. The book sold more than a million copies. Decades later Highsmith acknowledged it as her work and wrote an afterword to a new edition of the book, retitled *Carol* (1991). Her second gay novel, *Found in the Street* (1986) depicted homosexual family relations during the AIDS plague. A third novel about homosexuality, *Small g,* published just before her death in 1995, chronicled relationships gone astray in a gay bar. While many of her novels had gay themes, Highsmith lived alone and refused to discuss her own sexual preferences.

In her nonfiction book *Plotting and Writing Suspense Fiction,* which appeared in 1966 under her own imprint, Highsmith states that "art has nothing to do with morality, convention, or moralizing." This comment led Russell Harrison, the author of the only critical book on Highsmith, to associate Highsmith with the existentialism of Jean-Paul Sartre and Albert Camus. Other scholars have argued that Highsmith's work reflects the psychological fears of middle-class life and the closeted world of 1950s American homosexuality. Graham Greene famously described Highsmith as the "poet of apprehension" in an introduction to one of her works. Additional traits displayed by her characters include a propensity for stalking, inability to differentiate between people and objects, and a casual attitude about murder.

Highsmith's fame rests primarily on her five-volume Tom Ripley series. In the first of these novels, *The Talented Mr. Ripley* (1955), she created the memorable title character, an imposter who invents an Ivy League education and elite social manners. Hired by a wealthy man to induce his son, Dickie Greenleaf, to return from idleness in Europe to work in the family business in the United States, Ripley at first insinuates himself into Greenleaf's circle of émigrés, then kills him when Greenleaf and his friends ultimately reject him. Ripley assumes Greenleaf's identity, forges a will bequeathing the victim's money to himself, and creates a new life of luxury. Two movies have been made of this book, René Clément's *Plein soleil* (*Purple Noon,* 1960) and Anthony Minghella's *The Talented Mr. Ripley* (1999). Highsmith continued the series in *Ripley Under Ground* (1970), in which Ripley counterfeits a dead painter's work and kills an art collector who threatens to expose him. A third novel in the series, *Ripley's Game* (1974), is a story of revenge; Wim Wenders's *Der Amerikanische freund* (*The American Friend,* 1977) is a film version of this novel. *The Boy Who Followed Ripley* (1980) is Highsmith's unsuccessful attempt to establish an heir to Ripley's evil talents; and the last, *Ripley Under Water* (1991) describes how a greedy American pursues the protagonist. The Ripley novels, argues the critic David Cochran, offer the hero as a mixture of the American success story and a cold-blooded, rationalist killer, through whose behavior Highsmith questions the means and legitimacy of American supremacy in the cold war.

Highsmith has generally been labeled as a crime and suspense novelist. She did not reject this description, noting that crime novels sold well and provided a good living. Since her death, however, many critics have agreed that Highsmith created her own genre, in which life is a trap with no escape. Her terror is more psychological than physically brutal. Though such acts as Ripley's murder of Dickie Greenleaf usually set the plot in motion, other novels include no violence. Yet the result is inevitably the same, the suffocation of the individual's spirit. Despite his triumphs over rivals, for example, Tom Ripley could never be described as happy, merely smug. Highsmith did not pursue artistic prose but preferred blunt, matter-of-fact language that seduces the reader into complicity with murder. At times she came close to political statements. In *The Cry of the Owl* (1962), a community turns against the hero, a turn of events critics have likened to McCarthyism.

Originally an attractive woman, Highsmith's features became more severe as she aged, perhaps because of her smoking habit. She moved to Europe permanently in 1961, living in England from 1963 to 1966, France from 1967 to 1982, and Switzerland from 1982 until her death. She enjoyed an isolated existence, preferring not to talk to other people. Visitors found her polite but reclusive. Her companions were cats; in her 1975 collection of short stories *The Animal-Lover's Book of Beastly Murders,* household pets torture their owners. Highsmith rarely visited the United States and her work has always sold far better in Europe than in her native land. She died alone in Locarno of lung cancer and aplastic anemia. She left no survivors and bequeathed her entire estate of $3 million to Yaddo. Highsmith's influence is strongest among writers who combine suspense with feminist and/or lesbian fiction, a fairly new genre.

★

The fullest discussion is Russell Harrison, *Patricia Highsmith* (1997). Useful articles include David Cochran, "'Some Torture That Perversely Eased': Patricia Highsmith and the Everyday Schizophrenia of American Life," *Clues* 18 (1997): 157–180; and Susannah Clapp, "The Simple Art of Murder," *New Yorker* (20 Dec. 1999). An obituary is in the *New York Times* (5 Feb. 1995).

GRAHAM RUSSELL HODGES

HILL, Julian Werner (*b.* 4 September 1904 in St. Louis, Missouri; *d.* 28 January 1996 in Hockessin, Delaware), Du Pont research chemist whose work in the 1930s led to the creation of nylon, one of the company's most versatile and lucrative products.

Hill was the son of Werner Kamlah Hill and Pearl Sames Reuther. He attended local schools and graduated from Washington University in St. Louis in 1924. Hill then earned a doctorate in organic chemistry from the Massachusetts Institute of Technology in 1928.

In 1928 Hill went to work for DuPont Company and became a member of the team studying the behavior of certain molecules that combine to form polymers as part of the efforts in pure research the company sponsored at the time. He and other DuPont scientists had reported progress in developing artificial silks like rayon, then coming into use. In 1930 Hill tried to synthesize larger polymers by changing the experimental conditions of his chemical reactions. He and his team accidentally came up with a concoction that the head of DuPont research, Wallace Hume Carothers, thought useless. However, Hill found that the material could be shaped into strands that were remarkably long and strong. His accidental discovery of this tough, taffylike compound revolutionized everyday life, and it proved its worth in many practical applications. Introduced at the 1939 World's Fair in New York City, the substance was named nylon. On 23 July 1934 Hill married Mary Louisa ("Polly") Butcher; they had three children.

Nylon's first practical application to a consumer product came in 1938, when the polymer was introduced as tooth-

Julian Hill reenacting his invention of nylon, 1948. HAGLEY MUSEUM AND LIBRARY

brush bristles. What made it a commercial success was its use in stockings, first sold to consumers in 1939. Similar to silk but far less expensive, nylon became the ideal replacement for the silk of stockings and other fashionable clothing. It was also used for fishing lines and surgical sutures.

When the United States entered World War II, the government used most of the nation's limited supplies of nylon for making parachutes, ropes, and many other military supplies. Since there was not enough nylon for both military and civilian uses, nylon stockings were rationed until the end of the war. During that time, nylon stockings became a valuable item of barter in Europe and achieved the status of an informal currency. Not until the early 1950s was there sufficient production capacity to provide enough of the material for other consumer and commercial uses. Because DuPont held the patent for nylon, Hill did not make a lot of money from his discovery.

Hill was a birdwatcher and wildlife lover, and he expressed his concern over nylon's effects on the environment. He played the violin and was an avid squash player. During the last years of his career Hill supervised DuPont's program giving aid to universities for research in physics and chemistry. He retired from DuPont in 1964. Hill died in Hockessin, at the Cokesbury Village retirement community, where he had lived for several years.

★

For further information on Hill see Charles R. Cornell, ed., *Biography Index: A Cumulative Index to Biographical Material in Books and Magazines, September 1995–August 1996* (1996); and *American Men and Women of Science,* 13th ed. (1976). An obituary is in the *New York Times* (1 Feb. 1996) and *Time* (12 Feb. 1996).

MARIA PACHECO

HISS, Alger (*b.* 11 November 1904 in Baltimore, Maryland; *d.* 15 November 1996 in New York City), U.S. State Department official and foundation president best known for his conviction in 1950 on perjury charges related to allegations that he had been an undercover agent for the Soviet Union during the 1930s and had delivered State Department documents and information to a Communist courier. From the earliest public charges of involvement in Soviet espionage in 1948 until his death almost a half-century later, Hiss denied the allegations against him.

Hiss was one of five children born to Mary Lavinia ("Minnie") Hughes, a homemaker, and Charles Alger Hiss, a Baltimore dry goods importer and jobber. His father died when Alger was two and a half years old. Hiss attended Baltimore's public schools, graduating from the public high school Baltimore City College in 1921 before entering Johns Hopkins University. After graduating from Johns Hopkins in 1926, Hiss entered Harvard Law School, where

Alger Hiss. LIBRARY OF CONGRESS

he served on the *Law Review.* Upon graduating in 1929 he clerked for the Supreme Court justice Oliver Wendell Holmes, Jr., and soon after assuming his new post he married Priscilla Fansler Hobson on 11 December 1929. Hobson brought with her a son from a previous marriage and the couple had one son together.

After Hiss completed his clerkship with Justice Holmes the family moved to Boston, where Hiss worked for the law firm of Choate, Hall and Stewart. They remained in Boston until 1932, when Hiss resigned to join Cotton and Franklin, a New York City corporate law firm. In New York both Hiss and his wife, like many others in that depression decade, became active in left-liberal reform political activities. In the spring of 1933 Alger Hiss accepted an invitation to join the staff of Jerome Frank, general counsel to one of President Franklin D. Roosevelt's liveliest agencies, the Agricultural Adjustment Administration (AAA). According to the testimony of, among others, Whittaker Chambers, a self-confessed former communist courier and Hiss's chief accuser, Hiss first took part in a secret communist "study group" of New Deal officials during his tenure at the AAA.

In July 1934 Hiss joined the legal staff of a Senate committee, chaired by Senator Gerald Nye, investigating the impact of foreign and domestic munitions makers on American policy during and after World War I. Hiss, Chambers, and their wives agreed that the two couples first met during this period, although they disputed the circumstances.

During the fall of 1936, after a brief stint at the Justice Department, Hiss, a tall, handsome man who bore a similarity to the actor James Stewart, began working at the State Department as an assistant to the Assistant Secretary Francis B. Sayre. Hiss rose rapidly in the department, in less than a decade becoming a trusted adviser to the secretary of state and other leading U.S. government officials. Chambers alleged and evidence confirmed to the satisfaction of a trial jury in 1950 that when Hiss reached the State Department in 1936 he began actively delivering State Department materials to Chambers while continuing a covert life, begun while he was with the Nye committee, as a Soviet agent.

Chambers severed his links with the communist underground in 1938 and, on various occasions over the next decade in interviews with Federal Bureau of Investigation (FBI) and State Department officials, named Hiss and others as former associates. Chambers's first interview took place on 23 August 1939 with Adolf A. Berle, Jr., then in charge of security matters at the State Department. Berle's notes of the discussion, a list of those named by Chambers, included the following reference: "*Alger Hiss*/Ass't to Sayre—CP—37/Member of the Underground Com.—/ Active."

Despite the information given to Berle, no formal investigation of Hiss occurred as he rose in State Department ranks. In 1944 Hiss joined the important, newly created Office of Special Political Affairs in a policy-making position concerned with postwar planning for international organizations. Hiss became director of the office in March 1945, by which time he had become a trusted aide to the Secretary of State Edward Stettinius. The previous month Hiss had accompanied Stettinius, President Roosevelt, and others in the U.S. delegation to the Yalta Conference. In April 1945 Hiss served as the U.S. coordinator and temporary secretary general of the United Nations organizing conference in San Francisco, the high point of his career at the State Department.

By that time, amidst growing postwar tensions in U.S.–Soviet relations, FBI and State Department security officials had begun investigations of Hiss based on the allegations made by Chambers and other informants. Hiss resigned from the State Department in 1946 to become president of the Carnegie Endowment for International Peace, his government career effectively sidetracked by the rumors and probes of alleged communist involvement. The allegations pursued Hiss to his new post. Despite continuing FBI interviews, the issue probably would have died for lack of evidence except for a hastily scheduled hearing of the controversial House Un-American Activities Committee (HUAC) on 3 August 1948. There Chambers testified as a reluctant witness, and Hiss became the focus of public attention.

The hearing had been called to try to confirm earlier testimony by another former Soviet agent, Elizabeth Bent-

ley, concerning allegations of communist spy rings in Washington. Chambers again named Hiss as having been involved in clandestine activities during the mid-1930s though not as an espionage agent. Hiss immediately demanded to be heard by the committee and appeared before HUAC two days later. He categorically denied either knowing Chambers or having participated in any way in communist activities. Several members of the committee, however, notably the young California representative Richard M. Nixon, decided to pursue the inquiry and determine whether Hiss or Chambers had told the truth concerning their personal relationship. Hiss denied one, while Chambers had testified in stunning detail of family visits, apartment loans, the gift of an automobile, and other aspects of the Hiss family life. During a heated and dramatic confrontation at the Commodore Hotel in New York City organized by Nixon on 17 August, Hiss acknowledged having known Chambers. But he insisted he knew Chambers as "George Crosley," a free-lance journalist whom Hiss claimed to have befriended briefly. According to Hiss, the impecunious "Crosley" abused his hospitality. Eight days later Hiss and Chambers repeated their respective accounts of the relationship before a televised HUAC hearing in Washington, D.C.

The matter might still have rested there had Hiss not challenged his accuser to repeat his allegations in a noncongressional forum, thereby opening him to a lawsuit. Chambers did just that during a *Meet the Press* radio interview on 27 August. A month later, on 27 September, Hiss filed suit in Baltimore against Chambers for slander. During pretrial depositions on 17 November, Chambers was challenged by Hiss's attorneys to produce evidence of Hiss's complicity in communist activities, and the issue shifted abruptly from credibility to espionage. Chambers handed over to Hiss's lawyers sixty-five pages of retyped State Department cables and dispatches covering the period from 5 January 1938 to 1 April 1938, the month Chambers left the communist underground. Chambers claimed that Hiss had given him these documents and four handwritten notes.

Both Hiss and Chambers were then summoned to testify before a grand jury in New York City, which was already investigating various allegations of Soviet espionage. On 2 December Chambers turned over to HUAC investigators at his Maryland farm two strips of developed film containing State Department documents from the same period as the typed and handwritten material previously handed over on 17 November. In addition he delivered three rolls of undeveloped film, two of which held Navy Department documents also from early 1938. More than any other factor, the dramatic appearance in November and early December of the typed documents, handwritten notes, and microfilm, which at the trials the prosecutor collectively called the "immutable witnesses," persuaded U.S. government attorneys to abandon an earlier plan to indict both Hiss and Chambers. Instead, they decided to indict Hiss alone. On 15 December the grand jury indicted Hiss on two counts of perjury for denying that he had given Chambers the purloined State Department documents and for denying having known Chambers during the period covered by the documents. The statute of limitations precluded indicting Hiss on the more serious charge of espionage assumed by the perjury indictments. Hiss pleaded not guilty on both counts.

Hiss's trial began on 31 May 1949 at the federal courthouse in Foley Square in Manhattan. The four principal witnesses at this trial and the one that followed—Alger Hiss, Priscilla Hiss, Whittaker Chambers, and Esther Chambers—spent many hours testifying and endured vigorous cross-examination. The defense argued that other communist agents at the State Department could have transferred the material in question to Chambers. Alternatively, the defense argued that Chambers, as "George Crosley," became fixated on Hiss, who rebuffed his friendship, and therefore Chambers was determined for malicious reasons to frame Hiss a decade later. Thomas Murphy, the main government prosecutor, focused both on the wealth of detail produced by Whittaker and Esther Chambers concerning their relationship with the Hiss's as fellow communists and, in the end, on the evidence of the documents—the so-called "immutable witnesses." The government's experts also showed, through other letters typed on the Woodstock typewriter that produced the sixty-five pages of State Department documents, that the machine was the same one owned and used by Hiss at the time.

On 7 July the jury deadlocked, eight for conviction and four for acquittal. A retrial began on 17 November 1949, exactly a year from the date that Chambers had submitted the typed and handwritten documents to Hiss's attorneys at the Baltimore slander trial. The second trial substantially replayed the first trial's basic arguments and evidence, although a defense effort to show with psychiatric testimony that Hiss's accuser, Chambers, was mentally unbalanced fell flat in the opinion of most observers. On 21 January 1950 the jury found Hiss guilty on both counts of perjury. All of Hiss's subsequent appeals for a new trial or for setting aside the verdict were rejected by appellate courts at the time and later. Hiss's verdict intensified the anticommunist mood of the country in 1950, as did the outbreak of the Korean War in June, Senator Joseph McCarthy's demagogic emergence that year, and a series of unrelated but dramatic spy trials regarding alleged atomic espionage.

On 22 March 1951 Hiss began serving his sentence at the Lewisburg, Pennsylvania, federal penitentiary. Still proclaiming his innocence when he left prison in 1954, Hiss spent several years working on a book he considered more a meticulous brief for the defense than a personal memoir,

In the Court of Public Opinion, published in 1957. In the decades that followed he was a popular, effective, and much-in-demand speaker at universities.

During the immediate postprison years Hiss held a series of jobs in small business. In 1959 he separated from his wife. In the decades that followed Hiss developed a devoted circle of friends and supporters, and he continued to live in New York City and to summer in the Hamptons. His major focus remained on arguing his innocence, and he cooperated with various authors by discussing the case and opening his papers. Hiss's greatest advantage "in the court of public opinion" remained his other chief adversary, Nixon, whose activities during the Watergate crisis revived interest for a time in Hiss's claims. Chambers, who had also remained obsessed with the case and had published a memoir, *Witness* (1952), died on 9 July 1961.

In August 1975 the Massachusetts Supreme Judicial Court approved Hiss's application for readmission to the bar without requiring from him any acknowledgement of guilt, a dramatic illustration of the public and legal mood at the time. "Mr. Nixon is sort of a press agent for me," Hiss observed in a 1973 interview. Nonetheless, as Nixon disappeared from public notice, various efforts by Hiss, his attorneys, and a dwindling number of defenders during the 1980s and 1990s to reopen legal proceedings or at least to rekindle public interest in the case failed to catch fire. Personally, however, Hiss's final decade appears to have been a happy one. After the death of his wife in 1984, Hiss married Isabel Johnson in 1985; they had no children. With his second wife, Hiss divided his life between residences in Manhattan and the Hamptons. As the journalist David Remnick wrote in 1986, Hiss was "a fixture on a certain level of the social circuit. His friends are editors, artists, musicians, civil liberties attorneys."

Had Hiss not been indicted and convicted on the charges he confronted in 1948–1950, he might have left a completely reputable but more modest legacy as a skilled attorney, promising New Deal bureaucrat, State Department official, and foundation president. Because of the legal case, however, both Hiss and his accuser Chambers emerged in their own time as icons in the demonologies and hagiographies of their opposing camps of supporters. The case lived on in American political debate, with conservatives invoking Hiss's presumed treachery to indict the Roosevelt and Truman administrations for tolerating such figures in their ranks.

For many liberals and radicals, on the other hand, the political loyalties of those who pictured Hiss as a subversive, including Chambers, Nixon, and J. Edgar Hoover, persuaded them that Hiss had somehow been an innocent victim of perjured testimony and concocted evidence. A plethora of conspiracy theories emerged. The assault on Hiss, his defenders argued, foreshadowed a larger effort by

Republicans to discredit New Deal liberalism and bipartisan internationalism. Both sides in time agreed that Hiss's conviction helped transform American public opinion on the question of communism in American government. "Without the Alger Hiss case," the historian Earl Latham correctly noted in his study of the McCarthy era spy probes, "the six-year controversy that followed might have been a much tamer affair and the Communist issue somewhat more tractable." In time, however, most though not all anticommunist liberals came to accept Hiss's guilt.

Why, then, has the case continued to have cultural and public resonance, even after the deaths of its protagonists? One of the most sensible answers to this question comes from Remnick, who wrote of Hiss in the *Washington Post Magazine* in 1986: "His persistence gives him the *possibility* of martyrdom, even if he is probably not one. It has helped him win friends, loyal defenders. Ambiguity has been a savior to him."

On 15 November 1996 Hiss died of emphysema in New York City. Extensive front-page obituaries filled the nation's newspapers the following day, most accepting his guilt, and Hiss's death was prominently reported on America's major television network news programs. Thus, although its major figures had died, the Hiss case and the issues it raised, both in substance and symbol, remained alive.

★

Hiss's *In the Court of Public Opinion* (1957) provides his retrospective brief for the defense, and his later work, *Recollections of a Life* (1988), gives a more revealing personal account. Hiss's son, Tony Hiss, discussed his parents and the case in *Laughing Last* (1977) and offered a fascinating view of Hiss's prison experiences in *The View from Alger's Window: A Son's Memoir* (1999). Two comprehensive and scholarly works that provide an overview of Hiss's life and an analysis of the Hiss case are Allen Weinstein, *Perjury: The Hiss-Chambers Case,* rev. ed. (1997), and Sam Tanenhaus, *Whittaker Chambers: A Biography* (1997). Both Weinstein and Tanenhaus argued that Chambers's account of his relationship with Hiss was substantially accurate and that Hiss was guilty of the perjury charges leveled against him. Alistair Cooke, *A Generation on Trial* (1952), is a balanced and informative narrative of the case by the most dispassionate observer of the two trials at the time. Two comprehensive books that argue Hiss's innocence are Meyer A. Zeligs, *Friendship and Fratricide* (1967), and John Chabot Smith, *Alger Hiss: The True Story* (1976). An obituary is in the *New York Times* (16 Nov. 1996).

ALLEN WEINSTEIN

HOBBY, Oveta Culp (*b.* 19 January 1905 in Killeen, Texas; *d.* 16 August 1995 in Houston, Texas), commander of the Women's Army Corps during World War II, first secretary of the Department of Health, Education, and Welfare, and publisher of the *Houston Post.*

Hobby was the second of seven children born to Isaac William ("Ike") Culp and Emma Elizabeth Hoover. She was a precocious child who visited her father's law office after school each day to read books and other literature, including the *Congressional Record,* which expanded her vocabulary. At age thirteen she had read the Bible three times and was designated the best speller in her class. Early evidence of an independent nature was her refusal to sign a Sunday school pledge against alcohol use because she refused to give her word regarding a subject on which she had not made a decision. When she was fourteen years old her father was elected a member of the Texas legislature and she accompanied him to Austin, beginning a lifelong association with politics.

Hobby graduated from Killeen High School at the top of her class and briefly considered a career in the theater after a Chautauqua manager, impressed with her dramatic reading, offered her a touring contract. Bowing to her parents' objections, she enrolled in Mary Hardin Baylor College in Belton, Texas, and became a cub reporter for the *Austin American Statesman.* In 1925 the speaker of the Texas House of Representatives asked Hobby, then age twenty, to become parliamentarian of the House. She served in the post until 1931 and later wrote *Mr. Chairman* (1937), a book on parliamentary law, and continued her studies at the University of Texas, though she did not graduate.

Hobby, who had been a clerk for the State Banking Commission before her appointment as parliamentarian, was active in the Democratic Club. She helped plan the

Oveta Culp Hobby *(left).*

party's national nominating convention in Houston in 1928 and worked for the election of Senator Tom Connally in his defeat of the Ku Klux Klan candidate, Earle B. Mayfield. She worked as an assistant to Houston's city attorney until released to resume her duties as parliamentarian of the Texas House, and ran unsuccessfully for a legislative post at the age of twenty-five. She was defeated partially because her opponent accused her of being "a parliamentarian and a Unitarian."

On 23 February 1931 she married William Pettus Hobby, who had served as governor of Texas from 1917 to 1921. The groom was fifty-three years of age and the bride twenty-six. She joined him at the *Houston Post-Dispatch,* then owned by former governor Ross Sterling. Later the Hobbys bought the newspaper and also acquired radio and television interests. By 1955 Hobby's career in journalism had included duties as book editor, assistant editor, executive vice president, and president. She also served as president of the League of Women Voters in Texas and was active as a board member of fine-arts organizations in Houston. The Hobbys were the parents of two children. Their son, William Pettus Hobby, Jr., served as lieutenant governor of Texas from 1973 to 1991.

In 1941 Hobby visited Washington to represent family interests before the Federal Communications Commission. While there, General David Searles asked her to organize women's activities for the army. She declined, but accepted a subsequent request that she help plan the Women's Interest Section, War Department Bureau of Public Relations. She visited British and French women's military auxiliaries at the request of General George Marshall to learn from their experiences. Hobby was in Chicago on a speaking engagement when Japanese air and naval forces attacked Pearl Harbor on 7 December 1941; General Marshall called her speech the first declaration of war against Japan. He then asked Hobby to prepare a list of names of women who could command a Women's Auxiliary Army Corps (renamed in 1943 the Women's Army Corp, or WACs.) He read the list, then said, "I'd rather you took the job." Hobby entered the army with the rank of major and eventually reached full colonel, though she admitted, "I never did learn to salute properly or master the thirty-inch stride." She endured slights from male soldiers. Army engineers refused to help her design barracks for WACs, and the quartermaster corps ignored her suggestions for uniforms. Despite reluctance by males to accept them, women were eventually qualified to perform 264 jobs in the military service, releasing hundreds of thousands of men for combat or combat-support duty. Though the WACs had a strength authorization of only 150,000, requests for their assignment reached 600,000.

Hobby resigned from the army in 1945 and returned to Houston as director of KPRC radio and KPRC-TV. She accepted positions on the boards of the American National Red Cross, the American Cancer Society, and the American Society of Newspaper Editors, among others, and was a member of the United Nations Commission on Freedom of Information and the Press in 1948.

Although a Democrat, she worked for the election of the Republican presidential candidate Thomas E. Dewey in 1948 and headed Democrats for Eisenhower in 1952. In January 1953 President Dwight D. Eisenhower appointed Hobby chairman of the Federal Security Agency and invited her to participate in Cabinet meetings. On 11 April 1953 Congress elevated the agency to Cabinet status and renamed it the Department of Health, Education, and Welfare. Hobby became the second woman to hold a Cabinet position and the first to hold that rank since the departure of Frances Perkins, Franklin D. Roosevelt's secretary of labor. Hobby's agency had a $17.7 billion annual budget (in 1953 dollars). During her term the Salk polio vaccine was introduced and there was a significant increase in federal funding for hospitals.

After thirty-one months in office, Hobby returned to Houston in 1955 because of her husband's declining health and resumed duties as president and editor of the *Houston Post.* She also accepted positions on the boards of Rice University, the Texas Heart Association, General Foods Corporation, and the Carnegie Commission on Educational Television. Hobby was named to the Texas Women's Hall of Fame in 1984. She died of a stroke and is buried in Glenwood Cemetery in Houston.

★

The best source is an article written by Hobby's son, William Pettus Hobby, Jr., for Ron Tyler et al., *The New Handbook of Texas,* vol. 3 (1996): 637–640. A biography appears in Ann Fears Crawford and Crystal Sasse Ragsdale, *Women in Texas* (1982). Hobby is discussed in Marguerite Johnston, *Houston, The Unknown City, 1836–1946* (1991). A biography published shortly after Hobby was named secretary of the Department of Health, Education, and Welfare appears in *Current Biography 1953.* Obituaries are in the *New York Times* (17 Aug. 1995) and the *Austin American Statesman* (19 Aug. 1995).

Archie P. McDonald

HOLMAN, Nathan ("Nat") (*b.* 19 October 1896 in New York City; *d.* 12 February 1995 in New York City), professional basketball player, college coach, and a pioneer of basketball who was elected to the Basketball Hall of Fame in 1964.

Holman was the fourth of ten children of Russian Jewish immigrants, Louis Holman and Mary Goldman. His father ran a small grocery, where Holman and his six brothers helped with stocking and shelving. Nat began playing basketball at a local settlement house on the Lower East Side of Manhattan, but he also participated in other sports; his enthusiasm for athletics was motivated by the example of

Nat Holman, *c.* 1934. © BETTMANN/CORBIS

his older brothers and also by his natural ability. At Commerce High School, Holman played four sports—basketball, football, soccer (as a goalie), and baseball (as a pitcher and shortstop).

After graduating from high school in 1913, Holman enrolled at Savage School of Physical Education. Rather than play college basketball, he immediately accepted an offer to play professional basketball for the Hoboken, New Jersey, team, where he scored twenty-three points in his first professional game. During his college years, Holman also played for New York's Knickerbocker Big Five, which paid him $5 a game, as well as for the professional teams of Greenville, New York, and Norwalk of the Connecticut League. He graduated from Savage with a B.S. degree in 1917 and took a position coaching the junior varsity basketball team at the City College of New York (CCNY) for the 1917–1918 season.

In the 1917–1918 season Holman played for independent teams in the New York City region when all the top leagues suspended play for World War I. From 1918 to 1919 he served in the navy. Holman then returned to coach at CCNY, where he also coached varsity soccer and taught courses in hygiene; at the age of twenty-three he was the youngest college coach in the United States. Meanwhile, he enrolled at New York University, where he earned a master's degree in physical education in 1920.

From 1919 to 1930 Holman led a double life as a player and a coach. In the 1919–1920 season Holman played for Jersey City of the Interstate League, Albany of the New York State League, Scranton of the Penn State League,

Germantown of the Eastern League, and with several independent New York City–based squads. His CCNY team went 13–3, playing mostly on Saturday nights, allowing him to travel to play professional games during the week.

During the 1920–1921 season, Holman's CCNY team went 11–4. That season he played once again for Germantown and Scranton and was also on the Westfield, Massachusetts, team of the Interstate League and the New York Whirlwinds, an independent team owned by the famous sports promoter Tex Rickard. As a professional player, Holman was known as a great ball handler, able to see the entire court and anticipate his teammates' movements. He was an excellent scorer—in 1920–1921 he led the Eastern League in scoring while with Germantown. He was also famous for being able to draw fouls on opponents. One promotional brochure from 1921 referred to him as "the cleverest man with a basketball playing today."

From 1921 to 1928 Holman played exclusively for the famous original Celtics team of New York, one of four teams enshrined in the Naismith Memorial Basketball Hall of Fame in Springfield, Massachusetts. During that time, the Celtics played in the Eastern League in 1921–1922, winning the championship, and the Metropolitan League in 1922–1923, compiling a 12–0 record before withdrawing from that league and returning to the Eastern League. When the Eastern League collapsed in January 1923, the Celtics barnstormed throughout the Northeast and Midwest, even engaging in a southeastern tour one year. The Celtics returned to league play in the American Basketball League (ABL) for the 1926–1927 and 1927–1928 seasons, winning the league championship both seasons. Playing as many as 200 games in a season, they won more than 90 percent.

After the 1927–1928 season the league broke up the Celtics; their great success discouraged fans in other cities and attendance at games not involving the Celtics dropped precipitously. In 1928–1929 Holman played for the New York Hakoahs, an all-Jewish squad competing in the ABL. In 1929–1930 Holman played his final season of professional basketball with the Chicago Bruins of the ABL.

All this time, Holman had been running a summer camp, Camp Scatico, in the Catskill Mountains northwest of New York City (he had purchased the camp in the early 1920s) as well as coaching at CCNY, where he had compiled a record of 134–40 in eleven years. When he was offered another job as director of health and physical education at a new Young Men's Hebrew Association (YMHA) in Manhattan, he chose to retire as a player at the age of thirty-three.

Holman continued to coach at CCNY, and in 1950 his squad performed a singular act, now impossible; it won both the National Collegiate Athletic Association (NCAA) and the National Invitational Tournament (NIT) titles.

The NIT was, at that time, the more prestigious tournament. The gold of this victory turned to dross the next year when it was discovered that players at many top colleges, including CCNY, had accepted bribes to shave points to help gamblers meet the point spread in many games. Though Holman was never accused and never knew anything of his players' behavior in the point fixing, the incident called his coaching into question and he was forced to resign in 1952. At CCNY'S request, he returned to coach again in the 1955–1956 and 1959–1960 seasons, compiling a total record at CCNY of 422 wins and 188 losses—one of college basketball's all-time best winning percentages. But the college had greatly deemphasized basketball following the scandals, and Holman never recovered from what he felt was his players' betrayal of him, their school, and the sport.

After his retirement in 1960, Holman continued to run Camp Scatico. He coached in Israel and became a goodwill ambassador for basketball and Israeli sports. He remained in contact with his players over the years, encouraging them to support sports for Israel and visiting with them at CCNY basketball games.

Holman had married late in life, wedding Ruth Jackson in 1945, and when his wife died at the age of fifty-two in 1967, he was devastated. In the last years of his life he resided at the Hebrew Home for the Aged in the Riverdale section of the Bronx. Reluctant to see many visitors, and having outlived his teammates, most of his family, and many of his players, he died on 12 February 1995 at the age of ninety-eight.

Holman was elected to the Basketball Hall of Fame in 1964 after being nominated by his longtime friend and teammate Joe Lapchick. Among the qualities that made Holman a legendary figure in the sport were his unprecedented analytical abilities regarding basketball: despite his critical nature and aloofness, no one ever questioned Holman's innovative genius as a player and a coach. He wrote four books on basketball that were widely read and praised, and his pioneering talents in the early days of the sport earned him the sobriquet "Mr. Basketball," by which he was known to fans of the game.

★

Although Holman did not write a full-length autobiography, his book *Scientific Basketball* (1922) contains a chapter on his early playing career. One of his other coaching books, *Holman on Basketball* (1950), includes his comments about the victories in the NCAA and NIT tournaments in 1950. Murray Nelson, *The Originals: The New York Celtics Invent Modern Basketball* (1999), is a lengthy study of the original Celtics from 1915 to 1928 with featured selections on each of the players, with emphasis on Holman and Joe Lapchick, the two best-known players. Bernard Postal, Jesse Silver, and Roy Silver, *Encyclopedia of Jews in Sports* (1955),

features a biography of Holman. Charles Rosen, *Scandals of '51: How the Gamblers Almost Killed College Basketball* (1978), is an examination of the college basketball point-shaving scandal of 1951; Holman's life and career are discussed in length. There is an obituary in the *New York Times* (13 Feb. 1995).

MURRY R. NELSON

HOOKER, Evelyn Gentry (*b.* 2 September 1907 in North Platte, Nebraska; *d.* 18 November 1996 in Santa Monica, California), psychologist whose groundbreaking research demonstrated that homosexuality is not a mental disorder.

Hooker was one of nine children born to Edward Gentry and Jessie Bethel, an impoverished farming couple in North Platte, Nebraska. When she was thirteen, she and her family loaded up their prairie schooner (one of her fondest childhood memories) and moved to Sterling, a small town in northeastern Colorado.

Admonished by her mother, who had only a third-grade education, to "get an education . . . they can never take it away from you," Hooker was determined to pursue college studies. Expecting to attend a teacher's college, she was encouraged by several faculty members to enroll at the University of Colorado at Boulder, which she did in 1924 with a tuition scholarship. Hooker became a psychology major under the tutelage of Karl Muenzinger, who offered Hooker an instructorship her senior year and became her adviser as she pursued a master's degree in psychology after being awarded a bachelor's degree in 1928. After earning a master's degree in psychology from the University of Colorado in 1930, Hooker was offered a teaching position there. Despite the fact that the nation was in the midst of the Great Depression and jobs were few, she refused the offer and decided to pursue doctoral studies. Hooker wanted to attend Yale University, but the chairman of the Colorado psychology department, a Yale graduate, refused to recommend a woman for admission. Hooker thus attended Johns Hopkins University and in 1932 received a Ph.D. in experimental psychology. After receiving her degree, Hooker joined the faculty of the Maryland College for Women and taught there until the fall of 1934, when she became ill with tuberculosis. Following a year's recuperation at an Arizona sanatorium, Hooker taught for a year at Whittier College near Palo Alto, California. She applied for a fellowship to study in Europe for a year, and in 1937, increasingly interested in clinical psychology, she attended the Berlin Institute of Psychotherapy. There Hooker lived with a Jewish family and saw firsthand the rise of Adolf Hitler and the persecution of select groups, which spawned her desire to "make her life count in helping to correct social injustice."

In 1939, after another year at Whittier, Hooker became

a research associate in the psychology department at the University of California at Los Angeles (UCLA). Except for a brief teaching stint at Bryn Mawr (1947–1948), Hooker remained at UCLA, where she conducted research and taught experimental and physiological psychology until her retirement from academic life in 1970.

While teaching an introductory course at UCLA in 1945, Hooker befriended one of her brightest students, a man named Sam From. Socializing outside the classroom, From introduced Hooker and her husband (she had married Donn Caldwell, a freelance writer, in 1941) to his circle of gay friends, both men and women, many of whom were among the intelligentsia of the day, including Christopher Isherwood and Stephen Spender. From urged Hooker to conduct research on homosexuals, contending that it was "her scientific duty to study people like us." Hooker had believed all the while that he and his friends were well-adjusted individuals, which contradicted the prevailing belief that homosexuality was a mental illness. Scientific curiosity prompted her to explore From's idea. She began to administer psychological tests to homosexual men whom From helped her recruit, but abandoned the project after divorcing Caldwell in 1947 and taking a teaching position at Bryn Mawr. She returned to California a year later, and in 1951 in London, England, married Edward Niles Hooker, distinguished professor of English at UCLA.

Determined to resume her study of homosexual men, and bolstered by the 1948 Kinsey Institute findings that homosexuality was more widespread than previously thought, in 1953 Hooker applied to the National Institute of Mental Health (NIMH) for a grant to study the adjustment of nonpathological homosexual men. The application, she was told by John Eberhart, chief of the NIMH grants division, was most unusual. After all, in the 1950s, at the height of the McCarthy era, homosexuality was considered to be a mental disorder by psychology professionals, a crime according to the law, and a sin in the eyes of the church. Moreover, there had been no scientific data gathered about homosexuals in settings other than prisons or mental institutions. Eberhart was persuaded by her proposal and awarded Hooker the NIMH grant.

Hooker recruited sixty male subjects (thirty homosexuals and thirty heterosexuals) whom she matched by age, socioeconomic status, and intelligence level. Each individual was given three projective personality tests widely used at the time—the Rorschach Test, the Thematic Apperception Test, and the Make-a-Picture-Story Test. Hooker submitted the results to three nationally recognized psychologists who were unaware of the subjects' sexual orientation. First, they evaluated each test for overall psychological adjustment; second, presented with pairs test results (of matched individuals), they attempted to distinguish the homosexual from heterosexual subjects. The results demon-

strated that in the Rorschach Test the judges could not reliably distinguish the homosexual men from the comparable heterosexual men. The other two tests elicited narratives that did identify homosexuals. But overall, the scientists could not identify any adjustment differences. Hooker presented her findings, "The Adjustment of the Male Overt Homosexual," at the American Psychological Association Convention on 30 August 1956 in Chicago, Illinois, and published them in the *Journal of Projective Techniques* the following year.

Hooker continued her research into the 1960s and, because of her recognition as a leading authority on homosexual behavior, was asked in 1967 by the NIMH to head its task force on homosexuality. The final report of the task force was issued on 10 October 1969 and recommended, among other things, the establishment of the Center for the Study of Sexual Behavior and the repeal of sodomy laws.

Hooker authored several scientific articles, many of which were published in the *Journal of Projective Techniques* and contributed to several books on homosexuality. In 1970 Hooker retired from research at UCLA and established a private clinical practice in Santa Monica, California. She died at the age of eighty-nine and was buried at Woodlawn Cemetery in Santa Monica, next to her husband Edward Hooker, who had died in 1957. There were no children from either of her marriages.

An imposing woman with a six-foot frame (she was often compared to Eleanor Roosevelt), Evelyn Hooker was described by many as a researcher with a keen intellect, a charismatic educator, and a compassionate individual with a compelling sense of humor. She is remembered most for her pioneering study of homosexual men that provided empirical evidence that homosexuals were not inherently abnormal. Her research was a major influence on the 1974 decision by the American Psychiatric Association to remove homosexuality from its official list of mental disorders (*Diagnostic and Statistical Manual of Mental Disorders,* 3d ed.), acting on the governing board's recommendation of December 1973. In 1975 the American Psychological Association resolved that homosexuality per se implied no mental impairment but rather was within the normal range of human behavior. Hooker received many accolades throughout her career, including the American Psychological Association Award for Distinguished Contributions to Psychology in the Public Interest, the association's highest honor, in 1991. The writer Eric Marcus called Hooker the "Rosa Parks of the gay rights movement"; she was also recognized by many gay rights organizations for her role in the changing societal attitudes about homosexuality.

★

The collection of Hooker's personal papers is housed in the Department of Special Collections, University Research Library, at the University of California, Los Angeles, and an autobiographical piece, "Reflections of a Forty-Year Exploration: A Scientific View on Homosexuality," appeared in *American Psychologist* 48, no. 4 (April 1993): 450–453. While there is no full-scale biography of Hooker, the work that, according to Hooker herself, "sums me up like nothing else" is the documentary *Changing Our Minds: The Story of Dr. Evelyn Hooker* (1992), produced by David Haugland and directed by Richard Schmiechen, which was nominated for an Academy Award in the Best Documentary Feature category. Several articles detail her life, including "The Grand Dame of Gay Liberation," *Los Angeles Times* (10 June 1990), and "Award for Distinguished Contributions to Psychology in the Public Interest: Evelyn Hooker," *American Psychologist* 47, no. 4 (1992): 501–503. An obituary is in the *New York Times* (22 Nov. 1996).

PAMELA W. BELLOWS

HORTON, Mildred Helen McAfee (*b.* 12 May 1900 in Parkville, Missouri; *d.* 2 September 1994 in Berlin, New Hampshire), educator, college president, and head of the WAVES in World War II.

One of three children of Harriet Brown, a homemaker, and the Reverend Cleland Boyd McAfee, Horton grew up in Missouri before attending Vassar College, where she played

Mildred McAfee Horton. WOMEN IN MILITARY SERVICE FOR AMERICA MEMORIAL FOUNDATION, INC.

hockey and baseball and was a member of the debating team. Vassar awarded her a B.A. degree in 1920. Horton's first position was as a teacher of English and French at Monticello Seminary in Godfrey, Illinois. In 1921 she taught the eighth grade at the Francis Parker School in Chicago, and in 1922 she was selected by the Fourth Presbyterian Church in Chicago to become director of girls' work. In 1923 she became acting professor of economics and sociology at Tusculum College in Greenville, Tennessee. In 1927 she was appointed professor of sociology and dean of women at Centre College in Danville, Kentucky, where she stayed until 1932. Horton obtained an M.A. degree from the University of Chicago in 1928. In 1932 she became the executive secretary of the Associate Alumnae of Vassar College, and in 1934 she was appointed dean of women at Oberlin College.

Horton's most prestigious move came in 1936, when, at the age of thirty-six, she became the seventh president of Wellesley College. Even though Horton said she would make no changes at Wellesley, she hoped that all persons in academic or nonacademic fields could obtain an education. An upholder of women's rights but not a feminist, she wanted to see that career patterns be made without sex discrimination and that marriage would not interfere with a woman's career. Horton was on the board of trustees of several schools and colleges, vice president of the Associated Boards of Christian Colleges in China, and a member of the Educational Advisory Committee for the Navy Training Program of the Bureau of Naval Personnel. By 1942 her work had gained national attention in such newspapers as the *New York Times* and such magazines as *Scholastic, Newsweek,* and *Time.*

In mid-1941, anticipating a shortage of men if the nation went to war, Joy Bright Hancock, a civilian employee, was sent by the navy's Bureau of Aeronautics to study how Canada utilized women in its armed forces. After canvassing the bureau chiefs, Rear Admiral Chester W. Nimitz, chief of the Bureau of Navigation (later Personnel), requested on 2 January 1942 that the secretary of the navy petition Congress for a women's reserve. Meanwhile, the navy obtained advice from colleges and universities that were training male reservists and civilian personnel. Particularly useful were the recommendations of an advisory committee chaired by Virginia Gildersleeve, dean of Barnard College, and a report made by Professor Elizabeth Reynard, who traveled around the United States and Canada investigating the type of work women did. Reynard came up with the name for the organization—Women Accepted for Voluntary Emergency Service (WAVES)—and Gildersleeve's committee suggested that it be headed by Horton.

On 30 July 1942 President Franklin D. Roosevelt signed PL 689, a bill that canceled the 1925 requirement that naval reservists be men and created a women's reserve which, unlike the WACs (Women's Army Corp), an auxiliary service, was independent. Women between the ages of twenty and thirty-five could apply. Taking leave from Wellesley on 3 August 1942, Horton was sworn in as lieutenant commander and was put in charge of the WAVES as the first permanent woman officer of the armed forces. With her engaging manner and excellent communication skills, Horton convinced old sea dogs of the value of women in navy work. She was a popular woman who did not drink or smoke—but she liked to dance and go to the movies. She directed an organization with 75,000 enlisted personnel and 12,000 officers. Confined initially to the United States, these women did what had traditionally been considered men's work for comparable pay. Horton helped the Navy Bureau of Personnel establish schools in colleges and universities in which candidates received two months of training. Smith College in Northampton, Massachusetts, and Mount Holyoke College at nearby South Hadley, Massachusetts, both trained officers. Oklahoma State University of Agriculture and Applied Science in Stillwater, Indiana University in Bloomington, and the University of Wisconsin at Madison were the first to train enlisted women.

WAVES were naval personnel first and women second. When Horton became head of the WAVES, she directed that the women could date only when on leave and use only minimal makeup. As per her directive, they were to follow the same rules about drinking that applied to men (no drinking while on duty, liberty, or leave), and they were also not allowed to smoke in public. With the aid of Gildersleeve's committee and women liaison officers in each naval district, Horton directed an administrative and technical program that trained women for thirty occupations. Ultimately, they served as flight instructors, truck drivers, weather observers, air-traffic controllers, maintenance workers, communications specialists, and Link trainer (teaching simulator) operators. Women at first clamored to join the WAVES, but by the end of 1942 a spirited recruitment campaign competed for personnel with the other branches of the armed services.

In 1945 Mildred McAfee married the Reverend Douglas Horton, who later became the dean of the Harvard Divinity School. That same year, she was awarded the Distinguished Service Medal. She resigned from the navy at the rank of captain in 1946 and returned to Wellesley as its president until 1949, when she became vice president of the National Council of Churches and president of the American Association of Colleges. The Reverend Horton died in 1968, leaving her with four stepchildren. She died of natural causes in Berlin and is buried in Randolph, New Hampshire. Her career with the navy helped unify the sexes in that service and improved women's position in general throughout the nation.

★

Horton's work as a teacher and educational administrator is covered in *Newsweek* (31 May 1923); *Time* (23 May 1925); and *Who's Who in America*, 1942–1943. The basic records of the WAVES are on microfilm (twenty reels) under the title of *United States. Assistant Chief of Naval Personnel for Women. The WAVES: Records of the Assistant Chief of Naval Personnel for Women, 1942–1972* (1991). The transcript of two extensive interviews of Horton by Dr. John T. Mason of the U.S. Naval Institute (1971) covers 115 pages and fully describes her objectives and results as the commander of the WAVES in *The Waves of World War II* (1971–1979). The origin of the WAVES, Horton's acceptance speech, the locations of the training schools for both officers and enlisted personnel, and the impact the WAVES had on World War II up to 1943 can be followed in Nancy Wilson Ross, *The WAVES: The Story of the Girls in Blue* (1943). Photographs and brief reports of the careers of WAVES for the period covered here are in the two volumes of *A Pictorial History of Navy Women, 1908–1988* (1990). An obituary is in the *New York Times* (4 Sept. 1994).

PAOLO E. COLETTA

HOWARD, James Howell (*b.* 8 April 1913 in Canton, China; *d.* 18 March 1995 in Bay Pines, Florida), fighter pilot who single-handedly defended thirty American B-17 bombers against thirty Luftwaffe fighters over Oschersleben, Germany, during World War II and became the only pilot in the European theater to win the Congressional Medal of Honor.

Howard was one of three children born to two American medical missionaries, Harvey James Howard, an eye surgeon, and Maude Irene Stroebel, a nurse. In childhood he yearned for adventure and once found it while on a hunting trip with his father, when he barely escaped Chinese bandits who held the elder Howard for ten weeks. When James was fourteen years old the family moved from China to Philadelphia, Pennsylvania, where he attended Haverford boarding school from 1927 to 1929. At Haverford, he was nicknamed "China" and was relieved when his father explained that—by *jus sanguinis,* right of blood—he was an American citizen like his classmates. He graduated in 1932 from John Burrows School in St. Louis, where the family had moved in 1927. He earned a B.A. degree in 1937 from Pomona College in Claremont, California. He was over six feet tall, slender, with blond hair and blue eyes.

At Pomona, Howard attended a talk by a naval aviation cadet recruiting aviation trainees. The talk steered Howard away from medicine to "something exciting and challenging" where he would "find romance and adventure." After graduation, and because of this talk, Howard went to Long Beach, California, for naval aviation training. He entered military service in December 1937 and began training in Pensacola, Florida. In January 1939, Howard completed

James H. Howard, 1944. © BETTMANN/CORBIS

this training and was assigned five months later to Fighting Squadron Seven on the aircraft carrier *U.S.S. Wasp* in Norfolk, Virginia. He eventually transferred to Fighting Squadron Six on the *U.S.S. Enterprise* in San Diego, California.

Howard left the Navy on 12 June 1941 to return to China and join its air force's American Volunteer Group—the Flying Tigers—to defend the Burma Road against Japan. He considered this "the opportunity of a lifetime" and a chance to "exercise some leadership and authority." In the Flying Tigers, Howard became a squadron leader under General Claire Chennault and flew a P-40 for $600–$750 per month plus a $500 bonus for each confirmed enemy aircraft destroyed. The Tigers, who were stationed at Toungoo and Kunming, Burma, began combat in December 1941 and fought Japanese Zeros, I-97s, and Ki-27s. In fifty-six missions, Howard destroyed six Japanese planes and became an ace over Burma and China. In ten weeks' fighting in Rangoon, Burma, the Tigers destroyed 217 Japanese planes, likely destroyed 43 more, and lost only sixteen P-40s and six pilots. Such victories bolstered America's hopes in spite of many Allied defeats elsewhere. The Tigers disbanded on 4 July 1942 to become the Twenty-third Fighter Group of the Fourteenth Army Air Force.

On 31 January 1943 Howard began active service in the 332nd Fighter Squadron, Fourth Air Force, U.S. Army Air Forces, stationed in Santa Ana, California. Later that spring Howard transferred to Hamilton Field near San Francisco, as a captain and commander of the 356th Fighter Squadron of the Ninth Air Force's 354th Fighter Group. In the 354th, he initially flew P-39s. From roughly July to October 1943, the 356th went to Salem, Oregon, so Howard could "galvanize this outfit into a fighting organization." In September 1943 Howard became a major.

Howard and the 354th moved to Boxted, England, in the fall of 1943, becoming the first Army Air Force unit in the European theater to be equipped with the new P-51 Mustangs, and calling itself the Pioneer Mustang Group. The 354th escorted Eighth Air Force B-17 and B-24 bombers on long-range missions into Germany and France. On these missions, P-51s replaced shorter-range P-38s and P-47s. German opponents of the 354th flew ME-109s and 110s, Focke Wulf 190s, and JU-88s. On 1 December 1943, the 354th flew its first mission. Several missions later, Howard flew into history.

On 11 January 1944, when the 354th escorted 600 B-17s and B-24s to bomb German aircraft factories, Howard became separated from his group during combat over Oschersleben, Germany. When thirty German fighters assailed thirty B-17s of the 401st Bombardment Group, he single-handedly attacked the fighters in *Ding Hao!*, his P-51, destroyed four of them, and scared others away in a frantic thirty-minute battle, saying afterward, "Today I was the hunter, not the hunted." No B-17s were lost. During the battle, the enemy was not Howard's only worry. He was dangerously low on fuel, three of his four guns malfunctioned, and B-17 "waist and tail gunners shot at anything that approached" from the rear. Since P-51s were new to Europe, had been kept secret, and resembled ME-109s, friendly fire was a threat. (Indeed, *Ding Hao!* suffered only one hit during the battle: a stray .50 caliber bullet from a B-17.) For psychological advantage over the enemy, pilots were trained never to turn away from a frontal attack but deliberately ram the enemy head-on. When a reporter asked why he took this risk, Howard facetiously replied, "I seen my duty and I done it." For this selfless act Major Howard received the nation's highest award for bravery, the Congressional Medal of Honor, on 27 June 1944. Howard eventually became an ace over Europe.

In February 1944 Howard became a lieutenant colonel and the 354th's commander. He was promoted to colonel on 29 March 1944 and later transferred to the Ninth Fighter Command at Uxbridge, England, to help supervise Normandy invasion operations. In November 1944 Howard returned home to command the Third Fighter Gunnery School at Pinellas, Florida. Because he wanted to leave the military and get married, he rejected an August 1945 request to become liaison officer to Chinese forces fighting communism. Howard left active duty on 30 November 1945 and became a brigadier general on 22 March 1948.

Civilian life caused Howard "years of anguish and adjustment." He married twice, first to Mary G. Balles in 1948, then to Florence Buteau several years later. He had one stepdaughter. Both marriages ended in divorce because Howard was impotent, a painful contrast to the obvious gallantry and manhood behind his combat heroics and a condition for which he was never medically treated. After the war, Howard was briefly chief of aeronautics for the city of St. Louis. In 1961 he formed Howard Research Corporation, which sold and installed intercom and telephone systems, primarily for the navy. It merged with Control Data Corporation in 1965, and Howard retired in 1977. He retired from the Air Force Reserve in 1966. Howard died of cancer at Bay Pines VA Medical Center and is buried in Arlington National Cemetery in Arlington, Virginia.

Howard's Medal of Honor signified that the dangers of aerial combat equaled that of fighting on the ground. A quiet, strict, rule-abiding man and a confident, expert dogfighter who destroyed enemy planes even while flying inverted, he stressed training and vigilant, disciplined flying from his comrades. He loved China and America and found adventure defending them.

★

Howard's memoir is *Roar of the Tiger* (1991), the source of the above quotes. The book contains several photos that include his childhood, the planes he flew, and the men with whom he served in the skies over Burma, China, and Europe. Howard is also covered in Walter P. Tracy, *St. Louis Leadership* (1944). Articles about Howard include John L. Frisbee's "One-Man Air Force," *Air Force Magazine* 66 (Nov. 1983): 127; Harold W. Bowman, "Little Friend," *Aerospace Historian* 30 (winter 1983): 235–239; and Timothy P. Barela, "I Seen My Duty, and I Done It," *Airman* 39 (Aug. 1995): 10–11. Bowman's article contains five photographs of Howard and B-17 formations over Germany, one in heavy flak. The congressional citation for Howard's Medal of Honor is in *Medal of Honor Recipients 1863–1994, vol. 2, World War II to Somalia* (1995) compiled by George Lang et al., and Kenneth N. Jordan, Sr., *Yesterday's Heroes: 433 Men of World War II Awarded the Medal of Honor 1941–1945* (1996). Obituaries are in the *New York Times* (22 Mar. 1995), *St. Louis Post-Dispatch* (23 Mar. 1995), *Los Angeles Times* (25 Mar. 1995), and *Air Force Times* (22 May 1995). The U.S. Air Force produced a seven-minute black-and-white film titled *One Man Air Force*.

GARY MASON CHURCH

HUGHES, Harold Everett (*b*. 10 February 1922 near Ida Grove, Iowa; *d*. 24 October 1996 in Glendale, Arizona), trucking executive, three-term governor of Iowa, and U.S. senator.

Hughes was one of two sons of Lewis C. Hughes, a farmer and bridge construction foreman, and Etta E. Kelly. His

Senator Harold Hughes, 1973. ASSOCIATED PRESS FILE

parents later operated a greenhouse and florist business. He graduated in 1940 from Ida Grove High School, where he was district singing champion as a bass-baritone, finished runner-up in a statewide tuba competition, won the 1938 state discus championship, and made right guard on the 1939 all-state football team.

Hughes attended the University of Iowa for one academic year (1940–1941) but dropped out to marry Eva Mae Mercer on 23 August 1941. They eventually had three daughters. Hughes worked with the Des Moines Parks Department until joining the U.S. Army in December 1942. During World War II, he fought as a combat rifleman in North Africa and Italy until contracting malaria. He received a medical discharge in July 1945.

Hughes found it hard to reconcile his combat experience with his religious beliefs, and he also suffered recurrent malarial attacks. After drinking heavily from 1946 to 1952 and nearly committing suicide, he joined Alcoholics Anonymous in 1954 and became a lay leader in the Methodist Church. Hughes drove a semitrailer for Hinrich's Truck Line of Ida Grove and managed its trucking line from 1950 to 1953. He then served as a field representative for the Iowa Motor Truck Association from 1953 to 1955.

Hughes founded the Iowa Better Trucking Bureau in 1955. He complained in 1957 to the Iowa State Commerce Commission about meager enforcement of state trucking laws, but the Republican-controlled group refused to investigate his complaints. Hughes switched his party affiliation from Republican to Democrat and was elected to the Iowa State Commerce Commission in 1958. He served from 1959 through 1962, making the commission appointive.

In 1962 Hughes upset the incumbent Republican, Norman Erbe, for the Iowa governor's seat by 40,000 votes. Strong Democratic organization, growing Republican dissatisfaction with Erbe, and the desire of Iowa voters to see the liquor laws revised brought Hughes victory. The only Democrat to win a state office in the traditionally Republican state that year, Hughes advocated permitting the sale of liquor by the drink in bars and restaurants rather than exclusively by the bottle in state-owned stores. In July 1963 the state legalized the sale of liquor by the drink.

Standing six feet, three inches tall, the rugged Hughes, who served as governor from 1963 through 1968, possessed a powerful evangelical speaking style. He built a bipartisan coalition, securing social legislation that urban lawmakers of both parties long had promoted. Hughes brought legislative breakthroughs in taxation formulas, reapportionment, public utility regulation, fair employment practices, and workmen's compensation increases.

Hughes was reelected governor in 1964 by 420,000 votes, the largest margin ever in Iowa, over Evan Hultman of Waterloo. This gave the Democrats control of both houses of the state legislature for the first time in three decades. Under Hughes's leadership, the General Assembly in 1965 and 1966 accomplished more than any legislature since 1846. It reorganized state government, reapportioned the legislature, directed that the legislature meet annually, and combined the governor and lieutenant governor on party tickets. It enacted legislation that the rural-dominated assemblies had blocked, abolishing capital punishment, creating a civil rights commission and a civil service system for state employees, giving more power to cities and counties, allowing county supervisors to establish public defenders, initiating prison reforms, founding an alcoholic treatment center, and establishing a state law enforcement academy. The General Assembly created a state withholding tax system, increased agricultural land tax credits to help relieve property taxes, and provided tax relief for the elderly. The legislature increased appropriations for schools, revamped secondary education guidelines, initiated four area community colleges, established educational radio and television programs, and inaugurated state scholarship programs for colleges and universities. It increased workmen's compensation and employment security benefits and controlled billboard advertising along state highways. Legislators increased taxes on income, cigarettes, gasoline, inheritances, and hotel and motel rooms.

In 1966 Hughes defeated William Murray of Ames to become the first Democratic governor in Iowa history to be elected to three terms. He launched the state into a new phase of social activism and convinced the divided legislature to reorganize the tax structure along more progressive lines. Hughes chaired the Democratic Governor's Conference from 1966 to 1968 and opposed President Lyndon B. Johnson's Vietnam policies by 1968. In 1968 he nominated Eugene McCarthy for president at the tumultuous Democratic National Convention in Chicago and helped reform the delegate-selection process, leading to the creation of the early Iowa presidential caucuses.

In 1968 Hughes ran for the U.S. Senate and defeated David Stanley by 4,200 votes. He served as assistant majority whip and on the Armed Services, Labor and Public Welfare, and Veterans' Affairs Committees. Hughes chaired the first congressional subcommittee on alcoholism and narcotics and secured funding for an alcoholism program in the Office of Economic Opportunity. He authored the federal Comprehensive Alcohol Abuse and Alcoholism Prevention, Treatment, and Rehabilitation Act of 1970, legislation that came to be known as the Hughes Act and that established the National Institute on Alcohol Abuse and Alcoholism. As chair of the Armed Services Subcommittee on Alcoholism and Drug Abuse, he persuaded the Department of Defense to recognize alcohol and drug abuse and provide treatment throughout the armed services. Hughes also served on the National Commission on Marijuana and Drug Abuse and sponsored legislation to prevent job discrimination against recovered alcoholics and drug patients. He added a provision for approval in the first Strategic Arms Limitations Talks (SALT I) that the United States should not develop a nuclear first-strike capacity and exposed the unauthorized bombing of North Vietnam and the secret bombing of Cambodia. He also authored an amendment forbidding covert Central Intelligence Agency operations in foreign countries without informing Congress, and secured reduction of military aid to South Vietnam.

Hughes did not seek reelection in 1974 and instead founded a religious retreat in Maryland. He served on the board of directors of the National Council on Alcoholism and chaired the National Commission on Alcoholism and Alcohol-Related Problems. Upon returning to Iowa in 1981, he started the Hughes Foundation and opened the Harold Hughes Center for Alcoholism and Drug Treatment in Des Moines. He considered running for governor in 1982 but withdrew when the press revealed that he had voted as a Maryland resident.

Hughes divorced his first wife in January 1987 and married Julianne Hol, his former secretary, six weeks later in Arizona. He died at home of complications from emphysema, and his remains were cremated.

Hughes, who overcame a battle with alcoholism to become a three-term Iowa governor, helped make the Democratic Party a competitive force in a state that had historically been dominated by Republicans and modernized and reformed state government. As a senator, he helped focus national attention on alcohol and drug abuse. The charismatic Hughes, noted for impressive oratory skills, quit politics at the height of his popularity to devote himself to lay religious work and open the Harold Hughes Center for Alcoholism Treatment.

★

The Harold E. Hughes papers are located at the University of Iowa Library in Iowa City. Harold E. Hughes with Dick Schneider, *Harold E. Hughes: The Man from Ida Grove* (1979), recounts his roles as governor and senator and his battle with alcoholism. *Current Biography 1963* describes his earlier career. James C. Larew, *A Party Reborn: The Democrats of Iowa 1950–1974* (1980), and "A Party Reborn: Harold Hughes and the Iowa Democrats," *Palimpsest* 59 (Sept.–Oct. 1978): 148–161, illuminate how Hughes revitalized the Iowa Democratic party. Other profiles of Hughes include Fletcher Knebel, "One Man's Triumph," *Look* (6 Oct. 1964); V. Bourjally, "Governor from Ida Grove," *New York Times Magazine* (26 Feb. 1957); L. L. King, "Evangelist from the Prairies," *Harper's* (Mar. 1969); and George Douth's serial publication *Leaders in Profile: The United States Senate* (1972): 130–134, and (1975): 114–122. Obituaries are in the *New York Times* and the *Des Moines Register* (both 25 Oct. 1996).

DAVID L. PORTER

HUNCKE, Herbert Edwin (*b.* 9 January 1915 in Greenfield, Massachusetts; *d.* 8 August 1996 in New York City), writer, outlaw, and legendary storyteller who introduced the writers of the Beat Generation to New York's underworld of sex, drugs, and crime, and whose use of the word "beat" lent the literary movement its name.

Herbert Huncke, 1985. CHRIS FELVER/ARCHIVE PHOTOS

Huncke was the oldest of two sons born to Herbert Spencer Huncke, an apprentice machinist at the Greenfield Tap and Die Company, and the sixteen-year-old Marguerite Bell, a homemaker. In 1919 the family moved to Detroit where Huncke's younger brother was born; two years later they settled in Chicago, where Huncke's father founded H. S. Huncke and Company, a machine-parts distributorship.

Raised in a middle-class household along Chicago's fashionable lakefront, Huncke's childhood was marred by his parents' constant arguments, which ultimately led to divorce as Huncke entered adolescence. He attended the local public schools but found Chicago's street life more alluring. He spent his sophomore year in high school in continuation school (a program that allowed students to drop out of the regular school program and attend school during evenings and weekends) while working as a messenger at the Union Trust and Savings Bank. A year later he quit school for good. He began hanging around Rush

Street, consorting with hustlers, drug addicts, and petty criminals connected with the Al Capone mob. Inspired by Francis Beeding's novel about drug smugglers, *The Little White Hag* (1926), he began using drugs himself and soon acquired a heroin habit.

A drug addict who had disgraced his family, Huncke left Chicago in the early 1930s, hitchhiking and riding freight trains all over the country. He stopped in New Orleans, Memphis, Tennessee; Galveston, Texas; East St. Louis, Illinois; and towns in California, hustling, stealing, and working odd jobs, including a brief stint in the Civilian Conservation Corps. Finally, in 1939, he arrived in New York City.

Huncke wound up in Times Square dead broke, but before long he was selling sex, dealing drugs, and stealing suitcases in the All American Bus Depot—doing whatever it took to survive. Caught breaking into a car on Thirty-fourth Street, he served six months as a prisoner on Hart's Island, where one of his jobs was to dig mass graves for persons whose families could not afford proper burial. Upon his release he returned to Times Square. Often homeless, he haunted the all-night cafeterias—Chase's, Bickford's, the Horn & Hardart automats—and the seedy bars along Eighth Avenue. He soon attracted the attention of the local police who dubbed him "The Creep." Alfred Kinsey, the sex researcher, also noticed Huncke. Meeting with him in the Angler bar at 674 Eighth Avenue, he recruited Huncke for his survey and agreed to pay him $2 for any acquaintances he might refer. In this way Beat authors William S. Burroughs, Allen Ginsberg, and Jack Kerouac became part of Kinsey's *Sexual Behavior in the Human Male* (1948).

World War II put a damper on Huncke's activities in Times Square. Motivated by high wartime wages and a romantic desire to go to sea, he joined the merchant marine. Ironically, while classified 4-F, Huncke served in the most dangerous of occupations and saw action in a war zone, supplying the troops at Normandy shortly after the Allied invasion.

In 1945 Huncke was living on Henry Street in lower Manhattan. One day his roommate Bob Brandenburg brought a distinguished-looking gentleman in a Chesterfield coat to their apartment. It was William S. Burroughs, seeking to dispose of a gun and some morphine Syrettes. He and Huncke became friendly and, when Burroughs moved into Joan Vollmer Adams's apartment at 419 West 115th Street, he brought Huncke around to meet Ginsberg and Kerouac, who were also living there. Huncke introduced the Columbia University intellectuals to a gritty underworld of drugs and criminality that seemed more authentic than academic life on Morningside Heights. They, in turn, provided Huncke, a gifted storyteller, with an appreciative audience.

Around Christmas 1946, Burroughs and Adams moved to New Waverly, Texas, where Burroughs hoped to grow marijuana. Huncke joined them in February 1947 and remained until October, when Neal Cassady drove Burroughs and Huncke back to New York with a jeep full of inferior pot. Except for a brief trip to Detroit, Huncke drifted around Times Square for the next fourteen months. The winter of 1948 was particularly harsh, as Huncke recalled in his autobiography: "I only wanted a place to live or die in out of the cold, not to be found a corpse crouched in the doorway." In February 1949, sick and exhausted, he arrived at Ginsberg's apartment at 1401 York Avenue.

Taking advantage of Ginsberg's hospitality, Huncke recovered his health. He soon teamed up with two friends, Jack Melody and Priscilla Arminger (also known as Vicki Russell), on a series of burglaries. The trio used Ginsberg's apartment to store their loot. On 21 April 1949, Melody and Arminger offered to drive Ginsberg to his brother's house on Long Island in a stolen car. Stopped by police

after making a wrong turn in Queens, Melody attempted to run down an officer. After a hectic chase, the car turned over on 205th Street. Ginsberg and Arminger escaped, but Melody was apprehended, and he led the police to Ginsberg's apartment, where everyone was arrested on charges of burglary and grand larceny. The others avoided jail time, but Huncke, with a prior record and little influence, was sentenced to five years in prison.

During the 1950s, when Ginsberg, Kerouac, and Burroughs were publishing books, becoming famous, and launching the Beat Generation, Huncke was doing time in such notorious New York State prisons as Sing Sing, Dannemora, and Riker's Island. By his own estimate, he spent about a dozen years of his life behind bars.

Paroled in 1959, Huncke found work in a glass-importing company on Seventeenth Street, off Fifth Avenue. After locating Ginsberg at 170 East Second Street, he moved into the building. Encouraged by Ginsberg, he gave his first reading at the Seven Arts Coffee Gallery at 596 Ninth Avenue. It was a good time. Friends were supportive of his writing and, although he continued to take drugs, he had enough money to support his habit. In 1964, arrested again for drug possession, Huncke spent six months on Riker's Island, but he was out in time to see the publication of his first book, *Huncke's Journal* (1965). In 1968 he appeared on the David Susskind show and published his story "Alvarez" in the October *Playboy*.

Around 1970, Huncke met Louis R. Cartwright, an aspiring photographer. Huncke, who considered himself to be bisexual, served as both lover and father figure to Cartwright. They took an apartment at 276 Henry Street in Brooklyn and remained together on and off for nearly twenty-five years. Huncke lived quietly in the 1970s and 1980s, entering a methadone treatment program, doing readings, and giving interviews to Beat Generation scholars. As a result, his work received more attention. In 1979 Pequod Press published *Elsie John and Joey Martinez,* a handsome edition of the Huncke stories "Elsie John" and "Joey Martinez." A year later, Cherry Valley Editions issued a collection of stories, *The Evening Sun Turned Crimson.* Finally, Paragon House released *Guilty of Everything* (1990), the autobiography Huncke had worked on for more than twenty years.

The 1990s saw Huncke back in Manhattan, first at an apartment at 269 East Seventh Street, then at the Chelsea Hotel, where he was supported by friends and admirers, including the Grateful Dead's Jerry Garcia. In January 1994 he fell and broke his shoulder and was hospitalized briefly at Cabrini Medical Center. Another blow came on 6 June 1994, when Cartwright was murdered on Second Avenue. Huncke was too grief-stricken to attend the funeral. Although his health was deteriorating, he read at the Lowell Celebrates Kerouac Festival on 6 October 1995 in Lowell,

Massachusetts, and at the University of Connecticut on 7 December 1995. At the age of 81 he died of congestive heart failure at Beth Israel Hospital. By his own request, Huncke was cremated without any formal rites.

Huncke's fame rests primarily on his appearance in numerous works by Beat Generation authors: He was Ancke in John Clellon Holmes's *Go* (1952), Herman in Burroughs's *Junkie: Confessions of an Unredeemed Drug Addict* (1953; 1977 edition was retitled *Junky*), and Elmo Hassel in Kerouac's *On The Road* (1957). A picaresque antihero, he represented an alternative to the conformist middle-class values the Beats heartily rejected. Since his writings appeared mostly in small-press publications, Huncke was less influential as an author than he was as a literary character. The publication of the *Herbert Huncke Reader* (1997) by William Morrow, however, may make his own writings more accessible and better appreciated.

★

Columbia University's Rare Books and Manuscript Division holds thirty notebooks and some early correspondence dating from 1946. The University of California, Berkeley, has corrected proofs of *Guilty of Everything: The Autobiography of Herbert Huncke* (1990), along with a transcript of a conversation between Huncke and his editor, Don Kennison. This autobiography is the most complete record of Huncke's life. Interviews containing biographical information are in *unspeakable visions of the individual*, 3, nos. 1–2 (1973): 3–15 and *Catching Up With Kerouac* (1984): 67–92. A profile by Michael T. Kaufman is in the *New York Times* (9 Dec. 1992). A tribute, edited by Benjamin Schafer and produced by Jerome Poynton, Huncke's literary executor, was published in connection with a memorial service held on 30 November 1996 at the Friends Meeting House at 221 East Fifteenth Street, New York City. Obituaries are in the *New York Times* (9 Aug. 1996) and the London *Independent* (16 Aug. 1996). *Huncke and Louis* (1999), a video documentary by Laki Vazakas, focuses on Huncke's relationship with Louis Cartwright. Huncke also appears in video clips in *Kerouac* (1985); *Burroughs: The Movie* (1985); *The Beat Generation, an American Dream* (1987); and *The Life and Times of Allen Ginsberg* (1993).

WILLIAM M. GARGAN

HUNTER, Howard William (*b.* 14 November 1907 in Boise, Idaho; *d.* 3 March 1995 in Salt Lake City, Utah), attorney and religious leader, best known as Prophet, Seer, Revelator, and president of the Church of Jesus Christ of Latter-day Saints (LDS), 1994–1995.

Hunter was born in a working-class family to John William Hunter, an inactive Episcopalian and railroad worker, and Nellie Marie Rasmussen, a granddaughter of Scandinavian Mormon immigrants and homemaker. He grew up in Boise and in a nearby rural area.

Nellie took Howard and his younger sister, Dorothy, to Boise's LDS, or Mormon, branch (small congregation), where she served in the children's and young women's auxiliaries. Although John would eventually join the LDS Church, his early religious views led him to oppose Howard's baptism at the usual age of eight. Therefore, Howard was not baptized until age twelve, an age when most Latter-day Saint boys are ordained to the priesthood. Howard was ordained shortly thereafter and was active in the Boy Scouts of America, reaching the rank of Eagle.

During his youth, Howard worked part-time and mastered a number of musical instruments. He attended Boise High School, from which he graduated in 1926. While there Howard organized an orchestra, "Hunter's Croonaders," which played for dances in Boise and nearby towns. In 1927 he booked the group on a cruise ship bound from Seattle to Asia. Thereafter, he promoted a dance club and worked in advertising.

In 1928 Hunter moved to Huntington Park, California, where he worked as a shoe salesman and orange packer until April 1928, when he landed a job with the Bank of Italy. In November 1930, after the Great Depression had begun, Hunter worked on bookkeeping for the conversion of the Bank of Italy into the Bank of America.

On 10 June 1931 Hunter married Clara May Jeffs in the Salt Lake LDS Temple. They became the parents of three children, one of whom died in infancy.

Settling first in Hermosa Beach, California, the Hunters moved later in 1931 to Inglewood, California, where Howard worked as assistant cashier at the First Exchange State Bank in Inglewood until the bank passed into receivership in January 1932. He worked at a series of jobs until January 1934, when he accepted an appointment in the title department of the Los Angeles County Flood Control District.

Because of the legal complexities of title work, Hunter enrolled in Southwestern University Law School in September 1935, while continuing to work full-time. He graduated cum laude and third in his class in June 1939 and was admitted to practice in January 1940. Hunter practiced law and worked part-time at the flood control district until 1945. He then devoted himself exclusively to his law practice and church work until 1959. He specialized in corporate, business, and probate law, and he served on the boards of more than two dozen companies.

In the meantime, Hunter accepted a series of increasingly more responsible church calls. In 1935 he directed the scouting program for the Hollywood LDS Stake (an administrative division consisting of approximately six to ten congregations, called wards, which are generally made up of from 250 to 500 members). He served on the Los Angeles Metropolitan Area Scout Council and chaired the com-

Howard Hunter, 1994. ASSOCIATED PRESS AP

mittee to finance construction of a chapel for the Inglewood Ward.

In 1936 the Hunters moved to Alhambra, California. In September 1940, at age thirty-two, Howard was ordained as bishop of the newly created El Sereno Ward of the Pasadena Stake. He served until November 1946. Hunter was then called as president of the High Priests Quorum (the highest office in the LDS priesthood) of the Pasadena Stake.

In 1948 the family moved to Arcadia, California, where they became members of the Las Flores Ward. In February 1950 Hunter was called as president of the Pasadena Stake. In this capacity he served as spiritual leader for 4,482 members in the six wards of the Pasadena area. He also served as chairman of the Southern California Regional Council of stake presidents.

In October 1959, after nine years of service as president of the Pasadena Stake, Hunter was at age fifty-one called to the Quorum of the Twelve Apostles, the second-highest governing body in the LDS Church. He continued to live in Southern California until April 1961, when he moved to Salt Lake City. Between 1959 and 1961 he commuted to Salt Lake City, attended to the administrative and spiritual duties required of one of the Twelve, and wound up his law practice.

As a member of the Twelve, his major responsibilities were to bear witness to the divinity of Jesus Christ and of his atonement, to make policy for the church, and to oversee the spiritual and temporal affairs of the church. In carrying out these responsibilities, Hunter visited stake conferences and served on the general welfare committee, the general priesthood committee, the missionary committee, the personnel committee, the Brigham Young University board of trustees, and the church board of education. He also advised the Sunday School (the teaching auxiliary for adults) and Primary (the teaching auxiliary for children) and reviewed clearances for divorced persons seeking to enter the temple. Additionally, Hunter served as president of the Genealogical Society (1964–1972), church historian (1970–1972), chair of the advisory board of the New World Archaeological Foundation (1961–1985), and president and chair of the board of the Polynesian Cultural Center in Laie, Hawaii (1965–1976). His wife Clara May died in 1983.

Hunter also began a round of visits to non-Mormon national and civic leaders and to LDS leaders and members throughout the world. He oversaw the construction of the Brigham Young University Center in Jerusalem (dedicated in 1989), a project opposed by ultra-orthodox Jews. The project succeeded largely because of the support of Jerusalem mayor Teddy Kollek, with whom Hunter and other church leaders developed a close relationship.

Although confined to a walker, crutches, or a wheelchair following back surgery in 1987, Hunter continued active church service. He was called as acting president of the Quorum of the Twelve Apostles in November 1985 and as permanent quorum president in June 1988. Hunter married Inis Bernice Egan Stanton on 12 April 1990. In June 1994, at age eighty-six, Hunter was ordained as president of the Church of Jesus Christ of Latter-day Saints. As president, he expanded the worldwide charitable work of the church and continued to promote the construction of temples. He served until his death nine months later of cancer at the age of eighty-seven. He is buried in Salt Lake City.

Hunter served as an apostle and church president during a time of enormous growth and change in the LDS Church. Between 1959 and 1994, Mormon Church membership increased from 1.6 million to 9 million members worldwide. At the same time, the church expanded from an organization with a majority of members in the Intermountain American West to a national and worldwide religion. Hunter was the only LDS church president who had neither been converted to the church as an adult, grown up in a family in which both parents were active members, nor lived before his call to the Twelve in an area where a sizable proportion of the population consisted of Latter-day Saints. In part because of this unusual background, Hunter—as a young man in Boise and as a bishop and stake president in Southern California—understood the need to develop good relations with less active members and with non-Mormons. All remember him as an inspiring, kind, and tolerant leader devoted to the promotion of harmony within the church and good relations with non-Mormons.

★

The Howard W. Hunter Journals, 1959 ff., are in the possession of the First Presidency of the Church of Jesus Christ of Latter-day Saints in Salt Lake City, Utah. They are not available for research. Eleanor Knowles, *Howard W. Hunter* (1994), is a favorable biography, but it was written before his death and before his service as president of the LDS Church, so it does not include important information on that service. Obituaries are in the *Deseret News* (3 Mar. 1995) and *New York Times* (4 Mar. 1995).

THOMAS G. ALEXANDER

I–J

IVES, Burl Icle Ivanhoe   (*b*. 14 June 1909 in Hunt, Illinois; *d*. 14 April 1995 in Anacortes, Washington), popular folksinger of the 1950s and 1960s and Academy Award–winning actor.

Ives was the youngest of six children of Frank Ives and Cordella White, tenant farmers in Illinois. Although they could trace their roots to Revolutionary America, the family lived on a very modest income during Ives's earliest years. In spite of their poverty, Ives had a childhood that was rich in music, and he learned hundreds of folk songs from his pipe-smoking, tobacco-chewing grandmother Kate White. Ives could not remember a time when he was not singing, and he was only four years old when he first sang for money: he received a quarter for singing "Barbara Allen" at a veterans' picnic.

By the time he was in high school, his family had become more financially secure with the purchase of a construction business in Newton, Illinois. Ives played fullback on the Newton High School football squad. After graduating in 1927 he went on to Eastern Illinois State Teachers College in Charleston. He hoped to become a football coach, but he was indifferent about his studies and left college in his third year to become an itinerant singer, using his warm tenor voice with a trace of vibrato. His travels took him to forty-six states as well as Canada and Mexico, performing under the name "Burl Ives, the Vagabond Lover." When he could not support himself by singing and playing the banjo, he did odd jobs. Along the way he added many new songs to his repertoire as he learned tunes from cowboys, lumberjacks, and hoboes.

Eventually Ives settled in Terre Haute, Indiana, where he gave college another try at the Indiana State Teachers College. He also worked at odd jobs, lined up a radio program, and played semiprofessional football. His singing instructor, Clara Bloomfield Lyon, convinced him to bypass college and go to New York City to break into show business.

In 1937 Ives moved into a $5-a-week apartment on the Upper West Side of Manhattan. At first booking agents considered his music too rustic, so he endured some lean times before making his Broadway debut in 1938 in the musical comedy *The Boys from Syracuse*. Rodgers and Hart placed him in the road company of *I Married an Angel* (1938). His Broadway exposure led to a four-month engagement at the Village Vanguard (1940) and a national radio show called *The Wayfarin' Stranger* on CBS. Ives was known for his bearish looks—he weighed nearly 300 pounds and stood six feet, three inches tall. In contrast, he had a distinctively honey-sweet singing voice that made him a favorite with generations of children as he defined songs such as "The Big Rock Candy Mountain," "Foggy, Foggy Dew," and "Frosty the Snowman."

In 1942 Ives was drafted into military service and served in Irving Berlin's production *This Is the Army* in New York. The following year he received a medical discharge, although he continued to entertain the troops. He also pro-

Burl Ives. © BETTMANN/CORBIS

directed both the play and the film, noted that he considered Ives the perfect choice for Big Daddy even though he did not have any formal training as an actor. That year turned out to be Ives's high-water mark in film. For his role as a patriarch in *The Big Country* (1958) he received an Academy Award for best supporting actor. Ives's banner year for record sales came in 1963 when "A Little Bitty Tear" and "A Funny Way of Laughing" appeared on the popular and country music charts. He also won a Grammy Award for the latter recording. On television, he narrated the 1964 production of *Rudolph the Red-Nosed Reindeer*. In 1971 Ives married Dorothy Koster, and the couple settled in Anacortes. Although he slowed his pace in the 1970s and 1980s, Ives still continued to entertain. He had a regular part on "The Lawyers" segment of the TV series *The Bold Ones* from 1970 to 1972 and appeared in the miniseries *Roots* in 1977. His last album of original music was released in 1993. Ives died in Anacortes from complications of mouth cancer. He was buried at the Mound Cemetery in Jasper County, Illinois.

Ultimately Ives succeeded in every form of entertainment he undertook, with more than thirty movies, 100 record albums, and appearances in thirteen Broadway productions. He is probably best known for his singing, as evinced by the poet Carl Sandburg, whose words about Ives are inscribed on the entertainer's tombstone: "The mightiest ballad singer of this or any other century."

★

Ives's biography is *Wayfaring Stranger* (1948). Among his other major writings are the *Burl Ives Song Book* (1953) and *Song in America: Our Musical Heritage* (1962). See also his *Tales of America* (1954). Information about the controversy with Pete Seeger can be found in Seeger's memoir, *How Can I Keep from Singing* (1981), written with David King Dunaway. For further reading about Ives's life, see *Current Biography 1960*. An article that focuses on Ives's recordings is in Neal Walters and Brian Mansfield, eds., *MusicHound Folk: The Essential Album Guide* (1998). An obituary is in the *New York Times* (15 Apr. 1995).

TERRY BALLARD

JACKSON, J(ohn) B(rinckerhoff) (*b.* 25 September 1909 in Dinard, France; *d.* 28 August 1996 in Santa Fe, New Mexico), author, editor, teacher, cultural geographer, and reader of the American landscape known for such essay collections as *A Sense of Place, a Sense of Time* (1994) and for championing an understanding of the "vernacular landscape," or the interactions between ordinary Americans and their everyday environments.

duced and starred in the Broadway revue *Sing Out, Sweet Land*, which won him a Donaldson Award as best supporting actor in the 1944–1945 season. One of the songs he included was "The Blue Tail Fly," which became his signature tune over the years.

Ives traveled to Hollywood and made his film debut in 1945 in an adaptation of the Will James novel *Smoky*. Later that year he performed his first major New York concert at Town Hall. On 6 December 1945 Ives married Helen Payne Ehrlich. They had one child before divorcing in 1971. Ives published his autobiography, *Wayfaring Stranger*, in 1948. Over the next decade he also produced a number of folk-song anthologies, collections of his short stories, and a book of verse for children.

In the early 1950s Ives testified before the House Un-American Activities Committee. He did cooperate with the investigators to some extent because he had become disillusioned with communists. This led to a bitter public feud with the folksinger Pete Seeger, who had admired Ives earlier in their careers.

In 1955 Elia Kazan cast Ives as an authoritarian but well-spoken small-town sheriff who has to deal with a troubled James Dean in *East of Eden*, then cast him as Big Daddy in the Broadway production of *Cat on a Hot Tin Roof*, a role he reprised on the screen in 1958. Kazan, who

Jackson was born in Dinard, France, to American parents, William Brinckerhoff Jackson and Alice Richardson Jackson. The Jackson family, including a brother and sister from his mother's first marriage, lived on and off in Europe and in the United States near Washington, D.C. The young Jackson was educated at Le Rosey boarding school in Switzerland and in Paris, and later at Choate and Deerfield Academy, while spending summers of his preparatory years on an uncle's sheep ranch near Wagon Mound, in eastern New Mexico.

Jackson entered college in 1928 with a year at the Experimental College of the University of Wisconsin in Madison, then transferred to Harvard University for the duration of his undergraduate work, where he graduated in 1932 with a degree in history and literature. After a year of graduate study at the Massachusetts Institute of Technology (MIT) School of Architecture, Jackson worked as a newspaper reporter for the *New Bedford Mercury*. In 1934 he enrolled briefly in a commercial drawing school in Vienna, Austria, then embarked upon an extended tour of Europe. During this period, he published a well-received novel, *Saints in Summertime* (1938), and several shorter works, all concerned with European politics and the rise of Nazism. Again in the United States by the late 1930s, Jackson worked on a ranch near Cimarron, New Mexico.

During World War II, Jackson enlisted in the First Cavalry Division and was transferred to Washington to begin training as an intelligence officer. He saw battle in North Africa and Sicily (where he was wounded in action), as well as in France and during the Battle of the Bulge. Assigned to combat intelligence beginning with the Normandy invasion, Jackson's task for the duration of the European campaign was to combine a variety of intelligence—maps, guidebooks, aerial photographs, local geographical literature, interviews, and prisoner interrogations—to interpret the enemy-held landscape that lay before the advancing American armies. Major Jackson was discharged in 1946, after which he returned to New Mexico and coleased a 10,000-acre ranch near Clines Corners, but a severe riding accident soon ended his ranching venture.

In 1951 Jackson founded the journal *Landscape,* in effect inaugurating a new field of inquiry on the American scene, one influenced by the French geographers and anthropologists he had read during and after the war. Originally carrying the subtitle *Human Geography of the Southwest* and later the more inclusive *Magazine of Human Geography,* Jackson created a forum for discussing the American physical landscape from a variety of perspectives and academic disciplines. In Jackson's seventeen years (1951–1968) as editor of *Landscape,* his central topic was human geography, or the human story as written in the material constructions of, and continuing alterations to, the land. To Jackson, the landscape was a rich source of information regarding American history and values, and he probed for overlooked cultural meanings latent in the evolution of commonplace sites

J. B. Jackson, 1974. © BETTMANN/CORBIS

such as backyards, garages, trailer parks, roadsides, and urban strips.

Known to many simply as "Brinck," Jackson began teaching in 1962 at the University of California at Berkeley and by 1969 was offering a class each semester at either Harvard or Berkeley while spending his summers in New Mexico. His courses on the history of the American cultural landscape, based largely on discoveries he made on countless motorcycle forays into country and city, were popular at both institutions over the next decade, where he typically taught between 600 and 700 students per year. After retiring from teaching in the late 1970s, he continued to lecture widely.

As an essayist of the American landscape, Jackson possessed a keen eye for detail and an eloquent prose style that purposely eschewed academic tone and structure. Jackson taught his readers to know the landscape not as simple scenery but as an historical and ever-changing organization of man-made space that lay open to valuable interpretation if one learned how to look, question, and connect material specifics to broader themes of American social history. His books include the collection *Landscapes: Selected Writings of J. B. Jackson* (1970); *American Space: The Centennial Years, 1865–1876* (1972); *The Necessity for Ruins* (1980); and *Discovering the Vernacular Landscape* (1984). In March 1995 Jackson won a PEN Award for his collection of essays *A Sense of Place, a Sense of Time* (1994). He also edited and contributed to a number of collections and journals, and in the spring of 1996 displayed his drawings in New York City and in Rhode Island. Jackson's *Landscape in Sight* was published posthumously in 1997.

A long-term resident of La Cienega, New Mexico, a village near Santa Fe, Jackson lived alone in a home he designed himself. Situated on six lush acres with a pond, orchard, and garden plot, the house itself was of simple adobe construction but bore New England and North African influences. The interior was unpretentious, hung with the owner's own drawings, watercolors, and oils. The kitchen was the fulcrum of activity in the Jackson house, where a steady stream of locals, friends, colleagues, students, and pilgrims was the norm. He never married.

After his retirement from lecturing in 1985, Jackson—a small, bald man perpetually dressed in casual attire—continued to write, but he also worked mornings at construction sites, gardens, and at a local service station. The unassuming day laborer quietly became a village benefactor, building the local community center and pool and paying for several village children to go to college. Jackson also left a $2 million bequest to the University of New Mexico, which now houses his papers and correspondence. Few were aware of his various generosities, and not even his closest friends seem to have known everything about the somewhat enigmatic man. Increasingly devout in the last years of his life, Jackson frequented his local parish and a small African-American church in Albuquerque. He died at age eighty-six in Santa Fe following a brief illness and is buried in the cemetery of the San Jose Catholic Church in La Cienega.

Because he was associated with a number of academic disciplines, Jackson and his work are difficult to classify in any conventional academic way. Among the fields he affected were history, architecture, geography, urban studies, environmental studies, literature, anthropology, and landscape architecture, yet his perspective was relentlessly multidisciplinary, and he was often at odds with (or ahead of) prevailing academic winds. He was criticized for his tolerance of ecological degradation or homogenization of the landscape, and he in turn criticized environmentalists for romanticizing the landscape and denying people—particularly marginalized people—an existence within it. His writing was sometimes discounted because it lacked the critical apparatus *de rigueur* in academe, yet it was clear that Jackson, his repeated modesty notwithstanding, had an impressive command of the multiple perspectives and

disciplines at play in his work. The only fair way to label him may be as an influential iconoclast with a unique and powerful voice, or as a thinker and writer who employed the sweeping multidisciplinarity of American studies. Certainly Jackson is crucial to the broad field of landscape studies: his elevation of the vernacular landscape and his appeal to academics and the lay public alike are far-reaching. Ultimately Jackson was a steady advocate for the common American landscape and the people whose story is written in and on it. He valued the less-attractive and passed-over components of the terrain and taught others to interpret this vital American cultural story. As Jackson states in the preface to one of his works, "The beauty that we see in the vernacular landscape is the image of our common humanity."

★

The collection of Jackson's papers and correspondence is in the Center for Southwest Research at the University of New Mexico. No full-length biography exists, and aside from Jackson's own published, occasionally autobiographical work, including that in *Landscape* magazine from 1951 to 1968, the following provide the best picture available of this complex man: Helen Lefkowitz Horowitz's opening essay "J. B. Jackson and the Discovery of the American Landscape" in the collection of Jackson's work she edited, *Landscape in Sight: Looking at America* (1997); D. W. Meinig's discussion of Jackson's work in *Landscape* magazine, "Reading the Landscape: An Appreciation of W. G. Hoskins and J. B. Jackson," in *The Interpretation of Ordinary Landscapes* (1979); Marc Treib's look at Jackson's New Mexican residence, "J. B. Jackson's Home Ground," in *Landscape Architecture* 78 (Apr.–May 1988), and Treib's "The Measure of Wisdom," an editorial homage to Jackson's life and influence, in the *Journal of the Society of Architectural Historians* 55 (Dec. 1996); a special issue of *Geographical Review* 88 (Oct. 1998) dedicated to Jackson and his connections to that discipline; obituaries from the *Santa Fe New Mexican* (30 Aug. 1996) and *New York Times* (31 Aug. 1996); and the 1988 documentaries *J. B. Jackson and the Love of Everyday Places*, produced by Robert Calo, and *Figure in a Landscape: A Conversation with J. B. Jackson*, produced by Janet Mendelsohn and Claire Marino.

ANDREW SMITH

JACOBS, Bernard B. (*b.* 13 June 1916 in New York City; *d.* 27 August 1996 in Roslyn, New York), lawyer and president of the Shubert Organization, the largest theatrical firm in the United States.

Bernard Jacobs was born in the neighborhood of Harlem, then largely Jewish, to Russian-Polish Jewish immigrants. His father and grandfather worked on the Lower East Side of Manhattan in the woolen waste business. Jacobs and his two older sisters and brother were raised in an Orthodox

Bernard B. Jacobs. THE SHUBERT ARCHIVE

home, and his father was president of the leading Jewish-Polish synagogue in Harlem. Although not religious, Jacobs was active in Jewish organizations and philanthropies throughout his life. He attended New York City Primary Schools 10 and 184. His family moved to the Upper West Side of Manhattan when he was thirteen. He attended DeWitt Clinton High School, graduated from New York University's Bronx campus in 1937 and received a law degree from Columbia University in 1940. He then went to work with his brother as his partner in a general law practice that mainly represented jewelers.

During World War II, Jacobs was sent to the U.S. Army Signal Corps' electronics school at Fort Monmouth, New Jersey, where he became an expert in VHF, or Very High Frequency, a fighter command control system. He then shipped to the South Pacific to help operate VHF equipment, but because there was no VHF equipment where he was stationed, he worked as a cryptographer and company clerk for three years in Australia.

After the war, Jacobs returned to work with his brother. He married Betty Shulman in 1946. They moved from Manhattan to Roslyn, Long Island, and had two children.

The Jacobses helped organize the first synagogue in Roslyn. They would return to Manhattan in 1980.

In 1958 Gerald Schoenfeld, the younger brother of one of Jacobs's closest college friends, invited him to become his partner as house counsel to the powerful Shubert Organization, which owned and operated sixteen theaters in New York and others in Washington, D.C., Philadelphia, Boston, and Los Angeles. In March 1958 Jacobs joined Schoenfeld in a partnership that was to last for nearly forty years.

Although from 1958 until 1972, Jacobs and Schoenfeld were the lawyers for the Shuberts, they were deeply involved in the day-to-day operations of the business. Both J. J. (Jacob J., the surviving Shubert brother) and his son and successor, John, worked closely with their attorneys. After John died suddenly in 1961, a distant relative, Lawrence Shubert Lawrence, Jr., took over the organization. Lawrence was an alcoholic and erratic, so Jacobs and Schoenfeld were, in effect, running the business. In 1972, with the help of the Shubert board of directors, they ousted Lawrence. At that time, Jacobs became president, and Schoenfeld chairman, of the largest and most powerful theater organization in the country. They disbanded their law firm in 1978.

Despite its influence and reach, the Shubert Organization in 1972 was close to bankruptcy, and Broadway was in decline. Denied a credit line from Morgan Guaranty Bank, which considered theater properties too specialized and theater productions to be speculative, Jacobs and Schoenfeld realized they needed to make major changes. Among other innovations, they computerized the box office operations and used television and radio advertising, which had not been done in the past. Most significantly, as Jacobs said in an interview in 1993, "When we became the controlling forces, we resolved that if you're not involved in production, you're going to have a lot of dark theaters all of the time."

Pippin, produced by Stuart Ostrow, was their first success, opening at the Imperial Theater in October 1972 and closing in June 1977. In 1975 Jacobs saw the off-Broadway production of Michael Bennett's *A Chorus Line* at Joseph Papp's New York Shakespeare Festival. Spotting a hit, he arranged for the production to move to the Shubert Theater. It opened in October 1975 and ran nearly fifteen years, the longest run of a Broadway show up to that time.

In the 1980s, buoyed and financed by the success of *A Chorus Line,* the Shubert Organization produced or housed a string of commercially successful musicals, from *Cats* at the Winter Garden Theater, which opened in October 1982 and passed *A Chorus Line*'s long run record (before finally closing in September 2000), to *The Phantom of the Opera, Les Misérables,* and *Miss Saigon.* They also produced many less commercial but critically praised works, including the

Pulitzer Prize–winning *Glengarry Glenn Ross* by David Mamet, *Sunday in the Park with George* by Stephen Sondheim, and *The Heidi Chronicles* by Wendy Wasserstein.

From 1961 until his death, Jacobs led all union negotiations for the League of American Theaters and Producers. During that time there were no strikes. He believed strongly that people were entitled to decent working conditions, a pension, and a fair wage. Management accused him of "giving away the store," but he was chosen to lead negotiations year after year. He was awarded a lifetime membership card from the Stagehands Union in 1992, the first person in management ever to receive this honor.

Although dour in appearance, Jacobs was warm and generous. He spoke bluntly and honestly and was respected for his integrity. Michael Bennett, creator of *A Chorus Line* and *Dreamgirls,* considered him a father figure. His contributions to the theater were significant: He was an adjunct professor of theater at Columbia University and the Yale School of Drama for many years; he initiated a program with New York City public schools to bring students to Wednesday matinees; and the philanthropic Shubert Foundation, under his presidency, gave millions in unrestricted grants to regional theater and arts organizations.

In 1986 Jacobs was diagnosed with global transient amnesia, an almost total but temporary loss of memory. For the next ten years there were rumors that his health was deteriorating, but he attended performances and remained active with the Schubert Organization and Foundation. In 1994 he was inducted into the Theater Hall of Fame. He died at Saint Francis Hospital in Roslyn, New York, of complications following heart bypass surgery. A tribute was held at the Majestic Theater on 15 October 1996, and he was posthumously awarded the Antoinette Perry ("Tony") Award for lifetime achievement in 1997.

As president for more than forty years of the largest and most powerful theater organization in the United States, Jacobs truly shaped American theater and quite possibly saved it. Although many found the crowd-pleasing, techno-fabulous shows of the 1980s and 1990s to be shallow and vacuous, it is clear that Broadway would not have survived without them. Jacobs defended these shows as good entertainment, and millions of theatergoers agreed. At the same time he used the foundation to make sure that quality theater flourished throughout the United States. He believed that all who worked in the theater deserved a living wage and made sure they had it. Jacobs was completely dedicated to the theater and those who made it possible.

★

There are no biographies of Bernard Jacobs. An interesting interview with Jacobs and Schoenfeld was printed in the *Dramatists Guild Quarterly* 25 (summer 1988): 13. The *New York Times* published a two-part series about the company's unusual tax status

(10 July 1994 and 11 July 1994). There are tributes to Jacobs in *Daily Variety* (28 Aug. 1996), the *New York Times* (15 Sept. 1996), *Theatre Week* (16 Sept. 1996), and *Newsday* (8 Oct. 1996). An obituary is in the *New York Times* (28 Aug. 1996). On 8 Apr. 1993 Jacobs was interviewed for the American Jewish Committee Oral History Project on Jews in the Theater. The transcript is in the Dorot Jewish Division of the New York Public Library. He was also interviewed for the New York Public Library's Theatre on Film and Tape Archive on 1 Nov. 1995. The videotape is located at the New York Public Library's Performing Arts Library.

SARA J. STEEN

JIMMY THE GREEK. *See* Snyder, Jimmy.

JOHNSON, Robert Edward (*b.* 13 August 1922 in Montgomery, Alabama; *d.* 27 December 1995 in Chicago, Illinois), pioneering black journalist and longtime associate publisher and executive editor of *Jet* magazine.

Johnson was the son of Robert and Delia (Davis) Johnson, about whom little personal information is known today. He had at least three brothers and one sister. The family moved from Montgomery to Birmingham, Alabama, during Robert's youth. In his early years, Johnson spent his spare time selling black newspapers to passersby in busy

Robert E. Johnson. PHOTO COURTESY OF JET MAGAZINE COPYRIGHT © 1991 JOHNSON PUBLISHING COMPANY

sections of Birmingham and by founding his high school newspaper, the *Westfield Trail Blazer*. By pursing these two endeavors, Johnson acquired an interest in black-oriented publications and skills in editorial work that would serve him throughout his life.

Following high school, Johnson, known as "Bob" to his friends, served in the U.S. Navy Reserves (USNR) from 1943 to 1946. While stationed at the Treasure Island Naval Base, Johnson actively sought and later received appointment as the first black editor of the installation's newspaper, the *Masthead,* because he wanted to turn it away from racist policies and cartoons.

In 1948 Johnson received a B.A. degree from historically black Morehouse College in Atlanta. While at Morehouse, he studied under the legendary educator Benjamin E. Mays, and he matriculated with future civil rights leader Martin Luther King, Jr. Meanwhile, Johnson edited the Morehouse student paper, the *Morehouse Maroon Tiger,* and worked as a stringer for national newspapers.

Also in 1948, Johnson joined the staff of the *Atlanta Daily World* and married Naomi Cole. The couple would have three children. Johnson earned an M.A. degree in journalism from Syracuse University in 1952. At the *Atlanta Daily World,* Johnson rose from reporter to city editor in only two years.

Johnson's service at the *Atlanta Daily World* caught the attention of John H. Johnson (no relation), founder of the mass-circulation *Negro Digest* (1942), *Ebony* (1945), and *Jet* (1951) magazines in Chicago. John H. Johnson hired Robert E. Johnson to work at *Jet* headquarters in Chicago in February 1953. While at *Jet,* Johnson rose from associate editor (1953–1954), to assistant managing editor (1954–1956), to managing editor (1956–1963), and finally to executive editor and associate publisher (1963–1995). Meanwhile, *Jet* magazine rose in circulation from 964,000 to 7.8 million within three decades. Johnson played a prominent role in making *Jet* one of black America's most widely read publications. By giving increased attention to social, cultural, and sporting events within the black community, Johnson was widely credited by journalists and nonjournalists alike for guiding *Jet* to this pinnacle of success.

Johnson's forty-three-year career with *Jet* propelled him into the ranks of nationally known black journalists. Starting with his on-the-scene coverage of the Montgomery bus boycott in 1955, sparked by Rosa Parks's defiance of city bus segregation laws, Johnson continued to give national attention in the pages of *Jet* magazine to racial issues throughout his career. Perhaps Johnson's greatest legacy to civil rights resulted from his being one of the first black journalists to chronicle the career of Martin Luther King, Jr., from King's ascendancy as a civil rights leader in Montgomery during the bus boycott to his tragic assassination in Memphis, Tennessee, in 1968. Johnson connected King

with *Jet*'s black readership through the copious use of photographs.

During his life Johnson maintained friendships with civil rights leader and political activist Jesse L. Jackson and with entertainers Duke Ellington, Michael Jackson, and Bill Cosby, with whom Johnson coauthored *Bill Cosby: In Words and Pictures* (1986). In 1972 Johnson was the only black journalist to travel with President Richard M. Nixon to Russia, Poland, Austria, and Iran, and in 1979 Johnson was one of the few senior journalists accompanying U.S. ambassador Andrew Young on a trade-mission tour of Africa. As with his other trips to Europe and Asia, Johnson related these experiences to his readership through columns, articles, and pictures in *Jet* magazine. In 1994 President Bill Clinton invited Johnson to participate in a White House ceremony for noted leaders of the 1960s civil rights era. The following year Johnson interviewed the controversial boxing figure Mike Tyson in prison in Indiana and became the only journalist allowed to accompany the former champion on his return to Harlem upon release from prison. The ensuing interview that Johnson conducted for *Jet/Ebony* remains a classic journalistic exposé of Tyson's tormented inner self. The Tyson interview coup capped the dynamic career of Johnson, who fell gravely ill shortly thereafter from prostate cancer, with which he was originally diagnosed in 1988.

Johnson died at his home in the Hyde Park neighborhood of Chicago at the age of seventy-three. Johnson's family held services for him at Rockefeller Chapel on the campus of the University of Chicago, where Johnson had been a member of University Church of Disciples of Christ, United Church of Christ. Notables at the service included Dillard University president Samuel DuBois Cook, Morehouse College president Walter E. Massey, comedian and activist Dick Gregory, Nation of Islam minister Louis Farrakhan, and longtime colleague and *Jet* publisher John H. Johnson. In his eulogy, the Reverend Jesse L. Jackson captured the spirit of Johnson's life when he characterized him as a "modern-day Griot . . . one of the great communicators of our time." Johnson is buried at Oak Woods Cemetery in Chicago.

Throughout his professional life, Johnson had been active in numerous civil rights and professional organizations, including the National Association for the Advancement of Colored People, the National Urban League, the Martin Luther King, Jr., Center for Nonviolent Social Change, Upward Bound, Operation Push, the DuSable Museum of African-American History, Alpha Kappa Delta, Sigma Delta Chi, Alpha Phi Alpha, the Chicago Association of Black Journalists, and the National Association of Black Journalists. Johnson was a trustee of Dillard University and received honorary degrees from Dillard, Morehouse College, Miles College, and Texas College.

★

Jet magazine is a good source for information on and articles by Johnson. John H. Johnson, *Succeeding Against the Odds* (1989), includes information about Robert E. Johnson's years at *Jet,* while Fred Powledge, *Free at Last? The Civil Rights Movement and the People Who Made It* (1992), provides a good backdrop to the critical events shaping Johnson's journalism while at *Jet.* Obituaries are in the *Detroit News* and *Chicago Sun-Times* (both 28 Dec. 1995).

IRVIN D. SOLOMON

JORDAN, Barbara Charline (*b.* 21 February 1936 in Houston, Texas; *d.* 17 January 1996 in Austin, Texas), first black southern woman in the United States Congress.

Jordan was the third of three daughters of Arlyne Patten Jordan and Benjamin Jordan. Her mother cleaned houses, and her father was a laborer and Baptist preacher. Both were well-known orators in the Good Hope Missionary Baptist Church in Houston. The year she was born, the church's minister helped found the Texas branch of the National Association for the Advancement of Colored People (NAACP). A Good Hope church member was plaintiff in the 1944 Supreme Court decision that forced Texas Democrats to allow black voters to participate in party pri-

Barbara Jordan, 1976. AP/WIDE WORLD PHOTOS

maries. Jordan's great-grandfather, Edward Patton, served as the only black member of the Texas House of Representatives from 1891 to 1893 and was one of the last black Republicans elected after Reconstruction in that state. Jordan's cousin, Dr. Thelma Patten, the first black female physician in Houston, presided at her birth. Her grandfather, John Ed Patten, used to read to her as they rode on his mule cart collecting junk for resale, and encouraged her to "travel up from segregation."

Jordan attended segregated schools in Houston. She was a champion debater for Phillis Wheatley High School and for Texas Southern University, which debated both black and white teams and once tied in competition with Harvard University. She became president of Delta Sigma Theta sorority and graduated magna cum laude in 1956 with a B.A. in political science. Her first experience in integrated classrooms was at Boston University Law School, where only six students in her class were black. One of her first white friends was the daughter of the chairman of the Democratic National Committee. She received her LL.B. in 1959 and passed the bar in both Massachusetts and Texas.

From 1960 to 1966 Jordan conducted a private legal practice from her parents' home in Houston and served as administrative assistant to a county judge. She worked in John F. Kennedy's 1960 presidential campaign, and made speeches in support of white liberal candidates, but lost her own races for the Texas legislature in 1962 and 1964. After the federal Civil Rights Act of 1964 and Voting Rights Act of 1965 enfranchised more black voters and a United States Supreme Court decision forced redistricting in Houston, Jordan was elected to the Texas state senate from the Eleventh District in 1966. She served in the sixtieth through the sixty-second legislative sessions in Austin, from 1967 through 1973, becoming the first black state senator in Texas since 1883, the first African-American female Texas legislator, and the only woman in the state senate during her two terms.

To the surprise of many, the serious-minded Jordan hosted parties, drank whiskey, played poker, traded votes, and quickly became popular with the other legislators. Nearly half the 150 bills Jordan introduced during her three terms in the legislature were signed into law. These included creation of a Texas Fair Employment Practices Commission; the state's first minimum-wage law; and increased workers' compensation coverage for on-the-job injuries. She successfully backed the Equal Legal Rights Amendment to the Texas Constitution as well as Texas's ratification of the Equal Rights Amendment to the U.S. Constitution. She also called in political favors to block bills that would harm her constituency in areas such as voting rights. Although she often voted with liberal members of the legislature, she did not let their caucus speak for her.

Her success came from studying the rules, learning the art of compromise, and working closely with the insiders who controlled the power structure, regardless of any disagreements on the issues. President Lyndon Johnson was one of her strong supporters, and her reciprocal support for him included withholding criticism regarding his Vietnam policies at the 1968 Democratic Convention, though she herself had come out against the war. Governor John Connally vetoed Jordan's appointment to the executive committee of the Texas Democratic party in 1964, yet she would eventually serve as a character witness during his trial for bribery and perjury in 1975. Connally's protégé, Lieutenant Governor Ben Barnes, appointed Jordan to fourteen committees in the Texas senate. She chaired the Labor and Management Relations Committee and was vice chair of two others, including the one that drew boundaries for a new Eighteenth U.S. Congressional District in her home county. In 1972 she ran for that seat and won, and before she left the Texas senate, she was elected president pro tempore and governor for a day.

One of President Johnson's last political acts before his death in 1973 was to advise Jordan to get on the House Judiciary Committee and to secure her appointment. She also served on the House Government Operations Committee. Jordan joined the Black Caucus but did not sit with its members on the floor, choosing instead a seat on the center aisle. She was also one of fourteen women in Congress, the largest number to serve up to that time. She joined other female legislators on several issues, winning an extension of the deadline for ratification of the Equal Rights Amendment but losing on federal Medicaid funding for abortions and Social Security benefits for homemakers. One of her first legislative victories in Congress was revising the Omnibus Crime Bill to increase the hiring of women and minorities as police officers. As a Texan she also represented a Mexican-American constituency. Against the will of almost all her old colleagues in Texas, she backed reauthorization of the 1965 Voting Rights Act, which was due to expire in 1975, and successfully extended its provisions to cover Texas and other states with five percent or more Hispanic population. She was successful in passing a law to protect consumers from price-fixing, and active in the Judiciary Committee's efforts to curb abuses by the federal intelligence agencies because she had been the target of the U.S. Army's domestic intelligence program in the 1960s.

Jordan is best known for her role in the confrontation between Congress and President Richard M. Nixon that led to the latter's resignation. Jordan's first speech in Congress, on 18 April 1973, analyzed the separation of powers and concluded that Nixon had trampled on the Constitution by refusing to spend money Congress appropriated, by bombing Indochina without consent of Congress, and by

forbidding members of his administration to appear before congressional committees.

That summer, Nixon's illegal campaign activities, including covering up break-ins and spying at the Democratic National Committee office in the Watergate building, came to light. The president defied the special prosecutor, the courts, and later Congress by refusing to turn over subpoenaed evidence. On 31 July 1973 the first impeachment resolution against Nixon for high crimes and misdemeanors was introduced in the House Judiciary Committee, and on 20 October, Nixon fired Special Prosecutor Archibald Cox, replacing him with a Houstonian whom Jordan knew and respected, Leon Jaworski. Jaworski gave information to the Judiciary Committee that enabled them to conduct a parallel investigation and learn that transcripts sent to the committee by the president had been distorted.

In July 1974 House Judiciary deliberations on impeachment were televised to the nation. Jordan spoke just before 9 P.M. on 25 July. She had studied the evidence, the Constitution, and the Federalist Papers to arrive at her decision. "I have finally been included in 'We, the People.' . . . My faith in the Constitution is whole, it is complete, it is total," she said. "I am not going to sit here and be an idle spectator to the diminution, the subversion, the destruction of the Constitution." Jordan explained to the public the meaning of impeachment and the ways that Nixon had set himself above the law and the Constitution.

The success of her speech set the stage for a series of votes in committee favoring impeachment on grounds including lying to investigators, subverting justice, paying hush money, and misusing the Federal Bureau of Investigation and the Central Intelligence Agency. Jordan also voted with a minority of committee members to impeach Nixon for tax evasion and the illegal bombing of Cambodia.

On 8 August, before the full House could vote on impeachment, Nixon resigned. His successor, President Gerald Ford, pardoned Nixon while Jordan was on a congressional delegation trip to China. As President, Ford vetoed many bills that Jordan considered important to her constituency, including public works jobs and day-care provisions for children.

In 1976 Jordan electrified the public with her televised keynote address at the Democratic National Convention, but she quashed a popular cry to nominate her for vice president and supported Democratic presidential nominee Jimmy Carter in his slim general election victory over Ford. Although Jordan expressed an interest in being appointed Carter's attorney general, such an offer was never made, and she declined to consider other posts such as United Nations ambassador.

Jordan learned in 1973 that she had multiple sclerosis, a progressive autoimmune disease. In her last session of

Congress, she focused on removing racial discrimination from all federal programs and preserving the Fifth Circuit Court of Appeals, which had done much to further civil rights. By the end of the session, Jordan was using a cane. Retiring from Congress in 1978, she returned to Austin to live with her longtime companion, Nancy Earl, and to teach at the Lyndon B. Johnson School of Public Affairs at the University of Texas at Austin. A year later, she had to use a wheelchair.

Over the next seventeen years, she gave many speeches; served on various corporate, nonprofit, and government boards; was ethics adviser to Texas governor Ann Richards from 1991 to 1995; and chaired President Bill Clinton's Commission on Immigration Reform from 1994 to 1996. She died of leukemia shortly before her sixtieth birthday. She was the first black person to be buried in the Texas State Cemetery in Austin.

Jordan was an inspiring orator, a consummate politician, and a champion of the political rights of the disenfranchised. Shortly before her death, she summed up her own motivation: "We cannot stand to have, in a democracy, any significant portion of the people who do not have a voice in what happens to them. . . . [W]e as a people, black, white, Asian, Hispanic, must keep scratching the surface until we get where we've got to be, and that's all inclusiveness for all people."

★

The collection of Barbara Jordan's papers is at Texas Southern University in Houston. Jordan's autobiography, written with Shelby Hearon, is *Barbara Jordan: A Self Portrait* (1979). The major biography of her is Mary Beth Rogers, *Barbara Jordan: American Hero* (1998). There is a major biographical essay on Jordan in Nancy Baker Jones and Ruthe Winegarten, *Capitol Women: Texas Female Legislators, 1923–1999* (2000). One of Jordan's last recorded interviews is included in a video, *Getting Where We've Got To Be! Women in the Texas Legislature, 1923–1999* (2000). The complete transcript of the interview is at the Archives for Research on Women and Gender, University of Texas at San Antonio. An obituary is in the *Houston Chronicle* (17 Jan. 1996).

RUTHE WINEGARTEN

JUDD, Donald Clarence (*b.* 3 June 1928 in Excelsior Springs, Missouri; *d.* 12 February 1994 in New York City), sculptor and founder of the minimalist movement, best known for his refined freestanding geometric sculptures made from industrial materials.

The son of Roy Clarence Judd, a Western Union executive, and Effie Cowsert, Judd was born in his grandparents' rural Missouri farmhouse. During his youth Judd's family moved frequently, finally settling in the mid-1940s in Westwood,

New Jersey, where he graduated from high school in 1946. After serving a stint in the U.S. Army, Judd returned to New Jersey and began investigating his childhood passion for art, commuting to the Art Students League in New York City in 1948. In the fall of 1949 he enrolled in Columbia University, where he studied philosophy and graduated with honors in 1953. In the evenings he continued to take courses at the Art Students League.

Judd's educational experience was a curious mixture: at Columbia he became interested in the empirical philosophy of David Hume, and at the Art Students League he was exposed to a curriculum that stressed representation and life drawing. In his art he would later reject outright the "illusionistic deceit" of representation in favor of an empirical, factual mode of expression. In his first one-person show at the Panoras Gallery in New York City in 1957, Judd exhibited some untitled paintings that eschewed representation in favor of an almost formless geometric investigation. Although the show was favorably reviewed, Judd decided in 1957 to return to Columbia as a graduate student in art history, studying with the influential critic and art historian Meyer Schapiro. Judd himself began writing critical reviews in 1959 for *Arts Magazine.* He remained on its staff until 1965, also contributing essays to *Art News* and *Art International,* and he continued to write extensively throughout the next three decades. In 1964 Judd married the dancer Julie Margaret Hughan Finch; they had two children before divorcing in the 1980s.

In a series of bluntly intellectual reviews, Judd became an outspoken advocate for a new type of art. He severely questioned the European artistic tradition of composition based on the balance and harmony of the discrete parts of a painting or a sculpture. Reacting strongly against subjectivity and emotionalism, he was among those who declared painting "finished." Judd came to believe in a non-metaphorical, autonomous, bare-bones type of art object—a pure object that could be appreciated solely for its essential formal properties of shape, color, surface, and volume. In 1964, in an important essay titled "Specific Objects" in *Arts Yearbook 1965,* Judd wrote: "The thing as a whole, its quality as a whole, is what is interesting." In 1965 the critic Barbara Rose, writing in *Art in America,* used the word "minimum" when she referred to this new art. By the late 1960s the term "minimalism" was in common use, but for his part, Judd preferred to call his objects "specific" and referred to himself as an "empiricist."

In the early 1960s, Judd abandoned painting and began making boxlike sculptures out of wood, metal, and Plexiglas. Inspired in part by the neutral, geometric forms he found in the paintings of Frank Stella, Judd utilized a clean, geometric language. Eventually he evolved a signature piece characterized by a five-sided box; groups of these were often arranged serially, either freestanding or

Donald Judd, 1992. © ERIC SANDER/GAMMA LIAISON

mounted on the wall. Following a successful solo show at Manhattan's Green Gallery (1963) in which he exhibited some plywood sculptures, Judd was able to have his work fabricated for him. Throughout the next two decades, he would send specific instructions to a manufacturing firm located in nearby Long Island City. These coolly elegant constructions, often made of copper and steel, would become synonymous with the minimalist movement.

In 1966 Judd joined the prestigious Leo Castelli Gallery in Manhattan, and in the 1980s the Paula Cooper Gallery represented him. Judd exhibited his work widely, both nationally and internationally. Major retrospectives of his work occurred at the Whitney Museum of Art in New York City in 1968 and in 1988 and 1989; at the Stedelijk Van Abbemmuseum, in Eindhoven, the Netherlands, in 1970; and at the Haags Gemeentemuseum, The Hague, in 1993 and 1994. In 1967 and 1976 he received National Endowment for the Arts grants and in 1968 he was awarded a Guggenheim fellowship.

In the early 1970s Judd purchased the 45,000-acre Ayala de Chinati Ranch overlooking the Rio Grande fifty miles south of Marfa, Texas. Over time Judd acquired seventeen buildings in and around Marfa, including the former 350-acre Fort D. A. Russell military post, which he renovated and converted into installation spaces for exhibiting his sculptures. The Marfa complex became Judd's work in progress over the next thirteen years. Outside the confines of the gallery Judd was able to realize his works on a grand scale. Particularly impressive are the large Fort Russell artillery sheds, in which Judd placed 100 aluminum box sculptures.

The 1980s were a decade of withdrawal and controversy for Judd. By 1985 he had removed himself from the New York City art scene and set up permanent residence in Texas, where he devoted his energies to the Marfa project and to a newfound passion for furniture design. In the same year, Judd became involved in a legal dispute with the Dia Art Foundation over funding for the Marfa project. Eventually a suit was avoided, and Dia and Judd joined forces to create the Chinati Foundation for the purpose of maintaining the Fort Russell exhibition spaces. In the late 1980s Judd reproached the Guggenheim Museum for acquiring artworks from the collection of Count Giuseppe Panza di Biumo. Judd claimed that Panza had fabricated his works, part of the acquisition, without his permission.

In his last years Judd traveled extensively with his companion, Marianne Stockebrand. He died of lymphoma at the age of sixty-five and was buried at his beloved Chinati ranch.

For more than thirty years Judd was the principle figure of the minimalist movement. His focused critical writings and spare geometric constructions profoundly influenced a generation of important sculptors and painters, including Richard Serra and Carl Andre. The rigorous ideas of minimalism put forward by Judd also found expression in dance, music, and the International Style in architecture.

Despite being often misunderstood by the general public, the vehemently antiexpressionistic, cool and precise artworks of Donald Judd profoundly informed general notions of what characterized "modern" in contemporary American art.

★

Donald Judd, *Complete Writings: 1959–1975* (1975) and *Complete Writings: 1975–1986* (1986) contain Judd's critical writings and artist statements. Barbara Haskell, *Donald Judd* (1988) is an exhibition catalog for Judd's 1988 retrospective at the Whitney Museum of American Art. Kenneth Baker, *Minimalism* (1988) is a primary source for information on the minimalist movement. The Tate Gallery Liverpool, *Minimalism* (1989), contains an anthology of quotations by critics and artists associated with the minimalist movement. An obituary is in the *New York Times* (13 Feb. 1994).

PETER SUCHECKI

JUDD, Walter Henry (*b.* 25 September 1898 in Rising City, Nebraska; *d.* 13 February 1994 in Mitchellville, Maryland), medical missionary to China who as a speaker and congressman urged American assistance to Nationalist China.

The sixth of seven children of Horace H. Judd, a lumberman, and the former Mary Elizabeth Greenslit, a teacher, Judd was born in a Nebraska town possessing a population of 499. After graduating from the local high school, he enrolled at the University of Nebraska in Lincoln in 1916. In 1918 he enlisted in the U.S. Army as a private, becoming a second lieutenant of field artillery the next year. After the war, Judd received his B.A. degree from the University of Nebraska in 1920 and his M.D. in 1923. He then interned at the university hospital in Lincoln in 1923 and 1924. Meanwhile, having pledged his life to missionary purposes, he spent a year as a traveling secretary for the Student Volunteer Movement, speaking in 100 college chapels and halls. In 1925 he went to China, and after a year of intense language study in Nanking was assigned to a remote town, Shaowu, in Fukien province, so far in the interior that it could only be reached by a ten-day boat trip up the Min River. There he remained until 1931, when persistent attacks of malaria forced his return to the United States. In a typical year he treated 8,000 patients at the clinic, conducted 10 major and 350 minor operations, and made 600 house calls. In 1927 he came close to being killed by an anti-British crowd that belatedly discovered he was an American. (That year a British police inspector in the International Settlement in Shanghai allowed Indian troops to fire on a mob, killing several Chinese, and throughout China anti-British feelings were high.)

After studying surgery at the Mayo Clinic in Rochester, Minnesota, from 1932 to 1934, Judd returned to China in

Walter H. Judd. ARCHIVE PHOTOS

1935, this time with his wife, the former Miriam Louise Barber, whom he had married in 1932. The couple eventually had three daughters. When the Japanese attacked China beginning in 1937, he sent the family home; he remained until 1938.

Upon Judd's return to the United States the second time, he worked to inform the American people of the danger of Japanese imperialism. From 1938 to 1940 he spoke to 1,600 audiences across the country, supporting himself and his family from a small legacy. In 1939 he testified to the Foreign Relations Committee of the United States Senate and the Foreign Affairs Committee of the House of Representatives. The next year he started a medical practice in Minneapolis, speaking to audiences in the evenings, and in 1942 he successfully ran for Congress from Minnesota's Fifth Congressional District.

Judd's twenty-year congressional career brought him to national attention, during which he took middle-of-the-road positions on domestic issues and liberal positions on foreign policy, espousing the United Nations (in 1957 he served as an American delegate to the General Assembly), the Truman Doctrine of 1947, the Marshall Plan, and the

North Atlantic Treaty Organization (NATO), as well as the Point Four program to send American technical aid to developing countries. He worked fervently to support Nationalist China and was instrumental in arranging $338 million in Marshall Plan appropriations for pre–Communist China and another $125 million to be spent at presidential discretion. Meanwhile, he had pushed for and obtained a quota for Chinese immigrants in 1943; he later pressed for the elimination of all racial-discriminatory clauses from immigration and exclusion laws in the McCarran-Walter Act of 1952. He supported the Korean War, although he opposed President Harry Truman's dismissal of General Douglas MacArthur in 1951.

With the return of the Republican Party to the White House in 1953 under President Dwight D. Eisenhower, Judd offered even more support for administration foreign policy, including China policy (unlike the average isolationist Republican adherent). In 1960 he was a candidate for nomination as vice president during the first presidential candidacy of Richard M. Nixon. That year Judd was the party keynote speaker, and to all appearances he set the convention on fire. In a bid for eastern support, however, Nixon chose as his running mate Henry Cabot Lodge, Jr. Nevertheless, Judd loyally worked for the Nixon-Lodge ticket. After his defeat by the Democrats, Nixon told Judd that the G.O.P. might have won with Judd.

Congressman Judd was taken aback when Nixon, becoming president in 1969, espoused recognition of Communist China. For years Judd had headed the Committee of One Million, which worked against admission of the Peking government to the United Nations. Judd's committee dissolved in 1971.

Upon his defeat for reelection in 1972, Judd continued his speeches and advocacy centering on East Asian issues and commanded much attention with articles in *Reader's Digest* and a radio program. In 1981 Ronald Reagan awarded him the Presidential Medal of Freedom. He continued to live in Washington rather than returning to Minneapolis, until in 1988 he entered an Episcopalian retirement home in Maryland, where he eventually died at the age of ninety-five. He is buried in Rising City, Nebraska.

Judd's face was scarred in youth by a physician who sought to cure his acne by use of X rays. The unfortunate treatment led to a lifelong battle with cancer, the disease from which he died. His medical ministry saved many lives. His political ministry may have been less successful, but he was an unforgettable figure to the millions who heard him speak and the many more millions who read his words or heard them quoted or cited. His biographer concluded, perhaps with exaggeration, that he was possessed of a monumental ego. Regardless, he was certainly voluble. During one political campaign, he told his campaign manager to station himself at the rear of a hall and signal him after thirty-five minutes. The manager did so. After forty-five he waved his arms. After fifty-seven the orator interrupted himself to say, "Why, my own campaign manager is even in the back of the room trying to shut me up. But I won't be shut up—I'm going to finish this speech!"

★

Judd's papers are mostly in the Hoover Institution in Palo Alto, California, with a small collection in the Minnesota Historical Society. The biography by Lee Edwards, *Missionary for Freedom: The Life and Times of Walter Judd* (1990), contains much description of national and international events. *Chronicles of a Statesman* (1980) is a compilation of Judd's speeches edited by Edward J. Rozek. Obituaries are in the *Washington Post* and *Minneapolis Star-Tribune* (both 15 Feb. 1994).

ROBERT H. FERRELL

JULIA, Raul Rafael Carlos (*b.* 9 March 1940 in San Juan, Puerto Rico; *d.* 24 October 1994 in Manhasset, New York), actor best known for the comedic role of Gomez Addams in *The Addams Family* (1991) and *Addams Family Values* (1993).

Julia was the oldest of four children born to Raul Julia, a prosperous restaurateur, and Olga Arcelay, a homemaker. At age five Julia attended a school taught by nuns who

Raul Julia. AP/WIDE WORLD PHOTOS

spoke mostly English, making Julia fluent in the language at an early age. The acting bug bit Julia when he was cast as the devil in a school play. The usually quiet and reserved little boy jumped on stage and recited his lines flawlessly.

From 1954 to 1958 Julia attended Colegio San Ignacio de Loyola, where he studied the plays of William Shakespeare. He appeared in every play the school produced during that time. After high school graduation in 1958, Julia enrolled in the Universidad de Puerto Rico, where he earned a bachelor's degree in the liberal arts in 1962. While in college he continued to act at local playhouses and nightclubs. After graduation his parents wanted Julia to become a lawyer, but Julia had other ideas. He became involved in theater.

While acting at a San Juan hotel, Julia caught the eye of Orson Bean, an actor and comedian from the United States, who convinced Julia that he should come to New York City to perfect his craft. Much to his parents chagrin, Julia decided to take Bean's advice. Prior to his departure, however, his brother died in a car accident. Although it was a painful time, Julia moved to New York in 1964.

In 1965 Julia married Magda Vasallo. He worked at a series of odd jobs, tutored people in Spanish, and accepted a stipend from his parents to make ends meet. His New York stage debut was in a 1965 off-Broadway production of *La vida es sueño* (Life Is a Dream). Later that year he appeared as Conrad Birdie in the musical *Bye Bye Birdie*. Julia began his long association with the theatrical producer Joseph Papp when he appeared in 1966 as MacDuff in a Spanish-language production of *Macbeth* with Papp's New York Shakespeare Festival. In 1967 Papp cast Julia as Demetrius in *Titus Adronicus*.

Julia made his Broadway debut in *The Cuban Thing* in 1968. Unfortunately, the play folded after only one performance. In 1969 Julia divorced Vasallo and met Merel Poloway, whom he married on 28 June 1976; Poloway and Julia had two children. Julia acted in *Indians* (1969) and *The Castro Complex* (1970) before having a watershed year in 1971, when a festival production of *Two Gentlemen of Verona* moved to Broadway. Julia garnered a Best Actor in a Musical Tony nomination for his lusty portrayal of Proteus. Julia made his feature film debut in *The Panic in Needle Park* (1971), a harsh, realistic study of drug addicts. He also dabbled in a bit of television work during this period, appearing as Rafael the Fixit Man on *Sesame Street*.

Julia's stage career continued to thrive through the 1970s. He starred on Broadway in a revival of *Where's Charley?* (1974), for which he received his second Tony nomination, and in the revival of *The Threepenny Opera* (1976–1977), for which he received his third Tony nomination. In 1978 he played Petruchio to Meryl Streep's Kate in *The Taming of the Shrew*. Julia received his fourth and final

Tony nomination in 1982 for his starring role in the musical *Nine*.

In 1977 Julia and Poloway began their long association with the Hunger Project, a charity dedicated to ending world hunger. Julia was the charity's spokesperson for seventeen years. In 1978 Julia had his first major film role in *The Eyes of Laura Mars*. But it was not until 1985 that his film and TV career took off, when he starred opposite William Hurt in the political prisoner drama *Kiss of the Spider Woman*. This movie brought both actors a joint award as best actor from the National Board of Review. That same year Julia starred as a detective in the film *Compromising Positions*. Other significant film roles followed with *The Morning After* (1986), *Trading Hearts* (1987), *Moon over Parador* (1988), *Tequila Sunrise* (1988), *Romero* (1989), and *Presumed Innocent* (1990). On television, he starred in the miniseries *Mussolini: The Untold Story* (1985) and the made-for-television movie *Onassis: The Richest Man in the World* (1988).

The 1990s were perhaps the best for Julia professionally, and it is ironic that he became ill at this time. In 1991 Julia landed the role of the dashing, yet ghoulish Gomez Addams in *The Addams Family*. He reprised this role in *Addams Family Values* (1993). Julia had his last starring role on Broadway as Don Quixote in the musical drama *Man of La Mancha* (1992). On television he played the environmental activist Chico Mendes in *The Burning Season* (1994), which became his most revered performance. For this role, he received a Golden Globe Award, a Screen Actors Guild Award, a Cable Ace Award, and the Emmy for outstanding lead actor in a miniseries or special. His last role was in the film *Street Fighter* (1994).

By the time Julia was filming *Street Fighter* and *The Burning Season,* he was battling stomach cancer. He died in a Manhasset hospital on Long Island, New York, from complications from a massive stroke. Although there were several tributes to Julia in New York, his final resting place was his homeland. Thousands of people lined the streets of San Juan, Puerto Rico, for his state funeral and burial.

It is much too easy to remember Raul Julia as the man who played Gomez Addams. First and foremost, he was a man of the theater. He also bridged the gap between being proud of his Puerto Rican heritage, yet transcending stereotypes. Finally, his philanthropic endeavors with the Hunger Project, which was renamed Raul Julia's Hunger Project after he died, are a lasting tribute to the man, the actor, and the humanitarian.

★

There is no full-length biography or autobiography of Julia, but two young adult biographies, *Raul Julia* (1994) by Rebecca Stefoff and *Raul Julia: Actor and Humanitarian* (1998) by Barbara C. Cruz, comprehensively cover the actor's career, personal life, and humanitarian contributions. *Raul Julia* (1995) by Frank Perez and Ann Weil is a clever and informative children's book about the actor, written for grades 3–6. Valuable articles about Julia include Alexandra Witchel, "Raul Julia: Kiss of Success," *Elle* (Nov. 1987), and Kevin Sweeney, "Raul Julia's Romero: A Flawed but Saintly Man," *Lerner Publications* (Sept. 1989). Obituaries appeared in *Knight-Ridder* (24 Oct. 1994), *Time* (7 Nov. 1994), and *People Weekly* (7 Nov. 1994).

KRISTAN GINTHER

K

KAPPEL, Frederick Russell (*b.* 14 January 1902 in Albert Lea, Minnesota; *d.* 10 November 1994 in Sarasota, Florida), president and chairman of AT&T who presided over the unprecedented expansion of the Bell Telephone System in the post–World War II period.

Frederick R. Kappel (rhymes with "apple") was the eldest of five children. His father, Frederick Albert Kappel, whose Swiss ancestors had been among Minnesota's pioneering families, owned a barbershop that doubled as a cigar emporium. His mother, Gertrude May Towle, was a homemaker. While an undergraduate at the University of Minnesota in Minneapolis, Kappel was a serviceman for the Southern Minnesota Gas and Electric Company; he also worked as a waiter. An accomplished musician, Kappel was a drummer in the University of Minnesota band and, to generate income during the school year, he moonlighted as a drummer for a dance band. An electrical engineering major, he earned a bachelor of science degree in 1924.

After graduation Kappel embarked upon a career in the communications industry and literally worked his way up the ladder a step at a time. His first position as a $25-a-week groundsman with the Northwestern Bell Telephone Company led, in the course of one year, to jobs as a lineman, splicer's assistant, circuit tester, switchman's apprentice, and interference engineer. In 1925 Kappel advanced to the position of inductive coordination engineer. Three years later he moved to the company's division of foreign wire relations. In the meantime, on 18 August 1927 he married Ruth Carolyn Ihm, whom he had met during their undergraduate days at the University of Minnesota. The couple had two children.

Following his marriage, Kappel's career continued to advance steadily. By 1929 he was a transmission and protection engineer. In 1933 he became a building and equipment engineer for Northwestern Bell. A year later Kappel was transferred to Omaha, Nebraska. After serving initially as regional engineer for the Nebraska and South Dakota service area, he was promoted to plant operations supervisor in Omaha in 1937. Two years later he became assistant vice president in charge of operations. After six years as vice president beginning in 1942, Kappel accepted a position with Northwestern Bell's parent company, American Telephone and Telegraph (AT&T).

In 1949, his first year at AT&T headquarters in New York City, Kappel advanced from assistant vice president for operations and engineering to vice president of the long lines department to vice president for operations and engineering. Five years later he was named president of Western Electric, AT&T's manufacturing subsidiary, which produced not only telephone equipment in its nearly two dozen plants but also components for the U.S. government's Nike missiles, a key element in the nation's cold war defense arsenal. Under Kappel's leadership, Western Electric also provided communications equipment for the Distant Early Warning (DEW) radar stations established

Frederick Kappel, 1966. ARCHIVE PHOTOS

in the Arctic to alert the U.S. military in the event that America's cold war foe, the Soviet Union, launched nuclear weapons. A hands-on manager, Kappel personally inspected Western Electric's work in the Arctic and paid regular visits to the company's far-flung plants. Approximately 50 percent of his time was spent in the field.

Beginning in 1956, when he was elected president of AT&T, Kappel supervised a $10 billion expansion of the Bell Telephone System necessitated by the insatiable post–World War II demand for phone service. To finance the expansion, an enormous bond issue and a major increase in the number of common stocks were required. The number of AT&T shareholders jumped from 1.5 million to more than 3 million during the time Kappel served as company president and then, beginning in 1961, as chairman. He also presided over the development and launching of TELSTAR communications satellites, something his daughter has called his most important achievement. The utilization of phone lines for data transmission, the expansion of direct distance dialing, and the laying of new overseas cables to Europe, the West Indies, Bermuda, Panama, the Philippines, Guam, Japan, and Hawaii also occurred during his tenure at AT&T.

All the while Kappel never lost sight of the fact that the company he headed was essentially a "people" business. In an address made at the annual meeting of the American Bar Association in 1964, he stated that the goal of AT&T

was "to make your service always more personal, more closely suited to your individual needs, more simple and easy for you to use." Two years later, when he received Pace University's Man in Management Award, Kappel shared his thoughts on business leadership. "I think leadership in a large organization must be exercised by many people, not by just a few," he said. "You cannot articulate goals in an ivory tower. . . . You have to get around, try things out, test, listen, and learn. If you want people to share your values, you have to share with them." Even before his retirement from AT&T in 1967, Kappel devoted time to public service and in the process imparted his philosophy of business leadership. In 1963, as chairman of the Business Council, an influential organization providing economic advice to the president of the United States, he called upon corporations to increase their number of minority employees. Appointed chairman of the Commission on Postal Organization by President Lyndon B. Johnson in 1967, Kappel also served as special mediator in a railroad conflict during the Johnson administration. Kappel was a governor of the United States Postal Service during the administration of President Richard M. Nixon and chairman of the Postal Service from 1972 to 1974. In the late 1960s Kappel returned to the corporate world. He served as chairman of the International Paper Company's board from 1969 to 1971. In 1971 and 1972 he was chairman of the company's executive committee. During his lifetime, Kappel was honored by the Economic Club of New York, which conferred its Gold Medal for Management upon him in 1959. Other awards included the Cross of Commander of the Postal Award of the Republic of France in 1962 and the Citation for Leadership in the Conquest of Space from the Salvation Army the same year. In 1963 Kappel was the recipient of the Silver Quill award from the National Business Publications Association. He received the Presidential Medal of Freedom in 1964 and the Hoover Medal in 1972. Kappel, who for many years lived in Bronxville, a suburb of New York City, died of Alzheimer's disease at the age of ninety-two. He is buried in Lakewood Cemetery in Minneapolis. He was predeceased by his first wife, Ruth, who died in 1974, and survived by his second wife, Alice McWhorter, whom he had married on 2 December 1978.

In the course of his long career in the communications industry, Kappel witnessed many changes, a considerable number of which he initiated, particularly during his tenure at Western Electric and AT&T, and presided over the unprecedented expansion of the Bell System during the period after World War II. That he accomplished as much as he did was not surprising, according to William G. Sharwell, vice president of administration and planning at AT&T, because "Frederick Kappel's most outstanding qualities were his drive and persistence. He was also a good motivator."

Kappel discusses his business philosophy in two books he wrote: *Vitality in a Business Enterprise* (1960) and *Business Purpose and Performance: Selections from Talks and Papers* (1964). Substantial biographical articles about Kappel appear in *Current Biography 1957* (1958) and Nelson Lichtenstein, ed., *Political Profiles: The Johnson Years* (1976). Kappel's business career is discussed in *Business Week* (28 Nov. 1953), *U.S. News and World Report* (28 Sept. 1956), *Newsweek* (1 Oct. 1956), and *Time* (1 Oct. 1956). An obituary is in the *New York Times* (12 Nov. 1994).

MARILYN E. WEIGOLD

KAY, Ulysses Simpson (*b.* 7 January 1917 in Tucson, Arizona; *d.* 20 May 1995 in Englewood, New Jersey), classically trained composer and professor who was among the first black American musicians to write music independent of folk traditions.

From an early age, Kay determined to be an accomplished musician, with encouragement from musically inclined relatives including his father, Ulysses S. Kay, a barber who sang in the family home, and his mother, Elizabeth Davis Kay, who sang at church and played piano. Especially influential was his uncle, the legendary cornetist and leader of the Creole Jazz Band, Joseph "King" Oliver, who urged

Ulysses Kay. © OSCAR WHITE/CORBIS

his nephew to study piano. Kay took piano lessons from the age of six through his college years. In his youth he also studied the violin, saxophone, and flute, performing in school ensembles and in a navy band during World War II. But well into adulthood he did not consider himself "a player."

At age seventeen he entered the University of Arizona, where he received a bachelor's degree in 1938. As an undergraduate he met the eminent composer William Grant Still, probably best known for his *Afro-American Symphony*. The Mississippi-born Still encouraged Kay's composition efforts, and the younger musician considered Still a major influence on his career. Kay received a master's degree in 1940 from the Eastman School of Music in Rochester, New York, where he studied composition with Bernard Rogers, another career influence, and with Howard Hanson. Kay continued study with Paul Hindemith at the Berkshire Festival at Tanglewood in Massachusetts and at Yale University (1941–1943). After his military service, Kay studied with Otto Luening at Columbia University (1946–1949). On 20 August 1949 Kay married Barbara Harrison, a teacher; they had three daughters.

Kay's work and residence overseas included three years in Italy (1949–1952), made possible by two Prix de Rome awards and a Fulbright scholarship. In 1958 he took part in a cultural exchange with the Soviet Union through the U.S. State Department. A music professor for more than twenty years, Kay taught at Boston University in 1965 and at the University of California at Los Angeles in 1966–1967. In 1968 he joined the faculty of the City University of New York's Herbert H. Lehman College, where he remained until retiring in 1988. For years Kay was also an editorial consultant for Broadcast Music, Inc.

Kay wrote more than 140 compositions scored primarily for orchestra, chorus, chamber groups, voice, and keyboard instruments. While some black American composers routinely incorporated spirituals, work songs, or other elements of black folk traditions into classical structures, Kay preferred not to follow suit. Comparatively few of his pieces draw attention to black traditions, among them *Lift Every Voice and Sing* (1952), scored for a big band–style orchestra and named for a hymn often called the black national anthem; *Fugitive Songs* (1950), an unpublished song group; and the opera *Frederick Douglass* (1985), created with librettist Donald Dorr. In both scholarly interviews and the public press, Kay has been quoted as saying he saw "nothing especially black" about his music, "other than its expressive content."

Nor could Kay's compositional career be considered terribly nationalistic, because he did not often incorporate American folk tunes or patriotic themes into his works, although he did write some music for the Bicentennial celebration of 1976. Still, some observers have detected a subtle

American flavor in his *Serenade for Orchestra* (1954) and *Umbrian Scene* (1963), due to their "optimistic character" and "unconstrained color and melody." Kay also wrote pieces inspired by monumental American historical figures, among them presidents Abraham Lincoln and John F. Kennedy and the explorer Admiral Richard E. Byrd.

Kay's choral and orchestral music was often inspired by literary or historical figures. One piece he mentioned as being personally significant to him was the 1966 symphonic essay *Markings,* inspired by writings of the United Nations secretary-general Dag Hammarskjold. Premiered by the Detroit Symphony Orchestra and performed by the New York Philharmonic and Cleveland Orchestra, *Markings* stood out to Kay because it is "big in scope as well as in expression" and "quite personal in terms of how it's worked out." *The International Dictionary of Black Composers* calls *Markings* prototypical of Kay's chromaticism, lyrical melodies, and potential for great tension.

In middle age Kay increasingly read poetry for inspiration for vocal and choral music. Text-based compositions include *Three Pieces After Blake* (1952) for soprano and orchestra, *Inscriptions from Whitman* (1963) for chorus and orchestra, *Emily Dickinson Set* (1964) for women's chorus, and *Stephen Crane Set* (1967) for chorus and orchestra. Other major orchestral works include *Of New Horizons: Overture* (1944), which was an early success premiered by the New York Philharmonic; *Concerto for Orchestra* (1948); *Theater Set* (1968), which was commissioned for the Atlanta Symphony; and *Southern Harmony: Four Aspects for Orchestra* (1975), inspired by nineteenth-century hymns.

Slightly built with glasses, close-cropped hair, and a receding hairline in later years, Kay and his wife lived for more than three decades in suburban Teaneck, New Jersey. He died in Englewood Hospital after a lengthy illness. The family attributed the cause to Parkinson's disease.

Historians who classify Kay's music sometimes head in decidedly different directions. Observations often depend on various periods in Kay's music. Hildred Roach, who wrote two volumes of profiles of black composers, sees "neo-baroque" structure and counterpoint in some of Kay's early works. Pieces from the 1940s and 1950s seem "neoclassical" to Samuel A. Floyd, Jr. Atonality in Kay's late works has been described both by Roach and by Kyle Gann of the *Village Voice*. Perhaps the former Harvard University professor Eileen Southern's description of Kay's "contemporary traditionalism," "neoromantic roots," and "crisp, dissonant" technique comes closest to the composer's intentions.

★

The music historian Nicolas Slonimsky's extensive detailing of Kay's life and work in his 1997 edition of *Baker's Biographical Dictionary of Twentieth-Century Classical Musicians* builds on material Slonimsky published forty years earlier in *American Composers Alliance (ACA) Bulletin.* Hildred Roach chronicled Kay's work and analyzed his music in her first volume of *Black American Music: Past and Present* (1973), then credited the composer for research for the second volume (1985). *The Black Composer Speaks* (1978), edited by the jazz composer David N. Baker and others for Indiana University's Afro-American Arts Institute, contains extensive commentary and analysis from Kay himself. Obituaries are in the *New York Times* and *Bergen* (New Jersey) *Record* (both 23 May 1995) and the *Washington Post* (28 May 1995).

WHITNEY SMITH

KELLY, Eugene Curran ("Gene") (*b.* 23 August 1912 in Pittsburgh, Pennsylvania; *d.* 2 February 1996 in Beverly Hills, California), dancer, actor, director, and choreographer who helped invent and extend the possibilities of the Hollywood musical.

Kelly was the third of five children born to James Patrick Joseph Kelly and Harriet Curran, second-generation Irish-Americans. The family lived in East Liberty, a working-class section of Pittsburgh. James Kelly was a $75-a-week traveling salesman for the Columbia Phonograph Company and was home only on weekends. He was an affable man of careful habits who adored his family and demanded their respect. Harriet Kelly taught her children the value of thrift and was strongly committed to their success. At the age of eight Kelly enrolled in a dance school where his mother worked as a receptionist. He was a good athlete. He enjoyed skating, played hockey, and loved baseball, gymnastics, and swimming. Small for his age, and annoyed with a "girl's name," Gene groused that dancing was "a girl's game."

Encouraged by their mother, the five Kelly children appeared in local talent shows. A younger brother, Fred, loved the limelight, but Kelly dreamed of becoming a shortstop for the Pittsburgh Pirates. At age ten he did a tap dance to the song "Toyland," from Victor Herbert's operetta *Babes in Toyland,* at the St. Raphael School and reluctantly took violin lessons. A respectable student at Peabody High School, Kelly performed in school shows and discovered at age fifteen that "girls loved dancers." He debated well and wrote for the school paper. In 1929 he enrolled at Pennsylvania State College, planning a career in journalism.

The stock market crash in the fall of 1929 cost James Kelly his job and brought Kelly home from college. The Kelly children went to work to keep the family financially afloat. Kelly dug ditches, laid bricks, pumped gas, and danced nights with Fred at local clubs and speakeasies. Audiences threw coins onto the stage. He found it humiliating, but it was a way to make $10. As a camp counselor

Gene Kelly, 1970. © Hulton-Deutsch Collection/Corbis

turned to Chicago, studied dance with a protégé of a Russian master, and danced at the city's World's Fair. He entered law school but left in less than one month. His enthusiasm for dance had become too great.

Over the next five years Kelly's dancing schools grew to 350 pupils. He performed with them at the Pittsburgh Playhouse and with his brother Fred in cap and gown shows with college players staged at the University of Pittsburgh. Gene's enthusiasm for ballet grew, but he turned down an offer to join the Ballet Russe de Monte Carlo because "I couldn't see doing *Swan Lake* for the next twenty years of my life." In the summer of 1937 he accepted an offer to choreograph a dance number on Broadway in New York City but returned to Pittsburgh when he found the producers only wanted him for the male chorus. A year later he took the advice of the choreographer Robert Alton and tried again.

Kelly's Broadway debut came in the chorus line of Cole Porter's *Leave It to Me.* He danced while Mary Martin sang "My Heart Belongs to Daddy." He had a bigger role in Harold Rome's *One for the Money.* In the summer of 1939 he worked as a choreographer with a Connecticut stock company and made friends with future collaborators Betty Comden and Adolph Green, who found the twenty-seven-year-old "outgoing, earthy, with something extra hidden away." He was a hit as Harry the Hoofer in William Saroyan's *The Time of Your Life,* which opened at the Booth Theater in October. Saroyan credited Kelly's tap dancing with helping to win the play a twenty-two-week run. For Kelly it was the beginning of realizing the common man through dance. The role won him the job of a choreographer at Billy Rose's Diamond Horseshoe dance club, where he met the sixteen-year-old dancer Betsy Blair, whom he married on 24 September 1941.

Meanwhile, however, Christmas Eve 1940 saw the Broadway opening of Rodgers and Hart's *Pal Joey,* starring Kelly as the sleazy song-and-dance man Joey Evans, a portrait critics found an exercise in "theater art." Kelly's "characterization through dance" included a classical ballet in the first act, followed by a Spanish tap dance in tango rhythm. Kelly's confident athleticism made a deep impression on audiences, and Louis B. Mayer, head of Metro-Goldwyn-Mayer (MGM), was impressed enough to offer Kelly a Hollywood contract, which he rejected in a disagreement over a screen test. Privately, Kelly wondered whether he was ready for films. He continued to star in the 270-performance run of *Pal Joey* by night while choreographing *Best Foot Forward* by day. Kelly eventually signed a contract with the independent Hollywood producer David O. Selznick and arrived in Hollywood on 11 November 1941.

For five months Kelly sat, because Selznick thought of Kelly as a dramatic actor. "Selznick didn't want to make musicals," Kelly recalled, and the young dancer had no

during the summer he taught dance and earned $150, enough to continue his education at the University of Pittsburgh. On weekends, beginning in 1931, he agreed to help his mother at a dance school she had started in Johnstown, Pennsylvania, sixty-five miles from Pittsburgh. Lessons cost fifty cents apiece, but some parents paid in potatoes and bread loaves. His debut as a choreographer came at Pittsburgh's Beth Shalom Synagogue with a production of *Revue of Revues* that made the temple $1,100. Students flocked to the classes he started at the synagogue.

The Gene Kelly Studio of the Dance opened in Johnstown in 1932 and developed a brisk business. One hundred fifty students, ages four to eighteen, danced the Black Bottom and Big Apple in summer shows that became a regional attraction. Apache dances and tap solos filled the seats. James Kelly ran the box office and Harriet kept the books. In 1933 Kelly graduated from the University of Pittsburgh with a degree in economics and planned to begin law school. But his dance schools in Pittsburgh and Johnstown were flourishing. In the summer of that year he re-interest in becoming a dramatic actor. Arthur Freed, a musical producer at MGM, had seen Kelly on Broadway and persuaded him to star opposite Judy Garland in *For Me and My Gal* (1942), playing a character not unlike that of *Pal Joey*'s Evans. The plot was thin but Kelly's dancing and Garland's singing made the film a hit. MGM bought Kelly's contract from Selznick at $1,000 a week for seven years. An added delight for Kelly was the birth of a daughter in October 1942.

Kelly's next four films at MGM (all 1943) were undistinguished. He supported Franchot Tone in a World War II drama, *Pilot No. 5,* backed up Red Skelton's slapstick in *DuBarry Was a Lady,* danced with a mop in *Thousands Cheer,* and was overly earnest in *The Cross of Lorraine.* MGM did not know how to cast him. And Kelly himself had not yet discovered what worked. "I fell in love with dancing for the movies," he observed, but quickly found that "what I did on stage didn't work in films." He wanted "to do something new in dance," to lift it out of being "a musical interlude," enabling it to "further the plot emotionally" by "expressing what the character felt in dance in a way that had meaning for the camera." Dance exploited three dimensions but film had only two. He found a way to attack the problem in *Cover Girl* (1944) by dancing a duet with his conscience, transforming a simple movie moment of lost love into a scene that expanded the limits of film art. Kelly and his doppelgänger start in unity and end in violent, competing leaps, jumps, and turns. Critics and audiences were equally enthusiastic. The film historian Tony Thomas summarized their sense that it marked "a major turning point in the history of the Hollywood musical."

Back at MGM and working with Stanley Donen, Kelly in a sailor suit danced memorably with Jerry the Mouse, a cartoon character, in *Anchors Aweigh* (1945), combining animation and live action in a performance that won him an Academy Award nomination for best actor. Costar Frank Sinatra got a dose of Kelly's "insane insistence on hard work" and was never better. In November 1944, with the film in post-production, Kelly joined the navy, serving eighteen months in special services without seeing combat. When he returned to Hollywood, the film *Ziegfeld Follies* (1946) was in release, featuring a dance duet he had done with Fred Astaire before enlisting. It highlighted the charming grace of one and the robust athleticism of the other. Kelly's dance creations with kids failed to make *Living in a Big Way* (released in 1947) a hit but won him praise from Martha Graham, whose work had long inspired him. Kelly broke an ankle while filming *Easter Parade* (1948) with Judy Garland, and Astaire was brought in to replace him. Kelly starred again with Garland in the period musical *The Pirate* (1948), directed by her husband, Vincente Minnelli. Critics praised Kelly's bravura performance, but au-

diences, Kelly realized, liked him better as a hoofer. His dance duet with Garland received raves, but the film did not do well at the box office. "You couldn't give it away with dishes," he later observed, after the film had become a cult classic. A similar swashbuckling style in *The Three Musketeers* (1948) did better at the box office.

Frustrated in his desire to bring *Cyrano de Bergerac* to the screen, Kelly instead brought modern ballet to a Hollywood film, when he and Vera-Ellen did "Slaughter on Tenth Avenue" in the star-studded *Words and Music* (1948). Kelly came up with the idea for *Take Me Out to the Ball Game* (1949) as a salute to the national pastime. He was reunited with Comden and Green as well as Sinatra. Kelly's steps in "Where Did You Get That Hat?" celebrate the Irish experience in America, and the number was one of his personal favorites. The ensemble was happily reunited in *On the Town* (1949), Kelly's directorial debut with Donen and the first movie musical to be shot on location. The outcome was an exuberant evocation of postwar American enthusiasm as it followed three sailors on a twenty-four-hour leave in New York City. Kelly's quick cutting captured the optimism of Leonard Bernstein's "New York, New York," while transforming the narrative possibilities of the movie musical. It liberated the musical from the studio back lot and became Kelly's favorite film.

Kelly's favorite dance was his highly inventive duet with a spread sheet of newspaper, ably accompanied by a squeaky floorboard, in *Summer Stock* (1950), his last film with Judy Garland. Arthur Freed's idea of linking Gershwin standards to the romantic life of an artist living abroad became *An American in Paris,* which won the Academy Award for best film of 1951 and was the most honored movie musical of its time. Highlights included Kelly's time-step shim-sham with Parisian street children to the tune of "I Got Rhythm" and his romantic pas de deux with Leslie Caron along the Seine to the strains of "Our Love Is Here to Stay." A seventeen-minute finale, staged by Kelly and director Minnelli, combined elements of modern and classical ballet, tap, and jitterbug. Kelly's creativity was recognized in a special Academy Award for furthering the art of filmmaking.

The brilliance of Kelly's next film, *Singin' in the Rain* (1952), was not immediately recognized because of its close proximity to *An American in Paris.* Kelly rated it below *On the Town,* but the affectionate send-up of Hollywood's conversion to sound, codirected by Kelly and Donen, has only grown in reputation over the years, making it almost certainly the most admired film musical ever made. Kelly thought his semiautobiographical "Gotta Sing! Gotta Dance!" would stop the show. Instead, it was the title tune, shot in a day and a half, which became the all-time best loved dance on film. The movie's record-shattering success at the box office should have signaled a golden age in making musicals, but in fact that age was nearly over. Threatened by television and stripped by court order of their profitable theaters, Hollywood studios were forced to cut back on production schedules. The teams that made musicals were quietly disbanded. Kelly spent eighteen months abroad, making three films that were quickly forgotten. A tight budget and an indifferent public doomed the Kelly-Minnelli collaboration in *Brigadoon* (1954). Kelly's collaboration with Donen and Comden and Green in *It's Always Fair Weather* (1955), complicated by the wide-frame CinemaScope, did little better. *Les Girls* (1957) would be Kelly's last starring role in a major musical.

Kelly's personal and professional life after the late 1950s was a long, if never fully satisfying, postscript. On 3 April 1957 his fifteen-year marriage to Betsy Blair ended in divorce. He married Jeannie Coyne, a longtime coworker from his MGM days, on 6 August 1960. They had two children. Coyne died of leukemia on 10 May 1973. In July 1990, Kelly married Patricia Ward, a scriptwriter.

Inherit the Wind (1960) was a good dramatic part for Kelly. He directed *Gigot* (1962) to good reviews and *Hello, Dolly!* (1969) to indifferent ones. Occasional television appearances in the 1960s and 1970s were affectionately received. After *Forty Carats* (1973) and *Xanadu* (1980) he stopped working as an onscreen actor. His appearances in *That's Entertainment!* (1974), *That's Entertainment, Part 2* (1976), and *That's Dancing!* (1985) celebrated the history of the movie musical in which he had played a leading role. On 7 March 1985 he received the prestigious Lifetime Achievement Award from the American Film Institute for "advancing the filmmaking art" and for work that "has stood the test of time." He told interviewers that, from the first, he had attempted to dance "the love, joy, and dreams" of the common man. The creative work of collaboration was his greatest joy. His only regret was that "dance careers are so short" he never had the chance "to do the many dances I still have up in my head." Weakened by a series of strokes in the mid-1990s, he died with his legacy firmly fixed as the great architect of the movie musical in the golden era of film.

★

A fire in 1983 at Kelly's Beverly Hills home destroyed many of his personal papers. Materials on his life are in the Gene Kelly Archives in the Department of Special Collections at Boston University. Kelly was interviewed at length by Clive Hirschhorn for *Gene Kelly: A Biography* (1974). Extensive interviews also are in Tony Thomas, *The Films of Gene Kelly, Song and Dance Man* (1974), and Jerome Delamater, *Dance in the Hollywood Musical* (1981). Retrospectives include Rudy Behlmer, "Gene Kelly Is One Dancer Who Can Also Act and Direct," *Films in Review* (Jan. 1964); David Shipman, *The Great Movie Stars: The International Years* (1972); Jeanine Basinger, *Gene Kelly* (1976); and Alvin Yud-

koff, *Gene Kelly: A Life of Dance and Dreams* (1999). Contextual works on Kelly's career and its significance include Lee Edward Stern, *The Movie Musical* (1974); Jane Feuer, *The Hollywood Musical* (1982); and Rick Altman, *The American Film Musical* (1987). An obituary is in the *New York Times* (3 Feb. 1996). He was interviewed in 1974 for "An Evening with Gene Kelly," a joint production of the British Broadcasting Company and MGM, and again in 1994 for *Reflections on the Silver Screen,* a series produced by the Library of Congress.

BRUCE J. EVENSEN

KENNEDY, Rose Elizabeth Fitzgerald (*b.* 22 July 1890 in Boston, Massachusetts; *d.* 22 January 1995 in Hyannis Port, Massachusetts), mother of President John F. Kennedy and matriarch of a political family that in a span of eighty years produced an ambassador, three United States senators, three congressmen, and a lieutenant governor, and with her encouragement directed its wealth and personal leadership to politics, public service, and a variety of philanthropic causes.

Rose Fitzgerald was the eldest of three daughters and three sons born to Mary Josephine Hannon and John Patrick "Honey Fitz" Fitzgerald, a wealthy businessman and powerful Democratic politician who served three terms in Congress (1895–1901) and seven years as mayor of Boston (1906, 1907, 1910–1914.) By her own account she had an

Rose Kennedy, 1963. ASSOCIATED PRESS CBS

idyllic childhood in which she was readily indulged by a doting father and an adored mother, both of whom taught her to value the family, Roman Catholicism, and her Irish heritage. Because her mother disliked the public role of a political wife, Rose, even as a toddler, accompanied her father to parades and local gatherings as he kept in touch with his constituents or campaigned for office.

She was educated in the public schools, graduating with honors from Dorchester High School in 1906 at the age of fifteen. Her dream was to go to Wellesley College, but her parents considered her too young and instead sent her to study at the Convent of the Sacred Heart in downtown Boston. At the end of the family's European tour in the summer of 1908, she and her sister Agnes remained at a convent school at Blumenthal in Holland on the Dutch-German border, where wealthy young women were trained for traditional roles as wives devoted to *kinder, kirche, und kucher* (children, church, and cooking). The following year, Rose entered the Sacred Heart Convent at Manhattanville on the Upper West Side of New York City, where she received a graduation certificate in 1910.

She returned to Boston to an active social life, courses at Boston University and the New England Conservatory of Music, and settlement work among the poor. She again joined Honey Fitz on his political rounds, sometimes serving as his translator when French or German dignitaries came to visit. On 7 October 1914, having overcome her father's objection to the match, she married Joseph Patrick Kennedy at a wedding mass, attended by their families, in the private chapel of William Cardinal O'Connell.

Joe Kennedy, she wrote, was the love of her life, and despite repeated separations during their years together and reports of his philandering that she refused to believe, he remained so until her death. They first met as children in Maine, where their families summered, and from the age of sixteen, she said, she was determined to be his wife. The son of P. J. Kennedy—a prominent Irish Catholic businessman and powerful Democratic ward boss who often clashed with Honey Fitz—he quickly made a name for himself among Boston's business leaders in the three years following his Harvard graduation. At twenty-five he was the youngest bank president in Massachusetts. Ambitious, willful, and, some said, ruthless, he was a gifted financier and over the next two decades, working long hours and often away from home, he amassed a fortune in banking, real estate, liquor distribution, Wall Street, and Hollywood, weathering the Great Depression with most of his wealth intact.

Rose Kennedy remained at home in Brookline, a Boston suburb, and later in the Riverdale neighborhood of the Bronx in New York City, giving birth to five daughters and four sons between 1915 and 1932 and overseeing their growth. She had been taught since childhood that motherhood was "the most beautiful station in life" and the family a sacred institution—concepts reinforced by her parents, her convent schooling, and especially her deep commitment to Roman Catholicism, which led her to a lifelong routine of daily mass and prayer. Among the lessons she passed on to her children were the principles that family came first; that each of them had a primary responsibility for the well-being of the others; and that they were obligated to develop their talents to the fullest and, because of the trust funds that each of them had, to make a positive contribution to society through some form of public service.

The family moved to New York in 1927 to escape the great social divide that continued to separate Boston's old-line Protestant families from the Irish Catholic newcomers, whatever their intelligence or wealth. Because of it, Rose Kennedy—among other slights—had been blackballed from membership in the Junior League, and her husband had been snubbed at Harvard and denied seats on the boards of Boston corporations. They were determined that their children would not face similar barriers, but they retained their ties to Massachusetts by purchasing a large summer home at Hyannis Port on Cape Cod.

In 1937 Kennedy accompanied her husband to England, where he served as U.S. ambassador to the Court of St. James, following a successful three years as the first chairman of the Securities and Exchange Commission and head of the Maritime Commission. It was a moment of political triumph—an Irish Catholic from Massachusetts in a post once occupied by John Adams and John Quincy Adams—that was soon marred by the ambassador's growing isolationism and his public statements that America and England should seek to coexist with the German dictator Adolf Hitler. Condemned by the British people as defeatist and pro-German, he resigned his appointment in February 1941, his public career effectively over and his dream of one day running for president destroyed.

The years 1941–1946 were difficult ones for Rose Kennedy. Her daughter Rosemary, who was diagnosed as mentally retarded (and on her father's orders, lobotomized), was placed in a nursing convent in the Midwest where she remained for the rest of her life. Her eldest son, Joseph Jr., was killed on a secret mission when his navy plane exploded over the English Channel in 1944 during World War II. A month later, her daughter Kathleen's English husband was killed in France; Kathleen herself died in 1946 in a plane crash. For a time, Rose Kennedy remained in her home at Hyannis Port, inconsolable in her grief; but in the end, she wrote, she found in her religion the strength to go on.

After the war, Kennedy and her husband settled into a pattern of separate lives; he in New York City or Palm Beach, Florida, she in Boston or on the cape. Ambitious as always for her children, she joined them in campaigning for John in his successful race for the House of Representatives (1946) and the Senate (1952). Popular with voters, she was a key figure in the 1960 presidential election, her children calling her the best campaigner in the family. Her proudest moment came with her son's inauguration as the thirty-fifth president of the United States in 1961. Robert Kennedy became the attorney general and Edward was elected to fill John's vacated Senate seat in 1962.

Her world fell apart once more when the president was assassinated on 22 November 1963, and yet again when Robert, then a U.S. senator from New York, was assassinated in Los Angeles in 1968 after winning four of five presidential primaries. Within a year, the ailing Joseph Kennedy was dead as well. Rose Kennedy withdrew into the family compound at Hyannis Port.

By 1974 she had completed her memoirs, *Times to Remember,* assigning the book's royalties to the Joseph P. Kennedy, Jr., Foundation to aid the mentally retarded. In 1984 she sustained the first in a series of debilitating strokes that left her partly paralyzed and confined to a wheelchair. She lived long enough to see two of her grandsons enter Congress, a third enter the Maryland legislature, and a granddaughter become lieutenant governor of Maryland. She was honored by a joint resolution of Congress and President George Bush on her 100th birthday.

Four years later, with members of her family at her bedside, she died at home of heart failure and complications from pneumonia. She is buried next to her husband in Hollyhood Cemetery, Brookline, Massachusetts.

Although some biographers of the Kennedys suggest that she was a cold and distant mother, obsessed by religion and driven by ambition, her surviving children in a letter to the *New York Times* categorically rejected that portrayal; she was, they wrote, a devoted and caring parent. Edward Kennedy had said as much at her 100th birthday party, calling her "the anchor of our family, the safe harbor to which we always came."

★

Rose Kennedy's papers are in the John F. Kennedy Library, Boston, Massachusetts. They cover the years 1896–1975 and include correspondence, family papers, and the drafts and proofs of her indispensable memoir, *Times to Remember* (1974). The family home at 83 Beale Street, Brookline, Massachusetts, is a National Historic Site, maintained by the National Park Service. The best biographical account of Rose Kennedy is Doris Kearns Goodwin, *The Fitzgeralds and the Kennedys: An American Saga* (1987); see also Richard Whalen, *The Founding Father* (1964), a biography of Joseph P. Kennedy. Barbara Gibson, *Life with Rose Kennedy: An Intimate Account* (1986), by her personal secretary in the 1970s, describes her years of declining health. Gibson, with Ted Schwarz, also wrote *Rose Kennedy and Her Family: The Best and Worst of Their Lives and Times* (1995). Other biographies include Gail

Cameron, *Rose: A Biography of Rose Fitzgerald Kennedy* (1971); Charles Hingham, *Rose: The Life and Times of Rose Fitzgerald Kennedy* (1995); and Cindy Adams and Susan Crimp, *Iron Rose: The Story of Rose Fitzgerald Kennedy and Her Dynasty* (1995). Obituaries are in the *New York Times* and *Boston Globe* (both 23 Jan. 1995).

ALLAN L. DAMON

KERR, Walter Francis (*b.* 8 July 1913 in Evanston, Illinois; *d.* 9 October 1996 in Dobbs Ferry, New York), Pulitzer Prize–winning drama critic and author.

One of four children born to Walter Sylvester Kerr, a construction foreman, and Esther Daugherty Kerr, the future drama critic of the *New York Times* began his career at the age of thirteen, writing for the Illinois weekly newsmagazine *Evanston Review*. As featured columnist in the junior section of the magazine, Kerr reviewed movies under the title "Junior Film Fans" until, two years into high school, he became the *Review*'s regular movie critic. Upon graduating from Evanston's St. George High School in 1931, he received a trip to Hollywood as a present from his parents. Throughout a long and distinguished career in the theater, it was the movies—and most notably silent comedy—that remained Kerr's most ardent preoccupation and in many ways the key to his mature thought.

From 1931 to 1933 Kerr attended DePaul University in Chicago on a four-year scholarship, which he was forced to relinquish for a full-time job due to the economic depression. Even so, he was able to find work in the film industry as a booking clerk for the Fox Film Company. At the same time, he was hired by the *Evanston Daily News-Index* to criticize films once or twice a week, a pace he was to maintain until he entered graduate school.

In 1935 he returned to college, this time at Northwestern University's School of Speech, a school noted for its drama department. Here, amidst a wide range of on-campus editorial involvements, he wrote two musicals and was publicity director of the university theater. He earned his B.S. in 1937 and an M.A. the following year. At Northwestern he received his tutelage in theory, playwriting, and history of the theater mainly from the distinguished drama teacher Hubert Heffner, who oversaw Kerr's master's thesis, a farce entitled *Christopher over Chaos*. This play, one of the 1939 winners of the Maxwell Anderson play contest at Stanford University, was eventually produced when Kerr was on the faculty of the Catholic University of America in Washington, D.C.

Kerr joined the newly formed drama department at Catholic University in 1938 after he met its founder, the Reverend Gilbert Hartke, at a meeting of the National Catholic Theater Conference in Chicago. Over the next

Walter Kerr *(right)* with Tennessee Williams at the Morosco Theatre, New York City, 1955. © BETTMANN/ CORBIS

eleven years, in addition to directing, writing, and adapting plays for the modern stage, Kerr lectured on dramaturgy and the history of the theater. In 1939, with Leo Brady, he wrote *Yankee Doodle Boy* about the life of George M. Cohan. In so doing, the pair originated a genre known as "musical biography," which Hollywood was to adopt for films about George Gershwin and other Tin Pan Alley greats. Their subsequent revue, *Count Me In,* was the first of Kerr's original works to reach Broadway, two of the other three coming in collaboration with his wife, the humorist Jean Kerr.

It was in 1941, while lecturing at Marywood College in Scranton, Pennsylvania, that Kerr attended a production of *Romeo and Juliet* and met the stage manager, a nineteen-year-old undergraduate named Jean Collins. For the next three summers, Collins studied at Catholic University, and on 16 August 1943, shortly after her graduation from Marywood, the two were married. Between 1944 and 1949, Kerr and his young wife pursued various theatrical ventures that would eventually take them beyond the university environment.

In 1944 they adapted Franz Werfel's historical novel *Song of Bernadette* for the amateur stage. In March 1946, three years after the release of the celebrated film of the same name, the play appeared on Broadway. By then Kerr's "musical biography" of American song, *Sing Out, Sweet Land,* had made the transition from university production

to Broadway opening to national tour. The couple then collaborated on a revue that arrived on Broadway in 1949 under the name *Touch and Go,* closing in London late the next year.

All of this activity was not without due appreciation, despite mixed results on the commercial front, and in mid-1949 the Kerrs took leave of Catholic University and what *Time* magazine called "the finest non-professional theater in the country" to make their way in New York City.

Although he did not abandon playwriting entirely, it was during this period that Kerr decided to devote himself primarily to criticism. In the fall of 1950 he took a job reviewing plays on a weekly basis for *Commonweal,* a well-regarded Catholic journal of opinion. One year later he succeeded Howard Barnes as drama critic for the *New York Herald-Tribune.* He had a fifteen-year run with the *Herald,* until it closed in 1966, whereupon he became drama critic for the *New York Times.* There he wrote weekly columns of a more substantial sort than would be possible for a newspaper critic writing daily. This choice played well into his strengths as a lecturer and scholar, while his experience in playwriting and directing gave him a detailed, sympathetic insight into what he was criticizing. He had a distinguished career with the *Times* until his retirement in 1983 at the age of seventy.

Over the intervening years, Kerr produced a prodigious body of work, including some three thousand reviews and essays before 1976. Substantial selections from his reviews saw republication as collections of essays, namely *Pieces at Eight* (1958); *Theatre in Spite of Itself* (1963); *Thirty Plays Hath November* (1969); *God on the Gymnasium Floor, and Other Theatrical Adventures* (1971); and *Journey to the Center of the Theater* (1979). All these collections show an unusual mixture of talent and learning, taste and principle, that to an even greater extent carries over to the full-length "theoretical" works that Kerr managed to write in addition to his journalistic pieces.

These works include the early book *How Not to Write a Play* (1955), drawn from Kerr's playwriting experiences during the Washington years; and *Criticism and Censorship* (1957), an extended lecture originally delivered at Marquette University. Then came his masterful treatment of the contemplative act in art and culture, published under the title *The Decline of Pleasure* (1962), and five years later another tour de force, *Tragedy and Comedy*, in which Kerr traced the complex interplay of these two ancient forms from their Greek roots down to the "pathos" of the modern stage. In 1975 he brought forth what is in many ways his signature work, *The Silent Clowns,* an affectionate journey through the technical intricacies and philosophical implications of silent film comedy. It was for these full-length works, as well as for his many years of opening-night reviews, that Kerr was honored with the Pulitzer Prize for criticism in 1978.

In 1990 the refurbished Ritz Theatre was renamed the Walter Kerr Theatre in his honor. The night following his death from pneumonia in a nursing home in 1996, the lights on Broadway were dimmed in his memory. He is buried in Greenwood Union Cemetery in Rye, New York.

In the midst of a rich and demanding career, Kerr married well and raised five sons and a daughter—a blessed life that perhaps explains the wholesomeness of his work. He was a many-sided man and had a sense of the Great Tradition, in philosophy no less than in drama. He could speak as tellingly about Periclean Athens as about the effect of Copernicus, Darwin, and Freud on the eclipse of genuine tragedy in our age. At the same time, he was open to the intellectual currents of the times, invoking an evolutionary model to illuminate both the nature of tragedy and the plight of a generation unduly constrained by an abstract sense of value and pleasure.

Nevertheless, comedy was Kerr's preferred theme, as his detractors were quick to point out. Even *Tragedy and Comedy* began as a book about comedy. At Kerr's hand, not only Falstaff but Shylock, too, reveal his true essence when seen from the perspective of the comic, understood as nature's limiting counterpoint to tragedy's expansive theme. From Kerr's perspective, Charlie Chaplin's ultimate limitation was that he had no limitation.

Kerr was that exceptional philosopher of culture who was both a real philosopher and a cultured man of his time. In fact, *The Decline of Pleasure* was cited as one of the top sixty spiritual books of the half-century. In the end Kerr wrote *grateful* prose: responsive, first of all, to a primordial presence, intellectually intuitive, thoroughly playful, witty and good-natured, the work of a man graciously pleased with his lot. As he said in concluding *The Decline of Pleasure,* "I am pleased in that instant when I discover that I am not alone. My joy, like the discovery, is profound."

★

The Walter and Jean Kerr Papers, covering the years 1929–1987, are at the State Historical Society Library at the University of Wisconsin at Madison. A detailed examination of Kerr's journalistic work was published by Roderick Bladel in *Walter Kerr: An Analysis of His Criticism* (1976). The text contains valuable biographical information but does not attempt to engage the longer works. The years leading up to Kerr's tenure with the *Herald-Tribune* are covered in great detail in *Current Biography* (1953). A respectful obituary, including excerpts from Kerr's more memorable reviews, is in the *New York Times* (10 Oct. 1996).

KENNETH M. BATINOVICH

KHAURY, Herbert Butros. *See* Tiny Tim.

KIENHOLZ, Edward Ralph (*b.* 23 October 1927 in Fairfield, Washington; *d.* 10 June 1994 in Sandpoint, Idaho), artist known for a highly personal form of sculptural installation art frequently characterized by complex and highly theatrical tableaux, typically involving found objects and mannequins and often exploring charged political and social themes.

Kienholz was the only son of Lawrence U. C. Kienholz, a farmer, and Ella Louise Eaton, a homemaker. In 1933 his parents adopted a girl, his only sibling. Growing up in rural Washington State, Kienholz learned carpentry, welding, and metalwork from his father. He attended high school in Fairfield, Washington, where he first showed an interest in art, often creating the sets for school plays. He graduated in 1945. Beginning in 1946, Kienholz traveled extensively for several years and held numerous odd jobs. He spent time in Montana, Oregon, Minnesota, Chicago, and Los Angeles, working variously as a used-car salesman, the manager of a dance band, a vacuum cleaner salesman, a builder, a window display designer, and an attendant at a mental hospital. Kienholz eventually returned to the Spokane, Washington, area. He briefly studied art at Whitworth College in Spokane and the Eastern Washington College of Education in nearby Cheney, Washington.

After another round of traveling during which he lived briefly in both Reno and Las Vegas, Nevada, Kienholz finally settled in Los Angeles in 1952; it was there that he made his name as an artist. Within a year Kienholz—who had continued to study and make art during his wander-

Edward Kienholz at the opening of the Park Place Gallery, 1965. COPY-RIGHT © BY FRED W. MCDARRAH

ings—began producing works in earnest, starting with wall-hanging painted reliefs to which he often applied color with a broom. His first one-man show took place in 1955 at Von's Café Galleria in the Laurel Canyon area of Los Angeles, and soon thereafter he began to arrange exhibitions of other southern California artists, often at small galleries he set up in neighborhood theaters.

Kienholz's increasing prominence as an artist and impresario in Los Angeles earned him an invitation in 1956 to serve as the producer of Los Angeles's Fourth Annual All-City Art Festival. His collaborator on the project was a young gallery owner named Walter Hopps, who had opened a space called the Syndell Studio in Brentwood in 1954, while still a student at the University of California at Los Angeles. The two soon began working as a team, and in 1957 they opened the Ferus Gallery on La Cienega Boulevard, which was a pioneering supporter of the work of the then-burgeoning California avant-garde, showing not only Kienholz but also artists such as Billy Al Bengston, Jay DeFeo, Richard Diebenkorn, and Robert Irwin.

Kienholz built a studio in the back room of Ferus, where he worked until 1958, when he sold his share in the gallery to Hopps and moved his home and studio to Laurel Canyon. There the additional room allowed his increasingly elaborate relief constructions to evolve into the fully three-dimensional, found-object-based works for which he be-

came famous. Over the next few years, Kienholz continued to develop his highly individual form of sculptural assemblage, gradually moving away from the wall-hanging form and toward totally freestanding arrangements of the kind first seen in works from 1959 like *Mother Sterling,* a dressmaker's dummy perched atop a wire cage holding dismembered doll parts, and *John Doe,* a store display mannequin cut in half, decorated with paint and other small sculptural items, and affixed to a baby stroller.

In the first few years of the 1960s, the peripatetic Kienholz, who had already been married and divorced twice, began to settle into something of a more stable life. He and his third wife, Mary Lynch, had two children during this time. Kienholz had a solo exhibition, curated by Hopps, at the Pasadena Art Museum in 1961, and was included in a survey, the Art of Assemblage, mounted by the Museum of Modern Art in New York. In 1962 the Ferus Gallery showed a revolutionary new work by Kienholz, an enormous walk-in installation called *Roxy's.* Named after a Nevada brothel, the work represented a startling progression for Kienholz. Moving on from his now-established concept of life-size, freestanding sculptural works, often involving manipulated mannequins, *Roxy's* is a fully formed environment. In its faithfully furnished rooms, viewers encounter the artist's large cast of characters, constructed from doll parts, found objects, and bits of machinery. *Roxy's* set the tone for one important strand of Kienholz's mature work—a highly theatrical mode of large-scale sculptural installation, typically addressing emotional, often controversial, subject matter—seen in his most well-known works, such as *The Beanery* (1965), *The State Hospital* (1966), *Sollie 17* (1979–1980), and *The Pedicord Apts.* (1982–1983).

During the remainder of the 1960s Kienholz's reputation continued to grow. His 1966 solo retrospective at the Los Angeles County Museum of Art caused a sensation when the county board of supervisors unsuccessfully attempted to close the show because of the content of works such as *Roxy's* and *Back Seat Dodge '38,* another life-size tableau depicting a man and a woman copulating in the backseat of an automobile. And in 1970 the eminent curator Pontus Hulten organized an exhibition of Kienholz's work, *11 + 11 Tableaux,* which toured major museums throughout Europe.

In 1972 Kienholz was married for a fifth and final time, to Nancy Reddin, the Los Angeles–born daughter of the city's chief of police and a real estate broker. Kienholz adopted her child. Reddin became Kienholz's collaborator on his subsequent work, which by now often included figures produced by the time-consuming and arduous process of making plaster casts of live subjects. In fact, in 1981 Kienholz announced that all works from the date of their marriage forward would contain the signatures of both him and his wife. The last twenty years of Kienholz's career was marked by almost continuous work and exhibitions. Splitting time after 1973 between Berlin and a summer home in Hope, Idaho, Kienholz and Reddin Kienholz received numerous solo shows at galleries and major museums around the world, including the Centre Georges Pompidou in Paris, the Louisiana Museum in Denmark, the San Francisco Museum of Modern Art, the Museum of Contemporary Art in Chicago, and the Walker Art Center in Minneapolis. Kienholz died of a heart attack at the Bonner General Hospital in Sandpoint, Idaho, at age sixty-six. He was buried at the top of nearby Howe Mountain in a 1940 Packard, with a dollar in his pocket, a deck of cards, a bottle of red wine, and the ashes of his beloved dog, Smash.

For all its success, Kienholz's idiosyncratic and highly personal work has probably been influential more for its experimental spirit than its form. His highly particularized, walk-in installations remain almost unique in the history of twentieth-century art for their mixture of large-scale theatricality and careful attention to poignant detail, while his use of found objects expanded the then-developing terrain of appropriation for generations of later artists. Although his work has struck some commentators as too broad and didactic, Kienholz's best pieces manage to strike a delicate balance between their often passionate political messages and their aesthetic qualities.

★

There are literally hundreds of catalogs, brochures, and articles related to the work of Kienholz. Although very few deal with the details of Kienholz's life, Edward and Nancy Reddin Kienholz, *Kienholz: A Retrospective*—published in 1996 to accompany the full-scale retrospective mounted that year by the Whitney Museum of American Art in New York—is by far the most comprehensive and includes a valuable biographical timeline compiled by the artist's widow. The Whitney catalog also includes a comprehensive selected bibliography of articles. Among other sources are Robert L. Pincus, *On a Scale That Competes with the World: The Art of Edward and Nancy Reddin Kienholz* (1990), and *Los Angeles Art Community: Group Portrait, Edward Kienholz*. See also the journalist Lawrence Wechsler's thirteen-hour interview with the artist for the Oral History Program at the University of California, Los Angeles, *Edward Kienholz: Oral History Transcript*, 2 vols. (1977). An obituary is in the *New York Times* (12 June 1994).

JEFFREY KASTNER

KIRBY, George (*b.* 24 June 1924? in Chicago, Illinois; *d.* 30 September 1995 in Las Vegas, Nevada), stand-up comedian and impressionist best known for his impressions of stars ranging from John Wayne to Ella Fitzgerald and for his dead-on takes of women.

Born in either 1923 or 1924, Kirby was the youngest son of a musical family. His mother was a singer and his father a musician. Kirby grew up on Garfield Street on Chicago's South Side, where Louis Armstrong, one of the first voices in Kirby's act, was his neighbor. He spent much of his childhood on the road with his parents in show business. He was often absent from school and dropped out of Wendell Phillips High School at the end of his sophomore year. He began working as a porter, then as a dishwasher at the Rhum Boogie club on Fifty-fifth Street on Chicago's South Side. He also worked as a substitute bartender at the famed DeLisa club, where the club's manager gave him the chance to perform on stage; he was subsequently booked for a year at the DeLisa.

Kirby served in the U.S. Army during World War II in Europe and the South Pacific, where he was wounded and received the Purple Heart. After serving in the army for three years, he returned to the DeLisa as a featured performer. He then left Chicago and headed to New York City, where he became a regular performer at the 845 club. In 1948 he performed in London at the London Casino with Sophie Tucker. Upon returning to the United States, he was managed by Charles Carpenter, who helped him to tour with other performers such as Cab Calloway, Earl Hines, Sarah Vaughan, and Billy Eckstine. In 1948 Kirby made his debut on Ed Sullivan's *Toast of the Town* program. For the remainder of the 1940s, he was a regular guest on many variety and talk shows, which gave him the name recognition he needed to perform at some of the best clubs and theaters in the country. He was one of the first African Americans to break long-standing racial barriers and perform in these places. By the end of the 1940s, Kirby's act had made the transition from black audiences to white audiences.

In 1952 Kirby, performing as a part of the Count Basie show, became one of the first black acts to play Las Vegas. During this time black entertainers were not allowed to sleep, gamble, or even change clothes in the hotels where they performed. At the peak of his success in the mid-1950s, Kirby began headlining in Las Vegas and began appearing on more television programs than any other African American comedian. This may have been because he did not have a risqué act and was more of a song-and-dance man. Near the end of the decade, Kirby developed a heroin addiction that halted his successful career. In 1958 he was arrested in a drug raid and was given three years' probation. Unable to kick the heroin habit, Kirby asked to be committed to the drug rehabilitation center at the U.S. Public Service Hospital in Lexington, Kentucky, for treatment.

In 1960, after being released from the rehabilitation center, Kirby began a comeback by performing for black audiences at places such as the famous Apollo Theatre in New York City's Harlem neighborhood. The club's owner Art Braggs and Sarah Vaughan were instrumental in helping Kirby resume his career. Braggs, owner of the Idlewild Re-

George Kirby *(center)* at a ribbon-cutting ceremony. (Edward Koch, mayor of New York City, is at right.)
CORBIS CORPORATION (NEW YORK)

view in Michigan, sent Kirby a plane ticket and pocket money while he was still in the hospital at Lexington to get to Michigan to appear at his club; Vaughan invited Kirby to New York City and surrendered her featured spot at the club Basin Street East on a night when a couple of dozen booking agents whom she had invited were at the club. In the early 1960s Kirby expanded his nightclub routine by incorporating his talents of singing, playing the piano, and telling anecdotes into his act. Kirby married his wife, Rosemary, in 1961; their marriage lasted until Kirby's death.

During the 1960s Kirby became a favorite in such places as Caesar's Palace and the Riviera in Las Vegas, Harrah's in Reno, Nevada, the Beverly Hills Motor Hotel in Los Angeles, the Shamrock in Houston, and the Americana Royal Box in New York City. William Rice wrote in the *Washington Post* (3 November 1967) that Kirby's "singing voice is excellent, his impressions are nearly flawless, his material is in perfect taste. As a Negro, he uses racial stories deftly and with a bemused eye for foibles of both whites and Negroes." Kirby made his motion-picture debut in *A Man Called Adam* (1966), and in 1967 he appeared in *Oh Dad, Poor Dad, Mama's Hung You in the Closet and I'm Feelin' So Sad.* Neither film fared well with audiences or critics. During this decade he made appearances on most of the major television variety shows. He also made a second trip to Australia, performing in Sydney and Melbourne clubs, entertained troops at army posts in Germany, and made six appearances at the famous Copacabana nightclub in New York City.

In 1972 Kirby was a regular on the television program the *Copycats,* a weekly show for established impressionists. He starred in his own variety series, *Half the George Kirby Comedy Hour,* which lasted for only part of the 1972–1973 season. He continued with club dates and television appearances and in 1975 starred in a situation comedy, *Rosenthal and Jones,* with Ned Glass, which lasted only a few episodes. With the call for more cutting-edge comedy that blended social satire with off-the-wall storytelling and sardonic jokes, it became harder for Kirby to get club bookings and television appearances. The lack of work caused Kirby to turn to drug dealing in an effort to save his home and catch up on bills. In 1977 he was convicted of selling drugs to an undercover police officer in Las Vegas. He was sentenced to ten years in a federal prison but served only three and a half years at Terminal Island, outside Los Angeles. After his release, he toured schools with an antidrug message to warn young people about the damage drugs can do. In 1982 Kirby again renewed his career on stage, this time performing at the Dangerfield's nightclub in New York.

Kirby was diagnosed with Parkinson's disease in the early 1990s. In 1995 an all-star tribute, "Friends of George Kirby," was held on 22 May 1995 at the Debbie Reynolds Hotel and Casino in Las Vegas to help pay for his medical expenses after his insurance ran out. Paralyzed for several months, Kirby died in a nursing home at the approximate age of seventy-one. He is buried at the Queen of Heaven Cemetery in Hillside, Illinois.

The multitalented Kirby, the man of a thousand voices, was instrumental in opening doors for many African American comedians. His secret to being a successful impressionist was not "just to try to sound like the other person but to become the other person, to feel the way the person does."

★

Good sources for biographical information about Kirby are *Current Biography* (1977); *Contemporary Black Biography,* vol. 14 (1997); and Ronald L. Smith, *The Stars of Stand-up Comedy: A Biographical Encyclopedia* (1986). Information on his career can be found in *Coronet* (May 1968) and *Jet* (8 May and 16 Oct. 1995). Obituaries are in the *Chicago Sun-Times* (1 Oct. 1995) and the *New York Times* and *Houston Chronicle* (both 2 Oct. 1995).

JOYCE K. THORNTON

KIRK, Russell Amos   (*b.* 19 October 1918 in Plymouth, Michigan; *d.* 29 April 1994 in Mecosta, Michigan), conservative man of letters noted for defining and articulating a traditionalist philosophy descended from Edmund Burke, paving the way for the post–World War II conservative movement in America.

The first of two children of Russell Andrew Kirk, a locomotive engineer, and Marjorie Rachel Pierce, a homemaker, Kirk was born and raised in the town of Plymouth,

Russell Kirk. AP/WIDE WORLD PHOTOS

some twenty miles west of Detroit. He was shy and bookish as a boy, given to long walks and discussions with his grandfather, Frank Pierce, a well-read community leader in Plymouth. Through these precocious talks with his grandfather, Kirk came to appreciate at an early age the works of Edmund Burke, Nathaniel Hawthorne, Robert Louis Stevenson, and other writers of centuries past, drawing upon Pierce's extensive personal library. At Plymouth High School, Kirk captained the debate team, which scored numerous wins throughout the state thanks in large part to Kirk's leadership and strong skills as a well-prepared debater.

In 1936 Kirk graduated from high school and enrolled in the Michigan State College of Agriculture and Applied Science, in East Lansing (later known as Michigan State University), where he studied history and literature. He received his B.A. in history in 1940. Kirk then went to Duke University, in Durham, North Carolina, where he earned a master's degree, writing his thesis on the fiery nineteenth-century conservative politician John Randolph of Roanoke. (This thesis, completed and accepted in 1941, was brought out ten years later as *Randolph of Roanoke: A Study in Conservative Thought,* becoming Kirk's first published book.) The year he spent at Duke and in the South impressed upon Kirk an abiding affection for the best of the traditionalist South: a strong sense of heritage and living history, a slower, more humane pace of life than that offered in America's big cities, and a life of conservative faith, lived close to the soil amid a largely agrarian setting.

Kirk was drafted into the U.S. Army and spent the duration assigned to the Chemical Warfare Service, stationed in the Utah desert. There, with relatively little to do, he read and contemplated the writings of Marcus Aurelius. Stoicism reminiscent of Aurelius became a firm element of Kirk's mindset. He also entered into a correspondence with Albert Jay Nock, a man of the right and founder of the respected periodical *The Freeman* (1920–1924), with Kirk coming to admire the self-styled "superfluous man" who had labored to reach America's thinkers through his writings and editorship. Having attained the rank of sergeant, Kirk left the service at the end of the war and returned to Michigan State, where he taught courses in the history of civilization. From 1948 through the early 1950s he spent roughly half of each year teaching in East Lansing and the other six months in Scotland, where he researched and wrote his doctoral dissertation at St. Andrews University in Edinburgh. His dissertation was accepted in 1952, with Kirk thus becoming the first American to earn the revered degree of D. Litt. from Scotland's oldest university. While he enjoyed tramping about Edinburgh and Scotland on long walking tours and conversing with Scottish writers and academics, his time at Michigan State became increasingly dissatisfying. Over time Kirk had come to disagree with the lowering of academic standards in order to attract more students. In 1953 Kirk resigned from Michigan State and moved to his family's ancestral home, "Piety Hill," in upstate Mecosta, Michigan. From this old farmhouse, Kirk set up to become a writer unattached to any institution of higher learning.

By this time he was established as a respected contributor to historical and literary journals in the United States and Britain, but in 1953 Kirk saw his star ascend even further. That year he met and began corresponding with the Anglo-American man of letters T. S. Eliot, with each man recognizing in the other a philosophical kindred spirit. That same year, the publisher Henry Regnery brought out Kirk's doctoral dissertation in the United States, titling it *The Conservative Mind: From Burke to Santayana*. Appearing at a time when the statist, liberal heritage of Franklin D. Roosevelt and Harry Truman was still very much alive, Kirk's book was hailed by reviewers as an intelligent and articulate history of ideas which identified, drew together, and illuminated the disparate strands of Anglo-American conservative thought from Burke through John Adams, Samuel Taylor Coleridge, James Russell Lowell, and many other political and literary figures. Subtitled in later editions "From Burke to Eliot," the book was widely and, for the most part, favorably reviewed in influential venues.

Over the next decade Kirk wrote a succession of books on conservative themes, articulating a conservatism grounded in the tradition of what his friend Eliot had termed "the permanent things"—those timeless norms that humanity ignores at its peril, including honor, character, humility, virtue, and other elements of the natural law, chief among them being prudence. The conservative statesman combines the disposition to preserve with a talent for effecting prudent change, as such change is the means of our preservation, wrote Kirk on numerous occasions—and the conservative layman is of like temperament. To make prudent change requires that conservative men or women possess what Burke called the "moral imagination," that faculty that descries man as a being flawed by passion, selfishness, and self-centeredness, yet beloved by God and made for eternity, for which he must be made fit through a combination of self-discipline and providential shaping and molding. Specifically, Kirk adopted certain key principles articulated by Burke, which the Burke scholar Peter J. Stanlis identified as belief in "moral natural law, prudence, legal prescription, limited power under constitutional law, normative appeals to Providence and religion, appeals to history and tradition as preceptors of experience and prudence, a defense of private and corporate property as essential to civil liberty, and respect for party government."

In 1955 Kirk began contributing a regular column on American education to William F. Buckley, Jr.'s new conservative magazine, *National Review*. This widely read column, "From the Academy," appeared in that periodical for the next twenty-five years, lambasting the harmful fads and the general lowering of standards in American education at all levels. Emulating Eliot and Nock, Kirk himself founded a periodical to reach American conservatism's thinking minority; *Modern Age* appeared in 1957, and he edited this quarterly for two years before turning over the review's editorial responsibilities to a successor. Almost immediately he founded another quarterly, *The University Bookman*, devoted almost entirely to reviews of books that would be of special interest to conservatives. Kirk edited this magazine from his library in Mecosta from 1960 until his death.

By the time Barry Goldwater ("Mr. Conservative," as he came to be called) was nominated as the Republican Party's presidential candidate in 1964, Kirk's national reputation had solidified: not only for his writings on politics and educational matters, but through a nationally distributed column called "To the Point" he wrote for the Los Angeles Times Syndicate. He also wrote a popular Gothic novel titled *Old House of Fear* (1961), which prompted a resurgence of interest in the genre of Gothic fiction, and a small number of ghost stories. In 1964 Kirk also took instruction in Roman Catholic doctrine and joined the Church, not long before he married Annette Yvonne Cecile Courtemanche, a Thomist, schoolteacher, and vivacious conservative activist from Springfield Gardens in the borough of Queens in New York City.

During the mid-1960s through the early 1970s, Kirk engaged in campus debates with such leftist icons as Abbie Hoffman, Tom Hayden, and William Kunstler, often with striking success in winning the respect of student audiences. He also published several books that were favorably reviewed, perhaps the best of these being *Enemies of the Permanent Things: Observations of Abnormity in Literature and Politics* (1969), a prolonged statement of literary principles and appraisal of contemporary writers. At Piety Hill, the Kirks opened their home to a steady succession of political refugees from communist nations, unwed mothers, hoboes in need of work, and other individuals who needed a place to stay and learn job skills before striking out again into the world at large. Also, beginning in the early 1970s, numerous college students also came to Piety Hill to study in Kirk's library, ask his advice, assist him in publishing *The University Bookman*, and write their own dissertations. Amid this crowded, mildly chaotic household, between 1967 and 1975, the Kirks welcomed four daughters into their lives.

In 1974 Kirk published the book that stands, with *The Conservative Mind*, as his most significant: a detailed history of America's cultural heritage called *The Roots of American Order*. In this work, Kirk traced the origins of four key elements of American order to four great cities: Athens, the source of America's reason and art; Rome, the source of America's law and sense of public order, Jerusalem, the fount of faith and pious submission; and London, the springhead of the concept of liberty under law. *The Roots of American Order* was widely praised by critics, with the English man of letters Malcolm Muggeridge writing that he could not imagine "how this so essential task of referring back to the origins of order as it has existed in North America could have been more lucidly, unpretentiously, unpedantically and yet informatively executed."

With the election of the conservative Ronald Reagan to the U.S. presidency in 1980, Kirk found himself an increasingly sought-after speaker at the Heritage Foundation in Washington, D.C., and at university campuses throughout the United States and Europe, as well as a sometime-visitor to the White House. Ironically, during this time of conservative ascendancy, his own books were reviewed with decreasing frequency, even among some right-wing publications. Although conservative columnists and speakers were in high demand, Kirk was sometimes forgotten as other, more media-savvy conservative speakers—really "neoconservatives," who tended to focus upon economics and American foreign policy—came to the forefront. Unlike many of his fellow conservatives, Kirk was a regionalist rather than a nationalist, an advocate of fair trade rather than free trade, a proponent of agrarian and small community life rather than a cosmopolitan one, a champion of the free-market economy on a humane scale rather than no-holds-barred laissez-faire capitalism, a believer in a prudent rather than an interventionist foreign policy, and a strong conservationist, believing that humankind is responsible for the stewardship of the earth, not the pillaging of it. Upon leaving office in 1989, Reagan, who had spoken of Kirk in glowing terms during his presidency, presented the conservative Michiganian with the Presidential Citizens Medal.

In the final years of his life, Kirk lectured frequently at the Heritage Foundation and elsewhere, and his publications tended to be collections of speeches, along with a pithy counterblast to the excesses of multiculturalism titled *America's British Culture* (1993). In early 1994, having learned that he had congestive heart failure and but a short time to live, he put the finishing touches on his long-anticipated memoir, *The Sword of Imagination: Memoirs of a Half-Century of Literary Conflict* (1995). He died peacefully at his Mecosta home on 29 April 1994. Kirk is buried in the cemetery of his local parish church, St. Michael's, in the nearby town of Remus.

As a founder of the post–World War II conservative movement in America, Kirk, held by "the permanent things," articulated these truths through both the well-turned essay and the well-told tale in an adept melding of the intellect and the imagination. The historian Wilfred McClay has written that Kirk defended American culture against those who would radically alter or replace it, while at the same time challenging many elements of that culture by comparing it to its classical and Judeo-Christian antecedents. The hallmark of Kirk's career was its uninterrupted consistency in terms of conveying much wisdom in an accessible manner. Of Kirk, Buckley has written, "It is . . . inconceivable to imagine an important, let alone hope for a dominant, conservative movement in America, without his labor."

★

Most of Kirk's private papers are on file at the Russell Kirk Center for Cultural Renewal in Mecosta, Michigan. Many details of his life are contained in his posthumously published memoir, *The Sword of Imagination* (1995). James E. Person, Jr., *Russell Kirk: A Critical Biography of a Conservative Mind* (1999), is a full-length biographical and critical study. Other important examinations of Kirk's life and accomplishments can be found in Bruce Frohnen, *Virtue and the Promise of Conservatism: The Legacy of Burke and Tocqueville* (1993); the Festschrift *The Unbought Grace of Life: Essays in Honor of Russell Kirk* (1994), edited by James E. Person; Wilfred M. McClay, "The Mystic Chords of Memory: Reclaiming American History," *Heritage Lecture* 550 (Heritage Foundation, 1995); and George H. Nash, *The Conservative Intellectual Movement in America Since 1945* (2d ed., 1997). Kirk's most important works include *The Conservative Mind* (1953; 7th rev. ed., 1986), *A Program for Conservatives* (1954; rev. ed., as *Prospects for Conservatives,* 1989), *Enemies of the Permanent Things: Observations of Abnormity in Literature and Politics* (1969), *The Roots of American Order* (1974), and *America's British Culture* (1993). A detailed primary and secondary bibliography is provided by Charles Brown's *Russell Kirk: A Bibliography* (1981). An obituary is in the *New York Times* (30 Apr. 1994).

JAMES E. PERSON, JR.

KIRSTEIN, Lincoln (*b.* 4 May 1907 in Rochester, New York; *d.* 5 January 1996 in New York City), writer, critic, arts patron, cofounder of the New York City Ballet, and indefatigable champion of choreographer George Balanchine, whom he brought to the United States in 1933.

Kirstein was one of two children born to Louis E. Kirstein and Rose Stein. A maverick in the true sense of the word, Kirstein was a towering figure in the history of American ballet. Dance was not his first love (from an early age he wrote poetry and painted), nor was it his only love (at one time or another he wrote about film, sculpture, and photography). But it was the one that remained a constant presence in his life from his teen years and to which he made a contribution that is almost incalculable. Born in Rochester to parents of German Jewish heritage, he grew

Lincoln Kirstein. LIBRARY OF CONGRESS

1930, the year he graduated from Harvard, he was a member of the junior advisory committee of the New York Museum of Modern Art, where in the 1930s he curated a controversial show on American mural art, arranged a retrospective of the sculptor Gaston Lachaise and the first major exhibition of Walker Evans's photographs, organized a Soviet film archive, and set up the country's first dance archive. In 1932 he published his first book, *Flesh Is Heir,* a thinly veiled autobiographical novel full of references to the Ballets Russes.

That celebrated company, which Serge Diaghilev founded and then directed from 1909 to 1929, inspired Kirstein's love of ballet. He first saw the company perform in 1916, when it toured the United States without its great star Vaslav Nijinsky. During the middle and late 1920s Kirstein kept up with the company on summer holidays in London. In New York Kirstein studied ballet with Michel Fokine, the Ballets Russes choreographer on whom Kirstein initially pinned his hopes for the development of a native American ballet. This was not to be. But Kirstein absorbed from the Ballets Russes the idea of ballet as an art of high seriousness, a feast for the eye, ear, and intellect, a mode of expression at once traditional but also modern, a form classical but open to experiment, and this model became his credo. In Diaghilev, a Napoleonic man of action with the soul of an artist and the taste of a connoisseur, he discovered a model for his own restless intelligence and ambition.

The turning point came in 1933, when Kirstein invited the Russian-born George Balanchine, Diaghilev's last in-house choreographer, to form a company in New York. Their partnership transformed American ballet from a popular curiosity or European import to a respected art and lasted until Balanchine's death in 1983. Initially they experienced more failures than successes. With the exception of the School of American Ballet, which opened its doors in 1934 and remained open into the twenty-first century, the companies they founded in the 1930s and the early 1940s quickly foundered. Of these none was more significant for Kirstein than Ballet Caravan. Founded in 1936, at the height of the Popular Front, this small touring company was an experiment in creating a repertory that was American in theme and modernist in form, a means of associating ballet with the country's emerging avant-garde. Although *Billy the Kid* (1938), with music by Aaron Copland and choreography by Eugene Loring, is the only Caravan work still performed, for Kirstein the experience of directing a ballet company proved invaluable.

From 1943 to 1945 Kirstein served in the U.S. Army, where among other duties he supervised the recovery of the massive collection of art looted by the Nazis in Alt Aussee, Germany. Within a year of his discharge as a private first class, he again teamed up with Balanchine to form Ballet

up in privileged circumstances in Boston, where his father, a partner in Filene's department store with a passion for American history, became a well-known philanthropist. Kirstein inherited his father's strong sense of civic responsibility together with his mother's love of the arts and from an early age used his wealth and other less tangible gifts to benefit a host of arts institutions.

Kirstein attended Phillips Exeter Academy from 1921 to 1922 and the Berkshire School from 1922 to 1924. Like so many future members of the eastern elite, he went on to Harvard University. There he found himself at the nerve center of a group that transformed the landscape of American cultural life. In 1926, with Varian Fry, he founded the *Hound & Horn,* a literary review that during its seven years of existence published Ezra Pound, T. S. Eliot, and Edmund Wilson as well as Kirstein's first major essay on dance, "The Diaghilev Period" (1930). In 1927, with John Walker III and Edward M. M. Warburg, he founded the Harvard Society for Contemporary Art, which exhibited works by artists such as Isamu Noguchi, Buckminster Fuller, Constantin Brancusi, and Alexander Calder. By

Society, a subscription-based organization that produced a host of new works, including two of Balanchine's masterpieces, *The Four Temperaments* (1946) and *Orpheus* (1948). Most of the money came from Kirstein, who had received a substantial inheritance. Spending lavishly, he commissioned designs from Noguchi and second-generation surrealists like Kurt Seligmann and Esteban Francés and music from Igor Stravinsky, Elliott Carter, John Cage, and Gian Carlo Menotti (for the opera *The Telephone,* 1947). By 1948, when Kirstein's funds were becoming rapidly depleted, Morton Baum, chairman of the executive committee of the New York City Center, came to the rescue by inviting the company to join the New York City Opera and City Center Orchestra as a constituent of this "people's" theater, opened only five years before by Mayor Fiorello La Guardia.

The New York City Ballet danced its first performance at City Center in 1948. Times were tough. Although the company now had a home, it was still penniless and needed a repertoire, an audience, dancers with polish, and regular seasons. Kirstein was in his element. He energetically sought out donors; pulled strings to arrange prestigious foreign tours; and found money for costumes, decors, new music, and even to underwrite productions by guest choreographers. In 1952 Kirstein became managing director of City Center and persuaded the Rockefeller Foundation Division of Humanities to appropriate $200,000 "to cover the costs of creative preparatory work on new productions in ballet and opera." Kirstein's friendship with Nelson Rockefeller, the future New York governor, dated back to the early 1930s. Amounting to fully half the sum allocated to the New York City Ballet, this was the first grant awarded to an American dance ensemble by a leading philanthropic institution. Nearly a dozen operas and ballets came to the stage thanks to Rockefeller largesse, including *The Nutcracker* (1954), the most expensive production the young company had ever mounted. Even as the New York City Opera began to chafe at Kirstein's high-handed ways, he began to dream of a City Center that was virtually a blueprint for what later became Lincoln Center, an institution housing all the performing arts as well as professional training facilities. Indeed within months of his resignation because of policy differences with the New York City Opera, Kirstein joined the committee headed by John D. Rockefeller III "to explore," as the *New York Times* reported, "the feasibility of an artistic set-up that would take in ballet, concerts, chamber music, drama, light opera and perhaps educational programs, as well as opera and symphony."

By 1955 Kirstein had laid his creative ambitions largely to rest. Instead, he turned his attention to strengthening the two institutions to which he dedicated his remaining years—the New York City Ballet and the School of American Ballet (SAB). It was his Herculean efforts and politicking that secured the publicly funded New York State Theater at Lincoln Center for the New York City Ballet, an accomplishment that earned him the enmity of the rest of the dance world. This was compounded by the series of Ford Foundation grants which, beginning in 1959 and continuing well into the 1970s, enabled the School of American Ballet to transform itself from a New York–based institution to a national one that recruited students from around the country. When the SAB relocated in the Juilliard School's new Lincoln Center studios, displacing Juilliard's own ballet program, it seemed to many that Kirstein exerted undue influence in high places. However, Kirstein's dream of creating a national American academy of ballet was finally realized when the SAB acquired its own quarters in the Rose Building along with dormitory facilities.

Even apart from the SAB and the New York City Ballet, Kirstein's contributions to dance were enormous. His writings form perhaps the most distinguished corpus of any American writer on dance. His *Dance: A Short History of Classic Theatrical Dancing,* published in 1935, is an extraordinary accomplishment for a twenty-eight-year-old, and it remained in print into the twenty-first century. *Movement and Metaphor: Four Centuries of Ballet,* published thirty-five years later in 1970, is a brilliant if idiosyncratic analysis of seminal works of dance history, while *Nijinsky Dancing* (1975) paid homage to the Ballets Russes icon who first excited Kirstein's interest in the male dancer. In books like *Blast at Ballet: A Corrective for the American Audience* (1938) and *Ballet Alphabet: A Primer for Laymen* (1939) he took on the Russians who dominated ballet of the period knowledgeably, fearlessly, and with punch. He was a prolific essayist, publishing not only in journals like *Theatre Arts* and *Modern Music* but also in left-wing periodicals such as the *Nation* and *New Theatre,* glossy magazines such as *Town and Country,* and despite his profound dislike of modern dance apart from Martha Graham, even in *Dance Observer,* its unofficial house organ. His essays of the 1930s, unlike his later ones for the *New York Review of Books,* were free of the crustiness that by the late 1970s sounded much like the jeremiads of neoconservatives traumatized by the Age of Aquarius.

From his father Kirstein inherited a sense of public service. To the New York Public Library's Dance Collection he donated thousands of volumes of Russian books, including a complete run of the *Annals of the Imperial Theatres* (1890–1917); nineteenth-century American dance manuals; rare French and Italian books; and all his diaries and papers. He donated the Ballet Caravan and American Ballet set and costume designs to the Museum of Modern Art and his collection of George Platt Lynes photographs, which commemorated nearly twenty years of work with Balanchine, to the Metropolitan Museum of Art. He was a founder of *Dance Index,* a quarterly published between 1942 and 1948 whose monographs, essays on Anna Pavlova, Nijinsky, and Isadora Duncan; on the designers Eugene Berman and Pavel Tchelitchew; on the romantic ballet by George Chaffee; on Marius Petipa and Lev Ivanov by the Soviet scholar Yury Slonimsky; and on nineteenth-century American dance by Lillian Moore bear reading. With covers by Joseph Cornell, *Dance Index* is visually as well as intellectually stimulating.

The visual arts were Kirstein's second love. Innumerable artists were recipients of his patronage, including Tchelitchew, about whom Kirstein published a book in 1994; Isamu Noguchi; Ben Shahn; Paul Cadmus; and Elie Nadelman. Although he was gay or bisexual, Kirstein married Paul Cadmus's sister Fidelma in 1941; they had no children. She died in 1991. Kirstein mounted numerous exhibitions, especially in his early years, and in many cases he wrote the accompanying catalogs. He loved photography and wrote presciently about the work of Evans, Henri Cartier-Bresson, and other modernists. In the 1940s he came under the sway of the surrealists, and when they were eclipsed by the overnight triumph of abstract expressionism, he denounced the new movement along with the Museum of Modern Art, which supported it, in a 1948 article written for *Harper's* magazine. In his insistence on the figurative, the erstwhile modernist turned his back on contemporary art.

A true man of letters, Kirstein wrote poetry, novels, plays, and volumes of reminiscences. However, he was more of a critic than a creative writer. His poetry, although competent, seldom sings, and his fiction lacks narrative energy and the gift for making characters come alive. Kirstein was not unaware of this. But it made him all the more cognizant of talent in others and all the more willing to support it. Kirstein's private acts of generosity were often unsung, but few were the artists, writers, or dancers among his acquaintance who did not receive small sums of cash to tide them over. He also extended such generosity to African Americans. The School of American Ballet welcomed its first black students at least as early as the mid-1940s, and by 1950 nearly a dozen were enrolled in the summer course. In 1965 Kirstein marched in Selma, Alabama, in support of civil rights. He died at the age of eighty-eight. He was cremated and his ashes were scattered.

Brilliant, controversial, single-minded, ever loyal, Kirstein did more than anyone else to make ballet an American art. He brought Balanchine to the United States, then struggled to make it possible for him to stay. He fought to build institutions that enabled his company, his work, and his school to survive. He used his wealth wisely and well to promote not only what he loved but also what in his high-toned Brahmin way he felt the country needed. Another patron of Kirstein's magnitude will be long in coming.

★

Kirstein's papers and diaries are in the Dance Collection, the New York Public Library for the Performing Arts. His major autobiographical works are *Thirty Years: Lincoln Kirstein's the New York City Ballet* (1978), *Quarry: A Collection in Lieu of Memoirs* (1986), and *Mosaic: Memoirs* (1994). The two major collections of Kirstein's writings are *Ballet: Bias, and Belief: "Three Pamphlets Collected" and Other Dance Writings of Lincoln Kirstein* (1983) and *By with to & From: A Lincoln Kirstein Reader*, edited by Nicholas Jenkins (1991). A detailed chronology of Kirstein's life is in Harvey Simmonds, Louis H. Silverstein, and Nancy Lassalle, comps., *Lincoln Kirstein, The Published Writings, 1922–1977: A First Bibliography* (1978), which is an invaluable guide to Kirstein's writings although it does not contain any publications from the last two decades of his life. No full-scale biography of Kirstein has been written, but Nicholas Fox Weber, *Patron Saints: Five Rebels Who Opened America to a New Art, 1928–1943* (1992), gives a good account of Kirstein's years prior to World War II, while Nancy Reynolds, "Diaghilev and Lincoln Kirstein," in *The Ballets Russes and Its World*, edited by Lynn Garafola and Nancy Van Norman Baer (1999), surveys his whole life and compares it to Diaghilev's. An obituary is in the *New York Times* (6 Jan. 1996).

LYNN GARAFOLA

KORSHAK, Sidney Roy (*b.* 6 June 1907 in Chicago, Illinois; *d.* 20 January 1996 in Beverly Hills, California), attorney associated with organized labor and organized crime who was a reputed Hollywood fixer.

Korshak was born on Chicago's West Side to Jewish refugee parents from Lithuania. He had one sibling, his brother Marshall. Korshak was an active student athlete in both high school and college. He received a bachelor of arts degree from the University of Wisconsin and later obtained his law degree from Chicago's DePaul University College of Law in 1930.

During his life Korshak was one of the most powerful men in Hollywood. He worked mostly behind the scenes and had the reputation of being the Mafia's man in Los Angeles. His power, according to government investigations, stemmed from his close ties to both powerful unions such as the International Brotherhood of Teamsters and to organized crime families. Because of these ties, Korshak became a force in both the entertainment and sports industries. His clients included Ronald Reagan, George Raft, Frank Sinatra, Madison Square Garden, the New York Rangers, the New York Knicks, Gulf and Western, the Hilton and Hyatt hotel chains, the Los Angeles Dodgers, and numerous Hollywood movie studios.

After Korshak graduated from DePaul, his first clients were members of Al Capone's Chicago mob. Korshak developed a reputation as someone the mobsters could trust

Sidney Korshak, 1957. © BETTMANN/CORBIS

Chicago lawyer. He soon mingled with the financial and cultural elite of Chicago. His ability to wear both masks successfully owed something to his skill in keeping a low profile. Korshak never drew attention to himself, rarely accompanied clients to court, and seldom was a party to any contract signing. He preferred to do his consulting in private. Financially successful, he and his wife lived in a luxury apartment on Lake Shore Drive in Chicago.

Playing the role of legitimate attorney, Korshak moved to Hollywood in the late 1940s (while retaining his Chicago residence) to be the Mafia's adviser to the movie industry. Over time, he became a force in both Hollywood and Las Vegas, with its gaming casinos. Both movie studios and the new hotels of Las Vegas needed his help to settle labor disputes. It was rumored, but never proven, that the unions threatened strikes to force hotels to deal with the mob. While Korshak's power was rarely visible, one example demonstrates the weight he pulled. During a Teamsters convention in 1961, Korshak arrived in Las Vegas to find that the powerful Teamster's chief Jimmy Hoffa occupied Korshak's usual presidential suite. A few hours later, Hoffa found himself in another room and Korshak was once again relaxing in his accustomed quarters.

In Hollywood, Korshak was an adviser and deal broker. He never actually practiced law in California because he never bothered to get his license. He kept no office and, as had always been his custom, left no paper trail. He preferred to work out of the corner table of Le Bistro, a fashionable Los Angeles restaurant of which he was a co-owner. One example of his influence concerns the making of the motion picture *The Godfather* (1972). When the producer, Robert Evans, was threatened by the mob, which did not want the movie made, he went to visit "Mr. K," who—for a fee—made the problem disappear. Evans, who eventually became the chief at Paramount Studios, later remembered that "one call from Mr. K and suddenly threats turned into smiles." Evans needed Korshak again to help land Al Pacino to play the role of Michael Corleone. Pacino was then under contract with MGM, which would not release him or allow him to work for Evans. Korshak made one call to Kirk Korkorian, the majority stockholder in MGM. Korkorian was then building a new MGM-Grand Hotel in Las Vegas. "I asked him if he wanted to finish building his hotel," Korshak reportedly told Evans. A simple threat from Korshak put Pacino in the movie. His ability to close deals such as this made him a multimillionaire by the time of his death. In 1960 Korshak and his wife moved into a luxurious house on Chalon Road in the Bel Air section of Los Angeles. When guests arrived, an armed guard greeted them at the door. Korshak died of natural causes and was buried in Beverly Hills, California.

Korshak counted among his friends Lew Wasserman, the head of MCA, and President Ronald Reagan. Reports

and soon he was advising them. Because many Chicago mobsters were involved in labor unions, Korshak quickly became an adviser on labor matters. He rose quickly in the mob organization. A 1942 investigation by the Internal Revenue Service reported that he was often the racketeers' key business adviser and negotiator. Later that same year, in a New York City extortion trial, a witness testified that Korshak was the Chicago mob's man in motion pictures and the unions involved in the industry.

During World War II, Korshak was in the U.S. Army, serving as a military instructor at Camp Lee, Virginia. While on leave he married Bernice Stewart in August 1943. They had three children.

After the war Korshak established himself in a law partnership with his brother, who was a player in the Chicago Democratic Party, holding elected and appointed offices at both the city and state levels. Their firm was able to attract hundreds of respectable clients mainly due to its connections with labor unions, Chicago politics, and the mob. For example, Sidney Korshak's mob connections allowed him to settle his clients' labor troubles with the truck drivers and hotel and restaurant employees unions (or create labor problems for his clients' competitors). These new clients allowed Korshak to remake himself into an upstanding

suggested that his relationships with the Democratic Party, through his brother, and the Republican Party, through the Teamsters and Reagan, helped keep him out of jail when so many others were convicted for less. The *New York Times* stated in his obituary that "it was a tribute to Sidney Korshak's success that he was never indicted."

★

There is no biography of Korshak and little secondary literature apart from Dan Moldea, *Dark Victory: Ronald Reagan, MCA, and the Mob* (1986), and Lester Velie, "The Capone Gang Muscles into Big-Time Politics," *Collier's* (30 Sept. 1950). Newspapers sometimes covered his activities. An example is Paul Steiger's article in the *Los Angeles Times* (15 Sept. 1968). See also the four-part, front-page series on Korshak by Seymour M. Hersh for the *New York Times* (27–30 June 1976). Nick Tosches, "The Man Who Kept the Secrets," *Vanity Fair* (Apr. 1997), appeared the year after Korshak's death. An obituary is in the *New York Times* (22 Jan. 1996).

RICHARD A. GREENWALD

KRIM, Arthur B. (*b.* 4 April 1910 in New York City; *d.* 21 September 1994 in New York City), attorney, entertainment industry executive, and discreet but influential presidential adviser with enormous behind-the-scenes impact.

Krim was one of three children of Morris Krim, a Russian immigrant who became a successful operator of a chain of cafeterias, and Rose Ocko. He grew up comfortably in suburban Mount Vernon, New York, and in high school he

Arthur B. Krim. ARCHIVE PHOTOS

was captain of the cross-country team and senior class president. Elected to Phi Beta Kappa at Columbia College, he graduated in 1930 with a B.A. degree. In 1932 he earned an LL.B. degree from Columbia University Law School. First in his class, he served in 1931–1932 as the law review editor in chief.

After graduation Krim joined Phillips and Nizer, entertainment law specialists. Admitted to the New York bar in 1933, he and his colleague Robert Benjamin became senior partners in the mid-1930s. The firm was renamed Phillips, Nizer, Benjamin, and Krim. Krim retained his law partnership until 1978. Thereafter until his death he was "of counsel." During World War II Krim served from 1942 to 1945 in the army, where he carried out special assignments both in the United States and the Pacific for the War Department and for the Army Services Forces, ultimately attaining the rank of lieutenant colonel.

In 1946 Krim became head of Eagle-Lion Films, a low-budget production venture of the British film mogul J. Arthur Rank and the American financier Robert Young. Circumstances hobbled the company's efforts. Eagle-Lion could not access the stars necessary to sell its product or enough first-run venues to show it. Moreover, the movie industry was suffering severe declines in attendance as competition for the leisure dollar intensified dramatically in postwar America. Krim, clashing repeatedly with Young, resigned in 1949.

In 1951 Krim and Benjamin assumed management of United Artists, a venerable film company founded in 1919 and headquartered in New York that at the time was on the verge of collapse. Krim, Benjamin, and their team would receive half the company's stock if they turned a profit in three years. With Krim as president and Benjamin as chairman, positions the men held until 1968, they did so in six months. Within six years they bought out the surviving founders and in 1957 took the company public, earning substantial sums for themselves. On 7 December 1958 Krim married the Italian-born Mathilde Galland, who became a medical leader in the fight against AIDS. They had one daughter.

Although Krim worked closely with Benjamin until the latter's death in 1979, Krim, known to many as "the Great White Father," was the dominant figure. The key to the company's profitability and artistic success lay in his ability to attract and retain independent producers. United Artists did not physically make movies. In return for a significant share of the profits and a hefty distribution fee, the company put up funding, handled distribution and publicity, and created what Krim called the proper "psychological climate." Autonomy for the independent producer was certainly not total. The producer had to reach agreement with United Artists on the story, cast, director, and budget before a project was approved. One producer recalled, "It's tough to get a commitment, . . . but once they're committed, you get more freedom." United Artists went from strength to strength, becoming by 1967 the largest movie producer-distributor in the world. That year the conglomerate Transamerica acquired it in a friendly takeover.

Krim, chairman of what now had become a subsidiary of the larger conglomerate, concentrated on other interests. In 1967 he became a trustee of Columbia University. Elected chairman in 1977, he served until he reached the mandatory retirement age in 1982. During the early 1960s he successfully raised funds for the Democratic Party, an activity he continued into the 1970s. Close to President Lyndon Johnson in the 1960s, Krim refused various posts but accepted an appointment in late 1968 as a "special consultant" in the Johnson administration's last months. Jack Valenti, a key Johnson aide, maintained that during the last two years of Johnson's presidency "there was no single individual in government . . . in whom Johnson reposed greater trust."

Partly because Krim focused on his interests outside United Artists, the firm suffered serious financial reverses in 1970. The situation changed when Krim returned to a more active role. In 1976 and 1977 United Artists led the industry in theatrical rentals and won Best Picture Academy Awards. Krim, chafing at Transamerica's restrictions on its subsidiaries, quietly tried for a spin-off. That failing, the usually discreet Krim undertook a carefully orchestrated public campaign. In early 1978 Krim, Benjamin, and three other top company executives resigned and organized Orion Pictures with Krim as chairman. Krim's power gradually diminished over the years. In 1982 Orion merged with Filmways, which also had diverse nonfilm interests, and became a public company.

For much of the 1980s Orion did well at the box office. In 1987 the company had the major share of domestic theatrical rentals. It also did well artistically. Krim's policy of "leave the talent alone" attracted creative filmmakers, one of whom said, "You can sleep nights if you have a deal with Arthur Krim." Orion's hits included Oscar winners; Woody Allen movies; critically acclaimed "niche" films, most of which were foreign; and the television series *Cagney and Lacey*. Overexpansion, excessive debt interest, and a series of expensive flops resulted in chapter eleven bankruptcy in December 1991, despite back-to-back Academy Award winners in 1990 and 1991. In April 1991 Krim assumed the honorary post of founding chairman; thirteen months later he resigned from Orion.

In failing health since undergoing heart surgery in 1993, Krim died in his Manhattan home. His honors included the Presidential Medal of Freedom (1969), the Jean Hersholt Humanitarian Award of the Academy of Motion Picture Arts and Sciences (1975), Columbia College's Alexander Hamilton Medal (1976), and an honorary doctorate

from Columbia University (1982). He is buried in New York City.

A short, stocky man, Krim exuded what one contemporary called a "calculated flexibility." Some considered him arrogant and autocratic, but overall his peers rated him favorably. At various times Krim was described as "the smartest man ever to work in the movie industry." Better known within the industry than to the public, he was noted for his discretion. A contemporary said, "You would never know from seeing Arthur Krim the amount of wealth he had or power." Once Krim and his associates approved a project, a producer worked in an atmosphere of creative autonomy. His management, especially at United Artists, resulted in a new freedom for filmmakers and a restructuring of the industry away from the traditional factory-style studio production.

★

The United Artists Collection at the Wisconsin Center for Film and Theater Research, State Historical Society of Wisconsin, Madison, houses considerable Krim material. Tino Balio, *United Artists: The Company that Changed the Film Industry* (1987), is based in part on extensive interviews with Krim. Capsule histories of Orion Pictures are in Jim Hillier, *The New Hollywood* (1992); Ephraim Katz, *The Film Encyclopedia,* 3d ed., revised by Fred Klein and Ronald Dean Nolen (1998); and Anthony Slide, *The New Historical Dictionary of the American Film Industry* (1998). Ronald Brownstein, *The Power and the Glitter: The Hollywood-Washington Connection* (1990), details Krim's political career. See also "The Derring-Doers of the Movie Business," *Fortune* (May 1958); "United Artists Script Call for Divorce," *Fortune* (16 Jan. 1978); and "Personalities: Real-Life Movie Melodrama," *New York Times* (22 July 1962). Obituaries are in the *New York Times* and *Los Angeles Times* (both 22 Sept. 1994) and *Columbia University Record* (30 Sept. 1994).

DANIEL J. LEAB

KROL, John Joseph (*b.* 26 October 1910 in Cleveland, Ohio; *d.* 3 March 1996 in Philadelphia, Pennsylvania), cardinal, archbishop of Philadelphia for twenty-seven years, and a leading churchman during a period that stretched from the Second Vatican Council to the end of the cold war.

Krol was the fourth of eight children born to a Polish immigrant couple, John Krol, a machinist who worked odd jobs as a carpenter, bricklayer, and plumber, and Anna Pietruszka Krol. The children all worked at an early age, and Krol could point to scars on each hand as proof of his having worked in a meat store at the age of nine and a box factory at the age of fifteen.

After graduating from Catholic elementary and secondary schools in Cleveland, Krol, at the age of seventeen, became a meat-cutter at Kroger, a chain food store, and soon rose to manager of the meat department. When a Lutheran colleague asked him religious questions, Krol began to peruse books of theology and was prompted to consider a vocation to the priesthood. Krol returned to school, St. Mary's College in Orchard Lake, Michigan, in 1931 and later entered St. Mary's Seminary. He continued to work as a meat-cutter during the summers to pay for his education and purposely took a job in a factory during his last summer so that he might better understand the labor his future parishioners ordinarily performed.

Krol was ordained to the priesthood on 20 February 1937 and served the next year as a parish priest. He was then sent to Rome, where he earned a licentiate in canon law at the Gregorianum. Krol visited relatives in Poland in the summer of 1939, just weeks before the Nazi invasion. He returned to the United States in 1940 as World War II engulfed Europe. He completed his doctorate in canon law at the Catholic University of America in Washington, D.C., in 1942 and then moved back to Cleveland, where he taught canon law at the local seminary and eventually was appointed to several archdiocesan administrative positions, including chancellor (1951). Krol was consecrated auxiliary bishop of Cleveland on 2 September 1953.

On 11 February 1961, Krol was appointed the tenth archbishop of Philadelphia. He entered a diocese that was several million dollars in debt, and he proved his administrative acumen by clearing away the debt within two years. Over the next fifteen years Krol opened thirty-four new parishes, as well as Newman Centers, designed to serve as gathering places for Catholics, at the major secular universities in his archdiocese. So strong was Krol's reputation as an administrator that he became the most prominent American churchman at the Second Vatican Council (1962–1965), largely in the capacity of an administrator rather than a theologian. He served first on the preparatory Committee on Bishops and Diocesan Government and then as undersecretary of the council, with responsibility for organizing the debates and votes of the attending prelates.

Krol was elevated to the cardinalate on 26 June 1967, the same year in which Karol Wojtyla, the archbishop of Cracow and future Pope John Paul II, became cardinal. According to Polish custom, a new cardinal makes a ceremonial entry into his hometown, and when Krol was denied a visa to make this journey to Siekierczyna, his father's village, Cardinal Wojtyla performed the ceremony on his behalf in a horse-drawn sleigh. When Wojtyla made his first trip to the United States in the fall of 1969, Krol was his host in Philadelphia, and the two men met again in 1976, when Wojtyla attended the International Eucharistic Congress in Philadelphia.

Cardinal John J. Krol. CAMERA PRESS LTD./ARCHIVE PHOTOS

Between 1971 and 1974, Krol was president of the National Conference of Catholic Bishops. He served on the committee that revised the Code of Canon Law (promulgated in 1983). In 1985, he was named one of three copresidents of the Extraordinary Synod of Bishops, a special council called to review the implementation of the reforms of the Second Vatican Council.

Cardinal Krol was a staunch defender of the Church in matters ranging from sexual ethics to international relations. He opposed state funding of artificial contraception and denounced *Roe* v. *Wade,* the Supreme Court ruling in 1973 that abrogated state laws against abortion. He argued for the return of prayer in public schools and supported public aid to nonpublic schools. Krol also advocated nuclear disarmament. He testified before the Senate Foreign Relations Committee on the matter in 1979 and helped formulate the American bishops' pastoral letter of 1983, *The Challenge of Peace.* Krol believed that the arms race had to be halted and nuclear weapons eventually banned, but he accepted the policy of deterrence as an intermediate step.

Despite his criticism of the arms race, Krol became a trusted adviser to President Ronald Reagan and his intelligence officials on the political situation in Poland. Because of his heritage and his position, Krol was well placed to explain Vatican views to the U.S. government and American policies to Pope John Paul II. In 1984 Krol offered prayers at the beginning of the Republican National Convention. Having already done the same in 1972, his public association with the Republican party and conservative politics was not new.

Cardinal Krol's reputation as a financial manager earned him a place on a select council of fifteen cardinals that was convoked in 1981 to reform the Vatican's methods of budgeting and accounting. In 1987 he and John Cardinal O'Connor of New York and Archbishop Theodore Mc-Carrick of Newark, New Jersey, founded the Papal Foundation, an independent trust developed to fund projects of particular interest to the pope. This foundation was intended as an American contribution to the effort to extricate the Vatican from financial problems experienced after the Church expanded its government and programs after Vatican Council II.

Krol remained active in the Papal Foundation after his retirement on 11 February 1988. In accordance with canon law, he submitted his resignation in 1985 on his seventy-fifth birthday, but the pope refused it. In the intervening years, however, Krol's health had deteriorated; he suffered from diabetes, with complications affecting his heart and kidneys.

On 14 February 1996 Krol was hospitalized for fluid in his lungs, the result of his continuing kidney problems. He died at home on 3 March at the age of eighty-five and is buried in Philadelphia in the crypt of the Cathedral Basilica of Saints Peter and Paul.

Cardinal Krol was foremost a legal and financial administrator, but he became an energetic defender of Catholicism at a time of cultural upheaval in the United States and religious change in the Church. He asserted the sanctity of life in discussions of both sexual morality and nuclear disarmament and exercised his influence on American and Vatican relations with communist Poland.

★

The Philadelphia Archdiocesan Historical Research Center at St. Charles Borromeo Seminary contains an archive of Cardinal Krol's papers and ancillary materials from his episcopacy. Krol explained the Church's view of disarmament in "The Catholic Bishops' Concern with Nuclear Armaments," *Nuclear Armament and Disarmament, Annals of the American Academy of Political and Social Science* 469 (Sept. 1983): 38–45. E. Michael Jones makes some use of archival material in *John Cardinal Krol and the Cultural Revolution* (1995). The archdiocesan newspaper *The Philadelphia Catholic Standard and Times* published special issues devoted to Krol (16 June 1977; 3 Apr. 1986), and the *National Catholic Reporter* published a profile (25 Oct. 1985). A memorial

was issued after his death, *His Eminence John Cardinal Krol* (1996). Obituaries are in the *New York Times* (4 Mar. 1996) and *National Catholic Reporter* (15 Mar. 1996).

ANDREW J. CARRIKER

KUHN, Margaret Eliza ("Maggie") (*b.* 3 August 1905 in Buffalo, New York; *d.* 22 April 1995 in Philadelphia, Pennsylvania), crusader against age discrimination who helped found the Gray Panthers, an activist group dedicated to improving the lives of older Americans.

Maggie Kuhn was the elder of Minnie Louise Kooman and Samuel Frederick Kuhn's two children. Her father managed the Memphis, Tennessee, office of the conservative Bradstreet Company (later Dun and Bradstreet), but both Maggie and her brother, Samuel Kooman, were born in their grandmother Kooman's Buffalo, New York, home because Minnie did not want to bear her children in the segregated South.

Samuel Kuhn's job took the family to Louisville, Kentucky (1910–1915), Cleveland (1915–1930), and finally Philadelphia (1930). Maggie attended schools in Cleveland and in 1926 graduated from Flora Stone Mather, the women's college of what is now Case Western Reserve Uni-

Maggie Kuhn. CORBIS CORPORATION (BELLEVUE)

versity, where she majored in English and took sociology courses from Charles Elmer Gehlke, a forceful proponent of community activism. He introduced her to the works of August Comte, Karl Marx, and Max Weber, and class visits to city jails, sweatshops, and slums made a lasting impression. Her first job was in Cleveland with the Young Women's Christian Association (YWCA), then an active advocate for working women and a champion of the notion that a strong group can empower the individual and change society. It marked the beginning of her long career in social activism. In 1929 the YWCA sent her to New York City for courses in social work and theology taught by the Christian activist and preacher Harry Emerson Fosdick and the theologian Reinhold Niebuhr at Columbia University Teacher's College and Union Theological Seminary.

For the next eleven years Kuhn worked in both Cleveland and Philadelphia for the YWCA, organizing social and educational programs for young women employed in factories and low-paying clerical jobs. At the beginning of World War II she moved to New York, where she worked from 1941 to 1945 coordinating United Service Organization (USO) programs to assist female defense plant workers working in abysmal conditions. Many of these women had no place to sleep for lack of housing, and at work they handled unsafe chemicals that made their hair fall out. Working with these women made Kuhn even more aware of the life experiences of the poor and socially marginal. After the war she worked briefly in Boston for the Unitarian Church (1948–1950) before returning to Philadelphia to care for her aging parents and to be near her brother, who was institutionalized with mental illness. She joined the national staff of the Presbyterian Church's Social Education and Action Department and edited its magazine, *Social Progress,* urging the church leadership to take a stand on desegregation, poverty, nuclear arms, and the aged. But in 1970, after twenty years of service and seven months before her sixty-fifth birthday, Kuhn was asked to retire.

Stunned and outraged, Kuhn joined with five friends and organized the Consultation of Older and Younger Adults for Social Change, setting up shop in 1970 in a converted janitor's closet in the basement of Philadelphia's Tabernacle Church. Kuhn insisted that the fledgling group represent all ages—not just the old—united by an interest in social change. Early causes included not only the elimination of mandatory retirement but also opposition to the Vietnam War. Kuhn abjured the term "senior citizen" ("old people are old," she said) and advocated the elderly's place at the table: "We'll do it with militancy, demonstrations, badges—anything." She encouraged older people to take control of their lives and to "speak out, even if your voice shakes."

By 1971 Kuhn had gained national attention. A melee at the White House gates between Kuhn's pickets and mounted police prompted the host of a New York television talk show, the Reverend Reuben Gums, to label them Gray Panthers. The name stuck. Kuhn appeared on Johnny Carson's *Tonight Show* and scolded the host for his "Aunt Blabby" portrayal, and she admonished President Gerald Ford at a White House meeting for calling her a "young lady." "I'm an old woman," she told him. By 1979 the group claimed 30,000 members, contributors, and supporters in thirty-two states, with 25 percent comprising Gray Panther "cubs," or members under the age of thirty.

The Panthers became a part of the contemporary counterculture. It ran joint campaigns with Ralph Nader's Retired Professional Action Group, the National Organization of Women, Hospice International, and the Union of Concerned Scientists, targeting nursing homes, the American Medical Association, the National Gerontological Society, and various courts, banks, and insurance companies. Spirited demonstrations and rallies called for the liberation of residents from unsafe nursing homes, an end to mandatory retirement, public ownership and control of utilities, elimination of the income cap on social security benefits, nuclear disarmament, prison reform, and a national health care program. In 1978 the *World Almanac* called her one of the world's most influential people, and the Gray Panthers were publishing their own newspaper, running radio programs in several cities, conducting a media watch to monitor press coverage of old people, and producing *Over Easy,* a public television program on social issues. In 1981 the Gray Panthers were recognized as a nongovernmental organization and given consultant status at the United Nations. It also opened an office in Washington, D.C.

On the local level Kuhn cowed the chief executive officer of Philadelphia's largest bank into granting no-fee money orders and free checking accounts and eased bank loan terms for people over sixty-five. Kuhn never married—"sheer luck," she said. In her eighties she boasted of love affairs with a married minister and a man fifty years her junior. She died in her sleep in the big stone Victorian twin house she shared with several young people, just one month before she was to have been honored by a White House Conference on Aging. She had endured two muggings, bouts of cancer, mastectomies, severe arthritis, osteoporosis, and a degenerative eye ailment. But in the end, her heart just stopped. She is buried in Ivy Hill Cemetery in Philadelphia.

A tiny, frail-looking woman who always maintained that she was born with activism in her blood, Maggie Kuhn was an inspirational speaker and persuasive in private conversation, described as "forceful yet gracious" by Sue Leary, her personal assistant. Kuhn's is the story of a fiercely independent woman who struggled to defend both the old and the oppressed and in the process covered a large part of the history of American social reform in the twentieth century. She came to age sixty-five at a time when gerontologists viewed the separation of the elderly—from work, families, and communities—as the norm. Kuhn challenged the stereotypical perception of old age, empowering the elderly to take on tough social issues of the day, ranging from housing to economic justice to national health care. She never tired of articulating her outrage at society's injustices or of fighting prejudice against the elderly. "Old people," she said, "are the only ones who have the sense of history and the time to do their jobs."

★

Papers, correspondence, photographs, and original files documenting Kuhn's activities and the Gray Panther organization from its inception to the mid-1990s are housed in the Urban Archives, Paley Library, Temple University, Philadelphia. Personal and professional papers and letters from childhood through retirement in 1970 are located in the Presbyterian Historical Archives, Philadelphia. Her autobiography, *No Stone Unturned: The Life and Times of Maggie Kuhn* (1991), written with Christina Long and Laura Quinn, details her upbringing and the forces that influenced the choices she made. Her outlook on age and ageism is the focus of *Maggie Kuhn on Aging* (1977), edited by Dieter Hessel. Obituaries are in the *New York Times* and *Washington Post* (both 23 April 1995). She is the subject of two film documentaries: *Maggie Kuhn: Wrinkled Radical* (1975), an interview with Studs Terkel; and *Maggie* (1994), a discussion of her intergenerational views.

MARTHA MONAGHAN CORPUS

KUHN, Thomas Samuel (*b.* 18 July 1922 in Cincinnati, Ohio; *d.* 17 June 1996 in Cambridge, Massachusetts), physicist turned historian and philosopher who transformed the study of the history and philosophy of science in the 1960s.

Kuhn was one of two children of Samuel L. Kuhn, an industrial engineer, and Minette Stroock Kuhn, a civic activist and professional editor; both were nonobservant Jews. When Kuhn was an infant, the family moved to New York City. The home atmosphere was politically liberal, and his parents sent him to "progressive" schools that encouraged pupils to think for themselves. In the mid-1930s—as the Great Depression gripped America, fascism threatened Europe, and Stalin tightened his control of the Soviet Union—Kuhn attended the progressive Hessian Hills School in Croton-on-Hudson, New York. There, he later recalled, "there were various radical left teachers all over." Young Kuhn participated in May Day marches and was an articulate pacifist, but as World War II approached, he changed his mind and supported U.S. intervention. In 1940 he entered Harvard University, where he majored in physics, served as an editor of the *Harvard Crimson,* and graduated summa cum laude in 1943 (a year early because of

Thomas S. Kuhn. COPYRIGHT © 2000 STANLEY ROWIN

wartime mobilization). During the war he worked on radar countermeasures at a U.S. laboratory in England and visited radar facilities on the Continent. He witnessed the liberation of Paris. Afterward, he returned to Harvard and pursued a doctorate in physics, although by this time he was more interested in philosophy, especially that of Kant.

The turning point in Kuhn's life came when he was befriended by Harvard president James B. Conant, who sought Kuhn's aid in developing a program to teach science to nonscience majors. The course would emphasize "case histories" of scientific research through the centuries. On a hot summer day in 1947, while doing research for the Conant course and reading Aristotle's *Physics,* Kuhn experienced an epiphany. To a modern scientist, Aristotle appears hopelessly antiquated, but Kuhn suddenly understood how the philosopher's physical notions made sense within the intellectual context of ancient Greece.

Kuhn compared this new understanding (a type of "empathetic historiography," that is, the effort to understand past cultures in their own terms rather than critiquing them by modern standards) to the gestalt switch cited by gestalt psychologists. A familiar example of a gestalt switch is a drawing of what appears to be ducks. Gaze at the sketch long enough, and suddenly they look like rabbits: What changes is not the raw data (the drawing) but rather one's perception of it. According to traditional historical accounts, science had advanced over the centuries by steadily accumulating raw data, in the manner advocated by the Elizabethan scholar-politician Francis Bacon. By contrast,

Kuhn realized that fundamental scientific revolutions may occur via reinterpretations of the same old data. His appreciation of the importance of such shifts in consciousness was strengthened when he read the works of Alexandre Koyré, who argued that Galileo's achievements owed more to the seventeenth-century astronomer's theoretical insights than to his celebrated physics experiments.

On 27 November 1948 Kuhn married Kathryn Muhs; they had three children. Kuhn received his M.S. degree in 1946 and his Ph.D. in 1949, both from Harvard. In 1951 he lectured on the nature of scientific change at the Boston Public Library. From 1952 to 1956 he was an assistant professor of general education and the history of science at Harvard.

In 1956 Kuhn accepted a teaching position at the University of California, Berkeley. His first book, *The Copernican Revolution: Planetary Astronomy in the Development of Western Thought* (1957), lucidly explained how in the sixteenth and seventeenth centuries astronomers abandoned the ancient astronomer Ptolemy's Earth-centered cosmology for the Sun-centered theory of Nicolaus Copernicus. Although Copernicus relied on the same observational data as Ptolemy, the former astronomer perceived a totally different arrangement of celestial bodies—another example of a gestalt switch.

Kuhn's most famous work, *The Structure of Scientific Revolutions* (1962), depicted the history of science as alternating periods of placid "puzzle-solving" and revolutionary changes of perspective, akin to gestalt switches that he dubbed "paradigm shifts." A mature scientific field operates with basic assumptions (in other word, paradigms, such as Ptolemaic or Copernican astronomy) that steer research in specific directions. No paradigm is all-explanatory: it always faces a number of "anomalies"—scientific observations or experimental results that challenge its underlying assumptions. (For example, pre-Copernican astronomers struggled for centuries to understand why planets moved in "anomalous" directions inconsistent with predictions of the Ptolemaic cosmology.) During a period of "normal science," researchers try to explain anomalies in a manner consistent with the paradigm—a process that Kuhn called "puzzle solving."

Over time, the accumulation of anomalies can become unbearable. Scientists struggle to "explain away" the anomalies in increasingly ad hoc ways. Rather than continue sticking with the old paradigm, a few scientists suggest radical alternatives. Most of these alternatives will fail, but one or more might offer real advantages, such as greater conciseness or predictive power. Eventually this new paradigm may displace the old one.

Does science progress? In that regard, Kuhn's most disturbing claim was that scientific paradigms are at least partly "incommensurable": one paradigm cannot necessar-

ily be treated as a special case subsumed by its successor. For example, the terminology of Newtonian physics cannot readily be translated into the terminology of its successor, Einsteinian physics. This is because terms such as "mass" and "force" have different meanings within each paradigm. (Kuhn's thinking here was indirectly inspired by the linguistic and anthropological ruminations of Ludwig Wittgenstein and Benjamin Lee Whorf.) True, progress occurs *within* a paradigm; scientists can accumulate more and more information that is compatible with the paradigm. But when science shifts from one paradigm to another, it is harder to say whether "progress" has occurred, for one paradigm's terms may be incommensurable with the other's. Hence, Kuhn suggested, comparing two paradigms is like comparing apples and aardvarks, and a scholar might reasonably question whether one paradigm is "truer" than its predecessor. Although tentative and vague, Kuhn's comments on incommensurability stirred excitement and controversy, for they appeared (on the surface, anyway) to question a cherished tenet of modernism: that science invariably progresses over the centuries. Indeed, Kuhn suggested (again, somewhat vaguely) that in certain time periods, science may move backward—in other words, *lose* "knowledge" by pursuing paradigms that prove to be blind alleys.

Kuhn's book became a best-seller by academic standards. About 750,000 copies were sold during his lifetime. His views especially intrigued social scientists, psychologists, and psychiatrists, who debated how (and whether) they should try to develop organizing paradigms for their conflict-bloodied fields. Kuhn's ideas also attracted attention from social critics of science, who gained attention in the 1960s and 1970s partly because of growing public concern about the high-tech Vietnam War, the nuclear arms race, and environmental destruction.

Kuhn also attracted critics. The philosopher Imre Lakatos accused Kuhn of attributing scientific change to "mob psychology." Another philosopher, Karl Popper, said Kuhn's view of "normal science" sanctioned a semiauthoritarian ethic of scientific research. According to Popper, Kuhnianism implied that scientists should blindly obey paradigmatic rules in hopes that these would lead, ironically, to revolutionary insights. To the contrary, Popper declared: scientists should openly challenge authority by proposing "outrageous" hypotheses to test and perhaps "falsify" orthodox ideas.

Upset, Kuhn insisted that both his admirers and critics had misinterpreted him. According to academic folklore, his postscript to the 1970 edition of *Structure* backed away from some of his earlier claims. However, a careful reading of the postscript suggests that he abandoned no crucial position.

Kuhn's status as the field's radical visionary was challenged by the rise of more overtly radical, colorful figures, such as the "episteme" theorist Michel Foucault and "anarchic epistemologist" Paul K. Feyerabend. Compared to them and the more recent postmodern scholars, Kuhn looked conservative, even orthodox.

A distinctly Kuhnian school never emerged. One reason is that some historians of science rejected Kuhn's model as being too vague or as irrelevant to most historical episodes of scientific change. Another reason is that Kuhn trained few doctoral students. Although he could become passionate and animated during intellectual discussion, he was a shy, chain-smoking loner who liked to cultivate his ideas at his own pace. By his own admission (in a 1995 interview), he tended to drive students away by insisting on rigorous intellectual standards.

Kuhn left Berkeley in 1964 for Princeton, where he was the M. Taylor Pyne Professor of Philosophy and History of Science until 1979. While at Princeton, he served as physics adviser on the editorial board of the *Dictionary of Scientific Biography*. In the latter part of his Princeton years, he published *The Essential Tension: Selected Studies in Scientific Tradition and Change* (1977) and the highly controversial *Black-Body Theory and the Quantum Discontinuity, 1894–1912* (1978), which questioned the standard account of Max Planck's discovery of the quantum nature of matter and energy.

In September 1978 Kuhn divorced Kathryn; the next year he became the Laurance S. Rockefeller Professor of Philosophy at the Massachusetts Institute of Technology. On 26 October 1982 he married Jehane Burns. In his last years he tried to complete a final book clarifying his views and answering his critics. The book was unfinished when he died from cancer of the bronchial tubes.

Thanks partly to Kuhn, the study of the history of science—once regarded as an academic backwater—became a respectable intellectual field in the late twentieth century. His views have been quoted (and misquoted) by thinkers across the intellectual spectrum, as Hegel's were in his heyday. Less happily for Kuhn, his ideas were co-opted by popular culture: the term "paradigm shift" has become a cliche from Main Street to Madison Avenue. In popular parlance, it refers to any radical shift of opinion or worldview.

★

Certain aspects of Kuhn's thinking were anticipated by other scholars, among them Ludwik Fleck in *Genesis and Development of a Scientific Fact* (original German edition, 1935); R. G. Collingwood in *Essay on Metaphysics* (1940); W. V. O. Quine in *Word and Object* (1960); and Stephen Toulmin in *Foresight and Understanding* (1961). Kuhn frankly discussed his life and work in an interview published as "A Discussion with Thomas S. Kuhn," which appears in the Greek scholarly journal *Neusis* 6 (spring-

summer 1997): 145–200. Important biographical material, including the possible role of psychoanalytic thought in influencing Kuhn's philosophical outlook, is in Jensine Andresen, "Crisis and Kuhn," *Isis* 90 (1999): S43–S67. The numerous detailed analyses of Kuhn's work include David A. Hollinger, "T. S. Kuhn's Theory of Science and Its Implications for History," *American Historical Review* (1973): 370, and Paul Hoyningen-Huene, *Reconstructing Scientific Revolutions: Thomas S. Kuhn's Philosophy of Science* (1993), both of which Kuhn regarded highly. Attacks on Kuhn appear in Imre Lakatos and Alan Musgrave, eds., *Criticism and the Growth of Knowledge* (1970); Steven Weinberg, "The Revolution That Didn't Happen," *New York Review of Books* (8 Oct. 1998); and Steve Fuller, *Thomas Kuhn: A Philosophical History for Our Times* (2000). A forceful reply to Fuller is David A. Hollinger, "Paradigms Lost," *New York Times Book Review* (28 May 2000). A profile of Kuhn in his last years is in John Horgan, *The End of Science* (1996). Obituaries are in the *New York Times* (19 June 1996) and *Washington Post* (20 June 1996). See also an insightful obituary by one of Kuhn's early students, John L. Heilbron, "Thomas Samuel Kuhn," *Isis* 89 (1998): 505–515.

KEAY DAVIDSON

KUNSTLER, William Moses (*b.* 7 July 1919 in New York City; *d.* 4 September 1995 in New York City), lawyer who gained national notoriety for his radical legal philosophy in the 1960s and, in the following decades, for his spirited defense of a broad range of accused anarchists, murderers, terrorists, social outcasts, and political pariahs.

A self-proclaimed radical and political outsider for much of his professional life, Kunstler grew up in the comfortable middle-class world of Manhattan's Upper West Side, the eldest of three children born to Monroe Bradford Kunstler, a proctologist, and Frances Mandelbaum, a homemaker. He was an indifferent student in his early public-school years and, in his words, a "rebellious" youth, but he graduated first in his class from DeWitt Clinton High School (Manhattan Annex) in 1937 and went on to Yale University, in New Haven, Connecticut, where he joined the swim team and took up boxing. In his senior year he was a co-author (with William Stone) of a privately printed volume of poetry, *Our Pleasant Vices,* and graduated in 1941 with a B.A. degree in French and membership in Phi Beta Kappa.

Kunstler enlisted in the U.S. Army on 3 September 1941 and served in the Pacific as an officer in the Signal Corps, participating in the 1944 invasion of Leyte in the Philippines and later in the occupation of Japan. He received the Bronze Star and was mustered out in March 1946 as a major. Before going overseas on 14 January 1943, he had married seventeen-year-old Lotte Rosenberger, a distant cousin and refugee from Germany; they had two daughters and divorced in 1976, the year in which he married Mar-

William Kunstler. ARCHIVE PHOTOS

garet Ratner, a lawyer, with whom he also had two daughters.

In the autumn of 1946, Kunstler, along with his brother Michael, was admitted under the GI Bill to a special two-year program at Columbia University Law School. To meet expenses, he wrote book reviews for the Sunday editions of the *New York Herald-Tribune* and the *New York Times* and taught a writing course in Columbia's School of General Studies (1946–1950). Graduating with an LL.B. in 1948 and admitted to the New York bar that same year, he began an executive training program at R. H. Macy, the huge New York City department store, but withdrew in 1949 to join his brother as a partner in Kunstler and Kunstler, specializing in matrimonial, estate, and family law.

As the firm's practice grew, Kunstler moved to Westchester County, New York, in 1950 and settled into the suburban round of commuting, work, and family. But, despite his rising fortunes, he was bored with the routine of everyday law and through the next decade devoted his spare hours and weekends to writing and teaching, which, he said, he found more fulfilling. Starting in 1950 he taught

law as an associate professor or lecturer at New York Law School (1949–1961, 1992), Pace Business School (1951–1960), the New School (1965–1966, 1970–1971, 1989), and Cooper Union (1986–1987), all in New York. He continued his freelance book reviewing and contributed essays to *Saturday Review* and *Atlantic Monthly,* among other magazines, and produced three books on the law: *The Law of Accidents* (1954), *First Degree* (1960), and *And Justice for All* (1963). Beginning in the late 1950s he wrote and narrated a number of scripts on famous trials for local radio stations in New York City and occasionally served as a radio host or panelist on programs dealing with legal questions or current events.

When he turned forty, Kunstler remained restless and uncertain about his professional life. But, he later wrote, his life changed forever when, on 15 June 1961, he was asked by the American Civil Liberties Union to fly to Mississippi as its representative among the Freedom Riders, young blacks and whites who were riding interstate buses to force integration of segregated transportation facilities in the South. Recalling the words of Oliver Wendell Holmes, Jr., that it was "required of a man to share the passion and action of his time," he agreed to go. Taking on Freedom Rider cases throughout the South on behalf of the Congress of Racial Equality, he became special counsel to Martin Luther King, Jr., and the Southern Christian Leadership Conference.

During the summer of 1961 Kunstler discovered an obscure federal statute from the Reconstruction era that permitted removal of certain cases from state to federal courts and successfully argued in federal court for its application in the contemporary South to prevent local courts from taking precipitous action against civil rights workers. That same year, Kunstler convinced the Fifth Circuit Court of Appeals, in a case involving a black journalist, to overturn on constitutional grounds a federal statute requiring a passport for reentry to the United States. These decisions, he said, proved to him that lawyering could make a difference and that he and the law could, in fact, play a role in changing society.

From the summer of 1961 onward, he became deeply involved in major cases seeking to desegregate schools and public facilities across the South and later in the North. He successfully appealed the convictions of black ministers involved in the bus boycotts in Birmingham, Alabama, and later defended student leaders like Stokely Carmichael (in Alabama, 1966) and H. Rap Brown (in Maryland, 1967) against charges of incitement to riot or insurrection. He challenged federal jury selection in the Southern District of New York (Westchester County, Manhattan, and the Bronx) on the ground that the method "systematically" excluded minorities.

Despite the demands of these and dozens of other cases,

Kunstler completed four well-received books: *Beyond a Reasonable Doubt* (1961), about the trial of Caryl Chessman, the so-called "Red Light Bandit" whose execution in California had stirred up international protests against the death penalty; *The Case for Courage: Ten Lawyers Who Risked Their Careers in the Cause of Justice* (1962); *The Minister and the Choir Singer* (1964), about the notorious Hall-Mills murder trial in 1922; and *Deep in My Heart* (1966), a memoir of his years with Dr. King.

By 1966 he had turned his attention to the war in Vietnam. As legal counsel to members of the antiwar movement and to radical groups on both coasts, he crisscrossed the country, often alone, sometimes with a team of lawyers, to aid clients whose ideologies ranged from anarchism to pacifism, including the Black Panthers in California (1966) and opponents of the draft in Maryland (1967). He was sentenced to prison in 1970 for contempt of court during the notorious Chicago Conspiracy trial, in which he defended eight radical protesters who had disrupted the Democratic National Convention in 1968. Indicted on federal charges of crossing state lines to incite violence, the defendants turned the courtroom into political theater. They and Kunstler repeatedly mocked the presiding judge, berated the prosecution with profane language, and delivered lengthy political harangues. All of them were acquitted of criminal conspiracy, five were found guilty of criminal incitement to violence, and all of them, including Kuntsler, were cited for contempt and "outrageous behavior." All were released pending appeals and in time were exonerated of all charges. In 1971 Kunstler was one of the independent observers called for by inmates at Attica prison in upstate New York during their bloody standoff with prison guards and later represented a number of them in court.

Kunstler became a familiar figure on television: a tall, angular man with a rich baritone voice, a craggy face, and flowing dark-brown (but graying) hair, his glasses characteristically pushed up on his forehead, given to provocative, often inflammatory, statements that got under the skin of his opponents. Some of his critics called him a publicity hound and questioned his penchant for trying cases by the seat of his pants, improvising as he went along. But even his critics found him eloquent, and many of them conceded that he won the majority of his cases through his superior legal skills and inventive application of the law rather than the histrionics he sometimes employed.

From 1970 until his death he continued to defend unpopular clients in high-profile criminal cases. Among the best known was his successful defense in 1987 of Larry Davis, a black drug dealer charged with the attempted murder of nine New York City policemen. Davis was acquitted on the principal complaint but was found guilty of the lesser charge of weapons possession and sentenced to four years in prison. Kuntsler created a furor in 1991 by winning an acquittal for an Islamic revolutionary, El Sayyid Nosair, accused of murdering Meir Kahane, leader of the militant Jewish Defense League in New York, and in 1993 by defending three resident aliens accused (and eventually found guilty) of the World Trade Center bombing in Lower Manhattan. Kunstler served briefly as attorney for Colin Ferguson, a black man who killed six commuters on a Long Island Railroad train in 1993. Kunstler and his associate Ronald L. Kuby unsuccessfully argued that Ferguson was innocent of criminal intent, having been driven to violence by "black rage" against white oppression. Ferguson subsequently chose to defend himself, dismissing Kuntsler and other court-appointed attorneys; he was found guilty on all counts in 1995 and sentenced to a term of 200 years.

Kuntsler's client list reflected his radical legal philosophy, which proceeded from the premise that American society and its legal system were corrupted by a racism so pervasive that all blacks and most minorities were denied political, economic, and social justice, that the criminal justice system was ultimately fashioned to keep the underclasses hobbled, and that the aim of government at every level was to eliminate dissent and opposition. He said it was his responsibility as a lawyer to expose the system and to defend the most socially undesirable from the overweening power of the state because all criminal trials were political in nature.

Kunstler claimed to represent many of his clients for free or for sharply reduced fees, because, he said, he had abandoned "the economic escalator" and had learned to live simply. He drew a small salary and travel expenses from the Center for Constitutional Rights, which he and other activist lawyers had set up in New York. He spread the story that his principal income came from lecture honorariums on college campuses and such money as his (now sporadic) writing and book reviewing might bring in. Kuby, who became his partner, told an interviewer that this was an exaggeration and that their firm had an income from fees. Kunstler's major asset at his death was his Federal row house in Greenwich Village, which he purchased in 1979 to use as his home and law office.

Kunstler dictated his autobiography to Sheila Isenberg, who shaped his narrative into *My Life as a Radical Lawyer* (1994). In 1995 he developed severe heart disease and received a pacemaker in August. He died a month later in Columbia-Presbyterian Hospital. Three thousand mourners filled the Cathedral of St. John the Divine for a memorial service. His remains were cremated and the ashes strewn across a mountain outcropping in the Catskills.

★

Kunstler's legal papers from the law firm of Kunstler and Kuby (1984–1995) and a collection of his articles from 1984 until his death are in the law offices of Ronald L. Kuby in New York. The bulk of his legal papers and his personal papers are held by his widow, Margaret Ratner. As a general rule, the legal papers are protected in perpetuity by the attorney-client privilege and are not accessible to researchers. His autobiography, *My Life as a Radical Lawyer* (1994), should be read with caution, because Kunstler was given to self-aggrandizement, invention, and exaggeration in telling his life story. David J. Langum, *William M. Kunstler: The Most Hated Lawyer in America* (1999), corrects some of its factual misstatements and challenges some of Kunstler's interpretations of events. See also Jeffrey Rosen, "The Trials of William Kunstler," *New York Times Book Review* (18 Sept. 1994). A convenient summary of Kunstler's political and legal philosophy is in "An Interview with William Kunstler," in Jonathan Black, ed., *Radical Lawyers: Their Role in the Movement and in the Courts* (1971). For Kunstler's role at Attica, see *Attica: The Official Report of the New York State Special Commission on Attica* (1972). For his role in the pivotal Chicago Conspiracy case, see J. Anthony Lukas, *The Barnyard Epithet and Other Obscenities: Notes on the Chicago Conspiracy Trial* (1970), and Tom Hayden, *Reunion: A Memoir* (1988). An obituary is in the *New York Times* (5 Sept. 1995).

ALLAN L. DAMON

Philip B. Kurland, 1973. © BETTMANN/CORBIS

KURLAND, Philip B.   (*b.* 22 October 1921 in Brooklyn, New York; *d.* 16 April 1996 in Chicago, Illinois), constitutional law expert who founded the *Supreme Court Review* and reviewed the Watergate transcripts for the Senate Judiciary Committee and concluded that they would support an impeachment charge against President Richard M. Nixon.

Kurland was one of two children of Archibald Kurland, a lawyer, and Estelle Polstein. After graduating from Erasmus Hall High School in Brooklyn, New York, in 1938, he received his B.A. degree from the University of Pennsylvania in 1942. In 1944 he earned an LL.B. from Harvard Law School, where he served as the president of the *Harvard Law Review*. He was a law clerk to Judge Jerome Frank of the U.S. Court of Appeals for the Second Circuit in 1944–1945 and in 1945–1946 to the Supreme Court justice Felix Frankfurter, with whom he formed a deep intellectual and personal bond. After working for the Justice Department and practicing law with Richard Wolfson in New York City from 1947 to 1950, Kurland moved to Chicago and joined the Northwestern University law faculty in 1950. In 1953 he moved to the University of Chicago, where he remained for the rest of his life. On 29 May 1954 he married Mary Jane Krensky; they had three daughters.

Kurland was at the center of sharp battles over the appropriate role of the U.S. Supreme Court during the 1950s and 1960s. "Don't shoot the piano player. He's doing his best," Kurland said in a 1964 critique of the Court. In 1969 he spoke of the Court's "essentially anti-democratic character" and opined that its justices were "full of the devil."

But gradually Kurland came to view the Constitution as a complex system that could not be reduced to any single component. His service as the chief consultant to the U.S. Senate Subcommittee on Separation of Powers from 1967 to 1974 under Senator Sam Ervin was central in this evolution. "If the history of the origins of our Constitution teach[es] us anything," Kurland wrote in 1970, "it must be that one great fear of the Constitution's makers was the danger of a strong and arbitrary executive." He reviewed the Watergate transcripts for Ervin, who chaired the Senate Watergate committee, and concluded that the transcripts would support an impeachment charge against President Richard M. Nixon.

In 1975 Kurland had a "real shot" at an appointment to the Supreme Court himself. Attorney General Edward Levi, a University of Chicago colleague and close friend, ran the selection process to replace Justice William O. Douglas for President Gerald Ford. But when Levi, who could have had the position himself, quietly mentioned Kurland within the administration, officials noted Kurland's aggressive positions on Congress's prerogatives and relative limitations on executive power. That concerned Levi, who backed off.

Kurland took a particular interest in religious issues. In a trailblazing article, "Of Church and State and the Supreme Court" in the 1961 *University of Chicago Law Review*, he proposed that the First Amendment's religious clauses "should be read as a single precept" forbidding government from using religion as "a standard for action or inaction." The Supreme Court cited Kurland's article in several opinions, and his reasoning gained increasing currency over the years.

Kurland grew so disenchanted with the academy during the turmoil of the late 1960s and early 1970s that he talked about leaving teaching to establish his own law firm, perhaps in New York City. He opened a 1971 book, *Mr. Justice Frankfurter and the Constitution,* a subject dear to him, speaking of "the academic community in which I try to work," and closed it by noting, "If not the man for this season, one may hope that he [Frankfurter] will be the man for the next one, if there is a next one." This bespoke Kurland's despair at the time. He estranged himself from the law school, viewing its concerns and faculty appointments dimly. In the mid-1970s, however, he began teaching law and humanities to undergraduates and was actively involved in undergraduate faculty affairs. It was not something Kurland did easily, given his sedentary nature and inclinations. From his new office on the eighth floor of the Harper Library, he said he "could now look down on the law school."

The essay was Kurland's favorite literary form, not the least reason being that it enabled him to show the fruits of his wide reading. *Watergate and the Constitution* (1978), a collection of essays and speeches, sparkles with vigor and insights into the greatest constitutional crisis since the Civil War to that date. Although Kurland said his tone was frequently "acerbic, ironic, sardonic, iconoclastic," all "appropriate to the subject matter," his judgments were more measured and understanding than previously, with a greater recognition of human folly and foibles. They were also more rooted in history.

Kurland collaborated with Ralph Lerner, at Lerner's suggestion, to edit *The Founders' Constitution* (1987), a five-volume set of primary documents that has aptly been called "the *Oxford English Dictionary* of American constitutional history." "If the Constitution is to be a viable instrument of governance," Kurland wrote in the introduction, "then it must (as it has to a great degree) cut itself free from its eighteenth-century moorings. The thought of the Founders, even to the extent it is discoverable, . . . cannot be binding." Nevertheless, their "principal objective" was "the preservation and advancement of individual liberty."

In 1987 Kurland adamantly opposed Robert Bork's nomination to the Supreme Court. He had worked with Bork, whom he had known since 1953. While most of his colleagues at the University of Chicago ardently supported the nomination, Kurland assisted the Senate Judiciary Committee in depicting Bork as a "Dr. Jekyll and Mr. Hyde" who shed a traditional legal approach to adopt "original intent," which was "merely a slogan," a vehicle to enable Bork to embrace more conservative views reflecting his "personal predilections." Kurland wrote a widely circulated article quoting Bork's earlier writings against his current views, and he testified before the Senate against the nominee, who was defeated.

Kurland's writings were "rather flavorful and pungent and filled with exciting alliteration," as one senator observed during the Bork hearings. Although he feigned an air of nonchalance and called himself a "trimmer," a skeptic rather than a believer, Kurland left little doubt where he stood. Increasingly he relied on the power of history to make his points. He frequently couched his seriousness in irony, with which history also abounded. Socially he often smiled sheepishly, for underneath, as friends put it, he was a "pussycat." Over time and especially in his later years he became more compassionate. His writing was no longer as carping, but he never lost his stinging wit. When a colleague observed, "No lawyer would," Kurland interrupted. "Stop right there," he said. "There is no way you can finish that sentence."

In 1960 Kurland founded the *Supreme Court Review,* which he edited until 1988. He felt he "made a mistake" in giving it up. He started researching a biography of Justice Robert H. Jackson but did not in any serious way pursue writing it, feeling he did not want to be a party to aspects of Jackson's private life. Starting in the 1970s, Kurland became counsel to a Chicago law firm, representing a variety of public and private clients. He worked on a collection of Justice Frankfurter's letters for several years before his death.

Kurland's first wife died in 1992, and he married Alice Hoag Bator on 12 February 1993. Kurland, who had a heart condition, died as the result of pneumonia.

Kurland gloried in having his opinion sought publicly, but he also prized a separate sphere in which "the private I" could flourish. As one of the most prominent constitutional commentators of his generation, Kurland continued the intellectual tradition of Frankfurter, "confident in the strength and security derived from the inquiring mind . . . unafraid of the uncertitudes," as he wrote of his mentor, and reveling in the joyous complexities of life.

★

Kurland's papers are in the Regenstein Library at the University of Chicago. His extensive correspondence with Frankfurter is in the Frankfurter papers at Harvard Law School and at the Library of Congress. Sources on Kurland include Mark Tushnet, "'Of Church and State and the Supreme Court': Kurland Revisited," *Supreme Court Review* (1989): 373; and Mark Gitenstein, *Matters of Principle* (1992). Tributes are in the *University of Chicago Law Review* 59 (1992) and 64 (1997). An obituary is in the *New York Times* (18 Apr. 1996).

ROGER K. NEWMAN

L

LAMONT, Corliss (*b.* 28 March 1902 in Englewood, New Jersey; *d.* 26 April 1995 in Ossining, New York), socialist author, teacher, humanist philosopher, and civil rights advocate.

Lamont was born into wealth. His father, Thomas William Lamont, was chairman of J. P. Morgan and Company, and in 1915 his parents rented the New York City residence of Franklin D. Roosevelt while the latter served as assistant secretary of the navy. Florence Haskell Corliss, Lamont's mother, donated the Lamont 125-acre estate in Palisades, New York, for the Lamont-Doherty Earth Observatory of Columbia University.

Lamont graduated from Phillips Exeter Academy in New Hampshire in 1920 and received his B.A. degree from Harvard University in 1924 with high honors. He attended Oxford University in England for one year and earned a Ph.D. in philosophy from Columbia University in 1932.

As a lifelong rebel, Lamont's initial cause was an attack on university clubs at Harvard. Then, at the start of his career at Columbia as a philosophy instructor, Lamont initiated help for Harvard women fired in a dispute over a new minimum-wage law. Lamont's leftward leanings continued in the 1930s, when he researched the Great Depression and coauthored a book on the Soviet Union, *Russia Day by Day*, with his first wife Margaret Hayes Irish. Although he initially praised the material progress achieved by the Soviet Union, which he observed firsthand during a visit to that country, eventually he became critical of Josef Stalin's repressive dictatorship. Lamont did not, however, lose faith in the communist system and believed that the Soviet Union needed time to develop democratic institutions similar to those in the West.

In 1953 Lamont's leftist views and activism led to a subpoena to appear before Senator Joseph McCarthy and the House Un-American Activities Committee. He testified that he was not and had never been a communist, and, though he did not invoke a Fifth Amendment privilege against self-incrimination, he would not discuss his political philosophy and associations. He claimed that as a private citizen, he was protected under First Amendment freedoms. Because of his testimony, Lamont was cited for contempt of Congress in federal court. A district court eventually dismissed the charge. The decision was unanimously upheld in 1955 by a circuit court, which effectively ended the case. The case was not decided on First Amendment rights but on the authority of McCarthy. It was a major victory in Lamont's career as a civil libertarian.

Another civil rights victory occurred in the late 1950s, when the U.S. State Department was ordered to issue a passport to Lamont after refusing to do so for nearly a decade. The reason he was given was that his travel abroad "would be contrary to the best interests of the United States." Lamont also won a suit against the U.S. Postmaster General in 1965. He charged that his First Amendment rights were violated when his mail, which included propaganda from the Chinese communist regime in Peking, was

Corliss Lamont, 1952. © BETTMANN/CORBIS

opened and withheld. The U.S. Supreme Court held that an anti-propaganda mail law was unconstitutional. Also in 1965, he won a lawsuit against the Central Intelligence Agency. The agency opened many letters that were mailed or received by him, including from his wife. A federal court held that "illegal prying into shared intimacies of husband and wife is despicable."

Lamont's connection of militancy and philosophy was on humanist principles and "not Christian service to an Improbable God, but service here and now to our fellow human beings." Lamont indicated that humanism is "a philosophy which works for the welfare and progress and happiness of all mankind." As a leading humanist and president of the American Humanist Association for many years, Lamont maintained that the humanist uses intelligence and the scientific method to solve problems. He wrote a standard text on the subject, *The Philosophy of Humanism,* in 1949.

Lamont was married to Margaret Hayes Irish in 1928. They divorced in 1962, and he married Helen Lamb. Lamb died in 1975, and Lamont married Beth Keehner on 24 July 1986.

During his career, Lamont taught philosophy at Harvard, Cornell, and Columbia universities and the New School for Social Research. Lamont endowed a chair in civil liberties at the Columbia University Law School and contributed to the construction of the Corliss Lamont Reading Room at the Rare Book and Manuscript Library at Columbia.

Lamont was a member of the board of directors of the American Civil Liberties Union for twenty-two years, as well as chairman of the National Emergency Civil Liberties Committee, which he helped found, for thirty years. He also served on the board of directors of the National Urban League, and he received the Gandhi Peace Award in 1981. He twice ran for the U.S. Senate, first on the American Labor Party ticket in 1952, receiving 10,000 votes, and then on the Independent Socialist ticket in 1958, receiving 49,000 votes.

Lamont was brown-haired and brown-eyed, weighed 145 pounds, and stood five feet eight and a half inches tall.

Lamont wrote pamphlets and letters on a variety of civil rights and humanist subjects, including his opposition to nuclear testing, the war in Vietnam, and the convictions of Julius and Ethel Rosenberg for atomic spying. The sixteen books written by Lamont include *Lover's Credo: Poems of Love*; *The Illusion of Immortality*; *Freedom of Choice Affirmed*; *Remembering John Masefield*; *A Lifetime of Dissent*; *A Humanist Funeral Service*; *A Humanist Wedding Service*; *Soviet Civilization*; *The Independent Mind*; *The Peoples of the Soviet Union*; and *You Might Like Socialism: A Way of Life for Modern Man*. He edited *Dear Corliss*; *Letters from Eminent Persons*; *Collected Poems of John Reed*; *Dialogue with John Dewey*; *Dialogue with George Santayana*; *The Trial of Elizabeth Gurley Flynn by the American Civil Liberties Union*; and *Man Answers Death*. He died of heart failure and is buried in Brookside Cemetery in Englewood, New Jersey.

As a humanist, author, civil libertarian, and fighter for causes he believed just, Lamont contributed to American principles of humanism, fairness, equality and justice, stating in *Yes to Life*, "My final word is . . . to keep on fighting for our fundamental principles and ideals."

★

Major autobiographical works by Lamont include *Yes to Life—Memoirs of Corliss Lamont* (1981) and *A Lifetime of Dissent* (1988). Appreciative articles after his death include Frederick Edwords, "Requiem for a Freedom Fighter," *Humanist* (July 1995). Obituaries are in the *New York Times* (28 Apr. 1995) and Manchester *Guardian* (19 May 1995).

MARTIN JAY STAHL

LAMOUR, Dorothy (*b.* 10 December 1914 in New Orleans, Louisiana; *d.* 22 September 1996 in Hollywood, California), one of the most popular film actresses and singers of the 1930s and 1940s, best known for her sarong-wearing roles and for her comedic collaboration with Bob Hope and Bing Crosby in their "Road" series of movies.

Dorothy Lamour was born Mary Leta Dorothy Slaton in the charity ward of New Orleans's Hotel Dieu Hospital,

Dorothy Lamour, 1986. THE KOBAL COLLECTION

the daughter of waitress Carmen Louise LaPorte and waiter John Watson Slaton. Named after a movie heroine, Dorothy showed promise early on as a performer, winning a basket of groceries at age five for singing and dancing on stage in a New Orleans movie house. Her parents eventually divorced, and Dorothy took the surname of her stepfather, Clarence Lambour. The family struggled financially, and at the age of fourteen Dorothy got permission from her mother to quit school so she could go to work.

At fifteen Lamour landed the role of Miss Louisiana in the traveling vaudeville show *The American Beauty*. She would win the real-life beauty queen title of "Miss New Orleans" in 1931. Upon moving to Chicago, she worked as an elevator operator for Marshall Field's department store on State Street and went on tour as a singer. The crooner Rudy Vallee helped the fledgling singer appear in 1931 at New York City's Stork Club, where she also met bandleader Herbie Kaye, whom she married on 10 May 1935; they divorced in May 1939. When a poster painter misspelled Lambour's name as "Lamour," she and Kaye decided they liked the look of it; she would delete the "b" for the rest of her career.

Lamour headed for Hollywood, where she signed a seven-year contract with Paramount Pictures. Her first film, *The Jungle Princess* (1936), provided her signature dress—a sarong, created by soon-to-be famed designer Edith Head. To go along with her sarong, Lamour sported her sultry thirty-inch-long locks, which her studio called "the longest tresses in the film colony."

"We sometimes worked a very hard sixteen to eighteen hour day, six days a week. (Of course that was B.U.—Before Unions)," Lamour later recalled in her memoir *My Side of the Road*. Besides the grueling schedule, there were also the menacing special effects she endured, as in her 1937 movie *The Hurricane,* also starring Mary Astor and Raymond Massey. "To make the great winds, the special effects department rigged up a half a dozen airplane engines with huge propellers. Then to make the wind whistle, they mixed a concoction of dried leaves and yellow sulfur, which photographed like dust, and flung it in front of the propellers," she later noted. "Each night after work, I was covered from head to foot with small nicks from the gale-swept leaves, and the sulfur didn't have the greatest effect on my eyes and throat."

Lamour survived the cinematic hurricane to earn $1,000 a week during the Depression years. She also earned a place on a "Greatest Discoveries" list from a newspaper poll that cited Judy Garland and Don Ameche in the top ten. When the Depression ended and World War II began, audiences wanted to see Lamour in escapist entertainment. Thus began her "Road" series of movies with the singer Bing Crosby and comedian Bob Hope. Their first, *Road to Singapore* (1939), spawned one of the most successful screen teams in Hollywood history. That year, in a swipe at her acting skills, the *Harvard Lampoon* placed her on its "worst" list, along with *The Wizard of Oz,* which was named "most colossal flop." Lamour, with her characteristic good humor, went on to share the same success as *The Wizard of Oz,* earning $150,000 per year by the late 1940s. Also during this period, she met the offscreen love of her life—Air Corps Lieutenant William Ross Howard III, whom she married on 7 April 1943; they remained happily married for more than three decades, until his death in 1978. They had two sons.

Lamour's career, fueled by her sex symbol status, skyrocketed throughout the 1940s. Paramount's direction to its cameramen was to "show as much of Lamour as the censors will permit—with or without the sarong." *Road to Singapore* was followed by *Road to Zanzibar* (1940), *Road to Morocco* (1942), and *Road to Utopia* (1944). Lamour also volunteered to go out on the road for the war effort, selling war bonds; on one twenty-five-city tour she sold $31,439,515 worth of bonds in just nine days, at a time when a movie ticket cost just forty cents or less. After the war ended, the "Road" pictures continued with *Road to Rio* (1947). Lamour moved from Paramount to RKO Pictures in 1947. In 1949 she won a victory for working mothers when she was hit with the cancellation of her contract by Howard Hughes's RKO Pictures. Given the official notice in the hospital the morning after giving birth to her second son, she resolved not to be victimized because of her pregnancy. From a countersuit, she was awarded more than $500,000 from RKO.

The "Road" movies went on in the 1950s with *Road to Bali* (1952). In *Road to Hong Kong* (1961), Lamour had a reduced role, with the female lead given to younger actress Joan Collins. It would be the last "Road" film. The 1960s were not kind to the aging actress.

"Sometimes show business associates can be very cruel," Lamour noted. "It was suddenly difficult for me to reach certain Hollywood people by phone—the same people for whom I had done so many favors when I was 'box office magic.' You know the routine: Someone would be 'in a meeting and simply couldn't be disturbed.' 'May I ask what this is about?' his secretary would say, or 'He's out of town, but when he returns I'll be sure to give him the message.'" Lamour cushioned the blow by settling for several years in Baltimore, the hometown of her husband. In Baltimore the couple concentrated on raising their sons.

Lamour continued her singing and acting career on stages across the country, not bitter about the cold shoulder she received from the film industry. As she put it in her 1980 autobiography: "I've often said that God has blessed me so much. I had a wonderful mother, a loving husband, . . . sons (and now two lovely daughters-in-law), and a fabulous career. What woman could ask for anything more? I've certainly had the best in life."

Lamour died at her Hollywood home of cardiac arrest at the age of eighty-one. She is buried in Forest Lawn Cemetery, Los Angeles.

The self-described "little girl from New Orleans who became Dorothy Lamour Howard" managed to create a balanced life for herself despite the 100-hour-plus Hollywood workweeks. She is remembered best for the light-hearted fare she offered America during grim years.

★

Lamour's memoir *My Side of the Road* (1980) traces the actress's life. Information about her career also appears in Joan Collins, *Past Imperfect* (1978), and Edward Maeder, *Hollywood and History* (1987). Obituaries are in the *New York Times* and *Los Angeles Times* (both 23 Sept. 1996).

ROBERT J. SMITH

LANCASTER, Burt(on) Stephen (*b.* 2 November 1913 in New York City; *d.* 20 October 1994 in Los Angeles, California), movie actor and one of the most successful independent star-producers of the post–World War II Hollywood era.

Lancaster was born in the family house on East 106th Street in the politically progressive, immigrant neighborhood of New York's East Harlem. He was the fourth and final child

Burt Lancaster. ARCHIVE PHOTOS

of James Lancaster, a postal worker, and Lizzie Lancaster, both second-generation Northern Ireland Protestants. A pugnacious scrapper as a child, Lancaster nevertheless loved to read. He dreamed of being a famous opera singer and performed in many amateur theatrical productions at the local Union Settlement Association. When, as a teenager, he shot up to his full adult height of 6 feet two inches, he came into his own as a handsome, graceful athlete.

An injury prevented Lancaster from starting college immediately after his graduation from DeWitt Clinton High School in 1930. Before entering New York University's School of Education in the fall of 1931, he developed a passion for acrobatics and started to perfect a parallel bar act in the gym of the local Union Settlement Association with his neighborhood pal, Nick Cuccia (later called Nick Cravat).

In the spring of 1933, in the depth of the Great Depression, the two young men left East Harlem to join the Kay Brothers Circus as acrobats. Thus began Lancaster's key exposure to and training in the American circus and in vaudeville that lasted until he was drafted into the U.S. Army in 1942. He and Cravat crisscrossed the country as part of a string of small "mud show" circus troupes and learned the hard craft and vigorous routine of live circus entertainment. In 1935 Lancaster married June Ernst, of a well-known family of circus aerialists; the relationship lasted barely two years. By the end of the decade, after two years (1935–1937) in the WPA Circus of the Federal Theater Project in New York, Lancaster was reduced to burlesque and vaudeville routines and quit the entertainment field in 1941 to work in Chicago's Marshall Field's department store as a salesman.

Lancaster served in Italy from 1942 to 1945 in the Twenty-first Special Service Division, a branch of the armed forces created to provide entertainment to the troops. Following General Mark Clark's Fifth Army up the Italian boot, he gained not only key exposure to seasoned theatrical performers but also a chance to observe American military attitudes and characters that would later provide essential background for some of his key postwar roles in such movies as *From Here to Eternity* (1953). He also met Norma Anderson, a USO performer from Wisconsin whom he would marry on 28 December 1946 and who would be the mother of all of his five children.

In September 1945 Lancaster arrived back in New York City and was immediately cast as a sergeant in Harry Brown's new "dugout drama," *A Sound of Hunting.* His serendipitous luck in being cast in a Broadway play, the immediate contract bids that streamed in from all the major Hollywood studios, his signing with Hal Wallis of Paramount Studios with an unusual outside option, his quick capitalizing on the option with independent Universal producer Mark Hellinger to appear in a movie version of the famous Ernest Hemingway short story "The Killers"—all these factors created one of the most famous star discovery stories in Hollywood history. Without ever having appeared in a major theatrical or movie production in his life, at the age of thirty-three in 1946, Lancaster was a star and remained so for the rest of his life.

The years from 1946 to 1960 were Lancaster's zenith years. One of the megastars of Hollywood, famous around the world for his blond hair, blazing blue eyes, chiseled white teeth, and physical power and grace, he was also a primary force in the explosively changing postwar movie industry. In 1947 he and his partner, Harold Hecht, formed Norma Productions (named for Lancaster's wife), an independent production company. As Hecht Lancaster and, from 1957, Hecht Hill Lancaster, the company allied with United Artists to become one of the most successful "indies" of the decade. In breakthrough pictures like *Marty* (1955), which was the first American film to win best picture at the Cannes Film Festival, *Apache* (1954), *Trapeze* (1956), *Sweet Smell of Success* (1957), and *Separate Tables* (1958), the company charted the course from the old Hollywood of studio vertical domination to the new world of star-driven independent production.

Using the international stardom earned through a remarkable range of movie choices, Lancaster crafted a balance of commercial and "art" films that he maintained

throughout his screen life. Up until 1960, when his independent company dissolved itself, he alternated between contracts with his original studio, Paramount (*Sorry, Wrong Number* [1948], *The Rainmaker* [1956], *Gunfight at the O.K. Corral* [1957]); with Warner Bros. (*The Flame and the Arrow* [1950], *The Crimson Pirate* [1952], *Jim Thorpe—All American* [1951]); and with Columbia (*From Here to Eternity,* for which he won his first Oscar nomination). Under the safer commercial umbrella of Paramount, he played some of the most ambitious early "stretch" parts through which he learned the craft of acting, including *Come Back, Little Sheba* (1952) and *The Rose Tattoo* (1955).

By the time Lancaster made *Elmer Gantry* (1960) with director Richard Brooks and won his first Academy Award, for his portrayal of the slick, huckster evangelist from Sinclair Lewis's 1920s novel, he was independent of any studio. He proceeded to make some of the movies for which he is most vividly remembered, deepening with each challenging role his redefinition of the popular idea of the movie star as a consistent persona. *Birdman of Alcatraz* (1962), for which he won his third Oscar nomination in the title role, reinforced in the public's mind Lancaster's reputation for making hard-hitting pictures cued to key issues of his time—in this case, prison reform. *Judgment at Nuremberg* (1961) vividly revived the memory of the Nazi Holocaust when the cold war had swept the memory out of public consciousness. For Luchino Visconti, Lancaster made *The Leopard* (1963), a lavish chronicle tracing the post-Garibaldi end of the Italian aristocracy in Lancaster's character, the Sicilian Prince of Salina. For John Frankenheimer, a director with whom he worked frequently in this era, Lancaster and frequent costar Kirk Douglas made *Seven Days in May* (1964), a cold war melodrama about a military attempt to take over the U.S. government, a movie made with the active cooperation of President John F. Kennedy and released shortly after his assassination.

Throughout these years, Lancaster worked hard to maintain some semblance of a normal family life. His wife and children routinely came on foreign locations with him up until the late 1950s. At the same time, he was well known for engaging in extramarital love affairs with costars such as Yvonne De Carlo, Deborah Kerr, and Katy Jurado; in the late 1940s he had a longer, more serious relationship with Shelley Winters. In 1969 Lancaster and Norma divorced; in 1964 he had begun a relationship with a movie hairdresser, Jackie Bone, that lasted almost twenty years. In his own fashion, Lancaster valued loyalty and maintained his old business partner, Nick Cravat, on his payroll for the rest of his life. His involvement with progressive political causes began with his active opposition to the House Un-American Activities Committee in 1947, continued with his quiet hiring and supporting of gray- and black-listed movie professionals such as Waldo Salt in the 1950s, and found mature expression from the 1960s on in such issues as civil rights, First Amendment rights, and, generally, in giving the disenfranchised equal access to mainstream American life. His was a complicated, fractious personality that mellowed as he got older. "Somewhere it has got to stop," he once said. "You've got to put down the sword."

The last third of Lancaster's life was marked by remarkable but overlooked performances in such films as *The Swimmer* (1968), *Ulzana's Raid* with director Robert Aldrich (1972), Visconti's *Conversation Piece* (1975), *1900* for Bernardo Bertolucci (1976), and *Buffalo Bill and the Indians, or Sitting Bull's History Lesson* (1976) for Robert Altman. But with *Atlantic City* (1981), directed by Louis Malle, Lancaster not only received his fourth Oscar nomination but the "comeback" recognition that, finally, he was a great actor.

With the physique and discipline of an athlete, Lancaster kept himself in play for decades. As he matured, his onscreen acting style became more contained but no less graceful. His body remained his instrument of style. The agile body that had been his trademark began to break down in the 1980s. After a quadruple heart bypass operation in 1983, he had to turn down a string of worthy parts (*Gorky Park, Kiss of the Spider Woman*) that would not come his way again. Nevertheless, he savored the chance to play thoughtful character roles in *Local Hero* (1983) and *Rocket Gibraltar* (1988). On 10 September 1990 he married Susie Martin, an actress and script supervisor he had met in 1984. Lancaster's last movie role was as Doc Graham in *Field of Dreams* (1989). His final piece of work was in *Separate but Equal*, the 1991 Emmy Award–winning ABC-TV multiseries about the 1954 U.S. Supreme Court school desegregation decision. In late 1990 Lancaster suffered a debilitating stroke, and four years later he died of a heart attack at the age of eighty in his home at Century City in Los Angeles. He is buried in Westwood Memorial Park, Los Angeles.

In a pivotal, transitional time in Hollywood—the 1950s—Lancaster challenged the industry's and the public's assumptions about movie stars. A true maverick of the movie business, he insisted his films match the tenor of his time. Moreover, he used his power as a star to set up and sustain an independent production company that similarly redefined the parameters of the movie business in one of its most chaotic decades. Lancaster is remembered by millions for a charismatic, disciplined energy on the screen and an expressive mastery of screen language that harks back to cinema's beginnings on the silent screen.

★

Lancaster's personal collection of the bound scripts of his movies is at the School of Cinema-Television, University of Southern California, Los Angeles. Material related to his film ca-

reer can be found at USC; the Wisconsin Center for Film and Theater Research, State Historical Society of Wisconsin, Madison, Wisconsin; the Academy of Motion Picture Arts and Sciences, Beverly Hills, California; and the Billy Rose Theater Collection, New York Public Library at Lincoln Center, New York City. The most recent and complete biography, written with the cooperation of Lancaster's widow, is Kate Buford, *Burt Lancaster: An American Life* (2000). The only significant retrospective periodical article is also by Buford: "Lancaster: Dance with the Leopard," *Film Comment* (Jan.–Feb. 1993). An obituary is in the *New York Times* (22 Oct. 1994).

KATE BUFORD

LANTZ, Walter (*b.* 27 April 1900 in New Rochelle, New York; *d.* 18 March 1994 in Burbank, California), animator noted for creating the cartoon character Woody Woodpecker.

Lantz was the first of the three children of Frank Lantz, a butcher, and Mary Gervasi. Both of Lantz's parents were Italian immigrants, and a U.S. immigrant official had changed the Old Country name Lanza to Lantz. Lantz became interested in drawing when he was a child. His relatives recalled that, at the age of four, he would sit on the sill in the bay window of his family's house drawing trees or birds or just copying comic strips from newspapers.

Walter Lantz with his creation Woody Woodpecker, 1967. © BETTMANN/ CORBIS

He finished a mail-order drawing course at the age of twelve. His father encouraged his talent.

Lantz began brushing with famous illustrators in his teens. At age fifteen he worked as an office boy in the art department of the *New York American* newspaper. He took night classes, and at age sixteen he was hired by the new Hearst animation studio. Two years later Lantz was made a full-time animator. However, the Hearst studio closed shortly after his promotion, and he worked on the "Mutt and Jeff" cartoon at other studios in New York City.

Lantz became a manager at the John R. Bray studios, creating the Dinky Doodle films that feature a boy named Dinky Doodle and a dog named Weakheart. He moved to Hollywood in 1927 and worked as a comedy writer for a few years. His career returned to cartoons in 1929, when Lantz, working with Universal Pictures, produced *Oswald, the Lucky Rabbit*. In the following years, famous animators, including Jack Hannah, Tex Avery, and Dicky Lundy worked for Lantz. His studio created his second most famous cartoon character, Andy Panda, in 1939.

The idea for Woody Woodpecker came to Lantz while he honeymooned with the actress Grace Stafford in 1940. As recounted in his biography, *The Walter Lantz Story* (1985), inspiration for Woody Woodpecker hit him whole in an irritating manner, as he was trying to rest in a lakeside cottage with his wife. "This one particular woodpecker kept pecking on our roof. I thought maybe he was pecking for enjoyment. He would come about four in the morning and Gracie would lean over in the bed and knock on the wall, just as a gag, and he'd knock back."

Grace Lantz suggested that her husband use the irritant as material. "I decided to take him into partnership," Lantz said. "If you can't fight 'em, join 'em." Woody Woodpecker was a hit when he appeared in the Andy Panda movie *Knock, Knock,* but his popularity skyrocketed in 1948 with the release of *The Woody Woodpecker Song*. It began with the famous laugh, "Ha-ha-ha-HAAA-ha. Ha-ha-ha-HAAA-ha. That's the Woody Woodpecker Song." Grace Lantz supplied the bird's voice for the song, which was nominated for an Academy Award as best song. Mel Blanc, noted for other cartoon voices, supplied the laugh.

A steady stream of Woody Woodpecker cartoons followed, and the redheaded maniac soon reached the top of the television cartoon popularity list alongside the likes of Bugs Bunny and Popeye. In 1959 the Los Angeles City Council honored Lantz as "one of America's most outstanding animated film cartoonists."

Lantz spent his final years in California accumulating accolades for his work. In 1979, three years after Lantz stopped making cartoons, he received an Academy Award for lifetime achievement for his contributions to the art of animation. In 1986 he was honored with a star on Hollywood's Walk of Fame. In 1993, one year after Grace Lantz

died at the age of eighty-eight, Lantz founded a $10,000 animation scholarship and prize in his name at the California Institute of the Arts in Valencia. He had no children and died of heart failure at age ninety-four.

A producer, comedy writer, and animator, Lantz proved his versatility in the entertainment industry. He was at the heart of cartoon making when color animation first became a force in the world of entertainment. His timeless Woody Woodpecker cartoons, with side characters such as Buzz Buzzard and Chilly Willy the Penguin, have been enjoyed by people who were not born until after Lantz died.

★

Joe Adamson, who wrote extensively about the Marx Brothers, authored the full-length biography *The Walter Lantz Story* (1985). Works about other famous cartoonists mention Lantz, including Leonard Maltin, *Of Mice and Magic: A History of American Animated Cartoons* (1980) and Jeff Lenburg, *The Great Cartoon Directors* (1983). Obituaries are in the *New York Times* and *Los Angeles Times* (both 23 Mar. 1994).

JEFFREY A. DIAMANT

LARSON, Jonathan (*b.* 4 February 1960 in Mount Vernon, New York; *d.* 25 January 1996 in New York City), composer, lyricist, and librettist of music for television, modern dance, and musical theater, best known as the author of the Pulitzer Prize–winning Broadway musical *Rent* (1996).

The son of Allan S. Larson, a direct-marketing executive, and Nanette Notarius, a homemaker, Larson grew up in suburban White Plains, New York, and learned to play the piano at an early age. While at White Plains High School, he took music theory and composition classes and played the tuba in the marching band. Meanwhile, he was involved in school and community theater. In the fall of 1978 he entered the acting conservatory at Adelphi University on a full-tuition scholarship, receiving a B.F.A. degree with honors in 1982. While planning to become an actor, he was equally interested in composing music; at Adelphi he collaborated on nine musicals, favoring the political cabaret. While still a senior, he sent a letter to the famed composer-lyricist Stephen Sondheim in praise of his work. Sondheim responded, inviting Larson over for a drink; thus commenced their friendship and Sondheim's mentoring, which lasted until Larson's death.

After graduation, Larson moved to Manhattan and began his life as a struggling artist. He pursued an acting career at first but soon turned his attention exclusively to composing music, moonlighting as a waiter to pay the bills. As his style and artistic vision evolved, Larson worked on diverse projects spanning the gamut of musical genres: children's film and television, modern dance, promotional video, musical theater, and book tapes. During these years

Jonathan Larson. ARCHIVE PHOTOS

he also formed lasting friendships, mostly with other artists living between privilege and poverty. People were drawn to Larson, a natural leader who was known for his lanky and graceful awkwardness, his dark curly hair, and his soulful eyes. He liked getting around New York City by bicycle, as a way of staying in touch with the urban pulse. On holidays, especially Thanksgiving, he hosted festive dinner parties at his loft, inviting new friends and old. While he loved tradition, Larson also kept up with current events, mostly by reading the newspaper. A devoted urbanite, Larson also loved the ocean and went there whenever he could.

The rock opera, however, was Larson's passion. He aspired to revive the tradition established in the 1960s with *Tommy, Hair,* and *Jesus Christ Superstar,* all of which hybridized musical form while also commenting on society's ills. Not limiting his inspiration to rock music, Larson cast his creative net widely for sources of material. His music, therefore, was eclectic; it drew not only from rock and roll but also from popular forms like show tunes, rap, jazz, salsa, and reggae, and classical forms like opera and the avant-garde.

In the late 1980s and early 1990s, Larson's creative output was prodigious. His productions included *Superbia* (1985–1991), a futuristic and dystopian musical based on

George Orwell's *1984* that was developed and performed at Playwrights Horizons with a Richard Rodgers grant; *Tick, Tick . . . Boom!* (1991), an autobiographical rock monologue he performed at the New York Theater Workshop; *J. P. Morgan Saves the Nation* (1995), an ironic event commissioned by the En Garde Arts Festival and set on the steps of the Federal Hall National Memorial on Wall Street; and *Rent* (1996), directed by Michael Greif and assisted by a Richard Rodgers production grant. During this time Larson earned various honors including a Stephen Sondheim Award (1989) presented at the American Musical Theater Festival and the Stanley Drama Award (1994) from Wagner College, Staten Island, New York.

According to Sondheim, Larson's greatest talent was "his sense of what is theatrical, of how you use music to tell a story, as opposed to writing a song." A keen observer of the world, Larson was good at establishing character through his lyrics (perhaps owing to his talent as an actor), and he used his songs to portray the existential adversity that individuals experience in their daily lives. Sometimes, he modeled his characters on historical figures (J. P. Morgan) or artistic prototypes (Mimi in *La Bohème*), but he often fashioned them on himself or people he knew like lovers, friends, or the denizens of Manhattan's subcultures and streets.

Rent was perhaps the clearest example of Larson's sensitivity, observational acumen, artistic eclecticism, and commitment to social commentary. Based loosely on *La Bohème* (1896) by Giacomo Puccini, it borrowed the opera's themes of bohemianism, plague, and doomed love. Yet Larson transported Puccini's story from the tuberculosis-ridden Left Bank in late nineteenth-century Paris to the AIDS-plagued East Village in late twentieth-century Manhattan to depict the paradoxes of capitalism. As he explained, "I analyzed [Puccini's] libretto, broke it down beat by beat," all the while thinking, "Who would these characters be in my world?" In fact, Larson based the characters in the musical on some of his many friends and its squalid setting on his own loft in lower Manhattan.

Rent evoked the hodgepodge of New York City's bohemian scene. As Margo Jefferson, theater critic for the *New York Times,* put it, it was a "montage of performance artists, abandoned buildings, upwardly mobile landlords, film makers and rock and roll bands; homeless people, policemen, drug dealers and drug addicts; free-thinking, free-form multiculturalism; homo-, hetero- and bisexuality, life-support groups and safe sex; privilege side by side with poverty and open-hearted exhilaration in the face of death and HIV." Unfortunately, Larson did not live to see the show open. Racked with abdominal and chest pain during dress rehearsals, he sought emergency treatment at two local hospitals. Each incorrectly diagnosed him as having the flu or food poisoning, respectively, gave him medicine to relieve the pain, and told him to rest. After the show's final dress rehearsal, Larson returned home, where he died of an undiagnosed aortic aneurysm. In December 1996 a New York State–directed inquiry found both hospitals negligent and were fined and publicly criticized for the poor quality of Larson's care. Larson was cremated and his ashes scattered at several of his favorite places.

Within weeks, the show became a hit—due in part to its soulful and driving soundtrack, its striking vision of young life on the edge, and its sense of the cultural moment. However, despite all that the show had to recommend it, the media focused most on the tragic irony of Larson's untimely death, making an unfortunate accident into a case of the uncanny. Within two months of opening, with a cast of virtual unknowns and advance ticket sales topping $6 million, *Rent* moved from the New York Theater Workshop off off Broadway to Broadway's prestigious Nederlander Theater. In 1996 the production won a host of honors, including the Pulitzer Prize for drama; Tony awards for best musical, musical score, book, and supporting actor; the New York Drama Critics Circle Award for best musical; Drama Desk awards for best musical, music, lyrics, book, featured actor in a musical, and arrangement; the Drama League Award for best musical; and Obie awards for outstanding book, lyrics, music, direction, and ensemble performance.

Meanwhile, commotion surrounded the production. Movie producers clamored for film rights to Larson's life story and libretto. Cast members signed recording and film contracts and appeared on national television. Lynn Thompson, Larson's dramaturg, filed a lawsuit demanding that she be recognized as coauthor (she eventually lost her case). Bloomingdale's, an upscale department store, opened a *Rent*-inspired clothing boutique. And the show began touring, playing to audiences on five continents by 2000.

The irony of *Rent*'s rags-to-riches story did not go unnoticed by critics like Ward Morehouse III of the *New York Post*, who wondered if "'Rent' [would] lose heart as it won success?" Others, like Michiko Kakutani of the *New York Times*, charged that *Rent* was little more than a "new brand of tourism that offered bourgeois audiences a voyeuristic peep at an alien subculture and let them go home feeling smug and with it."

Yet its critics' cynicism never eclipsed *Rent*'s powerful and enduring portrayal of despair and hope embodied by its characters, nor did it succeed in trivializing Larson's vision of social trouble amidst a culture of growing prosperity.

★

The Larson family maintains an archive of materials such as manuscripts, correspondence, and demo recordings. *Rent by Jonathan Larson* (1997), with text and interviews by Evelyn McDonnell with Katherine Silberger, documents Larson's life and work. For an account of Larson's early career, see Barry Singer's profile in *New York* magazine (21 June 1993) and John Istel, "Rescuing the Musical," *Village Voice* (4 July 1995). Articles published in 1996, the year of Larson's death, include Anthony Tommasini, "A Composer's Death Echoes in His Musical," *New York Times* (11 Feb. 1996); Michael Feingold, "Long Term Lease," *Village Voice* (20 Feb. 1996); Margo Jefferson, "'Rent' Is Brilliant and Messy All at Once," *New York Times* (25 Feb. 1996); Jack Kroll, "A Downtown 'La Bohème,'" *Newsweek* (26 Feb. 1996); Ward Morehouse III, "'Rent' Losing Heart as It Wins Success?" *New York Post* (22 Mar. 1996); Jack Kroll, "Love Among the Ruins," *Newsweek* (13 May 1996); Gregory Beals and Yahlin Chang, "The World of 'Rent,'" *Newsweek* (13 May 1996); David Lipsky, profile of Larson, *US* magazine (Nov. 1996); and Elizabeth Rosenthal, "2 Hospitals Fined in Wake of Death of 'Rent' Creator," *New York Times* (13 Dec. 1996). An obituary of Larson is in the *New York Times* (26 Jan. 1996).

REBEKAH J. KOWAL

LASCH, Christopher (*b.* 1 June 1932 in Omaha, Nebraska; *d.* 14 February 1994 in Pittsford, New York), social critic and historian who attacked the modern culture of consumerism and narcissism and who, though he remained a political leftist, sharply critiqued what he saw as the self-indulgence of the American Left.

Lasch was the son of Robert Lasch, a newspaper editorialist for the *Omaha World Herald,* and Zora Schaupp, a part-time social worker and professor with a Ph.D. in philosophy. Lasch was brought up as a liberal and Midwest progressive, traditions he professionally debated in his writings, but he continued to characterize himself as a liberal throughout his life.

His family, which included one sister, moved to Barrington, Illinois, shortly after he was born. At Barrington High School, from which he graduated in 1950, Lasch edited the school paper and was politically engaged on behalf of the Progressive Party candidate Henry Wallace's 1948 campaign for the U.S. presidency. He gained a scholarship to the University of Chicago but chose to attend Harvard, from which he graduated in 1954 with summa cum laude honors in history. He went on to Columbia University in New York City, where he gained an M.A. degree in history in 1955 and a Ph.D. in 1961 under the guidance of the New Deal historian William E. Leuchtenburg. His first book, *The American Liberals and the Russian Revolution* (1962), grew out of his dissertation.

Also while at Columbia, in 1956 Lasch married Nell Commager, daughter of the eminent historian Henry Steele Commager. She became an accomplished potter, and together they raised four children. Lasch taught at Williams

Christopher Lasch. AP/WIDE WORLD PHOTOS

College in Williamstown, Massachusetts, and Roosevelt University in Chicago while finishing his doctorate. He moved to the University of Iowa, where within four years he became a full professor. He then went on to Northwestern University in Evanston, Illinois, in 1966. He began teaching at the University of Rochester in New York in 1970 and remained there until his death in 1994. In 1979 he was named the Don Alonzo Watson Professor of History, and in 1985 he became chairman of a department that was rated one of the best in the nation.

His first book established something of a pattern, delineating the fault lines in liberals' perception of the 1917 Russian Revolution as the establishment of an earthly paradise—a belief so strong that they dared make only faint criticisms of Soviet brutality. Lasch's reputation as an intellectual of substance was enhanced with his second book, *The New Radicalism in America (1889–1963): The Intellectual as a Social Type* (1965), in which he examined the careers of social activists such as Jane Addams. In the book, he developed the idea, derived from his studies of Karl Marx and Sigmund Freud, that religion lay at the base of progressive ideas and was a source of weakness in them, encouraging the perversion of education into a means of social control rather than of broadening and enhancing the life of the mind.

American radicals came up for further criticism in Lasch's *The Agony of the American Left* (1969), in which he chastised American leftists for what he saw as their infatuation with personal liberation and vague notions of wholesale revolution. He believed that liberals had become tied to the society of corporate greed and had unwittingly used education to lead the middle classes into greater depths of materialism. Lasch did not merely curse the darkness of misguided thought, however, but attempted to counter the misguided progressive notions of the Left with ideas of his own.

In addition, Lasch became concerned with a society of individuals absorbed in self but incapable of establishing control over their own personal lives. The weakness of faith, community values, personal discipline, and family structure became the stuff of his next three books, *Haven in a Heartless World: The Family Besieged* (1977); *The Culture of Narcissism* (1979), his most commercially successful work; and *The Minimal Self* (1984). His *Haven* was significant in that it coldly illuminated the role of educated elites, allied with the forces of corporate capitalism, in crippling and depersonalizing the individual. The family in Lasch's view was subverted by a communal acquiescence to elements contributing to its breakdown, including divorce, single parenthood, the substitution of day care for traditional childraising, and forms of social disarray celebrated as evidence of diversity in a supposedly revolutionary society.

The Culture of Narcissism continued themes outlined in *Haven,* this time by critiquing Americans' emphasis on self-gratification. Perhaps surprisingly, given its attack on contemporary ways of life, the book became a best-seller and earned the admiration of President Jimmy Carter. The latter consulted with Lasch in 1979 on the topic of "America's crisis of confidence," and the result was Carter's widely criticized "malaise" speech. Lasch, too, increasingly found himself under attack both from the Left and the Right. Conservatives, while they may have admired his emphasis on the family, rejected his attacks on capitalism.

As he had done earlier in *The New Radicalism,* Lasch examined the work of famous social critics and activists in *The True and Only Heaven: Progress and Its Critics* (1991). This time he used Thomas Carlyle, Reinhold Niebuhr, Orestes Brownson, Jonathan Edwards, and Martin Luther King Jr. to display the value of religious purpose in public life. Again he took liberals to task, portraying the civil rights movement of the 1960s as a victim of liberal sociological and scientific arguments, and contrasting these with the moral and spiritual vigor of King's principles. He was chosen to write the introduction to the fiftieth anniversary edition of Richard Hofstadter's *The American Political Tradition: And the Men Who Made It*; the introduction established much of what history as an intellectual exercise meant to Lasch.

Lasch's final work, *The Revolt of the Elites and the Betrayal of Democracy*, published in 1995 after his death from renal cancer, took up issues that included the erosion of the middle class, the betrayal of democracy, the role of global capitalism and its impact on social divisiveness, and the revolt of new elites against the verities of common life. With the help of his historian daughter, Elizabeth Lasch-Quinn, Lasch devoted his final year to assembling a series of essays on the role of women in society, and in 1997 these became *Women and the Common Life: Love, Marriage, and Feminism*. He is buried in Pittsford, New York.

Lasch stands as one of the most profound and original intellectual historians of his time. A courageous thinker, he did not shy from the obligation to seek out the meanings behind historical developments and the need to discern the underlying ideas that propelled society. He was an engaged critic, a man who retained the ability to stand apart from and above the arguments he developed, while maintaining a passion for his cause.

★

Lasch's papers are at the University of Rochester. Interviews with Lasch include Casey Blake and Christopher Phelps, "History and Social Criticism: Conversations with Christopher Lasch," *Journal of American History* (Mar. 1994), and Richard W. Fox, "An Interview with Christopher Lasch," *Intellectual History Newsletter* (Sept. 1994). Articles on Lasch and his work include Jean Bethke Elshtain, "The Life and Work of Christopher Lasch: An American Story," *Salmagundi* (spring–summer 1995); Robert Coles, "Remembering Christopher Lasch," *New Oxford Review* (Sept. 1994); Jackson Lears, "The Man Who Knew Too Much," *New Republic* (Oct. 1995); and James Seaton, "The Gift of Christopher Lasch," *First Things* (Aug.–Sept. 1994). An obituary is in the *New York Times* (15 Feb. 1994).

JACK J. CARDOSO

LASKER, Mary Woodward (*b*. 30 November 1900 in Watertown, Wisconsin; *d*. 21 February 1994 in Greenwich, Connecticut), philanthropist who championed medical research against cancer and heart disease.

Lasker was one of two daughters of Frank Elwin Woodward, a prominent banker, and Sara Johnson Woodward. Her sister, Alice Fordyce, later worked with her in her medical research foundation. Chronic ear infections in Mary's childhood first aroused her interest in medical issues. She studied art history at the University of Wisconsin and at Radcliffe College, where she graduated in 1923. Woodward also pursued studies at Oxford.

Following seven years as an art dealer at the Reinhardt Galleries in New York City, Woodward changed profes-

Mary Lasker, 1979. AP/WIDE WORLD PHOTOS

sions and opened Hollywood Patterns, which sold dress patterns. Out of her work in art came a personal collection that featured works by Miró and Renoir, which she sold in later life to fund her philanthropy.

In 1926 she married Paul Reinhardt. Their childless marriage ended in divorce in 1934, and in 1939 Woodward met Albert Lasker, a retired advertising executive interested in medical research. They were married in June 1940 and had no children. Their joint interest in medical issues led in 1942 to the creation of the Albert and Mary Lasker Foundation, which provided annual awards beginning in 1944 to physicians for pursuing research on major diseases. The Lasker Awards became a major and highly coveted medical prize. During the 1940s the Laskers revitalized the dormant American Cancer Society and used it to lobby Washington for additional research funds.

Albert Lasker died of abdominal cancer in 1952, and his widow became more intensely concerned with medical research during the 1950s. A lifelong Democrat, she used her political contributions shrewdly to establish alliances with such key lawmakers as John Fogarty, an important House member from Rhode Island, and Senator Lister Hill, an Alabaman who chaired the Senate committee overseeing health issues. Her influence was exercised through these political surrogates, whom she called her "Little Lambs," and her own panels such as the National Health Education Committee. She bombarded legislators with letters and clippings about the money that medical research required, and she recruited skilled operatives such as Michael Gorman to do legwork for her on Capitol Hill. In her statements, she often compared the paltry amount spent on medical issues with the hundreds of millions of dollars Americans spent annually on chewing gum.

At the same time, Lasker also promoted beautification causes. In New York City, she arranged tree plantings along Park Avenue. "Flowers in a city are like lipstick on a woman," she said. "You have to have some color." Lasker was a major contributor to Lady Bird Johnson's campaign to reshape Washington's appearance in the 1960s. Her money helped underwrite trees and flowers for the First Lady's work, and the two women forged a productive partnership. But Lasker always maintained that she was primarily interested in medical research.

Her achievements included creation of the National Heart Institute in 1948 during the administration of President Harry Truman, increased funding for the National Institutes of Health in the 1950s, and the establishment of the President's Commission on Heart Disease, Cancer, and Strokes during Lyndon Johnson's presidency. As President John F. Kennedy said, "if you really want to know about what needs to be done in medical research in America, have a talk with Mary Lasker."

Lasker's lobbying work culminated in the passage of the legislation that declared a "war on cancer" in 1971. With Republican President Richard Nixon determined to cut funding for the National Institutes of Health, Lasker faced the prospect of serious reductions in her special causes. Lasker had no special access to Nixon and his inner circle, so she turned first to shaping public opinion. She created the Citizens Committee for the Conquest of Cancer in December 1969. The panel ran newspaper ads saying, "Mr. Nixon: You Can Cure Cancer." To increase the pressure on the president, she turned to Elmer Bobst, head of the drug company Warner Lambert, an old friend of hers and Nixon's.

A final element of her campaign came when Senator Edward M. Kennedy of Massachusetts was named chairman of a key health subcommittee in January 1971. Anxious to deny Kennedy the chance to use the cancer issue if he ran for president in 1972, Nixon came out for "an intensive campaign to find a cure for cancer" in his 1971 State of the Union speech. When the National Cancer Act stalled in the Senate, Lasker used her friendship with the popular advice columnist Ann Landers to stimulate a flood of mail to senators on behalf of the measure. The National Cancer Act became law in December 1971, and the resulting "war on cancer" was an enduring legacy of Mary Lasker's political skills.

In her later years, Lasker received numerous honors for her philanthropic work. Congress created the Mary Woodward Lasker Center for Health Research and Education at the National Institutes for Health in 1984. Five years later, she received a congressional gold medal for her work, and President George Bush called her "a woman who has focused an enormous amount of energy on finding solutions to life-threatening diseases." Lasker continued her activities well into her tenth decade, but she succumbed to heart failure in February 1994. Tributes poured in from the scientific, medical, and political communities. She had been the major public advocate for funding medical research for more than half a century, and she exercised a unique influence on both Congress and the presidency during her heyday in the 1950s and 1960s. As Dr. Michael DeBakey, one of her close associates, put it, "Mary Lasker is an institution unto herself."

★

The Mary Lasker Papers are at Columbia University and contain her extensive oral history. Information about her work is also available at the Harry Truman, Dwight D. Eisenhower, John F. Kennedy, and Lyndon B. Johnson presidential libraries, as well as the Richard Nixon Presidential Papers project. The Richard Neuberger Papers at the University of Oregon, the John Fogarty Papers at Providence College, and the Lister Hill Papers at the University of Alabama at Birmingham are invaluable. For general accounts of her life, see Nadine Brozan, "Health Care Lobbyist on a National Scale: Mary Lasker," *New York Times* (21 Nov. 1985); and Gary Cohen, "Mary and Her 'Little Lambs' Launch a War," *U.S. News and World Report* (5 Feb. 1996), which looks back to the origins of the war on cancer. For assessments of her career, see Richard A. Rettig, *Cancer Crusade: The Story of the National Cancer Act of 1971* (1977); Clarence G. Lasby, "The War on Disease," in Robert A. Divine, ed., *The Johnson Years,* vol. 2 (1987); and Lewis L. Gould, *Lady Bird Johnson and the Environment* (1988). An obituary is in the *New York Times* (23 Feb. 1994).

LEWIS L. GOULD

LEARY, Timothy Francis (*b.* 22 October 1920 in Springfield, Massachusetts; *d.* 31 May 1996 in Beverly Hills, California), psychologist, writer, advocate of LSD (lysergic acid diethylamide) and other hallucinogenic drugs as a means of expanding consciousness, and author of the phrase "tune in, turn on, drop out," which captured the spirit of the hippie movement in America during the 1960s.

Leary was the only child of Timothy Leary, Sr., a U.S. Army captain and sometime dentist, and Abigail Ferris, a teacher. Leary grew up Irish Catholic in the medium-sized industrial city of Springfield, Massachusetts, where he was exposed to the fiercely religious, family-oriented, traditional moralistic attitudes of the Ferris clan and the "sexy, fun-loving, and self-oriented" inclinations of the Leary line. Timothy, Sr., nicknamed "Tote," was a colorful alcoholic who often recited Shakespeare, Poe, Keats, and other great

Timothy Leary. ARCHIVE PHOTOS

poets while intoxicated and was "a disdainer of the conventional way." Leary's greatest influence came from his father's side of the family, from whom he learned how to "be happy" by asserting his individuality. By the age of ten, Leary was reading eight to ten books a week and adopting the advice of his grandfather (a wealthy retired doctor also named Timothy): "Never do anything like anyone else. Be one of a kind!" Leary's grandfather died when Leary was thirteen. Shortly thereafter, when a large inheritance never materialized, Leary's father got drunk and abandoned the family to make a new life for himself performing dentistry in Boston, working construction in South America, then traveling as a steward on transatlantic ships. It was twenty-three years before Leary saw his father again.

Leary was already rebelling against authority by the time he attended Classical High School in Springfield, so much that no one would write him a recommendation for college. His mother pulled strings to get him accepted into the Jesuit College of Holy Cross, in Worcester, Massachusetts, which he attended from 1938 to 1940. Leary considered these first years of education "unfortunate." In 1940 Leary was accepted into West Point, based on his excellent test scores, but a drinking incident involving upperclassmen

prompted the Cadet Honor Committee to punish Leary by demanding that no one speak to him. Leary was quickly acquitted of the charges, but the resentful committee maintained the punishment for nine months. Leary agreed to leave West Point in his sophomore year (1941), on the condition that the honor committee publicly proclaim his innocence. A prepared statement was read to cheering crowds in the dining hall, and Leary left West Point. He was accepted into the University of Alabama in 1942, where he majored in psychology. Shortly after beginning studies there, he was expelled for spending the night in the girl's dormitory. Losing his deferment over the incident, he was called up just after Christmas in 1942 and was sent to Fort Eustis, Virginia, for basic training. Because the military needed psychologists, they offered anyone with a psychology background the opportunity to return to school. While in the army he returned to the University of Alabama, where he completed his undergraduate degree in psychology (1943). He was transferred to the Army Medical Corps hospital in Butler, Pennsylvania, where he continued training in clinical psychology. It was there he met his first wife, Marianne Busch; they were married on 12 December 1944. In 1946 he earned an M.S. degree in psychology from Washington State University. The Learys moved to Berkeley, California, in 1946, and had two children, Susan and Jack. Leary received his Ph.D. in psychology from the University of California at Berkeley in 1950 and taught there as an assistant professor from 1950 to 1955, when he was appointed as director of psychological research at Kaiser Foundation Hospital in Oakland, California. Although Leary's professional career was doing well, his home life was turbulent. He and Marianne both drank heavily and frequently argued. In October 1955 Marianne, who suffered from postpartum depression after the birth of Susan, committed suicide by closing herself in the garage with the car running. Leary found her body on the morning of his thirty-fifth birthday.

In 1957 Leary published his first book, *The Interpersonal Diagnosis of Personality*, which was well received. The work questioned the efficacy of traditional psychotherapeutic methods. Disillusioned with a profession that "didn't seem to work," Leary quit his position at Berkeley and spent some time in Europe living on a small research grant. In Europe he received a visit from Frank Barron, a previous Berkeley colleague, who told Leary about his religious experience after eating "sacred mushrooms" in Mexico. Ironically, Leary warned Barron that he would lose credibility if he continued experimenting with the hallucinogenic fungus. During 1959, while living in Florence, Leary interviewed with David McClelland, then director of the Harvard Center for Personality Research. McClelland was impressed with Leary, and in 1960 Leary became a lecturer at Harvard. In the summer of that same year, while vacationing in Cuernavaca, Mexico, an anthropologist from the University of Mexico offered Leary some of the mushrooms described by Barron. Leary tried them and had a life-altering experience, during which he concluded that reality was merely "social fabrication." Leary received permission from Harvard to perform research into the psychological effects of psilocybin. Leary experimented with psychedelics, using graduate students, divinity students, and select prisoners at Concord State Prison as subjects. Leary also began working with Richard Alpert, an assistant professor at Harvard who also experimented with the mind-expanding properties of hallucinogenic drugs. Alpert later achieved recognition as Baba Ram Dass, an advocate of Eastern philosophy and religion.

When Michael Hollingshead, a British philosophy student, exposed Leary to LSD, Leary said he had "the most shattering experience of . . . [his] life," and the focus of his research shifted to LSD. Leary "turned on" many notable literary figures, antiwar protestors, musicians, and artists to psychedelics, such as Aldous Huxley, Allen Ginsberg, William S. Burroughs, Jack Kerouac, Thelonious Monk, and Abbie Hoffman. By 1962 Leary and Alpert's LSD experiments had gained international attention. But many parents and conservative colleagues, who were upset that Leary was giving drugs to students, put pressure on Harvard, and the university sought to gain tighter supervision over the experiments. The Narcotics Bureau became involved, and the Central Intelligence Agency began tracking Leary's activities. Leary objected to the loss of control, and in 1963 he and Alpert were dismissed from their positions at Harvard. Both continued their experimentation with psychedelic drugs on a 4,000-acre, sixty-four-room estate owned by William Mellon Hitchcock in Millbrook, New York. In 1964 Leary married his second wife, Nena Von Schlebrugge, a model. Shortly thereafter, Leary and Alpert fell into discord over how Millbrook was being run and went separate ways. In 1967 Leary and Nena divorced, and on 11 November of that year Leary married Rosemary Woodruff, an actress.

As the government developed new antidrug policies, it became more difficult for Leary to continue his experimentation unhindered. When he took Rosemary Woodruff and his two children to Mexico for a vacation, they were denied entrance into the country. On their way back home, the police in Laredo, Texas, found ten dollars worth of marijuana on his daughter, Susan. Leary took the blame for the drug and was sentenced to thirty years. Susan was sentenced to five. Leary's popularity among young antiestablishment types soared, while President Richard Nixon dubbed him the "most dangerous man in America." Meanwhile, in 1965, after a trip to India, Leary formed the League of Spiritual Discovery and sought constitutional protection for the use of LSD as a religious sacrament. In

1966 G. Gordon Liddy, then assistant prosecutor for the State of New York, led a raid on Millbrook. Shortly after the raid, the Millbrook era ended.

Under the guidance of Marshall McLuhan, Leary sought to counter the increasingly militant antidrug movement and garner public support for LSD. Leary constructed a smiling on-camera image that associated LSD with positive qualities, such as intelligence, creativity, and religious revelation. It was around this time that Leary coined his most famous phrase, "tune in, turn on, drop out." According to Leary, "tune in" meant to "activate your neural and genetic equipment," "turn on" meant to "interact harmoniously with the world around you," and "drop out" meant to engage in "an active selective and graceful process of detachment from involuntary or unconscious commitments." The more general understanding of the phrase, particularly by the establishment and the media was that the phrase meant drop out of school and get high.

The family moved to Laguna Beach, California. While his Texas conviction was still on appeal, Leary got involved in the antiwar movement and recorded music with Jimi Hendrix, Stephen Stills, and Buddy Miles. Leary sang along when John Lennon and Yoko Ono sang "Give Peace a Chance" to the media from their honeymoon bed. In 1969 Leary made a failed bid for governor of California. The Beatles song "Come Together" was written by John Lennon for the occasion.

Leary's Texas conviction was finally overturned by the Supreme Court, but his legal problems were not over. He was arrested in California for possession of two roaches (the stubs of marijuana joints) and sentenced to ten years. The crime usually warranted six months probation. Leary was sent to a minimum security prison in San Luis Obispo, California, while he sought an appeal to the conviction. At the age of forty-nine, feeling persecuted by Nixon and the government, Leary escaped prison and sought asylum with the Black Panther leader Eldridge Cleaver in Algiers. But Cleaver considered Leary a security risk and put him and Rosemary under house arrest, so the couple fled to Switzerland. When the Swiss government refused him asylum, he fled to Afghanistan, where he was arrested at the Kabul airport.

Leary and Rosemary separated in October 1971. From 1972 to 1976 Leary spent time in many prisons. After his release Leary went to Hollywood, California. On 18 December 1978 Leary married his fourth wife, Barbara Chase, and he helped raise Zachary, her son from a previous marriage. Leary spent the 1980s lecturing at colleges. For one series of lectures in 1982, he shared the stage with his former nemesis, G. Gordon Liddy. In 1983 Leary formed Futique, a software company, and exhibited strong interest in the Internet and virtual reality. Leary believed technology would take up where the psychedelic movement of the 1960s had left off.

In 1990 Leary's daughter, Susan Leary Martino, hanged herself in a Los Angeles jail, which hit Leary hard. Barbara left Leary in 1992. Three years later Leary learned he had inoperable prostate cancer. He remarried Rosemary Woodruff on 21 March 1995 and embraced the act of dying with the same enthusiasm that had fueled many of his previous endeavors. Leary passed away quietly in his sleep a little after midnight on 31 May 1996. He died a twentieth-century icon surrounded by loved ones. His ashes were shot into space on a Spanish satellite in 1997. His final words were, "Why not?"

★

Leary's autobiography, *Flashbacks* (1983), covers his life from birth to 1983. Several of his early essays are collected in *Politics of Ecstasy* (1968), and *High Priest* (1968) includes details about his days at Millbrook. Robert Forte's *Timothy Leary: Outside Looking In* (1999) collects the views of those close to Leary. Valuable coverage also appears in Laura Mansnerus, "At Death's Door, the Message Is Tune In, Turn On, Drop Out," *New York Times* (26 Nov. 1995), and "Terminal Man," *Los Angeles Times* (28 Aug. 1995). Obituaries are in the *New York Times* and *Washington Post* (both 1 June 1996) and *Rolling Stone* (11 July 1996).

KEVIN ALEXANDER BOON

LEBOW, Fred (*b.* 3 June 1932 in Arad, Romania; *d.* 9 October 1994 in New York City), founder of the New York City Marathon who transformed the race into the world's most popular marathon.

Lebow was born Fischl Efraim Lebowitz, one of seven children in an Orthodox Jewish family in the Transylvania region of Romania, near the Hungarian border. His father ran a wholesale produce business, and the family survived the Nazi occupation during World War II but scattered in advance of the postwar Soviet takeover.

As a teenager, Lebowitz made his way through Hungary, Czechoslovakia, and Ireland before arriving in New York City with his brother Michael in December 1949. Soon afterward, he changed his surname. Although Lebow claimed that he smuggled sugar and diamonds from continental Europe to England and Ireland during his years on the move, family members disputed the story. His brother said that the two studied in Orthodox Jewish rabbinical seminaries (yeshivas) in Czechoslovakia and Ireland and later in Brooklyn. After brief stays in Kansas City and Cleveland, where he ran a nightclub, Lebow returned to New York City in the early 1950s. He studied for a short time at Manhattan's Fashion Institute of Technology before starting a business in the Garment District, specializing in moderately priced imitations of fashionable designer wear.

Fred Lebow with Gretta Waitz at the 1992 New York City Marathon. © REUTERS/CORBIS

Lebow took up running when his friend and tennis partner Brian Crawford challenged him to a race around the Central Park Reservoir. Although he kept only an eleven-minute-per-mile pace around the 1.6-mile loop, Lebow defeated Crawford and was hooked. With no wife or children and no other hobbies to occupy his time, running became Lebow's obsession. In the late 1960s he joined the handful of runners who then made up the New York Road Runners Club (NYRRC), and in 1970 he invested $300 to bankroll the first New York City Marathon, a four-loop race around Central Park in which he participated. The cash went to buy soft drinks for the 127 runners and inexpensive watches for the winners.

In 1973 Lebow became president of NYRRC, and in 1976 he executed the move that would catapult the New York City Marathon to greatness, dropping the Central Park course in favor of a route that went through all five of the city's boroughs. The marathon instantly went from just another footrace to a 26.2-mile-long celebration of the city, and the number of participants surged to more than 25,000. While the older Boston Marathon demanded that its entrants meet tough qualifying standards, the New York

City Marathon was open to anyone fit enough to run the distance.

Lebow's ego was as much a key to the race's success as were his boundless energy and ambassadorial enthusiasm for running. As longtime friend and fellow runner George Hirsch wrote, "Fred was the perfect person to put running on the map, a blend of priest of our sport and P. T. Barnum-style promoter. One without the other would not have worked." In his early years of running the marathon, Lebow alone negotiated with sponsors and city agencies, dealt with the media, and issued invitations to elite runners, whom he personally picked up when they arrived at the airport. With that kind of dedication came strong opinions, and Lebow feuded publicly with marathon star Bill Rodgers, who said that New York did not pay enough, and with other leaders in the sport. "People devoted to a single cause are usually a little crazy," said the New York Commissioner of Parks and Recreation Henry Stern. "That's what you expect and you don't judge them by normal standards. . . . If you're asking me if New York City is better off because Fred Lebow is around, the answer is yes."

Although the marathon was his passion, Lebow was the force behind other high-profile NYRRC events, including the Fifth Avenue Mile and a race up the Empire State Building's 1,550 steps. By the early 1990s the club's membership had grown from a few hundred to more than 30,000.

In 1990 Lebow was diagnosed with lymphoma of the brain, for which he underwent chemotherapy, and in 1991 he had surgery to remove a malignant tumor from his thyroid gland at Mount Sinai Hospital. The cancer went into remission, and though Lebow at first used a cane to walk the corridors of the hospital, he later ran in Central Park.

In 1992 Lebow—who had run in sixty-eight other marathons but not the five-borough New York City Marathon for which he was most famous—ran the race for the first time. Cheered by thousands, he and his escort, nine-time women's champion Grete Waitz, finished in five hours, thirty-two minutes, thirty-four seconds. At the Central Park finish, Lebow embraced Waitz, then kneeled and kissed the finish line, joking, "I never believed so many people would watch a miserable runner two hours behind."

It was his last marathon. The cancer returned early in 1994 and eventually forced Lebow to stop running. That August, in a special Central Park ceremony, he was inducted into the National Track and Field Hall of Fame. Lebow died at his home on New York's Upper East Side less than a month before the twenty-fifth running of the New York City Marathon. He is buried in Mount Carmel Cemetery in Queens, New York.

If Frank Shorter's 1972 gold medal in the Olympic marathon sparked the running boom and Jim Fixx's *Complete Book of Running* helped bring the sport to the masses, it was Fred Lebow who led the masses to the marathon. While the Boston Marathon remained only for those swift enough to meet its tough qualifying standards, Lebow's New York City Marathon was a people's race, embracing the city and its energetic diversity. Lebow's 1992 run was one of the most inspirational moments in the history of the sport.

★

A collection of Lebow's papers and memorabilia is housed in the library of the New York Road Runners Club. Lebow's thoughts on running, particularly its importance in his battle with cancer, can be found throughout *The New York Road Runners Club Complete Book of Running* (1992). George Hirsch wrote a tribute to Lebow, "The Visionary," in *Runner's World* (Jan. 1995). Obituaries are in the *New York Times* (10 and 13 Oct. 1994) and the *Houston Chronicle* (10 Oct. 1994).

TIM WHITMIRE

LEE, J(oseph) Bracken ("Brack") (*b.* 7 January 1899 in Price, Utah; *d.* 20 October 1996 in Salt Lake City, Utah), mayor of Price, Utah (1936–1947), governor of Utah (1949–1957), and mayor of Salt Lake City (1960–1972), best known for his conservative politics, tax protests, and ambivalent attitudes toward education.

The son of Arthur James Lee, an insurance and real estate salesman, and Ida May Leiter, a homemaker, Bracken attended school in Price, Utah, and in Fruita, Colorado. Lee attended Carbon County High School in Price, but left school two months before graduation to enlist in the army after the U.S. entry into World War I in April 1917. He was stationed in California during the war and served until March 1919, leaving as a sergeant. He then joined his father in an insurance and real estate business, managing and eventually owning the firm.

On 20 September 1920 Lee married Nellie Amelia Pace, a Latter-day Saint (Mormon). They had one child. Nellie died in 1926. On 23 February 1928 Lee married Margaret Ethel Draper. They had three children. Although Lee's wife and children belonged to the Church of Jesus Christ of Latter-day Saints (LDS), Lee belonged to no church. He was an active Mason.

In the early 1930s, Lee entered politics. A Republican in an overwhelmingly Democratic stronghold, Lee ran in 1931 for mayor of Price, an eastern Utah coal-mining city with a population of five thousand. He was soundly defeated. In 1935 he won by two votes. He served six two-year terms (1936–1947) and along the way eliminated the city's property tax. The city paid for services from 1943 to 1946 through the sale of electricity and water systems owned prior to Lee's incumbency. He concentrated on construct-

Perhaps Lee's most persistent controversies resulted from his efforts to reduce school expenditures. He carried on a running dispute with the State Superintendent of Public Instruction E. Allen Bateman. In 1948, just before Lee became governor, the national expenditure per school child was $179.43, while Utah spent $179.40. In 1957, at the end of Lee's two terms, the national expenditure had increased to $300 while Utah's stood at $258, or 86 percent of the national level. In addition, the salaries of Utah's teachers had dropped behind the national and regional averages. Despite a provision in the state's constitution requiring uniform school funding throughout Utah, Lee tried unsuccessfully to end both state aid for school construction and state acceptance of federal aid.

Lee carried on a number of other campaigns. He tried to remove commission members appointed by his predecessor, although their statutory terms allowed them to continue serving. He fought battles against lawyers, the Dwight D. Eisenhower administration, the United Nations, Utah Supreme Court Chief Justice James H. Wolfe, and Utah senator Elbert D. Thomas, a Democrat. On the other hand, he supported the Republican Wisconsin senator Joseph R. McCarthy and his anticommunist campaign. Lee conducted a persistent struggle to end the income tax and to repeal the Sixteenth Amendment, which permitted the federal government to levy such a tax. In 1955 and 1956 he refused to pay a portion of his income tax in protest against foreign aid. The Internal Revenue Service attached his bank account to recover the taxes.

Lee tried generally to maintain good relations with members of the LDS Church's general authorities, and especially with J. Reuben Clark, a counselor in the church's First Presidency. As an economy measure, he unsuccessfully proposed the return of Weber, Snow, and Dixie Junior Colleges to the LDS Church, which had donated them to the state in the 1930s. On the other hand, he vetoed a Sunday closing bill that Mormons and other Christian groups supported.

Lee's alienation from Republican moderates led to the defeat of his third-term bid by George D. Clyde in the 1956 Republican primary. In October, Lee launched a somewhat belated independent reelection bid, but ran third in the race. In 1958 he ran again as an independent in a three-way senatorial race with Republican incumbent Arthur V. Watkins and Democrat Frank E. Moss, who was the winner. Lee challenged incumbent Senator Wallace F. Bennett in the 1962 Republican primary; he dropped out of the race after Bennett defeated him. Lee failed to win sufficient support at a Republican state convention to qualify for the Republican primary for governor in 1964.

Meanwhile, in 1959, following his defeat by Moss, Lee won election as mayor of Salt Lake City. He served three four-year terms. At the time, Salt Lake City operated under

Governor J. Bracken Lee, 1950. ASSOCIATED PRESS

ing a civic auditorium and city hall, in part with assistance from the federal Works Progress Administration and additions to the water and street systems. Lee also carried on a running battle with the state liquor control commission agents and other state agencies.

Lee failed in an attempt to obtain the Republican nomination for governor in 1940. He won the Republican nomination for U.S. representative in 1942 and for governor in 1944, but lost both general elections. In 1948, however, Lee won the governorship of Utah in a hotly contested election, becoming the first Republican to serve as the state's governor since 1925. He was reelected in 1952.

Although taking office in a state free of debt, Lee moved rapidly to cut the state's budget. In continuing battles with educators and with the legislature, he saved money by reorganizing the liquor commission and cutting expenditures for education and public works, in part through the line-item veto. Lee reduced property and income taxes and the levy for school equalization. Although all people received some tax reductions, the principal benefits went to corporations like the Kennecott Copper Company and the Denver and Rio Grande Railroad.

a commission system, and the mayor had no more power than the other four commissioners. Lee wanted to supervise the city's finance department, but the commissioners voted to assign him to the more controversial public safety post.

In 1960, shortly after his inauguration, Lee generated a public storm by removing the police chief, W. Cleon Skousen, an anticommunist crusader. Lee locked horns with Skousen over a reduction in the police department budget that Lee had mandated and the commission approved, department policies, and Skousen's management style. After Skousen's removal, the commission agreed to change Lee's assignment to the finance department. Lee promoted public works but opposed urban renewal and the fluoridation of Salt Lake City's water. He opposed the construction of a sports arena and convention center in downtown Salt Lake City and battled over vice prosecution and finance with Commissioner James L. Barker.

Lee left public life in 1972 at age seventy-three. He died of old age in a Salt Lake City retirement home at the age of ninety-seven and is buried in Salt Lake City.

Lee was the most controversial governor in Utah's history and may have well been the state's most controversial political figure. His battles against E. Allen Bateman, W. Cleon Skousen, James L. Barker, James Wolfe, Elbert Thomas, fluoridation, and the IRS, bestow on him little lasting credit. He gained considerable support for his campaign to cut taxes on the state and city levels. Nevertheless, his tax-cutting campaigns damaged Utah's public, technical, and higher education. On the other hand, time has demonstrated the wisdom of his battles against urban redevelopment to remove minorities and the poor in favor of upscale businesses.

★

Lee's correspondence as governor from 1946 to 1957 is at the Utah State Archives in Salt Lake City, Utah. His mayoral papers from 1948 to 1972 are in the Marriott Library, University of Utah, Salt Lake City, Utah. Dennis L. Lythgoe, *Let 'Em Holler: A Political Biography of J. Bracken Lee* (1982), is an excellent biography for which the author received Lee's assistance. An obituary is in the *Salt Lake Tribune* (21 Oct. 1996).

THOMAS G. ALEXANDER

LELYVELD, Arthur Joseph (*b.* 6 February 1913 in New York City; *d.* 15 April 1996 in Beachwood, Ohio), rabbi and leader in the Reform movement who championed social causes, especially Zionism and civil rights.

The only child of Edward Joseph, a hosiery salesman, and Dora Cohen, a homemaker, Lelyveld exhibited tremendous energy and motivation for learning from an early age. He and his family lived in Manhattan, where he attended George Washington High School. He was greatly influ-

Rabbi Arthur J. Lelyveld. COURTESY FAIRMOUNT TEMPLE, BEACHWOOD, OHIO

enced in his childhood by his maternal grandfather, a rabbi who had immigrated to the United States from Europe. Although his immediate family was not religiously observant, both of his parents were supportive of his decision to become a rabbi.

Entering Columbia University at age fifteen, Lelyveld supported himself by playing banjo and guitar in three bands, all under the name Arthur J. Lelyveld and the Columbia Ramblers. While in college, he became the first Jewish editor of the campus newspaper, the *Columbia Daily Spectator,* as well as a director of the glee club and a member of the wrestling team. In 1933 Lelyveld graduated Phi Beta Kappa, and on 26 December of the same year he married Toby Bookholtz. They had three children and divorced in 1964. Later that year, on 5 December, he married Teela Stovsky. They had two children, one of whom predeceased Lelyveld.

Although he confessed to an interest in journalism, Lelyveld felt a calling to the rabbinate. In 1939 he graduated from Hebrew Union College with a master of Hebrew letters degree. The Lelyvelds moved from New York to Hamilton, Ohio, where he became rabbi at congregation B'nai Israel. He stayed there until 1941, when he moved to Omaha, Nebraska, to serve as the rabbi of Temple Israel.

Always an ardent Zionist, Lelyveld left the ministry in 1944 to work for the Committee on Unity for Palestine as its executive director. In this capacity, he had the opportunity to meet with President Harry S. Truman to promote the idea of a Jewish state in Palestine. During Lelyveld's lifetime, he made more than thirty trips to Israel and received numerous awards for his efforts on behalf of the Jewish state. In 1946 he left the committee to work for B'nai B'rith Hillel Foundations, first as associate national director and later as national director. In 1956 he served as the executive vice president of the America-Israel Cultural Foundation.

Lelyveld moved to Cleveland in 1958 to become the rabbi at Fairmount Temple. While there, he added several innovations to the services, lectures, and prayers. For example, he hired the first female cantor in Cleveland, instituted special services for families, and included Tisha B'Av and Selichor as holidays of observance. Although he was ordained in the Reform movement, Lelyveld retained many traditional observances, which were apparent in the way his synagogue was run. Breaking from Reform traditions, Lelyveld chose to attend an Orthodox synagogue on the second day of Jewish High Holidays.

A renowned orator, Lelyveld also became a leader in the civil rights movement. After officiating at the funeral of the slain twenty-year-old civil rights worker Andrew Goodman, the son of friends, Lelyveld joined other Cleveland clergy on a voter registration drive in Hattiesburg, Mississippi, in the summer of 1964. He served as a minister-counselor to the Council of Federated Organizations under the auspices of the Commission on Race and Religion of the National Council of Churches. Returning from voter registration work one evening, Lelyveld, then fifty-one, was severely beaten by segregationists. The National Association for the Advancement of Colored People (NAACP) later awarded him its Distinguished Service Award for this mission.

Lelyveld also spoke at the funeral of David R. Berger, a former Cleveland resident who became a weight lifter and who was murdered with other Israeli Olympic athletes by Palestinian terrorists in Munich, Germany, in 1972. Lelyveld, continuing to believe in nonviolent protest, rejected the idea of retaliation voiced by some militant Jewish extremist groups.

Although an unassuming man, Lelyveld nevertheless gained a reputation for being a leader among his peers. During his tenure as senior rabbi, he took top leadership positions in many national organizations. From 1966 to 1972 he served as president of the American Jewish Congress. He also served as president of the Central Conference of American Rabbis (1975–1977) and of the Synagogue Council of America (1979–1981). His volunteerism and leadership were prominent at the local level as well. In 1963 he was the general chairman of the Cleveland Jewish Welfare Fund campaign. During the 1960s he served on the executive committee of the Cleveland NAACP and as president of the Cleveland Board of Rabbis.

Lelyveld was the author of two books: *Atheism Is Dead* (1963) and *The Steadfast Stream: An Introduction to Jewish Social Values* (1995). He contributed chapters to several books, including *The Universal Jewish Encyclopedia* (1939–1941) and *Retrospect and Prospect: Position of the Jew in the Modern World* (1964). Lelyveld also contributed articles and reviews to numerous journals.

After retiring in 1986, Lelyveld became an adjunct professor of religion at Case Western Reserve University in Cleveland. He was also the Bernard Rich Hollander Lecturer in Jewish Thought at John Carroll University in University Heights, Ohio. Lelyveld said that because of his love of learning, he always considered himself a student rather than a teacher. He enjoyed almost ten years of active retirement before he died of a brain tumor in 1996. He was buried in Cleveland according to Orthodox procedures.

Lelyveld's unwavering commitment to social justice influenced his actions and inspired those who met him. At the core of this commitment was his quest to become a more learned and pious Jew. "There's a certain ambivalence among people in minority groups," he said. "Some tend to become escapists. Others are drawn more into the group. My psychological tendency all through life has been to become more and more a Jew. It's my philosophy that the more integrated I become, the better human being I'll be."

★

The collection of Lelyveld's manuscripts and personal papers is held at the Western Reserve Historical Society. Information regarding his Jewish philosophies can be found in Mark Raphael, *Profiles in American Judaism* (1984). Information about his accomplishments can be found in the *Encyclopedia Judaica* (1986). An obituary is in the *New York Times* (16 Apr. 1996).

MOLLY JALENAK WEXLER

LEVITT, William Jaird (*b.* 11 February 1907 in Brooklyn, New York; *d.* 28 January 1994 in Manhasset, New York), builder and developer best known for his Levittowns, postwar suburban subdivisions in New York, Pennsylvania, and New Jersey.

Levitt was one of two sons born to Abraham Levitt, a real estate lawyer, and Pauline Biederman. He entered New York University in 1924 but left without graduating in 1927 to join his father's law firm. Levitt's 1929 marriage to Rhoda

William Levitt. ARCHIVE PHOTOS

Kirshner, with whom he had two sons, ended in divorce in 1959. In the same year, he married Alice Kenny, who he divorced in 1969, once again marrying before the year was out, this time to Simone Korchin.

When a client defaulted on a land deal in 1929, Levitt's father formed Levitt and Sons to develop the property. William Levitt managed the firm, while his brother Alfred designed the houses. In the 1930s they built several developments on former estates in Manhasset, Long Island, and deeded the mansions to the residents for use as clubhouses. The Levitts's nearby "Miracle Mile" shopping center lured suburban branches of Manhattan department stores to the community.

In 1941 the Levitts built 2,350 defense housing units at Norfolk, Virginia. Of these, 1,600 were slab-based worker houses, constructed in assembly-line fashion. It was here that Levitt conceived the idea for his Levittown project. He later served at Pearl Harbor in Hawaii as a lieutenant with the naval construction battalions, the Seabees; meanwhile, at home, the firm took options on 1,000 acres on Long Island's Hempstead Plains. In 1946, with the war over and a housing shortage underway, Levitt and Sons purchased additional land to complete their holdings and announced plans to build affordable housing for veterans.

The plans met with considerable opposition from local community, political, and labor leaders concerned with the rudimentary nature of the houses and the use of concrete slabs and labor-saving new materials. Levitt launched a public-relations campaign around the themes of patriotism and social justice, and in May 1947 house-hungry veterans filled the local town hall, successfully demanding the nec-

essary changes to the building codes. In July, Levitt broke ground for what would become Levittown, a mass-produced subdivision of four-room Cape Cod houses.

Levitt reduced construction to about twenty-six steps, each of which was the responsibility of a different crew. He called this method his "on-site factory." Hiring workers as subcontractors, Levitt circumvented the unions, paying workers by the unit rather than the hour and speeding production to a completion rate of thirty houses a day. He favored skilled laborers over craftsmen and used prefabricated elements wherever possible; nonetheless, the Levittown homes, which sold for under $8,000, included appliances such as washers and dryers, refrigerators, and even television sets.

By the time the Federal Housing Administration (FHA) withdrew its support from rental housing in 1948, to encourage home ownership among the working class, Levittown consisted of 4,000 houses. To fund the next phase, Levitt sold most of the houses to his tenants. The remainder were sold, along with his management company, to a nonprofit organization in Pennsylvania (a private school) to treat his income from the development as a capital gain rather than the more highly taxed income from rents.

The 1949–1951 models, built only for sale, had a new exterior with the same concrete slabs, four rooms and bath, and expansion attics that could be turned into additional bedrooms. These ranch-style houses sold faster than Levitt's crews could build them. In 1952 Levittown comprised 17,447 houses with a community center, nine swimming pools, seven village greens, and land set aside for houses of worship.

Levittown was severely criticized for its mass-produced houses, the conformity of the lifestyle they imposed, and the resulting influx of working-class families into formerly middle-class suburbs. Levitt's racially covenanted deeds—which conformed to the FHA standards of the times—were also controversial. It was his policy not to sell houses to blacks, which he explained by saying that if a black family bought a house at one of his Levittown developments, this would lead to a decrease in purchases by white families. He told the *Saturday Evening Post* in 1954, "As a company, our position is simply this: we can solve a housing problem, or we can solve a racial problem. But we cannot combine the two."

Levitt also built Levittowns in Pennsylvania and New Jersey, where, still stinging from the criticism of the first Levittown, he varied the designs and aimed for a more affluent market. After cancer surgery in 1959, Levitt went on to build in Maryland and Puerto Rico as well as Las Vegas and Chicago. In 1963 he returned to Long Island to build another series of mid-priced developments in Suffolk County.

Levitt's French branch, Levitt-France, built Chez Levitt

outside of Paris in 1964 after the French government eased mortgage regulations. As with the early Manhasset developments, Chez Levitt included a former chateau converted to a community center, a park, tennis courts, and a swimming pool. But the French effort was less successful than its American prototype, in part because European purchasers demanded amenities that added considerably to the sale price.

In 1968 he sold Levitt and Sons to International Telephone and Telegraph (ITT) for $92 million in stock. Levitt and Sons became the Levitt Corporation, with Levitt as a consultant. Under the terms of the agreement, Levitt could not build in the United States for ten years. Doing business as Levitt Industries, Inc., Levitt invested in other fields, including an engine factory in Israel and a chain of drugstores in New England. He also experimented with "panelization," a form of prefabrication in which house walls were wired, plumbed, and painted in the factory for assembly at the site. His projects were heavily leveraged, using ITT stock as collateral. In 1972 a major downturn in construction caused financial problems for ITT, and Levitt's ITT stock fell, eventually losing more than 90 percent of its value. In 1974 ITT was ordered to divest some of its holdings, including Levitt Corporation, which languished in receivership until 1978, when it was sold to Starrett Housing Corporation.

After being invited to develop housing in Nigeria in 1977, Levitt withdrew from the project, believing that it would fail, probably because of the instability of Nigeria's government and its economy. Ironically, he then turned his attention to what would become a far more volatile foreign market. In 1977 he began a project of 11,600 garden apartments outside Tehran, Iran. With the shah's overthrow in 1979, Levitt was deported and the project halted. He unsuccessfully sued the Iranian government for $34 million in lost revenues.

When his agreement to abstain from building in the United States expired in 1977, Levitt formed International Community Corporation and announced a new Levittown to be built near Orlando, Florida. Starrett immediately sued Levitt for infringing on its rights to the Levittown credentials. As a result, Levitt was forbidden to use any references to Levittown or its history in advertising and publicity. He subsequently changed the development's name to Williamsburg. The Williamsburg project ran into serious problems when roof tiles, purchased from Australia, began to leak. Complaints to Orange County officials resulted in a 1980 moratorium on building permits, pending repairs to the houses. As the first 1,000 of the planned 9,000 dwellings at Williamsburg reached completion in 1981, Levitt's already tenuous finances headed toward legal disaster. He was charged with illegally transferring millions of dollars from the family's tax-exempt foundation (established by his

father in 1949) between 1974 and 1980, and with misleading the foundation's board of directors. The court ordered him to pay $10 million in punitive damages and $4 million in interest. In 1987 Levitt resigned from the foundation.

From 1982 through 1986, Levitt, no longer considered a good banking risk, kept his business alive by moving money from project to project. He used sizable deposits on projected houses to build units for which money had already been paid. In 1984 the Williamsburg developments failed amid accusations that he had transferred business funds to personal needs. Undaunted, Levitt announced a third Florida project on 7,000 acres outside Orlando. Poinciana Park's 26,000 houses promised to become the world's largest development.

In 1985 Levitt's silent partner, Old Court Savings and Loan, failed. The Maryland bank was placed in receivership, curtailing Levitt's access to financing. The receiver determined that continued association with Levitt's name and lost credibility would negatively impact the Poinciana Park project's marketability, but Levitt continued to advertise the development. Fourteen months later, with no construction underway, more than 3,000 deposits had been received. Despite the legal ban on promotion of his association with Levittown, the reputation of his earlier developments had drawn a stream of deposits.

In 1986 Levitt was forced to liquidate all of his assets, including his Mill Neck estate on Long Island's north shore, to pay his creditors. Many of these were contractors, now on the brink of bankruptcy, who had worked with him since his Levittown years. The Orlando Williamsburg property was sold with only 2,000 of the proposed units built, and the Tampa Williamsburg development was foreclosed with only 124 of its proposed 4,500 houses completed.

In 1987 Levitt was found guilty of using deposit money to fund the advertising and overhead expenses for the projects. Unable to repay $12 million to Old Court Savings and Loan, he lost the Poinciana property. New York's attorney general sued for the return of the deposits to dissatisfied New Yorkers and barred Levitt from selling houses in the state. Levitt settled the suit in 1987, agreeing to repay the foundation $11 million, of which only $7.7 million had been paid by 1990, when he unsuccessfully requested relief from the court. He also returned $434,000 in deposits. Levitt was accused of having used additional millions from the foundation to pay his Florida debts.

Still planning to rebuild his business, Levitt died of kidney failure at age eighty-six in Manhasset's North Shore University Hospital, a clinic funded by his foundation during the good years. He is buried in Mount Ararat Cemetery in North Lindenhurst, Long Island. His last known residence was a rented condominium.

William Levitt has been alternately credited with inventing the American suburb and blamed for suburban sprawl. Neither view is entirely accurate: he was a businessman who provided what the market demanded. His skill was in clever adaptation of the ideas of others, innovations suited to the business climate of a time and place. Despite the poor judgment of his later years, for most of his career he managed to earn handsome profits, and in turn his foundation generously funded charitable causes. Throughout his troubled years, Levitt returned to Levittown and the affordable houses he had provided for young families. He strove to recapture his early success with venture after venture. Neither the heroic figure of his early years nor the villain of his later ones, Levitt was an entrepreneur for whom the times and the rules of the game had changed.

★

Levitt's clippings files, along with a number of photographs and maps of his developments, are on deposit in the Long Island Studies Institute at Hofstra University. The best sources of information about him can be found in books and dissertations about his early communities. John Liell's *Levittown: A Study in Community Planning and Development* (1952) was the first serious study of the Long Island Levittown. Herbert Gans mounted a spirited defense of Levitt and his Levittowns in *The Levittowners: Ways of Life and Politics in a New Suburban Community* (1967), and Jean Buhr's *The Meaning of Levittown* (1988) addressed the social phenomenon of the postwar subdivision. In *Expanding the American Dream: Building and Rebuilding Levittown,* Barbara Kelly examines the transition of Levittown from working-class to middle-class housing. A profile of Levitt at the height of his success can be found in *Current Biography* (1956). Numerous articles on Levitt appeared in *Newsday* over the years, and obituaries are in the *New York Times, New York Post,* and *Newsday* (all 30 Jan. 1994).

BARBARA M. KELLY

LUENING, Otto Clarence (*b.* 15 June 1900 in Milwaukee, Wisconsin; *d.* 2 September 1996 in New York City), composer, flutist, and educator who influenced the course of twentieth-century American music through his tireless advocacy on behalf of his fellow composers and his pathbreaking work in electronic music.

Luening was the youngest of the seven children of Eugene Luening and Emma Jacobs. The family was of distinguished German lineage; both his parents were educated at the German-English Academy in Milwaukee, which was founded by Luening's paternal grandfather. His mother was a singer, and his father was a pianist, singer, and conductor who had studied at the Leipzig Conservatory and sung under Richard Wagner. He served as the director of the Milwaukee Musical Society from 1879 to 1904.

Otto Luening, 1956. AP/WIDE WORLD PHOTOS

Luening grew up on the family farm in Wauwatosa, Wisconsin. He demonstrated musical prowess at a young age and basically taught himself piano. When Luening was four years old, his father began to supervise his piano studies, although he initially discouraged his son from a career in music. In his autobiography Luening recounts his father saying, "I do not want any of my children to be a musician. . . . An artist's life is much too difficult in the United States." Luening composed two small piano pieces, his first musical compositions, at the age of six.

In 1909 the Luenings sold the farm and moved to Madison, Wisconsin, where Eugene Luening assumed a teaching position at the University of Wisconsin School of Music. This proved to be a less-than-satisfactory situation, and in 1912 Eugene Luening made the decision to take his wife and Otto with him to Munich to pursue musical opportunities. The move to Munich coincided with young Luening's graduation from the seventh grade and marked the end of his formal education.

In Munich, Luening received private tutoring in languages, literature, and history. He frequented museums, attended concerts, and in general continued his self-education. In 1913 he began private flute studies with Alois Schellhorn and in 1915 enrolled in the Staatliche Hochschule für Musik as its youngest student. He continued to compose and made his concert debut as a flutist in 1916.

When the United States broke off diplomatic relations with Germany in 1917, Luening and his sister Helene moved to Zurich. He continued his musical work at the Zurich Conservatory, where he studied theory, conducting, and score reading with Philipp Jarnach, a former pupil of the composer and pianist Ferruccio Busoni. His studies in Zurich were subsidized by Edith Rockefeller McCormick, who had supported the work of Jarnach and James Joyce. Luening also supported himself by playing percussion and flute in the Zurich Tonhalle Orchestra. In this position he had the opportunity to perform under such conductors as Richard Strauss and Arthur Nikisch. During this time Jarnach introduced him to Busoni, who was very supportive of Luening's compositional work. Luening met Joyce in 1918, and he performed with Joyce's theatrical company during the 1918 and 1919 seasons under the stage name of James P. Cleveland.

Luening returned to the United States in 1920, settling in Chicago at McCormick's suggestion. He studied with Wilhelm Middleschulte, a major Bach scholar. In general, Luening found the musical environment in Chicago to be disappointing following his years in Europe. To support himself he played in movie house orchestras, taught music theory, arranged gospel hymns, and conducted choral societies. McCormick continued to encourage his compositional work and arranged for private performances of some of his works at her home. Luening was one of the founders of the American Grand Opera Company in Chicago, which was dedicated to performances of works in English. He conducted the premiere performance of Charles Wakefield Cadman's opera *Shanewis* with the company in 1922.

In 1924 Luening's work *Sextet* (1918) was recommended to the committee of the United States section of the International Society for Contemporary Music. Among the committee members was the composer and Eastman School of Music director Howard Hanson, who offered Luening a position in the opera department of the Eastman School in Rochester, New York, beginning in 1925. Luening stayed at the Eastman School through 1928. He coached singers, handled a myriad of administrative duties in the opera department, and served as the assistant conductor and eventually conductor of the Rochester American Opera Company. During his time at Eastman he met Ethel Codd, a Canadian-born singer. They were married on 19 April 1927.

In June 1928 Luening and his wife left the United States for a year's stay in Cologne, in part to further Ethel's career in German opera houses and to reestablish contact with Jarnach, who was an important faculty member at the Co-

logne Conservatory. Luening hoped to find work as a conductor or teacher. However, he found the environment in depressed, pre-Nazi Germany to be very different from what he experienced during his teenage years in Munich. His application for a Guggenheim Fellowship was denied, and he and Ethel returned to the United States in 1929 and settled in New York City.

Luening did receive a Guggenheim Fellowship the following year, which enabled him to write his opera *Evangeline,* based on Henry Wadsworth Longfellow's narrative poem about the expulsion of the Acadians from Nova Scotia by the English. He and Ethel traveled to Nova Scotia as well as to Louisiana to experience Acadian culture firsthand. Luening did not complete *Evangeline* until 1947; it premiered at Columbia University in 1948.

Luening was a member of the faculty of the University of Arizona at Tucson from 1932 to 1934. In 1934 he was invited to join the faculty of the newly created Bennington College in Vermont. While at Bennington he developed the music department's programs, encouraging exposure to and awareness of new American works. He invited such prominent figures as the poet Carl Sandburg (whom he had originally met in Tucson) and the composers Paul Hindemith, Carl Ruggles, and Henry Cowell to the Bennington campus for special guest residencies.

Luening was involved with music projects of the Works Progress Administration from 1935 to 1939, continuing to encourage the promotion and performance of American music. In the late 1930s and early 1940s, he helped to organize music festivals at Bennington and elsewhere. He became increasingly involved with administrative activities to promote contemporary American works and was a founding member of several key music organizations, including the American Music Center (1939), the American Composers Alliance (1938), and the nonprofit recording company Composers Recordings (1954).

In 1944 Luening was appointed to the position of musical director of Brander Matthews Hall at Columbia University, where he conducted the premieres of several American operas, including his own *Evangeline*. He also taught at Barnard College, Columbia's undergraduate institution for women, where he served as the chairman of the music department from 1944 to 1948. Luening taught at Barnard until 1964 and at Columbia until 1968, when he was named professor emeritus and music chairman of the School for the Arts. He retired from Columbia in 1970 and taught at the Juilliard School from 1971 to 1973.

Luening became involved with electronic music during his years at Columbia University. His 1952 works for flute on tape, *Fantasy in Space, Invention in Twelve Tones,* and *Low Speed,* were among the earliest electronic music compositions. He cofounded the Columbia-Princeton Electronic Music Center with the composers Vladimir Ussachevsky, Milton Babbitt, and Roger Sessions in 1959; it was one of the first electronic music laboratories in the United States.

Following Luening's retirement from his academic posts, he remained active as a composer, administrator, writer, and spokesman on contemporary American composition. During his lifetime he composed more than three hundred works, many of which are characterized by their creative juxtapositions of musical styles. Among his many prominent composition students were Chou Wen-Chung, John Corigliano, Mario Davidovsky, Charles Dodge, Ezra Laderman, Seymour Shifrin, and Charles Wuorinen. He received numerous honors and awards, commissions, and honorary degrees, including three Guggenheim Fellowships, the Brandeis University Creative Arts Award (1981), and the first American Composers Alliance (ACA) Laurel Leaf Award (1985).

Luening and Ethel Codd were divorced in 1959, following a lengthy and difficult separation. On 5 September 1959, he married pianist Catherine Johnson Brunson. Luening had no children from either marriage. He died at age ninety-six.

Luening's openness to exploring new paths in his compositions and his understated yet indefatigable advocacy of American works had a profound influence on the development of twentieth-century musical life. He was a consummate musician who was highly respected by all who were privileged to work with him.

★

Luening's papers are at the New York Public Library for the Performing Arts in New York City. His autobiography, *The Odyssey of an American Composer* (1980), provides a detailed description of his life and career. The other major book-length work about Luening is Ralph Hartstock, *Otto Luening: A Bio-Bibliography* (1991), which includes citations to hundreds of articles about the composer and his works through 1989, as well as a list of his compositions (through 1986), a discography, and a list of his own writings. An obituary is in the *New York Times* (5 Sept. 1996). An unpublished oral history is available in the Oral History Collection of Columbia University in New York City.

JANE GOTTLIEB

LUPINO, Ida   (*b.* 4 February 1918 in London, England; *d.* 3 August 1995 in Burbank, California), actress and director known for her vivid performances in many films and, in later years, for her direction of socially relevant movies.

Lupino was the daughter of Stanley Lupino, a star of the London musical stage and a member of an illustrious theatrical family originating in Renaissance Italy. Lupino's mother, Connie O'Shea, was a popular dancer known professionally as Connie Emerald, and other family members

Ida Lupino. THE KOBAL COLLECTION

were also prominent theatrical performers. Her father's cousin, Lupino Lane, appeared in and occasionally directed popular two-reel comedies and feature films in England and America.

With her younger sister, Lupino attended Clarence House, an elite boarding school for girls in a Brighton suburb. Early on it became clear that she was destined to follow in her parents' theatrical footsteps. In January 1932, when she was nearly fourteen, she enrolled in the Royal Academy of Dramatic Arts, where she was active in school productions. Not long afterward, Lupino won her first movie role, playing the ingenue lead in a minor British movie called *Her First Affaire* (1933). Subsequently, she appeared in vapid roles in a number of equally minor films. Armed with a contract from Paramount Pictures, Lupino left for America in August 1933.

At Paramount, Lupino was at first expected to play the lead in a new production of *Alice in Wonderland*, but she was judged too sophisticated for the role. Instead, she was cast as a spirited ingenue in lightweight films, including *Paris in Spring* (1935), *Anything Goes* (1936), and *Artists and Models* (1937). Only one of these films had any distinction —the director Rouben Mamoulian's *Gay Desperado* (1936), a clever musical spoof of American gangster films. Her best opportunity came when she won the role of Bessie Broke in *The Light That Failed* (1939), based on Rudyard Kipling's novel. Lupino gave a riveting performance as the headstrong Cockney girl who vindictively destroys the last painting by the blinded artist (Ronald Colman) for whom she had modeled. In November 1938 the actress married a fellow actor, Louis Hayward.

Lupino began a new phase of her acting career in May 1940 when she signed a contract with Warner Brothers. Her first role at the studio was among her best. In *They Drive By Night* (1940), she played Lana Carlsen, the flashy, treacherous wife of a trucking boss (played by Alan Hale), who tries to frame a driver (played by George Raft) for a murder she committed. She was equally effective as the loyal moll to Humphrey Bogart's ill-fated gangster in *High Sierra* (1941) and as an escaped convict trapped aboard Edward G. Robinson's doom-laden ship in *The Sea Wolf* (1941). One of her finest roles, however, came when she was loaned to Columbia Pictures for *Ladies in Retirement* (1941), adapted from the stage play. As Ellen Creed, a housekeeper who murders her employer to keep her retarded sisters from being evicted from her employer's home, Lupino gave an intense but firmly controlled performance.

Back at Warner Brothers, she took a role that won her the New York Film Critics Award as the year's best actress. In *The Hard Way* (1942), she excelled as Helen Chernen, a hard-as-nails woman who ruthlessly controls her younger sister's theatrical career. Other roles at Warner Brothers were less felicitous: she played Emily Brontë in *Devotion* (made in 1943 but released in 1946), a fanciful version of the lives of the Brontë sisters; an Englishwoman caught up in World War II in *In Our Time* (1944); and a tough-minded but generous nightclub singer in *The Man I Love* (1946). During World War II, Lupino participated actively in war work. She divorced Louis Hayward in 1945. Early in 1947 Lupino terminated her contract with Warner Brothers. Her first freelance role, as a nightclub singer in *Road House* (1948)—in which she did her own singing—took advantage of her special combination of toughness and vulnerability. The year 1948 also marked major changes in her personal life—in June she became an American citizen, and six weeks later she married Collier Young, then an executive assistant to Harry Cohn, the head of Columbia Pictures.

The following year Lupino took a new direction in her film career. Joining with her husband and a writer-producer named Anson Bond, she formed a new production company, first known as Emerald Productions and then as The Filmmakers. The primary goal of the company was to cover adult themes not explored by other filmmakers. Their second film, *Not Wanted* (1949), dealing with unwed motherhood, was directed largely by Lupino, after Elmer Clifton, the director of record, suffered a mild heart attack. The actress received her first full credit as director of the company's next film, *Never Fear* (later retitled *The Young Lovers,* 1950), centering on a dancer (portrayed by Sally Forrest) stricken with polio. With The Filmmakers now under the banner of RKO, Lupino also directed *Outrage* (1950), which dealt with the controversial subject of rape, and *Hard, Fast and Beautiful* (1951), with Claire Trevor as the domineering mother of a tennis star played by Sally Forrest. Lupino continued to act in films, appearing in *Woman in Hiding* (1950), *On Dangerous Ground* (1952), and *Beware My Lovely* (1952). After divorcing Collier Young in 1951, she married actor Howard Duff in October of the same year. Their daughter was born in April 1952.

Throughout the 1950s Lupino worked steadily as both actor and director (and often as writer and producer) in films and television. She starred in such movies as *Private Hell 36* (1954), *Women's Prison* (1955), and *The Big Knife* (1955). In 1953, with *The Bigamist,* she became the first woman to direct herself in a new motion picture. On television she appeared as one of the rotating stars on *Four Star Playhouse* (1952–1956), and for two seasons (1957–1958) she costarred with Howard Duff in a situation comedy entitled *Mr. Adams and Eve.* Duff and Lupino separated in 1972, but they remained married until 1984. In later years, Lupino was active in television as a director and, occasionally, a producer and also made appearances in films, most notably as Steve McQueen's mother in *Junior Bonner* (1972). Although she remained dedicated to her family and friends, she became increasingly reclusive as her health declined. She died of a stroke at her home in Burbank, California, at the age of seventy-seven. She was cremated and her ashes were sent to her residence.

An actress whose best performances bristled with energy and passion, Ida Lupino was also a notable director who dared to deal with then controversial themes in her films. She wore both hats with skill and pride, paving the way for other achieving women in the world of motion pictures.

★

Books on Lupino include Jerry Vermilye, *Ida Lupino* (1977), and William Donati, *Ida Lupino: A Biography* (1996). An interview with Lupino by Graham Fuller appears in *Interview* (Oct. 1990). Obituaries are in the *New York Times* (5 Aug. 1995) and *Variety* (14 Aug. 1995).

TED SENNETT

M

McGUIRE, Francis Joseph ("Frank") (*b.* 6 November 1913 in New York City; *d.* 11 October 1994 in West Columbia, South Carolina), coach who helped bring big-time college basketball to the South, winning a national title in 1957 with an undefeated North Carolina team.

The thirteenth child of Robert McGuire, a New York City police officer, and Anne Lynch McGuire, a homemaker, Frank McGuire grew up in Greenwich Village and was a standout athlete at Saint Francis Xavier High School. At Saint John's University, he captained the baseball and basketball teams as a senior. He received his B.S. degree in 1936. Starting in 1936, McGuire worked as a teacher and coach at Saint Xavier while playing five seasons in the American Basketball League, a forerunner to the National Basketball Association. In 1941 he married Patricia Johnson, with whom he had three children.

After serving as a U.S. Navy officer during World War II (he did not see combat), McGuire returned to Saint John's in 1947 as the school's baseball and basketball coach. In baseball, he led the Redmen to the final round of the 1949 College World Series, while in basketball he coached the team to the 1952 national championship game, where the Redmen fell to Kansas.

A smooth talker and fine dresser, known for the alligator shoes he wore during games, McGuire seemed a perfect fit in New York City. But in 1951 McGuire and his wife Pat had a son, Frank Jr., who was mentally retarded and had

cerebral palsy. It was difficult to care for Frankie in the McGuires' small apartment, and in 1953 McGuire left to coach basketball at the University of North Carolina in Chapel Hill.

McGuire immediately became a rival to Everett Case of North Carolina State in Raleigh, the coach who had built the state's first college basketball program with national ambitions. To counter Case's pipeline that brought top players from Indiana to Raleigh, McGuire established an "underground railroad" from New York City to Chapel Hill. The coaches soon became bitter on-court rivals, though McGuire later said they were good friends away from the game. In 1953 Case and McGuire moved their schools from the Southern Conference to the new Atlantic Coast Conference (ACC), joining "Tobacco Road" rivals Duke and Wake Forest in a nine-team league that would become the nation's college basketball showcase.

McGuire's 1956–1957 team was his greatest. All five starters—Lennie Rosenbluth, Pete Brennan, Joe Quigg, Bob Cunningham, and Tommy Kearns—were from the New York City area, and they rolled through their schedule. By the time they reached the Final Four in Kansas City, Missouri, the Tar Heels were 30–0. They won the national title with a thrilling pair of triple-overtime victories, the first over Michigan State in the national semifinals. In the championship game, the Tar Heels faced Kansas and the Jayhawks' seven-foot star center, Wilt Chamberlain. McGuire set an against-all-odds tone for the game by

Frank McGuire, 1957. © BETTMANN/CORBIS

sending Kearns, at five-foot-ten, to jump for the opening tip against Chamberlain. In the third overtime, Quigg made a pair of free throws with six seconds left, then batted away a final pass intended for Chamberlain to secure a Tar Heels 54–53 win.

McGuire stayed at North Carolina through the 1960–1961 season, after which he left to coach the NBA's Philadelphia Warriors. There, his star was Chamberlain, who later said that McGuire's even-keeled approach to coaching changed his life. During the 1961–1962 season, Chamberlain scored 100 points in a game, a record that still stands.

When the Warriors moved to San Francisco the following season, McGuire declined to go. After two years working in public relations in the New York City area, he returned to coaching in 1964 with South Carolina, an ACC doormat. Given a mandate to build a national power by school officials, McGuire succeeded. In 1971 the Gamecocks won the ACC tournament title, 52–51 over North Carolina, and earned a trip to the NCAA tournament, the first of four straight NCAA appearances. Buoyed by McGuire's success at building interest in basketball in a traditionally football-oriented state, South Carolina opened the 12,400-seat Carolina Coliseum in 1968. The arena would later be named in McGuire's honor. Gamecock bas-

ketball became a South Carolina obsession, and cars bore bumper stickers reading "McGuire for Governor."

Amid the acclamation, there were problems. In 1967 the Gamecocks were placed on a two-year probation because of the way they were paying the tuition of top recruit Mike Grosso. And in 1972 athletic director Paul Dietzel moved South Carolina to the football-dominated Southeastern Conference, a move McGuire opposed. "The ACC is the most important league in basketball history. You don't just pull up and leave something like that if you're ever lucky enough to be in it in the first place," he later said.

McGuire was ousted at South Carolina after the 1979–1980 season. His 283 wins there were the most in school history, and with 164 wins at North Carolina and 102 at Saint John's, the National Basketball Hall of Fame member (inducted in 1977) was the first college coach ever to win 100 games at three different schools. In all, McGuire won 724 games in his career.

McGuire retired to Columbia, South Carolina, with his second wife, Jane Henderson, whom he married on 3 June 1972, following his wife Pat's death from cancer in 1967. In addition to Frank Jr., he had two daughters, both from his first marriage. In 1992 he suffered a stroke; he died of complications two years later at the age of eighty. He is buried in Saint Peter's Cemetery in Columbia, South Carolina.

McGuire helped transform college basketball from a regional game, dominated by schools from the Northeast and Midwest, to a national game. In building college basketball in the South, both at North Carolina and South Carolina, he is rivaled in influence only by Kentucky's Adolph Rupp. The perfect season of McGuire's 1956–1957 North Carolina team helped make basketball a passion in that state, and that team's triple-overtime championship upset of Kansas is remembered as one of the sport's greatest games.

★

There are no full-length biographies of McGuire, although he figures prominently in Joe Menzer's *Four Corners: How UNC, N.C. State, Duke, and Wake Forest Made North Carolina the Center of the Basketball Universe* (1999). A lengthy *Sports Illustrated* feature by Frank Deford, "A Team That Was Blessed" (29 Mar. 1982), recounts North Carolina's perfect 1956–1957 season. The *Columbia* (South Carolina) *State* featured extensive coverage of McGuire following his death, though with an emphasis on his South Carolina years. Obituaries are in the *New York Times, Boston Globe,* and *Los Angeles Times* (all 12 Oct. 1994).

TIM WHITMIRE

McNEILL, Don(ald) Thomas (*b.* 23 December 1907 in Galena, Illinois; *d.* 7 May 1996 in Evanston, Illinois), host of the radio show the *Breakfast Club,* one of the longest-running programs in radio network history.

Don McNeill was born in Galena, Illinois, but he grew up mainly in Sheboygan, Wisconsin. In 1926 he entered Marquette University in Milwaukee to study journalism, hoping to become a newspaper editorial cartoonist. But during his sophomore year, with the failure of his father's furniture manufacturing business, he found it necessary to look for a job to pay his way through college. The position he found was as an announcer at a Milwaukee radio station, at a salary of $15 a week. He also worked as radio editor of the Milwaukee *Sentinel,* which was the newspaper that owned the station. The job did not last long. Years later, McNeill recalled that the "manager fired me and said I had no future in radio." In 1930 he received a B.Phil. degree from Marquette.

After graduating from college, McNeill took a position in Louisville, Kentucky, as a staff announcer for a local radio station. There, he met Van Fleming, a singer with whom he formed a radio comedy team called "Don and Van, the Two Professors." They met with success in Louisville, but when they lost their sponsor they headed for San Francisco, where their routine was broadcast over several NBC outlets on the West Coast. When they were unable to get enough work to sustain themselves, the team broke up and McNeill headed back to the Midwest.

In September 1931 he married Katharine (Kay) Bennett,

Don McNeill with Ilene Woods on his *Breakfast Club* program. ARCHIVE PHOTOS

a Marquette University classmate whom he had met at the college's annual Christmas party. The couple moved to New York City, where McNeill looked for a job in radio. Unsuccessful in his quest, McNeill and his wife returned to Milwaukee. A short while later, he went to Chicago alone to look for a position. In 1932 he auditioned for master of ceremonies and writer for the *Pepper Pot,* an early-morning NBC Blue Network Chicago-based network program that was not doing well. He was hired for a $50-a-week salary. The station also had him working as a writer for *Saturday Jamboree,* a weekly one-hour program, as well as announcing schedules five days a week. His wife joined him in the Chicago area, where they remained for the rest of their lives.

The first thing McNeill did was to change the name of the *Pepper Pot* to the *Breakfast Club;* he also organized it into four segments that were designated "calls to breakfast." The show premiered on 23 June 1933, and after preparing the script for the next two months, McNeill asked the network for permission to run the program without a script. Because they thought the *Breakfast Club* had a small audience, they acquiesced. For the rest of its many years on the air, except for commercials and musical selections, the show essentially was unrehearsed and extemporaneous. The formula worked, and the *Breakfast Club* was a huge success. At its peak it was broadcast on more than 400 stations and listened to by an estimated four and a half million people. Each year McNeill received more than a million pieces of mail from his audience, and much of the content of the show came from these letters.

The *Breakfast Club* aired five mornings a week for the next thirty-five years. Beginning in 1937, it was broadcast before a live audience, sometimes from the Drake Hotel, the Terrace Casino in the New Morrison Hotel, and other Chicago locations. McNeill involved his audience in the show by interviewing some of its members and by getting them up and marching them around the studio—called a march around the breakfast table—to introduce each of the four calls to breakfast. Tickets to the program were in great demand not only in Chicago but in other locations as well when he took the show on tour for a month each year. Members of the program's regular cast were Fran Allison (later famous for work on the television puppet show *Kukla, Fran, and Ollie*), Sam Cowling (comedian), Eddie Ballantine (conductor), and Carol Richards and Dick Noel (vocalists). Some of the famous guests who appeared on the *Breakfast Club* were Patti Page, Johnny Desmond, Joe Louis, Thomas Hart Benton, Jane Russell, Groucho Marx, Danny Kaye, Gary Cooper, Jerry Lewis, Bob Hope, Ginger Rogers, and James Stewart. Jim and Marian Jordan, who were later to achieve fame as "Fibber McGee and Molly," appeared as "Toots and Chickie." McNeill's wife and their three sons often were heard, especially in a Christmas-season holiday show that aired for many years.

During World War II McNeill broadcast a series of interviews with workers in the factories producing military goods, and he introduced "Prayer Time" as a feature on the show, in which listeners were asked to join in silent prayer, "each in his own words, each in his own way, for a world united in peace." This feature proved popular, and it was retained from then on.

On 22 February 1954 the *Breakfast Club* was brought to television as a simulcast. McNeill did not work well in the new medium, and while the show was televised for a few years, it was not successful. The radio audience declined in the 1960s and fewer stations carried it, which meant fewer sponsors. On 27 December 1968, after nearly 7,500 broadcasts, one of the longest-running programs in the history of network radio came to an end. McNeill signed off in his usual way, with the words "Be good to yourself."

After retirement McNeill continued to live in his home in Winnetka, Illinois. He taught communication arts at Marquette and Notre Dame universities, represented a Florida land development company, served as a director of the Sears Foundation, and was on the advisory boards of Marquette, Notre Dame, and Loyola University of Chicago. He died of heart failure at Evanston Hospital in Illinois at the age of eighty-eight. He is buried in All Saints Cemetery in River Grove, Illinois.

Don McNeill was not only one of the most popular and successful personalities from the golden age of radio, he also was an important innovator. The format he developed for the *Breakfast Club* often has been credited for laying the groundwork for popular late-night television talk and entertainment shows such as the *Tonight Show*.

★

The papers of Don McNeill are located at Marquette University in Milwaukee, Wisconsin. While there are no biographies of McNeill or full-length studies of the *Breakfast Club,* substantial information can be found in John Dunning, *Tune in Yesterday: The Ultimate Encyclopedia of Old-Time Radio, 1925–1976* (1976), and in *Current Biography* (1949). Obituaries are in the *New York Times* and *Chicago Sun-Times* (both 8 May 1996) and the *Los Angeles Times* (9 May 1996).

IVAN D. STEEN

McQUEEN, Thelma ("Butterfly") (*b.* 8 January 1911 in Tampa, Florida; *d.* 22 December 1995 in Augusta, Georgia), character actress legendary for her role as the maid Prissy in the 1939 movie *Gone with the Wind*.

McQueen was the only child of a stevedore, Wallace McQueen, and a domestic worker, Mary Richardson. Deserted by her father at the age of five, Thelma lived with an aunt in Augusta until her mother found employment in Harlem in New York City. She attended school in Tampa

Butterfly McQueen. LIBRARY OF CONGRESS

and Augusta, and completed her high school education in suburban Babylon on Long Island, New York. She developed an interest in performing while reciting passages from the Bible in school. She briefly studied nursing at the Lincoln Training School in the Bronx, before quitting in 1935 to pursue a stage career. She joined Venezuela Jones's Harlem-based Youth Theatre Group and studied dancing with Katherine Dunham, Geoffrey Holder, and Janet Collins.

McQueen made her stage debut as part of the Butterfly Ballet in Venezuela Jones's off-Broadway production of *Swingin' the Dream* in 1935. She was dubbed "Butterfly" during the production, and the name remained with her throughout her life. She made her Broadway debut in New York in the George Abbott production of *Brown Sugar* (1937). The show ran for only four performances, but McQueen's contribution was favorably reviewed and Abbott next cast her in *Brother Rat* (1937) and *What A Life* (1938).

Her screen career began in 1939 when she was cast in the role of Scarlett O'Hara's maid Prissy in *Gone with the Wind*. Playing a fourteen-year-old slave girl, McQueen delivers one of the most famous lines in cinema history, made especially memorable by her high-pitched voice and convincing hysteria: "Lawdy Miz Scarlett, I don't know nothin' 'bout birthin' babies." The author Donald Bogle wrote that "Butterfly could take a big scene and condense it into the tiniest of lyrical poems." Because the movie premiered in an all-white theater, McQueen could not attend the opening. Although unhappy about playing such a stereotyped character, McQueen realized that she was taking part in a legendary film that might open up other opportunities to her as an actress. Her appearance in the film brought her not only fame but criticism later from people who considered the role demeaning. She appeared in a second film in 1939, *The Women*, which was also a box office success.

Her subsequent screen appearances were, for the most part, based on the Prissy role; she repeated the squeaky-voiced foolish maids in *Affectionately Yours* (1941), *I Dood It* (1943), *Mildred Pierce* and *Flame of the Barbary Coast* (both 1945), and *Duel in the Sun* (1946). She also appeared in the 1943 musical *Cabin in the Sky*. By the late 1940s, however, her film career was languishing, primarily because she refused to accept any more maid parts. She left Hollywood and returned to New York, where she attended City College, taking courses in political science, Spanish, drama, and dance.

The decades of the 1950s and 1960s were lean years for McQueen. For a brief period (1950–1952) she played Oriole, the dizzy neighbor on the television series *Beulah*. In 1951 she staged a one-woman show at Carnegie Hall. In 1956 she was in the unsuccessful all-black play *The World's My Oyster,* and in 1957 she appeared on stage in an off-Broadway production of Molière's comedy *The School for Wives* and in a television production of Marc Connelly's all-black biblical drama *The Green Pastures*. Meanwhile, she worked at various nonacting jobs as a factory worker, a dishwasher, and a companion, among others, to sustain herself. She moved to Augusta, Georgia, in 1957, where she had her own radio show, opened a restaurant, took a nursing course at the Georgia Medical School, and managed a community service club for black children.

McQueen returned to the Harlem stage in the role of Ora in *The Athenian Touch* in 1964. Her next theater appearance was in the off-Broadway production of *Curley McDimple* (1968). She made two other appearances in the 1960s: her own musical, *McQueen and Friends,* and the Abbott production of *Three Men on a Horse*. In the 1970s she returned to films with a cameo role in *The Phynx* (1970) and a small role in *Amazing Grace* (1974). In 1975 she was inducted into the Black Filmmakers Hall of Fame. That same year, at the age of sixty-four, McQueen received a bachelor of arts degree in political science from the City College of New York, the culmination of coursework she had undertaken at several colleges starting in 1946. In 1976

she staged her second one-woman show, *Prissy in Person*. In 1978 she put together a New York nightclub act and in 1979 won an Emmy for her role in the children's television special *The Seven Wishes of Joanna Peabody*.

In 1980 McQueen sued the Greyhound Bus Lines after being roughed up by security guards who accused her of being a pickpocket based on her appearance. In the 1980s she had a small role in *The Mosquito Coast* (1986), roles in the television documentary series *Our World* (1987) and in two television movies, *The Adventures of Huckleberry Finn* (1981) and *Polly* (1989), and a cameo role in the Sam Irwin film *Stiff* (1989). With the fiftieth anniversary celebration of *Gone with the Wind,* McQueen was again in the limelight.

"My main job is community work," McQueen once said. "Show business is only my hobby." Never having married, she worked as a volunteer in the offices of city politicians and served as playground supervisor at an elementary school (P.S. 153) in Harlem, worked for racial equality, animal rights, environmental protection, and urban beautification. An atheist who felt strongly about the separation of church and state, McQueen was also a member of the Freedom from Religion Foundation.

McQueen died at the Augusta Regional Medical Center on 23 December 1995 from burns covering over 70 percent of her body, which she received in a house fire. Her body was donated for medical research.

In the 1950s and 1960s McQueen began to refuse roles that exploited racial stereotyping, and she became publicly assertive about the rights of African Americans to a "just" representation in the cinema, a brave stance that likely accounts for the way her career came to a virtual standstill during that era. A selfless person whose integrity was often in conflict with the roles she was offered, McQueen was a proud and independent woman whose reputation as an actress centers on her portrayal of the fragile and hysterical Prissy in *Gone with the Wind*.

★

A good source of information on McQueen's career can be found in Donald Bogle, *Toms, Coons, Mulattoes, Mammies, and Bucks: An Interpretative History of Blacks in American Film* (1973). Most biographical information on McQueen is found in short entries in many biographical sources, newspapers, and magazines. Longer biographical sketches can be found in *Contemporary Black Biography*, vol. 6 (1994), *Encyclopedia of World Biography,* 2d ed., vol. 10 (1998), and Jessie Carney Smith, ed., *Notable Black American Women* (1992). The volume edited by Smith also gives a good analysis of her film and theater roles. An interview with McQueen appeared in *People* (1 Dec. 1986). Obituaries are in the *Washington Post, Atlanta Daily World,* and *New York Times* (all 23 Dec. 1995).

JOYCE K. THORNTON

McRAE, Carmen Mercedes (*b.* 8 April 1920 in New York City; *d.* 10 November 1994 in Beverly Hills, California), jazz singer known for her impeccable phrasing, melodic invention, and dramatic interpretation of lyrics.

McRae was the daughter of Jamaican immigrants, Osmond "Oscar" McRae, a health club manager, and Evadne McRae, a homemaker. She was their only child, although she had three half-siblings. McRae grew up in the Bronx and Manhattan, where she attended Julia Richman High School. Her parents hoped she would become a concert pianist and gave her five years of classical piano lessons. She later said: "That experience of studying music is what put me where I am today."

But McRae preferred popular music and jazz. She idolized Billie Holiday, whom she had heard on recordings and at Harlem's famed Apollo Theater. As a teenager McRae won a talent contest at the Apollo, which attracted the attention of songwriter Irene Kitchings, then married to the jazz pianist Teddy Wilson. Billie Holiday often sang with Wilson's band, and Kitchings introduced McRae to Holiday. They became friends, and in 1939 Holiday recorded McRae's song "Dream of Life." McRae later told

Carmen McRae. ARCHIVE PHOTOS

the *New York Times* reporter John S. Wilson, "If Billie Holiday had never existed, I probably wouldn't have, either."

McRae's musical ambition did not win immediate success. So, at her parents' urging, she took a secretarial course and worked for two years as a secretary in Washington, D.C., during World War II. Between 1940 and 1946 she did brief stints as a singer with bands led by Benny Carter, Count Basie, and Earl "Fatha" Hines. During this period she married and divorced the bebop drummer Kenny Clarke. From 1946 to 1947 she sang with Mercer Ellington's band for eighteen months, recording with them as Carmen Clarke.

For a time in 1948 she lived with the comedian George Kirby in Chicago. After the relationship ended, she found work in a Chicago nightclub as intermission pianist-singer. She later told Arthur Taylor, "I realized that my piano playing was very limited . . . [so] I hired a piano and rehearsed every day until my repertoire grew bigger." Her three and a half years in Chicago convinced her that she could earn a living by playing and singing.

In 1952 she returned to New York City as an intermission pianist at Minton's Playhouse, the legendary Harlem club where jazz musicians honed their craft. This led to her first job as a standup singer with Tony Scott's quartet, which drew national attention in a *Down Beat* magazine review in 1953. That year she cut two singles with the Larry Elgart Orchestra and recorded with the jazz accordionist Mat Mathews.

In 1954 she cut her first albums, *Easy to Love* and *Carmen McRae,* and a *Down Beat* poll named her as the best new female singer of that year. In 1955, having tied Ella Fitzgerald for Best Female Vocalist in a *Metronome* magazine poll, she signed with Decca and recorded seven albums on that label between 1955 and 1958. Will Friedland cites *Torchy* (1955), *Blue Moon* (1956), and *Afterglow* (1957) as jazz classics. It was around this time that McRae married the bassist Ike Isaacs, but they soon divorced.

The year 1961 was particularly productive. McRae recorded "Take Five" with Dave Brubeck, whose wife, Iona, wrote the lyrics, and an album with the Dave Brubeck Quartet and Louis Armstrong, *The Real Ambassadors.* That year also marked the beginning of a fruitful eight-year musical partnership with pianist Norman Simmons, who wrote the arrangements for her landmark album *Lover Man* (recorded in 1961 and released in 1962), a tribute to Billie Holiday. Simmons admired McRae's artistry, describing her as down-to-earth but musically demanding with a strong personality. "She's a great storyteller," he said, "[and] the key to it is her romance with words and syllables and her understanding of lyrics."

In 1967 McRae moved to Beverly Hills, California. In 1968 the jazz critic Ralph J. Gleason featured McRae on his *Jazz Casual* television series. Gleason admired her ability to mesmerize an audience and termed her public performances "a one-woman exercise in dramatic art [with] a quality of intimacy [such that] the lyrics become a story, they literally come to life." McRae rarely accompanied herself on piano, saying, "It's hell to concentrate on two things at a time," but in 1973 she recorded a live solo album in Tokyo, *As Time Goes By*. On 28 March 1980 she and her trio performed at New York City's Carnegie Hall in a concert featuring Mel Tormé and other jazz masters.

In a project that grew out of her friendship with Thelonious Monk during the 1960s, she sought and received permission from Monk's family to record the lyrics to his melodies. Due to the complexity of Monk's music, McRae considered *Carmen Sings Monk*, recorded in 1988 in San Francisco, one of her most challenging projects, and critics deemed it her best work in a decade. Her final album was *Sarah—Dedicated to You* (1991), a tribute to her friend and fellow jazz singer Sarah Vaughan. Between 1960 and 1990 McRae performed at elite jazz clubs throughout the United States, appeared at international jazz festivals, and toured Europe and Japan. She recorded more than forty albums as leader and appeared on others with such artists as Betty Carter, George Shearing, and Duke Ellington.

Her film appearances include *The Square Jungle* (1955), *The Subterraneans* (1960), *Hotel* (1967), and *JoJo Dancer, Your Life is Calling* (1986), as well as one episode of the television series *Roots* (1978) and the documentaries *Tribute to Billie Holiday* (1979), *Thelonious Monk: Music in Monk's Time* (1985), and *Carmen McRae—Live* (1986).

Even while based in California, McRae appeared regularly at the Blue Note in New York City. A lifelong smoker who refused to quit, she suffered a respiratory failure after performing there in 1991 and never sang in public again. In 1994 she received a Jazz Masters Award from the National Endowment for the Arts, which cited "her instinctive feeling for rhythm, her skillful vocal technique, her innovative scat singing."

McRae died in Beverly Hills from complications of a stroke suffered a month earlier. Her remains were cremated. She had no children.

Although Carmen McRae never attained the heights of popularity achieved by Ella Fitzgerald, Sarah Vaughan, and Billie Holiday, many regarded her as their artistic equal. She was nominated for a Grammy Award six times but never won. Nonetheless, she inspired many young jazz singers, and musicians and critics alike recognized her superb musicianship and evocative interpretation of lyrics.

★

Arthur Taylor, *Notes and Tones* (1982), contains a lengthy interview with McRae. Valuable coverage is in Ralph J. Gleason, *Celebrating the Duke: And Louis, Bessie, Billie, Bird, Carmen, Miles,*

Dizzy, and Other Heroes (1975); Leslie Gourse, *Louis' Children: American Jazz Singers* (1984); and Will Friedwald, *Jazz Singing: America's Great Voices from Bessie Smith to Bebop and Beyond* (1990). Several magazine articles are helpful: James T. Jones IV, "Carmen McRae: Cut the Crap," *Down Beat* (June 1991); Frank Alkyer, "Jazz On Campus: Jazz Educators Invade Boston," *Down Beat* (April 1994); Dave Helland, "The End of Three Vocal Eras: Farewell to Cab Calloway, Antonio Carlos Jobim, and Carmen McRae," *Down Beat* (Mar. 1995); and "McRae and Jamal Named Masters of Jazz by NEA," *Jet* (17 Jan. 1994). See also John S. Wilson, "Carmen McRae Salutes Billie Holiday," *New York Times* (14 Dec. 1979), and Stephen Holden, "Carmen McRae Gives Voice to the Melodies of Thelonious Monk," *New York Times* (2 May 1990). Numerous McRae recordings have been reissued on compact disk. An obituary is in the *New York Times* (12 Nov. 1994).

SUSAN FLEET

MANCINI, Henry Nicola (*b*. 16 April 1924 in Cleveland, Ohio; *d*. 14 June 1994 in Los Angeles, California), composer, conductor, and arranger whose music enhanced hundreds of movies and television shows over a career that spanned more than four decades.

Mancini, who grew up in Aliquippa, Pennsylvania, was the only child of Quinto Mancini, a steelworker, and Anna

Henry Mancini. ARCHIVE PHOTOS

Pece, a homemaker. An amateur musician, the elder Mancini encouraged Henry to study the flute and piccolo at an early age. Mancini later attributed much of his success to his father's stern admonitions to maintain a rigorous regimen of practice. As a youngster, Mancini went to see Cecil B. de Mille's movie *The Crusades* (1935), which included a captivating musical score by Rudolph Copp. Intrigued, Mancini resolved to become a film composer. "I've always felt," Mancini said, "there was magic on a movie screen, seeing that bunch of light pouring out of the projector and creating images for you." He graduated from Aliquippa High School in 1942 and enrolled at Carnegie Institute of Technology. After a year, Mancini transferred and went on to study music at the Juilliard School of Music in New York City (1943).

Mancini was drafted into the U.S. Army in 1943. He served in the Army Air Corps, but his musical talent caught the attention of his officers and they had him work as an arranger for service bands. Mancini met the members of Glenn Miller's Army Air Corps Band, though not Miller himself. After his discharge from the Army in 1946, Mancini joined the new Glenn Miller Band, which was reorganized after Miller's death in 1944, as a pianist and arranger. In 1947 Mancini quit the band and relocated to Hollywood. He met and married the singer Virginia ("Ginny") O'Connor. They had a son and twin daughters. From 1947 to 1952 Mancini acquired invaluable experience from scoring music played on radio programs. He also continued his musical training, by studying composition.

In 1952 he became a staff composer and arranger for Universal Studios. After working on many films, including *It Came from Outer Space* (1953) and *The Creature from the Black Lagoon* (1954), he received his first complete scoring assignments for *The Glenn Miller Story* (1954) and *The Benny Goodman Story* (1956). He received an Academy Award nomination for his score for *The Glenn Miller Story*. He also provided a score for Orson Welles's *Touch of Evil* (1958).

In 1958 he left Universal. That year, the television producer-director Blake Edwards hired Mancini to write the score for *Peter Gunn,* which became a hit detective series. Mancini produced a memorable score that established him as a leader in his craft. His *Peter Gunn* theme song employed a guitar and piano played in unison in a manner that produced what Mancini described as "a sinister effect with some frightened saxophones and some shouting brass." This theme song's "use of the jazz idiom, applied dramatically to the story," Mancini said, "put music on everybody's mind as far as TV is concerned."

The *Peter Gunn* score received an Emmy Award nomination for best musical score of the year in 1958. RCA-Victor produced a record album, *The Music from "Peter Gunn"* (1958), for which Mancini won two Grammy Awards in 1958, for best album and best arrangement. *Music from "Peter Gunn"* sold more than a million copies, as did a sequel release, *More Music from "Peter Gunn"* (1959).

In 1960 Mancini wrote the musical score for *Mr. Lucky,* another Blake Edwards–produced TV detective show. The series became a hit, and a record album, *Music from Mr. Lucky,* sold very well, netting Mancini two additional Grammy Awards, for best arrangement and best orchestral performance. Mancini won yet another Grammy Award in 1960 for his album *The Blues and the Beat.*

That year he returned to the motion-picture industry as a freelance composer. He wrote the musical scores for a string of successful movies encompassing a range of genres. These included *The Great Impostor* (1961), *Bachelor in Paradise* (1961), *Breakfast at Tiffany's* (1961), *Hatari!* (1962), *Days of Wines and Roses* (1962), *Charade* (1963), *The Pink Panther* (1964), *Love Story* (1970), *That's Entertainment* (1974), *The Great Waldo Pepper* (1975), *10* (1979), *Victor/Victoria* (1982), *The Glass Menagerie* (1987), and *Son of the Pink Panther* (1993). Mancini also continued to write music for television shows, including *Newhart, Remington Steele,* and the 1983 miniseries *The Thorn Birds.*

In his career Mancini produced eighty-five record albums. He also formed and led an orchestra, the Mancini Pops. He established music-education scholarships and he wrote a textbook, *Sounds and Scores: A Practical Guide to Professional Orchestration* (1973). His autobiography, *Did They Mention the Music?,* appeared in 1989.

Mancini received much critical acclaim for his work. He received seventy Grammy nominations and won the award twenty times. He won Academy Awards for the scores of *Breakfast at Tiffany's* and *Victor/Victoria* and for the songs "Moon River" and "Days of Wine and Roses." He also earned seventeen other Academy Award nominations. Mancini received more than twenty Emmy Awards for his television music.

For all his acclaim, the earnest, kindly-looking Mancini always remained a self-effacing, modest individual, who made and kept many friends in the music industry. He liked to say that he "never trusted this thing called success." He died of pancreatic cancer at the age of seventy. Mancini's ashes were scattered off the coast of Malibu, California, and in Vail, Colorado, which his daughter Felice described as the "two places he loved most."

Mancini set a high standard that few of his contemporaries could equal. He left a rich and prodigious body of musical work. Future generations of movie-watchers are certain to rediscover and enjoy the films of which his music was such an important part.

★

Mancini's autobiography, written with Gene Lees, is *Did They Mention the Music?* (1989). William Darby and Jack Du Bois,

American Film Music: Major Composers, Techniques, Trends, 1915–1990 (1991), includes a chapter on Mancini. See also Tony Thomas, *Music for the Movies* (1973), and Tony Thomas, *Film Score: The View from the Podiums* (1979). Obituaries are in the *New York Times* (15 June 1994) and *Down Beat* (Sept. 1994).

IRINA BELENKY

MANTLE, Mickey Charles   (*b.* 20 October 1931 in Spavinaw, Oklahoma; *d.* 13 August 1995 in Dallas, Texas), baseball superstar who played center field for the New York Yankees in succession to Joe DiMaggio, earning fame for his "tape-measure" home runs and as the best power-hitting switch hitter (right- and left-handed) in the history of the game.

Mantle's mother, Lovell Richardson, was a homemaker. His father Elvin, known as "Mutt," was a part-time baseball player and a fanatical fan of the St. Louis Cardinals. He named his eldest child (there would be four others) for an idol of his youth, Mickey Cochrane, the renowned catcher-slugger of the Philadelphia Athletics and later player-manager of the Detroit Tigers. Mutt Mantle lost his job with a paving company as the Great Depression deepened. After a stint as a tenant farmer, he moved the family

Mickey Mantle. ARCHIVE PHOTOS

from Spavinaw to Commerce, Oklahoma, where he found work as a shoveler for a zinc and lead company. Beginning when Mickey was only a toddler, Mutt Mantle would come home before nightfall and patiently teach his son how to swing a baseball bat—both right-handed and left-handed—until it was too dark to see. He aimed to make Mickey the player he wished to have been himself. Meanwhile, Mickey's approving mother waited with dinner on the table. Mantle liked to recall that his mother sewed every baseball uniform he wore until he was fitted for Yankee pinstripes.

Mickey played Little League baseball as a shortstop, and in a few years was on the baseball and football teams at Commerce High School. In a football game there in 1946, he was kicked in the left shin and suffered a bruise that led to osteomyelitis, a fulminating bone disease that eventually required five operations to control. The affected limb, however, had been permanently weakened, and the long series of leg injuries that would plague his professional career had begun.

While playing semiprofessional baseball with the Baxter Springs Whiz Kids, Mantle drew the attention of Tom Greenwade, a scout for the Yankees who was riveted by the home runs he saw fly off Mantle's bat—from both sides of the plate. When Mantle graduated from high school in 1949, Greenwade signed him to a Yankee contract. The eighteen-year-old Mickey received a bonus of $1,100 on top of $400 for the remainder of the summer. The prize prospect was sent to the Yankees' Class D team in Independence, Kansas, where he continued to play shortstop. While hitting .313 in eighty-nine games, he committed forty-seven errors. Still, his speed on the bases as well as his slugging earned him a promotion the following year to the Yankees' Class C team in the Western Association, the Joplin (Missouri) Miners. There he batted .383, with 199 hits and 326 total bases, but he continued to field erratically, committing fifty-five errors in 137 games, mostly by making wild throws. In September 1950 the Yankees called him up to "The Show," as the big leagues were familiarly known, and he joined the team in St. Louis at Sportsman's Park. He was touted as the likely eventual successor to Phil Rizzuto, the team's sterling shortstop. By design, Mantle did not get into a single game. He was simply to sit on the bench to watch and learn. Mantle was awed by his new teammates; he barely could bring himself even to look at DiMaggio, whom he had worshiped for most of his young years, let alone talk to him.

In 1951, at the age of nineteen, Mantle was in Phoenix for spring training with the Yankees, and on opening day at Yankee Stadium, Casey Stengel, the manager, stationed him in right field, alongside DiMaggio in center field. "Joltin'" Joe was starting what would be the final season of his scintillating career. The visiting team was the Boston

Red Sox, whose right fielder was Ted Williams, the incomparable "Splendid Splinter." Mantle felt keenly the intense pressure of both the company he was in and the cheering fans who had heard he was a kind of superman. Two months into the season, because he was striking out too much—in one game he fanned five times—the team sent him down to their top farm team, the Kansas City Blues, in the American Association. There he was assigned to play center field, in anticipation of his succeeding DiMaggio. Mantle burned up the American Association with his home run hitting. After forty games the Yankees called him up, and he finished his rookie season with a .267 batting average and thirteen home runs in ninety-six games.

On 23 December 1951 Mantle and Merlyn Louise Johnson, his long-time steady girlfriend, were married at her parents' home in Picher, Oklahoma. They had four children. Nationally, the war in Korea was holding public attention, and Mantle was eligible for the military draft. Eyebrows were raised—and he felt the criticism deeply—when he was excused as 4F because of his osteomyelitis, even though on the diamond he seemed as fit as anybody.

As the regular center fielder in 1952, Mantle quickly established himself as worthy of comparison with the other luminous New York center fielders, Duke Snider of the Brooklyn Dodgers and Willie Mays of the New York Giants. Mantle combined power at the plate with outstanding speed on the bases. A teammate said: "With his one good leg he could outrun everyone." In 1952 he hit .311, including twenty-three home runs in 142 games. His prowess was only just developing. In 1955 Mantle led the league in home runs with thirty-seven. The following year he won the Triple Crown, leading the league in average (.353), home runs (fifty-two), and runs batted in (130). Three times he was the American League's Most Valuable Player (1956, 1957, and 1962), and four times he led the league in home runs (1955, 1956, 1958, and 1960). In 1961, driving out fifty-four homers, he was second to Roger Maris, his teammate, who broke Babe Ruth's long-standing record of sixty homers by striking sixty-one.

From 1952 to 1965 Mantle was named to the league's All-Star team. In two All-Star games he smacked homers. In 1962 he won the Gold Glove Award for his fielding. In his eighteen-year career he hammered out 536 home runs, placing him eighth on the all-time list (373 were struck left-handed and 163 right-handed). He had delivered 2,415 hits—including 344 doubles and 72 triples, and had averaged .300 or better at bat in each of ten years. His lifetime batting average was .298. He would always regret that he had not corralled enough additional hits to be a .300 lifetime batter. Five times he topped the American League in walks and six times in runs scored. In his first fourteen seasons with the Yankees, Mantle helped lead the team to twelve World Series, serving as the anchor of the most suc-

cessful team in the history of American sports. His eighteen home runs in the sixty-five World Series games in which he played is the Mount Everest of slugging achievement. Moreover, his forty-two runs scored, forty-three bases on balls, 123 total bases, and forty runs batted in are also World Series records.

The heights Mantle might have reached had he not been injury-prone can only be conjectured. No one ever loved to play baseball more than he did, but practically from the beginning of his professional life he played with his knees or legs bound in bandages. The first injury came in the World Series of 1951, when Mantle was a rookie. Running after a fly ball that Willie Mays had hit, he stopped short to allow DiMaggio to catch it and tripped on a lawn sprinkler head, ripping up ligaments in his right knee. In his years as a Yankee he had seven operations, six on his knees. In 1963 in Baltimore he broke his left foot scaling a mesh fence in pursuit of a hit ball. His shoulder also once required serious surgical repair. Despite his considerable infirmities, however, Mantle holds the record for Yankee games played (2,401) and times at bat (8,102). In his last years as a Yankee, Mantle played first base to help save his ailing legs.

No longer able to bear the pain and punishment of regular play on damaged knees, Mantle decided to quit during spring training in 1969. He was elected to the National Baseball Hall of Fame in 1974, the first year of his eligibility. The Yankees retired the number 7 he had worn so brilliantly, enshrining him in succession to the team's royal lineage: Babe Ruth (number 3), Lou Gehrig (number 4) and DiMaggio (number 5).

Mantle threw right-handed, and although he made an asset of his remarkable speed, he was only somewhat better than average with the glove. Still, he thrilled crowds everywhere with the power he generated at the plate and the distance his best blows traveled. Batting right-handed in 1953, he drove a ball 565 feet over a fifty-five-foot fence at Griffith Stadium in Washington, D.C. No one has ever driven a ball out of Yankee Stadium, yet twice, batting left-handed, he sent prodigious wallops crashing off the filigree facade in right field at the top of the famous ballpark, 500 feet away and 108 feet high—only a few feet short of clearing the roof. An unassuming, even naive man who never crowed about his skills, he said in self-deprecation at his induction into the Hall of Fame: "I also broke Ruth's record for strikeouts. He struck out only 1,500 times. I struck out 1,710 times."

In retirement Mantle lent his name and prestige to a restaurant and sports bar in New York City, where he often could be seen responding to the endless questions of his admirers. Located on Central Park South near the St. Moritz Hotel where he had stayed when he played ball, it provided a substantial income for him. An earlier enterprise, a chain of restaurants named Mickey Mantle's Country Cooking had failed in 1969 because his partners apparently cheated him. When he took a well-paying job in 1983 as a greeter in an Atlantic City casino, as Willie Mays had done, he, like Mays, was suspended from baseball by the commissioner of baseball because their duties suggested they were associated with gambling. Both suspensions were lifted after two years.

"The Mick," as his fans and friends referred to him affectionately, stood just under six feet tall and at the zenith of his career weighed 195 pounds. In addition to being well-muscled, he had been a blond, freckle-faced, handsome young man made to order for a matinee idol. Still, he was no all-American type: there was too much Peck's Bad Boy in him, and his behavior could be embarrassing and dismaying. Beginning early in his career, more often than not in the company of Whitey Ford, the peerless pitching star of the Yankees, and Billy Martin, an irrepressible infielder of the team, Mantle was carousing in the nightlife of New York and other cities on the American League circuit. Bearing playground-sounding first names, the three nevertheless went around calling one another "Slick," as if to seal their friendship like a band of adolescent pranksters. They drank heavily and incessantly, oftentimes arriving at Yankee Stadium notably hungover. After Billy Martin was involved in a drunken brawl at the Copacabana, a popular nightclub in Manhattan, he was traded away. The Yankee management regarded him as exerting a bad influence on his two buddies. Mantle's willingness to live on the edge may have owed something to his conviction that Hodgkin's disease, the genetic debility that had taken the life of every male Mantle before the age of forty—including his father—would claim him early, too. In the event, it was his third son, Billy, who fell victim to the ailment and subsequently died of a heart attack at the age of thirty-six.

As the years passed, Mantle continued his boozing and lived as an alcoholic in a constant haze. Nonetheless, after the death of Billy and perhaps also the realization that he was not going to die as he thought he was fated to, Mantle seems to have recognized that continuing his life with the bottle was going to kill him. At the urging of his surviving children, David, Danny, and Mickey, Jr., and his friend Pat Summerall, a well-known sports broadcaster, he turned himself in for addiction treatment at the Betty Ford Center in Rancho Mirage, California. He emerged determined never to drink again, and in the next year and a half he seemed a new man.

Mantle's resolve, though, came too late, for his once powerful body had begun to come apart. His doctors determined that his liver, which his heavy drinking had put under constant strain, was now ravaged not only by cirrhosis, but also by hepatitis and cancer, and that if he was to survive he required a liver replacement. He underwent transplant surgery on 8 June 1995 at Baylor University Medical Center in Dallas. A question that remained unanswered was whether this beloved national figure had received preference for the donor liver over other eligible candidates. Many people wondered also why a man whose disability was largely self-inflicted should have had access to a scarce organ. He developed anemia as a result of the chemotherapy that he underwent, and when he was hospitalized again on 28 July, it was discovered that the cancer had invaded his entire body. His surgeon said that had he known the cancer had spread beyond the liver, he would not have allowed the transplant.

In the days remaining to him, Mantle directed that a Mickey Mantle Foundation be established to encourage the donation of tissue and organs for transplants. He involved himself, too, in a fund-raiser for children affected by the Oklahoma City bombing. In a news conference on 11 July 1995, Mantle confessed that he was a poor role model for the country's youth, although he had never posed as one. He had squandered his body, he confessed ashamedly. "God gave me the ability to play baseball. God gave me everything. For the kids out there . . . don't be like me." He died with his wife and three surviving sons at his bedside. Mickey and Merlyn Mantle had been estranged from each other for many years, with him living with his agent Greer Johnson, said to be his mistress. After funeral services—televised nationally—at Lovers Lane United Methodist Church in Dallas on 15 August 1995, Mantle was buried in a crypt near his son in Sparkman-Hillcrest Memorial Park, also in Dallas.

The continued enthusiasm for Mantle memorabilia in the years following his death testifies to the hold he had on the American imagination. Recognizing the value of his name and reputation, his family created Four M Enterprises to license products bearing his picture and signature. In a publicized court action, the Mantle family failed to prevent Greer Johnson from auctioning off some of Mantle's intimate personal possessions. Mickey Mantle had realized in his life story the dream that millions of youngsters of his time had of becoming a stellar player on the country's premier baseball team, leading it to victory year after year, and electrifying the nation each fall with herculean feats performed before awed World Series crowds. That dream will always remain a bright and shining piece of Americana to which Mantle's name must always be attached.

★

Mantle produced a spate of autobiographical accounts of his life. The first was Mickey Mantle, as told to Ben Epstein, *Mickey Mantle Story* (1953). Then came Mickey Mantle and Robert W. Creamer, *The Quality of Courage* (1964, reprint 1999). The best is Mickey Mantle with Herb Gluck, *The Mick: Mickey Mantle* (1985). Additional tidbits are in Mickey Mantle and Phil Pepe, *My Fa-*

vorite Summer (1956); Whitey Ford, Mickey Mantle, and Joseph Durso, *Whitey and Mickey: A Joint Autobiography of the Yankee Years* (1977); and Mickey Mantle, with Mickey Herskowitz, *All My Octobers: My Memories of Twelve World Series When the Yankees Ruled Baseball* (1994). Throughout his career Mantle was the subject of a stream of hagiographic sportswriting. Examples are Gene Schoor, *Mickey Mantle of the Yankees* (1959); Dick Schaap, *Mickey Mantle: The Indispensable Yankee* (1961); Milton J. Shapiro, *Mickey Mantle: Yankee Slugger* (1962); and Al Silverman, *Mickey Mantle: Mister Yankee* (1963). The year Mantle died came David Falkner, *The Last Hero: The Life of Mickey Mantle* (1995); Mickey Herskowitz, *Mickey Mantle: An Appreciation* (1995); and Robert Creamer, *Mickey Mantle Remembered: Stories Excerpted from the Pages of Sports Illustrated* (1995). The flow of books continued: Gene Schoor, *The Illustrated History of Mickey Mantle* (1996); Maury Allen, *Memories of the Mick* (1997); Phil Berger, *Mickey Mantle* (1998); Larry Canale, *Mickey Mantle: The Yankee Years, The Classic Photography of Ozzie Sweet* (1998); and David S. Nuttall, *Mickey Mantle's Greatest Hits* (1998). A revelation of some of the unsavory hijinks of Mantle and his cohorts is in Jim Bouton, *Ball Four* (1970, reprint 1990). A collective appreciation of New York City's greatest center fielders is Donald Honig, *Mays, Mantle, Snider: A Celebration* (1987). An FBI file of documents on Mickey Mantle was released in 1998. Steve Wulf, "Superman in Pinstripes, 1931–1995," *Time* (21 Aug. 1995), is a sentimental appreciative evaluation. An obituary is in the *New York Times* (14 Aug. 1995).

HENRY F. GRAFF

MARTIN, Dean (*b.* 7 June 1917 in Steubenville, Ohio; *d.* 25 December 1995 in Los Angeles, California), singer, actor, and comedian who prospered in nightclubs, recordings, radio, television, and films for more than thirty years in the post–World War II era.

Martin was born Dino Paul Crocetti, one of two children of Gaetano Crocetti, an Italian immigrant barber, and Angela Barra, a homemaker. He dropped out of Wells High School in the tenth grade and held various jobs in his late teens and early twenties before he began to gain notice for his singing. His first notable professional job as a singer came with the Sammy Watkins Band in Cleveland in 1940 and lasted until September 1943, when he went solo in the wake of Frank Sinatra's success as a solo artist. Martin struggled for several years, but in July 1946 he teamed up with the comedian Jerry Lewis to create the enormously successful music-and-comedy act Martin and Lewis. By 1948 they were playing the country's top nightclubs, had made their television debut, and had been signed to Capitol Records and Paramount Pictures.

Martin scored his first top ten hit in March 1949 with

Dean Martin. AP/WIDE WORLD PHOTOS

"Powder Your Face With Sunshine (Smile! Smile! Smile!)." The following month, the team launched its radio series *The Martin and Lewis Show,* which ran through 1953. The duo's first film, *My Friend Irma,* opened in September 1949, followed by *My Friend Irma Goes West* in August 1950. In September *The Colgate Comedy Hour* began running on NBC-TV on Sunday nights; Martin and Lewis hosted it about once a month through the end of 1955.

The team was most successful in movies, starring in a series of film vehicles that found Lewis clowning maniacally while Martin acted as straight man, romantic interest, and singer. *At War with the Army* (1950), *That's My Boy* (1951), *Sailor Beware* (1951), and *Jumping Jacks* (1952), were among the highest-grossing films of their time. The success continued with the four Martin and Lewis films of 1953, *The Stooge, Scared Stiff, The Caddy,* and *Money from Home. The Caddy* gave Martin a second top ten hit with "That's Amore," which also sold a million copies, helping establish him as a serious singer apart from his comic partnership.

The pace of filmmaking slowed after 1953, as Martin and Lewis began to make two films a year, one for the summer and another for Christmas release, a pattern they followed in 1954 with *Living It Up,* based on the Jule Styne–Bob Hilliard Broadway musical *Hazel Flagg,* and *Three Ring Circus;* in 1955 with *You're Never Too Young* and *Artists And Models;* and in 1956 with *Pardners* and *Hol-*

lywood or Bust. Martin scored his biggest hit on records so far in January 1956, when his recording of "Memories Are Made of This" topped the charts and sold one million copies. Emboldened by this independent success and increasingly bored and frustrated in his partnership with Jerry Lewis, Martin quit the team. Martin and Lewis performed together for the last time on 25 July 1956, the tenth anniversary of their first performance, at the Copacabana nightclub in New York City.

Early predictions for Martin and Lewis as solo performers had Lewis succeeding but not Martin, forecasts that at first seemed borne out by the failure of Martin's first film without Lewis, *Ten Thousand Bedrooms* (1957), and by his inability to come up with a follow-up hit to "Memories Are Made of This." But Martin turned things around in 1958, drawing critical respect for his acting in the dramatic film *The Young Lions* in April and reaching the top ten in May with "Return to Me." These successes established him as an entertainer in his own right, and over the next five years he devoted much of his time to film acting, appearing in a wide variety of movies including dramas (*Some Came Running,* 1959; *Career,* 1959; *Ada,* 1961; and *Toys in the Attic,* 1963); Westerns (*Rio Bravo,* 1959); comedies (*Who Was that Lady?,* 1960; *All in a Night's Work,* 1961; *Who's Got the Action?,* 1962; and *Who's Been Sleeping in My Bed?,* 1963); musicals (*Bells Are Ringing,* 1960; *What a Way to Go!,* 1964; and *Kiss Me, Stupid,* 1964); and a series of films with the so-called "rat pack" of his friends including Frank Sinatra and Sammy Davis, Jr. (*Ocean's Eleven,* 1960; *Sergeants Three,* 1962; *Four For Texas,* 1963; and *Robin and the Seven Hoods,* 1964).

Martin devoted less attention to his recording career, although he switched from Capitol Records to the Sinatra-founded Reprise label in 1962. But in the spring of 1964, Reprise released Martin's recording of "Everybody Loves Somebody," which had been given an arrangement reminiscent of 1950s rock and roll. That summer the record hit number one and became a million-seller, reestablishing him as an important recording artist. His follow-up single, "The Door Is Still Open to My Heart," hit the top ten, as did "I Will" in 1965. He continued to reach the singles charts through the end of the decade, and in the same period had twelve gold-selling albums: *Everybody Loves Somebody, Dream with Dean,* and *The Door Is Still Open to My Heart* (all in 1964); *Dean Martin Hits Again, (Remember Me) I'm the One Who Loves You,* and *Houston* (all in 1965); *Somewhere There's a Someone* and *The Dean Martin Christmas Album* (both in 1966); *Welcome to My World* (1967); *Dean Martin's Greatest Hits! Vol. 1* and *Vol. 2* (both in 1968); and *Gentle on My Mind* (1969).

Martin's success on records led to his own television variety series, *The Dean Martin Show,* which premiered in September 1965 and became one of the highest-rated programs on the air; it ran regularly until 1974. The series did not prevent Martin from making movies, and he continued to vary the kinds of films he appeared in, including Westerns (*The Sons of Katie Elder,* 1965; *Texas Across the River,* 1966; *Bandolero!,* 1968); comedies (*Marriage on the Rocks,* 1965; *How to Save a Marriage—And Ruin Your Life,* 1968); dramas (*Rough Night in Jericho,* 1967; *Five Card Stud,* 1968); and a series of James Bond spoofs in which he played a spy named Matt Helm (*The Silencers,* 1966; *Murderers' Row,* 1966; *The Ambushers,* 1967; and *The Wrecking Crew,* 1969).

Martin became less active in the first half of the 1970s. His film roles diminished to a handful (*Airport,* 1970; *Something Big,* 1972; *Showdown,* 1973; *Mr. Ricco,* 1975), his TV show subsided to a series of specials after the 1973–1974 season, and he stopped recording regularly after 1974. In the early 1980s he worked occasionally, appearing in the films *The Cannonball Run* (1981) and *Cannonball Run II* (1984), cutting the country album *The Nashville Sessions,* released in 1983, and appearing as a regular on the 1985 TV series *Half-Nelson.* He also made live appearances, but after he dropped out of a joint tour with Frank Sinatra and Sammy Davis, Jr., reportedly due to health problems and particularly after the death in a plane crash of his son Dean Paul Martin, Jr., both in 1987, he virtually retired. He died eight years later of acute respiratory failure and is buried in the Sanctuary of Love site in the Westwood Village Memorial Park in Los Angeles.

Martin was married and divorced three times. On 2 October 1941 he wed Elizabeth Ann MacDonald, with whom he had four children. They were divorced in August 1949, and Martin married Jeanne Beigger, a model, on 1 September 1949; they had three children. He was divorced for a second time in March 1973 and on 24 April 1973 married Catherine Mae Hawn, a beautician, adopting her daughter from a previous marriage. Their divorce became final in 1977.

In his prime Martin was six feet tall with a trim build. Ruggedly handsome (he sported a broken nose from his days as a pugilist), he had light brown eyes and a full head of curly dark hair. As a performer, Dean Martin followed in the footsteps of Bing Crosby, adopting a similar relaxed persona that extended to his apparently effortless singing and matter-of-fact acting. At the same time, he was in the tradition of Italian-American singers, led by Frank Sinatra, that dominated the postwar pop music scene; in fact, he was more Italian than most, singing many songs in the language. But unlike the cool but sincere Crosby and the hot and sometimes brooding Sinatra, Martin, perhaps as a legacy of his decade-long comedy partnership with Jerry Lewis, brought an offhandedly ironic style to his work. Despite a busy schedule that included an average of two to three films a year for twenty years, recordings, radio and television shows, and personal appearances, he affected a drunken, playboy demeanor, often singing parody lyrics to his songs (carefully crafted for him by Sammy Cahn) and sending himself up. One of his most convincing film roles, in *Kiss Me, Stupid,* found him playing a singer much like himself, or rather, much like the thoughtless star he pretended to be. Martin's charm was that he always seemed to be suggesting that life was an elaborate joke, one that he and his audience were in on. When he could no longer maintain the pose of insouciance that was at the core of his image, he abandoned his career, living as a virtual recluse in his later years. But his work continues to charm decades after it was fabricated.

★

The first attempt to capture Dean Martin between book covers was Arthur Marx's 1974 dual biography, *Everybody Loves Somebody Sometime (Especially Himself): The Story of Dean Martin and Jerry Lewis.* In 1992 Nick Tosches published the unauthorized *Dino: Living High in the Dirty Business of Dreams,* which was exhaustively researched but also composed in overheated prose. No authorized biography has been published, but the best, most thorough account of Martin's career through 1961 is by John Chintala and is found in the two hardcover books accompanying the boxed-set collections of Martin's recordings up to that year and issued by the German Bear Family Records label, *Memories Are Made of This* (1997) and *Return to Me* (1998). Chintala is also the author of a thorough reference book, *Dean Martin: A Complete Guide to the "Total Entertainer,"* (1998). The "rat pack" aspect of Martin's career is treated in Shawn Levy's *Rat Pack Confidential: Frank, Dean, Sammy, Peter, Joey, and the Last Great Showbiz Party* (1998). An obituary is in the *New York Times* (26 Dec. 1995).

WILLIAM J. RUHLMANN

MAXWELL, Vera Huppé (*b.* 22 April 1901 in New York City; *d.* 15 January 1995 in Rincon, Puerto Rico), fashion designer whose classic designs were at the forefront of the women's sportswear revolution of the post–World War II era.

Maxwell was one of three children of Bernard Alexander Huppé, a former aide-de-camp to Emperor Franz Joseph, and Irma Torges Honthumb, a homemaker. Because her parents, who came from Vienna, Austria, frequently traveled, Vera gained early impressions of Europe that were later reflected in her designs. At the age of ten she was in Vienna admiring the handsome uniforms of the Hussars, details of which she later interpreted in her "fencing" jacket.

Back in the United States, Vera Huppé was a student in public and private schools in the Bronx. She attended Leonia High School in New Jersey for one year, then entered the Metropolitan Opera School of Ballet in New York City. In 1919 she became a member of the Metropolitan

Vera Maxwell, 1947. © BETTMANN/CORBIS

Opera Ballet and danced professionally until her marriage on 21 October 1924 to Raymond J. Maxwell, who worked on Wall Street. They had one son.

Maxwell stopped dancing and found employment as a model for wholesale fashion houses on Seventh Avenue during the 1920s. From this exposure to the garment business, Maxwell learned about clothing construction, sketching, and design. She made clothes for herself and for other models who were her friends. The clothes she wore were noticed by one of the buyers at Best and Company, who encouraged Maxwell to become a professional designer.

Around 1925 Maxwell visited London, England, where she found garments designed by Coco Chanel to be profoundly inspiring. Like Chanel, Maxwell believed that clothes should be comfortable enough to move around in without constricting or pulling. From the beginning of her designing career, Maxwell created tweedy, man-tailored clothes for women. Chanel became her idol, so much so that later Maxwell was dubbed the "American Chanel."

In 1929 Maxwell began modeling riding habits for manufacturers and also suits and coats for Linker and Klein in New York, who eventually employed her as a designer. She also began designing separates. One ensemble consisted of a reddish-brown tweed riding jacket paired with a gray skirt, a combination based on the classic British men's outfit of a Harris tweed jacket and Oxford-gray, wool-flannel trousers. Other sportswear manufacturers for which Maxwell designed were Adler and Adler, Max Milstein, and Glenhunt. The 1930s were a period when women's fashions were developing into modern sportswear, a movement in which Maxwell was in the forefront.

In 1935 Maxwell designed the "skirt dress," which had the look of a suit but avoided the problem of blouses pulling out of skirts by pairing a sheath dress with a jacket or coat; this design became a classic in American fashion. Also in 1935, Maxwell invented her "Weekend Wardrobe," a practical and ingenious collection of separate pieces. Inspired by Albert Einstein's collarless tweed jacket, Maxwell designed a woman's version in 1935—her own "Einstein Jacket," to be worn with a gray flannel skirt. By 1937 Maxwell worked for Brows, Jacobson, and Linde, creating tailored clothes for active women engaged not only in riding and skiing but who appreciated casual playclothes and separates: slacks, skirts, jackets, and shorts. Also that year, Maxwell's marriage ended in divorce. She married architect Carlisle H. Johnson on 17 November 1938.

By 1940 Maxwell had already designed her "fencing suit," and the "Reefer suit" was in her collection as well. This latter suit was for daytime wear and consisted of a slim coat worn over a matching skirt and a simple blouse. Because economy of fabric was characteristic of Maxwell's designs even before World War II, when restrictions on use of materials for clothes came into effect, Maxwell easily adjusted to them. She mainly worked in the silhouette that became most associated with the 1940s: broad-shouldered and narrow everywhere else. She created functional clothes for women involved in the war effort. One outstanding example was cotton overalls, the first women's jumpsuits, which Maxwell designed for factory workers in the Sperry Gyroscope Corporation.

Again deriving inspiration from menswear, in 1942 Maxwell designed a suit jacket for women that was based on a lumberjack's shirt, complete with envelope-style patch pockets. This was also the year when Maxwell introduced peasant and ethnic looks into her collection. Shorts were worn with simple tops and Peruvian jackets or with jackets fastened with crocheted buttons. A slit-sided, braid-edged mandarin coat was among Maxwell's innovations. After the war ended, Maxwell softened the silhouette of her designs, showing pinched waists and more fullness in skirts.

Maxwell's second marriage ended in divorce in 1945. In 1947 Vera Maxwell, Inc., offering "Vera Maxwell Originals," opened. Maxwell did almost everything herself, working as president of the company, designer, public relations manager, and fabric buyer. The hard work paid off, as she became regarded as one of the leading sportswear designers, taking her place among the renowned Claire McCardell, Tina Leser, Claire Potter, Tom Brigance, and Sydney Wragge.

Maxwell's clients appreciated the practicality and creativity of sportswear as well as the relatively moderate price compared to haute couture. During the 1950s Vera Maxwell Originals ensembles cost $125 for a three-piece suit, $245 for a dress and coat duo. An example of her philosophy of practical fashion was the "original flight suit," a tweed coat with a plastic-lined pocket that could be used to store toiletries during a flight. This coat was paired with pants and a wool jersey blouse. Fluid jersey fabric was also used for wrap-tied blouses. Another use for jersey was for a long evening dress, worn with a long tweed coat. The three-piece vested suit for women, the Chesterfield coat worn with slacks, and the print dress paired with matching print-lined coat were among Maxwell's innovations during this time. Home sewers could make Vera Maxwell two-piece suits for themselves thanks to Spadea's American Designer Pattern series in the 1950s.

In 1951 Maxwell won the prestigious Coty American Fashion Critics' Award. She continued to design classics like the princess coat dress, the fencing dress, and cotton dresses with matching linen coats. Maxwell made frequent buying trips abroad to bring back fine wools from Austria, silk prints from Italy, and handwoven silks from India. Among Maxwell's loyal clients were Grace Kelly, Mrs. Leonard Bernstein, dancer Martha Graham, Pat Nixon, and actress Lillian Gish. Princess Grace was an especially good friend whom Maxwell often visited in Monaco. By 1960 Vera Maxwell Originals were sold in 700 stores throughout the United States.

In 1961 Maxwell staged a well-received twenty-five-year retrospective of her work at her Seventh Avenue salon. Many of her earlier designs compared well with her newer designs, and sometimes the two were difficult to tell apart. In 1962 she received the New York Fashion Designers Award. Maturing along with her clients during the 1960s, Maxwell ignored the miniskirt fashions and created conservative outfits in interesting fabrics or colors, but providing more coverage. In 1964 a collection of American Indian–inspired designs was a devastating failure, and Maxwell took a break from designing.

During her hiatus, Maxwell continued to show retrospective collections of her designs to women's groups and dared fashion critics to guess the year when the clothes were designed. She also taught at the Parsons School of Design in New York, lectured and judged student work at the Fashion Institute of Technology, and acted as a consultant. By 1970 only 200 stores in the United States continued to carry Vera Maxwell clothing, but that same year a retrospective of her designs was held at the Smithsonian Institution in Washington, D.C.

Encouraged by the enthusiasm that greeted this retrospective, Maxwell renewed her active role in fashion. In May 1970 she asked Morton Milstein, nephew of Max Milstein, to become a partner in her business. A fashion show at a tea held in her honor at B. Altman and Company in New York marked Maxwell's comeback in the fall of 1970. In 1971 Maxwell made extensive use of the new miracle textile, Ultrasuede, which she employed for coats, suits, and dresses. Ultrasuede is an easy-care fabric that took color well and could be used year-round without the special care required by real suede.

In 1972 Maxwell showed a collection including classic knit coats over pants or dresses and sleeveless, slit-sided "Paletot" Ultrasuede coats. The "Speed Suit," so named because it was a stretch dress with an elasticized waist that could be quickly pulled over the head, was Maxwell's revolutionary fashion contribution in 1974. In various lengths it became a staple in Maxwell's collections thereafter. It has been said that the Speed Suit was an inspiration to Donna Karan's fashion philosophy.

Maxwell attributed the longevity of her designs and her business to a devotion to "style" rather than "fashion," creating classics that could be worn for years. Another reason for the popularity of her originals was her recognition that there are many different sizes and shapes of women. Her "misses" sizes went up to size twenty, and there were collections for petite women under five feet tall. The Vera Maxwell Fashion Gallery in the Museum of the City of New York was dedicated in 1981.

Maxwell stayed active in the community; an opera lover, she was a member of the Metropolitan Opera Guild. In 1985 she closed her business, which had been headquartered at 530 Seventh Avenue in New York City. Nevertheless, the following year Maxwell designed a collection of dresses, coats, and sportswear for the Peter Lynne Division of Gulf Enterprises. In 1992 Maxwell sold her Manhattan apartment to live with her son in Gilgo Beach, Long Island. During one of their winter vacations in Rincon, Puerto Rico, Maxwell died of a stroke at the age of ninety-three.

★

Examples of Vera Maxwell Originals are in the collection of the Museum of the City of New York. Sometimes garments by Maxwell appear for sale on the Internet. Caroline Rennolds Milbank traced Maxwell's career in *Couture: The Great Designers* (1985) and in *New York Fashion: The Evolution of American Style* (1989). A biographical essay appeared in *Current Biography* (1977), and costume historian Jean Druesedow wrote a critical essay on Maxwell's contribution to fashion in *Contemporary Fashion* (1995). Obituaries are in the *New York Times* (20 Jan. 1995) and *Los Angeles Times* (21 Jan. 1995).

THERESE DUZINKIEWICZ BAKER

MAY, Rollo Reece (*b.* 21 April 1909 in Ada, Ohio; *d.* 22 October 1994 in Tiburon, California), innovative philosopher, psychotherapist, and writer regarded as a founder of American existentialist psychotherapy.

May was the second of six children and the eldest son of Earl Tuttle, a Young Men's Christian Associations field secretary, and Matie Boughton May, a homemaker. May grew up in Michigan in a family that had "more than its share of troubles." May said that he felt closer to his father (who traveled often) than to his mother. She had named him after "Little Rollo," a hero in nineteenth-century children's books. In a *New York Post* interview in 1972, May stated that he hated his "sissy" name and felt that his mother did not find him "acceptable." He later described his parents as "austere disciplinarians and anti-intellectuals" and portrayed their relationship as "discordant" and the precursor for his interest in psychology and counseling. His oldest sister was frequently psychotic and spent time in mental hospitals. Because his family moved often during his childhood, May repeatedly had to make new friends and viewed himself as a loner. He enjoyed athletics, especially swimming, and this ability helped him to be accepted by other kids. Throughout his life, surroundings were very important to his sense of well being.

From 1926 to 1928 May attended Michigan State College of Agriculture and Applied Science (now Michigan State University). He was more interested in literature than agriculture, so he started a magazine devoted to this subject. He then transferred to Oberlin College in Ohio, where the

Rollo May, 1974. ARCHIVE PHOTOS

liberal arts were the college's primary focus. May earned an A.B. degree in English from Oberlin in 1930, minoring in Greek history and literature. He also developed a strong interest in art. From 1930 to 1933 he taught English at Anatoluia College in Salonika, Greece. During vacations, he visited and took seminars from Alfred Adler, whom he grew to admire greatly, toured Eastern Europe, and took painting lessons with Joseph Binder.

In 1933 May returned to the United States and became a student adviser and counselor at Oberlin from 1934 to 1936. He then enrolled at the Union Theological Seminary in New York City in 1936. He studied with and was heavily influenced by Paul Tillich and Reinhold Niebuhr. He earned a B.D. degree cum laude in 1938 and was married on 5 June 1938 to Florence DeFrees. They had three children and divorced in 1968. He married again in 1971, to Ingrid Schoell, whom he divorced in 1975. In 1988 he married Georgia Lee Miller Johnson. May pointed to his parents' problems as a partial answer for his failed marriages.

May was a Congregationalist minister from 1938 to 1940 in New Jersey. His lectures on counseling and personality adjustment were published as his first book, *The Art of Counseling: How to Gain and Give Mental Health* (1939), which was well regarded. May decided he would better serve people as a psychologist and resigned to study psychology at Columbia University in New York City. While working on his dissertation in 1942 and still counseling, May was diagnosed with tuberculosis. His personal struggle against death solidified his views on existentialism. While recuperating in upstate New York for almost two years, May wrote *The Meaning of Anxiety* (1950), which he considered the "watershed" event of his career. He stressed that anxiety can be a positive, motivating force for social and personal development, and that people can use their inner resources for life choices. Upon his own recovery, he graduated summa cum laude with a Ph.D. in clinical psychology, the first ever bestowed by Columbia, in 1949. For the next thirty years he lectured widely and was a visiting professor at Harvard, Yale, Brooklyn College, New York University, and the University of California at Santa Cruz.

From 1943 to 1944 he worked as a counselor at the William Alanson White Institute of Psychiatry, Psychoanalysis, and Psychology in New York City; he became a faculty member in 1948 and a fellow in 1952. In 1946 he started a private practice. He also taught at the New School for Social Research in New York City from 1955 to 1975. In 1953 May published his second book, *Man's Search for Himself*. Written in laymen's terms, it was a popular and critical success and established May as a leader of American existentialism. In 1969 May published another best-seller, *Love and Will*, which portrayed his personal struggle with love and relationships. The theme was Western society's struggle with new questions about sex, marriage, and morality. He continued to popularize self-realization, the idea that within certain limits individuals have freedom of choice.

By the early 1960s May had become a leader in challenging behaviorism and psychoanalysis. He "defected" from biological determinism by stressing unique conscious elements in individual psychology. After moving to California in 1975, he resumed his private practice as a therapist. He also served in various capacities at the Saybrook Institute of the California School of Professional Psychology. More books and ideas followed: *Power and Innocence: A Search for the Sources of Violence* (1972), *The Courage to Create* (1975), *My Quest for Beauty* (1985), and *The Cry for Myth* (1991). May was a prolific writer and thinker who wrote more than fifteen books, many of which are directly related to his personal life and growth as a person. He was the recipient of the American Psychological Association's Gold Medal for his distinguished career in psychology, Phi Beta Kappa's Ralph Waldo Emerson Award, and the Whole Life Humanitarian Award. He died of congestive heart failure at the age of eighty-five in Tiburon, California. His remains were cremated and his ashes were scattered on the East and West Coasts.

May's faith in humans to solve their problems, "his treatment of anxiety as a positive challenge," and his focus on self-fulfillment contributed to and popularized these ideas. His work helped link the fields of psychology and religion and concerned itself with ways in which people can grow.

★

Many of May's books contain information about his life and career. Critical studies of his work include Clement Reeves, *The Psychology of Rollo May* (1977) and F. Rabinowitz, G. Good, and L. Cozad, "Rollo May: A Man of Meaning and Myth," *Journal of Counseling and Development* 67 (Apr. 1989): 436–441. For posthumous summaries of his work, see J. F. T. Bugenthal, "Rollo May (1909–1994)," *American Psychologist* 51 (Apr. 1996): 418–419; R. H. Abzug, "Rollo May as Friend to Man," *Journal of Humanistic Psychology* 36 (spring 1996): 17–22; R. J. De Carvalho, "Rollo R. May (1909–1994): A Biographical Sketch," *Journal of Humanistic Psychology* 36 (spring 1996): 8–16; and J. F. T. Bugenthal, "Aristophanes, William James, Rollo May, and Our Dog Dickens," *Humanistic Psychologist* 24 (1996): 221–230. See also the conversation between May and Carl Rogers in *Carl Rogers: Dialogues* (1989). Obituaries are in the *New York Times* and *Los Angeles Times* (both 24 Oct. 1994), the *Washington Post* (25 Oct. 1994), and the Chicago *Tribune* (6 Nov. 1994).

GWYNETH H. CROWLEY

MEADOWS, Audrey (*b.* 8 February 1922 in Wuchang, China; *d.* 3 February 1996 in Los Angeles, California), singer and actress best known for her portrayal of Alice Kramden in the 1950s comedy series *The Honeymooners*.

Meadows was the youngest of four children of Francis James Meadows Cotter, an Episcopal minister, and his wife, Ida. Published sources vary on her birthdate, most giving 1925 or 1926; the year 1922 is suggested by her Social Security file. She spent her early years in China, where her parents were missionaries. At the age of five, Meadows and her family moved back to the United States when her father was appointed rector of St. John's Protestant Episcopal Cathedral in Providence, Rhode Island.

Reared in New England, Audrey was educated at Miss Hill's School in Great Barrington, Massachusetts. Aspiring to become an opera singer, she took an early interest in entertainment. At the age of sixteen she made her debut at Carnegie Hall in New York City as a coloratura soprano singer. At the urging of her older sister Jayne, a film actress later married to Steve Allen, Meadows decided to steer her career into acting. She performed in summer stock and some Broadway productions including *High Button Shoes*.

During World War II Meadows performed in Mike Todd's production of *Mexican Hayride*, touring the South Pacific with the USO. In 1951 she joined radio celebrities Bob Elliott and Ray Goulding on their television show the *Bob and Ray Show*. The only woman in the cast, Meadows had to keep up with the comic duo while playing all of the female roles. In one episode, she sang an opera aria while standing on her head.

During her run on the *Bob and Ray Show*, Meadows also appeared on Broadway. She starred in the musical *Top Banana*, in which she played opposite Broadway great Phil Silvers. In 1952, while preparing to take the show on the road, Meadows was asked by her manager to suggest a replacement for blacklisted actress Pert Kelton on Jackie Gleason's variety show. After suggesting many actresses, it dawned on Meadows that she should try out for the part.

When Jackie Gleason rejected the actress for being too young and too pretty to play Alice Kramden, a working-class housewife from Bensonhurst, Brooklyn, a furious Meadows decided to take matters into her own hands. She called photographer Bill Mark to take pictures of her in her apartment wearing a frumpy housedress with her hair in rollers and her face without makeup. She then persuaded her manager to show Gleason the pictures. Upon seeing the photos, Gleason, unaware that he was looking at the same woman whom he had recently turned down for the role, declared that Alice Kramden had been found! Later, when Gleason learned that the attractive young woman he had met earlier and the dowdy housewife in the photos were indeed the same person, he offered Meadows the part without an audition.

With Meadows on board, the *Jackie Gleason Show* attracted a wide audience, and *The Honeymooners* became the most popular sketch of the show. In 1955 CBS ordered more episodes of *The Honeymooners,* and the skit became a series. For the next five seasons, the television audience came to know her as Alice Kramden. In 1954 her portrayal of this tough, sarcastic, no-nonsense Brooklyn housewife earned her an Emmy for best supporting actress in a comedy series. Her ability to memorize every character's lines, to retain her composure, and to improvise whenever anything went awry on the live television show earned her the nickname "Rock Of" (as in Gibraltar), as Gleason lovingly referred to her. Unsatisfied with the scripts for the 1956–1957 season, Gleason decided to cancel the sitcom and return to his one-hour variety show, featuring *The Honeymooners*. However, this time, *The Honeymooners* was a musical.

When it came time to negotiate her contract, Meadows proved to be a woman with sharp business acumen. Along with her attorneys, Mortimer Becker and her brother Ed Cotter, Meadows negotiated a deal that gave her a significant salary increase as well as residuals—a percentage of future syndication profits—for her participation in *The Honeymooners*. This deal proved extremely lucrative; reruns of *The Honeymooners* have been broadcast since the show's original run ended.

In her personal life, a 1956 marriage to wealthy Washington realtor Ralph Rouse ended in divorce after two years.

Audrey Meadows with her dog, Sugar, 1994. AP PHOTO/CHRIS PIZZELLO

In 1961 she made another attempt at marriage when she married Continental Airlines CEO Robert F. Six. Meadows cut back on her acting career to accompany her husband on business trips around the world. Later, Meadows became a member of the airline's board of directors. The couple had homes in New York City, Beverly Hills, and Denver. The marriage lasted for twenty-five years until Six died in 1986. Meadows had no children.

In addition to *The Honeymooners,* Meadows guest-starred on a variety of television shows, such as *Alfred Hitchcock Presents, Kraft TV Theatre, Checkmate, Wagon Train, Sid Caesar's* television specials, and several *Honeymooners* reunions. In addition, she appeared on several Broadway shows and a few films, including *That Touch of Mink* (1962), where she played a supporting role opposite Cary Grant and Doris Day, and *Take Her She's Mine* (1963). She also had a recurring role as Ted Knight's mother-in-law on the television sitcom *Too Close for Comfort.*

During *The Honeymooners* run, Meadows developed a close friendship with Jackie Gleason. In 1994, as a response to biographies of Gleason that she felt misrepresented him, Meadows published her memoirs, *Love, Alice: My Life as a Honeymooner.* The book is a tribute to Gleason and describes him as she knew him: kind, loving, intelligent, and professional.

A heavy smoker, Meadows was diagnosed with cancer in 1996. She kept her condition a secret from her family, including her sister, Jayne, who learned about her illness a few days before her death. Meadows died in her sister's arms five days before her seventieth birthday. She is buried at Holy Cross Cemetery in Culver City, California.

Throughout her career, Audrey Meadows showed the depths of her talent from the myriad characters she played. However, her fans will remember her as the sassy Alice Kramden. Meadows was a trailblazer who paved the way for women on television. A person of dignity and grace, she is remembered by those who knew her well as a loving sister, aunt, and friend. Fans, however, will always remember her as what Jackie Gleason called her on the show: "The Greatest."

★

Meadows wrote a memoir with Joe Daley, *Love Alice: My Life as a Honeymooner* (1994), which is an autobiographical account of her time on the comedy show. For a tribute to her that details her life story, see "Diamond in the Rough," *People Weekly* (16 Feb. 1996). Her life story and accomplishments can also be found in the 1958 yearbook and Apr. 1996 issue of *Current Biography.* Obituaries are in the *New York Times* and *Daily News* (both 5 Feb. 1996); *Variety* and *U.S. News and World Report* (both 19 Feb. 1996); and *TV Guide* (24 Feb. 1996).

SABINE LOUISSAINT

MERRILL, James Ingram (*b.* 3 March 1926 in New York City; *d.* 6 February 1995 in Tucson, Arizona), writer who published a memoir, a collection of essays, two novels, and two plays but whose reputation rests principally on his fifteen books of verse, including *The Changing Light at Sandover* (1982).

Merrill was the youngest son of Charles Edward Merrill, a founding partner of the equities brokerage firm Merrill Lynch, Pierce, Fenner, and Smith, and his second wife, Hellen Ingram, a Jacksonville, Florida, newspaper reporter and socialite. He had a half brother and a stepsister by his mother's second marriage to Colonel William Plummer. Merrill grew up in resplendent surroundings, first in an elegant federal-style brownstone at 18 West Eleventh Street in New York City and later at the sumptuous Southampton estate the "Orchard" on Long Island. Merrill was rich at the age of five, "whether I liked it or not," he later wrote, and never lived on his writing income.

Merrill's parents separated during the summer of 1937. Two of his frequently anthologized poems, "The Broken Home" and "Lost in Translation," deal directly with the anguish of his childhood and home, a metaphor often recapitulated in his verse, according to the critic David Kalstone. After his parents' divorce, Merrill and his mother

James Merrill. AP/WIDE WORLD PHOTOS

returned to New York City. From 1939 to 1943 Merrill attended the Lawrenceville School near Princeton, New Jersey, where he worked on the literary magazine's staff. Although he had penned his first poems at the age of eight, a friendly rivalry with his classmate Frederick Buechner, the author of *A Long Day's Dying* (1950), spurred Merrill to dedicate his life to writing. He could not be deterred by his father, who eventually came to appreciate his son's dedication. Merrill's father privately published the young poet's first collection of juvenilia in 1942 to his son's surprise and later chagrin.

Merrill said in an interview that he cared about music long before he concerned himself with literature. In 1939 he heard the complete cycle of Richard Wagner's *The Ring of the Nibelung*, and those performances initiated him into a lifelong passion for opera. Merrill claimed his true education occurred at the old Metropolitan Opera house, where he heard many of the twentieth century's great singers.

Merrill entered his father's alma mater, Amherst College, in 1943. His studies were interrupted by the draft in 1944. Because demobilization had begun, Merrill was not deployed in Europe, and after his discharge in 1945, he returned to Amherst. He had a romantic relationship with a teacher, the Greek poet and translator Kimon Friar, which scandalized his parents. Merrill dedicated the privately printed collection *The Black Swan and Other Poems* to Friar in 1946.

Merrill graduated from Amherst summa cum laude with a B.A. degree in 1947. He wrote his thesis on the French novelist Marcel Proust and published poems in the *Kenyon Review*. An early appearance in *Poetry* in 1946 garnered Merrill the Oscar Blumenthal Prize in 1947. He taught at Bard College for a year. Culling the best poems from *The Black Swan* into a manuscript, he submitted it to one publisher, Alfred A. Knopf. He learned of the acceptance of *First Poems* (1951) shortly before he sailed for Europe in March 1950. Merrill traveled the Continent for two and a half years and later chronicled his odyssey in the memoir *A Different Person* (1993). This poignant account of the life of the gay expatriate in the 1950s is colloquy between the dapper young poet and his older self from the vantage point of experience and years.

With the publication of *First Poems,* Merrill marked the formal beginning of his long career, distinguishing himself among the poets of his generation with his technical virtuosity and stylistic brilliance. In retrospect this early collection and the next, *The Country of a Thousand Years of Peace and Other Poems* (1959), in part an elegiac tribute to the Dutch poet Hans Lodeizen, whom Merrill knew at Amherst, exhibit a reticence reflective of the suffocating political and cultural climate of the United States in the 1950s. Like his contemporaries, Merrill eventually wrote more autobiographical verse. Influenced by the Proustian concept that memory harbors patterns of childhood experience that a writer is fated to revisit, Merrill explored his past and articulated the details of his formative years with peerless imagination and intellect, molding them into an art that held a mirror not only to himself but to his age.

In the 1950s Merrill experimented with other literary forms. *The Bait,* a one-act play, premiered in New York in 1953. *The Immortal Husband,* a three-act, modern retelling of the Greek myth of Tithonus and Aurora, premiered in 1955. Both plays were directed by Herbert Machiz and produced by John Bernard Myers for the Artists' Theatre. In 1956 Merrill published his first novel, *The Seraglio,* a roman à clef about his father. *The (Diblos) Notebook,* published in 1965, grew out of his sojourns in Greece.

At the premier of *The Bait,* Merrill met his lifelong companion David Jackson. In 1954 Merrill and Jackson moved to the coastal village of Stonington, Connecticut, retreating from the literary scene of New York City. In 1956 they bought a home together, and Merrill's collection *Water Street* (1962), a seminal work in his artistic development, is named for its address. With *Water Street,* Merrill proclaimed his poetic vocation as the "need to make some kind of house / Out of the life lived, out of the love spent." In 1959 Merrill bought a house in Athens, Greece, and for twenty years he and Jackson divided their time between the two cities.

At the time of his father's death in 1956, Merrill funded the Ingram Merrill Foundation with a portion of his inheritance. From its inception to its cessation of activities in 1996, the foundation awarded millions of dollars of grants and prizes to writers, musicians, and visual artists. In 1966 the state of Connecticut named Merrill its first poet laureate.

Minutes before noon on Friday, 6 March 1970, Merrill's childhood home at 18 West Eleventh Street attained a grim notoriety when dynamite stored in the basement of the premises by the radical group the Weathermen accidentally detonated, killing three bomb makers. Cathlyn Wilkerson, the daughter of the building's owner and a member of the group, escaped the rubble and remained a fugitive for a decade. Characteristically, Merrill registered his shock at his "vainly exploded" former home with a poem named for the address. It was published in *Braving the Elements* (1972) and won the Bollingen Prize in poetry.

Merrill and Jackson began experimenting with a homemade Ouji board and chipped willowware teacup in 1955, and in the 1970s Merrill conceived of a long narrative poem based on the voluminous transcripts of the couple's conversations with their personal pantheon of friends, mentors, and spirits. "The Book of Ephraim," which recounts twenty years of conversations with their favorite voice, first appeared in the Pulitzer Prize–winning collection *Divine Comedies* in 1976. It was followed by *Mirabell: Books of Number* (1978), which won Merrill's second National Book Award, and *Scripts for the Pageant* (1980), which won the National Book Critics Circle Award in poetry for 1983. With an epilogue titled "Coda: The Higher Keys," Merrill published the entire trilogy in one volume, *The Changing Light at Sandover,* in 1982 to the delight of his admirers and the bewilderment of the skeptics, who poured over its cosmogonic revelations, its melange of science and occult, and its portrait of the couple's relationship.

Merrill's other works include *Nights and Days* (1966), for which he won his first National Book Award in 1967; *The Fire Screen* (1969); *Late Settings* (1985); and *The Inner Room* (1988), which garnered the first Bobbitt National Prize for Poetry awarded by the Library of Congress.

In February 1995, while vacationing in Tucson, Merrill was admitted to the hospital for acute HIV-related pancreatitis. He died of cardiac arrest at the Arizona Health Sciences Center in Tucson. His ashes are interred in Stonington Cemetery, Stonington, Connecticut. *A Scattering of Salts,* his last book of poetry, was published a month following his death.

Revered by fellow poets and readers alike for his peerless mastery of an eclectic mix of poetic forms, his affinity for paradox and pun, his great tonal range, his urbanity and wit, few twentieth-century poets achieved a genuine metamorphosis of the autobiographical into art. Calling him "one of our indispensable poets" in 1972, the critic Helen Vendler noted that his lyric poems were "autobiographical without being 'confessional.'" But the zenith of his imaginative powers remains his eccentric magnum opus *The Changing Light at Sandover*, which the poet J. D. McClatchy names "with the possible exception of Whitman's 'Song of Myself' America's strangest and grandest poem."

★

Merrill's papers reside in the collection of the James M. Olin Library of Washington University in St. Louis, Missouri. The essential text on Merrill remains his memoir, *A Different Person* (1993). Stephen Yenser, *The Consuming Myth: The Work of James Merrill* (1987), is an exhaustive study of Merrill's art. David Kalstone, *Five Temperaments* (1977), is an intuitive and well-written analysis of the autobiographical impulse in Merrill's work and the work of four contemporaries. Two superb collections of essays on Merrill's work are Harold Bloom, ed., *James Merrill* (1985), and David Lehman and Charles Berger, eds., *James Merrill: Essays in Criticism* (1983). Interviews with Merrill are in *Paris Review* (Summer 1982), and *Saturday Review of the Arts* (2 Dec. 1972). Helen Vendler's review of *A Scattering of Salts* in the *New York Review of Books* (11 May 1995) is an excellent piece of scholarship. Among the numerous tributes to Merrill after his death, J. D.

McClatchy's piece for the *New Yorker* (27 Mar. 1995) is exceptional. Obituaries are in the *New York Times* (7 Feb. 1995) and *Time* (20 Feb. 1995).

WILLIAM STERLING WALKER

MINNESOTA FATS (Rudolph Walter Wanderone, Jr.)

(*b*. 19 January 1913? in Brooklyn Heights, New York; *d*. 18 January 1996 in Nashville, Tennessee), pool hustler who popularized the game in the 1960s.

Wanderone, called "Roodle" as a youngster by his adoring family, was the only son of four children born to Rudolph Walter Wanderone, Sr., a merchant seaman and later a plumbing and heating contractor, and Rosa Bergin Wanderone, a homemaker. Wanderone later revealed only scanty details of his early life, and much of what he did

Minnesota Fats, 1990. ASSOCIATED PRESS AP

reveal turned out to be mythical. Thus, there is not much of a factual historical record.

His birth date is an example of Wanderone's taking liberties with facts. The most universally agreed date is 1913, but at other times he gave 1914 and 1900 as the actual year. He called the variations "my baseball age," after a practice of professional athletes who took a year or more off their ages as they got older. He also claimed to have sailed around the world six times, surviving two shipwrecks.

Wanderone traced his early interest in pool to the fact that when he was two years old his uncle, in the absence of Wanderone's seafaring father, often took him to poolrooms and placed him on vacant tables. Said Wanderone, "A pool table was my crib." He also claimed to have pulled his first pool hustle when he was only six and "won a bag of gumdrops from a ten year old." He also said of his early childhood, "I've been eating like a sultan since I was two days old. I had a mother and three sisters who worshiped me, and they would plop me in a bed with a jillion satin pillows and spray me with exotic perfumes and lilac water and then they would shoot me the grapes."

Leaving school in the eighth grade, Wanderone made several trips to Europe with his father and claimed to have studied under a national champion pool player from Switzerland. In the 1920s there were hundreds of thousands of pool tables all across the nation, and 5,000 poolrooms in New York City alone. The game was primarily a "gentlemen's" form of recreation. There were bets made, to be sure, but these were friendly wagers to add interest to the competition. However, as the Great Depression descended upon the nation, a new type of competitor came on the scene—the hustler. Here was a player interested only in winning money, and almost any means of doing so was acceptable to the hustler. "Lemonading," or disguising one's true ability as a player, was one method; losing a match on purpose was another. So, too, was "sharking," the practice of distracting an opponent to break his concentration. Wanderone used all these at one time or another.

Wanderone, who weighed 300 pounds and stood five feet ten inches tall, soon came to be known as "New York Fats," "Brooklyn Fats," or "Broadway Fats." He immodestly proclaimed a dislike for "an honest day's work" and was quoted as saying he "never picked up anything heavier than a silver dollar." As he traveled much of the country in large Cadillacs that became his signature, his wife—a waitress named Evelyn Inez, whom he met in southern Illinois and married on 7 May 1941—was expected to do all the driving, handle the luggage, and even change flat tires. The less-than-courtly Wanderone said, "Change a tire? I'd rather change cars."

Speaking in the vernacular, as he often did, Wanderone said he "never lost a game when the 'cheese' [money] was

on the table." Evelyn verified this, saying, "Fatty tended to be just good enough to win." He told of a 1930s match in Chicago with the three-cushion billiards champ Arthur Thurnblad that began as a $100,000, fifty-point game. Heavy interest and heavy betting "jacked it up" (poolroom lingo for raising the bet) to $250,000. According to Wanderone, "Thurnblad didn't have a 'bean' [a dollar]," while Wanderone reached into his jacket pocket and spread 250 $1,000 bills on the table. Again according to Wanderone, he gained a large and early lead of 10 to 15 points and won the match, 50–32. "When it was over," he said, "I collected my money and went out to get something to eat. That's all there was to it." Pool folklore says that Wanderone always had between $200,000 and $300,000 in crisp bills in the trunk of his Cadillac.

Although unpolished in some ways, Wanderone reminded opponents to watch their language when Evelyn— he always called her "Eva-line"—accompanied him to poolrooms, which she often did. He was said to have been an easy touch when asked for a loan, seldom getting repaid. He also was a lover of animals, keeping at one time twenty-seven cats, fourteen dogs, and a groundhog. While making a good living, Wanderone lost a considerable amount due to his inability to stay away from the dice tables.

Wanderone's reputation was greatly enhanced after 1961, when the film version of Walter Tevis's novel *The Hustler* appeared. Playing opposite Paul Newman, Jackie Gleason portrayed the character "Minnesota Fats." Despite Gleason's dapper onscreen appearance—he played in a coat, tie, and vest, even sporting a boutonnière—the rumpled and disheveled Wanderone claimed that the character was based on him. To bolster his claim, he began billing himself as "Minnesota Fats."

Wanderone engaged in a celebrated public rivalry with the perennial billiards champion Willie Mosconi, who won thirteen national billiards championships between 1940 and 1956. Mosconi extended countless invitations to settle the issue of who was the better player in head-to-head competition. Fats never accepted but did continue to fan the flames of the feud. Finally in 1978, Fats and Mosconi were matched on an ABC-TV *Wide World of Sports* show, with Howard Cosell as emcee. Fats lost by a wide margin to the gentlemanly Mosconi.

The new "Minnesota Fats" persona led to Wanderone's first structured, full-time job, working for a billiard equipment company. Personal appearances and the accompanying travel created tensions at home, and he and Evelyn divorced in 1985. He moved from Dowell, Illinois, where he had lived for years, to Nashville, where he lived in a subsidized celebrity suite in the Hermitage Hotel. His days were spent feeding pigeons in a nearby park, his nights rubber-stamping his "autograph" in Music City honky-tonks.

Fear of being declared incompetent and institutionalized led him to marry twenty-seven-year-old Theresa Ward Bell, a nurse, in 1992. She, his only survivor, provided round-the-clock care until his death. He died of heart failure and is buried in Hermitage Gardens in Hermitage, Tennessee, a suburb of Nashville.

Whether or not he was the inspiration for the Gleason character in *The Hustler*, Wanderone remained the consummate pool hustler. His role in pool history is best described by the writer George Fels: "He was once a very good—but far from great—player. He was certainly a champion storyteller."

★

Wanderone's autobiography is *The Bank Shot and Other Great Robberies*, written with Tom Fox (1966). Fred Walther, *Minnesota Fats—Never Behind the Eight Ball* (1998), is an informative biography. George Fels, "Where the Boys Were," *Sports Heritage* (Mar./Apr. 1987) further discusses Wanderone and the pool scene of the 1930s. An obituary is in the *New York Times* (19 Jan. 1996).

JIM CAMPBELL

MITCHELL, Joseph Quincy (*b.* 27 July 1908 near Iona, North Carolina; *d.* 24 May 1996 in New York City), literary journalist who brought dignity and poetry to the lives of the eccentric and obscure people he wrote about.

Mitchell, one of three children of Averette Nance Mitchell, a cotton and tobacco farmer and trader, and Elizabeth

Joseph Mitchell, 1994. ASSOCIATED PRESS AP

Amanda Parker, a homemaker, grew up in Fairmont, a small town in southeastern North Carolina, and attended Fairmont High School. From 1925 to 1929 he studied at the University of North Carolina at Chapel Hill, where he developed an interest in literature and the goal of becoming a writer. In 1929 he submitted an article about tobacco to the *New York Herald Tribune,* which published it. Inspired, he left school and moved to New York City; he arrived four days before the stock market crash. He got a job as a reporter for the *New York World,* moved to the *New York Herald Tribune* in 1930, and landed at the *New York World-Telegram* in 1931. On 27 February 1931 he married Therese Dagny Engelsted Jacobsen, who died in 1980. They had two children.

Although he covered the Lindbergh kidnapping trial and other major stories, Mitchell's regular beat was human-interest features rather than hard news. He quickly became known for his ability to capture the rhythms of his subjects' speech, a gift recognized in the title of a 1938 collection of his articles, *My Ears Are Bent*. Reviewing the book in the *New Yorker,* Clifton Fadiman wrote, "I guess he must be about the best interviewer in the world, though on the surface it seems he does nothing but let people talk."

Mitchell, a gracious man who habitually dressed in dark Brooks Brothers suits, began contributing to the *New Yorker* in 1933, with an article about Elkton, Maryland, where more marriages were performed than in any other city in the country. He joined the weekly's staff in 1938 and embarked on a series of articles about (as Mitchell later described his subjects) "visionaries, obsessives, imposters, fanatics, lost souls, the-end-is-near street preachers, old Gypsy queens, and out-and-out freak-show freaks." Most of these early pieces were collected in the book *McSorley's Wonderful Saloon* (1943). The somewhat ironic title referred to Mitchell's article about a New York City barroom where, in winter, the elderly regulars "grab the chairs nearest the stove and sit in them, as motionless as barnacles, until around six, when they yawn, stretch, and start for the door, insulated with ale against the dreadful loneliness of the old and alone."

Along with his good friend A. J. Liebling and other *New Yorker* colleagues, Mitchell, an ardent admirer of James Joyce and other modernist writers, viewed journalism as a branch of literature, no less prone to artistry because it happened to be true. His articles displayed deftly drawn characters, a rich and subtle prose, and often a penetrating psychological symbolism. Reviewing one of his later books, the critic Stanley Edgar Hyman wrote that Mitchell "is a reporter only in the sense that Defoe is a reporter."

In 1944 Mitchell published a *New Yorker* profile of a ninety-three-year-old retired house-wrecking contractor named Hugh G. Flood, and followed it with two more articles. When the pieces were collected in *Old Mr. Flood*

(1948), Mitchell wrote in an author's note, "Mr. Flood is not one man; combined in him are aspects of several old men who work or hang out in Fulton Fish Market, or who did so in the past." Mr. Flood represented the only time Mitchell indulged in a "composite" character. Indeed, all his subsequent writing was strictly factual.

In the late 1940s and the 1950s, Mitchell's articles grew longer and more intricate, and tended to focus less on eccentric personalities than on the natural and man-made landscapes of New York City and its environs. (Long before the phrases gained currency, he was interested in and wrote about ecology and historic preservation.) These pieces were collected in *The Bottom of the Harbor* (1959).

As the shape of his writing changed, Mitchell took more and more time to produce each piece. He worked five years on "Joe Gould's Secret," a long profile that was published in the *New Yorker* in 1964 and as a book of the same title the following year. Gould, "an odd and penniless and unemployable little man who came to the city in 1916 and ducked and dodged and held on as hard as he could for over thirty-five years," had been one of Mitchell's profile subjects in the 1940s. He was a Greenwich Village eccentric whose fame was based on his claim that he had written the longest unpublished literary work in existence, a document he called "An Oral History of Our Time." Mitchell's earlier portrait essentially took Gould at face value, but as its title suggests, "Joe Gould's Secret" probed more deeply. In Mitchell's characteristically indirect way, it confronted such issues as the mutual dependency between authors and their subjects and the intricacies of self-deception.

More than two decades passed after "Joe Gould's Secret," and still Mitchell did not produce another piece of writing. Long gaps between his publications were now assumed and Mitchell, a courtly and reticent man, occasionally made vague references to ongoing projects, so it took his editors and readers a long time to realize that there would be no more articles. While Mitchell never publicly announced his retirement, he seemed to tacitly acknowledge it when he allowed the publication in 1992 of *Up in the Old Hotel*, a collection of virtually all his *New Yorker* pieces. (At that time all his previous books were out of print.) The book was a critical and commercial success, and served to introduce Mitchell's work to at least two generations of new and appreciative readers. His awards included the North Carolina medal for literature in 1984 and the Brendan Gill Prize of the Municipal Art Society in 1993.

Mitchell died of cancer at the age of eighty-seven in New York City. He was buried in the family plot in North Carolina.

While sometimes named as a forerunner to the New Journalism of the 1960s, Mitchell's work was too idiosyncratic, too self-effacing, and probably too subtle to be a direct influence on many. However, thanks to the continued availability and popularity of *Up in the Old Hotel,* he continues to provide an example of a writer who magnificently distilled the literature of fact.

★

There is no biography or full-length critical study of Mitchell. Information about him can be found in Norman Sims, ed., *Literary Journalism in the Twentieth Century* (1990); Thomas Kunkel, *Genius in Disguise: Harold Ross of the New Yorker* (1995); and Ben Yagoda, *About Town: The New Yorker and the World It Made* (2000). Mitchell gave interviews to all three authors. Illuminating articles include Noel Perrin, "Paragon of Reporters: Joseph Mitchell," *Sewanee Review* 91, no. 2 (1983): 167–184; William Zinsser, "Journeys with Joseph Mitchell," *American Scholar* 62, no. 1 (1993): 132–138; and Mark Singer, "Joe Mitchell's Secret," *New Yorker* (22 Feb. and 1 Mar. 1999). The *New Yorker* published a memorial to Mitchell (10 June 1996). An obituary is in the *New York Times* (25 May 1996).

BEN YAGODA

MITFORD, Jessica ("Decca") (*b.* 11 September 1917 in Batsford, Gloucestershire, England; *d.* 23 July 1996 in Oakland, California), prolific author and social and political commentator on American culture, best known for her work *The American Way of Death* (1963), a biting exposé of the funeral industry.

Mitford was the youngest of seven children born to Lord Redesdale (David Bertram Mitford) and Lady Redesdale (Sydney Bowles Mitford), a well-known and rather eccentric family in England. Her parents did not believe girls should be formally educated, so their one son was sent to school but their six daughters were schooled at home, albeit idiosyncratically. The Mitford's vast library had strikingly different effects on the sisters: Diana married Sir Oswald Mosley, a leader of Britain's Fascists; Unity became a disciple of Adolf Hitler; Nancy became a famous novelist, best known for her fictitious autobiographies, most notably *The Pursuit of Love;* and Jessica (known as "Decca") eventually joined the Communist Party. Although she was close with most of her siblings, Decca described her childhood as unhappy, to the point where she started saving her money in what she called her "running away" fund.

At the age of seventeen, Mitford did leave her family, running off with her leftist cousin Esmond Romilly, a nephew of Winston Churchill. In 1936 the pair eloped to Spain to support the front against fascism, then moved to London, where their first child, a girl, was born. At four months of age, the child succumbed to an outbreak of measles. The couple moved to New York in 1939. In 1941 Romilly, who had joined the Canadian Air Force, was killed

Jessica Mitford, 1979. Express Newspapers/985/Archive Photos

when his plane went down over the North Sea, leaving Mitford pregnant and alone.

Mitford moved to be with her friends Clifford and Virginia Durr in Washington, D.C., where she was raising her daughter Constancia and working for the Office of Price Administration as an investigator when she met Bob Treuhaft, a labor attorney. She and Treuhaft moved to San Francisco and were married in 1943. In 1944 Mitford became a U.S. citizen, and shortly thereafter the two joined the American Communist Party. Ever active, Mitford was a fund-raiser and educator within the party. She and Treuhaft relocated to Oakland, California, in 1947, and their son, Benjamin, was born. (They later had a second son, but he died at the age of eleven after being hit by a bus.) In 1949 Mitford began working for the Civil Rights Congress (CRC), determined to champion the rights of African Americans.

In 1951 the House Committee on Un-American Activities subpoenaed Mitford due to her "identified communist" status, and in 1953 both Mitford and Treuhaft were subpoenaed. The interrogations brought about the end of the CRC, so Mitford began working for the *San Francisco Chronicle* as a telephone solicitor. Her reputation as a communist dogged her, however, and she was fired. With no hopes of escaping her communist label, Mitford turned to writing.

Her first work, *Lifeitselfmanship* (1956), was a privately published, wittily constructed exposé of the Communist Party and its jargon. Mitford felt that the party was becoming disorganized, and she resigned in 1958, although she continued to espouse the party's basic tenets until she died. Her second literary effort, *Daughters and Rebels* (published as *Hons and Rebels* in England), appeared in 1960. This autobiographical book details her childhood and her marriage and travels with Romilly and humorously attacks the lifestyle of the English upper class.

Her third, and most famous, book, *The American Way of Death* (1963), was a best-seller for more than a year. Her first investigative study, it skillfully deconstructed the funeral industry, exposing price inflation, tactics that prey upon the poor, and the inhumane antics of funeral directors. The book enjoyed phenomenal success and was made into a CBS television documentary.

Her other books, although not as successful as *The American Way of Death,* attracted much attention and critical acclaim. *The Trial of Dr. Spock* (1969) analyzed the government's accusation of five defendants for their role as draft evaders and for denouncing the Selective Service Administration; *Kind and Unusual Punishment: The Prison Business* (1973) criticized the prison industry, finding fault with every aspect including parole, the treatment of inmates, and the brutality of officers; and *A Fine Old Conflict* (1977), her second autobiographical foray, detailed her communist days and early life with Treuhaft.

Poison Penmanship: The Gentle Art of Muckraking (1979) gathered together several of Mitford's articles. Of particular interest is one story chronicling Mitford's semester of teaching at San Jose State University as a distinguished professor of sociology in 1973. The university attempted to extract a loyalty oath, demanded her fingerprints, and requested that the word "muckraking" be deleted from her syllabus. She refused, ultimately teaching without pay and taking the university to court. Mitford then turned to memoir, producing *Faces of Philip: A Memoir of Philip Toynbee* (1984) and *Grace Had an English Heart* (1989), but eventually returned to her love, investigative journalism, with *The American Way of Birth* (1992). She also wrote articles for several publications including *Esquire,* the *San Francisco Chronicle, Life,* and the *Nation.*

Mitford died of lung cancer in Oakland. True to form, she left detailed instructions requesting a highly elaborate, expensive funeral. She was cremated. At the time of her death, Mitford was preparing a revision of *The American Way of Death;* it came out posthumously in 1998.

Jessica Mitford was a highly spirited, intelligent person dedicated to exposing hypocrisy and championing the causes of the underdog. Her interests ranged from birth to death, but all were based upon one tenet—her passion for social justice. Mitford was fond of remarking, "You may not be able to change the world, but at least you can embarrass the guilty," a lesson she attempted to teach all of her readers with each work she constructed.

★

Most of Mitford's manuscripts and personal papers are stored at the Harry Ransom Humanities Research Center at the University of Texas at Austin; some are housed at Ohio State University. Her first autobiography, *Daughters and Rebels* (1960), traces the years 1917 until 1941, and her second one, *A Fine Old Conflict* (1977) traces her years in the Communist Party. Jessica Benedict wrote *Portraits in Print: A Collection of Profiles and the Stories Behind Them* (1991), interviews of many well-known authors, including Mitford, with a commentary by each author. Mitford's nephew Jonathan Guinness and his daughter, Catherine, wrote *The House of Mitford: Portrait of a Family* (1984), a tome chronicling the Mitford heritage and offering in-depth coverage of the sisters' lives. An obituary appears in the *New York Times* (24 July 1996).

SHARON L. DECKER

MOLNAR, Charles Edwin (*b.* 14 March 1935 in Newark, New Jersey; *d.* 13 December 1996 in Sunnyvale, California), computer scientist who codesigned the machine considered the world's first personal computer.

Molnar was the only child of Louis Molnar, who was born in Nógrádszakal, Hungary, and Mildred Knelly, a native of New Jersey. His father worked in a mattress factory, and his mother was a secretary. His interests included music, furniture building, hiking, and canoeing. After graduating from Perth Amboy High School in 1952, Molnar entered Rutgers University in New Brunswick, New Jersey, and received a B.S. degree in 1956 and an M.S. degree in 1957. Both degrees were in electrical engineering. He married Donna Addicott on 31 August 1957. They had two sons. Molnar earned a doctorate in electrical engineering from the Massachusetts Institute of Technology (MIT) in Cambridge, Massachusetts, in 1965. His dissertation concerned the mechanics of the inner ear and how it translates auditory signals into neural responses.

From 1957 to 1961 Molnar was a staff associate with the Lincoln Laboratory at MIT. He was in the U.S. Air Force from 1961 to 1964 and assigned as a lieutenant to Hanscom Field in Lexington, Massachusetts, which was adjacent to the laboratory. Although assigned to Hanscom, he was allowed to work at the lab because the air force was interested in his research. In 1962 he worked with a team of designers led by Wesley A. Clark in developing the Laboratory Instrument Computer (LINC). The LINC, which Molnar used in his dissertation work, featured a keyboard with an alphanumeric-graphical display unit for interactive uses and a block-addressed tape unit—which operated like the later diskette units—with pocket-sized reels that captured both data, in either digital or analog form, and programs prepared on-line by the user. The machine, one of the few unclassified projects at the laboratory in the early l960s, had a basic operating system with a small display, and the programs were stored on a magnetic tape. Doctors and medical researchers were expected to use the self-contained machine, which was relatively small and inexpensive for its day and was specifically designed for individual use. The Institute of Electrical and Electronics Engineers (IEEE) Computer Society acknowledged it as the first personal computer.

The LINC was of insignificant power compared to later personal computers, and at the time many scientists believed in time-sharing computers. The LINC project received a grant from the National Institutes of Health, and Molnar's group placed twenty machines, early prototypes of the computer, in various biomedical research laboratories. In 1965 the Digital Equipment Corporation introduced the computer commercially.

Molnar and Clark obtained a patent in August 1972 for using cable television lines to send data and computer programs from central computers to less expensive bedside terminals in intensive care units. Under the direction of Molnar and Clark, Macromodules, a set of computer building blocks, were designed and fabricated. The primary goal was to simplify the task of building computer systems. Designing a computer system consisted of drawing a flow chart, then plugging modules into a structure that supplied power, cooling, and most connections, and finally connecting cables in one-to-one correspondence with the flow chart. Unlike most computer systems, macromodular systems operated without fixed timing. Molnar went on to develop radical improvements in the theory and practice of such asynchronous systems design. Eventually, computer systems were developed from these modules for use in molecular graphics, drug design, and detection of cardiac arrhythmias from electrocardiograms.

In 1965 Molnar became an associate professor of physiology and biophysics at Washington University in St. Louis, where he stayed for thirty years. He collaborated with Russell R. Pfeiffer in 1966 to establish the Sensory Biophysics Laboratory in the physiology department of the university. They investigated the functioning of the cochlea, the sensory organ of hearing. Molnar became an associate professor of electrical engineering in 1967 and was an associate director of the Computer Systems Laboratory from 1967 to 1972. He became a professor of physics and electrical engineering in 1971 and the director of the Computer Systems Laboratory in 1972.

In 1983 Molnar established the Institute for Biomedical Computing, which increased interest in biomedical computing within the Schools of Engineering and Medicine, and he became the institute's director. His efforts to bridge the cultural gap between the schools were successful because of his fundamental research, ranging from computer design to auditory physiology, which drew on his previous dissertation work. He remained the institute's director until 1992.

Molnar was a member of the Board of Regents of the National Library of Medicine from 1980 to 1984. He and Clark received the 1983 Director's Award from the National Institutes of Health for their work on the LINC. Molnar also received the 1985 Jacob Javits Distinguished Neuroscience Investigator Award from the National Institutes of Health. An award for the best paper bridging theory and practice was named after Molnar at the Async 97, the third international symposium on advanced research in asynchronous circuits and systems, held in Eindhoven, the Netherlands. Molnar was also a visiting professor at the University of Chile, the California Institute of Technology, the University of North Carolina at Chapel Hill, Eindhoven University of Technology, and the University of Waterloo in Belgium, making extended visits to each institution.

In 1995 Molnar left Washington University to become a senior research fellow and director of the Science Office at Sun Microsystems in Mountain View, California, where he had been consulting since 1990. The LINC was retired in 1996.

Molnar was a charismatic individual, six feet one inch tall with dark hair that grayed early. He died at the age of sixty-one of complications from diabetes and high blood pressure. According to his wishes, his body was donated to science at the San Francisco Medical Center.

Molnar had a worldwide reputation as a pioneer in self-timed computer system theory, a design approach for ultra-fast computers. He was a curious researcher, and his discoveries helped usher in the computer age.

★

For further information on Molnar, see J. A. N. Lee's article in *IEEE Annals of the History of Computing* 21, no. 3 (1999): 67–69, and Tom Verhoeff, ed., *Encyclopedia of Delay-Insensitive Systems* (1995–1998). An obituary is in the *New York Times* (16 Dec. 1996).

MARTIN JAY STAHL

MONETTE, Paul Landry   (*b.* 16 October 1945 in Lawrence, Massachusetts; *d.* 10 February 1995 in West Hollywood, California), autobiographer, poet, and novelist who wrote two influential works on modern American gay life.

Monette, the son of Paul Monette, a truck driver and dispatcher for a coal company, and Jackie Monette, began his memoir *Becoming a Man: Half a Life Story* (1992) with his unhappy childhood in Andover, Massachusetts, fifteen

Paul Monette, after winning a National Book Award for *Becoming a Man: Half a Life Story*, 1992. ASSOCIATED PRESS AP

miles north of Boston. He felt "invisible," not only because he struggled with his homosexuality, of which he became aware at an early age, but also because his parents focused their attention on his younger brother, Robert, who was born unable to walk.

Despite his unhappiness, Monette's wit and charm made him popular at school. He won scholarships to the Phillips Academy in Andover, from which he graduated in 1963, and to Yale University, where he majored in English and started writing poetry. The summer before his senior year in college Monette went to Cambridge University in England on a fellowship and then traveled in Europe. During that summer he wrote his first novel, "The Beautiful Brick Day," which was not published. Monette maintained a high profile at Yale, but he felt emotionally isolated, experiencing what he described as an "extended nervous breakdown." Although he found refuge in writing poetry, Monette wrote in *Becoming a Man*, "I would have gladly given up being a writer if I could've been queer out loud."

After receiving a B.A. degree in 1967, Monette stayed at Yale for another year on a Carnegie Teaching Fellowship.

For the next two years he taught eleventh grade at Cheshire Academy in central Connecticut, leaving after a sexual relationship with a male student became a near scandal. From 1970 to 1976 Monette lived in Boston and taught at Milton Academy and Pine Manor College. His sexual conflict reached its height in the early 1970s, when he dated several women and underwent therapy, neither of which eased his torment. He finally accepted his homosexuality in 1974, when he met and fell in love with Roger Horwitz, a Harvard-educated attorney who also had a Ph.D. in comparative literature.

Monette's poetry collection *The Carpenter at the Asylum* was published in 1975, and he stopped teaching in 1976 to write a novel. Two years later, in 1978, *Taking Care of Mrs. Carroll,* the first of Monette's six published novels, appeared. The novel's explicit gay themes forced him to come out to his parents. In 1977 Monette and Horwitz moved to Los Angeles, where Monette embarked on a full-time writing career. None of his screenplays was produced, but he published novelizations of hit movies, including *Scarface* (1983).

Monette and Horwitz spent some ten good years together, surviving a "ruinous affair" Monette had with another man in 1981. Horwitz was diagnosed with AIDS in March 1985. *Borrowed Time: An AIDS Memoir* (1988) chronicles Horwitz's diagnosis through his death from cryptococcal meningitis in October 1986. There were occasional moments of hope. On the "front lines" of the AIDS battle, Horwitz was among the first to try every new drug rumored to be promising. These twenty months, however, were marked mainly by his deteriorating health and repeated hospitalizations, a battery of drugs and intravenous injections, an eye infection that left him nearly blind, and the deaths from AIDS of numerous friends and acquaintances.

Unsparingly documenting Monette's personal tragedy, *Borrowed Time* humanizes the fear, anger, love, sorrow, and enormous loss of the AIDS epidemic. Nominated in 1989 for the National Book Critics Circle Award for biography, the memoir joins Randy Shilts's reportage *And the Band Played On* (1987) as one of the most important and widely read books about the epidemic. Monette also memorialized Horwitz in a volume of poetry, *Love Alone: 18 Elegies for Rog* (1988). This volume and much of his other poetry are collected in *West of Yesterday, East of Summer* (1994). AIDS also transformed Monette's fiction. His earlier novels are lighter genre exercises with gay protagonists, the comic *Taking Care of Mrs. Carroll* and the 1982 mystery *Lightfall,* for example. His later novels, *Afterlife* (1990) and *Halfway Home* (1991), are more serious political considerations of how AIDS altered gay men's lives.

In contrast to the invisibility he felt in his youth, Monette was one of the most visible spokespersons in the fight against AIDS, even as his own health began to fail from the disease in the early 1990s. In his writings, speeches, and television and radio appearances, he expressed anger and frustration at the indifference of the government and the media and the generally slow response to the health crisis. Raised an Episcopalian, Monette became an atheist and a vocal critic of organized religion, especially of the Vatican. He often spoke in favor of the radical AIDS protest movement.

In 1993 *Becoming a Man* won the National Book Award for nonfiction. In a tribute to Monette in the *Los Angeles Times* on 19 February 1995, Robert Dawidoff called *Becoming a Man* "the ultimate coming-out story, that genre so central to gay and lesbian literature." Monette wanted to be identified as a gay writer. He once told a reporter: "You have to understand that I spent twenty years being turned down because my work was considered 'too gay.' Which I came to regard as a compliment, and proof I was on the right track" (*Last Watch of the Night,* 1994). In addition to novels, autobiographies, and poetry, Monette's prolific output included a play, *Just the Summers* (unproduced and unpublished), and a fable, *Sanctuary: A Tale of Life in the Woods,* published posthumously in 1997.

After losing another companion, a Hollywood casting agent named Stephen F. Kolzak, in 1990, Monette developed a relationship with Winston Wilde, a general contractor. Monette died of AIDS complications in 1995. He is buried at Forest Lawn in Los Angeles, next to Horwitz.

Monette's two memoirs are testimonials to the major themes of the modern gay American experience, coming out and AIDS. His mission, he told an audience at the State University of New York at Oswego when he received an honorary degree in 1992, was "to serve witness to the calamity that has befallen my brothers."

★

Monette's papers are at the Department of Special Collections at the University of California, Los Angeles, Library. Monette's two memoirs and *Last Watch of the Night: Essays Too Personal and Otherwise* (1994) give the most complete biographical details of the writer's life, although for privacy Monette changed certain names in these books. Obituaries are in the *Los Angeles Times* and *New York Times* (both 12 Feb. 1995). A 1997 documentary written and directed by Monte Bramer, *Paul Monette: The Brink of Summer's End,* includes footage of Monette's last years.

JEFFREY H. CHEN

MONROE, William Smith ("Bill") (*b.* 13 September 1911 in Rosine, Kentucky; *d.* 9 September 1996 in Springfield, Tennessee), the "father of bluegrass music," whose distinctive mandolin playing, high-pitched tenor voice, and songwriting skills made him a driving force in country music.

Monroe was the youngest of eight children. His father, James Buchanan "Buck" Monroe, was a step dancer as well as a farmer, and his mother, Malissa Vandiver, played the fiddle, accordion, and harmonica and sang songs and ballads. Bill's brothers Harry and Birch played fiddle, while another brother, Charlie, and a sister, Bertha, were guitarists. Monroe began playing mandolin when he was nine years old. As a youth he was cross-eyed, and at age eleven he dropped out of school partially because of his poor eyesight. Both parents died at about this time, and Monroe moved in with his fiddle-playing uncle, Pendleton Vandiver. He began accompanying his Uncle Pen at local dances, playing the guitar. Another early influence was a local black musician, Arthur Schultz, who played blues guitar.

After their parents' deaths, Monroe's elder brothers moved north in search of work. Birch and Charlie ended up working in an oil refinery in East Chicago, Indiana. When he was eighteen years old, Bill decided to join them there. They worked at the refinery by day while playing musical jobs at night and on weekends. However, it was their dancing skills that first got them a full-time job. All three brothers were talented "buck" dancers, performing in the traditional flat-foot clogging style. They were hired in 1932 by the Chicago radio station WLS, sponsors of the *National Barn Dance* show (the major competitor to Nashville's *Grand Ole Opry*), to tour with the radio show's road company as dancers. Local radio work as musicians followed, and then, in 1934, an offer came from the patent medicine makers Texas Crystals to tour in support of their product, a natural laxative. Birch retired at this point, preferring the regular refinery work to life on the road. On 18 October 1935 Monroe married Carolyn Brown; they had two children and divorced on 2 August 1960.

Now called the Monroe Brothers, Charlie and Bill began working at a series of radio stations. In 1936 they made their first recordings for Bluebird, the budget division of RCA, and also signed up with the *Crazy Barn Dance,* a radio show out of Charlotte, North Carolina, sponsored by the archrival of Texas Crystals, Crazy Water Crystals. The brothers' recordings were popular, thanks to Charlie's relaxed, warm vocals and Bill's lightning-fast mandolin playing and high-tenor harmonies. They recorded about sixty songs for Bluebird before 1938, when they split up. Charlie then formed his own band, the Kentucky Pardners, and Bill went out on his own.

After briefly working in Little Rock, Arkansas, and Atlanta, Monroe got his big break in 1939 when he was invited to sing on the *Grand Ole Opry*. Monroe's backup band, first known as the Kentuckians, now became the Blue Grass (later Bluegrass) Boys (after Kentucky's motto, the "bluegrass state"). The first song he sang on the *Opry* was his version of Jimmie Rodgers's classic "Mule Skinner

Blues"; the audience and the announcer, George D. Hay, were bowled over. Monroe remained a "member" of the radio show for the rest of his life.

Monroe participated in several *Opry* road tours in the early 1940s and continued to record. The war led to a break in recording and some disruptions in the personnel of Monroe's bands, but he managed to stay on the road. He also played a role in promoting amateur baseball, often hiring musicians for their sports abilities as much as musical ones. The band would arrive in a town and challenge a local team to a contest on the baseball diamond, then entertain the crowd between innings and after the game. Monroe profited from the fees he collected as both a baseball manager and a musician. From the 1940s to the early 1960s, Monroe had a long-running relationship with Bessie Lee Maudlin, who played bass in his band. He married Della Scivers Streeter on 24 April 1985, but the marriage only lasted until 21 November 1988. Streeter, the daughter of a man who booked dates for him in Florida, was considerably younger than Monroe.

In 1945 Monroe put together the classic form of his Blue Grass Boys. The guitarist Lester Flatt and the banjo player Earl Scruggs (later famous as Flatt and Scruggs), along with the fiddler Chubby Wise and the bass player Howard Watts (known by his stage name of Cedric Rainwater), joined Monroe in a five-piece ensemble that became the model for all bluegrass bands to follow. Monroe's instrumental virtuosity met its match in the playing of Earl Scruggs, who pioneered what came to be known as bluegrass banjo picking, or three-finger style. Monroe signed with Columbia Records, and beginning in 1946 the band enjoyed several country hits, including "Kentucky Waltz" (which reached number 3), the classic "Footprints in the Snow" (number 5), and Monroe's most famous song, "Blue Moon of Kentucky." The piece was originally recorded in waltz time, but Elvis Presley made it famous as a rollicking piece of country boogie when he recorded it in 1954 and performed it on the *Grand Ole Opry* in his sole appearance there. Monroe approved of Elvis's version and thereafter introduced the song in waltz time and ended it in Elvis's souped-up manner.

The late 1940s was a period of change for Monroe. Flatt and Scruggs left in 1948 to form their own group, modeled closely after Monroe's band. He was so angry that he refused to speak to them for decades afterward, although eventually they reconciled. Annoyed when Columbia signed a similar-sounding group, the Stanley Brothers, to their roster, Monroe left the label in 1950, signing with Decca Records, where he remained for the balance of his career. The singer and guitarist Jimmie Martin joined the band about this time, and through the 1950s Monroe nurtured the careers of several future bluegrass talents, including Martin, Sonny Osborne, Vassar Clements, and Kenny

Baker. In 1951 Monroe bought some land in rural Indiana near Bean Blossom, developed it as a recreational area, and held annual bluegrass festivals there beginning in 1967. In 1953 he was seriously injured in an automobile accident and had to stop performing for a time. After his recovery Monroe worked steadily through the 1950s, both on the *Opry* and on the road. He scored his last Top 30 country-chart hits with the lively instrumental "Scotland" (1958) and the vocal "Gotta Travel On" (1959).

The folk-music revival of the late 1950s and early 1960s gave a boost to Monroe's career. The mandolinist Ralph Rinzler, who played with a folk-revival bluegrass group called the Greenbriar Boys, convinced Monroe to allow him to be his manager. Rinzler arranged for Monroe to play at urban folk festivals, beginning with a festival held in 1963 in Chicago. He also arranged for Monroe's 1950s-era recordings (many issued only on 45s) to be reissued on LP albums. Younger musicians, including the banjo player Bill Keith and guitarist Peter Rowan, joined Monroe's band during this period. In 1969 Monroe recorded a classic album in honor of his Uncle Pen. Featuring the fiddle tunes he had learned as a youth, it was perhaps the best work of his later career.

Numerous honors came to Monroe in the last decades of his life. In 1969 he was made an honorary Kentucky colonel for his contributions to his home state's culture. He was inducted into the Country Music Hall of Fame a year later and elected to the Nashville Songwriters Association International Hall of Fame in 1971. In 1982 he received a National Heritage Fellowship and in 1989 won the first Grammy awarded for bluegrass music. In 1985 he made a cameo appearance in the music video for Ricky Skaggs's hit "Country Boy," flat-foot clogging on a New York City subway train. In 1995 he was awarded the National Medal of Arts.

Monroe continued to perform and tour despite failing health. In 1980 he successfully battled cancer, and in 1991 he had a double coronary-bypass operation. After suffering a stroke in spring 1996, however, he was placed in a hospice, where he died the following September. Monroe is buried in Rosine, Kentucky.

Monroe virtually created bluegrass music. His bands from 1946 onward defined its instrumentation, repertoire, and overall sound. Moreover, he wrote many of the songs that have become bluegrass classics, from "Blue Moon of Kentucky" to such classic instrumentals as "Rawhide," "Scotland," and "Wheel Hoss." Steadfast in his convictions, he refused to record with slick strings or fancy vocal accompaniments. Despite changing styles in country music, he remained a popular and admired entertainer until his death.

★

A full biography is Richard D. Smith, *Can't You Hear Me Callin': The Life of Bill Monroe, Father of Bluegrass* (2000). Jim Rooney's *Bossmen* (1971) features a large section on Monroe, mostly based on firsthand interviews. One chapter of *The Stars of Country Music* (1975), edited by Bill C. Malone and Judith McCullogh, is devoted to Monroe. Neil V. Rosenberg compiled a discography of Monroe for the Country Music Foundation in 1974. Ralph Rinzler conducted an extensive interview that was published as "Bill Monroe: The Daddy of Blue Grass Music" in *Sing Out!* 13, no. 1 (1963), which helped introduce him to a new audience. Bear Family Records of Germany has issued Monroe's complete recordings from 1950 to 1980 in three large boxed sets, including some documentation of his life and career. An obituary is in the *New York Times* (10 Sept. 1996).

RICHARD CARLIN

MONTGOMERY, Elizabeth (*b.* 15 April 1933 in Los Angeles, California; *d.* 18 May 1995 in Los Angeles, California), versatile television actress best known as Samantha, the supernatural housewife on *Bewitched* (1964–1972), as well as for a wide range of made-for-television movies.

Montgomery was one of two children born to cinematic leading man Robert Montgomery and his first wife, actress Elizabeth Bryan-Allan. She grew up in a privileged environment, graduating from the Spence School in New York City in 1951. She attended the American Academy of Dramatic Arts from 1951 to 1953 but acted while studying,

Elizabeth Montgomery, posing for the television show *Bewitched*, 1964. ASSOCIATED PRESS AP

making her television debut in the drama "Top Secret" from her father's anthology program, *Robert Montgomery Presents,* in December 1951.

Montgomery's famous father showed no enthusiasm about her following in his footsteps. "It wasn't that he never gave me any encouragement," she later said. "It's that he was entirely unsuccessful in trying to discourage me. . . . He was my most severe critic, but also a true friend."

In October 1953 the young actress opened on Broadway in *Late Love,* for which she was voted the most promising newcomer of the 1953–1954 season by *Theater World.* She seldom returned to the stage, however, concentrating instead on television. One source lists her as appearing in some 250 programs in the 1950s and 1960s, including two seasons in the summer repertory company of *Robert Montgomery Presents* and an Emmy-nominated guest appearance as a gangster's moll on *The Untouchables* in 1960. She also made a few films, appearing in *The Court Martial of Billy Mitchell* (1955), *Johnny Cool* (1963), *Who's Been Sleeping in My Bed?* (1963), and *How to Stuff a Wild Bikini* (1965).

In 1954 Montgomery married Frederick Gallatin Cammann, characterized by one writer as a "blue-blooded New Yorker." They were divorced in 1955. In 1957 she married actor Gig Young, with whom she appeared in a 1961 television version of *The Spiral Staircase.* She divorced Young in 1963 to wed film and television director William Asher.

Asher told Herbie J. Pilato, author of *Bewitched Forever,* that his bride did not want to work after marriage: she feared the separation that film work entailed, and the pair hoped to have children. (They had three: William, Jr., in 1964, Robert in 1965, and Rebecca Elizabeth in 1969.) He suggested that they collaborate on a television series, and the result was *Bewitched,* for which he served as principal director and producer.

The show ran from 1964 to 1972 and became one of the most enduring comedies of American television by playing both on the theme of conflicts between spouses with different backgrounds (à la *I Love Lucy*) and on the science-fiction/supernatural motif so popular at that time (*The Munsters, My Favorite Martian*). Its protagonist, witch Samantha Stephens, dwells uneasily in suburban Connecticut with her mortal advertising-executive husband, Darrin (Dick York, replaced in 1969 by Dick Sargent), who wishes to rule the domestic roost. In order to maintain marital harmony, Samantha vows not to use her supernatural powers. Her vow is foiled again and again, however. Sometimes the cause of disruption is one of her witch relatives, most often her mother Endora, played with panache by Agnes Moorehead. Sometimes Samantha uses witchcraft to help Darrin's career. She is usually penitent about breaking the rules, and the couple reconciles at the episode's end.

Later critics interpreted Samantha's dilemma in a feminist light, seeing the repression of her magical powers as emblematic of the submission of the average American housewife. In general, contemporary critics did not stress this angle, though Isaac Asimov did suggest in a humorous 1969 *TV Guide* article that Darrin's obvious fear of Samantha's powers did not bode well for American husbands.

In 1972, after selling well in syndication and making money for the Ashers, who owned a percentage of the profits for the program as well as those for related merchandise, *Bewitched* filmed its final episode. Montgomery went on to concentrate on made-for-television movies.

She spent the rest of her career making such films, including *A Case of Rape* (1974), *The Legend of Lizzie Borden* (1975), *The Awakening Land* (1978), *The Black Widow Murders* (1993), and *The Corpse Had a Familiar Face* (1994). She played seductresses, victims, killers, journalists, and pioneer women. Unafraid to take chances, Montgomery was proud of her groundbreaking role in *A Killing Affair* (1977), in which she played a white detective who falls in love with her married African-American partner.

In 1974 Montgomery divorced Asher, beginning a long-term romantic relationship with actor Robert Foxworth, an occasional costar. The two married in 1993. Her final television movie, *Deadline for Murder,* was broadcast a week before her death from colon cancer. Her family disposed of her remains privately.

Montgomery charmed fans with her deft hand at comedy in *Bewitched*; nevertheless, she was proudest of the later work she brought to the small screen. "I'm not trying to put *Bewitched* down," she said in the 1980s. "It's just that I've reached another plateau in the type of work I want to do. It's like a man working all his life as a gardener and suddenly waking up to the fact that he wants to be a landscape architect. I want to act—believe me—because that's what I do best."

In a 1996 memorial piece in the *Advocate,* Bruce Vilanch explained, "As the traditional women's audience abandoned [movie] theaters for the most part, the guys running the networks noticed that that very audience was watching a lot of TV. A versatile TV star like [Montgomery] could play the full range of roles once available to studio actors such as Susan Hayward and Joan Fontaine if she was willing to do them on TV. And so she did. She was the first."

★

Profiles of Montgomery include Herbie J. Pilato, *Bewitched Forever* (1996). See also Tim Brooks, *Complete Directory of Prime Time TV Stars* (1987), and Ronald L. Smith, *Sweethearts of '60s TV* (1989). Other profiles include Alvin J. Marill, "The Television Scene," *Films in Review* (Feb. 1981), and Bruce Vilanch, "Magic Moments," the *Advocate* (25 June 1996). Asimov's article, "Husbands, Beware!," ran in *TV Guide* (22 Mar. 1969). An obituary is in the *New York Times* (19 May 1995).

TINKY "DAKOTA" WEISBLAT

MORGAN, Henry (*b.* 31 March 1915 in New York City; *d.* 19 May 1994 in New York City), radio announcer and wit who became a popular panelist on television game shows.

Morgan was born Henry Lerner von Ost, Jr., the son of the German Jewish Henry von Ost (né Henry Ost), vice president of a New York bank, and Eva Lerner, a homemaker. He had a younger brother and was a first cousin of the songwriter Alan Jay Lerner. His parents divorced when he was fourteen.

Morgan attended elementary school at New York's P.S. 169, then the High School of Commerce. For his last two years of high school, his mother sent him to Harrisburg Academy in Harrisburg, Pennsylvania. Upon his graduation in 1931, he went to work as a page at radio station WMCA in New York. After two years, he was given an announcing job, but shortly thereafter he was fired for insubordination, a theme that would recur in his career.

In the 1930s he moved around the country, working for radio stations. In 1933 he was let go by WCAU in Philadelphia, Pennsylvania, for including the name of the radio station's owner in a missing persons story. From there, he went to Duluth, Minnesota, where he was chief announcer, program director, and host of a WEBC show called *Strictly Masculine,* and then to Boston, Massachusetts, and *House*

Henry Morgan, 1963. © BETTMANN/CORBIS

Party on WNAC. While working there, Morgan took courses at Suffolk Law School. One day in 1940 he insisted that be excused from work to take a law exam. He was fired instead.

He returned to New York City, where he became a staff announcer with WOR. He was soon given his own Saturday morning show, *Meet Mr. Morgan.* In 1942 the show was renamed *Here's Morgan* and moved to the evenings, first three times a week, then six. In these jobs he honed his trademark approach of mocking his show's sponsors. Of a namesake candy bar, he said, "Oh! Henry is a meal in itself. But if you eat three meals of Oh! Henrys a day, your teeth will fall out."

Morgan's broadcasting career was interrupted by World War II. He enlisted in the Army Air Corps in 1942, underwent flight training, and was discharged in the fall of 1945. He returned to civilian life and switched radio stations, to WABC, in 1946. On 17 August of that year he married the actress Isobel Gibbs. The marriage soon ended in divorce.

In 1946–1947, *Here's Morgan* was a weekly half-hour show, sponsored by the Eversharp Company, a manufacturer of razor blades. On one show, he asked parents to leave the room and then encouraged the children in the audience to run away from home and become smugglers. At the end of 1946 Morgan was named "Most Promising Star of Tomorrow" by *Motion Picture Daily* and "Outstanding Radio Star of the Year" in *Billboard*'s poll of radio editors. But Eversharp tired of his remarks and fired him in December 1947.

Morgan was also a popular actor in summer stock, in such plays as *The Man Who Came to Dinner* and *The Teahouse of the August Moon.* In 1948 he starred in his first movie, *So This Is New York.* In 1952, however, Morgan was named in "Red Channels," a list of supposedly communist or procommunist performers, and he soon was all but unemployable. Morgan insisted that he was apolitical and that if he had appeared at any communist-front rallies, it was only because he thought they were good causes. (In his book *Here's Morgan,* he mentions that his first wife was friendly toward some communist or communist-front organizations.) Eventually, he was cleared, and in the late 1950s he began appearing as a guest panelist on the game show *What's My Line.*

In 1963 he stepped into the role he is best known for, as a panelist on *I've Got a Secret,* a game show in which celebrity panelists questioned guests in an attempt to guess their "secrets." He remained with the show for fourteen years, also finding time to appear in summer stock and do voice-overs for commercials. In 1969 he played a supporting role in the television comedy series *My World, and Welcome to It,* a critical success that did not last long. On 31 March

1978 he married Karen Sorenson, and they remained married until his death.

In his later years, Morgan was ill and out of the public eye. Having smoked three packs of cigarettes a day for most of his life, Morgan stopped making cigarette commercials in 1969 and began imploring others to give up smoking, while admitting that he could not. Suffering from heart trouble and lung cancer, he wrote an obituary for himself, ascribing his demise to, among other things, 3,000 quarts of beer, 7,000 quarts of liquor, and 1,296,000 cigarettes. He died of lung cancer at his home in New York City, survived by his wife and by Steve Robinson, a son from another liaison.

Morgan's greatest contribution was his insouciant and irreverent wit. Proudly basing his approach on that of his friends Robert Benchley and Fred Allen, he was given to remarks like, "There came the time, as it must in every organization, for the man with the money to fire the man with the idea." Since Morgan, there has been a school of advertising that uses frankness and self-mockery to sell its products, an approach almost unknown before him, although, unlike him, others have rarely given the impression that they might actually mean the mockery.

★

Morgan told his own story in *Here's Morgan,* published shortly after his death in 1994. The book is a rambling account, filled with nostalgia for the New York of his childhood, irritable complaints about the general decline of the world around him, and the settling of old scores, particularly with his first wife. It also contains much of the wit for which he gained his reputation. An obituary is in the *New York Times* (20 May 1994).

ARTHUR D. HLAVATY

MORISON, Elting Elmore (*b.* 14 December 1909 in Milwaukee, Wisconsin; *d.* 20 April 1995 in Peterborough, New Hampshire), educator and historian who believed "that science, technology, and a liberal education were indivisible."

Morison was one of three sons of George Abbot Morison, who rose to the position of vice president of the Bucyrus Erie Company, and Amelia Huntley Elmore. Morison attended Loomis School in Connecticut, graduating in 1928. Continuing his education at Harvard University, he earned an A.B. degree in 1933 and an M.A. degree in 1937. He taught at St. Mark's School and at the Wooster School before accepting a position as an assistant dean at Harvard that he held from 1935 to 1937. He married Anne Hitchcock Sims in June 1935. They had three children.

Between 1937 and 1941 Morison lived at a family home in Peterborough, New Hampshire, where he wrote his first book, *Admiral Sims and the Modern American Navy*. The book was published in 1942, a few months after the Japanese attack on Pearl Harbor, and Morison knew his subject well. His wife was the admiral's youngest daughter. This book won the American Historical Association's John H. Dunning Prize as the outstanding book of that year. Morison served in the navy reserve from 1942 to 1946, leaving with the rank of lieutenant commander.

In 1946 Morison began his affiliation with the Massachusetts Institute of Technology (MIT) as an assistant professor of English in the Department of Humanities. Promoted to associate professor in 1949, in 1953 he was appointed the professor of industrial history in the Sloan School of Management and director of a program designed to analyze technological change, including the history of science, technology, and industrial development. At MIT, which Morison described as a "large, fascinating imaginative, energetic institution, not like any other," he established his place in the history of technology. In 1948 he became director of the Theodore Roosevelt Research Project and edited the eight-volume *The Letters of Theodore Roosevelt* (1958). In 1960 Morison published the book he liked most, *Turmoil and Tradition: A Study of the Life and Times of Henry L. Stimson,* which won the Frances Parkman Prize of the Society of American Historians.

During the 1960s, in addition to performing his writing and academic duties, he served as a consultant and chairman of the social science committee for Educational Services, Inc. In that position he helped redesign social studies curricula for primary and secondary schools. In 1962 he was elected vice president of the Edward MacDowell Association, the parent organization of the MacDowell Colony in Peterborough, New Hampshire. He also served as a consultant to the Houghton Mifflin Publishing Company and to the Research and Development Board of the U.S. Department of Defense. In 1966 he was elected to the Board of Trustees of Hampshire College. In 1969 Morison was a member of the Pounds Review Panel on special laboratories at MIT and served as chairman of the New Hampshire state committee of the National Endowment for the Humanities.

Morison and his wife divorced in 1965, and he moved to Yale University that year. A year later he became master of Timothy Dwight College, a professor of history and American studies, and director of the Scholars of the House Program at Yale. He married Elizabeth Forbes Tilghman in 1967. At Yale he worked to convey his concept that humanities and the sciences should be taught together. In 1972 Morison returned to MIT as the Killian Class of 1926 Professor in the School of Humanities and Social Science. He became the founding spirit and intellectual guide of the MIT Program in Science, Technology, and Society (STS), which complemented MIT's traditional training in science and engineering with a historically informed, sophisticated understanding of the surrounding society and culture.

After retiring in 1975, Morison, six feet tall and slim, soft-spoken with a warm smile and bright eyes, traveled extensively, but he remained active at MIT in the 1980s as professor emeritus. He was twice, in 1976 and 1980, an overseas fellow at the Churchill School in Britain, and he spoke at numerous universities and conferences worldwide. Returning from a visit to Epcot in Orlando, Florida, he expressed his disappointment with the "technical problems" and the shallowness of the exhibits. He and his wife collaborated on the *250th Anniversary History of New Hampshire*.

Among his other accomplishments, Morison helped establish the *American Heritage* technology series; edited *The American Style* (1958), a series of papers on the history of international affairs in the United States; and wrote *Men, Machines, and Modern Times* (1966), which won the Academy of Management's McKinsey Award. His last major book, *From Know-How to Nowhere*, was published in 1974. Morison was a fellow of the American Academy of Arts and Sciences and a member of the American Historical Association and Phi Beta Kappa. He spent his last years in Peterborough at his family home, where he enjoyed the "country life." He died there after a long illness. He is buried in Pine Hill Cemetery in Peterborough.

Morison's theories have influenced most schools that teach engineering or the sciences. In September 1963 he articulated his belief that universities are the only hope to bring people and technology into sync: "Universities can do it, but they must first reorganize themselves by allowing artists and scientists to mingle," and that today's scientific world can only deal with human needs "when poets and scientists could meet with mutual understanding."

★

The MIT Museum has materials on Morison's life and work, including press releases and a vertical file of biographical sketches. An interview with Morison by Hal Bowser, "Technology and the Human Dimension," is in *American Heritage* (Summer 1985). Several papers presented at a conference to honor Morison at MIT were published in *Technology and Culture* 37 (Oct. 1996): 864–879. Obituaries are in *Tech Talk* (28 Apr. 1995), the *New York Times* (25 Apr. 1995), and the *Boston Globe* (22 Apr. 1995).

JOAN GOODBODY

MULLIGAN, Gerald Joseph ("Gerry")   (*b.* 6 April 1927 in New York City; *d.* 20 January 1996 in Darien, Connecticut), composer, arranger, baritone saxophonist, bandleader, and pioneer of the Cool School of jazz.

Mulligan was born in the borough of Queens in New York City. His father, a management engineer, moved the family

Gerry Mulligan. ASSOCIATED PRESS AP

frequently, but in 1944 they settled in Philadelphia, where Mulligan spent his adolescence and received his early education. Both parents played piano, and Mulligan first took lessons on piano and ocarina. He studied clarinet and the basics of arranging with Sam Correnti in Reading, Pennsylvania, but was largely self-taught, and continued his musical education informally.

Mulligan quit high school after his third year and began his professional career at age seventeen, selling arrangements for radio bands and playing with East Coast bands led by Harvey Marburger and Chuck Gordon (1944–1945), Alex Bartha, and George Paxton (1945). He did musical arrangements for the radio band led by Johnny Warrington (1945), which performed on WCAU in Philadelphia, and later toured with Tommy Tucker, arranging and playing alto saxophone. He then took a regular job as an arranger with WCAU's house band, led by Elliot Lawrence.

Encouraged by his friend Charlie Parker, Mulligan moved to New York City in 1946, and at age nineteen he found high-profile work arranging and filling in on alto sax for Gene Krupa's band (1946–1947). For Krupa he composed a big hit, "Disc Jockey Jump," and an arrangement of "How High the Moon." Through bandleader Claude Thornhill, with whom he recorded, he met arranger Gil Evans, who introduced him to rising stars in the jazz world, including the pianist John Lewis and trumpeter Miles Davis. Mulligan took part in rehearsal sessions at Evans's apartment in New York City. He found a home in the small-ensemble format, collaborating with Davis's "Birth of the Cool" nine-piece ensemble (1948–1950). Their album, *The Complete Birth of the Cool* (1948), featured original Mulligan compositions, including the innovative "Jeru," and several arrangements, including one of Davis's "Boplicity." Mulligan played a number of exceptional baritone saxophone solos on the album.

After relocating in 1950 to Los Angeles, where he had a brief association with bandleader Stan Kenton, Mulligan recorded *Gerry Mulligan All Stars* (1951) with his own ten-piece band. The following year he formed his first pianoless quartet with trumpeter Chet Baker, bassist Bob Whitlock, and drummer Chico Hamilton. (The lineup changed over time: Baker was followed by John Eardley, by valve trombonist Bob Brookmeyer, and then by trumpeter Art Farmer.) In 1952, with Baker on trumpet, the Gerry Mulligan Quartet first recorded on the World Pacific label. Their overnight success helped establish the West Coast sound in jazz, and the quartet played regularly to large audiences at the Haig in Los Angeles from 1952 to 1954. The absence of a dominant chord instrument, such as piano or guitar, was a marked departure from the era's standard jazz ensemble and allowed Mulligan to improvise a new aesthetic in two-part horn counterpoint, first with Baker and later with Brookmeyer and others.

Mulligan was jailed briefly in 1953 for a narcotics offense and returned to New York City after his release in 1954. In the early 1950s his quartet made frequent tours of Europe and in 1954 played to great popular and critical acclaim at the Salle Playel in Paris. A fixture on the international jazz scene, Mulligan was exceptionally prolific throughout his career and was one of the biggest draws in jazz from the early 1950s through the early 1990s. He performed at the first Newport Jazz Festival (1954) and at most major jazz festivals through the early 1990s. His growing popularity led to a feature about him in *Time* magazine in 1953.

In 1954 Mulligan led a sextet that included Earley and tenor saxophonist Zoot Sims. They toured the United States and Europe (1955–1958) and recorded three albums for Mercury Records that were notable for their exceptional solos. The successful *Gerry Mulligan Songbook,* released in 1957, featured his compositions for other saxophonists, including Sims, Al Cohn, and Lee Konitz. Mulligan recorded with Thelonious Monk and Stan Getz in 1957, and with Ben Webster in 1959. In 1958 he formed a group with Art Farmer, and in New York City in 1960 he established the thirteen-piece Concert Jazz Band, which toured Europe. *Gerry Mulligan and the Concert Jazz Band Live* (1960) includes a scoring of the standard "You Took Advantage of Me." The band's *Live at the Village Vanguard* (1960) features the ballad "Come Rain or Come Shine" and the swinging "Blueport" with Clark Terry.

Mulligan played the part of the beatnik priest in the film *The Subterraneans* (1960), was on the soundtrack of *The Hot Rock* (1972), and appeared in other films. Following a 1964 tour of Japan, Mulligan returned to the small-group format, leading a quintet (1966–1968) that included piano, guitar, bass, and drums. In 1966 Mulligan collaborated with Bill Holman on *Music for Baritone Saxophone and Orchestra,* which premiered with the Los Angeles Neophonic Orchestra. He won the *Down Beat* magazine readers' poll for best baritone saxophone from 1966 to 1975. Mulligan became active as a sideman, and from 1968 to 1972 he appeared as the guest soloist on five albums for the Dave Brubeck Trio.

After a hiatus of more than five years, in 1971 Mulligan recorded *The Age of Steam* (1972), a breakthrough album that included electric bass and electric piano. In 1974 he was an artist-in-residence at the University of Miami. A series of acclaimed reunion concerts with Chet Baker in 1974 and 1975, including one at Carnegie Hall, yielded a recording of exceptional range and depth. He formed a sextet with Dave Samuels that played in New York City and in Italy (1974–1977) before reforming the Concert Jazz Band in 1978. He also collaborated, in 1974, with Argentine composer Astor Piazzolla.

The 1980s were a productive decade for Mulligan, with regular appearances at jazz festivals and clubs and a fine recording in *Gerry Mulligan Meets Scott Hamilton: Soft Lights and Sweet Music* (1986). Earlier in the decade he formed a twenty-piece big band. Mulligan won a Grammy Award for his recording *Walk on the Water* (1981), as well as the Connecticut Arts Award (1982) and the Viotti Prize (1984). He was a recipient of the Yale University Duke Ellington Fellowship (1988) and was inducted into the Philadelphia Museum Association Hall of Fame (1990). In 1992 he recorded *Re-Birth of the Cool,* which revisited his sessions with Davis from the early 1950s, this time with a different lineup. He died from complications after surgery for a knee infection at age sixty-eight.

Mulligan was married several times, first to Jeffie Lee Boyd in 1953. The marriage was annulled, and in May of that year he married Arlyne Brown, with whom he had a son. They divorced in March 1959, and Mulligan later married the actress Judy Holliday. After Holliday died in 1965, Mulligan married another actress, Sandy Dennis. This marriage ended in divorce in 1976, and he later married Contessa Franca Rota.

A major artist who helped define the Cool School of

jazz, Mulligan remained a prolific composer and player for nearly fifty years. With more than 100 albums to his credit, he recorded and performed with many of the twentieth century's greatest jazz musicians, from small combos to big bands, often but not always using the piano-less format. Although Mulligan earned his early reputation as an articulate arranger, over time he became best known as a baritone saxophonist of exceptional melodic range.

As an instrumentalist—in addition to his trademark baritone saxophone, he played tenor and soprano sax, clarinet, and piano—Mulligan's elegant improvisational style evoked a wispy lighthearted lyricism, and his thoughtful phrasings were short in excess and long in measured understatement. Original compositions from his 1950s quartets, such as "Line for Lyons," "Walking Shoes," and "Song for Strayhorn," along with his popular perennial rendition of "My Funny Valentine," retain their vitality and reveal a distinctive artistry. Outstanding albums include the classic early sessions with Chet Baker, as well as *What Is There to Say?* (1959), *Two of a Mind* (1962), *Night Lights* (1963), and *Something Borrowed, Something Blue* (1966).

★

Valuable sources include A. Morgan and Raymond Horricks, *Gerry Mulligan: A Biography, Appreciation, Record Survey, and Discography* (1958); J. Burns, "Gerry Mulligan: The Formative Years," *Jazz and Blues* 1, no. 1 (1972): 9; and L. Tomkins, "The Classic Interview: Gerry Mulligan," *CI* 24, no. 10 (1987): 16. Jerome Klinkowitz, *Listen, Gerry Mulligan: An Aural Narrative in Jazz* (1991), provides a detailed discography. An obituary is in the *New York Times* (21 Jan. 1996).

JONATHAN G. ARETAKIS

MUSKIE, Edmund Sixtus (*b.* 28 March 1914 in Rumford, Maine; *d.* 26 March 1996 in Washington, D.C.), U.S. senator, vice presidential nominee, presidential candidate, and secretary of state whose legislative legacy was a landmark series of laws renewing and protecting the environment.

A tall, plainspoken New Englander whose regional accent and cadences remained unchanged throughout his life, Muskie was one of two sons and four daughters born to Stephen Marciszewski, a tailor, and Josephine Czarnecki. His mother came from a Polish-American family in Buffalo, New York, and his father was a Polish immigrant who officially simplified his surname to Muskie when he was naturalized as a citizen of the United States. The second-oldest child, Muskie was educated in the local public schools, graduating from Stephens High School in Rumford as valedictorian—and high-scoring center on the basketball team—in 1932. His father taught him carpentry and sewing, each a lifelong hobby for Muskie, and he de-

Edmund S. Muskie. LIBRARY OF CONGRESS

veloped an enduring love of the outdoors, returning regularly to his vacation home in Kennebunk, Maine, to hunt, fish, and sail.

Muskie worked his way through Bates College in Lewiston, Maine, supplementing his scholarship by waiting tables in the dining hall and at resort hotels in the summer. "The only Democrat on campus," as he said later, he was chosen class president, became a champion debater, and won election to Phi Beta Kappa. He earned a B.A. in history, graduating cum laude in 1936, and went on to Cornell Law School, again on scholarship, graduating with an LL.B. in 1939. Admitted to the Maine bar that same year, he set up practice in the small south-central Maine city of Waterville.

When America entered World War II, Muskie became an officer in the U.S. Navy (1942) and as a lieutenant junior grade served on destroyer escorts in the Atlantic and the Pacific. In 1945 he resumed his fledgling law practice in Waterville and, like many other returning veterans, entered local and state politics. Over the next decade, he almost single-handedly revived Maine's moribund Democratic Party. He was elected to the Maine House of Representatives (1946) and at the conclusion of his first term in 1947—

the legislature then met only in odd-numbered years—ran unsuccessfully for the mayoralty of Waterville. He was the Democratic floor leader of the state legislature in 1949 and quickly won the respect of the Republican majority, who found him intelligent, cooperative, and a man of his word. In 1951 he resigned from the legislature to become district director for Maine in the Office of Price Stabilization, a position he held until 1952, when he resigned to become a Democratic national committeeman. He married Jane Frances Gray, a bookkeeper for a local women's shop, on 29 May 1948. They had two sons and three daughters

In 1954, running on a platform that emphasized a need for change in leadership and economic policies (including new roads, incentives to attract industry, and higher pay for teachers), Muskie scored a personal triumph in the race for governor of Maine, emerging victorious over the Republican incumbent to become the first Democrat elected to the state's highest office in twenty years, and the first Roman Catholic ever to hold it in his own right. (There had been an interim appointment of a Roman Catholic in 1843 to complete the term of a governor who resigned to enter the U.S. Senate.) His reelection in 1956 was equally impressive, but, as in 1954, he faced a Republican majority in the legislature and was forced to pursue his legislative agenda with diplomacy and moderation.

As governor, Muskie gained a reputation for integrity, common sense, and the ability to work with his opponents. He was known as well for a ferocious temper that remained famously short-fused until his death. Despite his outbursts—some of his supporters claimed they were staged for dramatic effect—he was admired for not holding grudges or putting on airs. Urged by his party to seek a third term as governor in 1958, he ran instead for the U.S. Senate, easily beating the incumbent to become the first Maine Democrat to serve in either house of Congress. He was not seriously challenged in any of his three bids for reelection.

As he began the first of his four terms in 1959, Muskie allied himself with the liberal wing of the Senate, earning the enmity of Lyndon Johnson, the Democratic minority leader, by refusing to support Johnson's successful effort to block a change in the chamber's filibuster rules that made it easier for the majority to end filibusters. In retaliation, Johnson denied Muskie his first three choices for important committee assignments and acted coolly toward him for the next several years. Yet after he became president, Johnson grudgingly admitted that Muskie had become "a real powerhouse," one of the few liberal Democrats who in his opinion had mastered the Senate's arcane rules and thus was able to challenge southern conservatives and Republicans in drafting and floor managing legislation.

Banished to the relatively minor Public Works Committee, Muskie used the appointment to make his mark in the Senate. He became an expert on environmental matters, in the process earning the nickname "Mr. Clean." He was chief sponsor and floor manager for the Clean Air Act of 1963, the Water Quality Act of 1965, and for Senate passage of a multimillion-dollar appropriation for pollution control in 1966. Throughout the next fourteen years, he beat back every effort to weaken the protections he helped put into place. He also played important roles in developing the Johnson administration's model cities program and antipoverty measures (1965–1966). A fiscal conservative, he took a continuing part in largely unsuccessful efforts to hold down government spending (especially on pork barrel items) and to secure a balanced budget. He sought to reshape the relations between the federal bureaucracy and the states by strengthening the role of state agencies in carrying out federal mandates, a concern that carried over into his retirement years. He saw no contradiction in his votes for federal expenditures he considered necessary to the nation's well-being. Thus, he was a leading figure in supporting increased federal aid to education, key civil rights measures, and Medicare, as well as a broad range of social legislation proposed by liberals during his Senate years. In contrast to many of his colleagues, he preferred to do his own reading on major issues rather than rely on his aides' research summaries.

The Democrats chose Muskie as their vice presidential candidate in Hubert Humphrey's run for the presidency in 1968. He had become the party's favorite for vice president largely because of his centrist position on Vietnam, the principal issue of the campaign and the source of bitter, sometimes violent, divisions in the American electorate. Neither "hawk" nor "dove," Muskie's calm, conciliatory approach to the voters led many commentators to conclude that he was a more credible candidate than either Humphrey or Richard Nixon, the Republican challenger. Had Muskie rather than Humphrey headed the ticket, many observers maintained, the Democrats might well have won the election that instead returned the Republicans to the White House by a narrow margin.

Muskie emerged from the 1968 election as the principal Democratic spokesman, well positioned as his party's candidate for president four years later. By January 1972 he was the clear front-runner, well ahead in the polls and seemingly unstoppable. But during the New Hampshire primary, the conservative *Manchester Union Leader,* owned by William Loeb, published an anonymous letter accusing Muskie of making ethnic slurs against the state's French Canadians, along with an article claiming that Jane Muskie was "unladylike" and given to excessive drinking and cursing. It was later revealed that these stories—both fabrications—had been planted by Kenneth W. Clawson, a Nixon aide, as part of "a dirty tricks" campaign to discredit Democrats. Muskie, exhausted from an extended multistate tour and visibly angry, went directly from the Manchester airport on a snowy Saturday to the *Union Leader* building, where he castigated the paper and its publisher. While defending his wife, he broke down and seemed to weep—though later he said the tears were melting snowflakes—and his campaign was effectively over. As reports of the incident spread, supporters abandoned him nationwide, and he suffered a drop in the polls. In April he withdrew from the race, saying that voters were looking for "a strong, steady man, and here I was [seeming] weak."

He returned to the Senate, retiring in 1980 to serve for eight months as President Jimmy Carter's secretary of state. His appointment received nearly unanimous bipartisan support (the two Republicans who voted against him did so in protest against Carter's foreign policy), but he was little more than custodian of the office. His principal achievement was helping secure the release of American hostages held in Iran.

Following the inauguration of President Ronald Reagan in 1981, Muskie resumed the practice of law as a Washington-based partner in the New York firm of Chadbourne and Parke. He served as chairman of the Nestlé Infant Formula Audit Commission assembled by Nestlé to monitor its compliance with international rules governing the sale of infant formula. He also sat on the president's special review board (1986–1987) that investigated charges that the Reagan administration had secretly sold arms to Iran and used the proceeds to finance opponents of the Sandinista government in Nicaragua. With McGeorge Bundy, he co-authored *Presidential Promises and Performance* (1980). He contributed chapters to several books, including "Congressional Overreaching in Foreign Policy," in Robert A. Goldwin and Robert A. Licht, eds., *Foreign Policy and the Constitution* (1990); and "The Carter Presidency and Foreign Policy," in Kenneth W. Thompson, ed., *The Carter Presidency: Fourteen Intimate Perspectives of Jimmy Carter* (1990). He also wrote *Exploring Cambodia: Issues and Reality in a Time of Transition; Findings and Recommendations from the Visit to Thailand, Vietnam, and Cambodia by Former Senator and Secretary of State Edmund S. Muskie* (1990).

Muskie was admitted to Georgetown University Hospital on 18 March 1996 for surgery to remove a blocked artery in his right leg. The surgery was successful, but within a week Muskie suffered a heart attack and died without regaining consciousness. He is buried in Arlington National Cemetery outside Washington, D.C.

During his years of public service, both in Maine and Washington, Muskie was widely admired for his flinty integrity, his intellectual powers, and his commitment to liberal issues. His legislative leadership helped secure the passage of key social and environmental programs during the unsettled political years of the Vietnam War, when he was seen as a man of reason and moderation. In a memorial tribute, President Bill Clinton called Muskie "a leader in the best sense . . . [who] spoke from his heart and acted with conviction."

★

Muskie's papers are in the Edmund S. Muskie Archives at Bates College, Lewiston, Maine. In addition to his personal papers, office files, and memorabilia, the archives include photographs, videotapes, motion-picture film, and audiotapes covering Muskie's public appearances as governor and senator. Muskie's only autobiographical work was his anecdotal memoir, *Journeys* (1972), published for his presidential campaign. Two political biographies written by sympathetic journalists on the eve of the 1972 elections—Theo Lippman, Jr., and Donald C. Hansen, *Muskie* (1971), and David Nevin, *Muskie of Maine* (1972)—transcend some of the limitations imposed by the authors' viewpoints, offering solid and generally balanced reporting. Katharine Whittemore's article, "Farewell to a Tailor's Son," in *Yankee Magazine* (Feb. 1997), features a number of photographs by Stephen O. Muskie, a professional photographer and one of Muskie's five children. See also William Lee Barnet, "An Analysis of the Rhetorical Effectiveness of the 1972 Presidential Primary Election Campaign of Senator Edmund S. Muskie," unpublished Ph.D. dissertation, University of Pittsburgh (1976); Bernard Asbell, *The Senate Nobody Knows* (1978); and James Gardner Ross, "As Maine Goes . . . The Early Years of Edmund Muskie," unpublished thesis, Bates College (1986). Posthumous appraisals by Muskie's colleagues are in United States Senate, *Memorial Tributes Delivered in Congress: Edmund S. Muskie, 1914–1996, Late a Senator from Maine* (1996). An obituary is in the *New York Times* (27 Mar. 1996).

ALLAN L. DAMON

N

NEARING, Helen Knothe (*b.* 23 February 1904 in New York City; *d.* 17 September 1995 near Harborside, Maine), author and advocate of organic farming and homesteading.

Helen Nearing was the daughter of Frank K. Knothe, a businessman, and Maria Obreen Knothe, and grew up in Ridgewood, New Jersey. The Knothes were intellectuals and philanthropists, with a broad range of interests and acquaintances. They were well educated, with interests in music, art, Eastern religion, and vegetarianism. Nearing acknowledged to an interviewer late in her life that these were unusual interests for the 1890s, and she felt that she had "picked" a family that was uniquely suited to her. She studied the violin and was considered a gifted and promising young musician. At age seventeen she chose to go to Europe to continue her musical studies instead of attending Vassar or Wellesley.

After her return from Europe, in 1927 Helen Knothe met Scott Nearing, a committed pacifist and critic of mainstream American life who had been dismissed from several academic positions because of his political and social beliefs. Knothe described herself as a "flibberty-gibberty" kind of person when she met Scott and believed that her real education began with the start of her life with him. Giving up her musical studies, she immersed herself in a new life of political and social activism, saying that there are many violinists but not many people involved in the kind of life she developed with Scott.

Knothe and Nearing lived together in New York City (Scott was married but separated from his wife, Nellie) and worked for the New York Public Library, doing research to support Scott's writing. By the early 1930s they had made a decision that they could live more simply and cheaply in the country. This decision was spurred by the United States' slide into depression and unemployment and the increasing grip of fascism on Western Europe. In 1932 they purchased a farm in Jamaica, Vermont, for $1,000. Unlike many American intellectuals who chose to leave the United States, Knothe and Nearing decided that they should stay in the United States and be part of developing an alternative social and economic system. Specifically, they had three goals: to develop an independent living for themselves, without the influence of businessmen, politicians, or educators; to improve their health and physical well-being; and to remove themselves as much as possible from social exploitation and work toward a new social and ethical order.

After the death of Nellie Nearing, Helen and Scott married on 12 December 1947. The Nearings built a stone house from Vermont native granite and established a simple, productive way of life, earning an income from making maple syrup. In 1952 they moved to Harborside, Maine, and established Forest Farm, which was originally 140 acres but gradually was sold down to four acres by the time of Helen's death. Stressing that they were committed to assisting people who were truly committed to establishing a simple life, not making a financial fortune for themselves,

Helen and Scott Nearing, 1970. © BETTMANN/CORBIS

the Nearings sold land (at 1938 prices) only to families committed to homesteading and living simply. As in Vermont, they built a stone house and developed a cash crop—in this case, blueberries. The blueberry farm was not as economically profitable as the maple syrup business, but it was not as time consuming, and, once again, the Nearings were interested in simplifying their lives and increasing their leisure time for writing and study.

In 1954 the Nearings published *Living the Good Life: How to Live Sanely and Simply in a Troubled World,* a description of their way of life in Vermont. This was followed by *Continuing the Good Life: Half a Century of Homesteading,* which was published in 1979. The couple wrote numerous other books dealing with the philosophy behind their life choices and providing practical homesteading information. Both Nearings were proponents of fasting and simple eating, and Helen also published an "anti-cookbook" called *Simple Food for the Good Life: An Alternative Cookbook* in 1980. The proceeds from the books were put toward publishing Scott's writings, which did not attract interest from mainstream publishers.

Forest Farm attracted huge numbers of visitors (up to 2,300 one summer), as the Nearings' writings became well-known and Americans' interest in alternative living and organic farming grew. Visiting hours were posted, but visiting was actually an open, informal process. The Nearings continued to live privately and simply, without a telephone

or most other conveniences considered essential by the society around them.

The Nearings chose not to avail themselves of conventional medicine and did not see doctors, relying instead on fasting and simple food for good health. Helen claimed that she had never had a headache. When a doctor did convince them to come in to the local hospital for tests, both were found to be in excellent health.

Scott Nearing died at home in 1983 at the age of one hundred, after making the decision to fast and end his own life. Helen continued to live at Forest Farm until her death in an auto accident near her home in 1995. She continued to entertain visitors and write until the end of her life, with an increasing interest in issues related to aging and dying. *Loving and Leaving the Good Life,* published in 1992, was the memoir of her life with her husband, chronicling a relationship that she considered completely harmonious. As she and Scott had decided, Forest Farm was maintained after their deaths as the Good Life Center, an educational retreat. She was cremated and her ashes were spread, together with Scott's, on the garden at Forest Farm.

Helen Nearing and her husband met the goals that they set for themselves when they left New York City in the 1930s, achieving economic self-sufficiency and a simple, healthy life and establishing a personal lifestyle based on their social and ethical principles. Their writings and personal example struck a chord with many others who were also searching for a simpler, less exploitative lifestyle. Their beliefs and life decisions anticipated the "back to nature" movement of the 1960s by more than thirty years and continue to inspire those interested in reinventing modern life.

★

Helen Nearing's papers are at the Thoreau Institute in Lincoln, Massachusetts. Her writings include *The Good Life Album of Helen and Scott Nearing* (1974), which contains numerous photographs; *Simple Food for the Good Life: An Alternative Cookbook* (1980); *Our Home Made of Stone: Building in Our Seventies and Nineties* (1983); and *Loving and Leaving the Good Life* (1992). With Scott Nearing she wrote *Living the Good Life: How to Live Sanely and Simply in a Troubled World* (1954), *Continuing the Good Life: Half a Century of Homesteading* (1979), and numerous practical books on aspects of organic farming. Her friend Ellen LaConte wrote the biographical volume *On Light Alone: A Guru Meditation on the Good Death of Helen Nearing* (1996). Two extensive interviews with Helen Nearing appear in *Whole Earth Review* (winter 1994) and *Mother Earth News* (June–July 1994).

MARTHA E. NELSON

NELSON, Harriet Hilliard (*b.* 18 July 1909 in Des Moines, Iowa; *d.* 2 October 1994 in Laguna Beach, California), actress characterized as the ideal American housewife and mother when she played herself on the long-running radio and television series the *Adventures of Ozzie and Harriet.*

Harriet Nelson with *(descending)* Ozzie, David, and Ricky, 1954. © BETT-MANN/CORBIS

The future Harriet Nelson was born Peggy Lou Snyder, the daughter of actor Roy Hilliard (whose real name was Snyder) and actress Hazel McNutt. The Hilliards ran and starred in a midwestern stock company; their only child was supposedly first brought on stage at the age of six months. She had her first speaking role at age three. Educated at Saint Agnes Academy in Kansas City, Missouri, she traveled and acted with her parents on vacations.

When Roy and Hazel Hilliard separated in 1925, Harriet Hilliard moved with her mother to New York City, where she studied with choreographer Chester Hale and danced in his Capitol Theatre Corps de Ballet. At age seventeen, she appeared on the New York stage in a musical farce titled *The Blonde Sinner.* This work led her to vaudeville, touring with comedians Bert Lahr and Ken Murray. For a brief time she also played straight woman to a comic named Roy Sedley, whom she married in 1930 and left after a year. The marriage was annulled in 1933.

Hilliard returned to New York in 1931 and worked at the Hollywood Restaurant as a singer, dancer, and mistress of ceremonies. There, in 1932, she was discovered by bandleader Ozzie Nelson, who decided that she would give his orchestra the little something extra it needed. Her voice was throaty and not terribly strong, but it pleased audiences, as did her blonde good looks and lively personality. As they

toured, Nelson busied himself writing humorous boy-girl duets to sing with her. Their onstage flirtation eventually expanded offstage, and they married in October 1935.

Shortly after the wedding, Harriet Hilliard (she would not adopt her husband's name professionally until the 1950s) appeared as the romantic lead in *Follow the Fleet,* a Fred Astaire–Ginger Rogers vehicle. Although her first film was her most important, she kept busy in Hollywood through the mid-1940s in minor pictures. She frequently returned to the Nelson home base in New York, appearing with Ozzie's band and giving birth to two children, David in 1936 and Eric ("Ricky") in 1940.

In between films and musical gigs, the Nelsons explored radio. In the 1930s they worked on Joe Penner's *Baker's Broadcast* and supplied music and comic dialogue for cartoonist Feg Murray. In 1941 they joined Red Skelton in Los Angeles for what proved to be one of the most popular offerings on radio. When Skelton was drafted into the army in 1944, the Nelsons proposed that they star as themselves in a program of their own. The *Adventures of Ozzie and Harriet* would endure in one form or another for the next twenty-two years.

The program began its radio run with a number of comic external characters, as well as the musical interludes that had made Ozzie and Harriet Nelson famous. Within a few years, however, the humor became one of situation, and slowly the singing was phased out. Writer/director Ozzie filled in the slack with scenes featuring "cute" things done and said by the Nelson children. At first child actors played David and Ricky, but in 1949 they began to portray themselves. In 1952 the Nelsons moved to television. Their program successfully courted the American postwar family audience and stayed on the air until 1966.

The Nelsons' stock in trade was their normality. Ozzie, Harriet, David, and Ricky (who came to be known as Rick when he launched a highly successful singing career in the 1950s) played themselves—a white middle-class family living in a California suburb. Their fictional characters were said to be based on their actual personalities, and many of their adventures drew on true-life experiences.

Harriet Hilliard Nelson's radio and TV character was a homebody: she later quipped, "Nobody recognizes me without an apron and a coffee pot in my hand." She dispensed wisdom as she dispensed food. She was smarter than the character her husband played—smart enough, in the wisdom of the day, not to reveal her smartness. Her character was reactive rather than active, saving Ozzie and the boys from the situations into which ego and/or youth propelled them. She could do almost anything—but what she chose to do was cook meals, vacuum, listen to her family's problems, and have an occasional afternoon out with the girls. The offscreen Harriet Nelson was harder to define than her onscreen counterpart, but accounts during the run of the program and after it stressed her devotion to her family.

When *Ozzie and Harriet* finally lost the ratings battle in 1966, the parents continued to act, particularly in regional theater. They made a brief return to television in the fall of 1973 in the syndicated program *Ozzie's Girls*, produced by David. Ozzie and Harriet again played themselves, renting out the rooms of their married sons to female college students. After one season, however, Ozzie Nelson contracted liver cancer and canceled production. He died in 1975.

His widow lived on for another twenty years, occasionally taking on jobs as a guest star on television. "[S]omehow," she told one reporter, "without working, you find you don't know who you are." She maintained her personal privacy through her son Rick's death in a plane crash in 1985; according to rumor she kept her family together during that difficult time. She died of heart failure, surrounded by family members, in 1994. She is buried in Forest Lawn Cemetery in Los Angeles.

Harriet Hilliard Nelson simultaneously reinforced and challenged the domestic female stereotype of mid-twentieth-century America, working hard at her portrayal of a housewife. Later generations would both admire and rebel against the calm, well-tailored image associated with the former

singer who became, as one journalist termed it, "the mother of all TV moms."

★

The New York Public Library's Billy Rose Theater Collection has clipping files on the Nelsons. Information on Nelson from her radio and TV heyday may be found in her article, as told to Cameron Shipp, "My Heart Belongs to My Three Men," *Woman's Home Companion* (June 1953); in a similar piece, as told to Stanley Gordon, "The Men in My Life," *Look* (11 Nov. 1958); and in *Current Biography* (1949). Later sources include Ozzie Nelson, *Ozzie* (1973); Philip Bashe, *Teenage Idol, Travelin' Man* (1992), a biography of Rick Nelson; and Jay Sharbutt, "Harriet's New Life Without Ozzie," *Washington Post* (23 Aug. 1976). Obituaries are in the *New York Times* and *New York Daily News* (both 4 Oct. 1994).

TINKY "DAKOTA" WEISBLAT

NILSSON, Harry Edward, III (*b*. 15 June 1941 in New York City; *d*. 15 January 1994 in Agoura Hills, California), one of the most original and quixotic singer-composers of the 1960s and 1970s.

Nilsson was the son of Harry E. Nilsson, Jr., and Betty Nilsson, a homemaker. His father abandoned the family in 1944. Nilsson spent most of his early childhood living in an apartment at 762 Jefferson Avenue in the Bushwick section of Brooklyn with his mother and half sister, his maternal grandparents, two uncles, an aunt, and a cousin. His

Harry Nilsson, 1990. © NEAL PRESTON/CORBIS

mother introduced him to songwriting, penning "Marchin' Down Broadway" and "Little Cowboy," which Nilsson later recorded.

In 1952 Betty Nilsson, Harry, and his half sister traveled by bus to San Bernardino, California, to live with relatives and then settled for four years in Colton, California. Their home life was chaotic. Nilsson had a total of six stepfathers; his mother drank heavily and left a trail of bad checks before returning east in June 1957 with her children to live with a sister and brother-in-law on Long Island, New York. Nilsson briefly prospered, making the high school basketball and baseball teams. In 1957 Betty and her daughter again left for Los Angeles. Nilsson stayed behind with his aunt and uncle to finish school, but after being fired from his job as a caddy in the summer of 1957, he decided to drop out of school and hitchhiked to California to rejoin his mother. Unfortunately, she was in prison, so Nilsson took a job at the Paramount Theater in Los Angeles while living with another aunt and uncle. During this period he listened intently to such entertainers as the Everly Brothers, Ray Charles, the Coasters, and the duo Jan and Dean.

After the Paramount Theater closed, Nilsson talked his way into a job as night supervisor in a bank's computer department, despite his lack of a high school diploma. In 1966 Nilsson and Diane Clatworthy had a son. Nilsson also visited his father in Florida, where the elder Nilsson was a baseball scout for the Cincinnati Reds.

Nilsson cut a few singles, wrote commercial jingles, and authored three songs for the legendary producer Phil Spector. In 1967 the pop group the Monkees recorded his first hit, "Cuddly Toy"; he then signed with RCA Records as a songwriter. That year Nilsson's initial RCA album, *Pandemonium Shadow Show* (1967), sold poorly. The Beatles changed his life by claiming that Nilsson was their favorite American singer, which was exceptional praise for an unknown artist.

Nilsson, whose light-colored hair and complexion led to the nickname "the White Rat," complicated his rise to success by refusing to perform in concerts. In early 1968 he traveled to London, where he befriended the Beatles and sat in on their *White Album* sessions. In the same year he wrote the entire score for the legendary psychedelic film *Skidoo,* which improbably starred Jackie Gleason, Carol Channing, and Groucho Marx in his last role. Nilsson's next individual album, *Aerial Ballet* (1968), included a Fred Neil composition, "Everybody's Talkin'." Nilsson's version was selected for the soundtrack of the Oscar-winning hit movie *Midnight Cowboy* (1969), which propelled the single to number six on the Billboard charts and led to Nilsson's Grammy Award for best male contemporary vocal performance that same year. His next album, *Harry* (1969), was commercially successful and featured the song "I Guess the Lord Must Be in New York City," which had been rejected for the *Midnight Cowboy* album.

Now established, Nilsson followed up with *Nilsson Sings Newman* (1970), composed of tunes by Randy Newman. A lovely blend of romance and irony, the album demonstrated perfect compatibility between singer and songwriter. In 1971 came an animated musical television special, *The Point,* which was later produced on Broadway. In 1971 Nilsson issued his best-selling album *Nilsson Schmilsson;* its emotional centerpiece was "Without You," a song written by a Beatles spin-off group, Badfinger. "Without You" became an international hit, won a Grammy in 1971, and demonstrated the extraordinary range of Nilsson's three-octave voice. The cover photograph showed a bearded Nilsson lighting a cigarette with his thumb, a joke borrowed from his idol, Stan Laurel, of the comedy team Laurel and Hardy. Nilsson followed this triumph with his less successful album *Son of Schmilsson* in 1972, which featured Nilsson's bathroom humor. The next year he worked first on a project with the Beatles' drummer, Ringo Starr, which resulted in a soundtrack for a dismal horror movie, *Son of Dracula* (1974). Nilsson next recorded his classic album *A Little Touch of Schmilsson in the Night* (1973). Featuring Nilsson's brilliant interpretations of classic Tin Pan Alley songs and arranged by the legendary Gordon Jenkins, best known for his work with Frank Sinatra, the album was an artistic triumph, though it generated tepid sales. Nilsson appeared on the cover of *Time* on 12 February 1973.

Nilsson's friendship with John Lennon proved mutually self-destructive. The pair made drunken scenes in Hollywood, disrupting a comeback concert for the Smothers Brothers at the Troubadour. Worried about bad press, RCA reneged on a $5 million contract for Nilsson, but Lennon used his influence to make the company honor it. Nilsson and Lennon then collaborated on an underrated album, *Pussy Cats* (1974). During the recording sessions, Nilsson ruptured a vocal cord. He hid his bleeding and pain, fearful that Lennon might cancel the production. The album was hardly the sensation expected of a Beatles' album. Nilsson's next collections, *Duit on Mon Dei* (1975) and the highly commercial . . . *That's the Way It Is* (1976), sold poorly. His personal life improved in 1977 when he married Una O'Keefe, whom he had met in Rumplemeyer's Ice Cream Parlor; they had six children.

Nilsson's last original album for RCA was *Knnillssonn* (1977), which he considered his best effort ever. The company antagonized him by issuing a *Greatest Hits* collection without his permission in 1978, and he sought successfully to leave the company. His last album of the decade was the soundtrack for the movie *Popeye* (1980). Nilsson recorded rarely during the 1980s. A 1980 album, *Flash Harry,* was issued only in Europe and Japan.

The assassination of John Lennon in 1980 inspired Nilsson to join the National Coalition to Ban Handguns (now known as the Coalition to Stop Gun Violence) and to lobby Congress to ban access to firearms. He formed Hawkeye Entertainment, a production company; later a company officer embezzled millions of dollars, which were never recovered. After being diagnosed with diabetes, Nilsson suffered a massive heart attack on Valentine's Day in 1993. He died of a second heart attack almost a year later.

Nilsson's quixotic career makes his influence indistinct. His extraordinary vocal range and multiple talents were unique. His impact on John Lennon is clear, but Paul McCartney's post-Beatles albums indicate the influence of Nilsson's original ballad compositions. Nilsson's albums anticipated the intersections of rock, classical pop, and movie themes, which became standard in the 1990s. His compositions commonly appear on soundtracks today.

★

There is little critical appraisal to date of Nilsson. Dawn Eden's article "One Last Touch of Nilsson" appeared in *Goldmine* 20 (29 Apr. 1994). Andrea Sheridan wrote a personal remembrance of Nilsson, which appeared in the Beatles fanzine *Good Day Sunshine,* no. 73 (spring 1994). Most of his albums are available on compact discs. Obituaries are in the *New York Times* (16 Jan. 1994) and *Manchester Guardian* (17 Jan. 1994).

GRAHAM RUSSELL HODGES

NISBET, Robert Alexander   (*b.* 30 September 1913 in Los Angeles, California; *d.* 9 September 1996 in Washington, D.C.), influential neoconservative social philosopher, historian, and author, who wrote extensively on the history of political philosophy, social development, and current events.

Nisbet was the son of Henry S. Nisbet, a lumberyard worker, and Cynthia Jenifer Nisbet. Raising their family in southern California and Macon, Georgia, in modest circumstances, the Nisbets relied on New Deal relief measures during the Great Depression of the 1930s. Nevertheless, influenced by the conservative values of these regions, Nisbet later credited some of his anti-statism to his youthful experience. His interest in learning, he said, was a reaction to the bleakness of growing up in the San Joaquin Valley.

Nisbet took his B.A. (1936), M.A. (1937), and Ph.D. (1939) degrees in sociology, all from the University of California at Berkeley. There he found the ordered, meritocratic, and hierarchical community that he loved, increasing his nostalgia for medieval social organizations so lacking in 1930s society. Though a supporter of the New Deal as a youth, he became, under the influence of his adviser, Frederick J. Teggart, a historical sociologist. His dissertation analyzed the traditionalist French sociologists Louis de Bonald and Robert de Lamennais.

Nisbet served two years in the Pacific theater of World War II, again finding comfort in the shared values and identity of a structured military community. Returning to Berkeley, he taught sociology until 1953. He served as dean of the College of Letters and Science at the University of California at Riverside from 1953 to 1963 and as vice chancellor from 1960 to 1963. He was a professor of sociology there from 1953 to 1972. He then moved to the University of Arizona, where he served as a professor of history and sociology from 1972 to 1974. He taught at Columbia University from 1974 to 1978, ending as the prestigious Albert Schweitzer Professor of the Humanities. (Nisbet always affirmed the humanistic roots of sociology in contrast to the quantitative emphasis that dominated the field.) He also served as a resident scholar at the conservative American Enterprise Institute in Washington, D.C., from 1978 to 1980, continuing as an adjunct scholar until 1986. In 1988 he was Jefferson Lecturer for the National Endowment for the Humanities. During the 1980s, he was viewed as a conservative sympathetic to the Ronald Reagan administration. He received numerous awards, such as a Guggenheim Fellowship (1963–1964) and the Berkeley Citation (1970) and was a frequent speaker nationally and internationally.

Among more than a dozen books, Nisbet published several that were particularly influential in the formation of neoconservatism: *The Quest for Community* (1953); *Twilight of Authority* (1975); *History of the Idea of Progress* (1980); *Prejudices: A Philosophical Dictionary* (1982); *Conservatism: Dream and Reality* (1986); *The Making of Modern Society* (1986); and *Roosevelt and Stalin: The Failed Courtship* (1989).

Under the influence of Edmund Burke and Alexis de Tocqueville, Nisbet saw the rise of the centralized, territorial state as the defining development in modern history. Since the medieval era, the West had suffered from a steady decline of institutions that mediate between the individual and the state. The gradual dissolving of traditional voluntary ties to neighborhood, family, church, and guild had the effect of liberating people from institutional authority. However, the actual consequence of modernization was atomized, alienated, isolated, and spiritually deprived humans—the twentieth century's "mass men." This isolation generated a longing for community, that was too often satisfied in the false, externally imposed order of the modern totalitarian state.

Three themes define Nisbet's essential thought. First, he analyzed social and political processes and institutions in societies past and present. For him, a healthy society, such as pre-Revolutionary Europe, possesses strong communal and familial structures. Morals and other fundamentals of life were regulated by clan, guild, church, and village, and in time were expressed in custom and ritual. However, philosophers such as Thomas Hobbes and Jean-Jacques Rousseau undermined the raison d'être of these natural, plural communities and their internal structures of legitimate power.

In his pivotal *The Social Philosophers* (1973), Nisbet analyzed the gradual decline of voluntary communities and the rise of the omnipresent state. Hobbes, in the seventeenth century, had argued that individuals were constantly in a state of competitive war with others, and that they needed an artificial external government to protect themselves. Individuals thus consigned rights to the state in return for protection. Rousseau, in the following century, posited a virtuous, pre-social man who had become twisted and vile only after society imposed on him such artificial restraints as private property. Rousseau proposed a "social contract" as the way out of the uncomfortable social conditioning that had ruined our natural harmony. The centralized government, an omnicompetent and unitary state, was thus designed to secure the liberties of each citizen and to resolve individual conflicts by subordinating associations to its general will. Hobbes and Rousseau, according to Nisbet, had tied radical atomistic individualism to the concentration of state power. For Nisbet, however, the modern centralized state complements and feeds on the anomie of alienated modern man, who lacks bearings, identity, and meaning. In this, he is in league with other modern critics of "mass man" such as Eric Hoffer and José Ortega y Gasset.

Nisbet's second general theme was his suspicion of abstract ideas and intellectual fashions. He particularly distrusted intellectual systems that make large claims and have substantial popular appeal—especially the modern totalitarian systems of Marx, Lenin, Trotsky, and Mao. In Nisbet's view such systems excused a host of sins in exchange for millennial perfection. Ever the independent, however, he also attacked the hubris and simplifications of more conservative thinkers as well. Nisbet found the inarticulate rhythms of human existence more trustworthy than large ideologies or systems. He was particularly hostile to psychohistory, sociobiology, futurology, and environmentalism, which he considered to be disguised millennial religions which often "bully by metaphor" those who fail to agree with their pretensions. Environmentalism, for example, he saw as on its way to becoming a "redemptive" successor to Nazism, socialism, and Marxism—secularized religions that had justified mass slaughter in service to a sanctified end. By contrast, in *Social Change and History* (1969) and *History of the Idea and Progress* (1980), Nisbet argued that social problems could be alleviated only by incremental, pragmatic steps. Although a respected conservative friendly to many of Reagan's positions, Nisbet was always an independent libertarian thinker and found fault with the efforts of some conservatives to regulate morals and thus enhance the power of the state.

His last set of common ideas was his underlying assumption that man's nature was flawed beyond total repair. Consistent with his conservative forebears, Nisbet saw ample empirical evidence for human sloth, ambition, vanity, tyranny, stupidity, cupidity, aggression, and fanaticism. He particularly found fault with the vanities and banalities of academic life after World War II. In *The Degradation of Academic Dogma* (1971), he excoriated the modern decline of learning, authority, reason, and the quest for truth. He deplored the lowering of academic standards and the proliferation of training rather than education. For the conservative and skeptical Nisbet, man's capacity for tyranny gave great importance to pluralistic society where natural and voluntary communities would minimize the power of the state.

Critics such as Herbert Marcuse, Richard Rorty, Herbert Gutman, and Marvin Harris faulted his ignoring the socioeconomic context of ideas in his focus on political philosophers as agents of change. Others found fault with his romanticization of traditional community life, pointing out that the state has no monopoly over coercion, which may also be exercised by some of the very institutions Nisbet praised.

Nevertheless, Nisbet's influence is undeniable. His early work on the importance of communities and his analyses of their decline anticipated such "civil society" theorists and communitarians as Garry Wills, Charles Taylor, Amitai Etzioni, and Robert Bellah. *The Quest for Community* appealed to counterculture radicals where participatory democracy would challenge impersonal, government bureaucracies.

Aside from his considerable scholarly legacy, Nisbet is remembered as a brilliant teacher who lectured with original insight and without notes. Despite his aristocratic bearing, enormous vocabulary, and erudition, students recall him as modest, unassuming, and fair-minded to his intellectual opponents. Nonetheless, Nisbet fretted over what he saw as the decline of authority and standards in higher education and was pleased to give up teaching in 1978. He married Emily P. Heron and the couple had two daughters before they divorced. His second wife, Caroline Burks Kirkpatrick, survived him. They had one child. Nisbet died in his sleep at the age of eighty-two after a long struggle with prostate cancer. He is buried in Washington D.C.

★

The Robert Nisbet papers (1949–1994) are at the Library of Congress (MMC-3681). They contain 1,500 manuscripts, letters, documents, book reviews, and speeches. For a view of Nisbet's personality, see Robert Perrin, "Robert Alexander Nisbet," *Proceedings of the American Philosophical Society* (Dec. 1999). For a revealing memoir of his academic career, see Robert Nisbet, *Teachers and Scholars: A Memoir of Berkeley in Depression and War* (1992). An excellent overview and assessment of Nisbet's thought from the perspective of conservatives is found in Brad Lowell Stone, "A True Sociologist: Robert Nisbet," in *The Intercollegiate Review* 33 (spring 1999). For a full-length discussion of Nisbet's place in modern conservative thought see George H. Nash, *The Conservative Intellectual Movement in America Since 1945* (1996). For a comparison of Nisbet's evaluation of community and the new communitarians, see Bruce Frohnen, "The Misdirected Quest for Community: Why Neighborhood Ties Remain Elusive," *Family Policy* (May–June 1999). For a discussion of Nisbet's ideas on social progress, see Gertrude Himmelfarb, *The New History and the Old: Critical Essays and Reappraisals* (1987). An obituary is in the *New York Times* (12 Sept. 1996).

ALFRED L. CASTLE

NIXON, Richard Milhous (*b.* 9 January 1913 in Yorba Linda, California; *d.* 22 April 1994 in New York City), thirty-seventh president of the United States (20 January 1969 to 9 August 1974) and one of the dominant figures of the post–World War II era. Because of the Watergate scandal, Nixon became the only president ever forced to resign his office.

Nixon was born in Yorba Linda, a tiny town in southern California, and grew up in nearby Whittier. The region's deep conservative temper would inform his political views, but the more important influences in his boyhood were psychological. From his early boyhood, he exhibited a combustible mix of intelligence and suspiciousness, ambition and rage—qualities that would become hallmarks of his political persona.

Nixon's father, Francis Anthony, known as Frank, was an Ohio-born Methodist who struggled in various jobs before eventually opening a successful grocery and gas station. Hot-tempered and prone to violence, Frank strictly enforced his will. In 1908 Frank married Hannah Milhous, a devout Quaker. Hannah was equally strong-willed in her own way, quietly preaching a stern ethical code. Nixon remembered his father as "a common man" or a "little man" and idealized his mother as a "saint."

The Nixons had five sons: Harold in 1909, Richard, Francis Donald (called Donald) in 1914, Arthur in 1918, and Edward in 1930. Two of them died young: Arthur from encephalitis in 1925, Harold from tuberculosis in 1933. Apart from these traumas, the family also faced financial hardship, though not dire poverty. Richard worked odd jobs until he finished law school and always bore a deep resentment toward the privileged and fortunate.

Diligent and precociously serious, Nixon excelled academically. After two years at Fullerton High School, he transferred to Whittier High School in 1928, from which he graduated third in his class in 1930. Though not a natural athlete, he played football, serving dutifully as a bench-

warmer; he fared better in drama and debating. In 1930 he enrolled at Whittier College where he continued these pursuits. He also founded a club there, called the "Orthogonians," to rival the established "Franklins," whose well-to-do members dominated campus life. In 1934 Nixon graduated second in his class, winning a scholarship to Duke Law School in North Carolina.

At Duke, Nixon maintained his reputation for assiduous work habits (he had an "iron butt," one friend remarked) and a saturnine demeanor (he was nicknamed "Gloomy Gus"). He lived abstemiously, residing at one point in an abandoned toolshed. Although he graduated third in his class in 1937, he failed to get a job at a New York firm or the FBI, to his lasting disappointment.

After law school, Nixon returned to Whittier to begin private practice. While acting in community theater there in 1938, he met Thelma Catherine ("Pat") Ryan, a schoolteacher, whom he courted doggedly, even chauffeuring her to dates with other men. His perseverance triumphed: they were married on 21 June 1940 in a Quaker ceremony.

In January 1942 the Nixons moved to Washington, D.C., where Richard joined the wartime Office of Price Administration. But federal bureaucracy frustrated him. That same year he entered the U.S. Navy as a lieutenant, serving first at an air station in Iowa, and then, in 1944, as a transport-control officer in the Pacific. He was not assigned to combat, though his base suffered Japanese attacks. He finished his service in January 1946 in Maryland, terminating navy contracts.

In September 1945 Nixon received a call from Herman Perry, a Whittier banker. Perry belonged to a group of southern California businessmen seeking a Republican candidate to challenge the incumbent Democrat Jerry Voorhis for the Twelfth District Congressional seat. Nixon leapt at Perry's offer to audition before the "Committee of One Hundred." He flew to California in November, where he impressed the local solons with his articulateness, feistiness and support for their anti–New Deal ideology. Portraying himself as a clean-cut veteran, a young father (Pat gave birth to a daughter, Tricia, on 21 February 1946), and spokesman of "the forgotten man," he won the Republican nomination in June 1946.

An underdog against Voorhis, Nixon campaigned aggressively. He secured endorsements from the mostly Republican local newspapers, including the powerful *Los Angeles Times*. Amid unemployment, labor unrest, and food shortages, he articulated the kind of anti–big government agenda that would become popular a generation later. Distorting his opponent's record, he attacked Voorhis—in speeches, advertisements, and a series of public debates—as a communist sympathizer or dupe. Nixon won the election with 57 percent of the vote, helping his party capture control of Congress.

Nixon distinguished himself among congressional freshmen. He helped draft the Taft-Hartley Act, which prevented unions from keeping closed shops. His experiences touring Europe with a congressional committee persuaded him that his party should abandon its isolationism for an active role in world affairs. As a member of the House Un-American Activities Committee, he cosponsored the Mundt-Nixon Bill restricting the freedoms of domestic Communist party members.

The summer of 1948 raised Nixon's profile. After the birth of a second daughter, Julie, on 5 July 1948, Nixon became embroiled in the case of Alger Hiss, a Democratic ex–State Department official who *Time* magazine editor Whittaker Chambers had charged was a communist spy. Hiss sued Chambers for slander, inaugurating a national drama. Nixon led the charge against Hiss, and when Chambers produced incriminating microfilm that he had stored in a pumpkin on his farm, Nixon was vindicated. Hiss eventually served time for perjury.

Nixon won reelection handily in 1948. In 1950 he ran for the Senate against Congresswoman Helen Gahagan Douglas, a stylish former actress and New Deal Democrat. With the help of Murray Chotiner, a pioneer in campaign strategy, Nixon again spotlighted communism (and made Douglas's gender a tacit issue) as he called his opponent "pink right down to her underwear." His campaign circulated a "pink sheet" comparing her voting record to that of a well-known communist congressman. Some anti-Semitic Nixon supporters also played up Douglas's marriage to the Jewish actor Melvyn Douglas. Douglas ran a poor campaign and lost badly. Her main contribution was to saddle Nixon with a lasting epithet: "Tricky Dick."

Now a rising star, Nixon became a favorite Republican speaker. In July 1952 General Dwight Eisenhower, the party's presidential nominee, chose Nixon as his running mate. In September, newspapers revealed that Nixon's California supporters maintained a fund to cover his professional expenses—possibly an illegal practice. Editorials demanded his withdrawal from the ticket. On 23 September, he delivered a televised speech defending himself, citing at one point a gift he had been given: a cocker spaniel for his daughters named Checkers. The "Checkers" speech galled liberals as maudlin and manipulative, but viewers overwhelmingly praised Nixon's sincerity. Eisenhower kept him on board, and the Republican ticket triumphed in November.

As vice president, Nixon maintained a higher profile than previous understudies. Letting Eisenhower abstain from direct political combat, Nixon barnstormed the country in 1954 and 1956 on his party's behalf (he remained Eisenhower's running mate in 1956 despite an abortive "Dump Nixon" boomlet). Liberals grew to loathe him for his red-baiting, his combativeness, his rhetorical devious-

ness, and what they considered his phoniness. Nixon's face became a household image. Caricatures mocked his pendulous jowls, his ski-jump nose, and his perennial five-o'clock shadow. Magazine profiles noted, often with criticism or condescension, his painstakingly rigid and clear speaking style, his social awkwardness, and his skill at attacking liberal elites.

Detested as he was in some circles, Nixon also commanded deep support. When crowds harassed him on his visit to South America in 1958, Americans back home cheered him as a patriot. In Moscow in 1959, he won praise for out-debating Soviet leader Nikita Khrushchev in a model U.S. kitchen, proclaiming the superiority of freedom and capitalism to Soviet communism. In the 1960 presidential race, he sewed up his party's nomination after placating his main rival, New York governor Nelson Rockefeller, by adopting many of the governor's liberal positions.

For the general election, the Democrats nominated the forty-three-year-old Massachusetts senator John F. Kennedy. The election thus matched up two young up-and-comers, a moderate Republican and a cold war liberal. More than ideology, style separated the candidates. Kennedy possessed the charm, grace, and wit that detractors felt Nixon lacked. In four televised debates—the first ever—Nixon's forensic skills flagged. Kennedy appeared cool and polished, while the ill-at-ease Nixon faltered, sweat streaking his pancake makeup in the first debate. Kennedy also outflanked Nixon on cold war politics, promising to aid anticommunist forces in Cuba, which Nixon refused to do (though he knew Eisenhower had begun such efforts). Kennedy won the election by a whisker, 49.7 to 49.5 percent. Nixon claimed that Kennedy "stole" the election, although no one ever substantiated the charge.

Nixon returned to California, where he wrote a well-received memoir, *Six Crises*. Still attracted to politics, he ran for governor against Edmund G. ("Pat") Brown in 1962. He again tried to label his opponent "soft on communism," but the Red Scare was over and his gambit failed. After Brown won, Nixon berated reporters and told them, "You won't have Nixon to kick around anymore, because, gentlemen, this is my last press conference." His career seemed finished. ABC News ran a special called "The Political Obituary of Richard Nixon."

In 1963 Nixon moved to New York City, joined a Wall Street law firm, and rebuilt his reputation within his party. By 1968 he had emerged as a presidential nominee acceptable to conservatives, who otherwise preferred California governor Ronald Reagan, and moderates, whose first choice was Michigan governor George Romney or Rockefeller. On 8 August 1968 Nixon accepted the nomination at the Republican convention in Miami. He returned to his theme of extolling the common man. Offering himself as an exemplar of the American Dream, he recalled, as a boy, "hear[ing] a train go by at night and . . . dream[ing] of faraway places"—suggesting that with his election he and the American people alike might reach their long-sought goals.

As a candidate, Nixon pledged to end the Vietnam War "with honor," without ever revealing his precise plan for doing so. He championed "law and order," a concise phrase promising toughness against rising crime, urban riots, and antiwar agitation. With a "Southern strategy" of conservative racial rhetoric, he sought to neutralize the third-party campaign of segregationist governor George Wallace of Alabama.

Aided by new media experts, Nixon in 1968 pioneered a television-era strategy of image making. He tightly controlled his television appearances and his contact with the press. Although analysts had been hailing a "new Nixon"—more mellow, less pugilistic—since the mid-1950s, the 1968 strategy convinced many that he had arrived. With the Democratic party a shambles after a riot-torn convention in Chicago, Nixon won a slim victory on 5 November 1968 over Vice President Hubert Humphrey (43.4 to 42.7 percent, with Wallace running third). The concern with image and public relations that Nixon exhibited in the campaign would dominate his presidency and usher in an era in national politics where such matters received enormous attention by politicians, journalists, and the public.

Nixon took the oath of office on 20 January 1969. He promised to end the war and heal domestic divisions. "The greatest honor history can bestow is the title of peacemaker," he said. From the start, however, his presidency witnessed not unity but increased discord.

The first president since Zachary Taylor to face a Congress controlled by the opposition party, Nixon could not dismantle Kennedy and Lyndon B. Johnson's Great Society as he had promised. Rather, with the public broadly endorsing government activism, Nixon pragmatically mixed concessions to the Democrats with high-profile efforts to thwart them. Staffing his administration with a mix of conservative ideologues and liberal policy wonks, he produced an inconsistent domestic record.

Prodded by his liberal adviser Daniel Patrick Moynihan, Nixon proposed as his first major domestic initiative a "Family Assistance Plan" on 8 August 1969. FAP would replace the existing welfare system with direct payments to poor families, eliminating the bureaucratic web of more complex social-service programs. Ultimately FAP was defeated by Republicans who rejected it as "big government" and Democrats who thought its provisions too stingy. Still, the Nixon administration and Congress expanded social services in other ways, from indexing Social Security benefits (to rise with inflation), to establishing Supplemental Security Income (a system for aiding disabled workers), to enlarging the food stamps program.

Nixon confronted an economy straining under the twin perils of inflation and unemployment (conditions that worsened after the 1973 oil crisis). Though a believer in laissez-faire economics, Nixon tried different remedies. In 1971 he declared, "Now I am a Keynesian" and on 15 August imposed a freeze on wages and prices; he lifted them when the recession began to threaten his reelection. Nixon also suspended the convertibility of dollars into gold to make American goods more competitive overseas, a historic change to the global economic system known as Bretton Woods. On business regulation, Nixon sometimes acceded to Democratic wishes, establishing the Environmental Protection Agency and the Occupational Safety and Health Administration; at other times, he pleased the business world, vetoing regulations and impounding funds (illegally, as the Supreme Court later ruled) that were earmarked for environmental and other programs.

Nixon likewise produced a mixed record on racial issues. Cultivating southerners and working-class ethnic whites, he denounced school busing and quotas in job hiring, and he eliminated Johnson's Office of Economic Opportunity. Yet he also enforced (albeit less vigorously than liberals wanted) Supreme Court mandates for southern school desegregation, and his Labor Department revived Johnson's plan to require affirmative action among government contractors. He battled Congress, unsuccessfully, in seeking to name to the Supreme Court two southern conservatives—part of a larger effort to undo the cultural revolution of the 1960s.

Conflict over social issues—civil liberties, student activism, minorities' and women's rights, drug use, and others—proved the most divisive of Nixon's presidency. Along with Vice President Spiro Agnew (dubbed "Nixon's Nixon"), the president defended those he called "Middle Americans" or the "Silent Majority." These working-class Americans resented students, intellectuals, professionals, the news media, and others who they felt were undermining traditional values. From his efforts to reshape the courts to his battles with the press (which also stemmed from longstanding personal hatreds), Nixon's denunciations of liberal elites provided a thread of continuity through a record of eclectic policies and positions.

Nixon's foreign policy also proved controversial. Ending the Vietnam War proved harder than he and Henry Kissinger, his top adviser, imagined. They first aimed to calm domestic dissent with a program of "Vietnamization," or training South Vietnamese soldiers to replace Americans. The policy, announced in 1969, along with changes in the draft a few months later, eased fears about American boys dying in an unpopular war. Yet dissent persisted. October and November 1969 saw massive antiwar demonstrations, the biggest in history.

Nixon countered on several fronts. His "Silent Majority" speech of 3 November 1969 successfully rallied support for his policies while stigmatizing antiwar protesters. He deftly manipulated the news media into portraying dissenters as dangerous radicals. His administration undertook covert actions, some of them illegal, such as surveillance, wiretaps, and infiltration to undermine the movement.

Meanwhile, owing partly to South Vietnamese intransigence, Kissinger faltered in the peace negotiations. Hoping to force concessions, Nixon escalated the war. In March 1969 he bombed enemy sanctuaries in Cambodia, a neutral country. On 30 April 1970 he announced an "incursion" into Cambodia, renewing antiwar protests (resulting in the National Guard's slaying of four students at Ohio's Kent State University). In February 1971 Nixon expanded the war into Laos. Periodic raids—notably the "Christmas bombing" of December 1972—devastated North Vietnam. Finally, on 27 January 1973 in Paris the combatants reached an armistice, on terms, critics noted, similar to those obtainable in 1969.

Nixon and Kissinger also sought to attain peace—and to shore up America's power in the world—through diplomacy with China and the Soviet Union. In July 1971 Nixon sent Kissinger on a secret mission to Beijing, and on 17 February 1972 he himself traveled to China. He began to reverse America's position on the legitimacy of the communist government, agreeing to admit "Red China" to the United Nations and to expel the Taiwanese delegation. Diplomatic relations commenced. Meanwhile, Nixon pursued a Strategic Arms Limitation Treaty with the Soviet Union, resulting in a freeze on certain nuclear missiles. On 12 May 1972 he and Soviet leader Leonid Brezhnev signed a twelve-point agreement establishing what was called "détente": a thaw in diplomatic as well as commercial relations between the superpowers. Other arms-control treaties ensued, including, most importantly, the Anti-Ballistic Missile (ABM) Treaty of 1972.

Elsewhere, Nixon's foreign-policy record consisted of troubleshooting. After an Arab attack on Israel on the Jewish holy day of Yom Kippur on 6 October 1973, Nixon delayed before responding with aid, endangering an American ally. In Chile, the administration supported a ruthless coup against a popularly elected socialist leader, installing a pro-Western dictator. Elsewhere, Nixon had to cope with conflicts between Greece and Turkey, India and Pakistan, and warring factions in Angola.

Above all, Nixon's presidency was known for the collection of crimes and scandals known as Watergate, the greatest constitutional crisis of the twentieth century. Watergate had its origins in the social conflicts of the 1960s; in Nixon's ambition, suspiciousness, and unscrupulousness; and in the growth after World War II of what historian Arthur M. Schlesinger, Jr., called the "imperial presidency."

Possessed of a Manichean worldview, Nixon viewed political opponents as personal enemies. Fiercely secretive, and convinced that the press was determined to harm him, he became incensed when information was leaked to reporters. Kissinger shared Nixon's penchant for secrecy. Starting in May 1969 and continuing through February 1971, they had the FBI tap the phones of various aides and newsmen—the first actions in what would be a long line of illegal and clandestine activities.

Nixon was able to undertake such action because of the growing power of the presidency. During the cold war, Nixon's predecessors had arrogated power to the office. They had countenanced illegal FBI and CIA surveillance and break-ins against potential subversives, justifying their actions under the increasingly broad rubric of "national security." During the cultural tumult of the 1960s, such practices, rooted in defending the nation against espionage by the Soviet Union, were applied to homegrown radical movements, such as antiwar and black activists.

Nixon accelerated such practices. He had an aide, Tom Charles Huston, devise a plan for coordinating domestic intelligence activities, and on 23 July 1970 he approved the "Huston Plan" to bring such intelligence, including a variety of illegal activities, under White House control. Nixon soon abandoned it, however, when FBI chief J. Edgar Hoover balked.

On 13 June 1971 the *New York Times* began publishing a secret Defense Department history of American involvement in Vietnam known as the *Pentagon Papers*. Nixon sued to stop their publication but lost. The incident prompted Nixon to organize a White House security team, informally called the "Plumbers' Unit," to crack down on leaks. Daniel Ellsberg, the official who had leaked the *Pentagon Papers,* was its first target. Nixon had the Plumbers burglarize Ellsberg's psychiatrist's office on 3 September 1971 to find incriminating information about him. (When this news became public in 1973, the judge overseeing Ellsberg's prosecution threw out the case.)

Other such practices, varying in severity from violations of the constitution to political chicanery ("dirty tricks"), proliferated as the 1972 election approached. Nixon considered firebombing the Brookings Institution, a liberal think tank. One administration official sought to assassinate the muckraking columnist Jack Anderson. Another aide forged cables to implicate President Kennedy in the 1963 assassination of South Vietnam's premier, Ngo Dinh Diem. A third counterfeited a letter to a newspaper attributing bigoted comments to Senator Edmund Muskie, the Democratic front-runner in the 1972 presidential race, leading Muskie to withdraw.

On 17 June 1972 five burglars, hired by the White House, were caught breaking into Democratic party headquarters in the Watergate Hotel in Washington, D.C. Five days later Nixon publicly denied any role in the break-in.

However, the day after that, 23 June, he ordered his Chief of Staff Bob Haldeman to have the CIA obstruct the FBI's investigation of Watergate. And on 29 June aides began paying "hush money" to the burglars.

The press, led by two young *Washington Post* reporters, Bob Woodward and Carl Bernstein, found evidence linking the burglars to the White House and to Nixon's reelection committee. Yet for a while the revelations did not dent Nixon's popularity. Nor did other scandals—such as a possibly illegal effort by International Telephone & Telegraph to settle an antitrust suit or shady campaign contributions from the dairy industry—endanger Nixon's reelection.

In the 1972 campaign, Nixon enjoyed great popularity after his diplomatic effort to Moscow and Beijing. He easily repulsed primary challenges for the Republican nomination from both the left and right wings of his party. He got a boost when an assassin shot and crippled George Wallace, eliminating him as potential competition. Meanwhile, the Democratic nominee, South Dakota senator George McGovern, ran on an unpopular left-wing platform. What was more, McGovern lost his best issue, ending the Vietnam War, when shortly before the election Kissinger announced (prematurely, it turned out) that "peace is at hand." On 7 November 1972 Nixon and Agnew won reelection, capturing every state but Massachusetts.

After the election, however, Nixon's fortunes nosedived. In January 1973, the Senate established a committee to investigate Watergate under the leadership of North Carolina Democrat Sam Ervin. Concurrently, the Watergate burglars went to trial. These hearings loosed a string of revelations about what Attorney General John Mitchell called the "White House horrors." Nixon's popularity plummeted.

Nixon tried to protect himself. On 15 April 1973 he met with his lawyer, John W. Dean III, to discuss how to keep the illegal White House activities under wraps. On 30 April, hoping to stem the tide, Nixon announced the resignations of Dean, Haldeman, and aide John Ehrlichman. He continued to deny any involvement in Watergate. Nonetheless, on 18 May, Attorney General Elliot Richardson appointed a special prosecutor, Archibald Cox of Harvard Law School, to investigate.

More revelations ensued. In June, Dean told the Ervin Committee that Nixon maintained an "Enemies List" of political foes, reporters, and even celebrities such as Bill Cosby and Joe Namath, on some of whom the Internal Revenue Service had conducted tax audits. Dean also revealed Nixon's role in the cover-up. In July, White House aide Alexander Butterfield disclosed that Nixon secretly taped his White House conversations. Both the Ervin Committee and Cox sought these important tapes, which Nixon refused to surrender. The protracted struggle consumed the summer.

On 20 October 1973 Nixon ordered Richardson to fire Cox. Instead, Richardson resigned, as did his deputy. The so-called Saturday Night Massacre prompted fears that Nixon might eventually try to hold onto power illegally. Cries arose for his impeachment.

Other scandals emerged that fall, worsening Nixon's position. Vice President Agnew, under investigation for tax evasion and taking bribes while governor of Maryland, resigned on 10 October 1973, and was replaced by House Minority Leader Gerald Ford. Nixon was also found to have underpaid, and possibly cheated, on his income taxes and to have used government funds to improve his homes. Investigators also found that someone had erased eighteen-and-a-half minutes of a key Watergate tape. His credibility suffering, Nixon told reporters on 17 November, "People have got to know whether or not their president is a crook. Well, I am not a crook."

On 6 February 1974 the House voted to have its Judiciary Committee begin an impeachment investigation. Leon Jaworski, the new special prosecutor, and the House committee both continued to subpoena White House tapes. On 29 April 1974 Nixon announced he would provide only edited transcripts. When released, they shocked the nation. Even with "expletives deleted," the conversations were full of foul-mouthed, bigoted, and vengeful talk.

Still seeking the tapes, Jaworski and the House took their case to the Supreme Court. On 24 July, the Court ruled 8–0 against Nixon. One tape, of the 23 June 1972 conversation—called the "smoking gun"—proved Nixon had obstructed justice. Nixon's support, even among Republicans, crumbled. On 27 July the House approved the first of three articles of impeachment. On 9 August 1974 Nixon resigned.

Historians would debate the significance of Watergate for decades. The standard view held that Nixon's crimes outstripped other presidents' misdeeds and that Watergate defined his presidency. Defenders of Nixon argued that the crisis should not have overshadowed his diplomatic or domestic achievements. Most agreed, however, that Nixon's historic resignation, and the acts that led to it, shook the nation. Americans came to view their president as a liar, a criminal, and in some cases a would-be dictator. Public faith in government and political leaders, weakened by Vietnam, further eroded.

Nixon retired to San Clemente, California. He was psychologically devastated by Watergate, and severely depressed. He also suffered from other medical problems, including a serious case of phlebitis that required surgery and hospitalization. He escaped prosecution because President Ford, on 8 September 1974, pardoned him completely.

During his physical and psychological recovery from Watergate, Nixon kept a low profile. In 1977 he conducted a series of televised interviews with the British talk-show

Richard Nixon leaves the White House after the Watergate scandal caused him to resign from the presidency, 9 August 1974. LIBRARY OF CONGRESS

host David Frost. He defended his behavior during Watergate, famously stating, "When the president does it, that means it is not illegal."

After his resignation, Nixon worked tirelessly to rehabilitate himself. He brought endless lawsuits against the federal government, trying to recover control of, or hinder the release of, papers and tapes from his administration. He wrote nine books defending his behavior and trying to burnish his image as a foreign policy sage. The most important was his memoir *RN* (1978). Other books offered his views on foreign policy or recounted anecdotes about various world leaders he had met. In 1980 he and Pat moved back to New York City and later to Saddle River, New Jersey. He entertained journalists at his home, and many began to write that Nixon had made a comeback. A cover story in *Newsweek* in 1986 declared "He's Back."

Nixon died on 22 April 1994, ten months after Pat had passed away. He had suffered a stroke days earlier. President Bill Clinton declared a national day of mourning. Nixon was buried beside Pat on the grounds of the Nixon Presidential Library and Birthplace in Yorba Linda, on the site where his first boyhood home had been. His funeral, on 27 April, was a media event. Clinton, Kissinger, and other national figures delivered eulogies; and commentators extolled his achievements in foreign policy. Yet Watergate, as analysts had predicted years earlier, dominated

the obituaries and discussions of his life and shaped his legacy.

In the years after his death, Nixon remained nothing if not controversial. Some historians began to revise their estimations of him, especially in the area of domestic policy, where he was reassessed as more of a liberal than contemporaries had realized. Yet the overriding image of Nixon in most people's minds was still that of "Tricky Dick." The image was reinforced by numerous references to Nixon in films, sitcoms, and the culture more generally, in which Nixon was invariably portrayed as sinister. The word "Nixonian" entered the language as a synonym for Machiavellian.

Nixon's legacy was manifold. His opening of relations with China changed global politics, and détente began an easing of the hostilities with the Soviet Union that, although temporarily reversed under President Ronald Reagan, ultimately helped clear the way toward normal relations. Nixon's domestic stewardship paradoxically both continued the Great Society in some respects while hastening its downfall in others.

More than policy, Nixon shaped American politics. He was one of the first and most successful practitioners of a strategy that mobilized a "Silent Majority" against out-of-touch liberal elites. Nixon used this approach, starting with his first congressional campaign, long before others did. After him, almost all successful Republican politicians, from Reagan to Speaker of the House Newt Gingrich, would similarly play on resentments toward federal spending and bureaucrats, permissive courts, and elites who seemed to favor racial minorities.

In the end, there is no escaping the fact that Nixon's greatest legacy was Watergate, which became the benchmark of political corruption. Afterward, whenever politicians became enmeshed in scandal, their misdeeds would be measured against Nixon's—allowing some of them, such as Reagan and Clinton, to emerge relatively unscathed, since their transgressions seemed to pale next to Watergate.

The American experience with Nixon also helped breed a profound cynicism toward politics and political leaders. Faith in public leadership began to decline with the Vietnam War. Nixon's continuation of the war fed the decline, and Watergate accelerated it. Nixon convinced many people that presidents were not heroes to be admired but criminals, liars, or at the very least opportunists who would say or do anything to get elected.

Nixon also fostered cynicism toward politics with his relentless focus on image making. This focus helped to create a political culture dominated by polling, advertising, and efforts to manipulate of the news media. As the public became hyper-aware of the extent to which politics had become a contest of political imagery, many people came to conclude all politics was devoid of real meaning.

During the first quarter century after World War II, Nixon was one of the central figures in American politics. During the next quarter century, virtually every aspect of the political culture bore his imprint. For this reason many analysts have called the postwar era the "Age of Nixon."

★

Some of Nixon's early papers and all of his post-presidential papers are at the Richard Nixon Library and Birthplace in Yorba Linda, California. Other pre-presidential papers are at the Pacific regional branch of the National Archives in Laguna Niguel, California. His presidential papers and tapes are at the Nixon Presidential Materials Project in College Park, Maryland. Published sources of primary documents include Bruce Oudes, *From the President: Richard Nixon's Secret Files* (1989), H. R. Haldeman, *The Haldeman Diaries: Inside the Nixon White House* (1994), and Stanley I. Kutler, *Abuse of Power: The New Nixon Tapes* (1997).

The published literature about Nixon is voluminous. Yet biographies covering his whole life, or most of it, are few. Stephen E. Ambrose's three-volume *Nixon* (1987, 1989, and 1991) remains a standard, basic work. Herbert Parmet, *Richard Nixon and His America* (1990), tracks Nixon's politics of resentment. Tom Wicker, *One of Us: Richard Nixon and the American Dream* (1991), is a thoughtful synthesis. Jonathan Aitken's *Nixon: A Life (1993)* is a flattering account written by a friend. Covering Nixon's early years are Roger Morris's massive, critical and beautifully written *Richard Milhous Nixon: The Rise of an American Politician* (1990) and Irwin F. Gellman's pro-Nixon *The Contender: Richard Nixon, the Congress Years* (1999). Fawn Brodie's *Richard Nixon: The Shaping of His Character* (1981), controversial for its psychoanalytic approach, remains provocative.

Studies of Nixon's presidency include the comprehensive, even-handed *The Presidency of Richard Nixon* by Melvin Small (1999) and the brashly revisionist *Nixon Reconsidered* by Joan Hoff (1994). On Watergate, the most reliable is Stanley I. Kutler, *The Wars of Watergate: The Last Crisis of Richard Nixon* (1990). Important accounts from the Nixon era include Bob Woodward and Carl Bernstein, *All the President's Men* (1974) and *The Final Days* (1976); J. Anthony Lukas, *Nightmare: The Underside of the Nixon Years* (1975); and Theodore H. White, *Breach of Faith: The Fall of Richard Nixon* (1975).

Important studies of one aspect or another of Nixon's life and career are Joe McGinniss, *The Selling of the President, 1968* (1969), Garry Wills, *Nixon Agonistes: The Crisis of the Self-Made Man* (1969), Daniel Patrick Moynihan, *The Politics of a Guaranteed Income: The Nixon Administration and the Family Assistance Plan* (1973), Arthur M. Schlesinger, Jr., *The Imperial Presidency* (1973), Joseph Spear, *Presidents and the Press: The Nixon Legacy* (1984), Michael Schudson, *Watergate in American Memory: How We Remember, Forget, and Reconstruct the Past* (1992), William Bundy, *Tangled Web: The Making of Foreign Policy in the Nixon Presidency*

(1998), and David Greenberg, *Nixon's Shadow* (2001). Nixon tells his side of the story in *Six Crises* (1962) and *RN: The Memoirs of Richard Nixon* (1978). Other valuable memoirs include William Safire, *Before the Fall: An Inside View of the Pre-Watergate White House* (1975), John Dean, *Blind Ambition: The White House Years* (1976), and Henry Kissinger, *White House Years* (1979) and *Years of Upheaval* (1982).

DAVID GREENBERG

NIZER, Louis (*b.* 6 February 1902 in London, England; *d.* 10 November 1994 in New York City), lawyer for prominent celebrities and businesses, specializing in entertainment and libel law, whose defense of CBS radio personality John Henry Faulk helped break the blacklist.

Nizer was the son of Joseph Nizer and Bella Bialestock. Joseph Nizer immigrated to the United States in 1904, brought the family over the following year, and opened the California Cleaning and Dyeing Establishment on Sumner Avenue in the Williamsburg section of Brooklyn, New York. The Nizers lived first in a single room behind the store, then in a few rooms upstairs, before they finally purchased the building. To help pay the mortgage, Louis worked nights with his mother scalloping lace and during summers worked at errand jobs.

Louis Nizer. AP/WIDE WORLD PHOTOS

Louis had an active childhood. He sang in the choir of the renowned cantor Josef "Yosele" Rosenblatt. At the age of ten, he began speaking to local crowds. Nizer attributed his later fame as an orator and toastmaster to the lessons he learned as a socialist soapbox speaker. During World War I he turned his oratory to Liberty Loan drives, making appeals during intermission at Broadway shows and ultimately earning a government certificate of merit. After graduating from Boys High School in Brooklyn, Nizer entered Columbia College in Manhattan. He was small, but his competitive spirit turned that to his advantage as coxswain on the rowing team and on the handball team. He joined Alpha Epsilon Pi, a Jewish fraternity, and twice won the George William Curtis Prize for excellence in the public delivery of English orations. Nizer graduated in 1922 and entered Columbia University Law School. In 1924 Nizer obtained an A.B. degree and was admitted to the bar in the State of New York.

From 1924 to 1926 Nizer worked for Emily Janoer, a Manhattan lawyer, serving dispossession summonses on her defaulting tenants for $7 a week. His first case, on behalf of property owners on Ellery Street in Brooklyn was brought against the City of New York. Dubbed the "pushcart case," it went to the New York State Court of Appeals, where he argued before Chief Justice Benjamin N. Cardozo and won. In 1926 Louis Phillips, who knew Nizer's parents from London, hired him for $20 a week and 50 percent of his clients' fees. Nizer was so successful he was offered an equal partnership in 1928, and the law firm of Phillips and Nizer (later Phillips, Nizer, Benjamin, Krim, and Ballon) was established. He was appointed executive secretary and attorney for the New York Film Board of Trade in 1928, thus beginning his long association with the entertainment industry. He held that post until 1994.

In the 1930s Nizer was an active member of the New York City mayor Fiorello H. LaGuardia's "kitchen cabinet." He also advised President Franklin D. Roosevelt. In July 1939 Nizer married Mildred Mantel Wollins, becoming stepfather to her two sons. They lived at 180 West Fifty-eighth Street in Manhattan.

During World War II, Nizer increased his national political profile with his book *What to Do with Germany* (1944), which advocated temporary suspension of German sovereignty, national or international trials of war criminals, return of stolen property, and a complete overhaul of Germany's education system. He turned down President Harry Truman's offer of an appointment to the federal bench and consistently declined the seat when it was offered by subsequent presidents. He also refused the position of attorney general. In the late 1940s Nizer was a vocal opponent of communism. In articles and radio programs, he advocated the registration of Communist Party members as foreign agents, abolishing the party, and drastically changing judicial procedures so that communists could be "firmly dealt with."

An ardent supporter of Adlai Stevenson's campaign for the presidency in 1952, Nizer served as a speechwriter and adviser. In 1955 he won a libel suit for the journalist Quentin Reynolds against columnist Westbrook Pegler, dramatized by Henry Denker as *A Case of Libel* (1963). In 1956 he took on his most famous case, that of John Henry Faulk, a CBS radio personality blacklisted for his opposition to AWARE, an anticommunist organization that "cleared" performers for sponsors. In 1962 Nizer proved that Faulk had been libeled, winning $3.5 million in damages (reduced on appeal), and thus helped to break the blacklist whereby persons with suspected communist affiliations were denied jobs in the entertainment industry. The trial was turned into a television movie, *Fear of Trial* (1975), with George C. Scott portraying Nizer. Nizer's attacks on blacklisting in the entertainment industry and his defense of Faulk may seem contradictory, given his virulent public attacks on communism, but this was typical of left-wing anticommunists of the McCarthy era who strongly championed noncommunist liberals while vigorously denouncing communism and communists.

Nizer's book *My Life in Court* (1961) spent seventy-two weeks on the *New York Times* best-seller list. It brought him national fame and influenced a generation in the legal profession. Many lawyers and judges have stated that the book inspired them to pursue law. In 1964 Nizer published his analysis of the Warren Commission Report regarding the assassination of President John F. Kennedy. He became a close adviser and speechwriter for President Lyndon Johnson. He was also a member of the Fair Campaign Practices Committee. In 1966 the astronaut Alan Shepard asked Nizer to represent NASA's astronauts in their personal affairs, which he did pro bono. From 1966 to 1994 Nizer served as general counsel for the Motion Picture Association of America. As such, he successfully argued on 15 April 1974 before the Supreme Court on behalf of Billy Jenkins, a theater manager in Albany, Georgia, who had been charged with public indecency for showing the film *Carnal Knowledge*. The case, *Jenkins v. Georgia*, helped establish the principle that juries do not have "unbridled discretion" to determine what is patently offensive. Only material displaying "hardcore sexual conduct" is prohibited. He conducted legal work for Armand Hammer and his Occidental Petroleum Corporation and served on the company's board of directors.

Nizer wrote a weekly column for the Chicago Tribune–New York News Syndicate from 1971 to 1972. *The Implosion Conspiracy* (1973), his analysis of the Rosenberg atomic spying case, led to an unsuccessful defamation suit by the sons of accused spies Julius and Ethel Rosenberg. Always active in politics, Nizer advised foreign leaders such as Indira Gandhi, as well as several Israeli prime ministers.

Nizer was called a Renaissance man. His songs for his grandchildren were issued as *Songs for You* (RCA); others were bought for film and television. He received a Grammy nomination for a recording analyzing Oliver Wendell Holmes's Supreme Court decisions. His oil paintings and caricatures were exhibited in various galleries and museums.

In the 1980s Nizer was still generating about $6 million in yearly billings. In 1993 his wife died. Working until ten days before his own death, Nizer succumbed to kidney failure at Beth Israel Hospital in New York City. He is buried in the Nizer family mausoleum in Washington Cemetery, Brooklyn, New York.

Devoted to the law and to his firm, Nizer was a short man with curly hair whose physical appearance belied his immense energy and dedication. His "A Lawyer's Prayer" starts, "Please, O God, give me good health with which to withstand the rigors of a most arduous profession—the law." For him the client always came first, and he often counseled against litigation if he felt it was against the client's best interest. He was meticulous and thorough.

"Yes, there's such a thing as luck in trial law, but it only comes at three o'clock in the morning," he explained. "You'll still find me in the library looking for luck at three o'clock in the morning." His courtroom demeanor was polite and disciplined, and he concentrated on issues, not personality. Nizer insisted on clarity in written and oral briefs and never memorized arguments. These qualities also served him well as a speaker, writer, and political adviser. Nizer was the prototype for the modern celebrity lawyer.

★

My Life in Court (1961) describes some of Nizer's most interesting cases. *Reflections Without Mirrors: An Autobiography of the Mind* (1978) is a more personal journey, detailing the story and philosophy of his life. Other profiles include *Current Biography* (1955) and *Contemporary Authors New Revision Series* 76 (1999). The inaugural lecture of the Carnegie Council on Ethics and International Affairs' annual Louis Nizer Lecture on Public Policy includes two tributes. Obituaries are in the *New York Times* and *Los Angeles Times* (both 11 Nov. 1994). Much of Nizer's artwork hangs in the offices of Phillips, Nizer, Benjamin, Krim and Ballon.

SHARONA A. LEVY

O

ODELL, Allan Gilbert (*b*. 6 May 1903 in Minneapolis, Minnesota; *d*. 17 January 1994 in Edina, Minnesota), businessman behind the ingenious scheme to advertise Burma-Shave brushless shaving cream with sets of roadside signs whose whimsical, rhyming jingles exploited America's growing love of the automobile, entertained travelers, and became a popular part of Americana.

Odell was the oldest of four children born to Clinton McDougal Odell, a lawyer, insurance agent, and businessman, and Amy Ford Hamley, a homemaker. He lived all his life in and around Minneapolis and grew up in his father's family home at 1815 Fremont Avenue South. Odell spent childhood summers at the family farm near Oxboro Heath, Minnesota, to avoid contagious disease epidemics. He was fond of poetry by elementary school. Odell attended West High School in Minneapolis and graduated in 1921. He was captain and starting end of the school's Twin Cities 1920 championship football team. In his prime, Odell stood six feet, one inch tall and weighed 220 pounds; he had brown hair and blue eyes.

In 1925, Odell graduated with a degree in business from the University of Minnesota in Minneapolis. While in college, Odell broke his nose playing football and then quit at his father's request. He subsequently lettered in basketball as student manager and was active in the Zeta Psi fraternity. As a college student, Odell worked summers as an assistant game warden to help study beavers in Minnesota's north woods. Soon after college graduation, Odell met Grace Miriam Evans on a blind date. They married in 1928 and had three sons. During subsequent summers, Odell returned to the north woods with his own family to camp and fish. In 1935, Odell moved to 4903 Bruce Avenue in Edina, Minnesota, a Minneapolis suburb, where he and his wife lived out their lives.

Odell eventually found a practical, though unconventional, outlet for poetry. In 1924, his father began a company to market and produce a smelly liniment that Odell's grandfather made. Odell joined the company in 1925. The original plant was at 2019 East Lake Street in Minneapolis. Since the liniment was meant to provide life and vigor and many of its oils came from Burma, the company was named Burma-Vita, meaning life from Burma. However, sales were weak and provided the Odells with little livelihood. To make a more profitable, widely appealing product, the Odells began to make Burma-Shave, a brushless shaving cream, to eliminate the drawbacks of traveling with a wet brush and mug. The formula for Burma-Shave was based upon the original brushless shaving cream from Britain, Lloyd's Euxesis. After hundreds of attempts, formula 143 gave a nice shave if aged a few months. Original marketing attempts failed, and the company floundered financially. Then Odell, fate, and the popularity of automobile travel came to the rescue.

While marketing Burma-Shave in Joliet, Illinois, Odell noticed a sequence of signs advertising a gas station along the road between Joliet and Aurora, Illinois. He thought similar signs might promote Burma-Shave. Despite initial opposition from his father and advertising executives, Odell persuaded his father to back his scheme with $200. With this start-up money, Odell bought used boards for the first crude signs. The Odells erected ten or twelve sets of signs in the fall of 1925 along Routes 61 and 65 out of Minneapolis. These first signs contained brief statements about Burma-Shave, but no jingles.

By early 1926, the first repeat orders arrived for Burma-Shave. However, the company was still struggling and sold a virtually unknown product. Nonetheless, Odell's father incorporated the company and quickly sold 49 percent of its stock, which allowed the company to open its first sign shop in 1926 to make signs containing jingles that Odell and his father wrote. The signs measured roughly twelve by thirty-six inches. Each set consisted of six signs eight to ten feet off the ground and spaced 100 feet apart along rural roads for easy reading at normal travel speeds of about thirty-five miles per hour. They were erected by employees known as PhDs, or posthole diggers. Signs were usually placed on land leased from farmers for $5 to $25 annually.

From 1926 to 1948, Odell was vice president and advertising manager of Burma-Vita. By the fall of 1926, the company had spent $25,000 on signs, and sales of Burma-Shave reached $68,000. In 1927, the advertising budget was $45,000, and sales doubled. By 1929, the company had spent $65,000 on signs, and sales doubled again. At its peak, the company grossed over $3 million annually. In 1940, a new Burma-Vita plant was built at 2318 Chestnut Avenue in Minneapolis, into which the company moved in 1941. In 1948, Odell became president and remained advertising manager.

By 1930, when Odell and his father ran short of new jingles, Odell created an annual jingle contest. Winning entries received $100. Some contests generated more than 50,000 entries, such as "If Harmony / Is What / You Crave / Then Get / A Tuba / Burma Shave." The roadside signs advertised two major themes: Burma-Shave and public service. The latter helped counter antibillboard sentiments. Minor themes included boy-girl relationships, World War II, travel, and farmers. In 1935, Odell wrote the first public-service jingle: "Keep Well / To the Right / Of the Oncoming Car / Get Your Close Shaves / From the Half-pound Jar." In the early 1950s, the sign campaign peaked with 7,000 sets in forty-five states and made the company appear much larger than it was. It never had more than thirty-five employees, and the signs were erected and maintained by a fleet of only eight trucks. The company used about 600 different jingles.

On 8 February 1963, Philip Morris Incorporated bought Burma-Vita, Odell retired, and his younger brother, Leonard, became president. Later that year, Philip Morris replaced the signs with more traditional advertisements. In 1966, Philip Morris moved Burma-Vita to New Jersey. It was bought out again by the American Safety Razor Company (a division of Philip Morris) in 1997, and Burma-Shave is still available. The last signs were removed from the roads in 1964. That same year the Odell family donated his favorite set to the Smithsonian Institution: "Within This Vale / Of Toil / And Sin / Your Head Grows Bald / But Not Your Chin / Burma-Shave." Odell died at home of natural causes at age ninety and is buried in Lakewood Cemetery in Minneapolis, Minnesota.

Odell was an ethical, loving, intelligent, and creative businessman and humanitarian who gave to such charities as the Salvation Army and the United Way. He was also a poet who expressed himself on stationary signs, not books, for readers in cars, not chairs. Rather than sell his poems directly, he used them to sell shaving cream. Consequently, he saved his family's company and gave customers such product-added values as humor, entertainment, safety advice, patriotism, and their own poetic outlet. His roadside rhymes broke with traditional advertising and drove Burma-Shave into America's culture and memory.

★

Two books that present the Burma-Shave story are Frank Rowsome, Jr., *The Verse by the Side of the Road: The Story of the Burma-Shave Signs and Jingles* (1965, 1991 edition with introduction by Robert Dole), and Bill Vossler, *Burma-Shave: The Rhymes, the Signs, the Times* (1997). Both contain hundreds of Burma-Shave jingles. Whereas Rowsome's book features many humorous black-and-white line drawings, Vossler's presents numerous black-and-white photographs of the people behind the company, other types of Burma-Shave advertisements, and the times that made the signs so successful. Vossler's book contains an index of key words found in the jingles. Obituaries are in Marvin Siegel, ed., *The Last Word: The* New York Times *Book of Obituaries and Farewells, A Celebration of Unusual Lives; The* New York Times *Biographical Service,* 25 (Jan. 1994); *World Herald* (15 Jan. 1994); the *Minneapolis/St. Paul Star Tribune* (19 Jan. 1994 and 1 Feb. 1994); *Omaha* (Nebraska) and *Arizona Republic* (both 27 Jan. 1994); and *U.S. News and World Report* (31 Jan. 1994). On his 24 January 1994 CBS radio show *The Osgood File*, Charles Osgood eulogized Odell in rhyme. Burma-Shave's story is also told in *The Signs and Rhymes of Burma-Shave* (1991), a fifty-three-minute, color videotape by Sentimental Productions. The video provides interviews with Odell family members, many of the jingles, and a glimpse of American culture—especially automobiles and clothing—during Burma-Shave's heyday.

GARY MASON CHURCH

O'HAIR, Madalyn Murray (*b.* 13 April 1919 in Pittsburgh, Pennsylvania; disappeared and presumed dead 1995?), atheist who successfully sued to prohibit prayer in public schools, and who gained notoriety for her spirited attacks against religion before mysteriously disappearing.

John Irvin Mays, a building contractor, and Lena Scholle Mays, baptized their daughter Madalyn in the Presbyterian Church and gave her what she later described as a happy and secure childhood. As a girl, she regularly attended church services and Sunday school. In 1929 her father lost his business as the Great Depression began. He sought work as a handyman and carpenter, traveling with his family from state to state.

O'Hair recalled that her first pangs of spiritual disbelief struck as an adolescent. She said she read the Bible from beginning to end when she was thirteen years of age and was shocked by the brutality in the Old Testament. She found the New Testament too fantastical.

As a young woman, she attended several colleges before eloping with John Roths in 1941. World War II soon separated them, with Roths serving in the Pacific and she, a cryptographer, in North Africa and Europe, where she had an affair and became pregnant by Army officer William J.

Madalyn Murray O'Hair, 1969. AP/WIDE WORLD PHOTOS

Murray. She and Roths divorced after the war. Though Murray refused to marry her, she took his name and gave it to her son, William Murray III. O'Hair then moved to Houston, where she attended the South Texas College of Law.

In Baltimore in 1954, she gave birth to Jon Garth Murray, by a different father. As with her older son, O'Hair had him baptized. Although she dabbled in left-wing politics, it was not until young William Murray complained about the recitation of the Lord's Prayer in his school that O'Hair found a cause to which she could devote her considerable energy and rhetorical talent.

In *Murray* v. *Curlett,* she sued the Baltimore schools, arguing that the prayers were unconstitutional. She lost in the state courts, but in 1963 the United States Supreme Court ruled 8–1 in her favor. Justice Tom C. Clark wrote for the majority that the recitation of prayers or Bible passages in public schools constitutes "religious exercises, required by the state in violation of the command of the First Amendment that the Government maintain strict neutrality, neither aiding nor opposing religion."

The landmark decision brought O'Hair notoriety that made her life both difficult and exciting. Although her case became combined with a similar Pennsylvania challenge called *Abington School District* v. *Schempp,* with one decision being rendered for both cases under the Abington name, it was the brash, publicity-seeking O'Hair who became known as the woman who removed prayer from public schools. She not only talked openly of her atheism as the case proceeded through the courts, but brashly condemned people of faith, acts for which she received death threats and hate mail. Her sons were beaten on several occasions, and she lost her job as a social worker.

But her defense of atheism in a country where only a tiny minority questioned the existence of God also gave her the attention she craved. O'Hair raised tempers in 1967 as the first guest on the *Phil Donahue* show, and made appearances on *Merv Griffin* and the *Tonight Show.* In televised debates she took on popular preachers and enjoyed calling herself "the most hated woman in America."

O'Hair made atheism her life's work, founding a monthly atheist magazine and several atheist organizations. She continued to file lawsuits to further extricate religion from public institutions, challenging the tax-exempt status of church lands as well as a juror's oath that required swearing belief in God and the use of the words "In God We Trust" on U.S. coins. These suits failed, but with others she succeeded in forcing several cities to remove the cross from their seals.

In 1964 O'Hair left Baltimore, where she faced assault charges after a confrontation with police. She and her teenaged children moved to Hawaii. There her oldest son fathered a daughter, Robin, whom she later adopted. From there they moved to Mexico, from whence she was deported to Texas. With her new husband, Richard O'Hair (whom she married on 18 October 1965), she made Austin the center of what she hoped would be a national movement.

American Atheists, the largest of her several organizations, grew to thirty chapters nationwide with a total membership of several thousand. She elaborated on her philosophy on her cable television program and weekly radio show, which was heard on 150 stations. In the 1970s and early part of the 1980s O'Hair prospered, successfully soliciting donations from wealthy anti-religionists. She, her son Jon, and her granddaughter Robin took turns serving as the presidents of a family of atheist groups. They lived together in a spacious home and drove around Austin in luxury cars.

But the threesome made enemies of their fellow atheists. O'Hair grew abusive in increasingly frequent tirades against employees. Some suspected that she pocketed much of the wealth she had convinced elderly patrons to will to American Atheists. Many who had worked for her questioned her conviction, called her a detriment to their cause, and formed their own atheist organizations. Meanwhile, O'Hair's older son left the family and became an evangelical Christian.

In 1993, fighting lawsuits and the Internal Revenue Service, the O'Hairs began making plans to flee to New Zealand, where a sympathizer offered to help them resettle. In September 1995 the three disappeared with $500,000 in gold coins after leaving a note on the door of American Atheists' headquarters stating that they were out of town on business.

Although the three O'Hairs had apparently been in the process of fleeing, authorities later determined that they were probably murdered. Despite extensive searches, their bodies were never found. Federal investigators have suggested that the O'Hairs were murdered in a plot masterminded by David Waters, a former American Atheists employee who had learned of their plan to liquidate their assets and leave the country. Without their bodies, authorities could not charge Waters, who denied killing them. In August 2000 Waters's friend Gary Karr was convicted on extortion, money laundering, and other charges related to the O'Hairs' disappearance. A third man associated with the crime, Danny Fry, was found dead shortly after the family was presumably murdered.

O'Hair's mysterious disappearance underscored her ambiguous life. The atheist thrust herself into the national spotlight to defend a constitutional principle and, drawing much of the nation's ire, helped force America to accept a wider separation of church and state. But O'Hair also succeeded, through her eccentric behavior and questionable financial dealings, in making the unpopular cause of atheism in America even more unpopular.

★

Madalyn Murray O'Hair authored several books and tracts, many of them published by her own American Atheist Press, including: *Why I Am an Atheist* (1965), *The American Atheist* (1967), and *Let Us Prey: An Atheist Looks at Church Wealth* (1970). For a popular profile of Murray at the height of her fame, see Jane Howard, "The Most Hated Woman in America," *Life* (19 June 1964). For an account of O'Hair's demise, see John MacCormack, "Missing and Presumed Dead," *Texas Monthly* (28 Dec. 1999).

LAUREN MARKOE

ONASSIS, Jacqueline Lee Bouvier Kennedy (*b.* 28 July 1929 in Southampton, New York; *d.* 19 May 1994 in New York City), first lady of the United States from 1961 to 1963, style-setter, and editor.

The woman eventually known to millions simply as "Jackie" was the daughter of the wealthy and socially prominent Janet Lee and John ("Jack") Vernou Bouvier III, a stockbroker. After her parents divorced in 1940, Jacqueline and her younger sister, Lee, resided with their mother but continued to see and be influenced by their

Jacqueline Kennedy Onassis, 1979. ASSOCIATED PRESS AP

father, who made no secret of his preference for glamorous women with a touch of mystery about them. After graduation from Miss Porter's School in Connecticut in 1947, Jacqueline completed two years at Vassar College, in Poughkeepsie, New York, took her junior year in Paris, and graduated from the George Washington University, in Washington, D.C., in 1951. Months later she had her own byline ("Inquiring Photographer") at the *Washington Times-Herald,* where she earned $42.50 a week.

In May 1952 she met John F. Kennedy, a Massachusetts congressman who was preparing to run for the U.S. Senate. They married on 12 September 1953 in St. Mary's Roman Catholic Church in Newport, Rhode Island. The bride, who had grown up in a family that prized personal reserve, began a long apprenticeship in adapting to the high-energy lifestyle for which the Kennedy clan was already known. The interests she had nurtured since childhood—writing poetry, drawing, horseback riding—contrasted dramatically with the strenuous contact sports and hearty noise levels of the Kennedys. After many disappointments in the early years of her marriage (pregnancies that ended in miscarriage or stillbirth; the spinal surgeries of her husband and his failure to win the vice-presidential nomination in 1956), her luck turned: a daughter, Caroline, was born on 27 November 1957.

In 1960 Jacqueline Kennedy got her first taste of a national campaign. She had never shown much interest in politics, and after announcing in July that she was pregnant, she made few public appearances but contributed to her husband's presidential victory by writing a column, "Campaign Wife," for the Democratic National Committee's newspaper and hosting a "television listening party" to watch the debates between her husband and his opponent, Vice President Richard Nixon. Her greatest value in the campaign resulted from her own personal popularity. As the youngest wife of a presidential nominee in many decades, she attracted much attention, and her glamour, her elegant and expensive clothes, and her witty way with words added to her mysterious allure.

Well before the November 1960 presidential victory, Jackie Kennedy began assembling a staff to assist her as first lady. Soon after the birth of John, Jr., on 25 November of that year, her social secretary, Letitia Baldrige, announced that the incoming first lady would work to restore the White House to its original splendor and make it a "showcase" for American artists and talent. To quell fears that this meant adding abstract art or altering the mansion's familiar appearance, the first lady's staff emphasized that contemporary culture would be represented by performing artists but that the public rooms would retain their Early American style. Some people speculated that such a project might add to the already elitist image of the wealthy Kennedys. Nevertheless, she persisted in her plan, although she

was, she admitted, "warned, begged, and practically threatened" to leave it alone.

With the help of experts, she arranged to borrow paintings from the nation's outstanding museums. To raise money for other acquisitions and for refurbishing the interior, she established the White House Historical Association, a nonprofit historical and educational organization that published and sold guidebooks. To protect the holdings of the White House and to encourage Americans to donate precious possessions, she encouraged Congress to pass legislation making furnishings of "artistic or historic importance" the "inalienable property" of the White House. A part-time curator from the Smithsonian began cataloging White House holdings, and valuable pieces once reserved for the pleasure of a few guests went on view for all tourists to see.

Despite some criticism that the changes were too "Frenchified" or costly, Kennedy earned wide praise. In early 1962 she conducted a televised tour of the White House, and when the program aired on 14 February, more than 46 million Americans watched, thus underlining the building's prominence as a national monument and the first lady's responsibility for overseeing its condition and use. The association of her popularity with historic preservation—a topic formerly deemed stodgy—helped change Americans' attitudes. The number of visitors to the White House mushroomed.

Not all changes in the White House were limited to the public areas. Intent on providing more comfortable quarters for her family, Kennedy installed a kitchen and dining room on the second floor so that her two young children could enjoy more privacy. Upstairs, she arranged for a schoolroom so that young Caroline did not have to leave the premises. A new playground on the South Lawn was shielded from easy public view.

The first president's wife born in the twentieth century, Jacqueline Kennedy approached the job of first lady in traditional terms but with an interesting public-relations twist. When questioned, she emphasized that her most important responsibility was ensuring her husband's comfort and their children's happiness—much as her nineteenth-century predecessors had done—but she showed a savvy respect for the value of good publicity. As a former reporter, she understood that people were curious about the presidential family, but, as her father's daughter, she cherished privacy and understood its value in adding to her image. After appointing her own press secretary (the first president's wife to do so), she relied heavily on Pierre Salinger, the president's press secretary, to keep reporters away from her and her children.

In her social role as first lady, Kennedy made headlines. She arranged an elegant dinner at George Washington's estate, Mount Vernon, and scheduled other parties to honor outstanding American performers and writers. She employed a French-born chef, René Verdon, who produced menus more representative of his home country than of hers. By abolishing the formal reception line and replacing the large banquet tables with tables for ten, she made evenings at the White House less formal. Despite her reputation as a big spender, she did not order new White House china, and she noted that her choice of inexpensive glassware from a West Virginia factory helped put people to work.

Popular both at home and abroad, Kennedy became a fashion icon, and millions of women copied her bouffant hairstyle, low-heeled pumps, and sleeveless sheath dresses. The "Jackie look" gained admirers across Europe and South America, and when she accompanied the president on trips outside the United States, she sometimes attracted more attention than he. In the spring of 1961, when she reportedly impressed Prime Minister Charles de Gaulle with her style and knowledge of French, John Kennedy introduced himself as "the man who accompanied Jacqueline Kennedy to Paris."

The first lady also traveled on her own, without the president, making forays with her children or her sister to parts of the world that she visited for her own pleasure. She thus helped accustom Americans to the idea that a president's wife had a life of her own, apart from the responsibilities of political spouse. In October 1963 she went to Greece to recover from the death of her infant son, Patrick Bouvier, born on 7 August of that year.

Soon after returning, Jackie agreed to accompany the president on a political trip to Texas. She had frequently not participated in public appearances, asking others to substitute for her and thus keeping much of her time for herself. But she made an exception in this case, and she was seated beside her husband in an open limousine when he was shot to death in Dallas on 22 November 1963. Less than two hours later, still wearing her bloodstained suit, she stood beside Lyndon B. Johnson as he took the inaugural oath. The presence of a presidential widow at such an event was unprecedented, but the photograph taken on that occasion (and widely reproduced) helped calm fears of Americans regarding the assassination of a president and the legitimate passing of power to his successor.

On the flight back to Washington, Mrs. Kennedy began planning the details of her husband's funeral, using many of the trappings that had made the funeral of Abraham Lincoln so dramatic. She specified that the catafalque upon which the coffin lay in the East Room duplicate that of Lincoln and that the funeral take place at St. Matthew's Cathedral, which was close enough so that the cortege could reach it on foot. Afterward, the young widow met privately with world leaders who had come to show their respect. Millions of people who watched the funeral on television could never forget the poignant image of her with her two young children.

Intent on assuring that her husband's short presidency would not be forgotten, she ordered that a plaque—inscribed with the number of days that "John Kennedy and his wife Jacqueline" lived there—be placed over the mantel in their White House bedroom. Only a week after the funeral, she spoke with the writer Theodore White and encouraged him to write about the Kennedy administration as "Camelot," a description that stuck, although several members of the Kennedy staff, including special assistant Arthur M. Schlesinger, Jr., insisted that it was inaccurate.

By early December, Jackie and her two children had left the White House (although Caroline continued her classes there until the end of the semester) and moved into a house in Georgetown owned by the wealthy and distinguished diplomat and New York governor Averell Harriman. Just months later, she purchased an apartment at 1040 Fifth Avenue in New York City, and she moved her family there in September 1964.

At age thirty-four, Jacqueline Kennedy faced a much longer widowhood than any of her predecessors, and she became the second (after Frances Cleveland) to remarry. Following the assassination of her brother-in-law Robert Kennedy in June 1968, she became more concerned about her own safety and that of her children. On 20 October 1968 she married the Greek tycoon Aristotle Onassis, whose enormous wealth provided the means to give them a safe haven outside the United States. Despite her safety concerns, she continued to keep her children in New York City schools and to live much of the year there. Many Americans objected to her remarriage on the grounds that Onassis's Greek citizenship, advanced age (he was twenty-three years her senior), and reputation for womanizing and aggressive business dealings made him unworthy of a woman widely viewed as a national icon. When he died in Paris on 15 March 1975, she was in New York City but issued a statement about how he had "meant a lot to her" and had "rescued" her at a time when her life "was engulfed with shadows." She inherited more than $20 million from his estate while the bulk went to his daughter, Christina.

Later that year Jacqueline Onassis started working at Viking Press in New York City but moved to Doubleday in 1978. Beginning as an associate editor, she eventually became a senior editor responsible for about a dozen books each year by authors that included Bill Moyers, Michael Jackson, and the Nobel Prize winner Naguib Mahfouz. She also served as a board member of the American Ballet Theatre and worked to save historic buildings, most notably New York City's Grand Central Station. She continued to nurture her first husband's legacy with her support for the John F. Kennedy Presidential Library in Boston.

Wherever she went, Onassis continued to attract attention. Escorted at first by a variety of prominent men, she had as her constant companion for the last twelve years of her life the Belgian-born diamond dealer Maurice Tempelsman. On walks in Central Park she was sometimes photographed with her young granddaughters, the children of Caroline Kennedy Schlossberg.

In early 1994 Onassis was diagnosed with non-Hodgkin's lymphoma, and she died at her Fifth Avenue apartment on 19 May. Although she had been a member of the nearby St. Thomas More Church, her funeral service took place at the larger St. Ignatius. Her son, John, Jr., who spoke at the service, noted that he and his sister had searched for the themes that shaped her life, and in the end they had selected three: love of words, emphasis on family, and desire for adventure. Burial followed at Arlington National Cemetery, in Arlington, Virginia, where her first husband and the two children who had predeceased them (infant Patrick and an unnamed stillborn daughter) were also buried.

The four-day auction of Onassis's personal effects at Sotheby's in New York in April 1996 resulted in "insane" buying and reaped more than $34 million, far more than predicted. But it was hardly unexpected, since she had fascinated Americans for nearly four decades with her signature style.

★

The John F. Kennedy Library is the chief repository of Onassis's papers, including several hundred boxes of White House social files and 200 oral-history transcripts containing references to her. On her early years, see John H. Davis, *The Bouviers: Portrait of an American Family* (1969). On the White House years, see Letitia Baldrige, *Of Diamonds and Diplomats* (1968); Carl Sferrazza Anthony, *First Ladies,* vol. 2 (1991); and James A. Abbott and Elaine M. Rice, *Designing Camelot* (1998). Following her death, authors interviewed people who knew her and now spoke more openly about her and about the Kennedy marriage; see Edward Klein, *All Too Human* (1996), and Christopher P. Andersen, *Jack and Jackie: Portrait of an American Marriage* (1996). A front-page obituary is in the *New York Times* (20 May 1994).

BETTY BOYD CAROLI

O'NEILL, Thomas Philip, Jr. ("Tip") (*b.* 9 December 1912 in North Cambridge, Massachusetts; *d.* 5 January 1994 in Boston, Massachusetts), Massachusetts congressman who served for nearly four decades in Washington, holding positions as Democratic Party whip, majority leader, and Speaker of the House.

O'Neill was a third generation Irish-American whose father, Thomas O'Neill, was a bricklayer and superintendent of sewers in Cambridge, Massachusetts, and whose mother, Rose Ann Tolan, died within months of his birth. O'Neill

Thomas P. "Tip" O'Neill. ARCHIVE PHOTOS

had three siblings and attended parochial schools, graduating from St. John's High School in 1931. During this time, he received his nickname, a reference to another O'Neill, a baseball player whose specialty was foul balls that encouraged opposing pitchers to miss the strike zone and walk him. O'Neill completed his education at Boston College, graduating with an A.B. degree in 1936.

During these formative years, he developed his political ideas. O'Neill had grown up in a world in which businesses regularly discouraged Irish applicants by displaying signs that read "NINA," meaning "no Irish need apply." As a cutter of grass on the Harvard campus, he deeply resented the privileged students of that institution. The ensuing Great Depression and New Deal programs of President Franklin D. Roosevelt convinced him that politics could change the prejudices and other ills of American society.

After a brief venture in insurance and real estate, O'Neill turned to politics. He was a Democrat because of family upbringing. As for Republicans, so one of his sons later said, he was tolerant, on the principle of "hate the sin, but love the sinner." The five O'Neill children—he married Mildred Anne Miller on 17 June 1941—spent summers on the beach at Plymouth, Massachusetts, and remembered running down to the water yelling, "Last one in is a Republican!"

O'Neill's political career began in college when he ran for the Cambridge City Council in a field of sixty candidates, of whom the top eight were elected. He finished ninth, having failed to campaign in his own neighborhood, whose votes he took for granted. His father thereupon told him, "All politics is local." A Mrs. O'Brien had announced she was going to vote for him, and he told her he had thought that surely she would do so, as she knew him so well. "Tom," she replied, "let me tell you something: people like to be asked." He never forgot those two comments, and often quoted them.

His rise in politics was slow but sure. Elected to the Massachusetts House of Representatives in 1936 and subsequently reelected, O'Neill became minority leader in 1947. When the Democrats for the first time since the Civil War obtained a majority in 1948, he became speaker. He put through a series of legislative acts that supported his social beliefs, among them a strengthening of the state's mental health institutions; a reduction in interest rates to prevent usury; workmen's compensation; doubling of teachers' salaries; benefits for veterans and for the elderly; and laws making it illegal to bar anyone from employment because of color, creed, or age. In 1952 he successfully ran for the congressional seat vacated by John F. Kennedy, who that year was elected to the Senate. The race against Michael LoPresti was a close one—the last close race of O'Neill's career. Arriving on the national scene early in 1953, the already much-experienced O'Neill took to Washington politics with gusto.

When he entered the House of Representatives it was an old-fashioned place dominated by the committee chairmen, mostly long-time southern congressmen. O'Neill dubbed them the "College of Cardinals." Newcomers and first-termers were expected to keep their mouths shut and speak when spoken to. O'Neill chose to attend the daily morning meetings of the Democratic whip, John W. McCormack, also from Boston. Because his family remained in Cambridge, O'Neill was able to devote virtually all of his time to his work. McCormack, who eventually became speaker, was a formal, prim man who took nothing to excess. He did not drink alcohol, and it was said of him that he did not even burn the candle at one end. McCormack regularly invited O'Neill to accompany him on his evening rounds to receptions. During O'Neill's second term, in an almost unheard-of appointment, McCormack placed him on the prestigious Rules Committee.

As a member of the committee, O'Neill undertook to enlighten his fellow House members about when bills were coming up and to remind them when they absolutely had to be present for a crucial vote. Over the years he came to prominence, mixing well with Republicans and exercising his skills as a manager of people by restraining committee chairmen such as the head of the Rules Committee, Howard W. Smith, "an arrogant son of a bitch"—in O'Neill's words—"and an ultraconservative who was no more a Democrat than the man in the moon." When a 1961 civil rights bill came up for vote, it so happened that Smith had to return to Virginia because a barn on his property there had burned. Speaker Sam Rayburn (with O'Neill's ardent support) enlarged the Rules Committee to fence in Smith, and thus prevented him from successfully opposing the legislative program put forth by the newly elected Democratic president, Kennedy.

Under Kennedy's successor, Lyndon B. Johnson, legislation passed because Johnson was his own whip and Congress duly responded. Although Johnson did O'Neill a service by ensuring that Secretary of Defense Robert S. McNamara did not close down the Boston Navy Yard, O'Neill did not feel obligated to return the favor by keeping silent in his opposition to U.S. involvement in the Vietnam War. This was a particularly audacious thing to do, in light of the fact that his working-class constituency was in favor of the war. Years later this act of conscience redounded to his credit when House liberals voted as a bloc in favor of his elevation to the speakership.

With the election of Republican Richard M. Nixon to the presidency in 1968, the task of Democratic House leaders became difficult. Several subsequent changes in House procedures were carried out largely in the Democratic caucus, changes such as a requirement of majority approval for the choice of committee chairmen and the chairmen of Appropriations Committee subcommittees. Regular meetings of the caucus provided a forum in which rank-and-file members could inform committee members of their views and in a few instances instruct them in their work.

In 1971 O'Neill became House whip. The next year, majority leader Hale Boggs of Louisiana disappeared in an airplane crash in Alaska, and some months later O'Neill took his place. During the election of 1972, the new majority leader took alarm over rumors of severe pressure on GOP members and even Democrats to make contributions to the Nixon campaign. Because of what O'Neill saw as the timidity of then-speaker Carl Albert of Oklahoma and of Judiciary Committee chairman Peter Rodino of New York, he came out strongly against Nixon and soon was supporting impeachment. He did not do this in preparation for the speakership, but it increased his popularity.

Upon the retirement of Albert, O'Neill was chosen speaker of the House in January 1977, and he immediately began to push for his own programs. His meeting with the Rules Committee, several members of which he appointed, was instructive. He told the committee on 24 February 1977, "I've committed myself as the leader of the party to the strongest ethics bill in the history of the country. And

I'm asking you, the Rules Committee, as the one hand-picked committee that's appointed by the Speaker." He went around the room and took pledges of support. All eleven committee Democrats voted for the O'Neill rule.

The speaker made himself available, in his office or on the floor, for any member wishing to talk with him, a procedure he described in his memoirs as serving as a confessor, letting members get things off their chests. His predecessor had considered such availability a waste of time.

O'Neill came to the speakership in the same month that President Jimmy Carter entered the White House, but O'Neill was always on awkward terms with the Carter administration. The new president submitted legislation without consulting the House leadership, and his assistants seemed arrogant to many legislators, often not answering members' telephone calls. Regarding Carter's chief of staff, Hamilton Jordan, O'Neill later wrote, "As far as Jordan was concerned, a House speaker was something you bought on sale at Radio Shack." He complained to President Carter, who in a signed photograph carefully thanked O'Neill for his political lessons.

Relations with the Republican president Ronald Reagan, inaugurated in 1981, were, if anything, worse. The victorious Republicans pushed through conservative programs diametrically opposed to O'Neill's worldview. O'Neill called the president "Herbert Hoover with a smile" and "a cheerleader for selfishness" and noted that the name of the Irish village Ballypooreen, from whence Reagan's family had come, meant "Valley of the Small Potatoes."

A large man, obese in his later years, possessed of a bulbous nose, yellowed white hair, and everlasting cigar, O'Neill stood out in a crowd. For years he roomed in Washington with Representative Edward P. Boland, Democrat of Massachusetts, his closest friend. Their refrigerator, it was said, was stocked almost exclusively with beer. When he became speaker, his wife moved to Washington, and they remained there after retirement, with a summer house on Cape Cod, Massachusetts.

O'Neill retired from Congress in 1987 at the end of his seventeenth term. Also in that year, and again in 1990, he had surgery for colon cancer. O'Neill, who often spoke candidly about the disease, died in his beloved Boston at the age of eighty-one. Down to the end, he displayed his joie de vivre. He is buried in Harwich Port, Massachusetts.

O'Neill's principal contribution to American politics was twofold. First was his extraordinary shrewdness, so evident in the storytelling in his memoirs and a book of stories published the year he died. The other contribution was his work in carrying on the New Deal tradition of the Democratic Party at a time when for some party members that tradition had lost its luster. As the president of Boston College, J. Donald Monan, said at his funeral mass, Tip O'Neill had a faith in who he was and where he came from—for him power was no attraction, only the desire to bring government help to people who needed it. He had a story for that, too. At a political dinner during his heyday of power he shared the rostrum with the two Massachusetts senators, Edward J. Kennedy and Edward Brooke. Two hundred people, he said, came up and asked Kennedy for his autograph; two hundred asked Brooke for his autograph; and twenty came up and asked Tip for jobs.

★

There are 685.5 linear feet of O'Neill papers, including 196.5 feet of artifacts, in the Boston College library. The only full-length account of O'Neill's life is Paul Clancy and Shirley Elder, *Tip: A Biography of Thomas P. O'Neill, Speaker of the House* (1980). The congressman's books are *Man of the House: The Life and Political Memoirs of Speaker Tip O'Neill* (1987), with William Novak, and *All Politics Is Local: And Other Rules of the Game* (1994), with Gary Hymel. There is an excellent obituary by Martin Tolchin in the *New York Times* (7 Jan. 1994).

ROBERT H. FERRELL

P-Q

PACKARD, David (*b*. 7 September 1912 in Pueblo, Colorado; *d*. 26 March 1996 in Palo Alto, California), electrical engineer and industrialist who substantially influenced the rise of the global electronics industry and new management practices in high-technology companies.

Packard was the son of Sperry Sidney Packard, an attorney, and Ella Lorna Graber, a high-school teacher. Packard had two siblings, a brother who died in infancy and a sister who died at age twenty. Educated in Pueblo public schools, Packard took an early interest in radio and other things electrical. He built a ham radio system and frequently visited the technicians at a small local radio station. While his parents had little direct interest in this area, both encouraged Packard. One area of mutual interest to Packard and his father was athletics. The six foot, six inch tall young man excelled at football, basketball, and track in high school and college. Although he was raised in a comfortable home, he was not immune to hardships in the steel town of Pueblo. As the Great Depression deepened, Packard's father was appointed as a bankruptcy judge for the area. Through the elder Packard's compassionate approach to cases, the young Packard absorbed a philosophy of helping one's community, which guided many of his actions in corporate social programs for his Hewlett-Packard (HP) employees, the communities with HP facilities, and the nation.

While on visit to Palo Alto, California, in the summer of 1929, Packard toured Stanford University. He decided to apply to Stanford to study electrical engineering, a career choice he had made several years earlier. He graduated from Centennial High School in Pueblo in 1930, and entered Stanford that fall. There he formed several influential and enduring relationships. Two of the most significant were those with Professor Frederick E. Terman, who served as dean and provost, and later became known as the "father" of "Silicon Valley," and with fellow student William R. Hewlett, with whom he later cofounded the Hewlett-Packard Corporation in 1939. Terman encouraged the two men in radio engineering and nurtured the growing bond between Packard and Hewlett.

On graduating from Stanford, with a B.A. degree in 1934, Packard entered an economy still mired in the Great Depression. He felt he could not take the risk of an uncertain income at the time and accepted a position with General Electric in Schenectady, New York. He joined the section that made mercury-vapor rectifier tubes for the control of spot and seam welding. This position provided training that was important to him later. Many tubes were failing quality-control tests. Engineers and production employees worked together to conduct tests and identify every cause of failure. Packard later reported that he "found the factory people eager to do the job right." Personal communication helped both groups to correct the problem. At HP, Packard spent much time on the floor talking to and

403

David Packard. LIBRARY OF CONGRESS

helping employees, hence increasing performance, productivity, and loyalty.

On 8 April 1938, Packard married Lucile Laura Salter; they had four children. A few months later, Terman arranged a fellowship for Packard to complete his engineering degree at Stanford (which required a fifth year of study). Packard obtained a leave from General Electric and returned to Stanford, where his friend Hewlett was also studying and where he earned an E.E. degree in 1939. While in the engineering program, Packard enrolled in business courses, believing that they would provide him with useful skills as he embarked that year on an electronics company with Hewlett.

With an initial investment of $538 and some used equipment, Packard and Hewlett responded to the requests of several electronics entrepreneurs in the area for custom products. They worked on a weight-reducing machine, an electronic harmonica tuner, and a bowling alley foul-line indicator. Their initial success, and HP's first product, was a resistance-stabilized audio oscillator designed by Hewlett

as part of a class exercise. It was the first low-cost method of generating high-quality audio frequencies needed in communications, geophysics, medicine, and defense work. By the end of 1939, they had sold eight audio oscillators to Disney Studios for use in making the film *Fantasia*. HP went on to develop a full line of audio-frequency-measuring instruments. Even in their first full year of business (1939), HP sales totaled $5,369 with a profit of $1,653, the start of a long trend of profit.

During World War II, HP continued to expand its product line and develop new products, especially those associated with the needs of others in the defense effort. Hewlett served in the U.S. Armed Forces and Packard ran the company. Many of the new electronic concepts spawned during the war in radio frequency and microwave engineering were put to good use in new products. With the end of the war and the drive to establish a new technology-based economy, HP was well positioned to thrive. Although there was an inevitable slowdown in the late 1940s, the company continued to stay profitable and take care of its employees. Hewlett stayed closer to the engineering side of the company, and Packard moved over more into the business side. Decisions were always made jointly. They maintained a close bond with Stanford and Terman, and attracted able people to the company as it expanded throughout the 1950s.

Packard believed that the company should only make products that contributed to the economy and the nation, not just the company's bottom line. They achieved this by knowing customer needs and building quality products. Most products were successful as a result of HP's policy of only becoming involved in areas they knew well. They began with electrical engineering equipment designed by Hewlett and Packard that performed better and were cheaper than those on the market in 1939. Beginning with an audio oscillator for use in communications, geophysics, and medicine, they added a full line of audio-frequency measuring instruments. They excelled in this line of products and slowly acquired companies whose lines of business were on the boundaries of the HP product line. As high technology changed, HP kept pace with the change, often directing it.

Three things contributed to the HP's spectacular growth after 1955. The first was the internationalization of operations. HP opened manufacturing plants in Europe and began a joint venture with a Japanese firm. A second was the acquisition of companies whose product lines bordered on those of HP. Often these were companies HP had decided not to compete with because their products were handled by the same agents, and marketing would have been adversely affected if competition for certain products intensified. The third was the initial public offering of HP stock in 1957. Publicly traded stock allowed HP to acquire other companies through a stock exchange, alleviating the need for cash and helping employees benefit from HP growth through a stock option plan.

From HP's beginning in the late 1930s, Packard and Hewlett paid keen attention to their employees' welfare. Packard and Hewlett frequently interacted with employees at their work stations; gave generous benefits packages (with far-reaching implications for the general industry); provided opportunities for employees to socialize outside of the work place; placed offices and officers in a way that enhanced and encouraged communication among workers; frequently evaluated of the goals of the entire work force; and established what came to be called "management by objectives Packard and Hewlett downplayed their own special status in the company and rarely used authority as a means of control. Employees were not released, even for poor performance. Instead, more suitable positions were found for them. In difficult economic times, HP did not lay off workers. Instead, everyone's time was reduced by some percentage to ensure a talented and dedicated work force at all times.

As the company grew, the founders needed additional personnel to manage the multi-dimensional company. They developed a list of corporate objectives, modified only slightly after broad consultation within the company, to guide the firm after their departure. The objectives encapsulated all the aims and policies of Packard and Hewlett for the company. Long before the partners approached retirement, they began to groom successors imbued with these ideals. This "HP way" became the model for other companies. Packard became a model in other ways as well. HP was not just a good place to work, it also became a good community partner. Gifts from the company to civic and social programs, encouragement of community participation by employees, and public service away from the company represented Packard's initial philanthropic contributions. As his personal wealth increased, he and his wife began sharing their largesse with other groups.

Packard's main residence after 1937 was in Palo Alto, having lived in only two homes there. In 1952 the Packard and Hewlett families decided to engage in a ranching partnership. They purchased a ranch south of San Jose, California, in an area called San Felipe. Later they added Los Huecos to the south of the original tract. Packard actually helped to build twenty miles of road on the land piloting his own bulldozer to level the way. Ranch land in Idaho and California's Central Valley came later still. The families used these tracts for vacations, hunting trips to which they often brought guests, cattle raising, and fishing, all favorite hobbies of Packard.

President Richard Nixon asked Packard to serve as deputy secretary of defense in late 1968. Packard accepted the position, at great personal financial sacrifice, because he considered it his civic responsibility. Some detractors, however, suspected him of having self-serving motives. During his three years in defense, Packard devoted himself to reforming costly procurement and management practices, played a prominent role in the administration's Vietnamization policy, oversaw daily departmental operations, and represented it to the National Security Council. He participated in such monumental discussions as the bailout of the Lockheed Corporation, the development of the B-1 bomber, and the government wage freeze, which he opposed for military personnel. After leaving the department, he continued to serve presidents in many capacities. Meanwhile, he shared his wealth with various educational and charitable organizations, mostly through the David and Lucile Packard Foundation he and his wife had established in 1964. Through this foundation, the Packards made extensive donations to scientific research, community organizations, education, health care, conservation, population projects, and the arts.

Packard received many awards and commendations for his work and donations, including six honorary degrees. He served at various times as a trustee of Stanford University, the Hoover Institution, Colorado College, and the American Enterprise Institute. He was a member of the White House Science Council, the Institute of Electrical and Electronics Engineers, and the American Management Association. He died of complications from pneumonia in Palo Alto, California.

★

Packard's view of his life's accomplishments can be found in his book *The HP Way: How Bill Hewlett and I Built Our Company* (1995). For a useful discussion of the Hewlett-Packard Company and "Silicon Valley," see Michael S. Malone, *The Big Score: The Billion Dollar Story of Silicon Valley* (1985). An obituary is in the *New York Times* (27 Mar. 1996).

ARTHUR L. NORBERG

PACKARD, Vance Oakley (*b.* 22 May 1914 in Granville Summit, Pennsylvania; *d.* 12 December 1996 on Martha's Vineyard, Massachusetts), writer, journalist, and social critic who introduced the phrase "hidden persuaders" with his book on motivational research methods used in advertising.

Packard was one of three children of Philip Joseph Packard, a farmer, and Mabel Case, a former schoolteacher. Methodist and Republican, his parents were frugal, hardworking, and abstemious. Nevertheless, their dairy farm failed. When Packard was ten, his father took a job as a farm superintendent in the Agriculture School at Pennsylvania State College (Penn State). Packard's inclination for writing surfaced in high school, where he edited his class year-

Vance Packard, 1977. AP/WIDE WORLD PHOTOS

book. He graduated in 1932. As an English major at Penn State, he wrote for both the literary magazine and the college newspaper and coedited the *Summer Collegian*. He contributed to the cost of his education by working part-time in both the college library and student union.

While in college, Packard was influenced by Willard Waller, a sociology professor whose progressive background included muckraking journalism. Waller encouraged his students to look for the reality beneath the surface. That training was to serve Packard well in the research and writing of his most important works.

Graduating from Penn State with a B.A. degree in 1936, Packard began work as a cub reporter for $15 a week at the *Centre Daily Times* in State College, Pennsylvania. Soon thereafter, he secured a scholarship at Columbia University's Graduate School of Journalism, from which he earned his M.A. degree in 1937. Packard's first writing job after Columbia was in Boston at the *Daily Record,* which hired him to write features about personalities. Packard now felt secure enough to propose marriage to Mamie Virginia Mathews, whom he had met when they were both undergraduates. Married on 25 November 1938, the couple had three children.

In 1938 the Associated Press (AP) feature service in New York City hired Packard to edit and write a weekly review, *The World This Week*. He remained at the AP until 1942, when he went to work for the Crowell-Collier Publishing Company as editor of the "interesting people" section of *American Magazine*. Within two years he became a staff writer, a post he held until the magazine went out of business in July 1956. The company then moved him over to

Collier's, but that magazine also ceased publication in December of the same year.

In 1941 Packard returned to Columbia's School of Journalism, where he taught as a part-time lecturer on reporting and photo editing until 1944. In 1945 he joined the faculty at New York University, where he lectured on magazine writing until 1957. He also began work on *How to Pick a Mate* (1946), which he coauthored with C. R. Adams, the director of the marriage counseling service at Penn State. His second book, *Animal I.Q.* (1950), dealt with experiments in animal psychology and countered ideas about animal intelligence and reasoning popular with pet owners and animal lovers. Voluminous and eclectic, his magazine articles treated topics as varied as education, science, national problems, travel, entertainment, food, and dieting. He also explored parent-child relations and family problems.

In the early 1950s, Packard began to collect material for the book that was to cast a spotlight on him. He was studying motivational research (MR), especially the work of Ernest Dichter, a psychoanalytic consultant to business and industry. He used more than fifteen hundred sources, read more than three million words, and produced *The Hidden Persuaders* (1957), a book about the way advertisers used MR to influence consumer purchase decisions subconsciously.

At a time when conspiracy theories abounded in America, Packard's book, which suggested that advertising methods could easily work their way on an unsuspecting public, hit a responsive chord. It became a best-seller and was the leading book on the nonfiction list for several weeks. Reviews helped popularize the book. A. C. Spectorsky, writing in the *New York Times,* called the book "frightening, entertaining and thought-stimulating." C. J. Rolo, the reviewer for the *Atlantic Monthly,* found in it "a wealth of documentation which is often appalling." And Charles Winick, in the *Christian Science Monitor,* found the book to be "of value in opening to fuller public view an important area in American life which deserves closer scrutiny than it has been getting."

The response to *The Hidden Persuaders* was not uniformly positive. Those aligned with the advertising industry and business took exception to Packard's conclusions and attacked the work on the basis that it lacked scholarly thoroughness. Leo Bogart wrote in *Management Review* that the book's lack of scholarly apparatus such as references might make it more interesting and readable, but "without such references, how can the reader judge how much of the findings should be taken literally and how much should be discounted as unsubstantiated or just plain wrong?"

Packard followed his phenomenal success with studies of other troublesome aspects of American life. *The Status Seekers* (1959) looked at the way the country was betraying its democratic foundations by dividing itself between haves and have-nots according to material possessions and rank. *The Waste Makers* (1960) explored "planned obsolescence," the means by which manufacturers created products whose usefulness or desirability faded quickly, allowing them to sell new and improved versions. In *The Pyramid Climbers* (1962), he put his skills to work analyzing the psychology of the American corporate structure and found there another negative influence on society. *The Naked Society* (1964) turned to a broader concern, exposing the threat to freedom inherent in modern information-gathering and surveillance techniques as well as in behavior modification methods. Shifting relations between the sexes were viewed in *The Sexual Wilderness* (1968). In *A Nation of Strangers* (1972), Packard linked the American freedom of mobility to a growing rootlessness in the nation. His final book, *Our Endangered Children* (1983), viewed the changes in the modern world, especially those leading to the disintegration of the family, as detrimental to childrearing.

Reaction to Packard's work passed through several stages. He was criticized by some contemporaries for having a Puritanical philosophy that condemned consumption and waste and advocated a simple life, while at the same time enjoying the fruits of an upper-class life in his comfortable New Canaan, Connecticut, home. In the 1990s his views went through a reevaluation, summarized by his biographer Daniel Horowitz, who notes that for the millions of Americans who "came to understand the imbalance between public and private needs," Packard's writings "promoted an animus against experts, attacked unquestioned growth, and emphasized the social and psychological costs of status and class" and "stressed the quest for meaningful work and for a more democratic workplace, addressed the perils of conformity in corporations and suburbs, questioned discrimination based on ethnicity, advocated consumer rights, and expressed concern for ecological balance and natural resources."

A Democrat and member of the Congregational Church, Packard served for a time on the New Canaan planning commission. He was also a member of the Society of Magazine Writers. He had blue eyes and brown hair, some of which he lost in later life. He stood five feet, nine inches tall and weighed about 180 pounds. In addition to his New Canaan home, he owned property on Chappaquiddick Island near Martha's Vineyard, where he loved sailing his small boat and where he died of a heart attack. He was cremated and the ashes were buried on Chappaquiddick Island.

★

Packard's papers, at the library at Pennsylvania State College, are mostly research notes, clippings, and various drafts of his major books The definitive biography of Packard is Daniel Horowitz, *Vance Packard and American Social Criticism* (1994). An obituary is in the *New York Times* (13 Dec. 1996).

Richard L. Tino

PARISH, Dorothy May Kinnicutt ("Sister Parish") (*b.* 15 July 1910 in Morristown, New Jersey; *d.* 8 September 1994 in Dark Harbor, Maine), one of the most influential interior designers of the twentieth century, whose most famous work was done for the Kennedy White House.

Parish was the daughter of stockbroker and antiques collector G. Hermann Kinnicutt and homemaker May Appleton Tuckerman. The only daughter, she grew up with three brothers. Her brother Frankie gave her the nickname "Sister," by which she was known her entire life. The family was privileged and owned homes in Morristown, New Jersey; New York City; Dark Harbor, Maine; and Paris. Her forebears included the famous Puritan leader Cotton Mather and Oliver Wolcott, a signer of the Declaration of Independence. The comfort in which she was reared would influence the types of clientele she served as a design professional. Her father graduated from Harvard and with his uncle formed the brokerage firm Kissell, Kinnicutt; later it merged with Kidder, Peabody and Company. In 1920 the family moved from Morristown to Mayfield in New Jersey, where her room was the only one decorated in a French style. This helped shape her decorating taste.

Parish's formal education was limited. She graduated from Miss Chapin's School in New York City after the eighth grade and attended the Foxcroft School in Middleburg, Virginia, from which she never graduated. According to Parish, efforts to broaden her education through fencing, dance lessons, and piano lessons proved fruitless; she described herself as "untalented and graceless."

In 1928 she had an epiphany while visiting the family apartment in Paris. "Something stirred in me," she later said. She went from room to room, seeing the place in "new, more careful ways. . . . I realized that a deep, abiding belief in all things inherited, and all things of lasting quality, had been awoken in me. I was finally beginning to understand beauty and the role it would play in my life."

On 14 February 1930 she married Henry "Harry" Parish II, a Harvard graduate and stockbroker. They had three children. In 1933, during the Great Depression, Harry came home and announced that his salary at work was being cut. His wife decided to help the family by starting her own decorating business. She went to Stroheim and Roman, a well-known fabrics firm, and was able to persuade the head of the company to sell her materials on credit. A few weeks later, she rented her first office, in Far Hills, New Jersey, for $35 a month. She named the firm

Mrs. Henry Parish 2d Interiors. When Parish began the business, individuals were seldom hired for decorating jobs; firms were employed. Her earliest clients came from her social set, which was an enormous boon to a young, inexperienced businesswoman. The first client at the Far Hills office had a decorating budget of $100,000 in the midst of the depression.

When World War II came, Parish closed her business, did volunteer work, and from 1941 to 1943 worked for the company Budget Decorators, then resurrected her own company. After the war she entered into an agreement with the British decorating firm Colefax and Fowler. They sent her furniture, which she sold in New York, and she sent them tassels and other accessories that were hard to get in postwar England. Sibyl Colefax, John Fowler, and Nancy Lancaster, all affiliated with the firm, were major influences on Parish.

In 1962 Parish hired Albert Hadley, a graduate of the Parsons School of Design, to assist her in the business. At that time she was considering retiring, but that changed with the engagement of Hadley. In 1964 he became a partner in the firm, and it became Parish-Hadley. His formal training and his leaner, more modernist style, combined with Parish's more "romantic" style, produced one of the most successful decorating businesses of the twentieth century.

Parish's signature style, the "American country style," included flowered chintz, crocheted throws, needlepoint pillows, mattress ticking for slipcovers and throw pillows, hooked rugs, rag rugs, and starched organdy. She used vibrant colors to brighten rooms; three of her favorites were robin's egg blue, coral, and shrimp. She painted walls in bold colors such as reds and yellows. She also utilized four-poster beds, painted floors, and hand-woven bedsteads in her decorating. These innovations replaced the dark, heavy furniture that was a trademark of the Victorian look.

Parish was admired for her skill in placement and the ease, warmth, and comfort that she brought to the rooms that she decorated. She preferred that her work have an "unstudied," even cluttered look, and she is said to have "felt" her way around a room. Parish admitted that the ability to reach into the past and reintroduce something that was good and beautiful was a trademark of innovation. She has been called "a force informing and articulating tastes in interior design." She also introduced "tea carting" into the decorating lexicon. She would enter a client's room and would fill up a teacart with any accessories that she deemed to be unsuitable. It did not matter how expensive they were, or how much the client valued them: they would be removed.

Parish gained greater visibility when Jacqueline Kennedy hired her as a consultant in the White House redecorating project. Other clients among the wealthy and pow-

erful included the William Paleys, Brooke Astor, Edith Haupt, Oscar de la Renta, Al and Tipper Gore, and Happy Rockefeller, as well as the Whitneys, Vanderbilts, Gettys, and Mellons. The firm's impressive array of alumni include David Anthony Easton, John Robert Moore II, William Hodgins, Mariette Himes Gomez, Mark Hampton, Kevin McNamara, Bunny Williams, and Libby Cameron. Parish herself received the title of charter member of the *Interior Design* Magazine Hall of Fame in 1985.

Sister Parish's impact on decorating can be summarized partly by the comments made in 1995 by Lou Gropp, editor of *House Beautiful*: "There is no question that Sister Parish was one of the biggest influences on decorating in the United States. . . . She dominated the decorating of the 1970s and '80s, and many of her ideas that were fresh and new in the 1970s are now in the mainstream of American decorating."

Parish died at the age of eighty-four from pneumonia complications. She is buried in Dark Harbor, Maine. The firm of Parish-Hadley continued for five years after her death, until Hadley closed it at the end of 1999.

★

Parish's daughter May Appleton Parish Bartlett compiled Parish's memoirs, as well as comments and tributes from friends, relatives, and clients, in *Sister: The Life of Legendary American Decorator, Mrs. Henry Parish II* (2000). *Parish-Hadley: Sixty Years of American Design* (1995), by Sister Parish, Albert Hadley, and Christopher Petkansas, is a good source on Parish's work, containing essays by Parish and Hadley as well as numerous examples of their decorating styles. Suzanne Trocme, *Influential Interiors* (1999), has profiles of important twentieth-century interior designers including Sister Parish. Articles of note include Jura Koncius and Patricia Dane Rogers, "Doyennes of Décor," *Washington Post* (20 Oct. 1994); Martin Filler, "Remembering Mrs. Parish: Sister's Legacy," *House Beautiful* (Jan. 1995); "Designer's Designer," *St. Louis Post-Dispatch* (17 Aug. 1995); Julie V. Iovine, "Albert Hadley Draws the Shades," *New York Times* (30 Sept. 1999); and Steven M. L. Aronson, "Sister Parish: The Doyenne's Unerring Eye for Warmth and Grace," *Architectural Digest* (Jan. 2000). Obituaries are in the *New York Times* (10 Sept. 1994), the *London Independent* (26 Sept. 1994), and *Interior Design* (Oct. 1994).

JENNIFER THOMPSON-FEUERHERD

PAULING, Linus Carl (*b.* 28 February 1901 in Portland, Oregon; *d.* 19 August 1994 in Big Sur, California), renowned chemist and peace activist and the only person to receive two unshared Nobel Prizes.

Pauling was born and raised in Oregon. His father, Herman Henry William Pauling, was a modestly successful,

Linus Pauling. AP/WIDE WORLD PHOTOS

self-taught druggist; his mother, Isabelle ("Belle") Darling, was the descendent of a pioneer family. Pauling's childhood was marked by tragedy, emotional isolation, and precocious independence. His father died when he was nine, leaving the small family, including Pauling's mother and two younger sisters, alone and with limited means. Belle Pauling, devastated by the death of her husband and with her health crippled by pernicious anemia, used most of the family's savings for a down payment on a boardinghouse on the edge of town. Driven by an anxious, often-bedridden mother, all three children worked at early ages to keep the house going.

After his father's death, Pauling withdrew into books and hobbies. An interest in insects and minerals was followed, at age thirteen, by a fascination with chemistry spurred by a friend's demonstration of simple home experiments using a toy chemistry set. Pauling gathered his father's old pharmacy books, wheedled glassware from a drugstore salesman, smuggled chemicals and equipment home from an abandoned smelter, and created a homemade "laboratory" in a corner of the boardinghouse's basement. Here he sought solace in learning the rules of chemistry and spent hours in free-form experimentation, much of it focused on the creation of substances capable of burning or exploding.

In high school a sympathetic chemistry teacher provided Pauling with special tutoring. This, combined with the at-tention of educated neighbors, helped the young man set his sights on college. By the time he was a high school senior, Pauling was self-confident enough to defy both his school principal, who refused to let him graduate early, and his mother, who wanted him to give up college in favor of a job in a local machine shop. At age sixteen he dropped out of high school and enrolled at Oregon Agricultural College (now Oregon State University), where he intended to pursue a degree in chemical engineering.

Away from home, Pauling blossomed. He quickly demonstrated that he knew more about chemistry than many of his professors. While still an undergraduate, he jumped at the chance to teach chemistry courses in the understaffed department, and he reaped two side benefits: greater access to current chemical journals, which he read avidly, learning the latest theories; and close proximity to dozens of young female students. One of the latter was an extremely bright and flirtatious Oregon girl named Ava Helen Miller. They were soon in love and married on 17 June 1923, a year after he received his B.S. degree from Oregon and after his first year in graduate school at the California Institute of Technology (Caltech). Miller remained a strong influence throughout his life.

Pauling developed an interest in the questions of how and why atoms bond together to make molecules, and Caltech, then a little-known, fledgling research institute, was a perfect place to study. He was one of the school's first chemistry graduate students, beneficiary of a program devised by the renowned and innovative chemical educator A. A. Noyes. Pauling's graduate work focused on a new and little-used analytical technique called X-ray crystallography, a complex and painstaking procedure in which beams of X rays were shot at crystals, the resulting scatter patterns visualized on photographs, and the patterns analyzed mathematically. If done correctly, the patterns indicated the positions of individual atoms in the crystal. Using this technique, researchers for the first time were able to map the distances and angles between individual atoms. The only problem was that the technique could only be used on very simple crystals. More complex substances yielded patterns too difficult to analyze. After a shaky start in the laboratory—Pauling's talents were always more theoretical than experimental—he mastered the technique and earned his Ph.D. in 1925. At Noyes's urging, he then spent fifteen months in Europe on a Guggenheim fellowship.

But knowing how atoms were arranged in molecules, something he could determine at least in simple cases with X-ray crystallography, was only half the story. Pauling also wanted to know the nature of the chemical bond that caused atoms to join together in certain ways and not others. To find the answer, he focused his studies on physics. His timing was propitious. In Europe a new and powerful advance in physics, quantum mechanics, was being born in the late 1920s, and Pauling was lucky enough to learn it from its creators, including Arnold Sommerfeld, Werner Heisenberg, Wolfgang Pauli, Niels Bohr, and Erwin Schrödinger.

After returning to Caltech as a young faculty member in 1927, Pauling embarked upon an extraordinary professional career, beginning the task of rebuilding chemistry on the foundation of quantum mechanics. His approach involved an intuitive mix of bold theory and empirical research, memorable lectures, persuasive papers, and best-selling textbooks. He was a communicator as well as an innovator. The new physics was mathematically challenging for all but a handful of chemists in the late 1920s, but Pauling knew how to simplify the math and describe results at a level chemists could quickly grasp.

He was also successful at discovering the structures of complex substances. Pauling used X-ray crystallography to gauge the distances and angles between atoms in simple crystals, then used the results as guides to what was or was not possible regarding more complex structures. By whittling down the possibilities, he was able to make highly educated guesses at structures for more complex substances. He would then toss the remaining theoretical structures in the wind of quantum mechanics, blowing away those that were not in accordance with the principles of the new physics. Once he eliminated as much chaff as possible, Pauling tested the best remaining structures by seeing how they looked, creating three-dimensional molecular models out of paper, wire, and wood. The single most plausible remaining structure he would test once again by predicting the ways it would behave, including its melting and boiling points and its X-ray patterns. If the model matched the qualities of the real molecule, he would publish his findings.

It was a brilliant approach and it worked. Pauling believed two things strongly: that rules of chemistry and physics determined how molecules were built, and that the structure of molecules explained their activity. He played both ends. Knowing the rules, he could eliminate and illuminate possible structures; knowing the structures, he could amend and refine the rules. His memory was prodigious and his approach independent. He appeared cognizant of few boundaries, dancing gracefully between physics and chemistry, laboratory results and theory. In a dazzling series of papers throughout the 1930s, Pauling made important advances in determining the structures of complex minerals as well as describing the chemical bond in quantum mechanical terms. This work was capped in 1939 with the publication of *The Nature of the Chemical Bond,* one of the most-cited texts in science history.

By then, at age thirty-eight, Pauling was a full professor; head of the chemistry division at Caltech; the youngest person ever elected to membership in the National Academy of Sciences; and father of three sons and a daughter.

In the mid-1930s Pauling took his research in a new direction. The Rockefeller Foundation at that time was directing significant funding toward defining the molecules essential to life. Lured by Rockefeller support, Pauling turned his attention to the structure of biomolecules, especially proteins such as hemoglobin and antibodies. These were gigantic structural problems, molecule orders of magnitude more complex than any Pauling had worked with before. But again his hard work, deep understanding of simpler chemical structures, and model-building approach brought him success. Over the next fifteen years he made important discoveries about hemoglobin, including tracking the cause of sickle-cell anemia to changes of a few atoms among many thousands. Pauling also studied antibodies, producing the most sophisticated work at the time regarding the structural relationship between antibody and antigen. In addition, he investigated enzymes and other proteins. The capstone of this work was the publication in May 1951 of seven papers detailing the structures of a number of proteins at the level of individual atoms.

Pauling developed the powerful idea that biological specificity (the precise matching of antibody and antigen, for example, or the ability of an enzyme to react with only one substrate) was due to complementarity, in which the shape of one molecule precisely fits another like a key in a lock. This structural insight was critical to the development of molecular biology. For his achievements in structural chemistry Pauling was awarded the 1954 Nobel Prize in Chemistry.

By then, however, Pauling's maverick temperament had made him well known for something other than science. At the urging of his wife, he began focusing on stopping the development and spread of atomic weapons. Many scientists shared Pauling's antinuclear sentiments, but few were as outspoken or perseverant. A proponent of world government and democratic socialism, Pauling had no qualms about attacking U.S. government policies he deemed wrong. Federal authorities responded by putting him under FBI surveillance, canceling research grants, refusing him a passport, and stripping him of his security clearance. Senator Joseph McCarthy accused him of being a communist, and the press smeared Pauling; still, he carried on.

By the late 1950s Pauling was a world leader in the peace movement. In 1957 and 1958 he and his wife gathered the signatures of some 11,000 scientists on a global petition to end nuclear weapons testing and presented it to the United Nations. He was finally rewarded: the day after the first nuclear test ban treaty went into effect on 10 October 1963, Pauling learned that he had won the Nobel Peace Prize. Instead of warm public support following the award, however, Pauling encountered criticism. The *New York Herald-Tribune* dubbed him a "placarding peacenik," and *Life* magazine called the prize "a weird insult from Norway." Many observers felt that President John F. Kennedy should have won the award instead.

During his years of political activism, Pauling's science foundered. Following a failed attempt to find a structure for deoxyribonucleic acid (DNA), he moved his research increasingly toward the study of what he termed "molecular medicine." Pauling believed that the body could be viewed as an array of chemical reactions. Optimal health, in his view, could thus be achieved if the reaction conditions were right and the proper molecules present in the proper amounts. He spent years trying to find a molecular basis for mental disease, ways to counter inborn metabolic conditions, and a theory of anesthesia. But here Pauling's theories outstripped the technology of the time: the complexity and subtlety of biochemical systems in living organisms required more sophisticated analytical tools than had yet been invented. Each of his lines of investigation, while promising, refused to yield definitive results. His only significant scientific success during this period was a theory, developed with Emile Zuckerkandl, outlining how tracking the differences in similar biomolecules (such as hemoglobins) between various species could be used as a clock to time evolutionary divergence. The "molecular clock" idea has since proven important for evolutionary biology.

His Caltech colleagues in the late 1950s began grumbling about Pauling's fruitless pursuit of medical findings instead of basic chemistry. The president of Caltech and a number of trustees were concerned about his reputation as a left-wing agitator. As a result, in the late 1950s Pauling lost the chairmanship of the Caltech chemistry division, along with a good deal of his laboratory space. It was an insult he never forgot. One week after winning the Nobel Peace Prize, Pauling announced that he was leaving Caltech.

He spent the next decade as an academic nomad, working at various think tanks and universities, never finding a suitable intellectual home. Pauling spent much of the 1960s working on unifying ideas, including a system of ethics based upon science, as well as a book on the molecular basis of civilization, but nothing was published.

In the late 1960s Pauling became interested in the health effects of a single vitamin, ascorbic acid or vitamin C, which some evidence indicated had beneficial effects on everything from the common cold to cancer, but his controversial and widely publicized claims were strongly criticized by the medical community. There is no doubt that his work helped change the nutritional habits of millions of people, and a growing body of evidence in later years underscored the importance of high doses of vitamins, including C, in promoting health. In 1973 Pauling cofounded a California research institute devoted to the study of the health effects of vitamin C and other nutrients. There he conducted research until his death from cancer at age ninety-three. He had long outlived Ava Helen, who died thirteen years earlier, on 7 December 1981.

Pauling had a substantial effect on the history of science. Modern chemistry owes a great deal to his ability to explain chemistry in quantum mechanical terms, and to successfully apply his strongly structural approach to the form and function of complex organic and inorganic molecules. Pauling's insights about the importance of complementarity between giant molecules as a basis for biological specificity became an important approach for the new field of molecular biology—a field in which Pauling can be rightly considered a founding father.

Using his scientific fame as a springboard for political activism, Pauling became an important figure in the worldwide peace movement of the 1950s. His perseverance in the face of persecution was admirable; his rallying of scientific opinion against atmospheric nuclear testing was critical in achieving public sentiment in favor of a test ban. But perhaps history will judge Pauling most kindly for his character rather than his deeds. Especially in the current era of bland, poll-based, middle-of-the-road politics, Pauling's maverick outspokenness and willingness to risk his career for what he thought to be right appears increasingly admirable.

★

Pauling's personal and scientific papers are available in the Oregon State University Special Collections in Corvallis, Oregon. Additional Pauling-related material is available in the archives of the California Institute of Technology. Several overviews of his life are available, including Thomas Hager, *Force of Nature: The Life of Linus Pauling* (1995) and *Linus Pauling and the Chemistry of Life* (1998); and Ted and Ben Goertzel, *Linus Pauling: A Life in Science and Politics* (1995). Also useful is Barbara Marinacci, ed., *Linus Pauling in His Own Words* (1995). Obituaries are in the *Los Angeles Times* (20 Aug. 1994), *New York Times* (21 Aug. 1994), and *Chicago Tribune* (28 Aug. 1994).

Thomas Hager

PEARL, Minnie (*b.* 25 October 1912 in Centerville, Tennessee; *d.* 4 March 1996 in Nashville, Tennessee), popular country music comedian and fifty-year member of Nashville's *Grand Ole Opry*.

Born Sarah Ophelia Colley, Minnie Pearl was the youngest of five daughters of Thomas. K. Colley, a prosperous lumberman, and Fannie Tate House, a well-born woman who was an accomplished amateur pianist and dedicated suffragist. The woman who built a career on hayseed humor

Minnie Pearl (in costume). AP/WIDE WORLD PHOTOS

and backwoods diction grew up in a home where the refinements of education and genteel southern culture were paramount values. From an early age she yearned for a career as a great dramatic actress. However, when she was a high-school senior, the stock market crash of 1929 derailed her hopes of majoring in drama at a prestigious college. She had to compromise by attending Ward-Belmont College in Nashville, a two-year women's finishing school with a highly regarded drama department.

Upon graduation in 1932, she had no socially acceptable choice but to return to Centerville and live with her parents. She opened a studio where she taught dramatics, piano, and dancing, but she was bored and discontented. In 1934, determined to seek a theatrical career, she applied to the Wayne B. Sewell Production Company, which organized theatrical productions in small towns using local talent under the direction of a Sewell-trained director. To her parents' dismay, she was accepted and left home to spend the next six years on the road, traveling from town to town in the rural South, putting on a show every ten days.

In January 1936 Colley was housed with an impoverished old woman in a remote region of Alabama who in her own words "had sixteen young'uns and never failed to make a crop." This endearing lady became the model for the personality of a country girl who would evolve into Minnie Pearl. The name Colley chose combined, she said, "two fine country names. . . . There was always an Aunt Minnie or a Cousin Pearl back where I came from." Near

Colley's childhood home, there was a freight railroad station where her father loaded his lumber. It was known as Grinder's Switch. Colley took this name as Minnie Pearl's hometown.

She began to use the character of Minnie Pearl as a publicity ploy to promote the productions she staged for Sewell. In 1939 she received an offer to do a paid performance as Minnie Pearl from a women's group in Aiken, South Carolina, where she had previously directed a Sewell production. Deciding that Minnie needed a costume to reinforce the portrayal, Colley found a cheap yellow organdy dress at a secondhand shop along with white cotton stockings and a tacky straw hat. She would later add black Mary Jane shoes and a $1.98 price tag on the hat.

When the Sewell Company went out of business in 1940, Cannon returned to Centerville. She ran an afterschool recreation program for the Depression-era Works Progress Administration, meanwhile developing the character of Minnie Pearl. A family friend wangled an audition for her with the manager of the Nashville radio station that broadcast the *Grand Ole Opry*. She was granted a one-shot spot on the show and scored an instant hit. Minnie Pearl received several hundred fan letters, and Colley was hired as a *Grand Ole Opry* regular, the first female member of the troupe. It was not Colley's dream of becoming a great dramatic actress, but it was a way out of Centerville.

Soon after Colley's debut, Roy Acuff, known as the King of the Opry, asked her to join his weekly road show, doing one-night stands and returning each Saturday night to Nashville to do the *Grand Ole Opry*. This grueling life on the road would be Colley's for the next twenty-seven years. Just before and during World War II, Colley toured with Pee Wee King, presenting shows at military bases throughout the United States, in Panama, and across Europe. Later she toured with Eddy Arnold and Rod Brasfield.

Shortly after the end of the war, she met Henry Cannon, a former Air Force pilot who later ran a charter airplane service. They were married on 23 February 1947. The new Mrs. Cannon decided to give up life on the road while keeping her career alive only with her Saturday night slot on the *Grand Ole Opry*. The high point of this period was a 1947 appearance at Carnegie Hall for two sold-out performances. Before a year had passed, Minnie Pearl was back on the road, often traveling with her coworkers in her husband's charter planes. Henry Cannon soon dropped his charter service and concentrated on flying his wife to her many engagements and managing her business affairs. The couple had no children, which Pearl referred to in her autobiography as the biggest disappointment of her life.

During the next two decades, she delivered Minnie Pearl's rousing opening greeting ("How-DEE! I'm just so proud to be here!") in nightclubs, theaters, and concert halls and at country fairs and rodeos. She appeared with such stars as Hank Williams and Elvis Presley. In addition, she guest-starred on numerous television variety shows, such as those hosted by Mike Douglas, Dinah Shore, and "Tennessee" Ernie Ford. In 1957 Pearl was featured on the popular biographical television show *This Is Your Life*. This helped lead to a regular twenty-two-year slot on the country comedy show *Hee Haw*.

In her later years, Pearl scaled back her public appearances and focused on civic activities and charitable endeavors, notably cancer research. In 1965 she was named Nashville Woman of the Year. In 1975 she was inducted into the Country Music Hall of Fame, the first comedian accorded this honor. A stroke in 1991 ended her public career and left her bedridden for nearly five years. She died in Nashville following a final series of strokes and was buried in Mount Hope Cemetery in Franklin, Tennessee.

Had Minnie Pearl been perceived merely as a caricature of a country bumpkin, her popularity could never have become as permanent and wide-ranging. Her genius was to create a character of such uncomplicated warmth and joyous silliness that she broadened the audience for country humor as well as for country music around the world.

★

Minnie Pearl: An Autobiography by Minnie Pearl with Joan Dew (1980), like its author, is straightforward but focused on the upbeat. *Behind Closed Doors: Talking with the Legends of Country Music* by Alanna Nash (1988) devotes a chapter to Pearl. *The Encyclopedia of Country Music,* edited by Paul Kingsbury, and compiled by the staff of the Country Music Hall of Fame and Museum (1998) furnishes helpful facts and dates in a sketch by Kingsbury. An obituary is in the *New York Times* (6 Mar. 1996).

NATALIE B. JALENAK

PENICK, Harvey Morrison (*b.* 23 October 1904 in Austin, Texas; *d.* 2 April 1995 in Austin), celebrated golf instructor and author whose students included Ben Crenshaw and Tom Kite.

Penick was one of three boys born to Daniel Penick, a municipal employee in the city of Austin, and Molly Miller. Penick received a minimal education in the Austin public schools and became a golf caddie at the age of eight, a role he took pride in all his life. When not yet thirteen years of age, he became an assistant professional at Austin Country Club. Upon graduating from high school in 1923, he became head professional at the club. In his many roles as greenskeeper, caddie master, clubmaker, and instructor, Penick was both witness to and participant in the transformation of golf. The year he became head professional, Walter Hagen broke the line that barred professionals from entering country clubs. Previously, golf professionals had

Harvey Penick, 1964. AP/WIDE WORLD PHOTOS

been regarded as ne'er-do-wells, but Hagen changed all that.

Penick played a respectable game of golf, which in Texas terms—given the likes of Jack Burke, Jimmy DeMaret, Bill Melhorn, and Ky Lafoon—was considerable. However, in 1930 Penick chose not to follow the itinerant life of the touring professional. His marriage on 27 December 1929 to Helen Holmes of Whitesboro, Texas, encouraged him to lead a settled life in Austin.

In his next career position, as coach for the University of Texas golf team, Penick often advised talented golfers about turning professional. Many of his players came from families with oil, banking, insurance, and real estate interests, but he cautioned them against chasing a profession that as late as the 1940s provided a precarious living at best. For Penick, the joy of golf was in the satisfaction to be gained from improvement, and his teaching style fit his temperament. His University of Texas teams won twenty Southwest Conference titles during his tenure from 1931 to 1963.

The Professional Golfers Association named its teacher of the year award the Harvey Penick Award, but Penick remained one of golf's best-kept secrets until at the age of eighty-eight, he showed Edwin "Bud" Shrake, a writer, notebooks that he had been keeping for more than sixty years. The ideas, tips, theories, anecdotes, and personal reminiscences that Penick penned in his "Little Red Book" soon became a phenomenon in both golf and publishing history. *Harvey Penick's Little Red Book: Lessons and Teachings from a Lifetime in Golf* (1992) became an instant success. Penick was overwhelmed when told that the advance for the book would be about $90,000. He thought it was money required of him, and suggested to Shrake that taking out another mortgage might be an answer. The book sold 1.3 million copies by 1995. The two men collaborated on three other works: *And If You Play Golf, You're My Friend* (1993); *For All Who Love the Game: Lessons and Teachings for Women* (1995); and *The Game for A Lifetime: More Lessons and Teachings* (1996). A video was also developed and marketed, and the Golfsmith firm of Texas developed a line of golf clubs according to his design.

Penick's common sense came through in the written word as though he were standing beside the reader. He cautioned the need to ease the tension in the elbow, showing three knuckles of the top hand in the gripping of the club, nipping a tee with the swing as practice, and putting negative thoughts from the mind at every stroke of the club. Penick had an instinct for recognizing the potential of his students. He had the ability to grasp what would and could work with each individual. His rule was never to attempt to change what worked naturally for a golfer despite the unorthodoxy of a particular technique.

The mythology, mystery, and romance of golf were never part of Penick's passion for the game. Building on sound fundamentals and reinforcing confidence in one's abilities were basics that transcended the mystical. He believed in the need of golfers to associate with better players. As for the role of providence, Penick advised Sandra Palmer, who called him while playing the U.S. Women's Open, "If God wants you to win, you will." She went on to win and to join the legendary women golfers who were his pupils, including Babe Didrikson Zaharias, Mickey Wright, Kathy Whitworth, Betsy Rawls, Cindy Figg-Currier, Betty Jameson, and the accomplished amateur Judy Bell, who became president of the U.S. Golf Association in 1996. Six of his women students became members of the Ladies Professional Golf Association Hall of Fame.

Penick's male students were even more numerous and included Don January, Tommy Aaron, Jimmy Thompson, Davis Love, Jr., and the latter's son, Davis Love III. Two former members of his university team, Tom Kite and Ben Crenshaw, went on to brilliant and lucrative careers in professional golf.

Penick severely cracked his spine when thrown from a golf cart in 1972, the year following his retirement as head professional at the Austin Country Club. He still gave private lessons, though degenerating arthritis crippled him and kept him in constant pain. He slept virtually sitting up in a downstairs bedroom in his house on the country club's course. A hospital stay in 1991 did little to alleviate his condition.

Kite, who had been Penick's pupil for twenty-nine years, had never won a major tournament and was forty-two years old in 1992. He was not invited to the Masters that year, though he had the best record of finishes in the preceding decade. Instead he took his game to Pebble Beach and the U.S. Open, where in wind, wet, and cold, he won the coveted national crown and had his wife, Christy, take the trophy to Penick in Austin as his gift for all his help over the years. Kite returned to Penick's sickbed in 1995, where the immobile and speechless Penick was told that Davis Love III had won in New Orleans and gained a spot in the Masters. Penick feebly raised his hands in applause at the news.

Crenshaw told Love to stay in Augusta to prepare for the Masters rather than follow him to Austin to be with Penick. Kite and Crenshaw were pallbearers at his funeral, and he was buried in Austin Memorial Park. One week later, Crenshaw was on the sixteenth fairway in a tie for the lead with Love who was already finished. Crenshaw went two under par in the final three holes, dropping to his knees on the eighteenth hole, the emotion of the events ovewhelming him. His tears were for Penick and what Penick meant to him personally and for the game of golf. Crenshaw went on to win the Masters the following week. As defender of the championship in 1996, Crenshaw invited Penick's wife, Helen, to be his special guest at the Masters. It was her first visit to the tournament.

★

In addition to Penick's own books, useful sources include Herbert Warren Wind, *The Story of American Golf: Its Champions and its Championships*, 2d ed. (1972), and Tom W. Kite with Mickey Herskowitz, *A Fairway to Heaven: My Lessons from Harvey Penick on Golf and Life* (1997). *Golf Digest* has several articles dealing with Penick, including Mickey Herskowitz, "Golf's Greatest Teacher of the Century" (Sept. 1985), and Don Wade, "The Wit and Wisdom of Harvey Penick" (July 1989). *Sports Illustrated* has a study of the 1995 Masters highlighting Ben Crenshaw in an article by Rick Reilly, "For You Harvey: Ben Crenshaw's Second Masters Win Was a Memorial to His Mentor" (17 Apr. 1995). An obituary is in the *New York Times* (4 Apr. 1995).

JACK J. CARDOSO

PEPPARD, George (*b.* 1 October 1928 in Detroit, Michigan; *d.* 8 May 1994 in Los Angeles, California), stage, screen, and television actor who established himself with his film role opposite Audrey Hepburn in *Breakfast at Tiffany's* (1961) and was the star of several popular television series.

Peppard was the only child of George Peppard, Sr., a building contractor, and Vernelle Rohrer, a voice teacher and opera singer. His parents were in their forties when he was born, his mother having had five miscarriages before him. After graduating from Dearborn High School in suburban Detroit, Peppard enrolled as an engineering student at Purdue University in Indiana, where he was one of the founders of the Purdue Playmakers. Then his father died suddenly. According to the actress Elizabeth Ashley, who was married to Peppard, he left Purdue, went home to Detroit, and finished the construction projects his father had failed to complete before dying; then he joined the Marine Corps. When he got out of the service, Peppard enrolled at Carnegie Tech (now Carnegie Mellon University) on the GI Bill. He earned his B.F.A. degree in 1955.

Peppard made his professional debut playing the male lead in Arthur Miller's *The Crucible* at the Pittsburgh Playhouse. While a college student, he performed in the Oregon Shakespeare Festival in 1952 and 1953. After graduating from Carnegie Tech, he enrolled in Lee Strasberg's Actor's Studio in New York City. During this time Peppard lived on Bleecker Street in a $40-a-month flat and worked part-time as a cab driver. His first Broadway appearance was in N. Richard Nash's *Girls of Summer* in 1956. While he earned favorable notices, the play was panned by all the major New York critics and closed after fifty-six performances. Peppard received favorable notices in his next Broadway appearance in *The Pleasure of His Company* (1958), which starred Cyril Ritchard and Cornelia Otis Skinner.

Peppard made his film debut in 1957 with Pat Hingle and Arthur Storch in *The Strange One*. Next he appeared in *Pork Chop Hill* in 1959. Peppard played leading roles in *Home from the Hill* and *The Subterraneans*, both in 1960. He received the National Board of Review Award for best supporting actor for *Home from the Hill*. In 1963 he first received top billing in *The Carpetbaggers*.

Peppard was memorable for his role opposite Audrey Hepburn in *Breakfast at Tiffany's* (1961), Blake Edwards's adaptation of Truman Capote's novella of the same title. According to Alexander Walker's biography of Hepburn, as a method actor Peppard approached his role as a technician and thoroughly analyzed the contours of his role. Walker further observed that *Breakfast at Tiffany's* was the first film in which Hepburn played opposite an actor who was her own age. The next year, Peppard was impressive as the young sheriff in John Ford's Oscar-winning epic *How the West Was Won*. He continued to enjoy success as an actor, although much of his later career consisted of more routine adventure films. According to Ashley, Peppard was talented, educated, and intelligent, but he had been shaped professionally at the end of the era of powerful Hollywood studios. Peppard, she wrote, was "caught between being an actor and being a movie star." In a film career spanning more than thirty years, he appeared in more than twenty-five motion pictures.

His earliest television roles included a memorable part in the CBS drama special *Bang the Drum Slowly,* starring Paul Newman, in 1956; *The Little Man of Alban,* with Julie Harris in 1959; and appearances on the *Hallmark Hall of Fame,* the *Alcoa Hour,* and *Alfred Hitchcock Presents.* Beginning in the 1970s Peppard did extensive TV work. After a modestly successful crime drama series, *Banacek* (1972–1974), he starred in a less successful medical drama, *Doctors' Hospital* (1975–1976). In 1978 he wrote, produced, and directed *Five Days from Home.* He had been cast in the part of Blake Carrington in *Dynasty* but was replaced by John Forsythe during the filming of the pilot. Peppard played his best-remembered TV series role as John (Hannibal) Smith, an army veteran leading a team of renegade soldiers of fortune on *The A-Team* (1983–1987). The show was successful in the ratings, although it was criticized for its violence. Peppard once told an interviewer that the role of Hannibal "is probably the best part I've had in my career. It was a good script, and a good script is hard to find." After *The A-Team* was canceled in 1987, Peppard returned to the stage and in 1990 appeared in *Love Letters,* opposite Elaine Stritch, in London's West End. In the early 1990s Peppard

George Peppard, *c.* 1960. Archive Photos

toured the United States in *Papa,* a one-man show based on the life and career of Ernest Hemingway.

In 1992, as a result of many years of heavy smoking, Peppard had a cancerous tumor removed from his lungs. He finally quit smoking. He was married six times to five women. He was twice married (first in 1966) to Elizabeth Ashley, his costar in *The Carpetbaggers* and with whom he had one son. Both marriages to Ashley ended in divorce. His other wives were Helen Davies (1954–1964; they had two children), Sherry Boucher (1975–1979), Alexis Adams (1984–1986), and Laura Taylor (1992), who survived him.

Although he spent most of his life as an actor, producer, and writer, in his later years he spent much of his time helping alcoholics and working for various charities. He died of respiratory complications due to pneumonia at the age of sixty-five and is buried at Northview Cemetery in Dearborn, Michigan.

★

Elizabeth Ashley's *Actress: Postcards from the Road* (1978) details her life with Peppard. Alexander Walker's biography of Audrey Hepburn, *Audrey: Her Real Story* (1994), references Peppard. He was profiled in *Current Biography* (1965). Obituaries are in the *Los Angeles Times* and *New York Times* (both 10 May 1994) and *Newsweek* (23 May 1994).

JOHN KARES SMITH

PERPICH, Rudolph George ("Rudy") (*b.* 27 June 1928 in Carson Lake, Minnesota; *d.* 21 September 1995 in Minnetonka, Minnesota), governor of Minnesota known for his unusual ideas, which earned him the sobriquet "Governor Goofy."

Perpich was one of several children of Anton and Mary Perpich. Anton Perpich immigrated to the United States from Croatia in 1920 and settled among the numerous Slavic miners on Minnesota's "Iron Range" in the vicinity of Duluth. His mother was born in the United States to Croatian parents. Although the language of the home was Serbo-Croatian, and thus young Perpich began school without knowing English, his parents emphasized the value of education. They inculcated in all their children the view that education was the way out of the marginal living conditions of the Iron Range. On 4 September 1954 Perpich married Delores ("Lola") Helen Simich; they had a son and a daughter.

Perpich attended nearby Hibbing Junior College and then, at the urging of his father, went on to earn a D.D.S. degree at the Marquette University School of Dentistry in Milwaukee, Wisconsin, in 1954. For several years following his graduation, he practiced dentistry in Minnesota, but he soon found his vocation in politics, being elected to Hibbing's school board shortly after his graduation from the

Rudy Perpich. ASSOCIATED PRESS

dental school. In 1962 he was elected to the state senate, where he served for eight years, together with two of his brothers, Tony, representing Pine City, and George, who represented Shoreview.

Throughout his life Perpich represented the progressive wing of Minnesota politics. He was a representative in the state senate, and he ran for lieutenant governor in 1970 on the ticket with Wendell Anderson as a member of the Democratic-Farmer-Labor Party, which was a coalition of liberal and progressive political groups in Minnesota and established in the 1930s. Perpich had been known to declare that no one would elect a Catholic of Slavic background from the Iron Range as governor and that his only hope of reaching that office was to back into it from the position of lieutenant governor.

That was precisely what happened. Anderson, although an effective governor, tired of the demands made on him in that role. When Walter Mondale, one of Minnesota's U.S. senators, was elected U.S. vice president in the successful campaign of Jimmy Carter in 1976, Anderson resigned as governor, and Perpich moved up to the governorship. He then appointed Anderson as Mondale's replacement in the U.S. Senate. But the voters were outraged, and turned both Perpich and Anderson out of office in 1978. Perpich had, however, tasted the fruits of political office, and after a few years in Europe as a representative of Control Data Corporation, he returned to Minnesota and won the 1982 Democratic-Farmer-Labor primary as a candidate for governor. He went on to win the general election. Perpich had numerous governmental reforms to his credit. Perhaps the most important of these were improvements in education. His predecessor had reformed the financing of education so that more funds flowed to schools that lacked the real estate tax base to support good education. Perpich expanded on this reform by getting the state legislature to approve "open enrollment," a system that generally allowed parents to enroll their children in the public school of their choice, whether or not they lived in that school district. He also pushed through a proposal to allow senior high school students to take college courses at one of the state-supported colleges or universities and at state expense. He worked hard to upgrade the academic standing of the University of Minnesota. Finally, he was instrumental in the construction of the new Minnesota History Center in St. Paul, part of the reconstruction of the capitol area into an aesthetically pleasing state "campus."

One of Perpich's major achievements was expanding the role of women in state government. He chose a woman to run as lieutenant governor in his successful campaign to recapture the governorship in 1982, and he appointed a number of women to important administrative positions in the state as well as to many of the state courts. It was on his watch that Minnesota passed a law requiring equal pay for women who did a comparable job. A special commission was created to determine the "comparability" of the jobs women did with those of men. His wife, Lola, helped him entertain his political associates in Slavic style.

Perpich was an avid promoter of the Minnesota business community. He scoured the country to find a developer prepared to build a giant mall, and the result was the Mall of America, the largest such development in the United States. Few believed him when he promised to attract the Super Bowl to Minnesota, but he succeeded in 1992. He was an indefatigable salesman of Minnesota, persuading numerous high-tech industries to relocate to the state. One of his strangest ideas was to help Minnesota's depressed Iron Range, the old mining district around Duluth, by persuading a company to start a chopsticks factory there, an idea he conceived to counterbalance the negative U.S.-Japan trade balance in the 1980 (this was not a successful business venture).

Perpich's sense of community with the underprivileged of society led him to champion the Native American tribes still living on reservations in Minnesota. Following a U.S. Supreme Court decision in 1987 authorizing the tribes to create their own businesses, as well as the Indian Gaming Control Act passed by Congress in 1988, Perpich became the point man for those Minnesota Indian tribes that wanted to open gaming casinos. As a result, eleven of the first thirteen Indian gaming casinos in the United States were located in Minnesota. Moreover, the compacts that Perpich as governor negotiated with the Indian tribes gave the latter a perpetual right to operate such facilities, in contrast to the more limited contracts agreed to in other states.

Following his victory in 1982, he won reelection in 1986. By 1990, however, the voters had tired of Perpich's flamboyant methods and turned him out of the governorship once again. He died of colon cancer at his Minnetonka home and is buried in Minneapolis's Lakewood Cemetery.

Perpich epitomized the American dream, coming from modest, immigrant-based origins and reaching the penultimate layer of government, leadership of a state. He was a flamboyant, leader, and though he earned the nickname "Governor Goofy"—an epithet applied by one of his political opponents and transferred to the national stage by *Newsweek* magazine—in retrospect he rates as one of the best leaders in the history of Minnesota.

★

There is no full-length biography of Perpich, but there is a small chapter on him in Jim Klobuchar's *Heroes Among Us: Uncommon Minnesotans* (1996). Some of his specific programs are treated in Daniel J. Elazar, Virginia Gray, and Wyman Spano, *Minnesota Politics and Government* (1999). His obituary in the *Minneapolis Star-Tribune* (22 Sept. 1995) contains numerous tributes to his accomplishments as governor from a variety of leading Minnesota politicians.

NANCY M. GORDON

PETERSON, Roger Tory (*b.* 28 August 1908 in Jamestown, New York; *d.* 28 July 1996 in Old Lyme, Connecticut), artist, writer, and naturalist who achieved world fame as an author, illustrator, and editor of nature books.

In his youth, Peterson displayed a spirited and rebellious independence. His father, Charles Gustav, had come from Sweden as a small child and worked as a craftsman in the furniture factories of Jamestown. Peterson's mother, Henrietta Bader, brought to western New York by her German immigrant parents, worked as a teacher and homemaker. Peterson had a younger sister. His passion for nature study began at age eleven; he had a particular, but not exclusive, interest in birds. He used existing published guides to birds, wildflowers, and butterflies, but he was critical of their inadequacies.

Peterson developed skills in writing and drawing while attending Jamestown High School. He graduated in 1925 and took a job applying decorative painting to furniture. In

Roger Tory Peterson in his studio in Old Lyme, Connecticut, 1993. ASSOCIATED PRESS AP

November he attended the annual meeting of the American Ornithological Union (AOU) at the American Museum of Natural History in New York City. There he met the well-known bird scholar Ludlow Griscom and the bird artists Louis Agassiz Fuertes and Francis Lee Jaques. Peterson had submitted two bird paintings to be shown at the meeting, and exhibited his work again at the 1926 meeting of the AOU in San Francisco, which he did not attend.

Peterson enrolled in New York City at the Art Students League in 1927 and 1928 and at the National Academy of Design from 1929 to 1931 to study drawing and painting. His pursuit of bird watching continued undiminished. He found in New York City a small group of young men who shared his passion for birds and joined their Bronx County Bird Club. He continued to paint furniture decorations to supplement his income.

During his student years, Peterson spent summers as a nature counselor at a summer camp in Maine, developing into an enthusiastic and effective teacher. This led in 1931 to his position as an art and natural history teacher at the Rivers Country Day School in suburban Brookline, Massachusetts. His association with the prosperous families that summered in Maine and favored private education had the effect of cultivating refined social graces and gentlemanly behavior in Peterson.

Peterson began writing and illustrating articles that were published in *Field and Stream* and *Nature Magazine*. His book *A Field Guide to the Birds* was published by the

Houghton Mifflin Company in 1934 and was an immediate success. His innovation, the Peterson System of bird identification, was based on similarities of form, size, and color, rather than on scientific relationships, that could be used by the amateur observer. The *Field Guide* went through four editions, and together with his *A Field Guide to the Western Birds* (1941), eventually sold more than seven million copies.

Suddenly in demand as a famous author, in 1934 Peterson joined the National Association of Audubon Societies, where he served as art editor of *Audubon* magazine until 1943. He also was the association's educational director and principal lecturer and writer. His first duties included redesigning and illustrating the Audubon publications; he also wrote many of their articles.

In 1935 the Audubon Societies established a camp in Hog Island, Maine, with Peterson playing a major role in planning the facilities and programs and becoming the bird instructor in 1936. Programs were offered to adult nature enthusiasts. Peterson and one of these students, Mildred Washington, were immediately attracted to each other and were married on 19 December 1936. Peterson suddenly found himself in the social register, having married a descendant of George Washington's family. They had no children.

Peterson undertook a heavy schedule of traveling and lecturing, and continued his writings on nature, producing magazine articles and the major book projects *Junior Book of Birds* (1939), *A Field Guide to the Western Birds*, and *Birds Over America* (1948). His career activities aggravated some basic incompatibilities in his marriage with Mildred, and they divorced in 1942.

Peterson married Barbara Coulter, a curator of the Audubon photo library, on 9 July 1943; they had two sons. During World War II, Peterson was drafted into the army, serving in the Corps of Engineers. From 1943 to 1945 his writing and illustration talents were used to produce military instruction manuals. He adapted the Peterson System of bird identification to the task of enemy plane spotting. Toward the war's end, he contributed to an Army Air Corps research project on the dosage effects of the insecticide DDT.

Peterson's abilities as a writer, lecturer, and illustrator of the beauties of nature found a vast international audience. His articles appeared in *Life* magazine and *National Geographic,* and he formed partnerships with overseas naturalists. His books with the British ornithologist James Fisher, *Wild America* (1955) and *A World of Birds* (1964), were milestones in nature publishing. The demand for his participation as a teacher and advocate for wildlife preservation took him to projects in eighty countries. From 1946 he was general editor of the Houghton Mifflin Peterson Guide Series, which ran to twenty-one volumes.

Barbara Coulter Peterson became an independently accomplished naturalist. Her custody of the family's home responsibilities was unavoidably lonely, and the marriage suffered and ended in divorce after thirty-two years, in 1976.

Peterson was considered handsome and never lacked for female attention. He was six feet tall and had an outdoorsman's trim and robust figure. In maturity, his white hair was full. He married Virginia Westervelt, a divorced neighbor in Old Lyme, Connecticut, on 8 April 1976.

In his later years, Peterson devoted his energy to gallery-type painting and produced a series of limited edition collector's prints of wildlife, particularly birds. He received many honors, including awards, honorary degrees, and memberships on the boards of major organizations, worldwide. He received the Geoffrey St. Hilaire Gold Medal from the French Natural History Society in 1958 and the Presidential Medal of Freedom in 1980.

Peterson died at his home in Old Lyme. His remains were cremated and buried on Great Island at the mouth of the Connecticut River. His name had long since become practically synonymous with bird watching. The ecologist Paul Ehrlich wrote: "In this century, no one has done more to promote an interest in living creatures than Roger Tory Peterson. . . . His greatest contribution to the preservation of biological diversity has been in getting tens of millions of people outdoors with Peterson's Field Guides in their pockets."

★

John C. Devlin and Grace Naismith, *The World of Roger Tory Peterson* (1977), is an authorized biography that is enhanced by Peterson's own illustrations and many anecdotes of close friends and associates. An obituary is in the *New York Times* (30 July 1996).

MICHAEL F. HAINES

POGUE, Forrest Carlisle (*b.* 17 September 1912 in Eddyville, Kentucky; *d.* 6 October 1996 in Murray, Kentucky), historian, educator, and biographer of George C. Marshall.

Pogue was the son of Forrest Carlisle Pogue and Frances Carter Pogue. His politically active grandfather Marion Pogue, a teacher, lawyer, farmer, and proprietor of a country store, had a large library and interviewed local residents and wrote articles about early local settlers for the county newspaper. Years later, Forrest Pogue said that his grandfather might have influenced him to become an oral historian. Young Pogue entered high school at the age of eleven, graduated at fourteen, and studied history with his grandfather for a year. He then entered Murray State College in Kentucky at sixteen, graduating in 1931. He received a M.A. degree from the University of Kentucky in 1932 when only nineteen years old and his Ph.D. in history

Forrest Pogue. AP/WIDE WORLD PHOTOS

from Clark University (Massachusetts) in 1939. He was an American Exchange Fellow at the Institut des Hautes Études Internationales at the University of Paris during the academic year 1937–1938. Pogue began his teaching career as an instructor at Western Kentucky State College in 1933, and he rose from instructor to associate professor at Murray State College between 1933 and 1942. He met his future wife, Christine Brown, an artist, when she was a student in one of his classes in the mid-1930s; years later they met again in Germany and were married on 4 September 1954. They had no children.

Drafted into the army in 1942, Pogue was digging a foxhole one day at Fort McClellan, Alabama, when his commanding officer received an order to "find a soldier with a Ph.D. in history." The order had come from Washington, and the bemused Pogue was asked by his immediate superiors if he was "playing politics"; he responded that he was not. He was selected as an army combat historian, first writing a training history of the Second Army, and later interviewing men who had gone ashore in Normandy on D-Day in June 1944 shortly after the invasion. He remained with front-line troops, fulfilling a variety of assignments, until the end of the war in Europe, earning a Bronze Arrowhead (for his participation in the invasion), four battle stars, and the Bronze Star and French Croix de Guerre for his "front-line interviewing."

Following the war Pogue served as a civilian historian with the army from 1945 to 1952 and as an operations research analyst at Johns Hopkins University under contract to the army from 1952 to 1954. His book *The Supreme Command* (1954), written at the request of General Dwight D. Eisenhower, was an official history of the wartime Supreme Headquarters, Allied Expeditionary Force. It was a critical success. Following his military affiliation, Pogue returned to Murray State as a professor of history between 1954 and 1956.

In 1956 he began nearly two decades with the George C. Marshall Research Foundation in Lexington, Virginia, first as director (1956–1964), then as director of the Marshall Library (1964–1974). Pogue made one stipulation in accepting the research directorship: that he be permitted to write the general's biography. (Marshall, who died in 1959, had refused to write an autobiography.) During his years with the foundation, Pogue embarked upon a balanced and definitive four-volume study of the wartime chief of staff. Based in large part on the many interviews he had done with Marshall, Pogue published *George C. Marshall: Education of a General* in 1963. *Ordeal and Hope* appeared in 1966, *Organizer of Victory* in 1973, and *Statesman* in 1987. Pogue was also the author of *The Meaning of Yalta* (1956), and he was a contributor to many other books, including *Command Decisions* (1960); *Total War and Cold War* (1962); *D-Day: The Normandy Invasion in Retrospect* (1970); *The*

Continuing Revolution (1975); *The War Lords* (1976); *Bicentennial History of the United States* (1977); and *The Marshall Plan in Germany* (1991). He was a contributing editor of *Guide to American Foreign Relations Since 1700* (1983).

From 1974 until his retirement in 1984, Pogue served as director of the Eisenhower Institute for Historical Research, an affiliate of the Smithsonian Institution, in Arlington, Virginia. In 1993 Pogue moved back to his native Kentucky, residing there until his death from the effects of a stroke. Between 1948 and 1974, Pogue filled a variety of lectureships at the U.S. Air Force Academy, the U.S. Military Academy, Virginia Military Institute, and George Washington University.

★

Pogue's personal library and much of the correspondence and other papers associated with his publications and other activities are located at the Forrest Pogue Special Collections Library, Murray State University, Murray, Kentucky. Another group of papers, having primarily to do with his work on the Marshall biography, is at the library of the George C. Marshall Memorial Foundation, Lexington, Virginia. See also H. Lew Wallace, "Forrest C. Pogue: A Biographical Sketch," *Filson Club History Quarterly* 60, no. 3 (July 1986): 373–402, which is based on discussions with Pogue. An obituary is in the *Washington Post* (8 Oct. 1996).

KEIR B. STERLING

PONNAMPERUMA, Cyril Andrew (*b.* 16 October 1923 in Galle, Ceylon, now Sri Lanka; *d.* 20 December 1994 in Washington, D.C.), chemist known for his work on the chemical basis of life and for showing that the basic building blocks of DNA and RNA can be synthesized outside living cells.

Ponnamperuma was one of five children born to Andrew Ponnamperuma and Grace Siriwardene. Both of his parents were educators, and they persuaded him to study philosophy. After attending local schools, Ponnamperuma received a B.A. in philosophy from the University of Madras in 1948. At that point he decided to change his field of study to chemistry. He earned a B.Sc. from the University of London in 1959. While pursuing this degree, he also worked as a research chemist and as a radiochemist. He married Valli Pal on 19 March 1955. They had one daughter. The family immigrated to the United States in 1959, and Ponnamperuma became a U.S. citizen in 1967.

Ponnamperuma entered the University of California at Berkeley in 1959 and received a Ph.D. in chemistry in 1962. While at Berkeley he worked as research associate at the Lawrence Radiation Laboratory, where he collaborated with Melvin Calvin, a Nobel laureate and experimenter in chemical evolution, the chemical paths by which life might have originated. This relationship led to Ponnamperuma's interest in chemical evolution.

Cyril Ponnamperuma. AP/WIDE WORLD PHOTOS

After earning his Ph.D., Ponnamperuma won a one-year fellowship from the National Academy of Sciences to be a research scientist at the National Aeronautics and Space Administration (NASA) Ames Research Center in Mountain View, California. After his fellowship ended, he remained at Ames as a research scientist until 1971. From 1965 to 1971 he served as the chief of the Chemical Evolution Branch. In 1971 he became a professor of chemistry and the director of the Laboratory of Chemical Evolution, an endeavor supported by the National Science Foundation and NASA, at the University of Maryland in College Park. He held these positions until his death.

Although trained as a chemist, Ponnamperuma expressed interest in chemical evolution, exobiology, geochemistry, and space sciences. In his research he explored the chemical paths by which life might have originated and exploited dramatic advances in molecular biology, astrophysics, and micropaleontology. Ponnamperuma constructed a convincing theory about a series of chemical reactions that gave rise to the precursors of life on Earth. To do this he built on the work of Harold Urey and Stanley Miller in the early 1950s. Urey and Miller had experi-

mented with a "primordial soup" concocted of the elements thought to have made up Earth's early atmosphere, that is, methane, ammonia, hydrogen, and water. By sending electrical sparks through the mixture, they detected the formation of amino acids. Ponnamperuma set up variations of these experiments in the early 1960s. He sent high-energy electrons and then ultraviolet (UV) light through the primordial soup used by Urey and Miller. He succeeded in creating large amounts of adenosine triphosphate (ATP), a substance that fuels cells. In later experiments with the same conditions Ponnamperuma and his group created the nucleotides that make up nucleic acids. In 1984 Ponnamperuma reported the creation of all five chemical bases of living matter in a single experiment of bombarding a primordial soup mixture with electricity.

Ponnamperuma also was active in the growing field of exobiology, the study of extraterrestrial life. He worked with samples of lunar soil and with information sent back from Mars by the unmanned probes *Viking, Pioneer,* and *Voyager* in the 1970s.

Ponnamperuma received numerous national and international awards and distinctions, including the 1993 Harold Urey Prize awarded by the Russian Academy of Creative Arts, various honorary degrees, and a distinguished visiting professorship with the Indian Atomic Energy Commission in 1967. He was a fellow of the Royal Institute of Chemistry and the Third World Academy of Scientists and a member of the American Chemical Society, the Astronomy Association, the American Society of Biological Chemists, the American Association for the Advancement of Science, the Geochemical Society, and the Radiation Research Society. Ponnamperuma was also a foreign member of the Indian National Science Academy in 1978, director of the Arthur C. Clarke Center in Sri Lanka from 1984 to 1986, science adviser to the president of Sri Lanka from 1984 until his death, and director of the Institute for Fundamental Studies in Sri Lanka from 1984 to 1991. A member of the International Society for the Study of the Origin of Life, he received its A. I. Oparin Gold Medal in 1980. Ponnamperuma was renowned for his efforts promoting science to underdeveloped countries. At the time of his death he was the director and founder of the North-South Center for Sustainable Development, created by the Third World Foundation. The center's mission is to facilitate the exchange of scientific information and technology between industrialized and developing countries.

Ponnamperuma's scholarly work includes editorships of the *Journal of Molecular Evolution* from 1970 to 1972 and of *Origins of Life* from 1973 to 1983. He contributed many articles to professional journals; authored the books *The Origins of Life* (1972) and *Cosmic Evolution,* with George B. Field and Gerrit L. Verschuur (1978); and edited the books *Limits of Life,* with Lynn Margulis (1980), and *Com-*

ets and the Origin of Life (1981). Ponnamperuma suffered cardiac arrest in his office and died shortly thereafter at Washington Adventist Hospital in Washington, D.C.

★

For further information on Ponnamperuma see Jacques Cattell Press, ed., *American Men and Women of Science: The Physical and Biological Sciences*, vol. 5, 14th ed. (1971); *Current Biography Yearbook* (1995); and Emily J. McMurray, ed., *Notable Twentieth-Century Scientists,* vol. 3 (1995). An obituary is in the *New York Times* (24 Dec. 1994).

MARIA PACHECO

PRAEGER, Frederick Amos   (*b.* 16 September 1915 in Vienna, Austria; *d.* 28 May 1994 in Boulder, Colorado), founder of a publishing company noted for its books on communism, art, and controversial issues.

Praeger was the only child born to Max Mayer Praeger, an Austrian publisher who also was the managing director of a newspaper, and Manya Foerster Praeger. He attended the University of Vienna's school of law and political science from 1933 to 1938. He also studied at the Sorbonne in Paris in 1934. As a student he was one of Austria's best runners, becoming Vienna's interscholastic champion in the 100-, 200-, and 400-meter races, and running on relay teams that set national records. He won eighty medals. As a Jew, he noted, "there was a symbolic satisfaction in literally running ahead of my anti-Semitic opponents."

From 1935 to 1938 he was associate editor of R. Loewit Verlag, the publishing house owned by his father. He was also a part-time sports writer. After Austria's annexation by Nazi Germany in 1938, he was arrested, and following his release from prison, Praeger immigrated to the United States.

He held thirty jobs in twenty states, including furniture-mover, short-order cook, jewelry salesman, and assistant manager of a group of Kansas City, Kansas, jewelry shops. He was naturalized as an American citizen in 1941. When World War II started, Praeger joined the United States Army as a private. He was a research and editorial assistant and military intelligence instructor, and participated in five European campaigns. He was awarded the Bronze Star and a field commission as a second lieutenant. Meanwhile the Holocaust that accompanied the war in Europe claimed the lives of his father and mother, who died in Nazi concentration camps at Auschwitz and Teriesenstadt, respectively.

Returning to the United States after the war, Praeger founded a book-export business. In 1950 he borrowed $4,000 from friends to publish two British analyses of international law, and although they sold only 1,500 copies

each, he considered the venture enough of a success that he founded Frederick A. Praeger, Inc., and Inter Books, Inc., a subsidiary responsible for some of his activities overseas.

Praeger accepted for publication a manuscript by Milovan Djilas, former vice president of Yugoslavia, after it had been rejected by several publishers in the West. Once an ardent communist, Djilas had become disillusioned with the system he had helped establish in Yugoslavia, and in *The New Class: An Analysis of the Communist System*—published by Praeger in 1957—he made the case that Communism had established a class structure even more rigid than the one it replaced. Part of the manuscript was sent to Praeger and the rest had to be smuggled out of Yugoslavia because Djilas was under arrest at the time. Unfortunately, Djilas was sentenced to seven additional years in prison for consenting to the book's publication. Praeger retained a United States attorney to represent Djilas at his hearing, but the lawyer could not obtain a visa to go to Yugoslavia. Djilas was eventually released in 1966.

Praeger received the Carey-Thomas Award in 1957 from R. R. Bowker Company for outstanding creative publishing in obtaining and offering the Djilas book. When he accepted the prize, he indicated that the book was a "professional dream of glory. I wanted to find an intellectual weapon of enormous explosive force, preferably written from inside the Communist orbit by a man . . . with a great name, integrity and determination to seek out truth and defend it—a weapon in the form of a book which could . . . be effective in the areas such as the Soviet orbit and the neutralist and uncommitted countries."

In 1957 Praeger also published *The Naked God: The Writer and the Communist Party* by Howard Fast, an author and former communist who had renounced his previous convictions. The company also published the early works of dissident Russian writer Aleksandr Solzhenitsyn, including *One Day in the Life of Ivan Denisovich* (1963).

In 1956 Praeger began another phase of his publishing interests when the firm issued an art book, *Picasso: A Study of His Work by Frank Elgar; A Biographical Study by Robert Maillard*, including reproductions in six colors and in black and white. The printing of 38,000 copies sold out, an impressive achievement for an art book. In 1958 Praeger and the Whitney Museum of American Art in New York City entered into an exclusive contract for Praeger to be the publisher and distributor of the museum's books. The following year he published *Four American Expressionists: Doris Caesar, Chaim Gross, Karl Knaths, Abraham Rattner* and *Zorach* for the museum.

In 1966 Praeger sold the publishing company to *Encyclopaedia Britannica,* and two years later he ended his last ties to the publishing house. He then returned to Vienna for six years and invested in publishing properties in Germany. When he returned to the United States, he moved to Boulder, Colorado, and founded the Westview Press in 1975. The company issued scholarly scientific and technical books in relatively inexpensive, unjacketed, camera-ready typewritten editions. He sold Westview in 1989 to SCS Communications, and he remained as publisher and vice chairman until his retirement in 1991. He was estimated to have published close to 10,000 titles during his lifetime.

Praeger was married three times and had four daughters. He married Cornelia E. Blach on 8 May 1946. They were divorced (she died in 1993), and he married Heloise Aronson. That marriage, too, ended, and on 18 December 1983 Praeger married Kellie Masterson. Physically he was five feet, eight inches tall, weighed 175 pounds, and had brown eyes and hair. He had no religious or political affiliations and was interested in skiing, tennis, swimming, and art.

Praeger, who experienced complications arising from a stroke, chose not to take nourishment and died as a result. He was cremated and his ashes scattered. After his death, the Westview Press donated money in his honor toward a full scholarship at the University of Denver Publishing Institute, of which he was one of the founders.

Praeger was interested in creating controversy in the international studies arena. He once said, "I have always tried to be unconventional, even a bit outrageous. I have also always been willing to pay the price. Being controversial, at times even unpopular, is the premium one pays for being different."

★

Profiles of Praeger include an article in *Current Biography* (1959) and an interview in *Publishers Weekly* (2 Apr. 1979). His obituary is in the *New York Times* (2 Apr. 1979).

MARTIN JAY STAHL

PREUS, Jacob Aall Ottesen, Jr. ("Jake") (*b*. 8 January 1920 in St. Paul, Minnesota; *d*. 13 August 1994 in Burnsville, Minnesota), church leader who guided the Lutheran Church–Missouri Synod through the most difficult crisis of its history.

Preus was the first of two surviving children born to Idella Haugen Preus, a homemaker, and Jacob ("Jake") A. O. Preus, a former Minnesota governor and state insurance commissioner. Preus was baptized into the Norwegian Lutheran Church in America, the successor to the Norwegian Synod founded by his great-grandfather. The synod had close ties to the Lutheran Church–Missouri Synod (LCMS), which was one of the more orthodox Lutheran church bodies in America. His father retired from Minnesota politics in the mid-1920s and moved the family from Minneapolis to Highland Park, Illinois, where he engaged in the insurance business. There they worshiped in a Mis-

Jacob Preus, 1977. AP/WIDE WORLD PHOTOS

souri Synod congregation, before eventually attending an orthodox church body set apart from the Norwegian Lutheran Church.

Preus remained a nominal member of the LCMS until he matriculated at Luther College, in Decorah, Iowa, in 1937. There they worshiped in an LCMS congregation, where Preus became a member by confirmation. His father's alma mater, Luther College, was founded and led by family members, including an uncle, O. J. H. Preus, who was president during Preus's undergraduate years. Preus studied classics and history, graduating magna cum laude in 1941. There he met his future wife, Delpha Holleque. He attended Luther Seminary in St. Paul with a military deferment from 1941 until graduation in 1945 and came under the influence of another uncle, the theology professor Herman Preus. A staunch conservative reputed to be a "closet Missourian," the uncle developed in both Jack (as Preus was known throughout his life) and his brother, Robert, a strict orthodox Lutheran perspective.

With this varied background, Preus referred to himself as having no synodical identity. Debating with others helped him establish his own theological perspective. Preus found himself uncomfortable with the Norwegian Lutheran Church as compared with the Missouri Synod of his youth. The Norwegian Lutheran Church embraced two barely reconciled forms of the doctrine of election (the act of being chosen by God for salvation). Herman Preus emphasized God's electing will, a cause Jack Preus pushed in public debates with the systematic theologian George Aus, who emphasized the role of human reason and will in coming to faith.

Preus's seminary experience did not make him a "Missourian," but it shaped his conservative outlook. His dispute with Aus led Preus to write a public letter after graduation accusing the seminary of false teaching. Eventually, he and his brother Robert joined the confessionally more "pure" Little Norwegian Synod. There he remained for more than a decade, raising a family, finishing his graduate work at the University of Minnesota (where he earned his Ph.D. in 1951), and serving the synod as pastor and teacher at Bethany College and Seminary in Mankato, Minnesota. Together the restive brothers pushed to suspend fellowship with the doctrinally "lax" Missouri Synod, even as they sought employment in one or another of the Missouri Synod's Concordia seminaries. Jack became professor of New Testament studies at Concordia Seminary in Springfield, Illinois, developing a reputation as a "politician" and eventually joined the school's administration, becoming president in 1962. By then he had become known as "the politician brother."

By 1963 Preus was taking critical note of divisions in the synod over scriptural authority. Moderate theologians increasingly criticized the synod's "Brief Statement," which embraced verbal inspiration and inerrancy. In published remarks Preus proposed a solution: complete surrender to Scripture, a willingness to forgive, and shunning of all politicking. Four years later Preus joined the ad hoc United Planning Council, along with a campaign to replace the synod president Oliver Harms with a conservative leader. By the time of the next convention in March 1969, Preus was a candidate for the job, and, in contrast to his earlier statements, he pursued the office with ardent politicking. The council appealed directly to delegates, though this was contrary to established church procedure. Preus won on the third ballot.

Over the next two years (the convention met biennially), Preus purged moderate leaders and began investigating "liberalism" at Concordia Seminary in St. Louis. "That godless men take [Scripture away] from us is terrifying," he observed, "but that theologians and pastors should deprive the church of the Scripture by destructive criticism is even more unspeakable." A moderate party led by the Concordia president John H. Tietjen challenged the conservatives in the "Battle of New Orleans" at the 1973 convention. Preus, though by now labeled a parvenu and an interloper, was reelected on the first ballot, 606 to 451, maintaining a three-to-two advantage in delegate support.

Following the convention Preus suspended Tietjen in January 1974. The seminary students went on strike, and the Concordia faculty voted to establish a seminary in exile called Seminex. Thus, they left the campus to the conservatives, who rebuilt its program, faculty, and student body. Leaders at the 1975 convention instructed Preus to dismiss district presidents who ordained Seminex graduates, and four were eventually removed. By February 1976 disheartened moderates withdrew, forming the Association of Evangelical Lutheran Churches, with some 100,000 members in 200 congregations. Preus was elected to a third term at Dallas in 1977, by then referring to the recent schism as "sad and unfortunate, certainly—but minimal compared to dire predictions."

Preus retired in 1981 but remained active on synod committees and as a scholar. A devoted husband and father of eight, Preus spent his retirement years in the company of his children. He developed heart problems in his later years and died laughing at one of his own jokes. Forty-eight family members followed the casket into the Concordia Seminary Chapel singing the beloved Norwegian Lutheran hymn "Behold a Host Arrayed in White," with its assuring line, "These are the saints who kept God's Word." Preus is buried at Concordia Cemetery in St. Louis.

On several occasions, Preus said that he regretted the party spirit and power plays "on both sides," but he never revised his own doctrinal position. Although the abuse of scriptural authority may have been a real issue for him, hindsight suggested that power politics marred its resolution. Opponents dismissed him as an outsider who never understood the Missouri Synod and criticized his legacy of authoritarian fundamentalism. Supporters saw him as a true "Missourian" who saved a conservative synod from liberals by establishing the peace and unity necessary for the church's mission. Like his father, Preus was a consummate politician not overawed by clergy in a church that sought a political solution to its problems.

★

For a study of Preus's years as synod president, see James E. Adams, *Preus of Missouri and the Great Lutheran Civil War* (1977). *The Lutherans of North America* (1980) provides an account of the church conflict. Obituaries are in the *Lutheran* and the *Lutheran Witness* (both Oct. 1994), as well as the *St. Louis Post-Dispatch* (15 Aug. 1994) and *Christian Century* (24 Aug. 1994).

ROBERT F. SCHOLZ

PRIMUS, Pearl Eileen (*b.* 29 November 1919 in Port-of-Spain, Trinidad; *d.* 29 October 1994 in New Rochelle, New York), anthropologist, lecturer, teacher, dancer, choreographer, and storyteller who pioneered the art of dance as a "social instrument" to promote multicultural harmony.

Primus's parents, Edward Primus and Emily Jackson, moved to the United States in 1921, when their daughter was two years old, determined to make a better life. Primus grew up in Manhattan and Brooklyn, New York, in a traditional Trinidadian and African household. The young Primus and her two brothers were shielded from many of the societal ills prevalent in American culture. In the home, the Primus children were taught racial tolerance and ethnic pride through the inculcation of educational, religious, and cultural values. Primus once said that she had three mothers: "I have the mother where I was born, Trinidad, my Caribbean home; America, where I was educated, and primed, and sometime deeply hurt . . . and then there's my mother, Africa, who polished me."

There is considerable evidence that the importance of education, the desire to help others, and the splendor of dance are knotted throughout Primus's life. As a young student, she excelled in academics and athletics at P.S. 94 and P.S. 136 and at Hunter High School in a program for the exceptionally gifted. In preparation for a career in medicine, she earned a bachelor's degree in biology and pre-medicine sciences in 1940 and a master's in psychology in 1943, both from Hunter College. Face to face with racial prejudice and unable to get a position as a laboratory tech-

Pearl Primus. AP/WIDE WORLD PHOTOS

nician to support her education, she turned to dance for employment. She was disappointed but not discouraged by the educational barriers she faced. (In 1978 she finally received a doctorate in anthropology when New York University granted her permission to dance her dissertation.)

Primus's dance career began in 1940, after she turned to the National Youth Administration looking for work. Placed without previous experience in their dance troupe, she soon demonstrated a talent that earned her a scholarship with the New Dance Group (NDG), a politically charged company in which she became the first African-American student in 1941. In February 1943 her first public concert made a strong impression at the New York City Young Men's Hebrew Association. The nightclub Cafe Society Downtown engaged her as an entertainer in April 1943; she performed there for ten months. That year the *New York Times* proclaimed her the "dance debutante of the year." A solo recital followed in April 1944, and in October, Primus headed a dance troupe that enjoyed a ten-day run on Broadway. In 1944 she was asked to entertain servicemen. She was awarded a certificate of merit in September 1944 for her service of unrelenting entertainment.

Primus joined the NDG faculty in 1942. The group sought to bring dance to oppressed peoples as a voice of protest against social and political concerns of the 1940s. The NDG and Primus became important forces in modern dance. *African Ceremony*, Primus's first choreographed dance, depicting a priest's fertility rite from the Congo, was researched under her NDG scholarship, and the group's doctrine of social consciousness encouraged Primus to express her cultural protest in an artistic manner. *Strange Fruit* (1943), a passionate poem about the horror of lynching by Lewis Allen, was choreographed into a dance of conflict by Primus using a lone white woman's response as the vehicle. The influence of Langston Hughes, the "poet laureate" of black Americans and a close friend, was also evidenced in *The Negro Speaks of Rivers* (1943), *Jim Crow Train* (1943), and *Michael, Row Your Boat Ashore* (1979), about the horror of the church bombings in Birmingham, Alabama. The long list of dances based on jazz, blues, and spirituals is also very impressive.

In 1944 Primus traveled south to meet and live with the poor people directly affected by bigotry and oppression. Working as a migrant, traveling on Jim Crow trains, worshiping in black churches, and eating traditional southern meals, she came to identify with their problems. Later that year, in an interview for *Afro-American,* Primus stated that northern artists were committed to helping the southern people with "education, culture, and strength to fight for democracy."

As a proud recipient of a Rosenwald fellowship, Primus traveled to Africa in 1948 to research the dance and artistic culture of her ancestors. She recorded her excitement in

"To the Lands of Drum Throb and Dance," an article for the *Washington Star* (17 December 1948), as she expressed her desire "to learn from them the basic truths of dance and life—to salvage for America the beauty, dignity and strength of a threatened culture, to bring back music, folklore, dances and to interpret them honestly for the audience."

As a direct result of her trip to Africa, she produced a record album, *Pearl Primus' Africa* (1971), consisting of legends, folktales, and proverbs of African villages expressed through song and music for the benefit of high school teachers. At the age of fifty-nine, in 1978, she was the first to introduce "dance anthropology" as a form of artistic expression in the teaching of cultural awareness. Even when Primus was not teaching, she was still a lifelong student of other cultures. In addition, she wrote many articles on dance for educators. As a consultant, she worked with the National Endowment for the Arts, the New York State Council on Arts, and the New York City Department of Parks and Recreation. *The Integration of Visual Forms and Anthropological Content for Use in Teaching Children About Cultures and Peoples of the World* (1968) was produced by Primus for the Office of Education in Washington, D.C. As an ethnologist, Primus worked with the New York University Anthropology Program; the Dance Enrichment Program at Spelman College in Atlanta, from which she received an honorary doctorate; the Newark Museum in New Jersey; and various exhibitions in New York City.

Married in 1954 to the dancer and choreographer Percival Borde, Primus was a frequent collaborator with him and other major dance figures until Borde died in 1979. They had one son, Onwin Borde, who eventually came to arrange the music for many of Primus's dance pieces.

Heads of state, poets, educators, compeers, and dignitaries around the world recognized Primus's achievements. In 1949 she received the Star of Africa from the government of Liberia, the highest honor of achievement given by that nation. In 1949 President Truman appointed Primus chairman of cultural activities and director of the African Center of Performing Arts. In 1991 President George Bush conferred the National Medal of Arts on Primus. Her love of dance and respect for multicultural understanding made Primus not only one of the world's greatest dancers but also one of the greatest humanitarians.

Primus ceased performing in the 1980s but continued to teach until her death. To fight racial injustice, some social leaders sought the energy of student sit-ins and boycotts; others, the doctrine of nonviolence and politics; and others the rhyme of song and poetry. Primus chose the movements and expressions in the art of dance. For a conscientious artist, dance was first and foremost a means to promote multicultural understanding. Education rather then entertainment was always the focus of her energy. All of her themes related to social issues that strengthened racial pride for blacks and for all ethnic groups.

★

An interview with Pearl Primus is in the *Amsterdam News* (21 June 1980). An early account of her career is in *Current Biography* (1944). Beverly Anne Hilsman Barber, "Pearl Primus: In Search of Her Roots" (Ph.D. diss., Florida State University, 1984), and Jean Ruth Glover, "Pearl Primus: Cross-Cultural Pioneer of American Dance" (M.A. thesis, American University, 1989), are excellent resources for research. See also "Pearl Primus, Ph.D., Returns," *New York Times* (18 Mar. 1979); "Pearl Primus: Spirit of the People," *Dance Magazine* (Dec. 1990); "Acrobatic Anthropologist," *Negro Digest* (Jan. 1948); and Julia Foulkes "Pearl in Our Midst: In Memoriam, Pearl Primus," *Dance Research Journal* 27 (spring 1995): 80–82. Obituaries are in *Dance* magazine (Feb. 1995) and the *New York Times* (31 Oct. 1994).

GLORIA GRANT ROBERSON

PULLER, Lewis Burwell, Jr. (*b.* 12 August 1945 in Camp Lejeune, North Carolina; *d.* 11 May 1994 in Mount Vernon, Virginia), military officer, lawyer, and recipient of a 1992 Pulitzer Prize for *Fortunate Son: The Autobiography of Lewis B. Puller, Jr.*

Puller was one of three children of Lieutenant General Lewis ("Chesty") Burwell Puller, then the most decorated U.S. marine in history, and Virginia Montague Evans, a fourth-grade teacher. In *Fortunate Son,* Puller describes being drawn to a military career by age six, while witnessing a military ceremony to award his father a fifth Navy Cross, the most ever awarded a marine and the nation's second-highest medal for valor. "I had first begun to grasp the concept of battlefield glory and with it sensed a commitment to a calling over which I would be powerless." After failing health forced Chesty to end his distinguished thirty-seven-year career in the Marine Corps, strangers came to the Pullers' rural Virginia home to pay respects to Puller's father. "I decided early on that I wanted men to feel toward me the way they felt toward my father," Puller wrote, "as throughout my youth I witnessed examples of hero worship toward him that would have befitted the denizens of Mount Olympus." Puller attended high school at Christchurch School and graduated in 1962. After graduating with a B.A. degree from the College of William and Mary in Williamsburg, Virginia, in 1967, Puller joined the Marine Corps. In August 1968 Puller married Linda Ford Todd ("Toddy"); they had two children.

Puller arrived in Vietnam in August 1968 as a second lieutenant and was assigned to the Second Battalion of the First Marine Regiment of the First Marine Division. As a platoon commander, he led patrols in a coastal plain, derisively called "the Riviera." On 11 October 1968, while

Lewis Puller, Jr., at the Vietman Veterans Memorial in Washington, D.C., 1991. AP/WIDE WORLD PHOTOS

engaged in firefight with North Vietnamese soldiers, he stepped on a booby-trapped 105-millimeter howitzer round. Puller wrote, "I had no idea that the pink mist that engulfed me had been caused by the vaporization of most of my right and left legs." Not realizing the extent of his injuries, he felt an elation that "I had finished serving my time in the hell of Vietnam." Looking back, Puller wrote, "I did not realize until much later that I had been forever set apart from the rest of mankind."

Less than three months after arriving in Vietnam, Puller left with two Purple Hearts, the Silver Star, the Navy Commendation Medal, and the Vietnam Cross of Gallantry. He had sustained massive injuries that nearly killed him, including the loss of his right leg to his torso and all of his left leg except six inches of thigh; he also lost the thumb and the little finger from his right hand and all fingers except the thumb and half of the forefinger on his left hand. Sent to the U.S. Naval Hospital in Philadelphia, he endured several surgeries and many months of physical and occupational therapy before being released in August 1970, nearly two years after his injuries.

In the fall of 1971, Lewis returned to the College of

William and Mary to attend the Marshall Wythe School of Law. On 11 October 1971, exactly three years after suffering combat injuries in Vietnam, his father died. His father's death and the Vietnam War haunted Puller for the remainder of his life. After passing the Virginia bar and graduating from law school in 1974, he worked in the general counsel's office of the Veterans Administration. In October 1974 he was detailed from his new job to present cases before the Presidential Clemency Board, convened by President Gerald Ford to review the cases of military deserters and civilian draft evaders. In April 1975 Puller was appointed to the Clemency Board, one of only four Vietnam veterans among the eighteen members. Leaving the Veterans Administration, he went to work for the Paralyzed Veterans of America in August 1976. In the fall of 1977, he volunteered to work on the political campaign of Charles Robb, who was running for lieutenant governor in Virginia. Puller then left his job with the Paralyzed Veterans of America to seek election to the U.S. House of Representatives from Virginia's First Congressional District. Running as a Democrat against the Republican incumbent Paul Trible, Puller lost badly, garnering only 34,419 votes (28 percent) to Trible's 88,048 ballots (72 percent). In October 1979 he went to work as an attorney in the Office of the General Counsel at the Department of Defense. After years of heavy drinking, Puller attempted suicide in 1979. On 5 September 1981 he joined Alcoholics Anonymous, embarking on more than a decade of sobriety.

In the mid-1980s, Puller began writing *Fortunate Son: The Autobiography of Lewis B. Puller, Jr.,* which was published in 1991. The book won the 1992 Pulitzer Prize for biography or autobiography. Puller viewed the book's principal themes as his relationship with his father, his reconciliation with his country, and the Vietnam War. Indeed, one of the subheads of the title is "The Healing of a Vietnam Veteran." Puller claimed the title *Fortunate Son* came from John Fogerty's same-titled, antiwar protest song of the late 1960s, explaining that "I sort of turned the song on its ear," since he viewed the title as an ode to his father. Puller took a leave of absence from the Department of Defense to work as writer-in-residence at George Mason University in Fairfax, Virginia, where he was at the time of his death in 1994.

On Memorial Day in 1992, Puller was a speaker at the Vietnam Veterans Memorial. In the fall of 1993 he made a journey of reconciliation to Vietnam to dedicate a school, for which he helped raise money, near the site where he had suffered his wounds. His wife was elected to the Virginia legislature in 1991. The couple separated in 1994, and Puller slipped from sobriety. He died at his home from a self-inflicted gunshot wound. He was buried with military honors at Arlington National Cemetery in Virginia.

As the son of the most celebrated U.S. marine, Puller

embraced the military life and paid a heavy sacrifice for his short stint in Vietnam. *Fortunate Son,* a tale of reconciliation, spoke to a generation of Americans who lived through the Vietnam War. "To the list of names of victims of the Vietnam War," claimed Toddy Puller, "add the name of Lewis Puller. He suffered terrible wounds that never really healed."

★

The University Archives at the College of William and Mary has a file on Puller. His autobiography is *Fortunate Son: The Autobiography of Lewis B. Puller, Jr.* (1991). Brian Lamb interviewed Puller for C-SPAN's *Booknotes* on 24 May 1992. The interview was published in *Booknotes: America's Finest Authors on Reading, Writing, and the Power of Ideas* (1997). The lives of Lewis and Toddy are briefly covered in Mary Jordan, "The Fight of Their Lives," *Washington Post* (1 July 1991), and Ken Cross, "Surviving Was the Easy Part," *People Weekly* (fall 1991). William Styron, "The Wreckage of an American War," *New York Times Book Review* (16 June 1991), provides an extensive review of *Fortunate Son.* Marylou Tousignant, "Puller's Vietnam Reconciliation Realized," *Washington Post* (20 Apr. 1995), discusses Puller's effort to build schools in Vietnam. Obituaries are in the *New York Times* (12 May 1994) and the *Washington Post* (17 May 1994).

PAUL A. FRISCH

QUARLES, Benjamin Arthur (*b.* 23 January 1904 in Boston, Massachusetts; *d.* 16 November 1996 at Cheverly, Maryland), renowned African American historian of the last half of the twentieth century.

Quarles was one of four children of Arthur Benedict Quarles, a waiter, and Margaret O'Brien, a homemaker. Quarles attended public schools in Boston and then matriculated at Shaw University in Raleigh, North Carolina, from which he earned a B.A. degree in 1931. He then entered the University of Wisconsin, which was noted for the excellence of its program in American history. There he earned an M.A. degree in 1933 and a Ph.D. in 1940. His dissertation was a scholarly examination of the life of the abolitionist Frederick Douglass.

Quarles began his professional career by returning to Shaw University, where he served as an instructor from 1934 until 1938, while still working on his doctorate. In 1938 he joined the history department of Dillard University in New Orleans as a professor of history. From 1946 until 1953, Quarles also served as a dean at Dillard. Moving in 1953 to Morgan State University in Maryland, he was a professor of history and chairman of the department of history until his official retirement in 1969. He then held the position of professor emeritus.

Quarles and his first wife, Vera Bullock, whom he married in 1937, were parents to one daughter. Vera died in 1951. Quarles then married Ruth Brett on 21 December 1952; they had one child, a daughter.

Quarles's dissertation became the topic of his first book, *Frederick Douglass* (1948). With its publication, he became a pioneer in African American history, following in the footsteps of the early twentieth-century pioneer of that subject, Carter G. Woodson. Woodson and W. E. B. DuBois (more noted as a sociologist), tried to find traces of the African American past, a subject of little interest to most Americans. Woodson wrote primarily for a black audience and tried to use his writings to help those of African descent to discover their rightful place in American history. Although Quarles continued the crisp narrative style of his predecessors, his work broke new ground and was aimed at his professional colleagues. Because of his patient and meticulous research, coupled with a fluid narrative style, Quarles enriched his profession.

In the aftermath of World War II, and the resulting desegregation of the American military in 1948, Quarles turned to his next book, *The Negro in the Civil War* (1953), his lasting monument as an historian. He followed this success with a scholarly work on black participation in an even earlier conflict, *The Negro in the American Revolution* (1961). However, the Civil War era remained Quarles's particular interest; at least three more of his published works focused on that era of American history.

In addition to these works, Quarles published a number of other books and scholarly articles. As black studies gained academic respectability, he teamed up with Leslie H. Fishel in 1967 to produce *The Negro American: A Documentary History* (in the third edition of the work, issued in 1976, "*Negro*" was changed to "*Black*"). The book is a standard text for African American history classes. Quarles also contributed regularly to scholarly journals.

Some historians have accused Quarles of having too optimistic a view of the African American experience and of not giving proper attention to urban riots and the entire civil rights movement of the 1960s. He was analytical rather than confrontational. Rather than quarrel with white people, he wanted to demonstrate, in a cool professional manner, that while liberty and equality were American myths, it was impossible to understand American history without a knowledge of the reality of life for African Americans.

Quarles was a member of the National Council for the Frederick Douglass Museum of African Art at the Smithsonian, served on the fellowship selection committee of the American Council of Learned Societies, was a member of the project advisory committee to Black Congressmembers, and served on the Department of the Army Historical Advisory Committee. In 1958 he was a Guggenheim fellow. Later, he served as a consultant to the Library of Congress. Sixteen different universities granted him honorary degrees.

He served on the building committee of the Amistad Research Center, a African American studies research center at Tulane University in New Orleans. Quarles died of heart failure in the Prince Georges Hospital in Cheverly.

During his career, Quarles was a punctual and popular teacher; on most occasions, his classes were overbooked. His students remember him as soft-spoken and always a gentleman. Because the nature of his scholarship and lectures were so often controversial, he avoided exaggeration and theatrics. There, too, one finds the roots of his attention to detail. The historian William Pierson said of Quarles that he "was incapable of meanness."

★

The Quarles papers are in the Beulah Davis special collections of the library at Morgan State University. There are no biographies of Quarles. An obituary is in the *New York Times* (20 Nov. 1996).

ART BARBEAU

QUINTANILLA PÉREZ, Selena. *See* Selena.

R

RAND, Paul (*b.* 15 August 1914 in Brooklyn, New York; *d.* 26 November 1996 in Norwalk, Connecticut), illustrator and seminal figure in American graphic design who was an inaugural inductee into the Art Director's Club of New York Hall of Fame.

Rand was born Peretz Rosenbaum, the son of Itzhak Yehuda Rosenbaum, a grocer, and Leah Rosenbaum, who had emigrated from Poland. Rand had an older sister and a twin brother. His brother died in an automobile accident when he was in his twenties. At the young age of three Rand showed a talent in art through his restless drawings, but his interest was discouraged in his Orthodox Jewish household. He attended New York City public elementary schools in the mornings and yeshivas in the afternoons. Later he attended Harren High School in Manhattan. In 1930 he convinced his father to give him $25 to enroll in night school classes at Pratt Institute in Brooklyn. In 1932 he received both his high school degree and an art certificate from Pratt. He enrolled in Parsons School of Design in Manhattan in 1932 and in 1939 in the Art Students League, where he studied under George Grosz, the celebrated figure in German expressionism.

Rand began his commercial design career as an assistant designer with the small firm of George Switzer in 1932. Around this time he changed his name to Paul Rand to eliminate confusion and misspellings of his given name.

Rand designed lettering and packaging for Switzer's clients, including the Squibb Pharmaceutical Company. In 1935 he left Switzer to start his own design studio in Manhattan. In about 1937 he was hired by *Apparel Arts Magazine* to design covers and editorial spreads, an assignment that quickly led to designing for the magazine's parent company, Esquire-Coronet. Rand designed spreads for fashion and gift editorials for *Esquire*. He was only twenty-three years old when these prestigious magazines made him their editorial designer.

Rand brought a personal vision and style to these publications. Working against the contemporary milieu in graphic design that stressed traditional, symmetrical narrative design, he pioneered designs built on dynamic equilibrium. He drew heavily on the visual language of contemporary European art movements, such as cubism, constructivism, and Bauhaus, and frequently incorporated collages and montages in his work. He found inspiration in contemporary European design magazines, such as the German-language *Gebrauchsgraphik*. An admirer of the work of the European artist Paul Klee, Rand grafted Klee's techniques with color, symbols, and icons into his own graphic designs.

In the use of type in graphic design, Rand was at the forefront of a new style marked by straightforward, honest, provocative type design and selection. Mainstream type design at the time relied heavily on typography gimmicks, such as bullet points, arrows, dingbats, ornate initials, and

Paul Rand. COURTESY MARION S. RAND

superficial ornamentation, to dress up ads and graphic design. Rand preferred tight, concise type. His design work was frequently on display and was cited as "what's new" by the Type Director's Club of New York and the Composing Room.

In the early 1940s Rand designed a series of covers for *Direction,* an arts and culture magazine. One cover in particular became a classic. Rand depicted a stark photograph of a barbed wire cross ranged against a bullet-hole-pocked wall with a mundane hang tag listing the issue's date and volume number and a casual, handwritten "Merry Christmas" wish.

In 1941 William H. Weintraub, a partner at Esquire-Coronet, started an advertising agency, William H. Weintraub Advertising, and Rand became its art director. Working with Bill Bernbach, who later formed the groundbreaking advertising agency Doyle Dane Bernbach, Rand represented Weintraub clients such as Dubonnet, Lee Hats, Disney Hats, El-Producto cigars, Kaiser-Frazer cars, and Orbach's department store. Rand's designs for Orbach's, which became ad alley classics, display a playful, witty charm that arises through the conversion of a familiar object into a charming yet commanding symbol. To keep his superstar on his staff, Weintraub agreed to let Rand work three days a week, and Rand spent two days a week freel-

ancing, illustrating books, and designing book covers for Knopf and other publishing houses.

Little is known about Rand's first marriage, an Orthodox union that may have been an arranged marriage. His second marriage, in 1949, was to Ann Binkley, who wrote children's books, many of which Rand illustrated. They had one daughter before divorcing in 1960. Rand set out on his own as a freelance designer in 1956. Through the late 1950s and the 1960s he attracted showcase clients such as UPS, IBM, Westinghouse, the ABC television network, and Cummins Engine. In this fruitful period he created his most enduring and memorable graphic designs. Rand's 1956 trademark design for IBM has been considered a seminal influence on the evolution of corporate graphic communications. Under Rand's direction the company's logo moved away from the slab serif block letters to the familiar striped IBM letters. Rand's responsibility extended to coordinating the worldwide implementation of the design.

Rand's design for UPS put those three letters inside a shield motif topped by a rectangular package tied with a string. It is probably the best example of Rand's ability to distill the essence of an amorphous, sprawling corporation into a strong, memorable, unique, disarmingly simple graphic. The logo remained in use into the twenty-first century.

During his freelance years Rand designed posters, book covers, magazine covers and layouts, and numerous corporate communications. He also illustrated many books, chiefly children's literature. In 1975 he married Marion Swannie, a manager of graphic design at IBM with whom Rand had worked.

In addition to designing, Rand held several teaching posts at art schools. From 1938 to 1942 he taught at Cooper Union in New York City, and he was an instructor at Pratt Institute in Brooklyn from 1946 to 1947. He taught at Yale University for various periods between 1956 and 1991 and was a professor of Yale's Summer Design Program in Brissago, Switzerland, between 1977 and 1996. He became professor emeritus at Yale in 1991. Rand died of cancer. He is buried in an Orthodox Jewish cemetery in Norwalk, Connecticut.

Rand's work was included in almost forty design exhibits and shows. The most significant were at the American Institute of Graphic Arts in 1958 and 1966; the Art Director's Club of New York in 1945 and 1954; the National Museum in Stockholm in 1947; the Contemporary Arts Museum in Boston in 1954; the Pratt Institute in 1960; the IBM Gallery in 1971; the Brooklyn Museum in 1972; the Royal Designer for Industry, Royal Society, London, in 1973; the Design Gallery 358 in Tokyo in 1986; the Universita Internazionale Dell'Arte in Florence in 1987; and the Ginza Graphic Gallery in Tokyo in 1992.

Rand was inducted into the Art Director's Club of New

York Hall of Fame in 1972, the inaugural year of the club's hall of fame. He received honorary degrees from Tama University in Tokyo in 1958, the Philadelphia College of Art in 1979, and in 1985 from the Parsons School of Design and Yale University. He was named a president's fellow at the Rhode Island School of Design in 1985. Rand's corporate graphic design work is included in the permanent collections of the Museum of Modern Art in New York City and the Smithsonian Institution and the Library of Congress in Washington, D.C.

Rand's design work borrowed heavily from avant-garde European art schools and introduced modernism to American commercial design. He possessed an uncanny ability to distill the essence of his subject matter into strong, sleek visual forms representing his subject's conceptual expression rather than its narrative expression. For example, contrast Rand's UPS logo against the RCA logo, which typifies an older style. The dog listening to a gramophone, with the line "He hears his master's voice," has several graphic elements (a dog, a gramophone, a line of type), while the UPS logo is simple, highly suggestive (the tied rectangle atop the shield), and requires no explanatory line.

★

Rand's papers are at Yale University. He wrote *Thoughts on Design* (1947, rev. ed. 1951), *Black in the Visual Arts* (1949), *The Trademarks of Paul Rand* (1960), *Paul Rand: A Designer's Art* (1985), *Design Form and Chaos* (1993), and *From Lascaux to Brooklyn* (1996). Steven Heller's biography *Paul Rand* (1999) covers Rand's career and includes an introduction by the witty advertising executive George Lois. See also Yusaku Kamekura, ed., *Paul Rand: His Work from 1946 to 1958* (1959), and Michael Corey, *Special Issue on Paul Rand*, Printing Salesman's Herald series no. 35 (1975). An obituary is in the *New York Times* (28 Nov. 1996).

WILLIAM J. MALONEY

RAY, Dixy Lee (*b.* 3 September 1914 in Tacoma, Washington; *d.* 2 January 1994 in Fox Island, Washington), governor of Washington State, chair of the U.S. Atomic Energy Commission, scientist, and author.

Ray was the second of five girls born to Alvis Marion Ray, a printer, and Frances Adams Ray, a homemaker. She was christened Margaret and was known as Dick (short for "that little Dickens") because she was a mischievous child. She did not like her original name and at age sixteen legally renamed herself Dixy Lee after a favorite region and the Civil War general Robert E. Lee, a distant relative.

When she was twelve, Ray climbed Mount Rainier, Washington's highest peak, becoming the youngest girl to climb the mountain. She graduated from Mills College in 1937 with a B.A. in zoology and earned an M.A. degree a

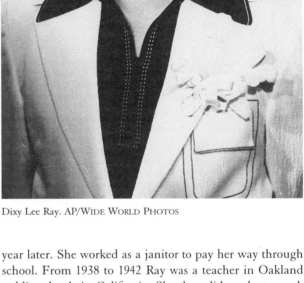

Dixy Lee Ray. AP/WIDE WORLD PHOTOS

year later. She worked as a janitor to pay her way through school. From 1938 to 1942 Ray was a teacher in Oakland public schools in California. She then did graduate work at Stanford University as a John Switzer fellow in 1942 and 1943 and as a Van Sicklen fellow from 1943 to 1945. She received her doctorate in zoology from Stanford in 1945.

Prior to beginning public service, Ray was an associate professor of zoology at the University of Washington from 1945 to 1972. She was also the director of the Pacific Science Center in Seattle from 1963 to 1972. The center was dedicated to improving the public understanding of science and actively developed exhibits, displays, demonstrations, and participation programs in many fields of science.

While at the University of Washington, Ray held many other scientific positions. From 1945 to 1960 she served as a member of the executive committee of the Friday Harbor Laboratories. She wrote the book *Marine Boring and Fouling Organisms* in 1959. From 1960 to 1962 she was a special consultant to the National Science Foundation in biological oceanography. Ray also was the chief scientist and visiting professor on the research ship *Te Vega*, sponsored by Stanford University, which explored the Indian Ocean in 1964. Ray received the William Clapp Award in marine biology in 1959 and in 1963 was elected a member of the

Danish Royal Society for Natural History. She was named Seattle Maritime Man of the Year in 1966.

Appointed a member of the U.S. Atomic Energy Commission (AEC) by President Richard M. Nixon in 1972, Ray in 1973 became that agency's first female director, only the third woman in history to head an independent regulatory agency. She was a strong advocate of nuclear power and aggressively moved to improve safety features for reactors. At one point in a television interview, she said that a 1965 AEC study on the consequences of a major nuclear power plant disaster included "speculative figures." Of its findings, which included estimates of 45,000 deaths, several hundred thousand injuries, and $17 billion worth of property damage resulting from such an incident, Ray stated that the figures were arrived at "if you imagine the worst possible kind of thing, that you don't have any safety backup . . . that there isn't any pressure vessel around the reactor, that there isn't any containment, that there isn't any building, and all these kinds of things." In 1974 she was charged by Ann Roosevelt of Friends of the Earth with making misleading statements regarding the study.

When the AEC was phased out and replaced with the Energy Research and Development Agency and the Nuclear Safety and Licensing Commission, Secretary of State Henry Kissinger in 1975 appointed Ray an assistant secretary of state for oceans and international environmental and scientific affairs. She complained that Kissinger gave her the cold shoulder, and in 1976 she returned to her home state to run for governor in the Democratic primary. In the primary she defeated Seattle mayor Wes Uhlman, and in the general election she defeated Representative John Spellman, an official in Seattle's King County. Elected to a four-year term, she thus became one of two women governors in the country (Ella Grasso of Connecticut was the other). However, her resource management policies put her at odds with the state's farmers, fishermen, and environmentalists, and she lost in the 1980 primary elections.

Known for her autocratic style, Ray insisted on loyalty at every level. She was five feet, four inches tall, weighed 165 pounds, and had amber eyes. She wore her hair closely cropped and favored tailored clothes. While in Washington, D.C., she lived in a custom-built, self-propelled motor home, and she took her two dogs to work with her. Ray never married.

In 1990 Ray and Louis Guzzo wrote *Trashing the Planet,* and in 1993 they collaborated on *Environmental Overkill: Whatever Happened to Common Sense.* The books concerned environmental stewardship, pollution, and the scientific and political realities of environmental issues. After her retirement from public life, Ray farmed on sixty-five acres of Washington's Fox Island, where she died of bronchitis. She is buried in Fox Island Cemetery.

Ray was a leading environmental policymaker who sought a balance between preservation of natural resources on the one hand and meeting the material needs of a modern population on the other. In her books and in her public life, she presented a conceptual framework radically different from that of mainstream environmentalists, who in her view tended to approach the natural world not from the intellectual perspective of scientists but with the sentimentality of romantics. Ray, by contrast, was a hard-edged thinker whose work presented a new and challenging contribution to the continuing debates over environmental issues.

★

Louis R. Guzzo wrote a biography of Ray, *Is It True What They Say About Dixie?* (1980). Assessments of Ray's work and career can be found in Iris Noble, *Contemporary Women Scientists of America* (1979), and Esther Stineman, *American Political Women: Contemporary and Historical Profiles* (1980). Profiles include "Dixy Rocks the Northwest," *Time* (12 Dec. 1977), and "Can Dixy Rise Again?" *Newsweek* (14 July 1980). Obituaries are in the *Washington Post* and *Los Angeles Times* (both 3 Jan. 1994).

Martin Jay Stahl

RAYE, Martha (*b.* 27 August 1916 in Butte, Montana; *d.* 19 October 1994 in Los Angeles, California), star of stage, screen, radio, television, and nightclubs noted for her distinguished service to the military.

Raye was born Margy Reed to the vaudevillians Peter Reed and Maybelle Hooper Reed. Two years later a brother, Douglas, nicknamed "Buddy," was born, as well as a sister, Melodye, a few years later. According to one of her biographers, her earliest memory was of the sound of applause echoing backstage for her mother and father. At three years old, Raye performed with her parents. From that time forward, she had no other ambition than to be a performer, and there are no records that she ever attended school.

Between 1919 and 1929 she performed with the Benny Davis Revue, the Ben Blue Company, and the Will Morrissey Company. She made her New York debut at the age of eighteen singing in the pit with the Paul Asch Orchestra at the Paramount Theater and later appeared at Keith's Eighty-sixth Street Theater, which was known for introducing vaudeville acts. "But you need a new name, for good luck," her mother told her. Opening a telephone directory, they came up with Martha Raye. Raye was canceled after only one performance at Keith's, but she appeared in clubs in and around New York. She began going nightly to Fifty-second Street to sing with Louis Prima and his band at the Famous Door. The Broadway producer Lew Brown was looking for a fresh face to open in his upcoming musical, *Calling All Stars,* and signed Raye to do the show.

Martha Raye. © BETTMANN/CORBIS

Calling All Stars opened in New York at the Hollywood Theater in December 1934, then moved to Boston. Although not successful in New York, the show lasted long enough for Raye to find other avenues for her talents as a singer, dancer, and comedian. She appeared in Earl Carroll's *Sketchbook Review* at the Winter Garden and then began singing in nightclubs in Chicago and New York. Along the way, she met Jimmy Durante and performed with him at the Casino de Paris in New York, where they were known as "the nose and the mouth."

Her big break came in 1935 in California after a guest appearance at the Trocadero in Hollywood, where the Paramount film director Norman Taurog signed her up for her first movie, *Rhythm on the Range*. The movie starred Bing Crosby and featured Raye singing "Mr. Paganini," which became her signature song. She appeared in fifteen films for Paramount from 1936 to 1940.

While her professional life was often successful, her personal life was not. While working on the Paramount lot, the twenty-year-old Raye met and married twenty-one-year-old makeup artist Hamilton "Buddy" Westmore. Three months later they filed for divorce. In 1938 she married the composer, arranger, and orchestra leader David Rose, but thirty-one months later, in 1941, they divorced. Fewer than five weeks after divorcing Rose, she married

Miami Beach hotel executive Neal Lang, but they divorced and she married dancer Nick Condos. On 26 July 1944 Raye gave birth to her only child, Melodye Condos. By 1954 she had divorced Condos and married dancer Edward Thomas Begley. She divorced Begley in 1956 and married policeman-bodyguard Robert O'Shea. Mark Harris, her last husband (whom she married in 1991), survived her. Although she and Condos divorced, he remained her personal manager until his death in 1988.

In her fifty years in show business, Raye performed in nightclubs, radio productions, theaters, movies, and television. She made twenty-six films, most memorably *Monsieur Verdoux* in 1947 with Charlie Chaplin and Billy Rose's *Jumbo* in 1962. She appeared in numerous Broadway productions including *Hold On to Your Hats* in 1940; the Broadway revival of *Annie Get Your Gun* in 1958; *Hello, Dolly* in 1967; and *No, No, Nanette* in 1972. She toured in productions of *Calamity Jane, Bells Are Ringing, Solid Gold Cadillac, Call Me Madam, Everybody Loves Opal*, and others. She starred in her own television show (1955–1956) and was featured in the series *McMillan and Wife* (1976–1977) and *Alice* (1982–1984). She also made countless television guest appearances.

Raye was devoted to entertaining military personnel, from World War II through the Vietnam years. The biographer Jean Maddern Pitrone observed that for Raye, serving the military was not a role but "a thorough immersion of self on behalf of a greater cause." Raye died of pneumonia after a series of strokes at Cedar-Sinai Medical Center in Los Angeles. She was seventy-eight. She is buried at Fort Bragg, North Carolina, with her "troops" from World War II, Korea, and Vietnam. She was interred in her Green Beret uniform, under a simple tombstone engraved "Martha Raye—Civilian."

Raye won many citations during her lifetime, most notably the Jean Hersholt Humanitarian Award from the Academy of Motion Picture Arts and Sciences in 1969 for "devoted and often dangerous work in entertaining troops in combat areas almost continuously since World War II." In 1993 President Bill Clinton awarded her the Presidential Medal of Freedom—the highest honor possible for an American civilian.

★

Noonie Fortin, a Vietnam-era veteran, wrote *Memories of Maggie: Martha Raye, A Legend Spanning Three Wars* (1999). Jean Maddern Pitrone's *Take It from the Big Mouth: The Life of Martha Raye* (1999) is a full-length biography. Raye is referenced in Anthony Slide's *The Encyclopedia of Vaudeville* (1994). She wrote the foreword to *A Piece of My Heart: The Stories of 26 American Women Who Served in Vietnam* (1985). An obituary is in *Variety* (24–30 Oct. 1994).

JOHN KARES SMITH

REDENBACHER, Orville (*b.* 16 July 1907 near Brazil, Indiana; *d.* 19 September 1995 in Coronado, California), agronomist and businessman known as the self-proclaimed "Popcorn King."

Redenbacher was one of four children of William Redenbacher, a farmer, and Julia Magdelena Dierdoff, a homemaker. According to his biographer, Len Sherman, Orville was named after the aviation pioneer Orville Wright because of William Redenbacher's respect for the Wright brothers and their accomplishments. The entire family helped maintain the farm. Young Redenbacher helped with the chores and by age ten was tending the straw blower on the threshing rig during harvest. Two years later he began raising corn—the crop that would one day make him famous. His parents allowed him to keep the money he earned from selling his crop in nearby Brazil and Terre Haute, Indiana.

Redenbacher was the first in his family to attend high school, traveling approximately fourteen miles from the

Orville Redenbacher, 1987. © GEORGE ROSE/GAMMA LIAISON

farm to Brazil, because they offered a vocational agriculture course. While in school he was a member of the Clay County 4-H club, becoming a team state champion in the dairy, poultry, egg, and corn categories. In individual competition, Redenbacher placed second in a national dairy competition held in Syracuse, New York. During this time he adopted the Clay County agricultural agent Horace Abbott as his mentor. He graduated from Brazil High School in 1924. Although Redenbacher had an appointment to the U.S. Military Academy at West Point, his love of agriculture led him instead to the School of Agriculture at Purdue University in West Lafayette, Indiana.

During his years at Purdue, Redenbacher played the sousaphone in the Purdue marching band, joined the track team, edited the student newspaper, participated in the local 4-H club, and joined Alpha Gamma Rho, a local fraternity. When he was not in school, Redenbacher earned tuition and board by working at the Purdue hog and cattle farms. In his senior year he met Corinne Rosemond Strate, a journalism student at Indiana University.

After receiving a B.S. degree from Purdue in June 1928, Redenbacher chose to teach vocational agriculture, biology, industrial arts, and seventh and eighth grade agriculture at the Fontanet (Indiana) High School. He chose to live in Fontanet because it was close to his parents' home in Brazil and only an hour car ride from Indiana University and his girlfriend, Corinne. They were married on 26 December 1928 and had three daughters.

Redenbacher's interest in popcorn was strengthened by his interaction with the hybrid corn seed specialist Arthur Brunson and George Christie, head of the Agricultural Experiment Station at Purdue. Both encouraged Redenbacher to continue the experiments he began on his parents' farm. In 1929 Redenbacher realized one of his dreams when his friend and mentor Abbott became an agent for Terre Haute and Vigo County and asked Redenbacher to take his place as the Clay County agricultural agent.

In 1932, when Abbott became the agent for Marion County, he asked Redenbacher to take his place as agent for Vigo County. Redenbacher gladly accepted the position and worked hard to improve the farmers' situation in Vigo. He pioneered the use of radio to broadcast crop reports and farm news. However, the Great Depression and drought conditions drove many farmers out of business, leaving Redenbacher discouraged. His fortunes changed when the owners of the Princeton Mining Company approached him about managing their 12,000-acre farm near Princeton, Indiana, in exchange for a home, a $4,500-a-year salary, and 10 percent of the farm's profits. Redenbacher had varied success with crops on the land, but it gave him the chance to test his hybrid corn seed and the hybrid popcorn seed he had developed at Purdue. By 1944 he was raising his popping corn for the supermarket industry as well as other crops on his farmland. In the late 1940s and 1950s, he became one of the first farmers to store liquid fertilizer, which he also produced and distributed, and to use it on his crops.

In 1940 Redenbacher formed a partnership with fellow Purdue graduate Charles Bowman. Together they purchased the George F. Chester and Son Seed Company and began to produce crop seeds (hybrid corn and others) for several large eastern agricultural businesses. When their business began to grow, Redenbacher moved his family to Valparaiso, Indiana. In 1953 he and Bowman went into business full-time. The company changed its name from Chester Hybrids to Chester, Inc., and was involved in a number of agricultural endeavors. Beginning in 1959 the partners, joined by another popcorn advocate, Carl Hartman, continued tinkering with hybrid popcorn seeds. In 1965, after years of experiments and cross-pollinating, they developed the hybrid corn seed that would make them famous. They sold it under the name RedBow, combining the names of the two principal originators of the hybrid corn seed and paying homage to Redenbacher's ever-present red bow tie.

Despite the fact that the three men had come up with a popcorn that was lighter and fluffier than most and left few unpopped kernels, RedBow was also more expensive, and many stores and businesses thought the investment was not worth the money. Redenbacher and his team nevertheless stood by their product, citing Redenbacher's belief, "Give the people a better product, and they'll beat a path to your door." They began to market RedBow themselves and, after consulting Gerson, Howe and Johnson, an advertising firm in Chicago, changed the name to Orville Redenbacher's Gourmet Popping Corn. Their marketing campaign featured Redenbacher himself, and the popcorn was first sold at Marshall Field's department store and specialty stores in the Midwest, where it attracted the attention of Blue Plate Foods, a subsidiary of Hunt-Wesson Foods, based in Fullerton, California.

In 1971, just as Redenbacher was about to realize his greatest triumph, Corinne died of a bleeding ulcer. In the next few years, Bowman and Redenbacher found that they could not keep up with the demands of their booming popcorn business. In 1976 they signed a deal with Hunt-Wesson that turned over their popcorn to the company in exchange for Redenbacher becoming the spokesperson. Redenbacher began a whirlwind tour of the United States promoting his gourmet popping corn. Meanwhile, he married family friend Nina Reder on 27 October 1971. She joined him in his cross-country tours and continued to do so until her death in 1991.

Hunt-Wesson renegotiated with Redenbacher and Bowman, agreeing to use the Redenbacher label into perpetuity. His gourmet popping corn continued to be one of the company's big sellers. Over the years, Hunt-Wesson was bought by a succession of companies, which all were committed to continue selling Redenbacher's popping corn.

Redenbacher presented himself just as he was—a folksy, honest, and friendly person. He appeared on many programs, including *CBS This Morning, Hee Haw,* and *Late Night with Conan O'Brien*. He made numerous television commercials about his product, including several with his grandson, Gary Fish-Redenbacher, and one with members of his family.

Redenbacher was also a philanthropist, working in President Dwight Eisenhower's People to People Program, which encouraged an exchange of ideas between people on an individual level. He visited 134 nations and eventually became the chairperson of the program. He was also a Kiwanis member and a supporter of 4-H and the Easter Seals Program. He and Gary supported the 1992 U.S. national volleyball teams and created the Orville Redenbacher's Second Start Scholarship Program, designed to help older students who wanted make a second start.

Redenbacher loved getting together with his extended family for visits and trips across the country. The family was in the midst of planning their next trip when he died of a heart attack in his apartment in Coronado, California, where he had moved in the mid-1970s, at the age of eighty-eight. His cremated ashes were scattered at sea.

★

Redenbacher's *Orville Redenbacher's Popcorn Book* (1984) contains recipes and brief autobiographical information. Redenbacher's biography, by Len Sherman, with Robert Topping, *Popcorn King: How Orville Redenbacher and His Popcorn Charmed America* (1996), provides a detailed recounting of the subject's life from birth to death. *People Weekly* (2 Oct. 1995) has a tribute to Redenbacher, with comments from Gary Fish-Redenbacher. See also Andrew Smith, *Popped Culture* (1999). Obituaries are in the *New York Times* and the *Chicago Tribune* (both 20 Sept. 1995).

BRIAN B. CARPENTER

RED THUNDER CLOUD (*b.* 30 May 1919 in Newport, Rhode Island; *d.* 6 January 1996 in Worcester, Massachusetts), singer, dancer, storyteller, and field researcher best known for his claim to be the last speaker of the Catawba language.

Born Cromwell Ashbie Hawkins West, Red Thunder Cloud was also known as Carlos Ashbie Hawk Westez, Carlos Westez, and Namo S. Hatiririe. He was the son of a druggist, Cromwell Payne West, and a homemaker, Roberta Hawkins West. Both were African Americans of Newport, Rhode Island. His father was born in Pennsylvania and his mother was born in Lynchburg, Virginia. Very little information can be found on Red Thunder Cloud's formative years. What is known and documented is that he

Red Thunder Cloud. Associated Press HO via Worcester Telegram & Gaze

was a descendant of a prominent African-American family of Baltimore. West's maternal grandfather was one of the first African-American lawyers of Baltimore and was a respected civic leader. His sister, Ada Fouche Williams, was a professor at the University of Maryland in Baltimore County. From 1935 to 1937 West was employed by the Newport City wharf as a watchman and later as a chauffeur.

For reasons that are unclear, West reinvented his identity and lived most of his life as Red Thunder Cloud of the Catawba tribe. Correspondence between West and Frank G. Speck, a professor of anthropology at the University of Pennsylvania, in 1938 stated that West was a sixteen-year-old Catawba Indian and a junior at Southampton High School on Long Island, New York. He petitioned Speck for help in learning more about his people and indicated that his fascination for Native American culture began when he was in the fourth grade. West stated further that he was brought up by the Narraganset Indians of Rhode Island and had lived with the Shinnecock tribe since 1937. West also told Speck that he had learned the Catawba language from his grandmother, Ada McMechen.

Speck believed Red Thunder Cloud to be a genuine Catawba Indian and proceeded to provide him with training in field methods of recording notes for ethnological studies. Red Thunder Cloud worked for Speck on small

projects, collecting ethnographic data and folklore among Long Island Indians. He also collected data on the Montauk, Shinnecock, and Mashpee tribes for George E. Heye of the Museum of American Indians. In December 1943 Red Thunder Cloud lived at the University of Pennsylvania for two weeks, providing information on the Catawba tribe, recording music, and aiding in ethnobotanical research. With a letter of introduction from Speck, Red Thunder Cloud made his first visit to the Catawba Reservation in Rock Hill, South Carolina, in February 1944. According to Chief Gilbert Blue of the Catawba tribe, Red Thunder Cloud studied with his grandfather, Chief Sam Blue, and Sally Gordon during his second visit to the reservation, which lasted for six months. When interviewed in 1957 by William C. Sturtevant, Chief Sam Blue and his daughter-in-law Lillian expressed doubts concerning Red Thunder Cloud's identity as a Catawba. They believed that he had learned the language from a book.

In a letter dated 25 October 1958, Red Thunder Cloud offered assistance to Sturtevant in making contact with Indian groups in the eastern United States. His correspondence revealed that his mother was Catawba and his father was from Tegucigalpa, Honduras, and came from Honduran and Puerto Rican parentage. Red Thunder Cloud also stated that he spoke Spanish and Portuguese as well as an array of Native American languages that included

Cayuga, Seneca, Mohawk, Narraganset, Micmac, Passamaquoddy, Penobscot, Creek, Choctaw, Sioux, and Winnebago. In addition, he was able to recognize other Indian languages when he heard them spoken. Foxx Ayers, a long-time Catawba friend of Red Thunder Cloud, stated that his friend's knowledge of the language was so good that he had trained his dog to answer only to Catawba commands.

Red Thunder Cloud's marriage to Jean Marilyn Miller (Pretty Pony) of the Blackfoot tribe was brief, although she frequently appeared with him at powwows and other Native American celebrations. He could also be seen at local fairs in New England, selling his herbal medicines under the name "Accabonac Princess American Teas."

Red Thunder Cloud's support of Native American causes was demonstrated by his involvement in Indian organizations, as well as his publication of a newsletter called the *Indian War Drum*. In 1964 and 1965 he worked with G. Hubert Matthews, professor at the Massachusetts Institute of Technology, to document the Catawba language. Together they published five texts in 1967. Matthews included in these books Red Thunder Cloud's family genealogy and named the Catawba relatives in his maternal line. In discussions with Matthews, Red Thunder Cloud gave the name of his mother's father as "Strong Eagle." The latter was a graduate of Yale Law School, Red Thunder Cloud said, and had died in 1941. He identified his mother's name as "Singing Dove."

Red Thunder Cloud died at St. Vincent's Hospital in Worcester at the age of seventy-six. At the time of his death, Leonor Pena, a close friend from Central Falls, Rhode Island, gave Red Thunder Cloud's name as Carlos Westez and included the alias Namos S. Hatiririe. She listed his occupation as shaman. His sister, as administrator to his will in probate court, gave his name as Cromwell Ashbie Hawkins West.

The noted linguist and ethnologist Goddard Ives of the Smithsonian Institution has validated suspicions of Red Thunder Cloud's identity by way of public documents, letters, and publications. He stated that "in spite of the negative issues surrounding Red Thunder Cloud's identity, he has made valuable contributions to the study of ethnography." Ives stated that even though Red Thunder Cloud's life was a "successful life-long masquerade," he contributed extensively to a greater understanding and protection of the Catawbas and other native cultures.

★

Red Thunder Cloud published five editions of *Indian War Drum*, three of which are located at the East Hampton Public Library in Southampton, New York. Correspondence between Frank G. Speck and Red Thunder Cloud, published by the *American Philosophical Society* (1938), as well as ethnographic studies on the Montauk and Shinnecock Indians of New York, are avail-

able in the Rare Eastern Indian Collection at the New York Public Library. Numerous articles have been written about Red Thunder Cloud, the most definitive of which is Goddard Ives, "The Identity of Red Thunder Cloud," *Society for the Study of the Indigenous Languages of the Americas* (Apr. 2000). An obituary is in the *New York Times* (8 Jan. 1996).

JOHNNIEQUE B. LOVE

REGNERY, Henry (*b.* 5 January 1912 in Hinsdale, Illinois; *d.* 18 June 1996 in Chicago, Illinois), conservative publisher who founded the Henry Regnery Company, which published books by William F. Buckley, Jr., Russell Kirk, Wyndham Lewis, and T. S. Eliot.

Regnery was born in a suburb of Chicago, the next to youngest of the five children of William Henry Regnery, a wealthy textile manufacturer of western German descent, and Frances Susan Thrasher, of English and Welsh descent. Although the family was Catholic and as an adult Regnery published Catholic books, he never made a commitment to the church. His memorial service was held in an Episcopal church. In 1929 Regnery entered the Armour Institute of Technology (later renamed the Illinois Institute of Technology) to study mechanical engineering. In 1931 he transferred to the Massachusetts Institute of Technology (MIT), where he took numerous humanities courses and received a B.S. degree in mathematics in 1934.

As the result of a friendship with a German exchange student, Regnery studied economics at the University of Bonn from 1934 to 1936. He later stated that he had little direct contact with the horrors of Nazism, then in its early stages, and that most of the people he met in Bonn were indifferent to or opposed to Nazism. In 1936 Regnery began doctoral studies in economics at Harvard, where he began to move toward a free-market position. Two years later he left Harvard with an M.A. degree, having decided to enter government service rather than teaching.

During the summer of 1937 Regnery held a temporary post in the Resettlement Administration, a New Deal agency involved with housing. From that position he gained employment with the American Friends Service Committee in connection with the development of a new community near Pittsburgh. While working there Regnery met Eleanor Scattergood, a member of an old Quaker family. They married on 12 November 1938 and subsequently had four children. In June 1941 Regnery returned to Illinois and entered the family textile business, Joanna Western Mills Company. He was an officer of this firm for six years and at one time was chairman of its board of directors. Nevertheless, he wrote in his memoirs that "Armour Institute of Technology convinced me that I would never be a businessman, MIT that I would never be a mathematician, Harvard Graduate School that I would never be a scholar, my father's business that I would never be a businessman."

During World War II, with the encouragement and financial assistance of his family, Regnery gradually entered publishing in 1944. He became a financial adviser for the newly established conservative weekly *Human Events,* headed by Felix Morley, whose books Regnery later published. In 1945 Regnery financed the publication of two pamphlets by the University of Chicago president Robert M. Hutchins. Regnery directed the publication of other pamphlets bearing the imprint Human Events, Inc., and covering various subjects and viewpoints. Many dealt with current events and foreign policy.

On 9 September 1947 the name of the nonprofit publishing organization headed by Regnery (Morley became president of Haverford College) changed from Human Events Associates to Henry Regnery Company. The first three books published under the new name were two highly critical examinations of the Allied occupation of Germany written by the left-wing British journalist Victor Gollancz and a book about "the sickness of the modern world" by the Swiss Catholic writer Max Picard. Six books, including works on history and philosophy, appeared in 1948, some of which were reviewed by the *Christian Science Monitor, Saturday Review,* and *American Historical Review.* However, that year the Internal Revenue Service denied the firm a tax exemption, forcing it to become a for-profit business. In 1948 Regnery began publishing Catholic religious works, later a major source of income for the company. Mortimer Brewster Smith's *And Madly Teach,* a criticism of progressive education, sold very well after it was favorably reviewed by *Time* magazine. By 1949 Regnery was publishing books for the University of Chicago's Great Books Program as well as books by Raymond Aron and Gabriel Marcel.

In 1951 Regnery published *God and Man at Yale* by William F. Buckley, Jr. The recent graduate contended that the faculty at Yale University and by implication at other elite American universities had come to be dominated by atheists and political leftists. Amid the ensuing uproar in the academic community, the University of Chicago canceled its publishing contract with Regnery. In 1953, to somewhat less controversy, Regnery published Russell Kirk's *The Conservative Mind: From Burke to Santayana,* a seminal work in American conservative thought. In later years Regnery published major works by other conservative authors, including Richard Weaver, Willmoore Kendall, and James Burnham, whom the more liberal-minded mainstream publishers, mostly in New York, would not touch. Although many of these books sold well, over the years much of the company's profits continued to come from Roman Catholic religious works. Thomas Aquinas, it was said, was Regnery's best-selling author. Regnery estab-

lished a quality paperback line called Gateway Editions. After 1960, for financial reasons, he began publishing books on baseball and civil service examinations.

In 1966 Regnery left the presidency of his firm but became chairman of the board of directors the following year. In 1977 he sold the firm, which was renamed Contemporary Books and published books on sports and automobile repairs. He established two new publishing houses in Washington, D.C.—Gateway Editions Limited and Regnery Publishers. Regnery headed these businesses until his retirement in 1983, when his son Alfred Regnery took over.

Regnery wrote *Memoirs of a Dissident Publisher* (1979). His book on intellectual life in Chicago, *Creative Chicago,* was published in 1993, and a collection of his essays, *A Few Reasonable Words* (1996), was published shortly before his death. Another essay collection, *Perfect Sowing: Reflections of a Bookman* (1999), was released posthumously. Regnery died in Chicago of complications from brain surgery and was buried in that city.

★

In addition to *Memoirs of a Dissident Publisher,* some information on Regnery's life is in his other books. An obituary is in the *New York Times* (23 June 1996).

STEPHEN A. STERTZ

RESTON, James Barrett (*b.* 3 November 1909 in Clydebank, Scotland; *d.* 6 December 1995 in Washington, D.C.), influential correspondent, columnist, Washington bureau chief, executive editor, and vice president of the *New York Times.*

Reston was the second of two children of James Reston, a machinist, and Johanna Irving, a homemaker. At the age of two, Reston emigrated with his family from Scotland to Dayton, Ohio, to escape poverty. Homesickness and a family quarrel soon sent them back to Scotland. They returned to the United States when Reston was eleven, and he was naturalized when his parents became citizens in 1927. He acquired his lifelong nickname, "Scotty," while a boy in Dayton. His devout Presbyterian mother hoped that he would grow up to preach to the heathen, and Reston later mused that he accomplished this by becoming a columnist.

Reston's father worked for Delco Remy, a subsidiary of General Motors, and after graduating in 1927 from Oakwood High School, Reston spent a year editing the factory newspaper, *Delco Doings.* He also caddied at a local golf course, where he met James Middleton Cox, the publisher of the Cox newspapers. In 1928 he entered the University of Illinois School of Journalism at Urbana-Champaign, where he was an indifferent student, devoting most of his attention to the golf team and sports reporting for the cam-

James Reston. LIBRARY OF CONGRESS

book *Prelude to Victory* (1942), he blamed Britain and the United States for having "underestimated the price of freedom" through appeasement, isolationism, and a lack of military preparedness. As a war correspondent, he tried to write as if sending a letter to a friend back home and displayed an ability to synthesize complex issues into straightforward prose. When undulant fever sent him home in 1940, Reston was assigned to the *New York Times* Washington bureau. In 1942 he took a leave of absence to run the U.S. Office of War Information operations in London. Later that year *Times* publisher Arthur Hays Sulzberger invited Reston to become his personal assistant and brought him on a mission to Moscow for the American Red Cross. Visiting the offices of the Soviet newspaper *Pravda,* Reston was startled to find that all of its "news" came over the wire from government offices. He resisted the notion of the press as an instrument of government and long struggled with defining the proper relations between reporters and officials.

A liberal internationalist, Reston saw journalism as a moral force for educating readers and furthering the public interest. His idealism and professionalism impressed Sulzberger, who insisted that Reston be reinstated in the *Times* Washington bureau, over the objections of its conservative bureau chief, Arthur Krock. Although Krock disapproved of Reston's desire to write news analysis instead of strictly objective reporting, he relented when he learned that Reston was considering writing a column for the rival *New York Herald-Tribune.* Reston became one of the first reporters at the *Times* with license to speculate on the mood in Washington and the motives of officials. In 1945 the Michigan Republican senator Arthur Vandenberg credited Reston with having influenced his celebrated speech announcing his abandonment of isolationism. Vandenberg kept Reston supplied with inside information from the State Department, bolstering his image as a "scoop artist," always eager to be first with a story.

Sent to gather news at the embassies, Reston covered the Dumbarton Oaks Conference that convened in 1945 in Washington to plan for the formation of the United Nations. Among members of the Nationalist Chinese delegation, he encountered a former apprentice at the *Times,* Chen Yi, who obliged him with copies of each nation's proposals. In 1945 the *Times* published one position paper each day, beating its competitors and outraging the assembled diplomats. The series won Reston his first Pulitzer Prize and promotion to diplomatic correspondent.

Short, stocky, and ruddy, Reston balanced his ample ability and self-confidence with humility and wry self-deprecation. He developed unparalleled access to the highest government officials in Republican and Democratic administrations alike, employing his wit, instinct, and em-

pus paper. When Reston's tuition check bounced in his senior year due to a bank failure, the university asked him to leave. He hastily secured a loan from Cox, who also promised him a job after graduation. On earning a B.S. degree in 1932, Reston began working as a sports reporter for Cox's *Springfield* (Ohio) *Daily News.* In 1933 Reston became a publicity agent for the Ohio State University athletic department and in 1934 for the Cincinnati Reds baseball club. He moved to New York City in 1934 as an Associated Press (AP) sportswriter. In 1935 he married his college sweetheart, Sarah Jane ("Sally") Fulton. They had three sons.

The AP sent Reston to London in 1937 to cover major sporting events and to report on the British Foreign Office during the off-season. His golfing skills helped him cultivate friendships with officials who kept him well informed. Impressed with his reporting, the *New York Times* London correspondent hired Reston as his assistant. He joined the staff of the *Times* on 1 September 1939, the day World War II began.

Covering the German blitz of London shaped Reston's worldview and sharpened his writing skills. In his wartime

pathy to coax out news. His sources cooperated out of respect for his talent, discretion, and prestigious news outlet.

In 1953, when the *Washington Post* sought to make Reston its editorial page editor, Krock stepped aside to allow him to become the *Times* Washington bureau chief. Reston recruited a talented team of reporters for the bureau, among them Russell Baker, Max Frankel, David Halberstam, Anthony Lewis, Neil Sheehan, and Tom Wicker. They became collectively known as "Scotty's Boys" and "Reston's Rangers." The bureau also included some able women reporters, Marjorie Hunter, Nan Robertson, and Eileen Shanahan, but Reston invited only the men to councils in his office and to lunch at the Metropolitan Club (which did not admit women). Beyond managing the bureau, he regularly wrote the *Times* lead stories from Washington and an editorial page column.

Reston often irritated presidents by publishing information before they wanted it released. He believed that in a democracy people had a right to know what their government was planning to do, and that the *Times* needed to anticipate developments rather than react after the fact. Various administrations also used him as a conduit. In 1955 the State Department covertly provided Reston with the Yalta Papers, which Secretary of State John Foster Dulles wanted published despite objections from the British. Reston's quest for such insider information required that he maintain confidences and sometimes suppress major stories. He learned that American U-2 planes were flying high-altitude reconnaissance missions over the Soviet Union but held back on publication until the Russians shot down one of the planes.

In 1961 *New York Times* reporter Tad Szulc uncovered evidence that the Central Intelligence Agency had trained a brigade of Cuban refugees to invade Fidel Castro's Cuba. Reston persuaded *Times* publisher Orvil Dryfoos to mute the story, over objections from the paper's editors. Reston reasoned that premature publication would more likely damage the *Times* than the invasion. Not even the failure of the Bay of Pigs invasion changed his mind, although afterward he called for greater press skepticism of government policies. President John F. Kennedy personally called Reston in 1962 to ask that the *Times* not publish an account of the Cuban Missile Crisis until after he had formally addressed the nation. Once again the *Times* complied.

Although he accepted U.S. leadership in the cold war against communism as an imperative, Reston never felt comfortable with the rationales offered for military intervention in Southeast Asia. After touring South Vietnam in 1965, he returned deeply disturbed over the war's futile brutality. President Lyndon B. Johnson tried to court his favor, but while Reston supported the social reforms of Johnson's Great Society, his criticism of the war soured their relationship. Johnson indignantly complained that

after Reston and the columnist Walter Lippmann turned against the war, the rest of the Washington press corps followed their lead.

Reston visited the People's Republic of China in 1971, months in advance of President Richard Nixon. His articles from Beijing included an account of his emergency appendectomy, aided by acupuncture. That year, the *New York Times* obtained a copy of the classified Pentagon Papers, a massively documented analysis of how the United States had gotten into the Vietnam War. Reston urged its publication and threatened that if the *Times* failed to act he would print the material in the *Vineyard Gazette,* the weekly Martha's Vineyard paper that his family had run since 1968. A court injunction halted the Pentagon Papers after the first installments appeared, but the U.S. Supreme Court, in *United States v. New York Times Company* (1971), rejected the government's attempt at prior restraint.

Reston stepped down as the bureau chief in 1964 to devote full attention to his thrice-a-week column, "Washington." In 1968, when editors in New York tried to remove his successor, Tom Wicker, and impose their own candidate to head the Washington bureau, Reston exerted his personal prestige and convinced Arthur Ochs Sulzberger, son of Arthur Hays Sulzberger, to reverse the decision. In the management shake-up that followed, Reston returned to New York as the executive editor, enabling him to sidetrack his opponents and facilitate a smoother transition in the Washington bureau. He reduced the semiofficial pronouncements that had filled the paper and emphasized thoughtful explanations of events. Although he commuted to Washington weekly, his column suffered. After eighteen months, he extracted himself from editing, became vice president for news coverage, and returned to Washington, where he wrote his column until his retirement in 1989.

Reston's other writings included the books *Walter Lippmann and His Times* (1959); *Sketches in the Sand* (1967); *The Artillery of the Press: Its Influence on American Foreign Policy* (1967); *The New York Times Report from Red China* (1971); and *Washington* (1986). He died of cancer in Washington, D.C.

During Reston's fifty years with the *New York Times,* influential readers at home and abroad paid close attention to his reporting. His critics considered him too intimate with top government officials, yet his columns held political leaders to high standards and pulled no punches whenever they disappointed him. One of the most respected journalists of his era, Reston encouraged a greater sense of responsibility in the press and relished its role as adversary.

★

Reston's papers are in the University of Illinois Library, Urbana-Champaign. His autobiography is *Deadline: A Memoir* (1991). Reviews of his career by colleagues at the *New York Times* include Arthur Krock, *Memoirs* (1968); Gay Talese, *The Kingdom and the Power* (1969); Bill Lawrence, *Six Presidents, Too Many Wars* (1972); Harrison Salisbury, *Without Fear or Favor* (1980); Russell Baker, *The Good Times* (1989); Nan Robertson, *The Girls in the Balcony* (1992); John Corry, *My Times* (1993); and Max Frankel, *The Times of My Life and My Life with the Times* (1999). An obituary is in the *New York Times* (8 Dec. 1995).

Donald A. Ritchie

REYNOLDS, Allie Pierce (*b.* 10 February 1915 in Bethany, Oklahoma; *d.* 26 December 1994 in Oklahoma City, Oklahoma), baseball player who, as the first American League pitcher to throw two no-hitters in one season, is considered one of the best big-game pitchers in baseball history.

Reynolds was one of three sons of David C. Reynolds, a Fundamentalist minister and evangelist who was three-eighths Creek Indian, and Mary S. Brooks, a homemaker. Reynolds's father became independently wealthy after oil was discovered on lands he had been allotted by the federal government. Having earned a divinity degree from a Nazarene college in Bethany, during the 1920s David Reynolds moved his family to Pasadena, California, then received a religious assignment in Hot Springs, Arkansas, and finally returned to Bethany to perform evangelistic missions.

Allie Reynolds played sandlot sports as a youngster but did not participate in organized baseball because of the restrictive Nazarene beliefs that proscribed Sunday athletic competition. When his father became pastor of a church in Oklahoma City in 1933, Reynolds transferred to Capitol

Hill High School, where he starred in football and track and field. After graduation in January 1935, he began working for an oil field pressure equipment firm but soon left the job and, through the assistance of his high school football coach, obtained a track scholarship to attend Oklahoma A&M College (now Oklahoma State University), in Stillwater. On 7 July 1935 Reynolds married Earlene Jones; the couple had three children.

At Oklahoma A&M, Reynolds played halfback and fullback on the football team from 1936 to 1938, gaining All–Missouri Valley Conference recognition, and ran sprints on the track team. A gifted athlete, he also threw the discus and the javelin to help build his frame from 140 to 200 pounds. During the spring of his junior year, he was asked by baseball coach Hank Iba to throw batting practice against the varsity. He so impressed Iba that he gained a place on the team and starred both on the mound and at bat. A three-sport letterman, Reynolds was proclaimed by the school's wrestling coach Ed Gallagher as the greatest natural athlete he had ever seen.

In 1939 Reynolds signed with the major league team the Cleveland Indians for $2,000 and a $200 a month no-cut contract. He advanced through the minor leagues from 1939 to 1942, playing for Springfield (Middle Atlantic League), Cedar Rapids (Three I League), and Wilkes-Barre (Eastern League), winning eighteen games and leading the league in strikeouts and earned-run averages for Cedar Rapids in 1942. Meanwhile, he made up his missing college credits via correspondence classes and received a B.S. degree in 1942. Late that season he appeared in two games for Cleveland. Classified 4-F as a result of a football-related

Allie Reynolds (*right*) and Casey Stengel. © Bettmann/Corbis

neck injury, Reynolds pitched for the Indians through the 1946 season, compiling a 51–47 record. During this time, he developed a reputation as a temperamental pitcher of unrealized potential who, by his own admission, was a hard thrower unable to pace himself.

The New York Yankees star outfielder Joe DiMaggio recommended that the team trade for Reynolds. On 19 October 1946 he was traded to the Yankees for Joe Gordon and Eddie Bockman. With the Yankees, Reynolds mastered the art of pitching and reached his greatest success, winning 131 games and losing only 60 between 1947 and 1954. Reynolds became a key component of the Yankees pitching staff that featured Vic Raschi, Ed Lopat, and Whitey Ford. He helped the team win six world championships during that span, including five in a row between 1949 and 1953. He won nineteen games in 1947 and led American League pitchers with a .708 winning percentage. In 1951 he won seventeen games, led the league with seven shutouts, and threw two no-hitters, the second of which included a classic confrontation with Ted Williams, who was retired for the final out. Reynolds won twenty games in 1952, leading the league with 6 shutouts, 160 strikeouts, and a 2.07 earned-run average. His heroics of 1951 earned him the Hickok Belt Award, recognizing the professional athlete of the year in 1952, a day after he received the New York Baseball Writers Association's Sid Mercer Award, given to the major league baseball player of the year.

Long before the era of specialization among pitchers, Reynolds was often called on to pitch in relief as well as his normal starting duties. His World Series statistics further reinforced his reputation for pitching best in crucial games. Reynolds had a 7–2 record with four saves while appearing in fifteen games. He ranks second in most series wins, third in strikeouts (62) and in saves and games pitched. He had a win and a save with an earned-run average of 0.87 in the 1950 World Series and won two games with a save and a 1.77 earned-run average in 1952. A proud, sensitive man whose courage and stamina had been questioned in his early years in the major leagues, Reynolds outpitched Don Newcombe to win 1–0 in the opening game of the World Series in 1949. Reynolds acquired the nickname "Chief" from New York sportswriters after being traded to the Yankees. After his second no-hitter in 1951, the Yankee broadcaster Mel Allen began to refer to him as "Superchief," after the Santa Fe Railroad luxury train that traveled from Chicago to Los Angeles.

From 1952 to 1954, Reynolds served as the American League player representative. Together with his National League counterpart, Ralph Kiner, Reynolds worked to increase the major league minimum salary, secure accountability for the players' pension fund, and set into motion the process whereby the first Major League Baseball Players Association was created in 1954. For several years he suffered from bone chips in his right elbow and in July 1953 suffered a painful back injury when the team bus struck an abutment. Reynolds rarely pitched pain-free thereafter, and he retired after records of 13–7 in 1953 and 13–4 in 1954. A six-time member of the American League all-star team, he concluded his thirteen-year major league career with 182 wins and 107 losses, 36 shutouts, 49 saves, and an earned-run average of 3.30.

Years before leaving baseball, Reynolds had planned to enter business. He spent several years managing his father's oil holdings, making financial investments, and gaining contacts within the petroleum industry. After retiring from baseball in 1954, he joined the Atlas Mud Company, a firm that serviced oil field drilling equipment. Within a year, he became the president of the company. Reynolds also established Reynolds Petroleum, and from 1980 to 1985 was the chairman of the board of the New Park Mid-Continental Drilling Company.

After his playing career ended, Reynolds became involved in raising funds for his alma mater, in many civic and charitable organizations, and in Native American causes. He was elected president of the minor league American Association from 1969 to 1971 and, with a number of Oklahoma City businessmen, bought the minor league Oklahoma City 89ers franchise in order to keep the team in that city. He and his wife were major contributors to a new baseball facility at Oklahoma State University, which was officially dedicated and named in his honor on 24 April 1982. He headed a program that developed youth baseball in Oklahoma and chaired several boards to raise funds to combat various diseases. In 1964 Reynolds ran unsuccessfully for the state senate on the Democratic Party ticket.

Reynolds was named the president of the American Indian Hall of Fame in 1978, helping that organization through financial difficulties to solvency. In 1984 he became the president of the Center of the American Indian and in 1986 was instrumental in the inauguration of Red Earth, a leading Native American cultural and arts exposition. He became active in Creek tribal affairs, helping utilize gaming profits to build a hospital and provide hospitalization insurance for tribal members. In 1991 Reynolds was elected to the Oklahoma Hall of Fame by the Oklahoma Heritage Association.

Reynolds's post-baseball career was marked by personal tragedy. In May 1978 he lost a son and a grandson in the crash of a private plane. His wife died of cancer in 1983. Reynolds died as a result of diabetes and lymphoma. A modest family man who shunned the spotlight, he was rightly regarded in his day as one of baseball's finest pitchers and one of the most dependable in a must-win situation. Although his pitching statistics are comparable with many pitchers in Baseball's Hall of Fame, at the beginning of the twenty-first century, he had not received serious consideration for induction.

★

Interviews with Reynolds are on file at the Oklahoma Historical Society archives. There is no full-length biography. Among the many books that cover the New York Yankees during his playing days are Peter Golenbock, *Dynasty* (1975); David Halberstam, *Summer of '49* (1989); and Tom Meany et al., *The Magnificent Yankees* (1953). In 1991 a group of Reynolds's friends and admirers put together a pamphlet hoping to advance his cause for Baseball Hall of Fame consideration; *The Pitch of the Superchief* (1991) includes highlights and statistical achievements of his baseball career and his many achievements outside it. The most comprehensive account of his baseball career and post-baseball exploits is Max J. Nichols, "Super Chief, Humble Man: The Life of Allie P. Reynolds," *Chronicles of Oklahoma* 73, no. 1 (spring 1995). Obituaries are in the *New York Times* (28 Dec. 1994) and *Daily Oklahoman* (31 Dec. 1994).

EDWARD J. TASSINARI

RICH, Charles Allan ("Charlie") (*b*. 14 December 1932 in Colt, Arkansas; *d*. 25 July 1995 in Hammond, Louisiana), country crooner nicknamed the "Silver Fox" who is best remembered for his 1973 number one hit, "Behind Closed Doors."

Rich was born to a family of cotton farmers. Both his father, Wallace Neville Rich, and mother, Helen Margaret West, were musical; his father sang in the church choir and his mother played organ. Rich was exposed to blues music by black sharecroppers as a youth. During his high school years he began playing saxophone in emulation of his then-idol, jazz musician Stan Kenton. After graduating from high school in Forrest City, Arkansas, where he met his future wife, Margaret Ann Greene, Rich attended the University of Arkansas for one year. He then enlisted in the Air Force and was stationed in Enid, Oklahoma. He wed Greene in 1952.

On his discharge Rich and his wife settled in Memphis, Tennessee, where Rich worked at local piano bars. He also formed a vocal group along with his wife called the Velvetones, which had a few local bookings. Margaret was a talented songwriter and later contributed some of Rich's best-loved songs to his repertoire, including 1969's "Life's Little Ups and Downs," which many critics have commented might have been a theme song for Rich's rocky career. Margaret also was the most important force behind his early career. Sometime around late 1957 or early 1958 she brought tapes of Rich's playing to Bill Justis, a producer and musician then working for Sam Phillips's Sun Records (original label of Elvis Presley, Jerry Lee Lewis, Carl Perkins, and Johnny Cash).

Charlie Rich. ARCHIVE PHOTOS

At first Phillips felt Rich's sound was too jazz-flavored to appeal to his country audience; however, by 1958 Rich was working regularly for Phillips as a session musician and songwriter. While appearing on records by Jerry Lee Lewis ("I'll Sail My Ship Alone," 1959) and supplying songs to Johnny Cash ("The Ways of A Woman in Love," 1959; "Thanks A Lot," 1960), Rich finally recorded his first record for Sun on his own in 1958. In 1960 he had his sole hit with the label, the rockabilly classic "Lonely Weekends," which reached the top twenty-five on the pop charts. However, alcoholism (which would plague him throughout his career) and a lack of a follow-up hit led him to leave the label by 1962. His wife briefly left him and Rich appeared to be at a career dead-end.

Rich spent most of the 1960s looking for a marketable sound. He first recorded for RCA in a jazz balladeer style, but failed to score any hits. In the middle of the decade he had a moderate novelty hit with the song "Mohair Sam" (commenting on the mop-topped Beatles' look of the 1960s) for the Smash label. Some critics feel he made his best country-styled recordings at this time, working with

Smash producer Jerry Kennedy, although none were hits at the time. Finally in 1967 the producer Billy Sherrill—who knew Rich from his days as a Sun studio engineer—signed Rich to Epic and began promoting him as a country songster. Rich scored some moderate hits during the late 1960s and early 1970s, finally reaching the top of the country charts in 1973 with the ballad "Behind Closed Doors," followed by the sugary "The Most Beautiful Girl." Thanks to his prematurely gray mane of hair, he gained his nickname the "Silver Fox" at about this time. Five more number one country hits followed in 1974, when he was voted "Entertainer of the Year" by the Country Music Association of America (CMA).

Rich's struggle with alcoholism again began to affect his career. In 1975 while appearing on the CMA's award program to announce the winner of that year's "Entertainer of the Year" award, he became angered when he read the slip of paper announcing that John Denver (a pop-oriented singer) had won the award. He dramatically set the envelope on fire, creating a furor in the country music community. Later he commented that he was "ill" at the time and should not have appeared on the program. Ironically, one of his earlier recordings made in the mid-1960s, "It's All Over Now," was re-released and was a minor country hit that year.

Rich's career continued to decline through the late 1970s and early 1980s. In 1976 in a shameless effort to appeal to the conservative country audience, he issued a string-drenched version of "America the Beautiful." He did nevertheless score a few hits. In 1977 he had the solo number one country hit "Rollin' with the Flow" followed by "On My Knees," a duet with Janie Fricke that also reached the top of the country charts a year later. His last work with Sherrill as the producer was a gospel album, recalling the songs of his youth. He recorded for United Artists in 1978 and 1979 and then for Electra in 1980. His last country chart song, "Are We Dreamin' the Same Dream?" in 1981, just missed reaching the top twenty-five. He did not record again until 1992. At that time, pop critic Peter Guralnick—a long-time fan of the singer who lamented his often poor recordings—produced what many critics feel was Rich's best album, and swan song, *Pictures and Paintings*. For the first time, his piano playing was highlighted and the accompaniment and song selection was good. Nonetheless, the album failed to produce any hits and Rich again lapsed into inactivity.

Rich's only son, Allan, was also a singer and songwriter. After attending a concert that Allan gave in Natchez, Mississippi, in July 1995, Rich and his wife checked into a motel in nearby Hammond, Louisiana, for the night on their way home to Memphis. That evening Rich suffered a blood clot on the lung that brought on a fatal heart attack. He is buried in Memphis.

Although Rich only enjoyed a short period of success, many felt he had the talent to be a true pop giant. His piano playing was soulful, combining elements of jazz, blues, and country, and his singing was heartfelt and warm (when it was not drowned in vocal choruses and strings). A shy, retiring man, he fumbled badly in managing his career, often being too willing to follow the commercial instincts of his producers. He nevertheless helped broaden the sound of country music, introducing elements of jazz and blues singing that are still heard today.

★

Judy Eron's thirty-one-page biography aimed at young readers, *Charlie Rich,* appeared in 1975, at the height of his country fame. Peter Guralnick's *Feel Like Going Home* (1971) and *Lost Highway* (1989) each feature a chapter-long portrait of Rich that are among the most sympathetic and revealing articles written about him. Colin Escott and Martin Hawkins's *Good Rockin' Tonight: Sun Records and the Birth of Rock 'n' Roll* (1992) also includes material on Rich. Obituaries are in the *New York Times* (26 July 1995) and *Billboard* (5 Aug. 1995).

RICHARD CARLIN

RIDDER, Eric (*b.* 1 July 1918 in Hewlett, New York; *d.* 23 July 1996 in Locust Valley, New York), publisher of the *Journal of Commerce* who expanded that historic newspaper's influence with its worldwide Commodities News Service and an Olympic gold medalist in sailing (1952) and America's Cup co-skipper (1964).

Ridder was the third of four children born to Joseph E. Ridder, a newspaper publisher, and Hedwig Schneider, who managed the household. He graduated from Portsmouth Priory in Portsmouth, Rhode Island, then attended Harvard College in 1936 and 1937. He followed his father into the family company, Ridder Publications, which his grandfather Herman Ridder had started in 1892 by acquiring the German-language *Staats-Zeitung* in New York City. The young Ridder began his professional career as the business manager of a newspaper, the *St. Paul Dispatch and Pioneer Press.* He married Ethelette Tucker in 1939. They had two children. During World War II, Ridder served in the U.S. Marine Corps in the Pacific and retired from the reserves as a colonel.

In 1946 Ridder became the general manager of the *Journal of Commerce,* a New York City newspaper founded in 1827 that specialized in shipping, trade, and transportation. The *Journal* had been bought by Ridder Publications in 1926. In 1954 Ridder and Ethelette divorced. He married Madeleine Graham in 1955. They had no children. She died in 1991.

In 1956 Ridder became the publisher of the *Journal of*

Eric Ridder, 1964. ASSOCIATED PRESS AP

Commerce and was instrumental in extending the newspaper's influence by starting the Commodities News Service, which could promptly distribute fast-changing business information. His work created a worldwide news reporting organization. In 1974 Ridder Publications merged with Knight Newspapers to become the international communications company Knight Ridder. After Ridder's retirement from the *Journal of Commerce* as chief executive officer and publisher in 1985, he served as a director of Knight Ridder until 1996. P. Anthony "Tony" Ridder, CEO of Knight Ridder, said after his cousin's death later in 1996, "Eric . . . had printer's ink in his veins for seventy-eight years."

Ridder was a prominent yachtsman. He won a gold medal as a member of the U.S. 6-meter class crew in the 1952 Olympic Games in Helsinki, Finland. In 1964 he set his sights on the America's Cup by joining the syndicate that raced the 12-meter yacht *Constellation*. Midway through the trials to select the American defender of the trophy, Ridder recognized that he was not the best helmsman available. He promoted the alternate helmsman, Bob Bavier, to co-skipper. Bavier went on to successfully defend

against the English challengers. Ridder accomplished his goal of having his crew win by setting aside his personal ambition of being an America's Cup helmsman.

During the 1970s and 1980s his two racing yachts—both named *Tempest* as a wry reference to his wife's nickname "Teapot"—were familiar sights on the East Coast ocean-racing circuit, a nonprofessional sport. Ridder was known as a quiet and focused skipper who left the organization of crew work to a loyal group of friends who raced with him season after season. Throughout his life he had an analytical nature and an athletic bearing. He was laconic but thoroughly enjoyed the camaraderie of the sport.

Ridder was instrumental in the creation of the South Street Seaport Museum. In 1967 he joined the board of trustees. The founders of the inchoate nonprofit institution had a narrow window of opportunity to secure a historically significant property on the East River in lower Manhattan before developers could expand the domain of Wall Street skyscrapers. The board accepted Ridder's offer to be treasurer and lend his efforts to the financial development of what became a prime educational and tourist attraction, consisting of significant sailing ships and exhibits on the maritime heritage of New York City. He was known to have proceeded through a lunch with a potential donor aboard one of the ships while public school children poked their heads through an open skylight above the businessmen's heads. Ridder believed that the museum was for children and refused to let anyone chase off the young spectators.

After the 1960s Ridder became fascinated with camping in the African bush. He shot game trophies on his early visits and had the heads hung on the walls of his house in suburban Locust Valley, New York. After a few safaris, he was content to go to East Africa each year to live simply, surrounded by the expansive landscape. One story of a visit involved a local hunter who was assisting Ridder. The hunter's cattle were stolen while he was away from his village, crushing his hopes of marriage. Ridder anonymously bought a replacement herd to facilitate the marriage.

Ridder died of pneumonia at his home in Locust Valley and was buried in the same town. He had been receiving treatment for a malignant tumor in the months before his death.

The printer's ink in Ridder's veins was mixed with saltwater. His accomplishments in business, sport, and philanthropy largely revolved around maritime enterprises. His life showed a keen interest in the past as well as the future; on the one hand, he helped preserve the historic waterfront in New York City, and on the other, he moved the *Journal of Commerce* from print to wire. He favored deeds over self-promotion. He chose his pursuits carefully, built a good team, and then decisively strove to make best use of the resources and people around him. When once asked by a sailor to explain a winning tactic in a sailboat race, Ridder replied with a knowing but unrevealing smile, "Sometimes I just do things I think I should."

★

Little has been written about Eric Ridder. In *A View from the Cockpit: Winning the America's Cup* (1965), Robert N. Bavier, Jr., chronicles the trials and tribulations of the 1964 America's Cup competition and gives insight into Ridder's approach to a challenge. The magazine *Lookout* (Feb.–Mar. 1983) published Ridder's thoughts on journalism's role in commerce in his article "Meat and Potatoes Journalism for Decision Makers." Obituaries are in *Media Daily* (24 July 1996) and the *New York Times* (29 July 1996).

SHEILA MCCURDY

RIESEL, Victor (*b.* 26 March 1913 in New York City; *d.* 4 January 1995 in New York City), syndicated labor columnist who crusaded against racketeers and communists and was blinded in an acid attack in 1956.

Riesel was born and raised on the Lower East Side of Manhattan, the oldest child of a Jewish garment-working fam-

Victor Riesel. ARCHIVE PHOTOS

ily. He had a sister and a half brother. His father, Nathan Riesel, led a small Manhattan union of skilled embroiderers and impressed upon Riesel the importance of unionism and the need to keep mobsters out. As a youngster Riesel witnessed numerous demonstrations and violent strikes, including incidents in which his father was beaten by thugs over control of the union.

While still attending Morris High School in the Bronx, Riesel began writing articles on labor matters in the United States and offering them for publication to overseas English-language newspapers. Following graduation at age fifteen in 1928, he took night classes in personnel and industrial relations at City College of New York, receiving his B.A. degree in 1940. During the 1930s, to pay for his education, he worked at a variety of jobs, including at a hat factory, a lace plant, and a steel mill. He also traveled through the industrial Midwest, taking jobs in mines and mills and reporting on labor conditions to newspapers in New York City and overseas. A wiry bantamweight, Riesel consistently stood up for "the little guy" against perceived exploitation.

Riesel's politics during this period were left of center. While vehemently opposed to communism, he supported the Congress of Industrial Organizations (CIO) and wrote in support of strongly pro–New Deal political candidates. As a result, while still taking classes at City College in 1939, he joined the staff of the left-wing *New Leader,* published in New York City. He wrote a column called "Heard on the Left," which assailed totalitarianism overseas and home-grown fascists of the Father Charles Coughlin school. Riesel briefly served as the managing editor for the *New Leader* before leaving to join the staff of the *New York Post,* then pro–New Deal, in 1942. His labor column in the *Post,* entitled "Inside Labor," ran six times a week and was syndicated to like-minded newspapers throughout the country. By this time he was married to Evelyn Lobelson; they had two children.

Following World War II, Riesel's politics began a shift to the right that continued for the rest of his life. In 1945 he left the *Post* and moved to William Randolph Hearst's *New York Daily Mirror,* taking his column with him. Access to the Hearst syndicate made Riesel's column nationally known, reprinted in more than 100 newspapers. His column hammered away at the presence of two perceived evils in the labor movement—communism and racketeers. His previous anticommunism became increasingly strident as the country entered the cold war and as the second red scare of the postwar period forced labor leaders to eschew support from communists and other left-wing organizers. Riesel's devoted anticommunism found him strong allies at high levels of power. J. Edgar Hoover, the director of the Federal Bureau of Investigation, regularly fed "scoops" to Riesel that were mutually beneficial.

Antiracketeering, however, was a newer theme in Riesel's writing, probably spurred by the death of his father in 1946. Riesel always attributed his father's death to compounded injuries suffered at the hands of thugs trying to wrest control of his father's union. As several major national unions were rocked by scandals in the 1950s, most notably the Teamsters and the International Longshoremen's Association, Riesel used his newspaper column and appearances on radio and television programs to assail the presence of organized crime in the labor movement.

Riesel's antiracketeering crusade apparently led to the most tragic incident in his career. In the early morning hours of 5 April 1956 an assailant threw acid in Riesel's face. While eventually able to make out dim shapes, Riesel never regained his sight. His assailant was later found murdered, and even though some co-conspirators were jailed, the intention behind the attack remained somewhat murky. The blinding incident created a national uproar and was the catalyst for the Senate investigation of racketeering in labor, beginning in 1957, from which the committee counsel Robert F. Kennedy made his assault on the Teamsters. Riesel's column was also more widely syndicated after the assault, reaching about 300 newspapers at its peak in the early 1960s, by which time it appeared five times a week.

After he was blinded, Riesel was chauffeured to and from his office and speaking engagements, and he continued to produce his column six days a week. Most of his work was done by telephone, after his wife or assistants read him the morning papers. He would call numerous contacts in government and labor and then type his column himself in the afternoon, which was fact-checked and typo corrected by his assistants.

Riesel continued to attack communism and labor racketeering until his retirement in 1990. He also served as an unofficial adviser on labor matters to the Republican presidents Richard M. Nixon and Ronald Reagan. Traveling extensively, even after the acid attack, Riesel was president of the Overseas Press Club of America from 1966 to 1980. He received numerous awards for journalistic excellence, including the Associated Press Editors Award for the fight for a free press. He was the second recipient of the Samuel Gompers Award and also received the U.S. Chamber of Commerce Greatest Living American Award. He died of a heart attack at the age of eighty-one and is buried in New Jersey.

For several decades after World War II, Riesel was the nation's best-known voice on labor matters. His syndicated column reached an estimated 23 million Americans, and his appearances, in his trademark dark glasses, on popular television programs like *Meet the Press* made his views widely circulated. His prose style was well suited to the short form of the daily column. He combined an eye for the personal anecdote that illuminated a larger issue with a zealot's focus on his main crusade, to rid labor unions of racketeers and communists. For many Americans, his stories were all they knew about labor unions. Consequently, he perhaps unwittingly contributed to the declining public favor for the labor movement in the cold war era. By the same token, his constant attacks on corrupt practices led to external government investigations as well as internal union housecleaning to the benefit of hundreds of thousands of union dues payers.

★

Riesel's personal papers are at the Tamiment Library and Robert F. Wagner Labor Archives of New York University. An obituary is in the *New York Times* (5 Jan. 1995).

MARK SANTANGELO

RIGGS, Robert Larimore ("Bobby") (*b.* 25 February 1918 in Los Angeles, California; *d.* 25 October 1995 in Leucadia, California), world champion tennis player who contested Billie Jean King in the most-watched tennis match ever, dubbed the "Battle of the Sexes."

One of seven children of Gideon Wright Riggs, a minister in the Church of Christ, and Agnes Jones, Riggs had two life-long passions from childhood: tennis and betting. Since he believed he performed best when betting on himself, his passions frequently intersected.

Riggs's introduction to tennis came by tagging along after an older brother who was trying out for the high school tennis team. On one such outing, he was discovered by Professor Esther Bartosh, an anatomy instructor at the University of Southern California and a highly ranked player in Los Angeles. She took twelve-year-old Bobby under her wing and showed him the basic grips and strokes of the game. After a few months under Bartosh's nurturing tutelage, Riggs began entering local tournaments, beginning a two-year winning streak in the thirteen and-under division. He went undefeated for four years of play at Franklin High School and was the first person to win California's state high school singles trophy three times.

At age seventeen Riggs became the national junior singles and doubles champion. Ready to test himself, he headed for the bigger East Coast grass tournaments, defying the request of the Southern California Tennis Association (with which he had a rancorous relationship) that he stay and defend his junior title. As it turned out, Riggs's game, peppered with spins and drop shots, was well-suited for grass, and he won the first grass-court tournament he entered. Soon the cocksure lobber declared his five-year plan: to rank in the top ten in 1936; to move up in 1937; to make the Davis Cup team in 1938; and to become the national amateur champion in 1939. Surprising everyone but himself, he accomplished each of these goals.

Bobby Riggs and Billie Jean King during a news conference to promote their "Battle of the Sexes" tennis match, 1973. ASSOCIATED PRESS AP

Riggs had an outstanding year in 1939. He captured the singles, doubles, and mixed doubles titles in his first appearance at Wimbledon, the world's most prestigious tennis tournament. He also collected nearly $108,000 from a London bookmaker with whom he had placed a bet on himself. Only two months later, Riggs followed up this trio of victories by winning the U.S. National Championships at Forest Hills in New York City.

Riggs's enthusiasm at turning pro after a second U.S. National Championship as an amateur in 1941 was dampened by World War II, which drafted many of the best tennis players and emptied the stadiums. Entering boot camp at Great Lakes Naval Training Station in 1943, Riggs spent two years in the navy, stationed in Hawaii and Guam. His time was spent mostly playing exhibition tennis matches.

Following World War II, Riggs resumed his tennis prominence, becoming co–vice president of the Professional Players Association; winning the 1946, 1947, and 1949 national professional singles titles, and participating in dozens of tournaments around the world. As the years passed, younger players stole the spotlight and the victories, so Riggs played less tennis and instead indulged his growing attraction to golf, a game even better suited to the betting that he so loved. Between 1953 and 1971 Riggs divided his time between his job as executive vice president of the American Photograph Corporation (his second wife's family business), playing golf, and betting on himself in tennis matches against "weekend players." Riggs's competitors, mostly middle-aged businessmen, devised unique handicapping rules in order to be competitive with the former

champ. For instance, Riggs might play tied to his doubles partner with rope, carrying an open umbrella or a weighted suitcase, or holding a dog's leash. He loved the challenge of such feats and usually found a way to win regardless of the obstacles.

As the burgeoning feminist movement gathered momentum in the early 1970s, Riggs incensed women around the country by his outspoken assertions of the inferiority of women's tennis. To prove his point he issued a $5,000 challenge to the top women players to face him on the court. The Australian Margaret Court was the first to accept his dare, but his decisive 6–2, 6–1 victory against her in a 1973 Mother's Day match only fueled his vocal assertions of male athletic prowess. Previously uninterested in playing him, the women's champion Billie Jean King now felt she had no choice but to face Riggs: "I kept thinking this was not about a tennis match, this was about social change."

The Riggs-King matchup, dubbed the "Battle of the Sexes," took place on 20 September 1973. It was a $100,000 winner-take-all match that set in motion frenzied media coverage that brought 30,492 spectators out to the Houston Astrodome and produced a record of 50 million worldwide viewers, the largest audience ever to witness a tennis match. The fifty-five-year-old Riggs entered the stadium in a chariot pulled by a group of buxom young women. Not to be outdone, King, twenty-nine, arrived atop a litter carried by college football players outfitted in mini-togas. Before the start of the contest, Riggs presented King with an oversized candy sucker, and King gave the self-proclaimed "male chauvinist pig" a live baby sow. In the end, King employed speed and endurance-testing rallies to defeat Riggs handily in straight sets, 6–4, 6–3, 6–3. This watershed match began a solid friendship between Riggs and King. More importantly, it is often credited for helping change America's perception of women and their abilities on and off the court.

At five feet eight inches tall and weighing 140 pounds during his prime, Riggs was small for a tennis player. However, he made up for any physical shortcomings with natural ability and an unending supply of self-confidence. He married Catherine Ann "Kay" Fischer on 1 September 1939. They had five sons and a daughter and divorced in the early 1950s. Riggs subsequently married Priscilla Wheelan; they were divorced in 1972. Nevertheless, his family life often took a backseat to the tours and tournaments that took him around the country. In the years following the King match, Riggs was active on the senior tennis circuit and participated in several more exhibition matches against women. Diagnosed with prostate cancer in 1988, he created the Bobby Riggs Tennis Foundation at Encinitas, California, in 1994 to display tennis memorabilia and to spread awareness about the disease. Riggs died of prostate cancer at age seventy-seven.

Despite his reputation as a hustler, Riggs was well liked and fair on the court. His abilities as a player were sometimes overshadowed by his bravura and stunts, but he was remembered by world champion player Jack Kramer as "the most underrated champion in the history of tennis." He was inducted into the Tennis Hall of Fame in 1967.

★

Riggs penned two autobiographies about his life in tennis: *Tennis Is My Racket* (1949) and (with George McGann) *Court Hustler* (1973). *The Game: My 40 Years in Tennis* (1979), by Riggs's friend and competitor Jack Kramer, includes personal anecdotes and an analysis of Riggs's tennis style. See also E. Digby Baltzell, *Sporting Gentlemen: Men's Tennis from the Age of Honor to the Cult of the Superstar* (1995). Obituaries are in the *New York Times* and the London *Guardian* (both 27 Oct. 1995).

CARRIE C. MCBRIDE

ROGERS, Ginger (*b.* 16 July 1911 in Independence, Missouri; *d.* 25 April 1995 in Rancho Mirage, California), Academy Award–winning actress best remembered for the movies she made with Fred Astaire.

Rogers was born Virginia Katherine McMath, the only surviving child of William Eddins McMath, an electrical engineer, and Lela Emogene Owens, a journalist. Her parents were divorced not long after her birth, and her mother got the upper hand in their bitter custodial dispute. Rogers's father kidnapped the child, and her mother used the incident to gain sole custody. During her early years Rogers lived for long periods with her grandparents in Kansas City, Missouri, as her mother traveled first to Hollywood and

Ginger Rogers, 1965. ASSOCIATED PRESS AP

later to New York to pursue opportunities as a screenwriter and then worked as a publicist for the U.S. Marine Corps after the United States entered World War I.

In May 1920 Rogers's mother married John Logan Rogers, and the family moved to Fort Worth, Texas. John Rogers worked for an insurance company, and Lela got a job as a reporter and drama critic for the *Fort Worth Record*. Ginger, nicknamed by a younger cousin who could not pronounce Virginia, attended the Fifth Ward Elementary School. Although John Rogers did not officially adopt Ginger, she began using his last name. She first thought about becoming an entertainer at age twelve, when she played the lead role in a school play, *The Death of St. Denis,* which her mother had written. "I started thinking how would it be on the stage, how would it be to be an entertainer," she said in an interview years later. "And I liked the idea."

In January 1926, at age fourteen, Rogers entered and won a statewide Charleston contest. First prize included a four-week engagement to perform on the local vaudeville circuit. Her mother helped her put together an act that was successful enough for them to continue on the vaudeville circuit throughout the South and Midwest. It was at this point that Rogers left school and her mother turned her formidable energy from her own career to that of her daughter. Until her death in 1977, Rogers's mother was instrumental in managing Rogers's career and in other ways as well. Both mother and daughter were devout Christian Scientists and strong Republicans.

On 29 March 1929, at age seventeen, Rogers married Edward Jackson Culpepper, a dancer and singer known on the vaudeville circuit as Jack Pepper. Her mother angrily returned to Fort Worth, and the marriage soon fell apart. Rogers and Culpepper separated for good after only a few months but did not officially divorce until July 1931. They had no children. Rogers was rejoined by her mother, whose own marriage had ended after she returned to Fort Worth.

In 1929 Rogers and her mother went to New York City, where Rogers landed a role in a Broadway musical, *Top Speed*. The show opened in December 1929 and ran for 102 performances. While she was still in *Top Speed,* Rogers began working for Paramount Pictures at Astoria Studios in Queens, New York. She did a series of musical short subjects with Rudy Vallee, then moved on to small roles in feature films. In her first feature, *Young Man of Manhattan* (1930), she uttered the memorable line, "Cigarette me, big boy." After *Top Speed* closed Rogers was offered the role of the postmistress in George Gershwin and Ira Gershwin's *Girl Crazy,* which opened on Broadway in October 1930 and ran for 272 performances. In that show she introduced the songs "But Not for Me" and "Embraceable You."

Shortly after the 6 June 1931 closing of *Girl Crazy,* Rogers and her mother traveled to Hollywood, where Rogers worked steadily but initially to little avail. She finally made a significant impact as the chorus girl Anytime Annie in *Forty-second Street* (1933). Then her song "We're in the Money" opened the movie *Gold Diggers of 1933* (1933). She landed a starring role in *Don't Bet on Love* (1933) with Lew Ayres, and not long before filming started they began dating. They married on 14 November 1934. They separated in May 1936 but did not divorce until 1940. They had no children.

In April 1933 RKO signed Rogers to a contract and cast her in the Dolores Del Rio musical *Flying down to Rio* (1933), in which she was paired with Fred Astaire, who had recently arrived from New York. Rogers and Astaire danced "The Carioca" with their foreheads pressed together, the highlight of the film. RKO began looking for another vehicle in which they could be paired, but Astaire first had to return to New York to star in Cole Porter's *The Gay Divorce* (1934). Rogers made another six movies, and when Astaire returned to Hollywood in late 1933, *The Gay Divorce* was revamped as a movie vehicle, *The Gay Divorcee* (1934), for Astaire and Rogers. They next were cast in supporting roles in *Roberta* (1935), then they starred in *Top Hat* (1935), *Follow the Fleet* (1936), *Swing Time* (1936), and *Shall We Dance* (1937).

The plots of most Astaire-Rogers films were slight, but composers like Porter, George Gershwin, Jerome Kern, and Irving Berlin wrote their music. Their dance numbers, choreographed by Astaire and the dancer-choreographer Hermes Pan, were exquisite. Most significantly, the combination of Astaire and Rogers was perhaps the most potent pairing in Hollywood history.

Rogers was five feet, five inches tall, and although her hair was naturally dark, she was usually blonde in her film roles. Her face was attractive and distinct, but not intimidating. While other stars often projected a chilly aura of glamour, Rogers came across as an ordinary girl—who wasn't quite ordinary. Perhaps her biggest strength was her ability to simultaneously project two contradictory personalities: down-to-earth yet special, and brassy yet sensitive.

Critics had a hard time explaining the impact of Astaire and Rogers as a pair. Katharine Hepburn offered one of the most famous explanations, "He gives her class, and she gives him sex." But their quality went further than that. Astaire and Rogers were believable as a couple. Away from Rogers, Astaire often seemed in a realm by himself. Rogers grounded him, and with her he came across as a real man with real emotions. John Mueller, author of *Astaire Dancing: The Musical Films* (1985), theorized that the special spark Rogers brought to her partnership with Astaire was her acting ability. Whatever the dance was intended to illustrate—enduring love or an initial spark of interest—she was a convincing actress who carried the viewers with her.

By the time Rogers and Astaire made *Carefree* (1938), however, both were restless. After *Shall We Dance,* Rogers had a breakthrough role in *Stage Door* (1937), easily holding her own as Hepburn's roommate, and she was anxious to prove that she could do more than musical comedy fluff. Astaire, long linked by the public mind to his original partner, his sister Adele Astaire, was unhappy to find himself in another semipermanent partnership. Consequently when Astaire and Rogers made *The Story of Vernon and Irene Castle* (1939), both felt it was their swan song.

Rogers also had an active social life during this time. Although she was officially married to Ayres until 1940, she had for all practical purposes been single since 1936, and she dated James Stewart, Cary Grant, George Gershwin, Alfred Vanderbilt, George Stevens, and Howard Hughes. After her divorce from Ayres, she was briefly engaged to Hughes.

After the Astaire-Rogers musical partnership ended, RKO cast Rogers in roles that showcased both her flair for comedy, such as *Bachelor Mother* (1939) and *Fifth Avenue Girl* (1939), and her dramatic ability, such as *Primrose Path* (1940). She quickly hit pay dirt, winning the 1940 Academy Award for best actress for her role in *Kitty Foyle* (1940).

Rogers's notable movies during the early 1940s include *Roxie Hart* (1942), in which she is a hungry-for-fame nightclub dancer; *The Major and the Minor* (1942), Billy Wilder's directing debut in which Rogers plays a woman who disguises herself as a twelve-year-old to save on rail fare; and *Lady in the Dark* (1944), the Kurt Weill–Ira Gershwin musical about a fashion magazine editor who undergoes psychoanalysis. In 1945 Rogers was listed as the highest-paid Hollywood star with earnings of $292,159. On 16 January 1943 she married the actor Jack Briggs, who was in the U.S. Marine Corps at the time. They had no children and divorced on 6 December 1949.

Rogers unexpectedly made one last movie with Astaire, *The Barkleys of Broadway* (1949), when she was brought in as a replacement for Judy Garland. It was Rogers and Astaire's only movie in color. In 1951 Rogers returned to Broadway in the comedy *Love and Let Love,* which ran for only three weeks. On 7 February 1953 she married Jacques Bergerac, a French actor and businessman. He starred with her in *Twist of Fate* (1954). They had no children and divorced on 9 July 1957.

As movie roles began to dry up, Rogers occasionally made television appearances and toured with a nightclub act. She also toured with *Annie Get Your Gun* (1960), *Bell, Book, and Candle* (1961), and *Calamity Jane* (1961). On 16 March 1961 she married G. William Marshall, an actor and producer. They had no children and divorced in 1967. It was Rogers's last marriage.

Rogers's last movie was *Harlow* (1965), in which she played Jean Harlow's mother. In 1965 she replaced Carol Channing in the hit Broadway musical *Hello, Dolly!* Rogers played Dolly Levi from 1965 to 1968, first on Broadway and then with the national touring company. She also starred in the London production of *Mame* in 1969–1970. From 1975 to 1979 she toured frequently with *The Ginger Rogers Show,* a musical revue featuring songs associated with her career.

During the 1980s Rogers began working on her autobiography, *Ginger: My Story,* published in 1991. By then her primary residence was a ranch in Oregon that she had purchased in 1940. In 1992 she was one of the recipients of the Fifteenth Annual Kennedy Center Honors for lifetime achievement. For a year before her death of a diabetic coma she was confined to a wheelchair. Rogers is buried in Oakland Memorial Park in Chatsworth, California.

Because of the effortless quality Rogers brought to her work, it is easy to underestimate her. But she was an actress who handled both comedy and drama with aplomb, a powerful singer who performed in Broadway musicals before onstage microphones came into use, and a dancer who held her own with Astaire. In fact the qualities that Rogers brought to her partnership with Astaire were so strong that it is difficult to think about Astaire without simultaneously thinking about Rogers.

★

Both the Lincoln Center branch of the New York Public Library and the Margaret Herrick Library of the Academy of Motion Pictures Arts and Sciences in Beverly Hills, California, have clippings files on Rogers. Her autobiography *Ginger: My Story* (1991)

is the most complete source, but it is in no sense a tell-all. A shorter, snippier, and lavishly illustrated biography is Sheridan Morley, *Shall We Dance: The Life of Ginger Rogers* (1995). For a survey of her movies see *Films in Review* (Mar. 1966). For an in-depth analysis of her dances with Astaire see Arlene Croce, *The Fred Astaire and Ginger Rogers Book* (1972), and John E. Mueller, *Astaire Dancing: The Musical Films* (1985). A detailed article on Rogers is in *Current Biography 1967.* An obituary is in the *New York Times* (26 Apr. 1995).

LYNN HOOGENBOOM

ROLAND, Gilbert (*b.* 11 December 1905 in Juarez, Mexico; *d.* 15 May 1994 in Beverly Hills, California), Mexican-American actor whose career spanned seven decades, from silent films to television, including eleven films as the legendary Cisco Kid.

Roland was born Luis Antonio Damasco de Alonso, the second of six children born to Don Francisco and Consuelo Alonso. Roland's father came from Spain and, following family tradition, trained as a matador. During the Mexican Revolution, when Pancho Villa occupied Juarez, allegedly threatening the lives of all Mexicans born in Spain, the

Gilbert Roland. CORBIS CORPORATION (BELLEVUE)

Alonso family moved to El Paso, Texas. Growing up in the barrios of El Paso, where he learned English, Roland helped support his family by selling newspapers. The young man also saw his first moving picture in El Paso and was captivated by the cinema. He later remarked, "As a child living near the Rio Grande, a great love came into my life. All my life I have loved all the people on the screen. It became an obsession."

At age thirteen or fourteen, Roland, hoping to find a career in film, hopped a train and headed to Hollywood, arriving in Los Angeles with $2.60 in his pocket. For the next several years, he survived by taking odd jobs, such as unloading ships at Catalina Island, but his passion for the cinema remained. Fearing that his Mexican name might hold back his fledgling career, Roland in 1922 chose his screen name by combining those of two performers he admired, actor John Gilbert and serial queen Ruth Roland. Earning $2 a day and a box lunch, Roland worked as an extra on such silent films as *Blood and Sand* (1922) and *The Phantom of the Opera* (1925).

Beginning to despair of breaking into the motion picture business, Roland was considering following family tradition and going to Spain to learn bullfighting when he was "discovered" by agent Ivan Kahn, who helped secure the aspiring Mexican actor a contract for the second lead in *The Plastic Age* (1925) opposite Clara Bow. In 1927 Roland secured his first leading role with *Camille* opposite Norma Talmadge. Through the late 1920s Roland was cast as the fiery "Latin lover," with lead roles in such films as *Rose of the Golden West* (1927), *The Woman Disputed* (1928), and *New York Nights* (1929).

Roland made the transition from silent films to sound, although in the 1930s his career as a leading man waned, and he appeared in more supporting roles. His film credits during the decade include *Resurrection* (1931) opposite Lupe Valez; *Call Her Savage* (1932), in which Roland portrayed a half-breed alongside Clara Bow; *She Done Him Wrong* (1933), in which Roland was cast as a South American gigolo opposite Mae West; *Thunder Trail* (1937), a Western melodrama; *The Last Train from Madrid* (1937), for which Roland received excellent reviews; the historical epic *Juarez* (1939); and *The Sea Hawk* (1940) with Errol Flynn. In addition, Roland made several Spanish-language features.

In 1941 Roland married the actress Constance Bennett, and the couple had two children before the marriage dissolved in the mid-1940s, allegedly because Bennett's stardom had exceeded that of her husband. In 1942 Roland became an American citizen, and he subsequently served as an intelligence officer in the Army Air Corps during World War II.

Returning to Hollywood after the war, Roland portrayed the Cisco Kid, based on a 1904 O. Henry short story entitled "The Caballero's Way," in a series of popular films for Monogram Studios. "My Cisco Kid might have been a bandit," Roland later said, "but he fought for the poor and was a civilized man in the true sense of the word." Referring to a scene in which Cisco was reading Shakespeare, Roland told the *Los Angeles Times,* "I wanted to make sure the Mexicano was not portrayed as an unwashed, uneducated, savage clown."

In 1949 Roland's career took an upward turn when the director John Huston tapped him to portray a Cuban revolutionary in *We Were Strangers,* for which the actor earned accolades from film critics. Roland flourished during the 1950s, as he was cast as a key supporting player in such films as *The Bullfighter and the Lady* (1951), in which he depicted an aging matador; *The Miracle of Our Lady of Fatima* (1952); director Vincente Minnelli's *The Bad and the Beautiful* (1952) opposite Lana Turner; *Thunder Bay* (1953) with James Stewart; *Underwater* (1955) opposite Jane Russell; *Three Violent People* (1956); and *The Big Circus* (1952), in which Roland portrayed a circus aerialist who walked over Niagara Falls. In 1954 he married Guillermina Cantu of Mexico City.

While sustaining his feature film career in the 1960s, 1970s, and 1980s, Roland also became a frequent guest star on television, appearing in the series *Zorro, Wagon Train, Medical Center, High Chaparral, Kung Fu, Hart to Hart,* and *The Sacketts.* Among his later film roles were John Ford's *Cheyenne Autumn* (1964), in which Roland played a Native American; *Any Gun Can Play* (1968); *Running Wild* (1973); *The Black Pearl* (1977); and *Islands in the Stream* (1978). His final performance in a feature film was as a Mexican patriarch in the Western *Barbarosa* (1982), with Willie Nelson. Roland also became an author, placing human-interest stories in such magazines as *Good Housekeeping* and *Reader's Digest.* In 1980 Roland was honored for his work as a Latin American in the entertainment industry with the Los Nosotros Golden Eagle Award. Diagnosed with cancer, he died at age eighty-eight in his home and was buried in Beverly Hills.

Roland's screen career spanned more than seventy years from the silent cinema to television, with more than 100 films to his credit. Ever conscious of his Mexican heritage, Roland was noted for working to assure that Hollywood offered positive screen images, rather than racial stereotypes, of Latin Americans.

★

Roland's life and career are chronicled in Gary D. Keller, *A Biographical Handbook of Hispanics and United States Film* (1997), and Luis Reyes and Peter Rubie, *Hispanics in Hollywood: An Encyclopedia of Film and Television* (1994). For an example of Roland's writing, see "Ten Things That Make My Heart Beat Faster," *Good Housekeeping* (Apr. 1956). Obituaries are in the *New York Times* (18 May 1994) and *Los Angeles Times* (17 May 1994).

RON BRILEY

ROME, Esther Rachel Seidman   (*b.* 8 September 1945 in Norwich, Connecticut; *d.* 24 June 1995 in Somerville, Massachusetts), women's health activist and writer best known as a coauthor of *Our Bodies, Ourselves* (1973) and *The New Our Bodies, Ourselves* (1984).

Rome was the daughter of Leo Seidman and Rose Deutsch Seidman and the granddaughter of immigrant retailers. Her father and his brother Abraham carried on the retail business as owners of two five-and-dime stores in Plainfield and Moosup, Connecticut. Her mother was a homemaker who reared two sons and two daughters. After graduating from Norwich Free Academy in 1962, Rome attended Brandeis University, graduating cum laude in 1966 with a B.A. degree in art. From Brandeis she went to the Harvard Graduate School of Education, where she earned an M.A. degree in teaching in 1968. She taught adolescents for one year following her Harvard studies. On 24 December 1967 she married Nathan Rome; the couple had two sons, Judah and Micah.

In the late 1960s, still in her mid-twenties, Esther Rome began her career as an advocate of change in the organization and delivery of women's health care. She focused on such issues as women's body image, the problematic nature of cosmetic surgery, nutrition and dietary needs, eating disorders, and sexually transmitted diseases. In all of her work, Rome argued that women's health-related problems were not simply medical issues, but involved cultural attitudes and ideals of womanhood as well. Rome was a strong critic of the medical system and of the popular media's treatment of women, especially the emphasis on weight loss, artificially achieved beauty, and reliance on "experts" for health care. She believed that women should be involved in their own health decisions and strongly advocated broad health education for women. Hence her participation with others in the Boston Women's Health Book Collective in the writing of *Our Bodies, Ourselves,* the first book of its kind, which attempted to give women the knowledge and confidence to take control of their own health-related needs.

The book, which Rome considered her greatest achievement, grew out of a workshop on women's health that she and other women attended in 1969. Several participants continued to meet to study women's health issues, publishing their collected notes in 1970 as *Women and Their Bodies.* This newsprint edition sold for 75 cents a copy and quickly became an underground hit. In 1971 the group changed the name of the book to *Our Bodies, Ourselves.* By 1973 the work had sold more than 250,000 copies, its success making possible a contract with Simon and Schuster, which published a new edition in that year. Because of its explicit photographs and plain language about women's sexuality, contraception, and reproductive matters, the work was criticized in conservative quarters. However, it reached a growing generation of feminists at a critical time, rapidly becoming a widely demanded and highly influential best-seller. It went on to a number of editions, by the late 1990s having sold over 4 million copies in some fifteen languages.

Following the publication of *Our Bodies, Ourselves,* Rome became an outspoken consumer advocate on several important women's health issues. She believed that government health agencies neglected women's interests, placing more emphasis on issues of relevance to men. For example, in the 1970s Rome understood that sexually transmitted diseases (STDs) were an important issue for women, but she recognized that the advice given about these diseases was mostly directed to men's experiences. To counter the bias in the literature and resources, Rome wrote what is believed to be the first STD-prevention pamphlet for women. True to her activist nature, she then crafted informative STD-prevention stickers that she distributed widely in women's public restrooms and other locations where women would see them.

In the 1980s Rome took on the issue of tampon safety, as it became apparent that tampons were associated with toxic shock syndrome. Even though it was known that lower-absorbency tampons were less dangerous, the then-current absorbency-rating system was meaningless, with products varying widely in their actual absorbency regardless of their labels. Rome's efforts led to legislation to require standardized absorbency ratings of tampons, so that women could choose lower-absorbency tampons with confidence.

In the 1990s Esther Rome served as a consumer representative on a Food and Drug Administration committee whose purpose was to study the potential dangers of silicone breast implants. Rome's determined work helped persuade the agency to implement a partial ban on the implants. After this effort, she led a support group for women who were experiencing health problems as a result of such implants. In addition to her activist work, Rome was an avid and creative gardener, and she also worked as a massage therapist.

In 1988, Rome was diagnosed with breast cancer. Although she followed the best medical advice of the time, her treatment was not successful. She spent the next seven years battling the disease, meanwhile never giving up on her work in behalf of women's health.

Rome's last major effort was the development of a book, *Sacrificing Our Selves for Love: Why Women Compromise Health and Self-Esteem—And How to Stop* (1996), coauthored with Jane Wegscheider Hyman. This book continues and expands upon many of the same topics Rome had worked on in the previous decades. These include the health risks of cosmetic surgery; starvation diets; domestic violence; and the role that women's desire to please others plays in their failure to reject risks to their health. Rome was working on this book until just shortly before her death at age forty-nine in her home. She is buried in B'nai B'rith Cemetery, Peabody, Massachusetts.

Rome and her colleagues of the Boston Women's Health Book Collective influenced millions of women through *Our Bodies, Ourselves* and its sequels. The central role she played in the development of this book is clear in the praise her colleagues have had for her work. Her advocacy of women's health concerns in many venues was likewise influential, leading to changes in law and practice and in women's own behaviors and attitudes toward their bodies. Rome was one of the first feminists of the 1970s to recognize the health risks of gender roles for women, and she worked tirelessly to educate and empower women so that they could take charge of their own health. She was one of twelve women memorialized in a mural in Cambridge, Massachusetts, in 1998 by the Women's Community Cancer Project of the Women's Center of Cambridge.

★

Several articles about Rome's life were published shortly after her death, including "Boston Women's Health Book Collective Remembers Esther," in *Sojourner: The Women's Forum* (Aug. 1995). An obituary is in the *Boston Globe* (25 June 1995).

BARBARA FINLAY

ROMERO, Cesar (*b.* 15 February 1907 in New York City; *d.* 1 January 1994 in Santa Monica, California), Cuban-American actor who appeared in more than 100 films and television shows from the 1930s to the 1990s, projecting the role of a tall, urbane, and handsome Latin lover. In the 1960s he was best known for his portrayal of the Joker in the *Batman* television series.

Romero was the son of an Italian-born sugar and machinery exporter, Cesar Julio Romero, and Maria Mantilla, a singer and concert pianist. On his maternal side, Romero's grandfather was José Martí y Perez (1853–1895), the Cuban patriot and writer. One of four children, Romero lived through difficult economic times when his father's exporting business floundered, yet his good looks and grooming made him popular at debutante parties. He was an indifferent student and did not graduate from high school.

In 1927, using the charm that made him popular on the party circuit, Romero began his career in show business as a ballroom dancer in New York City theaters and nightclubs. Generating attention with his fancy footwork, Romero soon appeared in Broadway productions. He was starring in the 1932 play *Dinner at Eight* when Metro-Goldwyn-Mayer (MGM) signed him to a film contract and cast him as a gigolo in *The Thin Man* (1934). His first featured role was in *British Agent* (1934). After MGM canceled his contract, Romero was signed by Universal (1934–

Cesar Romero. ARCHIVE PHOTOS

1936) and cast in such films as *Diamond Jim* (1935), *The Good Fairy* (1935), and *15 Maiden Lane* (1936). In 1937 he was signed by Darryl F. Zanuck, who had formed Twentieth Century–Fox. There the "Latin from Manhattan," as Romero often described himself, served as a contract player for fifteen years.

In the late 1930s Romero appeared with the child star Shirley Temple in *Wee Willie Winkie* (1937) and *The Little Princess* (1939). In addition, he became the first Latin actor to play the Cisco Kid—earlier Ciscos were portrayed by Anglos such as Warner Baxter—in films such as *The Return of the Cisco Kid* (1939) and *Viva Cisco Kid* (1940). The early 1940s found Romero cast as a supporting character in musical romances such as *Weekend in Havana* (1941); *Tall, Dark, and Handsome* (1941); and *Springtime in the Rockies* (1942).

Romero's film career was interrupted in the mid-1940s, when the actor enlisted for a three-year stint in the U.S. Coast Guard. He rose to the rank of chief boatswain's mate, the highest noncommissioned rank in the service, and was frequently used as a public spokesman urging American workers to increase production and support for the armed forces during World War II.

Following his military service, Twentieth Century–Fox sent Romero and Tyrone Power on a goodwill tour of South America, where the Latin actor was well received. Appearing opposite such actresses as Carmen Miranda and Betty Grable, Romero resumed his career in romantic musicals with *Carnival in Costa Rica* (1947) and *The Beautiful Blonde from Bashful Bend* (1949). Romero's favorite role was in *Captain from Castile* (1947), in which he was cast as the conquistador Hernán Cortés.

In 1950 the actor's contract with Fox expired, but as a freelance performer Romero continued to appear in feature films throughout the 1950s, 1960s, and 1970s. While many of these films were less than memorable, among Romero's credits are *Vera Cruz* (1954), with Gary Cooper and Burt Lancaster; the Oscar-winning *Around the World in 80 Days* (1956); *Ocean's Eleven* (1960), with Frank Sinatra and the rest of Hollywood's "Rat Pack"; *Donovan's Reef,* with John Wayne (directed by John Ford, 1963); and Disney's *The Computer Wore Tennis Shoes* (1970). His final feature film was *Mortuary Academy* (1991).

While Hollywood struggled in adapting to the challenge of television, Romero made a smooth transition to the new medium, appearing in a variety of roles for comic, dramatic, and Western shows from the 1950s through the 1980s. In addition to a featured role as the urbane, mysterious foreign courier in the syndicated series *Passport to Danger* (1954–1956), Romero was a frequent guest star on such popular television fare as *Zorro, Bonanza, Playhouse 90, Wagon Train, Fantasy Island, The Love Boat,* and the variety shows of Milton Berle, Dinah Shore, and Red Skelton. But Romero is probably best known for his characterization of the comic villain the Joker in the campy mid-1960s show *Batman.* Jack Nicholson borrowed from Romero in reprising the character for director Tim Burton's motion picture *Batman* (1989). Romero was also cast in a recurring role as the Greek shipping magnate Nick Stavros, opposite Jane Wyman, in the popular 1980s series *Falcon Crest.*

As his film career wound down in the 1970s and 1980s, Romero became a popular actor and dancer on the dinner theater circuit, in addition to maintaining an active presence in Hollywood social circles. Although he never married, Romero in his later years continued to cultivate his image as a romantic figure, commenting at age eighty-six, "I can't date women my own age any more—I hate going to cemeteries. So I look for the younger breed. I take them dining and dancing and by the end of an evening they're bushwhacked, whereas I still want to go on to the next nightclub."

In the 1980s and 1990s Romero received numerous lifetime achievement awards for his work and his contributions to the Latin community. In 1984 he was recognized with a career achievement prize at the Hollywood International Celebrity Awards Banquet and a Nosotros Golden Eagle Award for work as a Latin American in the entertainment industry. In 1991 he received the Imagen Hispanic Media Prize, and in 1992 he accepted the Beverly Hills Chamber of Commerce Will Rogers Memorial Award. Remaining active well into his eighties, Romero was hospitalized in late 1993 for severe bronchitis and pneumonia and died at age eighty-six due to complications from a blood clot. He is buried in Santa Monica.

Romero's film and television performances spanned more than sixty years, with more than 100 film roles and numerous television appearances to his credit. While many of his films cast Romero in the stereotypical role of a romantic Latin lover, his work in *Captain from Castile* and the *Batman* television series demonstrated the range of an actor who was capable of strong dramatic and comic performances. In an industry where Anglo actors were often assigned Latin roles, Romero's real Latin presence served as an important corrective.

★

Romero's life and career are chronicled in Gary D. Keller, *A Biographical Handbook of Hispanics and United States Film* (1997), and Luis Reyes and Peter Rubie, *Hispanics in Hollywood: An Encyclopedia of Film and Television* (1994). Romero's work as the Joker in the *Batman* series is featured in Joel Eisner, *The Official Batman Batbook* (1986). Obituaries are in the *New York Times* and *Los Angeles Times* (both 3 Jan. 1994).

RON BRILEY

ROMNEY, George Wilcken (*b.* 8 July 1907 in Colonia Dublan, Chihuahua, Mexico; *d.* 26 July 1995 in Bloomfield Hills, Michigan), three-term Republican governor of Michigan and businessperson whose auto industry innovations rescued American Motors Corporation from bankruptcy and began a national trend toward compact cars.

Romney was only five years of age when Mexican rebels forced his family and other Mormon colonists from their homes in Chihuahua, Mexico. His parents, Gaskell Romney, a carpenter and contractor, and Anna Pratt, moved their family of seven children, six sons and one daughter, five times before settling permanently in Salt Lake City, Utah, in the fall of 1921. Romney later worked in his father's construction business and attended Roosevelt Junior High School. From 1922 to 1926 he attended Latter-day Saints University, a high school and junior college. During this time Romney met Lenore LaFount, and they married on 2 July 1931 after a long and complicated courtship. They had four children. Following his graduation from Latter-day Saints University, Romney served two years as a missionary in Great Britain. He then returned to Salt Lake City and briefly attended the University of Utah.

In 1929 Romney moved to Washington, D.C., with his brother Miles Romney in part to attend George Washington University but largely to be near Lenore, whose family had moved there while he was abroad. He enrolled in night classes and worked as a tariff specialist for the Dem-

George Romney. AP/WIDE WORLD PHOTOS

ocratic senator David I. Walsh of Massachusetts. Although he had planned to attend the Harvard School of Business Administration, Romney in 1930 joined the Aluminum Company of America (Alcoa) as a salesman in Los Angeles. In 1932 he became Alcoa's representative in Washington. He also served as the Washington representative of the Aluminum Wares Association, a position that, through informal contact with Pyke Johnson, the executive vice president and general manager of the Automobile Manufacturers' Association (AMA), led Romney into the automotive industry.

Some of Romney's Washington friends found him naive in 1939, but Johnson saw a man who was "hard-headed . . . honest . . . loyal," a man with "good ideas . . . [who] could work with others and get a job done." In that year Johnson hired Romney to manage the AMA's Detroit office. In 1942 Romney became the association's general manager, and between 1942 and 1946 he oversaw the industry's changeover from civilian to military vehicles. As managing director for the Automotive Council for War Production, Romney orchestrated the cooperative and coordinated the efforts of all the companies involved in the automotive industry. He also helped form the Detroit Vic-

tory Council, which assisted workers with housing, transportation, and other home front problems.

In 1948, at the invitation of the chairman, George Mason, Romney joined Nash-Kelvinator as Mason's special assistant. The offer attracted Romney because it allowed him to learn the "inside" of automobile manufacturing from Mason, who had been employed in the industry since 1913. Romney was elected vice president in 1950 and executive vice president and director in 1953. Nash-Kelvinator merged with the Hudson Motor Car Company in 1954, forming the American Motors Corporation. When Mason died shortly after the merger, Romney was elected to succeed Mason as chairman, president, and general manager of the new corporation.

Under Mason's leadership Nash had begun experimenting with small, economical passenger cars, an effort Romney wholeheartedly endorsed and continued to the point of discontinuing all models but the Rambler. In 1957 Romney pitted the "compact" of American Motors against the "gas-guzzling dinosaurs" of the Big Three automakers and "exuded so much enthusiasm and confidence" that members of the newly formed policy committee "hardly realized the impossible odds" they were up against. In debt from its inception, American Motors first began to make money in 1958, and in 1959 the company saw a profit of more than $60 million.

With American Motors on its feet, Romney began turning his attention to Michigan's political and economic struggles. Inspired by the success of the Detroit Citizens Advisory Council on School Needs, which he had chaired in 1957–1958, Romney organized Citizens for Michigan, a nonpartisan initiative that ultimately led to Michigan's 1962 constitutional convention and to Romney's entrance in the 1962 gubernatorial race. Romney was shunned by Republican Party conservatives, but his "liberal" stand on civil rights, taxation, and social welfare appealed to moderates in both parties. He won by 78,000 votes over the incumbent John B. Swainson to become Michigan's first Republican governor in fourteen years.

Romney was reelected in 1964 and 1966 and throughout his three terms he focused on getting Michigan out of its "sorry and tangled mess," brought on, he asserted, by "selfish and partisan" politics. In 1963 voters approved a new state constitution. Michigan's economy was improving, and unemployment was decreasing. Romney worked successfully with a Democratic legislature in 1964–1965, and by 1966 he had so gained the respect of the Republican Party that his landslide victory brought with it one Republican senator and five Republican representatives.

In the national polls and media Romney was hailed as a "winner" and the Republicans' "best chance" to defeat President Lyndon B. Johnson in 1968. On 18 November 1967 Romney announced his candidacy for president. He campaigned vigorously but dropped out of the race in February 1968, two weeks before the New Hampshire primary. Richard Nixon easily won the Republican nomination for the nation's highest office.

Named secretary of the Department of Housing and Urban Development in President Nixon's cabinet in 1969, Romney left that post in 1972 to return to private life, where he felt he could more effectively address social issues. In 1974 he joined the National Center for Voluntary Action as chairman of the board. He briefly returned to politics in 1994 to campaign on behalf of his son Mitt Romney, who ran unsuccessfully against the Massachusetts senator Edward M. Kennedy for that U.S. Senate seat.

Romney remained active throughout his life, regularly enjoying swimming, dancing, and early morning golf. A tall, robust, energetic, and athletic man, he was a capable handyman, sportsman, gardener, and landscape designer. He died of a heart attack at the age of eighty-eight while exercising at his home in Bloomfield Hills.

A devout Mormon, Romney never let professional pressures intrude on either his family life or his religious convictions. Consequently, his deeply held views on family, individual responsibility, integrity, and hard work were often deemed "corny" and simplistic. Yet his gubernatorial performance won statewide approval. He served on the advisory boards and committees of more than a dozen organizations; received state and national awards and citations from numerous business, religious, educational, charitable, and civic groups; and was granted thirteen honorary degrees. In 1996 the Points of Light Foundation established the Romney Volunteer Center Excellence Award to honor Romney's commitment to community service in every aspect of society. As the biographer Clark R. Mollenhoff concluded, Romney was "a man most of us would like to have as a friend or neighbor . . . a man who could be trusted with our most precious possessions . . . a man easy to follow . . . and a man always willing to carry his share of the load."

★

Romney's personal and gubernatorial papers, including visual and audio materials, are in the Bentley Historical Library, University of Michigan. The Michigan Library and Historical Center in Lansing holds proclamations and constitutional convention records. Tom Mahoney, *The Story of George Romney: Builder, Salesman, Crusader* (1960), profiles Romney's business successes. Three biographies trace Romney's early life through his gubernatorial career: D. Duane Angel, *Romney: A Political Biography* (1967); George T. Harris, *Romney's Way: A Man and an Idea* (1967); and Clark R. Mollenhoff, *George Romney: Mormon in Politics* (1968). Obituaries are in the *New York Times, Detroit News,* and *Washington Post* (all 27 July 1995).

MARILYN MCLAUGHLIN

ROSTEN, Norman   (*b.* 1 January 1914 in New York City; *d.* 7 March 1995 in New York City), poet, playwright, novelist, and first poet laureate of Brooklyn who is best known for his play *Mister Johnson* (1956) and his nonfiction work *Marilyn: An Untold Story* (1973).

Rosten, one of four children born to the immigrants Louis Rosten, a farmer, and Celia Rosten, grew up in the small town of Hurleyville, New York. Deciding to follow in his father's footsteps, Rosten entered the Agricultural College at Cornell University in 1931. He studied there for six months, until a fire destroyed the family farm and the Rostens moved to Coney Island in Brooklyn, New York. The "wintry seascapes and the throbbing summer carnival" of his new home made a lasting impression on the farm boy, who soon developed a love affair with Brooklyn life.

His career as a farmer ended, Rosten enrolled in Brooklyn College, where he joined the staff of the college newspaper, wrote sonnets and short stories, and was exposed to the works of Carl Sandburg, Archibald MacLeish, and John Steinbeck. Rosten also became involved with the antifascist and labor movements on campus. After graduating in 1935

Norman Rosten strolling along the Brooklyn Heights Promenade, 1979. AP/WIDE WORLD PHOTOS

with a B.A. degree in English, he continued his studies at New York University, earning an M.A. degree in 1936. During this period he supported himself working as a garage mechanic with an eye on pursuing a literary career. With this in mind, Rosten submitted an "imitation Chekhov play about Brooklyn peasants" to the University of Michigan, earning him a playwriting scholarship for 1937–1938. At Michigan, Rosten experimented with verse plays and received the prestigious Avery Hopwood Award in poetry and drama. His play *This Proud Pilgrimage,* which premiered in January 1938 in Ann Arbor, Michigan, and was produced off-Broadway in 1942, won the 1942 National Theatre Conference Award. He also met Arthur Miller, a fellow student at Michigan. They were lifelong friends and for a time neighbors in Brooklyn Heights. Rosten also met Hedda Rowinski, a psychologist and freelance writer from Connecticut. They married in 1940 and had one child. In 1951 Rosten published *Songs for Patricia,* a collection of poems inspired by his daughter.

Returning to New York in 1939, Rosten found employment at the New York Federal Theatre and began to write verse plays for radio, including portraits of American literary figures for *Cavalcade of America.* His success on radio did not translate well to Broadway, however, where *First Stop to Heaven* opened to poor reviews in 1941. He returned to radio and achieved instant fame with his verse "Ballad of Bataan," recorded by both Alfred Lunt and Orson Welles. The poem was aired on more than 800 radio stations and in army recruitment campaigns. Spurred by his strong belief in the Allied cause, Rosten made further literary contributions to the war effort, including his *Lunch Hour Follies,* performed in war-production factories. He also wrote radio scripts, such as "The Unholy Three," for the wartime series *Day of Reckoning.*

Rosten's work in radio earned him an award from the American Academy of Arts and Letters in 1945 for the "exploration of the Radio as a new medium for poetry." This was not the first award he received for his poetry. In 1940 he won the Yale Series of Younger Poets Award for *Return Again, Traveler,* a poem inspired by a cross-country hitchhiking trip. In 1941–1942, on a Guggenheim fellowship, Rosten completed *The Fourth Decade and Other Poems.* In 1944 his antifascist poems from this collection were reprinted in *Seven Poets in Search of an Answer,* a compilation of poems dealing with the issues of freedom and liberty.

Rosten believed that poetry "should neither exhaust nor confuse, but invigorate and clarify." He wrote poetry for the people in everyday American language. Miller commented that *Big Road* (1946), Rosten's epic poem about the building of the Alcan Highway during World War II, is a "rare book that the people will make great. It speaks to

them and for them, and always beautifully." In all, Rosten published seven books of poetry.

Rosten's greatest success was *Mister Johnson,* which opened on Broadway in 1956 and in London in 1960. Based on the 1939 novel by Joyce Cary, this play centered on the tragic story of a Nigerian civil servant in British West Africa. In 1966 two more of Rosten's plays premiered off-Broadway, *The Golden Door* and *Come Slowly Eden: A Portrait of Emily Dickinson.* However, by the late 1960s he had abandoned playwriting, concluding that the political climate of the time created public distrust of the spoken word and consequently of the play as a form of theater. For Rosten only spectacles remained, and all theater had become theatrics.

In 1962 Rosten wrote the screenplay for Miller's drama *A View from the Bridge.* Through his friendship with Miller he came to know Miller's third wife, Marilyn Monroe. In 1973 Rosten wrote her biography, *Marilyn: An Untold Story,* considered by many an honest retelling of her tragic life. Later he wrote the libretto for Erza Laderman's opera *Marilyn,* which premiered at the New York City Opera in 1993.

In 1979, the same year his *Selected Poems* was published, Rosten was named the poet laureate of Brooklyn by the borough president Howard Golden, thus becoming the first person to hold this title. Brooklyn featured prominently in many of Rosten's works, including *Under the Boardwalk* (1968), his critically acclaimed novel about coming of age in Coney Island, and *Over and Out* (1972), a humorous tale about a Brooklyn writer. His experiences as a longtime resident of Brooklyn Heights inspired his *Neighborhood Tales* (1986), a melding of neighborhood facts with fiction.

By the 1990s Rosten was a local icon, honored by both the borough he loved and by Brooklyn College, where he was first exposed to literature. Right up to the end Rosten remained active, continuing to write and travel widely. He reveled in the recognition of academia when the University of Arkansas Press reprinted *Under the Boardwalk,* hailing it as "a neglected classic." When Rosten died of congestive heart failure, three memorials in New York City celebrated his life and career. His remains were cremated and are in the possession of his family.

Through his numerous poems, plays, stories, and essays Rosten sought to impart a vision of society in the vernacular. His work represents a genuine view of twentieth-century America, from his narrative poems of war and the Great Depression to his explorations of cultural icons and popular mythology.

★

Material relating to the Avery Hopwood Award and typescripts of Rosten's early plays are in the Harlan Hatcher Graduate Library at the University of Michigan. Brooklyn College of the City University of New York has a small collection of Rosten's papers, most notably the drafts of *Big Road* and *Mister Johnson*. An obituary is in the *New York Times* (9 Mar. 1995).

MARIANNE LaBATTO

ROTH, Henry (*b.* 8 February 1906 in Tysmenica, Galicia, Austro-Hungarian Empire, now Ukraine; *d.* 13 October 1995 in Albuquerque, New Mexico), author of *Call It Sleep* (1934), a compelling autobiographical novel about immigrant life in New York City, who is known also for his sixty-year writer's block and its eventual resolution.

Roth was the son of Herman Roth, a waiter, and Leah Farb. Brought to this country by his mother in about 1907, when she came to join her husband, Roth grew up in the Brownsville neighborhood in Brooklyn, on the Lower East Side of New York City, and in Harlem. The move from the familiar Jewish Lower East Side to Italian Harlem had a long-lasting effect on Roth, who, feeling displaced, resorted to reading. He attended the prestigious Stuyvesant High School around 1921 but graduated in 1924 from DeWitt Clinton High School and in 1928 from the City College of New York, all in Manhattan. As a freshman in college Roth wrote "Impressions of a Plumber," which was published in *Lavender,* the college literary magazine. A more significant influence was Eda Lou Walton, an English professor twelve years his senior. By 1928 Roth was living with Walton, who, according to Roth "was both mistress and mother." She introduced him to her intellectual friends but, more importantly, supported him for three or four years while he wrote *Call It Sleep.* Roth broke with Walton in 1938.

Dedicated to Walton, *Call It Sleep* was published in 1934 by Ballou. It was praised as a moving first novel about New York's Lower East Side in the early twentieth century. Showing influences of James Joyce and Mark Twain, it is powerful ghetto literature in its realism, sexual boldness, and use of language and speech. In the book, young David Schearl experiences life with his violent father, gentle mother, sexually obliging sister and cousin, and neighbors. It is a tale of redemption that catches the dialects and languages of the area and the era. Yiddish, David's home language, is rendered in accurate English, whereas English is conveyed in the colorful accents and grammar of the immigrants and the streets. Roth destroyed his second, already contracted novel, but in 1936 the short "If We Had Bacon" was published in the periodical *Signatures.* A communist since 1933, Roth believed his writing had to serve that cause and felt alienated from his religious and familial roots. He lapsed into an extended writer's block.

In 1938 at Yaddo, the artist's colony in Saratoga Springs in upstate New York, Roth met Muriel Parker, a musician and teacher he called his "savior." They married in 1939 and had two sons. No longer able to write, Roth held a variety of jobs, including substitute teacher at Theodore Roosevelt High School in the Bronx, Works Progress Administration (WPA) worker, and tool grinder. The family moved to Cambridge, Massachusetts, in 1945 and to Maine in 1946, first to Center Montville and then to a farm near Augusta. In Augusta, Roth worked as a psychiatric attendant at a state hospital, a teacher, a math and Latin tutor, and a breeder of geese and ducks.

Alfred Kazin and Leslie Fiedler included *Call It Sleep* on the *American Scholar*'s 1956 list of "The Most Neglected Books of the Past 25 Years." Consequently, Pageant Books republished it in 1960, and the paperback reprint by Avon in 1964, thirty years after the title's original publication, became a best-seller. Irving Howe's review marked the first time a review of a paperback reprint reached the front page of the *New York Times Book Review*. In 1965 Roth received the Townsend Harris Medal of the Alumni Association of City College and a National Arts and Letters grant, so he and Muriel went to Spain. Despite this acclaim, Roth was still a one-book writer. However, he had not been totally withdrawn. Among his published works were the stories "Broker" (1939), "Somebody Always Grabs the Purple" (1940), and "Petey and Yotsie and Marco" (1956), which appeared in the *New Yorker.* The 1967 Six-Day War between Israel and Arab nations inspired a "rebirth" in Roth, turning him from communism back to Judaism, and the Roths traveled to Israel. In 1968 Roth was writer in residence on the D. H. Lawrence ranch in New Mexico, and that year the family moved to New Mexico. Roth finally began another novel in the late 1970s. Mario Materassi, who had translated *Call It Sleep* into Italian, worked with Roth to collect his writing and statements from 1925 to 1987 into *Shifting Landscape* (1987). Upon receiving the Nonino International Prize in Percoto, Italy, in 1987 for *Call It Sleep*, Roth explained in his acceptance speech that when a writer was detached from the milieu of "his greatest sense of belonging," he lost "his originality; his creativity comes to an end."

After sixty years of "silence," Roth produced four more novels, published collectively as *Mercy of a Rude Stream* by St. Martins and later in paperback by Picado. Like *Call It Sleep,* the story is autobiographical, but this time the protagonist, Ira Stigman, is less of a victim. The individual titles, each with a Yiddish glossary, are *A Star Shines over Mt. Morris Park* (1994); *A Diving Rock on the Hudson* (1995); *From Bondage* (1996), winner of the Isaac Bashevis Singer Prize in Literature; and *Requiem for Harlem* (1998). The books are written in two voices, shown in different print. One is the voice of a young person, and the other is the voice of Ecclesias, a computer voicing an older Ira's perspective. Some critics say the novels lack the literary quality of *Call It Sleep,* while others recognize the extraordinary ability of an aged author to capture the emotions of youth.

Roth was awarded honorary doctorates from the University of New Mexico and Hebrew Union College–Jewish Institute of Religion, and he posthumously received a lifetime achievement award from Hadassah. When Muriel, who had returned to composing, died of congestive heart failure in 1990, Roth moved out of their trailer to another dwelling in Albuquerque. Ever self-deprecating and plagued by severe rheumatoid arthritis, the once stocky Roth continued to work on *Mercy of a Rude Stream.* He died at Lovelace Hospital in Albuquerque. The Museum of the City of New York celebrated Henry Roth Day on 29 February 1996. Known for turning autobiography into art in *Call It Sleep,* a boy's view of Jewish immigrant life in New York City, Roth rebounded from a sixty-year writer's block to produce the multivolume *Mercy of a Rude Stream.* In addition to generating further speculation about his personal life, these vivid novels portray the voices of an American era.

★

Roth's papers are at Boston University's Mugar Memorial Library, the New York Public Library, and the American Jewish Historical Society in New York City. His *Shifting Landscape: A Composite, 1925–1987* (1987), contains thirty-one interviews, correspondence, essays, and short stories that illuminate Roth's emotional state and his political views. In Bonnie Lyons, *Henry Roth, the Man and His Work* (1976), a close reading of *Call It Sleep* is supplemented by sections on Roth's life, career, influences, other writing, and an interview. An obituary is in the *New York Times* (15 Oct. 1995).

RACHEL SHOR

ROUSE, James Wilson (*b.* 26 April 1914 in Easton, Maryland; *d.* 9 April 1996 in Columbia, Maryland), real-estate developer who worked on regional shopping centers, suburban communities, urban festival markets, and inner-city restoration efforts.

Rouse was the youngest of five children of Willard G. Rouse, a canned-foods broker, and Lydia Robinson, a homemaker. Although his father owned a prosperous business, Rouse was encouraged to rise early and tend his own garden, selling the vegetables to local grocers. He also worked as a golf caddie, factory worker, and Fuller Brush salesman. He attended Easton High School, where he was president of his student council and the school newspaper, and finished his studies at the Tome School in Fort Deposit, Maryland, in 1930.

James W. Rouse, 1966. AP/WIDE WORLD PHOTOS

Rouse's parents both died while he was in high school, and he lost the family house when the bank foreclosed on the mortgage. He studied briefly at the University of Hawaii and then at the University of Virginia, but financial difficulties forced him to leave college in 1933 and work as a garage attendant in Baltimore. He began studying law during night classes at the University of Maryland and worked as a law clerk with the Federal Housing Administration.

In 1936 Rouse went to work at the Title Guarantee and Trust Company of Baltimore as head of its new mortgage department. After receiving his law degree in 1937, he joined the real-estate appraiser Hunter Moss in opening a mortgage banking business, the Moss-Rouse Company, specializing in FHA-approved loans for one-family homes.

On 3 May 1941 Rouse married Elizabeth J. Winstead. They had three children and were divorced in 1972. Rouse subsequently married Patricia Traugott Rixey, a former housing commissioner of Norfolk, Virginia, in 1974.

Rouse joined the Naval Reserve as a lieutenant in 1942 and was assigned to the Naval Air Intelligence staff of the Commander of the Air Force Pacific Fleet. He was discharged in 1945 with the rank of lieutenant commander. Rouse then returned to Baltimore and expanded his business operations to include the underwriting of apartment houses and shopping centers. In 1954 he bought out his partner and renamed the firm James W. Rouse and Company.

During the postwar years Rouse was also active as a

government adviser. He served as chair of the Mayor's Advisory Committee on Housing in Baltimore from 1949 to 1952 and as subcommittee chair of President Dwight D. Eisenhower's Advisory Committee on Government Housing Policies and Programs in 1953. His work led to the drafting of the 1954 Federal Housing Act, and he purportedly coined the phrase "urban renewal." In 1955 he and Nathaniel Keith coauthored *No Slums in Ten Years,* which called for an ambitious (and unfulfilled) government program to redevelop Washington, D.C., using the new federal law. Rouse also was a founder of the Greater Baltimore Committee and worked on the Maryland State Commission, which drafted legislation setting up a regional planning agency for Baltimore and its suburbs.

Meanwhile, Rouse led his company into planning and constructing regional shopping centers in the new suburbs. His first large shopping mall was Harundale, built in 1958 on the outskirts of Baltimore, followed by the Cherry Hill Mall in New Jersey in 1961. By the end of the decade, he had developed more than a dozen malls.

In the mid-1960s, in response to criticism that suburban "sprawl" was architecturally monotonous as well as segregated by race and social class, Rouse turned his attention to the design and construction of large-scale suburban planned communities. Purchasing 14,000 acres in rural Howard County between Baltimore and Washington, he built the community of Columbia, which contained seven suburban "villages"—clusters of single-family houses and garden apartments—set within a system of roads, schools, and other public facilities. The first homes went on sale in 1967, and Rouse specified that 20 percent were to be sold to African Americans. It eventually housed 56,000 residents. Although the "new city" of Columbia gained much attention and praise as an antidote to unplanned and segregated suburban sprawl, it was only a mild financial success. It had to be refinanced during the 1974–1975 recession, and Rouse later canceled plans for similar developments in Shelby Farms, Tennessee, and Wye Island, Maryland.

At the same time, Rouse recognized that the postwar migration to the suburbs had "sucked the blood out of the central cities and left some of the urban basket cases we see today." Seeking a way to redevelop abandoned commercial centers, he and the architect Benjamin Thompson created the concept of a "festival marketplace," a unified area of new shops, restaurants, and restored historic buildings that would attract suburbanites and tourists. The first festival market was in Boston. Based upon a renovated Faneuil Hall and adjacent Quincy Market (opened August 1976) it received critical praise and was an immediate financial success. It was followed by the Gallery in Philadelphia (opened August 1977) and Harborplace at Baltimore's Inner Harbor (opened July 1980). New York City mayor Edward Koch then asked Rouse to develop the South Street Seaport complex (opened 1983). The Rouse Company later developed plans for similar efforts in San Francisco, St. Louis, Milwaukee, and other cities. Rouse specified that a minimum proportion of the businesses would be run by African American and inner-city residents. The festival marketplace concept succeeded in the nation's largest cities but failed in smaller ones, such as Richmond, Virginia, and Toledo, Ohio, leading one analyst to note that "street jugglers and candle shops cannot solve every city's economic woes."

In 1979 Rouse resigned as chief executive officer of the Rouse Company but continued as part-time chairman of the board until 1981. Thereafter he concentrated his energies upon his newly created Enterprise Foundation, which focused on the redevelopment of inner-city neighborhoods. Initially the foundation emphasized replacing and upgrading the urban housing stock, but it later shifted its attention to social aspects of urban life such as education, employment training, medical help, and anticrime programs. Rouse also worked with Jubilee Housing, Inc., which encouraged housing rehabilitation in Washington, D.C., and with the Urban Wildlife Research Center.

On 29 September 1995, President Bill Clinton awarded Rouse the Presidential Medal of Freedom for his efforts to "heal the torn-out heart" of America's cities. During his final year Rouse underwent chemotherapy for lymphoma; he died as a result of complications from amyotrophic lateral sclerosis. His handwritten instructions for his memorial service said that funerals should be joyous events, since he believed that "I have just left on my trip to my next life." He is buried at Columbia Memorial Park.

Rouse pioneered several concepts that altered the face of urban and suburban America: regional shopping centers, planned communities, and festival marketplaces. Although regional shopping centers continue to dominate the suburban landscape, planned communities proved to have large capital requirements and relatively low profit margins. Festival marketplaces showed uneven results, with the greatest success in large cities with preexisting tourist draws. His influence is evident in hundreds of cities and towns across the United States.

★

Rouse's papers are at the Columbia Archives, Columbia, Maryland. His life and work are discussed in Gurney Breckenfeld, *Columbia and the New Cities* (1971). Ellen Uzelac, "The Chosen," *Baltimore Magazine* (May 1997) focuses upon Rouse's legacy for the Enterprise Foundation. See also J. W. Anderson, "A Brand New City for Maryland," *Harper's* (Nov. 1964); Gurney Breckenfeld, "Jim Rouse Shows How to Give Downtown Retailing New Life," *Fortune* (10 April 1978); "Shopping Centers Downtown: Roundtable on Rouse," *Progressive Architecture* (July 1981); Robert K. Landers, "The Conscience of James Rouse," *Historic Preser-*

vation (Dec. 1985); "Jim Rouse, A Life Well Lived," *Network News* (June 1996); John Bancroft, "A Visionary Lender-Developer," *Real Estate Finance Today* (23 Dec. 1996); and Jon Goss, "Disquiet on the Waterfront: Reflections on Nostalgia and Utopia in the Urban Archetypes of Festival Marketplaces," *Urban Geography* 17 (1996). Obituaries are in the *New York Times* (17 Apr. 1996), *Washington Post* (17 Apr. 1996), and *Time* (22 Apr. 1996).

STEPHEN G. MARSHALL

ROZELLE, Alvin Roy ("Pete") (*b.* 1 March 1926 in South Gate, California; *d.* 6 December 1996 in Rancho Santa Fe, California), commissioner of the National Football League who turned professional football into the most popular sport in the United States.

Alvin Rozelle, given the nickname "Pete" at age five by an uncle, was the only child of Raymond Rozelle, a grocer who later became a purchasing agent for Alcoa Aluminum, and Hazel Healey, a housewife. He was raised in Lynwood, like South Gate, a section of Los Angeles. The tall, thin youngster played tennis and basketball in high school but was too slight to participate in the sport over which he would later have so much influence.

Rozelle served three years in the Navy during World War II before enrolling at Compton Junior College in 1946. During his junior college days, he served as director of athletic news, but more importantly, he was a sports "stringer" (a writer/reporter) for local Los Angeles newspapers.

After two years at Compton, Rozelle completed his edu-

Pete Rozelle. COURTESY PRO FOOTBALL HALL OF FAME

cation at the University of San Francisco (USF) in 1950. He worked as sports information director during his time at USF and stayed on in the post for two years after graduation. Meanwhile, he married June Marilyn Coupe in 1949. They had one daughter.

Rozelle joined the Los Angeles Rams of the National Football League (NFL) as public relations director in 1952. In 1955 he left the Rams, fully intending not to return to football. He joined a public-relations firm whose major account was the 1956 Olympics, which were being staged in Melbourne, Australia. However, the Rams, by offering Rozelle the title and position of general manager, lured him back in 1957. For three years he was a solid front-office man but gave no real indication of the vision and greatness to come.

When NFL Commissioner Bert Bell died in November 1959, a new commissioner was needed. The choices were Austin Gunsel, league treasurer and then acting president, and Marshall Leahy, league legal counsel. Each had supporters among the league owners, though neither had enough votes to be elected. Rams owner Daniel F. Reeves proposed Rozelle as a compromise, a conciliatory deal that was eventually accepted. Meanwhile, to stay out of sight of the media, Rozelle waited in the men's room of Miami's Kenilworth Hotel, site of the marathon (twenty-three ballots) meetings, while the negotiations were in progress. Each time the door to the rest room opened, Rozelle went to the sink and washed his hands. When he was announced as the new czar of football, the thirty-three-year-old Rozelle quipped, "At least I come to the job with clean hands."

Rozelle soon moved the NFL headquarters from a small office in Bala-Cynwyd, a suburb of Philadelphia, to Park Avenue in New York City, home to all the major television networks. Rozelle was immediately confronted with a rival league, the American Football League (AFL).

Commissioner Bell had blacked out home games in local markets and had taken the championship game to a national audience via television. However, Rozelle had even greater vision. When he took over, the league's twelve teams each negotiated their own separate television deals. Rozelle quickly negotiated a league-wide agreement. Rozelle espoused "League Think," a concept whereby all teams did what was best for the league as a whole. This concept became his mantra. In 1962 he forced rival networks to bid for television rights, driving the price higher than ever imagined. To further enhance the stability of the league, Rozelle dictated that all teams would share the sizable television market equally. Thus, for example, the New York Giants, Chicago Bears, and Los Angeles Rams would receive the same television coverage as the Green Bay Packers, despite the vast discrepancy between their markets, consisting of millions of viewers in the larger cities compared to Green Bay's thousands. Vince Lombardi, the Packers' dynastic championship coach of the 1960s, was so appreciative of Rozelle's efforts that he said, "What Pete Rozelle did with television receipts probably saved football in Green Bay."

As commissioner, Rozelle was quickly tested by fire. In the spring of 1963 he had to suspend two of the NFL's biggest stars, Paul Hornung and Alex Karras, for admitted gambling. Later, after President John F. Kennedy was assassinated in November of that year, Rozelle elected to have NFL teams play, while the AFL canceled its games. Rozelle was roundly criticized, and he later called the action "the most regrettable decision I ever made."

Rozelle's public-relations background served him well. He continually worked at polishing the NFL's image and had the league's teams do likewise. Through entities such as NFL Films and NFL Properties, the league was marketed and merchandised like no other sports organization.

ABC's *Monday Night Football*, another of Rozelle's innovations, attracted millions to NFL football who would not normally have been interested, and it changed both the viewing habits of a nation and the programming of other networks. The league became an international attraction, and NFL teams played in such far-flung venues as England, Japan, Mexico, and Canada. A tie-in was established between the NFL and the United Way, and NFL Charities was created to distribute revenue from sales of NFL merchandise to charitable causes; monetary contributions ultimately totaled in the many millions. Perhaps Rozelle's most significant accomplishment was the creation of the Super Bowl, after he helped effect a merger in 1966 between the NFL and AFL. The world championship game came to be regarded as sports' greatest one-day event.

While the NFL was running smoothly on the field, not all was peaceful off the field. In 1982 maverick owner Al Davis of the Oakland Raiders sought to move his team to Los Angeles. Rozelle preached "League Think." But Davis was not converted and took his team to Los Angeles and the league to court. A jury sided with Davis and the Raiders moved, becoming the first team in more than two decades to do so. Others followed in subsequent years.

The league continued to prosper, but Rozelle tired of constant bickering among a new breed of owners, labor strife, and litigation. Somewhat surprisingly, he resigned in March 1989. Meanwhile, having divorced his first wife in 1972, he married Carrie Cook. They spent their retirement years in Rancho Santa Fe. Rozelle, who was elected to the Pro Football Hall of Fame in 1985, had an office in Southern California and continued to work as a consultant with the NFL. He suffered from brain cancer the last several years of his life and succumbed to the disease on 6 December 1996. Memorial services were held in January 1997 in New York City and Los Angeles.

Rozelle's impact on American sports is undeniable. The growth of the NFL from twelve teams in 1960, barely worth a million dollars each, to twenty-eight teams in his time, each worth several hundred million, is a credit to his leadership. In 1999 the *Sporting News* named him "the most powerful person in sports for the 20th Century." Wellington Mara, owner of the New York Giants, said, "He moved the NFL from the back page to the front page, from daytime to primetime." Rozelle, when asked to sum up his thirty-year tenure, simply said, "I did my best." Few would argue.

★

Extensive mentions of Rozelle's life and career can be found in the following books: Hamilton "Tex" Maule, *The Game* (1963); Jim Byrne, *The $1 League* (1986); David Harris, *The League* (1986); Bob St. John, *Tex* (1988); and Dan E. Modea, *Interference* (1989). An obituary is in the *New York Times* (7 Dec. 1996).

JIM CAMPBELL

RÓZSA, Miklós (*b.* 18 April 1907 in Budapest, Hungary; *d.* 27 July 1995 in Los Angeles, California), composer whose urgently exotic music enriched the concerto literature and the soundtracks of such films as *The Thief of Bagdad, Double Indemnity, Spellbound,* and *Ben-Hur* (1959).

Rózsa was the elder of two children of Gyula Rózsa, the owner of a small shoe factory, and Regina Berkovits, a musician. Born in Budapest but raised partly on the family's estate in northern hill country, Rózsa showed an early affinity for music and could compose before he could write words. Influenced by the nationalist school of Béla Bartók and Zoltán Kodály, Rózsa promoted their still-unfamiliar modern music while studying at the *Realgymnasium* (secondary school) in Budapest.

Against his father's wishes, Rózsa steered a musical course. Compromising, he agreed to study chemistry at the University of Leipzig if he could also pursue musical studies there. Quickly enthralled by that German city with its culture of Johann Sebastian Bach and Felix Mendelssohn, and freed from what he regarded as a provincial and oppressive Hungarian atmosphere, Rózsa soon emerged as a promising composition student who was then allowed to transfer to the Leipzig Conservatory. There, in 1927 and 1928, he presented his first chamber compositions, a String Trio and a Piano Quintet. These earned Rózsa high regard and a publishing contract with Breitkopf and Härtel. Soon he essayed an hour-long symphony, for which he was unable to secure a performance. Disappointed, he suppressed the piece for sixty-three years.

Rózsa graduated with honors in 1929 and moved to Paris three years later. There he composed the shorter orchestral works that made his European reputation: *Theme, Variations, and Finale* (1933) and *Three Hungarian Sketches*

Miklós Rózsa. INDIANA UNIVERSITY NEWS BUREAU

(1938). For these compositions he received the Hungarian Franz Joseph Prize in both 1937 and 1938. Although he enjoyed growing esteem and the friendship of the Swiss composer Arthur Honegger, Rózsa was still unable to make a living except by providing lightweight pastiches for cinema intermissions. The intensely serious Rózsa detested these assignments and wrote the tunes under such pseudonyms as "Nic Tomay."

Fortune smiled on Rózsa when he moved to London in 1935. The Markova-Dolin Ballet commissioned a folk-pastiche score, called *Hungaria,* which enjoyed a successful run. Rózsa also became associated with the émigré film producer Alexander Korda, whose London Films nurtured many Hungarian talents. Rózsa's first film score was *Knight Without Armour* (1936), and soon he was a regular composer for Korda. The elaborate Technicolor fantasy *The Thief of Bagdad* (1940), with its lavish and exotically colored score, brought him international attention, including the first of his sixteen Academy Award nominations from Hollywood. When production of this film was interrupted by the outbreak of World War II, the entire company moved to California in 1940. Rózsa stayed there, becoming an American citizen in 1946.

Following another exotic Korda fantasy, *The Jungle Book* (1942), Rózsa began to introduce a darker and more modernistic idiom to Hollywood films. Billy Wilder's *Double Indemnity* (1944) initiated a more mature kind of filmmaking that eventually came to be called film noir. Rózsa's accompaniment—terse, angular, violent, and close to his concert idiom—was disliked by the studio's music director but proved to be an immense help to this influential picture. *Spellbound* (1945), about a schizophrenic psychiatrist, and *The Lost Weekend* (1945), a grim depiction of the horrors of alcoholism, also achieved great success, partly based on Rózsa's introduction of an electronic instrument called the theremin, and partly owing to the familiarity of themes from *Spellbound,* which Cole Porter's publishing company popularized as the *Spellbound Concerto.* Both scores were nominated for the 1945 Academy Award. When Rózsa won for *Spellbound* (*The Lost Weekend* was judged best picture), he had reached the top of his profession.

Throughout the remainder of the 1940s Rózsa became the dominant musical voice for stories of crime and psychosis. His titles of this period, chiefly for Universal and Paramount, are a virtual catalog of film noir: *The Killers* (1946), *A Double Life* (1947; Academy Award), *The Strange Love of Martha Ivers* (1946), *Brute Force* (1947), *Secret Beyond the Door* (1947), *The Naked City* (1948), *Criss Cross* (1948), *Kiss the Blood off My Hands* (1948), *The Asphalt Jungle* (1950). After Rózsa signed a contract with Metro-Goldwyn-Mayer (MGM), which lasted from 1949 to 1963, his assignments tended toward historical subjects and his music toward increased color and romanticism in such films as *Madame Bovary* (1949), *Ivanhoe* (1952), *Knights of the Round Table* (1953), *Young Bess* (1953), *Julius Caesar* (1953), and *Lust for Life* (1956).

Two scores stand out from the MGM period. *Quo Vadis* (1951) afforded Rózsa the opportunity to return to Europe and research the music of ancient Rome to a degree never before attempted in a historical picture. *Ben-Hur* (1959) mined deeply in this vein while adding darker music of Judaic character. This rich tapestry of dramatic leitmotivs and Roman marches earned Rózsa his third Oscar and has been honored as a film music classic ever since. The blend of adventure story and religious imagery touched sensibilities around the world. Until the time of his death Rózsa received letters from young people who had been deeply affected by the music of *Ben-Hur.* At least one of them, the English musicologist Christopher Palmer, was later inspired to undertake a musical career.

Ensconced as the screen voice of antiquity and legend, Rózsa followed with comparably gigantic scores for *King of Kings* (1961), *El Cid* (1961), and *Sodom and Gomorrah* (1962), all written within three years of *Ben-Hur* in an astonishing burst of creative energy. By that time, however, Rózsa suddenly found his music out of fashion in a Hollywood that was inclining toward youth-oriented popular tunes.

In August 1943 Rózsa married Margaret Finlason; they had two children. (Little is known of an earlier German marriage to Emma Sauerbrey that ended in divorce in 1939). During his first decade in America, as Rózsa worked to establish his career and family, he produced little music outside of films. He did teach, however, and in 1945 inaugurated America's first university-based film composition course at the University of Southern California, where he continued to teach for some twenty years. A lean String Quartet (1950), composed in the wake of *Quo Vadis,* served to cleanse his musical palate, and Rózsa's rediscovery of his European roots led to renewed concert activity. Leasing a modest cottage on the Ligurian coast of Italy, he began a determined "double life" by composing personal works there every summer. The 1953 Violin Concerto, introduced by Jascha Heifetz, was his greatest success. Amid a total of some fifty chamber, orchestral, and choral works (amid his nearly 100 films), his most prominent scores were the concertos for Violin and Cello (*Sinfonia Concertante,* 1966), Piano (1967), Cello (1968), and Viola (1979). These works earned the support of distinguished soloists and have been recorded several times. Critical response to them was mixed. The young rebel of Budapest was now seen as a conservative—and one who noisily rejected the prevailing academic serial orthodoxy of the day. (In *King of Kings* he went so far as to assign a twelve-tone theme to the devil.) By the 1960s Rózsa found himself branded as a competent craftsman rather than an original talent. Concert fashion had turned away at the very moment he was embracing absolute music. Hollywood experience was seen as tainting any composer who succeeded there, and film music itself was completely ignored by the critical establishment.

In the 1970s, however, Rózsa was rediscovered by a new generation of filmmakers to whom he represented the last link to a classic age of moviemaking. The New Wave director Alain Resnais even brought him back to Paris for *Providence* (1977), for which Rózsa received the César award from the French film academy. His last score was *Dead Men Don't Wear Plaid* (1982), a farcical homage to the very noir genre that Rózsa himself had helped to create forty years earlier. A stroke ended Rózsa's film career in 1982, and he struggled to compose for solo instruments until failing eyesight finally stilled his pen in 1988. By then, others were attending to the revival and re-recording of both his film and concert music. The long-suppressed Symphony was recorded in 1993. Rózsa societies were established in several countries in recognition of the extraordinary impact his music exerted on people around the world. Immobilized during his final years, Rózsa found himself lionized by a Hollywood that he had disdained but of which he was now perceived as an avatar. He died of heart failure and is buried in Forest Lawn Cemetery beneath the Hollywood Hills, where he had lived since 1944. At his funeral a band of musicians sounded the "Parade of the Charioteers" from *Ben-Hur.* In the words of journalist Robert Horton, "If we went back in a time machine to ancient Rome and heard their actual music, we'd probably complain that it didn't sound like Miklós Rózsa."

★

Rózsa's papers are at the George Arents Research Library of Syracuse University. His *Életem történeteiből* (1980) is an informal series of anecdotes related to the harpsichordist János Sebestyén for broadcast in Hungary. The formal memoir *Double Life* (1982, 1989), written with Christopher Palmer, displays a mellow and distanced view of his twin musical careers. Palmer, an influential English musicologist whose career was partly inspired by Rózsa, became the composer's assistant and advocate during his last two decades. His sleeve notes for numerous recordings are a valuable source, as is the monograph *Miklós Rózsa: A Sketch of His Life and Work* (1975). Valuable biographical information is in a dissertation by Steven D. Wescott: "Miklós Rózsa: A Portrait of the Composer as Seen Through an Analysis of His Early Works" (University of Minnesota, 1990). Accounts of the composer's activities in later years, together with discographies, reminiscences, and reviews, appear in the Miklós Rózsa Society's *Pro Musica Sana* (1972–). For Rózsa's place in the history of Hollywood film music see Tony Thomas, *Music for the Movies* (1973) and *Film Score: The View from the Podium* (1979); William Darby and Jack Du Bois, *American Film Music* (1990); and Christopher Palmer, *The Composer in Hollywood* (1990). Obituaries are in the *Los Angeles Times* (28 July 1995) and *New York Times* (28 and 29 July 1995).

JOHN FITZPATRICK

RUBIN, Jerry Clyde (*b.* 14 July 1938 in Cincinnati, Ohio; *d.* 28 November 1994 in Los Angeles, California), 1960s radical, antiwar protester, and cofounder of the Youth International Party (popularly known as the Yippies). He was best known as a defendant in the 1968 Chicago Seven trial and for his theatrical use of the media, especially relating to the anti–Vietnam War movement.

Rubin was born in Cincinnati, the son of Robert Rubin, a truck driver turned union organizer, and Esther Katz, a homemaker. Shortly after his birth, the family moved to New York City, where Robert operated a small candy store. In 1944 Robert joined the merchant marine, and Esther returned to Cincinnati, where she became a secretary. After the elder Rubin returned from World War II, he began working as a truck driver and the family lived mostly with Esther's parents, who gave their grandson considerable attention. After failing the entrance exam requirements at the exclusive Walnut Hills High School in 1950, Rubin at-

Jerry Rubin. ARCHIVE PHOTOS

tended Samuel Ach Junior High School. Two years later he met the admission standards of Walnut Hills. He excelled as a sportswriter on the staff of *Chatterbox,* the school newspaper, for which he served as coeditor in his senior year. He used the paper to voice his negative opinion of high school fraternities.

Following graduation in 1956, Rubin worked for the *Cincinnati Post* for the summer before entering Oberlin College. He left in 1957 when the *Post* offered him a full-time position as sportswriter. He also carried a full load at the University of Cincinnati, graduating with a degree in history in 1961. Afterward, he left for India to attend graduate school at the University of Lucknow. En route he learned of his father's death and returned home. Upon his return, Rubin assumed guardianship of his fourteen-year-old brother, since his mother had died in 1960. His parents, who had inherited money from Esther's parents, had left him a sizable trust, much of it in stock; in a stroke of irony, this income enabled him to become a radical protestor who often railed against capitalism. In June 1962, Rubin, along with his brother, went to Israel, where they attended school. Rubin studied sociology at Hebrew University but did not graduate. After only one year they returned to the United States; Rubin had decided to attend graduate school at the University of California at Berkeley.

After six weeks there, Rubin joined a group of radicals and journeyed illegally to Cuba, which he viewed as a land of idealism. Arriving back in Berkeley, he became active in the Free Speech Movement and in 1965 helped organize the Vietnam Day Committee against growing American involvement in Vietnam. The organization sponsored teach-ins, organized marches, and protested the transportation of troops through Berkeley, an early sign that the antiwar movement had intensified. At that time, Rubin adopted the street-theater tactics that made him famous. He also shed his clean-cut appearance and began to sport a beard and long hair. In like manner, his personality underwent a transformation; he began to make such bold and memorable statements as "Don't trust anyone over thirty."

Subpoenaed by the House Committee on Un-American Activities in 1966 for his Vietnam War protest in Berkeley, Rubin appeared dressed as a Revolutionary War soldier to show that protest was American. He believed it was his right to question the country's leadership, especially its commitment to the Vietnam War. He was not called to testify and was arrested for his actions. In 1967, Rubin campaigned to elect a pig as president of the United States and protested capitalism by dropping dollar bills onto the floor of the New York Stock Exchange. On 31 January 1967, he, along with Abbie Hoffman and Paul Krassner, cofounded the Youth International Party. Their most publicized demonstration came at the 1968 Democratic National Convention in Chicago (Rubin was a vice presidential candidate on the Peace and Freedom ticket). It resulted in the arrest of Rubin, along with seven others, for conspiracy to incite violence and riot. During the trial, the group became known as the Chicago Seven, because one of the eight original defendants was tried separately. The accused group filled the court proceedings with mockery and unruliness. Five of the seven defendants, including Rubin, were convicted of riot provocation instead of conspiracy. An appeals court later overturned the convictions.

Afterward, Rubin toured college campuses lecturing and working on his first book, *Do It!: Scenarios of the Revolution* (1970). In the summer of 1970, he served a sixty-day sentence in Chicago's Cook County Jail for his role in the 1968 Chicago convention demonstration. While he was incarcerated, he wrote *We Are Everywhere* (1971). Both of these books were political statements of the 1960s, filled with the revolutionary language and radical thought of the times. In 1972 he coauthored *Vote* with Abbie Hoffman and Ed Sanders, which supported the Democratic presidential candidacy of George McGovern. In the early 1970s, Rubin found himself falling from the spotlight as the Vietnam War ended. In 1976, he published *Growing Up at Thirty-seven,* an autobiographical account of the changes he had experienced in the early 1970s. During this time he took part in self-awareness programs and continued to lecture.

In the late 1970s he worked as a therapist for the Fischer-Hoffman psychic therapy clinic, which was not a physical clinic but a self-help process he taught everywhere in the country.

Rubin married Mimi Leonard in 1978; they lived on the Upper East Side of Manhattan and had two children. In 1980 he denounced his anticapitalist beliefs and worked briefly for the Wall Street firm of John Muir and Company. He then promoted networking until 1991, when he moved from New York to Los Angeles. where he began working for Omnitrition International, marketing nutritional products. His marriage ended in divorce in 1992. On 14 November 1994, an automobile struck him in Los Angeles; injuries sustained in the accident led to cardiac arrest two weeks later. He is buried at Hillside Memorial Park in Los Angeles.

In the 1960s, Rubin understood that the antiwar movement depended on the media. In the 1970s he proved that he had the ability to adapt to changing times. In a 1980 article in the *New York Times,* he proclaimed that he still held many of his values and beliefs of the 1960s. He stated that money is power and that to develop power one needed to control money. In a 1993 interview with Ron Chepesiuk, he declared that money could be a tool for positive action and that he had not realized its value in the 1960s. Rubin understood that in present-day society it is easier to reform the system from within. His belief that he had made a difference in the 1960s never left him. Furthermore, he thought that the 1990s would be a decade of change, when the generation of the 1960s came to power in business, government, and politics. Consequently, he believed that he was doing his part by embracing the system and joining the business world.

★

See Rubin's *Growing Up at Thirty-seven* (1976), which is packed with information but lacks specific dates. Rubin's *New York Times* article of 30 July 1980, "Guess Who's Coming to Wall Street," covers well the changes he underwent through the 1960s and 1970s. Ron Chepesiuk, *Sixties Radicals, Then and Now: Candid Conversations with Those Who Shaped the Era* (1995), has a short interview with Rubin. Paul Krassner, *Confessions of a Raving, Unconfined Nut* (1993), includes a useful chapter titled "The Rise and Fall of the Yippie Empire." For a social history of the 1960s, see Todd Gitlin, *The Sixties: Years of Hope, Days of Rage* (rev. ed., 1993). *Esquire* (Nov. 1969) has an article by J. Anthony Lukas, "The Making of a Yippie," that contains information about Rubin's early family life and career. The *Los Angeles Times* (29 Nov. 1994) provides a short but informative tribute to Rubin. See also the article "He Didn't Need a Weatherman" in *People* (Dec. 1994), which pays tribute to Rubin's ability to adapt to the times. An obituary is in the *New York Times* (30 Nov. 1994).

BARRETT RICHARDSON

RUDOLPH, Wilma Glodean (*b.* 23 June 1940 in Saint Bethlehem, Tennessee; *d.* 12 November 1994 in Brentwood, Tennessee), athlete, executive, and winner of three Olympic gold medals.

Rudolph was the twentieth of twenty-two children of Eddie B. Rudolph and Blanche Pettus. Her father already had fourteen children when he married Blanche. While Wilma was an infant, her parents moved the family to Kellogg Street in nearby Clarksville. Eddie worked on the railroad and as a handyman. He and Blanche, who worked as a maid in homes of white families, raised the children in a disciplined Baptist family with a love of education.

Rudolph was a premature infant, who suffered many childhood diseases: pneumonia, scarlet fever, and then polio. With her mother, she often rode the segregated bus to Nashville to receive medical treatments. She was unable to walk until fitted with a leg brace at the age of eight. But her condition improved rapidly, and by eleven she was playing basketball barefoot. She studied at the Cobb School for Negroes, where her teachers gradually transformed Rudolph into a self-confident person, encouraging her to excel in life without any excuses. At the new all-black Burt High School, Rudolph participated in basketball and track. At

Wilma Rudolph with her Olympic gold medal for the 200-meter dash at the 1960 games in Rome. © BETTMANN/CORBIS

age thirteen, six feet tall and weighing only eighty-nine pounds, she won all her races at 50, 75, 100, and 200 meters. As a basketball player she scored over 800 points during her sophomore year of high school alone.

In 1954 at the Negro Schools Championship game in Nashville, a referee named Edward Stanley Temple noticed the skinny-legged youngster. Temple was the women's track coach at Tennessee State University (TSU) in Nashville, and he invited Rudolph to attend his summer track camp, where he had the girls run five miles a day on the university's farm roads, which helped build endurance and confidence. Mae Faggs, a five-foot-tall Olympic medalist at TSU helped Coach Temple to develop and chaperone young Rudolph. Students nicknamed the girls "Mutt and Jeff." Copying Rudolph's former high school coach, Clinton Gray, others affectionately called Rudolph "skeeter" because of her tall, skinny physique and quick "movements like a mosquito." Rudolph recalled: "I remember the year 1954 when I had just begun to find out that young girls were involved in sports." That year the fourteen-year-old Rudolph accompanied her high school track team to a meet at Tuskegee Institute in Alabama, and, although she did not win any of her events, she was emboldened by the spectacle of women competing.

In 1955 Rudolph returned to Temple's summer camp. In August the team participated in the National Amateur Athletic Union (AAU) races in Philadelphia, where Rudolph won all her races. They had to travel in automobiles, take along sack lunches from the university's cafeteria, and sleep wherever they could in the Jim Crow South. In October Rudolph accompanied Temple and five of his runners to Washington, D.C., for the U.S. Olympic team trials. TSU became the first institution to have six members qualify for Olympic competition; it was the first time that all four members of the American women's relay team originated from the same university. They won four bronze medals and one silver at the 1956 games in Melbourne, Australia.

Rudolph became a student at TSU in the fall of 1958, when some work aid was provided to pay the tuition and fees. (TSU offered neither scholarships for the athletes nor even a decent university coaching salary for Temple.) Training facilities were limited at this "Negro" institution. In lieu of an indoor track, the athletes ran through the corridors of Kean Hall, careful to hit the double swinging doors without hurting themselves. Yet, with sheer endurance and determination, Rudolph and the Tigerbelles (the TSU team) performed superbly. In the summer of 1959 Rudolph and her teammates won the relays at the Pan American Games in Chicago. Rudolph participated in the National AAU meet in Corpus Christi, Texas, in 1960, and won the 100-meter and 200-meter, thereby qualifying for

the 400-meter relay in the Olympic trials at Texas Christian University weeks later.

It was at the 1960 Olympics in Rome that Rudolph and the American women's track team won world fame. Tigerbelles comprised nearly a third of the members on the American team. Rudolph received three gold medals for winning at 100 meters and 200 meters and in the 400-meter relay. She became the first American woman to win three gold medals in a single Olympiad. Despite the lack of resources, Rudolph and her fellow Tigerbelles had won with guts and determination. Temple said: "I was bursting all the buttons on my shirt. . . . Rudolph became such a celebrity she couldn't leave the compound without creating a mob scene." The Africans and the French called her "the Black Pearl" and "the Black Gazelle." On 14 September 1960 Temple took his team to the British Empire Games in London, where Rudolph won all her events. All over Europe the team was acclaimed by crowds. In Clarksville, Blanche and Eddie Rudolph beamed with pride when the citizens sponsored a parade and banquet to welcome Rudolph home. There were honors from the governor of Tennessee, the Nashville *Banner,* and *Sport* magazine. She traveled to Chicago, Philadelphia, Atlanta, and Washington, D.C., where she was honored by President John F. Kennedy. But it was noted that in Clarksville the Shoney's restaurant still refused to serve African Americans, including Rudolph.

In 1961 Rudolph received the Sullivan Award as top amateur athlete in America. She was voted AAU All-American in 1956, 1957, 1959, 1960, 1961, and 1962. This was significant in the turbulent decade when America was in the midst of the movement for civil rights. Rudolph became the first woman and first African American to be invited to run in the New York Athletic Club Track Meet, an invitation that opened the door for other women to gain admittance into the club. She ran against the Russians in Madison Square Garden, and made goodwill tours of Africa and Japan.

Amid all the acclaim, Rudolph did not neglect her education. She joined Delta Sigma Theta sorority and received a bachelor's degree in elementary education in 1963. On 14 October 1961 Rudolph married William Ward; the couple were divorced the next year. On 20 July 1963 Rudolph married a high school sweetheart and TSU basketball star, Robert Eldridge. They had four children and were divorced in 1981. In 1965 the couple moved to Evansville, Indiana, when Rudolph became the director of a community center there. Later, she managed youth programs for the Job Corps in Boston and then in Maine, and by 1967 she was working with Vice President Hubert Humphrey to develop Operation Champion to provide sports training for inner-city children. In 1972 she provided television broadcast commentary for the Munich Olympic Games.

In later years Rudolph held a variety of public service positions. She worked with the Job Corps in St. Louis and served as a teacher in Detroit. In 1975 Rudolph became assistant director of the Youth Foundation in Chicago. Rudolph worked with the Watts Community Action Committee in California, and in Indianapolis for ten years before deciding to move the family back to Clarksville in 1977 before returning to Detroit. In 1992 she made her final move to Nashville, where she became a vice president with Baptist Hospital. Rudolph also became president of the Wilma Rudolph Foundation to help children overcome difficult life circumstances as she had done.

Late honors included induction into the Tennessee Sports Hall of Fame (1967) and the Black Athletes Hall of Fame (1974). In 1980 TSU named its indoor track for Wilma Rudolph, and in 1993 a section of U.S. Highway 79 in Clarksville became Wilma Rudolph Boulevard. In 1994, she was inducted into the National Women's Hall of Fame. Then, Wilma Rudolph was diagnosed with brain and lung cancer. She seldom appeared in public, except for quiet and personal walks around the old track with the retired Coach Temple. "If there's something I want to talk about, I just end up at his track," she said to a local newspaper.

At age fifty-four Rudolph died quietly in her Nashville home. Four thousand mourners filled TSU's Kean Hall for the memorial service. Rudolph's funeral was held at Clarksville's First Baptist Church, and the state flag was lowered all across Tennessee. Wilma Rudolph became one of America's greatest heroes. From a segregated, working class background, a once-sickly African American child became America's greatest female athlete. Surely, she resented the bitter taste of racism. Yet, Rudolph was always quiet, reserved, dignified, friendly, and humble. Nevertheless, despite the challenges in her life, she brought grace and respect to the sport of women's track and field and honor for her country.

★

Papers on Rudolph and Edward S. Temple are collected at the Brown-Daniel Library at Tennessee State University. *Wilma: The Story of Wilma Rudolph* (1977) is an autobiography, written with Martin Ralbovsky. (Bud Greenspan's dramatized film version appeared on television the same year.) Biographies include Tom Biracree, *Wilma Rudolph* (1988), and Linda Jacobs, *Wilma Rudolph: Run for Glory* (1975). See also Martha W. Plowden, *Olympic Black Women* (1996), and Edward S. Temple, *Only the Pure in Heart Survive* (1980). The story of TSU athletics and the Tigerbelles is told in Dwight Lewis and Susan Thomas, *A Will to Win* (1983). Reference resources include *Notable Black Ameri-*

can Women (1992) and the *Tennessee Encyclopedia of History and Culture* (1998). An obituary is in the *New York Times* (13 Nov. 1994).

BOBBY L. LOVETT

RUSK, (David) Dean (*b.* 9 February 1909 in Cherokee County, Georgia; *d.* 20 December 1994 in Athens, Georgia), fifty-fourth secretary of state, serving from 1961 to 1969 in the administrations of John F. Kennedy and Lyndon B. Johnson; he was the most articulate defender of United States participation in the Vietnam War and thus became a major target of the antiwar protest movement.

Rusk, whose paternal forebears had emigrated from Northern Ireland around 1795, grew up in poverty, later often vying jocularly with Lyndon Johnson as to which of them came from the poorer household. Rusk's mother was Elizabeth ("Fanny") Clotfelter, whose father came from the Black Forest region of Germany and whose mother was born in Ireland, attended a normal school in Milledgeville, Georgia, and was a teacher. His father, Robert Hugh Rusk, attended Davidson College in Davidson, North Carolina, but did not graduate. Later he enrolled in Louisville Theological Seminary and was ordained a Presbyterian minister; however, a throat ailment prevented him pursuing a career

Dean Rusk. UNITED NATIONS

in the pulpit. After a disastrous period as a farmer, he became a postman in order to support his family.

Rusk was the second youngest of five children. He liked to say that the name Dean, by which he preferred to be called, was taken from that of the horse which had carried to the Rusk house the doctor who delivered him. When Rusk was a young boy the family moved to Atlanta, where he graduated from Boys' High School. He graduated magna cum laude from Davidson College in 1931. As a Rhodes scholar at Saint John's College at Oxford University, he took a master of arts degree in 1934. This had been a formative time for the young "southern Yank," as he would style himself, for he traveled to Germany and witnessed some of the shattering events of the 1930s, including the rise of Hitler. In Berlin in March 1933 he watched the burning of the Reichstag building by the Nazis. Returning to the United States, he taught government and the relatively new subject of international relations at Mills College in Oakland, California, from 1934 to 1940, and became dean of the faculty in 1938. At the same time he studied law at the University of California at Berkeley. Meanwhile, he was courting Virginia Wynifred Foisie of Seattle, one of his students, to whom he was married on 19 June 1937. They had three children. Although Rusk participated in the American peace movement and felt an affinity to the Quakers, he held a reserve army commission as a result of eight years of ROTC training. In December 1940 he was called to active duty as a captain. After brief service with the Thirtieth Infantry Battalion of the Third Division, he was ordered to Washington and assigned to the military intelligence branch of the army general staff, where his focus was on Asian issues. In 1943 Rusk, now a major, was sent to New Delhi, India, to join the staff of General Joseph W. Stilwell, commander of the China-Burma-India Theater. By the end of the following year Rusk had been designated deputy chief of staff for the entire theater, and was a full colonel. He remained in the army until February 1946, concluding his tour of duty in the Operations Division of the War Department General Staff in Washington, D.C. He had been awarded the Legion of Merit medal with oak leaf cluster.

In 1946 while still at the War Department, Rusk was posted briefly to the Department of State as assistant chief of the division of international security affairs. He then became special assistant to the secretary of war, Robert P. Patterson, who was immersed in postwar defense issues. At the invitation of the secretary of state General George C. Marshall, Rusk joined the Department of State in 1947 to head the Office of Special Political Affairs, commonly called "the UN desk." Rusk regarded Marshall as "the most extraordinary man I ever knew." From him, he learned the art of delegating authority and of relying on well-chosen staff for analysis and proposals. Under Marshall, Rusk also

reinforced his belief in liberal internationalism and his obstinate faith in what the United States could provide in leadership and substance to the rest of the world. Rusk was unshakably committed to the idea that in a nuclear age, survival required absolute dependence on international law. Against some of the hardheaded "realists" in the department, Rusk remained an idealist in the tradition of Woodrow Wilson. Above all, as the cold war developed, he came to believe that unless Communism was confronted with firm and active commitment, the world would once again face what he called "the sorry experience of the 1930s." He recalled from his days at Oxford the fierce debates over how to deal with fascist aggression, and ever in his mind was the lesson that timid leadership, including especially the sellout of Czechoslovakia to Hitler at Munich in 1938, had opened the way to world war. This history would provide the framework for his view that the North Vietnamese assault on South Vietnam was a replay of a shameful story that this time must have a different ending.

On the eve of the Korean War in 1950, after a brief period as deputy undersecretary of state, Rusk became assistant secretary of state for Far Eastern affairs. He resolutely supported the war while opposing General Douglas MacArthur's stated fervor to expand the conflict across the Yalu River into China. The outcome of the conflict was inconclusive. In time, however, a prosperous South Korea allied to the United States offered a claim of success, and a few years later encouraged policymakers to think that the struggle in Vietnam provided a repeat opportunity. In conversation, Rusk himself would occasionally say "Korea" when he meant "Vietnam."

Rusk became president of the Rockefeller Foundation in 1952, calling it "the best job in America." While sympathetic to a variety of creative proposals, he aimed especially to direct funds to third world countries, which he considered to constitute "a time bomb for the whole human race." He remained at the foundation until President John F. Kennedy appointed him secretary of state in 1961. Kennedy did not know Rusk before naming him but was taken by his reserved, gentlemanly manner. Kennedy acted upon Dean Acheson's strong recommendation of Rusk for the post. The president had also concluded that he would aim to unofficially be his own secretary of state anyhow.

During his earlier service at the Department of State, Rusk's peers had known him as a splendid administrator, a remarkably deft explainer of policy, and a man able to testify brilliantly before congressional committees. Rusk was also somewhat of a loner who, in discussion, showed a unique ability to give people the impression that he agreed with them, even as he kept his counsel, reluctant to show his own hand. It would infuriate Rusk later when the historian Arthur Schlesinger, Jr., a member of the Kennedy administration, described Rusk as sitting at policy meetings silent "like a Buddha." Kennedy and Rusk came to work together harmoniously, although they were never close. The president relied for advice more on his special assistant for national security affairs, McGeorge Bundy, who carefully avoided seeming to usurp Rusk's authority.

The first great crisis of the administration was the disastrous invasion of the Bay of Pigs in Cuba in 1961 by Cuban exiles backed by the United States. Rusk later said that even though he publicly supported the undertaking out of loyalty to the new president, in advising him privately he opposed it. Playing the good soldier, he restrained himself from afterwards making this fact public. Later that year he earned Kennedy's respectful admiration as a negotiator by helping defuse the Berlin crisis created when the Soviet Union, in a tense showdown between the president and Nikita Khrushchev, aimed to limit Western access to the former German capital by erecting what would become the infamous Berlin Wall, cutting off the western and eastern portions of the city from each other.

In the even graver crisis in the fall of 1962, when the installation by the Soviet Union of missiles in Cuba appeared to threaten a nuclear confrontation between the two superpowers, Rusk did not provide the leadership expected of him. In the deliberations of ExCom (Executive Committee of the National Security Council), the ad hoc group of advisers that Kennedy assembled to counsel him in that moment of agonizing decision, Rusk appeared notably passive. To the dismay of some of those present, including Dean Acheson, Rusk refused to commit himself as to the course of action he favored, and was absent from some of the meetings—possibly to convey to the public that the State Department was in a business-as-usual mode.

Rusk later insisted that his place was to weigh all options before taking a stand, or, as he further explained, to "hold himself in reserve" before making a recommendation. It is noteworthy that the president never expressed dissatisfaction to Rusk over his performance. In the end, Rusk supported the proposal of Secretary of Defense Robert S. McNamara to put a partial naval blockade around Cuba. When the emergency was resolved on 28 October 1962, even as the nation and the world held its breath, Rusk whispered words to his confreres that earned him a place in Bartlett's *Familiar Quotations:* "We were eyeball to eyeball, and the other fellow just blinked." Subsequently, Rusk helped to bring about the partial Nuclear Test Ban Treaty in 1963.

The accession of Lyndon B. Johnson to the presidency in 1963 significantly changed Rusk's role. Johnson liked and admired Rusk both as a fellow southerner and as a loyal servant; the two had a warm and trusting relationship. Both had felt like outsiders in Kennedy's brief era, and often were treated as such. Kennedy was known to be displeased with Rusk's administration of the State Department

and was said to be planning to replace him in a second term. Rusk, for his part, had been uncomfortable with Kennedy's style of governing. Kennedy, he said, "sought ideas from any source," so that cabinet meetings were "seminar-like discussions." On the other hand, Rusk was pleased to note, Johnson relied "on the statutory responsibility of cabinet officers." Leaning heavily on each other for support as the American involvement in Vietnam—begun under President Dwight D. Eisenhower and expanded under President Kennedy—became full-fledged war in the summer of 1965, Johnson and Rusk defended the American effort unequivocally.

Although Johnson privately had misgivings about the war almost from the beginning of his presidency, Rusk never wavered in his position, private and public, that the waging of the war was indispensable to America's future. Memorably, he made this argument in February 1966 before the Senate Committee on Foreign Relations chaired by Senator J. William Fulbright of Arkansas, who had broken with the administration on the Vietnam issue and become one of the most vocal critics of the war. Rusk's contention was that the United States was obligated under the Southeast Asia Treaty to be fighting in Vietnam. "When you go into an alliance," he argued, "you have to mean it." At risk, he said, was not only the word of the United States, which must remain inviolable, but also the grim possibility of a larger and wider war with China or the Soviet Union. At the weekly Tuesday lunches that Johnson held in the private quarters of the White House with his chief aides—now often known as the Tuesday Cabinet—where Vietnam strategy was planned and sometimes even bombing targets were designated, Rusk was a powerful presence.

The president's gratitude to Rusk was unbounded. But Rusk became a leading target of the antiwar protests that erupted on college campuses and elsewhere around the country. By the end of Johnson's time in the White House, Rusk was a reviled symbol of the debacle in Vietnam and he hardly ever left Washington, lest he stir up violent demonstrations. Rusk would say, though, that as a government official he had always been treated respectfully wherever he went, and had even autographed a protester's placard reading "Rusk, go home." As the war increasingly offended people everywhere, Rusk's loyalty to Johnson remained unflinching. When it was time to end the war, far short of America's stated goal of establishing a non-Communist South Vietnam, it was Rusk who helped maneuver the president to opt for an end to the bombing of North Vietnam, which opened the way at last to negotiations ending the combat. Rusk never wavered in his conviction that the principles for which the war was fought were right, and he would in the end declare: "There is nothing I can say now that would diminish my share of responsibility. I live with that, and others can make of it what they will."

When Rusk left Washington in 1969 as the Republicans and President Richard Nixon took on the Vietnam issue, the former secretary was physically and mentally exhausted. Stomach pains that had beset him since 1965 persisted, and he was clinically depressed. He accepted a position as Sibley Professor of International Law at the University of Georgia, although there was considerable opposition to his appointment. Thus, he was teaching once again—this time a few miles from where he was born. When students addressed him as "Mr. Secretary," he turned them aside, saying he was simply "Professor." He retired in 1984.

Rusk stood six feet, one inch tall and weighed 200 pounds. He was a courtly, gracious, and unpretentious man whose broad, bald head was made to order for political cartoonists. His ideals and demeanor had been formed as a boy when he read books in the Rover Boys series and "rags-to-riches" stories. His personal integrity was beyond question and he regarded his word as his bond. As a public servant, his dedication and devotion to duty were legendary. He remains respected for having been a powerful voice of the free world in its long "twilight struggle" with the Soviet Union. If in the end this cold warrior became for a time a political pariah because of his support of the Vietnam War, his democratic liberalism remained undamaged. As a soldier he had earnestly participated in the effort to end segregation in the military and when he lived in suburban Scarsdale, New York, during his time with the Rockefeller Foundation, he refused to join the town's most prominent country club because its membership was closed to African Americans and Jews. In his days at the University of Georgia, he took a leading role in the Black Students Alliance, serving as its faculty adviser.

In retirement his health gradually declined, and he died of congestive heart failure with his family around him. After services at the Athens First Presbyterian Church he was buried in Oconee Hill Cemetery in Athens.

★

The Dean Rusk collections at the University of Georgia library in Athens, the John Fitzgerald Kennedy Presidential Library in Boston, and the Lyndon Baines Johnson Library in Austin, Texas, contain documents on Rusk's career and oral histories provided by Rusk himself and some of his contemporaries. Rusk's speeches, press conferences, and television appearances are contained in successive volumes of the *Department of State Bulletin.* Some of his early addresses are reprinted in Ernest K. Lindley, ed., *The Winds of Freedom* (1963). Rusk's autobiographical account (as told to Richard Rusk), *As I Saw It* (1990), edited by Daniel S. Papp, is especially rich on Rusk's early life and career. Three books tell the story of his public life: Warren I. Cohen, *Dean Rusk* (1980); Thomas J. Schoenbaum, *Waging War and Peace: Dean Rusk in the Truman, Kennedy, and Johnson Years* (1988); and Thomas W. Zeiler, *Dean Rusk: Defending the American Mission Abroad* (2000). Cohen is somewhat more critical of Rusk's handling of the Vietnam War than is Schoenbaum. Zeiler offers the advantage of a post–cold war perspective. Important collateral books are Henry F. Graff, *The Tuesday Cabinet: Deliberation and Decision on Peace and War Under Lyndon B. Johnson* (1970), based on extensive extemporaneous conversations between the author and the president's principal advisers, including Rusk, and two classics on the war itself: George C. Herring, *America's Longest War: The United States and Vietnam, 1950–1975* (3d ed., 1996), and Robert D. Schulzinger, *A Time for War, The United States and Vietnam, 1941–1975* (1997). The best censorious account of the Johnson-Rusk policies is Lloyd C. Gardner, *Pay Any Price: Lyndon Johnson and the Wars for Vietnam* (1995). More sympathetic is Frank E. Vandiver, *Shadows of Vietnam: Lyndon Johnson's Wars* (1997). Robert S. McNamara, with Brian VanDeMark, *In Retrospect: The Tragedy and Lessons of Vietnam* (1995), tries—with more than a little mea culpa by the former secretary of defense—to explain what went wrong in the making of policy. On the missile crisis, the best source is Robert A. Divine, ed., *The Cuban Missile Crisis* (second edition, 1988). But to see the Soviet viewpoint, consult James G. Blight and David A. Welch, *On the Brink: Americans and Soviets Reexamine the Cuban Missile Crisis* (1990). Indispensable are the transcribed proceedings of ExCom meetings in Ernest D. May and Philip D. Zelikow, *The Kennedy Tapes: Inside the White House During the Cuban Missile Crisis,* although the glaring inaccuracy of some of the important transcriptions is pointed out in Sheldon M. Stern, "What JFK Really Said," *Atlantic Monthly* (May 2000). An obituary is in the *New York Times* (22 Dec. 1994).

HENRY F. GRAFF

S

SAGAN, Carl Edward (*b.* 9 November 1934 in Brooklyn, New York; *d.* 20 December 1996 in Seattle, Washington), astronomer and Pulitzer Prize–winning author whose visibility as a television personality made him one of the most recognized scientists of the twentieth century.

Sagan was the first of two children born to Samuel Sagan, a garment cutter, and Rachel Molly Gruber, a homemaker. Both parents were Jewish immigrants to Brooklyn. A family visit to the 1939 New York World's Fair sparked Sagan's interest in science. By adolescence, he was an aficionado of science fiction and had resolved to become an astronomer. The family moved to Rahway, New Jersey, about 1948. After graduating from Rahway High School in 1951, Sagan attended the University of Chicago (B.A., 1954, with honors; B.S. in physics, 1955; M.S. in physics, 1956). He did graduate work at the university's Yerkes Observatory in Williams Bay, Wisconsin, earning a Ph.D. in astronomy and astrophysics in 1960. At the University of Chicago, Sagan met Lynn Alexander, a fellow student, whom he married in 1957. Later that year they established a residence in Madison, Wisconsin. They had two children. The couple were argumentative and often miserable, and they divorced in 1964.

While attending the university, Sagan also met such prominent scientists as the geneticist Hermann Muller, the chemist Harold Urey, the planetary astronomer Gerard Kuiper, and the geneticist Joshua Lederberg. All became friends and mentors. Lederberg was to play a particularly crucial role in Sagan's career. As a proponent of "exobiology" (the study of life beyond the earth), Lederberg recognized that the space program would bring this speculative field into the realm of positive science. Sagan fully shared Lederberg's enthusiasm for exobiology. After the Soviet Union's 1957 launching of Sputnik, Lederberg helped Sagan obtain a post as experimenter on the National Aeronautics and Space Administration's (NASA) Mariner missions to Venus. This was the first of a string of scientific and advisory roles with the space agency that Sagan held throughout his career.

The most important part of Sagan's doctoral thesis concerned the planet Venus. Some had suggested that the cloud-shrouded planet had oceans and life. Opposing this view were microwave readings implying that the planet was far too hot for liquid water, yet the planet's proximity to the sun could not itself account for such high temperatures. Sagan explained the measured high temperatures as the consequence of a greenhouse effect, in which atmospheric gases prevented thermal radiation from escaping efficiently into space. The idea was not new, and no definitive model was then possible, but Sagan became a leading advocate of the model, which was ultimately proved correct.

Sagan occupied posts as Miller Research Fellow at Berkeley (1960–1962) and Visiting Assistant Professor of Genetics at Stanford (1962–1963). In 1961, he was the youngest of the eleven scientists attending the Green Bank

Carl Sagan. LIBRARY OF CONGRESS

meeting organized by the radio astronomer Frank Drake. The meeting's subject was the possibility of radio communication with extraterrestrial intelligent life-forms. Those in attendance estimated the number of intelligent species in the galaxy using the latest thinking on the origin of life. They came up with an estimate of between 1,000 and 100 million technologically advanced species. The meeting helped spur serious efforts to pick up interstellar signals.

Sagan moved east to Cambridge, Massachusetts, to accept a position as lecturer and assistant professor of astronomy at Harvard (1962–1968), also working as a researcher at the Smithsonian Astrophysical Observatory. At Harvard his attention turned to the planet Mars, then considered by many (including Sagan) to be a plausible abode of life. The principal evidence for life on Mars was the planet's seasonal changes. Telescopic observers had long reported that the planet's dark regions appeared to darken or expand during the Martian summer and lighten or contract in the winter. Sagan's teacher Kuiper theorized that this was the result of seasonal growth and decline of vegetation. Sagan provided a convincing nonbiological explanation. In a model developed with his colleague James Pollack, he argued that the dark regions were Martian highlands. Seasonal winds blow light-colored dust into the highlands, covering the darker rock and changing its telescopic appearance; in the opposite season, the wind scours the highlands of dust, uncovering the dark rock. Sagan was one of the few American scientists to cultivate U.S.-Soviet ties throughout the cold war. He wrote *Intelligent Life in the Universe* (U.S. publication, 1966) with a prominent Soviet astrophysicist, I. S. Shklovskii.

In 1968, Sagan married Linda Salzman; they had one son. In his personal life Sagan was charismatic, egotistical, and occasionally temperamental. A workaholic, he was often an inattentive father. Sagan was politically liberal and spoke out on human rights issues privately and publicly. He supported the legalization of marijuana, which he used and credited for some of his scientific inspirations.

Sagan was passed over for tenure at Harvard. His former mentor Harold Urey gave him a scathingly negative review, faulting his penchant for speculation at the expense of solid results. Frustrated by his stalled advancement, Sagan accepted a post in 1968 as associate professor of astronomy and space sciences at Cornell University in Ithaca, New York, where he spent the rest of his career. He become full professor of astronomy and space sciences in 1971 and occupied an endowed chair, the David Duncan Professorship of Astronomy and Space Sciences. Sagan was also director of Cornell's Laboratory for Planetary Studies and (from 1968 to 1979) editor in chief of the journal *Icarus*. In his years at Cornell, Sagan became an influential figure at NASA. In 1969 Sagan and his colleague Frank Drake helped design a plaque, carried aboard the Pioneer spacecraft, containing a symbolic message to hypothetical extraterrestrials that might find it.

In a 1972 article in *Science,* Sagan and George Mullen proposed a gradually declining greenhouse effect as a way of resolving the "faint sun paradox." Astrophysical considerations imply that the primordial sun must have been much fainter and cooler than it is today, yet the geologic record suggests that the earth has always been warm enough to have liquid water, which is presumably a condition for life. Sagan's original and quantitative analysis of the issue was highly influential.

Sagan meanwhile played a key role in NASA's 1976 Viking lander mission to Mars. He served on the imaging team that designed and operated a camera capable of taking panoramic color images from the Martian surface—probably Viking's single most important instrument. Sagan also had close ties with the teams devising instruments for the detection of microbial life and served as a publicist for the mission through his television appearances. Viking was a resounding success: both landers set safely down and returned impressively detailed photographs and other data. The biology instruments were confused by an unexpectedly active surface chemistry. Ultimately, their results were judged not to support the existence of life. That was a disappointment to Sagan (who had not discounted the possibility of creatures large enough to photograph).

In the 1970s Sagan launched a second career as popularizer of science. He became a fixture of space-related news coverage and popular talk shows. He was a master of the sound bite; even his distinctive enunciation commanded attention. Sagan's 1977 book *The Dragons of Eden: Speculations on the Evolution of Human Intelligence* won a Pulitzer Prize. The jury called it "as easily a work of philosophy as it is of science." After his work with the Viking mission, Sagan turned his attention to *Cosmos* (1980), a graphically innovative television series and book deftly blending astronomy, cultural history, and informed speculation. *Cosmos* became the highest-rated series ever made for American public television. Winning both Emmy and Peabody Awards, it eventually was seen by a reported half billion viewers in sixty nations. But Sagan often found himself the focus of colleagues' misgivings about the popularization of science. Such attitudes led to a veto of Sagan's 1992 election to the National Academy of Sciences.

Ann Druyan, a collaborator on the *Cosmos* series, became Sagan's third wife. They married in 1981, a month after Sagan's bitter divorce from Salzman became final. This third marriage was the happiest and produced two children. Sagan's later works include a novel, *Contact* (1985), which was made into a 1997 motion picture; *Shadows of Forgotten Ancestors: A Search for Who We Are* (with Ann Druyan, 1992); and *The Demon-Haunted World: Science as a Candle in the Dark* (1996). In the latter book Sagan was a skeptical but open-minded critic of such popular obsessions as UFOs, alien abductions, and paranormal phenomena.

In 1980 Sagan cofounded the Planetary Society, the largest space-interest organization in the world. He was an activist for social and education issues and nuclear arms reduction. In a 1983 article written with four colleagues for *Science*, he claimed that the smoke and dust of a nuclear war would result in a catastrophic cooling of the global climate whose effects might approach those of the nuclear detonations themselves. These claims of "nuclear winter" were bitterly contested both by political opponents and by specialists who charged that estimates had been skewed in order to produce the dire predictions. In the late 1980s, with funding from the filmmaker Steven Spielberg, Sagan and the physicist Paul Horowitz collaborated on a full-sky survey intended to detect any interstellar signals from extraterrestrial beings. It found no repeating signals within its range of sensitivity. Sagan died of complications from myelodysplasia, a bone marrow disease. He is buried at Lakeview Cemetery in Ithaca.

Sagan is best remembered for his skill in bringing science to the masses. His gift for language and his ease before the television cameras rarely have been equaled by a working scientist. Sagan's public career has tended to overshadow his scientific achievements, which were nonetheless varied and numerous (more than 300 scientific articles). The most personal phase of Sagan's research comprised his diverse attempts to establish the existence of extraterrestrial life. Of all the talented people drawn to exobiology in the early years of the space age, Sagan alone pursued the field in all its varied aspects. In all cases, of course, the results were negative. But Sagan tested ideas of fundamental importance held by many of the best scientists of his time. We are left with a universe in which life seems rarer than many had supposed at the start of the space age. As Sagan himself maintained, that, too, is worth knowing.

★

The principal biographical sources are Keay Davidson, *Carl Sagan: A Life* (1999) and William Poundstone, *Carl Sagan: A Life in the Cosmos* (1999), both of which contain extensive bibliographies. Daniel Cohen, *Carl Sagan: Superstar Scientist* (1987), written for young readers, was the only book-length biography published in Sagan's lifetime. From the 1970s onward, Sagan's career was covered extensively in the general press. Particularly notable are Henry S. F. Cooper, Jr.'s two-part profile for the *New Yorker,* "A Resonance with Something Alive" (21 June 1976): 39–83 and (28 June 1976): 30–61 and two pieces by Timothy Ferris for *Rolling Stone,* "A Conversation with Carl Sagan of the Mars Mariner Project" (7 June 1973): 26–30, and "The Odyssey and the Ecstasy" (7 Apr. 1977): 56–65. There is an obituary in the *New York Times* (21 Dec. 1996).

WILLIAM POUNDSTONE

SALK, Jonas Edward (*b.* 28 October 1914 in New York City; *d.* 23 June 1995 in La Jolla, California), medical researcher who became an international hero on 12 April 1955, when it was announced that he and his staff had developed the first successful vaccine against polio.

The oldest of three sons of Daniel B. Salk and Doris Press was raised in East Harlem in Manhattan, and the Crotona section of the Bronx, then havens for immigrant Jewish families. He graduated from Townsend Harris High School, a selective school for academically talented students. He then received his B.S. degree from the College of the City of New York (1934) and his M.D. degree from the New York University School of Medicine (1939). His father worked as a designer of ladies' blouses and neckwear.

During a summer spent working at a laboratory in Woods Hole, Massachusetts, Salk met Donna Lindsay, a graduate of Smith College who was studying at the New York School of Social Work. They were married on 9 June 1939, the day after Salk's graduation from medical school, and had three sons.

Early in his medical training, Salk, who was slender, soft-spoken, and meticulous, decided he preferred laboratory research to the clinical practice of medicine. During

Jonas Salk. AP/WIDE WORLD PHOTOS

his final year in medical school, he worked in the laboratory of Thomas Francis, Jr., where he first studied the inactivation of influenza virus with ultraviolet light. This was his introduction to the new science of virus research, which was to occupy much of the rest of his career. It was also a confirmation of his conviction, unusual at the time, that it was possible to be immunized against a viral disease without suffering even a mild natural infection.

After his internship at New York City's Mount Sinai Hospital (1940–1942), Salk had difficulty finding an acceptable residency or research fellowship, partly because of the anti-Semitism that still pervaded many medical and scientific centers. Eager to find a position that would enable him to continue research during World War II, Salk moved in 1942 to Ann Arbor, Michigan, where his mentor Thomas Francis was now leading the University of Michigan's new School of Public Health.

From 1942 to 1947, under grants from the U.S. Army Epidemiological Board and the National Foundation for Infantile Paralysis, Salk worked on the preparation of influenza vaccines; on procedures for measuring the effect of vaccines on individual subjects; and on studies of the effectiveness of mass vaccination against epidemics of influenza A and influenza B. The army's interest was in finding a way to prevent a recurrence of the deadly influenza pandemic that had killed so many soldiers in 1918, but Salk's studies also provided the foundation for his subsequent work on developing a vaccine against poliomyelitis and in handling the equally difficult task of showing that such a vaccine had a measurable effect and could be used to control epidemics.

In 1947 Salk left Ann Arbor to direct the Virus Research Laboratory at the University of Pittsburgh. From his earliest work on influenza at the University of Michigan, much of Salk's research had been funded by the National Foundation for Infantile Paralysis, better known as the March of Dimes. After he moved to Pittsburgh, Salk became more centrally involved in polio research, first joining several other laboratories around the country in a program to type polio virus samples in order to determine how many strains of the virus existed, and then working to develop a vaccine using inactivated, or "killed," virus along the same principles of vaccines he had developed for influenza.

A scourge of the twentieth century, polio became an epidemic disease only when advances in hygiene prevented infants from being exposed to the virus, through open sewers and privies, at an age when most could survive infection with few effects because they were still protected by maternal antibodies. Without this early immunizing exposure, people were much more vulnerable to later, more serious infections. After the first large epidemic of 1916, polio swept across the United States and other countries in outbreaks that seemed to strike at random, mainly in the summer and fall. Although fewer than ten percent of victims died, many more were paralyzed, unable to move their arms or legs or to breathe without the help of artificial respirators called "iron lungs." The most famous polio survivor was Franklin D. Roosevelt, elected president in 1932 despite being paralyzed in 1921 at age thirty-nine. Most of the victims, however, were children.

In 1951 Salk met Basil O'Connor, the autocratic, hard-headed, self-made Wall Street lawyer who was the founding president of the National Foundation for Infantile Paralysis. Despite the considerable difference in age and background, Salk and O'Connor developed a strong friendship and respect for each other's talents. O'Connor had taken on the polio cause when his former law partner, Franklin D. Roosevelt, had asked him to manage the therapeutic spa at Warm Springs, Georgia, and he was always more interested in practical results than in the sometimes slow progress of science. By 1953, after a summer of 58,000 cases of polio in the United States, O'Connor was willing to devote millions of National Foundation dollars to producing and testing Salk's vaccine, even when his scientific advisory panels urged delays.

Between April and July 1954 more than 1.8 million schoolchildren participated in the national field trial of what became known as the Salk polio vaccine. Almost 450,000 children in the first, second, and third grades received vaccines. Another 150,000 received an inert placebo, and 1.2 million children served as observed controls, their health carefully recorded over the next summer to provide data on how their experience differed from those who had been vaccinated. Added to these young volunteers were some 20,000 doctors; 40,000 nurses; 14,000 school principals; 50,000 teachers; and 200,000 lay volunteers whose participation made the Salk vaccine field trial not only the largest ever held, but also the largest nonmilitary mobilization in American history.

The work of evaluating the vaccine took another nine months, in a special Vaccine Evaluation Center led by Thomas Francis, Jr., and staffed with statisticians and epidemiologists on loan from the U.S. Census Bureau and Public Health Service.

On 12 April 1955 Salk returned to Ann Arbor with his family for a large public meeting convened to announce the results. After Francis declared the Salk vaccine safe, effective, and potent, it was immediately licensed for commercial distribution by the Department of Health, Education, and Welfare. This was essentially the first government oversight of what had been a private medical experiment conducted and financed by the March of Dimes, which also spent $9 million to guarantee adequate vaccine supplies in the days just after the announcement. During a live television interview from Ann Arbor (a rarity in the early days of television), journalist Edward R. Murrow asked who owned the patent to the new vaccine. Salk answered, "Well, the people, I would say. There is no patent. Could you patent the sun?"

Salk was immediately swept up in an international flood of publicity, including a trip to the White House to be publicly thanked by President Dwight D. Eisenhower on behalf of all the parents and grandparents of the world. Within weeks, however, the vaccination program was marred by a manufacturing error that left live virus in some vaccine produced by Cutter Laboratories, causing 204 cases of vaccine-associated poliomyelitis, most of them paralytic, as well as eleven deaths. All vaccinations were halted until the problem was identified and corrected. Despite the resulting loss of confidence and momentum, vaccination programs for children resumed by late summer 1955, and by the following year enough vaccine was available for all age groups to get the full series of three shots. By 1960, the year before the introduction of the Sabin vaccine and long before all Americans were vaccinated, cases of paralytic poliomyelitis in the United States dropped from an average of 135 per million people to a rate of twenty-six per million.

Salk's global celebrity did not endear him to his scientific colleagues, many of whom dismissed the scientific work behind the killed-virus vaccine as "cookbook virology," or else cast doubts on the long-term effectiveness of any immunization that did not include natural infection. Although Salk received countless scientific, humanitarian, and academic awards over the next forty years, he was never elected to the National Academy of Sciences or awarded the Nobel Prize, two honors that were much discussed in the triumphant period after 1955.

Salk's chief scientific rival was Albert Sabin (1906–1993), whose polio research was also supported by the National Foundation. Sabin sought an oral vaccine made from weakened, or attenuated, strains of live virus. In the early 1950s he worked tirelessly to postpone and discredit the field trial of the Salk vaccine, although he later served on the committee that recommended licensing in 1955. After a 1959 field trial in the Soviet Union, Sabin's live-virus oral vaccine was introduced in the United States in 1961, amidst a vast publicity campaign that encouraged all people, including those who had received the Salk vaccine shots, to be revaccinated. Although both men insisted their rivalry was confined to differing convictions about immunology, few failed to notice how galling it was for each that Sabin's vaccine was the one most commonly used after 1960, while Salk's name was far more famous.

For the rest of his life, Salk campaigned to reinstate the killed-virus vaccine as the immunization of choice, working to refine the manufacturing process and arguing, with eventual success, that his vaccine was safer and just as effective. In January 2000 the Centers for Disease Control and Prevention recommended that use of the oral vaccine be phased out and that it be replaced with a version of Salk's killed-virus vaccine. Thanks to new standards of risk-assessment, even the relatively low number of cases of paralytic polio caused by the Sabin vaccine—approximately ten a year—had become unacceptable.

After the approval of his polio vaccine, Salk had expected to return to research, but he found his career interrupted by the demands of fame and the responsibilities of directing the Salk Institute for Biological Studies, a new research center in La Jolla, California, intended to bring together scientists and humanists to share ideas for the greater enhancement of humankind. Financed largely by the March of Dimes, which insisted on naming the center after its most famous grantee, the Salk Institute was founded in 1960 and formally opened in 1963, housed in an imposing group of concrete buildings designed by Louis Kahn on a magnificent site overlooking the Pacific Ocean.

The Salks moved to La Jolla in 1960 but were divorced in 1968. On 29 June 1970 Salk married Francoise Gilot, a painter most famous as the former mistress of the artist Pablo Picasso, with whom she already had two children.

After his second marriage, Salk turned to writing to explain his philosophical ideas. In *Man Unfolding* (1972) and *The Survival of the Wisest* (1973), Salk theorized that human history was at a turning point when rising population would end and a new kind of wisdom, based on cooperation, would become as essential to human survival as strength or intelligence had been in the past. He also felt that human development could be anticipated by a few exceptionally gifted people who were prepared, intellectually and psychologically, to seize the evolutionary moment and make unique contributions to the progress of humanity. He saw himself as one of these gifted seers and told interviewers, "There have to be people who are ahead of their time, and that is my fate."

Although Salk maintained a laboratory at the Salk Institute and conducted research in cancer and multiple sclerosis during the late 1960s and 1970s, he was not able to repeat his earlier triumph, and he retired from his laboratory in 1984. Despite a history of heart disease, he returned to virus research in 1987, when he cofounded the Immune Response Corporation to pursue a typically novel approach to managing AIDS. Rather than seeking a vaccine that would prevent the disease, Salk believed that treatment with inactivated HIV could enable those already infected to resist the secondary infections that were most often fatal. He died of heart disease at the age of eighty.

The near-global conquest of polio was a great medical triumph. But the success of Salk's vaccine was also a turning point in public acceptance of mass programs for medicine and other forms of public welfare, and even for the space program, whose backers often referred to the polio vaccine program as a model for their own massive enterprise. Equally significant, the Salk vaccine inaugurated an era of vaccine research against a host of childhood maladies and created the first generation of children, now parents and grandparents, who had little or no experience with epidemic disease. Salk said in 1995, "what had the most profound effect was the freedom from fear."

★

A wealth of material is available in the Jonas Salk Collection, University Library, University of California, San Diego; the Thomas Francis Collection, Bentley Historical Library, University of Michigan; and the March of Dimes archives. Valuable book-length sources include Richard Carter, *Breakthrough: The Saga of Jonas Salk* (1965); John Paul, *A History of Poliomyelitis* (1971); Jane S. Smith, *Patenting the Sun: Polio and the Salk Vaccine* (1990); and Nina Seavey, Jane S. Smith, and Paul Wagner, *A Paralyzing Fear: The Triumph over Polio in America* (1998). An obituary is in the *New York Times* (24 Jun. 1995).

JANE S. SMITH

SALVI, John C., III (*b.* 2 March 1972 in Salem, Massachusetts; *d.* 29 November 1996 in Walpole, Massachusetts), religious fanatic and aspiring hairdresser who murdered two women and wounded five other people in attacks on two abortion clinics in Brookline, Massachusetts. Considered mentally ill by his family and his attorneys, he was convicted of murder and sent to a maximum security prison where he took his own life.

Salvi was the only child of John C. Salvi, Jr., a dental technician, and Anne Marie Salvi, a choir director and piano teacher. He grew up in Ipswich, Massachusetts, where his family was active in the French Canadian parish of Saint Stanislaus Roman Catholic Church. Salvi attended parochial schools and served as an altar boy at Saint Stanislaus until he was thirteen years old, when his father moved the family to Naples, Florida, and Salvi switched to public high school.

While in Florida, Salvi began showing signs of emotional instability. By many accounts his family life was turbulent and fraught with arguments between the teenager and his parents. Far from typical family disagreements, these arguments were bitter and troubling, punctuated by several serious incidents. In 1991 Salvi was the prime arson

John Salvi in a Massachusetts courtoom, 1995. ASSOCIATED PRESS AP

suspect in a fire that destroyed a storage-space business owned by his father, but the senior Salvi refused to pursue the investigation of his son. Salvi's high school years were further marked by car accidents and at least two brushes with the law over suspicious fires. His father later conceded that even he considered the boy to be a troubled person.

After high school Salvi spent a short time at Edison Community College in Florida, then bounced from job to job, eventually drifting back to New England in 1992. He lived with relatives in Ipswich until finding an apartment of his own in Everett, Massachusetts. Later, Salvi moved to Hampton Beach, New Hampshire, where he found a condominium with low off-season rental rates. During his years in Hampton Beach, Salvi attended hairdressing school and worked part-time sweeping floors at a salon. His coworkers described him as quiet and extremely religious, refusing to work on Sundays and prone to quoting scripture.

When his parents visited him at Christmas in 1994, Salvi and his father fell into an argument revolving around the elder Salvi's disapproval of his son's decision to pursue a career as a hairdresser. Still angry at Christmas mass on 24 December, Salvi created a scene by stepping in front of the congregation at Saint Elizabeth's Church in Seabrook, Massachusetts, and ranting about the problems of the Catholic Church and its failures to see the true meaning of Christ.

Earlier in 1994 Salvi had purchased a .22-caliber rifle and ammunition from a gun shop in Salisbury, Massachusetts. On 30 December 1994, armed with this rifle, he opened fire in two Brookline abortion clinics, killing two women and wounding five other people. At the time the shooting was considered the worst attack on abortion providers in the nation's history. He struck first around 10:00 A.M. at the Planned Parenthood clinic on Beacon Street, killing the receptionist and wounding three other people. Ten minutes later he walked into the Preterm Health Services clinic two miles away on the same street, killing the receptionist there as well and wounding two other people. At the Preterm clinic, while trading gunfire with a security guard, Salvi dropped a black duffel bag in which police later found a receipt containing his name and address.

After the attacks Salvi returned briefly to his apartment in Hampton Beach, then headed south to Norfolk, Virginia, where he shot through the rear door of the Hillcrest abortion clinic. There police arrested him. He was arraigned at the Norfolk District Court on one felony count of shooting a weapon into an occupied building. While in jail in Virginia, Salvi rebuffed opportunities to confess to the Brookline abortion clinic slayings but repeatedly asked for newspapers and seemed obsessed with the publicity surrounding the shootings. The Virginia felony charge was eventually deferred so that he could be returned to Massachusetts, where he was charged with two counts of transporting a firearm across state lines with intent to commit a felony and unlawful flight from Massachusetts to avoid state prosecution in the Brookline clinic shootings. Finally, Salvi was charged with two counts of murder and five counts of armed assault with attempt to murder for the attacks at the Brookline abortion clinics.

Although he was not affiliated with any antiabortion organization, Salvi was known to have met with leaders of Massachusetts Citizens for Life, and he took part in at least one prayer vigil in front of the Planned Parenthood clinic in Brookline. He also had some contact with the Reverend Donald Spitz, head of the Pro-Life Virginia antiabortion group that rallied in support of Salvi outside the Norfolk jail in which he was held. While living in Everett, Salvi sometimes stood in front of the Immaculate Conception Roman Catholic Church and handed out antiabortion pamphlets and photographs of fetuses. The bumper of his pickup truck sported a picture of an aborted fetus and antiabortion slogans.

However, Salvi's attorneys turned attention away from abortion as the central issue and convinced him to answer the murder charges with a plea of not guilty by reason of insanity. During his first night in the Massachusetts jail, Salvi wrote a rambling, sometimes incoherent, statement that was immediately released to the press. In this statement he railed against the persecution of Catholics by the Freemasons and other groups and accused Norfolk City Jail officials of tampering with his food. "If convicted of the charges I am accused of I wish to receive the death penalty," he wrote. "If I am not proven guilty upon release I will become a catholic priest."

His attorneys attempted to have Salvi declared incompetent to stand trial, saying he was unable to help with his own defense and portraying him as schizophrenic, irrational, and possessed of a single-minded obsession to publicly make known his views on the persecution of Catholics. Dr. Phillip Resnick, a psychiatrist and professor at Case Western Reserve Medical School in Cleveland, and two other psychiatrists called by the defense testified that they believed Salvi was delusional and incompetent. In opposition, Joel Haycock, a psychiatrist from Bridgewater State Hospital, where Salvi was held during the trial, stated in court that the accused was manipulative and intelligent and was duping his defense team. On 24 August 1995 Salvi was found competent to stand trial by Norfolk Superior Court Judge Barbara Dortch-Okara.

Although Salvi displayed evidence of mental illness, the prosecution successfully demonstrated that he understood the criminality of his actions in Brookline, especially considering that he seemed to have carefully planned for the attacks, acquiring weapons and practicing with them at a local firing range. He also fled the scene of the crime, an act that experts testified is rarely done by psychotic murderers. On 18 March 1996 Salvi was convicted of first-degree murder and sentenced to two consecutive life terms in prison without the possibility of parole. He was first imprisoned at the Massachusetts Correctional Institution at Concord, then later moved to the state's maximum security prison in Walpole.

Salvi's uncle, Gerard Trudel, with whom Salvi had once lived, visited with Salvi on Thanksgiving Day, 28 November 1996, and found him to be unkempt, distant, and confused. Salvi's family had pleaded to have him placed in a hospital instead of prison and feared for his well-being. However, he was not considered mentally ill by Walpole prison officials and received no mental health treatment there. Early on 29 November, the morning following his uncle's visit, Salvi was found dead under his bed, his hands and feet tied with shoelaces and a plastic bag over his head, tied at the neck. His death was declared a suicide.

Salvi's suicide prompted several Massachusetts lawmakers, including State Representative Kay Khan, a Democrat from Newton, to introduce legislation that would increase funding for mental health services for inmates. In addition, State Senator James P. Jajuga, a Democrat from Methuen, filed legislation that he had been pushing for years to allow defendants the option of pleading "guilty but insane" to crimes they are charged with.

Psychiatrists for both the prosecution and defense agreed that Salvi was mentally ill. However, juries are often loath to turn in a verdict of not guilty by reason of insanity in murder cases because defendants can eventually be released if they are considered cured of mental illness. Legislation for the "guilty but insane" verdict would call for sentencing that includes original placement in a mental health facility, then transfer to prison if the patient is cured of mental illness.

Salvi came into the public eye as a symbol of the violence surrounding abortion and its foes. By the end of his trial and his life, he brought to the fore the forgotten issue of mentally ill criminals and the treatment many feel they need but do not receive.

★

Numerous articles from the *Boston Globe* (30 Dec. 1994–1 Dec. 1996) cover the crimes, the trial, and Salvi's death from beginning to end. The PBS documentary "Frontline: Murder on 'Abortion Row'" (6 Feb. 1996) includes transcripts of Salvi's psychiatric interview with Dr. Resnick and the competency hearing, along with information about the trial and the insanity defense.

NAN POLLOT

SARTON, May (*b.* 3 May 1912 in Wondelgem, Belgium; *d.* 16 July 1995 in York, Maine), poet, novelist, and memoirist whose journals depicting the rewards and sorrows of living alone won her an enthusiastic following.

Sarton was the only child of Belgian-born George Sarton, a distinguished historian of science and founder of the journal *Isis,* and an English mother, Mabel Elwes, a designer of textiles and furniture. After fleeing the German invasion of Belgium in 1914, the Sartons finally settled in Cambridge, Massachusetts, where George taught part-time at Harvard University while also receiving financial support for his private scholarship from the Carnegie Institution. May Sarton attended the progressive Shady Hill Elementary School and the Cambridge High and Latin School. Poetry and the theater were her passions. During the summers she attended the Gloucester School of the Little Theatre and, managing to meet Eva Le Gallienne backstage in Boston, so impressed the great actress that she invited the seventeen-year-old Sarton to join an apprentice group connected to her Civic Repertory Theatre in New York. By 1932 Sarton was managing the apprentices, an effort that failed in 1935, defeated both by the Great Depression and Sarton's keener interest in writing poetry.

During these New York theater years, Sarton fell in love with Grace Daly, the first of many lesbian lovers who were crucial to her poetic creation, because for Sarton the loved one served as muse. Her love for Daly, as well as for her adored mentor, the Belgian poet Jean Dominique, inspired *Encounter in April,* published in 1937. Visiting England shortly after the appearance of this first collection, Sarton made friends with the novelist Elizabeth Bowen, the biologist Julian Huxley and his wife Juliette, and S. S. Koteliansky, a reader for Cresset Press in London, which (as did Houghton Mifflin in America) published Sarton's first novel, *The Single Hound* (1938), and her second book of poems, *Inner Landscape* (1939). Reviews were mixed in England and few in America.

Back home, her beloved Europe torn by World War II, Sarton lectured at colleges across the United States, promoting her own work and writing the poems that were eventually published in *The Lion and the Rose* (1948). Back in Cambridge, however, money was a constant problem; she was still dependent on her father and was living at home. Through the influence of the poet Muriel Rukeyser, Sarton got a job with the Office of War Information in New York City, but by 1944, dissatisfied, she returned to Cambridge to finish her novel *The Bridge of Years* (1946), an homage to family friends in Belgium with whom she had lived during a year of study abroad, when she was twelve.

Meanwhile, Sarton met Judith ("Judy") Matlack, a teacher and the only woman with whom the volatile writer would ever establish a home; they shared a small house at 14 Wright Street in Cambridge. Her love for Matlack, however, did not prevent Sarton from leaving for frequent trips to Europe and engaging in even more frequent love affairs during their twelve-year union. Her novel *Shadow of a Man* (1950), for example, explores in the guise of a male protag-

May Sarton. CORBIS CORPORATION (BELLEVUE)

onist her passion for Juliette Huxley; *A Shower of Summer Days* (1952) her relationship with Elizabeth Bowen; *The Land of Silence* (1953) an affair in Belgium with Eugénie Du Bois. This latter collection of poems was blasted by John Ciardi in a review in the *Nation* that devastated Sarton.

Mabel Sarton died in 1950. With new seriousness Sarton undertook *Faithful Are the Wounds* (1955), a novel about the intellectual liberal as a scapegoat (based on the actual suicide of a Harvard professor) that was nominated for a National Book Award. George Sarton died in 1956, leaving his daughter the family home at Channing Place and a modest inheritance that meant Sarton was no longer forced to supplement her writing income with lecture tours and part-time teaching.

Shortly after the publication of *Faithful Are the Wounds*, Sarton began a liaison with Cora DuBois, a Harvard professor of anthropology, that ended her union with Matlack. In 1958 Sarton sold her parents' home in Cambridge and bought and moved into a house in the village of Nelson, New Hampshire, hoping to be alone with DuBois; the affair, however, ended in mutual recrimination. From 1960 to 1968, commuting back to Massachusetts, Sarton taught for one-year appointments at Wellesley College, an experience recreated in the novel *The Small Room* (1961). Her next novel, published in 1965, proved far more important to her career. *Mrs. Stevens Hears the Mermaids Singing*, Sarton's coming-out novel about a bisexual writer who cele-

brates her androgynous creativity, brought her a new readership, establishing her as a literary voice in the growing feminist, gay, and civil rights movements.

But the town of Nelson proved perhaps her best inspiration. In *Plant Dreaming Deep* (1968), an idealized version of her everyday existence, Sarton described the spiritual riches of living alone in an isolated village. The journal won her a legion of fans that multiplied with the publication of the franker *Journal of a Solitude* in 1973. Nelson was also the setting for the novel *Kinds of Love* (1970), though a series of love affairs as well as the turmoil of the 1960s inspired the poems of *A Grain of Mustard Seed* (1971) and *A Durable Fire* (1972). Her increasingly chaotic private life finally drove Sarton to seek the help of a psychiatrist, Marynia Farnham. But she fell in love with Farnham, and the relationship ended so disastrously that Sarton fled Nelson in 1973 to Wild Knoll, a rented house near the sea in York, Maine.

During the 1970s and 1980s, Sarton's popularity as a performer of her own poetry grew; standing ovations became the norm. Meanwhile, in response to her journals, fan mail poured in. Complaining of the burden, she nevertheless drove eagerly to the post office to collect her mail and answered every letter. Sarton continued to write poetry to new muses—*Halfway to Silence* (1980), *Letters from Maine* (1984), *The Silence Now* (1988)—and novels, among them *As We Are Now* (1973), *Crucial Conversations* (1975), *A Reckoning* (1978), *The Magnificent Spinster* (1985), and

The Education of Harriet Hatfield (1989). But in these later years she won her broadest and most enthusiastic audience through her journals: *The House by the Sea* (1977), *Recovering* (1980), *At Seventy* (1984), *After the Stroke* (1988), *Endgame* (1992), *Encore* (1993), and *At Eighty-two* (1996). Sarton died at home in York of metastasized breast cancer on 16 July 1995; she is buried in Nelson Cemetery.

Besides short stories, magazine articles, and children's books; May Sarton wrote fifteen books of poetry, nineteen novels, two memoirs, and nine journals. Love was often her theme—"to be in love is to be alive," she said—yet solitude, loneliness, frustration, the quest for identity, and the struggle to achieve spiritual balance are equally important subjects. She persistently refused to identify herself as a "lesbian writer," correctly arguing that her work had universal appeal. Sarton is an important writer because her best work had, and has, the power to change lives.

★

Norton published Sarton's *Collected Poems: 1930–1993* in 1993 and continues to keep her work in print. Her writing has been collected in *Selected Poems of May Sarton* (1978), *Writings on Writing* (1980), *Sarton Selected: An Anthology of the Journals, Novels, and Poems of May Sarton* (1991), and *May Sarton: Among the Usual Days* (1993). Susan Sherman, ed., *May Sarton: Selected Letters, 1916–1954* (1997) is the first volume of a projected multivolume set of Sarton's collected letters. Sarton wrote two memoirs, *I Knew a Phoenix* (1959) and *A World of Light* (1976). Margot Peters wrote the authorized *May Sarton: A Biography* (1997). Obituaries are in the *Boston Globe* and *New York Times* (both 18 July 1995). Sarton talks about her life and work in *World of Light: Portrait of May Sarton* (1980), a documentary film produced and directed by Marita Simpson and Martha Wheelock.

MARGOT PETERS

SAVALAS, Aristoteles ("Telly") (*b.* 21 January 1923 in Garden City, New York; *d.* 22 January 1994 in Universal City, California), actor best known for the title character in the television series *Kojak* (1973–1978), which earned him an Emmy Award in 1974.

Savalas was the second of five children born to the Greek immigrants Nicholas Savalas, a businessman and restaurant owner who lost his wealth in the stock market crash of 1929, and Christina Kapsallis, a noted painter whose work was exhibited around the world. The family was proud of their Greek heritage and imbued the sons with a strong sense of tradition and family loyalty. The Savalas family relied on each other in good times and bad. The young Savalas learned to be resourceful and creative, honing his acting skills at a young age in an effort to help his family. One family legend contends that the young boy learned to convince angry bill collectors that his parents

Telly Savalas, 1988. THE KOBAL COLLECTION

were not home. Another anecdote claims that Savalas got a job as a bus driver when he was only twelve years old. He posed as a twenty-year-old at bus driver school but was eventually betrayed by his squeaky voice.

Savalas served in World War II for three years and was trained to be a medic, although he never left the country due to injuries from a car accident. After he was discharged in 1944 he enrolled at Columbia University, where he took classes in psychology. Although he was fascinated by the role of psychology in human behavior, it did not translate into an inspired academic career, and he never graduated. In 1950 he married Katharine Nicolaides; they had one child. In 1955 Savalas took a position with the U.S. Information Service producing and hosting the radio series *Your Voice of America*. Part of his job involved interviewing celebrities, providing his first interaction with professional actors. He also discovered a penchant for performance. Savalas then became involved in local theater, first producing and then directing at the Stamford Playhouse in suburban Connecticut. Success was not immediate, however, and Savalas and his young family struggled to make ends meet. He and his first wife divorced, and in 1960 Savalas married Marilyn Gardner. They had two children.

Savalas's transition into acting occurred when he auditioned for the part of a Greek judge in a television show in 1958. Pretending he was an immigrant with broken English, he won the part. His first film role was in *The Young Savages* (1961), directed by John Frankenheimer and starring Burt Lancaster. Savalas's gritty portrayal of a detective in Harlem impressed Lancaster, who insisted the relative newcomer be cast in his next project, *The Birdman of Alcatraz* (1962). In that film Savalas played a sadistic convict so chillingly that he earned an Academy Award nomination for best supporting actor in 1962. Savalas broke the mold in many ways. He was not classically handsome, he was untrained, and he did not even break into acting until he was in his mid-thirties. But his charisma was powerful. While he did not win the Academy Award, his film career thrived. For a decade he averaged three films a year, totaling thirty-two credits between 1961 and 1973. He continued to impress audiences and critics alike. Some of his principal appearances were in *Cape Fear* (1961), *Genghis Khan* (1965), *Battle of the Bulge* (1965), *Beau Geste* (1966), *The Dirty Dozen* (1967), *The Scalphunters* (1968), and *Kelly's Heroes* (1970). He shaved his head for his role as Pontius Pilate in *The Greatest Story Ever Told* (1964). Savalas's shiny bald head became his signature, lending even more visual intrigue to the burly man with the prominent nose and protruding ears.

While Savalas's film career was notable, his television portrayal of Theo Kojak, the hard-boiled cop with heart, earned him his greatest recognition and fame. When he was approached about playing Kojak, a tough New York City cop, Savalas initially balked, fearing he would get bored playing one role. But the show's producer Abby Mann was convinced that Savalas was the man for the job. "He's exciting, enormously talented, one of the most sensitive performers around. He has brute power, which he releases with no seeming effort. Yet gentleness and compassion underscore his style. And Telly's perfect for TV—he needs no preparation," Mann commented in *TV Guide*. Savalas agreed to do the CBS pilot for *Kojak*, "The Marcus-Nelson Murders" (1973), based on two real-life murders in New York City. He then played the title role in the series from 1973 to 1978 and won an Emmy Award for best actor in 1974. That same year he and Gardner divorced. Around this time he and the actress Sally Adams had a son together.

Savalas lent many personal touches to Kojak's character. Kojak was a proud Greek, and in keeping with Savalas's family loyalty, his brother George Savalas played Detective Stavros. In addition to his signature bald head, crowned by a black hat when shaking down criminals on the streets, Kojak demonstrated a weakness for lollipops and used the lyrical catch phrase "who loves ya, baby?" while solving tough crimes. Savalas described the Kojak character as "tough but with feelings . . . the kind of guy who might kick a hooker in the tail if he had to, but they'd understand each other, because maybe they grew up on the same kind of block."

After *Kojak* completed its run in 1978, Savalas embarked on an ill-fated singing career and continued to act in film and on television. In 1984 he married Julie Howland, with whom he had two children. He briefly reprised the Kojak character in 1984, and he did his final television and film work in 1987. About that time he experienced symptoms of prostate (bladder by some accounts) cancer, and he spent the last few years of his life quietly, mostly surrounded by his family. He died in his suite at the Sheraton-Universal Hotel in Universal City, California, one day after his seventy-first birthday. He is buried in Hollywood Hills, California.

The lessons Savalas learned from his family, through the Great Depression, and on the streets of New York City bred a particular sensitivity that informed his acting. He once said, "Even with the crazies I've played, I've always tried to give some dimension to their insanity."

★

Numerous sources have articles and entries on Savalas, including *International Motion Picture Almanac* (1992), *Who's Who in Entertainment* (1992), David Ragan, *Who's Who in Hollywood* (1992), and *Contemporary Theatre, Film, and Television* (1994). Informative interviews with Savalas are in the *New York Times* (7 Oct. 1973), *TV Guide* (20 Oct. 1973), *Playgirl* (June 1974), and *People* (1 July 1974). An obituary is in the *New York Times* (23 Jan. 1994).

LIANN E. TSOUKAS

SAVIO, Mario (*b.* 8 December 1942 in New York City; *d.* 6 November 1996 in Sebastopol, California), student activist who rose to national prominence in 1964 as the leader of the Free Speech Movement at the University of California at Berkeley, which became regarded as the precursor and model for student activism of the 1960s.

The son of an Italian immigrant machine-punch operator, Savio was raised in the borough of Queens in New York City. An outstanding student, he was a finalist in the Westinghouse Science Talent Search Scholarship competition and graduated first in his class of 1,200 students at Martin Van Buren High School. He won a scholarship to Manhattan College and briefly attended Queens College before transferring to the University of California at Berkeley as a philosophy major in 1963. Savio joined the civil rights movement and volunteered for the Freedom Summer Project, organized by a national coalition of civil rights groups in Mississippi during the summer of 1964. He was deeply influenced by the moral courage of poor black sharecroppers who confronted intimidation and abuse while attempting to register to vote.

Upon returning to Berkeley in the fall of 1964, Savio became the leader of the campus chapter of the Friends of

Mario Savio during a Berkeley protest, 1964. ARCHIVE PHOTOS

the Student Non-Violent Coordinating Committee (SNCC) and, along with other civil rights and student activists, embarked on a collision course with restrictive new regulations imposed by Berkeley's chancellor Clark Kerr that barred political activity and solicitation on the university's campus. The Free Speech Movement (FSM) was a broad coalition of civil rights, Marxist, and even conservative groups, including Students for Goldwater (Barry Goldwater was the Republican presidential candidate that year), united by an insistence on free political expression on campus. Hampered in his private life by a stammer, Savio was a brilliant orator when speaking before a crowd, using logic, philosophical argument, and moral passion to sway his audience.

The FSM movement culminated in a massive rally on the steps of Sproul Hall, the university administration building, on 2 December 1964. In largely extemporaneous remarks, Savio addressed 5,000 students on the necessity of civil disobedience to protest the university's ban on political expression. His attack on the impersonalization of mass society in general, and mass education in particular, became an instant, almost folkloric expression of the youthful alienation and rebellion of the 1960s. Savio proclaimed:

"There is a time when the operation of the machine becomes so odious, makes you so sick at heart, that you can't take part; you can't even tacitly take part, and you've got to put your bodies upon the gears and upon the wheels, upon the levers, upon all the apparatus and you've got to make it stop. And you've got to indicate to the people who run it, to the people who own it, that unless you're free, the machine will be prevented from working at all." In the largest mass arrest in California history, nearly 800 student sit-in demonstrators were taken into custody by police, triggering campus-wide indignation. Six days later, on 8 December 1964, a previously complacent Berkeley faculty voted 824 to 115 to reverse the administration's policy and restore free political expression to campus life. However, student leaders still faced suspensions and criminal trials for their civil disobedience. Savio himself was suspended from the university and served four months in jail.

Savio received considerable media attention, including profiles in the *New York Times* and *Life* magazine, but he was uncomfortable with the notoriety and celebrity he had achieved. He resigned from the FSM, left Berkeley with his wife Suzanne Goldberg, also an FSM leader, and moved to Great Britain to study, retreating from the limelight and assuming only peripheral involvement in the antiwar movement of the late 1960s and early 1970s. Later, he returned to the Berkeley area and held a series of odd jobs as a bartender and bookstore clerk. His continuing political activism included running as a Peace and Freedom Party candidate for the California state senate in 1969 and helping to found Barry Commoner's Citizen Party in 1980. After his marriage to Goldberg ended in divorce, he married Lynne Hollander, also an FSM veteran, in 1980 and returned to college, graduating from San Francisco State University (SFSU) in 1984 with a bachelor's degree in physics and Phi Beta Kappa and summa cum laude honors. He taught at private schools in the San Francisco area until earning a master's degree in physics in 1989 at SFSU, after which he began teaching physics at Sonoma State University in Rohnert Park, California. He also taught courses in philosophy and logic and a seminar on science and poetry. In his later years, Savio opposed anti–affirmative action and anti-immigrant measures on the California ballot, and worked with students to oppose a California state university tuition increase. He experienced heart failure while moving furniture at home and slipped into a coma before dying a month before his fifty-fourth birthday. He had three sons: Nadav, Daniel, and Stefan.

Savio's life and personality were emblematic of the social ferment of the 1960s, and he has been hailed by many activist veterans as a source of inspiration in their lives. Over the years the Berkeley administration reconciled itself to the legacy of Savio and the FSM. In 1998 the university accepted a $3.5 million alumni gift to the library to create a Mario Savio Book Fund and an FSM cybercafe, as well as digitizing the FSM archives.

★

Savio's views on student activism can be found in a profile in the *New York Times* (9 Dec. 1964); A. H. Raskin's report in the *New York Times Magazine* (14 Feb. 1965); J. Fincher's *Life* magazine interview (16 Feb. 1965); and Savio's introduction to Hal Draper's *Berkeley: The New Student Revolt* (1965). A more reflective view can be found in Savio's graduation address at the Sidwell Friends School in Washington, D.C. (1988), available at the Free Speech Movement web page, which also provides the full text of Savio's key speeches and articles, a bibliography of his speeches, writings, and interviews, and tributes to Savio. Obituaries are in the *San Francisco Chronicle* (7 Nov. 1996) and *New York Times* and *Washington Post* (both 8 Nov. 1996).

JERRY BORNSTEIN

SCALI, John Alfred (*b.* 27 April 1918 in Canton, Ohio; *d.* 9 October 1995 in Washington, D.C.), journalist, consultant on foreign affairs information policy to President Richard M. Nixon, and U.S. ambassador to the United Nations best known for his role in the Cuban missile crisis.

Scali was the first of the four children of the Italian immigrants Paul M. Scali, who operated two bowling alleys, and Lucy Leone. Scali played basketball and tennis at Can-

John Scali, 1974. AP/WIDE WORLD PHOTOS

ton's McKinley High School, graduating in 1937. He remained in Canton, working and attending Kent State University for two years after his family moved to the Boston area. Following his family to Massachusetts, Scali majored in journalism at Boston University and worked on the student newspaper, serving as editor in chief during his senior year. After earning a bachelor's degree in 1942, he briefly reported for the *Boston Herald* before accepting a position with the Boston bureau of United Press. When he failed to secure an assignment as a war correspondent, Scali, whose poor vision precluded military service, joined Associated Press (AP), which assigned him to cover the war in Europe. Before the end of the conflict he was transferred to AP's Washington bureau. On 30 August 1945 he married Helen Lauinger Glock. The couple had three daughters.

As a correspondent covering the State Department, Scali frequently accompanied officials overseas. In 1959 he positioned himself between the Soviet premier Nikita Khrushchev and Vice President Richard Nixon during the "kitchen debate" in Moscow. After seventeen years with AP, Scali accepted a position as diplomatic correspondent for ABC Television in 1961. On 26 October of the following year, during the Cuban missile crisis, Alexsandr S. Fomin, a senior Soviet intelligence agent, told Scali that his country was prepared to remove its missiles from Cuba and supply no other offensive weapons in exchange for an American pledge not to invade the island nation. The ABC correspondent relayed Fomin's proposal to Secretary of State Dean Rusk. The arrival of a letter from Khrushchev with a similar proposal hours later seemed to confirm the validity of the Fomin-Scali conduit between Moscow and Washington and offered the first hope for a peaceful solution to the crisis. That hope dimmed the next day with the arrival of a second letter demanding removal of U.S. intermediate-range missiles from Turkey. Rusk asked Scali to contact Fomin to discover why Khrushchev had changed his original proposal. At the meeting the newsman accused Fomin of a "double cross" and suggested that an American invasion of Cuba was imminent.

Until the late 1980s it was believed that Scali's scathing tone prompted the Soviets to strike a bargain based on Fomin's initial proposal. Information from Russian sources has revealed that Fomin acted without authorization from the Kremlin and suggests that other channels of communication were more important in resolving the crisis. American officials at the time, however, believed that Fomin spoke for Khrushchev and gave serious consideration to his exchange with Scali. Ironically, Scali agreed not to report what would have been the biggest story of his career so the Kennedy administration might make future use of his connection to Fomin. After the assassination of President John F. Kennedy, other reporters revealed Scali's role in the crisis.

As combat in Vietnam escalated, ABC asked Scali to anchor a weekly series, *ABC Scope: The Vietnam War*. The program examined the conflict in greater depth than was possible on evening newscasts. Scali continued to cover the State Department, and his question concerning a claim that the 1968 Tet offensive constituted a major Vietcong defeat prompted Secretary of State Rusk to demand, "Whose side are you on, anyway?" Scali recalled that Rusk later apologized, but the ABC correspondent, like many Americans, was coming to believe that the nation should extricate itself from Vietnam.

Scali, a registered Democrat who had not voted for Nixon and who had publicly denounced Vice President Spiro Agnew's diatribes against the press, surprised his colleagues in 1971 by accepting the president's invitation to join the administration as a special media consultant. Concerning Nixon's Vietnam policy Scali said, "I believe he is headed in the right direction—namely out." *Time* magazine concluded, "Even if Scali can't solve Nixon's image problem, he should be able to relieve [Henry] Kissinger of the burden of being the only swinger in the White House" (19 April 1971). Scali's "freewheeling lifestyle" and acerbic personality alienated some administration officials, including Nixon's chief architect of foreign policy, Henry Kissinger. Nonetheless, during his tenure Scali accompanied Nixon on most of his foreign travels, arranged television coverage of the trip to China, and helped orchestrate press coverage for state visits of foreign leaders.

In 1973 Scali's first marriage ended in divorce, and on 4 March he married Denise St. Germaine. Less than two weeks earlier, on 20 February 1973, he had replaced George Bush as the U.S. ambassador to the United Nations. Despite criticism that the appointment of a journalist reflected a downgrading of the UN position, Scali did "a far better job than most people who knew him expected him to do," John Osborne commented in an article in the *New Republic* (24 May 1975). During his tenure as ambassador Scali cast or threatened vetoes in the Security Council to block action the United States opposed, walked a diplomatic tightrope during the Yom Kippur War of 1973, and on 6 December 1974 delivered a scathing address in which he criticized the "tyranny of the majority," warning third-world nations recently admitted to the UN that their irresponsible behavior threatened the organization's stability.

In 1975 Daniel Patrick Moynihan replaced Scali at the UN, and Scali returned to ABC News as senior correspondent, a position he held until his retirement in 1993. Scali, who had undergone triple bypass surgery in 1973, died of a heart ailment two years after his retirement. He is buried at Arlington National Cemetery.

Although Scali could not restore Nixon's credibility, he did bring the same dedication to his government positions that characterized his career as a newsman. Before accepting Nixon's invitation to join the administration, Scali told the president, "If I deal with my news colleagues, I must be able to speak truthfully." Despite administration stonewalling of the press over the Watergate scandal, Scali maintained his reputation and integrity. Osborne called him "a first-rate journalist, . . . better versed in foreign affairs than most political appointees." Even Kissinger said, "John Scali has been one of our more effective UN ambassadors." Although Scali was reluctant to lie even for his country, his willingness to give up the story of a lifetime during the Cuban missile crisis left no doubt that he placed national interests above scooping the opposition. No doubt ever existed about the answer to Rusk's question. Scali was on America's side.

★

The best source on Scali is a sketch in *Current Biography* (1973). After his death an obituary in *Current Biography Yearbook* (1996) recapitulated and updated the earlier piece. Bill Monroe, "Rusk to John Scali: 'Whose Side Are You On?'" *Washington Journalism Review* (Jan.–Feb. 1991), gives both sides of the Rusk-Scali confrontation. Soviet accounts of the Cuban missile crisis that became available after glasnost challenge interpretations of Scali's role based solely on American sources. Raymond L. Garthoff, "Cuban Missile Crisis: The Soviet Story," *Foreign Policy* 72 (1988): 61–80, surveys older interpretations and the Soviet view. Articles on Scali's government service that sketch his background and qualifications include "Recruiting the Opposition," *Time* (19 Apr. 1971); "Nixon's New Voice," *Newsweek* (19 Apr. 1971); "Nixon's U.N. Nominee," *New York Times* (19 Dec. 1972); and "Moynihan Is Selected to Replace Scali," *New York Times* (21 Apr. 1975). John Osborne, "Moynihan and Scali," *New Republic* (24 May 1975), briefly evaluates Scali's UN career. Obituaries are in the *New York Times* and *Washington Post* (both 10 Oct. 1995).

BRAD AGNEW

SCARRY, Richard McClure (*b.* 5 June 1919 in Boston, Massachusetts; *d.* 30 April 1994 in Gstaad, Switzerland), author and illustrator of more than 250 children's books, which have sold more than 100 million copies in thirty languages.

Scarry was one of five children born into the comfortable Boston home of John James Scarry, who successfully operated a small chain of department stores, and Barbara McClure, a homemaker. John Scarry taught his children the value of keeping regular hours and working hard. The lesson initially appeared lost on Richard, who seemed to lack direction and self-discipline. The Green Meadow stories and nature lore of Thornton Burgess made a deep impression on his imaginative landscape, along with Harrison Cady's illustrations of Buster Bear, Bobby the Raccoon, Little Joe Otter, Danny the Meadow Mouse, and all the inhabitants of Paddy the Beaver's Pond. Richard was particularly fond of explanatory stories found in the Mother West Wind "How," "Why," and "Where" series.

Scarry's curiosity did not extend to the classroom. He was an unenthusiastic student and took five years to finish high school, graduating in 1938. At his father's urging he enrolled in the Boston Business School, but the art of making money didn't engage him. Instead, he studied drawing and painting from 1938 to 1941 at the Boston Museum School of Fine Arts. He was attracted to the unorthodox art of Alexander Archipenko and practiced drawing "dinner-table art for the tired businessman" at Archipenko's art school in Woodstock, New York. At Eliot O'Hara's Watercolor School in Gooserocks Beach, Maine, Scarry painted clouds and crowds and remembered "fourteen lessons in making the brush behave."

Scarry's acute myopia didn't stop the U.S. Army from drafting him in World War II. He trained as a radio repairman but served throughout the war as art director in the Morale Services Section, based in North Africa, Italy, and France, and he rose to the rank of captain. Meanwhile, his military work making maps and graphic designs sharpened his skills as an illustrator. After separating from the service in 1946 he moved to New York City to become a freelance commercial artist. Golden Press put him to work illustrating Joan Hubbard's children's book *The Boss of the Barnyard*. The assignments that followed, in which he illustrated the works of other authors, were not altogether to Scarry's liking. He found it repetitive, "dull, cut and dried, and without lightness."

One assignment Scarry did find to his liking was working with Patricia ("Patsy") Murphy, a children's-book author from Vancouver, British Columbia. She could write but couldn't illustrate. He could illustrate but found writing laborious. They married two weeks after first meeting on 7 September 1949, when Scarry proposed in a telegram. "Must move grand piano," it read. "Heavy. Come immediately." The couple disdained urban living and settled on a farm in Ridgefield, Connecticut, where they collaborated on children's books and on starting a family. Their only son, Richard McClure Scarry, was born in 1953 and was nicknamed "Huck" by his father because of his resemblance to Mark Twain's adolescent hero. Like his father, he would become an author of children's books.

Scarry's career as both author and illustrator began in 1951, the year that Golden Press published *The Great Big Car and Truck Book*. What would become his delightful cast of animal characters plays only a supporting role in this tome to suburban sprawl. A tabby cat proudly escorts her kittens across an intersection while a smiling police officer holds up traffic. In another scene, a spotted dog reaches over from the backseat of a convertible as a smartly dressed housewife extends a treat. The same attention to detail that would later enthrall a generation of preschoolers

can first be seen in these pages. A "hi-test" fill-up at the Blue Star service station involves a cleaned windshield, a tire-pressure check, and a friendly wave from a tanker-truck driver. Scarry's busy workmen are a testament to America's can-do postwar positivism. A telephone company crew strings poles newly pounded into place. A coal-truck team happily makes its rounds. A postman collects six-cent airmail, and the driver for Daisy's Flower Shop hurries off to a delivery. Kids and cars and men in uniform abound.

Scarry wrote and drew in relative obscurity for a dozen years. His most popular work during the decade was the *Tinker and Tanker* series that took a rabbit and a hippopotamus out West, through Africa, up in space, and to a construction site. The Scarrys moved in the 1960s to suburban Westport, Connecticut, where Scarry, in his third-floor studio, worked with daily diligence on his ideas for a benign animal kingdom. The breakthrough came in *Richard Scarry's Best Word Book Ever* (1963), a four-million-seller that depicted 1,400 objects of everyday life arranged in thematic groupings. Humanized animals ride tricycles, build with blocks, race with scooters, construct sand castles, rock horses, drink tea, run to catch electric trains, and fight with toy soldiers. On other pages, twenty-eight recurring animal characters play instruments in an orchestra, kindly compete in games, bake cakes, go to doctors, safely navigate through busy city streets, and say goodnight.

Busy, Busy World (1965) and *What Do People Do All Day?* (1968) became best-sellers and Scarry's personal favorites. The first finds his cast of characters embroiled in thirty-three international adventures, laced with gentle slapstick humor in which "only dignity suffers." The other finds Huckle Cat, Lowly Worm, Farmer Goat, Sergeant Murphy, and Mayor Fox framing houses, piping water, digging coal, grading roads, and baking bread. Together these intensely active texts depict a crowded and comical world celebrating Scarry's ideal of self-worth achieved through the world of work. His creature kingdom helps to make the moral universal in application. "Children can identify more closely with pictures of animals than they can with pictures of another child," he told *Publishers Weekly* in 1969. They had no difficulty imagining "an anteater who is a painter and a goat who is an Indian."

In the late 1960s the Scarrys moved to Gstaad so that Scarry could be near his beloved ski slopes. Each morning at eight he would arrive at his studio in Lausanne and there continue the eagerly awaited adventures of Hilda the Hippo, the accident-prone Mr. Frumble, Bananas Gorilla, the endlessly patient bear-teacher Miss Honey, and the plaid-Tyrolean-cap-wearing Lowly Worm. *The Great Pie Robbery* (1969), *ABC Word Book* (1971), *Richard Scarry's Best Stories Ever* (1971), *Silly Stories* (1973), and *Richard Scarry's Please and Thank You Book* (1973) cemented his worldwide readership and reputation. *Richard Scarry's*

Great Steamboat Mystery received the Edgar Allan Poe Award for best mystery book of 1975.

By the mid-1970s and 1980s, Scarry was a millionaire, and his busy creatures had become a burgeoning multimedia industry, adapted for records, computer software, and television. Feminists decried Scarryland's socialization of active boys and passive girls. The author admitted "I like mothers to wear aprons" and promised "when father washes dishes he wears an apron too." Later tales took Ms. Mouse out of the kitchen and made her a painter, plumber, mechanic, and firefighter. Her friend Flossie joined the police force. Concessions were made to environmentalists as well. In *Richard Scarry's Great Big Air Book* (1971), Father Cat's fine suit is spoiled by air pollution he has had a "hand" in making.

Scarry took his opportunities to educate seriously. "It's a precious thing to be communicating to children," he believed, "helping them discover the gift of language and thought." In nearly a half-century of writing and illustrating for children he had won a vast audience by never "talking above them or beneath them." Young readers wanted to learn about their world and how it worked, just as he had as a dreaming adolescent. He had found that "you have to speak to them within the framework of their learning and experience" in a language that they could understand.

Critics of bourgeois culture complained that Scarry socialized kids into thinking that only production brought personal satisfaction. Scarry's purpose, however, was to demystify a world that could appear both capricious and enigmatic to young eyes. He treated his devoted readers with respect and infinite care. Those readers paid Scarry the highest compliment. At the time of his death from a heart attack, eight of the fifty best-selling children's books of all time were books by Richard Scarry.

★

The Kerlan Collection at the University of Minnesota has primary materials from the life and career of Richard Scarry. Ole Risom and Walter Retan have written an appreciation of the author's life, *The Busy, Busy World of Richard Scarry* (1997). An affectionate treatment of his contribution to children's literature is Julie Berg, *Richard Scarry/Richard Scarry* (1994). Bobbie Burch Lemontt has put the author's work in critical perspective in "Richard Scarry," an article in Glenn E. Estes, ed., *American Writers for Children Since 1960: Poets, Illustrators, and Nonfiction Authors,* vol. 61, *Dictionary of Literary Biography* (1987). Rob Wilder offers context in "Richard Scarry: The Wizard of Busytown," *Parents'* magazine (Aug. 1980). Scarry's analysis of his own work appears in Justin Wintle and Emma Fisher, *The Pied Pipers: Interviews with the Influential Creators of Children's Literature* (1974). An article capturing the illustrator in his workplace is Arthur Bell, "Richard Scarry's Best Switzerland Ever," *Publishers Weekly* (20 Oct. 1969). An obituary is in the *New York Times* (3 May 1994).

BRUCE J. EVENSEN

SCHAPIRO, Meyer (*b.* 23 September 1904 in Šiauliai, Lithuania; *d.* 3 March 1996 in New York City), American art historian who transformed studies of medieval and modern art and studies of the social and moral situation of the artist in the world.

Schapiro, one of the two surviving sons of Nathan Menachem Schapiro and Fanny Adelman, immigrated with his family to the United States in 1907. Nathan Schapiro had arrived in the United States the previous year; as a Hebrew teacher he saved enough money to send for his family, and he subsequently became a jobber in the paper-and-twine business. Schapiro and his brother, Morris, grew up in Brooklyn, New York, where he was first exposed to art in evening classes at the Hebrew Education Society Settlement House. He continued his training at the art school of the Brooklyn Museum of Art. At Boys High School, from which he graduated in 1920, he excelled in mathematics and Latin, while his political awareness and ideological commitment were developed through the Young Peoples Socialist League. He entered Columbia College in 1920, at the age of sixteen, and pursued a broad course of study, including Latin, modern languages, literature, anthropology, philosophy, mathematics, and art history. That intellectual range informed and characterized his work throughout his career. Receiving his A.B. in 1924, he continued his graduate studies at Columbia, studying especially with the anthropologist Franz Boas and the philosopher John Dewey. In 1929 Schapiro submitted his dissertation for a Ph.D., the first in fine arts and archae-

Meyer Schapiro, 1978. COPYRIGHT © BY FRED W. McDARRAH

ology awarded by Columbia. Parts of his dissertation, "The Romanesque Sculpture of Moissac," were published in the *Art Bulletin* in 1931 and opened entirely new critical perspectives for the study of medieval art.

A fellowship from the Carnegie Corporation enabled Schapiro to travel widely in Europe and the Near East in 1926 and 1927, viewing a vast range of art and preparing the foundations for his subsequent work. In 1928 he married Lillian Milgram; they had two children. In 1928 Schapiro also began teaching at Columbia, where he spent his entire career. He rose through the professional ranks at a surprisingly slow pace, suggesting lingering anti-Semitism. He was finally honored as University Professor in 1965, and he became University Professor Emeritus upon his retirement in 1973. In 1966 and 1967 Schapiro delivered the Charles Eliot Norton Lectures at Harvard, in 1968 he was Slade Professor of Art at Oxford, and in 1974 he was visiting lecturer at the Collège de France in Paris. Elected a member of the National Institute of Arts and Letters in 1976, he was awarded a five-year MacArthur Foundation Fellowship in 1987.

Throughout his career Schapiro moved between the Columbia campus on Morningside Heights and his home neighborhood in Greenwich Village, or between the university and the city, a pattern that typified his engagement in the worlds of the intellect and politics. From the late 1930s and through the 1940s he lectured as well at the New School for Social Research, thereby reaching the wider community of the New York City art world, especially the artists, in the years when the city was becoming the most dynamic center of contemporary art.

Committed to socialist ideals and anti-Stalinism, Schapiro played an active intellectual and moral role in the Marxist cultural politics of the 1930s. He was close to the émigré members of the Frankfurt school at the Institute for Social Research, and in 1939 he went to Paris to persuade the cultural critic and philosopher Walter Benjamin to accept an invitation to join them in New York City. Benjamin, however, declined. Close as well to the surrealists in exile, Schapiro mediated between those representatives of continental culture and young American artists, such as Robert Motherwell, who came to Columbia in 1940 to study with Schapiro. A trained artist, Schapiro respected artists and was close to them. In 1952 his comments to Willem de Kooning rescued one major monument of the new American painting *Woman, I* (1952).

As an art historian Schapiro moved between the medieval and the modern. His engagement with modern art opened him to phenomena in older art that had hitherto been ignored or not comprehended by a too generalized or limited art historiography. He recognized in Romanesque sculpture and in modern paintings problems of "perfection, coherence, and unity of form and content," which he made the subject of an essay in 1966. Bringing to each art a

searching precision of analysis, he was attentive to the nuanced decisions, conscious and unconscious, of the sculptors of Moissac, Souillac, and Silos. With that same close, critical attention, he discerned the creativity of the individual brush stroke and the constructive function of color in the art of the impressionists Pablo Picasso and Henri Matisse.

The larger aim of Schapiro's project might be termed the reclamation of the artist in and from history. Within the larger official field of medieval church art and its dominant hierarchic structures, he sought the signs of artistic self-awareness and independent artistic virtuosity at the margins of the field. In medieval art he tended to reduce this to a conflict between the religious and the secular. Seeking the explicitly "artistic character" of works of medieval art, in "On the Aesthetic Attitude in Romanesque Art" (included in *Art and Thought: Essays in Honor of A. K. Coomaraswamy,* 1947) Schapiro argued for the emergence within church art of a new kind of artistic autonomy. Invoking the "aestheticism" of troubadour poetry, he set out in effect to secularize the achievements of the medieval artist and to isolate the artist's professional ambition and skill.

Schapiro's method was one of close and sympathetic stylistic description. From the expressive physiognomy of the work of art, discerned in accordance with what he termed "general psychological laws," emerged a persona of its creator. The artists he discovered in history were embedded in and conditioned by larger material and ideological realities. Their prospects were hardly unlimited. It was precisely the dialectic of that tension between the individual and the social that attracted him, and that tension reflected the complexities of his own personal conflicts and commitments, including his Jewishness and his socialist beliefs. He deliberately rejected religion as a barrier to intellectual freedom and remained committed to socialism.

At the first American Artists' Congress against War and Fascism in 1936, Schapiro delivered a paper, "The Social Bases of Art." Refusing "to reduce art to economics or sociology or politics," he insisted rather on the distinctive nature and conditions of art, which has "its own conditions which distinguish it from other activities. It operates with its own special materials and according to general psychological laws." He went on to define the marginal situation of the artist in modern society, that is, his or her professional isolation. "Yet helpless as he is to act on the world, he shows in his art an astonishing ingenuity and joy in transforming the shapes of familiar things."

In 1937 in the *Marxist Quarterly,* of which he was a founding editor, Schapiro published an article on the "Nature of Abstract Art." Responding to the 1936 exhibition *Cubism and Abstract Art* at the Museum of Modern Art in New York City, Schapiro resisted its formalist assumption of the independence of modern abstract art from modern historical realities. He insisted instead on the moral dimensions of that art and its intimate rapport with the values of modern bourgeois life. As a student he had been inspired by the writings of Roger Fry, and his essay revealed a critical sensibility that joined the aesthetic perception of the studio with a Marxist vision grounded in social and material realities. Schapiro's essay established an entirely new basis for the understanding of modern art that acknowledged it as part of a larger world of social life. He made the bourgeois art of impressionism more intelligible and more interesting, and he demonstrated "the burden of contemporary experience" inherent in abstract art. "It bears within itself at almost every point the mark of the changing material and psychological conditions surrounding modern culture."

The assumed correlation of form and meaning allowed Schapiro to move easily between the large and small dimensions of style or between the work of art as a manifestation of shared social values and the most personal expression. He identified the work intimately with its maker, especially in his studies of Vincent van Gogh and Paul Cézanne. Although responsive to the possibilities of psychoanalytic theory, he was critical of Sigmund Freud's essay on Leonardo da Vinci for its narrow focus and Freud's failure to recognize the contributing conditions of the larger social world and cultural conventions.

Schapiro searched for the operational principles that distinguish art, and his main concern as a scholar was with periods when the basic elements of image making were subject to fundamental pressures and reevaluation. His language was characterized by candor, clarity of thought, directness, and even simplicity of expression. Regardless of the specific examples that occasioned his comments, he was sure of the absolute, fundamental nature of his theme, although his demonstrations were more suggestive than assertive. The markers of his argument are references to the essentials of the art: frame and field, figure and ground, and mimetic and nonmimetic. However, he never presented such basic terms as abstractions or as absolute values. Schapiro refused to subordinate the artist's freedom to the laws of art. He insisted on freedom, even if it were latent rather than actual.

This attitude made it difficult for Schapiro to accept the great descriptive and explanatory models of the earlier generation of theorists he admired for their intellectual ambition. In a magisterial article, "Style," published in *Anthropology Today* in 1953, Schapiro reviewed the efforts of the earlier theorists, including the stylistic polarities postulated by Heinrich Wölfflin, the cyclical pattern conceived by Paul Frankl, the phenomenological duality of Alois Riegl, and the progressive stages of Emanuel Löwy. He found each wanting, and he found wanting the crude application of Marx to the explanation of style by the forms of social life.

"A theory of style adequate to the psychological and historical problems has still to be created," Schapiro concluded somewhat wistfully. "It waits for a deeper knowledge of the principles of form construction and expression and for a unified theory of the processes of social life in which the practical means of life as well as emotional behavior are comprised." That open conclusion reveals his hopes as a scholar committed to the search for fundamental truths and his frustration as a man whose political ideals remained unrealized.

★

Lillian Milgram Schapiro, comp., *Meyer Schapiro: The Bibliography* (1995), is a bibliography of Schapiro's work published during his lifetime. Many of his studies, unpublished lectures, and papers are reprinted in Meyer Schapiro, *Selected Papers,* Vol. 1, *Romanesque Art* (1977), Vol. 2, *Modern Art, Nineteenth and Twentieth Centuries* (1978), Vol. 3, *Late Antique, Early Christian, and Mediaeval Art* (1979), and Vol. 4, *Theory and Philosophy of Art: Style, Artist, and Society* (1994). Other posthumous publications of Schapiro's lectures include *Words, Script, and Pictures: Semiotic of Visual Language* (1996), *Impressionism: Reflections and Perceptions* (1997), and *The Unity of Picasso's Art* (2000). Meyer Schapiro, *Worldview in Painting—Art and Society* (1999), includes several texts of Schapiro's early political and social commentary from the 1930s, especially in regard to the position of art and the artists in the modern world. Schapiro's development as an artist is documented in Lillian Milgram Schapiro and Daniel Esterman, eds., *Meyer Schapiro: His Painting, Drawing, and Sculpture* (2000). A full biographical treatment is Helen Epstein, "Meyer Schapiro: 'A Passion to Know and Make Known,'" *Art News* 82 (May 1983 and summer 1983). Evaluations of Schapiro's achievement are "On the Work of Meyer Schapiro," *Social Research: An International Quarterly of the Social Sciences* 45, no. 1 (1978), and in the *Oxford Art Journal* 17, no. 1 (1994). An obituary is in the *New York Times* (4 Mar. 1996).

DAVID ROSAND

SCHNEERSON, Menachem Mendel (*b.* 18 April 1902 in Nikolayev, Russia (now Ukraine); *d.* 12 June 1994 in New York City), the seventh Lubavitcher Rebbe (rabbi), who was considered the spiritual leader of the Chabad branch of Hasidim from 1950 until his death and was regarded by many of his followers as the Messiah.

Schneerson was the eldest of three sons born to Rabbi Levi Isaac Schneerson and Chana Yanovsky and was named for his great-grandfather, the third Grand Rabbi of Lubavitch, Russia. His father, a direct descendant of Rabbi Schneur Zalman of Liady, Russia—the founder of Chabad Hasidism (the school of thought that gives emphasis to wisdom, knowledge, and understanding in the study of the Torah)—served as chief rabbi of the Russian city of Yekaterinoslav (now Dnepropetrovsk) when the family moved there

Menachem Mendel Schneerson during morning prayers in Brooklyn, New York, 1992. AP Photo/Mike Ablans

in 1905. In December 1928, in Warsaw, Poland, Menachem Schneerson wed his distant cousin, Chaya Mushka Schneersohn, the daughter of the sixth Lubavitcher Rebbe (Lubavitcher Hasidim are a sect of Hasidic Jews who follow the virtues of Chabad), Rabbi Yosef I. Schneersohn; they had no children. After his marriage, the young Rabbi Schneerson followed an unusual course of study for a Hasidic rabbi. He studied mathematics and science at the University of Berlin and continued with his studies at the Sorbonne and at a Parisian engineering college until 1938. Faced with the spread of Nazism in Europe, Schneerson and his wife emigrated from France to the United States in 1941, where they joined Chaya's father, who had settled in the Crown Heights section of Brooklyn in 1940. Once in the United States, Schneerson began to rebuild the Lubavitcher community, which had witnessed its center in Poland and its followers decimated by the Nazis. (The Lubavitcher Hasidim are ultra-Orthodox Jews who strictly observe the laws of the Torah. They keep kosher, do not travel on the Sabbath or major Jewish holidays, and generally devote their leisure time to the study of the Torah. Many of them are professionals, although most do not pursue a college education because it takes time away from the study of the Torah.)

In 1942 Schneerson was appointed the director of Lubavitch publishing, known as Kehot Publication Society, and Lubavitch educational activities, known as the Merkos Linonei Chinuch. He also headed up Machne Israel, the social services organization. Following Rabbi Yosef Schneersohn's death, Schneerson, in 1951, was formally installed as the seventh Lubavitcher Rebbe.

As rebbe, Schneerson reached out to assimilated Jews and received support from non-Hasidic and even non-Orthodox Jews. With their assistance, Schneerson launched an ambitious program of disseminating the "Lubavitch way," or specifically Chabad Hasidism, among all sectors of American and world Jewry. Under his leadership, the Lubavitch set up Hebrew day schools in various cities in the United States and Canada. By the early 1970s, the Lubavitch movement was establishing so-called Chabad houses throughout America, which served as synagogues, schools, and drug-counseling centers, with the objective of reaching out to college-age youth. In 1990, there were more than 250 such houses throughout the country. In addition, the Lubavitch movement launched an extensive media campaign to spread its message. For example, they published textbooks and periodicals and broadcast the rebbe's speeches over radio and cable television.

Aside from promoting the teaching of this kind of ultra-Orthodox Judaism, Schneerson also organized the Baal Teshuva movement, an organization that helped tens of thousands of American Jews return to their faith. Schneerson's views were formulated in lengthy weekly discourses on a diverse range of subjects, including Hasidism, rabbinic thought, and political issues. His discourses usually were presented at the *Farbrengen,* or gatherings, before his followers on the Sabbath and Jewish holidays. These gatherings were held at his headquarters at 770 Eastern Parkway in the Crown Heights section of Brooklyn, which consists primarily of a population of Hispanics, African Americans, and Hasidic Jews. (The Eastern Parkway address is now the headquarters of the worldwide Lubavitcher movement and was the rebbe's home until his death.) In addition, Schneerson was a highly regarded rabbinic scholar whose opinion on Jewish law was widely sought throughout the world of Orthodox Judaism.

Although he eschewed ecumenical dialogue, Schneerson taught that Gentiles were crucial for the world's redemption. Not interested in converting Christians to Judaism, he encouraged non-Jews to observe the seven Noahide Commandments, believing that the Jews were ultimately responsible for the moral welfare of their Gentile brethren. (As listed in the bible, the Noahide Commandments include the belief in God; prohibitions on murder, thievery, illicit sexual relations, using God's name in vain, and eating a portion of a living animal; as well as the commandment to establish a just system of law. All human beings are bound by these commandments.) Through his writings and public statements, he also advocated a moment of silence in the public schools and favored federal aid to religious schools.

Although he never set foot on Israeli soil, Schneerson was a major political force and a firm supporter of the Jewish state. He adopted a rigid position on the question of Israel's occupied territories, believing that the Bible and Jewish law prohibited the return of these lands. He opposed the Camp David accords (1979), which returned the Sinai to Egypt as part of the overall peace between Israel and Egypt. In the spring of 1990, during the Israeli elections, Schneerson urged select Orthodox members of the Israeli parliament, the Knesset, not to help the Labor Party form a government that would have supported the Baker plan (sponsored by the United States and named after Secretary of State James Baker), which called for a peace conference to negotiate the question of Palestinian autonomy. Subsequently, Schneerson condemned the Oslo accords (1993), which he feared would lead Israel to cede land to the Palestinians.

Following Schneerson's death in 1994, his followers opposed Shimon Peres, who had promised to continue the peace process initiated by the assassinated prime minister Yitzhak Rabin. On the eve of the 1996 Israeli election, the Lubavitch movement put up thousands of posters with the words "Bibi Is Good for the Jews." Benjamin ("Bibi") Netanyahu was the head of the Conservative Likud Party that believed in slowing down the policy of Land for Peace, a policy that Schneerson believed would scuttle the peace process. Netanyahu became prime minister, defeating the Labor Party candidate, Shimon Peres. Schneerson also failed to persuade the Knesset to change Israel's Law of Return (the law that states that any Jewish person can attain automatic Israeli citizenship), so that conversions performed by non-Orthodox rabbis would be invalidated. (Orthodox Jews do not accept conversions by non-Orthodox Jews because they are believed to deviate from the laws of the Torah.) Ironically, many of Schneerson's opponents on this issue were Reform and Conservative Jewish leaders in the United States, some of whom were financial backers of the Lubavitch movement.

In the 1980s, Schneerson came under attack by an array of Orthodox rabbinical leaders for fostering a cult of personality and for implying that he was the Messiah. By the 1980s, Schneerson's campaigns and speeches had become marked by a messianic fervor. Indeed, the semiofficial Lubavitch motto was "We Want Messiah Now." In the months before his death, the Lubavitch movement was di-

vided between those followers who believed he was the Messiah, though he had mildly discouraged such belief, and those who wanted to put an end to such speculation.

As Schneerson grew older and suffered a heart attack (in 1976), speculation grew as to who would succeed the childless rebbe. He had given no indication concerning how to handle the problem of succession. In 1994 Schneerson died of complications resulting from a stroke; he is buried in Old Montefiore Cemetery in Queens, New York. At the time of his death he had not designated a successor as spiritual leader, and there was considerable discussion among the Lubavitcher about whether there even would be a successor—at the beginning of the twenty-first century, there was still no successor. (The movement has split between those who believe that Schneerson will return as the Messiah and those who think this is a form of heresy.)

Under his charismatic leadership, Rabbi Schneerson transformed the Lubavitch movement from an obscure ultra-Orthodox sect into the fastest-growing and most influential Hasidic group in the United States as well as a major force in American Jewish life. At the end of the twentieth century, the Lubavitch movement numbered about 200,000 followers around the world, with an estimated $100 million a year in contributions.

★

There is no biography of Rabbi Schneerson. The bulk of his homilies, sermons, lectures, and writings are in Hebrew and has not been translated into English. One work in English that provides the reader with the flavor of Schneerson's thought is his *Toward A Meaningful Life: The Wisdom of the Rebbe,* adapted by Rabbi Simon Jacobson (1995). Magazine articles on Schneerson include "The Oracle of Crown Heights," by Michael Specter, *New York Times Magazine* (15 Mar. 1992), and "Rabbi Menachem Schneerson: Waiting for the Rebbe," by Clyde Haberman, *New York Times Magazine* (1 Jan. 1995). An obituary is in the *New York Times* (13 June 1994). For general information on Hasidism, see Lis Harris, *Holy Days: The World of a Hasidic Family* (1985), and William Shaffir, *Life in a Religious Community: The Lubavitcher Chassidim in Montreal* (1974).

JACK R. FISCHEL

SCHULTZ, David Lesky ("Dave") (*b.* 6 June 1959 in Palo Alto, California; *d.* 26 January 1996 in Newtown Square, Pennsylvania), Olympic and collegiate wrestling champion, and worldwide "ambassador" for the sport.

Schultz was one of four children of Philip Gary, a counselor, and Jean St. Germain, a costume designer. As a first grader, he had trouble reading and was not up to the level of other students. Yet, as his father recalled, while the other youngsters were reading their first primers, David was singing "Greensleaves," the old English folk song, "at the top

Dave Schultz. ASSOCIATED PRESS AP

of his lungs." Amazingly, the bright six-year-old knew all of the words to the English air.

Larger than most children his age, Schultz compensated for his learning difficulties (later diagnosed as dyslexia) by being tough and intimidating his fellow grade-school pupils. When his contemporaries caught up to him physically, he took up wrestling as a way of maintaining his domination.

Living in Palo Alto, California, Schultz as a high school freshman ventured into the Stanford University wrestling practice facility and told college senior Chris Horpel that he wanted to learn as much as he could about the sport. Horpel was too old, too talented, and too large to engage in any real workout with the fourteen-year-old Schultz, but he was intrigued by how the youngster popped right up after being tossed on his back. Nothing seemed to discourage Schultz. His tenacity and infectious personality captured Horpel, and the college senior forged a friendship with Schultz that would last a lifetime.

Perhaps because of the hard lessons learned from Horpel, Schultz showed promise as a high school wrestler at Palo Alto High School. He won the California state championship at 165 pounds as a senior in 1977, after placing fourth in the state as a sophomore and junior. In fact,

Schultz, always a team player, moved up two weight classes to enhance the chances of his Palo Alto squad.

Heavily recruited by colleges, Schultz committed to Oklahoma State. As a 150-pound freshman, he earned All-America status and placed third in the NCAA national championship tournament. Close to his younger brother Mark, also an outstanding wrestler and three-time NCAA champion, Schultz transferred to the University of California, Los Angeles (UCLA), where Mark had matriculated. Not long after Schultz arrived on campus, UCLA dropped the sport. Both brothers then went to the University of Oklahoma. After sitting out for a year because of the NCAA's transfer rule, Schultz resumed his grappling career in 1981 as a 158-pounder. Again he earned All-America honors, again placing third in the nation. As a college senior in 1982, Schultz moved up another weight class to 167 pounds. This move was the culmination of a stellar college career, and Schultz was crowned national champion. The same year—on Valentine's Day—he married Nancy Lynn Stoffel, a former gymnast at Oklahoma State who transferred to the University of Oklahoma after an injury. The couple had a son and a daughter.

Schultz enjoyed an international reputation. Fluent in seven languages—quite an accomplishment considering his learning disability—he traveled abroad frequently. Successful American wrestlers were known abroad for their strength and stamina, but Schultz did not fit the mold. He was not a great athlete; he simply worked extremely hard, soaking up as much wrestling knowledge as he could. He was so impressed with the skill of Soviet wrestlers that he adopted their style—standing as they stood, moving as they moved. His ability as a communicator won him admirers among international competitors and was especially revered in countries where wrestling is held in high esteem: Bulgaria, Iran, the former Soviet Union, and Turkey.

One of the most prestigious foreign events is the Tbilisi tournament, held in what was then the Soviet republic of Georgia. Schultz twice won an international championship there, whereas no other American grappler had ever won more than one title. He continued to wrestle and win many other international tournaments: eight times he won "open" freestyle titles and twice won Greco-Roman senior national titles.

Schultz's devotion to the sport continued well past college graduation. In 1984 he won the Olympic trials and the right to represent the United States in the summer Olympics as a welterweight (163 pounds) freestyle wrestler. In Los Angeles he won the coveted Olympic gold medal. The only defending world champion freestyler to take part in the 1984 Olympics, Schultz won his title match by a pin and won five other matches by a combined score of 42–2. A day after his win, his brother Mark also won Olympic gold as a middleweight.

The wrestler continued his training, seeking further Olympic gold, but in both the 1988 and 1992 Olympic trials finals, he lost to Kenny Monday. Yet after Monday won a gold medal at the 1988 games in Seoul, South Korea, Schultz came down out of the stands, hoisted him to his shoulders, and paraded him around the mat. It was an act typical of the exuberant Schultz.

Ranked as the nation's number one 163-pounder in 1995, Schultz coveted a second Olympic gold medal. In the mid-1990s he accepted an invitation to train, with all expenses paid and even a salary, at Foxcatcher, the 800-acre estate of the chemical fortune heir John E. du Pont in suburban Philadelphia. Schultz lived on the grounds with his family. Du Pont, who started, coached, and endowed the wrestling program at nearby Villanova University, was viewed by many as eccentric, and by others as unstable. Friends pleaded with Schultz to leave Foxcatcher as du Pont became more delusional. His old friend Chris Horpel tried to entice him to return to coaching at Stanford—Schultz had also coached at Wisconsin—but Schultz stayed.

One Friday afternoon as Schultz was installing a car radio, Nancy heard gunshots. She rushed outside to see her husband lying mortally wounded in the driveway. Du Pont sat, gun in hand, in his luxury car. He fired another shot into Schultz's body, then drove away. Du Pont returned home and staged a forty-eight-hour siege before police took him into custody. He was later found innocent of murder charges by reason of insanity (he was said to be disillusioned and to hear voices) and institutionalized. Schultz was cremated and his ashes sent to the family's Foster City, California, home.

His widow, Nancy, began the Dave Schultz Wrestling Foundation to train wrestlers for international and Olympic competition. Schultz was inducted posthumously into the National Wrestling Hall of Fame, and his memory is further perpetuated by the Dave Schultz Memorial International Wrestling Tournament.

Dave Schultz became a wrestling icon through dogged determination and a desire to make himself the best wrestler he could be. His Olympic coach Joe Seay summed up Schultz and his influence with these words: "David was the greatest ambassador the sport has ever had."

★

There is no biography of Dave Schultz; however, his career and wrestling are touched on in *The New York Times Encyclopedia of Sports*, edited by Gene Brown (1979); *The Olympic Games* by Peter Arnold (1984); and *The Complete Book of the Olympics* by David Wallechinsky (1992). News articles about his murder and its aftermath appeared in the *New York Times* editions of 27 Jan., 30 Jan., 4 Feb., and 12 Mar. 1996.

JIM CAMPBELL

SCHWINGER, Julian Seymour (*b.* 12 February 1918 in New York City; *d.* 16 July 1994 in Los Angeles, California), theoretical physicist and Nobel laureate primarily responsible for the development of the field of quantum electrodynamics (QED), with applications to an extremely broad range of theoretical and experimental investigations in atomic, nuclear, and high-energy physics as well as other fields.

Schwinger was born to Benjamin Schwinger, a dress designer and manufacturer, and Belle Rosenfeld Schwinger. He attended Townsend Harris High School and at age fourteen entered the College of the City of New York (CCNY). He later transferred to Columbia University in New York City with the support of I. I. Rabi, a Nobel laureate in physics, graduating in 1936 at seventeen years of age. Schwinger then did graduate work at the University of Wisconsin, Purdue University in Indiana, and Columbia and completed his Ph.D. at Columbia in 1939.

Julian Schwinger. LIBRARY OF CONGRESS

Following this, Schwinger pursued postdoctoral studies at the University of California, Berkeley, with J. R. Oppenheimer, remaining there until 1941. At that point he went back to Purdue University, leaving there in 1943 as an assistant professor. He joined the University of Chicago's metallurgical laboratory and worked on the development of the atomic bomb, then moved to the Massachusetts Institute of Technology (MIT) and worked on radar systems. After World War II he became a member of the Harvard University faculty in 1945, and was promoted to full professor in 1947 as one of the youngest persons ever to reach that rank at Harvard. In June of that same year he married Clarice Carol; they had no children. He was appointed to the Higgins Chair at Harvard in 1966, then moved to the University of California, Los Angeles, in 1973. He spent a year at the State University of New York at Stony Brook as visiting professor in 1967. Among his doctoral students at Harvard were Ben Mottelson and Sheldon Glashow, both Nobel laureates.

Regarded as the prime mover in the development of quantum electrodynamics, Schwinger contributed to quantum field theory, elementary particle physics (including the two-neutrino concept), and the unification of electromagnetic and weak interactions (which led to Glashow's Nobel Prize–winning research). All these concepts have proved crucial to our understanding of modern physics, the structure of matter, and the interaction of radiation with matter. He pointed out the singular importance of Green's Functions in the mathematical problems of the day in his lecture upon receiving an honorary degree at Nottingham, England, entitled "The Greening of Quantum Field Theory: George and I." Schwinger also made contributions to the understanding of microwave wave-guides and the connection of microwave scattering theory and nuclear scattering. Schwinger's central standing in the theory of quantum electrodynamics led the editors of Physical Review Letters to suggest (with tongue in cheek) that contributions to this field should begin with the phrase "According to Schwinger. . . ."

The development of quantum mechanics in the 1900s by Erwin Schrödinger, Werner Heisenberg, Niels Bohr, Wolfgang Pauli, and others had led physicists to an understanding of many, but not nearly all, phenomena associated with atomic and molecular structure. A central issue of interest was the interaction of electrons and electromagnetic forces, which was treated by Paul Dirac in 1927. Dirac's treatment explained many of the interactions but also introduced some staggering difficulties. The interactions involved interchanges between electrons and short-lived photons. These were so short-lived, in fact, that according to the Heisenberg uncertainty principle the energy and mass of these so-called virtual photons approached an infinite limit; but the mass and charge of the electron were

small, providing an unavoidable conflict between theory and experimental results.

In addition, although the theory at that time provided good agreement with experimental results, the development of better experimental techniques began to reveal discrepancies between theory and experiment so great that physicists could not ignore them. Prior to the work of Schwinger (and Richard Feynman and Sin-Itiro Tomonaga), the annoying infinities were treated by a process that essentially replaced the terms by their known values.

The work of Schwinger and Tomonaga developed an approach that placed the process, called renormalization, on a basis with which physicists could be comfortable. The results were found to agree with the experimental data within the limits of precision of the experiments. The development also led to an understanding of such effects as the Lamb Shift in the energy levels of hydrogen, and a correction to the magnetic moment of the electron.

C. N. Yang, in a tribute to Schwinger, said that Schwinger made it possible for physicists to "climb the peak" of understanding renormalization. Schwinger received the Albert Einstein Prize (with Kurt Gödel) in 1951, the National Science Medal in 1964, and the Nobel Prize in physics (with Tomonaga and Feynman) in 1965.

★

An extensive list of Schwinger's publications can be found in *Julian Schwinger, the Physicist, the Teacher, and the Man*, edited by Y. Jack Ng (1996). Obituaries are in the *Los Angeles Times* (19 July 1994) and the *New York Times* (20 July 1994), and a remembrance by Jeremy Bernstein is in the *American Scholar* (Sept. 1995).

D. P. MALONE

SCOTT, Hugh Doggett, Jr. (*b.* 11 November 1900 in Fredericksburg, Virginia; *d.* 21 July 1994 in Falls Church, Virginia), three-term U.S. senator from Pennsylvania, Senate Republican leader during the Nixon and Ford administrations, and prominent member of his party's moderate wing.

Scott, the only child of Hugh Doggett Scott, Sr., a banker, and Jane Lee Lewis, was born on an estate that once had belonged to George Washington. Although Scott became a strong voice for civil rights, one of his great-grandfathers fought for the Confederacy in the Civil War. Scott once noted that, since his ancestors had emigrated from England in 1621, a politician had emerged in his family "every other generation," among them President Zachary Taylor. Scott said he became interested in a political career during his youth, when he watched committee hearings in the Virginia House of Delegates. His father remarried after the death of Scott's mother and had two more children.

Hugh Scott. ASSOCIATED PRESS AP

After attending public elementary and secondary schools in Fredericksburg, Scott received a bachelor's degree from Randolph-Macon College in Ashland, Virginia, in 1919 and a law degree from the University of Virginia in Charlottesville in 1922. To help pay for his studies, he clerked in a retail store and worked on construction crews. In 1922 Scott moved to Philadelphia, Pennsylvania, where he entered a law practice with his uncle Edwin O. Lewis. Scott married Marian Huntington Chase on 12 April 1924. They had one daughter. From 1926 until 1941 he served as an assistant district attorney in Philadelphia and prosecuted more than 20,000 cases. During this period Scott became active in Republican politics.

Scott, who was of medium height, grew a mustache as a young man to make himself look older. He wore horn-rimmed glasses and was a pipe smoker with a collection of several hundred pipes.

Scott was elected to the U.S. House of Representatives in 1940 from a northwest Philadelphia congressional district. He served until 1959 except for a two-year interval when he was defeated in 1944. He won back the congres-

sional seat in 1946. During the two-year interval, Scott served in the U.S. Navy in the central and western Pacific during World War II and was discharged on 9 April 1946 with the rank of commander.

As a member of the House, Scott voted for the abolition of the poll tax and supported lend-lease aid to Britain prior to U.S. entry into World War II, the Truman Doctrine, the Marshall Plan, and the Taft-Hartley Act. He also backed the Twenty-second Amendment limiting presidential tenures to two terms.

Scott, a shrewd strategist and tactician, played a major role in presidential politics for more than a generation. In 1940 he was among the organizers who helped Wendell L. Willkie win the presidential nomination. Eight years later Scott was chosen by the presidential nominee Thomas E. Dewey as the Republican national chairman. "I recommended a vigorous campaign and was very much startled when Dewey told me his other advisers had recommended a low-key campaign and that he never mention Truman by name," Scott recalled in a 1973 interview. Shortly after Dewey's loss, Senator Robert A. Taft of Ohio tried to make Scott the scapegoat and called for his recall as chairman. At a showdown meeting of the national committee, Scott insisted that Dewey's play-it-safe strategy had been a mistake. By a narrow margin, he survived a no-confidence vote. Scott resigned as chairman in August 1949.

While General Dwight D. Eisenhower was serving in France as supreme commander of the North Atlantic Treaty Organization (NATO), Scott went to Paris in 1951 and urged Eisenhower to seek the 1952 Republican presidential nomination. "He was very definitely in the inner circle," Milton S. Eisenhower said in 1975. "My brother paid a great deal of attention to his suggestions." Following Dwight Eisenhower's election as president, Scott remained among his stalwart allies. On congressional roll calls he voted with Eisenhower 97 percent of the time.

Offended by Senator Joseph R. McCarthy's wild charges and reckless vilification of public figures, Scott denounced his fellow Republican as a "noisy obstructionist" and "grandstander." As a member of the House Rules Committee, Scott proposed a "fair-play code" that would have allowed witnesses before congressional committees to testify in their own behalf and to have the right to cross-examine their accusers. The Republican congressional leadership blocked Scott's initiative, however.

Elected to the U.S. Senate in 1958, Scott became the first Pennsylvanian to win three terms by popular vote. During the Democratic administrations of Presidents John F. Kennedy and Lyndon B. Johnson, Scott provided key bipartisan support for the Nuclear Test Ban Treaty, the Civil Rights Act of 1964, and the Voting Rights Act of 1965. He was also an early supporter of U.S. military intervention in Vietnam, although he became disillusioned with the war during the Nixon administration.

In January 1969 Scott was elected Senate minority whip with the support of the party's moderate wing and over the opposition of the Republican leader Everett M. Dirksen. When Dirksen died in September of that year, Scott moved up to the minority leadership and held this position until his retirement in 1977. He was the first liberal Republican to hold the party floor leadership since World War II. Scott opposed President Richard M. Nixon's nomination of Judge Clement Haynsworth to the Supreme Court and the administration's efforts to weaken the Voting Rights Act.

During the Watergate scandal Scott defended Nixon but also urged him to make public all tapes of his White House conversations. Following the release of these tapes, mandated by a court order, Scott was appalled when they disclosed that Nixon had planned the cover-up. After Scott and Senator Barry Goldwater told Nixon that he was certain to be impeached, the president decided to resign.

Scott had a more collegial relationship with President Gerald R. Ford, having spent five years as Ford's partner in the Republican congressional leadership when Ford was the House minority leader. Scott was influential in Ford's selection of Nelson A. Rockefeller for the vice presidency. In 1976 Scott chose not to seek reelection after he was accused of accepting $45,000 from lobbyists for the Gulf Oil Corporation. Scott said the funds had been for his campaign and denied that the money had gone to personal use. A federal probe was dropped when Scott announced his retirement.

On leaving the Senate, he practiced law in Washington, D.C., and his clients included the governments of Japan, Pakistan, and Thailand. He was appointed by President Jimmy Carter as a cochair of a committee that revised the Panama Canal treaties. Scott retired from his law practice in 1987 and two years later was appointed by Senate Majority Leader Robert C. Byrd as a member of the Commission on the Bicentennial of the United States Senate. In his final years, he had Parkinson's disease and suffered a major stroke. He died of a heart attack at Goodwin House West, a retirement home, at the age of ninety-three. He is buried in Arlington National Cemetery in Arlington, Virginia.

Scott, who was a skillful builder of coalitions, was an articulate spokesman for his party. As a Senate leader, he put the national interest above narrow partisanship and was respected by colleagues in Democratic and Republican parties alike.

★

The Scott papers are at the University of Virginia in Charlottesville. Scott wrote two memoirs, *How to Go into Politics* (1949) and *Come to the Party* (1968). He is profiled in Steve Neal, "The Artful Dodger," *Philadelphia Inquirer Sunday Magazine* (29 Apr.

1973); and in Steve Neal, "Can Hugh Scott Tough It Out," *Nation* (29 Nov. 1975). An obituary is in the *New York Times* (23 July 1994).

STEVE NEAL

SCRIBNER, Charles, Jr. (*b.* 13 July 1921 in Quogue, Long Island, New York; *d.* 11 November 1995 in New York City), book publisher and head of the family publishing company Charles Scribner's Sons for more than three decades.

Charles Scribner, Jr., was the younger of two children, and the only son, of Charles Scribner III, president of the publishing house of Scribners from 1932 to 1952, and Vera Gordon Bloodgood, a socialite and horsewoman. He came from a distinguished line of publishers: his great-grandfather, the original Charles Scribner (1821–1871), founded the publishing house in 1846 that became Charles Scribner's Sons, one of the preeminent literary publishers in nineteenth-century America. His grandfather, the second Charles Scribner (1854–1930), not only ran the publishing company for more than fifty years but also donated the funds to start Princeton University Press in 1906, becoming its first president.

Charles, Jr., grew up at "Dew Hollow," the family home in Far Hills, New Jersey, and at the age of thirteen was sent to St. Paul's School in Concord, New Hampshire. He entered Princeton University in 1939, was elected to Phi Beta Kappa in his junior year, and graduated in 1943, thereupon joining the U.S. Navy's cryptanalysis group in Washington, D.C., where he served until 1946.

That same year he joined the family business, and his first task was dealing with the Scribner author Ernest Hemingway on an illustrated edition of *A Farewell to Arms*. Though Hemingway did not care for the illustrations, he got along well with the younger Scribner, establishing a relationship that was to enrich both of their careers.

Scribner married (Dorothy) Joan Sunderland on 16 July 1949. They had three sons, Charles, Blair, and John. After a brief stint back in Washington with the navy during the Korean War, Scribner was called back to the company on the sudden death of his father in 1952. Within a few months he was elected president.

When he began in 1946, the house that had made F. Scott Fitzgerald, Hemingway, and Thomas Wolfe household names was, in Scribner's words, "high in reputation and low in performance and profitability." Recognizing that publishing the fiction of first-time authors was risky, he saw that Scribners was losing an opportunity in the booming postwar educational market by not reissuing the classics of their standard authors. He undertook an ambitious program of reissuing older titles in quality paperback editions during the 1950s.

Charles Scribner, 1970. PHOTOGRAPH BY HELEN MARCUS/COURTESY OF CHARLES SCRIBNER III

In the case of Hemingway, this meant that the house was able to reissue all of his titles under the Scribner imprint by the time *The Old Man and the Sea* appeared in 1952, contributing significantly to that writer's financial security. After Hemingway's death in 1961, Scribner supported the firm's posthumous publication of his work. He was a trustee of the Ernest Hemingway Foundation and an honorary member of the Ernest Hemingway Society, and was often invited to speak to scholars and other groups about his years of working with Hemingway and the Hemingway heirs.

Scribner had been interested in the sciences since college, and he recognized the need for and potential profitability of a major reference program. He came up with the idea of publishing the *Dictionary of Scientific Biography,* the sixteen volumes of which Scribners released serially from 1970 to 1980. The success of this enterprise led to the firm's publishing the five-volume *Dictionary of the History of Ideas* in 1973–1974. Scribner referred to these projects as "the most important single contribution I have made to Scribners as editor and publisher," and they were the foundation of a significant scholarly reference publishing program. In 1976 he was awarded the Curtis Benjamin Award for Creative Publishing from the Association of American Publishers for the *Dictionary of the History of Ideas.* The *Dictionary of Scientific Biography* was awarded the American

Library Association's prestigious Dartmouth Medal in 1981.

The company faced a number of financial challenges in the late 1970s. In an effort to combine forces and share resources, Scribners merged with two publishers, Atheneum Publishers (in 1978) and Rawson, Wade (in 1982). In the aftermath of these acquisitions, Scribner, having become chairman of Scribner Book Companies (in 1977), felt somewhat beset with bank loans and debt, and the landmark Scribner Bookstore at Fifth Avenue and Forty-eighth Street, operating since 1913, was costing the Scribner family $500,000 a year. In 1984, in what he described as "a series of wrenching decisions," Scribner sold both the store and the building. Recognizing that he would be forced to sell or be taken over by another company, Scribner in 1984 merged the family company with Macmillan Publishing Company. He retired as chairman of the Scribner Book Companies in 1986. When Robert Maxwell purchased Macmillan in 1988, the Scribner stock was worth thirty-six times what it had been at the time Scribner took over in 1952.

In the mid-1980s Scribner began to experience difficulties with his vision, rendering him unable to drive a car, or even to read and write for a time. It was determined that he was suffering from *spatial, visual, simul agnosia,* called the Holmes syndrome, caused by nerve degeneration in the brain, the symptoms of which are similar to a stroke. He was eventually able to cope with everyday tasks and resume his literary and scientific interests. In his last years Scribner published two books of autobiography. He died of pneumonia on 11 November 1995, in New York City, and is buried in Woodlawn Cemetery in the Bronx.

Scribner was a devoted family man, a publisher with the sensibilities of a scholar and teacher, and an entertaining writer. He was awarded an honorary M.A. degree from Princeton in 1966 and an honorary Doctor of Literature degree from Bucknell University in 1983. He was elected president of Princeton University Press in 1957 (serving until 1968), having been a trustee of the press since 1949, and served as a trustee of both the university and its press from 1969 to 1979. He served as president of the American Book Publishers Council from 1966 to 1968 and in an advisory capacity on a number of committees, among them the Editorial Advisory Committee of *The Writings of Albert Einstein*. He was a member of the American Philosophical Society, and a vestryman and senior warden of St. Bartholomew's (Episcopal) Church in New York City. He lived with his family in New Jersey and on the Upper East Side of Manhattan.

Scribner was often described as a gentleman and was recalled in a memorial after his death as a person of "unshakeable integrity." He believed strongly in the value of the arts, saying that they were important for "self-cultivation and spiritual enrichment." He was interested in language and believed that clear writing had the power to "reshape the mind"; he loved learning and the life of the mind, and described his interest in the history of science as "an intellectual adventure."

★

In 1967 the papers of Charles Scribner's Sons were deeded to the Firestone Library at Princeton University to begin a publishing archive; in 1996 the library presented an exhibition celebrating the company's 150th anniversary entitled "The Company of Writers: Charles Scribner's Sons 1846–1996." The booklet, produced by the library to accompany this exhibition, includes several memoirs of Charles Scribner, Jr., as well as a chronology of significant events in the history of the publishing company. Scribner's two memoirs are *In the Company of Writers: A Life in Publishing* (1990) and *In the Web of Ideas: The Education of a Publisher* (1993). The first covers mainly the events in his life and his experiences as head of the family publishing house; the second is an intellectual autobiography. His other writings demonstrate the wide scope of his interests. His natural curiosity about Einstein and relativity led him to publish "Henri Poincaré and the Theory of Relativity" in the *American Journal of Physics* (1964). In reading Marcel Proust, he was struck by the number of scientific images the author used, and he wrote "Scientific Imagery in Proust," published in *Proceedings of the American Philosophical Society* in 1990. In

addition to editing two Hemingway anthologies, he wrote a children's book, *The Devil's Bridge* (1978). His skill with German and French was good enough that he published a translation of *Hänsel and Gretel;* a book of satirical German essays, *Doppelfinten,* by Gabriel Laub (1977); and a book of French mathematical and logical puzzles, *Le Jardin du Sphinx,* by Pierre Berloquin (1982), all done, as he said, "as exercises to help keep my reading knowledge green." An obituary is in the *New York Times* (13 Nov. 1995).

PETER COVENEY

SELDES, George Henry (*b.* 16 November 1890 in Alliance [now Vineland], New Jersey; *d.* 2 July 1995 in Windsor, Vermont), crusading journalist and author best known for his untiring press criticism and commitment to a free, unfettered press.

Seldes was one of two sons born to George Sergius Seldes and Anna Verna Saphro. They operated a family farm and ran the post office in Alliance, New Jersey, a Jewish utopian community. Seldes's father, a pharmacist, moved to nearby Philadelphia, Pennsylvania, to earn more money when the children were young. Seldes's mother died when Seldes was six, and family members raised the boys.

In 1907 Seldes joined his father and stepmother in Pittsburgh so he could attend a large city high school. He failed his junior year, quit school, and worked briefly in his father's drugstore. In 1909 he got a job at the *Pittsburgh Leader* earning $3.50 a week. In 1912, at his brother Gilbert's urging, he took a leave of absence and enrolled in a nondegree program at Harvard University for a year. Seldes then returned to Pittsburgh and in 1914 became night editor of the *Pittsburgh Post.* In 1916, during World War I, he went to London to work for the United Press.

In 1917 Seldes operated a one-person bureau office in Paris for the *Chicago Tribune Army Edition.* With the arrival in France of the American Expeditionary Force, Seldes joined General John Pershing's Army Press Section, a small group that included some of America's greatest journalists.

Seldes remained in Europe after the war and began a distinguished career as a foreign correspondent for the *Chicago Tribune.* He sought stories involving political change, class conflicts, and ideological leaders, including Leon Trostky, Nikolai Lenin, Benito Mussolini, and Adolf Hitler. He was expelled from Russia in 1921 when he attempted to write uncensored stories, and he was expelled from Italy in 1925 when he linked Mussolini to the murder of a political rival.

The *Chicago Tribune* made Seldes a roving correspondent for eastern Europe, and he traveled extensively from Berlin to Baghdad. He went to Mexico in 1927 to write a series about Mexico–U.S. relations and oil, but the *Chicago Tribune* publisher Robert McCormick censored the stories.

George Seldes. AP/WIDE WORLD PHOTOS

Seldes quit the paper the following year and remained in France painting and writing books.

Seldes's first book, *You Can't Print That! The Truth Behind the News* (1929), shared details about stories Seldes could not get published as a journalist. He followed with books about the Vatican and the world armament industry and a well-regarded biography of Mussolini, *Sawdust Caesar* (1935). Two important books on the newspaper industry, then the dominant media, established Seldes's reputation for press criticism. The books, *Freedom of the Press* (1935) and *Lords of the Press* (1938), set out in detail Seldes's conclusions that American journalism withheld critical information from the public. In 1932 Seldes married Helen Larkin Wiesman, an American living and studying in Paris. Although Wiesman was fifteen years younger than Seldes, they shared similar political views. They had no children.

In 1937 the couple covered the Spanish Civil War for the liberal *New York Post*. Francisco Franco's victory left Seldes distraught, in part because he saw the American press as sympathetic to the dictator, who won with military support from Italy and Germany. Seldes's next three books, though written about the United States, had strong political themes: the attack on civil liberties by the political right, the Catholic Church's ties to fascist organizations, and red-baiting.

In 1940 Seldes started *In Fact*, a four-page newsletter devoted to press criticism and investigative reporting. He accepted no advertising. At its peak its 176,000 subscribers exceeded the circulation of other leading liberal journals, such as the *Nation* and the *New Republic*. Seldes wrote stories other papers ignored. The tone of the publication was frank, critical, and matter-of-fact. With only a small staff he mined government reports and investigations and found major stories in overlooked scientific reports and professional journals.

In 1941 Seldes began publishing articles about new scientific studies on smoking and health. His first story stated simply, "Smoking shortens life." Over the next decade *In Fact* published nearly 100 articles on tobacco and its health hazards and the failure of the mainstream press, because the tobacco industry was a major advertiser, to report on the issue. Seldes, a small wiry man, had stopped smoking in 1931, to which, along with not drinking and matrimonial faithfulness, he later credited his long life.

Seldes came under harsh political attack and public vilification after World War II when Senator Joseph McCarthy accused him of being a communist. The charges were false, but *In Fact* lost circulation and closed in 1950 after publishing 521 issues. *In Fact* had carried on an earlier muckraking tradition, attacking big money and big business. The publication spawned greater press criticism and scrutiny, as reflected in A. J. Liebling's "Wayward Press" column in the *New Yorker* and the weekly that the journalist I. F. Stone started, with Seldes's assistance, in 1953.

Seldes ultimately wrote twenty-one books. His later volumes included *The Great Quotations* (1960) and *The Great Thoughts* (1985), compilations of ideas that he had collected on thousands of index cards during years of reading, writing, and interviewing. His wife died in 1979, when Seldes was eighty-eight years old. He continued living in his rural Vermont home, relying on the help of his friends and neighbors. He lived to enjoy recognition for his work late in his life. In 1982 he received a George Polk Award for lifetime contributions to journalism. His autobiography, *Witness to a Century* (1987), published when he was ninety-six, revived his professional reputation, as did the Academy Award–nominated documentary *Tell the Truth and Run*, completed in 1996, a year after his death.

Seldes died in Mount Ascutney Hospital and Health Center in Windsor. He was cremated, and his ashes were buried in the front yard of his longtime home in Hartland Four Corners, Vermont, next to those of his wife.

Seldes's untiring press criticism helped reshape modern journalism practices and ethics. He emphasized "telling the truth" by reporting accurately and fairly and not censoring information. Timely and needed, his criticisms came as many cities and towns lost competing newspapers and massive corporate media monopolies replaced earlier press barons.

★

Papers, manuscripts, and photographs from Seldes's later career (1940–1971) are in the Annenberg Rare Book and Manuscript Library at the University of Pennsylvania. Seldes loved to write about himself and his journalistic exploits, but his most thorough effort was his autobiography *Witness to a Century: Encounters with the Noted, the Notorious, and the Three SOBs* (1987). His significant writings are reprinted in Randolph T. Holhut, *The George Seldes Reader* (1994). The elderly Seldes is interviewed at length in the Rick Goldsmith documentary *Tell the Truth and Run* (1996). Obituaries are in the *New York Times* (3 July 1995) and the *Washington Post* (4 July 1995).

BRENT SCHONDELMEYER

SELENA (*b.* 16 April 1971 in Lake Jackson, Texas; *d.* 31 March 1995 in Corpus Christi, Texas), tejana (Texas Mexican) singer murdered at age twenty-three, just as she attained international fame and fortune.

Selena Quintanilla Pérez was one of the three children of Abraham ("Abe") Quintanilla, Jr., a singer, and Marcella Samora, a homemaker. Growing up in a devout Jehovah's Witness household, Selena and her siblings spent most of their early years in and around Lake Jackson and Corpus Christi, Texas, moving constantly from home to home. Selena's father held a series of menial, short-term, and usually dead-end jobs that barely fed the family and paid the rent. His energy and passion were spent listening to and arranging his own music and teaching his children how to sing and play musical instruments.

Known to friends as "Abe," Selena's father had dreamed of a life as a singer and music producer since about the age of eleven. In 1957, when he was only fourteen years of age, Abe joined the Dions, a three-person band, along with Seff Perales and Bobby Lira. Singing four-part harmonies in three parts and imitating the popular doo-wop style of Dion and the Belmonts, the Dions performed at sock hops, weddings, and proms throughout South Texas. By 1961, when the Dions temporarily disbanded because Abe was drafted into the military, they had recorded ten singles and were enjoying local musical fame. Discharged from the service in 1964, Abe returned with his family to Corpus Christi to resume his musical career. At the behest of local record producers, the Dions changed their name to Los Dinos and started singing in Spanish for Texas Mexican audiences. But despite twenty-six recordings, the group developed only a local following. Frustrated, Abe quit the band in 1969 and moved to Lake Jackson, where his parents lived.

Selena. AP/WIDE WORLD PHOTOS

Having failed as a singer, Abe poured his energy into his children, hoping that someday they would become music stars. By the time Selena was six years old Abe had organized his children into a garage band. Selena sang, accompanied by her brother "AB" on bass guitar and her sister Suzette on the drums. Many who heard Selena sing at this young age realized her potential. By age eight she was winning talent contests at county fairs and with her siblings was performing at weddings, birthdays, and parties.

In 1980 Abraham Quintanilla opened the Papa Gayo restaurant in Lake Jackson, primarily as a singing venue for his nine-year-old daughter Selena. The restaurant failed in March 1981, but it sparked Selena's singing career in South Texas. Word spread of her Spanish-language *música tejana* and Los Dinos family band, which in 1980 expanded, adding Rena Dcarman on keyboard and Rodney Pyeatt on guitar.

Impressed by Selena's voice, Freddie Martínez, the

owner of Freddie Records in Corpus Christi, produced her first singles in 1983. Those recordings later appeared as a cassette album titled *Selena y los Dinos* (1984) and was eventually reissued in compact disc as *Mis Primeras Grabaciones* (1995). In 1983 Dearman and Pyeatt left Los Dinos. They were replaced by Mike Dean on keyboard and Del Balint on guitar, who in 1985 were replaced by Ricky Vela and Roger García.

When Selena was fifteen years old, two of her 1986 recordings, "Dame Un Beso" and "A Million to One," became regional hits, receiving considerable radio play throughout Texas and earning her a magazine cover story in *Tejano Entertainer*. The following year she was named Female Entertainer of the Year at the Tejano Music Awards in San Antonio on the basis of those two songs. The release of her rendition of the Mexican song "La Bamba" in the summer of 1987 garnered a national audience when the recording hit the *Billboard* Latin chart on 8 August and ultimately rose to number twenty. Two years later Selena was named Female Entertainer of the Year and Female Vocalist of the Year at the 1989 Tejano Music Awards. A lucrative recording contract with Capitol–EMI Latin Records followed shortly, as did an extensive endorsement contract with Coca-Cola.

Executives at Capitol–EMI Latin Records believed that for Selena to become a star of global fame she first had to break into the international Spanish-language market in Latin America. Then she would return to the United States with English crossover songs. With her 1990 hit "Baila Esta Cumbia" on her album *Ven Conmigo,* Selena did just that, getting considerable airplay in Mexico. In addition her revealing outfits quickly transformed her into a popular sex symbol, the Madonna-like singing sensation of the Spanish-speaking world. A sultry siren with cinnamon-colored skin, Selena accentuated her well-proportioned figure with tight-fitting leather pants and bejeweled bustiers that left her midriff exposed.

During production of *Ven Conmigo,* Chris Pérez was hired to play guitar with Selena and Los Dinos. Before long Selena was smitten by him. Pérez and Selena clandestinely married on 2 April 1992, knowing that her father would object because marriage might lessen her sex appeal among fans.

Ven Conmigo became a major recording success. Selling some 300,000 copies, it brought Selena a fan club headed by Yolanda Saldivar and enough cash to begin a clothing and jewelry design line, Fashions by Selena. By 1992 Saldivar had become Selena's confidante and manager of Selena, Etc., a salon and boutique that opened in Corpus Christi early in 1994. Also in 1994 her album *Selena Live* won a Grammy in the Best Mexican American Performance category and quickly sold more than 2 million copies, gaining a double platinum award. Her next album,

Amor Prohibido, climbed to the top of the *Billboard* Latin fifty chart and stayed there for forty-eight weeks, winning quadruple platinum honors.

While Selena sold an unprecedented number of albums and garnered awards, fans, and prestigious engagements, her boutique and fashion designs were failing. Martín Gómez, Selena's designer, complained to Abe that Saldivar was seriously mismanaging the business and perhaps even embezzling company funds. Concerned about these allegations, Abe confronted Saldivar on 9 March 1995 and demanded her resignation. She refused. The next day Saldivar purchased a .38-caliber revolver in response to Abe's threats.

By 30 March 1995 Selena was convinced that she had to fire her close friend. She called Saldivar, who was staying at the Days Inn in Corpus Christi, and demanded a meeting to transfer all business records. Saldivar handed over only a portion of them. When Selena discovered that crucial ledgers were missing, she confronted Saldivar the next morning, 31 March, and they quarreled at the Days Inn. Saldivar pulled out her gun and pointed it at her own head. Frightened by the gun, Selena fled the room, and as she did a bullet hit her right shoulder. Saldivar claimed that the gun went off accidentally. Two hours later, at 1:05 P.M., Selena was pronounced dead from internal bleeding and cardiac arrest. She is buried in Corpus Christi.

At the Days Inn, Saldivar barricaded herself in the cab of her truck for ten hours, pointing a gun at her head. She claimed the shooting was accidental and denounced Abraham Quintanilla as responsible for Selena's shooting. In her statement to police later that night, Saldivar claimed that her relationship with Selena had soured in February 1995, when Abe told Selena "that I was a lesbian [and] . . . that I was stealing money from the company."

A massive outpouring of popular sentiment followed for the tejana pop star whose career was so tragically cut short at the age of twenty-three. In late November 1995 Saldivar was found guilty of Selena's murder and was sentenced to life in prison. Selena's posthumous album brought her the crossover English audience she had long sought. *Dreaming of You,* which includes "Bidi Bidi Bom Bom," "Techno-cumbia," "Dreaming of You," and "I Could Fall in Love," sold more than 3 million copies to become a best-seller. Her tragic death brought her the international fame she had worked for all her life.

★

For further information on Selena see Gordon Randolph Willey, *Selena* (1993); Himilce Novas and Rosemary Silva, *Remembering Selena: A Tribute in Pictures and Words* (Recordando a Selena: Un tributo en palabras) (1995); Barbara J. Marvis, *Contemporary American Success Stories: Famous People of Hispanic Heritage* (1996); Joe Nick Patoski, *Selena: Como la Flor* (1996);

María Celeste Arrarás, *Selena's Secret: The Revealing Story Behind Her Tragic Death* (1997); Marvis, *Selena* (1998); and Veda Boyd Jones, *Selena* (1999). An obituary is in the *New York Times* (1 Apr. 1995). Gregory Nava directed the movie *Selena* (1997). EMI–Latin produced the videocassette *Selena Remembered* (1997), and Wendy Greene and Rachel Hanfling produced the videocassette *American Justice: Selena, Murder of a Star* (1998).

RAMÓN A. GUTIÉRREZ

SHAKUR, Tupac Amaru (*b.* 16 June 1971 in Brooklyn, New York; *d.* 13 September 1996 in Las Vegas, Nevada), actor and an originator of the musical style called "gangsta rap," celebrated for his songs about the black inner city.

Shakur's mother, Afeni Shakur (born Alice Faye Williams), was a member of the Black Panther Party, a radical political organization. His father, William M. Garland, also belonged to the party. At the time of Tupac Shakur's conception, Afeni Shakur was married to Lumumba Abdul Shakur, another member of the Black Panthers, who had been incarcerated. Upon hearing of her pregnancy, Lumumba divorced her. During the pregnancy, Afeni Shakur was imprisoned in the Women's House of Detention in New York City's Greenwich Village, and she was subsequently acquitted of conspiracy charges involving a bombing. Afeni Shakur and her young son Tupac suffered financial hardship and moved frequently between 1975 and 1983, living in the Bronx, Harlem, and occasionally in homeless shelters.

Because of this urban-nomadic life, Shakur made no long-term boyhood friendships. "I was crying all the time," he later recalled in an interview. "My major thing was I

Tupac Shakur. AP/WIDE WORLD PHOTOS

couldn't fit in, because I was from everywhere. I didn't have no buddies that I grew up with." When the boy asked about the name of his father, Afeni Shakur would tell her son that she did not know who his father was. This lack of knowledge tormented the youth.

In September 1983 twelve-year-old Shakur was offered a role in the 127th Street Ensemble, a theater group in Harlem. He portrayed Travis in the play *A Raisin in the Sun.* He took to acting and felt that through his life experiences, performing came easily to him.

Meanwhile, his mother had become hooked on crack cocaine. Her lover, known simply as "Legs," encouraged her addiction. Shakur "adopted" Legs as a surrogate father, but Legs died of a crack-induced heart attack at age forty-one.

Trying to make a fresh start in Baltimore, Shakur's mother enrolled him in that city's School for the Arts. He studied acting and ballet. He had already written a rap song under the name "M.C. New York." Shakur's teachers recognized the confidence and talent that would later serve him as a successful actor. Shakur remembered in an interview one teacher's effort to provide some guidance: "Some old white guy, and I was a little black kid from the ghetto. It was beyond him to help me." Before Shakur could graduate, his family moved to Marin City, California. He never went back to school. "Leaving that [Baltimore] school affected me so much," Shakur commented. "Even now, I see that as the point where I got off track."

Yet in a few years Shakur would be on tour as a dancer-rapper for the group Digital Underground. In 1991 he made his recording debut with Digital Underground on the album *This Is an EP Release.* The album was later certified gold. *2Pacalypse Now,* released in November 1991, was hailed as a departure for R&B music and it catapulted Shakur to national recognition. On the album, he rapped to black youth about the world they knew, while a gunshot backbeat kicked with rhythm. There were narratives about teen pregnancy, gang banging, selling drugs, and about being cooped up too long in someone else's dream. It was the voice of truth to restless and oppressed African American men at the end of the twentieth century.

At this time he formed a philosophy called "Thug Life" and had those words, an acronym containing a vulgarism, tattooed in huge letters across his pelvis. The philosophy contends that the hatred of children ruins everyone's life. He felt that thugs were essentially unloved and were victims who had no choice but to carry guns to protect what little they had. On his back was tattooed the words "Laugh Now, Cry Later." This was meant to scare anyone who felt that they could backstab Shakur and get away with it. Through these expressions, he sought to protect all that he had from being taken by a world he did not trust. When questioned as to why he became a "thug," he answered, "Because if I don't, I'll lose everything I have. Who else is going to love me but the thugs?"

In 1992 Tupac earned praise for his big-screen debut in the movie *Juice*. In April 1993, amid other run-ins with police, the rap singer was arrested in Lansing, Michigan, for swinging a baseball bat at another performer during a concert. He was sentenced to ten days in jail. Shakur's many scrapes with the law did not adversely affect record sales, and his *Strictly 4 My N.I.G.G.A.Z.* (1993) went platinum. Also in 1993, the movie *Poetic Justice*, starring singer Janet Jackson and Shakur, was released. At Halloween of that year, Shakur was arrested for allegedly shooting two off-duty Atlanta police officers. These charges were eventually dropped.

Then, just eighteen days later, Shakur was picked up in New York City on sexual abuse charges after a teenage girl was attacked in a posh Manhattan hotel. On 10 March 1994 Shakur was sentenced to fifteen days in jail for punching the director Allen Hughes. That year, moviegoers saw Shakur playing a troubled drug dealer in *Above the Rim*. His real-life troubles continued in 1994, as he was shot and robbed in a Times Square recording studio. The case remained unsolved, and in early 1995 Shakur started his sentence in New York's Rikers Island penitentiary for his sexual-abuse conviction. While behind bars, he learned that his new album *Me Against the World* had hit number one on *Billboard* magazine's pop charts. On 29 April 1995 he married Keisha Morris while incarcerated, but the couple soon became estranged.

In prison, Shakur abandoned his violent philosophy, saying, "If Thug Life is real, then let somebody else represent it, because I'm tired of it. I represented it too much." In October 1995 Death Row Records executive Marion "Suge" Knight paid a $1.4 million bond to release Shakur from prison. The performer immediately flew to Los Angeles to sign a recording contract with Death Row, and soon afterward released rap's first double CD, *All Eyez on Me*.

Back in New York for the MTV Music Video Awards on 4 September 1996, Shakur managed to get into a scuffle. Three days later, on 7 September 1996, he was shot four times in the chest after leaving a Mike Tyson boxing match in Las Vegas. At five foot ten and 168 pounds, the twenty-five-year-old Shakur was diminutive compared to the massive 300-pound "Suge" Knight, who rode in the car with him that evening. Shakur's shooting was rumored to be part of a long turf war between Knight and Bad Boy Records' Sean "Puffy" Combs; this could not be substantiated, however, as the gunman was not found. Shakur was rushed to University Medical Center, where his right lung was removed. Six days after the shooting, Shakur was pronounced dead. His body was cremated.

Shakur's death allegedly created an all-out war between the reigning gangsta rap record companies, Combs's Bad Boy Records in New York City and Knight's Death Row Records in Los Angeles. Six months after Shakur's death, Biggie Smalls, also known as Notorious B.I.G., a 400-pound gangsta rapper with Bad Boy Records, was gunned down outside of Petersen's Automotive Museum in Los Angeles. In early 1997 Knight was sentenced to nine years in prison for probation violation in connection with a fight. Fans, sickened by the violence promoted by this music and its impresarios, turned to other music and forms of entertainment. The bad-boy glamour had vanished in gun smoke.

Shakur's use of lyrics laced with violent, sexual, and profane language, and his self-portrayal as a gangster and an outlaw, helped sell several million records, making him one of the most popular—and tragic—musicians of the 1990s. As the Reverend Jesse Jackson commented after Shakur's murder, "Sometimes the lure of violent culture is so magnetic that even when one overcomes it with material success, it continues to call. Tupac just couldn't break the cycle."

★

Vibe Editors, *Tupac Shakur* (1997), chronicles the rise and fall of the rap star. See also Katy Scott, *The Killing of Tupac Shakur* (1997); Armond White, *Rebel for the Hell of It: The Life of Tupac Shakur* (1997); *Newsweek* (1 Sept. 1997) and *Spin* (Apr. 2000). Obituaries are in the *Los Angeles Times* and *New York Times* (both 14 Sept. 1996).

LOUISE CONTINELLI

SHARKEY, Jack (*b.* 26 October 1902 in Binghamton, New York, *d.* 17 August 1994 in Beverly, Massachusetts), heavyweight boxing champion in the early 1930s.

Born Joseph Paul Zukauskas (often spelled Cukoschay), the son of Lithuanian immigrants, Sharkey attended school only through the eighth grade. His first job was shoveling coal for a box factory. From his earliest youth, his ambition was to become a sailor, and as a fourteen-year-old he made the first of several unsuccessful attempts to enlist in the U.S. Navy. In 1920 he was finally inducted into the navy and was stationed in Newport, Rhode Island.

During his stint at Newport, Zukauskas showed that he could fight. "I was pretty big for eighteen," he later recalled. "The Navy taught me that a fellow who can't take care of himself doesn't belong in hard-hitting company." He won nineteen of twenty bouts during his military boxing career, becoming known as one of the toughest men in the navy before his honorable discharge on 23 February 1924. A Boston fight manager, Johnny Buckley, then signed him to a professional contract.

In an era when the fight game was dominated by Irish

Jack Sharkey. © BETTMANN/CORBIS

American boxers, Zukauskas in 1924 took the ring name of Jack Sharkey in honor of two of his favorite fighters, Tom Sharkey and the heavyweight champion Jack Dempsey. Sharkey rose quickly in the heavyweight ranks, making his professional debut in the winter of 1924 with a one-round knockout over Billy Muldoon in Boston. His first major victory was a ten-round decision in June 1924 over veteran heavyweight Floyd Johnson. Over the next thirteen years, he compiled a record of thirty-eight victories, thirteen defeats, three draws, and one no-decision. In his boxing career, he earned more than $1.5 million. "Sharkey was one of the colorful men of the period," *Ring* magazine's Nat Fleischer wrote in 1949. "Brash and self-confident, he regarded all opponents as his inferiors in fighting qualities and felt that he could whip any heavyweight in the world."

In the fall of 1926 Sharkey took on the decade's two most prominent African American heavyweights. On 21 September he won a ten-round decision over George Godfrey in Boston. Then, on 12 October, he met the great Harry Wills at Ebbets Field in Brooklyn. Sharkey outpunched Wills and was well ahead on points when he won on a foul in the thirteenth round. Because both Dempsey and Gene Tunney were avoiding the black fighters, Sharkey's victories over Godfrey and Wills made him an instant contender.

Sharkey's next big fight was a 20 May 1927 heavyweight elimination bout with Jim Maloney at Yankee Stadium. A seven-to-five underdog, Sharkey stopped Maloney in the fifth round. The promoter Tex Rickard then signed Sharkey to fight Dempsey on 21 July 1927 at Yankee Stadium. Eight years younger than Dempsey, Sharkey was the two-to-one favorite. Before the fight, he vowed, "I am going in there to knock out Jack Dempsey."

In the first round, Sharkey looked as if he might deliver on that promise. Hitting Dempsey with sharp combinations, he split and bloodied the former champion's lower lip. And, as the round ended, Sharkey staggered Dempsey with a powerful left to the jaw. Though Dempsey fought back in the next round, his punches had little impact. Sharkey opened a cut over Dempsey's left eye in the third round and closed the former champion's right eye in the fourth round. "I thought I had him," Sharkey said. "I knew it was just a matter of time." "Sharkey gave me living hell for the first five rounds," Dempsey wrote in his 1960 autobiography. "During this stretch he was as good a fighter as I've ever seen. He moved like a good middleweight. . . . I thought he was going to knock me out. He couldn't miss with his left."

In the sixth round, Dempsey rallied with body punches. When Sharkey got hit below the belt in the seventh round, he complained to the referee Jack O'Sullivan. Despite a warning from O'Sullivan, Dempsey hit Sharkey four times in the same area. As Sharkey tried to get the referee's attention, Dempsey landed a left hook to the jaw. Sharkey fell to the canvas, and Dempsey was declared the winner by knockout. Sharkey's manager protested the decision, wanting to file an appeal, but Sharkey accepted the verdict. "Aw, shut up," Sharkey told his manager. "It's all in the game."

Ironically, Sharkey lost his first championship fight under similar circumstances. On 12 June 1930, he met Max Schmeling for the heavyweight title left vacant by Tunney's retirement. Sharkey dominated the first three rounds at the Madison Square Garden bowl in Long Island City, New York. In the fourth round, he knocked out Schmeling with a right to the body. But the German claimed that he had been fouled and ring officials concurred. Schmeling thus became the first heavyweight to win the championship on a foul.

On 21 June 1932 Sharkey gained the world championship by a controversial split decision in his rematch with Schmeling. Though Sharkey moved into an early lead, Schmeling had him in trouble in the middle rounds and held his own in the later rounds. At the end of the fifteenth round, Sharkey was awarded a majority decision. Schmeling's manager Joe Jacobs lamented, "We was robbed." A majority of sportswriters agreed with that assessment.

Sharkey's reign was brief. On 29 June 1933 he defended his title against the giant Primo Carnera. It was their second meeting: Sharkey had won a lopsided decision over Carnera in 1931. "I had to fight him but I had no respect for him," Sharkey recalled years later. "He had a head as big as a squash and I knew I could hit him any time I wanted. But when I got in the ring with him I realized he had improved." In the sixth round, Sharkey jolted the challenger with two rights to the chin. But Carnera responded with a right uppercut to the chin that dropped Sharkey for the count.

His last big fight, on 18 August 1936 at Yankee Stadium, was against Joe Louis, who knocked out Sharkey in the third round. Sharkey, who retired after the Louis bout, was inducted into the Boxing Hall of Fame in 1980 and the International Boxing Hall of Fame in 1994. He was the only heavyweight to have faced both Dempsey and Louis.

Sharkey married Dorothy Pike of Epping, New Hampshire, in 1924. Their marriage produced three children and lasted until Dorothy's death in 1992. After retiring, Sharkey lived in Epping, where he was an active outdoorsman. The baseball star Ted Williams was among his regular fishing companions.

★

There are profiles of Sharkey in Nat Fleischer, *The Heavyweight Championship* (1949), and John D. McCallum, *The World Heavyweight Boxing Championship* (1974). Dempsey recalls his bout with Sharkey in his autobiography *Dempsey* (1960). An obituary is in the *New York Times* (19 Aug. 1994).

STEVE NEAL

SHILS, Edward Albert (*b.* 1 July 1910 in Springfield, Massachusetts; *d.* 23 January 1995 in Chicago, Illinois), sociologist noted for his work on civil society, the culture of academia, and his efforts to make sociology more relevant to mainstream audiences.

Shils was the son of Eastern European Jewish immigrants. His father was a cigar maker, first in Springfield, Massachusetts, and then in Philadelphia, Pennsylvania. Shils and his two brothers viewed the "City of Brotherly Love" as their own intellectual playground, exploring neighborhoods, libraries, and museums with equal fascination. As an undergraduate, Shils attended the University of Pennsylvania, where he majored in French literature while reading widely in European philosophy, especially the works of German social theorists Georg Simmel, Ferdinand Tonnies, and Max Weber. He graduated with a B.A. degree in foreign languages in 1931. Both at home and in his university studies, Shils learned to appreciate an international

perspective on life and thought. Such preparation provided him with, as one of his friends has written, a "deep even intimate knowledge of several national cultures without ever losing touch with his own." Shils married twice, divorced twice, and was survived by one son, Adam.

Interested in the composition of societies, Shils ventured into the field of social work following his graduation from college. His travels took him to Chicago and ultimately to that city's distinguished university. At the University of Chicago, Shils became a research assistant to professors probing the dimensions of the then-emerging academic field of sociology. There he studied under and became a colleague of sociologist Robert E. Park, economist Frank H. Knight, and economic historian John U. Nef. Shils never completed his graduate work at the University of Chicago, but he did become a faculty member—a position he kept until his retirement from the Department of Sociology and the Committee on Social Thought as a distinguished professor in 1985.

During World War II, Shils was member of the Office of Strategic Services (OSS) and was deployed by the British government to interrogate captured German soldiers. Shils chose not to pursue a life in the military, but he did put to good use his facility with the German language. He became America's foremost translator and teacher of the giants of modern German social thought—Max Weber and Karl Mannheim. Shils helped make their work, as well as that of Emile Durkheim, accessible to the English-reading public.

In fact, Shils became a bridge between the academic worlds of the United States and Europe. Starting in 1946, he held joint appointments with the London School of Economics and, later, Peterhouse, Cambridge, for most of his scholarly career. As a member of an elite international club of academics, Shils became a guiding force behind the creation of the *Bulletin of the Atomic Scientists*. As with many of his intellectual endeavors, Shils's association with the scientists who had helped create the first atomic weapons was based on the belief that intellectuals must help the public understand issues that, however abstract and difficult, were significant to its welfare.

Shils was a public intellectual. He coauthored with the Harvard sociologist Talcott Parsons a major treatise on sociology entitled *Toward a General Theory of Action* (1951). Their study was an attempt to understand society as a network of interconnected individuals, groups, and interests. For much of his career, Shils worked to uncover and nourish those characteristics that would unite rather than divide societies and groups within societies. At the center of Shils's theories about civil society was the idea of civility—regarded as the glue that holds myriad social elements together. Shils's writing on that topic suggests that he was

508

concerned as much with the people affected by such ideas as with the theories behind them.

Shils maintained that among the important uses of higher education was the ability to inculcate the virtues of civil society among the younger generation. To Shils, universities had a vital role to play in the ordering of societies as both an intellectual authority and a training ground for future leaders in public policy. To advance that notion, he founded the journal *Minerva: A Review of Science, Learning and Policy* in 1962. He edited the quarterly until his death in 1995, and it reflected his deep concern for the connection between the work done by scientists on university campuses and its implications for government policy. Not surprisingly, Shils was unsympathetic to the protests and violent outbursts by students on campuses across the United States and around the world in the late 1960s and early 1970s. He and Edward Levi, president of the University of Chicago, refused to decentralize the university or allow students to turn the campus into a battleground.

Shils died without completing a masterwork upon which to base his scholarly reputation. He did, however, leave behind a mountain of essays and articles that have been collected in four separate volumes, published in 1972, 1975, 1980, and 1997. He was a member of the editorial boards of a number of important journals, including *Bulletin of the Atomic Scientists, Minerva, Encounter, Government and Opposition,* and *American Scholar.* Shils also wrote an important book, *The Torment of Secrecy* (1956), in which he did a commendable job of dissecting the dubious nature of McCarthyism without soft-pedaling the dangers of communism. Shils was an intelligent and fervent anticommunist who was a member of the Congress of Cultural Freedom, an organization born of cold war tensions and devoted to the battle for the minds of Western intellectuals.

Beside his appointments at distinguished universities, Shils also delivered the Jefferson Lectures in 1979 at the request of the National Endowment for the Humanities. His topic, "Government and Universities in the United States," emphasized a theme that ran through much of his career. He was also awarded the International Balzan Prize in 1983—an award that is the equivalent of the Nobel Prize for those fields not considered by the Nobel committee. As well as being friends with many of the most important intellectuals throughout Europe and India (a place Shils visited from 1955 through 1967), he also became close with Pope John Paul II during his participation in seminars at the papal retreat at Castel Gandolfo, Italy. Shils was a gourmet, a voracious reader of literature—his favorite authors included Charles Dickens, Honoré de Balzac, Willa Cather, and especially Joseph Conrad—and a dedicated mentor to students of all ages from all over the world.

★

To date there are no full-length biographies of Shils. One reason for this might be that researchers will not have access to Shils's papers, housed in the Department of Special Collections at the University of Chicago, until 2020, and will not be allowed to see the entire collection until 2045. But since Shils was a prolific writer, he has a sizable collection of work in the public sphere, including: *The Intellectuals Between Tradition and Modernity: The Indian Situation* (1961); *The Intellectuals and the Powers and Other Essays* (1972); *Center and Periphery: Essays in Macrosociology* (1975); *The Calling of Sociology and Other Essays on the Pursuit of Learning* (1980); *Tradition* (1981); *The Constitution of Society* (1982); *The Academic Ethic* (1983); and three collections of essays that appeared in 1997: *The Calling of Education: The Academic Ethic and Other Essays on Higher Education; The Order of Liberal Learning: Essays on the Contemporary University;* and *The Virtues of Civility: Selected Essays on Liberalism, Tradition, and Civil Society.* See also Philip G. Altbach, "Edward Shils and the American University," *Society* 36 (Mar./Apr. 1999): 68–73; Joseph Epstein, "My Friend Edward," *American Scholar* 64 (summer 1995): 371–386; and Saul Bellow's thinly veiled fictional portrait of Shils in his book about Allan Bloom entitled *Ravelstein* (2000). An obituary is in the *New York Times* (26 Jan. 1995).

RAYMOND J. HABERSKI, JR.

SHILTS, Randy Martin (*b.* 8 August 1951 in Davenport, Iowa; *d.* 17 February 1994 in Guerneville, California), journalist, author, and prominent spokesperson on gay issues best known for his chronicle of the AIDS crisis *And the Band Played On* (1987).

Shilts, the third of six sons born to Bud Shilts, a salesman of prefabricated housing, and Norma Shilts, spent most of his youth in the Chicago suburb of Aurora. Raised in the Methodist church, he was a conservative youth who founded a Young Americans for Freedom chapter in his high school. He left home at the age of eighteen and enrolled at Portland (Oregon) Community College. In 1972 Shilts publicly "came out" as gay and became interested in journalism. He then transferred to the University of Oregon, where he served as managing editor of the campus newspaper and as head of the Eugene Gay People's Alliance. He received his B.S. degree with a major in journalism in 1975. Failing to find employment, because of homophobia he believed, following graduation he served briefly as the Northwest correspondent for the *Advocate,* a national gay magazine. Shilts then moved to San Francisco, where he continued as a staff writer for the magazine and helped enhance its reporting on national issues. From 1977 to 1980 he was a reporter for the San Francisco public television station KQED and simultaneously contributed to Oakland's independent television station KTVU.

In 1981 Shilts was hired as a staff reporter by the *San*

Randy Shilts. © JERRY BAUER

Francisco Chronicle, thereby becoming the first openly gay reporter assigned to gay issues on a major metropolitan newspaper. Covering the AIDS crisis virtually from its beginning in mid-1981, when the epidemic was known as a mysterious "gay-related immune deficiency" (GRID), Shilts was instrumental in leading the *Chronicle,* alone among major dailies, to cite the disease in its obituaries. He also became active in San Francisco gay political circles and in 1982 published his first book, *The Mayor of Castro Street: The Life and Times of Harvey Milk,* a biography of the gay San Francisco city supervisor who was assassinated along with Mayor George Moscone in November 1978. This book drew national attention to Shilts and was made into a documentary video in 1993.

As the AIDS crisis worsened in the 1980s, decimating San Francisco's large gay community, Shilts turned his attention almost exclusively to the disease, producing well-documented articles and stirring human interest stories on its victims. His perspective made him controversial among gay activists, as he criticized gay leaders for treating the disease as a public relations problem. Shilts campaigned against homosexual promiscuity, taking a prominent part in the fight to close San Francisco's gay bathhouses as a health hazard. The bathhouses were closed in October 1984. In 1987 Shilts's research and observations were pub-

lished in his second book, *And the Band Played On: Politics, People, and the AIDS Epidemic,* which was an immediate success. A finalist for the National Book Award, it won for Shilts the American Society of Journalists and Authors Outstanding Author Award of 1988 as well as several other prizes. Although the book's major message was that the U.S. government had neglected the epidemic because of homophobic attitudes in high places, readers paid at least as much attention to the subtheme that gays themselves had failed to deal responsibly with the spread of the disease.

The book generated further controversy due to Shilts's claim to have tracked down "Patient Zero," a French airline attendant who had supposedly contracted the disease in Africa. This claim was never verified and in fact was later discredited by public health experts. Nonetheless, both political conservatives and the media seized on Shilts's message that the gay community had somehow failed in its responsibility to combat the health crisis, and he became a favored "gay spokesperson" for the media.

The mid-1980s were difficult for Shilts. His mother, with whom he had been close, died in 1983. He was also under increasing criticism from his peers, and AIDS continued to ravage gay communities in major American cities. In 1986 he submitted to medical tests to see if he had contracted the AIDS virus but deliberately waited to hear the results until after he had finished *And the Band Played On.* On the day he finished the manuscript he checked. The medical results were positive. He was now a "victim" of the crisis about which he wrote. Shilts's health remained good for the next several years, as he took AZT and other drugs commonly prescribed for AIDS.

Shilts remained controversial among gay activists in the late 1980s and early 1990s for taking positions against the radical AIDS activist group ACT-UP (AIDS Coalition to Unleash Power) and against "outing," the practice of exposing prominent public figures who were secretly homosexual. Shilts's last journalistic crusade was in favor of permitting gay men and women to serve in the U.S. armed forces. Continuing his writing through the difficult last months of his illness, he finished *Conduct Unbecoming: Gays and Lesbians in the U.S. Military* (1993). Although the book was on best-seller lists for several weeks, Shilts was again criticized, this time for refusing to "out" his sources who were military officers.

Shilts developed full-blown AIDS before finishing his last book. On Memorial Day 1993 he engaged in a commitment ceremony with his lover Barry Barbieri, a film student. That year Shilts was diagnosed with Kaposi's sarcoma, a disease common in AIDS patients, and he was mostly homebound thereafter. He died at home in February 1994, just days after a published report indicated that the number of AIDS cases in San Francisco had peaked in 1992 and was declining.

During his lifetime, Shilts was frequently criticized by other gay activists for his insistence on emphasizing his responsibilities as a professional journalist over his genuine political commitment to advancing gay and lesbian rights. In his refusal to conceal the hesitancy of gay leaders to acknowledge AIDS in its early manifestations and his opposition to the practice of "outing" of living persons, he remained faithful to journalistic ethics as he understood them. At the time of his death, however—even though his politics remained controversial (perhaps even suspect) in the opinion of many gay activists—Randy Shilts was recognized as the writer who had set the standards by which gay journalism would thenceforth be judged.

★

Shilts's personal papers, including drafts of books, copies of his journalistic articles, research subject files, and some correspondence, are in the James C. Hormel Gay and Lesbian Center at the San Francisco Public Library. A good overview of much of his work and influence is in James Kinsella, *Covering the Plague: AIDS and the American Media* (1989). The most useful brief biographical essay is by Joseph M. Eagan, "Randy Shilts," in *Outstanding Lives: Profiles of Lesbians and Gay Men*, edited by Michael Bronski (1997). Informative obituaries are in the *San Francisco Chronicle, Los Angeles Times,* and *New York Times* (all 18 Feb. 1994).

GARY W. REICHARD

SHORE, Dinah (*b.* 29 February 1916 in Winchester, Tennessee; *d.* 24 February 1994 in Beverly Hills, California), influential singer, actress, and talk-show host whose stellar career spanned five decades.

Born Fannie Rose Shore, she was the second child of Solomon A. Shore, proprietor of a dry goods store, and Anna Stein, homemaker, both Russian Jewish immigrants. When Shore was six years old, the family moved to Nashville, Tennessee, where her father invested in a large department store and made a comfortable living. Shore attended Hume-Fogg High School, where she was a cheerleader and was voted "most popular girl." Although she wanted to sing with a big band, Shore agreed to finish her education and graduated with a degree in sociology from Vanderbilt University in 1938. Because her father refused to finance her pursuit of a singing career, Shore sold her photographic equipment, netting $253.75, and headed for New York City in June 1938.

Although she had sung on a local radio station, WSM in Nashville, and had taken a few singing lessons, Shore had no real experience in the entertainment world. She was determined to become a singer, but even though she managed to get auditions with big band leaders Tommy Dorsey,

Dinah Shore.

Benny Goodman, and Woody Herman, no one wanted a "bobby soxer" who had had no formal training. At an audition for WNEW, a local radio station, Shore sang "Dinah" in a slow swing style, as opposed to the usual upbeat style, and although her voice was not powerful, it was rich. The producers were impressed but could not remember her name, so they called her Dinah. Shore had always hated the name Fanny and decided to adopt the name the producers had inadvertently given her. In 1944 she legally changed her name.

Shore and another unknown named Frank Sinatra were assigned duets at WNEW, but the animosity between them was obvious even to a radio audience. The show was revamped and neither was rehired. Finally, in January 1939 Shore was hired to sing with Leo Reisman's orchestra in Brooklyn for $75 a week. The review in *Variety* was mixed: "nicely gowned, sells a song passably and has an unaffected ease of manner, but doesn't pile up much of a wallop for the windup."

Ben Bernie of CBS hired Shore for his network show *The Half and Half Tobacco Hour,* but she was fired two weeks later because the sponsor said she sang "too slowly . . . too softly . . . with a funny accent." In February 1940 NBC began a show for blues and jazz fans, *The Chamber Music Society of Lower Basin Street,* which consisted of barrel-house, boogie-woogie, and blues music. Shore's appearance on this show made her a national radio star before she left to join the *Eddie Cantor Show* in September. Her fame was assured because Cantor was the biggest name in radio. She introduced a song called "Yes, My Darling Daughter" and then recorded it, selling 500,000 records, an amazing feat at the time. Then followed "Blues in the Night," another big seller. *Motion Picture Daily* named Shore the best female vocalist of 1941, and NBC promptly gave her a fifteen-minute show on Sundays that ran through 1942. She had become the top singer in America.

Eddie Cantor moved his show to Los Angeles in 1942, taking Shore with him. She became active in the Stage Door Canteen, an organization for entertaining servicemen, and eventually she toured England and France, singing for soldiers in camps and hospitals. One newspaper reported that Shore was "unquestionably the favorite entertainer of 10 million American fighting men." At one of the canteen shows, she met George Montgomery, a real-life Montana cowboy who starred in Westerns; they fell in love and married in Las Vegas, Nevada on 5 December 1943. Montgomery was a corporal in the army at the time and was sent to San Antonio, Texas, three days after their elopement.

Warner Brothers signed Shore for a movie with Cantor, *Thank Your Lucky Stars* (1943), but first did a complete makeover on her. Her jet-black hair was dyed a honey blond and restyled, and her olive skin lightened with makeup. After plastic surgery to reshape her nose, along with caps on her teeth, Shore was "unrecognizable" to herself and said that for the first time in her life, she felt pretty. Her second film, *Up in Arms* (1944) with Danny Kaye, was typical wartime entertainment like its predecessor, with blockbuster stars singing popular tunes. Shore made two more similar movies and after the end of World War II filmed three more movies: *Fun and Fancy Free* (1947), *Till the Clouds Roll By* (1948), and *Aaron Slick from Punkin' Crick* (1952). In the last of these, she finally had a speaking, not just singing, role. The movie was a flop, so Shore "retired" from films but continued as a singer. By 1947 she had sold over 6 million records.

Her daughter Melissa Ann was born on 4 January 1948, and Shore enjoyed being a wife and mother. Five years later she and George adopted a son, John David. They became known in Hollywood as "the perfect family."

In 1949 NBC invited Shore to New York to appear on the *Ed Wynn Show* on television. Both the show and Shore were a success, and she never again considered radio or movies: her relaxed and informal style was perfect for the "intimate" medium. In 1951 Chevrolet sponsored a twice-weekly, fifteen-minute show starring Shore; on the first night, there were thirty seconds left to fill, so the producer suggested she chat for a moment and then blow the audience a kiss. She did, and the kiss became her trademark. Shore loved the spontaneity of live television, and in 1957 the show was expanded to a one-hour, weekly offering. It quickly became one of the most popular programs on tele-

vision. In 1958 Shore won the first of ten Emmys. The show ran through 1961.

The Montgomerys moved from Encino to Beverly Hills, California, so that Shore could spend more time with her family. Her career had skyrocketed, but that of her husband had declined. Shore loved to entertain, but Montgomery wanted only to ride his horses. There were arguments over money, and in May 1962 "the perfect couple" divorced. Shore moved with her children to Palm Springs, California, and threw herself into sports, especially golf and tennis, playing at least one of the sports every day. Her frequent tennis partner was a building contractor, Maurice F. Smith, whom she married on 26 May 1963. Unfortunately, the marriage was a fiasco, and Shore found herself divorced once again, in 1964. Determined never to marry again, Shore devoted herself to her children, sports, painting, and occasional singing appearances.

Her frustration that women golfers made about one-sixth as much money as their male counterparts, and that single women were not allowed to play at country clubs, gave Shore the impetus to publicize and popularize the game for women. In 1970 Colgate toothpaste sponsored the Colgate–Dinah Shore Ladies Professional Golf Association Tournament. By 1976 it garnered more attention than the men's U.S. Open, and the money ratio had been cut to one-third. The tournament subsequently became known as the "Dinah Shore Classic."

When her daughter married in 1969 and her son went off to boarding school in Connecticut, Shore was "at loose ends," as she later said. Her manager, Henry Jaffe, suggested that she try a talk show, since these were the new rage. Therefore, in August 1970 *Dinah's Place* first aired on NBC. The format was easygoing and comfortable: Shore offered homemaker tips, and she and celebrity guests cooked favorite recipes. Even Frank Sinatra, her former antagonist at WNEW, prepared his favorite Italian meal. Shore purposely wished to discuss light rather than heavy topics and avoided controversial subjects. The program was an instant runaway hit.

Little did Shore suspect that one of her guests, the actor Burt Reynolds, would become the love of her life. Reynolds was twenty years younger than Shore, and the press had a field day with the "reverse May/December" affair. By the end of 1971, the entire country was aware of the controversial romance, which lasted until 1976.

In July 1974 NBC canceled *Dinah's Place*, but CBS wooed Shore, and her new show *Dinah!* aired three months later, on 21 October. Shore later hosted *Dinah and Friends* (1979–1984), and then a weekly cable show on the Nashville Network, *A Conversation with Dinah* (1989–1991). She continued to work in television, hosting specials and making guest appearances, until just before her death from cancer at her home in Beverly Hills. She is buried in Hillside Memorial Park, Culver City, California.

Dinah Shore became America's radio sweetheart in 1940 and reigned as the nation's television queen for almost forty years. In addition to her smooth voice and singing style, her success owed much to the fact that she was never pretentious but simply remained herself in front of the cameras. Her relaxed and informal southern ways charmed all who knew her, especially the public. Upon hearing of Shore's death, Reynolds stated, "She is the only person I ever knew who had nothing bad to say about anyone."

★

Shore wrote the foreword to *The Best of the Music Makers* (1979) by George T. Simon, as well as three cookbooks: *Someone's in the Kitchen with Dinah* (1971), *The Dinah Shore Cookbook* (1983), and *The Dinah Shore American Kitchen* (1990). She cooperated with Bruce Cassiday for his biography, *Dinah!* (1979). There are myriad newspaper and magazine articles about Shore; see also Burt Reynolds's autobiography, *My Life* (1994), in which he calls Shore the "sunshine of my life." Obituaries are in the *New York Times* and *Los Angeles Times* (both 25 Feb. 1994), *Variety* (28 Feb. 1994), *Daily Telegraph* (London) (1 Mar. 1994), and *Billboard* (12 Mar. 1994).

ELAINE MCMAHON GOOD

SIEGEL, Jerome ("Jerry") (*b.* 17 October 1914 in Cleveland, Ohio; *d.* 28 January 1996 in Los Angeles, California), comic book writer and editor best known for creating the character Superman, with Joe Shuster.

Siegel was the youngest of six children born to Michael Siegel and Sarah Fine, Russian immigrants who managed a tailor shop and dry cleaning establishment. School did not come easily for Siegel, but working in a printing plant supplemented his family income and encouraged his fascination with writing. This interest led him to submit stories to pulp magazines under the pseudonym Bernard J. Kenton and to self-publish a science fiction fanzine, *Cosmic Stories,* at the age of fourteen. Siegel met Joe Shuster at Glenville High School in 1931, and their shared passion for comic strips led to the creation of their own. Siegel wrote and Shuster drew a Tarzan parody, *Goober the Mighty,* in their school newspaper, the *Glenville Torch.* They also self-published a fanzine, *Science Fiction: The Advance Guard of Future Civilization* (October 1932); "The Reign of the Superman" first appeared in the third issue, January 1933. The Superman character was originally a villain, but Siegel and Shuster soon recognized the character's potential as a hero and, in 1934, tried to sell it as a comic book to Consolidated Book Publishers in Chicago, and later as a comic strip to the major newspaper syndicates, though without success. The pair produced other strips such as *Steve Walsh,*

Jerry Siegel with the Royal typewriter he used to write his first Superman stories. ASSOCIATED PRESS HO

Snoopy and Smiley, Reggie Van Twerp, and *Interplanetary Police,* but they, too, generated little interest.

In 1935 Siegel and Shuster's first professional work, a swashbuckling adventure called *Henri Duval* and a magic strip, *Dr. Occult,* appeared in *New Fun Comics* #6 (October 1935), published by National Allied Publishing, a firm that would become National Periodicals and ultimately DC Comics. Siegel and Shuster followed with *Federal Men* in National's *New Comics* #2 (January 1936) and *Slam Bradley* for *Detective Comics* #1 (March 1937). The latter was the team's first major success, becoming the first original comic book character to run in more than 100 continuous stories. Siegel drew additional income by writing for the *Cleveland Shopping News* and serving as editor/publisher of the *Dental Review.*

Then, in 1938 DC Comics published Superman in *Action Comics* #1. Their original strip came to the attention of Sheldon Mayer, editor/artist for the McClure syndicate. He showed it to chief editor M.C. Gaines, who rejected it as ill-suited to the newspapers but passed it on to Vincent Sullivan, editor of *Action Comics.* In a move that would have a profound effect on copyright and trademark issues, Siegel and Shuster signed the standard contract, turning over all rights to the character for $130 (roughly $10 a page for the first story), and worked exclusively for DC for the next ten years. The work gave the team financial independence. On 18 June 1939, Siegel married Bella Lifshitz; they later had a son, Michael.

On 16 January 1939, the McClure Syndicate debuted Superman in four newspapers and in November added a Sunday feature. By 1941 the strip was carried in over 300 newspapers with a circulation of over 20 million readers. *Action Comics* sold 900,000 issues per month in 1941, while the subsequent title, *Superman,* sold over 1,250,000; the comics together grossed $950,000 a year. Siegel and Shuster earned $500 per thirteen-page story plus a small percent of merchandising, sharing an estimated annual income of $150,000. Siegel alone developed other characters, such as the Spectre for *More Fun Comics* #52 (February 1940), the Star Spangled Kid in *Action Comics* #40 (September 1941), and Robotman in *Star Spangled Comics* #7 (April 1942).

Siegel was drafted into the United States Army in 1943. He served as a private in the Thirty-Ninth Special Service Corps and as an editor for *Stars and Stripes,* but still managed to write Superman stories for DC. When he returned in 1945, he found that DC had published one of his characters, Superboy, in *More Fun Comics* #101 (January/February 1945) without the partnership's permission. The team sued in April 1947 to regain the rights to the Superman/Superboy character, to cancel their newspaper contract with McClure, and to recover an estimated $5,000,000 worth of lost revenue. A $400,000 settlement was reached out of court, but with it Siegel and Shuster lost all claim on Superman and Superboy. Moreover, their names were taken off the strips and their DC contract was terminated.

Siegel and Shuster turned to Vincent Sullivan and Magazine Enterprises to create *Funnyman,* but it lasted only one year, and the Siegel and Shuster partnership ended. This troubling time also saw the end of Siegel's first marriage. As the Superman lawsuit was pending, Siegel's wife, Bella, was granted a divorce on 7 October 1948. Siegel had become reacquainted with Joan Kovacs who, under the professional name Joanne Carter, had posed as the original model for Lois Lane in 1937. On 14 October, Siegel and Carter were married in Cleveland; they had a daughter, Laura, and their marriage lasted until Siegel's death.

In 1950 Siegel became the editor of the Ziff-Davis publishing house and scripted their most successful title, *G.I. Joe.* But another Siegel work, *Kid Cowboy,* and other titles were less profitable, and by 1953 he was once again freelancing, writing *Joe Yank* (1953–1954) at Standard Comics and *Nature Boy* (1956–1957) for Charlton. He was rehired by DC in 1959 to write stories for the *Legion of Super-Heroes, Adam Strange,* and *Superman,* but received no published credit. In the mid-1960s he went to Archie Comics and penned stories for *Mandrake the Magician* and the *Phantom* (both 1966–1967) for Charlton, and finished his comics career early in the 1970s working for Marvel on the *X-Men, Human Torch,* and *Kazar.* By 1975 he had moved to California, where he worked as a mailroom clerk and typist.

Throughout the 1960s and 1970s Siegel wrote frequently to DC, arguing that the copyright on the original Superman contract had run out in 1963 and that the rights should be reassigned to him and Shuster. When Warner Brothers, which purchased DC in 1968, began to plan a Superman feature film in 1977, Siegel took his protest to the media. Embarrassed by the resulting outcry and fearful of a negative impact on their production, Warner settled out of court, paying Siegel and Shuster $20,000 a year. Jerry Siegel died of congestive heart failure in Los Angeles at the Daniel Freeman Memorial Hospital on 28 January 1996. His remains were cremated.

Siegel's outstanding contribution was in his early work with Shuster, creating and defining the superhero genre in American mass culture. Superman became the template for dozens of imitators in all realms of mass media, impacting the use of marketing and merchandising, and affecting radio, television, the movies, publishing, and even the stage. Siegel himself became an important figure in the struggle for writers' and artists' rights in graphic publishing; in part because of his efforts, marketing and creative rights for artists have drastically changed for the better.

★

The growing field of media studies research has produced several excellent examinations of Siegel and Shuster's work. Les Daniels's informative *Superman: The Complete History* (1998) is highly recommended, as are Ron Goulart's two volumes, *The Encyclopedia of American Comics* (1990) and *Over Fifty Years of American Comic Books* (1991). See also Maurice Horn, *The World Encyclopedia of Comics* (1976); Mike Benton, *The Comic Book in America* (1989); and Paul Sassiene, *The Comic Book* (1994). DC Comics has also published several reprint volumes of Siegel and Shuster's work that offer informative introductions, notably *The Superman Archives* (1989); *The Golden Age of Superman* (1993); *Superman: The Daily Strips* (1998); and *Superman: The Sunday Classics* (1998). An entry on Siegel also appeared in the 1944 *Supplement to Who's Who in America.* An obituary is in the *New York Times* (30 Jan. 1996).

PATRICK A. TRIMBLE

SIMPSON, Adele Smithline (*b.* 28 December 1903 in New York City; *d.* 23 August 1995 in Greenwich, Connecticut), fashion designer and chairperson of Adele Simpson, Inc., a Seventh Avenue manufacturer and wholesaler of ready-to-wear women's clothes.

Adele Smithline was the youngest of five daughters born to Jacob Smithline, a tailor, and Ella Bloch, a homemaker, both immigrants from Riga, Latvia. She lived with her family at 27 East 69th Street in New York City. After graduating from Wadleigh High School in 1920, she enrolled in the Pratt Institute in Brooklyn, New York, and received her degree in 1924.

Adele Simpson, 1974. AP/WIDE WORLD PHOTOS

Simpson's design career was launched in 1923, when she was hired by her sister Anna's employer, Sigmund Kaski, a partner in the New York firm of Ben Gershel, Inc., a manufacturer of coats and suits. Initially an assistant, she became a designer in 1924, earning a salary of $30,000. She was made head designer in 1926, but she moved to another New York firm, William Bass, Inc., in 1927 as its chief designer. She married Wesley Simpson, a textile executive, on 8 October 1930. They resided in a townhouse on East 79th Street in New York City and a country estate in Greenwich, Connecticut, where they raised their two children.

As more than a third of America's garment manufacturers went out of business between 1929 and 1933, Simpson was fortunate to be employed. U.S. manufacturers benefited from the new, lower import duties during the Depression, and Paris couturiers, unable to compete, enabled American designers to dictate fashion, albeit with department store labels rather than those of designers. Dorothy Shaver, president of Lord and Taylor, a New York department store, changed this practice in 1932, when she began a promotion of clothing with the designers' names on the labels. Adele Simpson was one of the first designers in the promotion. In 1934 Simpson became chief designer at Mary Lee Fashions, at 530 Seventh Avenue, where she

designed under her own label. When the owner Alfred W. Lasher retired in 1949, she purchased the company, which she ran with Eleanor Graham, long-time designer associate, and Joseph Immerman, one of the most famous production experts in the wholesale dress industry at the time. She changed the company's name to Adele Simpson, Inc., and was its chief designer and president. In 1978 she stopped designing but stayed on as chairman, passing the management of the firm to her daughter, Joan, and son-in-law Richard Raines, and left the designing to Donald Hobson. She retired in 1985. During her active employment at the company, Simpson oversaw the operation of twelve factories, selecting fabrics, designing many of the clothes, and presenting the annual collection to buyers. She was even one of the first to present her fashions on tours of midwestern and southern cities.

Simpson was recognized for her designs as well as for her use of fabrics. She was the recipient of the Neiman Marcus Fashion Award in 1946 for distinguished service in the field of fashion and the Coty Fashion Award in 1947. The 1950s brought her further recognition with the first Cotton Council Award in 1953, for using cotton, even for full-skirted evening gowns, and making it part of a high-fashion statement, and in 1958 with a salute from the International Silk Association for her fine use of silk surah in evening dresses and "doeskin," a silk and wool blend, in suits. She was twice the recipient of the Woolens and Worsteds of America Citation.

One of her most notable fashions of the 1950s was the cotton chemise dress she called the "skimmer," because it "skims over the woman . . . touching here, releasing there, involving her body-in-movement as part of the design." This dress was Simpson's adaptation of a beltless French design and was worn either with a belt behind for a tighter fit or a belt in front for a looser one. She thought that a woman would want to feel some fit and thus stressed inner construction with built-in bodices. Other preferred designs were the town costume, a dress with matching coat, and a suit with lining and blouse of the same fabric. Her clothes were totally coordinated, such as a red and tweed suit paired with "tweed" beads, bar pins she designed, and necklaces for her collarless suits or dresses. She chose hats, gloves, shoes, and even nylon stockings for a totally seamless effect. She even consulted with accessory manufacturers regarding colors and fabrics before selecting her own.

Simpson's phrase "pace, race, space" captured the need for women to move fast, unencumbered by pinched waists and accentuated busts, and she designed clothes that women could step into rather than put on over their heads. Her styles included zouave skirts, slenderized trapeze coats, and luxurious Venetian brocade empire-styled dresses in blue and red, inspired by carnations for pattern and color.

She was proud that all her fabrics were made in America, even the "Venetian brocade."

In 1964 Simpson was the first manufacturer of the Givenchy special collection for Bloomingdale's. Unlike her friend Pauline Trigère, who objected to Parisian couture setting the styles for the United States and to the pirating of styles by other designers, Simpson also made American ready-to-wear interpretations of French haute couture, and did not object to being copied herself: "You might just as well go out of business if they stop copying you. It really means that you aren't making clothes that are good enough to steal." Cheap copies, she maintained, could not duplicate the effect of fine fabrics and workmanship.

The 1970s marked a return to elegance but the midcalf-length skirt posed a problem for American designers, who were reluctant to follow the Parisian trend, finding the longer lengths dowdy. Simpson compromised by adopting the "midi" for evening but keeping daytime dresses shorter. From November 1978 to February 1979, 104 of her costumes were displayed at the Fashion Institute of Technology in New York City. On that occasion she also lectured on how she adapted exotic costumes to contemporary clothing: a Yemenite bride's outfit into tunic and pants; a Turkish caftan robe into hot pants; a Kenyan leopard-printed chiffon into a miniskirt. Neither avant-garde, like Yves St. Laurent, nor outré, like Rudi Gernreich, Simpson nonetheless thought "fashion should not make mice or wrens of women." She said, "Color may be a shout or a whisper . . . monochrome or a blaze of pattern . . . [it] is the mood of design," Simpson said, maintaining that color had to be suited to the type and shape of the dress—"inevitable color"—whereas fabric was "a means of relaxing or tensing a line . . . fluid or firm." She described a black-dyed Argentine lamb—broadtail processed—"as fragile as a butterfly's wing—but . . . tough and practical." Her fabrics, usually lightweight and sensual, were mostly "pure," rather than synthetic, during the 1950s and 1960s, but in the 1970s and 1980s she used viscose, nylon, and acetate for her designs, as did the Parisian couturiers.

Simpson's husband died in 1976. In 1978 she ceased to design but stayed on as chairperson of the board. She retired in 1985 and died of a heart attack in Greenwich, Connecticut, where she is buried.

Expressions of Simpson's philosophy of fashion include, "fashion is failure if not functional," "evolution, not revolution," and "know what your customer is doing and thinking." She had three criteria for her collections: trend-consciousness but with taste; appeal to men; and investment value. Frequently described as ladylike, her designs were moderately priced for their category. Her clientele included the first ladies Mamie Eisenhower, Patricia Nixon, Lady Bird Johnson, Rosalynn Carter, and Barbara Bush. Her designs were also sold to the best retailers nationwide, including Saks Fifth Avenue, Bloomingdale's, Bergdorf Goodman, Garfinckel's, Neiman Marcus, Meyer's, and Sakowitz. She combined design with marketability, aware of her responsibility for keeping her factories functioning.

★

The Simpson collection, including costumes, books, scrapbooks of newspaper clippings, photos of designs, fabrics, and 1,500 artifacts, was given to the Fashion Institute of Technology in New York City. The printed fashion items are in the Special Collections Division of its library. Information about Simpson's career appears in Catherine Houck, *Fashion Encyclopedia: An Essential Guide to Everything You Need to Know about Clothes* (1982), and Eleanor Lambert, *World of Fashion* (1976). Robert Riley's *1001 Treasures of Design* is a catalogue of the 104 items shown in the 1978 exhibition at the Fashion Institute of Technology. Robert Riley's video of Adele Simpson's lecture-fashion show (16 Oct. 1978) reveals how the designer adapted foreign costumes to current fashion. An obituary is in the *New York Times* (24 Aug. 1995).

BARBARA L. GERBER

SLONIMSKY, Nicolas (Nikolai Leonidovich) (*b.* 27 April 1894 in St. Petersburg, Russia; *d.* 25 December 1995 in Los Angeles, California), witty and erudite musical lexicographer, and sometime composer and conductor of avant-garde works, best remembered for writing four editions of *Baker's Biographical Dictionary of Musicians* (1958–1992). He is also celebrated for having championed the early works of Charles Ives and other American composers.

Slonimsky was the son of Leonid Slonimsky, an economist and writer, and Faina Vengerova. He began studying piano at the age of six, under the tutelage of his aunt, Isabelle Vengerova, who went on to be one of the great piano teachers of the twentieth century. He enrolled at the Saint Petersburg Conservatory and studied harmony and orchestration there from 1910 to 1914, when he was drafted into the Russian army at the beginning of World War I. Following the Russian Revolution of 1917, Slonimsky began working as a rehearsal pianist, first in Kiev (in 1919) and then in Yalta (in 1920), where he also taught at the conservatory. In 1921 he fled Russia and went to Turkey as a stowaway on a steamer; he remained there for a time, performing as a silent film and café pianist, and then worked his way through Bulgaria bound for France. By late 1921 he had arrived in Paris, where he became secretary and rehearsal pianist to the famed conductor Serge Koussevitzky.

In 1923 Slonimsky was offered a position at the Eastman School of Music in Rochester, New York. He served as an opera coach there for two years, and then rejoined Koussevitzky, now working in Boston, assisting the conductor through 1927. Settling in Boston, Slonimsky began a freelance career as a newspaper critic, beginning with the *Bos-*

Nicolas Slonimsky. COURTESY OF ELECTRA YOURKE

ton *Evening Transcript,* and as a conductor. In 1927 he formed the Chamber Orchestra of Boston specifically to perform modern works; the group premiered compositions by Edgar Varèse, Henry Cowell, and Charles Ives, among others. Ives, pleased by Slonimsky's premiere performance of his *Three Places in New England* at New York City's Town Hall on 10 January 1931, sponsored a European tour by the conductor later that year. In 1931 Slonimsky also became a U.S. citizen and, on 30 July, wed Dorothy Adlow, then the art critic for the *Christian Science Monitor.* The couple had one child. Slonimsky continued to conduct concerts of modern music on his return to the United States, including the world premiere of Varèse's *Ionisation* (6 March 1933). The work was dedicated to Slonimsky by the composer; it was also recorded by Columbia Records under Slonimsky's direction. This recording was said to be used by U.S. scientists at Los Alamos as background music while they were working on the atomic bomb. It was also used by the dance choreographer Hanya Holm for her dance *Trend* (1937).

In 1933 Slonimsky was hired by the Los Angeles Philharmonic to conduct a series of concerts at the Hollywood Bowl. However, he failed to take into account the conservative tastes of the audience that was then the backbone of support for the orchestra. After conducting a single program of new music, the reaction was so strongly negative

that Slonimsky was let go. Disillusioned, he abandoned his career as a conductor to focus on writing about music.

In 1937 Slonimsky produced the first installment of what would prove to be one of the most important chronicles of twentieth-century music, titled *Music Since 1900.* He went on to oversee the work through five editions (1937–1994) that carried it to 1992. More than a chronology, the volume is packed with the witty observations and critical acumen that characterized all of Slonimsky's writing. In 1946 he took over the editorship of the *International Cyclopedia of Music and Musicians,* overseeing the fourth through eighth editions of that work (1946–1958). He is best known, however, for his longtime editorship of *Baker's Biographical Dictionary of Musicians,* which he compiled and wrote for in its fifth through eighth editions (1958–1992). Slonimsky's work for the dictionary led to comparisons between him and Samuel Johnson, the witty eighteenth-century English writer and critic; indeed, Slonimsky's entries are full of sharp writing that would have made Johnson proud. Slonimsky was a bloodhound for musical facts; priding himself on his research; he went so far as to write the Vienna weather bureau to establish—once and for all—whether it snowed the day Mozart was buried. (It was, in fact, a sunny day.)

An early champion of Latin American composers, Slonimsky traveled to South America in 1941 to obtain information about contemporary music there; that trip formed the basis for his 1945 book, *Music of Latin America.* A series of articles for the *Christian Science Monitor* introducing music for children became the basis for *The Road to Music* (1947). That same year his monumental work, *The Thesaurus of Scales and Melodic Patterns,* "an inventory of all conceivable and inconceivable tonal combinations," was published; it later found favor among jazz musicians (most notably John Coltrane), who used it to inspire their improvisations. Beginning in the mid-1940s, Slonimsky wrote a regular column of musical anecdotes for *Étude* magazine; some of the columns were collected in *A Thing Or Two About Music* (1948). A few years later, he compiled bad reviews of musical classics, *The Lexicon of Musical Invective* (1952), which revealed the scorn, abuse, and disdain suffered by Brahms, Liszt, Berlioz, Beethoven, and other greats at the hands of their contemporary critics.

In 1962 and 1963, Slonimsky traveled through Eastern Europe on a tour sponsored by the U.S. State Department. After his wife's death in 1964, Slonimsky relocated to Los Angeles, where he joined the faculty of the University of California at Los Angeles (UCLA). However, three years later he was forced to retire at age seventy. He remained in Los Angeles, occasionally lecturing on music but focusing his efforts on updating and rewriting *Baker's.* In the early 1980s, he was befriended by the rock musician Frank

Zappa, who presented Slonimsky as the opening act for a Zappa concert at the Santa Monica Coliseum in 1981.

Although never a serious composer, Slonimsky wrote and published numerous works for piano, voice, and chamber groups. Usually, his music was playful or clever, but his stylistic range was broad, including sentimental ballads written in the 1920s; a tricky series for solo piano titled *Studies in Black and White* (1928), in which the left hand plays on the black keys and the right hand on the white; and musical settings for poetry and epitaphs (such as *Gravestones in Hancock, New Hampshire,* 1945). In 1925 he composed a series of humorous settings of newspaper ads of the period, including "Make This a Day of Pepsodent," "No More Shiny Nose," and "Children Cry for Castoria"; in later life, he would take credit for composing the first singing commercials, although these songs were never used commercially. He wrote an orchestral piece for children, *My Toy Balloon* (1942), based on a Brazilian children's song and still in the pop orchestral repertory, and Yellowstone Park Suite (1951). In 1965 Slonimsky composed a short choral work, playfully called *the Möbius Strip-Tease,* a "perpetual vocal canon notated on a Möbius band to be revolved around the singer's head," which was premiered at UCLA. Among his later works are the *Minitudes* (1971–1977), fifty short piano pieces illustrating different, often humorous, takes on classical themes and forms.

In 1992 Slonimsky returned to Russia to celebrate his ninety-eighth birthday in his native Saint Petersburg, a visit captured in a television documentary of his life. His music was played at a music festival, and he gave seminars to admiring students eager to learn of modern Western music from an insider.

Slonimsky was a lively, gregarious original, with a prodigious memory, addicted to arcana, an enthusiastic performer, and a media favorite from the time he won $30,000 on a television quiz show in 1956. Radio stations in Los Angeles and San Francisco regularly invited him for sessions of anecdote and opinion, which he expressed in vivid, slightly accented English. As he aged, Slonimsky became increasingly rotund; his angular countenance eventually rounded out into a pleasant face with twinkling eyes conveying a mischievous character.

Slonimsky remained active, working until his 100th year; he died quietly on Christmas Day, having reached the venerable age of 101. His remains were cremated.

★

Slonimsky's papers are deposited at the Music Division of the Library of Congress, Washington, D.C. Many letters from prominent composers to Slonimsky are included in the appendix to his *Music Since 1900* (5th ed. 1994), including correspondence with Charles Ives. Slonimsky wrote an autobiography, *Perfect Pitch* (1988), which includes many charming stories about his life and his interaction with composers and performers. He also wrote a quirky autobiography of himself for *Baker's Biographical Dictionary of Musicians,* 8th ed. (1992). Lawrence Wechsler wrote a two-part profile of Slonimsky that appeared in the *New Yorker* (Nov. 1986). Obituaries appear in the *New York Times* (27 Dec. 1995), the *New Yorker* (15 Jan. 1996), and *Opera News* (13 Apr. 1996).

RICHARD CARLIN
ELECTRA YOURKE

SMITH, Margaret Chase (*b.* 14 December 1897 in Skowhegan, Maine; *d.* 29 May 1995 in Skowhegan, Maine), Republican congresswoman from Maine, the first woman to serve in both houses of Congress, and the first woman to seek the nomination of a major political party for the presidency of the United States.

Margaret Madeline Chase was the eldest of six children of George Emery Chase and Caroline Murray Chase. Two brothers died in early childhood, leaving one brother and three sisters. Her father, a barber plagued by migraine headaches, worked sporadically. Her mother waited tables and labored in a shoe factory. When she was old enough, Margaret contributed to the family income by clerking at a variety store and working as a night operator for the telephone company.

Margaret Chase Smith. AP/WIDE WORLD PHOTOS

Following her graduation from high school in 1916, she briefly taught in a one-room rural school, then took a series of clerical jobs in her hometown, progressively earning more salary and higher status. At the same time, she became deeply involved in women's clubs, particularly the Federation of Business and Political Women's Club, where she discovered a community of achievement-oriented young women like herself who were training for public life. She founded the local chapter in 1922, and by 1925 was president of the Maine State Federation. During her tenure, she earned a statewide reputation as smart and competent. In 1926 she also began cultivating her interest in party politics through membership in the Skowhegan Republican Committee, later serving as the organization's secretary. In 1930 she was elected to the Maine State Republican Committee.

Chase remained unmarried into her thirties, but she had been "keeping company" with a prominent local politician, Clyde Harold Smith, since she was eighteen. Smith was first selectman of Skowhegan, a position comparable to mayor, from 1915 to 1932. He also concurrently held a series of state offices, while managing several local businesses. Smith had hired Chase for a brief assignment (to record the town inventory list) while she was still in high school. Over the next decade and a half, the couple, separated in age by twenty-two years, shared Sunday drives, picnics, and occasional political rallies. Smith, a divorced man, married Margaret Chase on 14 May 1930.

Smith wished to cap his long public career with a run for governor. However, he never realized this goal, largely due to intrastate politics. In 1936 he won election to Congress from Maine's Second District. Margaret Smith worked as her husband's campaign manager and secretary and, when his health began to fail shortly after they arrived in Washington, as his liaison to Maine. In April 1940, just days before the filing deadline for reelection to his third term, Clyde Smith suffered a heart attack. Before he died on 8 April, he dictated a press release that urged his constituents to "support the candidate of my choice, my wife and my partner in public life, Margaret Chase Smith." Despite significant opposition from Maine Republicans, Mrs. Smith, buoyed by the power base they had built together, won his unexpired seat and the next full term that fall.

Representative Smith swiftly established her independence from party orthodoxy by approving President Roosevelt's defense policies and favoring Social Security and labor measures. After her reelection in 1942, she won appointment to the House Naval Affairs Committee, a key committee in wartime, especially for Maine with its huge shipbuilding industry. As she worked on a variety of military and home-front issues, she represented women in the media, the committee room, and the House floor, articulating the contradictions between women's new wartime roles and aspirations and traditional attitudes about the status of women. These same circumstances also enhanced Smith's ability to surmount contradictions of her own, especially the need to remain ladylike while demonstrating that she was tough enough to handle the hard issues. Her expertise in military affairs and consistent advocacy of a strong national defense policy affirmed that reputation and shaped her congressional career.

Many of her efforts during the war were on behalf of military women, securing rank and regular military status for nurses and ultimately for women in all the armed services. Because policy is collectively made, it is often impossible to assess the impact of one member of Congress on the progress of a particular piece of legislation. The Women's Armed Services Integration Act of 1948 was an exception. Smith relentlessly pressed the issue, resurrecting it over several congresses, and once held out twenty-six to one against the entire Armed Services Committee to force the measure to the floor and eventual passage.

Throughout her years in the House, Smith built a reputation for independence and rectitude. The widespread perception that she did not adhere to party ideology, but considered each issue on its own merits and then voted based on her convictions, made her enormously popular with the voters in Maine, who placed a high value upon individualism and self-reliance.

In 1948 Smith risked her safe seat in the House to run for the U.S. Senate, a first for a woman. She had the able assistance and support of William C. Lewis, Jr., legislative counsel to the Naval Affairs Committee. He managed her successful campaign and afterward signed on as her administrative assistant, a post he held until she left office in 1973. Lewis had the legal education Smith lacked. Her reputation for sagacity owed much to his careful briefings. They were intensely devoted to one another, though neither was willing to risk the political price for marriage, as he was fifteen years her junior. Lewis remained her companion until he died of a heart attack in 1982.

Although Smith's election to the Senate was greeted with great expectation of imminent political equity for women, she served most of her twenty-four years as the only woman. She continued her work on defense committees, much of it dealing with reserve measures and officer promotions. She seldom made important speeches or took the lead on issues. Instead, she built a reputation for hard work and perfect attendance, moderation and probity, and for attacking extremism on both the political left and right. The most dramatic example of this was her riveting "Declaration of Conscience" speech against the depredations of Senator Joseph McCarthy in 1950. Although the speech attracted favorable national attention, it did little to restrain McCarthy, who was not censured by his peers until four years later.

Senator Smith, having accumulated substantial seniority and power on major committees and a positive national resume, launched a bid for the Republican nomination for president in 1964. Unable to compete with her millionaire opponents, chiefly Barry Goldwater and Nelson Rockefeller, she turned self-righteously away from money politics, a strategy that had long worked well for her in Maine. She refused to leave her post in the Senate, campaigning only on weekends, and returned all contributions. Her greatest handicap, though, was her sex, and she found it impossible to overcome the inherent dichotomy between being a lady and being a leader. She defensively insisted that women were people and that she expected people to vote for her record while disregarding her sex. But those around her recognized little else. She ran in New Hampshire and Illinois, then faded to an amusing sideshow. In July, at San Francisco's Cow Palace, Smith gathered twenty-seven first-ballot votes, thus becoming the first woman placed in nomination for the presidency of the United States by a major political party.

Smith continued on in the Senate, where seniority had elevated her to the ranking member on two key committees, Armed Services and Appropriations. As the Vietnam War escalated, she never wavered from her firm defense policy, despite increasing entreaties from her constituents. In 1970 she made a second "Declaration of Conscience," criticizing the extremist tactics of student militants as well as the attempts of the Nixon administration to repress dissent.

To the surprise of many, Smith lost her bid for a fifth term in 1972 to Second District Representative William Hathaway, who charged that she was out of step with her state and too old at seventy-four to continue to serve effectively. After three years as a visiting professor for the Woodrow Wilson Fellowship Foundation, Smith returned to her hometown, where she and Lewis established a research library. She devoted her final years to the Margaret Chase Smith Library, while a sympathetic media gradually transformed her into a symbol of all that was good about a Maine that was rapidly fading away. She died at home on 29 May 1995 following a massive stroke. She was ninety-seven.

Senator Smith was the first to breach several important barriers to higher office for women, serving effectively in a male institution for thirty-three years. Though her effectiveness was largely dependent upon the approval of male colleagues, and that approval was often dependent upon her ability to minimize her gender identity, she carved out a career for herself without violating that precept. Her diminutive size was belied by a strong chin and an iron will. Smith personified a powerful woman of moral courage and integrity. As a consequence, she advanced opportunities for all women who aspire to public office.

★

The Margaret Chase Smith Library in Skowhegan, Maine, contains over 300,000 documents, 3,000 photographs, dozens of audio and videotapes, 43 volumes of statements and speeches, and nearly 500 scrapbooks of clippings and personal items. Smith's memoir, *Declaration of Conscience* (1972), edited by William C. Lewis, Jr., is a collection of essays and speeches rather than an autobiography. Biographies of Smith include Patricia Ward Wallace, *Politics of Conscience: A Biography of Margaret Chase Smith* (1995); Patricia L. Schmidt, *Margaret Chase Smith: Beyond Convention* (1996); and Janann Sherman, *No Place for a Woman: A Life of Senator Margaret Chase Smith* (2000). Earlier biographies by Frank Graham, Jr., *Margaret Chase Smith: Woman of Courage* (1964), and Alice Fleming, *The Senator from Maine: Margaret Chase Smith* (1969), deal primarily with her public persona. A detailed survey of Smith's most significant legislation, the Women's Armed Services Integration Act of 1948, appears in Janann Sherman, "'They Either Need These Women or They Do Not': Margaret Chase Smith and the Fight for Regular Status for Women in the Military," *Journal of Military History* 54 (Jan. 1990): 47–78. An obituary of Smith is in the *New York Times* (30 May 1995).

JANANN SHERMAN

SMITH, (Charles) Page (Ward) (*b.* 6 September 1917 in Baltimore, Maryland; *d.* 28 August 1995 in Santa Cruz, California), historian, author, and founding provost of Cowell College, first college of the University of California at Santa Cruz.

Page Smith was the son of William Ward Smith, a native of New York, an aspiring but generally unsuccessful politician, businessman, and farmer, briefly secretary to New York governor Nathan Miller. His mother was Ellen West Smith, a banker's daughter. Page had one brother, John, born when he was five years old.

Smith attended the Gilman School, a private boys' school in Baltimore, and Dartmouth College, from which he graduated with a B.A. in 1940. He then enlisted, with a group of college friends, in the Civilian Conservation Corps. Smith was drafted into the United States Army in 1941, in the first draft call, and assigned to the Twenty-Ninth Infantry Division. He was selected to attend one of the early officer candidate classes at the Infantry School at Fort Benning, Georgia, and, as a newly commissioned second lieutenant, his first assignment was as a mortar instructor at the Infantry School.

On 11 July 1942, at Fort Benning, Smith married artist Eloise Pickard of Durham, North Carolina, whom he met after buying one of her paintings while he was on maneuvers in North Carolina. During the fifty-three years of their marriage, the Smiths reared four children, Ellen Davidson, Carter Smith, Anne Easley, and Eliot Smith.

In 1942 First Lieutenant Smith was assigned to command of Company C of the Tenth Mountain Division, and the newlyweds moved to Colorado. The Tenth Division fought in Italy, where in the battle of Mount Belvedere, Smith was seriously wounded; he was subsequently awarded a Bronze Star and discharged from service with the rank of captain. He enrolled in the history department at Harvard University and, with Eloise and his children, moved to Cambridge, Massachusetts. In 1948 Smith received a master of arts degree and continued his studies in American history under Samuel Eliot Morison, for whom he was a graduate assistant. Smith received a Ph.D. in 1951 and then a fellowship at the Institute of Early American History and Culture in Williamsburg, Virginia, and appointment as an instructor at the College of William and Mary, also in Williamsburg.

In 1953 the Smiths moved from Williamsburg to Los Angeles, where Page became an assistant professor in the history department of the University of California at Los Angeles (UCLA). Smith remained there until 1964, when Dean E. McHenry, a former UCLA colleague and now chancellor of the University of California's new campus at Santa Cruz (UC Santa Cruz), invited Smith to become provost of Cowell College, the first college of UC Santa Cruz.

The new campus, beautifully situated in the redwoods above town and with a panoramic view of Monterey Bay, provided an opportunity for several innovations that were of interest to Smith. Most important were the residential colleges, of which six were initially planned, and subordination of traditional grades to what was called a "Narrative Evaluation System," the introduction of which was a matter of great interest to Smith. This system was admired by most students and a number of faculty members, who felt that, compared to letter grades, it provided a more accurate reflection of the quality of a student's work. However, it was time-consuming, both for instructors and for transcript-readers, and professional schools complained of the difficulty in relating narrative evaluations to their quantitative admission standards. The university's academic senate later voted to depend more on letter grades, although narrative evaluation was not entirely abandoned.

Smith continued as provost of Cowell College until 1969, when he gave up his administrative responsibilities to return to teaching history. However, in June 1973 he resigned from the university to protest its failure to award tenure to Paul Lee, a friend and an unpublished assistant professor of religious studies. The Smiths had in 1969 moved from the Cowell provost's house to a country house on Pine Flat Road in nearby Bonny Doon, where they kept horses and chickens. Smith, Paul Lee, and Mary Holmes, an admired art historian who had joined Smith from UCLA, established what they called the Penny University,

which gathered once a week at Cafe Pergolesi in downtown Santa Cruz to discuss the meaning of life and other subjects. Smith also collaborated with Paul Lee to organize the William James Association, which concerned itself with homeless people and (at Eloise's suggestion) with teaching art to children and prisoners.

During this period, Smith devoted much of his time to writing. He began his People's History of the United States, ultimately an eight-volume series distributed by the Book-of-the-Month Club. His Harvard mentor, Samuel Eliot Morison, called the first two volumes (*A New Age Now Begins: A People's History of the American Revolution,* 1976) "a great and magnificent work," praising its narrative style in particular.

Smith published more than a score of substantial books. The first was his biography of James Wilson (1956), followed in 1962 by the two-volume *John Adams,* which won both the Bancroft Award and the Kenneth Roberts Memorial Award. In 1964 came *The Historian and History,* and in 1966 *As a City upon a Hill: The Town in American History.* In 1970 it was *Daughters of the Promised Land: Women in American History.*

Smith was fond of chickens, of which the Pine Flat ranch had a substantial flock. He discovered a kindred spirit in Professor Charles Daniel, a biologist with whom Smith coauthored *The Chicken Book* (1975). That year Smith also published *A Letter from My Father: The Strange, Intimate Correspondence of W. Ward Smith to His Son, Page Smith,* another anomaly in the progression of Smith's scholarly historiography. In his introduction to this one-volume abridgment of 10,000 manuscript pages, Smith wrote:

> It was my father's strange conceit to write me a letter, the writing of which extended over a period of more than thirty years, and which, ultimately, reached ten thousand pages in length, a total of over two and a half million words.

Although the letter recalled Ward Smith's business and political endeavors, its greatest emphasis was in detailed description of his sexual adventures; women apparently found him irresistible. His son Page debated for some time whether to destroy it or publish it, but the historiographer finally triumphed.

In 1978 he published *The Constitution: A Documentary and Narrative History.* The next twelve years were devoted to the completion of the People's History, except for the appearance of *Dissenting Opinions* (1984), comprising twenty-nine essays on history and education, and *Killing the Spirit: Higher Education in America* (1990), a sharply critical account of the evolution of American universities. Smith published two additional books in 1995, *Democracy on Trial: Japanese-American Evacuation and Relocation in World War II* and *Old Age Is Another Country: A Traveller's*

Guide; the latter was the outgrowth of a weekly column, "Coming of Age," that Smith wrote for the entertainment of the elderly and published in the *San Francisco Examiner.*

Smith died of leukemia on 28 August 1995, two days after his wife, Eloise, succumbed to cancer. Friends attending their joint funeral filled and surrounded the Calvary Episcopal Church in Santa Cruz.

★

Smith's papers are being gathered in the research library at UCLA. Smith's introduction to *Dissenting Opinions* (1984) and his introduction and afterword in *A Letter from My Father* (1975) provide useful personal detail. Before his death, Smith had composed a brief obituary, which is included in a longer piece published in the *Santa Cruz Sentinel* (29 Aug. 1995). Other obituaries appear in the *Los Angeles Times* and *New York Times* (both 29 Aug. 1995). The UC Santa Cruz library has an oral history of Smith's early years in Santa Cruz.

DAVID W. HERON

SMITH, Robert Weston. *See* Wolfman Jack.

SNELL, George Davis (*b.* 19 December 1903 in Bradford, Massachusetts; *d.* 6 June 1996 in Bar Harbor, Maine), immunogeneticist whose pioneering research on the human immune system paved the way for organ transplantation and earned him a Nobel Prize.

Snell was the youngest of three children of Cullen Bryant Snell and Katharine Merrill Davis. His father was secretary of a Young Men's Christian Association for many years; later, the elder Snell invented and marketed a device for winding induction coils used in motorboat engines. The family moved to suburban Brookline, Massachusetts, when Snell was four, and he and his brother and sister grew up in a home built by his great-grandfather. Snell attended the Brookline public schools and favored science and mathematics. He loved sports and played in his high school band, a reflection of the musical inclination of his entire family.

From 1922 to 1926 Snell attended Dartmouth College in Hanover, New Hampshire, earning a B.S. degree in biology. He then began graduate studies at Harvard University, working with Professor William Castle, one of the first American biologists to research Mendelian inheritance in mammals. Snell completed his M.S. in 1928 and was granted a Ph.D. in 1930. He wrote his doctoral dissertation on linkage in mice (that is, the means by which two or more genes on a chromosome are interrelated).

While completing his doctoral degree at Harvard, from 1929 to 1930, Snell taught zoology at Dartmouth College. The following academic year, Snell taught zoology at Brown University in Providence, Rhode Island. Then, in 1931 he accepted a National Research Council fellowship at the University of Texas at Austin, where he worked with

George Snell, 1980. ASSOCIATED PRESS AP

the prominent geneticist Hermann J. Muller. Muller would later win a Nobel Prize for showing that X rays could induce mutations in the common fruit fly. In his own research, Snell demonstrated for the first time that mice subjected to X rays often exhibited chromosomal damage.

From 1933 to 1934 Snell was an assistant professor at Washington University in St. Louis, but his time in Austin had convinced him that research was his true calling. In 1935 he accepted a position as a research associate at the Roscoe B. Jackson Memorial Laboratory in Bar Harbor, Maine. The Jackson Laboratory, founded by the geneticist Clarence Cook Little, was a center for study on mammalian genetics and renowned for its program on mouse genetics. At first, Snell continued his research with X rays and mice. Later, he helped develop a standardized gene nomenclature for mice. Then, in the early 1940s he shifted his attention to transplantation genetics.

Scientists knew that certain genes controlled the body's acceptance or rejection of tissue transplants, but the precise genes had not been isolated or identified. Snell set out to find these "histocompatibility" genes, as he called them. In a complicated procedure, he took two inbred lines of laboratory mice that did not accept grafts from each other and repeatedly crossbred them. After many generations, he had two strains of mice that were genetically identical except for the genes that controlled transplant rejection. Snell called the genes he had isolated the "histocompatibility locus." The mice Snell had bred, which he called "congenic," had made it possible to follow the effects of a single gene in a constant genetic background. Snell's breeding of these so-called congenic mice was a new and important contribution to genetics research.

In 1946 Peter Gorer of Guy's Hospital in London, England, joined Snell in his research at the Jackson Laboratory. Years earlier, Gorer had identified a blood protein, which he named Antigen-II, that was related to graft rejection in mice. Snell and Gorer quickly discovered that Snell's histocompatibility locus and Gorer's Antigen-II were one and the same and combined their nomenclature to call the gene Histocompatibility Two, or H-2. By the mid-1950s Snell identified a group of about ten loci that actually control transplant resistance. The H-2 locus was, in reality, a group of closely linked genes. These genes would become known as the major histocompatibility complex, or MHC.

In the late 1950s scientists discovered that humans also possess a major histocompatibility complex. The immunogeneticist Jean Dausset identified the first human histocompatibility protein and hypothesized correctly that there was a single set of MHC genes in humans that corresponded to the H-2 system in the mouse. In 1969 Baruj Benacerraf found that genes within the MHC determine whether or not the body can produce an immunological response to a foreign substance. He and other scientists determined, in the mid-1970s, that MHC products help white blood cells distinguish normal body cells from abnormal or foreign cells. In 1980 the Nobel Prize for physiology or medicine was awarded jointly to Snell, Dausset, and Benacerraf "for their discoveries concerning genetically determined structures on the cell surface that regulate immunologic reactions." Their work was a chronological sequence over several decades, and Snell's contribution was discovering "the genetic factors that determine the possibilities of transplanting tissues from one individual to another."

Snell's career at the Jackson Laboratory spanned nearly forty years. His later research focused on the role the MHC plays in relation to tumor resistance and cancer. He retired in 1973, having achieved the rank of senior staff scientist emeritus. Even after retirement, Snell frequently visited the lab. He also spent time writing on science, philosophy, and ethics.

In addition to the Nobel Prize, Snell's many awards included the Bertner Foundation Award (1962), the Gregor Mendel Medal of the Czechoslovakian Academy of Sciences (1967), the Gairdner Foundation International Award (1976), and the Wolf Prize in medicine (1978). He was a member of the American Academy of Arts and Sciences, the National Academy of Sciences, and the Transplantation Society. Snell wrote *Search for a Rational Ethic* (1988) and coauthored *Histocompatibility* (1976) with Dausset and Stanley Nathenson. Snell was also editor of *The Biology of the Laboratory Mouse* (1941) and from 1947 until 1980 was editor of the journal *Immunogenetics.*

On 28 July 1937 Snell married Rhoda Carson. The couple had three sons, Thomas, Roy, and Peter. Snell was a physically slight man, with reserved blue eyes behind thin-rimmed glasses. His personality was described as modest and shy. At work, Snell was diligent, precise, and patient. At home, he enjoyed his vegetable garden and tended it with the same exacting care as he did his work. Snell lived out his years in Bar Harbor, where he had spent most of his adult life as a quintessential New Englander.

Snell's pioneering research earned him the unofficial title "father of modern immunogenetics." Because of his work, doctors can predict compatibility in human organ transplants, giving hope to many where there was none before.

★

Articles about Snell and his work include "3 Cell Researchers Win Medicine Nobel," *New York Times* (11 Oct. 1980); "1980 Nobel Prize in Physiology or Medicine," *Science* (7 Nov. 1980); and "Portrait: Dr. George D. Snell: The Maine Hunter in White Coat," *Life* (Feb. 1981). Biographical sketches appear in *Nobel Prize Winners* (1987) and *Contemporary Authors,* vol. 106 (1982). An obituary is in the *New York Times* (8 June 1996).

Victoria Tamborrino

SNYDER, Jimmy ("Jimmy the Greek") (*b.* 9 September 1919 in Steubenville, Ohio; *d.* 21 April 1996 in Las Vegas, Nevada), oddsmaker and sportscaster who brought gambling to American television by predicting outcomes on CBS-TV's *NFL Today* pregame football show.

Jimmy the Greek was born Demetrios Synodinos, the son of George Synodinos, owner of a grocery store. His mother, Sultania, was killed by his uncle when Jimmy was only ten years old. His uncle was angry, and one afternoon he shot his wife as well as Jimmy's mother and then killed himself. Soon after his mother's death, the family moved from Jimmy's home in Steubenville, Ohio, to Kios, Greece, where Jimmy's relatives lived and were an influential family. George Synodinos remarried in Kios to Agnes, the woman on the island who seemed to show the greatest interest in his children. In 1932, when Jimmy was thirteen years old, his family returned to Steubenville, where Jimmy

"Jimmy the Greek" Snyder, 1971. © BETTMANN/CORBIS

would make his first bet at a local candy and cigar store. By tenth grade Jimmy had dropped out of high school and had begun a long career as a gambler.

In the 1930s Steubenville was a great place for a gambler to learn the "ins and outs" of the gambling world. The town had eleven bookmaking establishments, and Jimmy began dealing craps at a nightclub casino, where he was exposed to a gambling education on everything from horses to cards, dice, and sporting games. By age nineteen Jimmy had decided that in order to succeed he should concentrate on one aspect of gambling and learn it well. Jimmy chose team sports. He believed that team sports could be researched so that knowledgeable predictions could be made. Jimmy was winning thousands of dollars in a single night, and his name became known throughout the gambling world.

In 1942, at age nineteen, Jimmy married his first wife, Pauline ("Sunny") Miles, with whom he had only gone on two dates prior to the wedding. This marriage did not last, and they were divorced two years later. Jimmy lost all of his money in the divorce settlement, although he did get custody of his daughter Victoria. Jimmy was married for a second time in 1952 to Joan Specht. His engagement to Joan came after a much longer courtship and lasted the rest of his life. With Joan, Jimmy had five children, three of whom died of cystic fibrosis at young ages. A son, Anthony, and a daughter, Stephanie, survived him.

In 1956 Jimmy moved to Nevada, where gambling was legal, and he began selling the odds on games to people all over the nation. Soon a federal law was passed that forbade

gambling information from being passed across state lines for the purpose of betting. Jimmy the Greek did not let the law stop his business, and after only a few months, he was under federal indictment in Salt Lake City, Utah. The investigation began with several businessmen in Salt Lake City. They then provided Jimmy's name when asked where they got their odds. In order to regain respect after the arrest, in 1961 Jimmy began writing one column a week in the *Las Vegas Sun,* presenting his odds on football, baseball, and even political elections. This column made Jimmy a celebrity in Las Vegas. By 1965 Jimmy had formed a public relations firm called Sports Unlimited. His firm landed large accounts, though Jimmy eventually dropped some of them to spend more time with his family. In 1976 Mike Pearl, the producer of CBS-TV's *NFL Today* show, hired Jimmy to predict the outcome of games on television. Joining Brent Musburger, Phyllis George, and Irv Cross on the show every Sunday afternoon, Jimmy utilized nineteen people on his payroll to prepare his segment for the program. The ratings for the show soared, and in the next decade Jimmy established himself as leading football analyst.

Unfortunately, on 15 January 1988 Jimmy gave an interview that would ruin his career and change the rest of his life. It was the fifty-ninth birthday of the slain civil rights leader Martin Luther King, Jr., and Jimmy was at a restaurant in Washington, D.C., spending the weekend covering the NFL championship game between the Minnesota Vikings and the Washington Redskins. A reporter in the restaurant who was doing a story on the progress made by blacks in sports approached Jimmy, who told the interviewer that he thought black athletes were superior to white athletes. He commented that during the American Civil War, "the slave owner would breed his big black with his big woman so that they would have a big black kid, that's where it all started." He also told the reporter that a black athlete was better than a white one because "he's been bred to be that way because of his thigh size and big size."

CBS fired Jimmy the Greek the day after his comments were made public, without allowing any sort of explanation to be made. Jimmy offered an apology but was ostracized and relegated to obscurity after the incident. He returned to gambling near the end of his life, spending many days at the racetrack. He died of heart failure in Las Vegas on 21 April 1996 and was buried in Steubenville, where he had grown up.

Jimmy the Greek was the most famous oddsmaker in the betting world, the person who first combined gambling with televised sports. He brought a new excitement to the pregame show and made sports betting a form of entertainment.

★

Jimmy the Greek's autobiography, *Jimmy the Greek by Himself* (1975), includes interesting anecdotes about his life. Ginger Wadsworth collaborated with Jimmy at the end of his life to write *Farewell Jimmy the Greek: Wizard of Odds* (1996). See also *Sports Illustrated,* "Goodbye to a Gambler" (29 Apr. 1996), which includes additional information on Jimmy the Greek. Obituaries are in the *New York Times, Las Vegas Review-Journal, Las Vegas Sun,* and *Newsday* (all 22 Apr. 1996).

LAUREN A. BRODSKY

SOUTHERN, Terry Marion, Jr. (*b.* 2 May 1924 in Alvarado, Texas; *d.* 29 October 1995 in New York City), satiric screenwriter, journalist, and novelist who wrote burlesques of the military, pornography, drugs, psychoanalysis, political leaders, and corporate culture that epitomized the antiauthoritarian spirit of the 1960s.

Southern was born on 2 May 1924 (although it is often reported as 1 May). He was the only child of Terry Marion Southern, a pharmacist, and Helen Simonds Southern, a dressmaker. In 1933 the family moved to Dallas, where Southern attended Sunset High School. Though outwardly conventional, playing football and baseball, at eleven he showed an interest in writing on unconventional subjects, revising an Edgar Allan Poe story "to make it wilder."

Graduating in 1941, Southern began a pre-med program at Southern Methodist University, but from 1943 to 1945 served as a U.S. Army lieutenant in Europe. At the end of World War II, determined to become a writer, he entered the University of Chicago, but he soon transferred

Terry Southern. CORBIS CORPORATION (BELLEVUE)

to what he later called "a groovier scene" at Northwestern University in Evanston, Illinois. After earning his B.A. degree in 1948, he enrolled at the Sorbonne in Paris.

In France, Southern joined the literary expatriates Mordecai Richler, Aram Avakian, William Styron, George Plimpton, and others. He wrote fiction, influenced by Franz Kafka, Louis-Ferdinand Céline, and Nathanael West, for newly founded journals such as *Merlin* and *Zero.* His story "The Accident" appeared in the first issue of the *Paris Review,* and his later work helped define that journal as a venue for new fiction.

Southern returned to New York City in 1952. There he met Carol Kauffman, a nursery school teacher, whom he married on 14 July 1956. They had one child, a son named Nile. Habitually poor, Southern at one point worked as a barge captain, hauling rocks on the Hudson River. In 1955 he was advisory editor to *Best American Short Stories,* and he made his first film, collaborating with David Burnett on a nine-minute short called "Candy Kisses." Also in that year he wrote "Twirling at Ole Miss," an account for *Esquire* of his visit to a summer institute for drum majorettes in Oxford, Mississippi. The piece was hailed by the journalist Tom Wolfe as an example of a revolutionary kind of personal journalism.

In Geneva, Switzerland, where Carol found work teaching for the United Nations Educational, Scientific, and Cultural Organization (UNESCO), the couple entertained the British novelist Henry Green, whose work influenced Southern's first novel, *Flash and Filigree,* published in England in 1958. The same year, the Olympia Press in Paris published his second novel, *Candy.* Written with Mason Hoffenberg and published under the pseudonym Maxwell Kenton, *Candy* is an exaggeratedly obscene version of *Candide* that sought, as Southern said of all his work, to "blast smugness" and "to astonish," not simply "to shock." Neither novel attracted the interest of American publishers, but in Britain Southern was commissioned to adapt Eugene O'Neill's play *Emperor Jones* for the BBC.

The following year he published *The Magic Christian,* about the exploits of wealthy Guy Grand, mischievous but benign, who liked to "make it hot" for the greedy and pompous. Southern's physician Jonathan Miller recommended the novel to the actor Peter Sellers, who gave a copy to director Stanley Kubrick. In 1962 Kubrick hired Southern to collaborate on a script that became *Dr. Strangelove, or How I Learned to Stop Worrying and Love the Bomb* (1964). The film won the British Screenwriters Award and the Writers' Guild Award for the best screenplay of 1964, as well as earning an Academy Award nomination.

In 1960 Southern moved to a farm outside East Canaan, Connecticut, which became his permanent home. His work appeared widely in *Evergreen Review, Harper's Bazaar, Argosy, Nugget, Playboy,* and the *New York Times.* In 1964, while his notoriety spread with the American publication of *Candy,* he began a long-term companionship with actress and dancer Gail Gerber. They had no children. Southern formally separated from Carol in 1965, and they were divorced in 1972.

At age forty, with the success of *Dr. Strangelove,* Southern entered a period of intense screenwriting, usually in collaboration. Three of his films appeared in 1965: *The Collector; The Loved One* (written with Christopher Isherwood); and *The Cincinnati Kid* (written with Ring Lardner, Jr., and director Norman Jewison). He also published *The Journal of "The Loved One,"* an account of the production of that film, with photographs by William Claxton.

While contributing to the screenplay for *Casino Royale* (1967), Southern published the collection of essays and stories that became his most enduring literary work, *Red-Dirt Marijuana and Other Tastes* (1967). His status as a symbol of the 1960s was assured that year when he appeared on the cover of the Beatles' album *Sgt. Pepper's Lonely Hearts Club Band.*

The following year, in addition to collaborating with Roger Vadim on the screenplay of *Barbarella* (1968),

Southern went on assignment for *Esquire* with William Burroughs and Jean Genet to cover the Chicago Democratic Convention. There, he and the poet Allan Ginsberg found themselves in the midst of violence between demonstrators and police. That year he also published his infamous essay "Blood of a Wig," a scurrilous fantasy of Lyndon B. Johnson's behavior on Air Force One after the 1963 assassination of President John F. Kennedy.

In 1969 Southern collaborated with Dennis Hopper and Peter Fonda in writing a script for the film *Easy Rider* (1969). Although the creative contributions of all three have been disputed, the film brought Southern a second Academy Award nomination. Following this project, he collaborated on the screenplay of *The Magic Christian* (1969).

Southern's fourth novel, *Blue Movie* (1970), was a satire of a Hollywood attempt to produce a "quality" pornographic film. Outside Hollywood that year, Southern worked with director Aram Avakian to adapt John Barth's novel *The End of the Road.*

In the 1970s, as the social climate grew less tolerant of satire, Southern's popularity declined. In addition, from 1970 to 1993 he struggled with the Internal Revenue Service (IRS) regarding payment of back taxes from the 1960s. Although he enjoyed intermittent periods of prosperity, he experienced financial difficulties for most of his remaining life.

Still Southern continued to write. He covered a Rolling Stones tour in 1972, worked with William Claxton on a teleplay (*Stop, Thief!,* 1975), published *The Donkey and the Darling* (1977) with lithographs by Larry Rivers, and in 1981 and 1982 worked as a staff writer for *Saturday Night Live.* In 1988 Southern collaborated with songwriter Harry Nilsson to film *The Telephone* with Whoopi Goldberg. At his death, some forty of his screenplays remained unproduced. From the late 1980s Southern taught popular screenwriting classes at New York University and at Columbia University in New York City.

Although the 1990s found Southern in ill health, the period also saw a renascence of his popularity. He produced the text of *The Early Stones: Legendary Photographs of a Band in the Making, 1963–1973* (1992); wrote a new semi-autobiographical novel, *Texas Summer* (1991); and finalized plans for the reissue of his four earlier novels. In the midst of promoting a new book, *Virgin: A History of the Virgin Record Company* (1996), he collapsed while walking to a screenwriting class at Columbia. He died of respiratory failure four days later, and his ashes were scattered over a pond near his home in East Canaan, Connecticut.

In his own eyes, Southern was, according to his son, "first and foremost, a political being." Others, however, saw him primarily as an influential stylist, a writer whose satire—always painted in extreme colors—developed astonishing situations with a journalist's ear for the colloquial.

One critic termed him "a serious, outrageously understated satirist and a quietly sophomoric Zen comedian." His fondness for collaboration, which he called "the purest form of writing," makes it difficult to assess his achievement. But he was unquestionably, as Dean Robert Fitzpatrick of Columbia said, "a truly independent voice and imaginative spirit and a generous mentor to young writers." Looking back over Southern's career, Brad Tyer in the *New York Times Book Review* observed: "From his vantage point as a literary hipster Mr. Southern used to cast a good-natured sneer at what he called the 'quality-lit game,' even as his work redefined what literature could include."

★

Terry Southern's extensive personal papers are held by Nile Southern, who also maintains a web site devoted to his father's work at www.terrysouthern.com. Links on this site include autobiographical reflections by Southern in Lee Hill, "Interview with a Grand Guy," *Backstory* 3 (1997), and Mike Golden, "Now Dig This: An Interview with Terry Southern," *Smoke Signals* (n.d.). For a brief appreciation of Southern's journalistic writings, see Tom Wolfe and E. W. Johnson, *The New Journalism* (1973). William Claxton presents a vivid personal portrait in *Photographic Memory* (2000). Articles on Southern include *Life* (21 Aug. 1964) and *New York Times Book Review* (16 Feb. 1992). Retrospectives are in the *New York Times* (12 Nov. 1995); *Village Voice* (26 Dec. 1995); *Time Out* (London) (9 Apr. 1997); *New Yorker* (22 and 29 June 1998); and *New Times* (11 Feb. and 4 Mar. 1999). Obituaries are in the *New York Times, Los Angeles Times, Hollywood Reporter,* and *Daily Variety* (all 31 Oct. 1995); and the *Times* (London) (1 Nov. 1995).

ALAN BUSTER

SPERRY, Roger Wolcott (*b.* 20 August 1913 in Hartford, Connecticut; *d.* 17 April 1994 in Pasadena, California), neuroscientist and Nobel Prize winner whose split-brain studies dramatically altered views of how the mind works.

Sperry, the elder of the two sons of Francis Bushnell Sperry, a banker, and Florence Kraemer, an assistant to the principal of a local high school, spent his childhood on a farm near Hartford, Connecticut, where he developed a lifelong passion for nature and the outdoors. Neither parent had much formal education. When Sperry was eleven years of age his father died, and the family moved to West Hartford, where Sperry attended William Hall High School, graduating in 1931. An all-star athlete and straight-A student, Sperry won a four-year scholarship to Oberlin College in Ohio, where he worked in the dining halls to cover his board. He graduated in 1935 with a bachelor's degree in English literature.

Sperry became interested in the subject of memory while he was studying at Oberlin. His decision to remain there

Roger Wolcott Sperry. LIBRARY OF CONGRESS

for a master's degree in psychology, which he received in 1937, was heavily influenced by the Oberlin psychology department's highly experimental and physiologically brain-oriented approach and the quality of its faculty, including Lawrence Cole, Louis Hartson, Homer Weaver, and Raymond H. Stetson, his adviser. A seminar talk by another graduate student on the work of Paul A. Weiss, one of the most influential biologists of his day, led Sperry to spend an extra year at Oberlin as a student-at-large, taking courses in the life sciences in preparation for Ph.D. work under Weiss at the University of Chicago.

At Chicago, Sperry mastered highly skilled neurological techniques, and he disproved a widely held theory about how the brain works that had been put forward by his doctoral adviser, Weiss. According to Weiss's theory, the huge neural network linking the sense organs and muscles to the brain begins as a bunch of casually connected nerve fibers, which are undifferentiated and unspecified, and becomes, after factoring in experience and learning, the highly coordinated, purposeful system seen in animals. The key ideas underlying this theory, based on meticulous experiments by Weiss that were misinterpreted, had to do with plasticity and interchangeability of function.

In a series of seminal papers published between 1941 and 1946, however, Sperry demonstrated unequivocally that what actually happens during an animal's development is just the opposite of that postulated by Weiss. Rather than being formed of interchangeable bits and pieces, the brain's circuits are largely hardwired, meaning that each nerve cell acquires its own chemical identity starting in early embryonic development. From then on the function of the cell is fixed and cannot be altered. Sperry's experiments involved surgical procedures, starting with rats. The results of his experiments showed that rearranging an animal's nerve connections produced inappropriate responses that could not be retrained.

Upon completing his doctorate in zoology in 1941 Sperry went to Harvard on a one-year National Research Fellowship and worked with Karl S. Lashley in psychology. In addition to continuing his experiments on the effects of surgical procedures involving peripheral nerves in rats and later in monkeys, Sperry started a new line of research on the selectivity of nerve growth in the visual system, using regeneration of the optic nerve in salamanders. When he surgically rotated the eyes 180 degrees before regeneration, the recovered vision of the animal was also rotated, and the animals saw the world upside down and reversed right to left. As Sperry later said, the animal responded "as if everything seen through one eye were being viewed through the opposite eye." Moreover, with their eyes inverted, no amount of retraining could restore correct vision to the animal. The experiments showed clearly that the nerves had grown selectively back to their original connections and offered compelling evidence, in Sperry's words, that nerves grow to specific connections "by intricate chemical codes under genetic control" and predetermination.

Shortly after Pearl Harbor was bombed by Japan in late 1941 Sperry moved to Orange Park, Florida, to continue his postdoctoral work with Lashley, who had left Harvard to become the director of the Yerkes Laboratories of Primate Biology. From 1942 to 1946 Sperry was a biology research fellow at Yerkes, where he continued his nerve-cross experiments on a variety of animals, including rats, fish, and monkeys. On rats Sperry showed that, if the nerve connections in the animal's hind feet were reversed, an electric shock to the right foot caused a reaction in the left foot and it could not be unlearned. He also continued his work on optic nerves and nerve growth using frogs and salamanders collected locally. From 1942 to 1945 Sperry's military service consisted of participation in the Nerve Injury Project, a medical research project organized by Weiss under the auspices of the Office of Scientific Research and Development. The project dealt with the surgical repair of peripheral nerve injuries. Sperry's demonstrations that nerve fibers are not interchangeable and that the design of the brain's machinery is set early in embryonic development had important consequences for human neurosurgery. Treatment protocols for nerve-damaged soldiers changed substantially after Sperry advised neurosurgeons of the group's findings in 1945.

In 1946 Sperry returned to the University of Chicago as an assistant professor in the department of anatomy. On 28 December 1949 he married Norma Gay Deupree, a biologist who was one of his many collaborators. They had two children. Soon after his marriage Sperry was diagnosed with tuberculosis, forcing him to spend part of 1950 in the Adirondack Mountains in upstate New York recovering from the disease. During this period he wrote a seminal essay, "Neurology and the Mind-Brain Problem," published in 1952 in the *American Scientist*. The article reflected his growing interest in the relationship between the brain and conscious experience. Returning to Chicago, Sperry taught human anatomy to medical students and worked on small tropical fish at Bimini in the Caribbean in the winter months. He started a scientific collaboration with Ronald Myers, a joint M.D. and Ph.D. student, on the corpus callosum, the fiber bridge between the two cerebral hemispheres, whose functions were a mystery to neurobiologists. In 1953 they reported that, when this brain structure was cut, the visual learning was divided in two by the surgery and the transfer of visual information between the two hemispheres ended. Split-brain research became one of Sperry's primary interests over the next decade.

In 1952 Sperry became section chief of neurological diseases and blindness at the National Institutes of Health and an associate professor of psychology at the University of Chicago. In 1954 he accepted an appointment at the California Institute of Technology (Caltech) as the Hixon Professor of Psychobiology. At Caltech, Sperry developed and extended the split-brain experiments with animals with the help of a long line of graduate students and postdoctoral students. In the early 1960s Sperry began studying the effects of brain splitting on perception, speech, and motor control in human beings whose hemispheres had been cut to control intractable epilepsy. With these patients Sperry discovered that the right hemisphere, like the left hemisphere where the speech center of the brain is located, had its own world of perception, memory, and consciousness. Sperry, who was of average height with a wiry build and piercing eyes that concealed a very shy personality, shared the 1981 Nobel Prize in medicine for his discoveries concerning the specialization of the cerebral hemispheres.

Beginning in 1965 Sperry published a great number of philosophical papers dealing with his own theory of mind and consciousness. He died in Pasadena, California, from a heart attack following a degenerative neuromuscular disease. He was cremated and his ashes were scattered in an undisclosed location.

A small amount of personal biographical material on Sperry is in the Oberlin College archives. Colwyn Trevarthen, ed., *Brain Circuits and Functions of the Mind* (1990), a collection of essays by Sperry's colleagues and former students, touches on many phases of his career and his personality and includes a complete bibliography of his writings. "Sperry on Consciousness," *Caltech News* (1988), is the closest thing to an autobiographical account of why he changed his thinking about scientific thought and human behavior in the mid-1960s. Personal glimpses of the man, his work habits, and his rich family life are scattered throughout "Paths in the Brain, Action of the Mind," *Neuropsychologia* 36 (Oct. 1998): 953–1096, a special issue devoted to Sperry and the main areas of his research by twelve colleagues who knew him professionally over a long time. See also "Roger Wolcott Sperry," in National Academy of Sciences, *Biographical Memoirs,* vol. 71 (1997). Obituaries are in the *New York Times* (20 Apr. 1994), *Trends in Neurosciences* 17 (1994): 402–404, and *American Psychologist* 50 (1995): 940–941.

JUDITH R. GOODSTEIN

STACY, Jess Alexandria (*b.* 11 August 1904 in Bird's Point, Missouri; *d.* 1 January 1995 in Los Angeles, California), jazz pianist prominent in big bands and combos of the Swing Era.

Originally named Jesse Alexander by his parents, Frederick Lee Stacy, a railroad engineer, and Sara ("Vada") Alexander, a seamstress, Stacy grew up along the banks of the

Jess Stacy, 1940s. FRANK DRIGGS COLLECTION/ARCHIVE PHOTOS

Mississippi River, which later washed away the town of his birth. Because the family lived in poverty in a railroad boxcar, he had to work at odd jobs during his school years at Malden and Cape Girardeau, Missouri. Largely self-taught to play the drums at age eleven and the piano at age twelve, he did receive some piano instruction in Cape Girardeau while he worked accompanying silent movies on the piano at a local theater. Stacy played both instruments in community and high school bands, at the same time discovering the jazz music of bands playing on visiting Streckfus Line river excursion boats. Especially instructive were the cornetist Louis Armstrong and the bandleader-pianist Fate Marable. In the summer of 1921, the year before he graduated from high school, Stacy played piano and the calliope on the steamer *Majestic.* Employed by local dance bands afloat and ashore, especially the band of Tony Catalano, he relished their jazz-inflected melodies and was especially inspired on one occasion when Bix Beiderbecke sat in on cornet and piano.

In 1924 Stacy moved to Chicago, then the focus of jazz music. But he had to be content over the next decade playing mostly with non-jazz dance orchestras. Such employment was necessary due to his marriage to Helen Robinson about 1926 and the birth of a son soon after. His major gigs were with the bands of Joe Kayser (1924–1926, 1928–1930), Floyd Town (1926–1928, 1933), Louis Panico (1929), and Paul Mares (1934–1935). His first recorded solo was with the Danny Altier band in 1928. He led his own quartet, Stacy's Aces, at dance marathons during 1930–1931, using the innovative jazz clarinetist Frank Teschemacher. Stacy became identified with such other white musicians of the "Chicago" style of hot swinging jazz as guitarist Eddie Condon, cornetist Muggsy Spanier, and drummer George Wettling, though Stacy was not a member of the inner circle of the so-called Austin High Gang players (white teenage boys from Austin and other Chicago high schools who went on to popularize the Chicago style). Freed from his marital obligations by divorce in 1934, Stacy was heard that year by the jazz promoter John Hammond while playing with the Frank Snyder orchestra at Chicago's Subway Cafe. The next year Hammond recommended him to the budding swing-band leader Benny Goodman.

Goodman hired Stacy in mid-July 1935, just one month before the band burst onto the national scene to inaugurate the Swing Era. In spite of the orchestra's often thunderous up-tempo arrangements and searing horn solos, Stacy fit in perfectly with a much more subdued but expert style of accompaniment and understated, lyrical piano solos that buoyed the band and dancers alike. Though capable of rollicking "barrelhouse" type solos, Stacy used rippling right-hand tremolos—inspired by Earl Hines—that were likened to sparkling bells to complement the reed or brass sections and female vocalists. The latter often resented his brilliant obligatos in fear of being overshadowed. Stacy's immense role in Goodman's success was crowned by a delicate and introspective two-minute, five-chorus solo that "stole the show" (Goodman's words) during the otherwise driving "Sing, Sing, Sing" finale number of the band's epic 16 January 1938 concert at New York's famed Carnegie Hall. The very next day Jess participated in the first hot jazz recordings of the new Commodore Record Company. When pianist Teddy Wilson left the Goodman Trio and Quartet early in 1939, Stacy replaced him (and played in the new Quintet) while continuing to accompany the full orchestra. Differences with Goodman, however, led Stacy to move to the Bob Crosby orchestra that summer.

Stacy was heard to even greater advantage in the Crosby band's arrangements and on many small group and piano solo records, often playing such compositions of his own as "Ec-stacy" and "Complainin'. " When the Crosby orchestra broke up in late 1942, Stacy rejoined Goodman until March 1944, when he moved to the Horace Heidt orchestra. Meanwhile, in 1943 he married the song stylist Lee Wiley, who persuaded him to form his own big band and make her its featured singer. From 1944 to 1946 the orchestra struggled along, lacking any jazz content, making no recordings, and plagued by the stormy marital relationship between the volatile Wiley and mild-mannered Stacy. Of the few small band recordings they made together the most memorable was "Down to Steamboat Tennessee" (1940). They also made appearances on several Eddie Condon radio broadcasts (1944–1945). They had no children and were divorced in 1948. Stacy made many small jazz group recordings in the Chicago style during the 1940s, played for the Goodman band again in 1946–1947, and settled in Los Angeles in 1948. He married Patricia Peck in 1950 (they had no children) and performed mostly in West Coast nightclubs until 1963, when he quit the music business in disgust after having lost any real audience for his piano style.

A major figure during the golden age of jazz music, Stacy created piano masterpieces in spite of a modest, self-effacing personality. Although he worked as a mail clerk for a cosmetics company from 1963 to 1969, he played at jazz concerts starting in 1966, cut solo albums for the Chiaroscuro label in 1974 and 1977, and in 1981 made his final recorded appearance, on Marian McPartland's *Piano Jazz* public radio program. He died of congestive heart failure and was cremated, his ashes buried in Los Angeles.

★

The authoritative biography and discography (including a CD of 1951 and 1953 sessions) is Derek Coller, *Jess Stacy: The Quiet Man of Jazz* (1997), based partly on Keith Keller, *Oh Jess! A Jazz Life* (1989). Whitney Balliett, *American Musicians* (1986) devotes a chapter to Stacy, who is also prominently discussed in Richard Sudhalter, *Lost Chords: White Musicians and Their Contribution to Jazz, 1915–1945* (1999). Stacy's famous "Sing, Sing, Sing" solo is on *Benny Goodman at Carnegie Hall* (Columbia Records), and his 1938–1944 small group and solo sessions are on *The Complete Commodore Jazz Recordings* (Mosaic). The Eddie Condon radio programs were issued on the Jazum label. Among several film appearances, Stacy is seen and heard to best advantage with Goodman in *Sweet and Lowdown* (1944) and with Wingy Manone in *Sarge Goes to College* (1947). An obituary is in the *New York Times* (4 Jan. 1995).

CLARK G. REYNOLDS

STENNIS, John Cornelius (*b*. 3 August 1901 in Kemper County, Mississippi; *d*. 23 April 1995 in Madison, Mississippi), United States senator from 1947 to 1989 who was the Senate's president pro tempore and who chaired the Senate Committee on Armed Services, the Senate Committee on Appropriations, and the Senate Select Committee on Standards and Conduct.

Stennis was the youngest of seven children of Hampton Howell, a farmer and merchant, and Cornelia Adams Stennis. He began his education in a one-room school at Kipling Crossroad and graduated from the Kemper County Agricultural High School in 1919. He attended Mississippi Agricultural and Mechanical College from 1919 to 1923, where he attained membership in Phi Beta Kappa and earned a B.S. degree. Stennis enrolled at the University of Virginia School of Law in 1923 and earned an LL.B. degree in 1928. On 24 December 1929 he married Coy Hines. They had a son and a daughter.

In 1928 Stennis was admitted to the bar, began practic-

John Stennis, 1967. © BETTMANN/CORBIS

ing law in the town of De Kalb, Mississippi, and was elected to the Mississippi House of Representatives from Kemper County. During his four-year term as a representative, he was chosen in 1931 as district attorney for the Sixteenth Judicial District. Four years later, he was renamed to the post without opposition. He was appointed circuit judge of the district in 1937 to fill a vacancy, was first elected in 1938, and was reelected in 1942 and 1946. In a special election held on 4 November 1947 to choose the successor to the late U.S. senator Theodore G. Bilbo, Stennis captured twenty-seven percent of the vote to prevail over four other Democratic candidates. Stennis stressed agricultural issues, avoided demagoguery on the race question, and promised Mississippians that "I will plough a straight furrow right down to the end of my row." This perennial slogan used in his six successful Senate campaigns captured the Presbyterian Stennis's Calvinistic devotion to duty, a dedication that propelled his senatorial career.

During the Harry S. Truman and Dwight D. Eisenhower presidential administrations, Stennis joined conservative southern Democrats in opposing liberal domestic policies and civil rights legislation. In 1956 Stennis helped author the "Southern Manifesto," which vowed resistance to the United States Supreme Court's school desegregation decision of 1954. He also voted against the Civil Rights Acts of 1957 and 1960.

A courtly and dignified man, Stennis gained a reputation for integrity that transcended party affiliation or the positions he took on particular issues. In 1954 he was made a member of the select committee to study censure charges against Republican senator Joseph R. McCarthy of Wisconsin and became the first Democratic senator to call for McCarthy's censure.

Stennis's rise to prominence as a spokesman on defense issues began with his appointment to the Senate Committee on Armed Services in 1951. Although a staunch anti-Communist who supported a strong national defense, he warned President Eisenhower against sending United States military support to the French in Indochina in 1954. Committee chairman Richard B. Russell placed Stennis on key subcommittees on manpower, military personnel, pay, and promotions that gave the junior senator the opportunity to develop expertise on a wide range of national defense matters. Stennis's Subcommittee on Real Estate and Military Construction discovered duplication and waste in the nation's developing missile defense program. Inspired by Stennis's detailed review of Pentagon weapons programs, Senator Russell attached an amendment to the Military Construction Act of 1959 requiring Congress to authorize selected weapons programs prior to appropriating funds. This initial authorization requirement was expanded over the next two decades to include the entire

defense budget and became the most important means for Congress to oversee national defense programs and policies.

Stennis's reputation among his Senate colleagues for fairness, integrity, and thoroughness continued to grow during the 1960s. After succeeding Lyndon B. Johnson as chairman of the powerful Preparedness Investigating Subcommittee, he conducted an investigation of the Pentagon's control over the public statements of military officers, a response to politically explosive charges that the Kennedy administration was "muzzling" anti-Communist military officers. In 1965 Stennis became the first chairman of the Select Committee on Standards and Conduct, and as chairman wrote the Senate's first code of ethics. In 1967 Stennis's committee investigated charges that Democratic senator Thomas J. Dodd of Connecticut had diverted campaign funds for personal use, and recommended that the Senate censure Dodd.

Stennis was a powerful ally of the building up of conventional military forces supported by presidents Kennedy and Johnson. Although skeptical of American military commitment to Vietnam, Stennis strongly supported approval of Johnson's Gulf of Tonkin Resolution, which served as the basis for further military action against North Vietnam. He also backed Johnson's deployment of ground forces to South Vietnam in the spring of 1965. Although Stennis supported vigorous action in Vietnam, he believed that the war there was weakening United States military strength worldwide and questioned the nation's ability to back up its various alliances and obligations. In the summer of 1967 Stennis jolted the White House by holding hearings critical of the administration's policy of restrictions and gradualism in its conduct of the air war. Although Stennis seemed to be pressuring President Johnson to escalate the conflict, he never broke publicly with the administration. When Johnson halted the bombing to pursue a negotiated settlement with North Vietnam in 1968, Stennis reluctantly supported the president.

Stennis was chairman of the Senate Committee on Armed Services from 1969 to 1981. Although inclined to support the major defense policies of the Nixon, Ford, and Carter administrations, he subjected Pentagon budgets and policies to scrutiny and critical examination. He expanded the scope of Congress's annual defense authorization requirement, built an expert committee staff, and developed procedures to monitor the progress of major weapons programs. Stennis was a master at maneuvering defense bills through the committee and was such a commanding presence on the floor of the Senate that a hush fell over the chamber when he spoke on defense matters. Despite a series of powerful challenges in the Senate to cut the defense budget and eliminate weapons, Stennis never lost a floor fight on a major weapons program during the 1970s. Although he defended the Nixon administration's Southeast

Asia policy, he became increasingly concerned that Congress's constitutional power to declare war had eroded. He became a principal sponsor of the War Powers Resolution of 1973, which set limits on the president's ability to commit troops abroad without congressional sanction.

On 30 January 1973 Stennis was shot twice and sustained near-fatal injuries during a holdup in front of his Washington, D.C., residence. The shooting removed him from the Senate until his seventy-second birthday on August 3. He made a remarkable physical comeback, but he never fully regained his energies. During the Watergate crisis that year, President Nixon sought refuge in the high esteem that Stennis enjoyed among his Senate colleagues, proposing that the senator authenticate the White House transcripts of tape recordings rather than submit them to the special prosecutor. Stennis agreed initially, but the plan collapsed from lack of widespread support.

After the Republicans gained a majority in the Senate in the 1980s, Stennis's power in the Senate waned. In 1982 he faced his first serious election challenge since 1947, and in the same year he supported civil rights legislation for the first time when he voted for an extension of the Voting Rights Act. When Democrats regained control of the Senate in the election of 1986, Stennis became chairman of the Senate Committee on Appropriations and was president pro tempore from 1987 to 1989.

When he left office on 3 January 1989, Stennis moved to the Mississippi State University campus at Starkville, where the John C. Stennis Institute of Government and the John C. Stennis Center for Public Service are located. The John C. Stennis Space Center at the National Aeronautics and Space Administration (NASA) laboratory near Bay St. Louis, Mississippi, and the Navy aircraft carrier USS *John C. Stennis* are also named after him. At the age of ninety-three, Stennis died of complications of pneumonia and is buried in De Kalb Cemetery in De Kalb, Mississippi.

Stennis became the preeminent voice on defense matters in the U.S. Senate during the 1970s and helped sustain the nation's military policies during the cold war. Although critics regarded him as too friendly to the Pentagon, Stennis did more than any senator in the twentieth century to establish the processes, procedures, and conditions for effective congressional scrutiny and oversight of the Department of Defense.

★

The John C. Stennis Papers are located at the Mitchell Memorial Library at Mississippi State University. Information on Stennis's role in defense issues can be found in the Records of the U.S. Senate, Record Group 46, Center for Legislative Archives, at the National Archives in Washington, D.C. With fellow senator J. William Fulbright, Stennis wrote *The Role of Congress in Foreign Policy* (1971). Also useful is Michael S. Downs, "Advise and Con-

sent: John Stennis and the Vietnam War, 1954–1973," *Journal of Mississippi History* (1993): 87–114. An obituary is in the *New York Times* (24 Apr. 1995).

RICHARD T. MCCULLEY

STEVENS, Brooks (*b.* 7 June 1911 in Milwaukee, Wisconsin; *d.* 4 January 1995 in Milwaukee, Wisconsin), pioneer in industrial design whose product designs for major U.S. corporations have become American icons.

Stevens was the son of William Stevens, a vice president and director of design and development with Cutler-Hammer, a Milwaukee electronics firm, and Sally Stevens, a homemaker. As a child, Brooks contracted polio, and while he was confined to bed, his father encouraged him to develop his talent for drawing.

After attending Milwaukee schools, including University School for precollege training, Brooks entered Cornell University in Ithaca, New York, in 1929, studying architecture. He left Cornell in 1933 without a degree because of the Great Depression and returned to Milwaukee. In 1934 he opened Brooks Stevens Design Associates, an industrial design studio. One of his first projects was creating a line of electrical controls and the corporate logo for the Cutler-Hammer firm. The early days as an industrial designer were extremely difficult. Stevens recalled that "I had to fight my way in to talk to anybody in the '30s. I had to justify not only myself, but my profession." Stevens prevailed, however, and won his first significant assignment from the farm tractor manufacturer Allis-Chalmers. He configured the tractor's exposed innards into a fine rounded form, molded the gas tank into a teardrop, and shaped two graceful fenders over the wheels. The design was an instant success and was so streamlined that farmers reportedly drove them to church.

Stevens undertook another early design project for his friend Ralph Evinrude, the outboard motor manufacturer. In 1934, he redesigned the engine, hiding the exposed loud motor under a sleek, streamlined cowling. Stevens went on to design many small boats for Evinrude.

Stevens's work on the first hot air clothes drier provides an understanding of the work of an industrial designer. In 1936 Hamilton Industries developed a prototype for a gas heated spin drier for household use. Essentially, it was a metal box with a simple on-off switch. "You can't sell this thing," Stevens told the developers. "It's just a sheet metal box!" Stevens designed a spin drier with a glass panel front door and added fluted panels and matching knobs. He then suggested that the company load the drier with brightly colored boxer shorts for demonstrations to retailers. The product took off, and the glass panel front door design on clothes driers has remained popular ever since. Stevens's work on the spin drier most aptly illustrates his own dictum that "I am a businessman-engineer-stylist—and in that order."

On 21 August 1937 Stevens married Alice Kopmeier. They had four children.

The futuristic designs shown at the 1939 World's Fair in New York City opened the eyes of American business-people to the possibilities of quality industrial design. However, industrial designers had to wait until after World War II, when corporations could devote production to consumer goods, to truly come into their own. Stevens rode the crest of this wave.

Throughout the 1940s and 1950s the output of Stevens's firm was prodigious. He designed portable grills, a side opening bread toaster, portable radios, lawn mowers, the wide-mouthed peanut butter jar, the Jeepster, Lawn Boy lawn mowers, the Steam-O-Matic electric steam iron, Mirro electric fryers, a line of enclosed bridge deck cruisers for Chris Craft, and many other familiar household products.

Some of Stevens's most renowned work was in the field of transportation. In 1949 he designed the Harley-Davidson Hydraglide motorcycle, and its front fender design was still used by the company's Heritage Classic series in the early twenty-first century.

Stevens's automotive industry clients included Kaiser-Frazier, for whom he designed passenger cars and the Excalibur, a two-seat sports car, of which 3,000 were produced. He designed the first postwar Jeepster for the company, and subsequent Jeep lines up to the 1980 Cherokee station wagons. He also worked for Studebaker, Packard, Willys-Overland, and the European car producers Alfa Romeo and Volkswagen. In total, Brooks Stevens Design Associates contributed forty-six designs between 1940 and 1980 for automotive clients.

Stevens created notable successes for railroads. For the Milwaukee Road, he designed every aspect for the transcontinental Hiawatha and Olympian Hiawatha trains from the sleek locomotives, dining cars, and aerodynamic Skytop Lounge car, down to the porters' uniforms and club car napkins.

Stevens also handled packaging and logo designs for corporations. Starting in 1942, he shaped Miller Beer's contemporary look, designing everything from the logo, to bottles (clear rather than brown), to the company's parade floats. Other logo designs included corporate identities for the 3M Company and for Allen Bradley. In all, Brooks Stevens Design Associates designed over 3,000 products for 585 clients during its founder's career. Eventually, the products designed by Stevens were sold across several continents and had a value of over $6 billion a year.

Probably the single most recognized Stevens design was the Wienermobile, a quirky hot dog on wheels that was an advertising gimmick for the Oscar Mayer Company. In 1958 Stevens redesigned the vehicle, adding buns to the body and a bubble cockpit for the driver. According to his son Kipp, it was one of Brooks Stevens's most signal achievements, since it "was designed as an advertising vehicle, and succeeded wildly in that regard." In 1944 Stevens became one of the founders of the Industrial Designers Society of America. The Society had over 8,500 members in the mid-1990s.

Stevens coined the phrase "planned obsolescence" in 1954, a phrase that "stirred up a storm in the trade, press, and with the consumer public." He did not use this phrase to mean designing products to wear out as their warranties expired. Rather, Stevens explained, the phrase signified giving a product a visual appeal that creates "the desire to own something a little sooner than necessary. We induce people to buy products, and then next year we deliberately introduce something that will make those products old-fashioned, out of date." Many postwar designers boasted that their spurring increased consumer buying was their contribution to the robust American economy.

Stevens's was the only major design firm located away from New York City and the East Coast, the center of the design industry. Stevens claimed that the abundant source of product manufacturers in the region was a reason he was so prolific.

For many years Stevens also taught design at the Milwaukee Institute of Art and Design (MIAD). In 1978 Stevens had open-heart surgery, and in 1979 he turned his design company over to his son Kipp but continued to teach at MIAD. In the 1980s he lost sight in one eye, and the residual effects of childhood polio confined him to a wheelchair. Through the 1980s, however, he continued to teach three days a week at MIAD.

Brooks Stevens died of heart failure on 4 January 1995. He is buried at Forest Home Cemetery in Milwaukee. Terrence J. Coffman, the president of the Milwaukee Institute of Art and Design, said at the time of Stevens's death, "He was a national treasure. His many designs in all areas of industrial design have been used and enjoyed by millions since the 1930s, and his contribution to the industrial design profession are inestimable."

★

The Brooks Stevens Gallery of Industrial Design at the Milwaukee Institute of Art and Design maintains a permanent collection of models of Stevens's automobiles, marine products, machine tools, household appliances, toys, farm and lawn equipment, and packaging. The bulk of his personal archives are at the Milwaukee Art Museum, which maintains an extensive photo file of his creations. Brooks Stevens Design Associates maintains a web site, www.brooksstevens.com. "Bringing Style to Life," in the *Washington Post* (19 Jan. 1995), discusses the development and everyday impact of the industrial design profession, and on Brooks Stevens's contributions to contemporary life. Obituaries are in the *Milwaukee Sentinel* (5 Jan. 1995) and the *New York Times* (7 Jan. 1995).

WILLIAM J. MALONEY

STIBITZ, George Robert (*b.* 30 April 1904 in York, Pennsylvania; *d.* 31 January 1995 in Hanover, New Hampshire), inventor of the modern digital computer.

In his early childhood, Stibitz's family moved from York, Pennsylvania, to Ohio, where he attended Moraine Park, an experimental school in Dayton. He then went on to Denison University, where he received his Ph.B. degree in 1926. After graduation, Stibitz moved to Schenectady, New York, where he combined work at the General Electric research laboratories with pursuit of an M.S. degree from Union College, which he obtained in 1927. Stibitz then attended Cornell University, where he earned his Ph.D. degree in mathematical physics in 1930.

Work was not easy to obtain in 1930, at the outset of the Great Depression, but Stibitz succeeded in getting a job as a mathematical consultant at Bell Telephone Laboratories. The job gave him an opportunity to tinker, a lifelong preoccupation. Stibitz would ultimately hold thirty-eight patents in his own name, including one for a stereophonic organ, along with numerous others held in the name of Bell Labs. In 1937 he was asked to study the magneto-mechanics of telephone relays, the electromechanical switches used to connect phone circuits. His focus quickly moved from the relays themselves to the binary circuits that the relays created, and to the many possible arithmetic calculations that were reducible to binary form. Finally, Stibitz decided to construct his own binary adding machine, combining several relays with flashlight bulbs and connecting them all with metal strips cut from a tobacco can.

Stibitz's Model K adding machine (so called because he built it at his kitchen table) used electromechanical relays as "gates." If the relays for the integers 5 and 3 were activated together, for instance, they would open the gate of the relay for 8, their sum, thus lighting the appropriate bulbs. A replica of this first crude machine is displayed at the Smithsonian Institution. Over the next two years, working with Samuel B. Williams, Stibitz created a far more sophisticated machine called the Complex Number Calculator, which could perform all four basic arithmetic operations, using both real and complex numbers. This machine, containing 450 telephone relays and ten crossbar switches, could divide two eight-place complex numbers in about half a minute. It could both read input from a teletypewriter and print the output the same way. It first operated on 8 January 1940 and was installed at Bell Labs'

main office in New York City, where it was linked to three teletypewriter "terminals." It took up about twenty cubic feet.

Later that year, Stibitz pulled off a public relations coup for his new machine. On 11 September 1940 the American Mathematical Society held a meeting at Dartmouth College in Hanover, New Hampshire, and Stibitz attended, bringing his teletypewriter. Telephoning New York City, Stibitz allowed the assembled mathematicians to pose arithmetic problems, which he then "downloaded" to his machine some 250 miles away. The answers printed out within seconds. This public demonstration of a working digital machine received wide publicity, and Bell Labs promptly renamed Stibitz's "calculator" the Model 1 Relay Computer.

Stibitz's demonstration did more than show how a digital computer could work; it displayed the principles of "remote entry" which would make the computer commercially viable. Particularly during the early decades of computing, when the huge machines took up entire rooms, the ability to access the mainframe (as it came to be called) through remote terminals was invaluable. Data could be entered at a laboratory, a workstation, or a job site; the calculations could be performed hundreds of miles away, at the home office; and the results could be displayed at a sales meeting, a production conference, or even at home.

During World War II Stibitz worked for the National Defense Research Committee (NDRC), joining with other early computer experts to help predict his infant specialty's future course of development. As with many experts during an industry's formative years, his predictions were wrong. Stibitz had gained tremendous success with computers based on electromechanical relays, whose inherent reliability made up for their relatively slow performance. He was understandably reluctant to back a new generation of computers based on speedy but unreliable electronic vacuum tubes. Indeed, until the commercial development of the transistor in the 1950s, electromechanical computers did retain a significant edge in reliability. But Stibitz and the rest of Subcommittee Z on High-Speed Computing (which grew out of the NDRC) failed to see the revolutionary potential of UNIVAC and other new designs, which hindsight would show to have laid the foundation of modern mainframe computing. The radical innovations that would make UNIVAC the first commercially successful mainframe computer, such as its use of high-speed magnetic tape rather than teletypewriter or paper tape for input and output, were dismissed as "details" in Subcommittee Z's final report.

Disappointed by his failure to influence government policy and by his apparent inability to reach useful conclusions about the emerging new computer technologies, Stibitz established himself as a private consultant in Burlington, Vermont. However, he continued to tinker, and in

1954 he developed a prototype of the minicomputer—a full-function machine the size of a desk rather than a room—a decade before this kind of computer would become popular. But never again would he experience that thrill of the years 1938–1940, when a brilliant idea met its ideal moment of opportunity.

At the age of sixty, Stibitz joined the Dartmouth Medical School, where he worked on applications of computers to biomedicine. He was given the rank of professor in 1966 and became professor emeritus in 1972, continuing his work there until 1983. During his later years, when most people are enjoying retirement, Stibitz worked on such subjects as the anatomy of the brain and the movement of drugs through the body, and he developed a mathematical model of the capillary interface, in which arterial blood gives up its oxygenated hemoglobin and becomes venous.

Stibitz married Dorothea Lamson in 1 September 1930 and had two daughters. He died at the age of ninety at his home in Hanover and is buried in that city.

Stibitz, who cut an imposing figure with his tall stature and long, lean face, was not the only member of his family to achieve long life; he was survived by a brother and two sisters. He was granted a form of happiness gained by few people: he was able to spend his life doing something he loved, gaining success and admiration in the process. His computers may appear crude to modern eyes, but Stibitz's electromechanical machines paved the way not only for the electronic computers that followed, but also—through his invention of remote job-entry—for the decentralized Internet-based culture of the modern world.

★

For more information on Stibitz, see Joel Shurkin, *Engines of the Mind* (1996). Stibitz's life and achievements are also memorialized in the web sites of the AT&T Labs Research History, administered by AT&T; the Bell Labs Museum, administered by Lucent Technologies; and the SHOT History of Computing, administered by the Computer History Association of California. An obituary is in the *New York Times* (2 Feb. 1995).

HARTLEY S. SPATT

STOKES, Carl Burton (*b.* 21 June 1927 in Cleveland, Ohio; *d.* 3 April 1996 in Cleveland, Ohio), first African American mayor of a major U.S. city, Cleveland, Ohio.

Born to laundry worker Charles Stokes, who died in Carl's infancy, and domestic laborer Louise Stone Stokes, Stokes grew up in poverty in Cleveland's predominantly African American inner city. His older brother Louis became a congressman who served from 1969 to 1999.

Stokes learned early how to box and hustle pool. He dropped out of East Technical High School at age seven-

Carl B. Stokes. LIBRARY OF CONGRESS

teen and served in the U.S. Army in Germany from 1945 to 1946. He then graduated from high school at age twenty. After attending West Virginia State College and Cleveland College of Western Reserve, he enrolled at the University of Minnesota in 1952, receiving his B.S. degree in law in 1954. He then went on to Cleveland Marshall School of Law, from which he graduated in 1956. In 1957 Stokes passed the Ohio bar examination and entered law practice with his brother.

Stokes held a series of patronage jobs, including Ohio Department of Liquor Control retail clerk in 1948 and enforcement officer in 1950; Cleveland Municipal Court probation officer from 1954 to 1958; and Cleveland assistant police prosecutor from 1958 to 1962. Meanwhile he entered Democratic Party politics.

Stokes was handsome, articulate, charming, and witty, and enjoyed fine suits and cigars. He married Edith Shirley Smith on 27 December 1951 and, although they separated a year and a half later, they did not divorce until 1955. They had no children. On 28 January 1958 he married Shirley Joann Edwards, with whom he had three children. They divorced in 1973, and on 3 January 1980 Stokes married Raija Kostadinov (Miss Finland, 1969). They adopted a daughter in 1988, divorced in 1993, then remarried three months before Stokes died.

After a narrow 1960 loss, Stokes in 1962 became the first African American Democrat elected as an Ohio state representative. He was reelected in 1964 and 1966. During this time he angered fellow Democrats—and pleased many Cleveland corporate leaders—by supporting Republican reapportionment and capital improvement plans he believed would help blacks.

In 1965 Stokes challenged the incumbent Democratic mayor Ralph Locher. Although only 34 percent of Cleveland's residents were black, they represented two-fifths of registered voters and were well mobilized by civil rights campaigns. Stokes filed as an independent in the general election, expecting whites to divide among three white candidates. Shunned by other black politicians, Stokes created his own inner-city campaign network of enthusiastic "Stokes Folks." Stokes also received help from some whites, drawn by civil rights and reform appeals. Stokes's bid fell short by a slim margin (87,858 to 85,716), but the 1965 run impressed big business and showed blacks that the Cleveland mayoralty was within their reach.

Conditions favored a second Stokes mayoral bid in 1967. A July 1966 race riot frightened many, and Mayor Locher angered blacks by neglecting their problems and demeaning civil rights activism. In January 1967 the federal government stopped funding urban renewal in Cleveland because the city had failed to complete earlier projects; hostile national press coverage ensued. African Americans wanted one of their own in City Hall; at the same time, corporate chiefs hoped Stokes would calm racial unrest, restore money from Washington, and halt Cleveland's economic decline.

Stokes ran against Locher in the 3 October 1967 Democratic primary. To African Americans, as one campaigner on Stokes's team recalled, "We sold blackness. . . . This was their opportunity to make black history." Among white people of Eastern European, Italian, and Irish backgrounds, Stokes stressed his qualifications and pledged he would be mayor for all. Stokes also courted white business leaders. His strategy worked: black turnout was high, and Stokes increased his share of the African American vote from 85 to 96 percent. Stokes quintupled his share in white wards to 15 percent, and Cleveland's elite delivered campaign donations and press endorsements. He defeated Locher soundly, 110,769 to 92,321.

In the 7 November 1967 general election, Stokes faced Seth Taft, grandson of President William Howard Taft and a member of Ohio's top Republican family. Unions helped Stokes, but white Democratic regulars did not. Stressing his party label and comparing his rise to that of European immigrants, Stokes nudged his vote in white wards from 15 to 19 percent. Meanwhile, black turnout climbed to 80 percent, and Stokes took 95 percent of the African American vote. With the slogan "Let's Do Cleveland Proud," Stokes barely edged Taft, 129,396 to 127,717.

During Stokes's two two-year terms, he gave minorities more city jobs and work in businesses contracting with Cleveland. He insisted that city contracts go to black businesses, and he forced banks to lend African Americans money. Stokes also secured urban development funds from corporations and the federal government. His "Cleveland: NOW!" crusade sought $177 million from federal, state, local, and private sources for jobs, housing, day care, health, and recreation. Stokes enforced housing codes, demolished slums, and built 5,500 public housing units. Finally, he made blacks feel part of government. But Stokes proved a better campaigner than mayor. Close aides left, saying that they could not work with him. Other top advisers and administrators departed due to scandals and conflicts. Critics decried Stokes's absences for paid speaking tours and campaign trips on behalf of black candidates. Relations with city council and the news media, good at first, soured, and Stokes's charm turned to angry outbursts.

Most of Stokes's difficulties, however, were not of his own making. African Americans lost patience with menial jobs, police abuse, and inferior segregated schools. After the assassination of the Reverend Martin Luther King on 4 April 1968, many in Cleveland feared ghetto residents would react violently. Stokes eased tensions by walking the street and speaking to people, and the local news media suppressed reports of violence. Three months later the city was less fortunate. On 23 July 1968 a gun battle between black nationalists and police in the black neighborhood of Glenville left seven dead (including three policemen) and fifteen injured. Arson and looting followed. For one night, Stokes excluded whites (including police) from Glenville, using black police and civilian patrols. No one else died, but white journalists and police were furious. Stokes suffered politically from his good relations with black nationalists. After reports that the nationalist leader Fred (Ahmed) Evans bought guns with Cleveland: NOW! funds, corporate donors deserted. Moreover, whites discovered that a black mayor could not necessarily prevent eruptions of racial violence.

Residents feared rising crime, so Stokes shifted some 200 police officers from desks to streets, hired more minority police, and tried to sensitize police to minorities. But most officers resisted change and civilian interference and remained prejudiced against African Americans, including the mayor. Meanwhile, a revolving door of police chiefs (four in four years) and public safety directors generated negative headlines. A civil service examination scandal in 1968 and 1969 involving Stokes's appointees also stained his image.

Stokes's housing and renewal plans met resistance. West Side whites balked at his Neighborhood Development Program and scattered-site public housing. Some tried to secede from Cleveland; many moved to suburbs. Class barriers also stymied Stokes. He wanted to build 277 units of owner-occupied housing for the poor in Lee-Seville, a middle-class black district. Intense protest there killed the proposal.

Inflation, reindustrialization, white flight, and rising demands for services eroded Cleveland's fiscal health. In 1968 the city council doubled the income tax to 1 percent. But in 1970 and 1971, voters spurned Stokes's pleas to hike the income tax rate to 1.8 or 1.6 percent. Meanwhile, pay for city workers rose, propelled by 1970 garbage and mass transit strikes. By 1971 Stokes faced a huge deficit and laid off city employees.

In 1969 Stokes narrowly won a second term, squeezing by the Republican county auditor Ralph Perk, 120,616 to 116,863. Once again, most white voters put race above party. Stokes recalled, "My second term was almost total war between . . . the mayor and everyone." In 1970 he and his brother Louis quit the local Democratic Party and launched the Twenty-first District Caucus, an independent black political force. White Democrats vowed to deny Stokes a third term. On 17 April 1971 Stokes announced he would not run again.

Stokes's post-mayoral career dimmed his reputation. In 1972 he moved to New York City as coanchor on the WNBC-TV evening news, and then worked as a WNBC reporter. Early reviews were unflattering. In 1980 he returned to Cleveland as a United Auto Workers legal counsel. His law partner ended their relationship and sued to evict Stokes in 1983. Cleveland voters elected Stokes a municipal court judge from 1983 to 1994 but denied his bids for a county judgeship in 1986 and city housing court in 1989. His colleagues chose him as presiding judge but then ousted him. Store employees caught Stokes shoplifting in 1988 and 1989, and the resulting news accounts were humiliating.

In 1994 he became the U.S. ambassador to Seychelles, but in June 1995 Stoke entered Cleveland Clinic for esophageal cancer treatment. He died there at age sixty-eight and was buried in Cleveland.

Stokes was the first black big-city mayor, a symbol of rising African American urban political power. He inspired other blacks, and his policy goals became theirs. However, three white ethnics succeeded him, so Stokes's local legacy was limited. Stokes showed that simply becoming mayor was not enough, for Cleveland's city council and bureaucracy blocked much of his agenda. Stokes stood for big-government liberalism when both white ethnics and young African Americans rejected it. He mounted an independent reform challenge to Democratic Party regulars. He also challenged older, more accommodating black politicians. Ghetto divisions between integrationists and revolutionaries ensnared him as well. Though many of his misfortunes were of his own making, Stokes's mayoralty shows how hard it was to govern cities in decline.

★

Stokes's papers are at the Western Reserve Historical Society, Cleveland. His autobiography is *Promises of Power: A Political Autobiography* (1973). Useful sources include Kenneth G. Weinberg, *Black Victory: Carl Stokes and the Winning of Cleveland* (1968); Estelle Zannes, *Checkmate in Cleveland: The Rhetoric of Confrontation During the Stokes Years* (1972); Philip W. Porter, *Cleveland: Confused City on a Seesaw* (1976); William E. Nelson, Jr., and Philip J. Meranto, *Electing Black Mayors: Political Action in the Black Community* (1977); and Leonard N. Moore, *The Limits of Black Power: Carl B. Stokes and Cleveland's African-American Community, 1945–1971* (doctoral dissertation, Ohio State University, 1998). Obituaries are in the *New York Times* (4 and 9 Apr. 1996) and *Washington Post* (4 Apr. 1996).

MICHAEL W. HOMEL

STRODE, Woodrow Wilson Woolwine ("Woody") (*b.* 28 July 1914 in Los Angeles, California; *d.* 31 December 1994 in Glendora, California), athlete who broke the color barrier in professional football in 1946 (a year before Jackie Robinson integrated major league baseball) and is regarded as having the first dignified role for a black actor in a feature motion picture.

Strode was one of two sons of Baylous Strode, Sr., a brick mason, and Rose Norris Strode, a homemaker; Baylous Jr. was the couple's only other child. Strode was tall and thin as a youngster, and his athletic ability did not materialize until he reached junior high school. After a growth spurt, he developed into a fine all-around athlete, earning all-city honors in football and all-state recognition in track and field at Thomas Jefferson High School in Los Angeles. His athletic ability interested several major colleges on the West Coast. He chose the University of California at Los Angeles (UCLA), at the time a relatively young institution that had recently moved to a new campus in the Westwood section of Los Angeles. In going to college, Strode fulfilled his father's wish that he "get an education."

During the late 1930s Jackie Robinson and Kenny Washington, also black athletes, were the bright stars on the UCLA gridiron, but Strode was also outstanding. It was at this time that Strode prepared for the decathlon (a ten-event track and field sport) in the 1936 Olympic trials.

Because of his muscular physique, Strode was asked to pose for an art class. He also caught the attention of the acclaimed German cinematographer Leni Riefenstahl, who took several still photographs of Strode and had him pose for a sculptor. The Nazi leader Adolf Hitler saw the photographs and sent Riefenstahl to America to film Strode. A painting of Strode was used, ironically—given Hitler's thoughts on Aryan supremacy—as part of the Berlin Olympic Festival in 1936.

When Strode finished his schooling at UCLA, the National Football League (NFL) was still an all-white organization. Blacks had no opportunity to play in the nation's only major professional football league. However, Strode and Washington did play with the Hollywood Bears of the Pacific Coast League, a minor league, and they actually earned more money than many NFL players.

During the late 1930s Strode and his UCLA teammate Washington began working in the service department at Warner Brothers Studio. After he left UCLA, Strode's contacts at Warner Brothers allowed him to secure small roles in motion pictures, including *Sundown* (1941), *Star-Spangled Rhythm* (1942), and *No Time for Love* (1943). But Strode was mainly an athlete during this time. When not playing football, he trained as a wrestler and won several professional matches. In 1941 he married Luana Kalaeloa, a Hawaiian princess. They later had two children: a son, Kalaeloa (known as Kalai), and a daughter, June.

When World War II broke out, Strode joined the U.S. Army Air Corps. He was stationed at March Field in Riverside, California, where he was a member of one of the top service football teams, the Fourth Air Corps Flyers. Commenting on Strode, Paul Stenn ("Stenko"), a ten-year NFL player, recalled, "I played along side of him—and he was good. I had played pro football and I can tell you Woody Strode was as good as the NFL players. He just needed a chance to prove it."

Strode got that chance after the war. When the Cleveland Rams moved their franchise to Los Angeles in 1946, they became the first major league team to play on the West Coast. The Rams wanted to play in Memorial Coliseum, a 100,000-seat stadium. Leaders of the black community reasoned that if the team was going to play in a public facility, then all Americans should be entitled to play on the team. Pressure was brought to bear, and in the spring of 1946 Strode and Washington signed on with the Rams, becoming the first blacks to play in the NFL since the league's pioneering days in the 1920s. Unfortunately, both Strode, then age thirty-two, and Washington, then twenty-nine, were past their athletic prime. Underutilized by the Rams, Strode caught only four passes for thirty-seven yards and was waived at the end of the 1946 season.

The next season, Strode signed with the Calgary Stampeders of the Canadian Football League. Age and football injuries caught up with him by 1950, and Strode returned to the United States to pursue a professional wrestling career in Los Angeles. The "movie crowd" often attended the wrestling matches, and this led to Strode's full-time acting career. A talent agent signed him, and he appeared in several movies that today would be known as "action" films. Strode often played the role of a gladiator or jungle warrior. He gained notoriety as a gladiator in the 1960 epic film *Spartacus*. That same year Strode starred in the title role of

Woody Strode. COURTESY PRO FOOTBALL HALL OF FAME

Sergeant Rutledge, a part that many consider to be the first dignified black character in American cinema. Strode continued to land meaningful roles throughout the 1960s and made films in Italy in the 1970s. He also made regular television appearances, ranging from a starring role in *Ramar of the Jungle* to a part in *The Quest.*

One of Strode's last major roles was in the 1984 film *The Cotton Club.* After he did several other feature films and a television movie (*A Gathering of Old Men,* 1987), Strode retired to a ranch in Glendora, California, with his second wife, Tina (Strode remarried on 10 May 1982 after Luana's death in 1980 from Parkinson's disease). Strode died on New Year's Eve, 1994, in Glendora of natural causes about a year after he was diagnosed with lung cancer. He was buried with full military honors in Riverside National Cemetery in California.

Strode was a versatile athlete who made his mark in the world of sports, but he is best remembered as one of the first blacks to integrate the modern NFL. He also left an important legacy of more than fifty feature films. His many significant roles opened the door for other black actors to follow—much like his role as a black pioneer in professional football led the way for future black athletes.

★

For information about Strode's athletic career see: Frank Cosentino, *Canadian Football* (1969); Myron Cope, *The Game That*

Was (1970); Arthur R. Ashe, Jr., *A Hard Road to Glory* (1988); and Woody Strode, with Sam Young, *Goal Dust* (1990). An obituary is in the *New York Times* (4 Jan. 1995).

JIM CAMPBELL

STYNE, Jule (*b.* 31 December 1905 in London, England; *d.* 20 September 1994 in New York City), composer noted for numerous scores for films and stage musicals and many hit songs.

Styne was born Julius Kerwin Stein; he changed the spelling of his last name in 1932 to avoid being confused with Doctor Julius Stein, who ran the Music Corporation of America (MCA), then a booking agency. Styne was the first of three children of Isadore Stein, an egg inspector, and Anna Kertman. They were Russians who had immigrated to England; in 1912 they moved to the United States, settling in Chicago. Styne was a child prodigy, performing as a piano soloist with several symphony orchestras in the Midwest by the age of nine. But by the time he was a teenager, he had abandoned classical music and was playing popular music in bands. In 1922 he graduated from Tuley High School, ending his formal schooling. He began writing music and enjoyed his first hit in 1927 with "Sunday" (cocredited to Ned Miller, Chester Conn, and Benny Krueger), through a recording by Cliff Edwards. In September of that year Styne married Ethel Pauline Rubenstein, with whom he had two children; they divorced in 1952. He married Margaret Ann Bissett Brown, a British model, on 4 June 1962, and they also had two children.

Jule Styne. ARCHIVE PHOTOS

In 1934 Styne moved to New York City, where he worked primarily as a vocal coach. In that capacity, he was hired by Twentieth Century–Fox in 1937 and moved to Hollywood. In 1940 he got a job as a songwriter with Republic Pictures, a maker of B-movies, especially Westerns. The song "Who Am I?" (with lyrics by Walter Bullock) from *Hit Parade of 1941* earned Styne his first Academy Award nomination. He was paired with lyricist Frank Loesser and moved to Paramount Pictures, where the two wrote "I Don't Want to Walk Without You," used in *Sweater Girl* (1942) and recorded for a Top Ten hit by Harry James.

Loesser began writing his own music, but Styne quickly teamed up with lyricist Sammy Cahn, with whom he formed one of the most successful songwriting partnerships of the 1940s. Their hits during the decade, written for films and independently, included "I've Heard That Song Before" from *Youth on Parade* and "It's Been a Long, Long Time," both recorded by Harry James; "Vict'ry Polka," recorded by Bing Crosby and the Andrews Sisters; "I'll Walk Alone," performed by Dinah Shore in *Follow the Boys* and subsequently recorded by her; "There Goes That Song Again" from *Carolina Blues,* recorded by Russ Morgan; "Let It Snow! Let It Snow! Let It Snow!," recorded by Vaughn Monroe; "It's Magic," performed by Doris Day in *Romance on the High Seas* and subsequently recorded by her; and "Saturday Night (Is the Loneliest Night of the Week)," "Five Minutes More," "The Things We Did Last Summer," "I Believe," and "Time after Time," all recorded by Frank Sinatra.

Styne and Cahn also teamed up for two stage musicals, 1944's *Glad to See You,* which closed out of town but contained the hit "Can't You Read Between the Lines?," recorded by Jimmy Dorsey, and *High Button Shoes* (1947), a hit that ran 727 performances. The team dissolved amicably at the end of the 1940s because Styne wanted to continue writing for Broadway, while Cahn preferred Hollywood. Styne moved to New York City and collaborated with Leo Robin on the songs for *Gentlemen Prefer Blondes* (1949), which ran 740 performances and made a star of Carol Channing, as well as spawning a Top Ten cast album that included "Diamonds Are a Girl's Best Friend." A 1953 film version starring Marilyn Monroe was also a success, though it retained only three songs from the score.

Styne turned producer with the 1951 musical *Make a Wish,* the songs for which were written by Hugh Martin. It was a flop, but later Styne productions, such as the 1952 revival of *Pal Joey* and the 1956 Sammy Davis, Jr., vehicle *Mr. Wonderful,* were hits. *Two on the Aisle* (1951), the next musical for which Styne served as composer, had a modest run of 279 performances and marked the start of his partnership with Betty Comden and Adolph Green. Next came *Hazel Flagg* (1953), with lyrics by Bob Hilliard; it ran only

190 performances but was adapted into the 1954 Dean Martin and Jerry Lewis film *Living It Up*.

Despite eight Academy Award nominations, Styne had never won an Oscar for best song until 1954, when he teamed with Sammy Cahn again to write "Three Coins in the Fountain" for the film of the same name. Frank Sinatra sang it on the soundtrack, while the Four Aces' recording was a million-copy seller. Back on Broadway, Styne, Comden, and Green wrote additional songs for a production of *Peter Pan* (1954) that had a basic score by Moose Charlap and Carolyn Leigh; starring Mary Martin, it was given a memorable television broadcast and is often revived. Styne again worked with Comden and Green on *Bells Are Ringing* (1956), which ran 924 performances and featured the hits "Just in Time" and "The Party's Over." Judy Holliday, who starred in the stage version, repeated her role in the 1960 film version opposite Dean Martin. *Say, Darling* (1958), another collaboration with Comden and Green, ran 332 performances.

Styne's most acclaimed score was that for *Gypsy* (1959), based on the memoirs of Gypsy Rose Lee and starring Ethel Merman. With lyrics by Stephen Sondheim, the songs included the hit "Small World" and the standard "Everything's Coming Up Roses." The show ran 702 performances, and the cast album, which spent two years on the charts, tied for the Grammy Award in its category. A film version was released in 1962. Returning to work with Comden and Green, Styne next composed the songs for *Do Re Mi* (1960), among them the hit "Make Someone Happy"; the show ran 400 performances. *Subways Are for Sleeping* (1961), again with Comden and Green, was less successful, running only 205 performances.

Styne scored the longest-running hit of his career with *Funny Girl* (1964), based on the life of the Ziegfeld Follies star Fanny Brice and starring twenty-one-year-old Barbra Streisand, which ran 1,348 performances. The songs, with lyrics by Bob Merrill, included "People," which Streisand recorded for a hit, and the Grammy Award–winning cast album reached the Top Ten and went gold. The 1968 film version of the show was that year's highest-grossing movie, and the soundtrack album sold a million copies.

Although Styne continued to write for the musical theater until his death thirty years later, *Funny Girl* was his last major success. Among his more successful later efforts, *Fade In—Fade Out*, written with Comden and Green and starring Carol Burnett, opened only two months after *Funny Girl* but ran only 271 performances; *Hallelujah, Baby!* (1967), again with Comden and Green, barely improved upon that record, though it won Tony Awards for best musical and best score; *Sugar* (1972), written with Bob Merrill, had a healthy run of 505 performances; and *Lorelei* (1974), a revised version of *Gentlemen Prefer Blondes*, ran 320 performances. *The Red Shoes* (1993), which ran briefly on Broadway, came less than a year before his death from heart failure.

Styne was a remarkably prolific song composer with a seemingly endless facility for catchy melodies and striking song structures. After an apprenticeship in Hollywood and Tin Pan Alley, he brought a theatrical flair to Broadway at a time when the subject matter of musicals was becoming increasingly somber. His best and most popular work was found in shows like *Gypsy* and *Funny Girl*, which were about show business itself and to which he contributed a knowing style that, like the lyrics, commented on the form of musical theater while celebrating it.

★

The sole biography of Styne is the authorized *Jule: The Story of Composer Jule Styne* (1979), by Theodore Taylor, an adequate popular biography, though not comprehensive. He is profiled in a chapter of Max Wilk's *They're Playing Our Song* (1973), to which he contributed the preface. Styne is much discussed in Sammy Cahn's autobiography, *I Should Care* (1974). David Ewen, *American Songwriters* (1987), has a good entry on Styne, and Didier C. Deutsch has a good essay accompanying the Columbia House Music Collection album *The Great American Composers: Jule Styne* (1991). There is an obituary on the front page of the *New York Times* (21 Sept. 1994).

WILLIAM J. RUHLMANN

SULLIVAN, Walter Seager, Jr. (*b*. 12 January 1918 in New York City; *d*. 19 March 1996 in Riverside, Connecticut), journalist who was the preeminent interpreter of scientific developments to the American public during the second half of the twentieth century.

Sullivan was the only son and the youngest of five children born to Walter Seager Sullivan, Sr., an insurance executive who was advertising manager of the *New York Times* under Adolph S. Ochs, and Jeanet Loomis, a talented composer and pianist. Music was an important part of his family, and cello playing, which he began at age five, remained an enduring passion for Sullivan. He graduated from Groton School in Groton, Massachusetts, in 1936 and was an English history major at Yale College, where he also pursued music studies. When he graduated with a B.A. degree in 1940, he was employed at the *New York Times* as a copy boy. When the United States entered World War II, he received a commission in the naval reserve. Sullivan served with distinction on the USS *Fletcher* in such decisive engagements as the third Battle of Savo Island off Guadalcanal in 1942. He won twelve combat medals and ended the war with the rank of lieutenant commander as captain of the USS *Overton*, a destroyer.

After Sullivan was discharged, the *New York Times* assigned him to cover the 1946 Operation Highjump to Antarctica commanded by Rear Admiral Richard E. Byrd. The experience fostered Sullivan's lifelong interest in that continent. Later, while on assignment to survey Pacific islands that had been the scene of fighting in World War II, he was sent to cover the civil war in China. On the way to the mainland, his plane crashed off the Philippine coast, and he suffered a broken rib. Sullivan then witnessed the closing months of the civil war in China and was one of the last Western reporters to visit the remote northwest province of Sinkiang before the Chinese Communists entered. He also reported on the early stages of the war in Korea. On 17 August 1950 he married Mary Barrett, the associate editor of the *China Weekly Review;* they had three children.

From 1952 to 1956 Sullivan headed the Berlin bureau of the *New York Times* and reported on the anticommunist uprisings in East Berlin in 1953, which he considered the first crack in the Soviet alliance, and the covert struggle between Western and Eastern intelligence operatives in the divided city. The newspaper shifted him to the science beat in 1956. As he later recalled, science writing "wasn't a profession when I started doing it. I was just another reporter who had moved from being a foreign reporter" (*Science Writers,* 1995, p. 13).

Sullivan tracked the preparations for the International Geophysical Year (IGY) in Antarctica. "I was hooked by the Antarctic," he remembered, "and I felt here was this continent and very little of it had ever been seen by any human eye" (*Science Writers,* 1995, p. 13). He provided extensive stories about the IGY's coordinated studies of the Earth's interior, atmosphere, and space from July 1957 to December 1958, and these writings marked his emergence as a major figure in science journalism. In October 1957 he brought the news of the Soviet launch of *Sputnik* to a meeting of scientists at the Soviet embassy in Washington. Sullivan won the George Polk Memorial Award for his work on the IGY. From that assignment also came two best-selling books, *Quest for a Continent* (1957), about Antarctica, and *Assault on the Unknown* (1961), about the International Geophysical Year itself. In all, Sullivan made seven visits to Antarctica, where a range of mountains thirty miles in length was named the Sullivan Range in honor of his journalistic work.

In 1962 the *New York Times* made Sullivan its science news editor, and in 1964 he became the science editor. During an era that saw the birth of space exploration and dramatic advances in science and technology, Sullivan pushed the newspaper to expand its coverage of scientific issues and discoveries. When Sullivan stepped down in 1987, the paper's commitment to science reporting had become securely established through the weekly *Science Times* and columns in the daily newspaper.

Sullivan's interests as science editor embraced many aspects of a field in which important discoveries occurred

regularly. In 1965 his reporting about the discovery of background radiation in the universe led scientists to remark that they had not realized the significance of their findings until reading his article. He wrote about the origins of plate tectonics, which led to his popular book *Continents in Motion: The New Earth Debate* (1974). He devoted much attention to the search for extraterrestrial intelligence, and his book *We Are Not Alone: The Search for Intelligent Life on Other Worlds* (1964) won the International Non-Fiction Prize. Updated editions of these books were published in 1991 and 1993. Sullivan's other books include *Science in the Twentieth Century* (1976), which he edited for the *New York Times; Black Holes: The Edge of Space, the End of Time* (1979); and *Landprints* (1984), about the geological history responsible for North American topography.

In his tenure with the *New York Times,* Sullivan commanded the respect of and ready access to the leading figures in American and world science. As a colleague said when Sullivan died, "Scientists knew and trusted and liked him" (John Wilford, *New York Times,* 23 Apr. 1996). A larger-than-life individual, Sullivan brought the style and élan of the globe-trotting foreign correspondent to science and infused his coverage of scientific revelations with an infectious aura of romance and adventure. Late in his life Sullivan portrayed Secretary of War Henry L. Stimson in a movie about the development of the atomic bomb. His foray into acting reflected the same willingness to stretch himself that he showed in journalism.

Sullivan retired as science editor in 1987 but remained an active writer and reporter until he was afflicted with the pancreatic cancer that killed him. He is buried in the Cemetery of the First Church of Round Hill in Greenwich, Connecticut. His career brought him many honors, including the Daly Medal of the American Geographical Society, the Distinguished Public Service Award of the National Science Foundation, and the Public Welfare Medal of the National Academy of Science, of which he was an honorary member. The American Geophysical Union named its annual prize for science writing for Sullivan.

In an age of rapid and often complex scientific advances, no reporter did more to make science understandable and meaningful to the American public than Sullivan. His *New York Times* colleague John Noble Wilford said Sullivan "set the pace for competitors and colleagues with inexhaustible energy, enthusiasm, and a keen sense of what was interesting and important—what was news" (*New York Times,* 23 Apr. 1996). For several generations Sullivan informed newspaper readers about scientific advancements that changed their lives.

★

Sullivan's personal papers were donated to Yale University. The archives of the *New York Times* contain much information about his professional career. Sullivan's own writings are extensive. "The Ship Ahead Just Disappeared," *New York Times Magazine* (7 May 1995), describes his World War II service in the Pacific. In addition to the books mentioned, Sullivan edited *America's Race for the Moon* (1962) and, with William C. Havard, *A Band of Prophets* (1982). He also wrote a number of children's books. "Walter S. Sullivan, Jr.," in *World Authors, 1975–1980*, edited by Vineta Colby (1985); and "Sullivan, Walter," in *1980 Current Biography* (1981), are informative brief treatments. An obituary is in the *New York Times* (20 Mar. 1996). "Walter Sullivan: A Different Time, a Different Style," *Science Writers* (summer and fall 1995), is a helpful oral history interview.

LEWIS L. GOULD

SUOMI, Verner Edward (*b.* 6 December 1915 in Eveleth, Minnesota; *d.* 30 July 1995 in Madison, Wisconsin), meteorologist, administrator, inventor, and educator known as the "father of satellite meteorology," who made numerous important contributions to the fields of meteorology, space science, and engineering.

Suomi was one of the seven children of John E. Suomi, a carpenter for one of the town's mining companies, and Anna Emelia Sundquist, a homemaker. Suomi attended local schools and worked as a public high school science and math teacher in Minnesota from 1937 to 1941 while

Verner Suomi. AP/WIDE WORLD PHOTOS

finishing his college education. He earned a bachelor's degree in engineering from Winona State College in 1938. On 10 August 1941 he married Paula Meyer; they had three children.

At the start of World War II, Suomi enrolled in a civil air patrol course and began studying meteorology. Later during the war he taught practical meteorology to pilots. In 1948 he joined the faculty at the University of Wisconsin at Madison in the department of atmospheric and oceanic sciences. His fascination with the subject prompted him to enroll in the University of Chicago's meteorology program. Suomi earned a Ph.D. in 1953. Suomi's activities at the university extended well beyond the classroom. In 1965 he became the cofounder and director of the Space Science and Engineering Center at the university, remaining director until his retirement in 1988. The center specializes in studies of the atmosphere of the Earth and other planets and in the construction of imaging tools for meteorologists and space scientists.

Suomi taught at the University of Wisconsin at Madison for his whole career, but during his tenure there he held various concurrent positions. Among others, he was associate program director of atmospheric science at the National Science Foundation in 1962, chief scientist with the U.S. Weather Bureau from 1964 to 1965, and chairman of the U.S. Commission Global Atmospheric Research Program from 1971 to 1974.

Suomi received numerous honors and awards, including the Meisinger Award from the American Meteorological Society in 1961; the Carl-Gustaf Rossby Research Medal, the highest honor bestowed on an atmospheric scientist by the American Meteorological Society, in 1968; a Presidential Citation in 1970; the Robert M. Losey Award in 1971; and the National Medal of Science in 1977. In 1983 he received the Franklin Medal from the Franklin Institute of Philadelphia, an award previously presented to Albert Einstein and Thomas Edison. Suomi was a member of the National Academy of Engineers; the American Academy for the Advancement of Science; the American Meteorological Society, of which he was president from 1968 to 1969; and the American Geophysics Union. He was a fellow of the American Academy of Arts and Sciences and a foreign member of the Finnish Academy of Science and Letters.

Suomi has been internationally recognized as the developer of the imaging technologies that made weather satellites possible. His research involved the development and improvement of meteorological satellites and environmental observation systems. His many inventions that transformed meteorology include the flat-plate radiometer, an instrument that measures the amount of heat coming into and leaving the Earth's atmosphere, which he developed in 1957–1960, before any weather satellite was launched into space; and the satellite spin-scan weather camera, arguably his most important invention, which took pictures of the Earth from a rapidly spinning satellite, invented in 1963. The resultant images displayed dynamic weather patterns, such as air motion, cloud growth, and atmospheric pollution, and began a revolution in weather forecasting. He also invented the balloon-borne radio altimeter with N. Levanon in 1968; the video display processing computer system with staff from the Space Science and Engineering Center in 1972; and McIDAS (Man-Computer Interactive Data Access System), the powerful interactive computer system that allows researchers and forecasters to access and manipulate satellite images, data, and other information. In addition Suomi pioneered the use of infrared technology in studying the atmospheres of the Earth, Venus, Jupiter, and Saturn. He initiated the use of space satellites to study weather on the Earth and other planets and in 1959 founded the Global Atmospheric Research Program to create a central, accessible location for the atmospheric data collected worldwide.

Suomi retired from formal teaching in 1986 but continued teaching an undergraduate meteorology course. A man of great charm, wit, and energy, he generated useful ideas and helped develop technology and foster interest in meteorology among several generations of students.

Suomi died of congestive heart failure at the age of seventy-nine. He is buried in southern Minnesota near his family home. An emeritus professor at the time of his death, he still worked as a research scientist at the Space Science and Engineering Center. The last week of his life he was working on a seasonde, a buoy-like instrument designed to measure the surface heat flux of the Atlantic Ocean.

★

For further information on Suomi see *American Men and Women of Science: The Physical and Biological Sciences*, vol. 6, 14th ed. (1979); *Who's Who in America*, 48th ed. (1994); Charles Cornell, ed., *Biography Index* (1996); and Emily J. McMurray, ed., *Notable Twentieth-Century Scientists,* vol. 4 (1995). An obituary is in the *New York Times* (1 Aug. 1995).

MARIA PACHECO

SWAYZE, John Cameron (*b.* 4 April 1906 in Wichita, Kansas; *d.* 15 August 1995 in Sarasota, Florida), radio and television newscaster who became a popular announcer, panel-show host, and commercial spokesman.

Swayze was the only child of Jesse Ernest Swayze, a traveling salesman with a degree in pharmacy, and Christine Cameron, a homemaker. Swayze graduated from Atchison High School in Kansas, where he excelled in drama and oratory. He attended the University of Kansas until 1929, when he left to attend drama school and to pursue an acting career in New York City. He met his wife, Beulah Mae, also a budding actress, at the school and married her in 1932, a union that lasted until his death; they had two children. Swayze used all three of his names professionally, in deference to his mother's Scottish background. The onset of the Great Depression discouraged a theater career, and Swayze moved to Kansas City, Missouri. He joined the *Kansas City Journal-Post* in 1930 as the city hall reporter and editor. Ironically, his broadcasting career started at the newspaper when he aired news bulletins for KMBC radio from the *Journal-Post* newsroom. He became a full-time newscaster at the station in 1940.

In 1945 Swayze was NBC's Hollywood–West Coast bureau chief. When NBC transferred him to New York City in 1947, he was a network radio newscaster. Later, he was a regular member on the television quiz show *Who Said That?*, hosted by Robert Trout. This turned out to be a popular program in which a panel of celebrities tried to identify the speakers of notable quotes from the preceding week. On Sundays, Swayze was master of ceremonies of *Watch the World,* a children's educational program.

In the spring of 1948 Swayze provided off-camera narration of *The Camel Newsreel Theatre,* a ten-minute featurette aired each weeknight at 7:50 P.M. This was a joint effort between NBC and Fox-Movietone Newsreels. Fox-Movietone provided newsreel film of the day's major events and NBC prepared a script, often written by Swayze himself, to accompany the images. Beginning in 1949, he opened the show, wearing his trademark carnation in his lapel, with "Ladies and gentlemen, a good evening to you" and by inviting the audience to join him in "hopscotching the world for headlines." The carnation, and the fact that he never wore the same tie two nights in a row, reflected his keen understanding that television is a medium for performers. Given his background and love for drama and oratory, he understood the craft of performance and how to apply it to this new technology. When doing his news broadcast from behind his desk once on a hot summer day, he rose from his chair to walk over to a weather map only to realize that from the waist down he was in blue jeans. He promptly sat down and the camera panned to the map. He closed the show with a warm, down-home "Well, that's the story folks! I'm John Cameron Swayze and I'm glad we could get together." His opening and closing became sound-bite classics. The program replaced the network's straight newsreel format and became the prototype for modern newscasts with live events and interviews from different cities. Swayze had a near-photographic memory. In an interview on 22 June 1979, Swayze proclaimed that, although he had a script on his desk in case of emergency, "I never 'read the news' in my whole life. I wrote my news and delivered my news."

The 1948 presidential conventions in Philadelphia pro-

John Swayze on NBC-TV. © BETTMANN/CORBIS

duced NBC's first superstar television anchorman. Swayze gave gavel-to-gavel on-camera coverage for all who had television sets between Boston, Massachusetts, and Richmond, Virginia. The rest of the country saw filmed highlights the next day. As the NBC anchor, Swayze continued to appear on-camera when his nightly newscast was changed to *The Camel News Caravan* and expanded from ten to fifteen minutes in early 1949. He was the *NBC Nightly News* anchor until 26 October 1956, when he was succeeded by Chet Huntley and David Brinkley. Toward the end of 1956 he worked with WABC radio. Also, Swayze hosted the *Armstrong Circle Theatre* (1955–1957) and played himself in *I, Mrs. Bibb* on the *Kraft Television Theatre* on 19 October 1955.

For twenty-three years Swayze was featured in Timex watch commercials, in which watches were subjected to all sorts of abuse and always emerged intact. Swayze would proclaim that "It takes a licking and keeps on ticking." In an interview on 22 June 1979, Swayze related the story of the now famous Timex ad. On the live *Steve Allen Show*, watches were strapped to three blades of an outboard-motor propeller and subjected to merciless whirring in a tankful of water. Two survived and one disappeared. Without missing a beat, Swayze told millions of viewers, "Ladies and gentlemen, I'm going to tell you, that watch is on the bottom of the tank right now. We'll show it to you next time." The camera switched to Allen, who said, "You think there'll be a next time, John?" Swayze told his interviewer, "What a line to hand me." Bulova had created the watch torture-test but dropped the idea. Timex, with Swayze, took the concept to enduring success for more than two decades.

Although *The Camel News Caravan* was sponsored by R. J. Reynolds Tobacco Company, Swayze did not smoke because he had been told by his doctors that it was bad for his health. Each week Reynolds would deliver a carton of Camels to his house where they accumulated and on occasion were given to friends. Swayze was required to have a lighted Camel cigarette in an ashtray on his desk while he was on the air so that the smoke would swirl upward on camera. At the end of the show, a camera would focus in on the cigarette as a getaway shot. One evening, just as the cameraman was about to do his job, Swayze realized that a careless stagehand had placed a rival brand cigarette, a lighted king-size Pall Mall, in the ashtray. Swayze flipped the errant cigarette out of camera range before millions of viewers (and Reynolds Tobacco) saw it.

In 1957 Swayze appeared in the cast of the *Westinghouse Studio One* live television drama *The Human Barrier,* a one-hour tribute to the U.S. Air Force featuring a history of military flight. Also in 1957, Swayze received the Alfred I. DuPont–Columbia University award for excellence in broadcast journalism.

In later years Swayze attempted various marketing ventures including neckties with his signature, a board game called "SWAYZE," and a paperback book entitled *The Art of Living* (1979). He died of natural causes at the age of ninety-nine and is buried in Greenwich, Connecticut.

John Cameron Swayze was a man who thought of himself as a serious newscaster. At his peak, he had an estimated 15 million nightly viewers. His son, John Cameron Swayze, Jr., said at the time of his father's death that he "managed to project a certain innocence, a feeling of promise, a genuine friendliness. . . . When he signed off with 'Glad we could get together,' he really meant it, and I think people understood that he meant it." Walter Cronkite said, "I'd like him to be remembered as a serious newsman. In later years he did the Timex commercials, so I'm afraid he'll be remembered as the guy who took watches down in the submarine."

★

Brief biographical material on Swayze was prepared by Dory DeAngelo and is located in Special Collections at the Kansas City, Missouri, Public Library. Tom Shales wrote an article for the *Washington Post* based on an interview with Swayze (22 June 1979) entitled "The Mighty Monarch of the Air; John Cameron Swayze—Newsman in Tune with Timex." The Museum of Television and Radio in New York City has numerous references to television and radio programs involving Swayze as an announcer, reporter, host, and actor, including *I, Mrs. Bibb* for the *Kraft Television Theatre,* which aired on NBC on 19 October 1955. David Brinkley discussed Swayze in an interview with Brian Lamb aired over C-SPAN's *Booknotes* (10 Dec. 1995). An obituary is in the *New York Times* (17 Aug. 1995). John Cameron Swayze, Jr., was generous in providing personal information about his father.

RICHARD A. COOK

T-V

TALMA, Louise Juliette (*b.* 31 October 1906 in Arcachon, France; *d.* 13 August 1996 near Saratoga Springs, New York), composer and professor of music who in 1974 became the first woman composer elected to the National Institute of Arts and Letters.

The daughter of American musicians, Talma was brought to the United States in 1914 and was raised and educated in New York City. Her father died when she was an infant; her mother, a singer, gave her her first piano lessons when she was five. From 1922 to 1930 Talma studied at the Institute of Musical Art (now the famed Juilliard School of Music), where she won the Seligman Prize for composition in 1927, 1928, and 1929. She earned her B.Mus. degree from New York University in 1931 and an M.A. from Columbia University in 1933. Concurrently, between 1926 and 1928, she spent summers at the American Conservatory in Fontainebleau, France, first as a piano student of Isidore Philipp, then, from 1928 on, studying harmony, counterpoint, fugue, composition, and the organ with Nadia Boulanger, who eventually persuaded Talma to become a composer and who remained her close friend and colleague. Two of Talma's compositions date from 1939: *Four-Handed Fun,* a perennial favorite piano piece; and *In Principio Erat Verbum,* for chorus and organ, based on the Gospel of Saint John. The latter won the Stovall Prize of the Fontainebleau conservatory.

Talma began her teaching career giving classes in theory and ear training at the Manhattan School of Music from 1926 to 1928, when she joined the faculty of Hunter College of the City of New York. Appointed a full professor in 1952, she taught music there until 1976 and was a professor emerita from then until 1979. She was the author of two textbooks: *Harmony for the College Student* (1966) and *Functional Harmony* (with James S. Harris and Robert Levin, 1970).

Her early music was neoclassical in style: spare, clear, and lyrical, much influenced by Stravinsky. And, according to the *New York Times* writer Allan Kozinn, her instrumental coloration often seemed to have more in common with Ravel and Messiaen than with contemporary American music. In her *Six Etudes for Piano* (1953–1954), however, Talma began to introduce twelve-tone elements. From then on, her music often combined serialism with an essential lyricism and tonality. Wary of committing herself to a rigorously repetitive serial style, she commented in a 1986 *New York Times* interview that music should, instead, "speak in human terms."

Notable among her more than forty major works are her settings of Biblical and secular texts, and English and French verse, in which the combination of voices and instruments is always, uniquely, respectful of the text. Such works include *The Divine Flame* (1946–1948), an oratorio composed for Robert Shaw and the Collegiate Chorale; *La Corona* (1954–1955), based on John Donne's *Holy Sonnets,* an a cappella work commissioned by the Illinois Wesleyan

Louise Talma, 1974. ASSOCIATED PRESS HO

University Collegiate Choir; *A Time to Remember* (1966–1967), a choral setting of texts from speeches by President Kennedy; and *The Tolling Bell* (1967–1969), verse by Shakespeare, Marlowe, and Donne set to music for baritone solo and orchestra. The composer herself described this latter work as "a somber piece, in the nature of an elegy to the fallen," her response to the political assassinations of the 1960s. The work was given its premiere by the Milwaukee Symphony Orchestra in 1969 and was dedicated by the composer to the MacDowell artists' colony in Peterboro, New Hampshire, where from the 1940s on she was a frequent resident and wrote much of her music.

Other major portions of Talma's oeuvre consisted of piano music—including two sonatas (composed in 1943 and 1944–1945) and the *Sonata for Violin and Piano* (1962) in honor of Boulanger's seventy-fifth birthday—and a number of chamber works. Among the latter were the quintet *Summer Sounds* (1969–1973) and *Ambient Air* (1980–1983), an evocation of the sounds of nature scored for flute, violin, cello, and piano. Many of these keyboard and chamber pieces have been recorded, as was her *Toccata for Orchestra* (1944). The last, incorporating some exuberant jazz passages, remains one of her best-known compositions.

Talma's three-act opera, *The Alcestiad,* with a libretto by Thornton Wilder (based on Greek legend), was given its premiere at the Schauspielhaus, Frankfurt am Main, in 1962, sung in German translation. It was the first work by a woman produced at a major European opera house. The first-night audience greeted it with a twenty-minute standing ovation for composer and librettist. Talma and Wilder had met at the MacDowell colony in 1952; three years later, at his request—and aided by a Senior Fulbright research grant in 1955–1956—she set about composing the score, which again combined tonal and serial elements. It was completed in 1960 and won the Marjorie Peabody Waite Award of the National Institute of Arts and Letters in recognition of her "personal, highly controlled and beautifully shaped music [that] has gained a new cogency and dramatic effectiveness."

Among the many other prizes accorded Talma's music were two Guggenheim fellowships, in 1946 and 1947; the French Government Prix d'Excellence de Composition, 1951; and, in 1963, the first Sibelius Medal for composition awarded to a woman. She held honorary doctorates from Hunter College (1983), Bard College (1984), and Saint Mary-of-the-Woods College (1991). Besides composing and teaching, Talma was vitally involved over the years in professional outreach—as a board member of the Edwin MacDowell Association (provider of financial assistance to young musicians), the League of Composers, the International Society for Contemporary Music, and the Fontainebleau Fine Arts and Music Association; and as a charter member of the American Society of University Composers.

The composer, who maintained an apartment in Manhattan often visited by her students, died at Yaddo, an artists' colony near Saratoga Springs, where she had been working on a song cycle with chamber music accompaniment. She had no survivors. She is buried in Gate of Heaven Cemetery in Hawthorne, New York.

Talma is remembered as an exacting teacher but an always sympathetic, generous guide with a rare ability to bring out the creative thinking of her students. By the terms of her will, she provided scholarships for aspiring artists to study at Fontainebleau and left a major endowment to the MacDowell colony. Often honored as "the first woman composer" to achieve certain milestones, Talma is now more appropriately recognized simply as one of the preeminent American composers of the twentieth century.

★

A collection of Talma's music manuscripts is housed in the Library of Congress, Washington, D.C. The entry on her in Jane Weiner LePage's *Women Composers, Conductors, and Musicians of the Twentieth Century: Selected Biographies* (1980) provides the fullest account of her career and an assessment of her contributions. The Louise Talma Society, dedicated to investigating her music and making it known to a larger public, maintains a web site that provides a chronological list of biographical facts, a bibliography of articles and books with reference to Talma's work, a list of her awards, and a transcript of an interview with the composer in 1995. An earlier interview appeared in the *New York Times* (19 Oct. 1986). A discography can be found in Jane Frasier's *Women Composers: A Discography* (1983). An obituary is in the *New York Times* (15 Aug. 1996).

ELEANOR F. WEDGE

TANDY, Jessica (*b.* 7 June 1909 in London, England; *d.* 11 September 1994 in Easton, Connecticut), actress whose sixty-seven-year career enriched both theater and screen in more than a hundred stage productions and twenty-five films.

Tandy was the third child and only daughter of Harry Tandy, a rope manufacturer and salesman who died of cancer when she was twelve, and Jessie Horspool, a headmistress at a school for retarded children who also taught night school and worked at clerical jobs after her husband's death. By the time she was a teenager, Tandy had decided to become an actress, a decision her mother supported "as a dignified way for her to break out of her bleak life." In 1924 Tandy began three years of drama training at the Ben Greet Academy of Acting in London. She made her professional debut in a tiny Soho theater when she was eighteen years old. After working in regional theater, she made her West End debut in *The Rumour* in 1929. Her 1932

Jessica Tandy. ARCHIVE PHOTOS

performance as Manuela in *Children in Uniform* established her as a talented actress. In the 1930s she appeared in more than two dozen contemporary plays, enhancing her reputation. In the British tradition, she sharpened her skills by acting in the classics, particularly Shakespeare. She began in *Twelfth Night,* first as Olivia (1930) and later as Viola on three different occasions, culminating in a 1937 Tyrone Guthrie production at the Old Vic also featuring Laurence Olivier. Her most unforgettable Shakespearean performance was as Ophelia opposite John Gielgud in the celebrated production of *Hamlet* (1934). In 1940 she returned to the Old Vic to appear with Gielgud as Cordelia in *King Lear* and Miranda in *The Tempest.*

In 1932 she married the well-known actor Jack Hawkins. They had one daughter. The couple divorced in 1940. The necessity of supporting her six-year-old daughter and the attraction of possible Hollywood jobs led her to immigrate to the United States. In 1954 she became a naturalized U.S. citizen. At first she struggled to make ends meet with a series of roles in lesser Broadway plays. She was so discouraged that she came close to abandoning her career. Her life changed after a well-to-do man-about-town and aspiring actor named Hume Cronyn appeared backstage. The couple married in 1942, after moving to Hollywood. The Cronyns had two children.

In Hollywood, Cronyn's career took off while Tandy languished in a variety of bit parts, generally as maids. (The one exception was the 1944 anti-Nazi melodrama *The Seventh Cross,* with Cronyn and Spencer Tracy.) She began to feel, as she later remembered, that "I had no talent and it was all a pipe dream. It was Hume who got me out of it."

Cronyn accomplished this by directing her in *Portrait of a Madonna,* a one-act drama by a little-known playwright, Tennessee Williams, in a small theater in Los Angeles. The glowing reviews led Williams to journey to California from New York City, where he was casting his new play, *A Streetcar Named Desire.* Williams recalled in his *Memoirs,* "It was instantly apparent to me that Jessica was Blanche." The play, which opened in New York in 1947, also starred Marlon Brando as Stanley Kowalski. It created an immediate sensation, winning ecstatic reviews, a Pulitzer Prize, and the Drama Critics Circle Award. Tandy won a Tony Award for her sensitive portrayal of Blanche DuBois, the fading southern belle. Brooks Atkinson in the *New York Times* was amazed by her "almost incredibly true" performance. The play ran for two years and Tandy then toured in it throughout the United States, although the starring role in the film version went to the more famous Vivien Leigh.

Tandy, however, was not one to dwell on disappointments. After a run as the title character in *Hilda Crane* (1950), directed by Cronyn, the couple decided that they wanted to act together again. In 1951 they appeared in *The*

Fourposter, a two-character comedy about the trials and tribulations of a thirty-five-year marriage. This was the first of ten joint appearances on Broadway and dozens of off-Broadway and regional productions. Collaborations included *A Delicate Balance* (1966); *The Gin Game* (1977), for which she won her second Tony; *Foxfire* (1982), which garnered her a third Tony; and *The Petition* (1986). Such high-profile hits led to their designation as the successors to Lunt and Fontaine as the first couple of the American theater. Asked how they tolerated so much togetherness in a fifty-two-year marriage, Tandy conceded, "It's hard sometimes, but we always manage to give ourselves space. We don't take the play home with us. We do make suggestions to each other, and if we don't agree we respect each other's view."

Tandy was always enthusiastic about regional theater. She and Cronyn were among the first to agree to perform at Tyrone Guthrie's repertory theater in Minneapolis in the 1960s. They also acted in the Shakespeare festivals in Stratford, Connecticut, and Stratford, Ontario. In 1983 Tandy played Amanda Wingfield in a revival of Tennessee Williams's *Glass Menagerie,* a performance, one critic warned his readers, to be passed up "only at your own peril."

Although Tandy disliked seeing herself in movies, she accepted a variety of roles in more than two dozen films to help support low-paying parts in off-Broadway and regional theaters. Her films included playing Cronyn's wife in the popular *Cocoon* (1984) and *Cocoon: The Return* (1988) and Cronyn's wife in **batteries not included* (1987), as well as a tour de force in *Fried Green Tomatoes* (1991), in which the eighty-two-year-old Tandy played an unconquerable eighty-two-year-old woman. The summit of her film career was her role in *Driving Miss Daisy* (1989) as a strongly independent elderly southern lady. In 1990 she won an Academy Award for her role, becoming the oldest person ever to do so. The following year she won an Emmy for her performance in the television adaptation of *Foxfire.*

She continued tackling demanding roles in her seventies and well into her eighties despite growing difficulties with stage fright and memorization, double-cataract surgery, cardiovascular problems, and even major surgery for cancer in 1991. She appeared in two more television movies and three more feature films after 1991. In 1994 she and Cronyn received a joint Tony Award for lifelong work in the theater. They had already been given the Kennedy Center Lifetime Achievement Award in 1988. She died at her home in Easton, Connecticut, of ovarian cancer.

Jessica Tandy always believed that in creating a role, "You have to get over 'how' you're doing it and know 'why' you're doing it." She succeeded in fashioning dozens of memorable characters on stage, screen, and television. A *New York Times* reviewer concluded, "Everything this ac-tress does is so pure and right that only poets, not theater critics, should be allowed to write about her."

★

For information about Tandy, see Hume Cronyn's autobiography *Bake My Brain* (1993). See also Milly S. Barranger, *Jessica Tandy: A Bio-Bibliography* (1991). Interviews with Tandy include those by Chris Chase, *New York Times* (24 Mar. 1974); Michael Kernan, *Washington Post* (23 Dec. 1982); Timothy White, *New York Times Magazine* (26 Dec. 1982); Samuel G. Freedman, *New York Times* (27 Nov. 1983); and Roy Newquist, *Showcase* (1966). A brief biography is in *Who's Who in the Theatre* (1981). An obituary is in the *New York Times* (12 Sept. 1994).

LOUISE A. MAYO

TAVOULAREAS, William Peter (*b.* 9 November 1919 in Brooklyn, New York; *d.* 13 January 1996 in Boca Raton, Florida), aggressive Mobil Oil Corporation president and chief operating officer.

Tavouraleas's father, Peter, was born in a small Greek village in 1892. The elder Tavoulareas, according to his son, "walked down his village mountain at the age of 16 and sailed by himself to America . . . he never saw Greece again." His father went on to become a small, successful restaurant entrepreneur. His mother, Mary Ralisi, a second-generation Italian, was "endlessly cooking and cleaning,

William P. Tavoulareas, 1974. AP/WIDE WORLD PHOTOS

endlessly concerned, but never tired." He had one sister. Tavoulareas received his B.B.A. in 1941 and his J.D. in 1948, both from St. John's University in New York City, and was admitted to the New York bar. While attending law school at night, he began working for the Mobil Oil Corporation as a junior accountant in 1947. Working for Mobil's Middle East concerns, he gained numerous opportunities for advancement once the company became aware that the Middle East had most of the Western world's oil supply.

Tavoulareas credited his 1959 appointment to head Mobil's first corporate-planning department as being his "big break." By 1961, he was in charge of Mobil International's planning section, which afforded him the opportunity to become personally acquainted with many powerful players in the oil industry. He was elected a director of the Mobil Oil Corporation in 1965, and by 1969 he was president and chief operating officer. His foresight, drive, deal making and negotiating skills, as well as his personal contacts, helped increase Mobil's 1969 revenues of $7.6 billion to nearly $70 billion when he retired in 1984.

Under Tavoulareas's guidance, Mobil's North American production increased as he was constantly on the "prowl" to purchase domestic reserves—"a cheaper way to increase output"—in the 1970s. Yet between 1970 and 1976, America's proven oil reserves fell by 27 percent and gas reserves by 24 percent. Mobil diversified and purchased the department store chain Montgomery Ward. This proved to be a mistake, and Mobil later sold the retailer for a big loss. Tavoulareas retired as president of Mobil Corporation on 1 November 1984 at the age of sixty-five.

Tavoulareas also served on the board of Georgetown University and as governor of the Society of New York Hospital. He was trustee of St. John's University, Georgetown University, and Athens College, Athens, Greece. He received an honorary degree (Doctor of Commercial Science) from his alma mater (St. John's University) in 1969 Until his death, he kept close ties with his Greek heritage. He died at age seventy-six from complications of a stroke suffered earlier (1995). His wife, Adele Maciejewska; two sons, Peter and William; a daughter, Patrice; and four grandchildren survived him.

Tavoulareas was a straightforward, fast-speaking individual—a sharp contrast with many major oil company executives of his era, who were known to speak with either the "drawl of the Southwest or the measured tones of the Ivy League." Following the OPEC oil embargo in 1974, the hard-hitting Tavoulareas challenged the idea that conserving oil alone would alleviate future shortages and dependency. He believed that the United States had plentiful energy resources and instead pointed the finger at political roadblocks that thwarted the development of gas and oil

deposits. His close ties with Saudi Arabian Sheik Ahmed Zaki Yamani, minister of petroleum and mineral resources (1962–1986) and an OPEC "moderate," along with his aggressive and sometimes unorthodox style, led to numerous confrontations with congressmen, environmentalists, and newspaper reporters.

On 30 November 1979, the *Washington Post* ran a story that alleged Tavoulareas had "set up his son" (eldest son Peter) in the London-based Atlas Maritime shipping industry. The article also inferred that he misused his position as Mobil's president as well as company assets. *Tavoulareas* v. *The Washington Post* was filed to defend his family's name. The case appeared on various court dockets until it reached the U.S. Supreme Court in 1989. The July 1982 federal jury found that he had indeed been libeled and awarded him a $2 million judgment. A 1985 appeals court upheld this verdict. This ruling reinforced newspaper industry fears that this case would lead to a wave of libel suits—inhibiting newspapers from doing tough investigative reporting. Tavoulareas ultimately lost in 1987, when the appellate court reversed the decision; the Supreme Court allowed that decision to stand.

In his 1985 book, *Fighting Back,* Tavoulareas recounted the six exhaustive and costly years of his lawsuit against the *Post* in which he initially fought to clear his family's name. He credited his hard-working immigrant father with passing on to him something that money could not buy: "a good, unblemished name." Later he took his struggle further—hoping in some small way to contribute to returning America to her initial path, "respect for the individual above all else." Neither derogatory remarks during the trials nor negative reviews of his book deterred him from pressing his legal case. Even the *Post* reporter Patrick Tyler, who wrote the 1979 story, was quoted as saying, "It is not every day you knock off one of the seven sisters (oil companies)." The two Mobil Oil presidents that followed Tavoulareas were also New Yorkers and considered "gritty, hard-edged characters who didn't go to Oxford or Harvard; tough, street-smart kids with very independent personalities." This is possibly Tavoulareas's chief legacy.

★

In addition to Tavoulareas's autobiographical account in *Fighting Back* (1985), consult Daniel Yergin's Pulitzer Prize–winning work, *The Prize: The Epic Quest For Oil, Money, and Power* (1991), an extensive history, analysis, and political outlook of the oil industry. See also Florence George Graves, "Starr Struck," *American Journalism Review* 3 (Apr. 1998): 1–7. Various newspaper articles regarding the lawsuit were published in the *New York Times* from 1979 through late 1982 including Jonathan Friendly, "Committee Aide's Work for Media is Challenged," *New York Times* (4 Jan. 1982); and Stuart Taylor, "Closing Arguments Are Made in *Washington Post* Libel Trial," *New York Times* (28 July 1982). See also Thomas Chayes, "Mobil Promotes One of Three in Race for Chief," *New York Times* (4 Feb. 1993). An obituary is in the *New York Times* (16 Jan. 1996).

ELLEN O'CONNELL BRASEL

TAX, Sol (*b.* 30 October 1907 in Chicago, Illinois; *d.* 4 January 1995 in Chicago, Illinois), anthropologist best known for his pioneering studies of Native American cultures; for founding the journal *Current Anthropology*; and for establishing the discipline of "action anthropology."

Tax was the third of four children born to Morris Paul Tax, a builder and inventor, and Kate Hanowit Tax, a homemaker. When he was a child, his family moved from the Russian Empire to Milwaukee, Wisconsin. Interested in political science and economics, Tax considered careers in politics and law. Even as a teenager, he knew that he wanted to help people to help themselves, a tenet at the core of action anthropology. He later reflected, "Physically small and shy, I compensated and had some success in helping like-minded peers to do together good things that we couldn't do separately."

After graduating from Riverside High School in Milwaukee, he enrolled at the University of Chicago in 1926 and later transferred to the University of Wisconsin–Madison. In 1928 he changed his major to anthropology upon the encouragement of the university's first anthropologist, Ralph Linton, who told the young student that there were only about fifty professional anthropologists in the United States at the time.

After receiving a Ph.B. degree in anthropology in 1931, Tax began his graduate studies at the University of Chicago. His major influences during this time were the anthropologists Robert Redfield and A. R. Radcliffe-Brown. The latter, a visiting professor from England whose expertise lay in kinship patterns, inspired Tax to turn his attention to the study of social organization among Native American tribes, particularly the Mesquakie (Fox) of Iowa. For the next three years, Tax conducted ethnographic research with the Mesquakie. His fieldwork provided the foundation for essays in the anthology *Social Anthropology of North American Tribes* (1937) as well as his doctoral dissertation. He was awarded his Ph.D. degree in 1935.

In 1934 Tax was hired as an ethnologist for the Carnegie Institution. In this capacity, he moved to Guatemala, where he would remain for the next seven years, studying the Maya Indians of the region. His wife, Gertrude Jospe Katz Tax—they married on 4 July 1933 and had two daughters—accompanied him and assisted with his fieldwork. Tax's mentor, Redfield, whose own research focused on the

Maya of the Yucatán, directed the study. Their correspondence was later published as *Fieldwork: The Correspondence of Robert Redfield and Sol Tax* (1991).

Tax's extensive Guatemalan fieldwork included studies of the economy, social relations, folk culture, and worldview of the indigenous peoples in the region. Several publications arose out of this work, most notably *Penny Capitalism: A Guatemalan Indian Economy* (1953). During this time, he was appointed a research associate with the University of Chicago (1940–1944).

In 1941 Tax moved to Mexico, where for the next four years he continued his studies of the Maya for the Carnegie Institution. He was a visiting professor at the National Institute of Anthropology and History in Mexico City from 1942 to 1943.

Upon his return to the United States in 1944, Tax became an associate professor at the University of Chicago, and in 1948 a full professor. He remained at the university until his retirement in 1974 and became professor emeritus in 1976. During his tenure, he held several administrative posts, including chairman of the anthropology department (1955–1958) and dean of the university extension (1963–1968).

Tax resumed his study of the Fox Indians of Iowa as director of the Fox Indian Project (1948–1962), supervising the fieldwork of graduate students. A turning point occurred when his students expressed their desire to help the Native Americans; however, they were divided over the best solution to challenges such as urbanization and assimilation. The anthropologists finally concluded that it was not their place to decide such matters; rather, they would place their knowledge at the service of the Mesquakie. Thus the seeds of action anthropology were sowed.

In 1952 Tax participated in the Wenner–Gren Foundation's International Symposium on Anthropology in New York and became the principal editor of *An Appraisal of Anthropology Today,* a collection of papers presented at the conference. His association with Wenner–Gren led to his becoming founding editor (1957–1974) of *Current Anthropology,* an international journal devoted to the exchange of ideas and information in all fields of anthropology.

Having devoted so much of his life to the study of Native American cultures, Tax was a natural choice to coordinate the American Indian Conference in Chicago in 1961, where approximately 700 Native American attendees drafted a "Declaration of Indian Purpose." In keeping with his principle of action anthropology, Tax resisted actively guiding or influencing the discussions, instead acting as a logistical coordinator. In the process, he gained a reputation as a leading advocate of self-determination for Native Americans. To him, the idea that the Indians be allowed to direct their own future was hardly radical. He said, "If you stop to think of it, the idea that they had never been asked, so to speak, 'What would you like to have happen to you?' is kind of a crazy thing."

Throughout most of his career, the indefatigable Tax simultaneously held posts in government, academia, and cultural and anthropological associations, while continuing his fieldwork and journalistic pursuits, striking a balance between the theoretical and practical aspects of his field. He served as associate editor (1948–1952), then editor (1953–1956) of the American Anthropological Association's journal, and was president of the association from 1958 to 1959. He was also president of the International Union of Anthropological and Ethnological Sciences (1968–1973), and directed the Carnegie Cross-Cultural Education Project (1962–1967) and the Smithsonian Institution's Center for the Study of Man (1968–1976).

Tax received the Viking Fund Medal and Award for anthropological achievements in 1962. In 1977 he was awarded both the Distinguished Service Award of the American Anthropological Association and the Bronislaw Malinowski Award of the Society for Applied Anthropology.

He died of a heart attack at the age of eighty-seven and was buried in Chicago.

Through a lifetime of helping others to help themselves, Tax inexorably altered the face of anthropology. As the founding editor of *Current Anthropology,* he was instrumental in establishing anthropology as a global discipline, maintaining a dialogue between anthropologists in all specialties, all over the world.

★

The Regenstein Library of the University of Chicago is home to the Sol Tax Papers, 147 linear feet of materials including correspondence, field notes, articles, papers, lecture notes, photographs, and memorabilia. The collection is cataloged in Jean M. O'Brien and Robert E. Moore, *Guide to the Sol Tax Papers* (1989). Additional material, particularly regarding the Fox Project and the 1961 American Indian Chicago Conference, is housed in the National Anthropological Archives at the Smithsonian Institution. In 1988 Tax recalled his career in an autobiographical essay, "Pride and Puzzlement: A Retro-introspective Record of 60 Years of Anthropology," *Annual Review of Anthropology* 17. Robert A. Rubinstein, "A Conversation with Sol Tax," *Current Anthropology* (Apr. 1991), contains excerpts from a series of 1986 interviews. Robert Hinshaw, ed., *Currents in Anthropology: Essays in Honor of Sol Tax* (1979), contains a preface charting Tax's career and essays by twenty-seven authors including both of Tax's daughters—Susan Tax Freeman, an anthropologist, and Marianna Tax Choldin, an authority on censorship and Soviet studies. Hinshaw also wrote a detailed essay on Tax in the *International Encyclopedia of the Social Sciences* (1979). Sam Stanley, "Community, Action, and

Continuity: A Narrative Vita of Sol Tax," *Current Anthropology* (Feb. 1996), contains a detailed examination of Tax's professional achievements. An obituary is in the *New York Times* (8 Jan. 1995).

BRENDA SCOTT ROYCE

TAYLOR, Peter Hillsman (*b.* 8 January 1917 in Trenton, Tennessee; *d.* 2 November 1994 in Charlottesville, Virginia), fiction writer regarded as one of America's enduring masters of the short story and winner of the Pulitzer Prize for his novel *A Summons to Memphis* (1986).

Taylor, the youngest of four children, was born on the ninth wedding anniversary of his parents, Matthew Hillsman Taylor, an insurance executive, and Katherine Baird Taylor, a homemaker. Both of his grandfathers were lawyers and politicians, and Taylor used the oratory of one, Robert Love Taylor, in his *Tennessee Day in St. Louis* (1957). Taylor's family moved from Trenton, Tennessee, to Nashville in 1924 and in 1926 to St. Louis, where his father became president of the Missouri State Life Insurance Company. Taylor enrolled in Miss Rossman's School, a private institution, and in 1929 he attended St. Louis Country Day School.

The family moved again in 1932, this time to Memphis. Taylor attended Memphis Central High School, from which he graduated in 1935. He won a scholarship to Columbia University in New York City, but his father vehemently objected to his accepting it because he wanted his son to attend Vanderbilt University, his alma mater. After a quarrel and a period of not speaking to his father, Taylor left home and worked his way to England on a freighter. He returned later in the year and took a job writing for the *Memphis Commercial-Appeal.*

In the spring of 1936 Taylor took courses under the poet and critic Allen Tate at Southwestern University. That fall Taylor enrolled in Vanderbilt University, where he studied with the poet and critic John Crowe Ransom. Taylor also became friends with his fellow student Randall Jarrell, who later became an important poet and critic. When Ransom moved on to Kenyon College in Ohio, Taylor dropped out of Vanderbilt University in 1937. For a time he sold real estate and wrote book reviews for the *Memphis Commercial-Appeal.* His first two short stories were published in *River,* a little magazine out of Oxford, Mississippi. In the fall of 1938 Taylor followed Ransom to Kenyon College and roomed with Robert Lowell. A poem by Taylor appeared in the *Kenyon Review* in 1939. Taylor graduated from the college with a B.A. degree in 1940 and enrolled for graduate study under Robert Penn Warren and Cleanth Brooks at Louisiana State University. His first mature story, "A Spin-

Peter Taylor. JERRY BAUER

ster's Tale," was published in *Southwest Review* that same year.

Taylor entered the U.S. Army in June 1941. He first served at Fort Ogethorpe, Georgia, and later served at Tidwell Camp in England as part of the Rail Transportation Corps. In 1942 he met Eleanor Ross, a poet from Norwood, North Carolina. They married six weeks later, on 4 June 1942, and subsequently had two children. Taylor was discharged from the army with the rank of sergeant in December 1945. That year he received the *Partisan Review* Award for "The Scoutmaster."

In 1946 Taylor worked briefly in publishing in New York City, then he began teaching at Women's College of the University of North Carolina in Greensboro (later the University of North Carolina at Greensboro). His first book, *A Long Fourth, and Other Stories* was published in March 1948. The first of a number of stories published in the *New Yorker* appeared on 6 November. He accepted a position as an assistant professor at Indiana University in 1948 but returned to the college in Greensboro in 1949.

After his first novel, *A Woman of Means,* appeared in 1950, Taylor was awarded a Guggenheim fellowship for 1950–1951. During the spring of 1952 he taught at the University of Chicago and received a National Institute of Arts

and Letters Award. That autumn he took an associate professorship at Kenyon College, and in 1953 he began a six-year period as advisory editor of the *Kenyon Review*. In 1954 Taylor published *The Widows of Thornton*. During 1955–1956 Taylor pursued research in Paris with a Fulbright grant. A comedy, *Tennessee Day in St. Louis,* premiered at Kenyon College in April and was published by Random House in 1957. Beginning in 1957 he worked as an associate professor at Ohio State University from January to June of each year.

Taylor's third story collection, *Happy Families Are All Alike,* appeared in 1959, and the story "Venus, Cupid, Folly, and Time" received the O. Henry Award First Prize. In 1960 he received a Ford Foundation fellowship at London's Royal Court Theatre and in 1963 rejoined the faculty at the University of North Carolina at Greensboro. A compendium, *Miss Leonora When Last Seen, and Fifteen Other Stories,* was issued in 1964, and a second play, *A Stand in the Mountains,* was published in 1968 in the *Kenyon Review*. The next year Taylor was inducted into the National Institute of Arts and Letters and his *Collected Stories* was published. In 1967 he became a professor of English at the University of Virginia in Charlottesville, where he directed the creative writing program for many years. *Presences: Seven Dramatic Pieces,* appeared in 1973.

Despite suffering a heart attack in 1974, Taylor remained productive. His later books include *In the Miro District and Other Stories* (1977), *The Old Forest and Other Stories* (1985), *A Summons to Memphis* (1986), *The Oracle at Stoneleigh Court* (1993), and a final novel, *In the Tennessee Country* (1994). His awards include the Gold Medal for the Short Story from the American Academy and Institute of Arts and Letters (1978), induction into the academy (1983), a $25,000 senior fellowship from the National Endowment for the Arts (1984), the PEN/Faulkner Award (1986), the Ritz Hemingway Prize for Fiction (1987), and the Pulitzer Prize for *A Summons to Memphis* (1987).

In July 1986 Taylor suffered a stroke, followed by several more in 1994. He died in the University of Virginia Hospital in Charlottesville at the age of seventy-seven. He is buried in Sewanee, Tennessee, next to his mentor Tate.

The author of several novels and plays, Taylor is best remembered as an American master of the short story. Short on dialogue and long on psychological and sociological acuity, his stories pack emotional power. He dealt with regional materials, making them universal. At least one critic compared his work to that of Anton Chekhov.

★

Taylor's papers are at Vanderbilt University. Hubert H. McAlexander, ed., *Conversations with Peter Taylor* (1987), gives many biographical and critical insights into Taylor, as does the first biographical chapter of Albert J. Griffith, *Peter Taylor,* rev.

ed. (1990). Other informative books are Hubert H. McAlexander, ed., *Critical Essays on Peter Taylor* (1993); C. Ralph Stephens and Lynda B. Salamon, eds., *The Craft of Peter Taylor* (1995); Catherine Clark Graham, *Southern Accents: The Fiction of Peter Taylor* (1994); and David M. Robinson, *World of Relations: The Achievement of Peter Taylor* (1998). Special issues of the *Sewanee Review* (1962), *Critique* (1967), *Shenandoah* (1977), and the *Journal of the Short Story in English* (1987) are devoted to Taylor. An obituary is in the *New York Times* (4 Nov. 1994).

ROBERT PHILLIPS

TEMIN, Howard Martin (*b.* 10 December 1934 in Philadelphia, Pennsylvania; *d.* 9 February 1994 in Madison, Wisconsin), virologist and professor of oncology who was a co-winner of the 1975 Nobel Prize in physiology or medicine for his research on "the interaction between tumor viruses and the genetic material of the cell."

Temin was the second of three sons born to Henry Temin, a lawyer, and Annette Lehman Temin. His mother was active in civic affairs, especially those involving education. Temin's interest in science became evident by the time he was fourteen years old; while a student at Central High School in Philadelphia, he spent summers doing research at the Jackson Laboratory in Bar Harbor, Maine. In 1951

Howard Temin, 1975. AP/WIDE WORLD PHOTOS

Temin began his college years at Swarthmore College in Pennsylvania, where he majored and minored in biology in the honors program. At the age of eighteen he published his first scientific paper. During the summer of 1953 he worked at the Institute for Cancer Research in Philadelphia. He graduated with a B.S. degree from Swarthmore in 1955.

In 1955, before he attended the California Institute of Technology (Caltech) in Pasadena, Temin once again spent his summer vacation doing research at the Jackson Laboratory. After a year and a half as an experimental embryology major, he became an animal virology major and worked in the laboratory of Professor Renato Dulbecco, with whom he would later share the 1975 Nobel Prize, along with David Baltimore. Professor Max Delbrück and Doctor Matthew Meselson both served as role models for Temin at Caltech as well. In 1958 Temin and Harry Rubin, a postdoctoral fellow in Dulbecco's laboratory, developed the first assay in vitro that could be reproduced for the quantitative measuring of viral growth, one that remains in use today for genetic studies of many oncogenic viruses in cell culture. Temin's doctoral dissertation was on the Rous sarcoma virus (RSV).

After earning his Ph.D. from Caltech in 1959, Temin remained in Dulbecco's lab for another year as a postdoctoral fellow. In that same year, he conducted the experiments that would lead to the formulation of the provirus hypothesis in 1964 for the Rous sarcoma virus. In 1960 he became an assistant professor at the McArdle Laboratory for Cancer Research at the University of Wisconsin Medical School, where he continued experimenting with the life cycle of RSV in chicken cells in culture. Temin, with genetic and biochemical findings, was able to support his assertion that RSV did indeed synthesize a DNA provirus from its own RNA. His hypothesis was regarded with disdain because at that time biologists were certain that only RNA could be formed from a DNA template; the reverse (DNA formed from RNA) was not thought possible. It was only in 1970, when Temin and Doctor Satoshi Mizutani, as well as Doctor David Baltimore (in separate labs), identified an enzyme, "reverse transcriptase," that synthesized DNA and used an RNA template, that Temin's provirus hypothesis was accepted.

While working as an assistant professor he married Rayla Greenberg, a population geneticist from Brooklyn, New York, on 27 May 1962. They had two daughters.

Temin held a number of positions at the McArdle Laboratory until his death in 1994. He was associate professor (1964–1969); professor of oncology (1969–1994); Wisconsin Alumni Research Foundation Professor of Cancer Research (1971–1994); American Cancer Society Professor of Viral Oncology and Cell Biology (1974–1994); Harold P. Rusch Professor of Cancer Research (1980–1994); and

Steenbock Professor of the Biological Sciences (1982–1994). Temin reached the pinnacle of success in 1975, however, when he received the Nobel Prize in physiology or medicine for the discovery of the reverse transcriptase enzyme, demonstrated by both Temin and Baltimore to be capable of making a DNA copy from an RNA template. Much of the work that Temin conducted on retroviruses became the germ of later research in developing vaccines and other preventive measures against both cancer and AIDS.

In addition Temin served on the editorial boards of several journals and earned many accolades, including: a Research Career Development Award from the National Cancer Institute (1964–1974); the U.S. Steel Award given by the National Academy of Sciences (1972); and the Enzyme Chemistry Award from the American Chemical Society (1973). In 1974 Temin received the Dyer Award from the National Institutes of Health, the G.H.A. Clowes Award from the American Association for Cancer Research, and the Albert Lasker Award for Basic Medical Research. The Lila Gruber Award from the American Academy of Dermatologists was presented to Temin in 1981. Other awards and honorary degrees include the Bitterman Memorial Award by the University of California at Berkeley (1984), the first Hilldale Award in the Biological Sciences at the University of Wisconsin at Madison (1986), and the National Medal of Science (1992).

Temin became a staunch supporter of nonsmokers, speaking extensively about the unhealthy effects of smoking on the body. A rare form of cancer called adenocarcinoma of the lung caused Temin's death at the age of fifty-nine. He is buried at the Forest Hill Cemetery in Madison.

Temin will be remembered not only for his groundbreaking work in the battle against cancer and AIDS through his research with retroviruses, but also as a reserved, family-oriented man. He always spoke out for what he believed to be right in an unassuming yet determined way. It is this selfless concern for human life, coupled with his extraordinary research talents, that earns him a place in history. The lakeshore bike-pedestrian path that Temin had been known to traverse each morning on his way to work has since been named after him.

★

The Kremers Reference Files, University Archives, University of Wisconsin at Madison, contains a folder with biographical material on Temin. The foreword to Geoffrey M. Cooper, Rayla Greenberg Temin, and Bill Sugden, eds., *The DNA Provirus: Howard Temin's Scientific Legacy* (1995) also provides information about Temin's life. He himself wrote a short autobiographical sketch for the Nobel Foundation after he won the Nobel Prize in 1975. An obituary is in the *Boston Globe* (11 Feb. 1994).

ADRIANA C. TOMASINO

Tiny Tim (Herbert Butros Khaury) (*b*. 12 April 1932 in New York City; *d*. 30 November 1996 in Minneapolis, Minnesota), songwriter, musicologist, and "lovable eccentric" best known for his appearances on television, dressed in outlandish costumes, playing the ukulele and singing his one hit, "Tiptoe Through the Tulips with Me," in falsetto.

Tiny Tim was the only child of immigrant parents Butros Khaury, a Lebanese textile worker, and Tillie Staff, an Orthodox Jew who worked in the garment industry. He grew up in Manhattan's Washington Heights neighborhood and showed an interest in music early. Tim dropped out of George Washington High School following his sophomore year. He enjoyed listening to Arthur Godfrey on the radio, and because Godfrey played the ukulele, Tim decided to try it. He also taught himself the guitar.

What he wanted to do was entertain. He played the guitar at parties in the Bronx and began to develop a reputation under the name Larry Love. Tim had a number of pseudonyms in accordance with his belief that changing a name was like changing luck. From 1950 to 1953 he sang on amateur nights at a number of clubs in New York and

Tiny Tim. ARCHIVE PHOTOS

New Jersey, but never won. In 1953 he had an inspiration to sing in a different voice from his pleasant baritone. One night at the Old Alliance Club amateur night he tried singing in a trembling falsetto, and his rendition of "You Are My Sunshine" took second place.

In 1958 Tim, using the name "Larry Love, the Singing Canary," was a regular at Hubert's Museum and Live Flea Circus, a "freak show" in New York City's Times Square. He left Hubert's in 1960 and changed his name to Darry Dover. In March 1962 he got a job at the Cafe Bizarre in Greenwich Village, working two nights a week at $10 per night. Although the job only lasted a month, other gigs in the Village followed. Tim's manager, George King, renamed him Sir Timothy Tims, but Tim could not master the English accent required by the "role," so King renamed him Tiny Tim, a comic touch for the six-foot, one-inch-tall singer.

His next engagement, in March 1963, was at the lesbian club Page Three. He was popular with the audience, and his falsetto versions of "I Feel Pretty" and "I Enjoy Being a Girl" invariably brought down the house. His act consisted of four numbers: three in his "high" voice and one duet with himself, using his own baritone and the falsetto. Tim stayed at Page Three until the police closed it in July 1965. On 5 December 1965 Tim did his act at yet another amateur show, at the Champagne Gallery, and won first prize. That same night Tim auditioned at The Scene and was hired for three months without pay.

In March 1966 he appeared on the *Merv Griffin Show*, singing "People Will Say We're in Love," one of his "duets." After a trip to California, Tim went back to The Scene and stayed there for the next year and a half. He got a small part playing himself in a documentary film, *You Are What You Eat* (1968), produced by Peter Yarrow of the musical group Peter, Paul and Mary. Yarrow brought Mo Ostin, an executive for Warner Brothers Reprise Records, to see Tim's act at The Scene. Ostin promptly signed him to a recording contract.

At last, Tiny Tim's career was beginning to move. In January 1968 he appeared in the first broadcast of *Laugh-In;* he eventually made several other appearances on the show. The fan mail was abundant and usually negative. His greatest television success, however, was on the *Tonight Show*. After his initial appearance in April 1968, his first album *God Bless Tiny Tim* (1968) sold more than 200,000 copies, and the single "Tiptoe Through the Tulips With Me" became a hit. On the *Tonight Show*, Tim became a favorite guest, appearing on an average of once every seven weeks. With his white face, long, stringy hair, exaggerated effeminate gestures, and odd topics of conversation, he was a complement to straight man Johnny Carson.

Tim met Victoria May Budinger, who was just seventeen years old, in June 1969 at a book signing at Wanamaker's in Philadelphia, Pennsylvania, for his book *Beautiful Things* (1969), a collection of his favorite sayings. He called all women "Miss" to show respect; thus she became "Miss Vicky." After Tim announced their engagement on the *Tonight Show*, Carson invited him to have the ceremony on television. At the wedding, which aired on 17 December 1969, some 10,000 tulips, imported from Holland, decorated the set. There were no commercials during the ceremony, whose viewing audience of 45 million was one of the largest in television history.

This was the high point of Tim's career. Once he started on the *Tonight Show,* Tim had many opportunities. In 1968 he appeared at the Royal Albert Hall in London, singing with a fifty-eight-piece orchestra, and won over a skeptical audience. A club engagement at Caesar's Palace in Las Vegas paid $50,000 for the first week. He and Miss Vicky appeared on the *Ed Sullivan Show,* and he toured England, Australia, and New Zealand. In 1970 he appeared at the Isle of Wight Festival, a rock festival on the Isle of Wight with the Who, The Doors, Joni Mitchell, and other superstars. His rendition of "There'll Always Be an England" can be seen in the "rockumentary" film *Message to Love: The Isle of Wight Festival* (1997).

But Tim's brief stardom was waning. In 1971 he was on the *Tonight Show* only twice, and his next appearance, in 1974, was labeled a "charity" booking by his biographer Harry Stein. Tim's personal life was also changing. He and Miss Vicky, who had one child, Tulip Victoria, were divorced in 1977. In June 1984 he married Jan Alweiss. That marriage also ended in divorce, and in August 1995 he married Susan Gardner.

Throughout the rest of his life, Tim tried to regain his fame. Unfortunately, the sideshow image of Tim, singing falsetto with his ukulele, was the image audiences wanted, not Tim the musicologist who had a remarkable knowledge of popular songs, gleaned from 78 r.p.m. records, Edison cylinders, and the music archives of the New York Public Library. In fact, Tim was described in a 1996 *Billboard* article as "a walking archive of music." He not only carried notebooks full of old songs but could imitate the recorded sounds of singers as diverse as Rudy Vallee, Al Jolson, Russ Columbo, and Ruth Etting. His knowledge of the history of recorded popular music was encyclopedic. In 1979 in Sydney, Australia, he sang a 135-minute, 133-song stream-of-consciousness history of recorded popular music, from the first songs recorded for the phonograph to the Bee Gees "Stayin' Alive."

In 1980 Tim's song "Tiptoe to the Gas Pumps," a response to the gas crisis, led to another appearance on the

Tonight Show, but not a return to stardom. He toured constantly, often on one-night stands, most often singing in his "real" baritone voice. In the late 1980s and the 1990s Tim became a feature on the *Howard Stern Show,* introducing a new generation to Tiny Tim. Dressed in his usual flamboyant style, he judged Stern's New Year's Rotten Eve Beauty Pageant in 1994.

Tim continued to record albums such as *Tiny Tim: The Eternal Troubadour* (1986) and *Rock* (1993), which includes his version of the AC/DC hit "Highway to Hell." In 1996 he did *Tiny Tim's Christmas Album,* with songs from the Beatles and Led Zeppelin, as well as old-fashioned Tin Pan Alley tunes. Reviews were good. While participating in a ukulele festival at the Montague Grange Hall in Massachusetts in September 1996, Tim collapsed on stage. Although diagnosed with congestive heart failure, he kept working. Always optimistic and trying to "make it" one more time, Tim said, in a June 1996 *People* magazine, "I'll go down to the grave always trying." He died from cardiac arrest after performing "Tiptoe Through the Tulips" at a benefit sponsored by the Minneapolis Woman's Club. Tim is buried in Lakewood Cemetery in Minneapolis.

Throughout his life, Tim wanted to please an audience. His love of music included performing as well as studying the great early singers and songs of popular music. He once said, "People have laughed at me my whole life," but did not see that as a bad thing. To be in front of an audience, whether as the butt of a joke or to sing a simple song, was everything to him.

★

A collection of Tiny Tim memorabilia is in the Tiny Tim Museum, housed in the store Fourteen Records, in Dallas, Texas. There is an unauthorized biography, Harry Stein's *Tiny Tim* (1976). Articles from his years of fame include "The Last Innocent," *Newsweek* (20 May 1968), and Alfred G. Aronowitz, "It's High Time Fame Came to Tiny Tim," *Life* (14 June 1968). Later articles are Robert Taylor, "The Amazing Tiny Tim," *Boston Globe* (30 July 1981), which discusses Tim as a showman and musicologist; David Gates, "Tiptoeing with Tiny Tim," *Newsweek* (3 Dec. 1984); and Mary Shaughnessy, "Tiny Tim Tiptoes On," *People* (15 Apr. 1985), which describes his lounge act. David Richards, "God Help Us Every One, Tiny Tim: Fame, Failure and the American Dream," *Washington Post* (19 Feb. 1995), is a lengthy article. Tributes include David Browne, "Tiny Phenom: The Archetypal Oddball Embodies Camp to the End," *Entertainment Weekly* (13 Dec. 1996), and Alex Tresniowski and Margaret Nelson, "Exit Singing," *People* (16 Dec. 1996). Obituaries are in the *Boston Globe, Daily Telegraph* (London), *New York Times,* and *Minneapolis Star Tribune* (all 2 Dec. 1996).

MARCIA B. DINNEEN

TRILLING, Diana Rubin (*b.* 21 July 1905 in New York City; *d.* 23 October 1996 in New York City), cultural and literary critic whose books, essays, and reviews explored the social, intellectual, and artistic questions of her time—the ideals and illusions of the American Old and New Left, the tastes and values of the middle class, and the achievements and shortcomings of American writers.

The youngest of three children of Eastern European Jewish parents, Trilling was raised in a prosperous, not religiously observant, Americanized household. Her father, Joseph Rubin, a hard-driving, no-nonsense striver, had fled from Russian Poland to avoid conscription; he began his business life selling macaroons and soon did well in the braid business. But when elaborate hats went out of fashion during World War I, he turned to manufacturing silk stockings, an enterprise that made the family comfortable enough to live in Larchmont, an upscale suburb of New York City where many middle class Jews lived. Trilling's mother, Sadie Helene Forbert, was an energetic housekeeper and gardener. In the late 1910s, the family moved to Brooklyn, where Trilling attended Erasmus Hall High School, graduating in 1921. She continued her studies at Radcliffe College—located as one might pick a name from telephone book and fondly desired because it was an all-women's college near a big city. She received good training in art

Diana Trilling. AP/WIDE WORLD PHOTOS

history and graduated cum laude from Radcliffe with a B.A. degree in 1925. But she claimed in her memoir, *The Beginning of the Journey: The Marriage of Diana and Lionel Trilling* (1993), to have learned little about world literature and thought. After college, Trilling studied singing and traveled with her father—her mother had died in 1926. In 1927 she met Lionel Trilling in a speakeasy; at the time he was a graduate student at Columbia University, teaching part-time at Hunter College. Their marriage in 1929 was inarguably the defining event of her life: with it came entrance into a world of literary culture, Marxist politics, and friendship with intellectuals and writers.

Psychological difficulties—especially fears of being alone and of asserting herself—as well as hyperthyroidism plagued Trilling during the 1930s and well into middle life. Nevertheless, in 1932 she began to be active in left-wing politics, engaging at first in "the women's work of revolution, stuffing and licking envelopes" for the National Committee for the Defense of Political Prisoners, a Communist front organization. She also spent the decade sharing her husband's problems. He had begun teaching in the English department at Columbia in 1932 but by 1936 had not secured his tenure. He was told that "as a Jew, a Marxist, and a Freudian" he was not welcome at the university and his contract would not be renewed. At that point he needed to distinguish himself in order to survive. She encouraged him to make a case for his teaching and literary potential. An avid reader and amateur editor, Trilling criticized his writing, perhaps sharpened his style, and unconsciously prepared for her own writing career. With the appearance of his book on Matthew Arnold in 1939, Lionel Trilling rose dramatically at Columbia and in the community of New York intellectuals—so much so that he was able to recommend his wife for a reviewing position at the leftist magazine *Nation* in 1941.

After a trial period writing small notices, Trilling got her own column and with it the obligation of reading what amounted to a novel a day for six and a half years. While she was not quite a full-fledged New York intellectual—a wife and a guest at literary gatherings rather than a peer—she began to build a reputation as an incisive critic of the novel in time of war. A 1978 collection of her essays for the *Nation, Reviewing the Forties,* reveals her talents and strong convictions about writing and politics. Having shed her Communist sympathies by the late 1930s, she cast a cold eye on books informed by Communist-sympathizing or pro-Soviet ideas; she wrote of "intellectual decency," which Stalinist writers of the period sacrificed to their cause. The reviews also embodied her literary standards—mastery of craftsmanship and freedom from ideology, sentimentality, and extreme subjectivity. She praised the playwright and fiction writer Christopher Isherwood's clarity and moral

sincerity and attacked the gothic elaboration and preciosity of Southern writers Truman Capote and Eudora Welty.

The critic Edmund Wilson took notice of her first long essay for the *Nation* and encouraged her to curtail her reviewing and instead develop her own ideas. She took his advice; by the late 1940s, after leaving her job at the *Nation*, she was moving between the world of women's magazines and the rarefied intellectual regions of *Partisan Review*. The latter publication—the standard-bearing magazine of the anti-Stalinist Left and the critical arm of literary modernism—eventually brought out her own unorthodox liberal evaluations of the U.S. State Department official Alger Hiss, who turned over state secrets to the Soviets; the American journalist and Soviet intelligence agent Whittaker Chambers; and the American physicist J. Robert Oppenheimer, who was instrumental in developing the atomic bomb. Her skeptical look at the politics of the postwar period—at deluded liberals and intense Communist-baiters—made her a controversial figure. The beginning of her fascination with the artist as rebel and battler with convention first yielded a long essay on the English novelist D. H. Lawrence for introduction to the Viking Portable series of edited classics (1947); the work became a bestseller. Meanwhile, she became the mother of James Trilling in 1948, and then as before the role of homemaker was central to her life.

In 1950, Trilling received a prestigious Guggenheim fellowship for a book on the American family, a project that was abandoned for steady essay writing in the 1950s. The decade also included a period as a columnist for the pro-labor, anticommunist *New Leader* (1957–1959) and more work on D. H. Lawrence, which resulted in a selected edition of his letters in 1958. In *Claremont Essays* (1964), she brought together long pieces about political and cultural life done from the late 1940s into the early 1960s. With pride in her social identity and locale, indicated by the title reference to her street on Manhattan's Upper West Side, she argued against a fashionable contemporary attitude—that society is hostile to the individual will. She wrote about such modern icons as Norman Mailer, Marilyn Monroe, and Allen Ginsberg, among others, and dealt with the theme of the disconnected self. Mailer is "messianic" rather than creative; Monroe is the prisoner of biology, not Hollywood; Ginsberg is a talented child trying to impress grown-ups. With a gift for evoking personalities in crisis, including a complex understanding of the intelligence as well as the extremism of larger-than-life artists and outsiders, Trilling measured these figures by her 1940s standards of artistic coherence and freedom from cant and destructive willfulness. Her verdicts were sensitive to the creative mission as well as critical of the illusions of hipsters, movie stars, and beatniks. Her defense of the mind and human community as against instinct and isolated individualism was her main enterprise from the 1960s to the end of her life.

Lionel Trilling, one of the most famous and honored intellectuals of the twentieth century, died in 1975, and Diana Trilling assumed the role of his editor once again, this time officially. She worked on the Uniform Edition of the writings of Lionel Trilling (1978–1980), including a new volume of uncollected pieces, *Speaking of Literature and Society*. Her own work continued to appear. *We Must March My Darlings* (1977) was Trilling's look at the Old Left's mistakes and the new counterculture's impact. She enraged the playwright Lillian Hellman and other old-time Marxist stalwarts and anti-anti-Communists by excoriating their ideas about Soviet virtue and American evil. As the wife of a famous professor and critic who had had his own troubles with an order-conservative Columbia, Trilling was sympathetic to one aspect of the 1968 student uprisings at Columbia of 1968: the critique of new power. But the New Left protestors who occupied buildings wanted fundamental changes in culture and values. Their goals were diffuse and anarchic compared to the Old Left's pursuit of political ends. This new generation seemed to be irresponsible and irrational. The book also reported on a stay at Radcliffe in 1971: she ironically identified a letdown of civilized standards and a general atmosphere of irresponsibility. In another vein, she found the classic 1969 counterculture film *Easy Rider* (written, produced, and starring Peter Fonda) no more than a romanticizing of the drug culture. On the topic of women's liberation, she was angry about the denial of women's "full humanity" in society and encouraged by the revolt against Madison Avenue images for women, but she lacked fervor and militancy. From 1977 to 1979 she received another tangible recognition of her work, a joint Rockefeller Foundation–National Endowment for the Humanities grant.

In 1980 Trilling found another theme to suit her essentially social imagination: the celebrated trial of the Madeira School headmistress Jean Harris for the murder of her lover, the "Scarsdale Diet" doctor Herman Tarnower. Covering the court case and bringing to bear on it her ideas of responsibility and integrity, she produced a richly textured account of pretensions, hypocrisies, and vulgarities. Harris is depicted as the prisoner of her class—an employee to the fashionable and a self-pitying woman desperate for a man of status. Tarnower, a cruel womanizer, is shown as a coarse, swaggering man despite his society airs. *Mrs. Harris: The Death of the Scarsdale Diet Doctor* (1981) has novelistic qualities and, as the *New York Times* critic Michiko Kakutani pointed out, rounds off the career of a fiction reviewer who was a keen observer of social nuance. The book was nominated for the Pulitzer Prize.

Trilling received a second Guggenheim in 1991 for her last book, the story of her marriage to Lionel. *The Beginning of the Journey* is a sweeping memoir of youth and maturity, love and friendship. It is also an intellectual's account of vivid ideas, characters, and crucial events. As the central figure, Lionel Trilling often appears as temperamental and filled with neurotic self-doubt, the great critic as would-be novelist and flawed personality. The cast of the book includes 1930s radicals, psychoanalysts, professors, critics, and editors. The backdrop is twentieth-century New York from the speakeasy days to Lionel's death in 1975. The events include the 1929 stock market crash, the rise of the Communist Party, and the impact of the Moscow trials of 1936–1939 with their forced confessions and the McCarthy hearings. Candid about her dissatisfactions—including condescension to women intellectuals and dishonesty and crude behavior among the brilliant and eloquent—she nevertheless celebrates the New York intelligentsia that grew to maturity in the 1930s and disappeared in her old age. This last book, dictated because of failing eyesight, was not Trilling's last publication. A lengthy article on Goronwy Rees, a British intellectual and Marxist of the 1930s, appeared in the *New Yorker* magazine in 1995. Rees had become a notable academic by the 1950s and feared his old friendship with Guy Burgess, the notorious Cambridge spy who had defected to Moscow in 1956; in a series of articles, he exposed Burgess and the intelligence network that supposedly protected him. Trilling's essay used Rees for her characteristic blend of intellectual analysis and memorable depiction of personality. Trilling died of cancer and is buried at Ferncliff Cemetery in Westchester, New York.

Diana Trilling combined an intensity about ideas with a commonsensical, middle-class attachment to moderation and decency. As a female writer in an essentially male world of letters, she refused the role of feminist spokesperson and forged an identity based on her personal reactions to books and contemporary manners and on her affinities with opinionated New York intellectuals. Her bracing, judgmental criticism was frankly moralistic and has earned her a modest but dignified place among American essayists and cultural commentators.

★

Valuable interview material with Diana Trilling in old age and the evaluation of her place among other women writers are available in David Laskin, *Partisans: Marriage, Politics, and Betrayal Among the New York Intellectuals* (2000). Norman Podhoretz, *Ex-Friends: Falling Out with Allen Ginsberg, Lionel and Diana Trilling, Lillian Hellman, Hannah Arendt, and Norman Mailer* (1999), offers a controversial and ultimately negative account of his own relationship with the Trillings, told from a neoconservative viewpoint. Ann Hulbert surveys major aspects of the Trillings' life together in her review of *The Beginning of the Journey* in the *New York Times Book Review* (24 Oct. 1993). Patricia Bosworth's "A Life of

Significant Contention," an informative and moving memorial essay in the *New York Times,* includes a series of interesting remarks Trilling made late in life (29 Dec. 1996). There is an obituary in the *New York Times* (25 Oct. 1996).

David Castronovo

TURNER, Lana   (*b.* 8 February 1920 in Wallace, Idaho; *d.* 29 June 1995 in Los Angeles, California), actress who epitomized glamour in Hollywood's golden years, despite an offscreen life touched by scandal.

Born Julia Jean Mildred Frances Turner in the small mining town of Wallace, Idaho, Turner was the only child of John Virgil Turner and Mildred Frances Cowan. After Julia (known as "Judy") was born, the family drifted from town to town, finally settling in San Francisco, where her parents eventually separated. Her father, a smooth-talking miner, gambler, and bootlegger, was murdered after an all-night crap game in San Francisco sometime around Christmas in 1930. When Turner was fifteen, she and her mother, a beautician, moved to Hollywood, where she attended Hollywood High School.

The legend that she was discovered while sipping a strawberry soda at Schwab's drugstore in Hollywood is not exactly true. In fact, she was drinking a Coca-Cola at the Top Hat Café across the street from her high school in January 1936 when she was spotted by W. R. ("Billy")

Lana Turner. The Kobal Collection

Wilkerson, publisher of the *Hollywood Reporter,* who asked her if she would like to appear in movies. After signing with the talent agency of Zeppo Marx (brother of the famous Marx Brothers comedy team), she won a bit role in *A Star Is Born* (1937) and even made a screen test for the role of Scarlett O'Hara in *Gone with the Wind.* Her big break came when she was cast as Mary Clay in Warner Brothers' production of *They Won't Forget* (1937). Playing a teenage girl whose murder sparks a firestorm of bigotry and lawlessness in a southern town, Turner sauntered down a street early in the film, wearing a skintight sweater and skirt. Her brief appearance prompted a barrage of publicity, and she became known as the "Sweater Girl." Although there are conflicting accounts, Turner claims that it was at this point that she changed her name from Judy to Lana.

After playing minuscule roles in *The Great Garrick* (1937) and *The Adventures of Marco Polo* (1938), Turner moved to Metro-Goldwyn-Mayer at the urging of Mervyn LeRoy, who had directed her in *They Won't Forget.* As moviegoers responded to her blonde beauty and her aura of innocent sexuality, her roles became increasingly prominent in such movies as *Love Finds Andy Hardy* (1938), *Rich Man, Poor Girl* (1938), and *Calling Dr. Kildare* (1939). She was soon starring in *These Glamour Girls* (1939), *Dancing Co-Ed* (1940), and *Two Girls on Broadway* (1940), films that relied more on her glamorous looks than on her modest acting ability. Her best role to date came in *Ziegfeld Girl* (1941), in which she played an ambitious chorus girl whose relentless search for stardom ends with her demise. During this early period of her career, Turner married twice, first in February 1940 to the bandleader Artie Shaw, whom she divorced only seven months later, and then in July 1942 to the restaurateur Stephen Crane, whom she divorced in 1944. Despite a contentious, much-publicized marital relationship with Crane, they had a daughter in July 1943.

As a major star in MGM's galaxy of players, Turner was frequently cast opposite the studio's most popular leading men, including Spencer Tracy (*Dr. Jekyll and Mr. Hyde,* 1941; *Cass Timberlane,* 1947), Robert Taylor (*Johnny Eager,* 1942), and Clark Gable. Gable was her most felicitous costar—his rugged masculinity played well against her kittenish, seductive ways in *Honky Tonk* (1941), *Somewhere I'll Find You* (1942), and *Homecoming* (1948). Other roles, in such films as *Weekend at the Waldorf* (1945), *Green Dolphin Street* (1947), and *The Three Musketeers* (1948), revealed a competent but unexceptional actress. After completing *The Three Musketeers,* Turner married the sportsman and millionaire Henry J. ("Bob") Topping in May 1948; they divorced in December 1952.

Only one of Turner's films in the 1940s was exceptional, and it featured one of her best performances. In *The Postman Always Rings Twice* (1946), adapted from James M.

Cain's novel, she played Cora, the seductive, scheming wife of an older man (Cecil Kellaway), who plots his murder in league with a drifter (John Garfield), whom she seduces. Dressed entirely in white as an ironic contrast to the utter blackness in her heart, Turner gave a full-throttle performance that riveted the audience's attention.

Turner's films in the 1950s were mostly mediocre, but she managed to retain her aura of Hollywood glamour, lavishly costumed in such movies as *The Merry Widow* (1952), *Latin Lovers* (1953), *The Prodigal* (1955), and *Diane* (1955). On loan to other studios, she appeared in *The Sea Chase* (Warner Brothers, 1955), opposite John Wayne, and *The Rains of Ranchipur* (Fox, 1955), a remake of *The Rains Came,* opposite Richard Burton. In MGM's *The Bad and the Beautiful* (1952), she gave what is arguably her best performance. As the alcoholic, jaded actress Georgia Lorrison, who is turned into a star and then discarded by the ruthless producer Kirk Douglas, she revealed the emotional fragility behind the Hollywood glitter. The scene in which she becomes hysterical as she drives away from her deceitful lover is one of her finest moments in film. In September 1953, Turner married her fourth husband, the actor Lex Barker, whom she divorced in July 1957. Around the same time, her contract with MGM came to an end.

In 1958, Turner became deeply involved in one of the most sensational crimes in Hollywood history. On an evening in April, her lover, the mobster Johnny Stompanato, allegedly threatened to disfigure her during a heated argument. Fearful for her mother's life, Turner's daughter, Cheryl, then fourteen, stabbed him to death with a carving knife. The crime, and the subsequent trial, prompted banner headlines in newspapers across the country. A jury exonerated Cheryl with a finding of justifiable homicide. Devastated by the event, Turner feared that her career was now at its lowest ebb.

She was bolstered, however, by the strongly favorable reaction to her performance in *Peyton Place* (1957), based on—and superior to—Grace Metalious's best-selling novel, which had been made before the Stompanato scandal but was released almost simultaneously with Cheryl's trial. Playing Constance MacKenzie, a repressed mother who finds new love in the secret-ridden town of Peyton Place, Turner gave a persuasive performance that won her an Academy Award nomination as Best Actress. Many of Turner's films in the late 1950s and 1960s reflected the public's perception of the actress as a woman with a troubled but active romantic life.

In *Portrait in Black* (1960), she conspired with her lover, Anthony Quinn, to murder her husband. In *By Love Possessed* (1961), she played a woman unhappily married to the wealthy Jason Robards, Jr., who begins a torrid affair with Efrem Zimbalist, Jr. *Love Has Many Faces* (1965) cast her as another rich, bored woman, this time with a shady past

and a beach boy lover (Hugh O'Brian). Turner's most successful films of this period, however, were glossy remakes of durable stories, such as *Imitation of Life* (1959) and *Madame X* (1966), which gave her the chance to stretch her acting ability. She also appeared in several comedy films, including *Bachelor in Paradise* (1961), with Bob Hope, and *Who's Got the Action?* (1962), with Dean Martin. During the 1960s, Turner, who enjoyed the company of men, continued her pattern of marriage and divorce: her husbands included the businessman and rancher Fred May (1960–1962), the producer Robert P. Eaton (1965–1969), and the nightclub hypnotist Ronald Dante (1969–1972).

Turner remained off the screen for three years; when she returned, the roles were few and far between, and the films were poor. In *The Big Cube* (1969), she played a mother at the mercy of her daughter's unscrupulous lover, and in *Persecution* (1973, also released as *Sheba* and *The Terror of Sheba*), she was a nasty woman ultimately murdered by her vengeful son. Her final film was called *Bittersweet Love* (1976). In her later years, she appeared occasionally on television, most notably in the series *The Survivors* (1969–1971), and also onstage in the comedy *Forty Carats*. She died in Los Angeles of throat cancer at the age of seventy-five and was cremated.

Over the years, Hollywood's "Golden Girl" may have been tarnished by scandal, and her offscreen life may have become fodder for tabloid headlines. Yet at the peak of her fame, she glowed with a radiance that virtually defined "movie star," and her blonde beauty was indisputably the stuff of dreams.

★

Lana Turner's autobiography, *Lana: The Lady, the Legend, the Truth,* was published in 1982. Other books on her life and career include Joe Morella and Edward Z. Epstein, *Lana: The Public and Private Lives of Miss Turner* (1971); Jeanine Basinger, *Lana Turner* (1976); Lou Valentino, *The Films of Lana Turner* (1976); and Jane Ellen Wayne, *Lana: The Life and Loves of Lana Turner* (1995). Turner's daughter, Cheryl Crane, related her own story in *Detour: A Hollywood Story,* written with Cliff Jahr (1988). An article by John Updike, "Legendary Lana," is in the *New Yorker* (12 Feb. 1996). Obituaries appear in the *New York Times* (1 July 1995) and *Variety* (10–16 July 1995).

TED SENNETT

URBAN, Matt Louis (*b.* 25 August 1919 in Buffalo, New York; *d.* 4 March 1995 in Holland, Michigan), military officer who was the most highly decorated American combat soldier of World War II and awarded the Medal of Honor for his actions in the Normandy campaign.

The third of four children (one of whom died in childhood) of Stanley Urbanowitz, a plumber of Polish descent, and

Matt Urban. AP/WIDE WORLD PHOTOS

Helen Urbanowitz, a homemaker, Matt L. Urbanowitz, a devout Catholic called "Matty" by friends and associates, grew up on Buffalo's East Side near the New York Central Railroad yards. At an early age, he abbreviated his last name to Urban. Attending Buffalo's East High School, he excelled as an athlete, lettering in three sports. In the fall of 1937 Urban enrolled at Cornell University, where he was inspired by his history professor, Fred Marcham. Prior to graduating, Urban competed on the university's intercollegiate boxing team and joined the army's Reserve Officers' Training Corps to pay for his education. In June 1941 Urban graduated with a bachelor of arts degree in history and government.

Urban received his commission as a second lieutenant in the United States Army on 22 May 1941 and moved to Fort Bragg, North Carolina, where he was assigned to the Sixtieth Regiment of the Ninth Infantry Division for basic training to prepare for Operation Torch, the invasion of North Africa.

The Sixtieth Regiment was part of the western task force that invaded French Morocco. Landing during the early morning hours of 8 November 1942, Urban's Company D sustained heavy casualties from the French Foreign Legion

defending Port Lyautey and its strategic airfield. After the war, Urban claimed that the motivation for his heroism was generated by the shock of holding in his hands the decapitated head of a dead comrade during this battle. With Morocco occupied by the Americans, the Ninth Division relocated by truck and train to the Tunisian front to reinforce the British at Thala in the aftermath of the Allied defeat at Kasserine Pass.

Urban fought at Maknassy Pass from 28 March to 9 April 1943. He single-handedly captured a German communications post in March 1943. Captain Urban's troops captured strategic enemy positions in the Sedjenane Valley and played a major role in the assault on Djebel Cheniti, which hastened the fall of Bizerte and the end of German resistance in Tunisia on 13 May. With the liberation of North Africa, Allied forces invaded Sicily as a precursor to the invasion of the Italian peninsula. As part of Operation Husky, the Ninth Division landed at Palermo, twenty-two days after the main American force breached Sicily's southeastern coast on 10 July. By this time Urban commanded Company F of the Sixtieth Regiment. Urban's unit was ordered to flank the Germans and take control of the territory overlooking the towns of Troina, Cesaro, and Randazzo. By doing so the Americans reached the Tortorici line, the last German line of defense on the island. Leading tethered pack mules over mountainous terrain on foot, Urban's company cleared the high ground used by the Germans for observation and long-range eighty-eight-millimeter artillery bombardment. With the fall of Randazzo, the Ninth Division reinforced the Third Division, which had made an amphibious landing at Brolo on 8 August. Messina and the island fell to the Allies on 17 August 1943.

From Sicily, the Ninth Division relocated to the British Isles, where it bivouacked near Winchester, England, one of the many staging areas for the D-day invasion of Normandy, launched on 6 June 1944. Having crossed the English Channel, troops of the Ninth loaded into Higgins landing craft near Utah Beach on 11 June to reinforce the Fourth Division. Moving inland, Urban's company encountered remnants of the German Panzer Lehr Division near Saint Mère-Église and Renouf on 14 June 1944. During the ensuing battle, Urban saw his bazooka gunner fall, a victim of enemy gunfire. Urban took up the weapon and, followed by an ammunition carrier, stalked two Mark IV tanks behind thick hedgerows, destroying both with devastating side shots. A third German tank nearby fired at Urban, wounding him in the left calf. Refusing evacuation, Urban ordered his men to rig a stretcher so that he could remain in combat. A bullet wound in the right forearm necessitated Urban's withdrawal to a hospital in southern England the next day.

On 25 July, Urban returned to France, where the Allied

advance had bogged down in hedgerow country, a labyrinth of small fields surrounded by rock walls laced with thick hedge growth, all of which bolstered the Germans' defense. By then General Omar Bradley, the commander of American ground forces, had devised a plan to take the offensive. Operation Cobra began with an aerial and artillery bombardment pulverizing a rectangular area three and one-half by one and one-half miles wide near the Periers-Saint-Lô Road. Urban's command was in close proximity to that area on the morning of 25 July 1944, the day of the offensive.

Upon his return to the front, Urban, walking with the support of a cane, found his men behind three stalled Sherman tanks. They were pinned down by lethal fire from a German antitank gun and a machine gun emplacement. One tank was burning. Urban heard cries for help from the second tank, from which he pulled a wounded man to safety; within seconds the vehicle burst into flames. The third tank had stopped, its turret gunner dead. Hobbling to it in a hail of gunfire, Urban climbed into the turret, ordering the driver forward. He manned the fifty-caliber machine gun, pouring devastating fire into the German gun emplacement. With the tank moving in the direction of the enemy, Urban's men rallied and captured the German position.

Eyeing the action through his binoculars, the battalion commander, Major Max Wolf, was so impressed with Urban's courage and leadership, he informed Sergeant Earl Evans that he would recommend Urban for the Medal of Honor. But Major Wolf was killed in action that same day. Remembering Wolf's words, Evans wrote a letter to the Pentagon dated 5 July 1945, which was forwarded first to the adjutant general of the army. The letter, however, was misplaced at the Pentagon. Still, Evans and Urban knew of the document's existence, and it was the basis of the latter's claim to the congressional medal. Meanwhile, on 3 September 1944, Urban was wounded for the seventh and final time when an enemy bullet pierced his throat, damaging his larynx. After twenty months of combat duty, he was medically discharged on 27 February 1946 with the rank of lieutenant colonel.

In October 1944 Urban began working as a writer for the military magazine *Liberty,* serving in that capacity until January 1946. After moving to Michigan in 1947, Urban was the executive director of the Monroe, Michigan, Community Center, until 1967. He then served as city recreation superintendent in Port Huron, Michigan, through 1974. After his marriage to Jennifer ("Jennie") Rockwell of Port Huron, he accepted a job as recreation director and Civic Center manager in Holland, Michigan. The couple had one child. Urban retired to devote more time to writing his autobiography, *The Matt Urban Story: Life and World War II Experiences* (1989). Urban's physique reflected the rigorous regimen of countless hours of roadwork throughout his life. He wore a neatly trimmed mustache and his eyes,

set beneath his auburn hair and broad forehead, exuded the confidence of a natural leader.

In July 1980 President Jimmy Carter awarded Urban the Medal of Honor in a White House ceremony after thirty-five years of bureaucratic oversight. This enabled Urban, who was decorated twenty-nine times for bravery, to surpass Audie Murphy as America's most highly decorated veteran of World War II. Urban died in 1995 from complications due to a collapsed lung. He is buried in section 7-A of Arlington National Cemetery, near the Memorial Amphitheater and the Tomb of the Unknowns.

★

Numerous obituaries, clippings describing Urban's celebrity status in the Holland community, and even Department of the Army personnel records can be found in the Hope College archives in Holland, Michigan. Information can also be found in the *Buffalo News* library in Buffalo, New York. Urban's autobiography, *The Matt Urban Story: Life and World War II Experiences* (1989), is a good place to begin a study of his life, although it is lacking in historical detail. The definitive history of the combat record of the Ninth Division is *Eight Stars to Victory: A History of the Veteran Ninth U.S. Infantry Division* (1948), by Captain Joseph B. Mittelman. An excellent bibliography is included in *Armies Corps, Divisions, and Separate Brigades* (2d ed., 1999), compiled by John B. Wilson. An obituary is in the *New York Times* (7 Mar. 1995).

JEAN W. GRIFFITH

VOLPE, John Anthony (*b.* 8 December 1908 in Wakefield, Massachusetts; *d.* 11 November 1994 in Salem, Massachusetts), building contractor and politician who founded a highly successful construction business and was elected governor of Massachusetts three times. He also served as secretary of transportation and became the first American of Italian descent to hold the post of ambassador to Italy.

Volpe was the third of seven children and the eldest of five sons of Vito Volpe, an itinerant plasterer, and Filomena Benedetto, a homemaker, both immigrants from the Abruzzi region of Italy. He grew up in Italian neighborhoods in Wakefield and nearby Malden, Massachusetts, and attended public schools. A good student who was especially proficient in mathematics, Volpe hoped to attend college. However, the death of his father's business partner forced him into the plastering trade full-time after graduating from Malden High School in 1926.

Volpe spent two unhappy years working with his father and others before enrolling at Wentworth Institute, a small engineering school in Boston, to study architectural construction. Upon graduating in 1930, he spurned a job offer from Stone and Webster, a large international engineering concern, and signed on with Frankini Brothers, a local con-

John A. Volpe, 1965. © BETTMANN/CORBIS

struction firm, where his chances for advancement seemed better. He rose from timekeeper to superintendent before the company succumbed to the Great Depression in 1932. After selling clothing and coal door-to-door for a few months, he cashed in a $300 insurance policy, borrowed another $200 from an uncle, and formed a partnership with Fred Grande, a bricklayer. Grande and Volpe began bidding on small construction jobs in March 1933. Their first success was a $1,287 addition to a heating plant in West Lynn, Massachusetts. On 18 June 1934, Volpe married his cousin Giovaninna ("Jennie") Benedetto, a psychiatric nurse; they had two children.

Volpe became the driving force of the business, finding the work, doing the estimating, and managing operations from an office in his parents' house. Propelled by his energy and skill (and low overhead), the fledgling company often underbid larger firms and was able to garner a significant share of the public works jobs available in eastern Massachusetts. By 1935 Grande and Volpe were winning lucrative contracts for larger projects—city and town halls and schools—and branching out into other New England states. They secured their first $1 million project in 1939 and subsequently expanded their operations all along the eastern seaboard with contracts for military projects.

In 1942 Volpe, who had become the sole owner, decided to close his company and join the war effort. As a navy lieutenant (junior grade), he trained African American sailors for construction battalions at Camp Peary, Virginia, and interviewed officer candidates for the Civil Engineer Corps in Washington, D.C. Discharged with the rank of lieutenant commander in 1946, he reopened the John A. Volpe Construction Company in time to participate in the post-

war building boom. Although most of the new construction of the period was housing, "monumental" projects of the kind that Volpe specialized in (college buildings, hospitals, and shopping centers) were also in demand. By 1953 he had offices in Washington, D.C., and Rome and assets of well over $1 million.

Having achieved business success and financial security, Volpe embarked upon a public career. An active Republican since the 1930s, he was named a party vice chairman in Massachusetts in 1951 as part of an effort to bring ethnic diversity to leadership positions traditionally dominated by Yankee Protestants. A year later he sought the Republican nomination for lieutenant governor at the state convention but withdrew in favor of a better-known candidate. Appointed the commissioner of public works by Governor Christian A. Herter in 1953, Volpe took over a department that was under constant attack for waste and corruption. He made its operations more businesslike and supervised $260.5 million worth of highway construction without a hint of scandal. In 1956 the U.S. secretary of commerce Sinclair Weeks asked Volpe to take charge of the newly inaugurated $50 billion federal interstate highway program. He declined, but agreed to serve as the interim Federal Highway Administrator for four and one-half months.

In 1958 Volpe's name surfaced as a possible candidate for governor after the sudden death of George Fingold, the Republican frontrunner, but he did not receive the nomination. Elected president of the Greater Boston Chamber of Commerce that same year, Volpe used the post to speak out on the important issues of government reorganization and taxation and position himself for the next election.

Capitalizing upon reports of malfeasance in the administration of Democrat Foster Furcolo, Volpe ran for governor on an anticorruption platform in 1960. Winning the Republican nomination, he pledged the "restoration of honor and competence" to state government and campaigned on the nonpartisan slogan "Vote the Man" to gain the support of independents and disaffected Democrats. Volpe defeated Joseph D. Ward by more than 138,000 votes even as Democrat John F. Kennedy was winning his home state by a landslide 510,000 votes in the presidential race. Volpe lost his reelection bid to the reform Democrat Endicott Peabody by 5,400 votes in 1962, but won a second term two years later, outpolling Lieutenant Governor Francis X. Bellotti, who had upset Peabody by 23,000 votes in a bitter Democratic primary. In 1966 Volpe won the state's first constitutionally mandated four-year term, defeating Edward J. McCormack by over 524,000 votes.

As governor, Volpe confronted overwhelming Democratic majorities in both houses of the state legislature. A moderate, he supported progressive policies in the areas of education, housing, mental health, welfare, and civil rights and had only relatively minor disagreements with the Democrats on budgetary matters. Bitter battles, however, were fought over the issues Volpe had exploited successfully in his election victories in 1960 and 1964. His first term (1961–1963) efforts to reorganize departments plagued by scandal and inefficiency were stymied by his partisan opponents. It was only after more evidence of maladministration came to light that the Democrats acquiesced to a Volpe proposal establishing a citizens' crime commission to investigate corrupt practices at the state and local levels in 1962. The commission, composed of six nonpoliticians, generated evidence that led to the indictment of a number of prominent officeholders. The anticorruption skirmish proved relatively tame in comparison to the struggle over the sales tax in his second term (1965–1967). Seeking to avert a financial crisis, Volpe proposed a 3 percent retail sales tax on selected goods to bring in needed revenue for state services and to provide property tax relief for cities and towns. Democratic leaders, who opposed the tax as regressive, defeated six versions of Volpe's bill before the persistent governor prevailed on his seventh try in March 1966. In November of that year his position was affirmed in a referendum vote by a five-to-one margin.

After his impressive reelection victory in 1966, Volpe waged a modest campaign to win a place on the Republican national ticket. At the 1968 Republican National Convention, he was seriously considered as a running mate for presidential nominee Richard M. Nixon, but Nixon and his advisers ultimately chose another ethnic governor, Spiro T. Agnew of Maryland, whose tough, law-and-order image was a better fit for their campaign's southern strategy. Following his election, Nixon named Volpe secretary of transportation.

With varying degrees of support from the White House, Volpe pursued an ambitious agenda and enjoyed a number of legislative triumphs during his tenure as transportation secretary. Most surprising were the former road builder's successful effort to increase funding for urban mass transit at the expense of highway construction and the creation of Railpax (later Amtrak), a semipublic corporation, to run the country's struggling passenger trains. He also secured a much-needed trust fund for the operation of airports and the airway system. The principal blemish on his record came in 1971, when Congress cut off funding for the development of the Supersonic Transport (SST), a costly and environmentally controversial high-speed airplane that Volpe had touted as the salvation of the slumping American aviation industry. Although he won strong White House backing for Railpax and the SST program, Volpe never established a close working relationship with the president and he disliked Nixon aides H. R. Haldeman and John Ehrlichman. Volpe resigned after the 1972 election and was appointed to fill the vacant post of ambassador to Italy.

At a time when anti-American demonstrations were common and the Italian Communist party was making significant gains in parliamentary elections, Volpe conducted what resembled a political campaign on behalf of his country and the NATO alliance. He traveled widely, made speeches in Italian, met with Catholic Church officials, local prefects, newspaper editors, and other opinion leaders, and received a generally favorable response. When he resigned in January 1977, Volpe could take pride in the fact that the Communists had been unsuccessful in securing a place in the coalitions that governed Italy in his four years as ambassador.

After leaving the ambassadorship, Volpe remained active. He served as president of the National Italian-American Foundation from 1977 to 1980, headed the American fund-raising effort for the relief of victims of a massive earthquake in southern Italy in 1980, and chaired a presidential commission on drunk driving in 1982. His panel's recommendation that a portion of federal highway funds be withheld from states that failed to raise the drinking age to twenty-one became law in 1984. Volpe died from the effects of a stroke and was buried in Forest Glade Cemetery in his native Wakefield.

A short (five feet, six and one-half inches tall), trim, devoutly Catholic, generous, and gregarious man, John Volpe involved himself in many charitable causes and belonged to numerous professional and fraternal organizations. Following his death, Volpe's Horatio Alger-like business success was noted and his courage and tenacity in the anticorruption and sales tax fights of the 1960s were lauded. But he was remembered primarily as an ethnic pioneer in Republican party politics. As a former associate put it: "He bridged the gap from the bocce player to the polo player."

★

Volpe's papers are housed in the Archives and Special Collections Department in Snell Library at Northeastern University in Boston; the Massachusetts State Archives in Boston has additional manuscript material. The official record of his governorship is Leslie G. Ainley, comp. and ed., *Addresses and Messages to the General Court, Proclamations, Public Addresses, Official Statements, and Correspondence of General Interest of His Excellency Governor John A. Volpe . . .*, 2 vols. (1962, 1970). Kathleen Kilgore, *John Volpe: The Life of an Immigrant's Son* (1987), is a biography written with Volpe's cooperation. Murray B. Levin (with George Blackwood), *The Compleat Politician: Political Strategy in Massachusetts* (1962), and Alec Barbrook, *God Save the Commonwealth: An Electoral History of Massachusetts* (1973), cover Bay State politics in the Volpe era. For Volpe's experience in the Nixon administration, see Rowland Evans, Jr., and Robert D. Novak, *Nixon in the White House: The Frustration of Power* (1971); Dan Rather and Gary Paul Gates, *The Palace Guard* (1974); and Alan L. Dean and James M. Beggs, "The Department of Transportation Comes of Age: The Nixon Years," *Presidential Studies Quarterly* (winter 1996). Obituaries are in the *Boston Globe,* the *Boston Herald,* and the *New York Times* (all 12 Nov. 1994).

RICHARD H. GENTILE

W-Z

WALCOTT, "Jersey Joe" (*b*. 31 January 1914 in Merchantville, New Jersey; *d*. 2 February 1994 in Camden, New Jersey), professional boxer who at age thirty-seven became the oldest fighter to win the sport's heavyweight championship title (1951), a record he retained until 1994.

Walcott was born Arnold Raymond Cream. His father, Joseph Arnold Cream, was an immigrant from the West Indian island of Barbados who worked as a laborer for the Pennsylvania Railroad. His mother, Ella Edna Amos, was a New Jersey native and homemaker. Walcott was the fifth of twelve children, and his father, who taught him the fundamentals of boxing, died when Walcott was fourteen. His formal education ended early, but he quickly acquired his pugilistic skills, later recalling that he and his pals "boxed up and down the street from morning to night. I fought as soon as I could walk. My father sparred open handed with me in the yard." Additionally, it was his father who impressed upon him the first commandment of the fight game: outsmart the other guy first.

By age eighteen Walcott was married to Lydia Talton, the daughter of a Baptist minister, with whom he had six children. Economic hardship befell Walcott early in the Great Depression years. After a variety of odd jobs (in a road crew, a soup factory, and an ice and coal truck), and after being forced to accept federal assistance, Walcott began to supplement his income by professional prizefighting. The local boxer Roxie Allen, impressed by Walcott's courage following a sparring session with him at Battling Mac's Gym in Camden, New Jersey, arranged for Walcott's professional debut. After knocking out Cowboy Wallace in the first round in Vineland, New Jersey, the underage Walcott (then sixteen) received $7.50 for his efforts. He adopted a new name in memory of his father's boyhood hero, Joe Walcott, the "Barbados Demon," a turn-of-the-century welterweight champion (1901–1906). "Jersey Joe" Walcott would run off a string of twelve consecutive victories, all in preliminary bouts, before suffering his initial setback.

Jack Blackburn, who later gained fame as the trainer of Joe Louis, recruited Walcott for his stable of Philadelphia-area fighters. Under Blackburn's tutelage, Walcott's distinctive cagey, deceptive style emerged. He learned his trademark step-back right-hand lead from Blackburn, whereby he feinted turning away only to pivot and "sneak in" a right-hand punch. Walcott fought a scant seven bouts from 1939 through the mid-1940s and later recalled that he was a "hungry fighter who took matches for coffee and cake" and was repeatedly refused bouts, as promoters told him "all-Dixie" cards sold few tickets. During World War II Walcott was employed as a "calker and chipper" at the Camden shipyard and also as a sparring partner for the new heavyweight champion, the "Brown Bomber," Joe Louis.

In 1945 and 1946 Walcott scored impressive wins over top competition, including Curtis Sheppard, Joe Baksi, Lee Oma, the second-ranked contender Jimmy Bivins, and the

"Jersey Joe" Walcott. © BETTMANN/CORBIS

rugged Joey Maxim. Sportswriters began to clamor for a world title shot for Walcott, by then a seventeen-year ring veteran. His opportunity came on 5 December 1947 against the aging champion Joe Louis at the old Madison Square Garden in New York City. Originally scheduled as an exhibition fight, it was later made into a title bout. Walcott was so lightly regarded at the time that he was an overwhelming ten-to-one underdog. The fight has since entered the pantheon of legendary bouts. After flooring the champion twice in the early rounds with lightning right-hand leads, Walcott lost a controversial and widely unpopular split decision. Sportswriter James P. Dawson noted in the *New York Times* that although the champ "retained his title, Louis was nearer dethronement than he had ever been in his ten-year reign as the world's premier boxer"; furthermore, "he was outmaneuvered, at times outboxed, always outthought, and generally made to look foolish." After the final bell rang, Louis, under the impression he had relinquished his title belt, fled the ring. He returned to learn that he had won and was overheard apologizing to his former sparring partner, "I'm sorry, Joe."

The legendary sports columnist Jimmy Cannon was quoted lamenting that if the "winner had not been a beloved American icon, the outrageous decision would have prompted a congressional investigation." Under instruc-

tions, Walcott had backpedaled the final two rounds, claiming, "they told me in my corner that I was way ahead and that all I had to do to win was to avoid any risk in the last round. If I had thought it was as close as it turned out, I'd have traded punch for punch in the fifteenth." Don Dunphy, the great ringside announcer, later mused on Walcott's retreating strategy: "It made me recall the criticism Billy Conn had received for mixing it up with Louis in the last couple of rounds. He'd lost. Walcott was criticized for not mixing it up and he lost, too." Walcott would lose another decision when his appeal to the New York State Athletic Commission was rejected within the week. In a June 1948 rematch at Yankee Stadium, Louis knocked out Walcott in the eleventh round and then retired from the ring.

In June 1949 Ezzard Charles defeated Walcott by decision in Chicago to capture the vacant National Boxing Association (NBA) heavyweight throne. In March 1951 he again defeated Walcott via decision, this time in Detroit. The boxing fraternity was puzzled over the announcement of a third Charles-Walcott bout, and the event took on the name the "Why Fight?" Why, wondered commentators, was Walcott receiving a fifth shot at a title that had eluded him in four previous attempts? Walcott's twenty-one-year dream came true on 18 July 1951 at Forbes Field in Pittsburgh. There he vindicated himself with a ferocious left hook to Charles's jaw that dropped the champ for the ten count. A six-to-one underdog prior to the fight, Walcott rewrote the record books with this historic victory. At the age of thirty-seven years and six months, he became the oldest man to win the heavyweight title; the former oldest titleholder was Ruby Bob Fitzsimmons, who was thirty-five when he leveled Gentleman Jim Corbett in Carson City, Nevada, in 1897. The following June, Walcott successfully defended his title, beating Charles by decision in Philadelphia.

Walcott's next title defense came against the wild-swinging and undefeated Rocky Marciano in an epic battle in Philadelphia's Municipal Stadium. The writer A. J. Liebling referred to the September 1952 struggle as "one of the stubbornest matches ever fought by heavyweights." In a bout that Marciano later said was the toughest of his career, Walcott dropped the young challenger in the opening round with his patented left hook; this was the first knockdown suffered by Marciano, the "Brockton Blockbuster," in forty-three fights. Dominating the bout and way ahead on points, Walcott seemed a certain winner by the late rounds. However, in what some ring historians consider the most famous right-hand punch in boxing history, Marciano's short, straight blow landed flush on the aging champion's jaw and Walcott crumbled to the ring floor, out cold. The epic thirteen-round fight is still considered one of the greatest title bouts of all time. Walcott retired from the ring after Marciano scored a first-round knockout in a rematch in Chicago the next year.

During his checkered career, Walcott, the superb ring technician and crafty counterpuncher, fought sixty-seven times for pay. He won thirty by knockout, eighteen by decision, and one by foul; he dropped eleven decisions, was knocked out six times, and fought one draw. He continues to hold the dubious distinction of having lost six heavyweight championship bouts, the most of any fighter in history. In 1994, forty-five-year-old George Foreman eclipsed Walcott's record as the oldest heavyweight champion by defeating Michael Moorer in Las Vegas for the crown.

Although Walcott earned over $1 million in purses, he lost most of it through poor investing. He was awarded the Edward J. Neil Trophy in 1951 as fighter of the year, and was elected to both the Ring Hall of Fame (1969) and the International Boxing Hall of Fame (1990). Overcoming his humble beginnings, Walcott was the picture of perseverance. A devout Christian, he credited his ring longevity to never having smoked or drunk alcohol. In addition, Philadelphia fight promoter J. Russell Peltz stated that Walcott endured hardships while overcoming racism, claiming, "he accepted a lot of what the black fighters had to accept . . . back in those days, it was like the Negro Leagues in baseball before Jackie Robinson. Black fighters had to fight among themselves. There were the occasional breakthrough like Joe Louis, but most of them never made it out of what was called the Chitlin' Circuit."

After his retirement, Walcott appeared in another role for which he is remembered, presiding as the referee in a bizarre ring spectacle: the March 1965 Muhammad Ali–Sonny Liston title rematch in Lewiston, Maine. In front of 2,400 fans in a converted high school hockey rink, Ali dropped Liston with what many ringside observers claimed to be a "phantom" punch in the first round. Ali, refusing to go to a neutral corner, delayed the start of the ten count over the fallen former champion. Walcott was startled and confused. He let the fight resume, but Nat Fleisher, publisher of *Ring* magazine, called out from his ringside seat that Liston had been down for the ten count. Subsequently, Walcott halted the contest and pandemonium ensued. The infamous fight has been shrouded in a cloud of controversy ever since.

In the 1980s Walcott became chairman of the New Jersey State Athletic Commission and, later, sheriff of Camden County, New Jersey, becoming the first African American to hold that position. Walcott died as a result of complications from diabetes at age eighty at Our Lady of Lourdes Medical Center in Camden. He is buried at the Sunset Memorial Park in Pennsauken, New Jersey. He was survived by all six of his children and many grandchildren.

★

Current Biography 1949 traces Walcott's childhood and early career. Bert Randolph Sugar, *100 Years of Boxing* (1982), and Jeffrey T. Sammons, *Beyond the Ring: The Role of Boxing in American Society* (1988), offer historical insights, biographical detail, and expert analysis. *Don Dunphy at Ringside* (1988) offers a breezy account of the Louis and Marciano fights by an expert ring analyst. The *New York Times* provides detailed and useful round-by-round accounts of his title fights against Joe Louis (6 Dec. 1947) and Ezzard Charles (19 July 1951). Numerous tributes appeared in various issues of the *Camden Courier-Post* following his funeral. There is an obituary in the *New York Times* (27 Feb. 1994).

JEFFREY S. ROSEN

WALKER, Junior (*b.* 14 June 1931, also stated as 1938 and 1942, in Blytheville, Arkansas; *d.* 23 November 1995 in Battle Creek, Michigan), the most influential and accessible rhythm-and-blues tenor saxophonist of the mid-1960s.

The childhood of Walker, born Oscar G. Mixon, is shrouded less in secrecy than it is in anonymity. His early childhood in southern Arkansas surely exposed him to the rich musical milieu of the South during the 1940s, including swing, blues, zydeco, New Orleans jazz, bluegrass, and country music

By the age of fourteen, Walker had moved with his mother, whose name is unknown, to South Bend, Indiana. During this time, he went by the name Autry De Walt. In South Bend, he met a saxophonist named George Mason, who ran a local jam session every Sunday. Walker attended frequently as a listener. When the band did not show up one Sunday, Mason offered an eager young Walker some free sax lessons, using the traditional call-and-response style of 1940s rhythm and blues. Mason would play a few notes on the tenor, and Walker would learn to repeat them on Mason's alto saxophone. Walker learned quickly—perhaps too quickly, because Mason abruptly suspended the lessons. Walker had to give back the borrowed alto, but he would never give up his love for the saxophone, which he always called the "crooked horn."

Walker's uncle, whose name is also unrecorded, was a retired saxophone player in Chicago. While visiting South Bend, the uncle gave him his old tenor saxophone. Within a year, Walker was playing nights with a local band in South Bend's juke joints, while working construction during the day.

Walker's mother arranged for a family trip to Elkhart, Indiana, the center for America's brass instrument manufacturing. The sole purpose of the trip was to allow her son to pick out a professional instrument. That handpicked saxophone remained Walker's favorite horn for all his life, so much so that he later had it gold-plated. By 1958 Walker

Junior Walker *(standing)* and the All Stars. FRANK DRIGGS COLLECTION/ARCHIVE PHOTOS

had started a bar band with his friend, drummer Billy Nicks. They called themselves the Jumping Jacks, then the Stix Nix. They moved to Battle Creek, Michigan. During this time, he changed his performing name to Junior Walker. Soon he assumed musical leadership of a struggling quartet, the original All Stars, which consisted of Walker on tenor sax and vocals, James Graves on drums, Willie Woods on guitar, and Vic Thomas on organ. By 1962 they were appearing at El Grotto in Battle Creek, a local bastion of soul music filtering up from the Memphis studios and clubs.

It was Johnny Bristol, a local singer and future Motown Records artist, who introduced Walker to a young Detroit producer, Harvey Fuqua, who agreed to record Walker on one of his microlabels, Harvey Records. Motown chief Berry Gordy soon purchased Fuqua's companies, as Motown Records rapidly expanded. Gordy released Walker's singles on a then-obscure Motown subsidiary label, Soul Records.

Walker's first attempt with Motown was a dance-craze song he wrote called "Shotgun." With little initial promotion, it quickly soared to the number-one position on the rhythm-and-blues charts, and then crossed over to number four on the pop charts. Between 1965 and 1972 Junior Walker and the All Stars enjoyed consistent studio success, placing fourteen songs in the R&B Top Twenty,

with eight of those crossing over to the Pop Top Twenty. At Motown's urging, the legendary bassist James Jemerson contributed his brilliantly crafted lines to many of Walker's recordings.

Despite his reluctance to sing—he once said, "I prefer playing to singing, 'cause I can't sing"—nearly all of Walker's mid-period Motown recordings featured his raspy vocals, in peculiar counterpoint to his soaring sax lines. Motown's producers insisted on adding string orchestras and background choruses into later All Stars recordings. Walker grew discouraged. Perhaps he felt that his rough-hewn, authentic music was becoming gentrified. Moreover, despite his success, Walker and his artistic vision were increasingly ignored by Motown, although he was the only instrumentalist at that label to record under his personal name rather than a group's.

Walker left Motown for a new label, Whitfield Records, in 1979 but was unsuccessful. In 1981 he soloed on the hit "Urgent" by the rock group Foreigner. Two years later, Walker signed again with Motown, now incorporating his son, Autry De Walt, Jr., into the All Stars as a drummer.

Walker spent his last fifteen years as a musician doing what he truly did best, touring and playing to his soul- and dance-oriented public. On the road, it was just Walker and his All Stars—no complex production values or layered background vocals or sweetening strings. After a tour in

1994 with the Temptations and the Four Tops, Walker weakened noticeably. He died some months later of cancer. He is buried at Oak Hill Cemetery in Battle Creek, renamed yet again, memorialized in stone as Junior "Shot Gun" Walker Mixon.

Walker once philosophically summed up his career: "I'm a road runner . . . I travel, I blow some. People dance, and I like it." Walker's roots lay in the blues, and so his performances, unlike those of his jazz contemporaries, had only the simple intents of excitement, emphasis, and consonant virtuosity. His great accessibility influenced every blues and funk saxophonist who followed him. Equally important was the All Stars' driving, impulsive, almost reckless sound, emulated by Steve Winwood, Mitch Ryder, and Spencer Davis among others. Walker's energy and artistry bridged two styles of disaffected early 1960s protest music—the instrumental, predominantly white surf music style and the predominantly black soul music style. He did all this while enjoying the greatest popularity of any mid-1960s instrumentalist.

★

Obituaries are in the *New York Times* and *Los Angeles Times* (both 25 Nov. 1995), *Entertainment Weekly* (8 Dec. 1995), *Billboard* magazine (9 Dec. 1995), and *Jet* magazine (11 Dec. 1995).

JAMES MCELWAINE

WANDERONE, Rudolf. *See* Minnesota Fats.

WELLEK, René Maria Eduard (*b.* 22 August 1903 in Vienna, Austria; *d.* 10 November 1995 in Hamden, Connecticut), comparativist scholar, literary theorist, and historian.

Wellek was the oldest of the three children of Bronislav Wellek, a Czech lawyer in the civil service of the Austro-Hungarian Empire, and Gabriele von Zelewsky, the daughter of a West Prussian nobleman of Polish origin. He grew up in Vienna in a rich aesthetic and linguistic atmosphere—his father an ardent Czech nationalist, opera reviewer, and singer of lieder and his mother a cultured woman who spoke German, French, Italian, and English. Young Wellek read voraciously, not only adventure stories but also encyclopedias and histories of geography, science, warfare, religion, and literature. He started Latin at age ten and Greek at thirteen, but a lingering case of scarlet fever so disrupted his studies that in 1916 he transferred from the classical *Gymnasium* (secondary school) to the *Realgymnasium* (nonclassical secondary school), where he was allowed to substitute English for Greek.

After the collapse of the Austro-Hungarian Empire, the Welleks settled in Prague in early 1919, where the schoolboy identified with the new Czechoslovakia. Although this little country with Western sympathies was a cultural crossroads, no English was taught at the *Realgymnasium*. Wel-

lek's passion for learning and literature, however, compelled him to read English literature at home, particularly Shakespeare and the Romantics. In 1922 Wellek entered Charles University (the Czech University of Prague) to study Germanic philology. He enjoyed particularly Vilém Mathesius's lectures on English literary history. In 1924 and 1925, Wellek spent several weeks in England preparing his first thesis (on the Scottish essayist and historian Thomas Carlyle) and began as an undergraduate to publish his scholarship in Czech books and periodicals. After earning his doctorate in 1926, he spent several years in America, as a fellow at Princeton University and then as a German instructor, first at Smith College and later at Princeton.

Back at Charles University in the fall of 1930, Wellek completed his second thesis, *Immanuel Kant in England: 1793–1838* (1931), a book that revealed the English poet and critic Samuel Taylor Coleridge to be less original than eclectic. From 1930 to 1935 Wellek lived in Prague, taught English as a *Privatdozent* (a lecturer not the regular faculty), joined Mathesius's famous Prague Linguistic Circle, translated English novels into Czech, and continued to publish in Czech journals. In 1932 he married Olga Brodská, an elementary schoolteacher from Moravia; they had one child.

Critically surveying the Russian formalists, the Czech structuralists, and the Cambridge theorists I. A. Richards, F. R. Leavis, and William Empson, Wellek further developed his considerable skill in textual analysis, formulation of theory, and reasoned evaluation. Since prospects for a professorship at Prague seemed remote, he taught Czech language and literature from 1935 to 1939 at the University of London. His important early paper "Theory of Literary History" (1936) in *Travaux du Cercle Linguistique de Prague* argues against merely accumulating facts about literature and advocates concentrating on literary works themselves, on bridging the gap between content and form.

Although many of Wellek's views coincided with those of Leavis, in 1937 Wellek charged the English critic with theoretical deficiency, which prompted Leavis to counter that Wellek was less an intuitive critic than an abstract philosopher. In England, under the auspices of the Czech Ministry of Education, Wellek not only taught and worked on his survey of English literary history but also gave more than eighty talks in and around London in defense of Czechoslovakia. After Hitler's troops marched into Prague in the spring of 1939, the Third Reich naturally halted Wellek's salary. Accepting the invitation of Norman Foerster, the director of the School of Letters at the University of Iowa, to join the English Department as a lecturer on a one-year appointment, Wellek moved into a house in Iowa City with his wife on 1 September 1939—the day World War II broke out in Europe. Debate also broke out in American universities at that time between scholars and critics, between those who favored facts about literature and those who preferred ideas. This entire debate seemed to Wellek a false dilemma, as his *Rise of English Literary History* (1941), rich in historical facts and literary ideas, clearly showed. Sensing the limitations of both the old positivism and the new humanism, Wellek sided with the American "New Critics" William K. Wimsatt, Cleanth Brooks, Allen Tate, and Robert Penn Warren while he maintained his broader European perspectives. With one of his colleagues at Iowa, Austin Warren, Wellek decided to write a book stressing the nature, function, form, and content of literature as well as its relationship to neighboring but distinct disciplines.

As director of the Language and Area Program in Czech from 1943 to 1944, Wellek turned out interpreters for the U.S. Army. After the war he and his wife considered returning to Prague with their infant son, but instead Wellek became a naturalized American citizen in the spring of 1946 and professor of Slavic and comparative literature at Yale in the fall. Although Wellek and Warren's *Theory of Literature* (1949) was not conceived as a textbook, this work showing the interdependency of literature generally and of theory, history, and criticism particularly became a vade mecum for graduate students at home and abroad and an academic best-seller in more than a score of translations. Whatever their social and political convictions, students and teachers of literature the world over came to understand more fully that "a literary work of art is not a simple object but rather a highly complex organization of a stratified character with multiple meanings and relationships."

Wellek spent most of the next forty-six years of his scholarly life writing (and publishing between 1955 and 1992) his monumental *History of Modern Criticism: 1750–1950,* an eight-volume survey of French, German, English, Italian, Spanish, Russian, Eastern European, and American critical argument. In 1952 he became Sterling Professor of Comparative Literature at Yale, and in 1960 he was named chairman of the Department of Comparative Literature. For his sixtieth birthday, the Czechoslovak Society of Arts and Sciences in America published his key Czech writings in English, *Essays on Czech Literature* (1963). His essays in *Concepts of Criticism* (1963) define problems of method and periodization, set ideals, and measure results. His essays in *Confrontations* (1965) on the intellectual and literary relations among Germany, England, and the United States prompted the Harvard literary scholar-critic Howard Mumford Jones to remark, "Wellek is the most erudite man in America."

Following the 1967 death of his first wife, in 1968 Wellek married Nonna D. Shaw, a Russian émigré and professor of comparative literature. Like his other books, his fourth collection of essays, *Discriminations* (1970), is indispensable reading for students of literature. During this time, Wellek continued his duties at Yale as a teacher and administrator, an editor and board member of literary journals, an officer in national and international conferences, a visiting professor at major universities in America and Europe, and a recipient of sixteen honorary degrees from such universities as Oxford, Harvard, Rome, and Munich. Retiring from Yale in 1972 at age sixty-nine, Wellek trusted that the diversity of students who had passed through his department had at least two things in common: "devotion to scholarship and complete freedom to follow their own bent." While still at work on his massive *History of Criticism,* Wellek published *Four Critics* (1981)—his lectures on Benedetto Croce, Paul Valéry, György Lukács, and Roman Ingarden—and *The Attack on Literature and Other Writings* (1982), his rapier-like defense of the Western aesthetic and literary tradition against postmodern deconstruction. He spent his last years dictating the final volumes of his *History* in a retirement home in Hamden, Connecticut, where he died of natural causes at age ninety-two. He is buried in New Haven's Grove Street Cemetery.

Recognized even by his detractors as the most eminent and learned exponent of comparative literature in the world, the fair-minded and gentlemanly Wellek inspired a generation of literary scholars.

★

Wellek's personal library is at the University of California, Irvine. Bibliographies of his copious books, articles, and reviews are in his *Concepts of Criticism* (1963), *Discriminations* (1970), and *The Attack on Literature and Other Writings* (1982). His memoir, "My Early Life," appears in *Contemporary Authors Autobiography Series,* 7 (1975): 205–226. Martin Bucco, *René Wellek* (1981), is a full-length critical biography. Journal articles include Thomas G. Winner and John P. Kasik, "René Wellek's Contribution to American Literary Scholarship," *Forum* 2 (1977): 21–31; Martin Bucco, "Profile of a Contemporary: René Wellek," *Wordsworth Circle,* 9 (1978), 269–274; Sarah Lawall, "René Wellek and Modern Literary Criticism," *Comparative Literature,* 40 (1988): 3–28; Peter Demetz, "Third Conversation with René Wellek," *Cross Currents: A Yearbook of Central European Culture* 11 (1992): 79–92. Joseph P. Strelka edited the two-volume *Literary Theory and Criticism: Festschrift in Honor of René Wellek* (1948). An obituary is in the *New York Times* (16 Feb. 1995).

MARTIN BUCCO

WEST, Cromwell Ashbie Hawkins. *See* Red Thunder Cloud.

WHITTEN, Jamie Lloyd (*b.* 18 April 1910 in Cascilla, Mississippi; *d.* 9 September 1995 in Oxford, Mississippi), Democratic congressman who set the record for length of service in the U.S. House of Representatives, who opposed the environmental movement, and who played a major role in shaping U.S. agricultural policies.

The older of the two children of Alymer Guy Whitten, a farmer and country-store owner, and Nettie Viola Early, Whitten grew up in rural Mississippi. He entered the University of Mississippi in 1927 but left after two years to become principal of a school in his home county at the age of nineteen. He returned to the university in 1930 to study law, but withdrew again after one year and ran successfully for the state legislature. Apparently one year of legal studies was sufficient, for he passed the state bar examination after his first year in the legislature.

In 1933 Whitten was elected district attorney for five counties. On 20 June 1940 he married Rebecca Thompson. They had a son and a daughter.

Whitten's long congressional career began with victory in a 1941 special election to fill an unexpired term. He joined the Democratic majority in the House of Representatives shortly before the Japanese bombing of Pearl Harbor in December 1941. He won reelection twenty-six times, establishing a record for years of service in the House before his retirement in 1995 after over fifty-three years on Capitol Hill.

Jamie L. Whitten. ASSOCIATED PRESS AP

In Congress, Whitten became a strong advocate of federal spending for agriculture, defense, and public works. Reflecting on his years in Washington toward the end of his career, Whitten attributed the prosperity of the United States to the policy of "meeting local problems with national policies." As a member of the budget-writing House Appropriations Committee, he was in a position to impact spending priorities for virtually all of his career.

The congressional seniority system, which awarded power to the longest-serving members of the majority party, combined with Whitten's remarkable political skills to make him one of Washington's most powerful individuals. Serving as chairman of the Agriculture Subcommittee of the House Appropriations Committee from 1949 to 1992 (except for 1953–1954, when the Republicans constituted the majority in the House), Whitten became widely known as "the permanent secretary of agriculture" because of his perennial influence over agriculture policies and the U.S. Department of Agriculture. He used his power to maintain the policies initiated under the New Deal, including crop subsidies, soil conservation programs, agricultural research, and rural infrastructure development.

Whitten viewed the environmental movement as a threat to American agriculture. Responding to Rachel Carson's groundbreaking attack on pesticides in her book *Silent Spring* (1962), he authored a book entitled *That We May Live*, published in 1966. In it, he argued that agricultural chemicals are essential to maintaining an abundant supply of food, and that environmental harm can be minimized through common-sense management. The book attracted scant notice, and most copies were bought by the agricultural chemical industry, which had supplied crucial assistance to Whitten in writing it.

As the Democratic Party embraced environmentalism, consumer rights, civil rights, and social welfare in the 1960s and 1970s, Whitten found himself increasingly marginalized within his party. An opponent of civil rights for the first half of his congressional career, Whitten began to modify his position only after the Voting Rights Act of 1965 enfranchised the large African-American minority in his district. In 1969 Whitten was savagely portrayed by journalist Nick Kotz as an inhumane racist willing to let the black agricultural workers of his district go hungry rather than permit the federal government to provide adequate food for them. Kotz contended that Whitten limited participation in the food stamp program to those who could pay and prevented government-sponsored investigations of the extent of hunger.

Whitten's marginalization within his party invited challenges to his power. The Democratic sweep in the post-Watergate election of 1974 brought a large number of reform-minded Democrats into the House of Representatives. The reformers set out to remake the House, and they achieved a notable victory when they won the right to elect committee and subcommittee chairmen by secret ballot. But when the reformers attempted to remove Whitten from his subcommittee chairmanship, old-fashioned political compromise saved his position: in a negotiated settlement, Whitten agreed to give up his subcommittee's recently acquired jurisdiction over environmental and consumer policy in exchange for retention of the chairmanship.

After this close call, Whitten began to reposition himself closer to the center of the congressional Democratic Party. "Conditions change," he told a reporter. "You go with conditions as they are, not like what they used to be." As he moved toward his party's center, Whitten revived his influence and began a climb that would take him to the zenith of his power.

In 1979 Whitten, who had almost lost his subcommittee chairmanship four years earlier, was elected chairman of the full Appropriations Committee. From his new post he was in a position to assist other members of Congress with the federal projects they wanted for their districts, and he used his power to aid former foes as well as friends with public works projects. Former Speaker of the House Tom Foley declared that "he has probably helped just about every member of this House with some special local need." He took care of his own district with agricultural subsidies, roads, health clinics, and federally financed research projects. His most notable public works achievement was the $1.8 billion Tennessee-Tombigbee Waterway, which created a barge route from the Tennessee River to the Gulf of Mexico, much of it running through Whitten's Mississippi district.

Health problems diminished Whitten's political effectiveness after he passed the age of eighty, and new members of the House became less inclined to accept his idiosyncrasies. When he had trouble conducting committee meetings and managing legislation on the floor after a rumored stroke, the Democratic caucus took away his committee and subcommittee chairmanships in 1992. In 1994 Whitten announced that he would not be a candidate for a twenty-eighth term. He and his wife left Washington for Charleston, Mississippi, in December 1994. He lived only nine months after his retirement. Death came from complications of chronic cardiac and renal disease. He is buried in Charleston's City Cemetery.

Whitten was a master of politics behind closed doors. When he found it necessary to bring legislative proposals to the light of public scrutiny, he skillfully resorted to vague language, mumbled speech, and strategic memory lapses to keep journalists and opponents off-balance. A master practitioner of traditional congressional politics, Whitten dominated agricultural policy for four decades. He assured a flow of federal dollars to his own district and built alliances by helping other members of the House with funding for their public works projects. Secure with his constituency,

Whitten slowly but successfully adapted to changes in Congress and the nation until his health undermined his capacity to fulfill his duties.

★

Whitten donated his papers to the University of Mississippi. Published accounts of his congressional career tend to portray him in an unfavorable light. These include Nick Kotz's *Let Them Eat Promises: The Politics of Hunger in America* (1969), a portion of which was reprinted as "Jamie Whitten: Permanent Secretary of Agriculture" in *Inside the System: A Washington Monthly Reader* (1970); as well as Anne Millet's *Jamie L. Whitten, Democratic Representative from Mississippi* (1972), part of the multivolume *Citizens Look at Congress,* prepared by the Ralph Nader Congress Project. An adulatory article, "Celebration of a Life Devoted to Public Service," was published in *Appalachia: Journal of the Appalachian Regional Commission* (winter 1992). The Mississippi Department of Archives and History in Jackson has a subject file on Whitten, consisting primarily of newspaper articles. An obituary is in the *New York Times* (10 Sept. 1995).

VAGN K. HANSEN

WIESNER, Jerome Bert (*b.* 30 May 1915 in Detroit, Michigan; *d.* 21 October 1994 in Watertown, Massachusetts), science adviser to President John F. Kennedy, president of the Massachusetts Institute of Technology (MIT), and outspoken advocate of nuclear arms control.

Wiesner, the son of Joseph Wiesner and Ida Freedman, dry goods shopkeepers in Dearborn, Michigan, was an inventive boy who worked throughout his youth selling newspapers, caddying at the local golf course, and tending bar. Always interested in technical systems, he once constructed his own telephone network to communicate with his friends in the community. He attended the public schools in Dearborn and graduated in 1932 from Fordson High School. He then enrolled in Michigan State Normal College in Ypsilanti before transferring to the University of Michigan at Ann Arbor, where he received a B.S. in electrical engineering in 1937. He continued at the University of Michigan and earned an M.Sc., also in electrical engineering, in 1938.

While still a student in Ann Arbor, Wiesner served as associate director of the University of Michigan's radio station. He also worked in the speech department developing electronic systems to aid in speech therapies, and he taught radio techniques each summer at the National Music Camp in Interlochen, Michigan. Wiesner remained at the University of Michigan until 1940, when he accepted a position as chief engineer of the acoustical and record laboratory at the Library of Congress, where he worked on sound recording preservation projects. Also in 1940 Wies-

Jerome Wiesner *(far left)* with colleagues at the Massachusetts Institute of Technology Research Laboratory of Electronics, 1948. ASSOCIATED PRESS MIT

ner married Laya Wainger; they had four children. Among his interesting activities with the Library of Congress, he traveled with the folklorists John Lomax and Alan Lomax to record folk songs in 1941.

As it did for many other scientists of Wiesner's generation, World War II defined the trajectory of Wiesner's career. In 1942 Wiesner joined the radiation laboratory at MIT, which was then engaged in top secret research on radar for the military. Because of his background in sound recording he proved invaluable in developing large, airborne early-warning radar systems. Later, in 1945 and 1946, Wiesner worked with the University of California's Los Alamos National Laboratory to develop instruments for the Bikini Atoll atomic bomb tests.

In the fall of 1946 Wiesner returned to MIT as an assistant professor of engineering. At the same time he pursued a Ph.D. at the University of Michigan, and he received both his degree and a full professorship at MIT in 1950. He spent the 1950s on the faculty at MIT and in 1952 he also began directing the Lincoln Laboratory.

During this period Wiesner's reputation for honesty, good sense, and moral vigor rose. He was increasingly called upon to assist national leaders in setting science and technology policy. Two areas especially sparked his involvement. The first was nuclear weapons and the deterrence theory current during the cold war with the Soviet Union. Wiesner favored a strong military capability for the United States but always argued for joint efforts to limit the number of nuclear warheads available to both sides. He be-

lieved, as he said in 1958, that a nuclear arms race results "in less security, not more, with each passing year." He asked the two rivals to maintain only "sufficient nuclear deterrence to provide protection . . . but not enough military power to assure the success of a surprise attack." Accordingly Wiesner participated in the Geneva summit of 1958 and the Pugwash conference of 1960, in both cases arguing in favor of strategic arms limitations. Wiesner had a significant impact on the Kennedy administration in the early 1960s, and the resulting Nuclear Test Ban Treaty of 1963 between the United States and the Soviet Union was an important early step toward strategic arms limitations.

The second area in which Wiesner played an especially important role was in the cold war rivalry in space flight. At the time of the Soviet successes of *Sputnik* in October 1957, President Dwight D. Eisenhower asked Wiesner to serve on a special science advisory committee charged with revamping the federal government's oversight of critical science and technology development efforts. Wiesner advocated the creation of the National Aeronautics and Space Administration (NASA) in 1958 and the consolidation of nonmilitary space flight activities under its leadership.

When President John F. Kennedy was preparing to take office in late 1960 he appointed an ad hoc committee headed by Wiesner to offer suggestions for American efforts in space. Wiesner, who later headed the President's Science Advisory Committee (PSAC) under Kennedy, concluded that the issue of "national prestige" was too great to allow the Soviet Union to lead the world in space efforts, therefore the United States had to enter the field in a substantive way. "Space exploration and exploits," he wrote in a 10 January 1961 report to the president-elect, "have captured the imagination of the peoples of the world. During the next few years the prestige of the United States will in part be determined by the leadership we demonstrate in space activities." Wiesner also emphasized the importance of practical nonmilitary applications of space technology, such as in communications, mapping, and weather satellites, and the necessity of keeping up the effort to exploit space for national security through such technologies as intercontinental ballistic missiles (ICBMs) and reconnaissance satellites. He tended to deemphasize the human space flight initiative for practical reasons. American launch vehicle technology, he argued, was not well developed, and the potential of placing an astronaut in space before the Soviets was slim. He thought human space flight was a high-risk enterprise with a low chance of success. Human space flight was also less likely to yield valuable scientific results, and the United States, Wiesner thought, should play to its strengths in space science where important results had already been achieved.

Kennedy only accepted part of what Wiesner recommended. The president was committed to conducting a vigorous space program and was more interested in human space flight than either his predecessor or his science adviser. This was partly because of the drama surrounding Project Mercury and the seven astronauts NASA was training. Wiesner had cautioned Kennedy about the hyperbole associated with human space flight. "Indeed, by having placed the highest national priority on the MERCURY program we have strengthened the popular belief that man in space is the most important aim for our non-military space effort," Wiesner wrote. "The manner in which this program has been publicized in our press has further crystallized such belief." Kennedy, nevertheless, recognized the tremendous public support arising from this program and wanted to ensure that it reflected favorably upon his administration.

Kennedy went further than Wiesner believed was warranted when, on 25 May 1961, he announced that the United States would land an American on the Moon by the end of the decade. Project Apollo became the vehicle for carrying out this mandate. Wiesner questioned implementing this decision, even after the commitment had been announced. For example, he objected to the inherent risk to the crew of the lunar-orbit rendezvous mode for conducting Apollo operations, the eventual method used to carry out the landings with a command module in orbit around the Moon while a small lander went to the surface. Responding to Wiesner's opposition, the NASA administrator backpedaled and stated that the decision was tentative and NASA would sponsor further studies.

The issue reached a climax at the Marshall Space Flight Center in September 1962, when President Kennedy, Wiesner, NASA administrator James E. Webb, and several other Washington figures visited Wernher von Braun. As the entourage viewed a mock-up of the massive *Saturn V* Moon rocket during a photo opportunity for the media, Kennedy nonchalantly mentioned to Braun, "I understand you and Jerry disagree about the right way to go to the moon." Braun acknowledged this disagreement, but when Wiesner began to explain his concern, Webb, who had been quiet until this point, began to argue with him "for being on the wrong side of the issue." The mode decision had been an uninteresting technical issue before, but thereafter it was a political concern hashed over in the press for days. The science adviser to the British prime minister Harold Macmillan had accompanied Wiesner on the trip, and he later asked Kennedy how the debate would turn out. The president responded that Wiesner would lose, "Webb's got all the money, and Jerry's only got me." Kennedy was right. Webb lined up political support in Washington for the lunar-orbit rendezvous mode and announced it as a final decision on 7 November 1962.

One other area of Wiesner's influence relative to Kennedy's policies on space flight was his efforts to make Project Apollo a joint mission with the Soviets. Rather than compete with the Soviet Union, Wiesner emphasized the possibilities of cooperation and thereby lessening cold war tensions. Indeed in the weeks preceding the Apollo decision the Kennedy administration quietly assessed the Soviet leadership's inclinations toward a cooperative approach to human space exploration. Although these "back channel" efforts did not produce any space agreements, the fact that President Kennedy pursued this track while simultaneously considering a competitive approach signified a newly appreciated depth to Kennedy's political acumen. The president publicly spoke about cooperating in space with the Soviets several times before May 1961, and afterward he pursued various forms of space cooperation, culminating less than a month before his death in 1963 with a call before the United Nations for a joint lunar mission. At every point Wiesner urged him to pursue such a cooperative strategy.

After the assassination of President Kennedy on 22 November 1963 Wiesner resigned from government service and returned to MIT. He became dean of the MIT School of Science in 1964 and provost in 1966. After the briefest of tenures as provost, he became president of MIT later in 1966 and served for nine years. A founding member of the International Foundation for the Survival and Development of Humanity, Wiesner retired from public life in 1975. He died of heart failure at his home.

★

A collection of Wiesner's papers is at the Massachusetts Institute of Technology in Boston. Another sizable collection of Wiesner materials is in the Kennedy Presidential Library in Boston. His autobiography is *Where Science and Politics Meet* (1965). For his role advocating nuclear disarmament see Abram Chayes and Jerome B. Wiesner, eds., *ABM: An Evaluation of the Decision to Deploy an Antiballistic Missile System* (1969). Wiesner's role as presidential science adviser is chronicled in James Everett Katz, *Presidential Politics and Science Policy* (1978); William T. Goldman, ed., *Science Advice to the President* (1980); W. Henry Lambright, *Presidential Management of Science and Technology* (1985); Goldman, ed., *Science and Technology Advice to the President, Congress, and Judiciary* (1988); and Gregg Herken, *Cardinal Choices: Presidential Science Advising from the Atomic Bomb to SDI* (1992). Obituaries are in the *New York Times* and the *Washington Post* (both 23 Oct. 1994).

ROGER D. LAUNIUS

WIGNER, Eugene Paul (*b.* 17 November 1902 in Budapest, Hungary, *d.* 1 January 1995 in Princeton, New Jersey), mathematical physicist who made numerous pioneering contributions to quantum mechanics and fundamental nuclear theory, for which he received the Nobel Prize in physics in 1963.

Eugene Paul (Jenó Pál in the Hungarian) Wigner was born in Budapest, the second of three children, to Anthony Wigner and Elizabeth Einhorn. His father ran a leather-making factory and both parents put a strong emphasis on education for their children. While attending Budapest Lutheran High School, Wigner was especially interested in physics and mathematics; however, after his high school graduation in 1920, practical concerns led him to enroll as a chemical engineering student at the Berlin Technische Hochschule (Institute of Technology) in Germany. He received an undergraduate degree in 1924 and a Ph.D. in chemical engineering in 1925 under the direction of another Hungarian scientist, Michael Polányi.

He returned to Budapest for one year to work in a leather-tanning factory but returned to Berlin in 1926 to take a post as a research assistant at the Technische Hochschule. This association began his first important exposure to the new field of quantum physics. Employing his exceptional mathematical aptitude he began exploring how group theory, a classical study first developed in the nineteenth century by the Norwegian mathematician Sophus Lie, might be applied to quantum mechanics. As the result of this work, Wigner was invited by the great German mathematician David Hilbert to join him at the University of Göttingen. At Göttingen, Wigner conducted his early investigations into the significant connection between rules of mathematical symmetry and corresponding conservation laws of physics—a connection that decisively influenced quantum mechanics and the growing understanding of nuclear structure.

In 1928 Wigner returned to the Technische Hochschule

Eugene Paul Wigner. ARCHIVE PHOTOS

as a lecturer, staying until 1930, when he emigrated to the United States to accept a position as an instructor in physics at Princeton University in New Jersey. Most of Wigner's career was spent in Princeton. During the period 1936–1938 he joined the University of Wisconsin as professor of physics. He returned to Princeton in 1938 and was named the Thomas D. Jones Professor of Mathematical Physics at the Palmer Physical Laboratories. Along with many other scientists during World War II, Wigner departed from his academic activities to apply himself to military research. Wigner was among the chief theoreticians under the leadership of Enrico Fermi in achieving the first nuclear chain reaction. Fermi, an Italian physicist with an extraordinary combination of abilities in both theoretical and experimental physics, had left his native country in 1938 because of the jeopardy he felt his Jewish wife could encounter under Benito Mussolini's fascist dictatorship.

The chain reaction was accomplished with a natural uranium-fueled, graphite-moderated assembly (an "atomic pile") in a squash court under the west stands of Stagg football field at the University of Chicago on 2 December 1942. The scientific team then sent a coded telephone message to the administration in Washington, D.C.: "the Italian navigator has just landed in the new world." Wigner toasted Fermi with a celebratory bottle of Chianti wine but later recalled in a more serious vein: "For some time we had known that we were about to unlock a giant. Still we could not escape an eerie feeling when we knew we had actually done it. We felt as I presume everyone feels who has done something that he knows will have far-reaching consequences which he cannot foresee."

This milestone in nuclear science—indeed in the history of mankind—had its origin in an earlier event in which Wigner had played a pivotal role. While in Berlin in the 1920s, Wigner had become friends with fellow scientists from Hungary, Leo Szilard and Edward Teller. At different times they each emigrated along with many other scientists from a Europe that was becoming dominated by Hitler, threatening the livelihood, freedom, and lives of Jews, intellectuals, and political adversaries. Szilard was the first to recognize the potentially serious problem created by the discovery of neutron-induced fission in the element uranium by the German chemists Otto Hahn, Fritz Strassman, and the Austrian-Jewish physicist Lise Meitner.

In 1939 Szilard enlisted Wigner and Teller to discuss the threat of an atomic bomb with Albert Einstein. They felt that only Einstein had sufficient prestige and influence to convey the urgency of the serious problem to President Franklin Delano Roosevelt. Einstein understood the problem at once and immediately signed the letter prepared by the Hungarian immigrants. Though Einstein played no subsequent role in atomic bomb development, his message to Roosevelt is regarded as the catalyst that led to the massive Manhattan Project, which resulted in the successful development of the uranium bomb that devastated Hiroshima on 6 August 1945 and the plutonium weapon that struck Nagasaki three days later, ending World War II.

Although Wigner, Szilard, and Teller had started the program and contributed importantly to technical phases of building the nuclear weapons subsequently used against Japan, they ultimately urged that the bomb not be used. They expressed their objections to the Hiroshima bombing in the form of a petition (written by Szilard) that received the signatures of sixty-seven other Manhattan Project scientists. The administration of Harry S. Truman nonetheless decided to drop the bomb.

From 1946 to 1948, before returning to Princeton, Wigner was director of research and development at the Clinton Laboratories in Oak Ridge, Tennessee (later to become Oak Ridge National Laboratory), a group of four hundred scientists and technical staff engaged in research and development under government contract. At the time, the reactors at the site were the principal source of radioactive isotopes for use in fundamental atomic research and for human applications in medical diagnosis using tracers and therapy in the treatment of cancer.

On 13 December 1963 Wigner shared the Nobel Prize in physics with Maria Goeppert Mayer and J. Hans D. Jensen for their separate discoveries in the theory of the nucleus and fundamental atomic particles. Unlike most Nobel scientific awards, which are generally given for unique single discoveries or inventions, the award to Wigner recognized his contributions to many different areas of nuclear physics over a period beginning in the late 1920s and extending for more than three decades.

Among Wigner's accomplishments was the recognition that symmetry principles explained patterns found in atomic and molecular spectra. Wigner's analysis of the application of mathematical group theory enabled physicists to understand relative stability or instability of nuclear isotopes having the same number of protons in the nucleus but different neutron numbers. Nearly a decade after he was awarded the Nobel Prize, Wigner's early group theory research was described as so farsighted that it was not immediately recognized for its importance as a pioneering advance in mathematical physics.

Interestingly referenced in the Nobel Prize presentation to Wigner was his law of the conservation of parity developed at Göttingen in 1928. The parity law states that particles emitted during a physical process should emanate from the left and right in equal numbers or equivalently that a nuclear process should be indistinguishable from its mirror image. The parity concept was not challenged until 1956 when it was disproved in certain so-called "weak decay" interactions in experiments by Tsung-Dao Lee of Columbia and Chen Ning Yang of Princeton. Lee and Yang were awarded the Nobel Prize in 1957 for their empirical refutation of Wigner's parity theory in this special case. The theory however remained substantially intact and along with other of Wigner's discoveries useful as a further guide in nuclear research.

Several aspects of Wigner's career outside of pure physics caused significant controversy. In the 1960s he pursued methods of protection against nuclear weapons effects which presumed that nuclear war might be survivable if suitable civil defense measures were taken. The advent of hydrogen bombs a thousand times more powerful than the atomic weapons employed against Japan made the defense measures advocated by Wigner questionable. Wigner also found himself among the minority of scientists who defended Edward Teller's critical testimony in a loyalty hearing that was influential in leading to J. Robert Oppenheimer, the scientific head of the Manhattan Project, losing his government secret security clearance in 1954. Wigner's public defense of Teller was more a case of personal confidence and trust in his long-time friend, rather than Wigner's own doubts about Oppenheimer's loyalty.

In 1936 Wigner married Amelia Z. Frank, who died in 1937. That year Wigner became a naturalized citizen of the

United States. In 1941 he married Mary Annette Wheeler, a professor of physics at Vassar College in Poughkeepsie, New York. They had two children. After his second wife's death in 1977, he married Eileen Hamilton in 1979, and they had a daughter. Wigner retired as professor emeritus from Princeton in 1971. He died of pneumonia at the age of ninety-two at the Medical Center in Princeton.

Along with the Nobel Prize, he was the recipient of honorary doctorate degrees from Princeton and twenty-six other colleges and universities in the United States, Europe, and Israel. In 1958 he received the U.S. Atomic Energy Commission Enrico Fermi Award and in 1972 the Albert Einstein Award. In 1990 he became the first recipient of the American Nuclear Society Award designated thereafter the Eugene P. Wigner Award. That same year, after the fall of the communist government in his native Hungary, he received the Order of the Banner of the Republic with Rubies, followed in 1994 by Hungary's highest honor, the Order of Merit "as an acknowledgment of his scientific career and of his outstanding achievements in the enrichment of universal human values." In his 1960 paper "The Unreasonable Effectiveness of Mathematics in the Natural Sciences," Wigner explained the importance of mathematics:

> The miracle of the appropriateness of the language of mathematics for the formulation of the laws of physics is a wonderful gift which we neither understand nor deserve. We should be grateful for it and hope that it will remain valid in future research and that it will extend, for better or for worse, to our pleasure even though perhaps also to our bafflement, to wide branches of learning.

★

The Eugene Paul Wigner Papers are held at Princeton University's library. His writings are being compiled in the eight-volume *Collected Works of Eugene Paul Wigner* (1993), edited by Arthur Wightman. See *The Recollections of Eugene P. Wigner as Told to Andrew Szanton* (1992) for Wigner's look back at his life and work. Wigner's sister Margit was married to the eminent English theoretician Paul Dirac, and in *Reminiscences About a Great Physicist: Paul Adrien Maurice Dirac* (1987), edited by Wigner together with Behram N. Kursunoglu, the point of view of one great scientist for another reveals much about the character of each of them. Richard P. Hewlett and Oscar E. Anderson, Jr., *The New World: A History of the United States Atomic Energy Commission,* vol. 1, *1939–1946,* and vol. 2, *1947–1952* (1962), is a journalistic account that gives prominent reference to Wigner's contributions to nuclear weapons and, later, reactor development. Also see G. Emch, "The Philosophy of Eugene P. Wigner," in *Classical and Quantum Systems* (1993). Tributes to Wigner in the months after his death appeared in *Current Science* 69 (1995): 375–385 and *Physics Today* 48, no. 12 (1995): 40–44. John Gibbon, *Q Is for Quantum: An Encyclopedia of Particle Physics* (1998), is a useful source for terminology and expositions of concepts in Wigner's

research as well as brief biographical information. An obituary is in the *New York Times* (4 Jan. 1995).

LEONARD R. SOLON

WILKINSON, Charles Burnham ("Bud") (*b.* 23 April 1916 in Minneapolis, Minnesota; *d.* 9 February 1994 in St. Louis, Missouri), football coach at the University of Oklahoma who set the national record for consecutive victories and who restored pride to the state of Oklahoma.

Wilkinson was one of three children (along with brother William and sister Florence) of Charles Patton Wilkinson, a real estate developer and mortgage broker, and Edith Lindbloom Wilkinson, a musically inclined housewife. Wilkinson's mother died when he was seven, a year after she was involved in a train wreck. Fortunately, Wilkinson's grandmother and aunt lived in houses adjacent to his father's and asserted a maternal influence on the young boy. One of Wilkinson's childhood playmates was Patty Berg, who later gained fame as a champion professional golfer.

In his teens Wilkinson enrolled at Shattuck Military Academy in Faribault, Minnesota, where he lettered in football, basketball, ice hockey, and baseball—the only four-sport letterman in his 1933 graduating class. He graduated cum laude and received awards for combining

Charles "Bud" Wilkinson. COURTESY PRO FOOTBALL HALL OF FAME

athletics and academics, and as the school's best all-around athlete.

Wilkinson entered the University of Minnesota in the fall of 1933 along with about 150 other freshmen football aspirants. As a sophomore in 1934, he came under the tutelage of coach Bernie Bierman, who led the Golden Gophers to three national championships during Wilkinson's varsity years at Minnesota (1934, 1935, and 1936). Bierman was a low-key, quiet coach, but his strong belief in football fundamentals, hard work, and sharp execution was not lost on his young lineman. As a six-foot-one-inch, 200-pounder, Wilkinson began his varsity career at guard; during his senior year he moved to quarterback (blocking back in the "single-wing") in Bierman's power-oriented system. He was a solid performer—an All-America choice in 1935—and was chosen to play in the traditional Chicago College All-Star game in the fall of 1937. He won the Big Ten Medal, symbolic of athletic (he also played golf and ice hockey) and academic excellence, at graduation.

During a trip to Carleton College to play hockey, Bud met his future wife, Mary Shifflett. They married on 20 August 1939 and had two sons—Patrick and Jay, the latter an All-America receiver at Duke University in the 1960s.

A considerable amount of tension existed between "C. P.," Wilkinson's strong-willed father, and Bud when Bud took a part-time coaching job at Syracuse University following graduation. C. P. felt that coaching was a waste of his son's considerable abilities. While coaching football, golf, and ice hockey, Wilkinson earned a master's degree in English—also his undergraduate major—in 1940. As part of a classroom assignment, he developed, and broadcast over radio, a fifteen-minute "coach's show."

Enlisting in 1942, Wilkinson was assigned to the U.S. Navy's pre-flight program at the University of Iowa in 1943, where he coached the Seahawks' service team. Don Faurot, of the University of Missouri, was the head coach, and Wilkinson and Jim Tatum were his assistants. Faurot devised the "split-T" formation, a quick-hitting, speed-oriented system, as opposed to the power and plodding of the more widely used "single-wing."

When the navy disbanded its pre-flight programs in 1944, Wilkinson was assigned as a hangar-deck officer on the aircraft carrier USS *Enterprise*. He saw intense action in the battle for Iwo Jima as a lieutenant commander.

After the war Faurot returned to Missouri, and Tatum, a University of North Carolina alumnus, became head coach at the University of Oklahoma in Norman. Wilkinson went to Oklahoma as Tatum's chief assistant. Tatum stayed only a year in Norman, and Wilkinson took over the Sooners in 1947. At thirty-one, he was head coach and athletic director at Oklahoma.

His Sooners were 7–2–2 in his first season, but they then embarked on a thirty-one-game winning streak that included two undefeated seasons, two bowl victories, and the

1950 national championship. During this time, Oklahoma president George L. Cross caused consternation in academic circles when he said, "I'm interested in building a university our football team can be proud of."

From 1951 to 1953 the Sooners had, for them, several "down" years—a record of 24–4–2. But the team rebounded in 1954 with a 10–0 season, and repeated in 1955 and 1956 with the same record and two more national championships. In 1957 the Sooners extended their winning streak to forty-seven games—the longest ever by a college football team. However, Notre Dame scored a shocking 7–0 upset victory over Oklahoma in Norman on 16 November, the eighth game of the 1957 season.

It was during this amazing winning streak that Wilkinson's Sooners captured the nation's imagination. His quick-hitting "split-T" team was also a "hurry-up" offensive machine. Players never sat on the bench; they stood during the entire game. As soon as a play was over, all eleven Sooners bounced up and were quickly ready to run the next play. Their opponents were seldom ready for what was coming next. A stickler for conditioning, Wilkinson's teams ran, and ran, and ran some more in practice. If a player weighed over 200 pounds, which few Sooners did, he was probably about six-feet-two inches or taller.

In addition to winning coach of the year honors in 1949, Wilkinson helped develop Sooner players Darrell Royal, Jack Mitchell, and Jim Owens, among others, into highly successful coaches. Halfback Billy Vessels won the 1952 Heisman Trophy, college football's highest individual honor. Just as importantly, Wilkinson racially integrated the Sooners' football team in 1957 when he played Prentice Gautt, an African American running back.

After the forty-seven-game winning streak ended, Wilkinson's team was good, but not the juggernaut they once were. To the end of his career at Oklahoma in 1963, his teams posted a 42–20–1 mark—certainly a fine record, but not what Wilkinson and Oklahomans were used to. Overall, his Oklahoma football record was an enviable 145–29–4.

In 1960 President John F. Kennedy recruited Wilkinson to head the President's Council on Physical Fitness. Spending considerable time in Washington, D.C., Wilkinson became intrigued by the political process. Friends convinced him to run for one of Oklahoma's senate seats in 1964, the same year he legally changed his name to Bud Wilkinson, perhaps to avoid being listed on the ballot as Charles B. Wilkinson. However, the charismatic coach, a Republican candidate, lost—a victim of Lyndon Johnson's Democratic landslide victory.

Beginning with a New Year's bowl game on 1 January 1965, Wilkinson started a long career as an NBC and ABC college football television analyst. He was well prepared, having been the first college coach to have his own television show (1952). In 1978, after a fifteen-year coaching hiatus, Wilkinson was a surprise choice as head coach of the St. Louis Cardinals of the National Football League (NFL). Unfortunately, Sooner magic never materialized with the Cardinals, and thirteen games into the 1979 season Wilkinson was released with a combined record of 9–20. He did, however, make an impression on the professional players. As Dan Dierdorf, a Pro Football Hall of Fame inductee, said, "Everyone on the Cardinals' team is enriched by the fact that for the rest of our lives we can say, 'I played for Bud Wilkinson.'"

During the Nixon administration, Wilkinson's organizational skills were put to use as a special consultant to the president. It was during this time that Wilkinson met Donna O'Donnahue, who shared his interest in politics and sports. After divorcing his first wife in 1974, Wilkinson married O'Donnahue on 18 November 1977.

Wilkinson returned to broadcasting and his business interests in 1980, but by 1986 his health began to decline. He suffered from congestive heart failure, and a series of strokes weakened him further. He died in St. Louis from complications of heart disease and strokes. He is buried in Oak Grove Cemetery in St. Louis.

Wilkinson was a man of dignity in a profession not noted for that trait. He was effective and efficient, and his success at Oklahoma is indisputable. When an entire state was looking for something to shed its "Grapes of Wrath" image, Wilkinson's near-invincible Sooners provided that. Jim Owens, an All-America end and later a great coach at the University of Washington, spoke for many of Wilkinson's players: "Bud was a man who knew what his job was, knew how to do it surpassingly well, and went about it quietly. He was no shouter, no bully, but you knew where you stood. He was honest, he was fair. He said he expected more from us than football. Above all, he said he expected us to work as diligently at our studies as at football." Wilkinson's charge to his players is something that is sorely needed in intercollegiate athletics today.

★

Charles "Bud" Wilkinson, *Oklahoma Split-T Football* (1952), is a technical coaching book. Jay Wilkinson, *Bud Wilkinson* (1994), is a biography written by his son with Gretchen Hirsch. Information about Wilkinson's life and career can be found in Edwin Pope, *Football's Greatest Coaches* (1955), and John D. McCallum, *Big Eight Football* (1979). There is an obituary in the *New York Times* (11 Feb. 1994).

JIM CAMPBELL

WOLFMAN JACK (Robert Weston Smith) (*b.* 21 January 1938 in Brooklyn, New York; *d.* 1 July 1995 in Belvidere, North Carolina), legendary radio personality, television host, actor, and commercial spokesperson.

Smith was the younger of two children of Anson Weston Smith, Jr., an Episcopal Sunday school teacher, writer, editor, and executive vice president of the *Financial World,* and Rosamund Small. His parents divorced while Smith was young. His father, who suffered financial losses during the Great Depression, sold shoes for a time, then started his own public relations consulting firm and wrote for the *Wall Street Transcript.* Both parents remarried and shared custody of Smith and his sister.

Smith later referred to himself as a "budding juvenile delinquent," and his father bought him a large transoceanic radio to keep him out of trouble. Smith became an avid fan of rhythm and blues (R&B) and the disc jockeys who promoted it, such as Philadelphia's "Jocko" Henderson, New York's "Dr. Jive," the "Moon Dog" Alan Freed (first in Cleveland and later at New York's WINS), and Nashville's "John R." Richbourg, who later became Smith's mentor. Smith began skipping school and to hang around at WNJR-AM, an R&B station in Newark, New Jersey, where he ran errands and learned a few radio basics. After being thrown out by his father, Smith sold encyclopedias and Fuller brushes door-to-door. His sister, Joan, intervened with their father to enable Smith to attend the National Academy of Broadcasting in Washington, D.C.

Upon graduation in 1960, Smith began working at WYOU-AM in Newport News, Virginia, where he played R&B music as "Daddy Jules" and sold ads for the station as Bob Smith. In 1961 he married Lucy ("Lou") Lamb. They had two children. When the station's format was changed from R&B to "beautiful music," Daddy Jules was forced to become "Roger Gordon and Music in Good Taste." In 1962 Smith moved to Shreveport, Louisiana, to manage the country music station KCIJ-AM and also served as the morning disc jockey, "Big Smith with the Records."

Smith had long been fascinated by the freewheeling radio stations that operated just south of the Mexican border, outside the jurisdiction of the U.S. government. Some of these "border blasters," for example, XERF-AM, broadcast at 250,000 watts, five times the U.S. limit. Consequently, their signals were picked up all over North America and at night even as far away as Europe and the Soviet Union. Many of these stations made high profits selling airtime to evangelical preachers from the United States who broadcast via tape and sold mail-order "cures" for people's ills.

In December 1963, longing to create his own on-air character and have more control over the music he played, Smith traveled to XERF in Ciudad Acuña, Mexico, just south of Del Rio, Texas, and walked into the middle of a labor dispute. Using both charm and money, Smith took control of the station with the backing of the workers' union and the *federales.* He then increased profits by raising the preachers' fees and put his newly created alter ego "Wolfman Jack" on the air every night.

In his trademark gravelly voice—he always refused to quit smoking unfiltered cigarettes for fear that his voice

"Wolfman Jack" *(right)*, 1975. ARCHIVE PHOTOS

would change—the Wolfman played R&B and early rock music, howling and yipping between songs, pounding on phone books, and using suggestive banter, telling listeners to "reach out and turn my knobs" and "get naked!" XERF's profitable empire was built on mail-order, where the jive-talking Wolfman sold Jesus figurines, posters, baby chicks, drug paraphernalia, and pills to improve sexual performance, lose weight, and even gain weight. Wolfman Jack's show was so popular and profitable that it continued on XERF via tape until 1966 and was also carried on the similarly powerful XERB, XELO, and XEG, even though Smith left Mexico after eight months. He moved to Minneapolis in 1964 to run station KUXL. Missing the excitement, however, he returned to border radio to run XERB, opening an office on Sunset Boulevard in Los Angeles in January 1966. His shows were taped a day in advance and sent over the border to be broadcast from the powerful transmitter in Rosarito Beach, Mexico. Smith lived the fast life of concerts, parties, and cocaine in Los Angeles, and XERB was a huge success until January 1971. At that time the Mexican government suddenly decided that its Catholic citizens should not be subjected to evangelization and banned the Pentecostal preachers, taking away 80 percent of the station's revenue.

The Wolfman then moved to the Los Angeles station KDAY-AM, a progressive station that could only pay a fraction of his former XERB income. Capitalizing on his fame, Wolfman edited his old XERB Wolfman Jack tapes and offered them to stations everywhere, inventing rock and roll radio syndication. He also appeared on Armed Forces Radio from 1970 until 1986. Thus, Wolfman Jack eventually was broadcast on more than 2,000 radio stations in fifty-three countries.

George Lucas, who grew up listening to XERB, cast Wolfman Jack to play himself in *American Graffiti* (1973), the first time many people outside California saw the face behind the voice. Many were surprised that he was not African American. No longer publicity shy, he was the host of NBC-TV's *The Midnight Special* from 1973 to 1981 and appeared on more than forty other network television shows. His legendary status was immortalized in numerous songs, including the Guess Who's "Clap for the Wolfman." Paid handsomely to join New York's WNBC-AM in August 1973, he moved back to California after only one year and concentrated on his syndicated radio show.

On television Wolfman hosted the syndicated *Wolfman Jack Show* in 1978–1979 and attempted an ill-fated animated Saturday morning show, *Wolfman Rock TV*, in 1984. In 1988 he began hosting the Nashville Network's *Rock 'n' Roll Palace*, which specialized in oldies groups and nostalgia acts, with whom he was closely identified in his late career, when he frequently made infomercials promoting music collections. In 1989 he settled in Belvidere, North Carolina. In 1995 he began hosting the weekly *Live from Planet Hollywood* radio show, broadcast from Washington, D.C., and heard on seventy-nine stations.

Overweight for many years, Wolfman Jack died of a heart attack at his home in Belvidere after returning from a publicity tour for his autobiography. He was cremated and his ashes inurned on his estate in Belvidere. He was posthumously inducted into the Radio Hall of Fame in 1996 and the National Association of Broadcasters (NAB) Broadcasting Hall of Fame in 1999. Always insisting that he was in "the happiness business," Wolfman Jack never used vulgarities on the radio, relying instead on attitude and double or even triple entendres. His enthusiastic style and fast-talking patter flourished when radio stations were driven by personalities rather than constrained by playlists.

★

Wolfman Jack looked back on his long career in *Have Mercy! Confessions of the Original Rock 'n' Roll Animal,* written with Byron Laursen (1995). Biographical profiles are in Wes Smith, *The Pied Pipers of Rock 'n' Roll: Radio Deejays of the 50s and 60s* (1989); Philip A. Lieberman, *Radio's Morning Show Personalities: Early Hour Broadcasters and Deejays from the 1920s to the 1990s* (1996); and John A. Garraty and Mark C. Carnes, eds., *American National Biography,* vol. 23 (1999). The Mexican radio stations are covered thoroughly in Gene Fowler and Bill Crawford, *Border Radio* (1987). Early profiles of Wolfman Jack include Dan Ford, "Wolfman Jack, from Cub to Howling Success," *Los Angeles Times* (3 Dec. 1972), and John Rockwell, "Wolfman Prowls the Ratings Front," *New York Times* (20 Nov. 1973). Notable stories and tributes are in the *Toronto Star* (2 July 1995), *Washington Post* (3 July 1995), and *Daily News* (5 July 1995). Obituaries are in the *Daily News* (2 July 1995), *Los Angeles Times* (2 July 1995), *New York Times* (2 July 1995), *Variety* (10 July 1995), *Billboard* (15 July 1995), and *Newsmakers* (1996).

JOHN A. DROBNICKI

WOOD, Evelyn Nielsen (*b.* 8 January 1909 in Logan, Utah; *d.* 26 August 1995 in Tucson, Arizona), educator and leading proponent of speed-reading.

Wood was the daughter of Elias Nielsen, the superintendent of the Logan Knitting Mills, and Rose Sirland Nielsen, who worked at the Logan Knitting Mills before her marriage. Wood had one brother. Wood entered the University of Utah in 1927 and received her bachelor's degree in English in 1929. On 12 June that year she married Myron Douglas Wood, a meat dealer and merchant. Members of the Church of Jesus Christ of Latter-day Saints, the Woods

had one daughter. Evelyn Wood taught English and biology at Weber College in Ogden, Utah, during the 1931–1932 school year. Returning to the University of Utah to pursue a master's degree in speech, she earned her M.A. degree in 1947.

Wood became interested in speed-reading techniques at the University of Utah after she turned in an eighty-page term paper to Professor C. Lowell Lees. Wood was stunned as she watched Lees read and grade her paper in less than ten minutes. As Lees discussed the paper with her, Wood found that he had not simply skimmed her paper. He described the paper's content in detail and discussed the paper's weaknesses as well. Wood was impressed. She asked Lees if she could time his reading of other materials. She discovered that Lee could read approximately 2,500 words per minute, an astounding rate. The average American reads about 250 to 300 words per minute. Lees could not explain how he had developed this skill, and Wood wondered if the average person could be trained to read at a faster rate.

Wood began to search for techniques to improve reading skills while working as a teacher and a girls' counselor from 1948 to 1957 at Jordan High School in Sandy, Utah. Working with troubled students who performed poorly in the classroom, she determined that a major factor in their lack of academic success was their inadequate reading skills. Believing that reading was the key to general scholastic achievement, Wood established Jordan High School's first remedial reading program. As the students' reading improved, so did their grades in other subjects and their discipline. Wood observed a strong correlation between the speed at which the students read and their ability to comprehend what they read.

Wood was a graduate student at Columbia University from 1956 to 1957. In 1958 she decided to seek out fast readers and see what traits they shared. She found fifty-three people who read from 1,500 to 6,000 words per minute and remembered what they had read. Her subjects ranged in age from their teens to their eighties and came from a variety of backgrounds. In observing these speed-readers, Wood found that they had several reading habits in common. Her subjects concentrated on the material and avoided rereading passages multiple times. They read complete ideas or groups of words at once rather than reading individual words one at a time. They also ran their eyes down the middle of a page rather than from left to right. Finally, they read materials on a wide variety of subjects efficiently. Wood was convinced that concentration was the key to the speed of these readers. Indeed, she argued that faster reading itself improved concentration and retention of knowledge because speed readers did not give their minds the opportunity to wander.

In trying to improve her own reading skills, Wood found

that her reading speed increased when she used her hand to guide her eyes down the page. Believing that this was a critical factor in the increase of her own reading speed to 2,700 words per minute, Wood noted that children use their fingers to mark their places when they first learn to read. Ironically, their teachers then require that they abandon this technique.

After Wood worked for two years as an instructor at the University of Utah, she and her husband established the Reading Dynamics Institute in Washington, D.C., in 1959. The institute's reading courses won widespread popularity, and Reading Dynamics courses soon were offered all over the United States and in other countries. Wood's speed-reading methods even received presidential endorsements. President John F. Kennedy believed in her program and sent White House staff members to her institute in Washington, President Richard Nixon sent thirty-five members of his administration to her courses, and President Jimmy Carter sent aides and was himself a student of Reading Dynamics.

Wood was an active teacher and researcher on the collegiate level as well. She taught reading at the University of Delaware in 1961 and at Texas Christian University in 1962, and she was a research specialist in reading at Brigham Young University from 1973 to 1974. In addition to her book *Reading Skills* (1958), coauthored with Marjorie Wescott Barrows of Jordan High School, Wood wrote several articles on reading education, including "A Breakthrough in Reading" (*International Reading Teacher*, 1961), "A New Approach to Speed Reading" (*Speed Reading, Practices and Procedures*, 1962), and "Speed Reading for Comprehension" (*Bulletin of the National Association of Secondary School Principals*, 1962).

The petite, soft-spoken Wood sold her Reading Dynamics business in 1967. While developing a remedial reading program for children in 1976, she suffered a severe and incapacitating stroke. After her husband died in 1987, she moved to Tucson, Arizona, to be with her daughter, Carolyn Davis Evans. Wood passed away at the age of eighty-six in Tucson. She is buried in Salt Lake City.

Wood's Reading Dynamics program has had its share of critics, who have argued that her techniques encourage readers to skim material. Wood maintained that a reader has to slow down somewhat to read difficult material and that students have to practice their speed-reading skills on a regular basis. Despite the criticism, Wood's name is synonymous with speed-reading.

★

Wood's papers are archived at the Utah State Historical Society. The collection includes instructional materials, correspondence, legal documents, photographs, and church-related documents. Although Wood did not publish her Reading Dynamics program in book form, Stanley D. Frank wrote *Remember Everything You Read: The Evelyn Wood Seven-Day Speed Reading and Learning Program* (1990), a study skills book based on Wood's speed-reading courses. Obituaries are in the *New York Times* and *Arizona Republic* (both 30 Aug. 1995).

KATHY S. MASON

YARBOROUGH, Ralph Webster (*b.* 8 June 1903 in Chandler, Texas; *d.* 27 January 1996 in Austin, Texas), U.S. senator (1957–1971), leader of liberal Democrats, attorney, district judge, conservationist, humanitarian, and orator.

Yarborough's story began in rural eastern Texas, where he was the seventh of nine children born to Charles Richard Yarborough, a farmer and justice of the peace, and Nannie Jane Spear, a homemaker. He attended local public schools in Chandler before transferring to Tyler High School in a nearby county; he graduated with honors in 1919. Yarborough spent one year at the United States Military Academy, traveled to Europe, and then worked in wheat fields in Oklahoma and Kansas and oil boomtowns in Texas. He taught in one-room schools while he attended Sam Houston State Teachers College in Huntsville, Texas, in 1921 to obtain state teacher's certification, He then worked his way through the University of Texas Law School (Austin), from which he graduated with highest honors in 1927. His

Ralph Yarborough, 1970. ASSOCIATED PRESS AP

hobbies included fishing, hunting, and collecting books and historic documents, and he had an avid interest in the Civil War. In June 1928 he married Opal Catherine Warren, his longtime sweetheart, after she told him, "I won't marry a man in politics." The couple moved to El Paso, where Yarborough practiced law in a prestigious West Texas firm. They had one child.

Newly elected as Texas attorney general, James Allred offered Yarborough a job in 1931. Yarborough's four years as an assistant attorney general placed him in the forefront of the state's efforts to protect public lands and resources. He gained statewide recognition for legal victories that preserved future oil and gas revenues for Texas public schools and universities. As a result of these decisions, the state's educational funds accumulated billions of dollars. One settlement alone generated more than $1 million for Texas, the second-largest legal judgment for the state.

Allred became governor of Texas in 1935 and rewarded his protégé with an appointment as a state district judge (1936–1940). Yarborough later decisively won election to the bench. He attempted to follow in Allred's footsteps but lost the Democratic nomination for attorney general in 1938. World War II interrupted his political career. He served in Europe in the Ninety-seventh Infantry Division under General George Patton's Third Army until the victory of the Allied forces in Europe in May of 1945. He then left for the Pacific, where General Douglas MacArthur, commander of U.S. forces in the Far East and, later, military governor of occupied Japan, appointed Yarborough as military governor for Honshu Province. By the time Yarborough was discharged as a lieutenant colonel in 1946, he had a Bronze Star, a Battle Star, and six other service medals.

The conservatism that replaced the prewar reform sentiments in Texas failed to alter Yarborough's views as he launched three unsuccessful races for governor in the 1950s. In doing so, he became the leader of liberal and reform Democrats in the state. Governor Allan Shivers, a conservative Democrat, survived two successive challenges from Yarborough. In the close 1954 race, Shivers used fears of communism, organized labor, and racial integration to fend off Yarborough's upset bid. In 1956 Shivers declined to run again, and U.S. senator Price Daniel, Sr., bested Yarborough in another controversial gubernatorial campaign.

Although he lost three successive races, Yarborough's popularity increased with each election. Victory finally came in the hard-fought 1957 special election to replace Daniel in the U.S. Senate. Yarborough prevailed over a crowded field of twenty-one candidates. A year later, Yarborough won a full term with his famous slogan, "Let's Put the Jam on the Lower Shelf So the Little People Can Reach It." His victories helped preserve majority leader Lyndon B. Johnson's slim hold on the Senate during the final years of the administration of President Dwight D. Eisenhower. But the two influential Texans clashed on legislation and personal issues, and Yarborough supported Senator John F. Kennedy over Johnson for the Democratic presidential nomination in 1960.

Yarborough's liberal social and economic views more closely resembled those of western and northern Democrats rather than traditional southern Democrats. When he first entered the Senate, Yarborough joined with Senate Majority Leader Johnson and two other senators from former Confederate states to pass the Civil Rights Bill of 1957. Later, Senator Yarborough supported President Johnson's historic 1964 Civil Rights Act and the 1965 Voting Rights Act. Yarborough earned the distinction of being the only senator from the Old South to favor every major civil rights bill from 1957 through 1970. He also coauthored the National Defense Education Act in 1958.

Because of his controversial positions, Yarborough often clashed with the Texas congressional delegation. Nonetheless, Yarborough sponsored more legislation than any senator ever elected from Texas. After President Kennedy's assassination in 1963, Yarborough and Johnson put aside most of their differences to achieve their common goals. Nearly every piece of legislation during the Johnson administration that involved education, health, labor, science, the environment, or veterans carried the name of Yarborough as a sponsor or earned his active support. His advocacy in these areas resulted in broad economic improvements nationwide and opened new doors of opportunity for millions of Americans. He ultimately broke with President Johnson, however, over the Vietnam War. Yarborough's antiwar statements, the rejection of the 1960s domestic reform agenda, and his own overconfidence led to a surprising loss to former congressman Lloyd Bentsen, Jr., in the 1970 Democratic primary. He died of heart failure and is buried in the state cemetery in Austin, Texas.

Yarborough, called "the People's Senator" for his accomplishments in the U.S. Senate, became the political leader of Texas liberals during the post–World War II era, when Texas and the South underwent dramatic political, social, and economic change. Yarborough's life offers a window into the changes in Texas and the nation during the twentieth century. His contributions to the political culture of Texas rival his legislative accomplishments. He followed the strong populist, antiestablishment streak that had survived since the era of Sam Houston (1793–1863), the U.S. senator and governor of Texas who was one of Yarborough's heroes. Along with preserving this legacy, Yarborough inspired two successive generations of Democratic officeholders. His large following rivaled that of his more famous counterpart, Lyndon Johnson. A litany of nationally recognized Texas leaders that included former governors Allan Shivers, Price Daniel, Sr., and John Connally as well as Lloyd Bentsen, Jr., sparred with him on everything from major policy issues to petty personal issues. His politics may have been controversial to some, but few questioned his integrity or his sincerity.

Yarborough reveled in the populist-styled traditions of the pretelevision political era. His oratorical skills combined with his keen mind served him in his whirlwind campaigns that often seemed more like old-time religious revivals. Beneath the public persona of a liberal politician working for reform was a private man driven by the urge to implant his vision in Texas and the rest of the nation. His intense devotion and desire sometimes exposed a temper that stung his closest advisers and staff members like a whip, yet he was usually courteous and friendly to everyone. Yarborough, who was of medium build, with wavy black hair and a wide smile, never tired of making speeches and shaking hands, a practice he continued until the final years of his life. With his tremendous yet melodious voice, Yarborough was fond of repeating a statement that represented his personal and political beliefs—"People are our greatest resource."

★

Ralph Yarborough's personal and Senate papers are located at the Center for American History at the University of Texas at Austin. Biographies include Patrick L. Cox, *The People's Senator: Ralph W. Yarborough* (2001), and William G. Phillips, *Yarborough of Texas* (1969), a campaign biography for the 1970 election. Evaluations of Yarborough's political role in Texas and the nation are provided in Chandler Davidson, *Race and Class in Texas Politics* (1990); George N. Green, *The Establishment in Texas Politics* (1979); and Kenneth E. Hendrickson, Jr., and Michael L. Collins, eds., *Profiles in Power: Twentieth-century Texans in Washington* (1993). Among many articles and publications by Ralph Yarborough are *Frank Dobie: Man and Friend* (1967) and "Lincoln as a Liberal Statesman," in *Lincoln for the Ages*, edited by Ralph G. Newman (rev. ed., 1964). Obituaries are in the *New York Times* (28 Jan. 1996) and *Texas Observer* (23 Feb. 1996).

PATRICK L. COX

ZELAZNY, Roger Joseph (*b.* 13 May 1937 in Cleveland, Ohio; *d.* 14 June 1995 in Santa Fe, New Mexico), science fiction and fantasy novel writer who made a major impression on the genre.

Zelazny was the only child of Joseph Frank Zelazny and Josephine Sweet. His father was a Polish immigrant who worked as a pattern maker for a typewriter company. Zelazny's childhood was spent in Euclid, a suburb of Cleveland, attending public school and spending much of his time reading. This early exposure to literature influenced him for the rest of his life; it was at this time that Zelazny was first exposed to the genre that he would later revolu-

tionize, science fiction. He became interested in writing humorous, fantastic stories as early as junior high school.

Zelazny's first published compositions were poems in a high school literary magazine, *Eucuyo*, for which he was later named editor. While still in high school, Zelazny submitted several pieces for publication to science fiction magazines but received only one acceptance, for the short story "Mr. Fuller's Revolt," which sold to *Literary Cavalcade* in 1954. He became somewhat discouraged and turned his attention to poetry.

His poetry won some recognition at Western Reserve University in Cleveland, where he twice won the Finlay Foster Poetry Prize. Oddly enough, he entered college intending to pursue a degree in psychology, reasoning that it would be more productive, but he changed his mind and graduated in 1959 with B.A. degree in English.

Better educated than most science fiction writers, Zelazny went on to graduate school at Columbia University, studying Elizabethan and Jacobean drama. In 1962 he began his rise to distinction. He finished a commitment to the Ohio National Guard, received his M.A. degree from Columbia, and sold two stories—"Passion Play" to *Amazing Stories* and "Horseman" to *Fantastic*. That same year he began working for the Social Security Administration as a claims agent to support himself and continuing to write part-time. In 1963 and 1964 he published numerous short stories, including "Graveyard Heart," "Lucifer," and "A Rose for Ecclesiastes," for which he received his first Hugo nomination.

The next year was more challenging. Zelazny and his fiancée, Sharon Steberl, were in an automobile accident, which postponed their wedding, and later that year, his father died unexpectedly. The couple was married on 5 December 1964, but they separated in 1965. After his separation, Zelazny was promoted to claims policy specialist and relocated to Baltimore. He met another Social Security employee, Judith Callahan, and married her on 20 September 1966, two months after his divorce from Steberl was finalized.

Putting the anguish caused by the failure of his marriage and the death of his father behind him, he received tremendous vindication for his efforts as a writer in 1966. He won two prestigious awards—the Hugo Award for " . . . And Call me Conrad" and the Nebula Award for both "He Who Shapes" and the "The Doors of His Face, the Lamps of His Mouth." He published his first novel-length works, *This Immortal,* the original version of " . . . And They Call me Conrad" and *The Dream Master,* which was based on "He Who Shapes" and expanded on the advice of editor Damon Knight.

Zelazny continued to be a prolific and much acclaimed writer through the 1960s and 1970s. He was nominated for the Hugo and Nebula Awards more than fifteen times. His book *Lord of Light,* published in 1967, won Zelazny his second Hugo and persuaded him to return to writing full-time. Quitting his job with the government worried him, and to compensate for the lack of regular income, he focused almost entirely on novel-length works—*Jack of Shadows* (1971), *To Die in Italbar* (1973), and *Doorways in the Sand* (1976). Most of his works are characterized by a certain whimsy or humor, bitter though it may be, and many of them are based on myth and folklore. *Lord of Light* was based on Hindu mythology, "Creatures of Light and Darkness" (1969) had Egyptian overtones, and "The Eye of the Cat" (1982) drew from Navajo folklore.

While Zelazny's short fiction is critically acclaimed, his Amber Chronicles are best known. Starting in 1970 with *Nine Princes in Amber,* he caught the imagination of the public with his whimsical and symbolic fantasy series. Subsequent volumes included *The Guns of Avalon* (1972), *Sign of the Unicorn* (1975), *The Hand of Oberon* (1976), and *The Courts of Chaos* (1978).

In 1975, in the midst of all of this writing, Zelazny moved to Santa Fe, New Mexico, with his wife, Judith, and his son, who was born in 1971; they had two more children. Zelazny periodically returned to the genre that he was most lauded for—short fiction. In 1976 he won the Nebula and the Hugo for "Home is the Hangman," and in 1980 he won the Balrog Award for "The Last Defender of Camelot." He also received Hugos for "Unicorn Variation" (in 1982), "24 Views of Mount Fuji, by Hokusai" (in 1986), and "Permafrost" (in 1987). His earlier works continued to gain recognition— the French edition of *The Isle of the Dead* won the Prix Apollo in 1972, and "Damnation Alley"

was made into a movie in 1977. While Zelazny's later works are considered subordinate to his early efforts by some science fiction scholars, they were still well received. He earned a Balrog Award and a Daicon Award for *Unicorn Variations* and the Locus Award for *Trumps of Doom* (1985).

Throughout his writing career, Zelazny is credited with a talent for experimentation in various styles and commended for the psychological, religious, and philosophical elements in his writing, hearkening back to his early education. He is also recognized for his form and chaos theory and for his mastery of the quest tale, which has inspired much commentary. His career ended with his death from colon cancer.

★

One of the most versatile and philosophical of science fiction and fantasy writers, Roger Zelazny died at the age of fifty-eight. He was a prolific writer and published more than 50 novels and 150 short stories during his career, gaining him international renown. His works were translated into many languages, among them French, Dutch, Italian, Spanish, German, Swedish, Greek, Hebrew, and Japanese. He also collaborated with such authors as Philip K. Dick, Fred Saberhagen, and Robert Sheckley. Biographies include Carl B. Yoke, *Roger Zelazny: Starmont Readers' Guide 2* (1979); Jane M. Lindskold, *Roger Zelazny* (1993); and Theodore Krulik, *Roger Zelazny* (1986). Journal articles include Richard Cowper, "A Rose Is a Rose Is a Rose: In Search of Roger Zelazny," *Foundation 11/12* (March 1977); and John Clute, "The Word from Space," London *Guardian* (20 June 1995).

WENDI ARANT KASPAR

DIRECTORY OF CONTRIBUTORS

AGNEW, BRAD
Northeastern State University, Tahlequah, Okla.
   Scali, John Alfred

ALEXANDER, THOMAS G.
Brigham Young University
   Hunter, Howard William
   Lee, J(oseph) Bracken ("Brack")

ANDERSEN, DAVID C.
Montpelier, Ohio
   Erikson, Erik Homburger

ARANT-KASPER, WENDI
Humanities Librarian, Texas A&M University
   Zelazny, Roger Joseph

ARETAKIS, JONATHAN G.
Editorial East, Pembroke, Maine
   Mulligan, Gerald Joseph ("Gerry")

BADER-BOREL, PHYLLIS
State University of New York at Albany
   Brodsky, Joseph

BAKER, THERESE DUZINKIEWICZ
Western Kentucky University
   Maxwell, Vera Huppé

BALLARD, TERRY L.
Librarian, Quinnipiac College
   Ives, Burl Icle Ivanhoe

BARBEAU, ART
West Liberty State College, West Virginia
   Foner, Philip Sheldon
   Quarles, Benjamin Arthur

BARTELIK, MAREK
Cooper Union for the Advancement of Science and Art
   Hansen, Al(fred) Earl

BATINOVICH, KENNETH M.
Engineer, Rancho Palos Verdes, Calif.
   Kerr, Walter Francis

BELENKY, IRINA
Graduate Student in History, Rutgers University
   Mancini, Henry Nicola

BELLOWS, PAMELA W.
Northwestern Connecticut Community College,
      Winsted, Conn.
   Hooker, Evelyn Gentry

BIRD, KAI
Independent Scholar and Journalist, Washington, D.C.
   Bundy, McGeorge

BLICKLEY, MARK A.
DeVry Institute of Technology, Long Island City, N.Y.
   Dickey, William Malcolm ("Bill")

BOON, KEVIN ALEXANDER
Pennsylvania State University
   Leary, Timothy Francis

BORNSTEIN, JERRY
Baruch College, City University of New York
   Savio, Mario

BOSKY, BERNADETTE LYNN
Writer and Instructor, Yonkers, N.Y.
   Bloch, Robert Albert
   Dahmer, Jeffrey Lionel
   Finney, Walter Braden ("Jack")
   Gacy, John Wayne, Jr.

BOULTIER, MELANI
San Ramon, Calif.
   Clurman, Richard Michael

BOYLES, MARY
University of North Carolina at Pembroke
   Gabor, Eva

BRASEL, ELLEN O'CONNELL
Marshall University, Huntington, W.Va.
   Tavoulareas, William Peter

BRILEY, RON
Sandia Preparatory School, Albuquerque, N.Mex.
   Roland, Gilbert
   Romero, Cesar

BRODSKY, LAUREN A.
Setauket, N.Y.
  Snyder, Jimmy ("Jimmy the Greek")
BUCCO, MARTIN
Colorado State University
  Wellek, René Maria Eduard
BUFORD, KATE
*Robinson, Lerer and Montgomery Strategic
    Communications, Irvington, N.Y.*
  Lancaster, Burt(on) Stephen
BULLWINKLE, DAVID
Haverford, Pa.
  Feyerabend, Paul Karl
BURKE, JOHN P.
University of Vermont
  Brownell, Herbert, Jr.
BUSTER, ALAN
Harvard-Westlake School, Los Angeles
  Berman, Pandro Samuel
  Southern, Terry Marion, Jr.
CALLAHAN, JOHN F.
Lewis & Clark College
  Ellison, Ralph Waldo
CAMPBELL, CYNTHIA L.
Memorial Art Gallery of the University of Rochester, N.Y.
  Burke, Selma Hortense
CAMPBELL, JIM
Bucknell University
  Conerly, Charles Albert ("Charlie"), Jr.
  Minnesota Fats (Rudolf Walter Wanderone, Jr.)
  Rozelle, Alvin Roy ("Pete")
  Schultz, David Lesky ("Dave")
  Strode, Woodrow Wilson Woolwine ("Woody")
  Wilkinson, Charles Burnham ("Bud")
CARDOSO, JACK J.
*Professor Emeritus, State University of New York College
    at Buffalo*
  Lasch, Christopher
  Penick, Harvey Morrison
CARDOSO, ROSEMARIE S.
Art Educator and Independent Scholar, Clarence, N.Y.
  Dzubas, Friedel Alfred
CARLIN, RICHARD
Senior Music Editor, Routledge Books
  Monroe, William Smith ("Bill")
  Rich, Charles Allan ("Charlie")
  Slonimsky, Nicolas (Nikolai Leonidovich)
CAROLI, BETTY BOYD
Historian, New York City
  Onassis, Jacqueline Lee Bouvier Kennedy

CARPENTER, BRIAN B.
Sterling C. Evans Library, Texas A&M University
  Grizzard, Lewis McDonald, Jr.
  Redenbacher, Orville
CARRIKER, ANDREW J.
Columbia University
  Krol, John Joseph
CARSTENSEN, FRED
University of Connecticut
  Baker, George Pierce
CASTLE, ALFRED L.
The Samuel N. and Mary Castle Foundation
  Curti, Merle Eugene
  Nisbet, Robert Alexander
CASTRONOVO, DAVID
Pace University
  Trilling, Diana Rubin
CHEN, JEFFREY H.
Cambridge University Press
  Monette, Paul Landry
CHURCH, GARY MASON
Sterling C. Evans Library, Texas A&M University
  Howard, James Howell
  Odell, Allan Gilbert
CICARELLI, JAMES
*Walter E. Heller College of Business Administration,
    Roosevelt University*
  DeBartolo, Edward John, Sr.
CICARELLI, JULIANNE
Freelance Writer, Arlington Heights, Ill.
  Cohen, Audrey C.
COBB, KENNETH R.
New York City Municipal Archives
  Corrigan, Douglas ("Wrong-Way Corrigan")
COLETTA, PAOLO E.
Professor Emeritus, United States Naval Academy (Retired)
  Burke, Arleigh Albert
  Horton, Mildred Helen McAfee
COLLIER, RICHARD L.
State University of New York at Albany
  Gordone, Charles
CONTINELLI, LOUISE
Ph.D. Candidate, University at Buffalo
  Shakur, Tupac Amaru
COOK, RICHARD A.
Port Washington, N.Y.
  Swayze, John Cameron
CORPUS, MARTHA MONAGHAN
Brooklyn College of the City University of New York
  Chadwick, Florence May
  Kuhn, Margaret Eliza ("Maggie")

590

COVENEY, PETER
Westport, Conn.
    Hemingway, Margaux
    Scribner, Charles, Jr.
COX, PATRICK L.
The Center for American History, University of Texas
    at Austin
    Yarborough, Ralph Webster
CROWLEY, GWYNETH H.
Texas A&M University Libraries
    May, Rollo Reece
DAMON, ALLAN L.
Horace Greeley High School, Chappaqua, N.Y.
    Belli, Melvin Mouron
    Kennedy, Rose Elizabeth Fitzgerald
    Kunstler, William Moses
    Muskie, Edmund Sixtus
DAVIDSON, KEAY
Science Writer, San Francisco Chronicle
    Kuhn, Thomas Samuel
DECKER, SHARON L.
State University of New York, Maritime College
    Mitford, Jessica ("Decca")
DIAMANT, JEFFREY A.
Parsippany, N.J.
    Lantz, Walter
DINNEEN, MARCIA B.
Bridgewater State College
University of Massachusetts at Dartmouth
    Clampitt, Amy Kathleen
    Tiny Tim (Herbert Butros Khaury)
DOENECKE, JUSTUS D.
New College of the University of South Florida, Sarasota
    Chamberlain, John Rensselaer
DOUGHERTY, DAVID C.
Director, Graduate Program in Modern Studies, Loyola
    College in Maryland
    Elkin, Stanley Lawrence
DROBNICKI, JOHN A.
York College Library, City University of New York
    Wolfman Jack (Robert Weston Smith)
ECKSTEIN, PETER
Ann Arbor, Mich.
    Eckert, J(ohn Adam) Presper, Jr.
EVENSEN, BRUCE J.
DePaul University
    Kelly, Eugene Curran ("Gene")
    Scarry, Richard McClure
FAFOUTIS, DEAN
Salisbury State University, Maryland
    Aspin, Les(lie), Jr.

FERRELL, ROBERT H.
Indiana University, Bloomington
    Ball, George Wildman
    Judd, Walter Henry
    O'Neill, Thomas Philip, Jr. ("Tip")
FEUERHERD, PETER
American Bible Society
    Gray, Barry
FINLAY, BARBARA
Texas A&M University
    Rome, Esther Rachel Seidman
FISCHEL, JACK R.
Millersville University
    Schneerson, Menachem Mendel
FITZPATRICK, JANE BRODSKY
Stephen B. Luce Library, State University of New York
    Maritime College
    Chen, Joyce
    Conover, Willis Clark, Jr.
    Furcolo, (John) Foster
FITZPATRICK, JOHN
Charles Scribner's Sons
Director, Miklós Rózsa Society
    Rózsa, Miklós
FLEET, SUSAN
Writer and Musician, Randolph, Mass.
    Elgart, Les(ter) Elliot
    McRae, Carmen Mercedes
FLEMING, THOMAS
New York City
    Fulbright, J(ames) William
FLYNN, JOSEPH G.
State University of New York College of Technology, Alfred
    Boyer, Ernest LeRoy, Sr.
FOLEY, MICHAEL S.
Widener University
    Garcia, Hector Perez
FRIED, RONALD K.
Television Producer, New York City
    Arcel, Ray
FRIGUGLIETTI, JAMES
Montana State University, Billings
    Hexter, J. H. ("Jack")
FRISCH, PAUL A.
Director of Library and Information Technology, State
    University of New York at Old Westbury
    Puller, Lewis Burwell, Jr.
GALGAN, MARY NAHON
Retired Librarian, Bronx, N.Y.
    Bernardin, Joseph Louis

GARAFOLA, LYNN
Writer and Editor, New York City
   Kirstein, Lincoln

GARGAN, WILLIAM M.
Brooklyn College of the City University of New York
   Bukowski, Charles
   Huncke, Herbert Edwin

GENTILE, RICHARD H.
Freelance Writer and Editor, South Easton, Mass.
   Volpe, John Anthony

GERBER, BARBARA L.
Brooklyn College of the City University of New York
   Simpson, Adele Smithline

GINTHER, KRISTAN
Writer, Los Angeles, Calif.
   Julia, Raul Rafael Carlos

GOOD, ELAINE MCMAHON
Nassau Community College, State University of New York
   Gould, Morton
   Shore, Dinah

GOODBODY, JOAN
Sterling C. Evans Library, Texas A&M University
   Morison, Elting Elmore

GOODSTEIN, JUDITH R.
California Institute of Technology
   Sperry, Roger Wolcott

GORDON, NANCY M.
Independent Scholar, Amherst, Mass.
   Herrnstein, Richard Julius
   Perpich, Rudolph George ("Rudy")

GOTTFRIED, MARTIN
Drama Critic and Author, New York City
   Burns, George

GOTTLIEB, JANE
The Juilliard School
   Luening, Otto Clarence

GOULD, LEWIS L.
University of Texas at Austin
   Ewell, Tom
   Lasker, Mary Woodward
   Sullivan, Walter Seager, Jr.

GRAFF, HENRY F.
Professor Emeritus, Columbia University
   Mantle, Mickey Charles
   Rusk, (David) Dean

GREENBERG, DAVID
Columbia University
Slate Magazine
   Nixon, Richard Milhous

GREENWALD, RICHARD A.
U.S. Merchant Marine Academy
   Korshak, Sidney Roy

GRIFFITH, JEAN W., JR.
Crowder College
   Urban, Matt Louis

GUTIÉRREZ, RAMÓN A.
University of California, San Diego
   Selena (Selena Quintanilla Pérez)

HABERSKI, RAYMOND J., JR.
Marian College, Indianapolis, Ind.
   Shils, Edward Albert

HAGER, THOMAS
University of Oregon
   Pauling, Linus Carl

HAINES, MICHAEL F.
Dominican College, Orangeburg, N.Y.
   Peterson, Roger Tory

HANSEN, VAGN K.
High Point University
   Whitten, Jamie Lloyd

HASENFUS, WILLIAM A.
Community College of Rhode Island
   Collins, John Frederick

HENRIQUES, DIANA B.
The New York Times
   Cornfeld, Bernard ("Bernie")

HERON, DAVID W.
University Librarian Emeritus, University of California, Santa Cruz
   Everson, William Oliver (Brother Antoninus)
   Smith, (Charles) Page (Ward)

HLAVATY, ARTHUR D.
Independent Scholar, Yonkers, N.Y.
   Condon, Richard Thomas
   Morgan, Henry

HODGES, GRAHAM RUSSELL
Colgate University
   Highsmith, (Mary) Patricia
   Nilsson, Harry Edward, II

HOMEL, MICHAEL W.
Ypsilanti, Mich.
   Stokes, Carl Burton

HOOGENBOOM, LYNN
Copy Editor, New York Times News Service
   Gonzalez, Richard Alonzo ("Pancho")
   Rogers, Ginger

JALENAK, NATALIE B.
Playhouse on the Square, Memphis, Tenn. (Retired)
   Blanton, (Leonard) Ray
   Pearl, Minnie (Sarah Ophelia Colley Cannon)

KALB, PETER R.
Middlebury College
   Eisenstaedt, Alfred

KASTNER, JEFFREY
Contributing Editor, Artnews
    Kienholz, Edward Ralph
KEEN, W. HUBERT
System Administration, State University of New York
    Cray, Seymour Roger
KELLY, BARBARA M.
Long Island Studies Institute at Hofstra University
    Levitt, William Jaird ("Bill")
KOTLOWSKI, DEAN J.
Salisbury State University, Maryland
    Cosell, Howard
    Finch, Robert Hutchinson
KOWAL, REBEKAH J.
Haverford College
    Larson, Jonathan
KRINGEN, TIMOTHY
Portland, Oreg.
    Chalk, (Oscar) Roy
LABATTO, MARIANNE
Brooklyn College of the City University of New York
    Rosten, Norman
LAMB, CHARLES M.
University at Buffalo, State University of New York
    Burger, Warren Earl
LANKEVICH, GEORGE J.
Professor of History Emeritus, City University of New York
    Bell, Terrel Howard
LAUNIUS, ROGER D.
*Chief Historian, National Aeronautics and Space
    Administration*
    Wiesner, Jerome Bert
LEAB, DANIEL J.
Seton Hall University
    Krim, Arthur B.
LEARY, WILLIAM M.
University of Georgia
    Colby, William Egan
LEITER, SAMUEL L.
*Brooklyn College and The Graduate Center, City University
    of New York*
    Abbott, George Francis
LEVY, SHARONA A.
*Borough of Manhattan Community College, City University
    of New York*
    Nizer, Louis
LOUGHRAN, ELLEN
Hunter College, City University of New York
    Coleman, James Samuel
    Factor, Max, Jr.

LOUISSAINT, SABINE
Writer, New York City
    Meadows, Audrey
LOVE, JOHNNIEQUE B.
Texas A&M University Libraries
    Ballantine, Ian Keith
    Red Thunder Cloud (Cromwell Ashbie Hawkins
    West)
LOVETT, BOBBY L.
Tennessee State University
    Rudolph, Wilma Glodean
LUFT, ERIC V. D.
*State University of New York Health Science Center
    at Syracuse*
    Church, Alonzo
McBRIDE, CARRIE C.
Writer, New York City
    Riggs, Robert Larimore ("Bobby")
McBRIDE, FRANCIS R.
Herrick Library, Alfred University
    Grace, J(oseph) Peter, Jr.
McCULLEY, RICHARD T.
National Archives
    Stennis, John Cornelius
McCURDY, SHEILA
State University of New York, Maritime College
    Ridder, Eric
McDONALD, ARCHIE P.
Regent's Professor, Stephen F. Austin State University
    Hobby, Oveta Culp
MACDONALD, GINA
Metairie, La.
    Clavell, James duMaresq
McELWAINE, JIM
Cos Cob, Conn.
    Calloway, Cab
    Walker, Junior
McLAUGHLIN, MARILYN
Earhart Foundation, Ann Arbor, Mich.
    Romney, George Wilcken
MALONE, D. P.
Williamsville, N.Y.
    Schwinger, Julian Seymour
MALONEY, WENDY HALL
Brooklyn College of the City University of New York
    Duke, Angier Biddle
MALONEY, WILLIAM J.
Writer, New York City
    Rand, Paul
    Stevens, Brooks

MARC, DAVID
S. I. Newhouse School of Public Communications,
Syracuse University
   Chancellor, John William

MARKOE, LAUREN
The Patriot Ledger, Quincy, Mass.
   O'Hair, Madalyn Murray

MARKOE, NANCY
Washington, D.C.
   Ginsberg, Mitchell Irving

MARKUSEN, BRUCE
Senior Researcher, National Baseball Hall of Fame
and Museum
   Finley, Charles Oscar ("Charlie")

MARSHALL, STEPHEN
Lincoln Park, N.J.
   Rouse, James Wilson

MASON, KATHY S.
Southwest Missouri State University
   Wood, Evelyn Nielsen

MASSEY, DANNY
Freelance Writer, New York City
   Delany, Annie Elizabeth ("Bessie")

MAYO, LOUISE A.
County College of Morris, Randolph, N.J.
   Bombeck, Erma Louise Fiste
   Tandy, Jessica

MUGLESTON, WILLIAM F.
Floyd College, Rome, Ga.
   Brooks, Cleanth

NEAL, STEVE
Chicago Sun-Times
   Agnew, Spiro Theodore
   Scott, Hugh Doggett, Jr.
   Sharkey, Jack

NELSON, MARTHA E.
State University of Agriculture and Technology at
Morrisville, N.Y.
   Nearing, Helen Knothe

NELSON, MURRY R.
Pennsylvania State University
   Holman, Nathan ("Nat")

NEWMAN, ROGER K.
School of Law, New York University
   Griswold, Erwin Nathaniel
   Kurland, Philip B.

NORBERG, ARTHUR
Charles Babbage Institute, Minneapolis, Minn.
   Packard, David

OHL, JOHN KENNEDY
Mesa Community College
   Boorda, Jeremy Michael ("Mike")

PACHECO, MARIA
Buffalo State College
   Anfinsen, Christian Boehmer
   Hill, Julian Werner
   Ponnamperuma, Cyril Andrew
   Suomi, Verner Edward

PERSON, JAMES E.
Northville, Mich.
   Kirk, Russell Amos

PESSAH, ROBERTA
Associate Professor, St. John's University
   Gellhorn, Walter

PETERS, MARGOT
University of Wisconsin–Whitewater
   Sarton, May

PETERS, SANDRA REDMOND
Southwest Missouri State University
   Candy, John Franklin

PHILLIPS, ROBERT
University of Houston
   Taylor, Peter Hillsman

PISPECKY, ROBERT
Spotswood High School, New Jersey
   Caesar, Irving

POLLOT, NAN
State University of New York College at Geneseo
   Salvi, John C., III

PORTER, DAVID L.
William Penn College
   Hughes, Harold Everett

POTTER, BARRETT G.
Professor Emeritus, State University of New York College
of Technology, Alfred
   Ellington, Mercer Kennedy
   Feather, Leonard Geoffrey

POUNDSTONE, WILLIAM
Author and Television Writer, Los Angeles, Calif.
   Sagan, Carl Edward

REDD, TINA
School of Drama, University of Washington
   Childress, Alice Herndon

REED, ROY R.
Professor Emeritus, University of Arkansas, Fayetteville
   Faubus, Orval Eugene

REICHARD, GARY W.
California State University, Long Beach
   Brown, Edmund Gerald ("Pat")
   Shilts, Randy Martin

REYNOLDS, CLARK G.
College of Charleston, S.C.
 Stacy, Jess Alexandria
RICHARDSON, BARRETT
Elk City, Okla.
 Rubin, Jerry Clyde
RITCHIE, DONALD A.
U.S. Senate Historical Office
 Reston, James Barrett
ROBERSON, GLORIA GRANT
Adelphi University
 Primus, Pearl Eileen
ROBERTS, PRISCILLA
University of Hong Kong
 Gilpatric, Roswell Leavitt
ROCCO, JOHN
State University of New York, Maritime College
 Cobain, Kurt Donald
 Garcia, Jerome John ("Jerry")
ROCKS, LAWRENCE
Long Island University
 Allen, Mel(vin)
ROME, ROMAN
State University of New York, Maritime College
 Brown, Ron(ald) Harmon
 Clay, Lucius DuBignon, Jr.
ROSAND, DAVID
*Meyer Schapiro Professor of Art History, Columbia
  University*
 Schapiro, Meyer
ROSEN, JEFFREY S.
Spotswood High School, New Jersey
 Walcott, "Jersey Joe"
ROYCE, BRENDA SCOTT
Freelance Writer and Editor, Los Angeles, Calif.
 Tax, Sol
RUHLMANN, WILLIAM J.
Writer, New York City
 Andrews, Maxene Angelyn
 Fitzgerald, Ella Jane
 Martin, Dean
 Styne, Jule
SANTANGELO, MARK
George Washington University
 Riesel, Victor
SAPIENZA, MADELINE
Independent Scholar, Washington, D.C.
 Colbert, Claudette
 Cotten, Joseph Cheshire
 Garson, Greer

SCHAFFER, THOMAS
Texas A&M University
 Broccoli, Albert Romolo ("Cubby")
SCHOLZ, ROBERT F.
Pastor, Holy Trinity Lutheran Church, New York City
 Preus, Jacob Aall Ottesen, Jr. ("Jake")
SCHONDELMEYER, BRENT
Journalist, Independence, Mo.
 Atanasoff, John Vincent
 Seldes, George Henry
SENNETT, TED
Author, Closter, N.J.
 Blaine, Vivian
 Lupino, Ida
 Turner, Lana
SEYEDIAN, MOJTABA
State University of New York, College at Fredonia
 Black, Fischer Sheffey
SHANNON, BILL
Sports Reporter, Associated Press, New York City
 Forte, Fulvio Chester, Jr. ("Chet")
SHERMAN, JANANN
University of Memphis
 Smith, Margaret Chase
SHOR, RACHEL
Queens Borough Public Library, New York City
 Roth, Henry
SMITH, ANDREW
Lafayette College
 Jackson, J(ohn) B(rinckerhoff)
SMITH, JANE S.
*Institute for Health Services Research and Policy Studies,
  Northwestern University*
 Salk, Jonas Edward
SMITH, JOHN KARES
State University of New York, Oswego
 Peppard, George
 Raye, Martha
SMITH, ROBERT J.
Writer, Clarence, N.Y.
 Furness, Elizabeth Mary ("Betty")
 Lamour, Dorothy
SMITH, WHITNEY
The Indianapolis Star
 Kay, Ulysses Simpson
SOLOMON, IRVIN D.
Florida Gulf Coast University
 Johnson, Robert Edward
SOLON, LEONARD R.
Physicist and Educator, Fort Pierce, Fla.
 Fowler, William Alfred
 Wigner, Eugene Paul

SPATT, HARTLEY S.
State University of New York, Maritime College
    Stibitz, George Robert
STAHL, MARTIN JAY
Empire State College
    Fisher, Avery Robert
    Lamont, Corliss
    Molnar, Charles Edwin
    Praeger, Frederick Amos
    Ray, Dixy Lee
STEEN, IVAN D.
State University of New York, Albany
    Harris, (Wanga) Phillip ("Phil")
    McNeill, Don(ald) Thomas
STEEN, SARA J.
Freelance Editor and Writer, Astoria, N.Y.
    Jacobs, Bernard B.
STENSTROM, CHRISTINE
LaGuardia Community College, City University of
    New York
    Graves, Nancy Stevenson
STERLING, KEIR B.
Command Historian, U.S. Army Combined Arms
    Support Command
    Dabney, Virginius
    Pogue, Forrest Carlisle
STERTZ, STEPHEN A.
Dowling College
    Regnery, Henry
SUCHECKI, PETER C.
Maine College of Art
    Hanson, Duane Elwood
    Judd, Donald Clarence
TAMBORRINO, VICTORIA
St. John's University, New York
    Snell, George Davis
TASSINARI, EDWARD J.
State University of New York, Maritime College
    Reynolds, Allie Pierce
TAYLOR, JON E.
Historian, Independence, Mo.
    Dandridge, Raymond Emmett ("Squatty")
    Day, Leon
THOMPSON-FEUERHERD, JENNIFER
New York Institute of Technology, Old Westbury, N.Y.
    Parish, Dorothy May Kinnicutt ("Sister")
THORNTON, JOYCE K.
Texas A&M University Libraries
    Kirby, George
    McQueen, Thelma ("Butterfly")

TINO, RICHARD L.
President, Tino Advertising and Public Relations
    Packard, Vance Oakley
TOMASINO, ADRIANA C.
Ph.D. Candidate, Graduate School and University Center,
    City University of New York
    Temin, Howard Martin
TRIMBLE, PATRICK A.
Pennsylvania State University
    Freleng, Isadore ("Friz")
    Hannah, John Frederick ("Jack")
    Siegel, Jerome ("Jerry")
TSOUKAS, LIANN E.
University of Pittsburgh
    Savalas, Aristoteles ("Telly")
TYE, LARRY
Boston Globe
    Bernays, Edward L.
UEBELHOR, TRACY STEVEN
University of Southern Indiana
    Benson, Ezra Taft
VANDOREN, SANDRA SHAFFER
Archivist, Balch Institute for Ethnic Studies, Philadelphia
    Hawkins, Frederick ("Erick")
VOIGT, JOHN
Berklee College of Music
    Cherry, Don(ald) Eugene
WALI, KAMESHWAR C.
Syracuse University
    Chandrasekhar, Subrahmanyan ("Chandra")
WALKER, WILLIAM STERLING
Freelance Writer, New York City
    Merrill, James Ingram
WATSON, MARY ANN
Eastern Michigan University
    Goode, Mal(vin) Russell
WEDGE, ELEANOR F.
Freelance Writer and Editor, New York City
    Francis, Sam(uel) Lewis
    Geldzahler, Henry
    Greenberg, Clement
    Talma, Louise Juliette
WEIGOLD, MARILYN E.
Pace University, Pleasantville, N.Y.
    Kappel, Frederick Russell
WEINSTEIN, ALLEN
Washington, D.C.
    Hiss, Alger
WEISBLAT, TINKY "DAKOTA"
Independent Scholar, Hawley, Mass.
    Montgomery, Elizabeth
    Nelson, Harriet Hilliard

WEXLER, MOLLY JALENAK
Memphis Jewish Federation
    Lelyveld, Arthur Joseph
WHITMIRE, TIM
Charlotte Observer
    Lebow, Fred
    McGuire, Francis Joseph ("Frank")
WINEGARTEN, RUTHE
Austin, Tex.
    Jordan, Barbara Charline

YAGODA, BEN
University of Delaware
    Mitchell, Joseph Quincy
YOURKE, ELECTRA
New York City
    Slonimsky, Nicolas (Nikolai Leonidovich)

OCCUPATIONS INDEX, VOLUMES 1–4

See also the Alphabetical List of Subjects beginning on p. 633.

	Volume		*Volume*
Actor (Film) (*continued*)		Reed, Donna	2
Greene, Lorne	2	Remick, Lee Ann	3
Hamilton, Margaret	1	Ritt, Martin	2
Hayworth, Rita	2	Rogers, Ginger	4
Hemingway, Margaux	4	Roland, Gilbert	4
Hepburn, Audrey Kathleen	3	Romero, Cesar	4
Holden, William	1	Savalas, Aristoteles ("Telly")	4
Houseman, John	2	Scott, (George) Randolph	2
Hudson, Rock (Roy Scherer, Jr.)	1	Shakur, Tupac Amaru	4
Huston, John	2	Shearer, (Edith) Norma	1
Ives, Burl Icle Ivanhoe	4	Shore, Dinah	4
Jessel, George Albert ("Georgie")	1	Silvers, Phil	1
Julia, Raul Rafael Carlos	4	Stanwyck, Barbara	2
Kaye, Danny	2	Strode, Woodrow Wilson Woolwine ("Woody")	4
Keeler, Ruby	3	Swanson, Gloria	1
Kelly, Eugene Curran ("Gene")	4	Tandy, Jessica	4
Kelly, Grace Patricia (Princess Grace)	1	Thomas, Danny	3
Lamour, Dorothy	4	Tierney, Gene Eliza	3
Lancaster, Burt(on) Stephen	4	Turner, Lana	4
Lanchester, Elsa	2	Webb, John Randolph ("Jack")	1
Landon, Michael	3	Weissmuller, John Peter ("Johnny")	1
Lawford, Peter Sydney Vaughn	1	Welles, Orson	1
Lenya, Lotte	1	Wood, Natalie	1
Lodge, John Davis	1	**Actor (Radio)**	
Loy, Myrna	3	Ace, Goodman	1
Lupino, Ida	4	Ameche, Don	3
McCrea, Joel Albert	2	Backus, James Gilmore ("Jim")	2
MacMurray, Fred(erick) Martin	3	Bellamy, Ralph Rexford	3
McQueen, Thelma ("Butterfly")	4	Blanc, Mel(vin) Jerome	2
MacRae, Gordon	2	Burns, George	4
Markham, Dewey ("Pigmeat")	1	Colbert, Claudette	4
Martin, Dean	4	Cotten, Joseph Cheshire	4
Marvin, Lee	2	Daniels, William Boone ("Billy")	2
Massey, Raymond Hart	1	Day, Dennis	2
Meeker, Ralph	2	Gosden, Freeman Fisher	1
Merman, Ethel	1	Goulding, Ray(mond) Walter	2
Milland, Ray	2	Harris, Wanga Phillip ("Phil")	4
Montgomery, Robert	1	Jessel, George Albert ("Georgie")	1
Murphy, George Lloyd	3	Livingstone, Mary	1
Negri, Pola	2	Martin, Dean	4
Nelson, Eric Hilliard ("Rick")	1	Raye, Martha	4
O'Brien, William Joseph, Jr. ("Pat")	1	Shore, Dinah	4
Page, Geraldine	2	Strasberg, Lee	1
Peppard, George	4	Webb, John Randolph ("Jack")	1
Perkins, Anthony	3	Welles, Orson	1
Phoenix, River Jude	3	**Actor (Stage)**	
Picon, Molly	3	Adler, Luther	1
Pidgeon, Walter	1	Adler, Stella	3
Powell, William Horatio	1	Albertson, Jack	1
Preston, Robert	2	Ameche, Don	3
Price, Vincent Leonard, Jr.	3	Anderson, Judith	3
Ray, Aldo	3	Astaire, Adele Marie	1

	Volume
Attwood, William Hollingsworth	2
Baldwin, Hanson Weightman	3
Bigart, Homer William	3
Bingham, (George) Barry, Sr.	2
Bishop, James Alonzo ("Jim")	2
Bombeck, Erma Louise Fiste	4
Broyard, Anatole Paul	2
Canham, Erwin Dain	1
Catledge, Turner	1
Childs, Marquis William	2
Dabney, Virginius	4
Daniels, Jonathan Worth	1
Dedmon, Emmett	1
Goode, Mal(vin) Russell	4
Graham, Sheilah	2
Grizzard, Lewis McDonald, Jr.	4
Harris, Sydney Justin	2
Hazlitt, Henry Stuart	3
Hearst, William Randolph, Jr.	3
Hemingway, Mary Welsh	2
Hobson, Laura Kean Zametkin	2
Huie, William Bradford	2
Kendrick, Alexander	3
Knight, John Shively	1
Kraft, Joseph	2
Lodge, Henry Cabot, Jr.	1
Lubell, Samuel	2
Mannes, Marya	2
Martin, John Bartlow	2
Maynard, Robert Clyve	3
Middleton, Drew	2
Pope, James Soule, Sr.	1
Reston, James Barrett	4
Riesel, Victor	4
Ryskind, Morrie	1
St. Johns, Adela Rogers	2
Salisbury, Harrison Evans	3
Seldes, George Henry	4
Shannon, William Vincent	2
Shilts, Randy Martin	4
Shirer, William Lawrence	3
Skolsky, Sidney	1
Stein, Aaron Marc	1
Stone, I(sidor) F(einstein) ("Izzy")	2
Sullivan, Walter Seager, Jr.	4
Sulzberger, Cyrus Leo	3
Sutton, Carol	1
Wechsler, James Arthur	1
Whitehead, Don(ald) Ford	1
Wilson, Earl	2

Journalist (Photographer)

Eisenstaedt, Alfred	4

Journalist (Political Commentator)

	Volume
Chancellor, John William	4
Dabney, Virginius	4
Janeway, Eliot	3
Kirk, Russell Amos	4
Lerner, Max	3
Maynard, Robert Clyve	3
Mitford, Jessica ("Decca")	4
Reston, James Barrett	4
Riesel, Victor	4
Scali, John Alfred	4

Journalist (Sportswriter)

Irish, Edward Simmons, Sr. ("Ned")	1
Kieran, John Francis	1
Smith, Walter Wellesley ("Red")	1
Whitaker, Rogers E(rnest) M(alcolm) ("E. M. Frimbo")	1

Judge. See Jurist.

Jurist

Baldwin, Raymond Earl	2
Brown, John R.	3
Burger, Warren Earl	4
Coleman, J(ames) P(lemon)	3
Ferguson, Homer Samuel	1
Fortas, Abe	1
Friendly, Henry Jacob	2
Gabel, Hortense Wittstein	2
Goldberg, Arthur Joseph	2
Haynsworth, Clement Furman, Jr.	2
Hofheinz, Roy Mark	1
Jessup, Philip Caryl	2
Kaufman, Irving Robert	3
McCree, Wade Hampton, Jr.	2
Marshall, Thurgood	3
Matthews, Burnita Shelton	2
Medina, Harold Raymond	2
Parsons, James Benton	3
Sirica, John Joseph	3
Smith, William French	2
Stewart, Potter	1
Wyzanski, Charles Edward, Jr.	2
Yarborough, Ralph Webster	4

Labor Leader

Abel, I(orwith) W(ilbur) ("Abe")	2
Beck, David	3
Boyle, William Anthony ("Tony")	1
Bridges, Harry	2
Chaikin, Sol (Chick)	3
Chávez, César Estrada	3
Curran, Joseph Edwin	1
de Mille, Agnes George	3
Dubinsky, David	1

ALPHABETICAL LIST OF SUBJECTS, VOLUMES 1–4

See also the Occupations Index beginning on p. 599.

Subject	Volume	Subject	Volume
Abbey, Edward Paul	2	Andrews, (Carver) Dana	3
Abbott, Berenice	3	Andrews, Maxene Angelyn	4
Abbott, George Francis	4	Anfinsen, Christian Boehmer	4
Abel, I(orwith) W(ilbur) ("Abe")	2	Angleton, James Jesus	2
Abernathy, Ralph David	2	Appling, Lucius Benjamin, Jr. ("Luke")	3
Abravanel, Maurice	3	Arcel, Ray	4
Accardo, Anthony ("Big Tuna")	3	Arden, Eve	2
Ace, Goodman	1	Arends, Leslie Cornelius	1
Acuff, Roy Claxton	3	Arlen, Harold	2
Adams, Ansel Easton	1	Armour, Norman	1
Adams, Harriet Stratemeyer	1	Armour, Richard Willard	2
Adams, (Llewellyn) Sherman	2	Armstrong, Herbert W.	2
Addams, Charles Samuel	2	Arnall, Ellis Gibbs	3
Adler, Luther	1	Arnaz, Desi	2
Adler, Stella	3	Arneson, Robert Carston	3
Agnew, Spiro Theodore	4	Arrau, Claudio	3
Aiken, George David	1	Arthur, Jean	3
Ailey, Alvin	2	Asch, Moses ("Moe")	2
Albertson, Jack	1	Ashe, Arthur Robert	3
Albion, Robert G.	1	Ashman, Howard Elliot	3
Albright, Horace Marden	2	Asimov, Isaac	3
Algren, Nelson	1	Aspin, Les(lie), Jr.	4
Allen, George Herbert	2	Astaire, Adele Marie	1
Allen, Mel(vin)	4	Astaire, Fred	2
Allison, Fran(ces)	2	Astor, Mary	2
Allott, Gordon Llewellyn	2	Atanasoff, John Vincent	4
Alsop, Joseph Wright, V	2	Atkinson, (Justin) Brooks	1
Alston, Walter Emmons	1	Attwood, William Hollingsworth	2
Alvarez, Luis Walter	2	Atwater, Harvey Leroy ("Lee")	3
Ameche, Don	3	Austin, John Paul	1
Anderson, Carl David, Jr.	3	Averill, Howard Earl ("Rock")	1
Anderson, George Whelan, Jr.	3	Axis Sally. *See* Gillars, Mildred Elizabeth Sisk.	
Anderson, Judith	3	Backus, James Gilmore ("Jim")	2
Anderson, Marian	3	Bacon, Ernst	2
Anderson, Robert Bernerd	2	Bailey, Pearl Mae	2

Subject	Volume
Gleason, Thomas William ("Teddy")	3
Gobel, George Leslie	3
Goddard, Paulette	2
Godfrey, Arthur (Morton)	1
Goffman, Erving Manual	1
Goldberg, Arthur Joseph	2
Golden, Harry	1
Goldman, Eric Frederick	2
Gonzalez, Richard Alonzo ("Pancho")	4
Goode, Mal(vin) Russell	4
Goodman, Benjamin David ("Benny")	2
Goodman, Percival	2
Goodrich, Frances	1
Goodson, Mark	3
Gordon, Dexter Keith	2
Gordon, Ruth	1
Gordone, Charles	4
Goren, Charles Henry	3
Gosden, Freeman Fisher	1
Gould, Chester	1
Gould, Morton	4
Goulding, Ray(mond) Walter	2
Grace, J(oseph) Peter, Jr.	4
Grace, Princess, of Monaco. *See* Kelly, Grace.	
Graham, Bill	3
Graham, John	3
Graham, Martha	3
Graham, Sheilah	2
Graham, William Patrick ("Billy")	3
Grange, Harold Edward ("Red")	3
Grant, Cary	2
Grasso, Ella Rosa Giovanna Oliva Tambussi	1
Graves, Nancy Stevenson	4
Gray, Barry	4
Graziano, Rocky	2
Green, Edith Starrett	2
Greenberg, Clement	4
Greenberg, Henry Benjamin ("Hank")	2
Greene, Lorne	2
Greer, William Alexander ("Sonny")	1
Grillo, Frank Raúl. *See* Machito.	
Grimes, Burleigh Arland	1
Griswold, Erwin Nathaniel	4
Grizzard, Lewis McDonald, Jr.	4
Groppi, James Edward	1
Grosvenor, Melville Bell	1
Grucci, Felix James, Sr. ("Pops")	3
Gruenther, Alfred Maximilian	1
Gruentzig, Andreas Roland	1
Grumman, Leroy Randle ("Roy")	1
Guthrie, Alfred Bertram, Jr.	3

Subject	Volume
Habib, Philip Charles	3
Hagen, John Peter	2
Hagerty, James Campbell	1
Haggar, Joseph Marion	2
Halas, George	1
Haldeman, H(arry) R(obbins)	3
Hale, Clara McBride ("Mother Hale")	3
Haley, Alex(ander) Murray Palmer	3
Haley, William John Clifton, Jr. ("Bill")	1
Hall, Joyce Clyde	1
Halleck, Charles Abraham	2
Halper, Albert	1
Halston (Roy Halston Frowick)	2
Hamilton, Margaret	1
Hammer, Armand	2
Hammond, E(dward) Cuyler	2
Hammond, John Henry, Jr.	2
Hancock, Joy Bright	2
Hanks, Nancy	1
Hannah, John Frederick ("Jack")	4
Hansen, Al(fred) Earl	4
Hanson, Duane Elwood	4
Hanson, Howard Harold	1
Harburg, Edgar Yipsel ("Yip")	1
Haring, Keith Allen	2
Harken, Dwight Emary	3
Harkness, Rebekah West	1
Harlow, Bryce Nathaniel	2
Harmon, Thomas Dudley	2
Harriman, W(illiam) Averell	2
Harrington, (Edward) Michael	2
Harris, Patricia Roberts Fitzgerald	1
Harris, (Wanga) Phillip ("Phil")	4
Harris, Sydney Justin	2
Hart, Marion Rice	2
Hartdegen, Stephen Joseph	2
Hartline, Haldan Keffer	1
Hartz, Louis	2
Hassenfeld, Stephen David	2
Hathaway, Starke Rosencrans	1
Haughton, Daniel Jeremiah	2
Haughton, William Robert ("Billy")	2
Hawkins, Erskine Ramsay	3
Hawkins, Frederick ("Erick")	4
Hayakawa, S(amuel) I(chiye)	3
Hayek, Friedrich August von	3
Hayes, Helen	3
Hayes, Wayne Woodrow ("Woody")	2
Haynsworth, Clement Furman, Jr.	2
Hays, (Lawrence) Brooks	1
Hays, Lee	1